PRENTICE HALL

AMERICA

PATHWAYS TO THE PRESENT

MODERN AMERICAN HISTORY

Andrew Cayton

Elisabeth Israels Perry

Linda Reed

Allan M. Winkler

PEARSON
Prentice
Hall

Needham, Massachusetts
Upper Saddle River, New Jersey

About the Authors

Andrew Cayton, Ph.D. Andrew Cayton is Distinguished Professor of History at Miami University in Oxford, Ohio. He received his B.A. in History from the University of Virginia and his M.A. and Ph.D. in American history from Brown University. A specialist in the history of the Early Republic and the Midwest, Dr. Cayton is the author of several books and articles, including *Frontier Indiana, Contact Points: American Frontiers from the Mohawk Valley to the Mississippi,* and *So Many Possibilities: A History of Ohio.*

Elisabeth Israels Perry, Ph.D. Elisabeth Israels Perry holds the John Francis Bannon Endowed Chair in History at Saint Louis University in St. Louis, Missouri. She received her Ph.D. in history from the University of California at Los Angeles. Dr. Perry's period of specialization is the late nineteenth and early twentieth centuries. She is the author of *Women in Action: Rebels and Reformers, 1920–1980.* Since 1987, she has directed five NEH Summer Seminars for Secondary School Teachers.

Linda Reed, Ph.D. Linda Reed is Associate Professor of History at the University of Houston. For nine years she directed the African American Studies Program. She received her B.S. from Alabama A & M University, her M.A. from the University of Alabama, and her Ph.D. from Indiana University. Dr. Reed's specialization is twentieth-century African American history, particularly the modern-day civil rights era. She is the author of *Simple Decency and Common Sense: The Conference Movement, 1938–1963.*

Allan M. Winkler, Ph.D. Allan M. Winkler is Distinguished Professor of History at Miami University in Ohio. He has also taught at Yale University and the University of Oregon and, for one year each, at the University of Helsinki in Finland, the University of Amsterdam in The Netherlands, and the University of Nairobi in Kenya. A prize-winning teacher, he is the author of seven books including *The Politics of Propaganda: The Office of War Information, 1942–1945* and *Life Under a Cloud: American Anxiety About the Atom.*

American Heritage® *American Heritage*® magazine was founded in 1954, and it quickly rose to the position it occupies today: the country's preeminent magazine of history and culture. Dedicated to presenting the past in incisive, entertaining narratives underpinned by scrupulous scholarship, *American Heritage* today goes to more than 300,000 subscribers and counts the country's very best writers and historians among its contributors. Its innovative use of historical illustration and its wide variety of subject matter have gained the publication scores of honors across more than forty years, among them National Magazine Awards.

American Heritage and My Brush with History are trademarks of American Heritage Inc. Their use is pursuant to a license agreement.

PEARSON
Prentice
Hall

ISBN 0-13-181547-4
2 3 4 5 6 7 8 9 10   07 06 05 04

Program Reviewers

HISTORIAN REVIEWERS

William Childs
Department of History
Ohio State University
Columbus, Ohio

Donald L. Fixico
Department of History
Western Michigan
    University
Kalamazoo, Michigan

George Forgie
Department of History
University of Texas
    at Austin
Austin, Texas

Mario Garcia
Department of History
University of California at
    Santa Barbara
Santa Barbara, California

Gerald Gill
Department of History
Tufts University
Medford, Massachusetts

Mark I. Greenberg
USF Florida Studies Center
University of South Florida
Tampa, Florida

Huping Ling
Division of Social Science
Truman State University
Kirksville, Missouri

John McKiernan-Gonzalez
Department of History
University of South Florida
Tampa, Florida

Roy Rosenzweig
Department of History
George Mason University
Fairfax, Virginia

Susan Smulyan
Department of
    American Civilization
Brown University
Providence, Rhode Island

TEACHER REVIEWERS

Suzanne P. Brock
Vestavia Hills High School
Birmingham, Alabama

Debra Brown
Eisenhower High School
Houston, Texas

Stephen Bullick
Mt. Lebanon
    School District
Pittsburgh, Pennsylvania

Alfred B. Cate, Jr.
Central High School,
Memphis City Schools
Memphis, Tennessee

Janet K. Chandler
Hamilton Southeastern
    High School
Fishers, Indiana

Lee Chase
Chesterfield County
    Public Schools
Chesterfield County,
Virginia

Vern Cobb
Okemos High School
Okemos, Michigan

Joyce Dixon Cooper
Sunset High School
Dallas I.S.D.
Dallas, Texas

Michael Jerry DaDurka
David Starr Jordan
    High School (LBUSD)
Long Beach, California

Mike Ferguson
Hebron High School
Lewisville, Texas

Robert Hasty
Lawrence Central
    High School
Indianapolis, Indiana

Robert C. McAdams
East Burke High School
Icard, North Carolina

Lawrence Moaton
Memphis City Schools
Memphis, Tennessee

Dr. Brent Muirhead
South Forsyth High School
Cumming, Georgia

Keith Denny Olmsted
Amon Carter Riverside
    High School
Fort Worth I.S.D.
Fort Worth, Texas

Debbie W. Powers
Fulton County
Atlanta, Georgia

Betsy Schmidt
Round Rock I.S.D.
Round Rock, Texas

Walter T. Thurnau
Southwestern Central
    High School
Jamestown, New York

Kevin Wheeler
Lamar High School
Houston, Texas

Barry Wilmoth
Lamar High School
Arlington, Texas

Judy Heckendorf Wood
Parkway West High School
Ballwin, Missouri

CONTENT CONSULTANTS

Senior Consultant
T. R. Fehrenbach
San Antonio, Texas
author, *Lone Star*

Senior Consultant
Herman Viola
Falls Church, Virginia
Curator emeritus,
Smithsonian Institution

**Curriculum and
Assessment Specialist**
Jan Moberley
Dallas, Texas

**Reading
Consultant**
Dr. Bonnie Armbruster
Professor of Education
University of Illinois at
    Urbana-Champaign
Urbana, Illinois

Constitution Consultant
William A. McClenaghan
Department of
    Political Science
Oregon State University
Beaverton, Oregon
author, *Magruder's
American Government*

Internet Consultant
Brent Muirhead
Teacher, Social Studies
    Department
South Forsyth
    High School
Cumming, Georgia

Holocaust Consultant
Marjorie B. Green
Director, Educational
    Policy & Programs
Anti-Defamation League
Los Angeles, California

PROGRAM ADVISORS

Michal Howden
Social Studies Consultant
Zionsville, Indiana

Joe Wieczorek
Social Studies Consultant
Baltimore, Maryland

Table of Contents

Unit 2: Building a Powerful Nation, 1850–1915. 152

I WANT YOU FOR U.S. ARMY
NEAREST RECRUITING STATION

Reference Section

Special Features

American Pathways

Thematic time tables clarify connections between events across time

AmericanHeritage®
MY BRUSH WITH HISTORY™

Eyewitness accounts from *American Heritage* magazine of ordinary Americans and extraordinary events

Geography & History

An in-depth look at the links between geography and history

TEST PREPARATION

Practice questions to help prepare for classroom exams and standardized assessment

Step-by-step lessons to learn and practice important skills

Focus on ...

■ CITIZENSHIP

■ CULTURE

COMPARING PRIMARY SOURCES

Primary source quotations on controversial issues of the period

COMPARING HISTORIANS' VIEWPOINTS

Respected historians debate events in our nation's history

BIOGRAPHIES

Profiles describing the lives and accomplishments of prominent Americans

NOTABLE PRESIDENTS

*1st President
1789–1797*

Biographies of some of the most highly respected Presidents

Fast Forward to Today

Key Documents

Primary Sources

Maps

Charts, Graphs, and Tables

American Pathways

Much of what you learn about American history can be better understood if you view events as part of a larger pattern. The themes described below and the American Pathways features throughout this book can help you identify the larger patterns and see the connections between events across time.

Go Online PHSchool.com **Creating a Study Guide** As you complete your course in American history, you can use the American Pathways features and the printable worksheets available at www.PHSchool.com to create your own thematic study guides.

▶ History

Fighting for Freedom and Democracy

Throughout the nation's history, Americans have risked their lives to protect their freedoms and to fight for democracy both at home and abroad. Use the American Pathways feature on pages 410–411 to help you trace specific events in the struggle to protect and defend these cherished ideals.

A cannon used in the Battle of Gettysburg

▶ Geography

The Expansion of the United States

Through a series of treaties, purchases, and warfare, the United States has grown from a small country bordering the Atlantic Ocean to one that stretches from the Atlantic to the Pacific, as well as north to Alaska and west to Hawaii. This vast territory has provided American citizens with many natural resources. Use the American Pathways feature on pages 148–149 to help you trace specific events in the expansion of the United States.

Advertisement for land in Iowa and Nebraska

A Hawaiian landscape

▶ Economics

Free Enterprise and the American Economy

The combination of abundant natural resources, an economic system that encourages individual initiative, and a political system that ensures private property rights has allowed hard-working Americans to build a strong and prosperous American economy. Use the American Pathways feature on pages 920–921 to help you trace specific events in the unfolding of our nation's economy.

Currency from the
Free Banking Era,
1837–1863

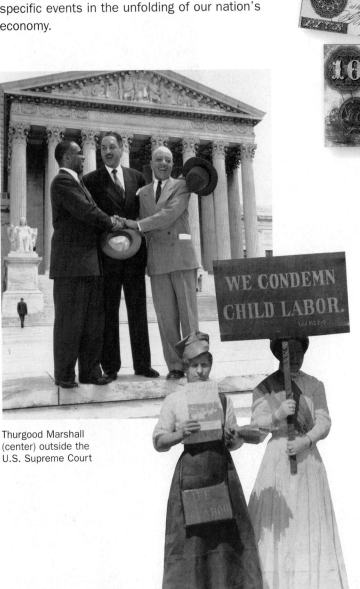

Thurgood Marshall
(center) outside the
U.S. Supreme Court

▶ Government

Federalism and States' Rights

The Framers of the Constitution based the American system of government on federalism, the sharing of power between the national, or federal, government and state governments. Throughout the nation's history, Americans have debated exactly which powers belong to the federal government and which belong to the states. Use the American Pathways feature on pages 196–197 to help you trace specific events in this ongoing debate.

Two women protesting child labor

►Citizenship

Expanding Civil Rights

The United States was founded on such ideals as equality and democratic representation. Throughout American history many groups, including women and African Americans, have fought for and won important civil rights. Use the American Pathways feature on pages 732–733 to trace the events surrounding various groups' struggles for civil rights.

An American suffragist

Dr. Martin Luther King, Jr.

►Culture

The Arts in America

In every period of their history, Americans have expressed their views in forms such as art, literature, films, and music. Use the American Pathways feature on pages 476–477 to help identify major contributions to the arts throughout American history.

Louis Armstrong's Hot Five jazz band and record labels from the 1920s

▶ Science and Technology

American Innovation in Technology

Innovations in science and technology have had an enormous impact on our nation's economy, standard of living, and quality of life. Use the American Pathways feature on pages 664–665 to identify important American inventions from the telephone to the microchip.

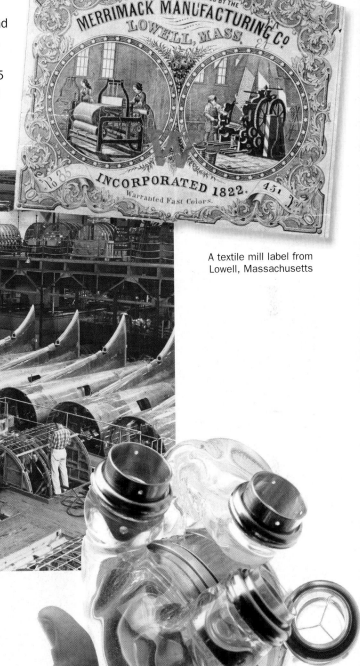

CLOTH MADE AND PRINTED BY THE
MERRIMACK MANUFACTURING CO
LOWELL, MASS.
INCORPORATED 1822.
Warranted Fast Colors.

A textile mill label from Lowell, Massachusetts

Boeing B-17 bomber production during the 1940s

An implantable replacement heart

The Five Geographic Themes

*L*ike history, geography can be divided into themes. Geographers use five themes, described below, to organize their study of the world. You will find these themes in the captions that accompany the maps in this textbook. In addition, a Geography and History feature in each unit explores one of the themes in greater depth.

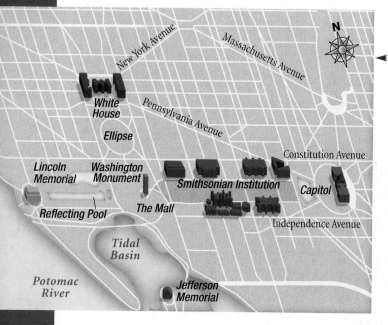

Location

The most basic of the geographic themes, location tells where a place is. Location can be expressed in two ways. Absolute location describes a place's position on the globe as determined by latitude and longitude. Relative location describes a place's position in relation to other places. While each place can have only one absolute location, its relative location can be expressed in a number of ways. For example, the relative location of the Smithsonian Institution can be described as "west of the Capitol," "at the Mall," or "east of the Washington Monument."

Place

Place describes the characteristics that make a location distinctive. There are two kinds of characteristics. Physical characteristics include landforms, vegetation, and climate. Human characteristics include the culture, economy, and government of the people who live in a place. Each place in the United States—indeed, on Earth—has a unique combination of physical and human characteristics.

Movement

People, goods, and ideas regularly travel from one place to another. Examples from American history include the continuing immigration of new Americans, the westward migration of Americans through the 1800s, and the spread of American ideals of individual liberty through the world following the American Revolution. Today's advances in communication and transportation make movement easier and more common than ever.

Regions

A region is any group of places with at least one common characteristic. Regions can be any size, and a single place can belong to several different regions. The city of San Diego, for example, is part of California (a political region), the Sunbelt (a demographic region), and the Pacific Rim (an economic region).

Human-Environment Interaction

Human-environment interaction explores the ways in which people use and modify their environment. The Brooklyn Bridge, the coal mines of West Virginia, the wheat fields of the Plains states, Hoover Dam—all are examples of Americans modifying their environment in order to produce or extract needed resources or to make movement more efficient.

Use This Book for Success

You can use this book as a tool to master United States history. Spend a few minutes to become familiar with the way the book is set up and learn how it can help you succeed in understanding the rich story of America.

Read for Content Mastery

Before You Read The sections in this book begin with Reading Focus questions. These questions point out important ideas in the section. Another helpful aid is the Target Reading Skill at the beginning of each section. The Target Reading Skills will help you master the section content by helping you to

• actively engage in making sense of the content;

• identify the structure of the text in each section; and

• organize information for learning.

As You Read Asking questions will help you gather evidence and gain knowledge. Suppose you are reading about World War I. You might ask: What events led up to the start of the war? Questions like this can be found in the margins of this book and are labeled "Reading Check." Use these questions to strengthen your understanding of new material.

After You Read The questions in the Section Assessment will help you understand what you read. Use these questions to assess yourself. Were your predictions on target? Did you find answers to your questions? Demonstrate your understanding by completing the Go Online activity.

Go Online
PHSchool.com

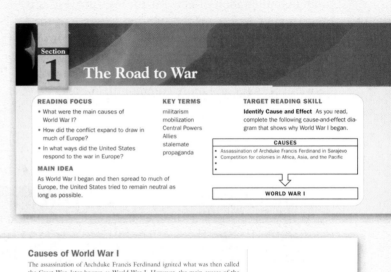

Section 1 — The Road to War

READING FOCUS
• What were the main causes of World War I?
• How did the conflict expand to draw in much of Europe?
• In what ways did the United States respond to the war in Europe?

MAIN IDEA
As World War I began and then spread to much of Europe, the United States tried to remain neutral as long as possible.

KEY TERMS
militarism
mobilization
Central Powers
Allies
stalemate
propaganda

TARGET READING SKILL
Identify Cause and Effect As you read, complete the following cause-and-effect diagram that shows why World War I began.

CAUSES
• Assassination of Archduke Francis Ferdinand in Sarajevo
• Competition for colonies in Africa, Asia, and the Pacific
•
•

↓

WORLD WAR I

Causes of World War I

The assassination of Archduke Francis Ferdinand ignited what was then called the Great War, later known as World War I. However, the main causes of the war existed well before 1914. Those causes included imperialism, militarism, nationalism, and a tangled system of alliances.

Imperialism A great scramble for colonies took place in the late 1800s. European powers rushed to claim the remaining uncolonized areas of the world, particularly in Africa, Asia, and the Pacific. Japan joined the roster of colonial powers when it won the Sino-Japanese War in 1895 and moved to acquire Korea, Taiwan, and territory on China's mainland.

By 1910, the most desirable colonies had been taken. Competition for th[e] lands that remained led to conflict among the powers of Europe. German[y] leaders envied Britain and France—two countries that had begun coloni[zing] early and controlled large, resource-rich empires. Leaders in Germany [and] other countries recognized that they could only expand in Africa by taking [it] away from other colonizers.

Militarism By the early 1900s in Europe, diplomacy had taken a back sea[t to] **militarism**. This policy involved aggressively building up a nation's arm[ed] forces in preparation for war and giving the military more authority over th[e] government and foreign policy. The great powers of Europe—Austria-Hungary, France, Germany, Great Britain, and Russia—all spent large sums of money on new weapons and warships for expanding their armed forces. Their endless planning for war made war much more likely.

Nationalism Two kinds of nationalism contributed to World War I. The first was the tendency for countries such as the great powers to act in their own

READING CHECK
How did competition for colonies help lead to war?

Section 1 — Assessment

READING COMPREHENSION

1. How did nationalism contribute to the start of World War I?
2. Which countries were known as the **Allies?** Which countries were known as the **Central Powers?**
3. What were two causes of the **stalemate** in the West?
4. What was the main reason that the United States stayed neutral at the start of World War I?

CRITICAL THINKING AND WRITING

5. **Checking Consistency** The alliance system in Europe was designed to maintain peace. Yet it seemed to make the conflict worse once the fighting began. Explain the apparent inconsistency.
6. **Writing to Persuade** Write an essay in which you express your support for the preparedness movement. Persuade your readers that the United States had no choice but to be ready to go to war.

Go Online
PHSchool.com
For: A poetry activity on World War I
Visit: PHSchool.com
Web Code: mrd-6191

Chapter 12 • Section 1   419

Develop Your Skills

Each chapter has a Skills for Life exercise. Use these exercises to learn and practice Social Studies skills. These skills will help you be successful in studying United States history. Complete the Applying the Chapter Skill activity at the end of every chapter to apply the skills you have learned.

Applying the Chapter Skill

Identifying Alternatives The United States chose to go to war with Germany in 1917 largely because of continued German submarine attacks on neutral shipping. Identify alternative solutions to this problem of U-boat attacks. Discuss your alternative in a written proposal to President Wilson.

Use the Internet to Explore

At the click of a mouse, the Internet offers you access to a wealth of United States history resources. Use the Go Online activities to research and learn more about key events and themes in United States history. By going to PHSchool.com on the Internet and entering the Web Codes printed in your book, you will find virtual field trips, interactive self-tests, and dozens of links to historical sites online.

Go Online PHSchool.com

For: A poetry activity on World War I
Visit: PHSchool.com
Web Code: mrd-6191

Prepare for Tests

This book helps you prepare for tests. Start by answering the questions at the end of every section and chapter. Go to PHSchool.com and enter the Web Code in your book to take the practice Self-Test. Then, use the Test Preparation pages at the end of the unit to check yourself further.

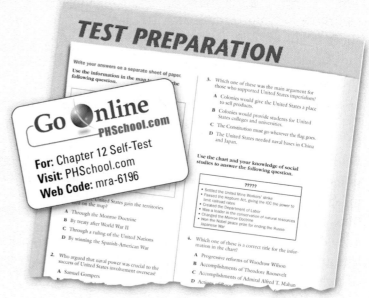

Go Online PHSchool.com

For: Chapter 12 Self-Test
Visit: PHSchool.com
Web Code: mra-6196

Reading Informational Texts

Reading a newspaper, a magazine, an Internet page, or a textbook is not the same as reading a novel. The purpose of reading nonfiction texts is to acquire new information. Researchers have shown that the **Target Reading Skills** presented below will help you get the most out of reading informational texts. You'll have chances to practice these skills and strategies throughout the book. Good luck!

Before You Read

Before you read an informational text, it's important to take the time to do some pre-reading. Here are some strategies for pre-reading an informational text.

Set a Purpose for Reading

It's important to have a goal in mind when you're reading your text. Preview the section you're about to read by reading the objectives and looking at the illustrations. Then write down a purpose for your reading such as "I'll learn about the history of ___," or "I'll find out about the causes of ___."

Predict

Another pre-reading strategy is to make a prediction about what you're preparing to learn. Do this by scanning the section headings and visuals. Then write down a prediction such as "I will find out what caused the American Revolution."

Ask Questions

Before you read a section ask a few questions that you'd like to answer while reading. Scan the section headings and illustrations and then jot down a few questions in a table. As you read, try to fill in answers to your questions. You don't need to use complete sentences.

Question	Answer
1. Why do people emigrate from their home country?	War, poverty, lack of food or jobs, persecution
2. What challenges do many immigrants face?	New language, new customs, finding jobs

Use Prior Knowledge

Research shows that if you connect the new information you're reading about to something you already know—your prior knowledge—you'll be more likely to remember the new information. After previewing a section, create a table like the one at right. Complete the chart as you read the section.

What I Know	What I Want to Know	What I Learned
Women have the right to vote.	When did women win the right to vote?	The 19th Amendment, guaranteeing women the right to vote, was a ratified in 1920.

As You Read

It's important to be an active reader. Here are some strategies to use while you're reading an informational text.

Reread or Read Ahead

If you don't understand a certain passage, reread it to look for connections among the words and sentences. Or try reading ahead to see if the ideas are clarified further on.

Paraphrase

To paraphrase is to restate information in your own words. Paraphrasing is a good way to check that you understand what you've read.

Original Paragraph	Paraphrase
Latin America's northern edge is marked by the boundary between the United States and Mexico. To the south, the region extends to the tip of the continent of South America.	Latin America extends from the U.S.-Mexico border in the north all the way to the southern tip of South America.

Summarize

Summarizing is another good way to check that you understand what you've read. To summarize is to restate the main ideas of a passage.

Original Paragraph	Summary
Electricity made from water power is called hydroelectricity. One way to build a hydroelectric plant is to dam a river. This creates a huge lake. When the dam gates open, water gushes from the lake to the river, turning a wheel that creates electricity.	Hydroelectricity is created when rushing water turns a wheel.

Identify Main Ideas and Details

A main idea is the most important point in a paragraph or section of text. Sometimes a main idea is stated directly, but other times you must determine it yourself by reading carefully. Main ideas are supported by details. Good readers pause occasionally to make sure they can identify the main idea. You can record main ideas and details in an outline format like the one shown here.

Main idea

The Constitution establishes our form of government, a republic. A republic is a government in which citizens elect their representatives. As the "supreme law of the land," the Constitution protects the rights of citizens by providing general rules that the national government and the state governments must follow.

Main idea

Details

The Constitution

I. Establishes our government, a republic
   A. Provides for citizens to elect representatives
   B. Is the "supreme law of the land"
   C. Protects rights of citizens
   D. Provides rules that national and state governments must follow

Use Context Clues

When you come across an unfamiliar word, you can sometimes figure out its meaning from clues in the surrounding words. For example, in the sentence "Some vendors sold bottled water," the word *sold* is a clue indicating that a vendor is someone who sells things.

Analyze Word Parts

When you come across an unfamiliar word, sometimes it's helpful to break the word into parts—its root, prefix, or suffix. For example, the prefix *in-* means "not." The word *injustice* means something that is "not just." Create a reference chart indicating the meanings of common prefixes and suffixes.

Persuasion

Writing that supports an opinion or position

① Select and Narrow Your Topic

Choose a topic that provokes an argument and has at least two sides. If there are too many pros and cons for the argument, consider narrowing your topic to cover only part of the debate.

② Consider Your Audience

The argument that you make in your writing should be targeted to the specific audience for your writing. Which argument is going to appeal most to your audience and persuade them to understand your point of view?

③ Gather Evidence

You'll need to include convincing examples in your essay. Begin by creating a graphic organizer that states your position at the top. Then in two columns list the pros and cons for your position. Consider interviewing experts on the topic. Even though your essay may focus on the pro arguments, it's important to predict and address the strongest arguments against your stand.

④ Write a First Draft

Begin by writing a strong thesis statement that clearly states the position you will prove. Continue by presenting the strongest arguments in favor of your position and acknowledging and refuting opposing arguments. Build a strong case by including facts, statistics, and comparisons, and by sharing personal experiences.

⑤ Revise and Proof

Check to make sure you have made a logical argument and that you have not oversimplified the argument. Try adding the following transition words to make your reasoning more obvious:

To show a contrast—*however, although, despite*
To point out a reason—*since, because, if*
To signal a conclusion—*therefore, consequently, so, then*

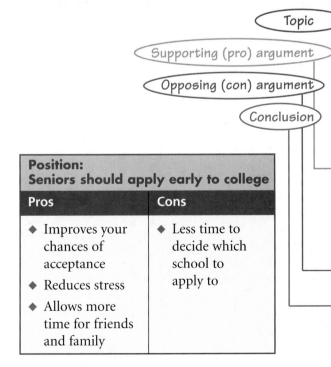

| Topic |
| Supporting (pro) argument |
| Opposing (con) argument |
| Conclusion |

Position: Seniors should apply early to college	
Pros	**Cons**
◆ Improves your chances of acceptance	◆ Less time to decide which school to apply to
◆ Reduces stress	
◆ Allows more time for friends and family	

Not Now, but Right Now!

It sneaks up on you at all hours of the day or night, a floating cloud of angst. Suddenly, a feeling bubbles up from the pit of your stomach, an achy, acidic feeling of panic. "Which college is the right college? Can I get in?" These fears are definitely part of your senior year experience, but two simple words hold the secret to reduced stress: Apply early. It is as simple as that. Apply early for college admissions and you will sleep easier at night.

Think for a moment of how the college admissions process works. Like a thousand cattle trying to pass through the same gate at once, vast numbers of people across the nation apply each year for a limited number of places at college. Academic records of applicants aside, admissions boards work on a first come, first served basis. The longer you wait to apply, the less likely you are to make the cut, no matter how qualified you may be.

Your senior year is a time of closing chapters, a time to enjoy the last days at home with friends and family, a time to remember the joys of childhood before jumping into the great unknown, adulthood. While waiting until the last minute to apply to college may give you more time to decide which schools to apply to, it will dramatically increase your stress. Take some pressure off yourself by getting applications in early. With just two simple words in mind, you can enjoy the sweet pleasures of the last year of high school in peace: Apply early.

Adapted from an essay by Jason Heflin, Lakeland, Florida

Exposition

Writing that explains a process, compares and contrasts, explains causes and effects, or explores solutions to a problem

❶ Identify and Narrow Your Topic

Expository writing is writing that explains something in detail. An essay might explain the similarities and differences between two or more subjects (compare and contrast), it might explain how one event causes another (cause and effect), or it might explain a problem and describe a solution.

❷ Gather Evidence

Create a graphic organizer that identifies details to include in your essay. Create a Venn Diagram for a compare-and-contrast essay, a diagram showing multiple causes and effects for a cause-and-effect essay, or a web for defining all the aspects of a problem and the possible solutions.

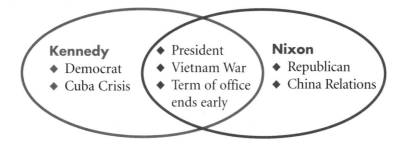

Kennedy
- Democrat
- Cuba Crisis

- President
- Vietnam War
- Term of office ends early

Nixon
- Republican
- China Relations

❸ Write Your First Draft

Write a strong topic sentence and then organize the body of your essay around your similarities and differences, causes and effects, or problem and solutions. Be sure to include convincing details, facts, and examples.

❹ Revise and Proof

Be sure you've included transition words between sentences and paragraphs:

Transitions to show similarities—*all, similarly, both, in the same way, closely related, equally*

Transitions that show differences—*on the other hand, in contrast, however, instead, yet*

John F. Kennedy and Richard Nixon ran for president of the United States against each other, yet both became president. Kennedy, a Democrat, was elected in 1960. He dealt with crises in Cuba and saw the beginnings of the Vietnam War. He was assassinated in 1963.

Nixon, a Republican, was elected in 1968. He opened relations with China and saw the end of the Vietnam War. Because of the Watergate scandal, he resigned from office in 1974.

Research Writing

Writing that presents research about a topic

1 Identify and Narrow Your Topic

Choose a topic you're interested in and make sure that it is not too broad a topic. For example, instead of writing a report on Panama, write about the Panama Canal. Ask yourself, What do I want to know about the topic?

2 Acquire Information

Locate and use several sources of information about the topic from the library, Internet, or an interview with someone knowledgeable. Before you use a source make sure that it is reliable and up-to-date. Take notes using an index card for each detail or subtopic and note which source the information was taken from. Use quotation marks when you copy the exact words from a source. Create a source index card for each resource, listing the author, the title, the publisher, and the place and date of publication.

3 Make an Outline

Use an outline to decide how to organize your report. Sort your index cards into the same order.

4 Write a First Draft

Write an introduction, body, and conclusion. Leave plenty of space between lines so you can go back and add details that you may have left out.

5 Revise and Proof

Be sure to include transition words between sentences and paragraphs.

To show a contrast–*however, although, despite*

To point out a reason–*since, because, if*

To signal a conclusion–*therefore, consequently, so, then*

Introduction

Building the Panama Canal

Ever since Christopher Columbus first explored the Isthmus of Panama, the Spanish had been looking for a water route through it. They wanted to be able to sail west from Spain to Asia without sailing around South America. However, it was not until 1914 that the dream became a reality.

Conclusion

It took eight years and more than 70,000 workers to build the Panama Canal. It remains one of the greatest engineering feats of modern times.

Writing for Assessment

Writing short answers, extended responses, or essays for a test

① Choose a Writing Prompt and Budget Time

In some testing situations you may be given a choice of writing prompts, or assignments. Before choosing, consider how much you know about a topic and how much a topic interests you. To budget time, allow about

1/4 time on preparing to write,

1/2 time writing a first draft,

1/4 time revising and editing.

② Carefully Analyze the Question or Writing Prompt

Pay special attention to key words that indicate exactly what you are supposed to do:

Explain—*Give a clear, complete account of how something works or why something happened.*

Compare and Contrast—*Provide details about how two or more things are alike and how they are different.*

Describe—*Provide vivid details to paint a word picture of a person, place, or thing.*

Argue, Convince, Support—*Take a position on an issue and present strong reasons to support your side of the issue.*

Summarize—*Provide the highlights or most important elements of a subject.*

Classify—*Group things into categories and define the categories using facts and examples.*

Persuade—*Provide convincing reasons to accept your position.*

> According to the author of the article, Chief Joseph was both a <u>peace chief</u> and a <u>military genius</u>. Use information from the article to <u>support this conclusion</u>.

③ Gather Details

Take a few minutes to divide your topic into subtopics. Jot down as many facts and details as you can for each subtopic. Create a graphic organizer to organize the details.

> **Prewriting List**
> **Peace Chief**
> ◆ traded peacefully with whites (1)
> ◆ "reluctantly" went to war (2)
> ◆ famous speech, "I will fight no more forever!" (3)
>
> **Military Genius**
> ◆ won battles with fewer warriors than white military (a)
> ◆ avoided capture for many months (b)
> ◆ led his people more than 1,000 miles (c)
> ◆ knew when to surrender for the good of his people (d)

④ Draft

Consider the best plan for organizing your essay. Use the organization you've selected to write your first draft.

◆ For a summary or explanation, organize your details in chronological order, as on a timeline.

◆ For a compare-and-contrast essay, present similarities first and then differences.

◆ For a persuasive essay, organize your points by order of importance.

> **Short-Answer Response:**
>
> Chief Joseph was known as a <u>peace chief</u> because he traded peacefully with whites for many years. (1) He went to war "reluctantly" after the government ordered his people to move to a reservation. (2) When he finally surrendered, he said in a famous speech, "I will fight no more forever."
>
> (3) Chief Joseph was also a <u>military genius</u>. He fought off government troops with fewer warriors than the white military, (a) and he avoided capture for many months. (b) He led his people more than 1,000 miles (c) before he made the decision to surrender.

⑤ Revise

Read your response to make sure

◆ the introduction includes a strong main idea sentence and presents subtopics.

◆ each paragraph focuses on a single topic.

◆ you've included transition words between sentences and paragraphs such as *first, for example, because,* and *for this reason.*

◆ you revise your word choice by replacing general words with specific ones.

⑥ Edit and Proof

Read your response to make sure each sentence

◆ contains a subject and a verb,

◆ begins with a capital letter, and

◆ ends with a period, question mark, or exclamation point.

Clean up any spelling or punctuation errors.

Evaluating Your Writing

Use this chart, or rubric, to evaluate your writing.

	Excellent	Good	Acceptable	Unacceptable
Purpose	Achieves purpose—to inform, persuade, or provide historical interpretation—very well	Informs, persuades, or provides historical interpretation reasonably well	Reader cannot easily tell if the purpose is to inform, persuade, or provide historical interpretation	Lacks purpose
Organization	Develops ideas in a very clear and logical way	Presents ideas in a reasonably well-organized way	Reader has difficulty following the organization	Lacks organization
Elaboration	Explains all ideas with facts and details	Explains most ideas with facts and details	Includes some supporting facts and details	Lacks supporting details
Use of Language	Uses excellent vocabulary and sentence structure with no errors in spelling, grammar, or punctuation	Uses good vocabulary and sentence structure with very few errors in spelling, grammar, or punctuation	Includes some errors in grammar, punctuation, and spelling	Includes many errors in grammar, punctuation, and spelling

1

Beginnings to 1861

"*I always consider the settlement of America with reverence and wonder, as the opening of a grand scene and design in providence. . . .*"

John Adams
Notes for "A Dissertation on the Canon and Feudal Law," 1765

This painting by Howard Chandler Christy shows George Washington presiding over the Constitutional Convention in Philadelphia, Pennsylvania, in 1787. ▶

Origins of a New Society,

To 1754

A modern replica of one of Columbus's ships

The signing of the Mayflower Compact

American Events

1492
Columbus sails to the Americas.

1565
The Spanish establish St. Augustine, in present-day Florida.

1570–1600
The Iroquois League, a confederation of Native American nations, is formed.

1607
The English establish Jamestown, Virginia.

1620
Pilgrims establish Plymouth Colony in present-day Massachusetts.

1475   **1525**   **1575**   **1625**

World Events

European slave raids begin in Africa.
1500

The Reformation begins.
1517

Samuel de Champlain establishes Quebec, New France.
1608

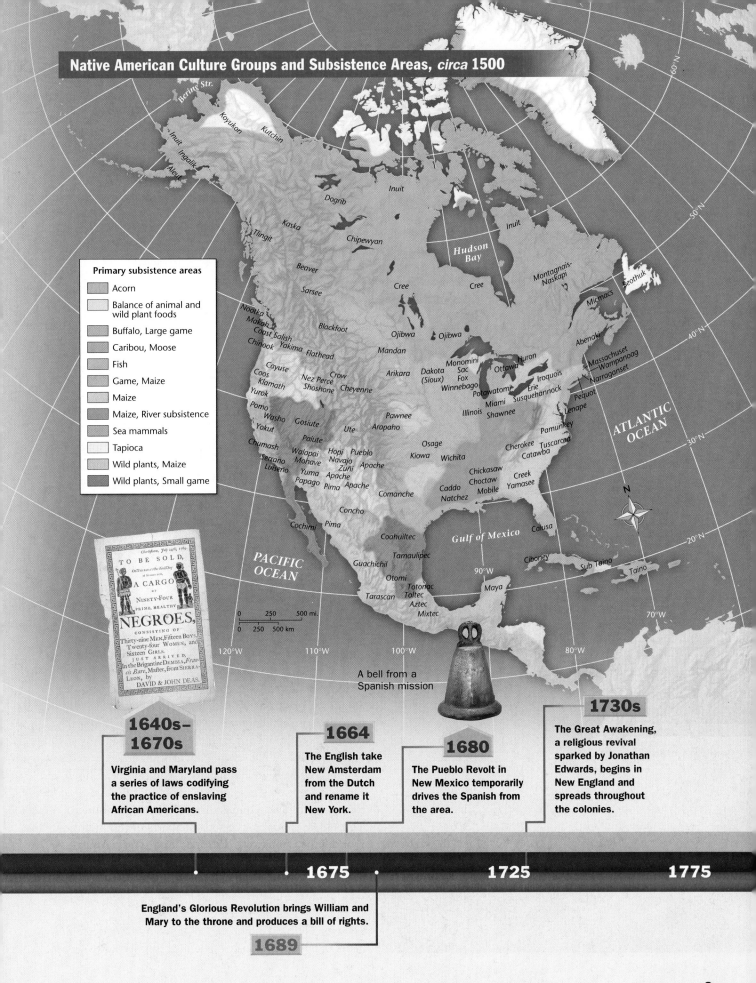

Native American Culture Groups and Subsistence Areas, *circa* 1500

Primary subsistence areas

- Acorn
- Balance of animal and wild plant foods
- Buffalo, Large game
- Caribou, Moose
- Fish
- Game, Maize
- Maize
- Maize, River subsistence
- Sea mammals
- Tapioca
- Wild plants, Maize
- Wild plants, Small game

Bering Str.

Inuit
Aleut
Ingalik
Koyukon
Kutchin
Dogrib
Kaska
Tlingit
Chipewyan
Beaver
Sarsee
Cree
Cree
Nootka
Makah
Coast Salish
Chinook
Yakima
Blackfoot
Flathead
Cayuse
Coos
Klamath
Nez Percé
Yurok
Shoshone
Crow
Cheyenne
Pomo
Washo
Gosiute
Yokut
Paiute
Ute
Chumash
Walapai
Hopi Pueblo
Mohave
Navajo
Serrano
Zuñi
Luiseño
Yuma
Apache
Papago
Pima Apache
Cochimi
Pima
Concho
Coahuiltec
Guachichil
Tamaulipec
Otomi
Tarascan
Totonac
Toltec
Aztec
Mixtec

Hudson Bay
Montagnais-Naskapi
Beothuk
Micmacs
Abenaki
Massachuset
Wampanoag
Narraganset
Pequot
Lenape
Pamunkey
Cherokee Tuscarora
Catawba
Creek
Yamasee
Calusa
Ciboney
Sub Taino
Taino

Ojibwa
Ojibwa
Mandan
Monomini
Dakota (Sioux)
Sac
Fox
Ottawa
Huron
Winnebago
Iroquois
Potawatomi
Erie
Miami
Susquehannock
Illinois
Shawnee
Arikara
Pawnee
Arapaho
Osage
Kiowa
Wichita
Chickasaw
Choctaw
Mobile
Caddo
Natchez
Comanche
Maya

ATLANTIC OCEAN
PACIFIC OCEAN
Gulf of Mexico

0 250 500 mi.
0 250 500 km

120°W 110°W 100°W 90°W 80°W 70°W
20°N 30°N 40°N 50°N 60°N

TO BE SOLD,
On THURSDAY the third Day
of August next,
A CARGO
of
NINETY-FOUR
PRIME, HEALTHY
NEGROES,
CONSISTING OF
Thirty-nine MEN, Fifteen Boys,
Twenty-four WOMEN, and
Sixteen GIRLS.
JUST ARRIVED,
In the Brigantine DEMBIA, *Fran-
cis Bare*, Master, from SIERRA-
LEON, by
DAVID & JOHN DEAS.

A bell from a Spanish mission

1640s–1670s

Virginia and Maryland pass a series of laws codifying the practice of enslaving African Americans.

1664

The English take New Amsterdam from the Dutch and rename it New York.

1680

The Pueblo Revolt in New Mexico temporarily drives the Spanish from the area.

1730s

The Great Awakening, a religious revival sparked by Jonathan Edwards, begins in New England and spreads throughout the colonies.

1675 1725 1775

England's Glorious Revolution brings William and Mary to the throne and produces a bill of rights.

1689

The Atlantic World

READING FOCUS

- What were the characteristics of the Native American world before the arrival of Columbus?

- What was life like in Europe during the Middle Ages and the Renaissance?

- What were the traditional societies of West Africa like?

- How did Columbus's voyages lead to the birth of the Atlantic World?

MAIN IDEA

Columbus's voyages to the Americas brought together and reshaped the differing cultures of the Americas, Europe, and West Africa.

KEY TERMS

migration
nomad
clan
barter
middle class
monarch
Magna Carta
Columbian Exchange
plantation

TARGET READING SKILL

Identify Supporting Details Copy the chart below. As you read, use the boxes to describe the three cultures before Columbus's voyages took place.

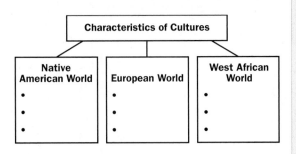

Setting the Scene A few hours after midnight on the morning of October 12, 1492, a sailor named Rodrigo de Triana spotted land. His ship, the *Pinta,* was part of an expedition authorized by Spain to find a water route to "the Indies" (India, China, and other Asian lands). The sailors thought they had reached their goal. Actually they were somewhere in the Caribbean Sea, probably approaching the island now called San Salvador. The source of their confusion was that Christopher Columbus, the expedition's leader, had underestimated the size of the earth. Columbus had probably realized his error, for he repeatedly misled the crew about the distance they had sailed. About two months after they had set sail, Columbus reported that the crew had lost patience, and that he encouraged them by "representing the profits they were about to acquire." He added that "having come so far, they had nothing to do but continue on to the Indies, till with the help of our Lord, they should arrive there." Two days later they sighted land.

Columbus was not the first European to reach the Americas. About 500 years earlier, Norsemen led by Leif Ericson had most likely sailed along the North American coast and probably stopped occasionally in present-day Maine and Newfoundland, Canada. Columbus's voyage had far greater importance, however, because of the explorers, conquerors, and settlers who followed him to the Western Hemisphere. Through Columbus, the separate parts of the Atlantic World—the Americas, Europe, and West Africa— became permanently linked. This would change forever the histories of the peoples on these continents.

This nineteenth-century American painting shows Columbus coming ashore in the Americas.

The Native American World

Today's Native Americans, or Indians, are descendants of the first people to live in the Americas. Many thousands of years ago, those first Americans arrived as part of a **migration,** or movement of people for the purpose of settling in a new place. They reached the Americas from Asia, most experts believe, by crossing what is now called the Bering Strait, a waterway off Alaska's west coast. During the last Ice Age, glaciers trapped much of the earth's ocean water in ice, causing sea levels to drop and exposing a "land bridge" that experts believe Asians crossed to reach North America.

Gradually the human population spread from the Arctic Circle to the southernmost tip of South America. Over thousands of years, Native American societies living in different regions developed a variety of distinct languages and cultures.

Native Peoples Across North America The North American continent varies greatly from region to region, and Native Americans adapted their ways of life to fit their local environments. The Inuit and Aleut peoples, for example, lived in the far north, on the coastal edges of North America. They were skilled at hunting on ice and snow. Other northern peoples, such as the Koyukon and Ingalik, were **nomads.** That is, they moved their homes regularly in search of food.

Native Americans of the Northwest Coast took advantage of the rich ocean fishing grounds nearby. In the Southwest, groups such as the Hopi and the Zuñi developed farming methods to suit their dry environment. Other southwestern groups, such as the Apache, were nomadic. In the center of the continent, Plains Indians traveled great distances on foot, hunting vast herds of buffalo that fulfilled many of their needs, from food to clothing to shelter.

In the Northeast, Indian peoples gathered wild plants and grew corn and other crops. They also hunted game such as deer, bear, and moose in the vast woodlands of the region. Native Americans of the Southeast included the Natchez, who settled the lower Mississippi River. Natchez towns included as many as several thousand inhabitants, who often built magnificent temples on raised mounds of earth.

Shared Customs and Beliefs Despite their cultural differences, Native American peoples had much in common. For example, many Native American societies were organized by kinship, or family relationships, rather than by social classes or by wealth or age. Individuals relied on their kin, or family, to fulfill many of their social needs, such as child care and education. Kinship groups were organized by clans. A **clan** is made up of groups of families who share a common ancestor.

Native American groups had similar religious beliefs. Indian peoples believed that the most powerful forces in the world are spiritual, and they followed traditional religious practices, or rituals, that recognized the power of these forces. Failure to perform these rituals, they believed, would cause disasters such as invasions, disease, or bad harvests. To preserve their beliefs and customs, Native Americans relied on oral history, or passing traditions from generation to generation by word of mouth. Elders told stories, sang songs, and provided instructions for ceremonies to young people, who later passed this knowledge on to their own children.

Trading Patterns Native American trading routes crisscrossed North America. For example, the Inuit traded copper from the Copper River in

VIEWING HISTORY This 1784 engraving shows a multifamily dwelling typical of the Nootka people of the Northwest Coast. **Analyzing Visual Information** *How does the engraving show the importance of fish in the Nootka diet?*

Focus on
GOVERNMENT

The Iroquois League Also called the Iroquois Confederacy or the Five Nations, the Iroquois League was a confederation of five tribes (Mohawk, Oneida, Onandaga, Cayuga, and Seneca) centered in present-day New York State. When the Tuscarora joined in 1722, it became known as the Six Nations.

According to tradition, the League was formed between 1570 and 1600 to put an end to constant warfare among the tribes and to provide a united force to withstand invasion. The League was governed by a council made up of clan and village chiefs. Voting in the council was by tribe, and a unanimous vote was required to declare war. The Iroquois were extremely successful in war, and subdued many of the neighboring tribes.

Following colonial settlement, the Iroquois traded beaver for firearms with the Europeans, and became important in the rivalry between French and British colonists. The confederacy was officially recognized by the British in 1722, and survived for more than 200 years.

southern Alaska for sharks' teeth collected by people living in coastal Washington. The Mohave of the Great Basin carried out **barter,** or trade, with people on the California coast, and then traded the coastal goods to the Pueblo in present-day Arizona and New Mexico.

Attitudes Toward the Land   One item that Native Americans never traded was land. In their view, the land could not be owned. They believed that people had a right to use land or to allow others to use it, but buying or selling land was unthinkable. Land, like all of nature, deserved respect. The Europeans who arrived in North America in the 1400s, however, had quite a different idea about land ownership. They frequently did not understand Indian attitudes and interpreted Native American references to land use to mean land ownership.

The European World

The voyages that brought Columbus and other Europeans to the Americas were a sign of Europe's rebirth. Between about A.D. 500 and 1300, a time known as the Middle Ages, or medieval period, Europeans had been too busy dealing with internal problems to give much thought to the world beyond their own continent.

The Early Middle Ages   The early part of the Middle Ages, roughly 500 to 1000, was marked by instability. Germanic tribes such as the Franks surged across the borders of the former Roman Empire. From the north, fierce Viking warriors came to loot and burn villages. In the south, the powerful Muslim empire spread from its birthplace in Arabia across North Africa and into what is now Spain. (The Muslim empire had arisen in the 600s, based on a new religion, Islam, inspired by the teachings of the prophet Muhammad.)

To protect themselves from these threats, Europeans created a political and economic system known as feudalism. Under feudalism, a powerful noble, or lord, divided his large landholdings among lesser lords. In return, they owed him military service and other favors. Peasants called serfs farmed the lord's manor, or estate, and gave him a portion of the harvest. They received his shelter and protection in return. Born into lifetime servitude, serfs had no education and knew little about the world outside the manor, which they were forbidden to leave.

The manor system produced everything a feudal society needed to survive. As a result, the trade links that had tied Europe to foreign lands during the Roman Empire largely died out.

Native American artists in present-day Kentucky created the beautiful stone mask (left). The Etowah neck ornament (right) is made of shell.

VIEWING HISTORY Asian spices were sold to Europeans in medieval marketplaces like this. **Drawing Conclusions** *What can you learn about medieval life from this marketplace?*

The Power of the Church   The Roman Catholic Church governed the spiritual life and daily activities of medieval Christians, both rich and poor. The head of the Church, the pope, claimed authority over emperors and kings, and often appointed them. The clergy, or Church officials who were authorized to perform religious ceremonies, often owned their own manors. Much of the clergy's power came from the fact that they were virtually the only educated people in medieval Europe. They alone could study the Bible and other holy writings of Christianity, so they controlled how the faith was communicated to the people. Christians were expected to obey Church authority completely.

After Muslims from Turkey seized Jerusalem, a city holy to both Christians and Muslims, the Church organized a series of military campaigns to retake the city. These holy wars, which took place between 1096 and 1291, were called the Crusades. The Crusaders failed to establish permanent Christian control of Jerusalem, but they did increase Europeans' awareness of the world beyond their borders. Returning home to Europe, Crusaders brought spices, fabrics, and other Asian goods they had looted in war. Europeans quickly developed a taste for these items, which helped revive Europe's trade with the outside world.

Signs of Change Meanwhile, Europe's economy had entered a period of new growth. New farming methods increased food supplies, which in turn led to population growth. More people, including runaway serfs, began moving to towns and cities that were growing up along trade routes. The growth of cities and trade in Europe created a new **middle class** of merchants, traders, and artisans who made and sold goods to the manors. It also revived the use of money, which had declined in the early part of the Middle Ages. Finally, it contributed to the eventual breakdown of the feudal system.

Europe's growing wealth also increased the power of **monarchs,** or those who rule over territories or states. Monarchs attracted the loyalty of the new middle class by protecting trade routes and keeping the peace. Strong monarchs sometimes clashed with one another. In 1066, the Duke of Normandy, who ruled a region in present-day France, conquered England. This event, called the Norman Conquest, led to a gradual blending of French and Anglo-Saxon cultures that became part of the English and American heritage.

Monarchs also clashed with their own nobles, sometimes over a king's attempts to impose heavy taxes. In 1215, England's King John, a weak and insensitive leader, was forced by his nobles to sign a document granting them various legal rights. That document, the **Magna Carta** or "Great Charter," not only shaped British government but also became the foundation for future American ideals of liberty and justice. One clause declared:

KEY DOCUMENTS
❝ *No freeman shall be arrested or imprisoned or dispossessed or . . . in any way harmed . . . except by the lawful judgment of his peers or by the law of the land.* ❞

—Magna Carta, 1215

Ambitious rulers such as King John also came into conflict with the Church. For a time, strong popes prevailed in these struggles, but by the 1200s, monarchies were growing stronger as papal supremacy declined.

The Renaissance Begins The 1300s in Italy signaled the beginning of a new era for Europe. Called the Renaissance, a French word meaning "rebirth," it was a time of enormous creativity and rapid change. The Renaissance spread throughout western Europe and peaked in the 1500s. It was a quest for knowledge in nearly every field of study, including art, literature, science, and philosophy.

Freed from the rigid thinking of the medieval past, Renaissance thinkers and artists rediscovered the art and learning of ancient Greece and Rome and of Muslim culture. They used reason and experimentation to explore the physical world and the individual's place in it. This philosophy is called humanism.

Marco Polo Europeans learned about Asia not only from the Crusaders, but also from a fascinating account of China written by Marco Polo. Born in the mid-1200s to a wealthy family of traders, Polo grew up in the Italian city of Venice. In 1271, when Polo was still a teenager, he left with his father and uncle on an overland journey to China. Their caravan is shown in the illustration below. They remained in China for more than 15 years. During this time, Polo saw many parts of that vast country while conducting business for China's emperor, Kublai Khan.

Polo returned to Italy in 1295, but he soon was briefly imprisoned in Genoa, a city that was a rival of Venice. There he dictated the story of his travels to a fellow prisoner. The book, commonly known as *The Travels of Marco Polo,* was a huge hit in Italy. Its descriptions of the wonders of Asia sent European merchants scrambling to set up trading missions to the East.

The Renaissance Man The idea of the Renaissance is embodied in what we now call the Renaissance man, the person who is skilled and knowledgeable in all the arts and sciences. This concept came from Leon Battista Alberti (1404–1472), who said that "a man can do all things if he will."

Today, Leonardo da Vinci (1452–1519) is regarded as the ultimate Renaissance man. He was a painter, sculptor, architect, and musician. His *Mona Lisa* (right) still fascinates viewers. In addition, Leonardo was a scientist and engineer; some of his inventions, such as a type of helicopter (below), were centuries ahead of their time. In his notebooks, Leonardo combined a spirit of scientific inquiry with extraordinary powers of observation and artistic skill. He studied anatomy in order to be a better sculptor—even dissecting corpses to view the muscles, skeleton, and organs—thus making contributions to both art and science.

The most admired art works of the Italian Renaissance, such as Michelangelo's sculpture of David and his paintings in the Sistine Chapel, and Leonardo da Vinci's *Mona Lisa*, depicted human beings and their emotions realistically.

The Renaissance Spreads North Eventually, the Renaissance spread northward from its Italian birthplace. By the late 1500s, it had reached much of Europe. Among the artists of this Northern Renaissance was the English playwright and poet William Shakespeare, generally regarded as the most gifted writer in history.

The works of writers like Shakespeare became available to many more Europeans thanks to the invention of the printing press. In 1455, Johann Gutenberg used a process involving movable metal type to produce a Bible. This invention set off a communications revolution over the next century, as some 200 million books came off European printing presses.

A large number of these books were Bibles, which now circulated among a wider audience. The printing revolution came at a time when critics, angry at corruption among the clergy, were calling for Church reform. In 1517, this criticism flared into a revolt known as the Reformation. A German monk named Martin Luther claimed that the Bible, not the Church, was the true authority in spiritual matters. Luther's followers called themselves Protestants because they protested Church authority.

The Rise of Nations During the Renaissance, government by local nobles and the Church gradually declined. Instead, monarchs began to combine smaller areas into the larger nation-states we know today. For the first time, Europeans began thinking of themselves as citizens of nations, such as France, England, or Portugal.

The young nations soon started competing for the highly profitable Asian trade, which had become important after the Crusades. In 1400, the only way to reach Asia was still by land, since Europeans did not have the technology to explore the faster sea route without becoming hopelessly lost. With the help of instruments developed by Renaissance scientists, however, long-range sea travel finally became possible. Sailors could use a compass to determine direction when neither the coastline nor the sun was visible. In addition, the astrolabe and the quadrant allowed ship captains to find their location far from visible land.

In 1418, Prince Henry of Portugal established a school for mariners. His seamen developed the final tool necessary for long-range voyages: the caravel, a ship that could sail against the wind as well as with it. In 1488, a navigator trained at this school, Bartolomeu Dias, sailed around the southern tip of Africa, the Cape of Good Hope. Nine years later, another Portuguese mariner, Vasco da Gama, sailed from Portugal to India. The first sea route from Europe to Asia was now open.

Portugal had a serious competitor, however. In 1469, Isabella of Castile and Ferdinand of Aragon were married, thereby uniting their two powerful kingdoms in what is present-day Spain. They launched a successful campaign to drive the Muslim empire out of Spain. Isabella also wanted to surpass Portugal in the race to explore new sea routes, and to bring Christianity to new lands. So, as her ships dropped anchor along the west coast of Africa, they carried not only trade goods but Christian missionaries as well.

The West African World

Europeans and Africans had first met in ancient times, when a wide trading network of land and sea routes thrived throughout the Mediterranean region. Much of this contact stopped during the Middle Ages, but it resumed during the Renaissance. European traders began to trade salt for gold from North African middlemen, who obtained it from their trading partners in the interior of West Africa. Europeans wanted to get around these middlemen and go directly to the sources of gold. This was the prize for which Portugal and Spain competed in the 1400s as their ships explored Africa's Atlantic coast.

Early relations between Europeans and West Africans were mostly peaceful. Portugal established trade ties with wealthy coastal kingdoms that produced much of the gold. The Portuguese built a string of forts along the coast for their ships to load and unload trade goods. Africans ran the trading operations and set their own prices. The Netherlands, France, and England soon launched expeditions to the region to set up similar trade arrangements.

West African Geography and Cultures   Like other peoples, West Africans adapted their culture to their geographic surroundings. Rain forests covered a large band of coastal land in the south. Some of the continent's earliest societies evolved in this resource-rich region, where people hunted, fished, mined, and farmed the land.

Farther north lay a wide expanse of savanna, or tropical grassland with scattered trees, where nomadic peoples hunted and raised livestock. Merchants did a brisk business obtaining gold and other goods from the forest regions and trading them to merchants in the north. The deserts of West Africa remained largely uninhabited. But scattered towns did arise at major watering holes, where camel caravans loaded with trade goods stopped to rest.

As in the Americas, West African societies were organized according to kinship groups. Often, all residents of a town or a city belonged to kinship groups that had a common ancestor. This type of organization is called a lineage. African lineage groups provided the types of support that clans did for Native Americans.

West Africans generally shared certain religious beliefs. They worshipped a Supreme Being, as well as many lesser gods and goddesses, or spirits. These spirits were thought to inhabit everything in the natural world, from animals to trees to stones. Humans also were thought to be living spirits both before and after death. Africans appealed to the spirits of their ancestors for help in their daily lives. Information about religious beliefs, as well as family stories and laws, were handed down from generation to generation through oral tradition. As in the Americas, oral histories gave kinship groups a sense of identity.

Kingdoms and Trade   Several well-established kingdoms ruled parts of West Africa for centuries. One was Benin, which arose in the late 1200s in the coastal forest. Artists left a record of their society in a series of bronze plaques that once decorated the palace of the king, or Oba. A European traveler who had visited the capital of Benin observed: "This city is about a league [three miles] long from gate to gate; it has no wall but is surrounded by a large moat, very wide and deep, which suffices for its defense. . . . Its houses are made of mud walls covered with palm leaves." The streets of Benin were wide and clean, and they led to a grand palace.

READING CHECK
Why did exploration by European mariners increase during this time?

Gold from the forest regions of West Africa was traded to other parts of Africa and to Europeans. This gold pendant was made by the Baule people.

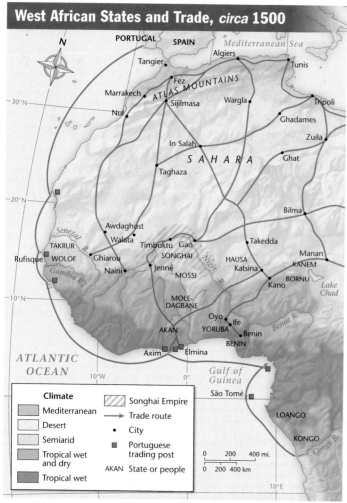

Climate

- Mediterranean
- Desert
- Semiarid
- Tropical wet and dry
- Tropical wet

Songhai Empire
→ Trade route
• City
■ Portuguese trading post
AKAN State or people

0 200 400 mi.
0 200 400 km

MAP SKILLS By 1500, extensive trade routes crisscrossed West Africa. *Movement Why do you think the Portuguese established their trading posts along Africa's west coast?*

Benin's wealth came from trade. The kingdom produced goods such as palm oil, ivory, and beautiful woods. Some of the finest artwork of the time came from Benin, especially sculpted heads created in a unique style. Before long, sculptors added figures with beards and helmets. These figures represented the Portuguese. A strong Oba had come to the throne in 1481, and had established friendly and profitable relations with the Portuguese.

Further west, between the coastal rain forest region and the Sahara, the Songhai empire thrived from the 1460s to 1591. Songhai's best-known monarch, Askia Muhammad, created a complex government with separate departments for defense, banking, and farming. A bureaucracy of paid officials enforced laws, collected taxes, negotiated with other nations, and kept the peace. Many trade caravans passed through Songhai—and paid heavy fees to do so.

Songhai's capital, Timbuktu, was a center of learning. Most of Timbuktu's scholars (like those in medieval Europe) studied religion. In Timbuktu, that religion was Islam, which had reached West Africa around 1050 through trade and by invasion from the north. Askia Muhammad, a devout Muslim, had made Songhai a Muslim empire. Yet most people, especially outside the cities, still followed traditional African beliefs.

Slavery in Africa Africans, like Europeans, believed in the private ownership of goods and property. Yet they differed from Europeans in their attitudes toward land and people. In Europe, land was scarce and thus very valuable. In Africa, labor was often valued more than land. The power of leaders was determined by the number of people they ruled, not the amount of land they controlled. Growing kingdoms such as Benin and Songhai needed increasing numbers of workers. As in many other societies, slaves provided the labor.

The most likely people to be enslaved in Africa were those who had been cut off from their lineage. Most slaves had probably been captured in war, although many were kidnapped in slave raids carried out by rival ethnic groups. Africans' concept of slavery differed from slavery as it developed in the Americas. In Africa, slaves became adopted members of the kinship group that enslaved them. They could marry into a lineage, even into the high ranks of society, and move out of their slave role. Children of slaves were not presumed to be born into slavery. Finally, slaves carried out a variety of roles, working as soldiers and administrators as well as laborers.

In the 1500s, Europeans began to exchange valuable goods, such as guns, for slaves sold by coastal societies such as Benin. Both sides profited greatly. The Africans obtained advanced technology, and the Europeans obtained labor for use in large farming operations in the Americas and elsewhere. As time wore on, however, Europeans demanded more and more slaves. Those who resisted dealing in the human cargo became themselves the victims of bloody slave raids.

The Birth of the Atlantic World

In January 1492, Spain's Queen Isabella and King Ferdinand authorized the Italian-born mariner Christopher Columbus to make contact with the people of "the lands of India." Much to his pleasure, they made him "High Admiral of the Ocean Sea and . . . Governor of the islands and continent which I should discover," as Columbus wrote later.

The Voyages of Columbus Columbus's commission appealed to his ambition, but the Spanish nobles and clergy also had reasons for wanting his voyage to succeed:

1. Columbus hoped to enrich his family and to gain honor and fame. He also planned to conquer non-Christian lands and convert their peoples to Christianity. Like many people of the time, he believed that other cultures and religions were inferior to his own, and he felt that God wanted him to bring Christianity to other lands.

2. Columbus's royal patrons shared his desire to spread Christianity, but they had economic motives as well. Muslims controlled the overland trade routes connecting Europe and Asia. Europeans wanted to bypass the Muslims and trade directly for eastern spices and herbs.

3. Portuguese sailors had found an eastern route to India by sailing around Africa. If the Spanish could find an easier, western route, they might gain an advantage in their rivalry with Portugal.

Shortly before sunrise on August 3, 1492, three ships under Columbus's command set sail from Spain. The *Niña, Pinta,* and *Santa Maria* reached the Americas roughly two months later. The Spanish received a warm welcome from the first Native Americans they met, the Tainos. Columbus collected the gifts given him by the Tainos—and took others by force—before returning to Spain. He also took back with him some Native Americans, whom he called "Indians" because he thought he had reached the Indies.

Upon his return to Spain, Columbus received the honors he had sought, including the governorship of present-day Hispaniola, an island in the Caribbean. Eventually, he made four voyages to the Americas. Columbus proved to be a far better admiral than governor. The Spanish settlers on Hispaniola complained to the Spanish government of harsh and unfair treatment. Columbus lost his governorship, as well as his prestige at court. And despite increasing evidence that he had found a new continent, he clung to his claim that he had reached the Indies. In 1506, Columbus died a disappointed man, never knowing how much he had changed the course of history.

The Impact of Columbus's Voyages Others, however, realized the importance of Columbus's findings. Beginning in 1499, the Italian seaman Amerigo Vespucci made several voyages along the coast of South America. He suggested that it might be a continent previously unknown to Europeans, "what we may rightly call a New World." In 1507, the German mapmaker Martin Waldseemüller read Vespucci's account and printed the first map showing the "New World" as separate from Asia. Waldseemüller named the unfamiliar lands "America," after Vespucci.

Columbus's voyages changed far more than maps. They also launched a new era of transatlantic trade known as the **Columbian Exchange.** European ships returned with exciting new foods from the Americas. The potato quickly became the new food of Europe's poor, helping to save them from famine. In return, Europeans brought to the Americas crops such as wheat, and domestic

Sounds of an Era

Listen to Columbus's description of his first voyage and other sounds from the era of exploration of the Americas.

Christopher Columbus was born Cristoforo Colombo in the Italian city of Genoa in 1451. His father was a merchant and worked in the wool industry, and his mother was the daughter of a wool weaver. Columbus wrote volumes about his voyages, yet we know little about his early life.

animals such as the cow and the horse. They also brought firearms and the wheel and axle. Finally, Europeans introduced their culture to the Americas, including European laws, languages, and customs.

One European import, however, caused immense suffering among Native Americans: disease. Explorers and soldiers infected the native populations with smallpox, typhus, measles, and other deadly diseases to which the Indians had not developed resistance. These diseases spread rapidly along the extensive Native American trade network, killing hundreds of thousands and weakening the social structure of Native American cultures.

Meanwhile, Europeans saw the New World as a source of wealth. Rival nations all wanted to gain land in the Americas. Resenting Spain's claim to the whole Western Hemisphere, Portugal sent a complaint to the pope. In 1494, at the urging of Pope Alexander, Portugal signed the Treaty of Tordesillas. It drew an imaginary line around the world called the Line of Demarcation. Spain was to rule over lands west of the line, including most of the Americas. Portugal would receive the rest, including Brazil. To this day, people in most of South America speak Spanish, but the language of Brazil is Portuguese.

Slave Labor in the Americas To produce the American foods that brought a high price in Europe, Portugal and Spain established large farms called **plantations.** At first, soldiers forced Native Americans to work on the plantations. Unaccustomed to that type of work and weakened by disease, these slaves did not provide a reliable labor force. Europeans then turned to West Africa.

The European settlers' enormous need for labor transformed the West African slave trade into an industry. Historians still debate the number of Africans who were abducted from their homeland and taken to the Americas, but it appears that some 9–11 million people were enslaved. Even such huge numbers, though, cannot portray the full horror of slavery. Slaves were regarded as mere property and were treated no better than farm animals. In the Americas, slavery was a lifetime sentence from which there was no escape. And in West Africa, the loss of many young and healthy people to the slave trade had a damaging effect on society for many years to come.

VIEWING HISTORY A Native American in Mexico drew this picture of a smallpox victim being comforted by a healer. The squiggle near the healer's mouth represents spoken words. **Recognizing Cause and Effect** Why do you think smallpox did so much damage to Indian populations throughout the Americas?

Section 1 Assessment

READING COMPREHENSION

1. (a) How were **clans** important in Native American societies? (b) How was lineage important in West African societies?

2. How were the rise of the **middle class** and the increased power of **monarchs** related?

3. What was the Renaissance?

4. What was the **Columbian Exchange?**

CRITICAL THINKING AND WRITING

5. Recognizing Bias What beliefs influenced Europeans' views of themselves and other cultures? How did these beliefs affect their actions?

6. Writing to Inform Explain how geography contributed to (a) the diversity of Native American peoples, (b) the rivalry between Spain and Portugal, and (c) the wealth of Songhai.

For: An activity on the Columbian Exchange
Visit: PHSchool.com
Web Code: mrd-0011

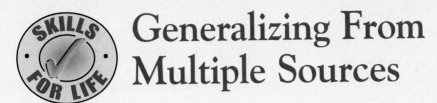

Generalizing From Multiple Sources

A generalization is a broad statement based on multiple examples or facts, often from various sources. Valid generalizations are useful for summing up information, but "sweeping generalizations"—those that are too broad and do not allow for exceptions—can be misleading. For example, you might generalize from your experience that *most* dogs like to be petted. But believing that *all* dogs *always* like to be petted could get you into serious trouble.

The time line and the quotation below relate to Christopher Columbus's effort to find financial backing for his first voyage. Friar Marchena, mentioned in the letter, was a priest whom Columbus had met in Spain.

1484 Columbus presents his proposal to King John II of Portugal.

1486 Columbus is summoned to the court of Ferdinand and Isabella of Spain.

1490–1491 Columbus and his brother request backing from the Italians, English, and French. All their requests are rejected.

| 1480 | • 1485 • | • | 1490 | • | 1495 |

1485 After a panel of experts reviews Columbus's calculations about the size of the earth and the ocean, they advise King John against supporting the venture.

1487 or 1488 Isabella's advisors recommend rejection of Columbus's proposal, again based on his calculations.

1492 Columbus again appears before Queen Isabella; again, her advisors reject his proposal, this time based on financial considerations. Before he reaches home, however, Columbus is overtaken by a messenger from the queen. She has reconsidered and agrees to finance the voyage.

LEARN THE SKILL

Use the following steps to make generalizations:

1. **Identify the main ideas of each source.** Consider both the information and the time period.

2. **List relevant facts.** Determine which facts in the sources support each main idea. You may find that some facts are not relevant to your topic.

3. **Find a common element.** Look for general trends, or a common thread, in the ideas stated in the sources. Also look for patterns or trends in the details and facts.

4. **Make a generalization.** "Add up" the facts and ideas in your sources to make a general statement. Be sure that you can support your generalization with facts and that it is not too broad. Valid generalizations often include words such as *many, most, often, usually, some, few,* and *sometimes.* Faulty generalizations may include words such as *all, none, always, never,* and *every.*

PRACTICE THE SKILL

Answer the following questions:

1. **(a)** What is the main idea of the time line? How do you know? **(b)** What time period does it cover? **(c)** What is the main idea of the excerpt? **(d)** What time period does the excerpt refer to?

2. **(a)** How many facts does the time line present to support its main idea? **(b)** What are two of those

Letter to the Spanish Monarchs

"Your majesties know that I spent seven years in the court pestering you for this; never in the whole time was there found a pilot, nor a sailor, nor a mariner, nor a philosopher, nor an expert in any other science who did not state that my enterprise was false, so I never found support from anyone, save father Friar Antonio de Marchena, beyond that of eternal God."

—Christopher Columbus, *circa* 1501

facts? **(c)** Describe how Columbus supports his main idea. **(d)** Is this support reliable? Explain.

3. **(a)** What main idea do both sources share? **(b)** How does the time line support the quotation and vice versa? In other words, what is the benefit of having these two kinds of sources?

4. What valid generalizations can you make about **(a)** Columbus, **(b)** his contemporaries, and **(c)** monarchs in the late 1400s?

APPLY THE SKILL

See the Chapter Review and Assessment for another opportunity to apply this skill.

European Colonization of the Americas

READING FOCUS

- How did the Spanish explore and build an empire in the Americas?
- What happened to the two earliest English colonies and why?
- What kinds of settlements did the French establish in North America?
- How were the New England, Middle, and Southern Colonies settled?

MAIN IDEA

After 1492, the Spanish began building an empire in the Americas, and in the 1600s, France established fur-trading posts in present-day Canada. In 1607, the English began establishing colonies along the Atlantic Coast.

KEY TERMS

conquistador
colony
missionary
charter
indentured servant
Puritans
Mayflower Compact
religious tolerance
proprietary colony

TARGET READING SKILL

Recognize Multiple Causes Copy the chart below. As you read, fill in the purposes of the settlements made by each nation.

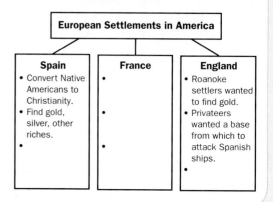

European Settlements in America		
Spain	**France**	**England**
• Convert Native Americans to Christianity. • Find gold, silver, other riches. •	• • •	• Roanoke settlers wanted to find gold. • Privateers wanted a base from which to attack Spanish ships.

VIEWING HISTORY This wood engraving shows the founding of St. Augustine. **Determining Relevance** *Why are the tasks shown here important to founding a colony?*

Setting the Scene On August 28, 1565, a Spanish force of 11 ships and roughly 2,000 men under the command of Pedro Menéndez de Avilés sailed into a bay in northeastern Florida. Because August 28 is the day the Catholic Church honors St. Augustine, Menéndez de Avilés named the bay St. Augustine. He also gave that name to a colony he established there.

A year earlier, France had built Fort Caroline to the north of St. Augustine. In fact, Menéndez de Avilés had been sent not just to build a Spanish colony but to eliminate the French one, which Spain's King Philip II saw as a threat to Spanish control of the region. With the help of two Native American guides, a force of Spanish soldiers marched to Fort Caroline. They destroyed the fort and killed its inhabitants. Many of the French were Protestants, and the Spanish hung the French bodies on trees with a sign saying "Not as Frenchmen, but as heretics." (A heretic is someone who holds religious beliefs opposed to those of the established church or religion.) While Fort Caroline had lasted only a year, St. Augustine has lasted to this day. It is the oldest continuously settled city in the United States.

The founding of St. Augustine illustrates several elements of Europe's colonization of the Americas. First, the competition among European powers for land in the Americas was sometimes violent. Second, Europeans were motivated not only by a desire for power and wealth, but by religious reasons as well. In addition, Native Americans were drawn into the conflicts among the Europeans. Later they would also fight the Europeans over land. Finally, like the city of St. Augustine, the European presence in the Americas was there to stay.

Building a Spanish Empire

The Spanish explorers of the Americas had three major motives for conquering the region. They wanted to spread the Christian religion, gain wealth, and win fame. In other words, they went to the Americas for "God, gold, and glory."

Spain's Major Explorers In the 50 years after Columbus's death, the discoveries of Spanish explorers greatly increased Europeans' knowledge about the lands from Florida in the East to the shores of the Pacific Ocean in the West.

Juan Ponce de León had only been in the Americas a few years when he heard tales of a spring that could make people young again. While searching in vain for this "fountain of youth," he explored and named Florida in 1513. Also in 1513, Vasco Núñez de Balboa led a group of Spaniards and Native Americans across the Isthmus of Panama. Balboa and his Spanish companions thus became the first known Europeans to see the Pacific Ocean from the American continent. And in 1519, Ferdinand Magellan, a Portuguese sailor who explored on behalf of Spain, began an historic expedition that eventually circumnavigated, or sailed around the entire earth. Unfortunately, Magellan himself died before the expedition was completed.

In 1519, Hernán Cortés was sent by the Spanish governor of Cuba to conquer the vast empire ruled by the Aztec people in Mexico. Located where Mexico City now stands, the Aztec capital, Tenochtitlán, had 150,000 to 300,000 inhabitants (perhaps more) and was one of the world's largest urban centers. The Aztecs governed some 10 to 12 million people. Cortés had only about 600 soldiers, but he also had thousands of allies among Native Americans who hated the Aztecs. Not only had the Aztecs conquered their neighbors, but they had also sacrificed untold numbers of them in religious ceremonies. By 1521, Cortés had destroyed Tenochtitlán and conquered one of the largest empires in the world.

Like Cortés, Francisco Pizarro was a **conquistador,** or Spanish conqueror of the Americas. He conquered the empire of the Incas, centered in present-day Peru, South America.

A Spanish Empire As the Spanish conquistadors explored and conquered, they also started settlements that they hoped would grow into **colonies,** areas settled by immigrants who continue to be ruled by their parent country. By the 1550s, the Spanish colonies amounted to a large empire in Mexico, Central America, South America, and the islands of the Caribbean Sea.

These colonies made the Spanish wealthy. Using the labor of enslaved Native Americans and Africans, the Spanish mined vast amounts of silver and gold from the mountains of Mexico and Peru. They also established farms and ranches that produced a variety of goods.

The Spanish dealt with Native Americans differently than did other European conquerors. They did not try to drive Indians out of their lands. Instead they forced them to become a part of the colonial economy. One method they used was known as the *encomienda* system, under which Native Americans were forced to work for the profit of an individual Spaniard. In return, the Spaniard was supposed to ensure the well-being of the workers.

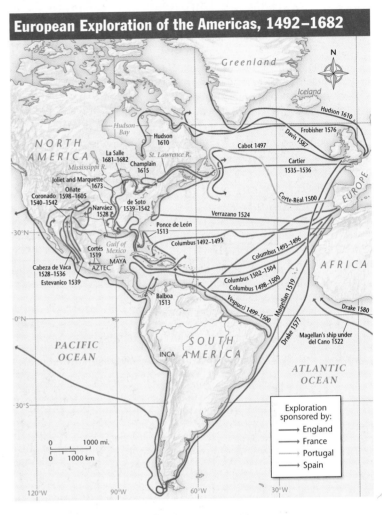

European Exploration of the Americas, 1492–1682

MAP SKILLS For more than a century after Columbus's voyages, explorers sailed on behalf of any power that would sponsor them. Cabot and Verrazano were Italian, and Hudson was English.
Movement *What nations sponsored Cabot, Verrazano, and Hudson?*

VIEWING HISTORY This painting of a missionary pierced by a lance depicts the Pueblo Revolt of 1680. **Recognizing Cause and Effect** *What caused the Pueblo Revolt?*

Because the Spanish and Native Americans lived together on the same land, in time a population arose that was a mixture of both peoples. They were called *mestizos,* which is Spanish for "mixed."

The Spanish Push North

Cortés and Pizarro strengthened Spain's grip on Mexico and Peru. Other conquistadors explored the southern parts of what would become the United States.

For example, the Spaniard Alvar Núñez Cabeza de Vaca and an enslaved African named Estevanico were part of an expedition that was shipwrecked in 1528 near present-day Galveston, Texas. With two other survivors, they wandered through the Gulf Coast region for eight years before being rescued. Estevanico later traveled into the American Southwest in search of seven golden cities that were rumored to exist there. Francisco Vásquez de Coronado, too, searched for the fabled golden cities. Between 1540 and 1542, he traveled through present-day Texas and pushed north as far as Kansas. In 1539, Hernán de Soto landed in Florida and traveled westward. He and his men were probably the first Spaniards to cross the Mississippi River.

Forts for Defense The regions explored by Cabeza de Vaca, Estevanico, de Soto, and others did not seem to offer much in riches or farming possibilities. For this reason, few of the approximately 450,000 Spanish immigrants to the Americas before 1650 settled in the lands that are now the United States.

As a result, the Spanish government tried to encourage settlement in certain neglected regions, such as the Southeast Coast. The Spanish built bases in Florida to protect their ships carrying silver and gold from Cuba to Spain. St. Augustine is the only Florida settlement that still survives. In the Southwest, the conquistador Juan de Oñate and several hundred settlers claimed an area they called New Mexico in 1598. (Spanish New Mexico included parts of present-day Arizona and Texas.) Finally, the Spanish began to consider settlements in California in the hopes of keeping their European rivals out of the region. Major efforts to colonize this region, however, did not begin until the 1700s.

Missionaries The Spanish settlements that eventually dotted the South and West were forts, or presidios, most of them occupied by a few soldiers. The survival of these Spanish outposts was due in large part to the hard work of a few dozen Catholic missionaries. **Missionaries** are people who are sent out by their church to teach people their religion. In North America, the missionaries converted Native Americans to Christianity and established dozens of missions—headquarters where the missionaries lived and worked.

Resistance to the Spanish Some Native Americans fiercely resisted the Spanish, but much of this resistance was disorganized. In New Mexico, however, the Pueblo people united in what is called the Pueblo Revolt of 1680. By the 1670s, widespread sickness and drought had reduced the Pueblo population. Seeking to reverse this decline, the Pueblo began to return to their traditional religious practices, which the Spanish had tried to stamp out. A religious leader named Popé inspired the Pueblo to revolt. In August 1680, with the help of their Apache allies, the Pueblo people in New Mexico rose up and drove the Spanish out of Santa Fe. Years passed before the Spanish were able to return and rebuild. Similar Native American rebellions also occurred in Florida.

English Colonization

In the race to take advantage of the opportunities in the Americas, the Spanish were soon far ahead. Among the other European nations, England was the most determined and, in time, the most successful.

English Explorers   Several explorers sailed to the Americas for England before the 1600s. Although none discovered fabulous riches as the Spanish had, they did greatly expand England's knowledge of the North American coast.

John Cabot was the first known explorer sailing for the English to cross the Atlantic. He may have reached present-day Newfoundland, Canada, in 1497. Sir Martin Frobisher made three voyages across the Atlantic Ocean in the 1500s. Like Cabot, he was searching for the Northwest Passage, a trade route to Asia that would go past or through the continent of North America. Henry Hudson explored for both the English and the Dutch. On his third voyage, in 1609, he explored the river later named for him in present-day New York. When he realized that it was not the Northwest Passage, he turned back. In 1610, he discovered present-day Hudson Bay.

Sir Francis Drake was the most famous of England's "sea dogs," or privateers. (A privateer is a privately owned ship, or the captain of such a ship, hired by a government to attack foreign ships.) Elizabeth I, the Protestant queen of England from 1558 to 1603, authorized the sea dogs to attack the ships of Catholic Spain. Drake's raids on St. Augustine and other Spanish port cities in the Americas severely weakened the finances of the Spanish empire. Earlier, during his 1577–1580 voyage around the world, Drake had made his way into San Francisco Bay and north along the Pacific coast of the present-day United States.

England's Sir Francis Drake became the first sea captain to sail his own ship around the globe.

The Roanoke Disaster   By Drake's time, the English had decided that they, like the Spanish, should have American colonies. They had several reasons:

1. Privateers were sailing far from England in search of riches. They wanted a base in the Americas from which they could attack Spanish ships and cities.
2. Europeans were still convinced that they could find a Northwest Passage through the Americas. When they did find such a passage, they reasoned, they would need supply stations in North America for their ships.
3. English merchants also wanted new markets. Some hoped that a growing population in the colonies would someday become buyers of English cloth and other products.
4. Some English people thought the Americas would be a good place to send those who could not find work or homes in England.

With these reasons in mind, the sea dog Sir Walter Raleigh tried twice to start a colony on Roanoke Island, off the coast of present-day North Carolina. Raleigh's first attempt, in 1585, ended when the starving settlers abandoned the colony and returned home. Two years later, there was a second attempt, and how it ended remains a mystery to this day. In 1590, a supply expedition from England found only empty buildings at the settlement. On a doorpost was carved the only clue to the settlers' fate—the word *Croatoan,* an early form of the name of a nearby Native American group. Whether the settlers joined the Indians, or fought them and were defeated, is not known.

The Jamestown Settlement   In 1606, several Englishmen made plans to establish another colony. They first had to obtain a **charter,** or certificate of permission, from the king. The charter allowed them to form what is now called a joint-stock company—a company funded and run by a group of investors who share the company's profits and losses. In 1607, the Virginia

READING CHECK

Why was the Roanoke colony settled, and what happened to it?

Company sent about a hundred colonists to Virginia, the region that Raleigh had reached and named two decades earlier. The settlers called their new village Jamestown in honor of their king, James I.

Jamestown nearly failed, for several reasons. First, most of the settlers were not used to doing the hard work required to start a settlement. Many had come to get rich quickly, so they ignored the daily tasks necessary for their survival and instead searched feverishly for gold. Second, the village was little better than a swamp swarming with disease-bearing mosquitoes. Lastly, the colony suffered from poor leadership. The settlers squabbled about minor matters even when they were in danger of starving. In early 1608, however, a brave and experienced soldier named John Smith emerged as a strong leader. Smith warned the settlers:

> 66 You must obey this now for a law, that he that will not work shall not eat . . . for the labors of thirty or forty honest and industrious men shall not be consumed to maintain a hundred and fifty idle loiterers. 99
> —John Smith

Unfortunately for the colonists, Smith soon left the Virginia colony because of an injury. The colony suffered from starvation and sickness for its first ten years. One particularly difficult period from October 1609 to March 1610 was remembered as the "Starving Time." Only the food and water provided by Native Americans kept the colonists alive.

King James made Virginia a royal colony in 1624 and appointed a governor to lead it. Beginning in 1614, Virginia also had a legislature, or lawmaking assembly made up of representatives from the colony. Although no one understood it in these terms at the time, this legislature, called the House of Burgesses, was the first example of limited self-government in the English colonies.

Growing Tobacco
During the difficult early years, one thing—tobacco—saved the Virginia colonists from failing completely. This plant was native to the Western Hemisphere. In 1614, colonist John Rolfe shipped some tobacco to Europe, where it quickly became popular. Soon tobacco was the basis of the colony's economy. In order to cash in on the tobacco boom, settlers carved out plantations on the banks of the James, York, Rappahannock, and Potomac rivers, and along the shores of Chesapeake Bay. They established their plantations close to waterways, so that they could grow and transport their tobacco more easily.

Labor for Plantations
Planters, as owners of these plantations were called, needed laborers to work their tobacco fields. One way to obtain these laborers was to promise them land when they arrived in the colony. Over time, the custom developed of giving each "head," or person who came to the colony, the right to fifty acres of land.

Many people, however, did not have the money for the voyage. To pay for the crossing, they became **indentured servants.** These people had to work for a master for a period of time, usually seven years, under a contract called an indenture. In return for their work, their master paid the cost of their voyage to Virginia and gave them food and shelter.

Historians estimate that between 100,000 and 150,000 men and women came as servants to work in the fields of Virginia and Maryland during the

VIEWING HISTORY This indentured servant is bundling and packing dried tobacco leaves. **Determining Relevance** *What was the relationship of tobacco to the need for inexpensive labor, such as indentured servants or slaves?*

1600s. Most of them were 18 to 22 years of age, unmarried, and poor. Among Virginia's indentured servants were some Africans, the first to settle in the present-day United States. The first group of about 20 Africans arrived in 1619, and their numbers remained small.

Pushing West As the population of Virginia increased, settlers pushed farther west in search of new farmland, causing clashes with the Native American inhabitants. These clashes led, in turn, to Bacon's Rebellion which showed that the frontier settlers were unwilling to tolerate a government that was not concerned about their interests.

The French in North America

The English were not the only Europeans interested in the East Coast of North America. The French, too, had been exploring the region for decades, in search of trading opportunities.

French Explorers One early French expedition was led by Giovanni da Verrazano, an Italian who sailed for the French. Searching for the Northwest Passage, he explored the coast of North America from present-day North Carolina to Newfoundland, and entered New York harbor in 1524. Jacques Cartier made three voyages to Canada (1534–1542). On the basis of Cartier's explorations, the French king claimed a region called New France. It included not only the land covered by present-day Canada, but also parts of what is now the northern United States.

In 1608, Samuel de Champlain founded the first successful French colony in North America at Quebec in present-day Canada. Champlain also mapped the Atlantic shores as far as Massachusetts, and traveled inland to present-day Lake Champlain (1609) and Lake Huron (1615).

The Fur Trade The French discovered that a product from North America, fur, could be sold for great gain in Europe. Clothing made from the skins of deer, beaver, and other animals became highly fashionable in Europe in the 1600s. Native Americans trapped these animals, collected their furs, and traded them to the French. The fur trade determined the shape of New France. By the late 1600s, it was a long, narrow colony stretching far into the interior of Canada, along the St. Lawrence River and the Great Lakes. New France clung to the waterways because, as in Virginia, water was vital for transporting goods.

English Colonies in New England

While the French were building the fur trade in New France, the English were beginning new colonies along the Atlantic Coast. Known as New England, this region included land that became the states of Connecticut, Rhode Island, Massachusetts, Vermont, New Hampshire, and Maine.

Plymouth Colony The first successful colony in New England was the result of religious conflicts in England. In 1534, England's King Henry VIII had broken with the Catholic Church and had founded the Anglican Church, England's national church. Some of the English, however, complained that the Anglican Church continued too many Catholic practices and traditions. Because they wanted what they considered a "purer" kind of church, they were called **Puritans.** Some Puritans started separate churches of their

Wampum belts, like this Iroquois example, served as currency in trade between Native Americans and Europeans.

own and were called Separatists. Both Puritans and Separatists were persecuted, or attacked because of their beliefs.

One group of Separatists, those who came to be called the Pilgrims, decided to make a new home in North America, where they hoped they would be free to worship as they wished. In 1620, a group of roughly 100 Pilgrims sailed to New England on the *Mayflower*. As the ship neared shore, some non-Separatists on board threatened to go off and live by themselves. Afraid that the group would break up, the Pilgrims made a compact, or agreement, called the **Mayflower Compact.** In it, the settlers agreed to obey all of their government's laws. As they put it:

KEY DOCUMENTS 66 *We . . . do . . . combine ourselves together into a civil body politic, for our better ordering and preservation . . . [and to] frame such just and equal laws . . . as shall be thought most [fitting] and convenient for the general good of the colony, unto which we promise all due . . . obedience.* 99

—The Mayflower Compact

The compact kept the Pilgrims together. It also showed that the Pilgrims expected to decide for themselves how they would be governed. One of the men who drew up the Mayflower Compact, William Bradford, went on to be elected governor of the colony 30 times between 1621 and 1656. He helped create a form of government in which the people guided their own affairs. Later this concept of self-government would become one of the founding principles of the United States.

VIEWING HISTORY The Pilgrims signed the Mayflower Compact while still aboard ship. **Determining Relevance** *How do you think this agreement helped the Pilgrims survive their initial hardships and eventually prosper?*

The Pilgrims settled near a harbor, and named their colony Plymouth after the English port from which they had sailed. Like the Jamestown settlers, the Pilgrims endured tremendous hardships. Half of them died in the first winter alone. The next summer, the colonists had the help of a Native American, Squanto, who taught them how to plant corn. Their plentiful harvest of corn led the settlers to hold a great feast of thanksgiving in the fall of 1621.

The Massachusetts Bay Colony In 1630, a thousand English settlers braved a voyage across the Atlantic to found the Massachusetts Bay Colony, just a few miles north of Plymouth. These were the first of a flood of colonists who came to New England in a movement called the Great Migration. By 1643, the Massachusetts Bay Colony had grown to roughly 20,000 people living in 20 towns, including its capital, Boston.

Many of these new settlers were Puritans hoping to live where they could worship as they wished. They did not, however, believe in **religious tolerance**—the idea that people of different religions should live in peace together. They had no desire to live among people who held beliefs different from their own. By law, everyone in the Massachusetts Bay Colony had to attend the Puritan Church and pay taxes to support it.

The Puritans believed that they were creating a new, pure society to serve the will of God. John Winthrop, a founder of the colony and later its governor, summarized the colonists' goals in 1630. To succeed, he said, "We must be knit together in this work, as one man. We must . . . make others' condition our own. . . . For we must consider that we shall be as a city upon a hill. The eyes of all people are upon us." Winthrop voiced a belief that many on board the ship, and many Americans since that time, have shared: America would be an example to people throughout the world.

The Puritans worked hard, not only for themselves but also for the common good. Each new town, for example, allotted a "common," or tract of land to be used by all. The colony was successful; children born in Massachusetts could be expected to live at least twice as long as children born in early Virginia. By 1700, New England was home to more than 93,000 people living fairly comfortable lives.

Yet life in the Puritans' "city on a hill" had its dark moments. In 1692, several girls and young women in Salem, Massachusetts, accused three townspeople of being witches. In the public uproar that followed, neighbors fearfully accused one another of dealing with the devil. As a result of the Salem witch trials, the Massachusetts authorities ordered 20 men and women to be executed. After a few months, however, the community regained its balance, and the trials and hangings came to an end.

Some historians believe that the witch trials reflected the colonists' fears about political changes taking place at the time. The year before the trials, England's new monarchs, William and Mary, had joined the Massachusetts Bay Colony and the Plymouth Colony into one. They were now a single royal colony, known as Massachusetts.

Other New England Colonies   As the population of New England increased, farmland in Massachusetts grew scarce. Some Puritans were given permission to establish new communities. In the mid-1630s, for example, the Puritan minister Thomas Hooker led a group of settlers from Massachusetts to Connecticut. Similarly, settlements in Maine and New Hampshire were populated by Puritans. New Hampshire became a separate colony in 1679. Maine was part of Massachusetts until it became a separate state in 1820.

Other people left Massachusetts because of religious conflicts with the colony's Puritan leaders. In 1635, for example, Roger Williams, a Separatist minister, was banished from Massachusetts. The next year he started a settlement called Providence, which later joined with several other Separatist communities to become the self-governing colony of Rhode Island. Roger Williams's colony was remarkable because it guaranteed religious tolerance to all settlers.

War With the Indians   English settlers pushed Native Americans out of their homelands during the 1600s, sparking several wars between the two groups. As one sachem, or Native American leader, explained:

> 66 *Our fathers had plenty of deer and skins, our plains were full of deer, as also our woods, and of turkies, and our coves full of fish and fowl. But these English having gotten our land, they with scythes cut down the grass, and with axes fell the trees; their cows and horses eat the grass, and their hogs spoil our clam banks, and we shall be starved.* 99
>
> —Miantonomo, 1642

The bloodiest of the wars between the English settlers and the Indians was called King Philip's War after King Philip (or Metacom), a leader of the Algonquin peoples of New England. In 1675, Metacom united Indian groups from Rhode Island to Maine in an attempt to drive out the English once and for all. He and his

BIOGRAPHY

Anne Hutchinson
1591–1643

Although Anne Hutchinson and her family moved from England to Boston to escape religious persecution and to join the community of Puritans living there, Hutchinson did not accept Puritan authority. She believed that it was wrong to obey the church if by doing so, a person felt he or she was disobeying God. Her home soon became a center for colonists who wanted to think for themselves. Critics of John Winthrop and the Massachusetts government gathered there, as did women who wanted to study the Bible.

The Puritan authorities called Hutchinson to trial in November 1637 to explain her actions. She skillfully defended herself with references to the law and the Bible. Still, the judges rejected her claim that her own beliefs about God could override the authority of Puritan laws and leaders. The court declared Hutchinson "unfit for society" and banished her from the colony.

Early the next year, the Hutchinsons settled in present-day Rhode Island. After the death of her husband, Anne Hutchinson and her children settled on Long Island Sound in New York where most of them were killed by Indians in 1643.

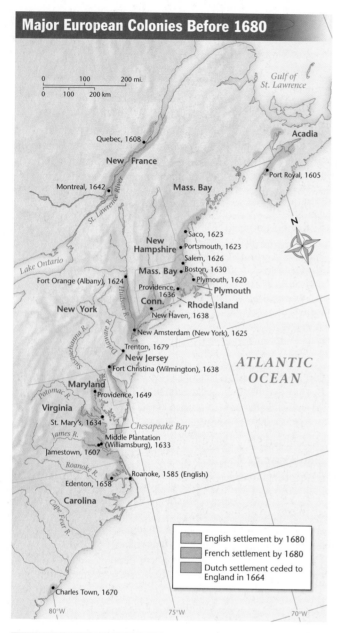

Major European Colonies Before 1680

0 100 200 mi.

0 100 200 km

Gulf of St. Lawrence

Quebec, 1608

New France

Montreal, 1642

Acadia

Port Royal, 1605

Mass. Bay

Lake Ontario

Fort Orange (Albany), 1624

Saco, 1623

New Hampshire

Portsmouth, 1623

Salem, 1626

Mass. Bay

Boston, 1630

Plymouth, 1620

Providence, 1636

Plymouth

New York

Conn.

Rhode Island

New Haven, 1638

New Amsterdam (New York), 1625

Trenton, 1679

New Jersey

Fort Christina (Wilmington), 1638

ATLANTIC OCEAN

Maryland

Providence, 1649

Virginia

St. Mary's, 1634

Chesapeake Bay

Middle Plantation (Williamsburg), 1633

Jamestown, 1607

Roanoke, 1585 (English)

Edenton, 1658

Carolina

Charles Town, 1670

80°W   75°W   70°W

English settlement by 1680
French settlement by 1680
Dutch settlement ceded to England in 1664

MAP SKILLS Both the French and the Dutch were more interested in the fur trade than they were in establishing permanent settlements. **Location** *How does the resulting settlement pattern of the French and Dutch differ from that of the English?*

warriors destroyed more than 20 English towns, attacked dozens of others, and killed about 2,000 settlers. The English struck back, killing or wounding about 4,000 Native Americans. By the war's end, Metacom was dead and the English conquest of the region was nearly complete. But Metacom and his allies had dealt New England settlers a severe blow from which they would not fully recover until the early 1700s.

The Middle Colonies

The colonies to the south of New England, called the Middle Colonies, included New York, New Jersey, Pennsylvania, and Delaware. They developed differently from the colonies in New England, in part because their settlers came from a variety of countries.

New York New York began in 1624 as the Dutch colony of New Netherland, in the Hudson and Delaware river valleys. (The Dutch came from Holland, also called the Netherlands.) The heart of the colony was the trading station of New Amsterdam, founded at the mouth of the Hudson River in 1625. The settlers built up a prosperous fur trade with Europe, and sold crops to other colonies. New Amsterdam became a port where the Dutch, Swedes, French, Germans, English and many others carried on peaceful business together. Some 18 different languages were spoken in its streets. Religious tolerance was a firm rule. The town even boasted the first synagogue, or house of Jewish worship, on the North American continent.

The prosperity of New Netherland attracted England's interest. In 1664, the English king, Charles II, declared that the entire region of the Dutch colonies belonged to his brother, the Duke of York. When the duke sent ships and soldiers to New Amsterdam to back up his claim, the Dutch were forced to give up New Netherland to the English, who renamed it New York.

The Other Middle Colonies The colony of New York was a **proprietary colony**—a colony granted by a king or queen to an individual or group who could make laws and rule it as they wished. (*Proprietor* means "owner.") The other Middle Colonies were also proprietary.

New Jersey was originally part of the Duke of York's charter. He transferred certain lands over to two English noblemen, and these lands were divided into East Jersey and West Jersey. In 1702, East and West Jersey became a single royal colony called New Jersey. Delaware began as a Swedish colony in 1638. The Dutch captured it from the Swedes, and then the Duke of York captured it from the Dutch. In 1682, he turned it over to the Englishman William Penn, who allowed Delaware to become a separate colony in 1704.

William Penn also owned the colony of Pennsylvania, which he established on land he had received from King Charles II in 1681. Like the Puritans, Penn saw his colony as a "Holy Experiment." Unlike the Puritans, he wanted to establish a society that practiced religious tolerance. Many of the colonists, like Penn himself, were Quakers, members of a Protestant group that had suffered persecution in England. Quakers believed firmly that all people should be treated as equals. Pennsylvania also attracted many non-Quaker settlers.

The Southern Colonies

In addition to Virginia, the Southern Colonies included Maryland, the Carolinas, and Georgia. All but Virginia began as proprietary colonies.

Maryland Maryland was first settled in 1634. It was created as a haven for Roman Catholics being persecuted in England, but Puritans outnumbered the Catholics from the very beginning. Therefore, the Maryland Toleration Act was passed to protect Catholics from persecution in the colony. This law was part of a general trend toward religious tolerance in the English colonies. The act was severely limited, however, in that it did not provide protection for non-Christians.

The planters of Maryland, like those in Virginia, grew prosperous during the 1600s by growing tobacco. And like the Virginians, they began to use enslaved Africans to work their fields. The Africans were brought to the colonies by slave traders. By 1704, roughly 15,000 of the 90,000 people in the two colonies were African slaves.

The royal charter of Carolina, 1663, includes the likeness of King Charles II.

The Carolinas King Charles II gave ownership of a region known as Carolina to a group of English noblemen in 1663. It was first split into North and South Carolina in 1712. In 1719, South Carolina became a royal colony. North Carolina became a royal colony in 1729. Both colonies thrived on tobacco profits and trade with Native Americans.

Georgia Although Georgia was set up like a proprietary colony in 1732, it was actually managed not by owners but by trustees. A trustee is someone entrusted to manage a business. The trustees, led by James Oglethorpe, wanted to create a haven for people who had been jailed in England because they could not pay their debts. At first, Oglethorpe and the trustees ruled Georgia strictly, barring slavery and liquor. Although Catholics could not live in Georgia, all Protestants were permitted. Gradually, however, the colonists forced the trustees to change their rules. Settlers were allowed to use and sell liquor, and enslaved Africans were brought in to work the land. After 20 years, the trustees gave their charter back to the king, and Georgia became a royal colony.

Section 2 Assessment

READING COMPREHENSION

1. What is a **colony**?

2. How was tobacco important to Virginia?

3. Why did each of these groups come to the Americas: (a) **missionaries**, (b) **Puritans**, and (c) **indentured servants**?

4. What is the importance of the **Mayflower Compact**?

CRITICAL THINKING AND WRITING

5. **Synthesizing Information** What role did religion play in the settlement of the Americas? How did religious tolerance—or the lack of it—affect the American colonies?

6. **Writing an Introduction** Write the introduction to an essay about the origins of the principle of self-government in the American colonies.

For: An activity on Jamestown
Visit: PHSchool.com
Web Code: mrd-0012

Growth of the American Colonies

READING FOCUS

- What were England's colonial policies?
- What were the origins of self-government in the colonies?
- What kinds of economies and social systems developed in the colonies?
- What were the lives of African Americans like in the different colonies?
- What tensions were caused by westward expansion and religious revivals?

MAIN IDEA

The English colonies developed diverse economies and prospered with little direct interference from England. Meanwhile, enslaved African Americans often suffered brutal treatment, and tensions developed with the French and Native Americans.

KEY TERMS

mercantilism
balance of trade
triangular trade
Middle Passage
immigrant
Great Awakening

TARGET READING SKILL

Recognize Multiple Causes Copy the web diagram below. As you read, fill in the circles with the reasons that the English colonies prospered during the mid-1600s and early 1700s.

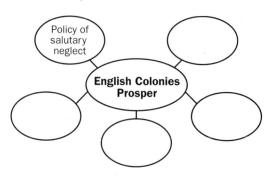

Setting the Scene Not quite 18 years old, and not very clean after a journey of several days, Benjamin Franklin arrived in the city of Philadelphia in October 1723. He had one dollar in his pocket. Franklin had quarreled with his brother (who was also his boss) and had left his home city of Boston to seek his fortune. He was determined to get ahead by improving himself. Franklin began by assembling a list of 13 virtues, including such qualities as temperance, frugality, and industry. He then set out to live by them. Each week, he decided, he would try to make one of the virtues part of his daily life. At the end of 13 weeks, he would repeat the cycle.

Although he did not succeed in mastering his virtues, Franklin did become America's best-known promoter of them. "Time is money"; "God helps them that helps themselves"; "Early to bed, early to rise, makes a man healthy, wealthy, and wise"—these and other famous sayings were published by Franklin. They helped convince American colonists of the economic opportunity available to them. According to Franklin, through hard work and clean living, a person from a humble background could prosper, maybe even become rich. In reality, this opportunity did not extend to all; enslaved African Americans in particular were excluded. Still, thanks to the labor of the colonists and the abundant resources of North America, England's American colonies grew in wealth, power, and self-confidence.

Young Benjamin Franklin is shown above, working as a printer's apprentice. A view of Philadelphia in approximately 1720 is shown below.

England's Colonial Policies

In the late 1600s and early 1700s, England prized its cluster of colonies on the Atlantic coast of North America for two reasons: The colonies supplied England with food and raw materials, and they bought large amounts of English goods. What's more, the colonists were, in general, loyal to their parent country. Thus, England got what it wanted from its colonies—raw materials and a place to sell its goods—by leaving them alone.

Mercantilism England's economic relationship with its colonies was based on a theory adopted by several western European nations in the 1600s. Called **mercantilism,** this theory held that a country should try to get and keep as much bullion, or gold and silver, as possible. The more gold and silver a country had, argued mercantilists, the wealthier and more powerful it would be.

For countries without sources of gold and silver like the mines Spain controlled in the Americas, the only way to obtain more bullion was through trade. If a country sold more goods to other countries than it bought from them, it would end up with more bullion. In other words, a country's **balance of trade,** or the difference in value between imports and exports, should show more exports than imports.

Mercantilists believed that a nation should have colonies where it could buy raw materials and sell products. The colonies should not be allowed to sell products to other nations or even to engage in manufacturing. The right to make goods for sale should be reserved exclusively for the parent country, since manufacturing was a major source of profit. What's more, to maintain control over trade and to increase profits, the parent country should require its colonies to use its ships for transporting their raw materials.

English rulers came to realize that the American colonies could provide raw materials such as tobacco, furs, and perhaps gold for England to sell to other countries. Furthermore, if the colonies had to buy England's manufactured goods, this exchange would greatly improve England's balance of trade. English leaders, therefore, set out to have as many colonies as possible, and to control colonial trade in order to provide the maximum profit to England.

Controlling Colonial Trade In 1660, England's King Charles II approved a stronger version of a previous law called the Navigation Act. Along with other legislation, the Navigation Act tightened control over colonial trade. The new laws required the colonies to sell certain goods, including sugar, tobacco, and cotton, only to England. Moreover, if colonists wanted to sell certain other goods to foreign countries, they had to take the crop or product to England first and pay a duty, or tax, on it. They also had to use English ships for some kinds of trade.

During the next two decades, England tried in several ways to tighten its control over the colonies. This effort peaked in 1686, when King James II attempted to take direct control over New York and the New England colonies by creating the Dominion of New England. This action abolished colonial legislatures within the Dominion and replaced them with a governor and a council appointed by the king.

Colonists up and down the Atlantic seaboard deeply resented the king's grab for power. They resented, too, the actions of Edmund Andros, whom James II had appointed governor of the Dominion. Andros collected taxes without the approval of the king or the colonists, and demanded payment of an annual land tax. He also declared a policy of religious tolerance, or respect for different religious beliefs. The Puritans saw these actions as blows to their freedom from English influence and their control over local religious matters.

VIEWING FINE ART This painting of Charles II hangs in the National Portrait Gallery, London. **Analyzing Visual Information** *What do you think the artist wanted to convey about the monarchy in general and about Charles II in particular? Explain.*

As part of the Glorious Revolution of 1688-1689, the English Parliament replaced James II with his daughter Mary and her husband William of Orange. New England citizens promptly held their own mini-rebellion against the Andros government, imprisoning the governor and his associates. William and Mary then dissolved the Dominion and reestablished the colonies that James had abolished. When they restored the Massachusetts charter, however, they revised the government to allow the king to appoint a royal governor. In 1707, another political change occurred when England joined with Scotland to form Great Britain.

Origins of Self-Government

As you recall, England had established three different types of colonies in North America: royal, proprietary, and charter. Over time, England transformed several of the charter and proprietary colonies into royal colonies and appointed royal governors for them. By the early 1700s, therefore, the colonial governments shared a similar pattern of government.

In most colonies, a governor appointed by the king acted as the chief executive. A colonial legislature served under the governor. Most colonial assemblies consisted of an advisory council, or upper house of prominent colonists appointed by the king, and a lower house elected by qualified voters. Only male landowners were allowed to vote. However, most adult white males did own land and thus could vote.

VIEWING HISTORY The law-making assemblies of the colonies, like the Virginia House of Burgesses shown here, continued the English tradition of strong local authority. **Drawing Conclusions** Why was setting the salaries for royal officials such an important power of colonial legislatures?

The colonial legislatures came to dominate the colonial governments. They passed laws regarding defense and taxation. Later they took over the job of setting salaries for royal officials. Even the governor's council came to be dominated by prominent local leaders who served the interests of the legislature rather than those of the royal government.

One reason the British government allowed its colonies freedom in governing themselves was that England had a long tradition of strong local government. Another reason was that the British government lacked the resources and the bureaucracy to enforce its wishes. Finally, the existing economy and politics of the colonists already served British interests, and the colonists considered themselves loyal subjects of the king. The British realized that the most salutary, or beneficial, policy toward their colonies was to "neglect," or leave them alone. (Thus, later historians would call British colonial policy during the early 1700s "salutary neglect.") One effect of the policy of salutary neglect was that Great Britain rarely enforced its own trade regulations, such as the Navigation Act. As a result, the colonies prospered, as did their trade with Britain, without much interference from their parent country.

Diverse Colonial Economies

By the early 1700s, the economic foundations of Britain's American colonies were in place. While the Spanish colonies focused on mining silver and growing sugar, and New France focused on the fur trade, the British regions of eastern North America developed diverse economies determined, in part, by local geography.

For the most part, English-speaking settlements continued to hug the Atlantic Ocean and the deep rivers that empty into it. Most commerce took place on water. Roads were little more than footpaths or rutted trails, so it was simply too costly and difficult to carry goods long distances over land. The Atlantic Ocean remained so vital to travel that there was more contact between

Boston and London than between Boston and Virginia.

The Southern Colonies In the Southern Colonies of Virginia, Maryland, South Carolina, North Carolina, and Georgia, the economy was based on growing staple crops—crops that are in constant demand. In Virginia and North Carolina, the staple crop was tobacco. In the warm and wet coastal regions of South Carolina and Georgia, it was rice. To produce these crops, planters needed huge amounts of land and labor but very little else. As a result, the South had fewer towns and merchants than other regions.

African slaves supplied most of the labor on tobacco and rice plantations. Virginia planters began to purchase large numbers of Africans in the late 1600s. By about 1750, enslaved Africans totaled 40 percent of the population. In South Carolina, Africans outnumbered Europeans throughout the 1700s.

The Middle Colonies From Maryland north to New York, the economy of the Middle Colonies was a mixture of farming and commerce. The rich, fertile soil produced profitable crops such as wheat, barley, and rye. New York and Philadelphia were already among the largest cities in North America. Growing numbers of merchants, traders, and craftspeople lived and worked there, and ships from all over the Atlantic World arrived regularly. New people arrived too, increasing the diversity of the populations of New York and Pennsylvania. These colonies included English, Dutch, French, Scots, Irish, Scotch-Irish, Germans, Swedes, Portuguese Jews, Welsh, Africans, and Native Americans.

The New England Colonies In the 1700s, the New England colonies were a region of small, self-sufficient farms and of towns dependent on long-distance trade. New England merchants hauled china, books, and cloth from England to the West Indies in the Caribbean Sea. From the Caribbean they brought sugar back to New England, where it was usually distilled into rum. They traded the rum and firearms for slaves in West Africa and then carried slaves to the West Indies for more sugar. This trade between three points in the Atlantic World—the Americas, Europe, and Africa—was called the **triangular trade.**

Life in Colonial America

Life was better for most white colonists than it would have been in Europe. They ate better, lived longer, and had more children to help them with their work. They also had many more opportunities to advance in wealth and status than average Europeans did. Many colonists earned a living by farming and fishing. Others were engaged in trade or were artisans.

At a very early age, boys from many families became apprentices, or persons placed under a legal contract to work for another person in exchange for learning a trade. Apprentices learned to make items such as silverware, furniture, pottery, and glassware. Some apprentices worked for printers, who gathered and circulated local news and information. One of the best-known printers of the 1700s

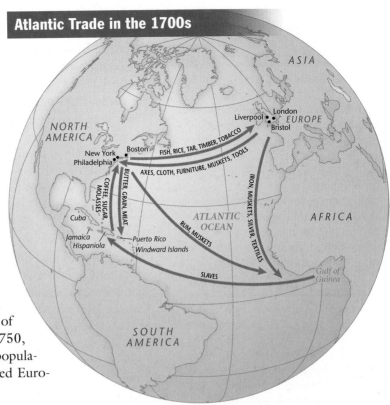

Atlantic Trade in the 1700s

MAP SKILLS This map shows the goods traded between the Americas, Europe, and Africa. *Movement How does the map illustrate why slavery was important to the New England and Middle Colonies even though few slaves lived and worked there?*

The Trial of Peter Zenger At the age of 13, John Peter Zenger emigrated from Germany to New York where he became indentured to a printer. After establishing his own printing business, in 1733 he launched the *New York Weekly Journal,* which often contained articles critical of the Royal Governor of New York. These criticisms led to Zenger's arrest for libel. Although he had not written the articles, Zenger was legally responsible for the contents of the paper he published.

After ten months in prison, Zenger was finally brought to trial in 1735. His attorney was Andrew Hamilton, who had also begun his life in America as an indentured servant but was now Speaker of the Philadelphia Assembly. Hamilton argued that the controversial articles were true and therefore could not be considered libelous. He further claimed that it was the duty of a publication to print the truth. Over the objections of the judges, Hamilton appealed to the jurors directly, and they found Zenger not guilty. The trial of Peter Zenger established truth as a defense against libel, and was a landmark victory for freedom of the press in the English colonies.

was Benjamin Franklin, who published several newspapers and magazines, as well as *Poor Richard's Almanac,* which was printed annually from 1732 to 1757. (An almanac is a book containing information such as calendars, weather predictions, proverbs, and advice.)

In colonial America, women juggled a number of duties that contributed to the well-being of their households and of the community. Women managed the tasks that kept a household operating, such as cooking, gardening, washing, cleaning, weaving cloth, and sewing. They supported one another by helping in childbirth and sharing equipment and tools. Women did not have political equality with men, however. Laws prevented them from voting, holding office, or serving on a jury. While many boys lacked the opportunity for schooling, young girls generally were not allowed to go to school—they were expected to learn everything they needed to know from their mothers at home.

During colonial times, most children received very little formal education. New England was an exception. Because the Puritans believed that everyone should be able to read the Bible, Massachusetts and Connecticut passed legislation in 1647 requiring communities to support local schools. As a result, literacy rates were higher in New England than anywhere else in British North America. Outside New England, if there were no schools in the area, parents taught their children at home. In the Southern Colonies, plantation owners often hired private instructors to teach their children.

Colonial colleges were primarily training grounds for ministers and lawyers; generally only the very wealthy attended. Up until the 1740s, there were only three colleges in the colonies, Harvard in Massachusetts (established in 1636), William and Mary in Virginia (1693), and Yale in Connecticut (1701).

African Americans in the Colonies

Not counting Native Americans, about one out of every five people living in British North America by the middle of the 1700s was of African descent. Most of these African Americans were enslaved.

One Person's Story As in the case of all immigrants, the experiences of African Americans in the colonies varied depending on where they lived. Yet the stories of Africans, uprooted from their homeland and sold into slavery, had many elements in common. One African who later told his story was Olaudah Equiano.

Born around 1745 in the country of Benin, Equiano was kidnapped at age 10. He was enslaved to a series of African masters, then sold and put aboard a British slave ship bound for the Americas. During the **Middle Passage,** Equiano witnessed many terrible scenes of suffering and cruelty. (The Middle Passage was one leg of the triangular trade between the Americas, Europe, and Africa. The term is also used to refer to the forced transport of slaves from Africa to the Americas.)

Equiano's ship finally arrived in the West Indies, where the Africans were sold at a public auction. Most went to work—and die—in the sugar plantations of the West Indies. Equiano noted that the sale separated families, leaving people grief-stricken and alone:

> 66 *In this manner, without scruple [concern], are relations and friends separated, most of them never to see each other again. I remember . . . there were several brothers who, in the sale, were sold in different lots; and it was very moving on this occasion to see and hear their*

Olaudah Equiano described the horrors of slavery from firsthand knowledge.

cries at parting. O, ye nominal Christians [Christians in name only]! might not an African ask you, Learned you this from your God, who says unto you, Do unto all men as you would men should do unto you?

—Olaudah Equiano

Slavery in the Colonies On the coastal plain of South Carolina and Georgia, called the low country, rice and indigo were grown most efficiently on large plantations with many slaves. High temperatures and dangerous diseases made life particularly difficult for the enslaved workers there, and they labored under especially brutal conditions. African Americans made up a large share of the population in South Carolina and Georgia. Wealthy planters often chose to spend most of their time away from their isolated estates, so slaves generally had regular contact with only a handful of white colonists.

In Virginia and Maryland, slaves made up a minority rather than a majority of the population, and relatively few of them had come directly from Africa. Slaves in these colonies performed many kinds of work. Cultivating tobacco, the major crop, did not take as much time as growing rice, so slaveowners put enslaved African Americans to work at other tasks. This led to more regular contact between African Americans and European Americans. The result was greater integration of European American and African American cultures than in South Carolina and Georgia. In the latter half of the 1700s, slaves in Virginia and Maryland blended the customs of African and European origin in everything from food and clothing to religion.

Some male slaves in Virginia even worked away from plantations as artisans or laborers in Richmond and other towns. As long as they sent back part of their wages to the plantations, they lived fairly independently of their owner's control. They were, however, still subject to harsh laws that controlled what they could do. In addition, their children were born enslaved.

About 400,000 African Americans lived in the Southern Colonies by the late 1700s. In contrast, there were only about 50,000 African Americans in the New England and Middle Colonies combined. These colonies had a more diverse economy, and their farms were much smaller than those in the Southern Colonies and did not require as many slaves for field work. It was more common to find slaves in this region working in the cities as cooks, housekeepers, or personal servants. Male slaves often worked in manufacturing and trade or as skilled artisans. They also worked in the forests as lumberjacks. Because shipbuilding and shipping were major economic activities, some African American men worked along the seacoast. As dockworkers, merchant sailors, fishermen, whalers, and privateers, they contributed to the growth of the Atlantic economy.

Slave Laws and Revolts Laws controlling the lives of slaves varied from region to region. Every colony passed its own slave laws, and revised them over time. Generally, slaves could not go aboard ships or ferries or leave their town limits without a written pass. Crimes for slaves ranged from owning hogs and carrying canes to disturbing the peace and striking a white person. Punishments included whipping, banishment to the West Indies, and death. Many of these laws also applied to free African Americans and to Native Americans.

READING CHECK

How did slavery develop in the various colonies?

Fast Forward to Today

The Gullah Language and Culture

In the 1700s, owners of rice plantations in the Sea Islands off the South Carolina and Georgia coasts imported slaves from West African rice-growing regions, including present-day Sierra Leone. The Sea Islands could be reached only by boat, and white planters did not want to live there. Thus, these isolated enslaved Africans were able to preserve their distinctive culture, as shown in the batik *Dawn to Dusk* by Frances Johnson.

The Gullah language that developed among these slaves and their descendants is a mixture of English and West African languages. For example, the Gullah "Dey fa go shum," is "They went to see her" in English.

When new roads linked the islands to the mainland in the 1960s, it was feared that the Gullah culture would die out. Today, however, there is renewed interest in preserving the Gullah language, and festivals celebrate Gullah storytelling, crafts, and cuisine.

? Do you think it is important to record and preserve distinctive historic dialects such as the Gullah language? Why or why not?

Laws restricting the movement of slaves made organizing slave rebellions extremely difficult. Because slaves could not travel or meet freely, they had only limited contact with slaves in other areas. A few early slave revolts are documented. In 1739, several dozen slaves near Charleston, South Carolina, killed more than 20 whites in what is known as the Stono Rebellion. The slaves burned an armory and began to march toward Spanish Florida, where a small colony of runaway slaves lived. Armed planters captured and killed the rebels. In New York City, brutal laws that were passed to control African Americans also led to rebellions.

More commonly, African Americans resisted slavery indirectly, by such acts as pretending to misunderstand orders or faking illness. In addition, strong African kinship networks helped people survive slavery and also helped preserve their traditions.

Free Blacks Not until after the American Revolution did the free black population in the Northern and Southern Colonies grow significantly. Some slave laws discouraged people from freeing slaves. Owners had to get permission from the legislature before they could do so. Some laws demanded that freed slaves leave a colony within six months of gaining freedom. Despite the obstacles, those slaves who earned money as artisans or laborers had the possibility of saving enough to purchase their freedom.

Free African Americans did much of the same work as enslaved African Americans. They were, however, probably worse off materially. Free blacks often endured poorer living conditions and more severe discrimination than slaves who were identified with specific white households. The rights of free blacks were also limited: they could not vote, testify in court against whites, or marry whites. They did not gain citizenship and voting rights until the ratification of the Fourteenth and Fifteenth Amendments after the Civil War. (See pages 207, 209.)

Sounds of an Era

Listen to a Gullah storyteller and other sounds relating to colonial life.

Emerging Tensions in the Colonies

By the mid-1700s, 13 prosperous British colonies hugged the Atlantic Coast. Colonial settlers had transformed the Atlantic colonies into a world of thriving farms, towns, and plantations. The success of the colonies came at a price, however. The growth of the colonies, both in population and territory, raised new issues in colonial life.

Western Expansion   In the mid-1700s, the colonial population increased rapidly, almost doubling every 25 years, as the birth rate grew faster than the death rate. The colonies also experienced a growth in the number of **immigrants,** or people who enter a new country to settle. While colonists continued to come from England, they also began to arrive from Ireland and Germany. Those people immigrating from Ireland were often called Scotch-Irish, because they had originally come from Scotland. As the population grew, the colonists began to feel crowded, especially in the smaller colonies of New England.

According to English custom, fathers tried to provide their sons with some land of their own. New Englanders now found it increasingly difficult to do so. Maintaining a family required about 45 acres, and since colonists were having many children, there was simply not enough fertile land to go around.

Clearly the colonies could not continue to flourish if forced to remain confined to the land along the Atlantic Ocean. By the mid-1700s, European settlers were moving into the interior of North America. Scotch-Irish and Germans settled central Pennsylvania and the Shenandoah Valley of Virginia. Farther to the north, colonists spread into the Mohawk River valley in New York and into the Connecticut River valley in present-day Vermont. In southern Pennsylvania and the Carolinas, settlements sprang up as far west as the Appalachian Mountains. In a few cases, settlers pushed through the Appalachians and began cultivating land in Indian territory.

Tensions With the French and Native Americans

The colonists' desire for more land raised tensions between the new settlers and those groups who already lived on the land—the French and the Indians. In the Ohio and Susquehanna River valleys, Native American groups, including the Delaware, the Shawnee, and the Huron, were moving west, too. As white settlers migrated into Native American territory, they forced the local Indians to relocate into lands already occupied by other Native American groups.

The French as well as the Native Americans were alarmed by the steady migration of the English settlers. In 1749, disturbed by the expansion of British trading posts in the Ohio Valley, the French sent defenders to strengthen the settlement of Detroit and to seize the Ohio Valley. Tensions continued to rise in the summer of 1752 when the French built Fort Presque Isle (where Erie, Pennsylvania, is now located) and attacked and killed the defenders of an English trading post in the valley.

COMPARING PRIMARY SOURCES
Expansion Into Native American Lands

Colonial efforts to purchase Native American lands in Pennsylvania created a difference of opinion.

Analyzing Viewpoints According to each speaker, what gives the land its value? How does each speaker characterize the actions and motives of the other? Do you think either or both are justified in their opinions? Explain your reasoning.

Opposed to Expansion

"We know our Lands are now more valuable. The white People think we do not know their Value; but we are sensible [aware] that the Land is everlasting, and the few Goods we receive for it are soon worn out and gone. . . . Besides, we are not well used [treated] with respect to the lands still unsold by us. Your people daily settle on these lands, and spoil our hunting. . . . Your horses and cows have eaten the grass our deer used to feed on."

—Canasatego, Iroquois leader, July 7, 1742

In Favor of Expansion

"It is very true that lands are of late becoming more valuable; but what rises their value? Is it not entirely owning to the industry and labor used by the white people in their cultivation and improvement? Had not they come among you, these lands would have been of no use to you, any further than to maintain you. . . . The value of the land is no more than it is worth in money."

—Governor George Thomas of Pennsylvania, July 7, 1742

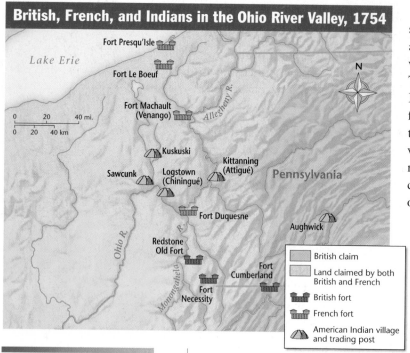

British, French, and Indians in the Ohio River Valley, 1754

Lake Erie

Fort Presqu'Isle

Fort Le Boeuf

Fort Machault
(Venango)

Allegheny R.

N

Kuskuski

Sawcunk

Logstown
(Chiningué)

Kittanning
(Attigué)

Pennsylvania

Fort Duquesne

Aughwick

Ohio R.

Redstone
Old Fort

Monongahela R.

Fort
Cumberland

Fort
Necessity

	British claim
	Land claimed by both British and French
	British fort
	French fort
	American Indian village and trading post

MAP SKILLS As English colonists pushed west, they came into conflict with both the French and the Indians. **Location** Which British forts are in disputed territory?

By the early 1750s, it was clear that some kind of explosion was rapidly approaching. The most likely setting was the western part of present-day Pennsylvania. There, the interests of the colonies of Pennsylvania and Virginia came into conflict with those of the Native Americans and the French. Whoever controlled the area where the Allegheny and Monongahela rivers meet to form the Ohio River could dominate the entire region. This was, in other words, an area worth fighting for.

Religious Tensions While tensions built along the outer edges of the British colonies, unrest was also increasing within them. Nowhere was this more obvious than in colonial religious life.

While the British colonies were overwhelmingly Protestant (aside from a small number of Jews in cities and some Catholics in Maryland), no single group of Protestants was more powerful than any other. Southern planters and northern merchants and professionals tended to belong to the Church of England. Most New Englanders were either Congregationalists or Presbyterians. Quakers were strong in Pennsylvania, as were Lutherans and Mennonites, while the Dutch Reformed Church thrived in the colony of New York.

In the early 1700s, many ministers, especially Congregationalists, believed that the colonists had fallen away from the faith of their Puritan ancestors. In the 1730s and 1740s, they led a series of revivals designed to renew religious enthusiasm and commitment. Known today as the **Great Awakening**, this revival of religious feeling was not a single event that began or ended at one specific time, nor did it take place in every colony. Most historians date the beginning of the Great Awakening to the great explosion of religious feeling that arose in the 1730s in response to the preaching of Jonathan Edwards, a Massachusetts minister.

News of Edwards's success spread throughout the colonies and even to Britain. It encouraged other ministers to increase their efforts to energize their followers. These ministers sought to remind people of the power of God and, at least in the beginning, to remind them of the authority of their ministers as well. In a well-known fiery sermon, "Sinners in the Hands of an Angry God," Edwards gave his congregation a terrifying picture of their situation:

> ❝ O sinner! Consider the fearful danger you are in: it is a great furnace of wrath, a wide and bottomless pit, full of the fire of wrath, that you are held over in the hand of that God, whose wrath is provoked and incensed as much against you, as against many of the damned in hell. You hang by a slender thread. ❞
>
> —Jonathan Edwards

Edwards would eventually be eclipsed in popularity by George Whitefield, a young English minister who toured the colonies seven times between 1738 and 1770. Whitefield's tour of New England in 1740 was a great triumph. In

Boston, he preached to vast crowds packed into churches. Later, he held open-air meetings at which thousands of listeners could hear his ringing sermons.

Effects of the Great Awakening   As time went on, the Great Awakening did more than revive people's religious convictions. It energized them to speak for themselves and to rely less on the traditional authority of ministers and books.

In some areas, the Great Awakening was led by ministers in established congregations. But many people flocked instead to revival leaders, such as Whitefield, who were itinerant, or traveling, preachers. If welcomed by the local minister, the itinerants would preach inside the church as a "visiting minister." If unwelcome, they preached in fields and barns to anyone who would come to hear their sermons. These ministers, some of whom had received little formal education, preached that anyone could have a personal relationship with Jesus. The infinitely great power of God did not put Him beyond the reach of ordinary people, they argued. Faith and sincerity, rather than wealth or education, were the major requirements needed to understand the Gospel.

One sign of the new religious independence brought about by the Great Awakening was the shift of many New Englanders to the Baptist faith in the 1740s and 1750s. In the South, both the Baptist and, later, the Methodist Churches drew new followers. The appeal of these two churches lay in their powerful, emotional ceremonies and their celebration of ordinary people. While some churches grew, others split when only part of the congregation embraced the new emotionalism. Some of these splinter groups were more tolerant of dissent, or difference of opinion, than the organizations from which they had split. This helped make religion in the colonies more democratic.

Although it was a religious movement, the Great Awakening had long-term social and political effects. Methodists and Baptists tended to be people at the middle or bottom of colonial society. When they claimed that individuals could act on their own faith and not rely on a minister or other authority, they were indirectly attacking the idea that some people are better than others. Such talk of equality would, in time, have revolutionary consequences.

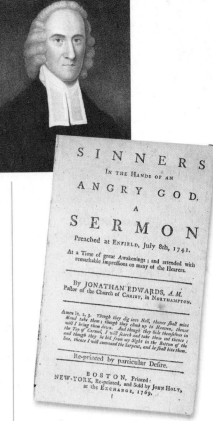

VIEWING HISTORY Jonathan Edwards, shown above, declared, "The bow of God's wrath is bent, and the arrow made ready on the string" in the sermon shown here. **Drawing Conclusions** *Why do you think so many people responded to this kind of preaching in the 1700s?*

Section 3 Assessment

READING COMPREHENSION

1. (a) What is **mercantilism?** (b) According to this theory, what kind of **balance of trade** is desirable?

2. What kinds of economies developed in the Southern, Middle, and New England Colonies?

3. What part did the **Middle Passage** play in the **triangular trade?**

4. What was the **Great Awakening?**

CRITICAL THINKING AND WRITING

5. **Identifying Central Issues** What situations, events, and policies began to lead toward a demand for self-government in the colonies?

6. **Writing a Letter** It is the mid-1700s, and you are moving west from one of the English colonies. Write a letter to a friend back home explaining why you are moving.

Go Online
PHSchool.com

For: An activity on the Gullah language
Visit: PHSchool.com
Web Code: mrd-0013

Review and Assessment

 *creating a* **CHAPTER SUMMARY**

Copy the web diagram (right) on a piece of paper. Complete it by adding examples of the development of self-government in the English colonies. Include English as well as colonial events. Add circles as needed.

interactive Textbook

For additional review and enrichment activities, see the interactive version of *America: Pathways to the Present*, available on the Web and on CD-ROM.

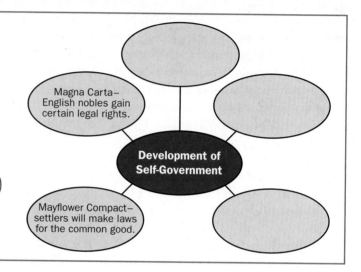

Magna Carta– English nobles gain certain legal rights.

Development of Self-Government

Mayflower Compact– settlers will make laws for the common good.

★ Reviewing Key Terms

For each of the terms below, write a sentence explaining how it relates to the creation of a new American society.

1. migration
2. clan
3. monarch
4. Columbian Exchange
5. colony
6. Mayflower Compact
7. religious tolerance
8. triangular trade
9. Middle Passage
10. Great Awakening

★ Reviewing Main Ideas

11. What are three characteristics shared by Native American cultures? (Section 1)
12. How did the Renaissance change Europe? (Section 1)
13. Describe one of the wealthy West African kingdoms of the 1400s. (Section 1)
14. How did Columbus's voyages affect Europe, West Africa, and the Native Americans? (Section 1)
15. What are three reasons the Spanish explored and settled in the Americas? (Section 2)
16. Describe the early years of (a) the Jamestown colony and (b) the first two settlements in Massachusetts. (Section 2)
17. How did the English acquire New York? (Section 2)

18. What was the policy of salutary neglect? (Section 3)
19. What kinds of economies developed in the different colonies? (Section 3)
20. Why did dependence on slave labor increase in the Southern Colonies? (Section 3)

★ Critical Thinking

21. **Demonstrating Reasoned Judgment** European nations competed first to find a sea route to Asia and later to conquer and settle the Americas. Do you think this competition was beneficial or harmful to the development of the Atlantic World? Explain your answer.
22. **Making Comparisons** Compare the ways that religion contributed to the founding of Spain's American colonies and the New England Colonies.
23. **Recognizing Ideologies** How was the European settlers' treatment of Native Americans and Africans similar? What do these actions tell you about the worldview of those Europeans?
24. **Recognizing Cause and Effect** How did geography help to determine the economies and social customs of the English colonies?
25. **Determining Relevance** Choose three events in English and colonial history that would later lead to the colonists' insistence on self-government, and explain their significance.

★ Standardized Test Prep

Analyzing Political Cartoons ▶

26. The topic of this modern-day cartoon is the current debate over immigration to the United States. Who does the man in the center represent?

  A illegal immigrants
  B Native Americans
  C Anglo Americans
  D recent immigrants

27. What historical events does the cartoonist want viewers to recall?

Analyzing Primary Sources

Columbus wrote to the Spanish monarchs, describing the first Native Americans the Spanish met. Read the excerpt from his letter, and answer the questions that follow.

> **❝** *They are so ingenuous [innocent] and free with all they have, that no one would believe it who has not seen it; of anything that they possess, if it be asked of them, they never say no; on the contrary, they invite you to share it and show as much love as if their hearts went with it.* **❞**
>
> —Letter from Columbus to the Spanish monarchs, 1493

28. Which statement BEST represents the meaning of the quotation?

  A The Tainos are innocent, generous, and cooperative.
  B The Tainos loved the Europeans.
  C The Tainos are loving but possessive.
  D The Tainos are just like the Spanish.

29. What conclusion do you think the king and queen probably drew from Columbus's description?

  F The Tainos should be treated the same way they treated Columbus.
  G Spain should leave the area and not come back.
  H The Tainos would provide no resistance to Spanish conquest.
  I The Tainos must be wiped out.

Test-Taking Tip

Note that Question 28 asks which statement BEST represents the meaning of the quotation. More than one answer may seem possible. You must determine which one *best* represents the *entire* quotation.

Applying the Chapter Skill

Generalizing From Multiple Sources Review the Skills for Life page and the chapter text about Columbus to make a new generalization about Columbus or the Spanish monarchs.

For: Chapter 1 Self-Test
Visit: PHSchool.com
Web Code: mra-0014

Geography & History

Colonial Settlements

Most early colonial settlements, particularly those in New England, consisted of tight clusters of houses, usually centered on a single church, or meetinghouse. Settlements often shared a mill where grain was ground. Near the center of many New England towns were commons, or commonly owned pastures, that were open to all townspeople. These shared spaces and institutions reflected the close-knit community spirit found in many early settlements.

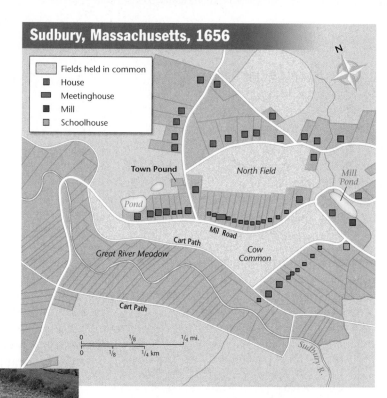

Sudbury, Massachusetts, 1656

- Fields held in common
- House
- Meetinghouse
- Mill
- Schoolhouse

Town Pound

North Field

Mill Pond

Pond

Mill Road

Cart Path

Great River Meadow

Cow Common

Cart Path

0   1/8   1/4 mi.
0   1/8   1/4 km

Sudbury R.

N

Geographic Connection How did the layout of colonial Sudbury, Massachusetts, reflect its physical geography and cultural values?

A Familiar Pattern

In many ways, these early settlements resembled villages where the settlers might have lived in England. This modern view of an English village shows a striking similarity in layout to colonial Sudbury.

Geographic Connection How is the geography of this English village similar to the geography of colonial Sudbury?

Reminders of Home

Colonial settlers not only patterned their settlements after villages in their homeland, they also brought treasured possessions with them. This chest was carried from England to Plymouth, Massachusetts, on the *Mayflower*.

36

Early Homes

In their first years in North America, settlers had to make do with small houses made of local wood with thatched (straw) roofs. These houses at Plimoth Plantation in Plymouth, Massachusetts, are part of a modern reconstruction of the first permanent English settlement in New England.

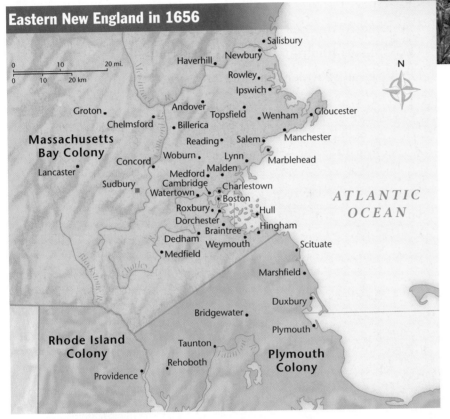

Eastern New England in 1656

Salisbury
Haverhill • Newbury
Rowley
Ipswich
Groton • Andover • Topsfield • Wenham • Gloucester
Chelmsford • Billerica
Massachusetts Bay Colony
Reading • Salem • Manchester
Woburn • Lynn • Marblehead
Concord • Medford • Malden
Lancaster • Cambridge • Charlestown
Sudbury • Watertown • Boston
Roxbury • Hull
Dorchester • Braintree • Hingham
Dedham • Weymouth • Scituate
Medfield
Marshfield
ATLANTIC OCEAN
Duxbury
Bridgewater • Plymouth
Rhode Island Colony
Taunton
Rehoboth • **Plymouth Colony**
Providence

0 10 20 mi.
0 10 20 km

N

The Colonial Frontier

This map shows the towns that existed near Sudbury when it was first settled. As you can see, Sudbury was near the edge of the area already settled by the English. Tightly clustered villages may have given English settlers a sense of security at the edge of a vast wilderness inhabited by peoples with different customs.

Geographic Connection Where were most of the settlements in eastern New England located in 1656?

A Culture Takes Root

As a new generation came of age, colonists abandoned some of the traditions of the old country to develop their own new regional cultures. This meetinghouse shows the elegant building style that gradually replaced the crude structures of the first settlers across New England. An increasingly self-confident population gathered in meetinghouses like this one to hear native-born preachers such as Cotton Mather, pictured here.

Balancing Liberty and Order
(1753–1820)

E pluribus unum—"from many, one"—was chosen as the nation's motto in 1776.

1776

The Declaration of Independence is signed.

1775

The Battles of Lexington and Concord signal the beginning of the Revolutionary War.

1781

The British surrender at Yorktown. The Articles of Confederation are approved.

American Events

1754

The French and Indian War begins.

1750   **1760**   **1770**   **1780**

World Events

The Seven Years' War begins in Europe.

1756

The Peruvians revolt against Spanish rule.

1780

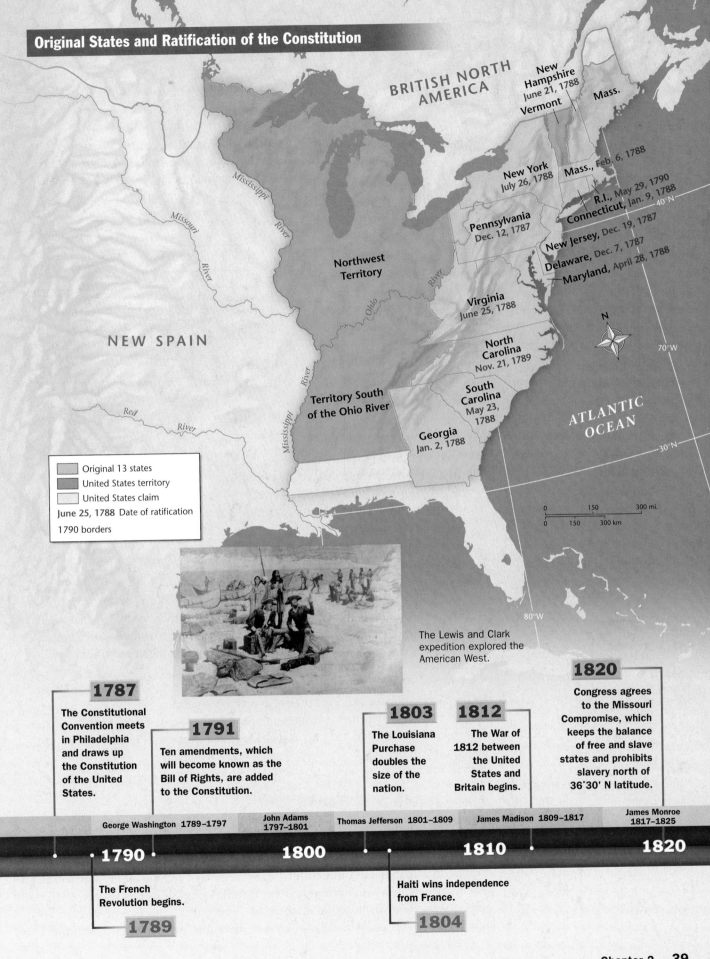

Original States and Ratification of the Constitution

BRITISH NORTH AMERICA

New Hampshire
June 21, 1788

Vermont

Mass.

New York
July 26, 1788

Mass., Feb. 6, 1788

R.I., May 29, 1790

Connecticut, Jan. 9, 1788

New Jersey, Dec. 19, 1787

Delaware, Dec. 7, 1787

Maryland, April 28, 1788

Pennsylvania
Dec. 12, 1787

Northwest Territory

NEW SPAIN

Mississippi River

Missouri River

Ohio River

Red River

Virginia
June 25, 1788

Territory South of the Ohio River

North Carolina
Nov. 21, 1789

South Carolina
May 23, 1788

Georgia
Jan. 2, 1788

ATLANTIC OCEAN

N

40°N

70°W

30°N

80°W

Original 13 states
United States territory
United States claim
June 25, 1788 Date of ratification
1790 borders

0   150   300 mi.
0   150   300 km

The Lewis and Clark expedition explored the American West.

1787

The Constitutional Convention meets in Philadelphia and draws up the Constitution of the United States.

1791

Ten amendments, which will become known as the Bill of Rights, are added to the Constitution.

1803

The Louisiana Purchase doubles the size of the nation.

1812

The War of 1812 between the United States and Britain begins.

1820

Congress agrees to the Missouri Compromise, which keeps the balance of free and slave states and prohibits slavery north of 36°30' N latitude.

George Washington 1789–1797

John Adams
1797–1801

Thomas Jefferson 1801–1809

James Madison 1809–1817

James Monroe
1817–1825

1790

1800

1810

1820

The French Revolution begins.

Haiti wins independence from France.

1789

1804

The Road to Independence

READING FOCUS

- What was the importance of the French and Indian War?

- What issues led to the Revolution?

- Why were the shots fired at Lexington and Concord "heard round the world"?

- What political ideas led to the Declaration of Independence?

- How did the colonists fight for and win independence?

MAIN IDEA

Ideas about equality and self-government, as well as grievances against the British, led to the outbreak of the Revolutionary War, in which the American colonies won their independence from Britain.

KEY TERMS

French and Indian War
boycott
Boston Massacre
First Continental Congress
Battles of Lexington and Concord
Revolutionary War
Declaration of Independence
patriotism

TARGET READING SKILL

Recognize Multiple Causes Copy the flowchart below. As you read, fill in the ideas and events that led to the American colonists declaring and winning their independence.

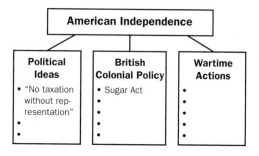

Setting the Scene

VIEWING FINE ART This depiction of Paul Revere's famous ride was done in the naïve, or folk art, style. **Drawing Inferences** *What idea do you think the artist wanted to convey?*

> " *Listen, my children, and you shall hear*
> *Of the midnight ride of Paul Revere,*
> *On the eighteenth of April, in Seventy-Five;*
> *Hardly a man is now alive*
> *Who remembers that famous day and year. . . .* "
> —Henry Wadsworth Longfellow, "Paul Revere's Ride"

Through Longfellow's famous poem, generations of young Americans have learned about the start of this nation's struggle for independence. On that night of April 18, 1775, Revere and other colonists warned the Massachusetts countryside of the approach of British soldiers. The next morning, colonial militia fought the British at Lexington and Concord.

The confrontations at Lexington and Concord were indeed the beginning of the Revolutionary War. Yet they also marked an ending—the end of a series of disagreements that drove Britain and its colonies further and further apart. For more than a decade, the two sides had argued over issues related to taxation and trade. Strangely, these issues arose in part from a tremendous victory for Britain and the colonies over a common enemy: France.

The French and Indian War

The rivalry among European nations for control of North America began soon after they started to explore and colonize the continent. While English colonists built their settlements along the eastern seacoast during the 1600s, the French explored farther inland—and claimed a vast region stretching all the way to the Rocky Mountains. Conflict erupted because the English claimed some of this territory also. An unsuccessful attempt by the English colonists of Virginia to take a French fort at the forks of the Ohio River in 1754 marked the beginning

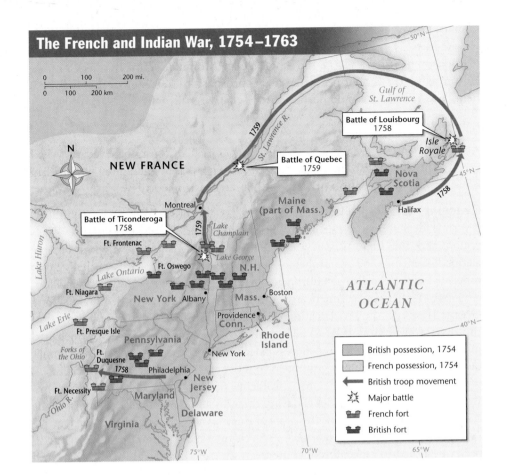

The French and Indian War, 1754–1763

of the **French and Indian War,** so-called because the British and their American colonists fought against the French and their Indian allies.

In June 1754, delegates from seven English colonies convened at Albany, New York, to work out a unified war effort in the northern colonies. Benjamin Franklin, a Pennsylvania delegate, offered an ambitious plan for a permanent union of the colonies. Named the Albany Plan of Union, it called for a grand council of delegates from each colony, elected by their colonial legislatures. Although the colonies rejected the plan, it did provide a model for the later government of the United States.

At first the war went poorly for the British. In 1758, however, British troops began to overwhelm French and Indian forces, and the French retreated into New France, or present-day Canada. The Iroquois, who had cleverly been playing each side against the other, now decided that the French cause was hopeless, and switched their support to the British.

In 1759, the British invaded New France. Their capture of Quebec proved to be the turning point of the war and led to more British victories in New France. In 1763, representatives of Great Britain, France, and France's ally Spain signed the Treaty of Paris, which ended the French and Indian War. In the treaty, France gave New France east of the Mississippi River to Britain, except for New Orleans and its environs, which France gave to Spain along with New France west of the Mississippi River. The British returned Cuba, captured during the war, to Spain in exchange for Florida.

Despite the victory, the French and Indian War seriously strained relations between Britain and the American colonists. The British thought the colonists did not provide enough support for the long and costly war that Britain had fought to protect them. For their part, the colonists were shocked by the weakness of British

READING CHECK

List the important events of the French and Indian War.

military tactics. They demanded to be led by colonial officers, which the British viewed as treason. Moreover, now that the French no longer held present-day Canada or the area west of the Appalachian Mountains, the colonists saw no reason why they should not expand and prosper on their own, without British help. These feelings would deepen the split between Britain and its colonies.

Issues Leading to the Revolution

At the end of the French and Indian War, British colonists believed they had every right to be regarded as full-fledged citizens of a great empire. The British, however, had no intention of treating their colonists as equals.

Changing British Policy As the French and Indian War drew to a close, British traders and land speculators showed increased interest in the Great Lakes region and the Ohio River valley. Native Americans in these areas became alarmed, and in 1763 a number of Indian peoples in the Great Lakes region rebelled against the British. Europeans named the uprising Pontiac's Rebellion, after one of the Native American leaders. To help restore peace, Britain's King George III issued the Proclamation of 1763. This order closed the region west of the Appalachian Mountains to all settlement by colonists. The area, which had just been given up by the French, was placed under the control of the British military. Nevertheless, colonists continued to move west into the forbidden territory.

The British, meanwhile, had problems of their own—financial problems. Britain had acquired huge debts during the war, and Parliament now felt that the colonists should pay some of the costs of their own government and defense.

The passage of the Sugar Act in 1764 marked the start of a new British policy designed to raise more income from the colonies. To enforce this tax and others, Parliament issued a flurry of rules. For example, smuggling cases were now to be tried in British, rather than colonial, courts. Under British law, such cases were decided by a judge alone, not by a jury. In addition, judges received a commission on all illegal cargoes and fines, which encouraged them to find

MAP SKILLS The French and Indian War drastically changed the political map and political future of North America. **Regions** *How did the relative size of European land claims in North America change between 1754 and 1763?*

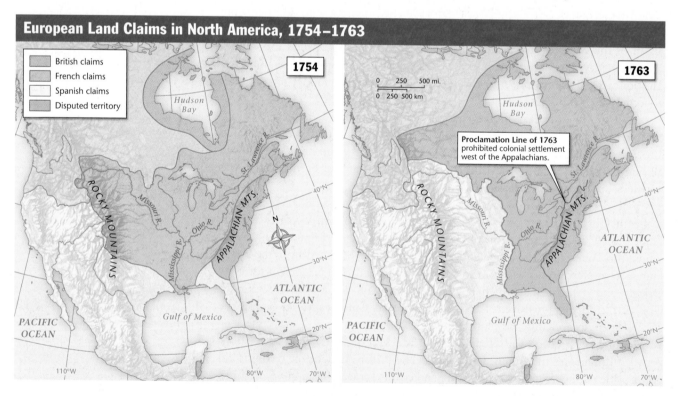

European Land Claims in North America, 1754–1763

British claims
French claims
Spanish claims
Disputed territory

1754

1763

0   250   500 mi.
0   250   500 km

Proclamation Line of 1763 prohibited colonial settlement west of the Appalachians.

accused smugglers guilty. The Quartering Act of 1765 required the colonies to provide housing and supplies for the British troops who remained in America after the French and Indian War. Although colonists complained about these British changes, most went along with them.

The Stamp Act Crisis   In March 1765, the British Parliament passed the Stamp Act. This law placed a tax on newspapers, legal documents, and most other printed materials. An official government stamp had to appear on these materials to show the tax had been paid. The Stamp Act marked the first time that the British government had taxed the colonists for the clear purpose of raising money. While the Sugar Act was really a way to raise money, too, it had been presented to the American colonists as a way to regulate trade. The colonists' reaction against the Stamp Act was widespread and extreme.

Colonists who poured their tea from this pot demonstrated their resistance to the Stamp Act.

In October 1765, delegates from nine colonies held what became known as the Stamp Act Congress. The main organizer of the meeting was James Otis of Massachusetts. As early as 1761, Otis had claimed that Britain had no right to force laws on the colonies because the colonists had no representatives in the British Parliament. In 1764, he had used the same "no taxation without representation" argument to protest the Sugar Act. Otis and other delegates now made this argument again in petitions, or letters, they sent to the king and Parliament. Colonists should have the same rights and liberties that the people of Great Britain enjoyed, the delegates argued.

In addition, colonial merchants and others organized a **boycott** of British goods. (A boycott is a refusal to buy certain products or use certain services.) Groups known as the Sons of Liberty and the Daughters of Liberty sprang up to enforce the boycott and to resist British policies in other ways. By November 1765, when the Stamp Act was to take effect, most stamp distributors had resigned or fled, leaving no one to sell the stamps. In Britain, merchants also protested as the colonists' boycott threatened their profitable trade with America. Parliament repealed the Stamp Act in March 1766.

VIEWING HISTORY Paul Revere created this engraving of the Boston Massacre to arouse anger toward the British. **Drawing Inferences** (a) Why do you think Revere depicted this aspect of the incident? (b) What part of the event might a British artist have chosen? Explain your reasoning.

Rising Tensions in the Colonies   The colonists celebrated wildly when news arrived that the Stamp Act had been repealed. Yet on the very day the Stamp Act was abolished, Parliament passed the Declaratory Act. This measure stated that Parliament had the authority to make laws that applied to the colonists "in all cases whatsoever."

In 1767, Parliament reasserted this authority by passing the Townshend Acts, which placed duties on certain imported goods, including glass and tea. The protests and violence began again. Trade duties were just as unacceptable to the colonists as direct taxes. Either way, the colonists were being taxed without their consent. Either way, Britain would use this money for the salaries of royal governors in America, who then would not have to turn to the colonial legislatures for their pay. This change would weaken the legislatures and undermine self-government in the colonies.

The growing hostility between the colonists and the British soon erupted into violence. In Boston, on the evening of March 5, 1770, an unruly crowd threatened a squad of British soldiers. The soldiers opened fire, leaving an African American named Crispus Attucks and four other colonists dead or dying in the snow. The incident, which became known as the **Boston Massacre,** added to an already tense situation.

"Remember the Ladies" Women were shut out of public debate in the 1700s, even when the subject of debate was how to create a free nation. Yet Abigail Adams made sure her voice was heard. To her husband, John, a member of the Continental Congress and later President of the United States, Abigail wrote in March 1776: "I long to hear that you have declared an independency—and by the way in the new Code of Laws which I suppose it will be necessary for you to make I desire you would Remember the Ladies, and be more generous and favorable to them than your ancestors. Do not put such unlimited power into the hands of the Husbands. Remember all Men would be tyrants if they could."

Abigail did not suggest that women be allowed to vote, an idea that was far too radical for that era. Instead, she urged that women be given greater opportunities for education.

Soon after the Boston Massacre, Parliament canceled the Townshend taxes. It kept only the duty on tea as a reminder of its authority over the colonies. While life in the colonies generally quieted down, some colonists continued to organize. In 1772, Samuel Adams, James Otis, and other Bostonians formed a Committee of Correspondence to coordinate resistance throughout the colonies. By 1774, nearly all the colonies had such committees.

In May 1773, Parliament passed the Tea Act, which gave the British East India Company the right to sell its tea in America without paying the normal taxes. Colonists had been smuggling much of their tea in order to avoid paying these taxes. The Tea Act would make the British East India Company's tea even less expensive than smuggled tea, thereby driving the American tea merchants out of business. Colonists, especially tea merchants, protested, and several colonial port cities refused to let ships carrying the tea dock in their harbors. On the night of December 16, 1773, a group of colonists disguised as Indians boarded three tea ships in Boston and threw the tea into the harbor. This act of protest became known as the Boston Tea Party.

To punish Boston and all of Massachusetts, in the spring of 1774, Parliament passed a series of harsh measures known as the Coercive Acts. The colonists labeled these laws the Intolerable Acts.

The First Continental Congress   Committees of Correspondence in several colonies called for a meeting to plan a united response to the Intolerable Acts. On September 5, 1774, the **First Continental Congress** convened in Philadelphia. The 56 delegates (including George Washington, Patrick Henry, Samuel Adams, and John Jay) came from every colony but Georgia, and they had a wide range of viewpoints. The First Continental Congress agreed to boycott English goods, and called on the people of all the English colonies to arm themselves and form militias. At the same time, the delegates made a direct appeal to the king:

> **KEY DOCUMENTS** " The foundation of English liberty, and of all free government, is a right of the people to participate in their legislative council: and as the English colonists are not represented, and . . . cannot properly be represented in the British parliament, they are entitled to a free and exclusive power of legislation in their several provincial legislatures, where their right of representation can alone be preserved. "
>
> —Declaration and Resolves of the First Continental Congress, 1774

On October 26, the Congress ended, though its members vowed to meet again in the spring if the crisis was not resolved. However, George III remained stubborn and firm. On November 18, he wrote, "The New England governments are in a state of rebellion, blows must decide."

The Shot Heard Round the World

The Americans that King George labeled "rebels" (they called themselves *Patriots*) followed the advice of the First Continental Congress. Massachusetts Patriots formed militias and began to gather guns and ammunition. A major stockpile of weapons was stored in Concord, a town about 20 miles from Boston.

Late at night on April 18, 1775, some 800 British troops moved out of Boston and marched toward Concord with orders to seize these supplies.

Boston Patriots learned of the plan and sent Paul Revere, William Dawes, and Dr. Samuel Prescott on horseback through the countryside to alert Patriot leaders. When the main British force reached Lexington, just east of Concord, they encountered 70 armed militia, known as minutemen, on the village green. Someone—no one knows who—fired a shot. The troops fired a volley into the militia. Within minutes, eight Americans lay dead on the green and another ten were wounded. The British then marched on to Concord, where they destroyed some of the militia's supplies.

As the British troops returned to Boston, thousands of Patriots gathered along the road to shoot at them from behind trees and stone walls. When the **Battles of Lexington and Concord** were over, what had seemed an easy British victory at dawn had turned into a costly defeat. More than one fourth of the British soldiers had been killed or wounded. The **Revolutionary War,** which became a war for American independence from Britain, had begun.

Just days before this fateful clash, Patrick Henry had warned his fellow Virginians to prepare for what was soon to come:

> ❝ *Gentlemen may cry, 'Peace! Peace!'—but there is no peace. . . . The next gale that sweeps from the north will bring to our ears the clash of resounding arms! . . . Is life so dear, or peace so sweet, as to be purchased at the price of chains and slavery? Forbid it, Almighty God! I know not what course others may take; but as for me, give me liberty or give me death!* ❞
>
> —Patrick Henry

Ralph Waldo Emerson noted the significance of the Battles of Lexington and Concord in his famous poem "Concord Hymn" : "Here once the embattled farmers stood, / And fired the shot heard round the world." The American Revolution would prove momentous not just for the participants but for the entire world.

Revolutionary Ideas

On one level, the American Revolution was a struggle for power between the American colonists and Great Britain over who would rule the colonies. However, the Revolution was also a struggle over ideas. The colonists were rethinking the proper relationship between citizens and their government.

Common Sense   Both levels of the Revolution were addressed in Thomas Paine's pamphlet *Common Sense,* which appeared in Philadelphia in January 1776. Paine's message to the colonists was blunt:

> **KEY DOCUMENTS** ❝ *The period of debate is closed. Arms as the last resource decide the contest. . . . Every thing that is right or natural pleads for separation. The blood of the slain, the weeping voice of nature cries, 'TIS TIME TO PART.* ❞
>
> —*Common Sense,* 1776

Within a year some 25 editions of *Common Sense* were sold. The pamphlet convinced many readers, including those who had favored a peaceful settlement of differences with Britain, to support a complete break instead.

The Declaration of Independence   *Common Sense* appeared while the Second Continental Congress was meeting in Philadelphia. Delegates included Benjamin Franklin, John Hancock, and Thomas Jefferson. In June 1776, the

This statue at the Old North Bridge in Concord, Massachusetts, honors the minutemen—those "embattled farmers" who "fired the shot heard round the world."

Congress decided it was time for the colonies to cut their ties with Britain. They appointed a committee to prepare a statement of the reasons for the separation—a **Declaration of Independence**—and chose Thomas Jefferson to draft it. (See the full text of the Declaration on the pages following this section.)

Jefferson's political ideas had been influenced by the Enlightenment, an eighteenth-century movement that emphasized science and reason as the keys to improving society. He also drew ideas from earlier political thinkers, such as the Englishman John Locke. Locke believed that people had natural rights—rights that belonged to them simply because they were human, not because kings or governments had granted them these rights. According to Locke's theory, people formed governments to protect their natural rights. If a government failed to act in the best interests of the people it governed, the people had the right to revolt and replace the government with a new one.

In the Declaration, Jefferson also stated that all people have inalienable rights, and that they have a right to change or overthrow a government that does not serve their best interests. He then listed the wrongs, or "repeated injuries," the colonists believed had been committed by the British king in an effort to establish "an absolute Tyranny." Therefore, Jefferson concluded, "these United Colonies are, and of Right ought to be Free and Independent States."

On July 4, the date now celebrated as Independence Day, delegates from 12 colonies approved the Declaration. Jefferson's document did much more than declare a nation's independence. It also defined the basic principles on which American government and society would rest. The United States would be a nation in which ordinary citizens would have a strong voice in their own government.

Fighting the Revolutionary War

By the time the Declaration of Independence was issued, Britain and the American colonists had been fighting for more than a year. The early military action centered in Boston.

The Siege of Boston Following the clashes at Lexington and Concord in April 1775, as many as 20,000 armed Patriots surrounded Boston and prevented the 6,000 British troops led by General Thomas Gage from quickly crushing the rebellion. The Patriots then turned their attention to gathering badly needed military equipment. In May, the Vermont militia's capture of Fort Ticonderoga in northern New York provided the Patriots with cannons and other supplies.

In June 1775, the Americans occupied two hills north of Boston. After two failed attempts, British troops succeeded in taking this strategic high ground. Their victory in the Battle of Bunker Hill came at a tremendous cost, however. Nearly 1,100 of 2,400 British soldiers had been killed or wounded. Patriot casualties—persons killed, wounded, or missing—amounted to around 400.

In January 1776, George Washington, whom the Congress had named commanding general of the Patriot forces, placed the cannons that had arrived from Fort Ticonderoga on Dorchester Heights. From there he could shell the British forces in Boston and the British ships in Boston harbor. The British could no longer defend their position and abandoned Boston in March 1776.

Strengths and Weaknesses Britain's main strength was its well-equipped, disciplined, and trained army. In addition, the British navy, the world's finest, provided support by transporting and landing troops and by protecting supply lines at sea. The British also received help from a number of sources. John Adams estimated that about one third of all colonists were Patriots; another third were Loyalists, or Tories as the Patriots called them; and the remaining third of

VIEWING HISTORY This eight pence colonial note is from an engraving made by Paul Revere. **Drawing Conclusions** *Why do you think Revere shows the minuteman holding both a sword and the Magna Carta?*

Americans were neutral in the war. Although Adams's estimate of Loyalists was probably high, roughly 50,000 Loyalists fought with the British army. Some African Americans, largely in the South, also helped Great Britain. The British promised freedom to all slaves who served their cause. Additional help came from Native Americans. Most Indian nations believed an American victory would be harmful to their interests. In addition, the British hired about 30,000 mercenaries, or foreign soldiers who fight for pay. They were called "Hessians" because most of their officers came from the German province of Hesse.

The British also had their problems, however. Many British citizens resented paying taxes to fight the war and sympathized with the Americans. British troops had to fight in hostile territory, and British commanders resisted adapting their tactics to conditions in America.

British weaknesses were, of course, American strengths. Patriot forces were fighting on their own territory, and many of their officers were familiar with the tactics that had worked in the French and Indian War. Even with the British promise of freedom, more African Americans served the Patriot cause than supported the British. Washington's army had some all-black units, but more often, African Americans served in white units.

On the other hand, for much of the war, the Americans lacked a well-supplied, stable, and effective fighting force. The Continental Congress lacked the power to force states to provide troops, money, and supplies. Experienced soldiers, their time of service up, would simply head home. Washington never could be sure how many troops he would have.

Fighting in the North   In the summer of 1776, British and German troops under General William Howe drove Washington's poorly trained and poorly equipped army out of New York City and into Pennsylvania. A young Patriot officer named Nathan Hale, who had volunteered to spy on the British, was

READING CHECK
What were British strengths during the Revolutionary War?

MAP SKILLS Fighting shifted south during the latter part of the war. **Movement** *How was General Washington able to trap the British at Yorktown?*

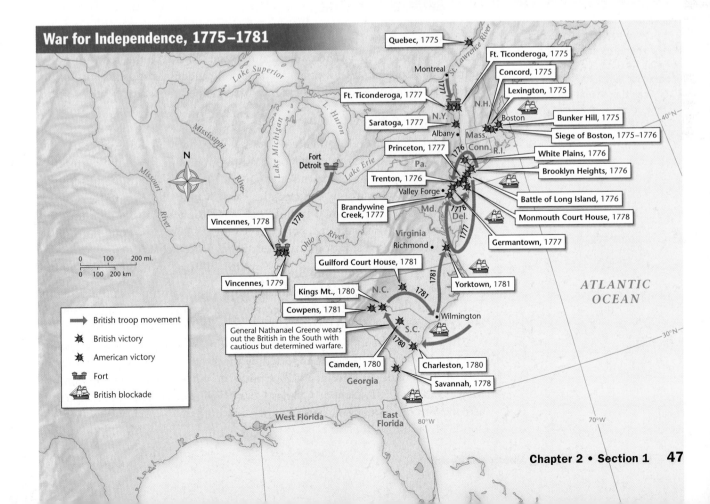

War for Independence, 1775–1781

Quebec, 1775
Ft. Ticonderoga, 1775
Montreal
Concord, 1775
Lexington, 1775
Ft. Ticonderoga, 1777
N.H.
Saratoga, 1777
Boston
Bunker Hill, 1775
N.Y.
Albany
Mass.
Siege of Boston, 1775–1776
Conn.
Princeton, 1777
R.I.
White Plains, 1776
Fort Detroit
Trenton, 1776
Pa.
Brooklyn Heights, 1776
Valley Forge
Battle of Long Island, 1776
Brandywine Creek, 1777
Md.
Del.
Monmouth Court House, 1778
Vincennes, 1778
Germantown, 1777
Virginia
Richmond
Guilford Court House, 1781
Yorktown, 1781
Vincennes, 1779
N.C.
ATLANTIC OCEAN
Kings Mt., 1780
Cowpens, 1781
Wilmington
General Nathanael Greene wears out the British in the South with cautious but determined warfare.
S.C.
Camden, 1780
Charleston, 1780
Georgia
Savannah, 1778
West Florida
East Florida

0   100   200 mi.
0   100   200 km

→ British troop movement
✸ British victory
✸ American victory
🏛 Fort
⛵ British blockade

caught. About to be hanged, he is said to have declared, "I only regret that I have but one life to lose for my country." Not all of Washington's soldiers felt that way, however. Many troops deserted, and by the winter of 1776, the entire Patriot cause seemed on the point of collapse.

Desperate times call for heroic measures, and Washington and his troops met the challenge. On Christmas night of 1776, Patriot troops were ferried across the ice-choked Delaware River in small boats. Early the next morning they surprised a force of Hessians in Trenton, New Jersey. Nearly the entire Hessian force was captured in the Battle of Trenton. The next month, a similar attack on nearby Princeton was also successful. These victories greatly boosted Patriot morale and convinced more Americans to support the Patriot cause.

In June 1777, General John Burgoyne led a British force from present-day Canada to northern New York in an effort to cut New England off from the rest of the colonies. At first, the Americans retreated, but at the same time the Continental Army and Patriot militias were assembling to confront the invaders. In mid-September the Americans won a series of victories around Saratoga, New York. Finally, on October 17, 1777, surrounded by a force now much larger than his own, Burgoyne surrendered his army. The Battle of Saratoga was the biggest American victory yet, and it marked the turning point of the war.

VIEWING FINE ART
Washington Crossing the Delaware by Emanuel Gottlieb Leutze is one of the most famous American paintings. **Analyzing Visual Information** *(a) How does the artist show the hardships of the crossing? (b) How does he indicate its heroism?*

Help From Abroad   Meanwhile, the Americans had been seeking help from France, and the victory at Saratoga finally convinced the French that the Americans had a real chance of winning the war. The alliance with France, signed on February 6, 1778, meant not only more supplies, but loans of money, French troops, and a navy. Even before France entered the war, the Marquis de Lafayette, a French nobleman, had volunteered to help the Patriots. So, too, had Polish military engineer Thaddeus Kosciusko and German Baron Friedrich von Steuben. A year later, Spain joined the war as France's ally.

Winning Independence

In the end, the British lost their colonies because the Americans had the determination to outlast their rulers. George Washington understood this better than anyone. He never gave up, no matter what the hardships. For example, Washington and his troops endured the harsh winter of 1777–1778 at Valley Forge, Pennsylvania, huddled in huts with few blankets, ragged clothing, and almost no food. Washington reported to Congress that nearly one third of his 10,000 soldiers were unfit for duty because they lacked coats or shoes.

Victories in the West and South   By late summer 1778, Patriot militia, with the help of French settlers, had captured all the British posts in present-day Indiana and Illinois. The American recapture of the fort at Vincennes strengthened the Patriots' claim to the Ohio River valley.

In 1779, the focus of the war shifted to the South, where the British hoped to draw on Loyalist sympathies. Supported by the Royal Navy, British forces seized Savannah, Georgia, in December 1778, and then Charleston, South Carolina, in May 1780. By 1781, General Charles Cornwallis had managed to set up camp at Yorktown, on a peninsula between the York and James rivers, and was waiting for the Royal Navy to arrive with reinforcements. Lafayette's troops blocked an overland escape from the peninsula.

Washington immediately recognized the opportunity to deal the British a fatal blow at Yorktown. He quickly moved a combined American-French force south from New York while the French fleet set up a blockade off the Virginia coast. When Washington's troops arrived to reinforce Lafayette, the Battle of Yorktown began. Cornwallis now faced an army more than twice the size of his own, blocking his escape from the peninsula. The French fleet prevented him from being reinforced or removed by sea. Escape was impossible. On October 19, 1781, Cornwallis surrendered to Washington.

American colonists pull down a statue of King George III.

The Treaty of Paris   In September 1783, the Treaty of Paris officially ended the Revolutionary War. In the treaty, Great Britain recognized the independence of the United States of America. The treaty also set the northern border between the United States and British Canada, and made the Mississippi River the boundary between the new United States and Spanish territory to the west, assuring the right to navigation on the river to both American and British citizens. Florida was returned to Spain, and the border between Florida and the United States was set.

The Impact of the Revolution   The Revolution did more than establish American independence. It also helped inspire Americans' **patriotism,** or love of their country. Patriotism is the passion that inspires a person to serve his or her country, either in defending it from invasion or protecting its rights and maintaining its laws and institutions. People who had made sacrifices during the Revolution, and especially those whose friends or relatives had given their lives in it, best understood the value of the freedom their country had earned.

The Revolution also spread the idea of liberty, at home and abroad. Jefferson's assertion that "all men are created equal" was a radical concept in a world that had long accepted the idea of human inequality. Jefferson, like most members of the Continental Congress, probably had no thought of applying this principle to people other than white men. However, he had set in motion a powerful idea that no one could long control. Over the next two centuries many groups in the United States, such as women and African Americans, would demand and win greater equality. At the same time, the principles for which the Patriots fought would also inspire people around the world—a process that continues to this day.

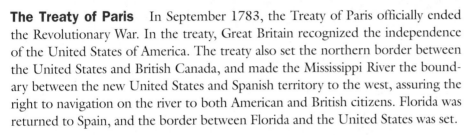

Section 1 Assessment

READING COMPREHENSION

1. What was the purpose of the colonists' **boycott** in 1765?
2. Describe the **First Continental Congress.**
3. Why were the **Battles of Lexington and Concord** important?
4. How did the **Revolutionary War** lead eventually to American **patriotism?**

CRITICAL THINKING AND WRITING

5. **Determining Relevance** How did the French and Indian War help set the stage for the American Revolution?
6. **Writing a News Story** It is 1776, and you are a journalist covering the Second Continental Congress. Write a story about the creation of the Declaration of Independence.

For: An activity on a key battle of the war
Visit: PHSchool.com
Web Code: mrd-0021

The Declaration of INDEPENDENCE

In Congress, July 4, 1776

THE UNANIMOUS DECLARATION OF THE THIRTEEN UNITED STATES OF AMERICA,

When in the Course of human events, it becomes necessary for one people to dissolve the political bands which have connected them with another, and to assume among the Powers of the earth, the separate and equal station to which the Laws of Nature and of Nature's God entitle them, a decent respect to the opinions of mankind requires that they should declare the causes which impel them to the separation.

We hold these truths to be self-evident, that all men are created equal, that they are endowed by their Creator with certain unalienable Rights, that among these are Life, Liberty and the pursuit of Happiness. That to secure these rights, Governments are instituted among Men, deriving their just powers from the consent of the governed, That whenever any Form of Government becomes destructive of these ends, it is the Right of the People to alter or to abolish it, and to institute new Government, laying its foundation on such principles and organizing its powers in such form, as to them shall seem most likely to effect their Safety and Happiness. Prudence, indeed, will dictate that Governments long established should not be changed for light and transient causes; and accordingly all experience hath shown, that mankind are more disposed to suffer, while evils are sufferable, than to right themselves by abolishing the forms to which they are accustomed. But when a long train of abuses and usurpations, pursuing invariably the same Object evinces a design to reduce them under absolute Despotism, it is their right, it is their duty, to throw off such Government, and to provide new Guards for their future security.—Such has been the patient sufferance of these Colonies; and such is now the necessity which constrains them to alter their former Systems of Government. The history of the present King of Great Britain is a history of repeated injuries and usurpations, all having in direct object the establishment of an absolute Tyranny over these States. To prove this, let Facts be submitted to a candid world.

He has refused his Assent to Laws, the most wholesome and necessary for the public good.

He has forbidden his Governors to pass Laws of immediate and pressing importance, unless suspended in their operation till his Assent should be obtained; and when so suspended, he has utterly neglected to attend to them.

He has refused to pass other Laws for the accommodation of large districts of people, unless those people would relinquish the right of Representation in the Legislature, a right inestimable to them and formidable to tyrants only.

He has called together legislative bodies at places unusual, uncomfortable, and distant from the depository of their Public Records, for the sole purpose of fatiguing them into compliance with his measures.

He has dissolved Representative Houses repeatedly, for opposing with manly firmness his invasions on the rights of the people.

He has refused for a long time, after such dissolutions, to cause others to be elected; whereby the Legislative powers, incapable of Annihilation, have returned to the People at large for their exercise; the State remaining in the mean time exposed to all the dangers of invasions from without, and convulsions within.

He has endeavored to prevent the population of these States; for that purpose obstructing the Laws for Naturalization of Foreigners; refusing to pass others to encourage their migration hither, and raising the conditions of new Appropriations of Lands.

He has obstructed the Administration of Justice, by refusing his Assent to Laws for establishing Judiciary powers.

He has made Judges dependent on his Will alone for the tenure of their offices, and the amount and payment of their salaries.

He has erected a multitude of New Offices, and sent hither swarms of Officers to harass our people and eat out their substance.

He has kept among us in time of peace, Standing Armies, without the Consent of our legislature.

He has affected to render the Military independent of and superior to the Civil power.

He has combined with others to subject us to a jurisdiction foreign to our constitutions, and unacknowledged by our laws; giving his Assent to their Acts of pretended Legislation:

For Quartering large bodies of armed troops among us:

For protecting them, by a mock Trial, from Punishment for any Murders which they should commit on the Inhabitants of these States:

For cutting off our Trade with all parts of the world:

For imposing Taxes on us without our Consent:

For depriving us in many cases, of the benefits of Trial by Jury:

For transporting us beyond Seas to be tried for pretended offenses:

For abolishing the free System of English Laws in a neighbouring Province, establishing therein an Arbitrary government, and enlarging its Boundaries so as to render it at once an example and fit instrument for introducing the same absolute rule into these Colonies:

For taking away our Charters, abolishing our most valuable Laws, and altering fundamentally the Forms of our Governments;

For suspending our own Legislature, and declaring themselves invested with Power to legislate for us in all cases whatsoever.

He has abdicated Government here, by declaring us out of his Protection, and waging War against us.

He has plundered our seas, ravaged our Coasts, burned our towns, and destroyed the lives of our people.

He is at this time transporting large Armies of foreign mercenaries to compleat the works of death, desolation and tyranny, already begun with circumstances of Cruelty and perfidy scarcely paralleled in the most barbarous ages, and totally unworthy the Head of a civilized nation.

He has constrained our fellow Citizens taken Captive on the high Seas to bear Arms against their Country, to become the executioners of their friends and Brethren, or to fall themselves by their Hands.

He has excited domestic insurrections amongst us, and has endeavored to bring on the inhabitants of our frontiers the merciless Indian Savages, whose known rule of warfare, is an undistinguished destruction of all ages, sexes, and conditions.

In every stage of these Oppressions We have Petitioned for Redress in the most humble terms. Our repeated Petitions have been answered only by repeated injury. A Prince, whose character is thus marked by every act which may define a Tyrant, is unfit to be the ruler of a free People.

Nor have We been wanting in attentions to our British brethren. We have warned them from time to time of attempts by their legislature to extend an unwarrantable jurisdiction over us. We have reminded them of the circumstances of our emigration and settlement here. We have appealed to their native justice and magnanimity, and we have conjured them by the ties of our common kindred to disavow these usurpations, which, would inevitably interrupt our connections and correspondence. They too have been deaf to the voice of Justice and of consanguinity. We must, therefore, acquiesce in the necessity, which denounces our Separation, and hold them, as we hold the rest of mankind, Enemies in War, in Peace Friends.

We, therefore, the Representatives of the United States of America, in General Congress, Assembled, appealing to the Supreme Judge of the world for the rectitude of our intentions, do, in the Name, and by the Authority of the good People of these Colonies, solemnly publish and declare, That these United Colonies are, and of Right ought to be Free and Independent States; that they are Absolved from all Allegiance to the British Crown, and that all political connection between them and the State of Great Britain, is and ought to be totally dissolved, and that as Free and Independent States, they have full Power to levy War, conclude Peace, contract Alliances, establish Commerce, and to do all other Acts and Things which Independent States may of right do. And for the support of this Declaration, with a firm reliance on the protection of Divine Providence, we mutually pledge to each other our Lives, our Fortunes and our sacred Honor.

JOHN HANCOCK
President of the Continental Congress 1775–1777

NEW HAMPSHIRE
Josiah Bartlett
William Whipple
Matthew Thornton

MASSACHUSETTS BAY
Samuel Adams
John Adams
Robert Treat Paine
Elbridge Gerry

RHODE ISLAND
Stephen Hopkins
William Ellery

CONNECTICUT
Roger Sherman
Samuel Huntington
William Williams
Oliver Wolcott

NEW YORK
William Floyd
Philip Livingston
Francis Lewis
Lewis Morris

NEW JERSEY
Richard Stockton
John Witherspoon
Francis Hopkinson
John Hart
Abraham Clark

DELAWARE
Caesar Rodney
George Read
Thomas McKean

MARYLAND
Samuel Chase
William Paca
Thomas Stone
Charles Carroll
of Carrollton

VIRGINIA
George Wythe
Richard Henry Lee
Thomas Jefferson
Benjamin Harrison
Thomas Nelson, Jr.
Francis Lightfoot Lee
Carter Braxton

PENNSYLVANIA
Robert Morris
Benjamin Rush
Benjamin Franklin
John Morton
George Clymer
James Smith
George Taylor
James Wilson
George Ross

NORTH CAROLINA
William Hooper
Joseph Hewes
John Penn

SOUTH CAROLINA
Edward Rutledge
Thomas Heyward, Jr.
Thomas Lynch, Jr.
Arthur Middleton

GEORGIA
Button Gwinnett
Lyman Hall
George Walton

Reviewing the Declaration

Vocabulary

Choose ten words in the Declaration with which you are unfamiliar. Look them up in the dictionary. Then, on a piece of paper, copy the sentence in the Declaration in which each unfamiliar word is used, and after the sentence write the definition of the unfamiliar word.

Comprehension

1. Which truths in the second paragraph are "self-evident"?

2. Name the three unalienable rights listed in the Declaration.

3. From what source do governments derive their "just powers"?

4. What right do people have when their government becomes destructive?

5. In the series of paragraphs beginning, "He has refused his Assent," to whom does the word "He" refer?

6. Which phrase in the Declaration expresses the colonists' opposition to taxation without representation?

7. According to the Declaration, what powers does the United States have "as Free and Independent States"?

8. List the colonies that the signers of the Declaration represented.

Critical Thinking

1. **Cause and Effect** Why do you think the colonists were unhappy with the fact that their judges' salaries were paid by the king?

2. **Drawing Conclusions** As Section 1 of this chapter explains, the Declaration was divided into four parts. Write down the first phrase of each of those four parts.

3. **Identifying Assumptions** Do you think that the statement "all men are created equal" was intended to apply to all human beings? Explain your reasoning.

4. **Recognizing Bias** What reference do you see to Native Americans? What attitudes toward Native Americans does this express?

5. **Drawing Conclusions** What evidence is there that the colonists had already unsuccessfully voiced concerns to the King?

Issues Past and Present

1. Write a letter to the Continental Congress from the perspective of a woman or an African American who has just read the Declaration in 1776. In your letter, comment on the Declaration's statement that "all men are created equal" and also express your attitude toward American independence.

2. What evidence in the Declaration is there of religious faith? How do you think this religious faith influenced the ideals expressed in the Declaration?

3. Examine the unalienable rights of individuals as stated in the Declaration. Do you think these rights are upheld today? Give examples to support your answer.

Analyzing Political Cartoons

1. This cartoon was published in 1779. (a) Read the caption and identify the horse. (b) Who is the master being thrown? (c) How do you know?

2. Examine the figure on the horse. (a) What is he holding? (b) What does it represent?

3. What is the cartoonist's overall message?

THE HORSE AMERICA, throwing his Master.

The Constitution of the United States

READING FOCUS

- How was the early government of the United States structured by the Articles of Confederation?

- What type of government structure did the Framers set up at the Constitutional Convention?

- How did the Federalists win the battle over ratification?

- How did Washington's administration set precedents for the new nation and provide for a new capital city?

MAIN IDEA

Some prominent Americans felt that the Articles of Confederation did not provide a strong enough national government. A new plan of government, the Constitution, was drafted at the Constitutional Convention. It was ratified after the promise was made to add a Bill of Rights.

KEY TERMS

Articles of Confederation
democracy
republic
United States Constitution
federal system of
    government
separation of powers
checks and balances
Federalists
anti-Federalists
Bill of Rights
administration

TARGET READING SKILL

Identify Cause and Effect Copy the chart below. As you read, list the problems of the Articles of Confederation and the ways in which the Constitution addressed them.

Problems of the Articles of Confederation	Solutions Provided by the Constitution
Government lacked the power to tax.	Congress has the power to tax.

This painting shows George Washington saying farewell to his officers after resigning his commission.

Setting the Scene On December 23, 1783, George Washington performed perhaps the most important act of his life: he voluntarily gave up power. The triumphant general was easily the country's most popular and best-known figure. Now that the Revolutionary War was over, many people expected him to move into a new role as head of the new nation, maybe even its king.

Washington, though, had other plans. Having helped Americans win their freedom from a king, he believed that the nation did not need another supreme ruler. In an act that stunned the world, he gave up his commission as commander of the American army and headed home to his estate at Mount Vernon, Virginia, to retire.

Early Government

Americans now faced a new challenge. Could they enjoy their hard-won freedoms without a strong, unified, national government? Could they keep their new liberty and maintain order at the same time? In short, what kind of government should a free people have?

The Continental Congress that had approved the Declaration of Independence in 1776 was simply a loose collection of delegates from 13 separate states. Almost no one wanted a powerful national government. Most people regarded Congress as only a wartime necessity.

Americans at that time generally thought of themselves as citizens of individual states, not of a nation. In fact, when referring to the United States, most Americans wrote "the United States *are*" (plural) rather than "the United States *is*" (singular) as people do today. They believed that the country as a whole

Washington Becomes President

On April 30, 1789, a crowd of thousands surrounded Federal Hall, an elegant building on New York City's Wall Street that served as the temporary home of the new government. Those within earshot listened as George Washington repeated the oath of office of President of the United States and kissed a Bible. The crowd then roared its approval.

Washington had been elected in early 1789 by a unanimous vote of the new electoral college. (*Unanimous* means having the agreement of everyone.) Massachusetts patriot John Adams, a leading Federalist, became Vice President.

Immediately, President Washington began selecting his Cabinet, the officials who head the major departments of the executive branch. Besides running their own agencies, Cabinet officers advise the President. Washington called on two of the nation's most respected patriots, Thomas Jefferson and Alexander Hamilton, to fill his most crucial Cabinet posts.

Jefferson was a logical choice to head the Department of State because he had just spent several years serving as ambassador to France, the closest ally of the United States. Alexander Hamilton, the new head of the Department of the Treasury, was a brilliant man who had served as private secretary to General Washington during the Revolution. Now Hamilton headed the government's largest department. In contrast to Jefferson, Hamilton believed that governmental power, properly used, could accomplish great things.

Despite the strong contrasts between Jefferson and Hamilton, the first months, even years, of the new government went fairly smoothly. The economic problems brought on by the war eased, and the adoption of the Constitution gave the nation much-needed stability.

READING CHECK

Where was Washington sworn in as President?

NOTABLE PRESIDENTS
George Washington

*1st President
1789–1797*

"The basis of our political systems is the right of the people to make and to alter their Constitutions of Government."

—**Farewell Address, 1796**

George Washington was not only the nation's first President, but also the person for whom the office was created. A former Virginia planter and surveyor, he had fought in the French and Indian War and had led the Continental Army during the Revolution. His leadership in the fight for independence made him the nation's leading public figure.

Washington was famous, too, for his honesty, dignity, and self-control. In 1787, the Framers of the Constitution were confident that he could be trusted with the enormous powers of the presidency. Washington's dignity and restraint as President eased many people's fears about the new government.

Washington could not, however, make the new government universally popular. Many Americans distrusted strong government, Hamilton's economic plans, and Washington's pro-British foreign policy. Convinced that Washington was leading the nation away from the ideals of the Revolution, they rallied behind Thomas Jefferson. Saddened that he could not prevent factions, Washington refused to run for a third term in 1796.

When Washington died, however, Americans joined together to honor his steadfast service to the nation, first as a general fighting a difficult war and later as a President seeking a workable balance between order and liberty.

Connecting to Today

Do you believe that dignity and restraint are as important for American Presidents today as they were in Washington's era? Explain your answer.

For: More on George Washington
Visit: PHSchool.com
Web Code: mrd-2057

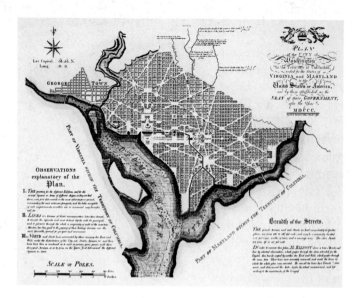

This 1792 engraving is based on L'Enfant's plan for Washington, D.C.

Washington knew that his every decision, every action, and every inaction as President would establish a precedent for how to govern. (A precedent is something done or said that becomes an example, rule, or tradition to be followed.) He worked to establish a tone of dignity in his term of office, or **administration.** (*Administration* can also refer to the members and agencies of the executive branch as a whole.) His own appearance and personality helped. More than six feet tall, Washington made an impressive figure. By nature he was solemn, reserved, and very formal.

Throughout his first term, Washington remained a popular figure, and in 1792 he won unanimous reelection. Reluctantly, he accepted. As you will read, though, his second administration would be marked by criticism and controversy.

Planning a Capital City

A new nation needed a new capital, one that could equal the beauty and stature of Europe's grand capital cities. The Residence Act of 1790 specified that the capital would be a 10-square-mile stretch of land on the Potomac River along the Maryland-Virginia border. At Jefferson's suggestion, Washington appointed Benjamin Banneker, an African American mathematician and inventor, to the commission to survey the city. Pierre-Charles L'Enfant, a French artist and architect who had fought for the United States during the Revolution, developed the plan for a spacious capital with broad streets laid out in an elegant, European-style pattern. The federal government moved to the new District of Columbia in 1800, decades before the plan was fully realized.

Today, Washington, D.C., with its great boulevards, marble buildings in the Roman style, and public monuments, is the most visible legacy of the Federalists' grand plans for the United States. It was meant to display the power and dignity of the new federal government that they had fought to build.

Section 2 Assessment

READING COMPREHENSION

1. What kind of government is (a) a **democracy,** (b) a **republic,** and (c) a **federal system of government?**

2. Explain how the **separation of powers** and the system of **checks and balances** affect government power.

3. What were the views of the **Federalists** and the **anti-Federalists?**

4. What is the **Bill of Rights?**

CRITICAL THINKING AND WRITING

5. **Distinguishing Fact From Opinion** Write two major facts about the kind of government set up by the Articles of Confederation. Then write an opinion about each of those facts.

6. **Writing a Letter to the Editor** It is 1787, and you are strongly in favor of (or strongly opposed to) ratification of the Constitution. Write a short letter to the editor expressing your views.

For: An activity on the Constitutional Convention
Visit: PHSchool.com
Web Code: mrd-0022

The Constitution
of the United States

THE SIX BASIC PRINCIPLES

The classic textbook *Magruder's American Government* outlines the six basic principles of the Constitution. Below is a description of these principles:

1 Popular Sovereignty

The Preamble to the Constitution begins with the bold phrase, "We the people . . ." These words announce that in the United States, the people are sovereign. The government receives its power from the people and can govern only with their consent.

2 Limited Government

Because the people are the ultimate source of all government power, the government has only as much authority as the people give it. Government's power is thus limited. Much of the Constitution, in fact, consists of specific limitations on government power.

3 Separation of Powers

Government power is not only limited, but also divided. The Constitution assigns certain powers to each of the three branches: the legislative (Congress), executive (President), and judicial (federal courts). This separation of government's powers was intended to prevent the misuse of power.

4 Checks and Balances

The system of checks and balances gives each of the three branches of government the ability to restrain the other two. Such a system makes government less efficient but also less likely to trample on the rights of citizens.

5 Judicial Review

Who decides whether an act of government violates the Constitution? Historically, the courts have filled this function. The principle of judicial review means that federal courts have the power to review acts of the federal government and to cancel any acts that are unconstitutional, or violate a provision in the Constitution.

6 Federalism

A federal system of government is one in which power is divided between a central government and smaller governments. This sharing of powers is intended to ensure that the central government is powerful enough to be effective, yet not so powerful as to threaten states or individuals.

PARTS OF THE CONSTITUTION

Preamble

A Note on the Text of the Constitution

The complete text of the Constitution, including amendments, appears on the pages that follow. Portions of the Constitution altered by later amendments or that no longer apply have been crossed out. Commentary appears in the outside column of each page.

PREAMBLE

We the People of the United States, in Order to form a more perfect Union, establish Justice, insure domestic Tranquility, provide for the common defence, promote the general Welfare, and secure the Blessings of Liberty to ourselves and our Posterity, do ordain and establish this Constitution for the United States of America.

Article I.

Section 1.

All legislative Powers herein granted shall be vested in a Congress of the United States, which shall consist of a Senate and House of Representatives.

Section 2.

1. The House of Representatives shall be composed of Members chosen every second Year by the People of the several States, and the Electors in each State shall have the Qualifications requisite for Electors of the most numerous Branch of the State Legislature.

2. No Person shall be a Representative who shall not have attained to the age of twenty-five Years, and been seven Years a Citizen of the United States, and who shall not, when elected, be an Inhabitant of that State in which he shall be chosen.

3. Representatives ~~and direct Taxes~~* shall be apportioned among the several States which may be included within this Union, according to their respective Numbers, ~~which shall be determined by adding to the whole Number of free Persons, including those bound to Service for a Term of Years and excluding Indians not taxed, three fifths of all other Persons.~~ The actual Enumeration shall be made within three Years after the first Meeting of the Congress of the United States, and within every subsequent term of ten Years, in such Manner as they shall by Law direct. The Number of Representatives shall not exceed one for every thirty Thousand, but each State shall have at Least one Representative; and, until such enumeration shall be made, the State of New Hampshire shall be entitled to choose three, Massachusetts eight, Rhode Island and Providence Plantations one, Connecticut five, New York

*The black lines indicate portions of the Constitution altered by subsequent amendments to the document.

The Preamble states the broad purposes the Constitution is intended to serve—to establish a government that provides for greater cooperation among the States, ensures justice and peace, provides for defense against foreign enemies, promotes the general well-being of the people, and secures liberty now and in the future. The phrase *We the People* emphasizes the twin concepts of popular sovereignty and of representative government.

LEGISLATIVE BRANCH

Section 1. Legislative Power; Congress

Congress, the nation's lawmaking body, is bicameral in form; that is, it is composed of two houses: the Senate and the House of Representatives. The Framers of the Constitution purposely separated the lawmaking power from the power to enforce the laws (Article II, the Executive Branch) and the power to interpret them (Article III, the Judicial Branch). This system of separation of powers is supplemented by a system of checks and balances; that is, in several provisions the Constitution gives to each of the three branches various powers with which it may restrain the actions of the other two branches.

Section 2. House of Representatives

Clause 1. Election Electors means voters. Members of the House of Representatives are elected every two years. Each State must permit the same persons to vote for United States representatives as it permits to vote for the members of the larger house of its own legislature. The 17th Amendment (1913) extends this requirement to the qualification of voters for United States senators.

Clause 2. Qualifications A member of the House of Representatives must be at least 25 years old, an American citizen for seven years, and a resident of the State he or she represents. In addition, political custom requires that a representative also reside in the district from which he or she is elected.

Clause 3. Apportionment The number of representatives each State is entitled to is based on its population, which is counted every 10 years in the census. Congress reapportions the seats among the States after each census. In the Reapportionment Act of 1929, Congress fixed the permanent size of the House at 435 members with each State having at least one representative. Today there is one House seat for approximately every 650,000 persons in the population.

The words "three-fifths of all other persons" referred to slaves and reflected the Three-Fifths Compromise reached by the Framers at Philadelphia in 1787; the phrase was made obsolete, was in effect repealed, by the 13th Amendment in 1865.

six, New Jersey four, Pennsylvania eight, Delaware one, Maryland six, Virginia ten, North Carolina five, South Carolina five, and Georgia three.

4. When vacancies happen in the Representation from any State, the Executive Authority thereof shall issue Writs of Election to fill such Vacancies.

5. The House of Representatives shall choose their Speaker and other Officers; and shall have the sole Power of Impeachment.

Clause 4. Vacancies The executive authority refers to the governor of a State. If a member leaves office or dies before the expiration of his or her term, the governor is to call a special election to fill the vacancy.

Clause 5. Officers; impeachment The House elects a Speaker, customarily chosen from the majority party in the House. Impeachment means accusation. The House has the exclusive power to impeach, or accuse, civil officers; the Senate (Article I, Section 3, Clause 6) has the exclusive power to try those impeached by the House.

Section 3. Senate

Clause 1. Composition, election, term Each State has two senators. Each serves for six years and has one vote. Originally, senators were not elected directly by the people, but by each State's legislature. The 17th Amendment, added in 1913, provides for the popular election of senators.

Clause 2. Classification The senators elected in 1788 were divided into three groups so that the Senate could become a "continuing body." One-third of the Senate's seats are up for election every two years.

The 17th Amendment provides that a Senate vacancy is to be filled at a special election called by the governor; State law may also permit the governor to appoint a successor to serve until that election is held.

Clause 3. Qualifications A senator must be at least 30 years old, a citizen for at least nine years, and a resident of the State from which elected.

Clause 4. Presiding officer The Vice President presides over the Senate, but may vote only to break a tie.

Clause 5. Other officers The Senate chooses its own officers, including a president pro tempore to preside when the Vice President is not there.

Clause 6. Impeachment trials The Senate conducts the trials of those officials impeached by the House. The Vice President presides unless the President is on trial, in which case the Chief Justice of the United States does so. A conviction requires the votes of two-thirds of the senators present.

No President has ever been convicted. In 1868 the House voted eleven articles of impeachment against

Section 3.

1. The Senate of the United States shall be composed of two Senators from each State ~~chosen by the Legislature thereof~~ for six Years; and each Senator shall have one Vote.

2. Immediately after they shall be assembled in Consequences of the first Election, they shall be divided, as equally as may be, into three Classes. The Seats of the Senators of the first Class shall be vacated at the Expiration of the second Year; of the second Class, at the Expiration of the fourth Year; and of the third Class, at the Expiration of the sixth Year; so that one-third may be chosen every second Year; ~~and if Vacancies happen by Resignation, or otherwise, during the Recess of the Legislature of any State, the Executive thereof may make temporary Appointments until the next Meeting of the Legislature, which shall then fill such Vacancies.~~

3. No Person shall be a Senator who shall not have attained to the Age of thirty Years, and been nine Years a Citizen of the United States, and who shall not, when elected, be an Inhabitant of that State for which he shall be chosen.

4. The Vice President of the United States shall be President of the Senate but shall have no Vote, unless they be equally divided.

5. The Senate shall choose their other Officers, and also a President pro tempore, in the Absence of the Vice President, or when he shall exercise the Office of President of the United States.

6. The Senate shall have the sole Power to try all Impeachments. When sitting for that Purpose, they shall be on Oath or Affirmation. When the President of the United States is tried, the Chief Justice shall preside: And no Person shall be convicted without the Concurrence of two thirds of the Members present.

7. Judgment in Cases of Impeachment shall not extend further than to removal from Office, and disqualification to hold and enjoy any Office of honor, Trust, or Profit under the United States: but the Party convicted shall nevertheless be liable and subject to Indictment, Trial, Judgment and Punishment, according to Law.

Section 4.

1. The Times, Places and Manner of holding Elections for Senators and Representatives, shall be prescribed in each State by the Legislature thereof; but the Congress may at any time by law make or alter such Regulations, except as to the Places of choosing Senators.

2. The Congress shall assemble at least once in every Year, and such Meeting shall be on the first Monday in December, unless they shall by Law appoint a different Day.

Section 5.

1. Each House shall be the Judge of the Elections, Returns and Qualifications of its own Members, and a Majority of each shall constitute a Quorum to do Business; but a smaller Number may adjourn from day to day, and may be authorized to compel the Attendance of absent Members, in such Manner, and under such Penalties, as each House may provide.

2. Each House may determine the Rules of its Proceedings, punish its Members for disorderly Behavior, and, with the Concurrence of two thirds, expel a Member.

3. Each House shall keep a Journal of its Proceedings, and from time to time publish the same, excepting such Parts as may in their Judgment require Secrecy; and the Yeas and Nays of the Members of either House on any question shall, at the Desire of one fifth of those Present, be entered on the Journal.

4. Neither House, during the Session of Congress, shall, without the Consent of the other, adjourn for more than three days, nor to any other Place than that in which the two Houses shall be sitting.

President Andrew Johnson, but the Senate fell one vote short of convicting him. In 1974 President Richard M. Nixon resigned the presidency in the face of almost certain impeachment by the House. The House brought two articles of impeachment against President Bill Clinton in late 1998. Neither charge was supported by even a simple majority vote in the Senate, on February 12, 1999.

Clause 7. Penalty on conviction The punishment of an official convicted in an impeachment case has always been removal from office. The Senate can also bar a convicted person from ever holding any federal office, but it is not required to do so. A convicted person can also be tried and punished in a regular court for any crime involved in the impeachment case.

Section 4. Elections and Meetings

Clause 1. Election In 1842 Congress required that representatives be elected from districts within each State with more than one seat in the House. The districts in each State are drawn by that State's legislature. Seven States now have only one seat in the House: Alaska, Delaware, Montana, North Dakota, South Dakota, Vermont, and Wyoming. The 1842 law also directed that representatives be elected in each State on the same day: the Tuesday after the first Monday in November of every even-numbered year. In 1914 Congress also set that same date for the election of senators.

Clause 2. Sessions Congress must meet at least once a year. The 20th Amendment (1933) changed the opening date to January 3.

Section 5. Legislative Proceedings

Clause 1. Admission of members; quorum In 1969 the Supreme Court held that the House cannot exclude any member-elect who satisfies the qualifications set out in Article I, Section 2, Clause 2.

A majority in the House (218 members) or Senate (51) constitutes a quorum. In practice, both houses often proceed with less than a quorum present. However, any member may raise a point of order (demand a "quorum call"). If a roll call then reveals less than a majority of the members present, that chamber must either adjourn or the sergeant at arms must be ordered to round up absent members.

Clause 2. Rules Each house has adopted detailed rules to guide its proceedings. Each house may discipline members for unacceptable conduct; expulsion requires a two-thirds vote.

Clause 3. Record Each house must keep and publish a record of its meetings. The *Congressional Record* is published for every day that either house of Congress is in session, and provides a written record of all that is said and done on the floor of each house each session.

Clause 4. Adjournment Once in session, neither house may suspend (recess) its work for more than three days without the approval of the other house. Both houses must always meet in the same location.

Section 6. Compensation, Immunities, and Disabilities of Members

Clause 1. Salaries; immunities Each house sets its members' salaries, paid by the United States; the 27th Amendment (1992) modified this pay-setting power. This provision establishes "legislative immunity." The purpose of this immunity is to allow members to speak and debate freely in Congress itself. Treason is strictly defined in Article III, Section 3. A felony is any serious crime. A breach of the peace is any indictable offense less than treason or a felony; this exemption from arrest is of little real importance today.

Clause 2. Restrictions on office holding No sitting member of either house may be appointed to an office in the executive or in the judicial branch if that position was created or its salary was increased during that member's current elected term. The second part of this clause—forbidding any person serving in either the executive or the judicial branch from also serving in Congress—reinforces the principle of separation of powers.

Section 7. Revenue Bills, President's Veto

Clause 1. Revenue bills All bills that raise money must originate in the House. However, the Senate has the power to amend any revenue bill sent to it from the lower house.

Clause 2. Enactment of laws; veto Once both houses have passed a bill, it must be sent to the President. The President may (1) sign the bill, thus making it law; (2) veto the bill, whereupon it must be returned to the house in which it originated; or (3) allow the bill to become law without signature, by not acting upon it within 10 days of its receipt from Congress, not counting Sundays. The President has a fourth option at the end of a congressional session: If he does not act on a measure within 10 days, and Congress adjourns during that period, the bill dies; the "pocket veto" has been applied to it. A presidential veto may be overridden by a two-thirds vote in each house.

Clause 3. Other measures This clause refers to joint resolutions, measures Congress often passes to deal with unusual, temporary, or ceremonial matters. A joint resolution passed by Congress and signed by the President has the force of law, just as a bill does. As a matter of custom, a joint resolution proposing an amendment to the Constitution is not submitted to the President for signature

Section 6.

1. The Senators and Representatives shall receive a Compensation for their Services, to be ascertained by Law, and paid out of the Treasury of the United States. They shall in all Cases, except Treason, Felony, and Breach of the Peace, be privileged from Arrest during their Attendance at the Session of their respective Houses, and in going to and returning from the same; and for any Speech or Debate in either House, they shall not be questioned in any other Place.

2. No Senator or Representative shall, during the Time for which he was elected, be appointed to any civil Office under the Authority of the United States, which shall have been created, or the Emoluments whereof shall have been increased during such time; and no Person holding any Office under the United States, shall be a Member of either House during his Continuance in Office.

Section 7.

1. All Bills for raising Revenue shall originate in the House of Representatives; but the Senate may propose or concur with amendments as on other Bills.

2. Every Bill which shall have passed the House of Representatives and the Senate, shall, before it become a law, be presented to the President of the United States: If he approve, he shall sign it, but if not he shall return it, with his Objections to that House in which it shall have originated, who shall enter the Objections at large on their Journal, and proceed to reconsider it. If after such Reconsideration two thirds of the House shall agree to pass the Bill, it shall be sent, together with the Objections, to the other House, by which it shall likewise be reconsidered, and if approved by two thirds of that House, it shall become a Law. But in all such Cases the Votes of both Houses shall be determined by Yeas and Nays, and the Names of the Persons voting for and against the Bill shall be entered on the Journal of each House respectively. If any Bill shall not be returned by the President within ten Days (Sunday excepted) after it shall have been presented to him, the Same shall be a law, in like Manner as if he had signed it, unless the Congress by their Adjournment, prevent its Return, in which Case it shall not be a Law.

3. Every Order, Resolution, or Vote to which the Concurrence of the Senate and House of Representatives may be necessary (except on a question of adjournment) shall be presented to the President of the United States; and before the Same shall take Effect, shall be approved by him, or, being disapproved by him, shall be repassed by two thirds of

the Senate and House of Representatives, according to the Rules and Limitations prescribed in the Case of a Bill.

Section 8.

The Congress shall have Power

1. To lay and collect Taxes, Duties, Imposts and Excises to pay the Debts and provide for the common Defence and general Welfare of the United States; but all Duties, Imposts and Excises, shall be uniform throughout the United States;

2. To borrow Money on the credit of the United States;

3. To regulate Commerce with foreign Nations, and among the several States, and with the Indian Tribes;

4. To establish an uniform Rule of Naturalization, and uniform Laws on the subject of Bankruptcies throughout the United States;

5. To coin Money, regulate the Value thereof, and of foreign Coin, and fix the Standard of Weights and Measures;

6. To provide for the Punishment of counterfeiting the Securities and current Coin of the United States;

7. To establish Post Offices and post Roads;

8. To promote the Progress of Science and useful Arts, by securing, for limited Times to Authors and Inventors the exclusive Right to their respective Writings and Discoveries;

9. To constitute Tribunals inferior to the supreme Court;

10. To define and punish Piracies and Felonies committed on the high Seas, and Offences against the Law of nations;

11. To declare War, grant Letters of Marque and Reprisal, and make Rules concerning Captures on Land and Water;

---

or veto. Concurrent and simple resolutions do not have the force of law and, therefore, are not submitted to the President.

Section 8. Powers of Congress

Clause 1. The 18 separate clauses in this section set out 27 of the many expressed powers the Constitution grants to Congress. In this clause Congress is given the power to levy and provide for the collection of various kinds of taxes, in order to finance the operations of the government. All federal taxes must be levied at the same rates throughout the country.

Clause 2. Congress has power to borrow money to help finance the government. Federal borrowing is most often done through the sale of bonds on which interest is paid. The Constitution does not limit the amount the government may borrow.

Clause 3. This clause, the Commerce Clause, gives Congress the power to regulate both foreign and interstate trade. Much of what Congress does, it does on the basis of its commerce power.

Clause 4. Congress has the exclusive power to determine how aliens may become citizens of the United States. Congress may also pass laws relating to bankruptcy.

Clause 5. Congress has the power to establish and require the use of uniform gauges of time, distance, weight, volume, area, and the like.

Clause 6. Congress has the power to make it a federal crime to falsify the coins, paper money, bonds, stamps, and the like of the United States.

Clause 7. Congress has the power to provide for and regulate the transportation and delivery of mail; "post offices" are those buildings and other places where mail is deposited for dispatch; "post roads" include all routes over or upon which mail is carried.

Clause 8. Congress has the power to provide for copyrights and patents. A copyright gives an author or composer the exclusive right to control the reproduction, publication, and sale of literary, musical, or other creative work. A patent gives a person the exclusive right to control the manufacture or sale of his or her invention.

Clause 9. Congress has the power to create the lower federal courts, all of the several federal courts that function beneath the Supreme Court.

Clause 10. Congress has the power to prohibit, as a federal crime: (1) certain acts committed outside the territorial jurisdiction of the United States, and (2) the commission within the United States of any wrong against any nation with which we are at peace.

Clause 11. Only Congress can declare war. However, the President, as commander in chief of the armed forces (Article II, Section 2, Clause 1), can make war without such

COMMENTARY

United States Constitution

a formal declaration. Letters of marque and reprisal are commissions authorizing private persons to outfit vessels (privateers) to capture and destroy enemy ships in time of war; they were forbidden in international law by the Declaration of Paris of 1856, and the United States has honored the ban since the Civil War.

Clauses 12 and 13. Congress has the power to provide for and maintain the nation's armed forces. It established the air force as an independent element of the armed forces in 1947, an exercise of its inherent powers in foreign relations and national defense. The two-year limit on spending for the army insures civilian control of the military.

Clause 14. Today these rules are set out in a lengthy, oft-amended law, the Uniform Code of Military Justice, passed by Congress in 1950.

Clauses 15 and 16. In the National Defense Act of 1916, Congress made each State's militia (volunteer army) a part of the National Guard. Today, Congress and the States cooperate in its maintenance. Ordinarily, each State's National Guard is under the command of that State's governor; but Congress has given the President the power to call any or all of those units into federal service when necessary.

Clause 17. In 1791 Congress accepted land grants from Maryland and Virginia and established the District of Columbia for the nation's capital. Assuming Virginia's grant would never be needed, Congress returned it in 1846. Today, the elected government of the District's 69 square miles operates under the authority of Congress. Congress also has the power to acquire other lands from the States for various federal purposes.

Clause 18. This is the Necessary and Proper Clause, also often called the Elastic Clause. It is the constitutional basis for the many and far-reaching implied powers of the Federal Government.

Section 9. Powers Denied to Congress

Clause 1. The phrase "such persons" referred to slaves. This provision was part of the Commerce Compromise, one of the bargains struck in the writing of the Constitution. Congress outlawed the slave trade in 1808.

Clause 2. A writ of habeas corpus, the "great writ of liberty," is a court order directing a sheriff, warden, or other public officer, or a private person, who is detaining another to "produce the body" of the one being held in order that the legality of the detention may be determined by the court.

Clause 3. A bill of attainder is a legislative act that inflicts punishment without a judicial trial. See Article I, Section 10, and Article III, Section 3, Clause 2. An *ex post facto* law is

12. To raise and support Armies; but no Appropriation of Money to that Use shall be for a longer Term than two Years;

13. To provide and maintain a Navy;

14. To make Rules for the Government and Regulation of the land and naval Forces;

15. To provide for calling forth the Militia to execute the Laws of the Union, suppress Insurrections and repel Invasions;

16. To provide for organizing, arming, and disciplining the Militia, and for governing such Part of them as may be employed in the Service of the United States, reserving to the States respectively the Appointment of the Officers, and the Authority of training the Militia according to the discipline prescribed by Congress;

17. To exercise exclusive Legislation in all Cases whatsoever, over such District (not exceeding ten Miles square) as may, by Cession of Particular States, and the Acceptance of Congress, become the Seat of the Government of the United States, and to exercise like Authority over all Places purchased by the Consent of the Legislature of the State in which the Same shall be, for the Erection of Forts, Magazines, Arsenals, Dockyards and other needful Buildings;—And

18. To make all Laws which shall be necessary and proper for carrying into Execution the foregoing Powers and all other Powers vested by this Constitution in the Government of the United States, or in any Department or Officer thereof.

Section 9.

1. The Migration or Importation of such Persons as any of the States now existing shall think proper to admit, shall not be prohibited by the Congress prior to the Year one thousand eight hundred and eight, but a Tax or duty may be imposed on such Importation, not exceeding ten dollars for each Person.

2. The Privilege of the Writ of Habeas Corpus shall not be suspended, unless when in Cases of Rebellion or Invasion the public safety may require it.

3. No Bill of Attainder or ex post facto Law shall be passed.

4. No Capitation, ~~or other direct, Tax~~ shall be laid, unless in Proportion to the Census of Enumeration hereinbefore directed to be taken.

5. No Tax or Duty shall be laid on Articles exported from any State.

6. No Preference shall be given by any Regulation of Commerce or Revenue to the Ports of one State over those of another: nor shall Vessels bound to, or from, one State, be obliged to enter, clear or pay Duties in another.

7. No Money shall be drawn from the Treasury, but in Consequence of Appropriations made by Law; and a regular Statement and Account of the Receipts and Expenditures of all public Money shall be published from time to time.

8. No Title of Nobility shall be granted by the United States: And no Person holding any Office of Profit or Trust under them, shall, without the Consent of the Congress, accept of any present, Emolument, Office, or Title, of any kind whatever, from any King, Prince, or foreign State.

Section 10.

1. No State shall enter into any Treaty, Alliance, or Confederation; grant Letters of Marque and Reprisal; coin Money; emit Bills of Credit; make any Thing but gold and silver Coin a Tender in Payment of Debts; pass any Bill of Attainder, ex post facto Law, or Law impairing the Obligation of Contracts, or grant any Title of Nobility.

2. No State shall, without the Consent of the Congress, lay any Imposts or Duties on Imports or Exports, except what may be absolutely necessary for executing its inspection Laws; and the net Produce of all Duties and Imposts, laid by any State on Imports or Exports, shall be for the Use of the Treasury of the United States; and all such Laws shall be subject to the Revision and Control of the Congress.

3. No State shall, without the Consent of Congress, lay any Duty of Tonnage, keep Troops, or Ships of War in time of Peace, enter into any Agreement or Compact with another State, or with a foreign Power, or engage in War, unless actually invaded, or in such imminent Danger as will not admit of delay.

any criminal law that operates retroactively to the disadvantage of the accused. See Article I, Section 10.

Clause 4. A capitation tax is literally a "head tax," a tax levied on each person in the population. A direct tax is one paid directly to the government by the taxpayer—for example, an income or a property tax; an indirect tax is one paid to another private party who then pays it to the government—for example, a sales tax. This provision was modified by the 16th Amendment (1913), giving Congress the power to levy "taxes on incomes, from whatever source derived."

Clause 5. This provision was a part of the Commerce Compromise made by the Framers in 1787. Congress has the power to tax imported goods, however.

Clause 6. All ports within the United States must be treated alike by Congress as it exercises its taxing and commerce powers. Congress cannot tax goods sent by water from one State to another, nor may it give the ports of one State any legal advantage over those of another.

Clause 7. This clause gives Congress its vastly important "power of the purse," a major check on presidential power. Federal money can be spent only in those amounts and for those purposes expressly authorized by an act of Congress. All federal income and spending must be accounted for, regularly and publicly.

Clause 8. This provision, preventing the establishment of a nobility, reflects the principle that "all men are created equal." It was also intended to discourage foreign attempts to bribe or otherwise corrupt officers of the government.

Section 10. Powers Denied to the States

Clause 1. The States are not sovereign governments and so cannot make agreements or otherwise negotiate with foreign states; the power to conduct foreign relations is an exclusive power of the National Government. The power to coin money is also an exclusive power of the National Government. Several powers forbidden to the National Government are here also forbidden to the States.

Clause 2. This provision relates to foreign, not interstate, commerce. Only Congress, not the States, can tax imports; and the States are, like Congress, forbidden the power to tax exports.

Clause 3. A duty of tonnage is a tax laid on ships according to their cargo capacity. Each State has a constitutional right to provide for and maintain a militia; but no State may keep a standing army or navy. The several restrictions here prevent the States from assuming powers that the Constitution elsewhere grants to the National Government.

EXECUTIVE BRANCH

Section 1. President and Vice President

Clause 1. Executive power, term This clause gives to the President the very broad "executive power," the power to enforce the laws and otherwise administer the public policies of the United States. It also sets the length of the presidential (and vice-presidential) term of office; see the 22nd Amendment (1951), which places a limit on presidential (but not vice-presidential) tenure.

Clause 2. Electoral college This clause establishes the "electoral college," although the Constitution does not use that term. It is a body of presidential electors chosen in each State, and it selects the President and Vice President every four years. The number of electors chosen in each State equals the number of senators and representatives that State has in Congress.

Clause 3. Election of President and Vice President This clause was replaced by the 12th Amendment in 1804.

Clause 4. Date Congress has set the date for the choosing of electors as the Tuesday after the first Monday in November every fourth year, and for the casting of electoral votes as the Monday after the second Wednesday in December of that year.

Clause 5. Qualifications The President must have been born a citizen of the United States, be at least 35 years old,

Article II

Section 1.

1. The executive Power shall be vested in a President of the United States of America. He shall hold his Office during the Term of four Years, and, together with the Vice President, chosen for the same Term, be elected as follows:

2. Each State shall appoint, in such Manner as the Legislature thereof may direct, a Number of Electors, equal to the whole Number of Senators and Representatives to which the State may be entitled in the Congress: but no Senator or Representative, or Person holding an Office of Trust or Profit, under the United States, shall be appointed an Elector.

3. ~~The Electors shall meet in their respective States, and vote by Ballot for two Persons, of whom one at least shall not be an Inhabitant of the same State with themselves. And they shall make a List of all the Persons voted for, and of the Number of Votes for each; which List they shall sign and certify, and transmit sealed to the Seat of the Government of the United States, directed to the President of the Senate. The President of the Senate shall, in the Presence of the Senate and House of Representatives, open all the Certificates, and the Votes shall then be counted. The Person having the greatest Number of Votes shall be the President, if such Number be a majority of the whole Number of Electors appointed; and if there be more than one who have such Majority, and have an equal Number of Votes, then, the House of Representatives shall immediately choose by Ballot one of them for President; and if no Person have a Majority, then from the five highest on the List the said House shall in like Manner choose the President. But in choosing the President, the Votes shall be taken by States, the Representatives from each State having one Vote; a quorum for this Purpose shall consist of a Member or Members from two thirds of the States, and a Majority of all the States shall be necessary to a Choice. In every Case, after the Choice of the President, the Person having the greatest Number of Votes of the Electors shall be the Vice President. But if there should remain two or more who have equal Votes, the Senate shall choose from them by Ballot the Vice President.~~

4. The Congress may determine the Time of choosing the Electors, and the Day on which they shall give their Votes; which Day shall be the same throughout the United States.

5. No Person except a natural born Citizen, or a Citizen of the United States, at the time of the Adoption of this

Constitution, shall be eligible to the Office of President; neither shall any person be eligible to that Office who shall not have attained to the Age of thirty-five Years, and been fourteen Years a Resident within the United States.

6. ~~In Case of the Removal of the President from Office, or of his Death, Resignation, or Inability to discharge the Powers and Duties of the said Office, the Same shall devolve on the Vice President,~~ and the Congress may by Law provide for the Case of Removal, Death, Resignation or Inability, both of the President and Vice President, declaring what Officer shall then act as President, and such Officer shall act accordingly, until the Disability be removed, or a President shall be elected.

7. The President shall, at stated Times, receive for his Services, a Compensation, which shall neither be increased nor diminished during the Period for which he shall have been elected, and he shall not receive within that Period any other Emolument from the United States, or any of them.

8. Before he enter on the Execution of his Office, he shall take the following Oath or Affirmation: "I do solemnly swear (or affirm) that I will faithfully execute the Office of President of the United States, and will to the best of my Ability, preserve, protect and defend the Constitution of the United States."

Section 2.

1. The President shall be Commander in Chief of the Army and Navy of the United States, and of the Militia of the several States, when called into the actual Service of the United States; he may require the Opinion, in writing, of the principal Officer in each of the executive Departments, upon any Subject relating to the Duties of their respective Offices, and he shall have Power to Grant Reprieves and Pardons for Offences against the United States, except in Cases of Impeachment.

2. He shall have Power, by and with the Advice and Consent of the Senate, to make Treaties, provided two thirds of the Senators present concur; and he shall nominate, and by and with the Advice and Consent of the Senate, shall appoint Ambassadors, other public Ministers and Consuls, Judges of the supreme Court, and all other Officers of the United States, whose Appointments are not herein otherwise provided for, and which shall be established by Law: but the Congress may by Law vest the Appointment of such

and have been a resident of the United States for at least 14 years.

Clause 6. Vacancy This clause was modified by the 25th Amendment (1967), which provides expressly for the succession of the Vice President, for the filling of a vacancy in the Vice Presidency, and for the determination of presidential inability.

Clause 7. Compensation The President now receives a salary of $400,000 and a taxable expense account of $50,000 a year. Those amounts cannot be changed during a presidential term; thus, Congress cannot use the President's compensation as a bargaining tool to influence executive decisions. The phrase "any other emolument" means, in effect, any valuable gift; it does not mean that the President cannot be provided with such benefits of office as the White House, extensive staff assistance, and much else.

Clause 8. Oath of office The chief justice of the United States regularly administers this oath or affirmation, but any judicial officer may do so. Thus, Calvin Coolidge was sworn into office in 1923 by his father, a justice of the peace in Vermont.

Section 2. President's Powers and Duties

Clause 1. Military, civil powers The President, a civilian, heads the nation's armed forces, a key element in the Constitution's insistence on civilian control of the military. The President's power to "require the opinion, in writing" provides the constitutional basis for the cabinet. The President's power to grant reprieves and pardons, the power of clemency, extends only to federal cases.

Clause 2. Treaties, appointments The President has the sole power to make treaties; to become effective, a treaty must be approved by a two-thirds vote in the Senate. In practice, the President can also make executive agreements with foreign governments; these pacts, which are frequently made and usually deal with routine matters, do not require Senate consent. The President appoints the principal officers of the executive branch and all federal judges; the "inferior officers" are those who hold lesser posts.

UNITED STATES CONSTITUTION

inferior Officers, as they think proper, in the President alone, in the Courts of Law, or in the Heads of Departments.

Clause 3. Recess appointments When the Senate is not in session, appointments that require Senate consent can be made by the President on a temporary basis, as "recess appointments."

3. The President shall have Power to fill up all Vacancies that may happen during the Recess of the Senate, by granting Commissions which shall expire at the End of their next Session.

Section 3. President's Powers and Duties

The President delivers a State of the Union Message to Congress soon after that body convenes each year. That message is delivered to the nation's lawmakers and, importantly, to the American people, as well. It is shortly followed by the proposed federal budget and an economic report; and the President may send special messages to Congress at any time. In all of these communications, Congress is urged to take those actions the Chief Executive finds to be in the national interest. The President also has the power: to call special sessions of Congress; to adjourn Congress if its two houses cannot agree for that purpose; to receive the diplomatic representatives of other governments; to insure the proper execution of all federal laws; and to empower federal officers to hold their posts and perform their duties.

Section 3.

He shall from time to time give to the Congress Information of the State of the Union, and recommend to their Consideration such Measures as he shall judge necessary and expedient; he may, on extraordinary Occasions, convene both Houses, or either of them, and in Case of Disagreement between them, with Respect to the Time of Adjournment, he may adjourn them to such Time as he shall think proper; he shall receive Ambassadors and other public Ministers; he shall take Care that the Laws be faithfully executed, and shall Commission all the Officers of the United States.

Section 4. Impeachment

The Constitution outlines the impeachment process in Article I, Section 2, Clause 5 and in Section 3, Clauses 6 and 7.

Section 4.

The President, Vice President and all Civil Officers of the United States, shall be removed from Office on Impeachment for and Conviction of, Treason, Bribery, or other high Crimes and Misdemeanors.

JUDICIAL BRANCH

Section 1. Courts, Terms of Office

The judicial power conferred here is the power of federal courts to hear and decide cases, disputes between the government and individuals and between private persons (parties). The Constitution creates only the Supreme Court of the United States; it gives to Congress the power to establish other, lower federal courts (Article I, Section 8, Clause 9) and to fix the size of the Supreme Court. The words "during good behavior" mean, in effect, for life.

Article III

Section 1.

The judicial Power of the United States, shall be vested in one supreme Court, and in such inferior Courts as the Congress may from time to time ordain and establish. The Judges, both of the supreme and inferior Courts, shall hold their Offices during good Behavior, and shall, at stated Times, receive for their Services, a Compensation, which shall not be diminished during their Continuance in Office.

Section 2. Jurisdiction

Clause 1. Cases to be heard This clause sets out the jurisdiction of the federal courts; that is, it identifies those cases that may be tried in those courts. The federal courts can hear and decide—have jurisdiction over—a case depending on either the subject matter or the parties involved in that case. The jurisdiction of the federal courts in cases involving States was substantially restricted by the 11th Amendment in 1795.

Section 2.

1. The judicial Power shall extend to all Cases, in Law and Equity, arising under this Constitution, the Laws of the United States, and Treaties made, or which shall be made, under their Authority;— to all Cases affecting Ambassadors, other public ministers, and Consuls;— to all Cases of Admiralty and maritime Jurisdiction;— to Controversies to which the United States shall be a Party;— to Controversies between two or more States;— ~~between a State and Citizens of another State;~~— between Citizens of different States;—

between Citizens of the same State claiming Lands under Grants of different States, ~~and between a State, or the Citizens thereof, and foreign States, Citizens, or Subjects.~~

2. In all Cases affecting Ambassadors, other public Ministers and Consuls, and those in which a State shall be a Party, the supreme Court shall have original Jurisdiction. In all the other Cases before mentioned, the supreme Court shall have appellate Jurisdiction, both as to Law and Fact, with such Exceptions, and under such Regulations as the Congress shall make.

3. The trial of all Crimes, except in Cases of Impeachment, shall be by Jury; and such Trial shall be held in the State where the said Crimes shall have been committed; but when not committed within any State, the Trial shall be at such Place or Places as the Congress may by Law have directed.

Section 3.

1. Treason against the United States shall consist only in levying War against them, or in adhering to their Enemies, giving them Aid and Comfort. No Person shall be convicted of Treason unless on the Testimony of two Witnesses to the same overt Act, or on Confession in open Court.

2. The Congress shall have Power to declare the Punishment of Treason, but no Attainder of Treason shall work Corruption of Blood, or Forfeiture except during the Life of the Person attainted.

Article IV

Section 1.

Full Faith and Credit shall be given in each State to the public Acts, Records, and judicial Proceedings of every other State. And the Congress may by general Laws prescribe the Manner in which such Acts, Records and Proceedings shall be proved, and the Effect thereof.

Section 2.

1. The Citizens of each State shall be entitled to all Privileges and Immunities of Citizens in the several States.

Clause 2. Supreme Court jurisdiction Original jurisdiction refers to the power of a court to hear a case in the first instance, not on appeal from a lower court. Appellate jurisdiction refers to a court's power to hear a case on appeal from a lower court, from the court in which the case was originally tried. This clause gives the Supreme Court both original and appellate jurisdiction. However, nearly all of the cases the High Court hears are brought to it on appeal from the lower federal courts and the highest State courts.

Clause 3. Jury trial in criminal cases A person accused of a federal crime is guaranteed the right to trial by jury in a federal court in the State where the crime was committed; see the 5th and 6th amendments. The right to trial by jury in serious criminal cases in the State courts is guaranteed by the 6th and 14th amendments.

Section 3. Treason

Clause 1. Definition Treason is the only crime defined in the Constitution. The Framers intended the very specific definition here to prevent the loose use of the charge of treason—for example, against persons who criticize the government. Treason can be committed only in time of war and only by a citizen or a resident alien.

Clause 2. Punishment Congress has provided that the punishment that a federal court may impose on a convicted traitor may range from a minimum of five years in prison and/or a $10,000 fine to a maximum of death; no person convicted of treason has ever been executed by the United States. No legal punishment can be imposed on the family or descendants of a convicted traitor. Congress has also made it a crime for any person (in either peace or wartime) to commit espionage or sabotage, to attempt to overthrow the government by force, or to conspire to do any of these things.

RELATIONS AMONG THE STATES
Section 1. Full Faith and Credit

Each State must recognize the validity of the laws, public records, and court decisions of every other State.

Section 2. Privileges and Immunities of Citizens

Clause 1. Residents of other States In effect, this clause means that no State may discriminate against the residents of other States; that is, a State's laws cannot draw unreasonable distinctions between its own residents and those of any of the other States. See Section 1 of the 14th Amendment.

Clause 2. Extradition The process of returning a fugitive to another State is known as "interstate rendition" or, more commonly, "extradition." Usually, that process works routinely; some extradition requests are contested however—especially in cases with racial or political overtones. A governor may refuse to extradite a fugitive; but the federal courts can compel an unwilling governor to obey this constitutional command.

Clause 3. Fugitive slaves This clause was nullified by the 13th Amendment, which abolished slavery in 1865.

Section 3. New States; Territories

Clause 1. New States Only Congress can admit new States to the Union. A new State may not be created by taking territory from an existing State without the consent of that State's legislature. Congress has admitted 37 States since the original 13 formed the Union. Five States—Vermont, Kentucky, Tennessee, Maine, and West Virginia—were created from parts of existing States. Texas was an independent republic before admission. California was admitted after being ceded to the United States by Mexico. Each of the other 30 States entered the Union only after a period of time as an organized territory of the United States.

Clause 2. Territory, property Congress has the power to make laws concerning the territories, other public lands, and all other property of the United States.

Section 4. Protection Afforded to States by the Nation

The Constitution does not define "a republican form of government," but the phrase is generally understood to mean a representative government. The Federal Government must also defend each State against attacks from outside its border and, at the request of a State's legislature or its governor, aid its efforts to put down internal disorders.

PROVISIONS FOR AMENDMENT

This section provides for the methods by which formal changes can be made in the Constitution. An amendment may be proposed in one of two ways: by a two-thirds vote in each house of Congress, or by a national convention called by Congress at the request of two-thirds of the State legislatures. A proposed amendment may be ratified in one of two ways: by three-fourths of the State legislatures, or by three-fourths of the States in conventions called for that purpose. Congress has the power to determine the method by which a proposed amendment may be ratified. The amendment process cannot be used to deny any State its equal representation in the

2. A Person charged in any State with Treason, Felony, or other Crime, who shall flee from justice, and be found in another State, shall on Demand of the executive Authority of the State from which he fled, be delivered up, to be removed to the State having Jurisdiction of the Crime.

3. ~~No Person held to Service or Labor in one State, under the Laws thereof, escaping into another, shall, in Consequence of any Law or Regulation therein, be discharged from Service or Labor, but shall be delivered up on Claim of the Party to whom such Service or Labor may be due.~~

Section 3.

1. New States may be admitted by the Congress into this Union; but no new State shall be formed or erected within the Jurisdiction of any other State; nor any State be formed by the Junction of two or more States, or Parts of States, without the Consent of the Legislatures of the States concerned as well as of the Congress.

2. The Congress shall have Power to dispose of and make all needful Rules and Regulations respecting the Territory or other Property belonging to the United States; and nothing in this Constitution shall be so construed as to Prejudice any Claims of the United States, or of any particular State.

Section 4.

The United States shall guarantee to every State in this Union a Republican Form of Government, and shall protect each of them against Invasion; and on Application of the Legislature, or of the Executive (when the Legislature cannot be convened) against domestic Violence.

Article V

The Congress, whenever two thirds of both Houses shall deem it necessary, shall propose Amendments to this Constitution, or, on the Application of the Legislatures of two thirds of the several States, shall call a Convention for proposing Amendments, which, in either Case, shall be valid to all Intents and Purposes, as Part of this Constitution, when ratified by the Legislatures of three fourths of the several States, or by Conventions in three fourths thereof, as the one or the other Mode of Ratification may be proposed by the Congress; Provided that no Amendment which may be made prior to the Year One thousand eight hundred and eight shall in any Manner affect the first and fourth Clauses in the Ninth section of the first Article; and that no State, without its Consent, shall be deprived of its equal Suffrage in the Senate.

Article VI

Section 1.

All Debts contracted and Engagements entered into, before the Adoption of this Constitution, shall be as valid against the United States under this Constitution, as under the Confederation.

Section 2.

This Constitution, and the Laws of the United States which shall be made in Pursuance thereof; and all Treaties made, or which shall be made, under the Authority of the United States, shall be the supreme Law of the Land; and the Judges in every State shall be bound thereby, anything in the constitution or Laws of any State to the Contrary notwithstanding.

Section 3.

The Senators and Representatives before mentioned, and the Members of the several State legislatures, and all executive and judicial Officers, both of the United States and of the several States, shall be bound by Oath or Affirmation, to support this Constitution; but no religious Test shall ever be required as a Qualification to any Office or public Trust under the the United States.

Article VII

The ratification of the Conventions of nine States, shall be sufficient for the Establishment of this Constitution between the States so ratifying the same.

Done in Convention by the Unanimous Consent of the States present the Seventeenth Day of September in the Year of our Lord one thousand seven hundred and Eighty-seven and of the Independence of the United States of America the twelfth. In witness whereof We have hereunto subscribed our Names.

United States Senate. To this point, 27 amendments have been adopted. To date, all of the amendments except the 21st Amendment were proposed by Congress and ratified by the State legislatures. Only the 21st Amendment was ratified by the convention method.

NATIONAL DEBTS, SUPREMACY OF NATIONAL LAW, OATH
Section 1. Validity of Debts

Congress had borrowed large sums of money during the Revolution and later during the Critical Period of the 1780s. This provision, a pledge that the new government would honor those debts, did much to create confidence in that government.

Section 2. Supremacy of National Law

This section sets out the Supremacy Clause, a specific declaration of the supremacy of federal law over any and all forms of State law. No State, including its local governments, may make or enforce any law that conflicts with any provision in the Constitution, an act of Congress, a treaty, or an order, rule, or regulation properly issued by the President or his subordinates in the executive branch.

Section 3. Oaths of Office

This provision reinforces the Supremacy Clause; all public officers, at every level in the United States, owe their first allegiance to the Constitution of the United States. No religious qualification can be imposed as a condition for holding any public office.

RATIFICATION OF CONSTITUTION

The proposed Constitution was signed by George Washington and 37 of his fellow Framers on September 17, 1787. (George Read of Delaware signed for himself and also for his absent colleague, John Dickinson.)

UNITED STATES CONSTITUTION

Attest: William Jackson,
SECRETARY
George Washington,
PRESIDENT AND DEPUTY
FROM VIRGINIA

NEW HAMPSHIRE
John Langdon
Nicholas Gilman

MASSACHUSETTS
Nathaniel Gorham
Rufus King

CONNECTICUT
William Samuel Johnson
Roger Sherman

NEW YORK
Alexander Hamilton

NEW JERSEY
William Livingston
David Brearley
William Paterson
Jonathan Dayton

PENNSYLVANIA
Benjamin Franklin
Thomas Mifflin
Robert Morris
George Clymer
Thomas Fitzsimons
Jared Ingersoll
James Wilson
Gouverneur Morris

DELAWARE
George Read
Gunning Bedford, Jr.
John Dickinson
Richard Bassett
Jacob Broom

MARYLAND
James McHenry
Dan of St. Thomas
Jenifer
Daniel Carroll

VIRGINIA
John Blair
James Madison, Jr.

NORTH CAROLINA
William Blount
Richard Dobbs Spaight
Hugh Williamson

SOUTH CAROLINA
John Rutledge
Charles Cotesworth
Pinckney
Charles Pinckney
Pierce Butler

GEORGIA
William Few
Abraham Baldwin

The first 10 amendments, the Bill of Rights, were each proposed by Congress on September 25, 1789, and ratified by the necessary three-fourths of the States on December 15, 1791. These amendments were originally intended to restrict the National Government—not the States. However, the Supreme Court has several times held that most of their provisions also apply to the States, through the 14th Amendment's Due Process Clause.

1st Amendment. Freedom of Religion, Speech, Press, Assembly, and Petition

The 1st Amendment sets out five basic liberties: The guarantee of freedom of religion is both a protection of religious thought and practice and a command of separation of church and state. The guarantees of freedom of speech and press assure to all persons a right to speak, publish, and otherwise express their views. The guarantees of the rights of assembly and petition protect the right to join with others in public meetings, political parties, interest groups, and other associations to discuss public affairs and influence public policy. None of these rights is guaranteed in absolute terms, however; like all other civil rights guarantees, each of them may be exercised only with regard to the rights of all other persons.

2nd Amendment. Bearing Arms

The right of the people to keep and bear arms was insured by the 2nd Amendment.

3rd Amendment. Quartering of Troops

This amendment was intended to prevent what had been common British practice in the colonial period; see the Declaration of Independence. This provision is of virtually no importance today.

4th Amendment. Searches and Seizures

The basic rule laid down by the 4th Amendment is this: Police officers have no general right to search for or seize evidence or seize (arrest) persons. Except in particular circumstances, they

AMENDMENTS

1st Amendment.

Congress shall make no law respecting an establishment of religion, or prohibiting the free exercise thereof, or abridging the freedom of speech, or of the press; or the right of the people peaceably to assemble, and to petition the Government for a redress of grievances.

2nd Amendment.

A well-regulated Militia being necessary to the security of a free State, the right of the people to keep and bear Arms, shall not be infringed.

3rd Amendment.

No Soldier shall, in time of peace be quartered in any house, without the consent of the Owner, nor, in time of war, but in a manner to be prescribed by law.

4th Amendment.

The right of the people to be secure in their persons, houses, papers, and effects, against unreasonable searches and seizures, shall not be violated, and no Warrants shall issue, but upon probable cause, supported by Oath or affirmation, and particularly describing the place to be searched, and the persons or things to be seized.

5th Amendment.

No person shall be held to answer for a capital, or otherwise infamous crime, unless on a presentment or indictment of a Grand Jury, except in cases arising in the land or naval forces, or in the Militia, when in actual service in time of War, or public danger; nor shall any person be subject for the same offence to be twice put in jeopardy of life or limb; nor shall be compelled in any criminal case to be a witness against himself, nor be deprived of life, liberty, or property, without due process of law; nor shall private property be taken for public use, without just compensation.

6th Amendment.

In all criminal prosecutions, the accused shall enjoy the right to a speedy and public trial, by an impartial jury of the State and district wherein the crime shall have been committed, which district shall have been previously ascertained by law, and to be informed of the nature and cause of the accusation; to be confronted with the witnesses against him; to have compulsory process for obtaining witnesses in his favor, and to have the Assistance of Counsel for his defence.

7th Amendment.

In Suits at common law, where the value in controversy shall exceed twenty dollars, the right of trial by jury shall be preserved, and no fact tried by a jury, shall be otherwise re-examined in any Court of the United States, than according to the rules of the common law.

8th Amendment.

Excessive bail shall not be required, nor excessive fines imposed, nor cruel and unusual punishment inflicted.

9th Amendment.

The enumeration in the Constitution, of certain rights, shall not be construed to deny or disparage others retained by the people.

must have a proper warrant (a court order) obtained with probable cause (on reasonable grounds). This guarantee is reinforced by the exclusionary rule, developed by the Supreme Court: Evidence gained as the result of an unlawful search or seizure cannot be used at the court trial of the person from whom it was seized.

5th Amendment. Criminal Proceedings; Due Process; Eminent Domain

A person can be tried for a serious federal crime only if he or she has been indicted (charged, accused of that crime) by a grand jury. No one may be subjected to double jeopardy—that is, tried twice for the same crime. All persons are protected against self-incrimination; no person can be legally compelled to answer any question in any governmental proceeding if that answer could lead to that person's prosecution. The 5th Amendment's Due Process Clause prohibits unfair, arbitrary actions by the Federal Government; a like prohibition is set out against the States in the 14th Amendment. Government may take private property for a legitimate public purpose; but when it exercises that power of eminent domain, it must pay a fair price for the property seized.

6th Amendment. Criminal Proceedings

A person accused of crime has the right to be tried in court without undue delay and by an impartial jury; see Article III, Section 2, Clause 3. The defendant must be informed of the charge upon which he or she is to be tried, has the right to cross-examine hostile witnesses, and has the right to require the testimony of favorable witnesses. The defendant also has the right to be represented by an attorney at every stage in the criminal process.

7th Amendment. Civil Trials

This amendment applies only to civil cases heard in federal courts. A civil case does not involve criminal matters; it is a dispute between private parties or between the government and a private party. The right to trial by jury is guaranteed in any civil case in a federal court if the amount of money involved in that case exceeds $20 (most cases today involve a much larger sum); that right may be waived (relinquished, put aside) if both parties agree to a bench trial (a trial by a judge, without a jury).

8th Amendment. Punishment for Crimes

Bail is the sum of money that a person accused of crime may be required to post (deposit with the court) as a guarantee that he or she will appear in court at the proper time. The amount of bail required and/or a fine imposed as punishment must bear a reasonable relationship to the seriousness of the crime involved in the case. The prohibition of cruel and unusual punishment forbids any punishment judged to be too harsh, too severe for the crime for which it is imposed.

9th Amendment. Unenumerated Rights

The fact that the Constitution sets out many civil rights guarantees, expressly provides for many protections against government, does not mean that there are not other rights also held by the people.

United States Constitution

10th Amendment. Powers Reserved to the States

This amendment identifies the area of power that may be exercised by the States. All of those powers the Constitution does not grant to the National Government, and at the same time does not forbid to the States, belong to each of the States, or to the people of each State.

11th Amendment. Suits Against States

Proposed by Congress March 4, 1794; ratified February 7, 1795, but official announcement of the ratification was delayed until January 8, 1798. This amendment repealed part of Article III, Section 2, Clause 1. No State may be sued in a federal court by a resident of another State or of a foreign country; the Supreme Court has long held that this provision also means that a State cannot be sued in a federal court by a foreign country or, more importantly, even by one of its own residents.

12th Amendment. Election of President and Vice President

Proposed by Congress December 9, 1803; ratified June 15, 1804. This amendment replaced Article II, Section 1, Clause 3. Originally, each elector cast two ballots, each for a different person for President. The person with the largest number of electoral votes, provided that number was a majority of the electors, was to become President; the person with the second highest number was to become Vice President. This arrangement produced an electoral vote tie between Thomas Jefferson and Aaron Burr in 1800; the House finally chose Jefferson as President in 1801. The 12th Amendment separated the balloting for President and Vice President; each elector now casts one ballot for someone as President and a second ballot for another person as Vice President. Note that the 20th Amendment changed the date set here (March 4) to January 20, and that the 23rd Amendment (1961) provides for electors from the District of Columbia. This amendment also provides that the Vice President must meet the same qualifications as those set out for the President in Article II, Section 1, Clause 5.

10th Amendment.

The powers not delegated to the United States by the Constitution, nor prohibited by it to the States, are reserved to the States respectively, or to the people.

11th Amendment.

The Judicial power of the United States shall not be construed to extend to any suit in law or equity, commenced or prosecuted against one of the United States by Citizens of another State, or by Citizens or Subjects of any Foreign State.

12th Amendment.

The Electors shall meet in their respective States and vote by ballot for President and Vice President, one of whom, at least, shall not be an inhabitant of the same State with themselves; they shall name in their ballots the person voted for as President, and in distinct ballots the person voted for as Vice President, and they shall make distinct lists of all persons voted for as President, and of all persons voted for as Vice President, and of the number of votes for each, which lists they shall sign and certify, and transmit sealed to the seat of the government of the United States, directed to the President of the Senate;— The President of the Senate shall, in the presence of the Senate and the House of Representatives, open all the certificates and the votes shall then be counted;— the person having the greatest Number of votes for President shall be the President, if such number be a majority of the whole number of Electors appointed; and if no person have such a majority, then, from the persons having the highest numbers not exceeding three on the list of those voted for as President, the House of Representatives shall choose immediately, by ballot, the President. But in choosing the President, the votes shall be taken by States, the representation from each State having one vote; a quorum for this purpose shall consist of a member or members from two thirds of the States, and a majority of all the States shall be necessary to a choice. And if the House of Representatives shall not choose a President whenever the right of choice shall devolve upon them, before the fourth day of March next following, then the Vice President shall act as President, as in case of death or other constitutional disability of the President. The person having the greatest number of votes as Vice President, shall be the Vice President, if such number be a majority of the whole number of Electors appointed, and if no person have a majority, then from the two highest numbers on the list, the Senate shall choose the Vice President; a quorum for the purpose shall consist of two thirds of the whole number of Senators, a majority of the whole number shall be necessary to a choice. But no person constitutionally ineligible to the office of President shall be eligible to that of Vice-President of the United States.

13th Amendment.

Section 1. Neither slavery nor involuntary servitude, except as a punishment for crime whereof the party shall have been duly convicted, shall exist within the United States, or any place subject to their jurisdiction.

Section 2. Congress shall have power to enforce this article by appropriate legislation.

14th Amendment.

Section 1. All persons born or naturalized in the United States and subject to the jurisdiction thereof, are citizens of the United States and of the State wherein they reside. No State shall make or enforce any law which shall abridge the privileges or immunities of citizens of the United States; nor shall any State deprive any person of life, liberty, or property, without due process of law; nor deny to any person within its jurisdiction the equal protection of the laws.

Section 2. Representatives shall be apportioned among the several States according to their respective numbers, counting the whole number of persons in each State, excluding Indians not taxed. But when the right to vote at any election for the choice of electors for President and Vice President of the United States, Representatives in Congress, the Executive and Judicial officers of a State, or the members of the Legislature thereof, is denied to any of the male inhabitants of such State, being twenty-one years of age and citizens of the United States, or in any way abridged, except for participation in rebellion, or other crime, the basis of representation therein shall be reduced in the proportion which the number of such male citizens shall bear to the whole number of male citizens twenty-one years of age in such State.

Section 3. No person shall be a Senator or Representative in Congress, or elector of President and

13th Amendment. Slavery and Involuntary Servitude

Proposed by Congress January 31, 1865; ratified December 6, 1865. This amendment forbids slavery in the United States and in any area under its control. It also forbids other forms of forced labor, except punishments for crime; but some forms of compulsory service are not prohibited—for example, service on juries or in the armed forces. Section 2 gives to Congress the power to carry out the provisions of Section 1 of this amendment.

14th Amendment. Rights of Citizens

Proposed by Congress June 13, 1866; ratified July 9, 1868. Section 1 defines citizenship. It provides for the acquisition of United States citizenship by birth or by naturalization. Citizenship at birth is determined according to the principle of *jus soli*—"the law of the soil," where born; naturalization is the legal process by which one acquires a new citizenship at some time after birth. Under certain circumstances, citizenship can also be gained at birth abroad, according to the principle of *jus sanguinis*—"the law of the blood," to whom born. This section also contains two major civil rights provisions: the Due Process Clause forbids a State (and its local governments) to act in any unfair or arbitrary way; the Equal Protection Clause forbids a State (and its local governments) to discriminate against, draw unreasonable distinctions between, persons.

Most of the rights set out against the National Government in the first eight amendments have been extended against the States (and their local governments) through Supreme Court decisions involving the 14th Amendment's Due Process Clause.

The first sentence here replaced Article I, Section 2, Clause 3, the Three-Fifths Compromise provision. Essentially, all persons in the United States are counted in each decennial census, the basis for the distribution of House seats. The balance of this section has never been enforced and is generally thought to be obsolete.

This section limited the President's power to pardon those persons who had led the Confederacy during the Civil War. Congress finally removed this disability in 1898.

Section 4 also dealt with matters directly related to the Civil War. It reaffirmed the public debt of the United States; but it invalidated, prohibited payment of, any debt contracted by the Confederate States and also prohibited any compensation of former slave owners.

15th Amendment. Right to Vote— Race, Color, Servitude

Proposed by Congress February 26, 1869; ratified February 3, 1870. The phrase "previous condition of servitude" refers to slavery. Note that this amendment does not guarantee the right to vote to African Americans, or to anyone else. Instead, it forbids the States from discriminating against any person on the grounds of his "race, color, or previous condition of servitude" in the setting of suffrage qualifications.

16th Amendment. Income Tax

Proposed by Congress July 12, 1909; ratified February 3, 1913. This amendment modified two provisions in Article I, Section 2, Clause 3, and Section 9, Clause 4. It gives to Congress the power to levy an income tax, a direct tax, without regard to the populations of any of the States.

17th Amendment. Popular Election of Senators

Proposed by Congress May 13, 1912; ratified April 8, 1913. This amendment repealed those portions of Article I, Section 3, Clauses 1 and 2 relating to the election of senators. Senators are now elected by the voters in each State. If a vacancy occurs, the governor of the State involved must call an election to fill the seat; the governor may appoint a senator to serve until the next election, if the State's legislature has authorized that step.

Vice President, or hold any office, civil or military, under the United States, or under any State, who, having previously taken an oath, as a member of Congress, or as an officer of the United States, or as a member of any State legislature, or as an executive or judicial officer of any State, to support the Constitution of the United States, shall have engaged in insurrection or rebellion against the same, or given aid or comfort to the enemies thereof. But Congress may, by a vote of two thirds of each House, remove such disability.

Section 4. The validity of the public debt of the United States, authorized by law, including debts incurred for payment of pensions and bounties for services in suppressing insurrection or rebellion, shall not be questioned. But neither the United States nor any State shall assume or pay any debt or obligation incurred in aid of insurrection or rebellion against the United States, or any claim for the loss or emancipation of any slave; but all such debts, obligations and claims shall be held illegal and void.

Section 5. The Congress shall have power to enforce, by appropriate legislation, the provisions of this article.

15th Amendment.

Section 1. The right of citizens of the United States to vote shall not be denied or abridged by the United States or by any State on account of race, color, or previous condition of servitude.

Section 2. The Congress shall have power to enforce this article by appropriate legislation.

16th Amendment.

The Congress shall have power to lay and collect taxes on incomes, from whatever source derived, without apportionment among the several States, and without regard to any census or enumeration.

17th Amendment.

The Senate of the United States shall be composed of two Senators from each State, elected by the people thereof, for six years; and each Senator shall have one vote. The electors in each State shall have the qualifications requisite for electors of the most numerous branch of the State legislatures.

When vacancies happen in the representation of any State in the Senate, the executive authority of such State shall issue writs of election to fill such vacancies: *Provided*, That the legislature of any State may empower the executive thereof to make temporary appointments until the people fill the vacancies by election as the legislature may direct.

This amendment shall not be so construed as to

affect the election or term of any Senator chosen before it becomes valid as part of the Constitution.

18th Amendment.

Section 1. After one year from the ratification of this article the manufacture, sale, or transportation of intoxicating liquors within, the importation thereof into, or the exportation thereof from the United States and all territory subject to the jurisdiction thereof for beverage purposes is hereby prohibited.

Section 2. The Congress and the several States shall have concurrent power to enforce this article by appropriate legislation.

Section 3. This article shall be inoperative unless it shall have been ratified as an amendment to the Constitution by the legislatures of the several States, as provided in the Constitution, within seven years of the date of the submission hereof to the States by Congress.

19th Amendment.

The right of citizens of the United States to vote shall not be denied or abridged by the United States or by any State on account of sex.

Congress shall have power to enforce this article by appropriate legislation.

20th Amendment.

Section 1. The terms of the President and Vice President shall end at noon on the 20th day of January, and the terms of Senators and Representatives at noon on the 3d day of January, of the years in which such terms would have ended if this article had not been ratified; and the terms of their successors shall then begin.

Section 2. The Congress shall assemble at least once in every year, and such meeting shall begin at noon on the 3d day of January, unless they shall by law appoint a different day.

Section 3. If, at the time fixed for the beginning of the term of the President, the President elect shall have died, the Vice President elect shall become President. If a President shall not have been chosen before the time fixed for the beginning of his term, or if the President-elect shall have failed to qualify, then the Vice President elect shall act as President until a President shall have qualified; and the Congress may by law provide for the case wherein neither a President elect nor a Vice President elect shall have qualified, declaring who shall then act as President, or the manner in which one who is to act shall be selected, and such

18th Amendment. Prohibition of Intoxicating Liquors

Proposed by Congress December 18, 1917; ratified January 16, 1919. This amendment outlawed the making, selling, transporting, importing, or exporting of alcoholic beverages in the United States. It was repealed in its entirety by the 21st Amendment in 1933.

19th Amendment. Equal Suffrage—Sex

Proposed by Congress June 4, 1919; ratified August 18, 1920. No person can be denied the right to vote in any election in the United States on account of his or her sex.

20th Amendment. Commencement of Terms; Sessions of Congress; Death or Disqualification of President-Elect

Proposed by Congress March 2, 1932; ratified January 23, 1933. The provisions of Sections 1 and 2 relating to Congress modified Article I, Section 4, Clause 2, and those provisions relating to the President, the 12th Amendment. The date on which the President and Vice President now take office was moved from March 4 to January 20. Similarly, the members of Congress now begin their terms on January 3. The 20th Amendment is sometimes called the "Lame Duck Amendment" because it shortened the period of time a member of Congress who was defeated for reelection (a "lame duck") remains in office.

This section deals with certain possibilities that were not covered by the presidential selection provisions of either Article II or the 12th Amendment. To this point, none of these situations has occurred. Note that there is neither a President-elect nor a Vice President-elect until the electoral votes have been counted by Congress, or, if the electoral college cannot decide the matter, the House has chosen a President or the Senate has chosen a Vice President.

Congress has not in fact ever passed such a law. See Section 2 of the 25th Amendment, regarding a vacancy in the vice presidency; that provision could some day have an impact here.

Section 5 set the date on which this amendment came into force.

Section 6 placed a time limit on the ratification process; note that a similar provision was written into the 18th, 21st, and 22nd amendments.

21st Amendment. Repeal of 18th Amendment

Proposed by Congress February 20, 1933; ratified December 5, 1933. This amendment repealed all of the 18th Amendment. Section 2 modifies the scope of the Federal Government's commerce power set out in Article I, Section 8, Clause 3; it gives to each State the power to regulate the transportation or importation and the distribution or use of intoxicating liquors in ways that would be unconstitutional in the case of any other commodity. The 21st Amendment is the only amendment Congress has thus far submitted to the States for ratification by conventions.

22nd Amendment. Presidential Tenure

Proposed by Congress March 24, 1947; ratified February 27, 1951. This amendment modified Article II, Section I, Clause 1. It stipulates that no President may serve more than two elected terms. But a President who has succeeded to the office beyond the midpoint in a term to which another President was originally elected may serve for more than eight years. In any case, however, a President may not serve more than 10 years. Prior to Franklin Roosevelt, who was elected to four terms, no President had served more than two full terms in office.

person shall act accordingly until a President or Vice President shall have qualified.

Section 4. The Congress may by law provide for the case of the death of any of the persons from whom the House of Representatives may choose a President whenever the right of choice shall have devolved upon them, and for the case of the death of any of the persons from whom the Senate may choose a Vice President whenever the right of choice shall have devolved upon them.

Section 5. Sections 1 and 2 shall take effect on the 15th day of October following the ratification of this article.

Section 6. This article shall be inoperative unless it shall have been ratified as an amendment to the Constitution by the legislatures of three fourths of the several States within seven years from the date of its submission.

21st Amendment.

Section 1. The eighteenth article of amendment to the Constitution of the United States is hereby repealed.

Section 2. The transportation or importation into any State, Territory, or possession of the United States for delivery or use therein of intoxicating liquors, in violation of the laws thereof, is hereby prohibited.

Section 3. This article shall be inoperative unless it shall have been ratified as an amendment to the Constitution by conventions in the several States, as provided in the Constitution, within seven years from the date of the submission hereof to the States by the Congress.

22nd Amendment.

Section 1. No person shall be elected to the office of the President more than twice, and no person who has held the office of President, or acted as President, for more than two years of a term to which some other person was elected President shall be elected to the office of the President more than once. But this Article shall not apply to any person holding the office of President, when this Article was proposed by the Congress, and shall not prevent any person who may be holding the office of President, or acting as President, during the term within which this Article becomes operative from holding the office of President or acting as President during the remainder of such term.

Section 2. This article shall be inoperative unless it shall have been ratified as an amendment to the Constitution by the legislatures of three fourths of the several states within seven years from the date of its submission to the States by the Congress.

23rd Amendment.

Section 1. The District constituting the seat of Government of the United States shall appoint in such manner as the Congress may direct:

A number of electors of President and Vice President equal to the whole number of Senators and Representatives in Congress to which the District would be entitled if it were a State, but in no event more than the least populous State; they shall be in addition to those appointed by the States, they shall be considered, for the purposes of the election of President and Vice President, to be electors appointed by a State; and they shall meet in the District and perform such duties as provided by the twelfth article of amendment.

Section 2. The Congress shall have power to enforce this article by appropriate legislation.

24th Amendment.

Section 1. The right of citizens of the United States to vote in any primary or other election for President or Vice President, for electors for President or Vice President, or for Senator or Representative in Congress, shall not be denied or abridged by the United States or any State by reason of failure to pay any poll tax or other tax.

Section 2. The Congress shall have power to enforce this article by appropriate legislation.

25th Amendment.

Section 1. In case of the removal of the President from office or of his death or resignation, the Vice President shall become President.

Section 2. Whenever there is a vacancy in the office of the Vice President, the President shall nominate a Vice President who shall take office upon confirmation by a majority vote of both Houses of Congress.

Section 3. Whenever the President transmits to the President *pro tempore* of the Senate and the Speaker of the House of Representatives his written declaration

23rd Amendment. Presidential Electors for the District of Columbia

Proposed by Congress June 16, 1960; ratified March 29, 1961. This amendment modified Article II, Section I, Clause 2 and the 12th Amendment. It included the voters of the District of Columbia in the presidential electorate; and provides that the District is to have the same number of electors as the least populous State—three electors—but no more than that number.

24th Amendment. Right to Vote in Federal Elections—Tax Payment

Proposed by Congress September 14, 1962; ratified January 23, 1964. This amendment outlawed the payment of any tax as a condition for taking part in the nomination or election of any federal officeholder.

25th Amendment. Presidential Succession, Vice Presidential Vacancy, Presidential Inability

Proposed by Congress July 6, 1965; ratified February 10, 1967. Section 1 revised the imprecise provision on presidential succession in Article II, Section 1, Clause 6. It wrote into the Constitution the precedent set by Vice President John Tyler, who became President on the death of William Henry Harrison in 1841.

Section 2 provides for the filling of a vacancy in the office of Vice President. Prior to its adoption, the office had been vacant on 16 occasions and had remained unfilled for the remainder of each term involved. When Spiro Agnew resigned the office in 1973, President Nixon selected Gerald Ford in accord with this provision; and, when President Nixon resigned in 1974, Gerald Ford became President and then chose Nelson Rockefeller as Vice President.

This section created a procedure for determining if a President is so incapacitated that he cannot perform the powers and duties of his office.

that he is unable to discharge the powers and duties of his office, and until he transmits to them a written declaration to the contrary, such powers and duties shall be discharged by the Vice President as Acting President.

Section 4. Whenever the Vice President and a majority of either the principal officers of the executive departments or of such other body as Congress may by law provide, transmit to the President *pro tempore* of the Senate and the Speaker of the House of Representatives their written declaration that the President is unable to discharge the powers and duties of his office, the Vice President shall immediately assume the powers and duties of the office as Acting President.

Thereafter, when the President transmits to the President *pro tempore* of the Senate and the Speaker of the House of Representatives his written declaration that no inability exists, he shall resume the powers and duties of his office unless the Vice President and a majority of either the principal officers of the executive department or of such other body as Congress may by law provide, transmit within four days to the President *pro tempore* of the Senate and the Speaker of the House of Representatives their written declaration that the President is unable to discharge the powers and duties of his office. Thereupon Congress shall decide the issue, assembling within forty-eight hours for that purpose if not in session. If the Congress, within twenty-one days after receipt of the latter written declaration, or, if Congress is not in session, within twenty-one days after Congress is required to assemble, determines by two-thirds vote of both Houses that the President is unable to discharge the powers and duties of his office, the Vice President shall continue to discharge the same as Acting President; otherwise, the President shall resume the powers and duties of his office.

Section 4 deals with the circumstance in which a President will not be able to determine the fact of incapacity. To this point, Congress has not established the "such other body" referred to here. This section contains the only typographical error in the Constitution; in its second paragraph, the word "department" should in fact read "departments."

26th Amendment.

Section 1. The right of citizens of the United States, who are eighteen years of age or older, to vote shall not be denied or abridged by the United States or by any State on account of age.

Section 2. The Congress shall have the power to enforce this article by appropriate legislation.

27th Amendment.

No law varying the compensation for the services of the Senators and Representatives, shall take effect, until an election of Representatives shall have intervened.

26th Amendment. Right to Vote—Age

Proposed by Congress March 23, 1971; ratified July 1, 1971. This amendment provides that the minimum age for voting in any election in the United States cannot be more than 18 years. (A State may set a minimum voting age of less than 18, however.)

27th Amendment. Congressional Pay

Proposed by Congress September 25, 1789; ratified May 7, 1992. This amendment modified Article I, Section 6, Clause 1. It limits Congress's power to fix the salaries of its members—by delaying the effectiveness of any increase in that pay until after the next regular congressional election.

much straitened for bread to supply the soldiers and firewood to keep them warm. This seems to be only one of the many calamities of war.

DEC. 30: A number of poor soldiers sick and wounded brought into town today, and lodged in the court-house; some of them in private houses. Today I hear several of our town's men have agreed to procure wood for the soldiers; but they found it was attended with considerable difficulty, as most of the wagons usually employed to bring in wood were pressed to take the soldiers' baggage.

DEC. 31: We have been told of an engagement between the two armies, in which it was said the English had 400 taken prisoners, and 300 killed and wounded. The report of the evening contradicts the above intelligence, and there is no certain account of a battle.

THE START OF A NEW YEAR

JANUARY 1, 1777: This New Year's day has not been ushered in with the usual ceremonies and rejoicing; indeed, I believe it will be the beginning of a sorrowful year to very many people. Yet the flatterer—hope—bids me look forward with confidence and trust in Him who can bring order out of this great confusion. I do not hear that any messengers have been in town from the camp.

JAN. 3: This morning between 8 and 9 o'clock we heard very distinctly a heavy firing of cannon. The sound came from toward Trenton. About noon a number of [American] soldiers, upwards of 1,000, came into town in great confusion with baggage and some cannon. From these soldiers we learn there was a smart engagement yesterday at Trenton, and that they left them engaged near Trenton Mill, but were not able to say which side was victorious. . . .

Several of those who lodged in Col. Cox's house last week returned tonight, and asked for the key, which I gave them. At about bedtime I went into the next house to see if the fires were safe, and my heart was melted with compassion to see such a number of my fellow creatures lying like swine on the floor, fast asleep, and many of them without even a blanket to cover them. It seems very strange to me that such a number should be allowed to come from the camp at the very time of the engagements, and I shrewdly suspect they have run away—for they can give no account why they came, nor where they are to march next.

JAN. 4: The accounts hourly coming in are so contradictory and various that we know not which to give credit to. We have heard our people have gained another victory [Battle of Princeton], that the English are fleeing before them, some at Brunswick, some at Princeton. We hear today that Sharp Delany, Anthony Morris, and others of the Philadelphia militia are killed, and that the Count Donop is numbered with the dead; if so, the Hessians have lost a brave and humane commander. The prisoners taken by our troops are sent to Lancaster jail. A number of sick and wounded were brought into town—calls upon us to extend a hand of charity towards them. Several of my soldiers left the next house, and returned to the place from whence they came. Upon my questioning them pretty close, I brought several to confess they had run away, being scared at the heavy firing on the 3rd. There were several innocent looking lads among them, and I sympathised with their mothers when I saw them preparing to return to the army.

Source: *Weathering the Storm: Women of the American Revolution* by Elizabeth Evan, Scribner's, 1975.

Understanding Primary Sources

1. What is a "flatterer"?
2. Why, given her situation, does Morris refer to hope as a "flatterer"?

American Heritage®

MY BRUSH WITH **HISTORY**™

Videotapes

For more information about the Revolutionary War, view "Diary of a Wartime Winter."

An Emerging New Nation
(1783–1861)

SECTION 1 Life in the New Nation
SECTION 2 The Market Revolution
SECTION 3 Religion and Reform
SECTION 4 The Coming of the Civil War

Covered wagons heading west

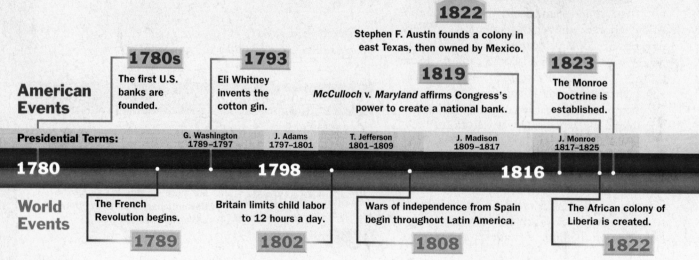

American Events

1780s
The first U.S. banks are founded.

1793
Eli Whitney invents the cotton gin.

1822
Stephen F. Austin founds a colony in east Texas, then owned by Mexico.

1819
McCulloch v. *Maryland* affirms Congress's power to create a national bank.

1823
The Monroe Doctrine is established.

Presidential Terms:
G. Washington 1789–1797
J. Adams 1797–1801
T. Jefferson 1801–1809
J. Madison 1809–1817
J. Monroe 1817–1825

1780

1798

1816

World Events

The French Revolution begins.
1789

Britain limits child labor to 12 hours a day.
1802

Wars of independence from Spain begin throughout Latin America.
1808

The African colony of Liberia is created.
1822

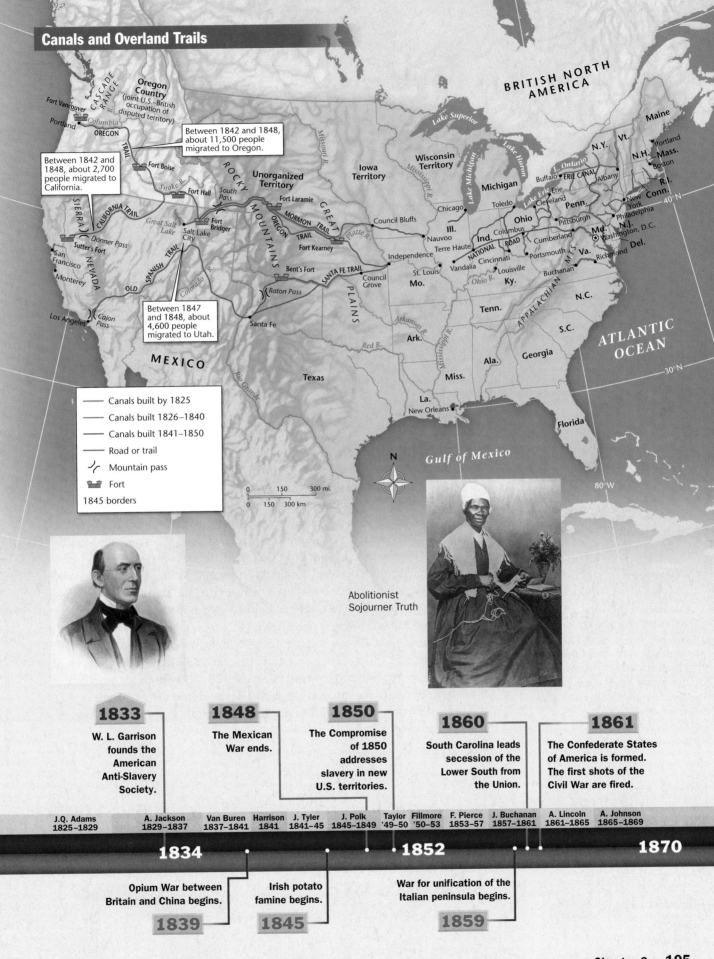

Canals and Overland Trails

BRITISH NORTH AMERICA

Oregon Country (joint U.S.–British occupation of disputed territory)

Between 1842 and 1848, about 11,500 people migrated to Oregon.

Between 1842 and 1848, about 2,700 people migrated to California.

Between 1847 and 1848, about 4,600 people migrated to Utah.

Fort Vancouver
Portland
OREGON
Fort Boise
Fort Hall
CASCADE RANGE
Columbia R.
Snake R.
ROCKY MOUNTAINS
South Pass
Unorganized Territory
Fort Laramie
Fort Bridger
MORMON TRAIL
OREGON TRAIL
Fort Kearney
Platte R.
Council Bluffs
Missouri R.
Iowa Territory
Wisconsin Territory
Lake Superior
Lake Michigan
Lake Huron
Michigan
Chicago
Toledo
Cleveland
Ohio
Columbus
Lake Erie
Buffalo
ERIE CANAL
Albany
N.Y.
Vt.
N.H.
Maine
Portland
Mass.
Boston
R.I.
Conn.
New York
Penn.
Pittsburgh
Philadelphia
N.J.
Md.
Del.
Washington, D.C.
NATIONAL ROAD
Cumberland
Portsmouth
Richmond
Va.
Buchanan
APPALACHIAN MTS.
N.C.
S.C.
Tenn.
Ala.
Georgia
Miss.
La.
New Orleans
Florida
ATLANTIC OCEAN
Gulf of Mexico

CALIFORNIA TRAIL
SIERRA NEVADA
Great Salt Lake
Salt Lake City
Donner Pass
Sutter's Fort
San Francisco
Monterey
OLD SPANISH TRAIL
Colorado R.
Cajon Pass
Los Angeles
Santa Fe
Raton Pass
SANTA FE TRAIL
Bent's Fort
GREAT PLAINS
Council Grove
Independence
St. Louis
Mo.
Nauvoo
Ill.
Ind.
Terre Haute
Vandalia
Cincinnati
Louisville
Ohio R.
Ky.
Arkansas R.
Ark.
Red R.
Rio Grande
Texas
MEXICO
Mississippi R.

N

40° N
30° N
80° W

Legend:
— Canals built by 1825
— Canals built 1826–1840
— Canals built 1841–1850
— Road or trail
⁁ Mountain pass
⌂ Fort
1845 borders

0   150   300 mi.
0   150   300 km

Abolitionist Sojourner Truth

Timeline

1833 W. L. Garrison founds the American Anti-Slavery Society.

1848 The Mexican War ends.

1850 The Compromise of 1850 addresses slavery in new U.S. territories.

1860 South Carolina leads secession of the Lower South from the Union.

1861 The Confederate States of America is formed. The first shots of the Civil War are fired.

J.Q. Adams 1825–1829
A. Jackson 1829–1837
Van Buren 1837–1841
Harrison 1841
J. Tyler 1841–45
J. Polk 1845–1849
Taylor '49–50
Fillmore '50–53
F. Pierce 1853–57
J. Buchanan 1857–1861
A. Lincoln 1861–1865
A. Johnson 1865–1869

1834   **1852**   **1870**

1839 Opium War between Britain and China begins.

1845 Irish potato famine begins.

1859 War for unification of the Italian peninsula begins.

Life in the New Nation

READING FOCUS

- How did America's growing and young population spur territorial expansion, and how did the United States gain Texas and the Oregon Country?

- How did a spirit of improvement, along with the Industrial Revolution and new transportation and communication, affect the nation's development?

- What were the key characteristics of the Second Great Awakening and of African American worship?

MAIN IDEA

In the early 1800s, the nation expanded south and westward. Innovations in industry brought great social change. A revival of religion resulted in new American forms of worship.

KEY TERMS

Adams-Onís Treaty
republican virtues
Industrial Revolution
interchangeable parts
cotton gin
Second Great Awakening
denomination
spirituals

TARGET READING SKILL

Identify Cause and Effect As you read, complete the following chart to show causes and effects of westward expansion in the early 1800s.

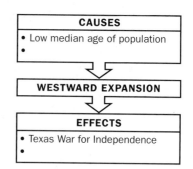

CAUSES
• Low median age of population
•

↓

WESTWARD EXPANSION

↓

EFFECTS
• Texas War for Independence
•

Setting the Scene Americans were moving west into new lands in the late 1700s and early 1800s. One of them, Daniel Boone, became a symbol of the personal qualities needed to explore and settle those lands: courage, practical know-how, and bottomless determination.

After spending several years exploring present-day Kentucky, Boone was hired in 1775 to cut the Wilderness Road through the Cumberland Gap, a low spot in the Appalachian Mountains. This road began in eastern Tennessee and ended in what is now Louisville, Kentucky. It became the main route to the lands west of the Appalachians for countless Americans, including Boone's own family.

During the American Revolution, Boone was captured by the Shawnee, who were allies of Britain. A few months later, Boone escaped to warn colonists of a coming attack by the British and Native Americans, which the colonists repelled.

After the war, Boone became a leading citizen of the Ohio Valley. He was a member of the Kentucky legislature as well as a hunter and a trapper. Moving west with the growing nation, he migrated to Missouri in 1799. When he died there in 1820, his fame as a bold and tough pioneer had spread across the nation.

VIEWING HISTORY The Cumberland Gap—the 1700s' equivalent of a new superhighway—opened the way westward for explorers and settlers. **Drawing Conclusions** *Using evidence from this picture, draw conclusions about the advantages and challenges of traveling through the Cumberland Gap.*

America's Population: Growing and Young

The westward surge of people symbolized by Daniel Boone was partly the result of a rapidly growing population. In 1780, about 2.7 million people lived in the original 13 states. By 1830, the population had grown to 12 million people in 24 states. Most of the growth came from an astonishing increase in the number of children born to each family. Between 1800 and 1849, the average American woman had about five children.

The large number of children meant that most of the population was young. The median age of Americans in 1820 was about 17. That is, half of the population was under the age of 17, and half was over that age. Young couples dreamed of working hard to make a good future. The place to make those dreams come true, many felt, was the area west of the Appalachian Mountains, a region known as trans-Appalachia.

Territorial Expansion

In the late 1780s, only a few hundred white Americans lived north of the Ohio River. By 1830, there were hundreds of thousands of Americans living in the region, which by then consisted of Michigan Territory and three new states: Ohio, Indiana, and Illinois.

Life on the Frontier   Most of the settlers in this region had traveled down the river from western Pennsylvania and Virginia, or northward from Kentucky and Tennessee. Entire families made the long and difficult journey, as an English traveler crossing the Appalachians in the spring of 1817 described:

> 66 *Old America seems to be breaking up and moving westward. We are seldom out of sight, as we travel on this grand track towards the Ohio, of family groups behind and before us, some [intending to go] to a particular spot, close to a brother perhaps, or [to] a friend who has gone before and reported well of the country.* 99
>
> —Morris Birkbeck

In the Northwest Territory, north of the Ohio River, slavery had been forbidden by the Northwest Ordinance of 1787. Supposedly, African Americans who gained their freedom could live in this region. Yet many settlers north of the Ohio did not want free African Americans in their states. In particular, they feared that blacks would compete for land and jobs. Therefore they made laws to discourage African Americans from moving in.

Focus on TECHNOLOGY

The Log Cabin One reason so many Americans left their homes and migrated westward may have been that they knew it would not be very difficult to build a new shelter. The typical log cabin took only a few days to build and required no expensive nails or spikes. (The builder cut notches in the logs to fit them together.) In fact, a pioneer could build a log cabin with no tools except an axe, and could even build a small cabin without help.

Many log cabins had only one room, with blankets or sheets hung from the ceiling to provide a bit of privacy. Glass windows were rare, since glass was both costly and difficult to transport. For floors, some cabins used wooden boards; others simply used packed earth.

Families generally saw their cabins as temporary homes while they cleared the surrounding fields for farming. In time, many built larger, more comfortable homes.

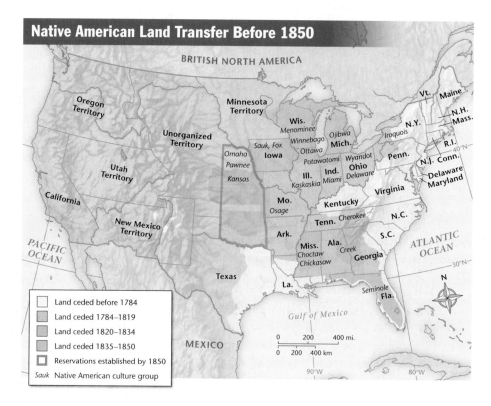

Native American Land Transfer Before 1850

BRITISH NORTH AMERICA

Oregon Territory

Minnesota Territory

Unorganized Territory

Wis.
Menominee
Winnebago
Ojibwa
Mich.
Ottawa

Sauk, Fox
Iowa
Potawatomi
Wyandot
Ohio
Delaware

Omaha
Pawnee

Ill.
Ind.
Miami

Kaskaskia

Penn.

Iroquois

Vt. Maine
N.H.
Mass.
N.Y.
R.I.
Conn.
N.J.
Delaware
Maryland

Utah Territory

Kansas

Mo.
Osage

Kentucky

Virginia

California

New Mexico Territory

Ark.

Tenn.
Cherokee

N.C.

S.C.

PACIFIC OCEAN

Miss.
Ala.
Choctaw
Chickasaw
Creek
Georgia

ATLANTIC OCEAN

Texas

La.

Seminole
Fla.

Gulf of Mexico

MEXICO

0   200   400 mi.
0   200   400 km

Seminole

Land ceded before 1784
Land ceded 1784–1819
Land ceded 1820–1834
Land ceded 1835–1850
Reservations established by 1850
Sauk Native American culture group

Focus on ECONOMICS

Florida Agriculture Americans streaming into northern Florida in the early 1800s found British settlers already working the land. Spain had allowed them to establish orange groves as well as cotton, rice, and indigo plantations, mainly along the coast. The American settlers brought their own plantation agriculture with them, planting cotton, tobacco, and corn. They also brought slaves to work the fields.

READING CHECK
How was the United States able to gain possession of Florida?

From the South, an estimated 98,000 southern slaves moved west with their owners between 1790 and 1810. Thousands more African Americans were brought directly from Africa or the West Indies. Native Americans gradually lost their land to the United States government in one treaty after another. As they lost their homelands, Indians were forced to make long, dangerous journeys to areas west of the Mississippi River.

Expansion Into Florida Thousands of settlers also flocked to the newly acquired land of Florida. Under the Pinckney Treaty of 1795, the southern boundary of the United States had been set at 31° N latitude, leaving Florida firmly in Spanish hands. However, Spain and the United States also agreed to control the Native Americans living within each country's territories and to prevent them from attacking the other country's territory.

During the 1810s, Spain was distracted by rebellions in its South American colonies and therefore paid little attention to its two colonies of East and West Florida. The Seminoles, a Native American group living in the Floridas, took advantage of the loose control and stepped up their raids on settlers in southern Georgia. The Seminoles also angered American officials by allowing escaped slaves to live among them.

Jackson and Florida The general in charge of protecting the settlers was the tough veteran of the War of 1812, Andrew Jackson. When told to put an end to the attacks, Jackson did so, by invading Florida. Within a few weeks Jackson claimed possession of the entire western part of the territory. Spain was outraged, and Congress threatened to condemn Jackson. Most Americans, however, applauded Jackson's move.

President Monroe and his Secretary of State, John Quincy Adams, decided to make the best of the situation. Refusing to apologize for Jackson's actions, Adams accused Spain of breaking the Pinckney Treaty by failing to control the Seminoles.

Spain reluctantly agreed to accept the loss of Florida. In 1819, Spain and the United States agreed on what has since been called the Transcontinental

Treaty, or the **Adams-Onís Treaty.** In the treaty, Spain gave up Florida, as well as its long-held claim on the Pacific Northwest. Now for the first time, the United States stretched from the Atlantic to the Pacific Ocean.

The Adams-Onís Treaty also fixed the boundary between the Louisiana Purchase and Spanish territory in the West. To settle the dispute over this boundary, the United States agreed to give up its claims to a huge territory in what is now the southwestern United States, including part of Texas.

Texas and Oregon Country

The United States government assumed that the lands of the Louisiana Purchase, which were located west of the Mississippi River, would remain part of "Indian Country." Thousands of Americans had other ideas.

Mexico and Texas   Mexico, which had won independence from Spain in 1821, encouraged trade with the United States. In 1822, Stephen F. Austin, a former member of the Missouri Territorial legislature, founded a colony of several hundred families in east Texas, in northern Mexico. By 1825, some 1,800 immigrants were living in Austin's colony. By 1835 their numbers exceeded 30,000.

As their numbers swelled, these Americans demanded more political control. In particular, they wanted slavery to be guaranteed under Mexican law. The newcomers called for the same rights from the Mexican government that they had possessed in the United States.

The Texas War for Independence   When General Antonio López de Santa Anna declared himself dictator of Mexico and stripped Texas of its rights of self-government, Texans became united in the cause of independence. In October 1835, these independence-minded settlers clashed with Mexican troops, beginning the Texas War for Independence.

Santa Anna led an army across the Rio Grande to subdue the rebellion. In February 1836, the Mexicans reached the Alamo, a walled mission in San Antonio that was occupied by Texans. Led by William Travis and James Bowie, the Texans hoped to slow the general's advance long enough to allow their fellow rebels to assemble an army. Under siege by a vastly larger Mexican force, Travis vowed "to sustain myself as long as possible and die like a soldier who never forgets what is due to his own honor or that of his country."

The courageous Texans inflicted heavy casualties, but the Mexicans eventually overwhelmed the Alamo and killed most of those inside. Two weeks later, Santa Anna ordered the killing of more than 300 Texan prisoners at Goliad. These two events enraged and energized Texans to mighty actions for their cause.

On March 2, 1836, the rebels formally declared the founding of an independent Republic of Texas. The following month, a Texan force led by Sam Houston and

MAP SKILLS After a stinging defeat at the Alamo, Texans led by Sam Houston (below) finally overcame the army of General Antonio López de Santa Anna at the Battle of San Jacinto. **Place** *Why was it crucial that Santa Anna be stopped at that point?*

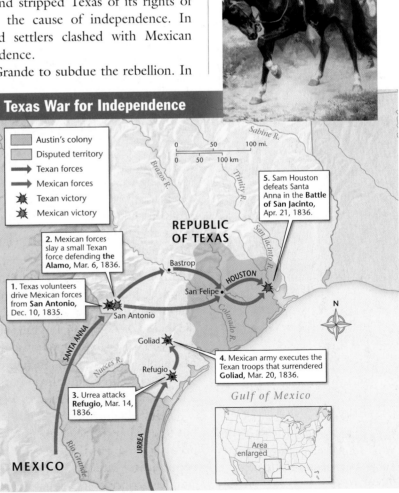

Texas War for Independence

Austin's colony
Disputed territory
Texan forces
Mexican forces
Texan victory
Mexican victory

0   50   100 mi.
0   50   100 km

Sabine R.
Brazos R.
Trinity R.
San Jacinto R.
Colorado R.
Nueces R.
Rio Grande

REPUBLIC OF TEXAS

5. Sam Houston defeats Santa Anna in the **Battle of San Jacinto,** Apr. 21, 1836.

2. Mexican forces slay a small Texan force defending **the Alamo,** Mar. 6, 1836.

Bastrop

HOUSTON

San Felipe

1. Texas volunteers drive Mexican forces from **San Antonio,** Dec. 10, 1835.

San Antonio

SANTA ANNA

Goliad

4. Mexican army executes the Texan troops that surrendered **Goliad,** Mar. 20, 1836.

Refugio

3. Urrea attacks **Refugio,** Mar. 14, 1836.

URREA

MEXICO

Gulf of Mexico

Area enlarged

N

shouting "Remember the Alamo!" routed Mexican troops at the San Jacinto River. The Texans captured Santa Anna and forced him to sign a treaty recognizing the Republic of Texas. In the fall of 1836, the citizens of Texas elected Sam Houston as their first president.

The Oregon Country   Far to the north of Texas, other Americans in the early 1820s were headed for a vast territory known as the Oregon Country, which stretched from northern California to the southern border of Alaska. In 1818, the United States and Britain signed a treaty agreeing to joint occupation of the Oregon Country.

Some of the first Americans to arrive were fur traders. Other newcomers were missionaries sent by churches back East to convert Native Americans to Christianity.

Starting in 1842, organized wagon trains carried masses of migrants to Oregon along Indian trails. Groups met at a small town in western Missouri called Independence. From there they began the 2,000-mile journey across the Great Plains and the Rocky Mountains along the Oregon Trail. Most came in search of land or trading opportunities.

By 1845, more than 5,000 Americans had migrated to the Oregon Country. In the Treaty of 1846, the United States and Great Britain agreed to divide the Oregon Country along the 49th parallel (line of latitude).

The movement west included the Mormons, the religious group founded by Joseph Smith in New York State. Harassed by their neighbors because of their beliefs, the Mormons migrated to Ohio and then to Missouri before settling in Nauvoo, Illinois, in 1839. But again they met with hostility. In 1844, after an angry mob killed Smith and his brother, the Mormons moved on. Under a new leader, Brigham Young, the group journeyed to the shores of the Great Salt Lake, then in Mexican territory. There they founded a permanent community that would become Salt Lake City, the capital of the state of Utah.

Westward migration brought about the creation of new cities, new territories, and ultimately, new states. In the mid-1800s, three western territories gained statehood: Iowa in 1846, Wisconsin in 1848, and Minnesota in 1858.

The Spirit of Improvement

Migrating westward was one way that Americans tried to make their lives better, but it was hardly the only one. The need to survive and the hope of making a profit led Americans in every part of the country to invent and innovate, or find new ways of doing things. This spirit of improvement partly reflects the ideals of the Enlightenment.

Improvement Through Education   Americans believed that the general condition of humankind could be improved through education. Educator Noah Webster, whose primary contribution to American education was the first major dictionary of American English, believed that a broad system of education was necessary to establish a national character. Many state constitutions encouraged free public education for all children. Even though few state governments actually provided free education in those early years, academies, or private high schools, often filled the gap.

Many Americans wanted their schools not just to teach academic subjects but to develop character by promoting certain virtues. The virtues the American people would need to govern themselves in the new republic were called **republican virtues.** They included self-reliance, industry, frugality, harmony, and the sacrifice of individual needs for the good of the community.

A historic marker along the Oregon Trail

READING CHECK
What "republican virtues" did some Americans seek to promote? Why?

The Role of Women In the early 1800s, Americans began to look to women to set the standard for republican virtues. After all, they reasoned, women were mothers, wives, and sometimes teachers. Thus women had a powerful influence on the men who would vote in, and govern, the nation. If women had such virtues as honesty, self-restraint, and discipline, they could teach these qualities to men.

To serve as examples of these virtues, women had to learn them first. In the late 1700s, most schools were for boys only. As people began to see the value of educating girls, many academies added "female departments" to help girls become "republican women." A republican woman was one who had the virtues that would help her contribute to the success of the republic.

The Industrial Revolution

Americans pursued profit with the same energy with which they pursued self-improvement. As the young republic expanded, Americans developed and profited from a variety of inventions that produced goods and materials faster and more cheaply.

Many of the inventions grew out of what is now known as the **Industrial Revolution.** This revolution was an ongoing effort over many decades to increase production by using machines powered by sources other than humans or animals. Several key British inventions sparked the Industrial Revolution in the 1700s. Among these was James Watt's steam engine, which harnessed the tremendous force given off by expanding steam.

The British jealously guarded all knowledge of their new technology. Anyone who knew about the design of these machines was forbidden to emigrate, or move out of the country.

New Technology Comes to America Britain's secrets and its technological lead were spoiled by a man named Samuel Slater, who emigrated to the United States in 1789 after working in Britain's advanced textile industry. Working in a clothier's shop in Pawtucket, Rhode Island, Slater reproduced the complicated machinery of the British mills in 1790. Slater and his partners went on to establish the nation's first successful textile mill, in 1793.

The Industrial Revolution in America

Date	Inventor	Invention or Innovation
1787	John Fitch	The first American steamboat
1790	Samuel Slater	Machinery for first U.S. textile mill
1794	Eli Whitney	The cotton gin patented
1795	Robert Fulton	The steam shovel (for digging canals)
1798	Eli Whitney	Mass production of muskets with standard measures and interchangeable parts
1807	Robert Fulton	The *Clermont*, the first commercially successful steamboat
1814	Francis C. Lowell	The first completely mechanized cotton mill
1820	William Underwood	The first U.S. canning factory
1826	Samuel Morey	An internal combustion engine
1828	Joseph Henry	The electromagnet

INTERPRETING CHARTS
The Industrial Revolution brought American advances in engineering, medicine, science agriculture, and technology. In fact, the word *technology* was coined in 1829.
Drawing Inferences *What aspects of American life did many of these advances affect?*

This woodcut shows two men operating machinery in an early textile mill. The machines are printing long sheets of a fabric called calico.

Others soon copied Slater's methods. By 1814, there were about 240 mills operating in the United States, most of them in Pennsylvania, New York, and New England.

Eli Whitney and Interchangeable Parts   Although the Industrial Revolution began in Great Britain, American inventors were not far behind. In 1798, Eli Whitney signed a contract with the federal government to make 10,000 guns in a little over two years. It was a bold promise. In those days, a gunmaker made parts for one gun at a time. The process took weeks, because each part fit only one gun.

Whitney realized that if all the parts were made exactly alike, they could be used on any of the guns. The gunmaker could assemble the parts rapidly, which would translate into higher production and greater profit. In fact, it took Whitney more than ten years to make the guns, and he had trouble making indentical parts. But he worked hard on his new system, and other inventors later perfected what is now called the system of **interchangeable parts,** in which all parts are made to an exact standard.

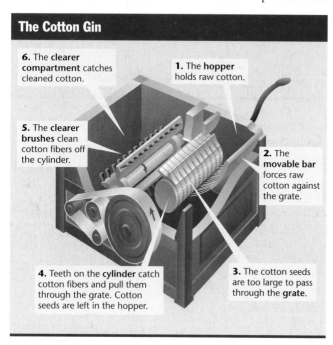

The Cotton Gin

6. The **clearer compartment** catches cleaned cotton.

1. The **hopper** holds raw cotton.

5. The **clearer brushes** clean cotton fibers off the cylinder.

2. The **movable bar** forces raw cotton against the grate.

4. Teeth on the **cylinder** catch cotton fibers and pull them through the grate. Cotton seeds are left in the hopper.

3. The cotton seeds are too large to pass through the **grate.**

INTERPRETING DIAGRAMS
By hand, a worker could clean (remove the seeds from) only one pound of cotton per day. However, with a hand-operated gin like the one shown here, a worker could clean 50 pounds of cotton per day. **Determining Relevance** *How did the invention of the cotton gin lead to the expansion of slavery?*

The Cotton Gin   While visiting a Georgia plantation in 1793, Whitney noted the time and effort needed to clean cotton seeds from the cotton fibers. Working by hand, a laborer could only clean one pound of cotton per day. Whitney devised a solution to the problem: the **cotton gin,** a machine that separates the seeds from raw cotton fibers. (The word *gin* means an "engine" or "machine.") With a gin operated by water power, one worker could now clean 1,000 pounds per day.

Whitney's invention had several important effects. Profit per pound of cotton skyrocketed, and with it the amount of cotton planted for harvest. United States cotton exports rose 6,000 percent between 1790 and 1815. Many southern planters began to depend on cotton as their only major crop, because it was so profitable. Planters began looking for new land where they could grow ever larger crops of cotton. They bought up and quickly settled large areas in Alabama, Mississippi, Louisiana, and finally Texas. These planters bought more enslaved Africans to work on the new and expanded cotton plantations. The enslaved population of the South more than doubled between 1790 and 1820, rising from 700,000 to 1.5 million.

The cotton gin helped keep the southern states a land of slavery and of farming, while the northern states became a land of free labor and of industry. In time, these fundamental differences between North and South would help lead to civil war.

Transportation and Communication

The Industrial Revolution was not the only "revolution" of the early 1800s in the United States. New technologies and new building projects produced a revolution in transportation.

Steam Power   Although James Watt had first used his steam engine to make textiles, American inventor Robert Fulton proved it could also be used to power a ship. His steamboat *Clermont* chugged up the Hudson River in 1807, demonstrating that a steamboat could travel against the current. Before long, hundreds of steamboats were plying the rivers of America's West. Steam power made it possible for western farmers and southern planters to ship their goods to markets around the world.

Canals   Since waterways were the cheapest way to carry goods, American innovators built artificial waterways, or canals. By 1840, the nation had some 3,000 miles of canals.

The best known of these canals, and the one that had the greatest impact, was the Erie Canal, which opened in 1825. Built by the state of New York, this 363-mile waterway connected the Hudson River with Lake Erie. People and goods could now travel easily between the Atlantic Coast and the Great Lakes. The Erie Canal thus speeded the development of the entire Great Lakes region. Farmers of that area could now ship their products to markets as far away as New York City and beyond.

Roads   Although canal building boomed in the young republic, it did not match road building. At first, roadbuilders had simply carved routes out of forests, throwing down the cut trees to surface the roadway. These roads were neither fast nor durable. The National, or Cumberland Road was built to last. Financed by the federal government, construction began in Cumberland, Maryland, in 1811. By the 1830s it had reached Columbus, Ohio, and later continued westward. Most of the new roads were privately built. Companies constructed highways and made a profit by collecting tolls.

Railroads   Several inventors in England and the United States adapted James Watt's steam engine technology to build a steam locomotive—a self-propelled vehicle used for pulling railroad cars. In 1828, construction on the first American railroad began in Baltimore, Maryland. It came to be known as the Baltimore and Ohio (B & O) line. By 1840, the nation had more than 3,300 miles of track on several different lines, more than any other country in the world.

Along with the revolution in transportation came advances in communication. The federal government led the way by greatly expanding its postal service. Regular mail delivery helped create a national network of information in the form of newspapers, magazines, and books.

By the 1820s, more than 500 newspapers and magazines of all sorts were being published daily in the United States. Advances in education had increased the nation's literacy rate. Newspapers and magazines now made information available to large numbers of people. Improved communication and the free exchange of ideas helped tie together the different parts of the country.

VIEWING HISTORY James Watt's steam engine (above) revolutionized transportation and manufacturing. The Erie Canal, shown below in a nineteenth-century woodcut, used mules to pull barges upstream. The canal made possible the shipping of goods from the nation's interior to the East Coast. **Determining Relevance** (a) What effect do you think such inventions and innovations had on Americans' view of the economy and of the country's future? (b) What modern-day advances have had similar effects?

VIEWING HISTORY From a makeshift pulpit, a speaker addresses a large crowd at a revival meeting. **Analyzing Visual Information** *How does the artist depict the atmosphere of this meeting?*

The Second Great Awakening

The 1790 census showed that only about 1 out of 10 Americans was a member of a church. Yet in the early 1800s, the pressures of a changing society led many people to renew their religious faith. The great religious movement of the early 1800s is known as the **Second Great Awakening.** Like the Great Awakening of the 1730s and 1740s, it took place among Protestant Christians.

The Second Great Awakening was democratic. Anyone, rich or poor, could win salvation if he or she chose to do so. Generally, the congregation, or the people of the church, was seen as more significant than its ministers.

One common feature of the Second Great Awakening was the revival. This was a gathering at which people were "revived," or brought back to a religious life, by listening to preachers and accepting belief in Jesus Christ. Revivals were also called camp meetings because they were often held outdoors in temporary shelters such as tents.

New Denominations   Partly as a result of the Second Great Awakening, during the early 1800s several Protestant **denominations,** or religious subgroups, experienced rapid growth. The United States soon had a greater variety of Christian denominations than any other nation.

One of the fastest-growing denominations was the Baptists. Unlike other denominations, which tend to baptize people as infants, Baptists believe that only those who were old enough to understand Christian beliefs should be baptized. (Baptism is a Christian ceremony by which a person is made a member of the church.) By 1850, Baptists were the nation's second-largest denomination.

Another denomination that gained many new members was the Methodists. The Methodists spread their message through a system of traveling ministers called circuit riders. Traveling on horseback in sweeping routes or "circuits" through the wilderness, these circuit riders won many new members. By 1850, the Methodists had become the largest Protestant denomination in the United States.

The Unitarians likewise gained strength during the Second Great Awakening. (Unitarianism is not an evangelical faith. The name *Unitarian* comes from the belief that God is a unity. Many other Christian groups believe that God is a trinity, or made up of three parts.) Unitarians believe that Jesus Christ was a human messenger of God, not divine himself. They see God not as a stern judge but as a loving father.

Focus on CULTURE

Awaiting the Advent Many ministers believed that America was leading the world into the millennium, or Earth's final thousand years of glory before the biblical Day of Judgment. They looked for signs of the coming event in everyday life.

Vermont farmer William Miller declared that Jesus Christ would return to the world in 1843. This return was called the Advent, or Second Coming. Miller preached that only those who believed in the Advent would be saved and go to heaven. He estimated that his followers, called Millerites, numbered from 50,000 to 100,000.

While the Advent did not arrive in 1843, Millerites continued to await Jesus' return. In the 1860s, they formed several churches, including the Seventh-day Adventist Church, which exists today.

Unitarianism took root not on the frontier, like other new denominations, but in New England.

Another region of great activity during the Second Great Awakening was central New York State. Here, in 1830, Joseph Smith published *The Book of Mormon*. The book foretold that God would soon restore a truer, simpler church, free of ministers. This was to take place not in the faraway Holy Land but in North America. Smith started a religion based on the book. He called it the Church of Jesus Christ of Latter-day Saints. In time, people began calling members of the church Mormons.

Women were extremely active in the Second Great Awakening. In part this may have reflected the loneliness and unhappiness of many women on the frontier. They worked together to help widows and orphans, to spread the Christian religion, or to improve conditions for mothers.

African American Worship

In the 1700s and early 1800s, Methodist and other evangelical churches included whites and blacks. As African Americans joined Christian churches, black and white religious traditions blended together. One example is the call-and-response method of worship, in which the congregation responds together to a statement made by one member. This is a feature of both older Protestant worship and African music.

Both white and black Christians also sang **spirituals,** or folk hymns. African American singers, however, often focused on themes that held a double meaning. For example, in the Bible, the Jewish people, called Israelites, had been kept in slavery under Egypt's pharaoh, or ruler, and were led out of Egypt to freedom by Moses. African Americans made this story a symbol for winning both spiritual salvation and freedom from physical slavery.

African Americans sometimes felt unwelcome in white-dominated churches. The tensions between whites and blacks increased as African Americans became more assertive about sharing in democratic liberty.

In several cities, African Americans started their own churches. In 1816, for example, 16 congregations joined to form the African Methodist Episcopal Church (AME). By 1831, the AME had 86 churches with about 8,000 members.

African American women preachers, such as Juliann Jane Tillman, found a voice within the African Methodist Episcopal Church (AME).

Section 1 Assessment

READING COMPREHENSION

1. Why was the population young and growing in the early 1800s?

2. Trace the causes and effects of (a) the westward migration of Native Americans; (b) the independence of Texas; (c) the **Adams-Onís Treaty.**

3. Name three inventions or innovations that changed early American life.

4. What new religious **denominations** arose during the **Second Great Awakening?**

CRITICAL THINKING AND WRITING

5. **Determining Relevance** How was the spirit of improvement related to the Industrial Revolution?

6. **Writing to Describe** Write an essay describing the changing role of American women as seen in (a) the call for republican virtues and (b) the Second Great Awakening.

For: An activity on the Erie Canal
Visit: PHSchool.com
Web Code: mrd-0031

READING FOCUS

- How did the economy expand in the early 1800s, and how did the northern and southern economies differ?
- What events of the early 1800s reflect the rise of nationalism in America?
- How did new opposition parties arise?
- What issues shaped the presidency of Andrew Jackson?

MAIN IDEA

In the early 1800s, manufacturing and banking expanded the U.S. economy. A sense of unified nationhood took hold, but growing regional differences began to challenge that unity.

KEY TERMS

Market Revolution
manufacturing
free enterprise system
capital
industrialization
strike
labor union
Monroe Doctrine
nullify
states' rights
secede
Trail of Tears

TARGET READING SKILL

Identify Cause and Effect As you read, complete the following chart to show causes and effects of the Market Revolution.

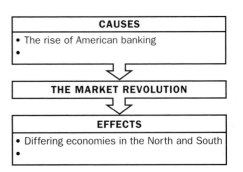

CAUSES
• The rise of American banking
•

⬇

THE MARKET REVOLUTION

⬇

EFFECTS
• Differing economies in the North and South
•

Setting the Scene On July 4, 1826, Americans celebrated the fiftieth anniversary of the Declaration of Independence with parades, cannon salutes, and speeches. It was a day to remember the achievements of the men and women who had won this nation's freedom.

Only after the celebrations were finished did many Americans learn that two of the greatest of those men, Thomas Jefferson and John Adams, had died that very day. Their deaths reminded Americans that the Revolutionary generation, for all its accomplishments, was now passing into history.

Not only were the men and women of the Revolutionary generation leaving the scene. The world they had lived in was disappearing as well.

An Expanding Economy

In the decades after the War of 1812, the American economy soared. While the United States remained mostly a nation of farmers, a new generation of Americans began buying and selling goods, borrowing and circulating money, and creating wealth. This change in the way Americans made, bought, and sold goods is known as the **Market Revolution.**

This cast metal weathervane, a symbol of American patriotism, dates to about 1800.

The Rise of Manufacturing The Market Revolution was fueled by the American genius for invention, which resulted in new and better ways to make and transport goods. Farmers started putting more and more frontier lands into the production of crops such as wheat and corn. Land in New England could then be put to other uses, such as **manufacturing,** or the making of products by machinery. The region's fast-moving rivers supplied power to the new machines in factories that sprang up in the early 1800s.

In 1813, a group of businessmen led by a Boston merchant named Francis Cabot Lowell built a factory in Waltham, Massachusetts, to manufacture textiles. Lowell's was the first truly centralized textile factory in the world. That is, all the tasks involved in making a product (in this case, cloth) were carried out in one place.

From the 1820s through the 1840s, manufacturing industries arose in New England and spread across the Northeast and parts of the Northwest Territory, such as the Ohio River valley. Manufacturing would soon become the backbone of the North's economy.

READING CHECK
What factors led to the rise in manufacturing?

The Free Enterprise System   The changes of the Market Revolution were based on a **free enterprise system.** This is an economic system characterized by private or corporate ownership of capital goods; investments that are determined by private decision rather than by state control; and determined in a free market. In a free enterprise economy, most property is owned by private individuals and companies. The operation of supply and demand decides how goods are produced and distributed. This system, also called capitalism, rewards people who can find better, faster, and more efficient ways of running their businesses. It encourages the creation of new industries, jobs, and wealth.

Generally these new jobs were located outside the home. In the past, most Americans had worked in the home or around the farm, making the food, clothing, and shelter they needed. Now more people began working in factories for a specific number of hours each day and for a certain amount of money.

As products became available and people worked for money, Americans began to shop. The relatively simple homes of the 1700s gave way to much more decorated homes in the 1800s.

The Rise of the Banking Industry   The Market Revolution could not have happened without large amounts of **capital,** or wealth that can be invested to produce goods and make money. Businesses used capital to buy land or to invest in money-making projects. Banks provided this capital.

The first real banks in the United States appeared in the 1780s and 1790s. By the 1830s, hundreds of new banks had been established.

Generally, a group of private investors would obtain a charter from the state to start a bank. The bank made money by charging interest for the loans it made. It made these loans using the money that customers deposited in the bank for safekeeping. Banks thus helped the economy grow by providing the money that businesses needed to expand.

However, banks often made bad loans to people who could not pay them back. Since (unlike today) the government did not require banks to keep a certain amount of cash on hand, banks sometimes lacked the cash to give to depositors who wanted to withdraw money. Customers would panic, rushing to the banks to get their money out before the banks went broke. As a result, the American economy experienced wild booms followed by panics, bank failures, and depressions.

As this bank note shows, people began earning a living outside the home in the early 1800s.

Bank Notes   The most common form of money in the early 1800s was the bank note, a piece of paper that banks issued to their customers. Similar to modern-day checks, bank notes were promises to pay specie (coins, mainly of gold or silver) on demand.

Because banks simply printed more bank notes whenever they needed money, the value of this money was unpredictable. A $100 bank note could be worth anything from $50 to $100 in specie, depending on the time and place its owner tried to cash it.

New England mill builders adopted a system of belts to harness river power. On the first floor cotton was combed; on the second floor, it was spun into thread; on the third, thread was woven into cloth; and on the fourth, the cloth was dressed, or finished. **Determining Relevance** *What effect did geography have on the location of a mill?*

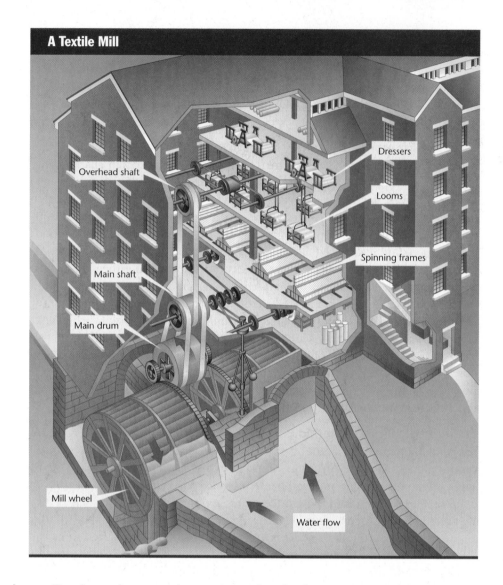

A Textile Mill

Dressers

Looms

Spinning frames

Overhead shaft

Main shaft

Main drum

Mill wheel

Water flow

Despite such economic growing pains, banks were essential to economic expansion. While different areas of the country grew at different rates, the United States as a whole achieved a new level of prosperity.

The Northern Economy

In the early 1800s, Americans became more aware that their nation had distinct regions or sections. The two main sections during this period were the North and the South.

One part of the North was the region north and west of the Ohio River, which historians call the Old Northwest. It included land that is now Ohio, Indiana, Illinois, Michigan, Wisconsin, and part of Minnesota. The other part was the Northeast, composed of New England and the states of New York, New Jersey, and Pennsylvania.

Northwest Farming, Northeast Industry The fertile fields of the Old Northwest were ideal for growing corn, wheat, and other grains. Grains could be sold or turned into other products. Many specialized businesses arose to handle the processing, transport, and selling of farm products.

Although most people in the Northeast still lived on farms, many others now worked in factories in urban areas. As more people came to the cities to work, the Northeast's population density, or the number of people living within a given space, rose as well. Between 1810 and 1840, the number of Americans living in cities jumped from about 6 percent of the total population to 12 percent. Much of that growth was in the Northeast.

Industrialization, or the growth of industry, increased rapidly. The mill town of Lowell, Massachusetts, founded in 1826, would become a booming industrial center. The Lowell mills hired young, unmarried women from New England farms to run the spinning and weaving machines. Women mill workers usually lived in boardinghouses established by the mill owners. Six days a week, twelve hours a day, they tended the machines. In the evening they might attend lectures or classes, or gather in sewing or reading circles.

The Rise of Labor Unions   The Lowell mills treated their employees much better than did other early industries. Most factory owners paid their employees little and did not provide benefits such as housing or food. Meanwhile, workers saw owners grow rich while they labored long hours for low wages. Workers had only one real weapon: a **strike,** or work stoppage. From 1834 through 1836, more than 150 strikes took place in the United States.

In 1834, workers also organized the first national labor union, the National Trades Union (NTU). A **labor union** is an organization of workers formed to protect their interests, usually by negotiating to resolve issues such as wages and working conditions. Close to 300,000 people joined the NTU or other labor unions in the 1830s, a large number for that period.

These early unions soon died out, however. Factory owners obtained court rulings that outlawed labor organizations. Workers were also hard hit by the economic depressions of 1837 and 1839, which caused higher unemployment and lower wages.

The Southern Economy

The South consisted of 6 of the original 13 states: Delaware, Maryland, Virginia (including what would become West Virginia), North Carolina, South Carolina, and Georgia. It also included newer states carved out of lands south of the Ohio River that stretched from the Appalachian Mountains to the Mississippi River: Kentucky, Tennessee, Alabama, Mississippi, Louisiana, and Arkansas.

This print shows workers loading and unloading cotton shipments at the port city of New Orleans in 1883.

A Rural Economy   While urban centers developed in the North, the South remained mostly a rural region of farms and countryside. Farmers enjoyed fertile soil, plentiful rain, and 200 to 290 frost-free days a year in which to grow crops.

The primary southern crop was cotton. Virginia and North Carolina were mainly tobacco states. Sugar and rice crops thrived in hot, wet places such as South Carolina. Kentucky developed a varied rural economy that included the breeding of thoroughbred horses.

The Slavery System   By 1804, all the northern states had either banned slavery or passed laws to end it gradually. The Constitution specified that Congress could not end the slave trade before 1808. In that year, Congress banned further importing of slaves.

Within the South, however, the slave trade increased sharply for the next half century due to population growth among people already enslaved. By

The issue of slavery opened up a bitter divide between the North and the South. The writers below present viewpoints on whether enslaved people wished to remain in slavery.

Analyzing Viewpoints Compare the main arguments made by the two writers.

In Support of Slavery

"A merrier being does not exist on the face of the globe than the Negro slave of the United States. They are happy and contented, and the master is much less cruel than is generally imagined. Why then . . . should we attempt to disturb his contentment by planting in his mind a vain and indefinite desire for liberty—something which he cannot understand?"

—Professor Thomas R. Dew, speech to the Virginia legislature, 1832

In Opposition to Slavery

"I thank God I am not property now, but am regarded as a man like yourself. . . . You may perhaps think hard of us for running away from slavery, but as for myself, I have but one apology to make for it, which is this: I have only to regret that I did not start at any early period."

—Henry Bibb, who escaped from slavery with his family, in a letter to his former master, 1844

1860, African American slaves made up more than half of the population of South Carolina and of Mississippi, as well as two fifths of the population in several other states.

Slave Revolts Only a small percentage of slaves managed to escape captivity or to win their freedom. Rebellions, especially on a large scale, stood little chance of success.

One attempt at a revolt was made by a former slave named Denmark Vesey. In 1822, he laid plans for the most ambitious slave revolt in American history. In a conspiracy that reportedly involved hundreds or even thousands of rebels, Vesey plotted to seize the city of Charleston. He was betrayed by some of his followers, however, and troops smashed the rebellion before it could get started. Thirty-five African Americans, including Vesey, were hanged.

Nine years later, Nat Turner, an African American preacher, carried out a violent uprising known as Turner's Rebellion. He led up to 70 slaves in raids on white families in southeastern Virginia. In attacks on four plantations, the rebels killed some 57 white people.

Eventually, local militia captured most of the rebels. The state of Virginia hanged about 20 of the slaves, including Turner. Crowds of frightened, angry whites rioted, killing about a hundred African Americans who had had no part in the revolt. Some southern states reacted to the Vesey and Turner rebellions by tightening restrictions on slaves.

The Rise of Nationalism

Eventually, the economic differences between the North and South would place great strains on the nation's unity. In the 1820s, though, the nation seemed to be pulling closer together. Americans began thinking of themselves as belonging to a country under a national government, instead of an association of states under separate governments. Reflecting this shift, a new generation of American leaders sought to exercise the powers of the federal government to unite the country.

Nationalism at Home After the War of 1812, the nation was weary of conflict. It adopted new nationalist policies to resolve political struggles at home and abroad. In domestic affairs, the Supreme Court under Chief Justice John Marshall made decisions in three key areas that strengthened the federal government's role in the economy.

The first decision supported the national bank. The Constitution did not specifically grant the federal government the right to charter a national bank. In 1819, the Supreme Court considered a case involving Maryland's attempt to wipe out the bank by levying heavy taxes on it. Maryland's action challenged Congress's authority to create such an institution. In *McCulloch* v. *Maryland*, Chief Justice Marshall ruled that Congress did have the authority to charter the bank. He based his argument on Article I, Section 8, which states that Congress

Nationalist Supreme Court Decisions, 1819–1824

Case	Issues	Outcomes
McCulloch v. Maryland (1819)	Does the government have the power to create a national bank? Do states have the right to tax institutions created by the federal government?	Reinforced (1) the doctrine of implied powers and (2) the principle of the power of the national government over state governments.
Dartmouth College v. Woodward (1819)	Was Dartmouth's contract protected by the Constitution? Was New Hampshire interfering with the contract?	Prevented state interference in business contracts. Gave stability to the economy by encouraging growth of corporations.
Gibbons v. Ogden (1824)	Who has the power to regulate interstate navigation, the states or the federal government?	Established the federal government's right to regulate all aspects of interstate commerce.

INTERPRETING CHARTS The Supreme Court under Chief Justice John Marshall made several decisions that greatly increased the authority of the federal government. **Drawing Inferences** *How do these decisions reflect the shift toward nationalism?*

has the right "to make all laws necessary and proper" for carrying out the powers granted it under the Constitution.

An 1819 ruling protected the legality of contracts. The Court barred New Hampshire from changing the charter of Dartmouth College. The college had been chartered during colonial times. In *Dartmouth College* v. *Woodward,* the Court ruled that states cannot interfere in such contracts. The long-term effect of the ruling was to protect business contracts, providing further stability to the economy.

In the 1824 case *Gibbons* v. *Ogden,* Chief Justice Marshall established the federal government's right to regulate commerce on interstate waterways. A man named Aaron Ogden had purchased a state license giving him exclusive rights to operate a New York–New Jersey steamboat line. When a competitor, Thomas Gibbons, started a business on the same route, Ogden sued him. Gibbons said he operated under federal license. Gibbons's victory gave the federal government authority over all types of interstate business.

Nationalism Abroad At the same time, American Presidents strengthened the nation's foreign policy. The new policies took shape under the leadership of President James Monroe and his Secretary of State, John Quincy Adams, the son of Abigail and John Adams.

In foreign policy, one of Monroe's main concerns was to ease tensions with Great Britain. In 1817, the United States and Britain signed the Rush-Bagot Agreement, in which both sides agreed to reduce the number of warships in the Great Lakes region. The following year, the two countries agreed to extend the northern border of the United States westward along 49° N latitude from Lake of the Woods to the Rocky Mountains.

A second concern for Monroe was that European countries might resume their efforts to colonize the Western Hemisphere. Monroe spelled out American policy on these urgent matters in an address to Congress on December 2, 1823. The speech established a policy that has been followed to some degree by every President since Monroe. The **Monroe Doctrine,** as it is called, had four main parts. First, the United States would not get involved in the internal affairs of European

Focus on CULTURE

Democracy in America One of the most influential books ever written about America was authored by a Frenchman. Alexis de Tocqueville wrote *Democracy in America* after spending nine months in the United States in 1831.

Tocqueville was struck by "the general equality of condition among the people." Compared to Europe, America had fewer very rich or very poor people and more who were in between. Also, Americans did not regard a wealthy person as being better than anyone else.

Yet equality had its drawbacks, Tocqueville warned. He knew of "no country in which there is so little . . . real freedom of discussion," since few Americans dared to disagree with the majority. Still, he hoped that Europeans would some day enjoy the liberty and equality he found in the United States.

countries nor take sides in wars among them. Second, America recognized the existing colonies and states in the Western Hemisphere and would not interfere with them. Third, America would not permit further colonization of the Western Hemisphere. Fourth, America would view any attempt by a European power to control any nation in the Western Hemisphere as a hostile action.

As President Monroe stated:

" *Our policy in regard to Europe . . . is, not to interfere in the internal concerns of any of its powers. . . . It is impossible that the allied [European] powers should extend their political system to any portion of either [the North American or South American] continent without endangering our peace and happiness. . . .* "

—The Monroe Doctrine speech by President James Monroe to Congress, December 2, 1823

The Rise of Opposition Parties

The elections of 1824 and 1828 were bitter battles. Yet out of these disputes arose new political parties that offered clear choices to voters.

The Election of 1824   In 1824, for the first time no presidential candidate could boast of having been a leader during the Revolution. Challenging John Quincy Adams were the brilliant political leader Henry Clay of Kentucky and war hero General Andrew Jackson of Tennessee.

Clay, former Speaker of the House and United States senator from Kentucky, was energetic and charming, with a magnificent gift for speech making. Andrew Jackson had served in the Senate in the 1790s and was a wealthy plantation owner near Nashville, Tennessee. His victories in the War of 1812 and his attacks on the Seminole Indians in Florida had won him widespread popularity.

In the 1824 election, Jackson won the most popular votes, but none of the candidates received the required majority of electoral college votes. Thus in February 1825, as the Constitution required, the House of Representatives voted to decide the election. Clay managed to swing Kentucky's votes to Adams to give him the victory. Just days later, Adams made Clay his Secretary of State. Furious Jackson supporters charged that Adams and Clay had made a "corrupt bargain" to deny Jackson the presidency.

New Political Parties Emerge   At every turn, Jackson's supporters in Congress blocked Adams' plans for public improvements and protective tariffs. Meanwhile Jackson prepared for the coming election— and for revenge.

Supporters of Adams and Clay adopted a new name: the National Republicans. They believed they were true to the Jeffersonian spirit of improvement. Jackson's followers called themselves Democrats. (Historians refer to them as Jacksonian Democrats.) They believed they were true to Jefferson's ideal of limited government.

Unlike most previous elections, the 1828 campaign offered voters a choice between candidates of sharply differing views. Jackson trounced Adams, winning 178 electoral votes to Adams's 83.

French writer Alexis de Tocqueville visited the United States three years later, in 1831. In his book, *Democracy in America,* he noted that "liberty is

READING CHECK
Why was the Monroe Doctrine a bold diplomatic move?

This first photograph of an American President shows John Quincy Adams—son of President John Adams and his wife, Abigail—in the 1840s.

generally born in stormy weather, growing with difficulty amid civil discords, and only when it is already old does one see the blessings it has brought." The rise of opposition parties in America would indeed produce "discords." But the party system would stir healthy debates and strengthen the democratic process.

The Presidency of Andrew Jackson

The rise of Andrew Jackson signaled several changes in American politics. Jackson was the first President from west of the Appalachian Mountains. He also came to the presidency not through party politics but on a wave of popular support. State laws requiring voters to be property holders had been repealed in the previous decade, and new states such as Indiana and Maine allowed all white adult men to vote. The votes cast for President tripled between 1824 and 1828, from roughly 356,000 to more than 1.1 million.

The Spoils System For many years, newly elected officials had given government jobs to friends and supporters. Although he did not originate this practice, known as patronage, Andrew Jackson made it official when he took office. However, during his eight years as President, Jackson actually removed fewer than one fifth of presidential appointees and other federal office holders and replaced them with Jacksonian Democrats. Patronage under Jackson became known as the *spoils system*. In this case, the spoils, or loot taken from a conquered enemy, were jobs for party supporters.

Jackson defended the spoils system on the grounds that any intelligent person could be a competent public official. He also argued that "rotation in office" would prevent a small group of wealthy, well-connected people from controlling the government.

Limited Government Jackson shared the beliefs of Americans who feared the power of the federal government. He attacked politicians whom he considered corrupt and laws that he thought would limit people's liberty. He used his veto power to restrict federal activity as much as possible, rejecting more acts of Congress than the six previous Presidents combined.

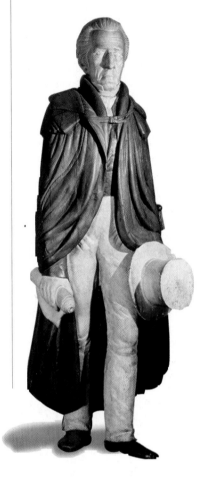

A navy ship bore this figurehead of Andrew Jackson in 1834.

The Tariff Crisis While Jackson sought to limit federal power, he did not shy away from strong federal action when he thought it necessary. In 1828, Congress had passed a high tariff to discourage foreign imports and encourage American manufacturing. The tariff benefited the industrial North but forced southerners to pay higher prices for manufactured goods. They called the import tax the "Tariff of Abominations." (*Abomination* refers to something especially horrible or monstrous.)

The tariff prompted South Carolina to declare that states had the right to judge when the federal government had exceeded its authority. The state maintained that in such cases, states could **nullify,** or reject, federal laws they judged to be unconstitutional.

South Carolina's nullification threat was based on a strict interpretation of states' rights. **States' rights** are the powers that the Constitution neither gives to the federal government nor denies to the states. The concept of states' rights is based on the constitutional principle of divided sovereignty between the federal government and the state government. In other words, each has its own powers that the other cannot take away.

The strict interpretation of states' rights that South Carolina endorsed is what some people call *state sovereignty*. The theory of state sovereignty maintains

Florida's Seminoles The name *Seminole* is thought to come from a Spanish word, *cimmarone,* meaning "runaway, or "wild one." The Seminoles had fled to Spanish Florida in the early 1700s when colonists pushed them off their lands in Georgia. True to their name, they later welcomed runaway slaves from the American South. Some of these black Seminoles lived among the Indians. Others set up villages nearby. The former slaves, with their knowledge of English language and culture, helped the Seminoles in their dealings with white settlers and government officials. The Seminoles waged three wars against U.S. forces before 1860. The first was fought to keep American authorities from capturing black Seminoles and returning them to slavery. The second and third were fought to resist attempts to force the Seminoles out of Florida under the Indian Removal Act.

that because states created the federal government, they have the right to nullify its acts and even to **secede,** or withdraw, from the Union if they wish to do so. In 1832, after the passage of yet another tariff, South Carolina declared the tariffs null and void, and threatened to secede if its nullification was not respected.

An enraged Jackson believed the state was defying the will of the people. At his urging, in 1833 Congress passed the Force Bill, which made it difficult for South Carolina to block federal collection of the tariff. Jackson threatened to send 50,000 federal troops to enforce the law.

The crisis eased when Congress reduced some of the import duties and South Carolina canceled its nullification act. Yet in an act of continued defiance, the state nullified the Force Bill at the same time.

Indian Relocation In the 1820s, wealthy plantation owners were buying up much of the best cotton-farming land in the South. Large and small planters alike wanted to expand westward into Native American lands. The Cherokee, Creek, Choctaw, Chickasaw, and Seminole peoples lived on about 100 million acres of fertile land in western parts of the Carolinas and in Georgia, Florida, Alabama, Mississippi, and Tennessee.

In 1830, Jackson encouraged Congress's passage of the Indian Removal Act, which authorized him to give Native Americans land in parts of the Louisiana Purchase in exchange for lands taken from them in the East.

In all, Jackson forcibly relocated about 100,000 members of the Five Tribes. For their 100 million acres of largely cultivated land, the Native Americans received about 32 million acres of prairie land in what is now Oklahoma.

In 1832, the Cherokees brought their case to the Supreme Court through a missionary from Vermont, Samuel Austin Worcester. In *Worcester v. Georgia,* Chief Justice John Marshall ruled that Georgia had no authority over Cherokee territory. Georgia, however, simply ignored the ruling, and Jackson backed the state. "John Marshall has made his decision. Now let him enforce it!" Jackson is said to have declared. Of course, the Court had no power to enforce its decisions.

In 1838, the United States Army rounded up more than 15,000 Cherokees. In a nightmare journey that the Cherokees called the **Trail of Tears,**

VIEWING HISTORY Jackson claimed that his Indian removal policy would "place a dense and civilized population in large tracts of country now occupied by a few savage hunters." **Analyzing Visual Information** *In this painting of the* Trail of Tears, *what difficulties does the artist suggest the displaced Indians faced under Jackson's policy?*

men, women, and children, most on foot, began a 116-day forced march westward. One out of every four Cherokees died of cold or disease on the journey.

The Bank War   Like many Americans, Jackson saw the Bank of the United States as a "monster" institution controlled by a small group of wealthy easterners. He blamed it for the Panic of 1819 and the hard times that had followed.

Under its charter, the Bank of the United States could only operate until 1836, unless Congress issued it a new charter. Supporters of the bank decided to recharter it four years early, in 1832. If Jackson vetoed the charter, Jackson's opponents planned to use that veto against him in the 1832 election. Jackson vetoed the bill anyway.

Jackson then won reelection in 1832 by a huge margin, defeating National Republican Henry Clay. In the process, a distinct two-party system was reestablished, consisting of Jackson's Democratic Party and the National Republicans. Later the National Republicans would take the name Whigs, after the party in the British parliament that had opposed the king in the 1700s. These American Whigs saw themselves as defenders of liberty against an executive so powerful they dubbed him "King Andrew I."

Jackson's Successors   In frail health, Jackson chose not to run for a third term in 1836. The next President, Martin Van Buren, whom Jackson had supported as a candidate, was not as popular as the general had been.

Weakened by panics in 1837 and 1839, the economy remained in poor shape in the 1840 election year. The Whig candidate, military hero William Henry Harrison, defeated Van Buren, only to be defeated himself by illness. Just one month after taking office, he died of pneumonia. Vice President John Tyler, who took over as President, was more of a Jacksonian Democrat than a Whig, and his term was largely one of fruitless quarreling between the parties.

INTERPRETING POLITICAL CARTOONS In this cartoon, Andrew Jackson drags Henry Clay behind him as he attacks the monster national bank. **Analyzing Visual Information** How does the artist suggest that the danger is imaginary?

 Sounds of an Era

Listen to reenactments of Native American history and Andrew Jackson on the bank war, as well as other sounds from the early 1800s.

Section 2 Assessment

READING COMPREHENSION

1. Describe the effects of **manufacturing** and **capital** on the U.S. economy.

2. How did America's **free enterprise system** affect the growing **Market Revolution?**

3. What two new political parties emerged in the 1820s, and how did their views differ?

4. How did President Jackson react to the tariff and Indian crises?

CRITICAL THINKING AND WRITING

5. **Making Comparisons** Compare the types of labor upon which economic activity was based in the North and in the South. How was labor a difficult issue in both regions?

6. **Writing to Inform** Trace the rise of nationalism in the early 1800s, and then explain how that sense of national unity yielded to regional rivalries.

For: An activity on 1800s census data
Visit: PHSchool.com
Web Code: mrd-0032

READING FOCUS

- How did religion and philosophy affect the growing American reform movement?

- What reform movements emerged in the early 1800s?

- How did the antislavery movement arise and grow?

- In what ways did women's roles change in the early 1800s?

- What factors caused growing social divisions in America?

MAIN IDEA

Powerful reform movements arose in the early 1800s. They transformed society and produced regional and ethnic tensions.

KEY TERMS

transcendentalism
temperance movement
abstinence
utopian community
abolitionist movement
Underground Railroad
Seneca Falls Convention
suffrage
discrimination

TARGET READING SKILL

Identify Main Ideas Copy the web diagram below. As you read, fill in the blank circles with types of reform movements and their leaders. Add more circles if needed.

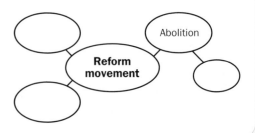

Setting the Scene In 1688, a group of Mennonites, a Christian sect of German immigrants, passed a resolution that stated:

> **❝** There is a saying, that we should do to all men like as we will be done ourselves; making no difference of what generation, descent, or colour they are. And those who steal or rob men, and those who buy or purchase them, are they not all alike? **❞**
>
> —Resolutions of Germantown Mennonites, 1688

This resolution, the earliest known protest against slavery in the colonies, shows the deep roots that reform movements have in American history. It also serves as an example of the strong ties that have existed between religious faith and social reform.

In the early decades of the 1800s, America's young cities experienced growing pains such as poverty, alcoholism, illiteracy, overcrowded housing, poor healthcare, and abuse of women. Because these growing pains occurred first in the urban North, it was there that powerful reform movements to address these problems first took hold.

VIEWING HISTORY After a string of personal tragedies, including a failed engagement in 1840 and the loss of his brother in 1842, Henry David Thoreau sought a quieter life at Walden Pond (below) in Massachusetts. **Drawing Inferences** *From what you know about economic and social trends taking place in the Northeast during this time, how might Thoreau's life at Walden Pond have represented a contrast from those trends?*

had already proclaimed an independent Republic of California. The settlers' flag pictured a grizzly bear and a single star, so the uprising became known as the Bear Flag Revolt. Frémont assumed control of the rebel forces and then drove the Mexican army out of northern California.

Another American force crossed into New Mexico. Meeting little resistance, it marched west to California to join Frémont. By January 1847, the United States had taken control of the territories of New Mexico and California.

Meanwhile, General Taylor had taken the war into Mexico, forcing Santa Anna to abandon the northeastern part of the country. Even worse for the Mexicans, General Winfield Scott captured the port city of Veracruz and marched his army of 10,000 men toward Mexico City. After fierce fighting, Scott defeated Santa Anna's forces and captured the Mexican capital on September 14, bringing the war to an end.

The Treaty of Guadalupe Hidalgo, signed on February 2, 1848, ended the war. Under its harsh terms, Mexico gave up its claim to Texas and recognized the Rio Grande as the southern border of Texas. Mexico also gave up New Mexico and California, which together made up more than two fifths of its territory. The United States paid Mexico $15 million.

In 1853, Mexico sold 30,000 square miles of what is now southern New Mexico and Arizona to the United States for $10 million. This land was known as the Gadsden Purchase. The 1846 division of Oregon, the Treaty of Guadalupe Hidalgo, and the Gadsden Purchase established the present-day boundaries of the continental United States.

Posters such as this, circulated by land dealers and other entrepreneurs in California, lured eager prospectors with visions of a gleaming land of gold.

The California Gold Rush Even as the United States was acquiring California from Mexico, Americans were starting to pour into the territory. In January 1848, gold was discovered in California. Word of the gold strike quickly spread throughout the country, and the California Gold Rush began.

California's population jumped from 14,000 residents in 1848 to 200,000 by 1852, as Americans—mostly unmarried men—rushed west. Immigrants, too, headed for California. By 1852, about 10 percent of Californians were Chinese. Chinese immigrants mainly labored in mines and as servants.

Indians and Western Migration Until the Mexican War, the United States had proclaimed all land west of the 95th meridian, or line of longitude, to be Indian Country. The migration of thousands of settlers into Indian Country, therefore, posed a problem. By the 1850s, the government increasingly saw the answer to that problem in the creation of reservations, or areas that the government sets aside for Native Americans who have lost their homelands. Many Native Americans refused to be herded onto reservations and fought to preserve their way of life.

Slavery in the Territories

A central issue facing Congress in the 1840s and 1850s was whether to allow slavery in the territories acquired from Mexico. In the short run, the Missouri Compromise of 1820 had maintained the balance in the Senate between slave and free states. The compromise did not, however, settle the issue of whether slavery would be legal in the western territories.

In 1846, the Wilmot Proviso came before Congress. The bill stated that slavery would not be permitted in any of the territory acquired from Mexico. Several times Congress rejected it, but Northerners continued to urge the bill's approval.

Focus on GOVERNMENT

Statehood for Florda The territory of Florida drafted a state constitution in 1838 and submitted it to Congress the next year. At the time, Florida had a population of 48,000, of which 21,000 were slaves. In keeping with the Missouri Compromise, Congress admitted new states to the Union in pairs, one slave and one free. In 1845, Florida entered the Union as a slave state, and Iowa entered the next year as a free state. Reflecting Florida's plantation economy, a planter named William Moseley was elected the state's first governor.

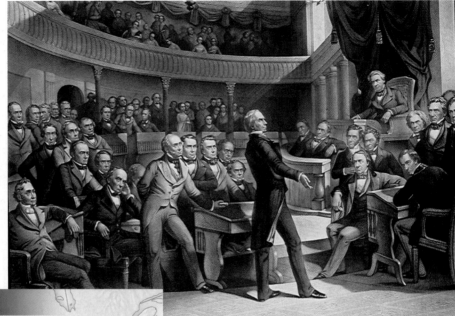

MAP SKILLS The painting at right depicts Senator Henry Clay leading a debate over the Compromise of 1850. Clay warned that a failure to compromise would lead to "furious" and "bloody" war. The compromise that resulted is shown in the map below. **Region** *What issues did the Compromise of 1850 attempt to address?*

The Compromise of 1850

BRITISH NORTH AMERICA

0   200   400 mi.

0   200 400 km

Oregon Territory

Minnesota Territory

Vt.

Me.

Wis.

Mich.

N.Y.

N.H.

Mass.

Iowa

Penn.

Utah Territory

Unorganized Territory

Ill.

Ind.

Ohio

N.J.

R.I.

Conn.

Calif.

Mo.

Ky.

Va.

Del.

Md.

New Mexico Territory

Indian Territory

Ark.

Tenn.

N.C.

S.C.

ATLANTIC OCEAN

Miss.

Ala.

Ga.

30°N

MEXICO

Texas

La.

Fla.

Gulf of Mexico

N

80°W

90°W

Legend:
- States and territories closed to slavery
- States and territory open to slavery
- Territories to vote on slavery

The Compromise of 1850

In 1850, the thousands of Americans who had rushed into California during the Gold Rush requested that California be admitted to the United States as a free state. This change would upset the fragile balance between free and slave states in the Senate.

Henry Clay of Kentucky proposed a plan that would become known as the **Compromise of 1850.** Seeking a middle ground on the slavery debate, Clay proposed five separate laws, two of which favored the North and two of which favored the South:

1. Congress would admit California into the Union as a free state.
2. The people of the New Mexico and Utah territories would decide for themselves whether to allow slavery.
3. Congress would abolish the sale of enslaved people, but not slavery, in Washington, D.C.
4. Texas would give up claims to New Mexico for $10 million.
5. A Fugitive Slave Act would order all citizens of the United States to assist in the return of escaped slaves and would deny a jury trial to escaped slaves.

Debating the Compromise

South Carolina's John C. Calhoun expressed the view of the South. The "great and primary" cause of the crisis, he said, was that the North now had "the exclusive power of controlling the Government" due to its larger population, which gave it more seats in the House and more votes in the electoral college.

Surprisingly, Daniel Webster of Massachusetts, who had opposed the extension of slavery, backed Clay's compromise. Webster argued that slavery would never be practical in New Mexico and that it was a constitutional duty to return fugitive slaves. Northern abolitionists and many of Webster's longtime supporters were furious.

Congress eventually passed the Compromise of 1850. Yet it brought only a brief period of calm.

Sounds of an Era

Listen to John C. Calhoun on the Compromise of 1850 and other sounds from the pre–Civil War era.

Differences Between North and South By the 1850s, many white Northerners had come to believe that slavery violated the basic principles of the United States and of the Christian religion. They did not necessarily believe that blacks and whites were equal. Many, in fact, were deeply prejudiced against African Americans. (A **prejudice** is an unreasonable, usually unfavorable, opinion of another group that is not based on fact.) Nevertheless, these people saw slavery as an evil that could not be tolerated.

The most popular antislavery statement of the period was a novel published in 1852 by Harriet Beecher Stowe, called *Uncle Tom's Cabin*. Through Stowe's novel, many northern readers saw the evils of slavery for the first time.

Many Southerners saw *Uncle Tom's Cabin* as a book of insulting lies. Most planters took a personal interest in the well-being of their slaves, they claimed, while Northern industrialists took no responsibility for their workers.

Yet the differences between North and South went deeper than attitudes toward slavery. The North was becoming still more urban, still more industrial than the South. In 1860, the North had 110,000 factories, compared to 20,000 in the South, and produced more than $1.6 billion worth of goods, compared to the South's $155 million. The North's population was more than twice as large as the South's.

New technology had a heavier impact on the North than on the South. For example, in 1860, the North had 70 percent of the nation's railroad track. The telegraph, patented by Samuel F. B. Morse in 1844, also was more widely used in the North. The telegraph allowed people to send messages over wire by using a code of short and long pulses of electricity.

The Kansas-Nebraska Act In January 1854, Senator Stephen Douglas of Illinois introduced the **Kansas-Nebraska Act,** which called for the creation of two new territories, Kansas and Nebraska. It also stated that the people in these territories would be permitted to decide whether slavery would be allowed there, a principle known as popular sovereignty. Since both Kansas and Nebraska lay north of 36° 30' N, which the Missouri Compromise had set as the boundary between slave and free territories, Douglas basically was calling for repeal of the Missouri Compromise.

Douglas knew his proposal would please Southerners. After all, it raised the possibility that Kansas and Nebraska might become slave states. He also thought that Northerners would assume that slavery would never take hold on the Great Plains (where cotton could not grow) and thus would back his proposal. Congress passed the Kansas-Nebraska Act, angering northern Democrats.

Changes in Political Parties

The continuing debate over slavery contributed to a breakdown of the party system during the early 1850s. By the end of the 1850s, the Whig Party had

Economic Advantages of the North and South

	Northern States	Southern States
Agriculture		
Corn (bushels)	✓ 446 million	280 million
Wheat (bushels)	✓ 132 million	31 million
Oats (bushels)	✓ 150 million	20 million
Cotton (bales)	4 thousand	✓ 5 million
Tobacco (pounds)	✓ 229 million	199 million
Rice (pounds)	50 thousand	✓ 187 million
Finance		
Bank Deposits	✓ $207 million	$47 million
Specie	✓ $56 million	$27 million
Livestock		
Horses	✓ 4.2 million	1.7 million
Donkeys and Mules	300 thousand	✓ 800 thousand
Milk Cows	✓ 5.7 million	2.7 million
Beef Cattle	6.6 million	✓ 7 million
Sheep	✓ 16 million	5 million
Swine	✓ 16.3 million	15.5 million
Manufacturing		
Number of Factories	✓ 110.1 thousand	20.6 thousand
Number of Workers	✓ 1.17 million	111 thousand
Value of Products	✓ $1.62 billion	$155 million
Population	✓ 21.5 million	9 million
Railroad Mileage	✓ 21.7 thousand miles	9 thousand miles

SOURCE: *The American Heritage Picture History of the Civil War*

INTERPRETING CHARTS The economic contrasts between the North and South were sharp, as this chart demonstrates. **Analyzing Visual Information** *Summarize the types of advantages held by the North and by the South.*

largely disappeared. Many northern Whigs abandoned the party because they were unhappy with its leaders' support of compromise on slavery.

Another issue that brought down the Whigs was the rise of the American Party, or the Know-Nothings. Its members promoted **nativism,** a movement to ensure that native-born Americans receive better treatment than immigrants. Nativism arose in response to a surge in immigration: Between 1846 and 1854, close to 3 million Europeans had arrived in the United States.

In 1849, fear about immigrants led to the formation of a secret nativist society called the Order of the Star-Spangled Banner. Members replied to questions about the organization with the answer, "I know nothing."

In 1854, nativists went public by forming the American Party, which became known as the Know-Nothings. It opposed Irish Catholic candidates and sought laws requiring immigrants to wait longer before they could become citizens.

Also in 1854, a group of antislavery Northerners launched a new Republican Party, the direct ancestor of today's Republican Party. Its members dedicated themselves to stopping the "Slave Power," or the South.

Worsening Tensions

Neither the Compromise of 1850 nor the Kansas-Nebraska Act brought North and South into a workable compromise over slavery. Events in the mid-1850s only worsened the situation.

"Bleeding Kansas" Under the Kansas-Nebraska Act, voters in Kansas would decide whether to become a free state or slave state. Antislavery groups in the Northeast sent more than a thousand New Englanders, known as free-soilers, to settle in Kansas to fight against slavery. Meanwhile, many proslavery settlers crossed into Kansas to vote illegally in territorial elections. By 1855, Kansas had an antislavery capital at Topeka and a proslavery capital at Lecompton. In 1856, tensions in Kansas escalated into violent raids and counter-raids that won the territory the grim nickname of "Bleeding Kansas."

The Election of 1856 In the 1856 presidential campaign, Democratic candidate James Buchanan supported the Compromise of 1850 and the Kansas-Nebraska Act. Republican John C. Frémont declared the federal government's right to restrict slavery in the territories and called for the admission of Kansas as a free state.

Buchanan won the election and pledged to his supporters in the South that he would stop "the agitation of the slavery issue" in the North. Buchanan hoped that the Supreme Court would use its power to resolve the issue for good.

The Dred Scott Decision In March 1857, the Supreme Court handed down one of the most controversial decisions in its history, *Scott v. Sandford*. The case had started when Dred Scott, an enslaved man living in Missouri, had filed suit against his owner. Scott argued that because he and his wife, Harriet, had once lived in states and territories where slavery was illegal, the couple was in fact free.

The Court under Chief Justice Roger Taney ruled 7 to 2 against Scott. The justices held that Scott, and therefore all slaves, were not citizens and therefore had no right to sue in court. The Court also ruled that living in a free territory

for a time had not made Scott free. Most important, the Court found that Congress had no power to ban slavery anywhere, including the territories, because slaves were private property. Antislavery forces were horrified by the Dred Scott decision.

The Lecompton Constitution In the fall of 1857, a small proslavery group in Kansas elected members to a convention to write their own constitution, which was required to attain statehood. Most Kansans were opposed to slavery and refused even to vote on the proslavery Lecompton constitution. The attempt to gain statehood failed, and for the time being, Kansas remained a territory where slavery was legal according to the Dred Scott decision. In reality, however, the free-soiler majority prohibited it.

The Lincoln-Douglas Debates

In 1858, Senator Stephen Douglas ran for reelection against a relatively unknown Republican, Abraham Lincoln. Born in Kentucky in 1809, Lincoln had studied law and worked at various jobs, including postmaster and rail splitter. In 1837, he settled in Springfield, Illinois, where he practiced law. He served one term in Congress in the 1840s.

Lincoln and Douglas conducted seven highly publicized debates on the issue of slavery in the territories. The debates highlighted two important principles in American government, majority rule and minority rights. Douglas supported popular sovereignty on issues including slavery. Lincoln did not believe that a majority should have the power to deny a minority of their rights to life, liberty, and the pursuit of happiness. Thus he opposed the extension of slavery to the territories. However, Lincoln did not propose forbidding slavery in the South because he thought the federal government did not have the power to do so. He hoped that if slavery were confined to the states in which it already existed, it would eventually die out.

In a now-famous speech, Lincoln foresaw the confrontation that the country would soon face over slavery. He stated:

> 66 *A house divided against itself cannot stand. I believe this government cannot endure, permanently half slave and half free. I do not expect the Union to be dissolved—I do not expect the house to fall—but I do expect it will cease to be divided. It will become all one thing, or all the other.* 99
>
> —Abraham Lincoln, speech in Springfield, Illinois, June 1858

Douglas won the election. Nevertheless, Lincoln earned a reputation for eloquence and moral commitment in the campaign that would serve him well just two years later.

A Nation Divided

Lincoln's "house divided" continued to be torn apart by violence. Furthermore, Lincoln himself would become the political issue that finally brought the house down.

"Bleeding Kansas," 1856

Nebraska Territory

Missouri

Capital of antislavery government

Capital of proslavery government

Lecompton · Kansas City
Topeka
Lawrence

Proslavery mob burns buildings in this largely abolitionist town, May 21.

Kansas Territory

Pottawatomie Massacre · Osawatomie

Osage R.

Area enlarged

Abolitionist John Brown and his sons massacre five proslavery settlers, May 24.

✸ Outbreak of violence

0 15 30 mi.
0 15 30 km

N

MAP SKILLS Outsiders from slave and free states tried to influence the political future of Kansas. In one election, some 5,000 proslavery Missourians crossed the border to vote. About four times as many votes were cast as there were registered Kansas voters. In violent clashes, some 200 people died. **Location** *(a) About how far did proslavery supporters from Kansas City, Missouri, have to travel to participate in the actions against abolitionists in Lawrence, Kansas? (b) About how far apart were the two Kansas capitals, and what effect might that have had on political tensions?*

READING CHECK
Describe the outcome(s) of the Lincoln-Douglas debates.

John Brown's Raid On October 16, 1859, the former Kansas raider John Brown and a small group of men attacked the federal arsenal at Harpers Ferry, Virginia. (An arsenal is a place where weapons are made or stored.) Brown and his followers hoped to seize the weapons and give them to enslaved people to start a slave uprising.

United States troops under the command of Colonel Robert E. Lee cornered and defeated Brown's men. Convicted of treason, Brown was sentenced to be hanged. Just before his execution, he wrote a note that would prove to be all too accurate:

> 66 *I John Brown am now quite certain that the crimes of this guilty land will never be purged away; but with Blood.* 99
>
> —John Brown

Northerners hailed Brown as a martyr to the cause of justice and celebrated him in song. Southerners denounced him as a tool of Republican abolitionists. In short, Brown's raid only deepened the divisions between North and South.

The Election of 1860 As 1860 began, it was clear that most Northerners would not accept leadership by a Southerner. Southerners would not accept a leader from the ranks of the antislavery Republicans in the North. A presidential election was looming. Could the Union survive it?

The Democratic Party met in Charleston, South Carolina, in April 1860 to nominate its candidate for President. Divided between Southern Democrats who wanted to protect slavery in the territories and Northern Democrats who stood by popular sovereignty, the party broke in two. Delegates from eight southern states left the convention and agreed to meet separately to nominate their own candidate.

Southern Democrats eventually chose John C. Breckinridge, who was committed to expanding slavery in the territories. Northern Democrats nominated Stephen Douglas of Illinois, who supported popular sovereignty.

In the meantime, moderate Southerners who had belonged to the Whig and American parties met in Baltimore to form their own new party. These Southerners, along with a few politicians from the **Border States** (Delaware, Maryland, Kentucky, and Missouri), formed the Constitutional Union Party. They chose John Bell of Tennessee, a moderate slaveholder, as their presidential nominee.

When the Republican Party convened in Chicago, it nominated Abraham Lincoln. Although he was little-known outside Illinois, Lincoln combined a firm stance against the spread of slavery with moderate views on slavery itself.

The November election made absolutely clear that there were no longer any national political parties. In the South, the race was between Bell and Breckinridge. (Lincoln's name did not even appear on many southern ballots.) In the North, voters chose between Lincoln and Douglas. Lincoln won every free state except New Jersey, which he split with Douglas. Breckinridge, meanwhile, won North Carolina, Arkansas, Delaware, Maryland, and the states of the Lower South—Texas, Louisiana, Mississippi, Alabama, Florida, Georgia, and South Carolina. Bell carried Tennessee, Kentucky, and Virginia. Douglas took Missouri.

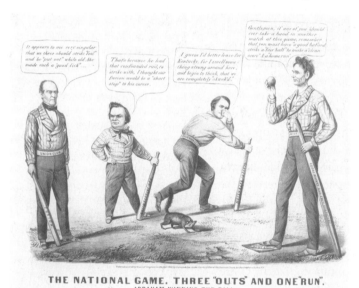

THE NATIONAL GAME. THREE "OUTS" AND ONE "RUN".
ABRAHAM WINNING THE BALL.

INTERPRETING CARTOONS
This cartoon shows Abraham Lincoln defeating his opponents in the 1860 election. In this baseball metaphor, Lincoln uses an iron rail to score a "home run," while his complaining opponents have only wooden baseball bats. **Drawing Inferences** *(a) What might the iron rail represent? (b) What overall point do you think the cartoonist is making?*

Lincoln captured the presidency without winning a single electoral vote in the South. While gaining only 39 percent of the popular vote, Lincoln had won 180 electoral votes—the majority he needed to win. His was a decisive victory, but a sectional one.

The Lower South Secedes   Southerners were outraged that a President could be elected without any southern electoral votes. The government of the nation, it seemed, had passed completely out of their hands. Wrote an Augusta, Georgia, newspaper editor:

> ❝ *[The Republican Party] stands forth today, hideous, revolting, loathsome, a menace not only to the Union of these states, but to Society, to Liberty, and to Law.* ❞
>
> —Augusta, Georgia, newspaper editor

Southern supporters of slavery called for the South to secede, or withdraw, from the Union. They argued that since the states had voluntarily joined the United States, they also could choose to leave it.

South Carolina left the Union officially on December 20, 1860. Over the next few weeks, six other states of the Lower South did the same. In early February 1861, delegates from the seven states met in Montgomery, Alabama. There they created a new nation, the **Confederate States of America,** also called the Confederacy. Jefferson Davis of Mississippi was elected its president.

The outgoing President, Buchanan, believed that secession was illegal but said he would not try to prevent it by force. Senator John J. Crittenden of Kentucky proposed a last-minute compromise by which slavery would be recognized in territories south of 36° 30' N. President-elect Lincoln opposed the plan, however, and convinced the Senate to reject it.

Other Americans proposed that the seceding states be allowed to go in peace. Many opposed this option, especially those who believed strongly in the Union. How could the United States continue to function as a country if its members could come and go as they pleased?

The government's response was in the hands of Abraham Lincoln, who took office in March 1861. Lincoln believed secession was wrong. He also was strongly committed to stopping the

Fast Forward to Today

Fort Sumter

Fort Sumter, South Carolina, was a symbol of national unity that President Lincoln wished to protect. Instead, the fort became the flash point that ripped apart the Union.

Construction of the fort, on an artificial island at the entrance to the Charleston Harbor, had begun in 1829. One Charleston newspaper described it in 1860 as a "most perfect specimen of civil and military engineering." But the structure was still incomplete and partially unprotected when it came under fire in 1861. Because the fort was built to protect the city from attack by sea, its 60 guns faced outward—not toward the Confederate outposts onshore

that shelled the fort, severely damaging it.

On April 14, 1865, four years to the day that Major Robert Anderson had surrendered the fort, the aging commander returned to raise the American flag above the fort.

In 1948, Fort Sumter was designated as a national monument. Today, tour boats take visitors on a harbor cruise out to the island and back to Charleston, a city whose antebellum charm and history attracts visitors from around the world.

? Why was Fort Sumter a flash point in tensions between the North and South?

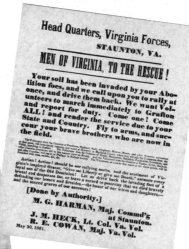

VIEWING HISTORY Civil War recruitment posters from the North (left) and South (right) urge their citizens to join the military. **Recognizing Ideologies** *To what emotions and beliefs do these posters appeal?*

expansion of slavery. Yet he did not want to be the one to start a civil war.

The War Starts   In January of 1861, prior to Lincoln's inauguration, a federal ship had been sent to supply Fort Sumter, a federal fort in the harbor of Charleston, South Carolina. Confederate forces had fired on the ship, forcing it to withdraw. Now federal soldiers under the command of Major Robert Anderson were running out of supplies. If Lincoln did not resupply the fort, it would have to be abandoned to the Confederates.

Lincoln struggled over a decision. To fight to keep the fort, or even to send new troops there, might make him responsible for starting the war. Yet to abandon the fort would mean acknowledging the authority of the Confederate government. He chose a middle course.

On April 6, Lincoln told the governor of South Carolina that he was sending food, but no soldiers or arms, to Fort Sumter. On April 10, before supplies could arrive, Confederate President Davis ordered General P.G.T. Beauregard to demand that Fort Sumter surrender. If Anderson refused, Beauregard was to take it by force. Anderson did refuse, and on April 12, 1861, Beauregard opened fire on the fort. After a 34-hour bombardment, Anderson surrendered Fort Sumter to Confederate troops on April 14.

By firing on federal property, the Confederate states had committed an act of open rebellion. As the defender of the Constitution, Lincoln had no choice but to respond. When he called for volunteers, Southerners saw his action as an act of war against them. The Upper South states of Virginia, North Carolina, Tennessee, and Arkansas now joined the Lower South in the Confederacy. For the time being, the four Border States remained uncommitted to either side.

The fighting at Fort Sumter in April 1861 proved that the division between the North and South could not be settled peacefully. Now a new question was raised: Could the Union be restored by force?

Section 4 Assessment

READING COMPREHENSION

1. How did **manifest destiny** lead the United States to **annex** Texas and fight the **Mexican War?**

2. Why did the **Compromise of 1850** and the **Kansas-Nebraska Act** fail to settle the slavery issue?

3. What trends led to the rise of **nativism,** and how did it influence party politics?

4. What events led to the creation of the **Confederate States of America** and to the outbreak of civil war?

CRITICAL THINKING AND WRITING

5. **Drawing Inferences** (a) What benefits did Texas gain by joining the Union? (b) What did it give up by becoming a state?

6. **Writing to Inform** Choose two major figures in this section who represent opposing views on slavery. Write a comparison of their views, goals, and tactics.

For: An analyzing primary sources activity
Visit: PHSchool.com
Web Code: mrd-0034

Analyzing Political Speeches

The goal of political speeches has always been to persuade listeners to take a particular view. Speeches can also serve as valuable evidence about historical figures and events. Political speakers use a variety of techniques. Sometimes they appeal to the listener's self-interest: "What I propose will make your life better." Sometimes they appeal to social conscience: "What I propose will benefit the community (or the nation, or the world)." Political speeches often appeal to patriotism.

Part of a speech Henry Clay made during the Senate debate over the Compromise of 1850 is shown below.

LEARN THE SKILL

Use the following steps to analyze political speeches:

1. **Identify the main topic of the speech and the speaker's position, or stand, on the issue.** Recall what you already know about the speaker, his or her political ideas, and the circumstances of the speech. Skim through the speech to get a general idea of its topic and purpose.

2. **Analyze the persuasive techniques the speaker uses.** Political speakers appeal to both the hearts and minds of their listeners. Evaluate the speaker's persuasiveness and how he or she achieves it. Be sure to consider the speaker's audience.

3. **Study the speech for clues about the historical period.** Look for hints about events and how people felt about those events, as well as the style of speeches at that time.

PRACTICE THE SKILL

Answer the following questions:

1. **(a)** Who is Henry Clay? Who is the audience for this speech? **(b)** What is the main topic of the speech? **(c)** What evidence in the speech tells you that Clay believes the compromise will work? **(d)** What is Clay's stand on the measure?

2. **(a)** What does Clay tell his listeners to "disregard" and "forget"? **(b)** Where in the speech does he appeal to reason? **(c)** Where in the speech does he appeal to patriotism? **(d)** How well do Clay's techniques suit his audience? **(e)** How would you evaluate the persuasiveness of this speech?

3. **(a)** Based on the speech, do you think that people in 1850 regarded the tensions between the North and the South as somewhat serious or very serious? Explain. **(b)** What does the excerpt tell you about the style of speeches during that period?

"I believe from the bottom of my soul that this measure is the reunion of the Union. And now let us disregard all resentments, all passions, all petty jealousies, all personal desires, all love of place, all hungering after the gilded crumbs which fall from the table of power. Let us forget popular fears, from whatever quarter they may spring. Let us . . . think alone of our God, our country, our conscience, and our glorious Union; that Union without which we shall be torn into hostile fragments, and sooner or later become the victims of military despotism, or foreign domination. . . .

What is an individual man? An atom, almost invisible without a magnifying glass—a mere speck upon the surface of the immense universe—not a second in time, compared to immeasurable, never-beginning, and never-ending eternity; a drop of water in the great deep, which evaporates and is borne off by the winds; a grain of sand, which is soon gathered to the dust from which it sprung. Shall a being so small, so petty, so fleeting, so evanescent [quick to disappear], oppose itself to the onward march of a great nation? . . . Let us look at our country and our cause; elevate ourselves to the dignity of pure and disinterested patriots, wise and enlightened statesmen, and save our country from all impending dangers. . . . What are we—what is any man worth who is not ready and willing to sacrifice himself for the benefit of his country when it is necessary?"

—Henry Clay, United States
Senator from Kentucky

APPLY THE SKILL

See the Chapter Review and Assessment for another opportunity to apply this skill.

creating a CHAPTER SUMMARY

Copy the chart (right) on a piece of paper and complete it by adding information about changes in early America. Some entries have been completed for you as examples.

For additional review and enrichment activities, see the interactive version of *America: Pathways to the Present*, available on the Web and on CD-ROM.

Type of Change	Effects on the North	Effects on the South
Westward expansion		
Market Revolution		
Reform movements		
Conflicts over slavery		

★ Reviewing Key Terms

For each of the terms below, write a sentence explaining how it relates to the growth of the United States from the late 1700s through the mid-1800s.

1. republican virtues
2. interchangeable parts
3. denomination
4. Market Revolution
5. free enterprise system
6. Monroe Doctrine
7. Trail of Tears
8. temperance movement
9. utopian communities
10. Seneca Falls Convention
11. suffrage
12. manifest destiny
13. Kansas-Nebraska Act
14. Confederate States of America

★ Reviewing Main Ideas

15. (a) How did the Industrial Revolution come to the United States? (b) How did it affect America's society and economy? (Section 1)

16. What attracted Americans to the Second Great Awakening? (Section 1)

17. What events led to Texas' independence and statehood? (Section 1)

18. How did economic growth in the North and in the South differ in terms of (a) major products and (b) the use of labor? (Section 2)

19. Give examples of nationalism in the early 1800s. (Section 2)

20. Explain President Jackson's response to the tariff crisis. (Section 2)

21. What were the main beliefs and goals of the transcendentalists? (Section 3)

22. How did the Underground Railroad operate? (Section 3)

23. Why was the Compromise of 1850 a failure? (Section 4)

24. Why did Lincoln's election prompt the secession of southern states? (Section 4)

★ Critical Thinking

25. **Determining Relevance** How did the invention of the cotton gin ultimately affect (a) North-South relations; (b) the slave trade; (c) Native Americans?

26. **Identifying Alternatives** With southern states seizing Indian lands illegally and white settlers pouring into these areas, how did President Jackson respond? How else might he have responded?

27. **Expressing Problems Clearly** Explain why the addition of Mexico's northern territories caused problems for the United States.

28. **Identifying Central Issues** Summarize the key issue in the dispute over Fort Sumter that led the United States into civil war.

★ Standardized Test Prep

Analyzing Political Cartoons ▶

29. This cartoon is titled "King Andrew the First" What is the cartoonist implying?

  A that President Jackson should be named king

  B that President Jackson's actions are justified

  C that President Jackson is abusing the powers of the Presidency outlined in the U.S. Constitution

  D that President Jackson did not believe in the veto power

30. One of the documents on the floor is labeled "Internal Improvements" and "U.S. Bank." The book in the foreground is labeled "Judiciary of the United States." To what do these items refer?

Analyzing Data

Refer to the chart entitled "Free and Enslaved Black Populations, 1820–1860" in Section 3 to answer these questions:

31. From 1820 to 1860, the enslaved black population increased by roughly how many people?

  A 4 million

  B 1 million

  C 1.5 million

  D 2.5 million

32. In 1860, how many times larger was the enslaved population than the free population?

  F two times

  G five times

  H eight times

  I eleven times

Test-Taking Tip

To find the correct answer to Question 31, determine which line on the graph shows the enslaved population. Then subtract the population in 1820 from the population in 1860 to find the answer.

Applying the Chapter Skill

Analyzing Political Speeches Summarize the excerpt below. (b) What techniques does Webster use to appeal to his audience?

> ❝ *When my eyes shall be turned to behold, for the last time, the sun in heaven, may I not see him shining on the broken and dishonored fragments of a once glorious Union. . . . Nor those . . . words of delusion and folly, Liberty first and Union afterwards . . . [but instead] Liberty and Union, now and forever, one and inseparable.* ❞
> —Senator Daniel Webster of Massachusetts

Go Online
PHSchool.com

For: Chapter 3 Self-Test
Visit: PHSchool.com
Web Code: mra-0035

American Pathways
GEOGRAPHY

The Expansion of the United States

From its start as 13 former British colonies along the Atlantic Coast, the United States expanded steadily westward. Explorers, trappers, and settlers pushed across the Appalachian Mountains, the Great Plains, and the Rocky Mountains all the way to the Pacific Coast and beyond. Through more than a century of treaties, purchases, and warfare, the nation grew to its present size.

1 Establishing the Original States

1607–1776 In the 1600s and 1700s, a mix of English, Dutch, Swedes, Germans, enslaved Africans, and others settled in colonies along the Atlantic Coast. These colonies later united to seek their independence from Great Britain and establish a new nation.

E pluribus unum—"from many, one"—was chosen as the nation's motto in 1776 (right).

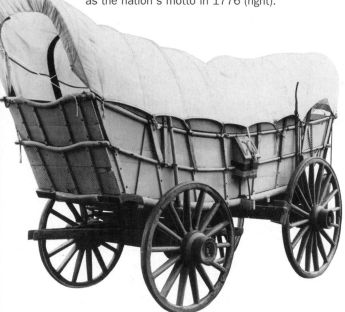

2 Crossing the Appalachians

1775–1830 As the population along the Atlantic Coast grew, Americans moved west to settle in the region between the Appalachian Mountains and the Mississippi River.

Covered wagons (left) carried settlers westward.

3 Moving Beyond the Mississippi

1803–1846 The Louisiana Purchase nearly doubled the size of the United States and gave Americans full control of the Mississippi River. Several groups explored the region in the early 1800s, but new settlements there remained sparse for many years. Most migrants who crossed the Mississippi in the mid-1800s had one goal in mind—reaching Oregon.

An advertisement for land in Iowa and Nebraska (above)

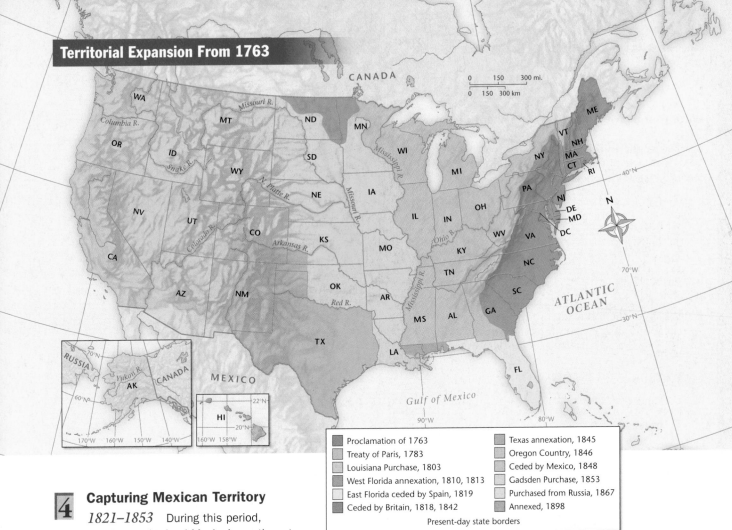

Territorial Expansion From 1763

CANADA

RUSSIA
AK
CANADA

MEXICO

Gulf of Mexico

ATLANTIC OCEAN

Legend:
- Proclamation of 1763
- Treaty of Paris, 1783
- Louisiana Purchase, 1803
- West Florida annexation, 1810, 1813
- East Florida ceded by Spain, 1819
- Ceded by Britain, 1818, 1842
- Texas annexation, 1845
- Oregon Country, 1846
- Ceded by Mexico, 1848
- Gadsden Purchase, 1853
- Purchased from Russia, 1867
- Annexed, 1898

Present-day state borders

4 Capturing Mexican Territory

1821–1853 During this period, Americans obtained Mexico's northern territories mainly through warfare. By 1853, they had established the boundaries of the continental United States as we now know them, fulfilling what many called the nation's "manifest destiny."

5 Acquiring Alaska and Hawaii

1867–1898 The United States expanded beyond its continental borders in the period following the Civil War, first with the purchase of Alaska in 1867 and later with the annexation of Hawaii in 1898.

A Hawaiian landscape (right)

6 Remaining a Mobile Society

1890–Present Streams of settlers moving west reflected the mobility of American society. Even after the nation's frontier ceased to exist, Americans continued to migrate, usually in search of a better life.

Continuity and Change

1. What circumstances drove Americans to leave their homes and settle in new places?
2. **Map Skills** What lands were included in the Gadsden Purchase in 1853?

For: A study guide on U.S. expansion
Visit: PHSchool.com
Web Code: mrd-1039

TEST PREPARATION

Write your answers on a separate sheet of paper.

1. Before the Europeans arrived in North America, which one of the following was never traded by the Native Americans?

   A Land

   B Fish

   C Minerals

   D Tools

2. Which of the following products was the first successful cash crop in the Jamestown Colony?

   A Fur

   B Tobacco

   C Wheat

   D Fish

Use the chart and your knowledge of social studies to answer the following question.

Early American Colonies
• Connecticut
• Maryland
• Massachusetts Bay
• Plymouth
• Rhode Island

3. What common experience did all of these colonies share?

   A All had farming on plantations.

   B All had economies based on tobacco.

   C All were established for religious reasons.

   D All were created to block Spanish expansion.

4. In the mid-1700s, Baptist and Methodist churches in North America increased their membership as a result of the

   A growth of American nationalism.

   B mercantilist policies of the British.

   C French and Indian War.

   D Great Awakening.

5. How was the Stamp Act different from all previous British laws for the colonies?

   A Its purpose was to raise money.

   B It applied only to cities along the coast.

   C It was supported by the French government.

   D It required each colony to create a post office.

6. Why was the Patriot victory at the Battle of Saratoga in the American Revolution a turning point in the war?

   A It caused the Native Americans in the Ohio Valley to join the Patriots.

   B It permitted George Washington to move his troops into Boston.

   C It guaranteed the Patriots control of the Atlantic Ocean.

   D It convinced the French government to aid the Patriots.

> **"It is . . . the duty of the judicial department to say what the law is."**
>
> —*Marbury* v. *Madison*, 1803

7. The *Marbury* decision by the United States Supreme Court is the basis for

   A implied powers.

   B a federal system of government.

   C separation of powers.

   D judicial review.

Use the information in the graph to answer the following question.

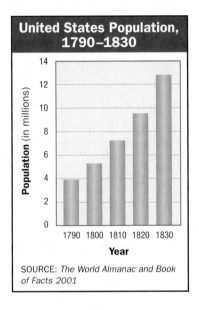

United States Population, 1790–1830

Population (in millions)

SOURCE: *The World Almanac and Book of Facts 2001*

8. The population trend shown in the bar graph was caused by

   A immigration from Europe.

   B a high birth rate.

   C migration from farms to cities.

   D conquering lands with many people.

9. Which one of the following statements about the Southern Colonies is correct?

   A Their economy was based on staple crops.

   B They were the center of American commerce and trade.

   C Most people lived on small, family-owned farms.

   D Most of the people came from Great Britain.

> "... that the American continents, by the free and independent condition which they have assumed and maintain, are henceforth not to be considered as subject for future colonization by any European power. ..."
>
> —President James Monroe,
> *Seventh annual message to Congress, December 2, 1823*

10. This quotation is the basis for the

   A *Gibbons* v. *Ogden* (1824) decision.

   B Adams-Onís Treaty.

   C Monroe Doctrine.

   D Missouri Compromise.

11. On the Underground Railroad, freedom came at the final destination

   A by the Great Lakes.

   B across the Ohio River.

   C in Massachusetts or Rhode Island.

   D in Canada.

Writing Practice

12. Describe the motives Columbus had for making his voyages.

13. Describe the effect of Eli Whitney's cotton gin on the United States.

14. Explain the economic differences between the Northern and Southern states preceding the Civil War.

Unit 2

Building a Powerful Nation (1850–1915)

"Up to our own day American history has been in a large degree the history of the colonization of the Great West. The existence of an area of free land, its continuous recession, and the advance of American settlement westward, explain American development."

Frederick Jackson Turner, 1893

An excursion party, awed by the new technologies of the era, stops to be photographed at Devil's Gate Bridge in Utah. ▶

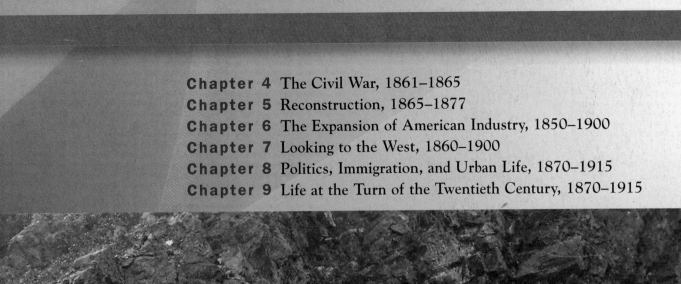

153

The Battle of Missionary Ridge, Tennessee

Civil War cannon

1861

The Confederate attack on Fort Sumter in April signals the start of the Civil War. The South wins the First Battle of Bull Run (Manassas).

1862

After the Battle of Antietam in September, the Confederate army under the command of General Robert E. Lee retreats into Virginia. In December, the Confederates defeat a Union army at Fredericksburg.

1863

The Emancipation Proclamation takes effect on January 1. In July, both sides suffer huge losses in the Union victory at Gettysburg. The Union gains control of the Mississippi River.

American Events

Presidential Terms: Abraham Lincoln 1861–1865

1861

1862

1863

World Events

Czar Alexander II emancipates Russian serfs.

Otto von Bismarck becomes prime minister of Prussia.

French emperor Napoleon III sets up the Austrian Archduke Maximilian as the emperor of Mexico.

1861

1862

1863

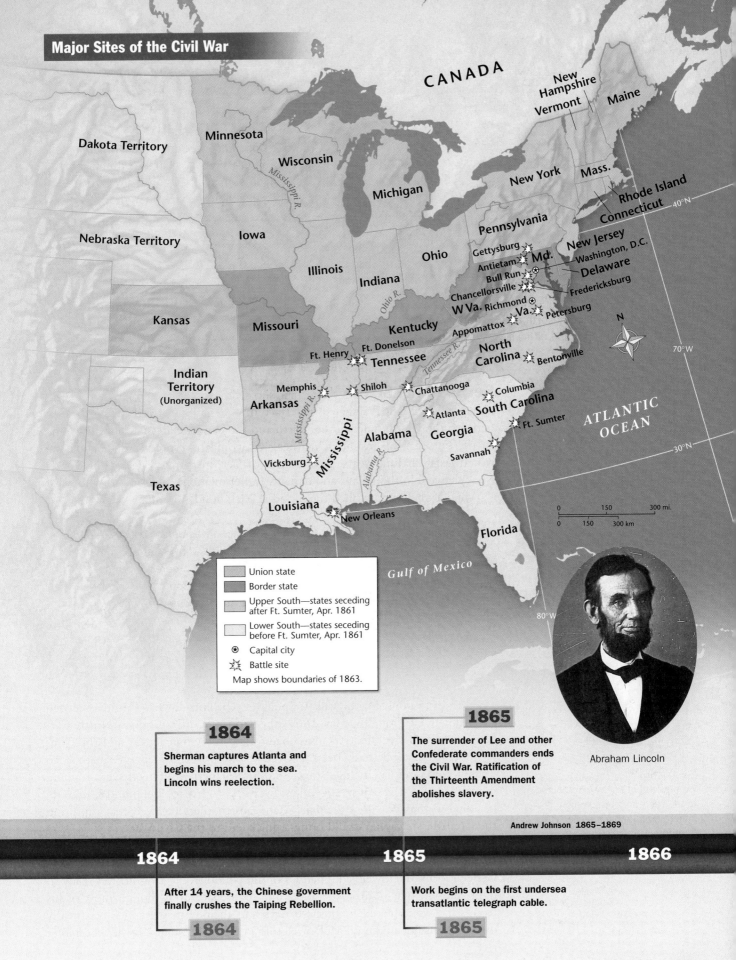

Major Sites of the Civil War

CANADA

Dakota Territory
Minnesota
Wisconsin
Michigan
New Hampshire
Vermont
Maine

Mississippi R.

Nebraska Territory
Iowa
New York
Mass.
Rhode Island
Connecticut

Illinois
Ohio
Pennsylvania
New Jersey
Washington, D.C.
Gettysburg
Md.
Delaware

Kansas
Indiana
Antietam
Bull Run
Fredericksburg

Missouri
Ohio R.
Chancellorsville
W Va.
Richmond
Va.
Petersburg

Kentucky
Appomattox

Ft. Donelson
Ft. Henry
Tennessee
Tennessee R.
North Carolina
Bentonville

Indian Territory (Unorganized)
Memphis
Shiloh
Chattanooga
Columbia

Arkansas
Mississippi R.
Atlanta
South Carolina
Ft. Sumter

ATLANTIC OCEAN

Mississippi
Alabama
Georgia

Alabama R.

Vicksburg

Savannah

Texas

Louisiana
New Orleans

Florida

Gulf of Mexico

N

70°W
40°N
30°N
80°W

| | 0 | 150 | 300 mi. |
| | 0 | 150 | 300 km |

Legend:
- Union state
- Border state
- Upper South—states seceding after Ft. Sumter, Apr. 1861
- Lower South—states seceding before Ft. Sumter, Apr. 1861
- ⊛ Capital city
- ✸ Battle site

Map shows boundaries of 1863.

1864

Sherman captures Atlanta and begins his march to the sea. Lincoln wins reelection.

1865

The surrender of Lee and other Confederate commanders ends the Civil War. Ratification of the Thirteenth Amendment abolishes slavery.

Abraham Lincoln

Andrew Johnson 1865–1869

1864 **1865** **1866**

After 14 years, the Chinese government finally crushes the Taiping Rebellion.

Work begins on the first undersea transatlantic telegraph cable.

1864 **1865**

From Bull Run to Antietam

READING FOCUS

- What was the significance of the First Battle of Bull Run?

- How did the North and the South prepare for war?

- Why were the battles in the West important?

- What was the outcome of each of the battles in the East in 1862?

MAIN IDEA

Bloody fighting during the first two years of the Civil War made it clear to both North and South that the struggle would be long and difficult.

KEY TERMS

Civil War
First Battle of
 Bull Run
casualty
war of attrition
shell
canister
Battle of Shiloh
Battle of Antietam

TARGET READING SKILL

Make Comparisons Copy the chart below. As you read this section, fill in the advantages of each side at the start of the Civil War. Also include the battles each side won.

Advantages/Battles Won	
North	**South**
More railroad track	First Battle of Bull Run

Setting the Scene The first shots fired on Fort Sumter, South Carolina, in April 1861 signaled the start of the nation's **Civil War**—the war between the Union states of the North and the Confederate states of the South. At the outbreak of hostilities, neither side would have predicted that the war would last four long years. As a matter of fact, in many places in the South, people were both jubilant and defiant. In her memoir, Sallie Hunt, who was a child at the time, recalled the mood in Richmond, Virginia:

> 66 *One spring day in April, 1861, all Richmond was astir. Schools were broken up, and knots of excited men gathered at every street corner. Sumter had been fired upon, and Lincoln had ordered the men of Virginia to rush upon their brethren of the South and put the rebellion down. Now 'the die was cast,' our lot was with theirs, and come weal [well-being] or woe, we would fight for independence. . . . [O]ur hearts swelled with pride to think we could say to our tyrants: 'Thus far shalt thou come, and no further.'* 99
>
> —Sallie Hunt

In response to the call to "put the rebellion down," Virginia seceded from the Union. By May 1861, the Upper South (Virginia, North Carolina, Tennessee, and Arkansas) had joined the Confederacy, and the Confederate capital had been moved from Montgomery, Alabama, to Richmond, Virginia. In July, some 35,000 Northern volunteers were training in Washington, D.C., just 100 miles away. "Forward to Richmond!" urged a headline in the *New York Tribune*. Many Northerners believed that capturing the Confederate capital would bring a quick end to the Civil War.

Women on both sides contributed to the war effort by sewing uniforms and other supplies. This Southern woman is making caps.

The First Battle of Bull Run

General Irvin McDowell, commander of the Union troops, was not yet ready to fight. He felt that he needed more time to prepare even though most of his troops had volunteered for just 90 days and their term of service was nearly over. "This is not an army," McDowell told President Lincoln. "It will take a long time to make an army." Despite this warning, Lincoln ordered his general into action.

On July 16, McDowell marched his poorly prepared army into Virginia. His objective was the town of Manassas, an important railroad junction southwest of Washington. Opposing him was a smaller Confederate force under General P.G.T. Beauregard, the officer who had captured Fort Sumter. The Confederates were camped along Bull Run, a stream that passed about four miles north of Manassas.

It took the Union army nearly four days to march the 25 miles to Manassas. Lack of training and discipline contributed to the soldiers' slow pace. As McDowell later explained, "They stopped every moment to pick blackberries or get water. . . . They would not keep in the ranks, order as much as you pleased." Meanwhile, Beauregard had no trouble keeping track of McDowell's progress. Accompanying the troops was a huge crowd of reporters, politicians, and other civilians from Washington, planning to picnic and watch the battle. They got a rude surprise.

McDowell's delays had allowed Beauregard to strengthen his army. Some 11,000 additional Confederate troops had been packed into freight cars and sped to the scene. (This was the first time in history that troops were moved by train.) When McDowell finally attacked on July 21, he faced a force nearly the size of his own army. But beyond the Confederate lines lay the road to the Confederate capital at Richmond.

After hours of hard fighting, the Union soldiers appeared to be winning. Their slow advance pushed the Southerners back. However, some Virginia soldiers commanded by General Thomas Jackson refused to give up. Seeing Jackson's men holding firm, another Confederate officer rallied his retreating troops, shouting: "Look! There is Jackson standing like a stone wall! Rally

VIEWING HISTORY This portrait of members of the U.S. Signal Corps is by the famous photographer Mathew Brady. **Making Inferences** *Judging by their expressions, what do these men think of their role in the Civil War?*

COMPARING PRIMARY SOURCES
The Aims of the Civil War

Throughout the years of quarreling between North and South, Southerners protested repeatedly that Northerners were trampling on their rights, including the right to own human beings as property.
Analyzing Viewpoints How did the war aims of each side reflect their quarrel, as described above?

The Aims of the South

"We have vainly endeavored to secure tranquillity and obtain respect for the rights to which we were entitled . . . . If . . . the integrity of our territory and jurisdiction [legal authority] be assailed [attacked], it will but remain for us, with firm resolve, to appeal to arms."
—*President Jefferson Davis, Inaugural Address, February 18, 1861*

The Aims of the North

"This war is not waged upon our part in any spirit of oppression, nor for any purpose of conquest or subjugation, nor purpose of overthrowing or interfering with the rights or established institutions of those [seceding] States, but to defend and maintain the supremacy of the Constitution and to preserve the Union."
—*House of Representatives, Crittenden Resolution, July 25, 1861*

West Virginia Statehood As early as 1776, there were divisions between the eastern and western parts of Virginia. Pioneers lived in the west, where both culture and geography discouraged slavery. Wealthy planters in the east depended on slave labor. Tax laws and the restriction of suffrage to men of property benefited the east and caused resentment in the west, where there was already talk of forming a separate state.

The Civil War only added to these differences. Western delegates walked out of Virginia's Secession Convention in April 1861, declaring secession an illegal attempt to overthrow the federal government. They formed a "Restored Government." In October, 39 western counties approved formation of a new Unionist state, and the Restored Government gave its permission. Congress approved West Virginia's entry into the Union on June 20, 1863, on the condition of gradual emancipation of slaves in the region.

behind the Virginians!" The Union advance was stopped, and "Stonewall" Jackson had earned his famous nickname.

Tired and discouraged, the Union forces began to fall back in late afternoon. Then a trainload of fresh Confederate troops arrived and launched a counterattack. The orderly Union retreat fell apart. Hundreds of soldiers dropped their weapons and ran north. They stampeded into the sightseers who had followed them to the battlefield. As the army disintegrated, soldiers and civilians were caught in a tangle of carriages, wagons, and horses on the narrow road. Terrified that the Confederate troops would catch them, they ran headlong for the safety of Washington, D.C. The Confederates, however, were too disorganized and exhausted to pursue the Union army.

The first major battle of the Civil War was over. It became known as the **First Battle of Bull Run,** because the following year another bloody battle occurred at almost exactly the same site. In the South, this engagement was known as the First Battle of Manassas. The First Battle of Bull Run was not a huge action. About 35,000 troops were involved on each side. The Union suffered about 2,900 **casualties,** the military term for those killed, wounded, captured, or missing in action. Confederate casualties were fewer than 2,000. Later battles would prove much more costly.

Preparing for War

Bull Run caused some Americans on both sides to suspect that winning the war might not be so easy. "The fat is in the fire now," wrote President Lincoln's private secretary. "The preparations for the war will be continued with increased vigor by the Government." Congress quickly authorized the President to raise a million three-year volunteers. In Richmond, a clerk in the Confederate War Department began to worry, "We are resting on our oars, while the enemy is drilling and equipping 500,000 or 600,000 men."

Strengths of the North and the South In several respects, the North was much better prepared for war than was the South. The North had more than twice as much railroad track as the South. This made the movement of troops, food, and supplies quicker and easier in the North. There were also more than twice as many factories in the North, so the Union was better able to produce the guns, ammunition, shoes, and other items needed for its army. The North's economy was well balanced between farming and industry, and the North had far more money in its banks than the South.

What's more, the North already had a functioning government and a small army and navy. Most importantly, two thirds of the nation's population lived in Union states. This made more men available to the Union army, while at the same time allowing for a sufficient labor force to remain behind for farm and factory work.

The Confederates had some advantages, too. Because most of the nation's military colleges were in the South, a majority of the nation's trained officers were Southerners, and they sided with the Confederacy. In addition, the Southern army did not need to initiate any military action to win the war. All they needed to do was maintain a defensive position and keep from being beaten. In contrast, to restore unity to the nation, the North would have to attack and conquer the South. Southerners had an additional advantage: they felt that they were fighting to preserve their way of life and, they believed, their right to self-government.

Patriotism was also important in the North. And there were strongly held beliefs about slavery. The abolitionist Harriet Beecher Stowe responded to the Union call to arms by writing, "This is a cause to die for, and—thanks be to God!—our young men embrace it." There were other reasons that people on both sides were eager to fight. Some enlisted for the adventure, and feared that the war would be over before they got a chance to participate.

READING CHECK What were the most important strengths of the North and the South?

Union Military Strategies After the fall of Fort Sumter, President Lincoln ordered a naval blockade of the seceded states. By shutting down the South's ports along the Atlantic Coast and the Gulf of Mexico, Lincoln hoped to keep the South from shipping its cotton to Europe. He also wanted to prevent Southerners from importing the manufactured goods they needed.

Lincoln's blockade was part of a strategy developed by General Winfield Scott, the hero of the Mexican War and commander of all U.S. troops in 1861. Scott realized that it would take a long time to raise and train an army that was big enough and strong enough to invade the South successfully. Instead, he proposed to choke off the Confederacy with the blockade and to use troops and gunboats to gain control of the Mississippi River, thus cutting the Confederacy in two. Scott believed these measures would pressure the South to seek peace and would restore the nation without a bloody war.

Northern newspapers sneered at Scott's strategy. They scornfully named it the Anaconda Plan, after a type of snake that coils around its victims and crushes them to death. Despite the Union defeat at Bull Run, political pressure for action and a quick victory remained strong in 1861. This public clamor for results led to several more attempts to capture Richmond. Seizing the Confederate capital was another important strategic goal of the Union.

Confederate War Strategies The South's basic war plan was to prepare and wait. Many Southerners hoped that Lincoln would let them go in peace. "All we ask is to be let alone," announced Confederate president Jefferson Davis, shortly after secession. He planned for a defensive war.

Southern strategy called for a **war of attrition.** In this type of war, one side inflicts continuous losses on the enemy in order to wear down its strength.

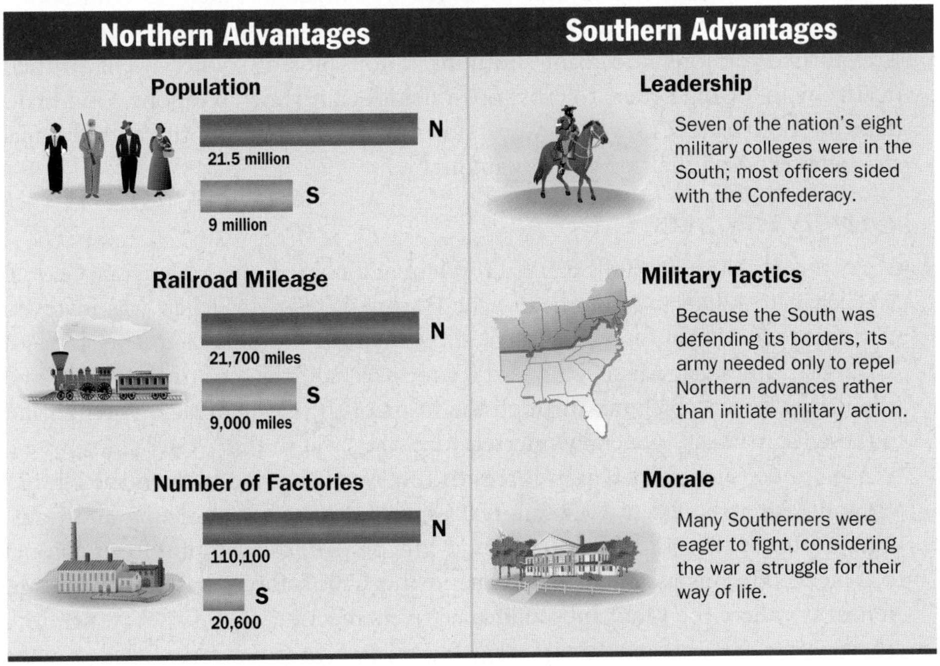

Northern Advantages
Population
N
21.5 million
S
9 million
Railroad Mileage
N
21,700 miles
S
9,000 miles
Number of Factories
N
110,100
S
20,600
Southern Advantages
Leadership
Seven of the nation's eight military colleges were in the South; most officers sided with the Confederacy.
Military Tactics
Because the South was defending its borders, its army needed only to repel Northern advances rather than initiate military action.
Morale
Many Southerners were eager to fight, considering the war a struggle for their way of life.

INTERPRETING DIAGRAMS
This diagram shows the advantages that the North and the South had at the start of the Civil War. **Analyzing Information** *The North and the South had different kinds of advantages. Explain the differences.*

Southerners counted on their forces being able to turn back Union attacks until Northerners lost the will to fight. However, this strategy did not take into account the North's tremendous advantage in resources. In the end, it was the North that waged a successful war of attrition against the South.

Southern strategy in another area also backfired. The South produced some 75 percent of the world's cotton, much of it supplying the textile mills of Great Britain and France. However, Confederate leaders convinced most Southern planters to stop exporting cotton. They believed that the sudden loss of Southern cotton would cause British and French industrial leaders to pressure their governments to help the South gain its independence in exchange for restoring the flow of cotton. Instead, the Europeans turned to India and Egypt for their cotton. By the time Southerners recognized the failure of this strategy, the Union blockade had become so effective that little cotton could get out. With no income from cotton exports, the South could not earn the money it needed to buy guns and maintain its armies.

Tactics and Technology For generations, European commanders had fought battles by concentrating their forces, assaulting a position, and driving the enemy away. The cannons and muskets they used were neither accurate nor capable of repeating fire very rapidly. Generals relied on masses of charging troops to overwhelm the enemy. Most Civil War generals had been trained in these methods and had seen them work well in the Mexican War.

The newer bullets (at right) were far more accurate than round musket balls like the one shown wedged in a soldier's shoulder plate.

By the time of the Civil War, however, gun makers knew that bullet-shaped ammunition drifted less as it flew through the air than a round ball, the older type of ammunition. They had also learned that rifling, a spiral groove cut on the inside of a gun barrel, would make a fired bullet pick up spin, causing it to travel farther and straighter. Older muskets, which had no rifling, were accurate only to about 100 yards. Bullets fired from rifles, as the new guns were called, hit targets at 500 yards. In addition, they could be reloaded and fired much faster than muskets.

Improvements in artillery were just as deadly. Instead of relying only on iron cannon balls, gunners could now fire **shells,** devices that exploded in the air or when they hit something. Artillery often fired **canister,** a special type of shell filled with bullets. This turned cannons into giant shotguns. Thousands of soldiers went to their deaths by following orders to cross open fields against such weapons. Commanders on both sides, however, were slow to recognize that these traditional strategies exposed their troops to slaughter.

War in the West

After the disaster at Bull Run, President Lincoln named General George McClellan to build and command a new army. While McClellan was involved with this task, Union forces in the West invaded the Confederacy. The states of Arkansas, Louisiana, Mississippi, and Tennessee held the key to control of the Mississippi River, which ran through the heart of the Confederacy. The fighting in these four states is generally referred to as the "war in the West."

The most successful Union forces in the West were led by General Ulysses S. Grant. After the fall of Fort Sumter, Grant's success at organizing and training a group of Illinois volunteers caused Lincoln to promote him from colonel to general. He was assigned to command the Union forces based in Paducah, Kentucky, where the Ohio and Tennessee rivers meet.

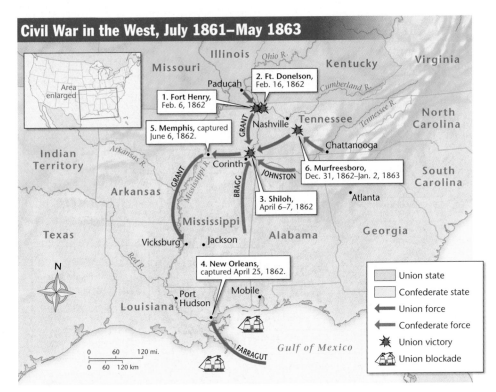

Civil War in the West, July 1861–May 1863

Illinois
Ohio R.
Missouri
Kentucky
Virginia
Paducah
2. Ft. Donelson, Feb. 16, 1862
1. Fort Henry, Feb. 6, 1862
Cumberland R.
5. Memphis, captured June 6, 1862.
Nashville
Tennessee
Tennessee R.
North Carolina
Area enlarged
Indian Territory
Arkansas R.
Corinth
Chattanooga
6. Murfreesboro, Dec. 31, 1862–Jan. 2, 1863
South Carolina
Arkansas
Mississippi R.
JOHNSTON
BRAGG
3. Shiloh, April 6–7, 1862
Atlanta
Georgia
Mississippi
Vicksburg
Jackson
Alabama
Texas
4. New Orleans, captured April 25, 1862.
Mobile
Port Hudson
Louisiana
Red R.
FARRAGUT
Gulf of Mexico

	Union state
	Confederate state
→	Union force
→	Confederate force
✸	Union victory
⛴	Union blockade

0   60   120 mi.
0   60   120 km

MAP SKILLS Union generals in the West focused their attention on the Mississippi River. "That Mississippi ruins us, if lost," worried Southern observer Mary Chesnut in 1862. **Place** *What two key cities on the Mississippi had the Union captured by the summer of 1862?*

Forts Henry and Donelson

In February 1862, Grant advanced south along the Tennessee River with more than 15,000 troops and several gunboats. Powered by steam and built to navigate shallow bodies of water, these gunboats were basically small floating forts fitted with cannons. Grant's objectives were Fort Henry and Fort Donelson, located just over the border in the Confederate state of Tennessee. The forts protected the Tennessee and Cumberland rivers, important water routes into the western Confederacy.

On February 6 the Union gunboats pounded Fort Henry into surrender before Grant's troops arrived. The general then marched his army east and attacked Fort Donelson on the Cumberland River. Following three days of shelling by the gunboats, Fort Donelson also gave up.

The battles caused a sensation in both the North and the South. Northerners rejoiced that at last the Union had an important victory. Southerners worried that loss of the forts exposed much of the region to attack. Indeed, Nashville soon fell to another Union army. Meanwhile, Grant and some 42,000 soldiers pushed farther south along the Tennessee River to threaten Mississippi and Alabama.

The Battle of Shiloh

In late March, Grant's army advanced toward Corinth, Mississippi, an important railroad center near the Tennessee-Mississippi border. Confederate general Albert Sidney Johnston gathered troops from throughout the region to halt the Union advance. By the time Grant's forces approached, Johnston had assembled an army of about 40,000 to oppose them. Grant, however, stopped at Pittsburg Landing, Tennessee, a small river town about 20 miles north of Corinth. Here he waited for more Union troops that General Don Carlos Buell was bringing from Nashville. Johnston decided to launch an attack against Grant's army before the Union force got any larger.

General Grant's demand for the "unconditional and immediate surrender" of Fort Donelson earned him the nickname "Unconditional Surrender Grant."

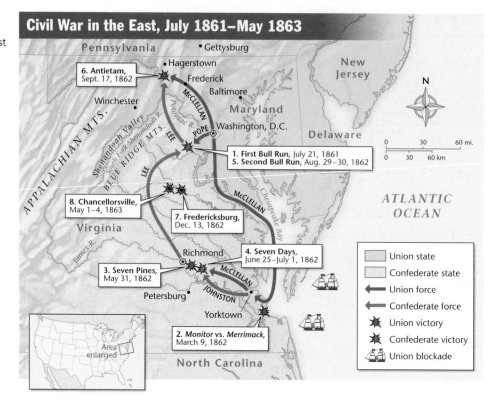

Civil War in the East, July 1861–May 1863

Pennsylvania • Gettysburg

New Jersey

6. Antietam, Sept. 17, 1862 • Hagerstown
Frederick
Baltimore
Winchester
Maryland
Washington, D.C.
Delaware

APPALACHIAN MTS.
Shenandoah Valley
South Fork Shenandoah R.
BLUE RIDGE MTS.
Potomac R.
McCLELLAN
POPE
LEE

ATLANTIC OCEAN

1. First Bull Run, July 21, 1861
5. Second Bull Run, Aug. 29–30, 1862

8. Chancellorsville, May 1–4, 1863
7. Fredericksburg, Dec. 13, 1862
Virginia
James R.
Richmond
4. Seven Days, June 25–July 1, 1862
3. Seven Pines, May 31, 1862
McCLELLAN
Petersburg •
JOHNSTON
Yorktown
2. Monitor vs. Merrimack, March 9, 1862
North Carolina

0   30   60 mi.
0   30   60 km

Area enlarged

Union state
Confederate state
← Union force
← Confederate force
Union victory
Confederate victory
Union blockade

On April 6, 1862, Johnston's forces surprised some of Grant's troops, who were camped at Shiloh Church outside Pittsburg Landing. Fighting quickly spread along a battle line six miles long. By the end of the first day of the **Battle of Shiloh**, the Southerners had driven the Union forces back, nearly into the Tennessee River. That night, some of Grant's officers advised a retreat before the Confederates could renew their attack the next day. "Retreat?" Grant scoffed. "No. I propose to attack at daylight and whip them."

Fortunately for Grant, Buell's troops arrived during the night. The next day, Union forces counter-attacked and defeated Johnston's army. However, the cost to both sides was very high. The Union suffered more than 13,000 casualties, the Confederates nearly 11,000. General Johnston was among the Confederate dead.

Shiloh was the bloodiest single battle that had taken place on the North American continent to that time. It shattered any remaining illusions either side had about the glory of war, and it destroyed Northern hopes that the Confederacy would soon be defeated.

Action on the Mississippi While Grant advanced into the Confederacy from the north, Union forces were also moving up the Mississippi River from the Gulf of Mexico. In late April 1862, a naval squadron commanded by David Farragut fought its way past two forts in the Louisiana swamps to force the surrender of New Orleans. Pushing upriver, Farragut soon captured Baton Rouge, Louisiana, and Natchez, Mississippi. In her diary, Southerner Mary Chesnut voiced her concerns about the Confederate losses: "Battle after battle—disaster after disaster . . . Are we not cut in two? . . . The reality is hideous."

On June 6, the Union navy seized Memphis, Tennessee. Only two major posts on the Mississippi River now remained in Confederate hands. These were Vicksburg, Mississippi, and Port Hudson, Louisiana. If Northern forces could find some way to capture them, the entire Mississippi River valley would finally be under Union control. The Confederacy would be split into two parts.

War in the East

While the Union army marched through the western Confederacy, Union warships maintained the blockade of Virginia's coast. The Confederates, however, had developed a secret weapon with which to fight the blockade. In early March 1862, a Confederate ship that resembled a floating barn roof steamed out of the James River. When the Union warships guarding the mouth of the river opened fire on the strange-looking vessel, their cannon shots bounced off it like rubber balls. In hours, the Confederate vessel destroyed or heavily damaged three of the most powerful ships in the Union navy.

The *Monitor* and the *Merrimack* Southerners had created the strange-looking vessel by bolting iron plates to an old wooden steamship called the *Merrimack*. (Although the ship was renamed the *Virginia*, it is still called the *Merrimack* in most historical accounts.) The Union's wooden navy was no match for this powerful ironclad warship. Northern leaders feared the new weapon might soon break apart the entire blockade.

Fortunately for the Union, early reports of the Confederates' work on the *Merrimack* had reached the North, and President Lincoln had ordered construction of a similar Union warship. It was made entirely of iron and was rushed to completion in about 100 days. Named the *Monitor*, it looked like a tin can on a raft.

On March 9, the *Monitor* arrived off the Virginia coast to confront the Confederate ironclad. Neither ship was able to do serious damage to the other. After several hours of fighting, the *Merrimack* finally withdrew. The two ships never met again. The Confederates blew up the *Merrimack* at its base in Norfolk, Virginia, in May 1862, rather than let it fall into Union hands. The following December, the *Monitor* sank in a storm. Their one encounter, however, changed the history of warfare. In a single day, the wooden navies of the world became obsolete.

The Peninsular Campaign When Union general George McClellan landed troops near Norfolk in May 1862, he was launching the North's second attempt to capture Richmond. At 36 years old, McClellan was young for a commanding general. However, he was an outstanding organizer, an excellent strategist, and was well liked by his troops. McClellan's great weakness was that he was very cautious and never seemed quite ready to fight. This irritated Lincoln and other Northern leaders, who were impatient to avenge the Union's defeat at Bull Run.

In March 1862, McClellan finally ordered the Army of the Potomac out of Washington. Because he thought that marching to Manassas again would be a mistake, he transported some 100,000 soldiers by boat to a peninsula southeast of Richmond. As the Union troops moved up the peninsula, they encountered some 15,000 Southerners at Yorktown, Virginia, about 60 miles from the Confederate capital.

Although the Confederate force was much smaller than his own, McClellan asked for more troops. Lincoln dispatched a stern message to his general:

VIEWING HISTORY At the center of this painting, the *Merrimack* and the *Monitor* exchange shots at close range. The *Minnesota*, which the *Monitor* was ordered to protect, sits grounded at right. **Drawing Conclusions** How did this single battle of the ironclads make traditional wooden warships like the *Minnesota* obsolete?

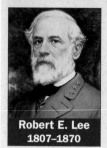

**Robert E. Lee
1807–1870**

A warm and charming Southern gentleman, Robert E. Lee came from an old and distinguished Virginia family. Among his relatives were two signers of the Declaration of Independence. In 1829, Lee graduated second in his class from West Point. Later he was recognized for outstanding service in the Mexican War.

When the Southern states seceded, Lincoln offered Lee the command of Union forces. Although he was opposed to slavery and secession, Lee refused, explaining "I cannot raise my hand against my birthplace, my home, my children." Instead, he resigned from the army and became the top military advisor to Confederate president Jefferson Davis. In May 1862, he took command of the Army of Northern Virginia, a post he held for the rest of the war. As a commander, Lee earned the loyalty and trust of his troops. Stonewall Jackson declared, "I would follow him onto the battlefield blindfolded."

> ❝ It is indispensable to you that you strike a blow. . . . The country will not fail to note—is now noting—that the present hesitation to move upon an entrenched enemy is but the story of Manassas repeated. . . . I have never written you . . . in greater kindness of feeling than now. . . . But you must act. ❞
>
> —President Lincoln

McClellan, however, did not act. He waited outside Yorktown for about a month. When he finally advanced, the defenders abandoned their positions and retreated toward Richmond. On May 31, as McClellan's army neared the capital, the Southerners suddenly turned and attacked. Although the North claimed victory at the Battle of Seven Pines, both sides suffered heavy casualties. Among the wounded was the Confederate commander, General Joseph Johnston. Command of his army now fell to Robert E. Lee. Like all great generals, Lee believed in good training and planning. However, he also understood that victory sometimes depends on the willingness to take chances.

The South Attacks

With McClellan's forces still threatening Richmond, Lee had his opportunity to take a chance. In early June he divided his 55,000-man army, sending several thousand troops to strengthen Stonewall Jackson's forces in western Virginia. The Seven Pines battle had cut McClellan's army to about 80,000 soldiers. Lee was gambling that the overly cautious McClellan, who was awaiting reinforcements, would not attack Richmond before the Confederates could act.

General Jackson then began a brilliant act of deception: He pretended to prepare for an attack on Washington. Lincoln responded by canceling the order for McClellan's additional troops, keeping them in Washington to protect the Union capital. Jackson then slipped away to join Lee outside Richmond. In late June their combined forces attacked McClellan's larger army in a series of encounters called the Seven Days' Battles. Although the Confederates lost more than 20,000 soldiers, 4,000 more than the Union, McClellan decided to retreat.

The Second Battle of Bull Run After McClellan's failure, Lincoln turned to General John Pope, who was organizing a new army outside Washington. The President ordered McClellan's troops back to Washington and put Pope in overall command. Lee knew that he must draw Pope's army into battle before McClellan's soldiers arrived and made the size of the Union force overwhelming.

Again, Lee divided his army. In late August he sent Jackson's troops north in a sweeping movement around Pope's position. After marching 50 miles in two days, they struck behind Pope's army and destroyed some of his supplies, which were stored at Manassas. Enraged, Pope ordered his 62,000 soldiers into action to smash Jackson. On August 29, while Pope's force was engaged, Lee also attacked it with the main body of the Confederate army.

The battle was fought on virtually the same ground where McDowell had been defeated the year before. And Pope's Union troops met the same fate at this Second Battle of Bull Run. After Pope's defeat, McClellan was returned to command. "We must use what tools we have," Lincoln said in defense of his decision. "If he can't fight himself, he excels in making others ready to fight."

The Battle of Antietam With Richmond no longer threatened, Lee decided that the time had come to invade the North. He hoped that a victory on Union soil would arouse European support for the South and turn Northern public opinion against the war. So, in early September 1862, Lee's army bypassed the Union troops guarding Washington and slipped into western Maryland. McClellan had no idea where the Confederates were. Then one of his soldiers found a copy of Lee's orders wrapped around some cigars near an abandoned Confederate camp. Now that he knew the enemy's strategy, McClellan crowed, "If I cannot whip Bobbie Lee, I will be willing to go home."

True to his nature, however, McClellan delayed some 16 hours before ordering his troops after Lee. This gave the Confederate general, who had learned that his plans were in enemy hands, time to prepare for the Union attack. The two armies met at Antietam Creek near Sharpsburg, Maryland, on September 17. Lee had about 40,000 troops, McClellan over 75,000, with nearly 25,000 more in reserve.

Union troops attacked throughout the day, suffering heavy losses. In the first three hours of fighting, some 12,000 soldiers from both sides were killed or wounded. By day's end Union casualties had grown to over 12,000. Lee's nearly 14,000 casualties amounted to more than a third of his army. The next day the battered Confederates retreated back into Virginia. Lincoln telegraphed McClellan, "Destroy the rebel army if possible." But the ever-cautious general did not take advantage of his opportunity to destroy Lee's army.

The **Battle of Antietam** became the bloodiest day of the Civil War. "God grant these things may soon end and peace be restored," wrote a Pennsylvania soldier after the battle. "Of this war I am heartily sick and tired."

VIEWING HISTORY This painting depicts two great Confederate generals: Robert E. Lee, left, and Stonewall Jackson. **Drawing Conclusions** *How does the artist show which general is in command?*

Section 1 Assessment

READING COMPREHENSION

1. Which side won the **First Battle of Bull Run?** Why?

2. What were the effects of the invention of new kinds of rifles, bullets, **shells,** and **canister?**

3. Briefly describe the war strategies of the North and the South.

4. Briefly describe the **Battle of Shiloh** and the **Battle of Antietam.**

CRITICAL THINKING AND WRITING

5. **Predicting Consequences** Choose one early Civil War battle that demonstrated the result of a lost opportunity, and describe what might have happened if a different decision had been made.

6. **Writing an Outline** Write an outline for a newspaper editorial of May 1861 in which you will argue why either the North or the South will easily win the Civil War.

Go Online
PHSchool.com

For: An activity on the Battle of Antietam
Visit: PHSchool.com
Web Code: mrd-4111

READING FOCUS

- How did wartime politics affect the Confederate and Union governments?

- How did the Emancipation Proclamation affect both the North and the South?

- What were the causes and effects of African Americans joining the Union army?

- What kinds of hardships befell the North and the South during the war?

MAIN IDEA

The Union and the Confederacy struggled to raise and support their armies and to provide for the well-being of their citizens. The Emancipation Proclamation had a profound effect on both those efforts.

KEY TERMS

draft
recognition
greenback
Copperhead
martial law
writ of *habeas corpus*
Emancipation
  Proclamation
contraband

TARGET READING SKILL

Summarize As you read, prepare an outline of the first part of this section. Use Roman numerals for the first two major headings, capital letters for subheads, and numbers for supporting details. Include responses to problems as shown in the sample below.

I. Politics in the South
  A. Mobilizing for War
    1. Not enough soldiers to fight/Lee calls for draft.
    2. _____
  B. _____
    1. _____
    2. _____

Setting the Scene

By early 1862, the "picnic" atmosphere evident at the beginning of the First Battle of Bull Run was gone. It was clear that the war was going to be neither quick nor easy, and that the resources of both sides would be severely strained. The South, for example, faced a crisis of manpower. As Grant moved toward Mississippi and McClellan's army threatened Richmond, many Confederate soldiers neared the end of their enlistments. Few seemed ready to reenlist. "If I live this twelve months out, I intend to try mighty hard to keep out [of the army]," pledged one Virginia soldier. A young Wisconsin boy who had run away to join the Union Army also had second thoughts:

> 66 *I want to say, as we lay there and the shells were flying all over us, my thoughts went back to my home, and I thought what a foolish boy I was to run away and get into such a mess as I was in. I would have been glad to have seen my father coming after me.* 99
>
> —Elisha Stockwell

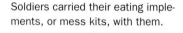

Soldiers carried their eating implements, or mess kits, with them.

Politics in the South

While both sides had to deal with the practical and political problems of a long and costly war, the South had a further difficulty. The branches and powers of the Confederate government were similar to those of the government of the United States. However, the framers of the Confederate constitution had made certain that it recognized states' rights and slavery—two of the main reasons for the South's secession from the Union. These two issues caused problems for the South throughout the war.

Like the government of the North, the Confederate government had to persuade individual citizens to sacrifice their personal interests for the common good. In addition, Confederate leaders had to find a way to build Southerners' loyalty to their new government. Furthermore, because the South had fewer resources than the North, its war effort depended more on making the best possible use of the resources it had. Since the Southern state governments were strong and sometimes fiercely independent, meeting these objectives would sometimes prove difficult.

Mobilizing for War   Fearing the war would be lost if there were not enough soldiers to fight, General Lee called for a **draft,** or required military service. Opponents of strong central government claimed that a draft violated the principles of states' rights that the South was fighting for. A Texas senator disagreed:

> 66 *Cease this child's play. . . . The enemy are in some portions of almost every state in the Confederacy . . . We need a large army. How are you going to get it? . . . No man has any individual rights, which come into conflict with the welfare of the country.* 99
> —Senator Louis Wigfall

Focus on
WORLD EVENTS

Britain and France While Britain and France had often been rivals and military foes, during the period preceding the American Civil War they had become allies. The two nations had fought on the same side in the Crimean War (1854–1856), and in 1860, Napoleon III of France had negotiated a treaty with Britain to lower tariffs levied on goods traded between them. What's more, by 1864, the German leader Bismarck was changing the balance of power in Europe and posing a threat to France.

In April 1862, the Confederate congress passed a draft law requiring three years of military service for white men ages 18 to 35. This automatically extended the service of all volunteers for two more years. After the horrible losses at Antietam, the upper age for the draft became 45. Later it was raised again to 50. The Confederate government also took charge of the South's economy. It determined how much wool, cotton, and leather should be produced, and seized control of Southern railroads from private owners. Farmers were required to contribute one tenth of their produce to the war effort.

To help raise money for the war, the Confederate congress imposed a tax on personal incomes. The Confederate government also authorized the army to seize male slaves for military labor. Though they were paid a monthly fee for borrowed slaves, planters resented this practice because it disrupted work on their plantations.

The Impact of States' Rights   Not all of the mobilization efforts described above were successful. A fierce commitment to states' rights worked against the Confederate government and harmed the war effort in many ways. You will recall that the national government under the Articles of Confederation had suffered similar difficulties, and was replaced by the Constitution when Americans of that time felt the need for a stronger central government. Many Americans, especially in the South, had continued to champion states' rights—both under the United States Constitution and under the new Confederacy. The governor of Georgia put it this way:

> 66 *I entered into this revolution . . . to sustain the rights of the states . . . and I am* still *a rebel . . . no matter who may be in power.* 99
> —Governor Joseph Brown

Many Southerners shared the governor's point of view. Local authorities sometimes refused to cooperate with draft officials. Whole counties in some states were ruled by armed bands of draft-dodgers and deserters. It is estimated that perhaps one quarter of Confederate men eligible for the draft failed to cooperate.

VIEWING FINE ART After operating for about 21 months, the Confederate privateer *Alabama* was finally sunk by the U.S.S. *Kearsarge* off the coast of France, as shown in this 1864 painting by Edouard Manet. **Determining Relevance** *Why was the South's ability to capture Union merchant vessels important to the Confederacy?*

"If we are defeated," warned an Atlanta newspaper, "it will be by the people at home."

Seeking Help From Europe Although the Union blockade effectively prevented Southern cotton from reaching Great Britain and France, Southerners continued to hope for British and French intervention in the war. In May 1861, the Confederate government sent representatives to both nations. Even though the Confederacy failed to gain **recognition,** or official acceptance as an independent nation, it did receive some help. Great Britain agreed to allow its ports to be used to build Confederate privateers. One of these vessels, the *Alabama,* captured more than 60 Northern merchant ships. In all, 11 British-built Confederate privateers forced most Union shipping from the high seas for much of the war.

Formal recognition of the Confederacy did seem possible for a time in 1862. Napoleon III, the ruler of France, had sent troops into Mexico, trying to rebuild a French empire in the Americas. He welcomed the idea of an independent Confederate States of America on Mexico's northern border. However, France would not openly support the Confederacy without Great Britain's cooperation.

British opinion about the war was divided. Some leaders clearly sympathized with the Southerners. Many believed an independent South would be a better market for British products. However, there was also strong anti-slavery feeling in Britain, and there were those who did not want to come to the aid of a slave-owning nation. Others questioned whether the Confederacy would be able to win the war. The British government adopted a wait-and-see attitude. To get foreign help, the South would first have to prove itself on the battlefield.

Politics in the North

After early losses to Confederate forces, President Lincoln and his government had to convince some Northern citizens that maintaining the Union was worth the sacrifices they were being asked to make. As in the South, efforts focused on raising troops and uniting the nation behind the war effort. In addition, the federal government found itself facing international crises as it worked to strengthen civilian support for the war.

Tensions With Great Britain British talks with the South aroused tensions between Great Britain and the United States. Late in 1861, Confederate president Davis again sent two representatives from the Confederacy to England and France. After evading the Union blockade, John Slidell and James Mason boarded the British mail ship *Trent* and steamed for Europe.

Soon a Union warship stopped the *Trent* in international waters, removed the two Confederate officials, and brought them to the United States. An outraged British government sent troops to Canada and threatened war unless Slidell and Mason were freed. President Lincoln ordered their release. "One war at a time," he said.

The Union vigorously protested Great Britain's support of the Confederacy. Lincoln demanded $19 million compensation from Great Britain for damages done by the privateers built in British ports, and for other British actions on the South's behalf. This demand strained relations between the United States and Great Britain for nearly a decade after the war.

READING CHECK
What caused tension between the Union and Great Britain?

Republicans in Control   With Southern Democrats out of the United States Congress, Republican lawmakers had little opposition. The Civil War Congresses thus became among the most active in American history. Republicans were able to pass a number of laws during the war that would have a lasting impact, even well after the South rejoined the Union.

For example, Southerners had long opposed building a rail line across the Great Plains. It was first proposed by Illinois senator Stephen Douglas in the early 1850s, in part to benefit Chicago by linking that city to the West. In July 1862, however, Congress passed the Pacific Railroad Act with little resistance. The law allowed the federal government to give land and money to companies for construction of a railroad line from Nebraska to the Pacific Coast. The Homestead Act, passed in the same year, offered free government land to people willing to settle on it.

The disappearance of Southern opposition also allowed Congress to raise tariff rates. The tariff became more a device to protect Northern industries than to provide revenue for the government. Union leaders turned to other means to raise money for the war.

Financial Measures   In 1861, the Republican-controlled Congress passed the first federal tax on income in American history. It collected 3 percent of the income of people earning more than $600 a year but less than $10,000, which is the equivalent of about $11,000 to $180,000 today. Those making more than $10,000 per year were taxed at 5 percent. The Internal Revenue Act of 1862 imposed taxes on items such as liquor, tobacco, medicine, and newspaper ads. Nearly all of these taxes ended when the war was over.

During the war, Congress also reformed the nation's banking system. Since 1832, when President Jackson vetoed the recharter of the Second Bank of the United States, Americans had relied on state banks. In 1862, Congress passed an act that created a national currency, called **greenbacks** because of their color. This paper money was not backed by gold, but was declared by Congress to be acceptable for legal payment of all public and private debts.

Opposition to the War   Like the South, the North instituted a draft in order to raise troops for what now looked like a longer, more difficult war. And like the Southern law, this March 1863 measure allowed the wealthy to buy their way out of military service. Riots broke out in the North after the draft law was passed. Mobs of whites in New York City vented their rage at the draft in July 1863. More than 100 people died during four days of destruction. At least 11 of the dead were African Americans, who seemed to be targeted by the rioters.

There was political opposition to the war as well. Although the Democrats remaining in Congress were too few to have much power, one group raised their voices in protest against the war. This group was nicknamed **Copperheads,** after a type of poisonous snake. These Democrats warned that Republican policies would bring a flood of freed slaves to the North. What's more, they predicted that these freed slaves

Focus on
GOVERNMENT

Civil War Conscription The Civil War marked the first time that conscription, or the draft, was instituted in the United States. Both sides used it to raise troops, and both sides used it unfairly. In the South, owners of 20 or more slaves were excused from serving. A Northerner could pay the government $300 to avoid service. In both the Union and the Confederacy, wealthy men could hire substitutes to fight in their place. No wonder many angry Southerners called the conflict "a rich man's war and a poor man's fight."

would take jobs away from whites. Radical Copperheads also tried to persuade Union soldiers to desert the army, and they urged other Northerners to resist the draft.

Emergency Wartime Actions   Like the government of the Confederacy, the United States government exercised great power during the Civil War. To silence the Copperheads and other opponents of the war, Lincoln resorted to extreme measures. He used the army to shut down opposition newspapers and denied others the use of the mails.

The border states provided a special set of problems. Four of them were slave states that remained—at least for the moment—in the Union. Because of their locations, the continued loyalty of Delaware, Maryland, Missouri, and Kentucky was critical to the North. Lincoln considered Delaware, where few citizens held slaves, to be secure. In nearby Maryland, however, support for secession was strong. In September 1861, Lincoln ordered that all "disloyal" members of the Maryland state legislature be arrested. This action prevented a vote on secession and assured that Washington would not be surrounded by the Confederacy.

The Union needed the loyalty of Kentucky and Missouri in order to keep control of the Ohio and Mississippi rivers. In Missouri, Lincoln supported an uprising aimed at overthrowing the pro-Confederate state government. To secure Kentucky, he put the state under **martial law** for part of the war. This is emergency rule by military authorities, during which some Bill of Rights

NOTABLE PRESIDENTS
Abraham Lincoln

"A house divided against itself cannot stand."
—Speech in 1858

Abraham Lincoln entered the White House with little experience in national politics. Before being elected in 1860, he had been a successful lawyer in Illinois and a one-term member of Congress. Nothing, however, could have prepared him for the extraordinary challenges he would face as President.

Lincoln confronted crises on every side. Southern states began seceding from the Union even before he took office. The border states had to be kept in the Union. Many Northerners who opposed secession did not want to fight the South, and white Northerners disagreed among themselves about slavery.

Lincoln's actions as President all pointed toward one goal: preserve the Union. He changed commanding generals again and again in a desperate search for one who could defeat the Confederate army. He suppressed freedom of speech and assembly. He issued the Emancipation Proclamation to free the slaves living behind Confederate lines, and in 1863 he called upon free blacks to join the Union army.

Along with his commitment to preserve the Union,

Lincoln's greatest strengths were his sense of compassion and his ability to express powerful ideas in simple yet moving language. In fact, his words have come to help define the Civil War, from his warning that "A house divided against itself cannot stand" to his hope in 1865 that Americans would face the future "with malice toward none, with charity for all." Lincoln did not live to work for the compassionate peace he favored, but he had done more than any other single person to preserve the Union at its time of greatest danger.

16th President 1861–1865

Connecting to Today
How important is it that a President be able to rally people behind a cause?

Go Online PHSchool.com   **For:** More on Abraham Lincoln
Visit: PHSchool.com
Web Code: mrd-4117

The Northern Economy In the North, the war hurt industries that depended heavily on Southern markets or Southern cotton. However, most Northern industries boomed. Unlike the Confederacy, the North had the farms and factories to produce nearly everything its army and civilian population needed. War-related industries fared especially well. Philip Armour made a fortune packaging pork to feed Union soldiers. Samuel Colt ran his factory night and day producing guns for the army.

As in the South, when men went off to war, women filled critical jobs in factories and on farms. Many factory owners preferred women employees because they could be paid less than male workers. This hiring practice kept wages down overall. Prices rose faster than pay during the war.

A few manufacturers made their profits even greater by selling the Union government inferior products: rusty rifles, boats that leaked, hats that dissolved in the rain. Uniforms made from compressed rags quickly fell apart. The soles came off some boots after a few miles of marching. Like the Southern profiteers, these manufacturers took shameful advantage of the needs of their countrymen.

Prison Camps Captured Confederate soldiers were sent to prison camps throughout the North, including Point Lookout in Maryland and Camp Chase in Ohio. The Ohio Penitentiary also housed some Confederate prisoners. The South's prison camps were located wherever there was room. Andersonville, its most notorious camp, was in a field in Georgia. Richmond's Libby Prison was a converted tobacco warehouse.

The North and the South generally treated their prisoners about the same. In most cases officers received better treatment than other prisoners. Andersonville was the exception. Built to hold 10,000 men, it eventually confined nearly 35,000 Northerners in a fenced, 26-acre open area. About 100 prisoners a day died, usually of starvation or exposure. The camp's commander was the only Confederate to be tried for war crimes after the South's defeat. He was convicted and hanged.

Medical Care While soldiers faced miserable conditions in prison camps, life was not much better in the battle camps. Health and medical conditions on both sides were frightful. About one in four Civil War soldiers did not survive the war, but it was disease that killed many of them. Poor nutrition and contaminated food led to dysentery and typhoid fever. Malaria, spread by mosquitoes, was also a killer. Many soldiers died of pneumonia.

A Union soldier was three times more likely to die in camp or in a hospital than he was to be killed on the battlefield. In fact, about one in five Union soldiers wounded in battle later died from their wounds. While most doctors were aware of the relationship between cleanliness and infection, they did not know how to sterilize their equipment. Surgeons sometimes went for days without even washing their instruments.

On both sides, thousands of women volunteered to care for the sick and wounded. Government clerk Clara Barton quit her job in order to provide supplies and first aid to Union troops in camp and during battle. Known to soldiers as the "angel of the battlefield," Barton continued her service after the war by founding the American Red Cross. Mental health reformer Dorothea Dix volunteered to organize and head the Union army's nursing corps. Nursing was a difficult task, as the following letter shows:

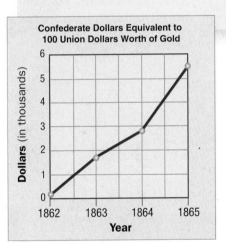

Focus on ECONOMICS

Inflation in the South As the war dragged on and Union armies advanced into the South, shortages and the falling value of Confederate currency caused almost unbelievable inflation. Inflation is a steady increase in prices over time. Even by late 1862, a bag of salt that had cost $2 before the war was selling for $60 in some places. Southerner Rose Frye remembered the price of calico going from 50 cents to $20 per yard, and paying $125 for shoes.

Another way to look at inflation is to compare the value of Confederate currency to $100 worth of gold as shown in this graph.

Confederate Dollars Equivalent to 100 Union Dollars Worth of Gold

Many women served as nurses in the wards of field hospitals. One nurse, Clara Barton (inset), was known as the "angel of the battlefield."

66 *I am very tired tonight; I have been in the field all day. There are no words in the English language to express the sufferings I witnessed today. The men lie on the ground; their clothes have been cut off them to dress their wounds; they . . . have nothing but hardtack to eat. . . . [F]our surgeons, none of whom were idle for fifteen minutes at a time, were busy all day amputating legs and arms. . . . I would get on first rate if they would not ask me to write to their wives; that I cannot do without crying, which is not pleasant to either party.* 99

—Cornelia Hancock

Some 4,000 women served as nurses for the Northern army. By the end of the war, nursing was no longer only a man's profession.

Sanitation in most army camps was nonexistent. Rubbish and rotting food littered the ground. Human waste and heaps of animal manure polluted water supplies. Epidemics of contagious diseases, such as mumps and measles, swept through camps. Sick lists were lengthy. At times only half the troops in a regiment were available for fighting.

The United States Sanitary Commission, created in June 1861, attempted to combat these problems. Thousands of volunteers, mostly women, inspected army hospitals and camps. They organized cleanups and provided advice about controlling infection, disease prevention, sewage disposal, and nutrition. Despite these and similar Confederate efforts, about twice as many soldiers on each side died from disease as from enemy gunfire.

Section 2 Assessment

READING COMPREHENSION

1. Describe the **draft** laws in the North and the South.

2. Who were the **Copperheads?**

3. How were **martial law** and the suspension of the **writ of *habeas corpus*** used to stifle dissent?

4. Why did Lincoln decide to issue the **Emancipation Proclamation?**

CRITICAL THINKING AND WRITING

5. **Comparing Points of View** Compare the quotes from Senator Louis Wigfall and Governor Joseph Brown. Given the measures President Lincoln used during the war, which position do you think he would have favored?

6. **Writing a List** Make a list of the effects of the Emancipation Proclamation in both the North and the South. Underline the two most important effects.

For: An activity on the constitutions of the U.S. and the Confederacy
Visit: PHSchool.com
Web Code: mrd-4112

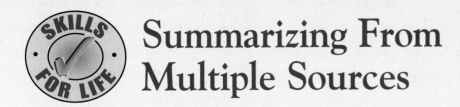

Summarizing From Multiple Sources

When you are doing research, you will often find two or more sources with information about one topic. Combining the main ideas of these sources into a single summary can provide a more complete picture of events than either source could alone. You can also use each source to test the reliability of the others: if the sources do not seem to agree, you should do further research to find out which ones provide the most reliable information.

In February 1865, General Sherman's army began marching through South Carolina, sparing little in its path. Dr. Samuel McGill, a resident of the state, made entries in his diary as the army advanced. Ten years later, in his memoirs, General Sherman would recall his own thinking at the time.

LEARN THE SKILL

Use the following steps to summarize from multiple sources:

1. **Find the main idea of each source.** Sometimes the main idea is stated by the writer, often in the first sentence of a paragraph. In other cases, you may have to use your judgment to identify the main idea from the details in the source.

2. **Identify supporting details in each source.** These include any facts, reasons, explanations, examples, or descriptions that helped you find each main idea.

3. **Write a summary of each source.** State or restate its main idea in your own words.

4. **Create a summary based on the main ideas of all the sources.** Use your own words to tie the sources' main ideas together. If possible, include a supporting detail from each source.

PRACTICE THE SKILL

Answer the following questions:

1. **(a)** Which sentence in Source A states the main idea of the two diary entries? **(b)** Which sentence in Source B provides the main idea of that excerpt?

2. **(a)** What actions are described in Source A? **(b)** How do they support the writer's sense of the mood of the people? **(c)** In Source B, what is the "power" that Sherman planned to use? **(d)** What was Sherman ready to do in order to use it?

3. **(a)** State the main idea of Source A in your own words. **(b)** State the main idea of Source B in your own words.

4. **(a)** What historical event links McGill's diary entries with the excerpt from Sherman's memoirs? **(b)** Do the two sources contradict or complement each other? Explain. **(c)** Drawing information from both sources, describe what happened in the Williamsburg District in 1865 and why it happened.

A

February 28, 1865: *"All is gloom and uncertainty, and preparations are being made for the worst. Furniture and provisions are hidden against pending raids. . . . It is feared famine will possess the land; our army is demoralized and the people panic stricken. . . . The power to do [act] has left us. . . . To fight longer seems to be madness; to submit tamely is dishonor."*

March 1, 1865: *"The whole country is in the wildest commotion and many are fleeing to the woods with their wives and daughters, while a few have gone to meet the advance and to give battle."*

—From the diary of Dr. Samuel McGill, Williamsburg District, South Carolina

B

"My aim then was, to whip the rebels, to humble their pride, to follow them to their inmost recesses [their inner selves], and make them fear and dread us. . . . It was to me manifest [obvious] that the soldiers and people of the South entertained a . . . fear of our . . . men. . . . [T]his was a power, and I intended to utilize it. . . . and therefore on them should fall the scourge of war in its worst form."

—William Tecumseh Sherman, *Memoirs, Vol. 2,* 1875

APPLY THE SKILL

See the Chapter Review and Assessment for another opportunity to apply this skill.

The Tide of War Turns

READING FOCUS

- What was the importance of Lee's victories at Fredericksburg and Chancellorsville?
- How did the Battles of Gettysburg and Vicksburg turn the tide of the war?
- Why was 1863 a pivotal year?
- What is the message of the Gettysburg Address?

MAIN IDEA

Despite Southern victories at Fredericksburg and Chancellorsville, the tide of war turned in the summer of 1863, when the North won at Gettysburg and Vicksburg.

KEY TERMS

Battle of Fredericksburg
Battle of Chancellorsville
Battle of Gettysburg
Pickett's Charge
siege
Gettysburg Address

TARGET READING SKILL

Identify Cause and Effect As you read, complete the following chart. For each battle, fill in the important officers, tell which side won, and write what you consider the most important reason for that side's victory.

Major Battles of 1863			
Battle	Union Officer	Confederate Officer	Victor/Why
Fredericksburg	Burnside	Lee	South/Burnside crossed right in front of Lee's army; kept charging into gunfire.

Setting the Scene

Civil War battles were noisy and smoky. Cannons boomed, rifles fired, men shouted, and the battlefield was wreathed in a haze of gunfire and dust. How did commanders communicate with their troops in this chaos? How did soldiers know when to advance, when to retreat, or even where their units were located? In the early years of the Civil War, it was the sound of the drumbeat that communicated orders. For that reason, drummer boys—usually only 12 to 16 years old—were so important that they were often purposely fired on by the enemy, and hundreds were killed in battle. One drummer boy who was wounded in action at Vicksburg received the Medal of Honor. Another boy described his experience this way:

> 66 *A cannon ball came bouncing across the corn field, kicking up dirt and dust each time it struck the earth. Many of the men in our company took shelter behind a stone wall, but I stood where I was and never stopped drumming. An officer came by on horseback and chastised the men, saying 'this boy puts you all to shame. Get up and move forward.' . . . Even when the fighting was at its fiercest and I was frightened, I stood straight and did as I was ordered. . . . I felt I had to be a good example for the others.* 99

—A Civil War drummer boy

Drummer boys were a vital part of the armies of both the North and the South.

Victories for General Lee

The Emancipation Proclamation may have renewed enthusiasm for the war among some Northerners, but the war still had to be won in the din and dust of the battlefield. When General George McClellan delayed in following up on his victory over Robert E. Lee at the Battle of Antietam, Lincoln again removed McClellan from command and replaced him with General Ambrose Burnside in November 1862. Sadly for Lincoln, Burnside was better known for his thick whiskers, the origin of the term "sideburns," than for his skills as a military strategist. He soon proved that his poor reputation was justified.

The Battle of Fredericksburg Knowing that McClellan had been fired for being too cautious, Burnside quickly advanced into Virginia. His plan was simple—to march his army of some 122,000 men straight toward Richmond. In response, Lee massed his army of nearly 79,000 at Fredericksburg, Virginia, on the south bank of the Rappahannock River. Lee spread his troops along a ridge called Marye's Heights, behind and overlooking the town.

Incredibly, instead of crossing the river out of range of the Confederate artillery, Burnside decided to cross directly in front of Lee's forces. "The enemy will be more surprised [by this move]," he explained. Lee was surprised—by the poor strategy of Burnside's plan.

Union troops poured across the river on specially constructed bridges and occupied the town. Lee let them cross. He knew that his artillery had the area well covered. Lee believed that if Burnside's army attacked, the Confederate forces could easily deal it a crushing defeat.

On December 13, 1862, the **Battle of Fredericksburg** began. Throughout the day Burnside ordered charge after charge into the Confederate gunfire. Some Union army units lost more than half their men. When the fighting ceased at nightfall, the Union had suffered nearly 13,000 casualties. Confederate losses were just over 5,000. A demoralized Burnside soon asked to be relieved of his command.

The Battle of Chancellorsville After accepting Burnside's resignation, a worried Lincoln turned to yet another general, Joseph "Fighting Joe" Hooker. General Hooker's plan was to move the Union army around Fredericksburg and attack the Confederates' strong defenses from behind. "May God have mercy on General Lee, for I will have none," Fighting Joe promised.

In late April 1863, Hooker put his plan into action. Leaving about a third of his 115,000-man army outside Fredericksburg, he marched the rest of his troops several miles upriver and slipped across the Rappahannock. Lee soon became aware of Hooker's actions. Confederate cavalry commanded by General J.E.B. "Jeb" Stuart discovered Hooker's force camped about ten miles west of Fredericksburg, near a road crossing called Chancellorsville.

Dividing his forces, Lee sent more than 40,000 Confederate soldiers westward to meet Hooker. About 10,000 troops remained in Fredericksburg. Lee ordered them to build many fires at night, so the enemy across the river would not realize that most of the army was gone.

The **Battle of Chancellorsville** began on May 1, 1863. When the Union troops started their march toward Fredericksburg, they suddenly saw Lee's army in front of them. After a brief clash, Fighting Joe ordered them to pull back into the thick woods and build defenses. The next day, when the Confederates did not attack, Hooker assumed they were in retreat. Instead, Lee had daringly divided his forces a second time. He sent General Stonewall Jackson and 26,000 men on a 12-mile march around the Union army for a late-afternoon attack on its right side. The movement of Jackson's troops was concealed by heavy woods that covered the area.

Again, Hooker was taken by surprise. The only warning was a wave of rabbits and deer that poured into the Union camp moments ahead of the Confederate charge. If darkness had not halted his attack, Jackson would have crushed the Union army. That night, Jackson and some other officers left the Confederate camp to scout the Union positions for a renewed attack. As they returned in

The Shenandoah Valley One of Stonewall Jackson's deadliest weapons was a detailed map of the Shenandoah Valley, a corridor about 150 miles long and 25 miles wide between the Blue Ridge Mountains and the Alleghenies. Southern armies were able to travel north through the Valley. Although forested, its slopes were not too steep or rocky for troops on foot or horseback, and the main road through the center of the Valley allowed even Robert E. Lee's large army to travel rapidly. What's more, the many gaps in the Blue Ridge Mountains and the pro-Confederate population permitted Southern forces to duck easily in and out of the Valley. However, Union forces that ventured there were harassed by armed raiders. Finally, the Shenandoah's splendid pastures and crops also supplied the Confederate Army with a much-needed source of food.

the darkness, some Confederate soldiers mistook them for enemies and opened fire. Three bullets hit Jackson, one shattering his left arm so badly that it had to be amputated.

On May 3, with Stuart now leading Jackson's command, the Confederate army completed its victory. On May 5, Hooker's badly beaten troops withdrew back across the river. Chancellorsville was Lee's most brilliant victory, but it was also his most costly one. On May 10, Jackson died of complications from his wounds. Stonewall Jackson was probably Lee's most brilliant general. His popularity with the troops was exceeded only by Lee's. His death deprived Lee of a man he called his "strong right arm."

The Battle of Gettysburg

The crushing defeats at Fredericksburg and Chancellorsville were the low point of the war for the Union. The mood in Washington was dark. Rumors swept the capital that Lincoln would resign as President. Some Northern leaders began to talk seriously of making peace with the South. "If there is a worse place than Hell," Lincoln said, "I am in it."

In June 1863, Lee marched his forces northward. The Union blockade and the South's lack of resources were beginning to weaken his army. With all the fighting in Virginia, supplies there had become scarce. Lee hoped to find some in Pennsylvania. More importantly, he hoped that a major Confederate victory on Northern soil would finally push the Union into giving up the war.

As Lincoln prepared to replace Hooker, the Union army moved north, too, staying between the Confederates and Washington. On July 1, some Confederate troops entered the town of Gettysburg, Pennsylvania. Many of them were barefoot, and a supply of shoes was rumored to be stored in the town. There the Confederates encountered a unit of Union cavalry and a fight developed. From this skirmish grew the greatest battle ever fought in North America, the three-day **Battle of Gettysburg.**

MAP SKILLS The Battle of Gettysburg was fought over three days. Notice the changes in troop positions over the course of the battle. **Human-Environment Interaction** How did each side attempt to use the terrain to gain an advantage?

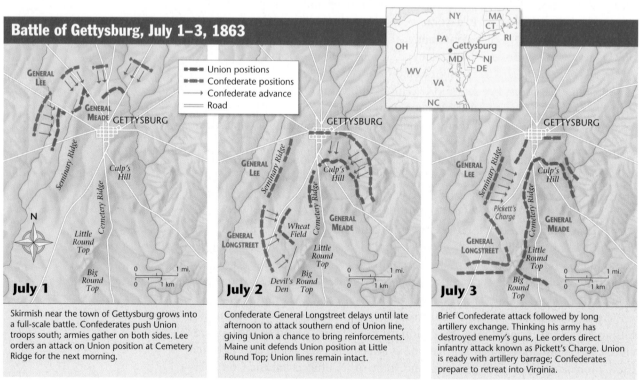

Battle of Gettysburg, July 1–3, 1863

Union positions
Confederate positions
Confederate advance
Road

July 1 Skirmish near the town of Gettysburg grows into a full-scale battle. Confederates push Union troops south; armies gather on both sides. Lee orders an attack on Union position at Cemetery Ridge for the next morning.

July 2 Confederate General Longstreet delays until late afternoon to attack southern end of Union line, giving Union a chance to bring reinforcements. Maine unit defends Union position at Little Round Top; Union lines remain intact.

July 3 Brief Confederate attack followed by long artillery exchange. Thinking his army has destroyed enemy's guns, Lee orders direct infantry attack known as Pickett's Charge. Union is ready with artillery barrage; Confederates prepare to retreat into Virginia.

July 1, 1863 Hearing the gunfire coming from Gettysburg, units of both armies rushed to the scene. At first, the Confederates outnumbered the Union forces. Fighting through the day, they pushed the Northerners back onto some hills south of town. Meanwhile, troops on both sides continued to gather. Among the Union soldiers to arrive that night was General George Meade, the new head of the Union army. He had been in command for less than a week.

Each army took up positions on a series of hills. Their lines stretched from the outskirts of town, in a southerly direction, for about four miles. The center of the Union line was a long hill called Cemetery Ridge. Another series of hills, called Seminary Ridge, was the center of the Confederate position. Between these two ridges was a large field several hundred yards wide.

That evening, Lee discussed his battle plan with General James Longstreet, his second-in-command since the death of Stonewall Jackson. Having won the day's fighting, and fresh from his victory at Chancellorsville, Lee's confidence was high. He proposed to continue the battle the next day. Longstreet advised against attacking such a strong Union position, but Lee had made up his mind. "The enemy is there," said Lee, pointing to Cemetery Ridge, "and I am going to attack him there." He ordered Longstreet to lead an attack on the southern end of the Union line the next morning.

July 2, 1863 Although a graduate of West Point, Longstreet preferred more peaceful endeavors. An accountant, he wanted to be in charge of the Confederate army's payroll. Lee made him a field commander instead. "Longstreet is a very good fighter when he . . . gets everything ready," Lee said of him, "but he is so slow."

On this second day of the battle, Longstreet was not ready to attack until about 4:00 P.M. His delays gave Meade the chance to bring up reinforcements. The battle raged into the early evening. Heavy fighting occurred in a peach orchard, a wheat field, and a mass of boulders known locally as the Devil's Den.

At one point, some Alabama soldiers noticed that one of the hills in the Union position, called Little Round Top, was almost undefended. They rushed to capture the hill. From it, Confederate artillery could have bombarded the Union lines. However, Union commanders also had noticed that Little Round Top was vulnerable. About 350 Maine soldiers under Colonel Joshua Chamberlain, a college professor before the war, were ordered to defend the position. They arrived on the hill just before the Alabamans' assault and then held off repeated attacks until they ran out of ammunition. Unwilling to give up, Chamberlain ordered a bayonet charge. The surprised Confederates retreated back down the hill. The Maine soldiers' heroic act likely saved the Union army from defeat. At the end of the day, the Union lines remained intact.

July 3, 1863 The third day of battle began with a brief Confederate attack on the north end of the Union line. Then the battlefield fell quiet. Finally, in the early afternoon, about 150 Confederate cannons began the heaviest artillery barrage of the war. Some Union generals thought the firing might be to protect a Confederate retreat. They were wrong. Lee had decided to risk everything on an infantry charge against the center of the Union position. As he had two days before, Longstreet opposed such a direct attack. Again Lee overruled him.

VIEWING HISTORY This lithograph shows part of the Battle of Gettysburg. **Drawing Inferences** *What can you tell about the military tactics of the battle from the picture?*

READING CHECK
Describe the battle for Little Round Top.

Fast Forward to Today

Photography and War

The Civil War was the first American conflict to be photographed. Mathew Brady and his team of photographers showed its grim realities to great effect.

The Vietnam War was the first to "invade" American homes via television, and the nightly news footage from Vietnam helped turn American public opinion against the war.

During the 2003 Iraq War, reporters were "embedded" into American military units. They traveled with their units, often reporting as combat took place.

? *Which of these images has the most impact on you, the viewer? Why? What do you learn about war from these images?*

After a two-hour artillery duel, the Union guns stopped returning fire. Thinking that the Confederate artillery had destroyed the enemy's guns, Longstreet reluctantly ordered the direct attack. Actually, the Union artillery commander had ceased fire only to save ammunition. Now, however, Northern soldiers on Cemetery Ridge saw nearly 15,000 Confederates, formed in a line a mile long and three rows deep, coming toward them.

Although this event is known in history as **Pickett's Charge**, General George Pickett was only one of three Southern commanders on the field that day. Each led an infantry division of about 5,000 men. As the Confederates marched across about a mile of open ground between the two ridges, the Union artillery resumed firing. Hundreds of canister shells rained down on the approaching soldiers, tearing huge gaps in their ranks. When the Southern troops closed to within about 200 yards of the Union lines, Northern soldiers poured rifle fire into those who remained standing.

Only a few hundred Confederates reached the Union lines—at a bend in a stone wall that became known as the Angle. A survivor described the fighting:

❝ *Men fire into each other's faces, not five feet apart. There are bayonet-thrusts, sabre-strokes, pistol-shots; . . . men going down on their hands and knees, spinning round like tops, throwing out their arms, falling; legless, armless, headless. There are ghastly heaps of dead men.* ❞

—Soldier at Gettysburg

In about 30 minutes it was over. Scarcely half the Confederate force returned to Seminary Ridge. Lee ordered Pickett to reform his division in case Meade counterattacked. "General Lee, I have no division," Pickett replied.

Pickett's Charge ended the bloodiest battle of the Civil War. Losses on both sides were staggering. The Union army of about 85,000 suffered over 23,000 casualties. Of some 75,000 Southerners, about 28,000 were casualties. For the second time, Lee had lost more than a third of his army. The next day, July 4, the Confederates began their retreat back to Virginia.

Vicksburg

While armies clashed in the East, a Union force in the West struggled to capture the city of Vicksburg, Mississippi. Only this stronghold and a fortress at Port Hudson, Louisiana, stood in the way of the Union's complete control of the Mississippi River. Vicksburg seemed safe from attack. It sat on a bluff, high above a sharp bend in the river. From this bluff, Confederate artillery could lob shells at any Union ships that approached the city. In addition, much of Vicksburg was surrounded by swamps. The only approach to the city over dry land was from the east, and Confederate forces held that territory.

Grant Attacks　The Union general who faced these difficult challenges was Ulysses S. Grant. Between December 1862 and April 1863, he made several attempts either to capture or to bypass the city. First, he sent General William Tecumseh Sherman and several thousand troops in an unsuccessful attack on Vicksburg from the north. Next he had his army dig a canal across the bend in the river, so Union boats could bypass the city's guns. However, the canal turned out to be too shallow. Then he tried to attack from the north by sending gunboats down another river. This too failed.

An attempt to approach the city through a swampy backwater called Steele's Bayou nearly ended in disaster. The Confederates cut down trees to slow the Union boats and fired on them from shore. Finally, Sherman's troops had to come and rescue the fleet.

By mid-April 1863, the ground had dried out enough for Grant to try a daring plan. He marched his army down the Louisiana side of the river and crossed into Mississippi south of Vicksburg. Then he moved east and attacked Jackson, the state capital. This maneuver

MAP SKILLS Lincoln called capturing Vicksburg "the key" to winning the war. Jefferson Davis considered the city to be "the nailhead that holds the South's two halves together." **Movement** *(a) Trace Grant's route on the map and explain the strategy behind it. (b) According to the painting, what made the attempt to attack the city by gunboat so difficult?*

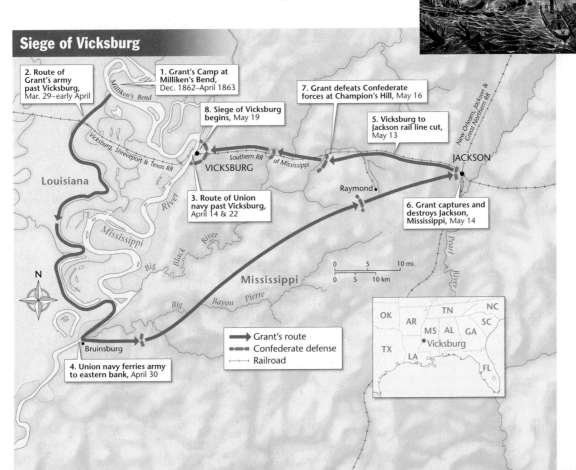

Siege of Vicksburg

2. Route of Grant's army past Vicksburg, Mar. 29–early April

1. Grant's Camp at Milliken's Bend, Dec. 1862–April 1863

8. Siege of Vicksburg begins, May 19

7. Grant defeats Confederate forces at Champion's Hill, May 16

5. Vicksburg to Jackson rail line cut, May 13

Milliken's Bend

New Orleans, Jackson & Great Northern RR

Vicksburg, Shreveport & Texas RR

Southern RR of Mississippi

VICKSBURG

JACKSON

Louisiana

3. Route of Union navy past Vicksburg, April 14 & 22

Raymond

6. Grant captures and destroys Jackson, Mississippi, May 14

Black River

Mississippi River

Big Black River

N

Big Bayou Pierre

Mississippi

Pearl River

0　5　10 mi.
0　5　10 km

Bruinsburg

4. Union navy ferries army to eastern bank, April 30

→ Grant's route
Confederate defense
Railroad

OK　AR　TN　NC
MS　AL　GA　SC
TX　　Vicksburg
LA　　　　FL

Life Underground A young mother described living in a cave during the siege of Vicksburg: "Our new habitation was an excavation made in the earth, a cave in the shape of a T. In one of the wings my bed fitted; the other I used as a kind of a dressing room. In this the earth had been cut down a foot or two below the floor of the main cave. I could stand erect here and when tired of sitting in other portions of my residence, I bowed myself into it and stood impassively resting at full height. Our quarters were close indeed, yet I was more comfortable than I expected I could have been under the earth.

"We were safe at least from fragments of shell—and they were flying in all directions—though no one seemed to think our cave any protection should a mortar shell happen to fall directly on top of the ground above us."

—Mary Ann Loughborough

Sounds of an Era

Listen to the Gettysburg Address and other sounds from the Civil War era.

drew out the Confederate forces from Vicksburg, commanded by General John Pemberton, to help defend the capital. Before they could arrive, Grant captured the city of Jackson. Then he turned his troops west to fight Pemberton.

On May 16, the two armies clashed at Champion's Hill, halfway between Jackson and Vicksburg. Although Grant won the battle, he could not trap Pemberton's army. The Confederates were able to retreat back to Vicksburg's fortifications. In late May, after two more unsuccessful attacks, Grant began a **siege,** a tactic in which an enemy is surrounded and starved in order to make it surrender.

The Siege of Vicksburg When Union cannons opened fire on Vicksburg from land and water, a bombardment began that would average 2,800 shells a day. For more than a month, the citizens of Vicksburg endured a nearly constant pounding from some 300 guns. The constant schedule of shelling took over everyday life.

To avoid being killed by the shells falling on their homes, residents dug caves in hillsides, some complete with furniture and attended by slaves. "It was living like plant roots," one cave dweller said. As the siege dragged on, residents and soldiers alike were reduced to eating horses, mules, and dogs. Rats appeared for sale in the city's butcher shops.

By late June, Confederate soldiers' daily rations were down to one biscuit and one piece of bacon per day. On July 4, some 30,000 Confederate troops marched out of Vicksburg and laid down their arms. Pemberton thought he could negotiate the best terms for the surrender on the day that celebrated the Union's independence.

The Importance of 1863

For the North, 1863 had begun disastrously. However, the Fourth of July, 1863, was for some the most joyous Independence Day since the first one 87 years earlier. For the first time, thousands of former slaves could truly celebrate American independence. The holiday marked the turning point of the Civil War.

In the West, Vicksburg was in Union hands. For a time, the people of that city had been sustained by the hope that President Jefferson Davis would send some of Lee's troops to rescue them. But Lee had no reinforcements to spare. His weakened army had begun its retreat into Virginia; it would never again seriously threaten Union soil. Four days later, Port Hudson surrendered to Union forces. The Mississippi River was now in Union hands, cutting the Confederacy in two. "The Father of Waters again goes unvexed [undisturbed] to the sea," announced Lincoln in Washington, D.C.

In Richmond there began to be serious talk of making peace. Although the war would continue for nearly two years more, for the first time the end seemed in sight.

The Gettysburg Address

On November 19, 1863, some 15,000 people gathered at Gettysburg. The occasion was the dedication of a cemetery to honor the Union soldiers who had died there just four months before. The featured guest was Edward Everett of Massachusetts, the most famous public speaker of the time. President Lincoln was invited to deliver "a few appropriate remarks" to help fill out the program.

Everett delivered a grand crowd-pleasing speech that lasted two hours. Then it was the President's turn to speak. In his raspy, high-pitched voice,

Lincoln delivered his remarks, which became known as the **Gettysburg Address.** In a short, two-minute speech he eloquently reminded listeners of the North's reason for fighting the Civil War: to preserve a young country unmatched by any other country in history in its commitment to the principles of freedom, equality, and self-government:

KEY DOCUMENTS ❝ *Fourscore and seven years ago our fathers brought forth on this continent, a new nation, conceived in Liberty, and dedicated to the proposition that all men are created equal.*

Now we are engaged in a great civil war, testing whether that nation, or any nation so conceived and so dedicated, can long endure. . . .

It is for us the living, rather, to be dedicated here to the unfinished work which they who fought here have thus far so nobly advanced. It is rather for us to be here dedicated to the great task remaining before us—that from these honored dead we take increased devotion to that cause for which they gave the last full measure of devotion—that we here highly resolve that these dead shall not have died in vain—that this nation, under God, shall have a new birth of freedom—and that government of the people, by the people, for the people, shall not perish from the earth. ❞

—Lincoln's Gettysburg Address,
November 19, 1863

VIEWING HISTORY "In times like the present," Lincoln said, "men should utter nothing for which they would not willingly be responsible through time. . . ." **Identifying Central Issues** *How do Lincoln's words at Gettysburg represent the noblest goals of the Union cause?*

In 1863, most Americans did not pay much attention to Lincoln's speech. Some thought it was too short and too simple. Lincoln's fellow speaker, Edward Everett, was an exception. He wrote to Lincoln the next day, "I wish I could flatter myself that I had come as near to the central idea of the occasion in two hours as you did in two minutes." Future generations have agreed with Everett. The Gettysburg Address has become one of the best-loved and most-quoted speeches in English. It expresses simply and eloquently both grief at the terrible cost of the war and the reasons for renewed efforts to preserve the Union and the noble principles for which it stands.

Section 3 Assessment

READING COMPREHENSION

1. Briefly describe the **Battle of Fredericksburg** and the **Battle of Chancellorsville.**

2. Why was the **Battle of Gettysburg** a turning point in the war?

3. What were three effects of Grant's **siege** of Vicksburg?

4. Summarize the main points of the **Gettysburg Address.**

CRITICAL THINKING AND WRITING

5. **Determining Relevance** How did the superior manpower of the North and its greater ability to produce both crops and manufactured goods begin to affect the war in 1863?

6. **Writing to Persuade** Which do you think was a more significant turning point: Vicksburg or Gettysburg? Write the opening paragraph of a persuasive essay supporting your choice.

Go Online PHSchool.com

For: An activity on Civil War soldiers
Visit: PHSchool.com
Web Code: mrd-4113

Devastation and New Freedom

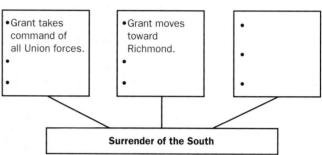

Setting the Scene In April 1865 the city of Richmond, which had welcomed the war with such enthusiasm four years earlier, was a very different place. The war was nearly over, and both the Confederate government and its army abandoned the city. While many Southern cities, towns, and farms were set ablaze by conquering Union armies, the fires in the Confederate capital were set by retreating Southern troops in an effort to keep stored provisions from falling into the hands of the enemy. One Union soldier described the scene as he approached the city:

Retreating Confederate troops and citizens flee their burning capital.

> 66 [I] looked down upon the grandest and most appalling sight that my eyes ever beheld. Richmond was literally a sea of flame, out of which the church steeples could be seen protruding here and there, while over all hung a canopy of dense black smoke, lighted up now and then by the bursting shells from the numerous arsenals scattered throughout the city. . . . The spacious capitol grounds afforded the only spot of refuge, and these were crowded with women and children, bearing in their arms and upon their heads their most cherished possessions. 99
> —R. B. Prescott

While there was certainly much destruction and misery, there were also pockets of rejoicing. African Americans joyously welcomed Union troops. Prescott went on to say that the freed slaves "hailed our appearance with the most extravagant expressions of joy. . . . 'God bless you' and 'Thank God, the Yankees have come' resounded on every side."

Grant Takes Command

At the beginning of 1864, the Confederates still hoped to keep the Union forces out of Richmond. Their war strategy was a simple one—to hold on. They knew that the North would have a presidential election in November. If the war dragged on and casualties mounted, some Southerners felt that Northern voters might replace Lincoln with a President willing to grant the South its independence. "If we can only subsist," wrote a Confederate official, "we may have peace."

At the same time, President Lincoln understood that his chances for reelection in 1864 depended on the Union's success on the battlefield. In March he summoned Ulysses S. Grant to Washington and gave him command of all Union forces. Grant's plan was to confront and crush the Confederate army and end the war before the November election.

Placing General William Tecumseh Sherman in charge in the West, Grant remained in the East to battle General Lee. He realized that Lee was running short of men and supplies. Grant now proposed to use the North's superiority in population and industry to wear down the Confederates. He ordered Sherman to do the same in the West.

Battle of the Wilderness In early May 1864, Grant moved south across the Rapidan River in Virginia with a force of some 115,000 men. Lee had about 64,000 troops. The Union army headed directly toward Richmond. Grant knew that to stop the Union advance, Lee would have to fight. In May and June the Union and Confederate armies clashed in three major battles. This was exactly what Grant wanted.

The fighting began on May 5 with the two-day **Battle of the Wilderness.** This battle occurred on virtually the same ground as the Battle of Chancellorsville the year before. The two armies met in a dense forest. The fighting was so heavy that the woods caught fire, causing many of the wounded to be burned to death. Unable to see in the smoke-filled forest, units got lost and fired on friendly soldiers, mistaking them for the enemy. One of these casualties was General Longstreet, Lee's second-in-command. He was accidentally shot and wounded by his own soldiers only three miles from where Stonewall Jackson had been shot the year before.

Grant took massive losses at the Battle of the Wilderness. However, instead of retreating as previous Union commanders had done after suffering heavy casualties, he moved his army around the Confederates and again headed south. Despite the high number of casualties, Union soldiers were proud that under Grant's leadership they would not retreat so easily.

Spotsylvania and Cold Harbor Two days later, on May 8, the Confederates caught up to the Union army near the little town of Spotsylvania Court House. The series of clashes that followed over nearly two weeks is called the **Battle of Spotsylvania.** The heaviest fighting took place on May 12. In some parts of the battlefield, the Union dead were piled four deep. When Northerners began to protest the huge loss of life, a determined Grant notified Lincoln, "I propose to fight it out on this line [course of action] if it takes all summer." Then he moved the Union army farther south.

In early June the armies clashed yet again at the **Battle of Cold Harbor,** just eight miles from Richmond. In a dawn attack on June 3, Grant launched two direct charges on the Confederates, who were behind strong fortifications. Some 7,000 Union soldiers fell—many in the first hour.

The Siege of Petersburg Unable to reach Richmond or defeat Lee's army, Grant moved his army around the capital and attacked Petersburg, a railroad center south of the city. He knew that if he could cut off shipments of food to Richmond, the city would have to surrender. However, the attack failed. In less than two months, Grant's army had suffered some 65,000 casualties. This toll

Focus on TECHNOLOGY

Civil War Submarine In 1864, the South had a secret weapon. Nothing like it had ever been seen before. It was the world's first successful military submarine, and the first such vessel to sink a ship in battle—something that would not happen again until World War I. Made from an old steam engine boiler, and cranked by hand, the Confederate *Hunley* was just 40 feet long. Once the craft submerged, the only light came from a candle. The flame would go out after about 25 minutes from lack of oxygen—a sign that the crew had better surface soon.

In February 1864, near Charleston, South Carolina, the *Hunley* rammed its torpedo into the *Housatonic,* and sank the Union ship. Then, mysteriously, the *Hunley* also sank. Now, in one of the largest recovery projects of its kind, the sub is being recovered and restored, and its crew of nine given heroes' burials.

READING CHECK
What happened at Spotsylvania and Cold Harbor?

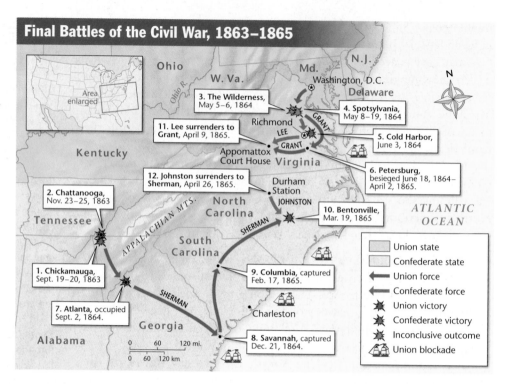

Final Battles of the Civil War, 1863–1865

Area enlarged

Ohio

W. Va.

N.J.

Washington, D.C.

Md.

Delaware

3. The Wilderness, May 5–6, 1864

4. Spotsylvania, May 8–19, 1864

Richmond

11. Lee surrenders to Grant, April 9, 1865.

LEE

GRANT

GRANT

5. Cold Harbor, June 3, 1864

Kentucky

Appomattox Court House

Virginia

6. Petersburg, besieged June 18, 1864– April 2, 1865.

12. Johnston surrenders to Sherman, April 26, 1865.

Durham Station

JOHNSTON

2. Chattanooga, Nov. 23–25, 1863

North Carolina

10. Bentonville, Mar. 19, 1865

ATLANTIC OCEAN

Tennessee

APPALACHIAN MTS.

South Carolina

1. Chickamauga, Sept. 19–20, 1863

SHERMAN

9. Columbia, captured Feb. 17, 1865.

7. Atlanta, occupied Sept. 2, 1864.

SHERMAN

Charleston

Georgia

Alabama

0   60   120 mi.

0   60   120 km

8. Savannah, captured Dec. 21, 1864.

Union state

Confederate state

Union force

Confederate force

Union victory

Confederate victory

Inconclusive outcome

Union blockade

Focus on
GEOGRAPHY

The Invasion of Florida With Union gunboats controlling the Mississippi River, the huge cattle herds of Texas were cut off from hungry Confederate armies in the East. The Confederacy looked to Florida's herds to fill the need for beef. Florida's cattle had to be driven from the central part of the state to rail lines in the north. President Lincoln, determined to block these shipments, ordered an invasion of Florida in 1864. Some 5,500 federal troops, including three regiments of African Americans, landed by sea at Jacksonville. In February, they marched westward 50 miles toward the railroad depot at Olustee. There, a slightly smaller Confederate force attacked the Union troops, who got trapped between a lake and cypress swamp. They defeated the Northerners in a six-hour battle and drove them back to Jacksonville, preserving the vital supply line. Three months after the battle of Olustee, the Union force withdrew from central Florida.

had a chilling effect on the surviving Union troops. At Cold Harbor, many soldiers pinned their names and addresses on their uniforms so their bodies could be identified.

Grant then turned to the tactic he had successfully used at Vicksburg. On June 18, 1864, he began the siege of Petersburg. Lee responded by building defenses. While he had lost many fewer men than Grant, it was becoming difficult for Lee to replace all of his casualties. He was willing to stay put and wait for the Northern election in November.

In the Shenandoah Grant recognized the importance of the Shenandoah Valley, both strategically and as a source of Southern supplies. In the summer of 1864, he told General Phil Sheridan, "Do all the damage to railroads and crops you can. . . . If the war is to last another year, we want the Shenandoah Valley to remain a barren waste." Sheridan carried out these orders to the letter.

In July 1864, one house that became a victim of Grant's policy belonged to Henrietta E. Lee. Her husband—the grandson of Revolutionary patriot and "rebel" Richard Henry Lee and a relative of Confederate General Robert E. Lee—was not at home. Henrietta Lee could not defend her home with weapons; all she had were words. She wrote the Union General a letter that began this way:

❝*General Hunter:*

Yesterday your underling, Captain Martindale, of the First New York Cavalry, executed your infamous order and burned my house. . . . the dwelling and every outbuilding, seven in number, with their contents, being burned. I, therefore, a helpless woman whom you have cruelly wronged, address you, a Major-General of the United States Army, and demand why this was done? What was my offence? My husband was absent—an exile. He has never been a politician or in any way engaged in the struggle now going on . . . The house was built by my father, a Revolutionary soldier, who served the whole seven years for your independence. There I was born; there the sacred dead repose. . . ."

—Henrietta Lee, July 20, 1864

READING CHECK

What was Grant's policy toward the Shenandoah Valley, and how was the policy carried out?

Little did Henrietta Lee know that this was just the beginning of the devastation of the South.

Sherman in Georgia

As Grant's army advanced against Lee, Sherman began to move south from Chattanooga, Tennessee, to threaten the city of Atlanta. Sherman's strategy was identical to Grant's in Virginia. He would force the main Confederate army in the West to attempt to stop his advance. If the Southern general took the bait, Sherman would destroy the enemy with his huge 98,000-man force. If the Confederates refused to fight, he would seize Atlanta, an important rail and industrial center.

The Capture of Atlanta   Sherman's opponent in Georgia was General Joseph Johnston, the Confederate commander who had been wounded at the Battle of Seven Pines in Virginia in 1862. Johnston's tactics were similar to Lee's. He would engage the Union force to block its progress. At the same time, he would not allow Sherman to deal him a crushing defeat. In this way, he hoped to delay Sherman from reaching Atlanta before the presidential elections could take place in the North.

Despite Johnston's best efforts, by mid-July 1864 the Union army was just a few miles from Atlanta. Wanting more aggressive action, Confederate president Jefferson Davis replaced Johnston with General James Hood.

The new commander gave Davis—and Sherman—exactly what they wanted. In late July, Hood engaged the Union force in a series of battles. With each clash the Southern army lost thousands of soldiers. Finally, with the Confederate forces reduced from some 62,000 to less than 45,000, General Hood retreated to Atlanta's strong defenses. Like Grant at Petersburg, Sherman laid siege to the city. Throughout the month of August, Sherman's forces bombarded Atlanta. In early September the Confederate army pulled out and left the city to the Union general's mercy.

Sherman Marches to the Sea   "War is cruelty," Sherman once wrote. "There is no use trying to reform it. The crueler it is, the sooner it will be over." It was from this viewpoint that the tough Ohio soldier conducted his military campaigns. Although a number of Union commanders considered Sherman to be mentally unstable, Grant stood by him. As a result, Sherman was fiercely loyal to his commander.

Now, Sherman convinced Grant to permit a daring move. Vowing to "make Georgia howl," in November 1864, Sherman led some 62,000 Union troops on a march to the sea to capture Savannah, Georgia. Before abandoning Atlanta, however, he ordered the city evacuated and then burned. After leaving Atlanta in ruins, Sherman's soldiers cut a

VIEWING HISTORY *General Sherman's March to the Sea* shows the destruction caused by the Union advance. **Drawing Inferences** *What kinds of destruction are the Union troops causing here? What are the strategic purposes of this destruction?*

nearly 300-mile-long path of destruction across Georgia. The Union troops destroyed bridges, factories, and railroad lines. They seized and slaughtered livestock. Grain that had recently been harvested for the Confederate troops went to Union soldiers instead.

As the Northerners approached Savannah, the small Confederate force there fled. On December 21, the Union army entered the city without a fight. "I beg to present you, as a Christmas gift, the city of Savannah," read General Sherman's message to Lincoln. For the President, it was the second piece of good news since the November election.

The Election of 1864

"I am going to be beaten," Lincoln said of his reelection chances in 1864, "and unless some great change takes place, badly beaten." Lincoln not only had to face a Democratic candidate, he also faced a brief challenge for the nomination of his own party. This challenge came from the Radical Republicans, those who were committed to emancipation and to "punishing" the South for the war. They were so angered when Lincoln pocket-vetoed the Wade-Davis Bill (which required stringent requirements for Southern states re-entering the Union), that they supported John C. Frémont for the nomination. Frémont eventually withdrew.

In an attempt to broaden Lincoln's appeal, the Republicans temporarily changed their name to the Union Party. They also dropped Vice President Hannibal Hamlin from the ticket and nominated Andrew Johnson of Tennessee to run with the President. Johnson was a Democrat and a pro-Union Southerner.

The Democrats nominated General George McClellan as their candidate. McClellan was only too happy to oppose Lincoln, who had twice fired him. The general was still loved by his soldiers, and Lincoln feared that McClellan would find wide support among the troops. McClellan promised that if elected, he would negotiate an end to the war.

Sherman's capture of Atlanta, however, changed the political climate in the North. Sensing that victory was near, Northerners became less willing to support a negotiated settlement. In November, with the help of ballots cast by Union soldiers, Lincoln won an easy victory, garnering 212 out of a possible 233 electoral votes.

A New Birth of Freedom

By reelecting Lincoln, voters showed not only their approval of his war policy, but also their increasing acceptance of his stand against slavery. Three months later, in February 1865, Congress joined Lincoln in that stand and passed the **Thirteenth Amendment** to the Constitution. It was ratified by the states and became law on December 18, 1865. In a few words, the amendment ended slavery in the United States forever:

KEY DOCUMENTS 66 *Neither slavery nor involuntary servitude, except as a punishment for crime whereof the party shall have been duly convicted, shall exist within the United States, or any place subject to their jurisdiction.* 99

—Thirteenth Amendment to the Constitution

In his Second Inaugural Address, in March 1865, Lincoln noted how slavery had divided the nation, but he also laid the groundwork for the effort to "bind up the nation's wounds."

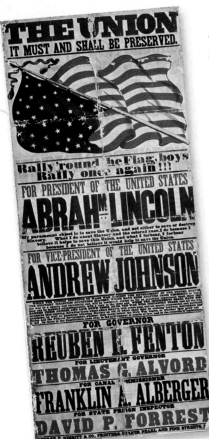

VIEWING HISTORY This campaign poster shows Lincoln running on the Union Party ticket. **Drawing Conclusions** *Do you think calling themselves the Union Party was a good strategy for the Republicans in 1864? Explain your answer.*

> " . . . It may seem strange that any men should dare ask a just God's assistance in wringing their bread from the sweat of other men's faces; but let us judge not that we be not judged. "
>
> —Lincoln's Second Inaugural, March 1865

As President Lincoln prepared to begin his second term, it was clear to most Northerners that the war was nearly over. Lincoln said, "Fondly do we hope, fervently do we pray, that this mighty scourge of war may speedily pass away."

The End of the War

As Grant strangled Richmond and Sherman prepared to move north from Savannah to join him, gloom deepened in the South. President Davis claimed that he had never really counted on McClellan's election, or on a negotiated peace. "The deep waters are closing over us," Mary Chesnut observed in her diary.

Sherman Moves North In February 1865, General Sherman's troops left Savannah and headed for South Carolina. Since it had been the first state to secede from the Union, many Northerners regarded South Carolina as the heart of the rebellion. "Here is where the treason began and, by God, here is where it shall end," wrote one Union soldier as the army marched northward.

Unlike Virginia and many other Confederate states, the Carolinas had seen relatively little fighting. Sherman had two goals as he moved toward Grant's position at Petersburg: to destroy the South's remaining resources and to crush Southerners' remaining will to fight. In South Carolina he did both. The Confederate army could do little but retreat in front of Sherman's advancing force. South Carolina was treated even more harshly than Georgia. In Georgia, for example, Union troops had burned very few of the houses that were in their path. In South Carolina, few houses were spared.

On February 17, the Union forces entered the state capital, Columbia. That night a fire burned nearly half of the city to the ground. Although no one could prove who started the fire, South Carolinians blamed Sherman's troops for the destruction. When the Union army moved into North Carolina, all demolition of civilian property ceased.

Surrender at Appomattox By April 1865, daily desertions had shrunk the Confederate army defending Richmond to fewer than 35,000 starving men. Realizing that he could no longer protect the city, on April 2 Lee tried to slip around Grant's army. He planned to unite his troops with those of General Johnston, who was retreating before Sherman's force in North Carolina. Lee hoped that together they would be able to continue the war.

Units of General Grant's army tracked the Confederates as they moved west. Each time Lee tried to turn his soldiers south, Grant's troops cut them off. On April 9, Lee's army arrived at the small Virginia town of Appomattox

Arlington National Cemetery

Arlington National Cemetery is located in Arlington, Virginia, across the Potomac River from Washington, D.C. This parcel of land once belonged to George Custis, who was the adopted son of George Washington.  After Custis's daughter Mary inherited the property, she married a young army officer named Robert E. Lee, and they lived in the mansion Custis had built. During the Civil War, the Union army seized the property and used the mansion as a headquarters. The land became a military cemetery in 1864. In an 1882 Supreme Court case, Lee's descendants finally succeeded in having the U.S. government declared a trespasser on their property. The next year, Congress appropriated $150,000 to buy the property from the Lee family. Today, Arlington is the final resting place for many of the nation's military dead, and the mansion serves as a memorial to Robert E. Lee.

? Given the circumstances of the Civil War, do you think the Union was justified in seizing this property? Explain.

After four years and more than 10,500 battles, the Civil War claimed a staggering number of casualties. **Drawing Conclusions** *How does the total number of Civil War dead compare to those killed in other U.S. wars? Why do you think this is so? How does the information in the pie chart help to explain the outcome of the war?*

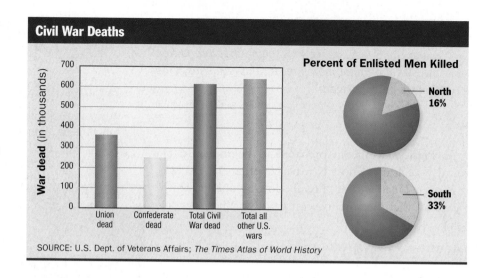

Civil War Deaths

Percent of Enlisted Men Killed

North 16%

South 33%

War dead (in thousands): 700, 600, 500, 400, 300, 200, 100, 0

Union dead | Confederate dead | Total Civil War dead | Total all other U.S. wars

SOURCE: U.S. Dept. of Veterans Affairs; *The Times Atlas of World History*

Court House. There, the Confederates were surrounded by a much larger Union force. Some of Lee's officers suggested that the army could scatter and continue to fight as **guerrillas**—soldiers who use surprise raids and hit-and-run tactics. Lee rejected this idea, fearing that it would bring more devastation to Virginia. Reluctantly he admitted, "There is nothing left for me to do but go and see General Grant, and I would rather die a thousand deaths." He knew the war was over.

That afternoon Lee and Grant met in a private home in the town. The house belonged to Wilmer McLean. He had not lived there long. In 1861, McLean had been living in Manassas, and the opening shots of the First Battle of Bull Run had landed in his front yard. To ensure the safety of his family, he had moved them away from the war—or so he thought—to the town of Appomattox Court House. Now the war was ending in his parlor.

When they met in McLean's house, General Lee was in his dress uniform, a sword at his side, and Grant was wearing his usual private's uniform, which was splattered with mud. They briefly chatted about the weather and their service in the Mexican War. Then Lee asked Grant about the terms of the surrender. These were generous. Southern soldiers could take their horses and mules and go home. They would not be punished as traitors so long as they obeyed the laws where they lived. Grant also offered to feed the starving Confederate army. After the two men signed the surrender papers, they talked for a few more minutes. Then Lee mounted his horse and rode away.

As news of the surrender spread through the Union army, soldiers began firing artillery salutes. Grant ordered the celebration stopped. He did not want rejoicing at the Southerners' misfortune because, as he pointed out, "the rebels are our countrymen again."

In the South, the news also met with mixed feelings. Nancy De Saussure recalled how she felt: "Joy and sorrow strove with each other. Joy in the hope of having my husband . . . return to me, but oh, such sorrow over our defeat!"

VIEWING HISTORY Lee surrenders to Grant at Appomattox Court House. **Making Inferences** *What do the expressions, dress, and other details of the two generals indicate about the surrender? Do you think the artist's sympathies were with the North or the South? Explain.*

Lincoln Is Assassinated

A few weeks after Lee's surrender, General Johnston surrendered to Sherman in North Carolina. Throughout May, other Confederate forces large and small also gave up.

Tragically, Abraham Lincoln did not live to see the official end of the war. Throughout the winter of 1864–1865, a group of Southern conspirators in Washington, D.C., had worked on a plan to aid the Confederacy. Led by John Wilkes Booth, a Maryland actor with strong Southern sympathies, the group plotted to kidnap Lincoln and exchange him for Confederate prisoners of war. After several unsuccessful attempts, Booth revised his plan. He assigned members of his group to kill top Union officials, including General Grant and Vice President Johnson. Booth himself would murder the President.

On April 14, 1865, Booth slipped into the back of the President's unguarded box at Ford's Theater in Washington, D.C. Inside, the President and Mrs. Lincoln were watching a play. Booth pulled out a pistol and shot Lincoln in the head. Leaping over the railing, he fell to the stage, breaking his leg in the process. Booth then limped off the stage and escaped out a back alley. The army tracked Booth to his hiding place in a tobacco barn in Virginia. When he refused to surrender, they set the barn on fire. In the confusion that followed, Booth was shot to death, either by a soldier or by himself.

Mortally wounded, the unconscious President was carried to a boardinghouse across the street from the theater. While doctors and family stood by helplessly, Lincoln lingered through the night. He died early the next morning without regaining consciousness.

In the North, citizens mourned for the loss of the President who had led them through the war. Lincoln's funeral train took 14 days to travel from the nation's capital to his hometown of Springfield, Illinois. As the procession passed through towns and cities, millions of people lined the tracks to show their respect.

Both the North and the South had suffered great losses during the war, but both also gained by it. They gained an undivided nation, a democracy that would continue to seek the equality Lincoln had promised for it. They also gained new fellow citizens—the African Americans who had broken the bonds of slavery and claimed their right to be free and equal, every one.

VIEWING HISTORY Lincoln's body was displayed in several major cities, including New York as shown here, on its way from Washington, D.C., to its resting place in Springfield, Illinois. **Drawing Conclusions** *Why do you think Lincoln was given such an elaborate funeral?*

Section 4 Assessment

READING COMPREHENSION

1. What did the **Battle of the Wilderness** reveal about Grant's strategy?
2. What happened at the **Battle of Spotsylvania** and the **Battle of Cold Harbor?**
3. What had the South hoped for in the election of 1864? Why did the election turn out differently?
4. What did the **Thirteenth Amendment** accomplish?
5. Who was John Wilkes Booth?

CRITICAL THINKING AND WRITING

6. **Analyzing Information** General Sherman said this about war: "The crueler it is, the sooner it will be over." Do you agree or disagree? Use examples from 1864 and 1865 to support your opinion.

7. **Writing an Editorial** Review the terms of surrender. Were they fair or too generous? Write the opening paragraph of an editorial stating your opinion.

For: An activity on the surrender at Appomattox
Visit: PHSchool.com
Web Code: mrd-4114

creating a CHAPTER SUMMARY

Copy the time line (right) on a piece of paper and complete it by adding the important military and political events of the Civil War. Include a brief explanation of why each event was important. You may need to continue on several sheets of paper.

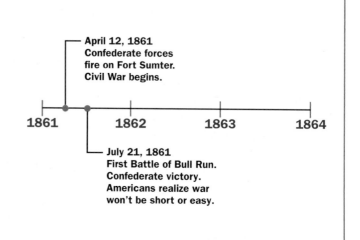

April 12, 1861
Confederate forces
fire on Fort Sumter.
Civil War begins.

| 1861 | 1862 | 1863 | 1864 |

July 21, 1861
First Battle of Bull Run.
Confederate victory.
Americans realize war
won't be short or easy.

For additional review and enrichment activities, see the interactive version of *America: Pathways to the Present*, available on the Web and on CD-ROM.

★ Reviewing Key Terms

For each of the terms below, write a sentence explaining how it relates to the Civil War.

1. First Battle of Bull Run
2. war of attrition
3. Battle of Antietam
4. Copperhead
5. martial law
6. writ of *habeas corpus*
7. contraband
8. Pickett's Charge
9. siege
10. Thirteenth Amendment

★ Reviewing Main Ideas

11. List three strengths of the North and three strengths of the South. (Section 1)

12. What gains did Union forces make in the western part of the Confederacy in the first two years of the war? (Section 1)

13. Summarize Union efforts to capture Richmond in 1861–1863. (Section 1)

14. How and why did the South seek help from Europe? (Section 2)

15. Briefly describe three emergency measures Lincoln took during the war. (Section 2)

16. How did the Emancipation Proclamation affect the war? (Section 2)

17. How was the South's economy affected by the war? (Section 2)

18. What was the significance of the Battle of Gettysburg? (Section 3)

19. Why did Vicksburg surrender, and what was the importance of this Union victory? (Section 3)

20. What were the immediate and the long-term effects of Sherman's march to the sea? (Section 4)

21. What events led to Lee's surrender? (Section 4)

★ Critical Thinking

22. **Making Comparisons** Compare the Union and Confederate military strategies.

23. **Predicting Consequences** How might the war have been different if Lincoln had appointed Grant to lead the Union forces in July 1861? Explain your answer.

24. **Testing Conclusions** Lincoln came to believe that the Union could not survive if slavery were preserved. Give evidence to support this conclusion.

25. **Synthesizing Information** Why did the Civil War cost so many more American lives than wars before or since?

★ Standardized Test Prep

Analyzing Political Cartoons ▶

26. In this cartoon, England and France look on as the Confederacy (left) and the Union (right) fight. What does the snake on the leg of the Union figure represent?

  A Confederate spies

  B Confederate army generals

  C Anti-war Democrats known as Copperheads

  D England and France

27. What is being trampled? What does it stand for?

28. What do you think the political leanings of the cartoonist are? Explain your answer.

Interpreting Data

Turn to the "Civil War Deaths" graphs on page 192.

29. Which statement BEST describes the number of Civil War dead?

  A More Confederate soldiers died than Union soldiers.

  B More soldiers died in the Civil War than in all other U.S. wars combined.

  C More Union soldiers died than Confederate soldiers.

  D Twice as many Union soldiers died as Confederate soldiers.

30. Which statement BEST describes the percent, or fraction, of the total number of enlisted men killed?

  F More than half of the soldiers who fought in the Civil War were killed.

  G A higher percentage of Confederate soldiers were killed than Union soldiers.

  H One third of all Union soldiers were killed.

  I More than a quarter of all Union soldiers were killed.

Test-Taking Tip

To answer Question 29, check each possible answer against the information on the bar graph until you determine which one is correct.

Applying the Chapter Skill

Summarizing From Multiple Sources Reread two descriptions of battle by young boys who served in the Civil War: the quotation from Elisha Stockwell at the beginning of Section 2 and the one from the drummer boy at the beginning of Section 3. Create a summary of the two sources that expresses how it felt to be in a Civil War battle.

For: Chapter 4 Self-Test

Visit: PHSchool.com

Web Code: mra-4115

American Pathways
GOVERNMENT

Federalism and States' Rights

The Framers of the Constitution based the American system of government on federalism, which is the sharing of power between the national, or federal, government and state governments. This system set up a struggle for power between the two levels of government. The Supreme Court has served as the referee in this ongoing contest, which reached its climax in the Civil War.

1 The Growth of Nationalism

1787–1828   The Constitution created a federal system of government that strengthened what had been a weak national government. In the early 1800s, a sense of nationalism, along with westward expansion, prompted Congress and the Supreme Court to become more involved in issues affecting the states.

2 Sectionalism and Civil War

1828–1865   Nationalism turned into sectionalism as the federal government's policies in support of business and trade benefited the industrial North more than the agricultural South. Southern states, demanding their states' rights, denounced tariffs imposed by the federal government as well as calls for the abolition of slavery. The inability to resolve sectional conflicts, especially the slavery issue, ignited the Civil War.

Industry in Whitneyville, Connecticut (above left), and growing cotton along the Mississippi River (below left)

3 Reconstruction

1865–1877   The federal government's power over the states peaked during Reconstruction, when Congress put the Southern states under military rule and set the conditions for their reentry into the Union.

Federal troops in Atlanta, Georgia (right)

4 Progressive Reforms

1890–1920   Cities and states often led the way in promoting Progressive reforms, which the federal government in some cases then applied to the entire nation. During this period, Congress took numerous actions to ensure the health and welfare of citizens and to prevent big businesses from limiting competition.

Two women protesting child labor (right)

5 From New Deal to Great Society

1932–1970   During the Great Depression, President Franklin Roosevelt's New Deal introduced many programs to assist the needy and regulate the economy. The federal government's involvement in areas formerly controlled by the states expanded.

6 The Civil Rights Movement

1954–1971   The Supreme Court, and later Congress, supported African Americans' efforts to secure their civil rights, despite firm resistance from state governments in the South.

Thurgood Marshall (left, center) outside the Supreme Court in Washington, D.C.

7 The Reagan Revolution

1980–Present   President Ronald Reagan sought to limit the size—and the power—of the federal government while giving more responsibility to the states. He focused especially on cutting taxes, reducing government regulations, and reforming social welfare programs. Reagan's view of government has influenced politics to the present day.

Continuity and Change

1. Why did Southern states dislike the tariffs that Congress imposed?
2. Has power been evenly balanced between the federal government and the state governments? Explain your answer.

For: A study guide on federalism and states' rights
Visit: PHSchool.com
Web Code: mrd-4129

197

Reconstruction
(1865–1877)

Andrew Johnson

Following the Civil War, the South faced the challenge of rebuilding.

American Events

1865
The Civil War ends, and Presidents Lincoln and Johnson put forth plans to pardon the South and restore the Union. The Thirteenth Amendment ends slavery.

1866
The Ku Klux Klan forms, using terror to maintain white supremacy in the South.

1867
Angered by the southern states' attempts to limit rights of African Americans, Congress takes over Reconstruction and places the South under military rule.

1868
The Fourteenth Amendment grants blacks citizenship.

1870
The Fifteenth Amendment gives blacks the right to vote, and Republicans, including hundreds of freedmen, are elected to public office in the South.

Presidential Terms: Abraham Lincoln 1861–1865   Andrew Johnson 1865–1869   Ulysses S. Grant 1869–1877

1863   **1866**   **1869**

World Events

Archduke Maximilian of Austria is made emperor of Mexico.

Russia sells Alaska to the United States.

The French-built Suez Canal opens in Egypt.

1864   **1867**   **1869**

Reuniting a War-Torn Nation

CANADA

Dakota Territory

Minnesota

Wisconsin

Michigan

New York

Maine

Vt.

N.H.

Mass.

Rhode Island

Connecticut

Nebraska Territory

Iowa

Mississippi R.

Missouri R.

Pennsylvania

New Jersey

Md.

Delaware

40°N

Colorado Territory

Kansas

Illinois

Indiana

Ohio

West Virginia

Virginia (1870)

N

70°W

Missouri

Ohio R.

Kentucky

North Carolina (1868)

Indian Territory (Unorganized)

Arkansas (1868)

Mississippi R.

Tennessee (1866)

Tennessee R.

South Carolina (1868)

ATLANTIC OCEAN

Red R.

Miss. (1870)

Alabama (1868)

Georgia (1870)

30°N

Texas (1870)

Louisiana (1868)

Florida (1868)

Gulf of Mexico

0   150   300 mi.

0   150   300 km

☐ Confederate states

☐ Other states and territories

(1868) Date of readmission to the Union

Map shows 1863 borders.

80°W

1872

By 1872, all southern states have established public schools based in part on the success of the Freedmen's Bureau schools.

1877

Reconstruction ends when President Hayes withdraws federal troops from the South and white Democrats regain control of southern politics.

Rutherford B. Hayes
1877–1881

1872

1875

1878

Britain legalizes labor unions.

1871

Slave markets are abolished in Zanzibar.

1873

Presidential Reconstruction

READING FOCUS

- What condition was the South in following the Civil War?
- How were Lincoln's and Johnson's Reconstruction plans similar?
- How did the newly freed slaves begin to rebuild their lives?

MAIN IDEA

Lincoln's and Johnson's Reconstruction plans focused on pardoning the Confederate states and restoring the Union quickly.

KEY TERMS

Reconstruction
pardon
Radical
  Republicans
pocket veto
Freedmen's
  Bureau

TARGET READING SKILL

Compare and Contrast Copy the diagram below. As you read, fill in the two circles with information about the two Presidents' Reconstruction plans. Place items that are similar in both plans in the area where the two circles overlap.

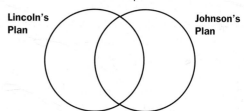

Lincoln's Plan   Johnson's Plan

Setting the Scene The Civil War was over, and throughout the summer and fall of 1865, the soldiers who had made up the great armies of the Union and the Confederacy headed home. One was former Confederate soldier Val C. Giles, of Texas:

> 66 *I reached home in Govalle, outside of Austin . . . after an absence of four years and five months. Father and mother were not expecting me and were not at home, but my dog, Brave, was on guard. . . . It was not a 'deep-mouth welcome' that greeted me as I drew near, but a gruff emphatic warning to keep out. 'Brave, old boy,' I said, 'don't you know me?' He cocked up one ear and looked at me sideways. It finally dawned on him who I was, and he . . . circled wildly all around me, expressing in his dumb way his delight at my return. . . . * 99
>
> —Val C. Giles

VIEWING HISTORY Many families eagerly awaited the return of loved ones at the end of the war. **Making Inferences** *What evidence is there in this photograph that this soldier's return home is an important event?*

Often the Confederate soldiers' homecomings contained as much sorrow as delight. Their cause had been defeated and their homes, in many cases, completely destroyed. Charleston, for example, was described by a journalist as a "city of ruins, of desolation, of vacant houses, of widowed women, of rotting wharves, of deserted warehouses, of weed-wild gardens, of miles of grass-grown streets, of acres of pitiful . . . barrenness."

Between 1865 and 1877, the federal government carried out a program to repair the damage to the South and restore the southern states to the Union. This program, known as **Reconstruction,** was hugely controversial at the time, and historians continue to debate its successes and failures to this day.

The War's Aftermath

At the start of Reconstruction, it was clear that the nation—especially the South—had been changed forever by the war. The changes reached into families and farms.

The Physical Toll War had destroyed two thirds of the South's shipping industry and about 9,000 miles of railroads. It had devoured farmland, farm buildings, and farm machinery; work animals and one third of all livestock; bridges, canals, and levees; and thousands of miles of roads. Factories, ports, and cities lay smoldering. The value of southern farm property had plunged by about 70 percent.

The Human Toll The Civil War destroyed a generation of young, healthy men—fathers, brothers, and husbands. The North lost 364,000 soldiers, including more than 38,000 African Americans. The South lost 260,000 soldiers, one fifth of its adult white men. One out of three southern men were killed or wounded. Many of the survivors were permanently scarred in mind or body. Fighting also resulted in countless civilian deaths. Children were made orphans; brides became widows.

VIEWING HISTORY This photograph of grave diggers by Alexander Gardner reminds viewers in grisly detail of the horrible human cost of the Civil War.

Southerners' Hardships The postwar South was made up of three major groups of people. Each group faced its own hardships and fears.

Black southerners Some 4 million freed people were starting their new lives in a poor region with slow economic activity. As slaves, they had received food and shelter, however inadequate. Now, after a lifetime of forced labor, many found themselves homeless, jobless, and hungry. Some freed slaves did choose to continue working on the plantations of their former masters. Others sought new jobs in the cities and in the West.

Plantation owners Planters lost slave labor worth about $3 billion. In addition, the Captured and Abandoned Property Act of 1863 allowed the federal government to seize $100 million in southern plantations and cotton. With worthless Confederate money, some farmers couldn't afford to hire workers. Others had to sell their property to cover debts.

Poor white southerners Many white laborers could not find work because of the new job competition from freedmen. Poor white families began migrating to frontier lands such as Mississippi and Texas to find new opportunities.

Punishment or Pardon? The fall of the Confederacy and the end of slavery raised difficult questions. How and when should southern states be allowed to resume their role in the Union? Should the South be punished for its actions, or be forgiven and allowed to recover quickly? Now that black southerners were free, would the races have equal rights? If so, how might those rights be protected? Did the Civil War itself point out a need for a stronger federal government? In Washington the debate over these questions launched new battles so fierce that some historians call Reconstruction an extension of the Civil War.

At stake were basic issues concerning the nation's political system. Yet it was not even clear which branch of government had the authority to decide these matters. On these key questions, the Constitution was silent. The Framers had made no provisions for solving the problems raised by the Civil War.

Sounds of an Era

Listen to "When Johnny Comes Marching Home Again" and other sounds from the Reconstruction period.

Lincoln's Reconstruction Plan

With no road map for the future, Lincoln had begun postwar planning as early as December 1863, when he proposed a Ten Percent Plan for Reconstruction. The plan was forgiving to the South:

1. It offered a **pardon,** an official forgiveness of a crime, to any Confederate who would take an oath of allegiance to the Union and accept federal policy on slavery.
2. It denied pardons to all Confederate military and government officials and to southerners who had killed African American war prisoners.
3. It permitted each state to hold a convention to create a new state constitution only after 10 percent of voters in the state had sworn allegiance to the Union.
4. States could then hold elections and resume full participation in the Union.

Lincoln's plan did not require the new constitutions to give voting rights to black Americans. Nor did it "readmit" southern states to the Union, since in Lincoln's view, their secession had not been constitutional. Lincoln set a tone of forgiveness for the postwar era in his Second Inaugural Address:

KEY DOCUMENTS

❝With malice toward none; with charity for all; with firmness in the right, as God gives us to see the right, let us strive on to finish the work we are in; to bind up the nation's wounds . . . to do all which may achieve and cherish a just, and a lasting peace, among ourselves, and with all nations.❞

—Lincoln's Second Inaugural Address, March 1865

Congress, however, saw Lincoln's Reconstruction plan as a threat to congressional authority. The Republican leadership warned that Lincoln "should confine himself to his executive duties—to obey and execute, not make the laws . . . and leave political reorganization to Congress."

Much of the opposition to Lincoln's plan for Reconstruction came from a group of congressmen from his own party. The group, known as the **Radical Republicans,** believed that the Civil War had been fought over the moral issue of slavery. The Radicals insisted that the main goal of Reconstruction should be a total restructuring of society to guarantee black people true equality.

The Radical Republicans viewed Lincoln's plan as too lenient. In July 1864 Congress passed its own, stricter Reconstruction plan, the Wade-Davis Act. Among its provisions, it required ex-Confederate men to take an oath of past and future loyalty and to swear that they had never willingly borne arms against the United States. Lincoln let the bill die in a **pocket veto.**

Lincoln's hopes came to a violent end just weeks after his second inauguration. As discussed in the previous chapter, Lincoln was murdered on April 14, 1865, by John Wilkes Booth. The assassination plunged the nation into grief and its politics into chaos.

Johnson's Reconstruction Plan

With Lincoln's death, Reconstruction was now in the hands of a one-time slave owner from the South: the former Vice President, Andrew Johnson. Born poor in North Carolina, Johnson grew up to become a tailor. He learned to read and write with the help of his wife and later entered politics in Tennessee as a Democrat.

Johnson had a profound hatred of rich planters and found strong voter support among poor white southerners. He served Tennessee first as governor, then in Congress. Johnson was the only southern senator to remain in Congress after secession. Hoping to attract Democratic voters, the Republican Party chose Johnson as Lincoln's running mate in 1864.

When Johnson took office in April 1865, Congress was in recess until December. During those eight months, Johnson pursued his own plan for the South. His plan, known as Presidential Reconstruction, included the following provisions:

1. It pardoned southerners who swore allegiance to the Union.
2. It permitted each state to hold a constitutional convention (without Lincoln's 10 percent allegiance requirement).
3. States were required to void secession, abolish slavery, and repudiate the Confederate debt.
4. States could then hold elections and rejoin the Union.

Presidential Reconstruction reflected the spirit of Lincoln's Ten Percent Plan but was more generous to the South. Although officially it denied pardons to all Confederate leaders, in reality Johnson often issued pardons to those who asked him personally. In 1865 alone, he pardoned 13,000 southerners.

The Taste of Freedom

As politicians debated, African Americans celebrated their new freedom. No longer were they treated as mere property, subject to the whims of white slave owners. The feeling was overwhelming. "Everybody went wild," said Charles Ames, a Georgia freedman. "We all felt like horses. . . . We was free. Just like that, we was free."

Booker T. Washington, a future leader in black education, was 9 years old when the news came: "[W]e were told that we were all free and could go when and where we pleased. My mother, who was standing by my side, leaned over and kissed her children, while tears of joy ran down her cheeks."

Focus on
GOVERNMENT

Pocket Veto *If Congress adjourns its session within ten days of submitting a bill to the President, and the President does not act, the bill dies. This is known as a pocket veto.*

The Historical Context In an effort to balance the powers of the President and the Congress, the Constitution grants the President the power to veto, or "refuse to sign," congressional legislation. Although it is rare, the House and Senate may pass a bill over the President's veto by a two-thirds vote of the members present in each house.

The Concept Today Most Presidents use the pocket veto frequently because Congress regularly passes a large number of measures in the closing days of its annual session.

READING CHECK
How did the Radical Republicans' Reconstruction plan differ from Lincoln and Johnson's plans?

Freedom brought new educational opportunities for African Americans both young and old. The young boy pictured below is holding a book furnished by the Freedmen's Bureau. **Drawing Inferences** *(a) Which person in the photograph to the right is the teacher? (b) What is the approximate age span of the students?*

Edmund Commander, after your boxes came

Freedom of Movement

During the war, enslaved people had simply walked away from the plantations upon hearing that a northern army was approaching. "Right off colored folks started on the move," said James, a freed cowhand from Texas. "They seemed to want to get closer to freedom, so they'd know what it was like—like it was a place or a city." Many freed people took to the roads looking for family members who had been torn from them by slavery. Not all were successful in finding loved ones, but many joyful reunions did occur.

Freedom to Own Land

Black leaders knew that emancipation—physical freedom—was only a start. True freedom would come only with economic independence, the ability to get ahead through hard work.

Freed people urged the federal government to redistribute southern land. They argued that they were entitled to the land that slaves had cleared and farmed for generations. A Virginia freedman put it this way: "We have a right to the land where we are located. For why? I tell you. Our wives, our children, our husbands, have been sold over and over again to purchase the lands we now locate upon; for that reason we have a divine right to the land."

Proposals to give white-owned land to freedmen got little political support. In 1865, Union general William Tecumseh Sherman had set up a land-distribution experiment in South Carolina. He divided confiscated coastal lands into 40-acre plots and gave them to black families. Soon the South buzzed with rumors that the government was going to give all freedmen "forty acres and a mule." Sherman's project was short-lived, however. President Johnson eventually returned much of the land to its original owners, forcing the freedmen out. In place of programs like Sherman's, small-scale, unofficial land redistribution took place. For example, in 1871 Amos Morel, a freedman who stayed on to work on the plantation where he had been enslaved in Georgia, used his wages to buy more than 400 acres of land. He sold pieces to other freedmen and later bought land for his daughter.

Focus on
CULTURE

Marriage and Family Upon gaining their freedom, African Americans could live together without fear of separation from their family members. Many legalized their marriages and adopted the children of deceased friends and relatives rather than send them to Freedmen's Bureau orphanages. Although a far higher percentage of black than white women and children continued to work outside their homes, African American families now had control of their own labor.

Freedom to Worship In their struggle to survive, African Americans looked to each other for help. New black organizations arose throughout the South. The most visible were churches. African Americans throughout the South formed their own churches. They also started thousands of voluntary groups, including mutual aid societies, debating clubs, drama societies, and trade associations.

Freedom to Learn Historians estimate that in 1860, nearly 90 percent of black adults were illiterate, partly because many southern states had banned educating slaves. One supporter of black education was Charlotte Forten, a wealthy black woman from Philadelphia. In 1862, after Union troops occupied Port Royal, South Carolina, Forten went there to teach. She observed:

> " I never before saw children so eager to learn. Coming to school is a constant delight and recreation to them. . . . Many of the grown people [also] are desirous of learning to read. It is wonderful how a people who have been so long crushed to the earth . . . can have so great a desire for knowledge, and such a capability for attaining it. "

—Charlotte Forten

Help came from several directions. White teachers, often young women, went south to start schools. Some freed people taught themselves and one another. Between 1865 and 1870, black educators founded 30 African American colleges.

The Freedmen's Bureau To help black southerners adjust to freedom, Congress created the **Freedmen's Bureau** in March 1865, just prior to Lincoln's death. It was the first major federal relief agency in United States history.

The Freedmen's Bureau lacked strong support in Congress, and the agency was largely dismantled in 1869. Yet in its short existence the bureau gave out clothing, medical supplies, and millions of meals to both black and white war refugees. More than 250,000 African American students received their first formal education in bureau schools.

Ho for Kansas!

Brethren, Friends, & Fellow Citizens:
I feel thankful to inform you that the
REAL ESTATE
AND
Homestead Association,
Will Leave Here the
15th of April, 1878,
In pursuit of Homes in the Southwestern Lands of America, at Transportation Rates, cheaper than ever was known before.
For full information inquire of
Benj. Singleton, better known as old Pap,
NO. 5 NORTH FRONT STREET.
Beware of Speculators and Adventurers, as it is a dangerous thing to fall in their hands.
Nashville, Tenn., March 18, 1878.

VIEWING HISTORY This ad from a Nashville, Tennessee, newspaper invites African Americans to emigrate to Kansas to find new homes. **Drawing Inferences** *(a) What can you infer were some of the chief obstacles to emigration for African Americans? (b) Who was Benjamin Singleton?*

Section 1 Assessment

READING COMPREHENSION

1. Why was a period of **Reconstruction** necessary following the end of the Civil War?

2. Who was **pardoned** under Johnson's Reconstruction plan?

3. Who were the **Radical Republicans?**

4. What was the **Freedmen's Bureau?**

CRITICAL THINKING AND WRITING

5. **Analyzing Information** Create a list of economic challenges that southerners faced after the Civil War.

6. **Writing an Outline** Create an outline for a persuasive essay in which you argue in favor of or against the redistribution of land from whites to blacks during Reconstruction.

Go Online
PHSchool.com

For: An activity on the Freedmen's Bureau
Visit: PHSchool.com
Web Code: mrd-4121

READING FOCUS

- How were black codes and the Four-teenth Amendment related?

- How did Congress's Reconstruction plan differ from Johnson's plan?

- What was the significance of the Fifteenth Amendment?

- Who supported the Republican govern-ments of the South?

MAIN IDEA

As southern states moved to limit freedmen's rights, Congress took over Reconstruction and passed new laws to protect African Americans' freedom.

KEY TERMS

black codes
Fourteenth
  Amendment
civil rights
impeach
Fifteenth
  Amendment
carpetbagger
scalawag

TARGET READING SKILL

Identify Cause and Effect Create a cause-and-effect diagram like the one below. As you read, fill in the chart with the causes and effects discussed in the section.

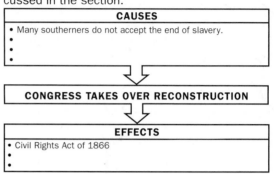

CAUSES
- Many southerners do not accept the end of slavery.
-
-

CONGRESS TAKES OVER RECONSTRUCTION

EFFECTS
- Civil Rights Act of 1866
-
-

Setting the Scene

For many African Americans, the initial surge of joy at gaining freedom quickly faded as they realized how many obstacles stood between them and true equality. Defeat in war had not changed the fact that white people still dominated southern society. As one white Georgian noted:

> 66 *[The freedman] has no land; he can make no crops. . . . He can scarcely get work anywhere but in the rice-fields and cotton planta-tions. . . . What sort of freedom is that?* 99

Under Johnson's plan for Reconstruction, former Confederates were par-doned, state governments were restored, and the white leaders of those govern-ments acted quickly to pass laws that severely restricted African Americans' newfound freedoms. These laws were known collectively as black codes.

Black Codes

One by one, southern states met Johnson's Reconstruction demands and were restored to the Union. The first order of business in these new, white-run governments was to enact **black codes**, laws that restricted freedmen's rights. The black codes established virtual slav-ery with provisions such as these:

Curfews Generally, black people could not gather after sunset.

Vagrancy laws Freedmen convicted of vagrancy—that is, not work-ing—could be fined, whipped, or sold for a year's labor.

Labor contracts Freedmen had to sign agreements in January for a year of work. Those who quit in the middle of a contract often lost all the wages they had earned.

Land restrictions Freed people could rent land or homes only in rural areas. This restriction forced them to live on plantations.

VIEWING HISTORY According to Florida's black codes, a freed-man without visible means of sup-port could be fined. If the fine was not paid, the freedman's services could be auctioned off, as shown here. **Drawing Conclusions** *How does this photograph support the claim that black codes established virtual slavery?*

The Fourteenth Amendment

Southern defiance of Reconstruction enraged northern Republicans in Congress who blamed President Johnson for southern Democrats' return to power. Determined to bypass Johnson and put an end to his Reconstruction plan, Congress used one of its greatest tools: the power to amend the Constitution.

In early 1866, Congress passed a Civil Rights Act that outlawed the black codes. Johnson vetoed the measure. As President, Johnson was head of the Republican Party. Yet instead of leading congressional Republicans, he often found himself at odds with them. As an unelected former Democrat, Johnson had no real mandate to govern. (A mandate is voter approval of a politician's policies that is implied when he or she wins an election.) Lack of a mandate greatly affected Johnson's ability to influence Congress.

Congress overrode the President's veto. Then it took further action. Concerned that courts might strike down the Civil Rights Act, Congress decided to build equal rights into the Constitution. In June 1866, Congress passed the **Fourteenth Amendment,** which was ratified by the states in 1868. The amendment was a turning point, and its effects have echoed throughout American history. The amendment states:

KEY DOCUMENTS 66 *All persons born or naturalized in the United States . . . are citizens of the United States and of the State wherein they reside. No State shall make or enforce any law which shall abridge the privileges or immunities of citizens of the United States; nor shall any State deprive any person of life, liberty, or property, without due process of law; nor deny to any person within its jurisdiction the equal protection of the laws. . . .* 99

—Fourteenth Amendment, Section 1

Radical Reconstruction

The congressional Republicans who drafted the Fourteenth Amendment consisted of two major groups. One group was the Radical Republicans. Radicals were small in number but increasingly influential. Most Republicans, however, saw themselves as moderates. In politics, a moderate is someone who supports the mainstream views of the party, not the more extreme positions.

Moderates and Radicals both opposed Johnson's Reconstruction policies, opposed the spread of black codes, and favored the expansion of the Republican Party in the South. But moderates were less enthusiastic over the Radicals' goal of granting African Americans their **civil rights,** citizens' personal liberties guaranteed by law, such as voting rights and equal treatment. (See Focus on Government.) Racial inequality was still common in the North, and moderates did not want to impose stricter laws on the South than those in the North.

The North Grows Impatient This reluctance to grant civil rights began to dissolve in early 1866, as word spread of new violence against African Americans. In April, the famous Civil War nurse Clara Barton gave graphic testimony in Congress about injured black victims she had treated. During the next three months, white rioters went on rampages against African Americans in Memphis, Tennessee; New Orleans, Louisiana; and New York City. White police sometimes joined in the stabbings, shootings, and hangings that killed hundreds.

Focus on GOVERNMENT

Civil Rights *The rights to which every citizen is entitled.*

The Historical Context The first Civil Rights Act, in 1866, guaranteed citizenship to African Americans. The second, in 1875, guaranteed them equal rights in public places. More fundamentally, in 1868, the Fourteenth Amendment made protection of civil rights part of the Constitution.

The Concept Today Violations of African Americans' civil rights continued and even increased following Reconstruction. Nearly a century later, the civil rights movement of the 1950s and 1960s fought to erase laws that discriminated against African Americans. Today it is illegal to discriminate on the basis of race.

READING CHECK
How did moderate Republicans in Congress differ from the Radical Republicans?

MAP SKILLS President Lincoln had hoped to restore southern state governments to "successful operation, with order prevailing and the Union reestablished," by December 1865. Under Radical Republican rule, however, this did not happen for more than a decade. Because of its adherence to Congressional demands, Tennessee was the only southern state not placed under northern military rule. **Place** (a) Which state was the first to rejoin the Union? (b) How do you think southerners reacted to military rule by northern generals?

Radical Rule of the South

Military District and Commander
- General Phillip Sheridan
- General Edward Ord
- General John Pope
- General Daniel Sickles
- General John Schofield
- (1868) Date of readmission to Union

Senator Charles Sumner of Massachusetts (top) and Thaddeus Stevens, a Congressman from Pennsylvania, were both leading spokesmen for the Radical Republicans in their fight to win civil rights for African Americans.

Despite public outrage against the brutality, Johnson continued to oppose equal rights for African Americans. In the 1866 congressional elections, he gave speeches urging states not to ratify the Fourteenth Amendment. Angry northern voters responded by sweeping Radical Republicans into Congress. Now, Radicals could put their own Reconstruction plans into action.

Strict Laws Imposed   Calling for "reform, not revenge," Radicals in Congress passed the Reconstruction Act of 1867. Historians note that this was indeed a "radical" act in American history. These are its key provisions:

1. It put the South under military rule, dividing it into five districts, each governed by a northern general. (See the map on this page.)
2. It ordered southern states to hold new elections for delegates to create new state constitutions.
3. It required states to allow all qualified male voters, including African Americans, to vote in the elections.
4. It temporarily barred those who had supported the Confederacy from voting.
5. It required southern states to guarantee equal rights to all citizens.
6. It required the states to ratify the Fourteenth Amendment.

Congress and the President   The stage was now set for a showdown that pitted President Johnson against two powerful Radical Republicans in Congress. Massachusetts Senator Charles Sumner, a founder of the Republican Party, was a passionate abolitionist who sought voting rights for black Americans. In the House, Johnson faced Thaddeus Stevens, a Pennsylvania congressman with a stern face and a personality to match. Stevens led the charge that threatened to bring down Johnson's presidency.

At face value, the contest was a test of wills between the President and his congressional adversaries. Yet it was also a power struggle between the legislative and executive branches of government, a test of the system of checks and balances established by the Constitution.

A Power Struggle   The crisis began in early 1868, when Johnson tried to fire Secretary of War Edwin Stanton, a Lincoln appointee. Johnson wanted Stanton removed because, under the new Reconstruction Act, Stanton, a friend of the Radicals, would preside over military rule of the South.

The firing of Stanton directly challenged the Tenure of Office Act just passed by Congress in 1867. The act placed limits on the President's power to hire and fire government officials. Under the Constitution, the President must seek Senate approval for candidates to fill certain jobs, such as Cabinet posts.

The Tenure of Office Act demanded that the Senate approve the firing of those officials as well, thereby limiting the President's power to create an administration to his own liking. The Command of the Army Act also took away the President's constitutional powers as commander in chief of the armed forces.

Johnson Is Impeached   Led by the fiery Stevens, the House found that Johnson's firing of Stanton was unconstitutional. On February 24, 1868, House members voted 126 to 47 to **impeach** him—to charge him with wrongdoing in office. The House drafted 11 articles of impeachment, including violation of the Tenure of Office Act and bringing "into disgrace, ridicule, hatred, contempt, and reproach the Congress of the United States." Johnson became the first President in United States history to be impeached.

As called for by the Constitution, the Senate tried President Andrew Johnson for "high crimes and misdemeanors." Chief Justice Salmon P. Chase presided over the proceedings. If two thirds of the senators were to vote for conviction, Johnson would become the only President ever removed from office. The historic vote took place on May 16, 1868. When all the "ayes" and "nays" were counted, Johnson had escaped by the closest of margins: one vote. The crisis set the precedent that only the most serious crimes, and not merely a partisan dispute with Congress, could remove a President from office.

Grant Is Elected   President Johnson, as the saying goes, "won the battle but lost the war." He served the remaining months of his term, but with no mandate and no real power. Rejected by the party that had never really embraced him, Johnson went back to Tennessee and regained his Senate seat—as a Democrat.

In the 1868 election, Republicans chose a trusted candidate who was one of their own: the victorious Civil War general, Ulysses S. Grant. In a close race, Grant beat Democrat Horatio Seymour, former governor of New York. Now, Congress and the President were allies, not enemies.

The Fifteenth Amendment

Across the South, meanwhile, freedmen were beginning to demand the rights of citizenship: to vote, to hold public office, to serve on juries, and to testify in court. In a letter to the Tennessee constitutional convention, Nashville freedmen eloquently presented the case for black voting rights:

> 66 If [freedmen] are good law-abiding citizens, praying for its [the nation's] prosperity, rejoicing in its progress, paying its taxes, fighting its battles, making its farms, mines, work-shops and commerce more productive, why deny them the right to have a voice in the election of its rulers? 99
>
> —The "black citizens of Nashville," January 9, 1865

The letter received no known response. Yet African Americans, and their supporters in Congress, pressed on.

President Johnson was the first President to be impeached by the House of Representatives. The Senate found Johnson innocent, and he was not removed from office.

**Blanche K. Bruce
1841–1898**

A boy born into slavery in 1841 could expect little more than a life of servitude. Blanche K. Bruce was more fortunate than some. Growing up in Virginia and Missouri, he shared a tutor with his master's son. Later he attended Oberlin College in Ohio, until his money ran out. Bruce then moved to Mississippi and began recruiting Republicans from among freedmen on the plantations. In 1871 he ran for sheriff of Bolivar County, Mississippi. Bruce won the sheriff's post, and later held other government jobs as well. As a public servant, he worked to ease racial and political tensions, earning respect from Radical and moderate Republicans— even white planters. In 1874 Bruce won election to the United States Senate.

READING CHECK

How did the Fifteenth Amendment influence the composition of southern state legislatures?

In February 1869, at the peak of Radical power, Congress passed the **Fifteenth Amendment** to the Constitution. It stated that no citizen may be denied the right to vote "by the United States or by any State on account of race, color, or previous condition of servitude." Ratified in March 1870, the Fifteenth Amendment was one of the enduring legacies of Reconstruction.

The Supreme Court added its weight to the federal Reconstruction effort in 1869. In *Texas* v. *White,* the Court ruled that it was illegal for any state to secede from the Union. The case also upheld Congress's right to restructure southern governments. The ruling added new support for federal power over states' rights.

The First Votes   Even before the Fifteenth Amendment was ratified, the military had begun to register freedmen under the Reconstruction Act of 1867. Nearly 735,000 African Americans joined the voting rolls and their electoral power transformed politics in the South.

In 1867 and 1868, voters in southern states chose delegates to draft new state constitutions. Nearly 80 percent of the newly registered African American voters went to the polls, while most registered white voters did not participate. As a result, one quarter of the more than 1,000 delegates elected to the ten state conventions were black. In two states where African Americans outnumbered whites, Louisiana and South Carolina, voters chose majority-black delegations.

These integrated conventions wrote new constitutions for their states. Provisions in the new constitutions guaranteed the civil rights of all residents, opened political office to individuals without regard to wealth, and set up a system of public schools and orphanages. Ten Reconstruction state governments quickly adopted the new constitutions.

Electing Black Leaders   In 1870, with federal troops stationed across the South and with the Fifteenth Amendment in place, southern black men proudly voted in legislative elections for the first time. Most voted Republican, while many angry white voters again stayed home.

The results were dramatic. Before the election, African American voters made up a majority in five states—Alabama, Florida, Louisiana, Mississippi, and South Carolina—and a substantial minority in the other states undergoing Reconstruction. The unique circumstances of the election swept Republicans, including hundreds of freedmen, into public office in the South.

More than 600 African Americans were elected to state legislatures. However, African Americans remained the minority in nearly every state house in the South. The sole exception was South Carolina, where black legislators controlled the lower house and even, for a short time, the state senate. Individual black leaders could rise to positions of power in state government through alliances with white Republicans.

Louisiana gained a black governor, P.B.S. Pinchback, who had settled in that state after fighting for the Union during the Civil War. During Reconstruction, Pinchback had served as a state senator and eventually became lieutenant governor and then governor in 1872.

Integrating the Capitol   The extension of the vote to freedmen led to the election of the first African Americans to the House of Representatives. Despite resistance from other representatives, their number gradually rose to eight by 1875.

In 1870, Hiram Revels of Mississippi became the first African American elected to the Senate. Four years later, Mississippi's state legislature sent to the Senate a former slave, Blanche K. Bruce. (See American Biography.) Louisiana chose P.B.S. Pinchback to represent it in the Senate, but other senators voted not to seat him in 1876. By that time, the climate in Washington, D.C., and the southern states had begun to shift against African American legislators.

The Republican South

During Radical Reconstruction, the Republican Party was a mixture of people who had little in common but a desire to prosper in the postwar South. This bloc of voters included freedmen and two other groups.

Carpetbaggers Northern Republicans who moved to the postwar South became known as **carpetbaggers.** Southerners gave them this insulting nickname, which referred to a type of cheap suitcase made from carpet scraps. The name implied that these northerners had stuffed some clothes into a carpetbag and rushed in to profit from southern misery.

A northerner's carpetbag

Carpetbaggers were often depicted as greedy men seeking to grab power or make a fast buck. Certainly the trainloads of northerners who disembarked in southern cities included some profiteers and swindlers. Yet historians point out that most carpetbaggers were honest, educated men. They included former union soldiers, black northerners, Freedmen's Bureau officials, businessmen, clergy, and political leaders.

Scalawags In the postwar South, to be white and a southerner and a Republican was to be seen as a traitor. Southerners had an unflattering name for white southern Republicans as well: **scalawag,** originally a Scottish word meaning "scrawny cattle." Some scalawags were former Whigs who had opposed secession. Some were small farmers who resented the planter class. Still others were former planters. Many scalawags, but not all, were poor.

Many southern whites, resenting the power of freedmen, carpetbaggers, and scalawags, criticized the Reconstruction governments as corrupt and incompetent. In reality, Reconstruction legislatures included honest men and dishonest men, qualified politicians and incompetent ones, literate men and a few illiterate ones. Today, most historians agree that these officials were no worse and no better than officials in other regions of the country at that time.

Section 2 Assessment

READING COMPREHENSION

1. Why were northern Republicans in Congress enraged by the **black codes** and the reports of violence against African Americans?

2. How did the moderate and Radical Republicans in Congress disagree over African American **civil rights?**

3. Who were the **carpetbaggers** and the **scalawags?**

CRITICAL THINKING AND WRITING

4. Drawing Conclusions How was the impeachment of Andrew Johnson a test of the Constitution's system of checks and balances?

5. Comparing Points of View Describe the gains made by African Americans under Radical Reconstruction governments in the South. How did white Democrats perceive Radical rule?

Go Online PHSchool.com

For: An activity on carpetbaggers
Visit: PHSchool.com
Web Code: mrd-4122

Birth of the "New South"

READING FOCUS

- How did farming in the South change after the Civil War?
- How did the growth of cities and industry begin to change the South's economy after the war?
- How was the money designated for Reconstruction projects used?

MAIN IDEA

The end of slavery brought about new patterns of agriculture in the South, while expansion of cities and industry led to limited economic growth.

KEY TERMS

sharecropping
tenant farming
infrastructure

TARGET READING SKILL

Identify Supporting Details Copy the chart below. As you read, fill in details about economic changes that occurred in the South during Reconstruction.

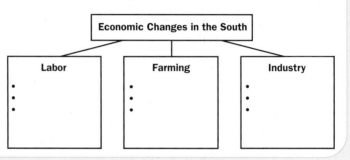

Economic Changes in the South

Labor	Farming	Industry
• • •	• • •	• • •

Setting the Scene Writing to a South Carolina newspaper late in 1865, a black soldier in the United States Army stated:

> ❝ *We have been faithful in the field . . . and think that we ought to be considered as men, and allowed a fair chance in the race of life. It has been said that a black man can not make his own living, but give us opportunities and we will show the whites that we will not come to them for any thing.* ❞
>
> —Black Union soldier

This demand for a "fair chance in the race of life" was echoed by freedmen across the South. For most of them, the key to that fair chance was land. "Give us our own land and we can take care of ourselves," said one freedman, "but without land, our old masters can hire us or starve us as they please."

As you read in Section 1, proposals to distribute formerly white-owned land to freedmen received little political support. Few freedmen had the money to buy their own land, and even those who did often found that whites refused to sell or rent land to them. As a result, most freedmen had little choice but to work the land of others. They soon discovered, in one freedman's words, that "No man can work another man's land [without getting] poorer and poorer every year."

One black family in Alabama learned this lesson the hard way. The Holtzclaw family worked on the cotton farm of a white planter. Every year at harvest time they received part of the cotton crop as payment for their work. Most years, however, the Holtzclaws' share of the harvest didn't earn them enough money to feed themselves. Some years the planter gave them nothing at all. To earn more money, Mrs. Holtzclaw worked as a cook, while Mr. Holtzclaw hauled logs at a sawmill for 60 cents a day. Their children waded knee-deep in swamps gathering anything edible. This was not the freedom they had hoped for.

VIEWING FINE ART Despite emancipation, the cotton still needed to be picked. This painting by Winslow Homer (1876) shows young women in the fields, probably working just as their mothers had before the war, except for some small wages. **Making Comparisons** *Compare the details in this painting to the photograph on the next page.*

Changes in Farming

The Holtzclaws were part of an economic reorganization in the "New South" of the 1870s. It was triggered by the ratification of the Thirteenth Amendment in 1865, which ended slavery and shook the economic foundations of the South.

The loss of slave labor raised grave questions for southern agriculture. Would cotton still be king? If so, who would work the plantations? Would freed people flee the South or stay? How would black emancipation affect the poor white laborers of the South? No one really knew.

Wanted: Workers Although the Civil War left southern plantations in tatters, the destruction was not permanent. Many planters had managed to hang on to their land, and others regained theirs after paying off their debt. Planters complained, however, that they couldn't find people willing to work for them. Nobody liked picking cotton in the blazing sun. It seemed too much like slavery. Workers often disappeared to look for better, higher-paying jobs. For instance, railroad workers in Virginia in the late 1860s earned $1.75 to $2 a day. Plantation wages came to 50 cents a day at best. Women in the fields earned as little as 6 cents a day. In simple terms, planters had land but no laborers, while freedmen had their own labor but no land. Out of these needs came new patterns of farming in the South.

Sharecropping The most common new farming arrangement was known as **sharecropping.** A sharecropping family, such as the Holtzclaws, farmed some portion of a planter's land. As payment, the family was promised a share of the crop at harvest time, generally one third or one half of the yield. The planter usually provided housing for the family.

Sharecroppers worked under close supervision and under the threat of harsh punishment. They could be fined for missing a single workday. After the harvest, some dishonest planters simply evicted the sharecroppers without pay. Others charged the families for housing and other expenses, so that the sharecroppers often wound up in debt at the end of the year. Since they could not leave before paying the debt, these sharecroppers were trapped on the plantation.

INTERPRETING DIAGRAMS
Whether white or black, most southern farmers remained poor in the years following the Civil War—as did this Florida family (below right), thought to be sharecroppers or tenant farmers. The chart (below left) shows the cycle of debt that poor families faced. **Drawing Conclusions** *How did farmers get caught in a cycle of debt?*

Sharecropping and the Cycle of Debt

1. Poor whites and freedmen have no jobs, no homes, and no money to buy land.

2. Poor whites and freedmen sign contracts to work a landlord's acreage in exchange for a part of the crop.

3. Landlord keeps track of the money that sharecroppers owe him for housing and food.

4. At harvest time, the sharecropper owes more to the landlord than his share of the crop is worth.

5. Sharecropper cannot leave the farm as long as he is in debt to the landlord.

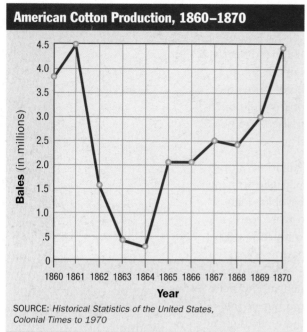

American Cotton Production, 1860–1870

Bales (in millions)

SOURCE: *Historical Statistics of the United States, Colonial Times to 1970*

INTERPRETING GRAPHS
Cotton production was the South's main economic activity until 1930.
Making Inferences *What accounts for the drop in production in the middle of this graph?*

READING CHECK
In what ways did the end of slavery change agriculture in the South?

Tenant Farming If a sharecropper saved enough money, he might try **tenant farming.** Like sharecroppers, tenant farmers did not own the land they farmed. Unlike sharecroppers, however, tenant farmers paid to rent the land, just as you might rent an apartment today. Tenants chose which crops to plant and when and how much to work. As a result, the tenant farmers had a higher social status than sharecroppers.

The Holtzclaws managed to move from sharecropping to tenant farming. They rented 40 acres of land. They bought a mule, a horse, and a team of oxen. William Holtzclaw was a child at the time. "We were so happy at the prospects of owning a wagon and a pair of mules, and having only our father for boss, that we shouted and leaped for joy," he later recalled.

Effects on the South Changes in farming during Reconstruction affected the long-term health of the South's economy in several important ways:

Changes in the labor force Before the Civil War, 90 percent of the South's cotton was harvested by African American slaves. By 1875, white laborers, mostly tenant farmers, picked 40 percent of the crop.

Emphasis on cash crops Sharecropping and tenant farming encouraged planters to grow cash crops, such as cotton, tobacco, and sugar cane, rather than food crops. The South's postwar cotton production soon surpassed prewar levels. As a result of the focus on cash crops, the South had to import much of its food.

Cycle of debt By the end of Reconstruction, rural poverty was deeply rooted in the South, among blacks and whites alike. Both groups remained in a cycle of debt, in which this year's profits went to pay last year's bills. The Southern Homestead Act of 1866 attempted to break that cycle by offering low-cost land to southerners, black or white, who would farm it. By 1874, black farmers in Georgia owned 350,000 acres. Still, most landless farmers could not afford to participate in the land-buying program. In the cotton states, only about one black family in 20 owned land after a decade of Reconstruction.

Rise of merchants Tenant farming created a new class of wealthy southerners: the merchants. Throughout the South, stores sprang up around plantations to sell supplies on credit. "We have stores at almost every crossroad," a journalist observed. By 1880, the South had more than 8,000 rural stores. Some merchants were honest; others were not. Landlords frequently ran their own stores and forced their tenants to buy there at high prices.

After four years of tenant farming, the Holtzclaws watched as creditors carted away everything they owned. "They came and took our corn and, finally, the vegetables from our little garden, as well as the chickens and the pig," Holtzclaw said. The family had no choice but to return to sharecropping.

Cities and Industry

Southerners who visited the North after the Civil War were astounded at how industrialized the North had become. The need for large-scale production of war supplies had turned small factories into big industries that dominated the North's economy. Industrialization had produced a new class of wage earners.

It had ignited city growth and generated wealth. Could all this happen in the South?

Some southern leaders saw a unique opportunity for their region. They urged the South to build a new, industrialized economy. One of the pro-business voices was that of Henry Grady, editor of the *Atlanta Constitution*. He called for a "New South" of growing cities and thriving industries.

The Growth of Cities Atlanta, the city so punished by Sherman's army, took Grady's advice. Only months after the war, the city was on its way to becoming a major metropolis of the South, as one observer noted:

> ❝ A new city is springing up with marvelous rapidity. The narrow and irregular and numerous streets are alive from morning till night . . . with a never-ending throng of . . . eager and excited and enterprising men, all bent on building and trading and swift fortune-making. ❞
> —Visitor to Atlanta, 1865

San Antonio, Texas, prospered following the Civil War as a mercantile and cattle center. This 1872 photo shows a view of the east side of Main Plaza.

A major focus of Reconstruction, and one of its greatest successes, was the rebuilding and extension of southern railroads. By 1872, southern railroads were totally rebuilt and about 3,300 miles of new track laid, a 40 percent increase. Railroads turned southern villages into towns, and towns into cities where businesses and trade could flourish. Commerce and population rose not only in Atlanta, but also in Richmond, Nashville, Memphis, Louisville, Little Rock, Montgomery, and Charlotte. On the western frontier, the Texas towns of Dallas, Houston, and Fort Worth were on the rise.

Limits of Industrial Growth Despite these changes, Reconstruction did not transform the South into an industrialized, urban region like the North. Most southern factories did not make finished goods such as furniture. They handled only the early, less profitable stages of manufacturing, such as producing lumber or pig iron. These items were shipped north to be made into finished products and then sold.

Most of the South's postwar industrial growth came from cotton mills. New factories began to spin and weave cotton into undyed fabric. The value of cotton mill production in South Carolina rose from about $713,000 in 1860 to nearly $3 million by 1880. However, the big profits went to northern companies that dyed the fabric and sold the finished product.

Funding Reconstruction

The Republicans who led Congress agreed with southern legislatures on the importance of promoting business. The strong conviction that the growth of business would bring better times for everyone was called the "gospel of prosperity." It guided the Reconstruction efforts of Congress and the Reconstruction legislatures throughout the 1870s.

Raising Money In a sense, the postwar South was one giant business opportunity. The region's **infrastructure,** the public property and services that a society uses, had to be almost completely rebuilt. That included roads, bridges, canals, railroads, and telegraph lines. In addition to the rebuilding effort, some states used Reconstruction funds

Focus on CITIZENSHIP

Achievements of Black Legislators
Thomas E. Miller defended the work of the South Carolina legislature in which he served: "We had built school

houses, established charitable institutions . . . rebuilt bridges and reestablished ferries. In short, we had reconstructed the State and placed it upon the road to prosperity." The lithograph above shows seven African Americans who were elected to the United States Congress.

"I BEG TO REPEAT THAT THESE FRAUDS ON THE GOVERNMENT SHALL BE PROBED TO THE VERY BOTTOM."

INTERPRETING POLITICAL CARTOONS This cartoon, which appeared in *Harper's Weekly* in 1876, poked fun at President Grant's promise to "get to the bottom" of the corruption in government. **Making Inferences** *What does the cartoon imply about Grant's ability to investigate and put an end to corruption?*

to expand services to their citizens. For instance, following the North's example, all southern states created public school systems by 1872.

Reconstruction legislatures poured money into infrastructure. Some of the money came from Congress and from private investors. The rest, however, was raised by levying heavy taxes on individuals, many of whom were still deeply in debt from the war. White southerners, both wealthy and poor, resented this added financial burden. Spending by Reconstruction legislatures added another $130 million to southern debt. What further angered southerners was evidence that much of this big spending for infrastructure was being lost to corruption.

Corruption The laws and business methods of an earlier era simply could not control corruption in a time of such massive change and growth. During Reconstruction, enormous sums of money changed hands rapidly in the form of fraudulent loans and grants. Participants in such schemes included blacks and whites, Republicans and Democrats, southerners and northern carpetbaggers. "You are mistaken if you suppose that all the evils . . . result from the carpetbaggers and negroes," a Louisiana man wrote to a northern fellow Democrat. Democrats and Republicans cooperated "whenever anything is proposed which promises to pay," he observed. The South Carolina legislature even gave $1,000 to the Speaker of the House to cover his loss on a horse race!

Scandal and corruption also reached to the White House. Late in Grant's first term, a scandal emerged involving the Credit Mobilier Company. Credit Mobilier had been set up by the owners of the Union Pacific Railroad to build their portion of the transcontinental railroad westward from Omaha. The Union Pacific gave the Credit Mobilier enormous sums of federal money. While some of this money paid for work, much of it went into the pockets of the Union Pacific officers and politicians who were bribed into ignoring the fraud.

Section 3 Assessment

READING COMPREHENSION

1. Why did planters have trouble finding people to work for them?
2. How did **sharecropping** and **tenant farming** differ?
3. How did railroads contribute to the growth of cities?
4. Why was southern industrial growth limited?
5. What were the sources of funding for Reconstruction programs?

CRITICAL THINKING AND WRITING

6. **Predicting Consequences** Why did sharecropping and tenant farming encourage planters to grow cash crops rather than food crops? What impact might this have had on people living in poverty?
7. **Creating an Outline** Create an outline for an essay in which you explain why the physical reconstruction of the South was necessary.

Go Online PHSchool.com

For: An activity on tenant farming
Visit: PHSchool.com
Web Code: mrd-4123

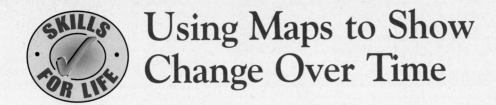

Using Maps to Show Change Over Time

Historians compare maps to help them identify changes over time. One far-reaching change that took place after the Civil War was the breakup of Southern plantations. The maps below show 2,000 acres of land before and after the Civil War.

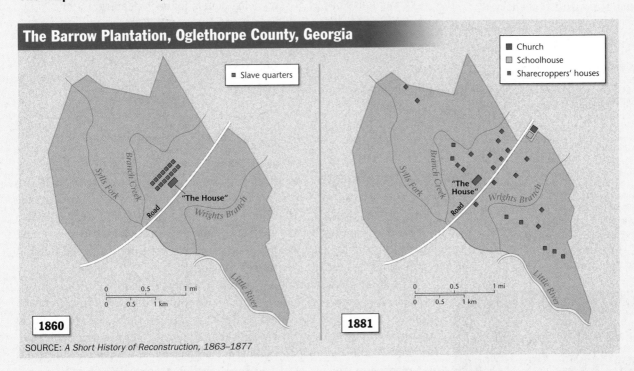

The Barrow Plantation, Oglethorpe County, Georgia

■ Slave quarters

■ Church
■ Schoolhouse
■ Sharecroppers' houses

1860

1881

SOURCE: *A Short History of Reconstruction, 1863–1877*

LEARN THE SKILL

Use the following steps to analyze maps for evidence of change over time:

1. **Identify the location and time periods of the maps.** Most maps are labeled with the location and subject. If a date is not included, historians can often determine the date based on the style and content of the map.

2. **Identify the subject of the maps.** Maps can include information about geographic features as well as man-made features, such as buildings and roads.

3. **Analyze the map key and scale.** The key identifies what different symbols and colors represent on the map. The scale helps you determine the actual distance between features shown on the map.

4. **Analyze the data on the maps.** Compare the data to draw conclusions about change over the time period the maps indicate. Also use what you already know about events in the time period.

PRACTICE THE SKILL

Answer the following questions:

1. **(a)** What specific area of land do both maps show? **(b)** What dates are given on the maps? How long a

time period is represented? **(c)** Is there anything unusual about the style of the maps? Explain.

2. **(a)** What geographic features are shown on both maps? **(b)** What man-made features are shown on each map? Are they the same on both maps?

3. **(a)** According to the key, what do the red squares on the 1860 map represent? **(b)** According to the key, what do the blue squares on the 1881 map represent? **(c)** How did the mapmaker show the difference between a church and a schoolhouse on the 1881 map? **(d)** What do you think the label "The House" means on each map? **(e)** On the 1881 map, approximately how far is "The House" from any other dwelling?

4. **(a)** How has the location of dwellings on the plantation changed during this time period? **(b)** What type of dwelling has disappeared? **(c)** What type of dwelling has been added? **(d)** What other new buildings have been added? **(e)** Summarize the changes to this plantation over time. What historical events helped produce these changes?

APPLY THE SKILL

See the Chapter Review and Assessment for another opportunity to apply this skill.

Section 4

The End of Reconstruction

READING FOCUS

- What tactics did the Ku Klux Klan use to spread terror throughout the South?
- Why did Reconstruction end?
- What were the major successes and failures of Reconstruction?

MAIN IDEA

In the 1870s, white Democrats regained power in the South, and white Republican interest in Reconstruction declined.

KEY TERMS

Enforcement Act of 1870
solid South
Compromise of 1877

TARGET READING SKILL

Identify Supporting Details Copy the web diagram below. As you read, fill in supporting details for each heading.

The End of Reconstruction — Reasons — Successes — Failures

Members of the Ku Klux Klan (pictured below) left miniature coffins like this, containing written death threats, at the doors of many freedmen and their white supporters.

Setting the Scene In 1866, six former Confederate soldiers living in Pulaski, Tennessee, decided to form a secret society. Someone suggested they name their group "Kuklos" (the Greek word for "circle"), and they voted to modify that to "Ku Klux Klan" (KKK). Members wore robes and masks and pretended to be the ghosts of Confederate soldiers, returned from the dead in search of revenge against the enemies of the South.

The Klan spread rapidly through the South, fueled by a blend of rage and fear over the Confederacy's defeat and toward the newly won freedom of black southerners. Klansmen pledged to "defend the social and political superiority" of whites against what they called the "aggressions of an inferior race." The membership consisted largely of ex-Confederate officials and plantation owners who had been excluded from politics. The group also attracted merchants, lawyers, and other professionals. While the Klan was supposed to be a secret society, most members' identities were well known in their communities.

In 1867, at a convention in Nashville, Tennessee, the Klan chose its first overall leader, or "grand wizard," Nathan Bedford Forrest. Before the war, Forrest had grown wealthy as a cotton planter and slave trader. During the war, he had become known as one of the Confederacy's most brilliant generals. He also had commanded the troops who captured Fort Pillow, Tennessee, in 1864, and then massacred more than 300 black Union soldiers as well as a number of black women and children.

As Reconstruction proceeded, Klan violence intensified. Arkansas Klansmen killed more than 300 Republicans, including a United States congressman, in 1868 alone. That year Klansmen murdered 1,000 people in Louisiana. Fully half of the adult white male population of New Orleans belonged to the KKK.

Spreading Terror

During Radical Reconstruction, the Klan sought to eliminate the Republican Party in the South by intimidating Republican voters, both white and black. The Klan's long-term goal was to keep African Americans in the role of submissive laborers.

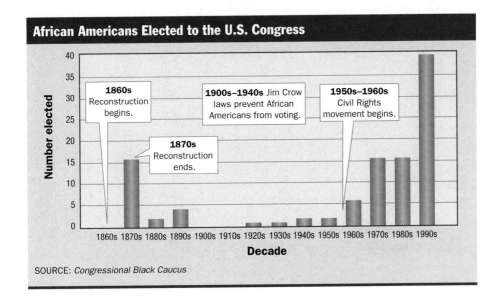

African Americans Elected to the U.S. Congress

1860s Reconstruction begins.

1870s Reconstruction ends.

1900s–1940s Jim Crow laws prevent African Americans from voting.

1950s–1960s Civil Rights movement begins.

Number elected (y-axis): 0 to 40

Decade (x-axis): 1860s 1870s 1880s 1890s 1900s 1910s 1920s 1930s 1940s 1950s 1960s 1970s 1980s 1990s

SOURCE: *Congressional Black Caucus*

The Klan's terror tactics varied from place to place. Often, horsemen in long robes and hoods appeared suddenly at night, carrying guns and whips. They encircled the homes of their victims, and planted huge burning crosses in their yards. People were dragged from their homes and harassed, tortured, kidnapped, or murdered.

Anyone who didn't share the Klan's goals and hatreds could be a victim: carpetbaggers, scalawags, freedmen who had become prosperous—even those who had merely learned to read. With chilling frequency, black women went to claim the dead bodies of their husbands and sons.

The Federal Response The violence kindled northern outrage. At President Grant's request, Congress passed a series of anti-Klan laws in 1870 and 1871. The **Enforcement Act of 1870** banned the use of terror, force, or bribery to prevent people from voting because of their race. Other laws banned the KKK entirely and strengthened military protection of voters and voting places.

Using troops, cavalry, and the power of the courts, the government arrested and tried thousands of Klansmen. Within a year the KKK was virtually wiped out. Still, the thinly spread federal army could not be everywhere at once. As federal troops gradually withdrew from the South, black suffrage all but ended.

Reconstruction Ends

President Grant, who won reelection in 1872, continued to pursue the goals of Reconstruction, sometimes with energy. However, the widespread corruption in his administration reminded voters of all that was wrong with Reconstruction.

A Dying Issue By the mid-1870s, white voters had grown weary of Republicans and their decade-long concern with Reconstruction. There were four main factors contributing to the end of Reconstruction:

Corruption Reconstruction legislatures, as well as Grant's administration, came to symbolize corruption, greed, and poor government.

The economy Reconstruction legislatures taxed and spent heavily, putting southern states deeper into debt. In addition, a nationwide economic

Focus on WORLD EVENTS

Alaska, the Midway Islands, and Mexico For the most part, Americans focused on rebuilding the nation during Reconstruction. Secretary of State William H. Seward, however, took a number of actions to expand the country's resources and trade. In 1867, Seward convinced the Senate to ratify his purchase of Alaska from Russia for $7.2 million. His opponents referred to Seward's purchase of Alaska's "walrus-covered icebergs" as "Seward's Folly." In an effort to expand trade with China, in 1867 Seward also annexed the Midway Islands, where coal-powered naval steamships could stop for refueling and repair on their voyages across the Pacific. Closer to home, Seward sent 50,000 American troops, who were already in Texas at the end of the Civil War, to the Mexican border to force the French to withdraw their troops from Mexico.

MAP SKILLS In the tarnished election of 1876, the electoral votes in three states under federal control were disputed, but went to Hayes when he promised to end Reconstruction. **Location** *In which states were election results disputed?*

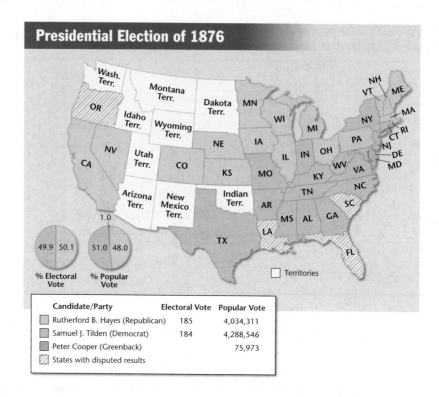

Presidential Election of 1876

% Electoral Vote	% Popular Vote
49.9 | 50.1	51.0 | 48.0

□ Territories

Candidate/Party	Electoral Vote	Popular Vote
▓ Rutherford B. Hayes (Republican)	185	4,034,311
▓ Samuel J. Tilden (Democrat)	184	4,288,546
▓ Peter Cooper (Greenback)		75,973
▨ States with disputed results		

downturn in 1873 diverted public attention from the movement for equal rights. In fact, white northern voters had never fully supported the Radical Republicans' goal of racial equality.

Violence As federal troops withdrew from the South, some white Democrats were freer to use violence and intimidation to prevent freedmen from voting. This allowed white southerners to regain control of state governments.

The Democrats return to power The era of Republican control of the South was coming to a close. In 1872, all but about 500 ex-Confederates had been pardoned. They combined with other white southerners to form a new bloc of Democratic voters known as the **solid South.** Democrats of the solid South blocked many federal Reconstruction policies and reversed many reforms of the Reconstruction legislatures.

Supreme Court Limits Scope of Amendments   The Supreme Court also played a role in bringing about the end of Reconstruction. In a series of cases, including the *Slaughterhouse Cases* in 1873, *United States* v. *Reese* in 1876, and *United States* v. *Cruikshank* in 1876, the Supreme Court narrowly interpreted the Fourteenth and Fifteenth amendments and placed the control of Americans' basic civil rights in the hands of the states. In short, the Court's decisions in these cases limited the federal government's ability to protect the civil and voting rights of African Americans.

The Compromise of 1877   Reconstruction politics took a final, sour turn in the presidential election of 1876. In that election, Republican Rutherford B. Hayes lost the popular vote to Democrat Samuel Tilden, who had the support of the solid South. The electoral vote, however, was disputed. The map above shows the results.

Hayes claimed victory based partly on wins in Florida, Louisiana, and South Carolina. Those states were still under Republican and federal control. Democrats submitted another set of tallies showing Tilden as the winner in those

READING CHECK
What factors contributed to the end of Reconstruction?

Successes and Failures of Reconstruction

Successes	Failures
Union is restored.	Many white southerners remain bitter toward the federal government and the Republican Party.
The South's economy grows and new wealth is created in the North.	The South is slow to industrialize.
Fourteenth and Fifteenth amendments guarantee African Americans the rights of citizenship, equal protection under the law, and suffrage.	After federal troops are withdrawn, southern state governments and terrorist organizations effectively deny African Americans the right to vote.
Freedmen's Bureau and other organizations help many black families obtain housing, jobs, and schooling.	Many black and white southerners remain caught in a cycle of poverty.
Southern states adopt a system of mandatory education.	Racist attitudes toward African Americans continue, in both the South and the North.

INTERPRETING TABLES
Until recently, many historians believed that Reconstruction was a dismal failure. Today most historians argue that the truth is more complex. The cartoon below shows President Hayes "plowing under" Reconstruction programs. **Drawing Conclusions** *Do you think Reconstruction was more of a success or a failure? Why?*

states, and thus in the presidential race. (The eligibility of one Republican elector from Oregon was also called into question.) Congress set up a special commission to resolve the election crisis. Not surprisingly, the commission, which included more Republicans than Democrats, named Hayes the victor. However, Democrats had enough strength in Congress to reject the commission's decision.

Finally the two parties made a deal. In what became known as the **Compromise of 1877,** the Democrats agreed to give Hayes the victory in the presidential election he had not clearly won. In return, the new President agreed to remove the remaining federal troops from southern states. He also agreed to support appropriations for rebuilding levees along the Mississippi River, and to give huge subsidies to southern railroads. The compromise opened the way for Democrats to regain control of southern politics and marked the end of Reconstruction.

Section 4 Assessment

READING COMPREHENSION

1. Why did Congress pass the **Enforcement Act of 1870?**

2. What four factors contributed to the end of Reconstruction?

3. What was the **solid South?**

4. What was the **Compromise of 1877?** Why do you think the two parties made this compromise?

CRITICAL THINKING AND WRITING

5. **Drawing Conclusions** Do you agree with historian Samuel Eliot Morison, who said that "the North may have won the war, but the white South won the peace"?

6. **Writing an Opinion** What was the most significant success of Reconstruction? What was the most significant failure? Write an outline for an essay in which you state your opinions.

For: An activity on the Election of 1876
Visit: PHSchool.com
Web Code: mrd-4124

creating a CHAPTER SUMMARY

Copy the chart (right) on a piece of paper, and then complete it by adding information about key legislation passed during Reconstruction. Some entries have been completed for you as examples.

For additional review and enrichment activities, see the interactive version of *America: Pathways to the Present*, available on the Web and on CD-ROM.

Major Reconstruction Legislation		
Date	**Legislation**	**Description**
1865	13th Amendment	Abolished slavery
1865, 1866	Freedmen's Bureau	Provided services for war refugees and newly freed people
1867	Reconstruction Acts	
1868	14th Amendment	
1870	15th Amendment	

★ Reviewing Key Terms

For each of the terms below, write a sentence explaining how it relates to the post-Civil War period.

1. Reconstruction
2. pardon
3. black codes
4. impeach
5. carpetbagger
6. scalawag
7. sharecropping
8. tenant farming
9. infrastructure
10. solid South

★ Reviewing Main Ideas

11. Name the three major problems the South faced at the end of the Civil War. (Section 1)

12. How did Lincoln's plan for Reconstruction compare to Johnson's plan? (Section 1)

13. How did African Americans try to improve their lives after emancipation? (Section 1)

14. Why did Johnson and Congress clash over Reconstruction? (Section 2)

15. How did Republicans gain control of southern governments? (Section 2)

16. In what ways were the new state constitutions different? (Section 2)

17. In what ways did the economy of the South change after the Civil War, and in what ways did it remain unchanged? (Section 3)

18. Why did Reconstruction end? (Section 4)

★ Critical Thinking

19. **Comparing Points of View** Evaluate Reconstruction from the point of view of (a) a black sharecropper, (b) an ex-Confederate, (c) a carpetbagger, (d) a Radical Republican.

20. **Identifying Assumptions** Congress accused President Johnson of abusing his presidential powers, and Johnson thought that Congress overstepped its authority in carrying out Radical Reconstruction. What differing assumptions led to these conclusions?

21. **Recognizing Ideologies** Why were the strong policies of Radical Reconstruction largely ineffective in changing the attitudes of white southerners toward African Americans?

22. **Identifying Central Issues** Refer to the political cartoon depicting corruption during Grant's presidency in Section 3. Conduct research to learn more about one of the scandals pictured in the cartoon, such as the Whiskey Fraud, Secretary of War W. W. Belknap's impeachment, or the Back Pay Grab. Write a summary of the scandal and explain its impact on Reconstruction.

★ Standardized Test Prep

Analyzing Political Cartoons ▶

23. This cartoon depicts President Grant riding in a carpetbag. The woman represents Southern Democrats. What do the soldiers represent?

   A Northerners angry with Grant's policy
   B The North's "bayonet rule" of the South
   C Southern opposition to Grant
   D Former Confederate generals

24. State the central message of this cartoon.

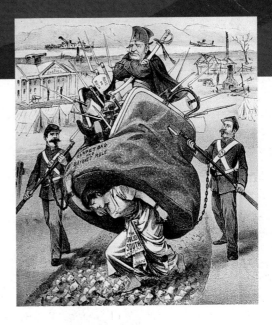

Analyzing Primary Sources

Read this excerpt, and then answer the questions that follow.

> ❝ If [freedmen] are good law-abiding citizens, praying for its [the nation's] prosperity, rejoicing in its progress, paying its taxes, fighting its battles, making its farms, mines, work-shops and commerce more productive, why deny them the right to have a voice in the election of its rulers? ❞
>
> —the "black citizens of Nashville," January 9, 1865

25. Which statement BEST represents the meaning of the quotation?

   A Freedmen are responsible citizens.
   B Freedmen deserve the right to vote because they earn money for the country.
   C Freedmen deserve the right to vote because they are fulfilling the responsibilities of citizenship.
   D Freedmen deserve to rule themselves.

26. What is the most likely reason the writers never received a response?

   F White Tennesseans did not want freedmen to vote.
   G White Tennesseans did not want freedman to become citizens.
   H White Tennesseans thought freedmen should have economic rights, not political rights.
   I White Tennesseans had already guaranteed freedmen the right to vote.

Test-Taking Tip

Question 25 asks you to choose which statement BEST represents the quotation. Several of the possible answers may seem correct, but one summarizes the entire quotation more thoroughly than the others.

Applying the Chapter Skill

Comparing Maps Over Time Refer to the maps on page 217. If the years of the maps were not labeled, would you be able to tell which map showed the plantation in 1860, and which showed the land in 1881? Explain your answer.

For: Chapter 5 Self-Test
Visit: PHSchool.com
Web Code: mra-4125

The Expansion of American Industry (1850–1900)

The steel-framed Syndicate Building in New York City

American Events

1856
The Bessemer process is patented, paving the way for the mass production of steel and a new industrial age in America.

1859
Edwin L. Drake strikes oil in Titusville, Pennsylvania, marking the first successful oil well and the beginning of the commercial use of oil.

1869
Workers finish construction on the transcontinental railroad, the first railroad to connect the east and west coasts.

Presidential Terms: Franklin Pierce 1853–1857   James Buchanan 1857–1861   Abraham Lincoln 1861–1865   Andrew Johnson 1865–1869   Ulysses S. Grant 1869–1877

1850   •**1860**•   •**1870**

World Events

Charles Darwin publishes *On the Origin of Species.*
1859

Louis Pasteur introduces pasteurization.
1861

The Suez Canal is completed.
1869

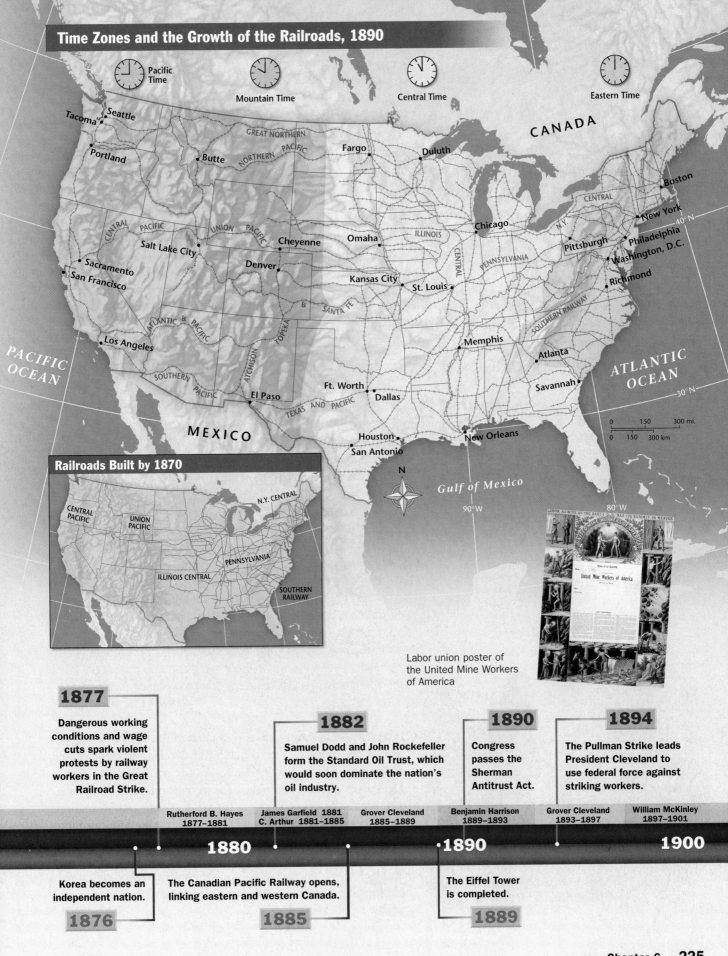

Time Zones and the Growth of the Railroads, 1890

Pacific Time

Mountain Time

Central Time

Eastern Time

CANADA

Tacoma
Seattle
Portland
Butte
GREAT NORTHERN
NORTHERN PACIFIC
Fargo
Duluth
Boston
CENTRAL
N.Y.
New York
40° N
CENTRAL PACIFIC
UNION PACIFIC
Salt Lake City
Cheyenne
Omaha
ILLINOIS
Chicago
Pittsburgh
Philadelphia
Washington, D.C.
Sacramento
San Francisco
Denver
Kansas City
St. Louis
CENTRAL
PENNSYLVANIA
Richmond
ATLANTIC & PACIFIC
& SANTA FE
Los Angeles
TOPEKA
ATCHISON
Memphis
SOUTHERN RAILWAY
Atlanta
PACIFIC OCEAN
SOUTHERN PACIFIC
El Paso
TEXAS AND PACIFIC
Ft. Worth
Dallas
Savannah
ATLANTIC OCEAN
30° N
MEXICO
Houston
San Antonio
New Orleans

0   150   300 mi.
0   150   300 km

N

Gulf of Mexico
90° W
80° W

Railroads Built by 1870

CENTRAL PACIFIC
UNION PACIFIC
N.Y. CENTRAL
PENNSYLVANIA
ILLINOIS CENTRAL
SOUTHERN RAILWAY

Labor union poster of
the United Mine Workers
of America

1877

Dangerous working
conditions and wage
cuts spark violent
protests by railway
workers in the Great
Railroad Strike.

1882

Samuel Dodd and John Rockefeller
form the Standard Oil Trust, which
would soon dominate the nation's
oil industry.

1890

Congress
passes the
Sherman
Antitrust Act.

1894

The Pullman Strike leads
President Cleveland to
use federal force against
striking workers.

Rutherford B. Hayes
1877–1881

James Garfield 1881
C. Arthur 1881–1885

Grover Cleveland
1885–1889

Benjamin Harrison
1889–1893

Grover Cleveland
1893–1897

William McKinley
1897–1901

1880

1890

1900

Korea becomes an
independent nation.

The Canadian Pacific Railway opens,
linking eastern and western Canada.

The Eiffel Tower
is completed.

1876

1885

1889

A Technological Revolution

READING FOCUS

- Why did people's daily lives change in the decades following the Civil War?

- How did advances in electric power and communication affect life for people and businesses?

- What effects did the development of railroads have on industrial growth?

- What was the impact of the Bessemer process on American culture?

MAIN IDEA

In the years after the Civil War, new technology revolutionized American life.

KEY TERMS

patent
productivity
transcontinental railroad
Bessemer process
mass production

TARGET READING SKILL

Understand Effects As you read, complete this table listing some of the major technological innovations of the decades following the Civil War and their impact on American life.

A Technological Revolution		
Technology	**Examples**	**Impact on Daily Life and Business**
Electric power	Refrigerator	Reduced food spoilage

Below, Samuel Morse sends the first successful telegraph message, using Morse code, from the Supreme Court in Washington, D.C. Morse code (inset) is still used today in amateur radio.

Setting the Scene Samuel Morse had worked for years on improving the telegraph and finally began to run out of money. Nearly broke, he anxiously awaited a bill to pass through Congress, which would provide him with funds to complete his work. The bill narrowly passed, to the surprise of many. Morse was greatly relieved. The next year he reached the climax of his success.

66 *And now at last the supreme moment had arrived. The line from Washington to Baltimore was completed, and on the 24th day of May, 1844, the company invited by the inventor . . . assembled to witness his triumph. True to his promise to Miss Annie Ellsworth, he had asked her to indite the first public message which should be flashed over the completed line, and she . . . chose the now historic words . . . 'What hath God wrought!' . . . Calmly he seated himself at the instrument and ticked off the inspired words in the dots and dashes of the Morse alphabet . . . the electromagnetic telegraph was no longer the wild dream of a visionary, but an accomplished fact.* 99

—Samuel F. B. Morse

Little did Americans know as they entered the second half of the nineteenth century what other "wild dreams" would become reality. Samuel Morse's first successful telegraph message sent in 1844 marked the beginning of a second industrial revolution. The United States was on the verge of a major transformation. In the years after the Civil War, the United States developed into an industrial powerhouse. Inventors and scientists, backed by business leaders, created an explosion of inventions and improvements. Their efforts brought about a technological revolution that energized American industry and forever changed people's daily lives.

Changes in Daily Life

Most Americans today can flip a switch for light, turn a faucet for water, and talk to a friend a thousand miles away just by pressing a few buttons. It is hard for us to imagine life without these conveniences. In 1865, however, daily life was vastly different.

Daily Life in 1865 Indoor electric lighting did not exist in 1865. Instead, the rising and setting of the sun dictated the rhythm of a day's work. After dark, people lit candles or oil lamps if they could afford them. If they could not, they simply went to sleep, to rise at the first light of dawn.

Think about summers without the benefits of refrigeration! Ice was available in 1865, but only at great cost. People sawed blocks of ice out of frozen ponds during the winter, packed them in sawdust, and stored them in icehouses for later use.

By modern standards, long-distance communication was agonizingly slow. In 1860, most mail from the East Coast took ten days to reach the Midwest and three weeks to get to the West. An immigrant living on the frontier would have to wait several months for news from relatives in Europe.

Investing in Technology By 1900, this picture of daily life had changed dramatically for millions of Americans. The post–Civil War years saw tremendous growth in new ideas and inventions. Between 1790 and 1860, the Patent and Trademark Office of the federal government issued just 36,000 **patents**—licenses that give an inventor the exclusive right to make, use, or sell an invention for a set period of time. In contrast, 500,000 patents were issued between 1860 and 1890 for inventions such as the typewriter, telephone, and phonograph.

European and American business leaders began to invest heavily in these new inventions. The combination of financial backing and American ingenuity helped create new industries and expand old ones. By 1900, Americans' standard of living was among the highest in the world. This achievement was a result of the nation's growing industrial **productivity**—the amount of goods and services created in a given period of time.

New Forms of Energy

The blossoming of American inventive genius in the late 1800s had a profound effect on millions of people's lives. For example, scientists began developing new uses for petroleum, including fuels that would help power new machines. Electricity proved to be another productive energy source. It led to many important advances in the nation's industrial development and changed people's eating, working, and even sleeping habits.

Drake Strikes Oil In 1858, the Pennsylvania Rock Oil Company sent Edwin L. Drake to Titusville, Pennsylvania, to drill for oil. The idea to drill for oil was new and many were skeptical of the project. Previously, oil had been obtained by either melting the fat from a whale or by digging large pits and waiting for oil to seep above ground—both of which were time-consuming and expensive. If the new method worked, it would be cheaper and more efficient.

READING CHECK
What were the benefits of Drake's new method of oil extraction?

After spending nearly a year raising money and building the equipment needed for the project, Drake finally set up an oil well and began drilling using a steam-powered engine. In 1859, just as nervous investors had decided to call off the project, Drake struck oil. Oil quickly became a major industry.

As new uses for oil began to appear, the oil business grew rapidly. Titusville soon became one of several boom towns in northwestern Pennsylvania. Oil refineries, which transformed crude oil into kerosene, sprang up around the country. A byproduct of this process, gasoline, would eventually make oil even more valuable. Until the invention of the automobile in the late 1880s, however, gasoline was seen as a waste product and simply thrown away.

Edison, a Master of Invention Thomas A. Edison helped make another new source of energy, electric power, widely available. Born in 1847, Edison grew up tinkering with electricity. While working for a New York company, he improved the stock tickers that sent stock and gold prices to other offices. When his boss awarded him a $40,000 bonus, the 23-year-old Edison left his job and set himself up as an inventor.

In 1876, Edison moved into his "invention factory" in Menlo Park, New Jersey. The young genius, who had never received any formal science training, claimed that he could turn out "a minor invention every ten days and a big thing every six months or so."

Edison then began experimenting with electric lighting. His goal was to develop affordable, in-home lighting to replace oil lamps and gaslights. Starting around 1879, Edison and his fellow inventors tried different ways to produce light within a sealed glass bulb. They needed to find a material that would glow without quickly burning up when heated with an electric current.

The team experimented with various threadlike filaments with little success. In 1880, they finally found a workable filament made of bamboo fiber. This filament glowed, Edison said, with "the most beautiful light ever seen."

Edison's favorite invention, the phonograph, shown above, recorded sounds on metal foil wrapped around a rotating cylinder. The first words Edison recorded and then replayed on his phonograph were "Mary had a little lamb." This wondrous machine, introduced in 1877, gained Edison the nickname the "Wizard of Menlo Park."

Until the early 1880s, people who wanted electricity had to produce it with their own generator. Hoping to provide affordable lighting to many customers, Edison developed the idea of a central power station. In 1882, to attract investors, Edison built a power plant that lit dozens of buildings in New York City. Investors were impressed, and Edison's idea spread. By 1890, power stations across the country provided electricity for lamps, fans, printing presses, and many other newly invented appliances.

Electricity Is Improved Other inventors later improved upon Edison's work. Lewis Latimer, the son of an escaped slave, patented an improved method for producing the filament in light bulbs. He worked in Edison's laboratories, where he helped develop new advances in electricity. Latimer later wrote a landmark book about electric lighting.

Another major advance for electric lighting came from inventor George Westinghouse. In 1885, Westinghouse began to experiment with a form of electricity called alternating current. Edison had used direct current, which was expensive to produce and could only travel a mile or two. Alternating current could be generated more cheaply and travel longer distances.

Westinghouse also used a device called a transformer to boost power levels at a station so that electricity could be sent over long distances. Another transformer at a distant substation could reduce power levels as needed. These aspects of Westinghouse's system made home use of electricity practical.

By the early 1890s, investors had used Edison's and Westinghouse's ideas and inventions to create two companies, General Electric and Westinghouse Electric. These companies' products encouraged the spread of the use of electricity. By 1898, nearly 3,000 power stations were lighting some 2 million light bulbs across the land.

Electricity's Impact on Business and Daily Life Electricity helped to improve the productivity of the business world and transform the nature of the workplace. Electric power was cheaper and more efficient than some previously existing power sources. For example, the electric sewing machine, first made in 1889, led to the rapid growth of the ready-made clothing industry. Before the electric sewing machine, workers had to physically push on a foot pedal to generate power. With electricity, a worker could produce more clothing in less time. As a result, the costs of producing each item of clothing decreased.

Rapidly growing industries, such as the ready-made clothing industry, opened up thousands of jobs for Americans looking for employment. Many of the country's new immigrants, especially women and children, found work making clothing in factories powered by electricity.

Household use of electric current revolutionized many aspects of daily life. To take but one example, electricity made the refrigerator possible. This invention reduced food spoilage and relieved the need to preserve foods by time-consuming means, such as smoking or salting.

Yet all Americans did not receive the benefits of electricity equally. Rural areas, especially, went without electricity for many decades. Even where electric power was available, many people could not afford the home appliances or other conveniences that ran on electricity.

Advances in Communications

In the late 1800s, thousands of people left their homes in Europe and the eastern United States to seek a new life in the West. One of the greatest hardships for these immigrants was leaving their loved ones behind. Would they ever hear from family and friends again? By 1900, thanks to many advances in communications, such fears of isolation had diminished.

The Telegraph The idea of sending messages over wires had occurred to inventors in the early 1700s. Several inventors actually set up working telegraph systems well before an American, Samuel F. B. Morse, took out a patent on telegraphy.

Morse may not have invented the telegraph, but he perfected it. He devised a code of short and long electrical impulses to represent the letters of the alphabet. Using this system, later called Morse code, he sent his first message in 1844. His success signaled the start of a communications revolution.

VIEWING HISTORY Here, visitors marvel at the electricity building, on display at the 1893 World's Columbian Exposition in Chicago. The building boasted more than 18,000 electric light bulbs and hosted other exhibits that showed the practical and entertainment value of electricity. **Drawing Conclusions** *Why do you think expositions such as this one were important? Who attended them?*

After the Civil War, several telegraph companies joined together to form the Western Union Telegraph Company. In 1870, Western Union had more than 100,000 miles of wire, over which some 9 million telegraph messages were transmitted. By 1900, the company owned more than 900,000 miles of wire and was sending roughly 63 million telegraph messages a year.

The Telephone   In 1871, Alexander Graham Bell of Scotland immigrated to Boston, Massachusetts, to teach people with hearing difficulties. After experimenting for several years with an electric current to transmit sounds, Bell patented the "talking telegraph" on March 7, 1876. He had just turned 29. In 1885, Bell and a group of partners set up the American Telephone and Telegraph Company to build long-distance telephone lines.

The earliest local phone lines could connect only two places, such as a home and a business. Soon central switchboards with operators could link an entire city. The first commercial telephone exchange began serving 21 customers on January 28, 1878, in New Haven, Connecticut. The next year President Rutherford B. Hayes had a telephone installed at the White House. By 1900, 1.5 million telephones were in use.

Railroads Create a National Network

In 1850, steam-powered ships still provided much of the nation's transportation. Over the following decades, however, improvements in train and track design, plus the construction of new rail lines, gave railroads a big boost.

Before the Civil War, most of the nation's railroad tracks were in short lines that connected neighboring cities, mainly in the East. Since there was no standard track width, or gauge, each train could only travel on certain tracks. As a result, goods and passengers often had to be moved to different trains, which caused costly delays. To make matters worse, train travel was dangerous. No system of standard signals existed, and train brakes were unreliable.

The Transcontinental Railroad   The rail business expanded greatly after the Civil War. The key event was the completion of the **transcontinental railroad,** a railway extending from coast to coast. When the project began in 1862, rail lines already reached from the East Coast to the Mississippi River. Now new rails were laid between Omaha, Nebraska, and Sacramento, California.

Because private investors did not see any likelihood of profit in building railroads beyond the line of settlement, the federal government stepped in to fund the completion of the transcontinental railroad. Members of Congress believed that the completion of a coast-to-coast railway would strengthen the country's economic infrastructure. Thus the federal government awarded huge loans and land grants to two private companies. The Central Pacific Railroad began laying track eastward out of Sacramento. The Union Pacific Railroad began work toward the west in Omaha.

Scholars disagree as to whether it was a good idea for the government to provide funds for this project. Many believe that the government gave a much needed boost to

Fast Forward to Today

The World Wide Web

The growth and influence of the Internet in the second half of the 1990s was a turning point in the nation's economy, similar in scope to the vast economic changes brought about by the telegraph and railroads in the late 1800s. Estimates show that from 1996 to 2001, the number of people using the Internet worldwide skyrocketed from 45 million to over 400 million. Also during that time, the amount of revenue generated by the Internet jumped from $2.9 billion to over $700 billion.

Just as in the late 1800s, the world of business and daily life at the end of the twentieth century changed drastically with the advent of new technologies resulting from the Internet. The Internet became the next step in a process that began with the telegraph and the railroads to connect people and ideas in faster, more efficient ways. Moving beyond telegraph wires and railroad tracks, the United States, and indeed the world, is now connected through an infinite and invisible World Wide Web.

?   **What other recent technological innovations have changed the world of communications? What do you think will be the next step in this process? Explain.**

the railroad industry when the private sector was hesitant to invest. However, others argue that the government should not have gotten involved. One reason is that railroads built with federal aid did not operate as efficiently and profitably as some built with little government assistance. For example, James J. Hill's Great Northern Railroad in the 1880s and 1890s had both lower rates and higher profits than railroads built with federal aid.

Most of the workers on the transcontinental railroad were immigrants. Irish workers on the Union Pacific line used pickaxes to dig and level rail beds across the Great Plains at the rate of up to 6 miles a day. Chinese workers brought to the United States by the Central Pacific chiseled, plowed, and dynamited their way through the Sierra Nevada. Workers took pride in their labor. One work crew set a record for putting down track—an amazing ten miles in one day.

Finally, after seven years of grueling physical labor, the two crews approached each other in what is now Utah. On May 10, 1869, at a place called Promontory Summit, Central Pacific president Leland Stanford raised his hammer to drive the final golden spike into position. A telegraph operator beside the track tapped out a message to crowds throughout the country: "Almost ready now. Hats off. Prayer is being offered. . . . Done!" The nation had its first transcontinental railroad.

Railroad Developments By 1870, railroads could carry goods and passengers from coast to coast, but they still had problems. Trains were often noisy, dirty, and uncomfortable for travelers. The huge engines, spewing smoke and cinders as they thundered through the countryside, sometimes aroused fear and distrust.

In spite of the problems, train travel continued to expand and improve. The various new technologies emerging at this time all aided in the development of the national railroad system. Steel rails replaced iron rails, and track gauges and signals became standardized. Railroad companies also took steps to improve safety. In 1869, George Westinghouse developed more effective air

READING CHECK

What types of problems did railroads have in the late 1800s?

VIEWING HISTORY Citadel Rock looms over the construction of the Union Pacific Railroad through Wyoming Territory in 1868. **Identifying Central Issues** *In what ways did the nation's growing transportation system help promote industrial growth?*

brakes. In 1887, Granville Woods patented a telegraph system for communicating with moving trains, thus reducing the risk of collision.

The growth of railroads also led to the development of many towns throughout the western part of the United States. Railroad owners, looking to expand their businesses and increase profits, began building towns near their railroads on land granted to them by the government.

Railroads and Time Zones Scheduling proved to be another problem for railroads. Throughout much of the 1800s, most towns set their clocks independently, according to solar time. But when trains started regular passenger service, time differences from town to town created confusion. So, in 1883, the railroads adopted a national system of time zones to improve scheduling. As a result, clocks in broad regions of the country showed the same time, a system we still use today.

Rail improvements such as this made life easier not only for passengers but also for businesses that shipped goods. By the end of the century, some 190,000 miles of rails linked businesses and their customers. Shipping costs dropped enormously. In 1865, shipping a barrel of flour from Chicago to New York cost $3.45. In 1895, it cost just 68 cents.

Railroads and Industry Although the development of canals, turnpikes, and steam-powered ships in the first half of the century had improved transportation, the transport of goods over long distances was still costly and inefficient. Railroads played a key role in revolutionizing business and industry in the United States in several ways.

A faster and more practical means of transporting goods Railroads were less limited by geographic and natural factors, such as poor weather conditions, than water transport was. Trains could travel at higher speeds and transport larger items in much greater quantities.

Lower costs of production Railroads were a cheaper way to transport goods. As shipping costs dropped, more goods could be sent at lower prices. As a result, businesses were able to receive the raw materials and resources needed to produce their products at much lower costs and in much less time.

Creation of national markets Higher speeds and lower costs now allowed a business to market and sell its finished products to locations nationwide, rather than just in a local region. Also, the resources needed to produce these goods could be obtained from anywhere in the country. These advances in commerce helped to link distant regions of the United States, furthering the national network of business, transportation, and communication.

A model for big business Because of the complexity and size of the railroad companies, with railroads came new administrative techniques for handling large numbers of workers and large quantities of materials and money. New methods of management also arose. The professional manager and the specialized department grew out of the railroad business.

Stimulation of other industries The growth of the railroad industry encouraged innovation in other industries. The replacement of iron rails with steel rails, for example, promoted the growth of the steel industry.

The Bessemer Process

Through the mid-1800s, the nation depended on iron for railroad rails and the frames of large buildings. But in the 1850s, Henry Bessemer in England and William Kelly in Kentucky independently developed a new process for making steel. In 1856, Bessemer received the first patent for the **Bessemer process.** Steel had long been produced by melting iron, adding carbon, and removing impurities. The Bessemer process made it much easier and cheaper to remove the impurities.

Locomotives, such as this Erie Locomotive from 1903, were an impressive sight to many Americans at the turn of the century.

Steel is lighter, stronger, and more flexible than iron. The Bessemer process made possible the **mass production,** or production in great amounts, of steel. As a result, a new age of building began. A majestic symbol of this new age that endures is the Brooklyn Bridge.

The Brooklyn Bridge   After the Civil War, New York City grew in size as well as population. Many people who worked on the island of Manhattan lived in nearby Brooklyn. The only way to travel between Brooklyn and Manhattan was by ferry across the East River. In winter, ice or winds often shut down the ferry service. Could a bridge high enough to clear river traffic be built across such a large distance? Engineer John A. Roebling, a German immigrant, thought it could.

Roebling designed a suspension bridge with thick steel cables suspended from high towers to hold up the main span. That span, arching 1,595 feet above the

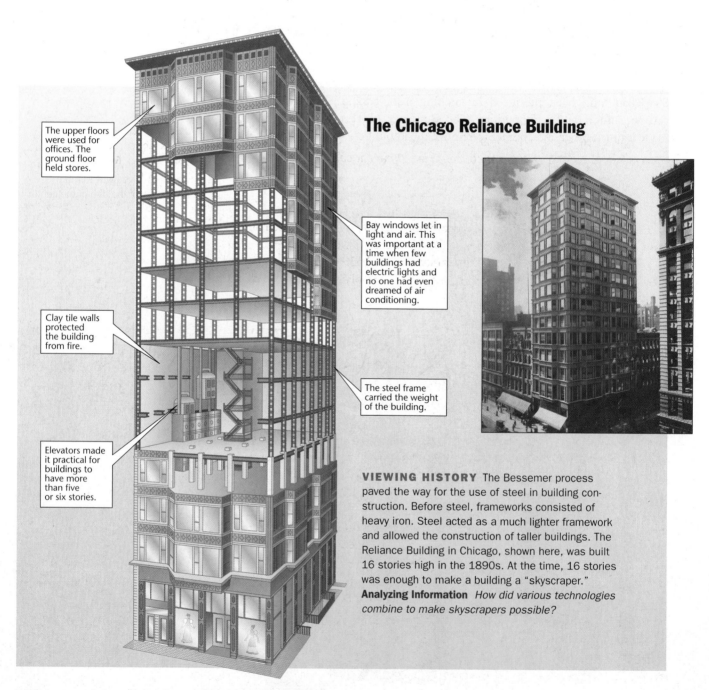

The Chicago Reliance Building

The upper floors were used for offices. The ground floor held stores.

Bay windows let in light and air. This was important at a time when few buildings had electric lights and no one had even dreamed of air conditioning.

Clay tile walls protected the building from fire.

The steel frame carried the weight of the building.

Elevators made it practical for buildings to have more than five or six stories.

VIEWING HISTORY The Bessemer process paved the way for the use of steel in building construction. Before steel, frameworks consisted of heavy iron. Steel acted as a much lighter framework and allowed the construction of taller buildings. The Reliance Building in Chicago, shown here, was built 16 stories high in the 1890s. At the time, 16 stories was enough to make a building a "skyscraper."
Analyzing Information *How did various technologies combine to make skyscrapers possible?*

river, would be the longest in the world. Roebling died shortly after construction of the Brooklyn Bridge began in 1869, so his son Washington took over the project. In 1872, after inspecting a foundation deep beneath the river, Washington became disabled by a severe attack of decompression sickness ("the bends"). Other disasters followed, from explosions and fires, to dishonest dealings by a steel-cable contractor.

A Symbol of American Success Despite these problems, the Brooklyn Bridge was completed and opened with a ceremony on May 24, 1883. In the keynote address, congressman and future New York City mayor Abram Hewitt remarked on this great triumph:

66 *It is not the work of any one man or any one age. It is the result of study, of the experience, and of the knowledge of many men in many ages. It is not merely a creation; it is a growth. It stands before us today as the sum and epitome of human knowledge; as the very heir of the ages; as the latest glory of centuries of patient observation, profound study and accumulated skill. . . .* 99

—Abram Stevens Hewitt

At nightfall, crowds gasped as electric light bulbs, which had been strung along the bridge, lit up the darkness and shimmered on the river below. The city celebrated with a magnificent fireworks display. Indeed, the entire United States celebrated, its inventive genius and hard work plainly visible for all the world to see.

VIEWING HISTORY This 1883 lithograph by Currier and Ives reveals the atmosphere of triumph and celebration that accompanied the opening of the Brooklyn Bridge. **Demonstrating Reasoned Judgment** *How do you think images such as this influenced people's perceptions of the changes taking place in society?*

Section 1 Assessment

READING COMPREHENSION

1. Why did the nation's industrial **productivity** rise in the late 1800s?

2. Why did the oil business change after Drake found oil in Pennsylvania?

3. How did inventions such as the light bulb and the telegraph change daily life in the late 1800s?

4. What were the advantages of building the **transcontinental railroad?**

5. What innovations did the **Bessemer process** encourage?

CRITICAL THINKING AND WRITING

6. **Determining Relevance** How did the system of patents encourage innovation and investment?

7. **Making Comparisons** Think of a modern convenience that you rely on. What benefits does this item bring to your life? Are there any drawbacks associated with this item?

8. **Writing a List** Create a list that compares the changes in business and daily life resulting from the telegraph and the railroad in the late 1800s with the changes resulting from the Internet in the late 1900s.

For: An activity on the Central Pacific Railroad
Visit: PHSchool.com
Web Code: mrd-5131

Using Cross-Sectional Maps

It is sometimes helpful to use more than one type of map to understand a particular piece of land. Physical-political maps show the land as if viewed from above, revealing distances across the surface. Cross-sectional maps show how the land would look if viewed from the side; they indicate the heights of mountains and valleys. The cross-sectional map below shows the changes in elevation along the route of the first transcontinental railroad. These changes posed a great challenge to workers building the railroad between 1862 and 1869.

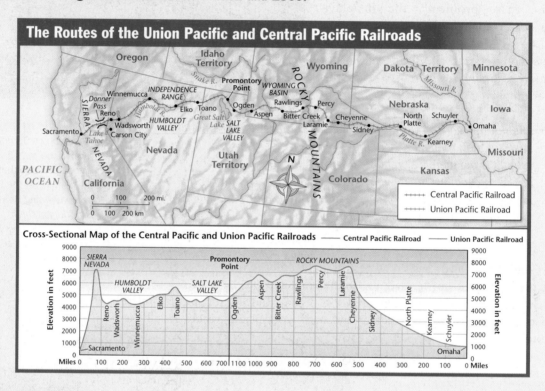

LEARN THE SKILL
Use the following steps to analyze a cross-sectional map:

1. **Study the region shown on both maps.** Compare the area covered and the elements shown on each map. Find several points that appear on both maps, and notice how they are depicted on each map.

2. **Analyze the information shown on the cross-sectional map.** Notice how changes in elevation are shown on the map (in this case, as the rising and falling of the green and red lines). Study the scale on the map, and notice both the distance covered across land and the elevation.

3. **Draw conclusions about the places or events depicted on the maps.** Use what you learn from both maps to better understand the landforms and the human activity in that area.

PRACTICE THE SKILL
Answer the following questions:

1. **(a)** Which landforms on the physical-political map correspond to those on the cross-sectional map?

Which landforms appear on only one map? **(b)** Does the cross-sectional map show the same land area as the physical-political map? Explain. **(c)** Does the cross-sectional map cover the same east-west distance as the physical-political map? Explain.

2. **(a)** What were the highest and lowest elevations of each railroad route? **(b)** Which 100-mile section on each route had the sharpest changes? **(c)** Which 100-mile section on each route had the most gradual changes? **(d)** How long was each route?

3. **(a)** How do the length and elevation changes of the two routes compare? **(b)** Which railroad workers faced the greatest challenge at the start of the project: those working east from Sacramento, or those working west from Omaha? Explain. **(c)** Which workers faced the greatest overall challenge? Explain.

APPLY THE SKILL
See the Chapter Review and Assessment for another opportunity to apply this skill.

The Growth of Big Business

READING FOCUS

- Why were American industrialists of the late 1800s called both "robber barons" and "captains of industry"?

- How did social Darwinism affect Americans' views on big business?

- In what ways did big businesses differ from smaller businesses?

- How did industrialists gain a competitive edge over their rivals?

MAIN IDEA

Big business created wealth for its owners and for the nation, but it also prompted controversy and concern over its methods.

KEY TERMS

social Darwinism
oligopoly
monopoly
cartel
vertical consolidation
economies of scale
horizontal consolidation
trust
Sherman Antitrust Act

TARGET READING SKILL

Identify Cause and Effect Copy the web diagram below. As you read, fill in examples relating to the growth of big business in the late 1800s.

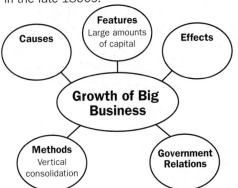

Setting the Scene

> 66 *A very important incident in my life occurred when one day in a train, a nice, farmer-looking gentleman approached me. . . . He pulled from a small green bag the model of the first sleeping car. This man was Mr. Woodruff, the inventor. Its value struck me like a flash. . . . [He] offered me an interest in the venture, which I promptly accepted. . . . I had not the money, and I did not see any way of getting it. But I finally decided to visit the local banker and ask him for a loan. . . . I really made my first considerable sum from this investment in the Woodruff Sleeping Car Company.* 99
>
> —Andrew Carnegie

Wall Street in New York City was a prominent financial center in the late 1800s.

One of the most successful of all business leaders and industrialists in the late 1800s was Andrew Carnegie. He came from humble beginnings, but quickly understood and embraced the concept that "money could make money." He just needed a way to find it. Carnegie had an eye for recognizing a good investment. Making wise and sometimes risky investments would soon make him one of the richest and most successful businessmen in the world.

The period of invention after the Civil War set the stage for great industrial growth. Still, more than technology would be needed to transform the United States. It would take shrewd businesspeople and many investors willing to gamble on new products. Without huge amounts of capital, businesses could not build factories or market their inventions. To succeed, business leaders often combined funds and resources to create large companies. Thus was born the age of big business.

Robber Barons or Captains of Industry?

Historians have used the terms "robber barons" and "captains of industry" to describe the powerful industrialists who established large businesses in the late 1800s. The two terms suggest strikingly different images.

"Robber barons" implies that the business leaders built their fortunes by stealing from the public. According to this view, they drained the country of its natural resources and persuaded public officials to interpret laws in their favor. At the same time, these industrialists ruthlessly drove their competitors to ruin. They paid their workers meager wages and forced them to toil under dangerous and unhealthful conditions.

The term "captains of industry," on the other hand, suggests that the business leaders served their nation in a positive way. This view credits them with increasing the supply of goods by building factories, raising productivity, and expanding markets. In addition, the giant industrialists created the jobs that enabled many Americans to buy new goods and raise their standard of living. They also established outstanding museums, libraries, and universities, many of which still serve the public today.

Most historians believe that both views of America's early big business leaders contain elements of truth. The big business railroad giants of the late 1800s, such as Cornelius Vanderbilt, Edward Harriman, and James J. Hill, all exhibited qualities of both "robber barons" and "captains of industry." Consider how the examples of John D. Rockefeller and Andrew Carnegie, two of the country's first great industrialists, reflect this dual nature.

Industrial growth required the contributions of both workers and business owners, as this illustration suggests.

John D. Rockefeller John D. Rockefeller was on his way to accumulating a great fortune when he formed the Standard Oil Company in 1870. Some of the methods Rockefeller used to gain control of a large share of the oil industry were called into question, as you will read later in this section.

By the end of his life, however, Rockefeller had given over $500 million to establish or improve charities and institutions that he believed would benefit humanity. His philanthropy helped found the University of Chicago and the Rockefeller Foundation, which gave aid to institutions working in the fields of public health, the arts, social research, and many others.

Carnegie's "Gospel of Wealth" Andrew Carnegie's story is similar to Rockefeller's. (See the American Biography on the next page.) While expanding his steel business, Carnegie became a major public figure. In his books and speeches, he preached a "gospel of wealth." The essence of his message was simple: People should be free to make as much money as they can. After they make it, however, they should give it away.

More than 80 percent of Carnegie's fortune went toward some form of education. By the turn of the century, Carnegie had donated the money for nearly 3,000 free public libraries worldwide, supported artistic and research institutes, and set up a fund to study how to abolish war. By the time he died in 1919, Carnegie had given away some $350 million.

Still, not everyone approved of Carnegie's methods. As you will read later in this chapter, workers at his steel plants protested against his company's labor practices. Many others questioned the motives behind his good works. In reply, Carnegie argued that the success of men like him helped the nation as a whole:

> *It will be a great mistake for the community to shoot the millionaires, for they are the bees that make the most honey, and contribute most to the hive even after they have gorged themselves full.*
>
> —Andrew Carnegie

Social Darwinism

In statements such as these, Carnegie also suggested that the wealthy were somehow the most valuable group in society. This idea, popular in the late 1800s, was inferred from Charles Darwin's theory of evolution, first published in 1859. According to Darwin, all animal life had evolved by a process of "natural selection," a process in which only the fittest survived to reproduce.

After Darwin's death, Herbert Spencer in England and William Graham Sumner in the United States promoted a philosophy called **social Darwinism** that extended Darwin's concept to human society. Social Darwinists argued that society should interfere with competition as little as possible, and they opposed government intervention to protect workers. They believed that if the government would stay out of the affairs of business, those who were most "fit" would succeed and become rich. Social Darwinists believed that society as a whole would benefit from the success of the fit and the weeding out of the unfit. Americans were divided on the issue of government interference in private business. The government, however, neither taxed businesses' profits nor regulated their relations with workers.

Business on a Larger Scale

Many factors combined to create a new kind of business in the United States in the late 1800s. Businesses grew to include much greater sums of money, more workers, and more products than had previously existed in American business. Several characteristics help to explain how big business differed from earlier forms of business in the United States.

Larger pools of capital The most basic feature of the new giant industries was the huge amount of money, or capital, needed to run them. In order to pay for new, expensive technology, and to run large plants across the country, entrepreneurs had to invest massive amounts of capital themselves or borrow huge sums from investors. The high start-up costs also limited the ability of smaller businesses to enter an industry.

Wider geographic span The advent of railroads and the telegraph aided the geographic expansion of businesses. Big businesses often had factories and sales offices in several different regions throughout the country.

Broader range of operations Prior to big business, most businesses in the United States were highly specialized. Big businesses often combined multiple operations. They were responsible for all or almost all the stages of production.

Revised role of ownership The increased scope of operations, workers, products, and money changed the nature of ownership and management. Owners had less of a connection to all aspects of their businesses because their businesses were simply too large. In most cases, owners would hire a "professional manager" to run their business. The manager had no ownership in the business, but was responsible for overseeing its operations.

New methods of management Innovations, such as more complex systems of accounting, were also necessary for controlling these large amounts of

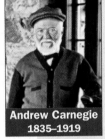

BIOGRAPHY

Andrew Carnegie 1835–1919

Born in Scotland in 1835, Andrew Carnegie knew something about the harsh side of industrialization. His father was a skilled weaver, but the invention of the power loom caused the market for skilled craftsworkers to collapse. Carnegie's family faced hard times. As a result, they immigrated to the United States in 1848, settling near Pittsburgh, Pennsylvania.

At 12 years old, Carnegie found work in a cotton mill at $1.20 a week. At age 18, he attained the post of secretary to the superintendent in the Pennsylvania Railroad Company. His boss there encouraged him to invest $500 in the Adams Express Company. Although this amount exceeded the available assets of his whole family, Carnegie's parents agreed to mortgage their house in order to come up with the money. He was amazed that he made money from this stock "without any attention." Carnegie had begun his career as a businessman.

READING CHECK
Why did owners hire managers to manage certain aspects of their business?

resources. As a result, big businesses developed new systems of formal, written rules and created specialized departments.

Gaining a Competitive Edge

In their efforts to compete and earn higher profits, industrialists used many methods, fair or unfair, to gain a competitive edge over their rivals. They attempted to pay as little as they could for raw materials, labor, and shipping, hoping to maintain the most efficient businesses in their industry.

New Market Structures The lure of gaining enormous profits from new booming industries attracted many investors and entrepreneurs. However, the start-up costs of creating certain types of businesses were high and, as a result, only a few companies could compete in those industries. A market structure such as this, which is dominated by only a few large, profitable firms, is called an **oligopoly.** Many industries today are oligopolies, such as those that produce breakfast cereals, cars, and household appliances.

Some companies set out to gain a **monopoly,** or complete control of a product or service. To do this, a business bought out its competitors or drove them out of business. Once consumers had no other place to turn for a given product or service, the sole remaining company would be free to raise its prices.

Toward the end of the 1800s, federal and state governments passed laws to prevent certain monopolistic practices. Those laws did not prevent or destroy all monopolies, however. One reason was that political leaders refused to attack the powerful business leaders.

Forming monopolies was not the only way to control an industry. Sometimes industrialists prospered by taking steps to limit competition with other firms. One way was to form a **cartel**—a loose association of businesses that make the same product. Members of the cartels agreed to limit the supply of their product and thus keep prices high.

Neither the monopolies nor the cartels were foolproof. Monopolies faced the threat of government action, and cartels tended to fall apart during hard economic times. To achieve a more reliable arrangement, industrialists came up with new strategies that would help them dominate their markets.

Carnegie Steel By the time he was 30, in 1865, Andrew Carnegie was making $50,000 a year, and he wanted to invest his wealth. The development of the Bessemer process persuaded Carnegie that steel would soon replace iron in many industries. During the early 1870s, near Pittsburgh, he founded the first steel plants to use the Bessemer process. These holdings would eventually grow into the Carnegie Steel Company, which he established in 1889.

Carnegie's business prospered. The company's wealth enabled him to make it even stronger. He soon had enough money to buy the companies that performed all the phases of steel production, from the mines that produced iron ore to the furnaces and mills that made pig iron and steel. He even bought the

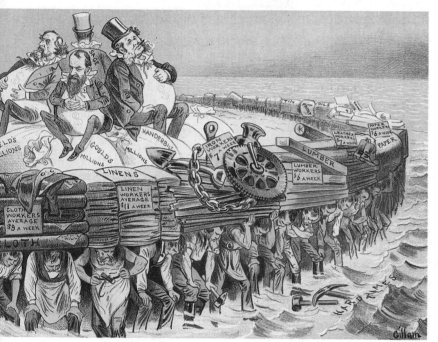

THE PROTECTORS OF OUR INDUSTRIES

INTERPRETING POLITICAL CARTOONS Some Americans were offended by the argument that business leaders protected jobs. **Drawing Conclusions** *What does this cartoon suggest about the relationship of workers to business leaders?*

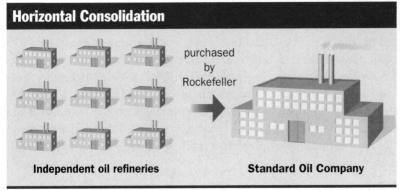

Independent oil refineries   purchased by Rockefeller   Standard Oil Company

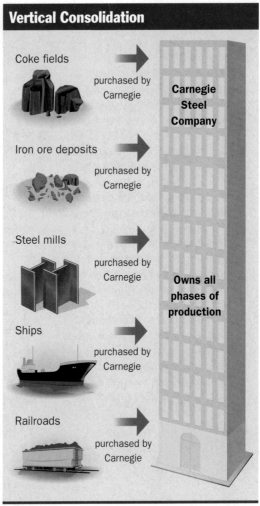

Coke fields — purchased by Carnegie

Iron ore deposits — purchased by Carnegie

Steel mills — purchased by Carnegie

Ships — purchased by Carnegie

Railroads — purchased by Carnegie

Carnegie Steel Company

Owns all phases of production

shipping and rail lines necessary to transport his products to market. Gaining control of the many different businesses that make up all phases of a product's development is known as **vertical consolidation.** (See diagram at right.)

This method of industrial control allowed Carnegie Steel to maintain very low production costs. This enabled Carnegie to cut his prices. He could charge less because of a phenomenon known as **economies of scale.** That is, as production increases, the cost of each item produced is lower. As Carnegie Steel expanded, its cost per item went down. Smaller companies were then at a disadvantage. Since they did not have the wealth to purchase all the phases of production, they were unable to cut their prices.

The Standard Oil Trust   Oil was another industry that was about to become huge. In 1859, when Edwin L. Drake discovered oil in Titusville, Pennsylvania, many new opportunities for oil arose. The new ease of attaining oil and oil's growing usefulness excited many wealthy businessmen, including John D. Rockefeller. He had become rich from a grain and meat partnership during the Civil War, and he saw the oil business as a way to become even richer. In 1863, Rockefeller built an oil refinery near Cleveland, Ohio. The refinery expanded rapidly. In 1870, Rockefeller and several associates formed the Standard Oil Company of Ohio.

The large size of Standard Oil helped Rockefeller cut some of his production costs. For example, Standard Oil did not need to use all of the railroad services that other companies used, such as insurance and storage. Therefore, Rockefeller was able to negotiate with railroad companies to obtain refunds on part of the cost of transporting his oil. As a result of these refunds, he could set Standard Oil's prices lower than those of his competitors. As Rockefeller's company sold more oil, he was able to undersell his competitors by charging even less.

Rockefeller knew that he could expand his business further. He figured that if he could own his competitors' oil refineries, he would be able to create a giant oil company that had even lower production costs. This is another method of industrial control, called **horizontal consolidation,** which involves the bringing together of many firms in the same business. (See diagram above.)

Rockefeller soon had enough money to buy out his competitors, but the law stood in his way. State laws prohibited one company from owning the stock of another. If Rockefeller were to "buy out" his competitors, he would in effect be owning their stock. State governments feared that this practice would reduce competition and restrain, or hold back, free trade.

INTERPRETING DIAGRAMS

Some companies grew more powerful through horizontal consolidation, in which companies simply bought competitors in their field (above left). Other companies grew more powerful through vertical consolidation, in which they controlled all the phases of production (above right). **Analyzing Information** *What problems might a business face when trying to compete with a company that has a vertical monopoly? With a company that has a horizontal monopoly?*

The Panic of 1893 In 1893, a period of business expansion suddenly ended, sending a severe shock to the economy. During the "Panic of 1893," hundreds of banks closed, and more than 15,000 businesses failed, sinking the economy into a four-year depression. The resulting unemployment caused widespread misery, especially among workers and their families.

How does such a panic happen? At some point, businesses may begin churning out more goods than consumers want or can afford. Then they have to lower prices in order to sell their products. To cover their losses, they often cut wages and lay off workers. In turn, investors begin to fear that key businesses, heavily in debt, might not be able to repay their loans. Investors rush to sell stock, stock prices fall, and companies go bankrupt.

Samuel Dodd, Rockefeller's lawyer, had an idea to get around this ban. In 1882, the owners of Standard Oil and the companies allied with it agreed to combine their operations. They would turn over their assets to a board of nine trustees. In return, they were promised a share of the profits of the new organization. The board of trustees, which Rockefeller controlled, managed the companies as a single unit called a **trust.**

In time, 40 companies joined the trust. Because the companies did not officially merge, they did not violate any laws. Rockefeller's trust, a new kind of monopoly, controlled a high percentage of the nation's oil-refining capacity.

The Government Response Many Americans were skeptical and wary of trusts and other large business organizations. Americans who feared that trusts were limiting industrial competition began to demand government action to break up these industrial giants.

Despite questions about their practices, the large industrialists found sympathy and support from many government officials and leaders. The government was hesitant to interfere with the actions of big business. After all, these firms contributed mightily to the country's rising level of wealth. By the turn of the century, such mammoth companies as American Telephone and Telegraph, Swift and Armour, General Electric, Westinghouse, and Dupont were some of America's greatest success stories.

Congress did pass a law, however, in 1890, in an attempt to limit the amount of control a business could have over an industry. The **Sherman Antitrust Act** outlawed any combination of companies that restrained interstate trade or commerce.

The act, however, proved ineffective against trusts for nearly 15 years. Its vague wording essentially meant that the courts had to determine what the law said. As a result, the courts, which were largely pro-business in their views, enforced the law infrequently. The law actually *aided* giant corporations when it was applied successfully against labor unions. Federal officials argued that labor unions restrained trade because workers were combining to gain an advantage.

Section 2 Assessment

READING COMPREHENSION

1. How did the theory of **social Darwinism** affect the government's relationship to big business?

2. What were some features of the new big businesses?

3. How did methods such as **vertical** and **horizontal consolidation,** and factors such as **economies of scale** help companies dominate their markets?

4. Why did the **Sherman Antitrust Act** seek to stop big business from forming **trusts?**

CRITICAL THINKING AND WRITING

5. **Making Comparisons** Andrew Carnegie and John D. Rockefeller were both giant industrialists. Compare and contrast the ways they entered into, controlled, and dominated their respective industries.

6. **Writing to Persuade** Create an outline for a persuasive essay in which you explain why you view the nation's early industrialists as either "robber barons" or "captains of industry."

For: An activity on Carnegie and Rockefeller
Visit: PHSchool.com
Web Code: mrd-5132

Industrialization and Workers

READING FOCUS

- What factors led to a growing American work force between 1860 and 1900?

- What was factory work like at the turn of the century?

- Why was it necessary for entire families to work?

MAIN IDEA

Industry relied on its laborers, who worked in low-paying, unskilled jobs and often in unsafe factories.

KEY TERMS

piecework
sweatshop
division of labor

TARGET READING SKILL

Understand Effects As you read, complete the following chart to show some of the positive and negative effects of industrialization on workers.

Effects of Industrialization		
Event/Aspect	**Positive Effects**	**Negative Effects**
Growing work force	Opens up many new jobs for immigrants and ex-farmers	Supply of workers drives wages down; whole families forced to work

Setting the Scene The abundant natural resources, inventive minds, and risk-taking entrepreneurs of the United States all contributed to the nation's industrial expansion. This expansion would not have been possible, however, without the millions of laborers who allowed the companies to succeed.

Sadie Frowne immigrated to the United States from Poland in 1899 when she was 13 years old. Her family, like so many others, hoped that America would provide greater opportunities for making money and living comfortably. Sadie began working in New York City, where she made skirts by machine.

> 66 *I was new at the work and the foreman scolded me a great deal. . . . I did not know at first that you must not look around and talk, and I made many mistakes with my sewing, so that I was often called a 'stupid animal.' . . . The machines go like mad all day, because the faster you work, the more money you get. Sometimes in my haste I get my finger caught and the needle goes right through it. It goes so quick, tho[ugh], that it does not hurt much. . . . We all have accidents like that. . . .* 99
>
> —Garment worker Sadie Frowne

VIEWING HISTORY Industrialization led to a growing work force and new work environment. **Identifying Central Issues** *How did industrial workers respond to their working conditions?*

The Growing Work Force

Around 14 million people immigrated to the United States between 1860 and 1900. Most came in the hope of finding work in the country's booming industrial centers. During the Civil War, when labor was scarce, the federal government encouraged immigration by passing the Contract Labor Act in 1864. This law allowed employers to enter into contracts with immigrants. Employers would pay the cost of their passage in return for immigrants' agreeing to work for a certain amount of time, up to a year. Employers soon began actively recruiting foreign laborers.

In another dramatic population shift, some 8 or 9 million Americans moved to cities during the late 1800s. Most of them fled poor economic conditions on the nation's farms. A long drought beginning in 1887, combined with

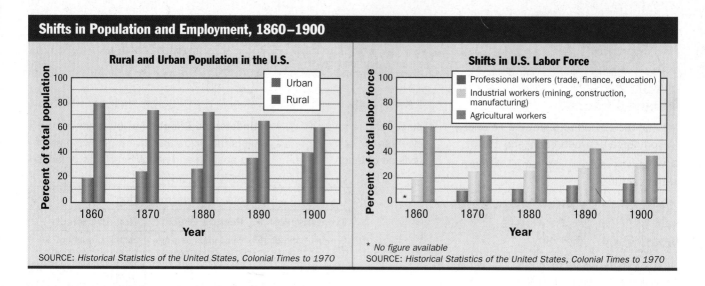

Shifts in Population and Employment, 1860–1900

Rural and Urban Population in the U.S.

Legend: ■ Urban ■ Rural

Y-axis: Percent of total population
X-axis: Year — 1860, 1870, 1880, 1890, 1900

SOURCE: *Historical Statistics of the United States, Colonial Times to 1970*

Shifts in U.S. Labor Force

Legend:
■ Professional workers (trade, finance, education)
■ Industrial workers (mining, construction, manufacturing)
■ Agricultural workers

Y-axis: Percent of total labor force
X-axis: Year — 1860, 1870, 1880, 1890, 1900

* No figure available

SOURCE: *Historical Statistics of the United States, Colonial Times to 1970*

INTERPRETING GRAPHS
Industrial growth in the mid- to late 1800s led to shifts in population and the work force. **Drawing Conclusions** *What do you think accounted for the rise in the percentage of professional workers?*

low prices and more competition from foreign wheat producers, left many farm families penniless. Plentiful work in the factories lured the former farmers, as did many of the new attractions of city life.

Factory Work

By 1860, most states had established a ten-hour workday, yet they rarely enforced it. Thus, most laborers worked twelve hours, six days a week—and even more when they had to meet production goals. An 1868 federal law granted government employees an eight-hour day, but this did not affect private industry.

In many industries, employers paid workers not by the time worked but by what they produced. Workers received a fixed amount for each finished piece they produced—for example, a few cents for a garment or a number of cigars. This system of **piecework** meant that those who worked the fastest and produced the most pieces earned the most money. Most piecework was performed in what came to be known as a **sweatshop**—a shop where employees worked long hours at low wages and under poor working conditions.

Increasing Efficiency In 1881, Frederick Winslow Taylor set out to improve worker efficiency in the steel plant where he was chief engineer. He began to study the workers, trying to see how much time they took to do various jobs. Then he broke down each task into a number of steps and determined how long each step should take. In the same way he also studied each motion needed in a task. The goal of Taylor's time and motion studies was to increase worker productivity and thereby increase profits.

Taylor used his studies as the foundation of an entire system for the scientific management of workers. In 1911, he described this system in his book, *The Principles of Scientific Management*:

> ❝ The work of every workman is fully planned out by the management at least one day in advance, and each man receives in most cases complete written instructions, describing in detail the task which he is to accomplish, as well as the means to be used in doing the work . . . and the exact time allowed for doing it. ❞
>
> —Frederick Winslow Taylor

Focus on TECHNOLOGY

Technology and the Arts The emergence of clanging, greasy machines at the end of the nineteenth century entirely changed the American landscape. Many Americans, including writers and artists, were delighted with the new machines and the human progress they represented. Nathaniel Hawthorne described trip hammers as "very pleasant objects to look at, working so massively as they do, and yet so accurately, chewing up, as it were, the hot iron, and fashioning it into shape, with a sort of mighty and gigantic gentleness in their mode of action."

Some employers had their own, unscientific methods of improving efficiency. They simply increased the speed of factory machines or gave each employee more work. Increases in productivity, however, did not always translate into higher pay for workers. On the contrary, greater factory efficiency often led to layoffs because businesses no longer needed as many workers. In addition, many workers felt that these methods gave owners too much control over their work. As a result, most workers came to resent them.

The Division of Labor Athough its goal was to increase worker productivity, the methods used in scientific management brought about a change in the relationship between the worker and the product he or she created. Artisans traditionally made a product from start to finish. Doing so required them to perform a variety of tasks. In contrast, factory workers usually performed only one small task, over and over, and rarely even saw the finished product. This **division of labor** into separate tasks proved to be efficient, but it took much of the joy out of the work.

The relationship between workers and owners also changed. In smaller businesses, owners and workers had day-to-day interactions with each other. Because of the large size of new big businesses, owners seldom even visited the factory floor where workers toiled. In the worst cases, the workers, called "hands" or "operatives," were viewed as interchangeable parts in a vast and impersonal machine. One factory manager in 1883 declared, "I regard my people as I regard my machinery. So long as they can do my work for what I choose to pay them, I keep them, getting out of them all I can."

The Work Environment Unlike farmers, who had more flexibility in the pace they worked, factory workers were ruled by the clock, which told them when to start, take any breaks, and stop work. In addition, discipline within the factory was strict. To make a profit, factory managers needed to run an efficient operation. Thus they might fine or fire workers for a range of offenses, such as being late, talking, or refusing to do a task.

Workplaces were not always safe. The noise of the machines could be deafening. Lighting and ventilation were often poor. Fatigue, faulty equipment, and careless training resulted in frequent fires and accidents. Despite the harsh conditions, employers suffered no shortage of labor. Factory work offered higher pay and more opportunities than most people could hope to find elsewhere.

Laboring in factories or mines and performing dangerous work was unhealthy for all workers. But it especially threatened growing children. Many children became stunted in both body and mind. In 1892, social reformer Jacob Riis explained the impact of factory work on children in a book titled *Children of the Poor.* Riis wrote that people who spent their whole childhood on the factory floor grew "to manhood and womanhood . . . with the years that should have prepared them for life's work gone in hopeless and profitless drudgery." Thanks to Riis and others, the practice of child labor came under broad attack in the 1890s and early 1900s, prompting states to begin curbing this practice through legislation.

VIEWING FINE ART John Ferguson Weir's painting *Gun Foundry* presents a vivid image of the nation's industrial might. **Drawing Inferences** *What does the painting suggest about the conditions faced by workers?*

Working Families

In the 1880s, children made up more than 5 percent of the industrial labor force. By the end of the 1800s, nearly one in five children between the ages of 10 and 16 was employed. For many households, children's wages meant the difference between going hungry or having food on the table.

As a result, children often left school at the age of 12 or 13 to work. Girls sometimes took factory jobs so that their brothers could stay in school. If a mother could not make money working at home, she might take a factory job, leaving her children with relatives or neighbors. If an adult became ill, died, or could not find or keep a job, children as young as 6 or 7 had to bring in cash.

In the 1800s, families in need relied on private charities. These charities could not afford to help everyone, however. They had limited resources, so only the neediest received the food, clothing, and shelter that charities had to offer. Except in rare cases, government did not provide public assistance. Unemployment insurance, for example, did not exist, so workers received no payments as a result of layoffs or factory closings. The popular theory of social Darwinism held that poverty resulted from personal weakness. Many thought that offering relief to the unemployed would encourage idleness.

VIEWING HISTORY Many children worked in hazardous conditions. The boys above worked in coal mines. The grime that covers their faces also clogged their lungs, leading to disease. The girl in the photo on the right operated dangerous machinery in a textile mill. **Drawing Conclusions** *How do you think Americans at the time reacted to photos such as these?*

Section 3 Assessment

READING COMPREHENSION

1. Why did the American work force grow in the late 1800s?

2. How did **piecework** change the nature of factory work?

3. What were the effects of Taylor's scientific management studies and the **division of labor** on workers?

4. Why did children work?

CRITICAL THINKING AND WRITING

5. Identifying Alternatives Although it differed from factory work, work on family farms was also difficult and dangerous. Explain what you think were the key differences between the two types of work.

6. Writing to Describe Prepare an outline for an essay describing the daily life of a typical factory worker.

For: An activity on labor conditions in the late 1800s
Visit: PHSchool.com
Web Code: mrd-5133

READING FOCUS

- What impact did industrialization have on the gulf between rich and poor?

- What were the goals of the early labor unions in the United States?

- Why did Eugene V. Debs organize the American Railway Union?

- What were the causes and outcomes of the major strikes in the late 1800s?

MAIN IDEA

In the late 1800s, workers organized labor unions to improve their wages and working conditions.

KEY TERMS

socialism
craft union
collective bargaining
industrial union
scab
anarchist
Haymarket Riot
Homestead Strike
Pullman Strike

TARGET READING SKILL

Identify Main Ideas As you read, complete the chart below, filling in the successes and failures of the labor unions.

Labor Unions	
Successes	**Failures**
The Knights of Labor protect railroad wages from being cut in 1885 through the use of the strike.	The Great Railroad Strike of 1877 turns violent, giving the public and the government a bad taste for unions.

Setting the Scene

" *What shall the workers do? Sit idly by and see the vast resources of nature and the human mind be utilized and monopolized for the benefit of the comparative few? No. The laborers must learn to think and act, and soon, too, that only by the power of organization, and common concert of action, can . . . their rights to life . . . be recognized, and liberty and rights secured.* "

—Samuel Gompers

Industrialization had lowered the prices of consumer goods, but in the late 1800s most factory workers did not earn enough to buy them. The successful entrepreneurs of the era had worked hard. Many, like Carnegie, had used their wealth to provide money for good works. Still, in hard times only the poor went hungry. Increasingly, working men and women took their complaints directly and forcefully to their employers.

Gulf Between Rich and Poor

In 1890, the richest 9 percent of Americans held nearly 75 percent of the national wealth. In the best of times, the average worker could earn only a few hundred dollars a year. Many workers resented the extravagant lifestyles of many factory owners. Poor families had little hope of relief when hard times hit. Some suffered in silence, trusting that tomorrow would be better. Others became politically active in an effort to improve their lives. A few of these individuals were drawn to the idea of **socialism,** which was then gaining popularity in Europe.

Socialism is an economic and political philosophy that favors public instead of private control

VIEWING HISTORY Many wealthy industrialists enjoyed great personal wealth and luxurious comforts (left). In stark contrast, many workers lived in crowded boarding houses (right). **Identifying Central Issues** *How did many workers respond to the contrast between the rich and poor?*

of the means of production. Socialists believe that society at large, not just private individuals, should take charge of a nation's wealth. That wealth, they say, should be distributed equally to everyone.

Socialism began in the 1830s as an idealistic movement. Early Socialists believed that people should cooperate, not compete, in producing goods. Socialism then grew more radical, reflecting the ideas of a German philosopher named Karl Marx. In 1848, Marx, along with Friedrich Engels, wrote a famous pamphlet called the *Communist Manifesto*. In it they denounced the capitalist economic system and predicted that workers would one day overturn it.

Most Americans opposed socialism. The wealthy saw it as a threat to their fortunes. Politicians saw it as a threat to public order. Americans in general, including most workers, saw it as a threat to the deeply rooted American ideals of private property, free enterprise, and individual liberty.

The Rise of Labor Unions

A small percentage of American workers became Socialists and called for greater government intervention in the economy. Far more workers, however, chose to work within the system by forming labor unions.

Early Labor Unions   The early years of industrialization had spawned a few labor unions, organized among workers in certain trades, such as construction and textile manufacturing. The first national labor organization was the National Trades Union, which was open to workers from all crafts. It survived only a few years before being destroyed by the panic and depression of 1837.

Strong local unions resurfaced after the Civil War. They began by providing help for their members in bad times, but soon became the means for expressing workers' demands to employers. These demands included shorter workdays, higher wages, and better working conditions.

National unions also began to reappear at this time. In Baltimore in 1866, labor activists formed the National Labor Union, representing some 60,000 members. In 1872, this union nominated a candidate for President. It failed, however, to survive a depression that began the following year. Indeed, unions in general suffered a steep decline in membership as a result of the poor economy.

Meeting posters and labor union badges such as these appeared around the country as labor unions grew more popular.

The Knights of Labor   Another national union, the Noble and Holy Order of the Knights of Labor, formed in Philadelphia in 1869. The Knights hoped to organize all working men and women, skilled and unskilled, into a single union. Membership included farmers and factory workers as well as shopkeepers and office workers. The union recruited African Americans, 60,000 of whom joined. After 1881, the union also recruited women members.

Under the leadership of former machinist Terence Powderly, the Knights pursued broad social reforms. These included equal pay for equal work, the eight-hour workday, and an end to child labor. They did not emphasize higher wages as their primary goal.

The leaders of the Knights preferred not to use the strike as a tool. Most members, however, differed with their leadership on this issue. In fact, it was a strike that helped the Knights achieve their greatest strength. In 1885, when

★ Standardized Test Prep

Analyzing Political Cartoons ▶

28. In the background of this cartoon, a concerned citizen tries to alert Uncle Sam to the dangerous scene in the foreground where a snake, symbolizing monopolies, threatens lady liberty. What does the position of the snake's tail symbolize?

   A The monopolies' control of Congress
   B Congress's struggle against monopolies
   C Anti-trust legislation
   D The end of monopoly control in the country

29. What is the cartoon's overall message?

Interpreting Data

Turn to the population and labor graphs in Section 3.

30. Which statement BEST summarizes the information shown in both graphs?

   A The rural population decreased between 1860 and 1900.
   B The number of agricultural workers and city dwellers rose between 1860 and 1900.
   C The percentage of professional workers decreased as people began moving away from farms.
   D As people moved to the cities, a higher percentage of the population became industrial or professional workers.

31. What was the main reason for shifts in population and employment in the late 1800s?

   F increasing immigration and decreasing farm prices
   G the lure of new attractions in the nation's growing cities
   H the growth of railroads and expansion of American industry
   I high wages and incentives offered by factory owners

Test-Taking Tip

To answer Question 30, study both of the bar graphs before looking at the possible answers. What is the overall trend in urban population? What is the overall trend in rural population? Choose the answer which summarizes the information in BOTH graphs.

Applying the Chapter Skill

Using Cross-Sectional Maps Use map resources to plot a route across the Appalachian Mountains from Raleigh, North Carolina, to Columbus, Ohio. Then draw a cross-sectional map of your route.

For: Chapter 6 Self-Test
Visit: PHSchool.com
Web Code: mra-5135

Looking to the West
(1860–1900)

Grand Canyon of the Yellowstone,
by Thomas Moran, 1872

Longhorn steer

A Ute settlement in the Great
Basin region

American Events

1862
Federal land grants ignite western settlement.

1867
Founding of Abilene, Kansas, spurs era of Texas cattle drives.

1872
Yellowstone National Park is created.

1876
Custer and his men are killed at Battle of Little Bighorn.

Presidential Terms: A. Lincoln 1861–1865   A. Johnson 1865–1869   U. S. Grant 1869–1877   R. Hayes 1877–1881

1860   **1870**

World Events

Swedish scientist Alfred Nobel invents dynamite.
1867

Canada begins forcing Indians onto reservations.
1871

Statehood in the West

CANADA

Washington
1889

Montana
1889

North Dakota
1889

Minnesota

Oregon
STATE OF OREGON
1859
1859

Idaho
1890

South Dakota
1889

40°N

Wyoming
1890

Nebraska
1867

Iowa

Nevada
1864

Utah
1896

Colorado
1876

Kansas
KANSAS
1861

Missouri

California
CALIFORNIA REPUBLIC
1850

Oklahoma
OKLAHOMA
1907

Arkansas

PACIFIC OCEAN

Arizona
1912

New Mexico
1912

30°N

120°W

Texas
1845

Louisiana

MEXICO

N

90°W

1890 Date of statehood

State flag today

0 100 200 mi.
0 100 200 km

1889

"Boomers" race to stake claims as tracts of Indian Territory open in Oklahoma.

1890

Wounded Knee Massacre marks the end of the Indian wars. The Sherman Silver Purchase Act aims to boost silver currency.

1896

Democratic presidential candidate William Jennings Bryan gives pro-silver "Cross of Gold" speech.

1887

The Dawes Act allots land to individual Indians.

J. Garfield 1881
C. Arthur 1881–1885

G. Cleveland 1885–1889

B. Harrison 1889–1893

G. Cleveland 1893–1897

W. McKinley 1897–1901

1880

1890

1900

Britain takes sole control of Egypt.

1882

Canada's transcontinental railroad completed despite uprising by Plains Indians.

1885

Russia's last czar, Nicholas II, begins his reign.

1894

Australian nationhood is approved by Britain.

1900

Moving West

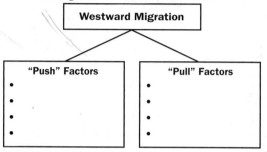

VIEWING HISTORY Buffalo dot the landscape today in South Dakota's Badlands National Park. Majestic prairie scenes like this greeted early settlers. **Expressing Problems Clearly** *To many newcomers, the first sight of the Great Plains was both dazzling and daunting. Explain this statement.*

Setting the Scene

At minus 50 degrees, a Montana winter night could turn a fatted steer into a furry icicle. In the Southwest, heat topping 110 degrees left the bleached bones of prospectors strewn across the desert. Describing the harsh winters of the open plains, one newspaper editor called western Kansas "a prairie where the cows give blue milk and the wind whips the long-tailed pigs to death."

After the Civil War, pioneers settled from the Mississippi River to the partly populated California coast. Newcomers from Vermont, or Kentucky, or Germany wrote home with fantastic tales of these strange lands:

> 66 *The wind was too fierce. . . . It actually blows the feathers off the chickens' backs. . . . I can't put up many pictures and things for everytime the door opens they all blow off the wall. . . . [W]e noticed how terrible loud everyone talks out here and now we find ourselves just shouting away at the top of our voices. . . . [U]nless you yell you can't be heard at all.* 99
> —South Dakota settler Mary Clark

Truly, you have to wonder: What moved people like Mary Clark to journey to this land of known and unknown dangers?

The Lure of the West

The settlers of the American West had many reasons for giving up their old, sometimes comfortable, lives for a new start in the wilderness. The West seized the American imagination. It kindled people's sense of adventure, their entrepreneurial spirit, and their appetite for profit and conquest.

When scholars study the reasons for major migrations, they look at what they call **push-pull factors**—events and conditions that either force (push) people to move elsewhere or strongly attract (pull) them to do so.

Push Factors Various conditions urged settlers westward. The Civil War had displaced thousands of farmers, former slaves, and other workers. Eastern farmland was increasingly costly, certainly for many African Americans or for impoverished immigrants. Failed entrepreneurs sought a second chance in a new location. Ethnic and religious repression caused both Americans (such as the Mormons) and Europeans to seek freedom in the West. The open spaces also sheltered outlaws on the run.

Yet the West was more than just a refuge for discouraged people and shady characters. The region offered temptations and adventures that lured—pulled—settlers westward.

Pull Factor: Government Incentives   Before the Civil War, disagreements between the North and South over the extension of slavery in the West delayed settlement in the region. During the war, with that issue eliminated, however, the federal government promoted western migration by giving away public lands—or selling them at rock-bottom prices.

Under the **Pacific Railway Acts** of 1862 and 1864, the government gave large land grants to the Union Pacific and Central Pacific railroads. The 1862 act granted every alternate section of public land to the amount of five alternate sections per mile on each side of the railroad. From 1850 to 1871, the railroads received more than 175 million acres of public land—an area more than one tenth the size of the whole United States and larger than the state of Texas.

Railroad expansion provided new avenues of migration into the American interior. The railroads sold portions of their land to arriving settlers at a handsome profit. Lands closest to the tracks drew the highest prices, because farmers and ranchers wanted to locate near railway stations.

To further encourage western settlement, Congress passed the **Morrill Land-Grant Act** of 1862. It gave state governments millions of acres of western lands, which the states could then sell to raise money for the creation of "land grant" colleges specializing in agriculture and mechanical arts. The states sold their land grants to bankers and **land speculators,** people who bought up large areas of land in the hope of selling it later for a profit.

The government program that really set the wagons rolling west was the **Homestead Act,** signed by President Lincoln in 1862. Under the act, for a small fee settlers could have 160 acres of land—a quarter-mile square—if they met certain conditions: They were at least 21 years old or the heads of families. They were American citizens or immigrants filing for citizenship. They built a house of a certain minimum size (usually 12 feet by 14 feet) on their claims and lived in it at least six months a year. Finally, they had to farm the land for five years in a row before claiming ownership.

The act created more than 372,000 farms. By 1900, settlers had filed 600,000 claims for more than 80 million acres under the Homestead Act.

Pull Factor: Private Property   A key incentive to western settlement was the availability of legally enforceable, transferable property rights. The Homestead Act and state and local laws helped to limit settlers' risks and avoid a total free-for-all. Miners, cattle ranchers, and farmers all received certain rights to land and possessions. Land parcels were measured, registered, and deeded. Cattle branding established ownership. Enforcement of water rights provided stable water sources for crops and for human and animal consumption.

In time, established American economic concepts of private property, private enterprise, and a free market extended across the continent. One editor, hoping to raise the standards of a rather lawless town, reminded his readers that

VIEWING HISTORY Settlers registered their claims at this land office in Round Pond, Oklahoma Territory. **Determining Relevance** *How did the surveying and registration of land claims encourage settlement and free enterprise in the West?*

"people who have money to invest go where they are protected by law."

Settlers From Far and Wide

New groups of settlers soon joined the mainly white easterners who first cut trails into the western wilderness. Cheap land and new jobs attracted people of other countries and ethnic groups. In growing towns and cities throughout the region, settlers spoke a rich mixture of languages and practiced a variety of customs.

European immigrants arrived in the middle 1800s, many seeking land to farm. Some German settlers established farms in the Great Plains. Other settled in Midwestern cities. They brought the Lutheran religion and a commitment to hard work and education. Scandinavian Lutherans settled the northern plains from Iowa to Minnesota to the Dakotas, many pursuing dairy farming.

Irish, Italians, European Jews, and Chinese tended to settle in concentrated communities, initially in West Coast cities. Eventually they gravitated to growing cities in the American interior, taking jobs in mining, railroad construction, and other trades. Ranching, mining, farm labor, and jobs in boom towns drew Americans and foreigners alike. Mexicans and Mexican Americans contributed to the growth of ranching.

After the Civil War, thousands of African Americans rode or even walked westward, often fleeing the violence and exploitation that followed Reconstruction. In 1879, Benjamin "Pap" Singleton led groups of southern blacks on a mass "Exodus," a trek inspired by the biblical account of the Israelites' flight from Egypt to a prophesied homeland. Hence, the settlers called themselves **Exodusters.** Some 50,000 or more Exodusters migrated west.

The Shifting Frontier

The "frontier" was not a line that moved westward in a unified motion. Various regions were settled at different times. Yet by 1890, settlements dotted the prairie every 10 miles or so. Towns gave rise to cities at a stunning pace. But one reality remained: The West was already occupied—by Native Americans.

Section 1 Assessment

READING COMPREHENSION

1. Why was the **Homestead Act** such a significant factor in the westward migration?

2. How did the **Pacific Railway Acts** influence Western settlement?

3. (a) What main groups of Americans and immigrants settled the West? (b) Describe the contrasting cultural influences they brought to the region.

CRITICAL THINKING AND WRITING

4. **Drawing Inferences** Why do you think some African Americans faced less discrimination in the West than they had experienced in the East?

5. **Writing to Inform** You were an unemployed eastern factory worker with a family who moved to Kansas. Write a letter to a friend back East, describing this new place and explaining why you made this risky move.

For: An activity on Exoduster towns
Visit: PHSchool.com
Web Code: mrd-5141

Conflict With Native Americans

READING FOCUS

- What caused changes in the life of the Plains Indians?

- How did government policies and battlefield challenges affect the Indian wars?

- What changes occurred in federal Indian policies by 1900?

MAIN IDEA

American expansion into the West led to the near destruction of Native American societies.

KEY TERMS

Great Plains
nomad
reservation
Battle of Little Bighorn
Ghost Dance
Massacre at Wounded Knee
assimilation
Dawes Act
boomers
sooners

TARGET READING SKILL

Understand Effects As you read, complete this chart, listing federal Indian policies in the West and their outcomes.

Federal Indian Policies	Results
Treaties	Often violated by U.S.

Setting the Scene Easterners called it "the Indian problem." What could and should be done with western Indians so that their lands could be used productively, as they saw it, for mining, ranching, and farming?

To Native Americans, the "problem" was a life-or-death battle. In the second half of the 1800s, they resisted an all-out assault on their warriors, their women and children, their homelands, their sources of food and shelter, and their ways of life. It was a race against time. They faced their fate in varying ways—with bloodthirsty anger, solemn faith, and cautious compromise. At last, when their time ran out, they faced resignation, fatigue, and heartbreak.

The Life of the Plains Indians

Long before eastern settlers arrived, changes had affected the lives of Native Americans on the **Great Plains,** the vast grassland between the Mississippi River and the Rocky Mountains. The changes blended with and altered traditions that had existed for generations.

Well into the 1800s, millions of buffalo ranged the Great Plains. These huge beasts provided life-sustaining supplies to the Plains Indians: meat, hides for making shelters and clothing, and a wealth of other uses. The opening of relations with French and American fur traders in the 1700s allowed the Plains Indians to exchange hides for guns, making buffalo hunting easier.

By the mid-1700s, horses' hooves thundered across the plains. The Spanish had brought horses to Mexico in the 1500s, and Native Americans obtained them through trading and raids. The impact of the horse on Native American culture was profound.

While many Indian nations continued to live mainly as farmers, hunters, and gatherers, others became **nomads.** These are people who travel from place to place, usually following available food sources, instead of living in one location. With horses, nomadic peoples were better able to carry their possessions as they followed the vast buffalo herds across the plains.

VIEWING FINE ART Artist George Catlin lived with the Plains Indians for years, producing more than 500 sketches and paintings of Native American life, including this work, *Buffalo Chase—Single Death.* **Analyzing Visual Information** *How does Catlin depict the equipment, skills, and character needed to hunt the buffalo?*

The arrival of the horse also brought upheaval. Warfare among Indian nations, to gain possessions or for conquest, rose to a new intensity when waged on horseback. Success in war brought wealth and prestige. The rise of warrior societies led to a decline in village life, as nomadic Native Americans raided more settled groups.

Indian Wars and Government Policy

Before the Civil War, Native Americans west of the Mississippi continued to inhabit their traditional homelands. An uneasy peace prevailed, punctured by occasional hostilities as workers laid railroad track deeper into Indian lands and as the California gold rush of 1848 drew wagon trains across the plains. By the 1860s, however, Americans had discovered that the interior concealed a treasure chest of resources. The battle for the West was on.

Causes of Clashes   Settlers' views of land and resource use contrasted sharply with Native American traditions. Many settlers felt justified in taking Indian land because, in their view, they would make it more productive. To Native Americans, the settlers were simply invaders. Increasing intrusions, especially into sacred lands, angered even chiefs who had welcomed the newcomers.

Making Treaties   Initially, the government tried to restrict the movements of nomadic Native Americans by negotiating treaties. Some treaties arranged for the federal purchase of Indian land, often for little in return. Other treaties restricted Native Americans to **reservations,** federal lands set aside for them.

The treaties produced misunderstandings and outright fraud. The government continued its longtime practice of designating as "tribes" groups that often had no single leadership or even related clans or traditions. Federal agents selected "chiefs" to sign treaties, but the signers often did not represent the majority of their people. Honest government agents negotiated some pacts in good faith; others had no intention of honoring the treaties. Some sought bribes or dealt violently with tribes until they signed. Indian signers often did not know that they were restricted to the reservations, and that they might be in danger if they left.

The federal Bureau of Indian Affairs (BIA), a part of the Interior Department, was supposed to manage the delivery of critical supplies to the reservations. But widespread corruption within the BIA and among its agents resulted in supplies being mishandled or stolen.

The government made some attempts to protect the reservations, but their poorly manned outposts were no match for waves of land-hungry settlers. Unscrupulous settlers stole land, killed buffalo, diverted water supplies, and attacked Indian camps. After a treaty violation in 1873, Kicking Bird, a Kiowa, declared: "I have taken the white man by the hand, thinking him to be a friend, but he is not a friend; government has deceived us. . . ."

Native Americans reacted in frustration and anger. Groups who disagreed with the treaties refused to obey. Acts of violence on both sides set off cycles of revenge that occurred with increasing brutality.

Battlefield Challenges

Federal lawmakers came to view the treaties as useless. In 1871, the government declared that it would make no more treaties and recognize no chiefs.

Focus on
GOVERNMENT

Acquiring Indian Lands From the 1860s to 1900, presidential administrations gained Native American lands however they could: through treaties, land purchases, forced relocation of Indians to reservations, wars—or simply looking the other way and letting settlers solve the problem. In 1875, after failed attempts to purchase the mineral-rich but sacred Black Hills of the Sioux, President Ulysses S. Grant gave General William T. Sherman the go-ahead for mining the treaty-protected territory. Sherman wrote that if the miners were to pour in, "I understand that the president and the Interior Department will wink at it." Word got out, and soon the hills were crawling with prospectors.

Inconclusive Battles   In 1865, one general urged the government to "finish this Indian war this season, so that it will stay finished." Yet the tragic conflicts would drag on for nearly three more decades.

Both sides lacked a coherent strategy along with the resources to achieve one. They reacted to each others' attacks in a long, exhausting dance of death. The Indians were outgunned, and suffered far more casualties. Yet in the end, they succumbed less to war than to disease and to lack of food and shelter.

The United States Army, spread across the South to monitor Reconstruction, had slim resources to send to the West. With infantry, cavalry, and artillery units spread thinly across the vast region, the Army could not build coordinated battle fronts. Battle lines constantly shifted as settlers moved into new areas. Most confrontations were small hit-and-run raids with few decisive outcomes. Still, experienced army generals managed to lead successful campaigns in some regions.

Indian warriors fought mostly on their own turf, employing tactics they had used against their traditional enemies for generations. Profit-seeking whites sold guns to the warriors. Native American groups made some alliances in attempts to defeat the intruders, but their efforts usually failed. Moreover, the army often pitted Indian groups against one another.

The Soldier's Life on the Frontier   Who would volunteer for this army? Living conditions: $13 a month; a leftover Civil War uniform; rotten food. Duties: build forts; drive settlers from reservations; escort the mail; stop gunfights; prevent liquor smuggling and stagecoach robberies; protect miners, railroad crews, and visiting politicians; and—occasionally—fight Indians. Hazards: smallpox, cholera, and flu; accidents; endless marching; and death in battle. In fact, thousands of recruits—former Civil War soldiers, freed slaves, jobless men—did join the frontier army. Unlike the typical Indian warrior, the average soldier on the plains rarely saw battle. Up to a third of the men deserted.

AMERICAN BIOGRAPHY

Chief Joseph 1840–1904

Born in 1840, *Hin-mah-too-yah-lat-kekt*, or "Thunder Rolling Down the Mountain," was better known by the name he got from his father, Joseph, a converted Christian. As his father lay dying in 1871, he made Joseph promise never to sell their scenic, fruitful homeland in the Northwest. The promise proved impossible to keep.

Forced to flee in 1877, the Nez Percé fought skillfully, but their chief found no joy in it. In his surrender speech, Joseph reportedly declared, "Hear me, my chiefs! I am tired. My heart is sick and sad. From where the sun now stands I will fight no more forever."

Chief Joseph's band was exiled to Indian Territory (Oklahoma), where all six of Joseph's children died. In 1885, the chief was returned to the modern-day state of Washington, but not to his father's land. He died in 1904 "of a broken heart," his doctor said.

Key Battles

Native Americans and the army met in battles throughout the interior West. In major engagements, the army usually prevailed.

The Sand Creek Massacre, 1864   The southern Cheyenne occupied the central plains, including parts of Colorado Territory. After some gruesome Cheyenne raids on wagon trains and settlements east of Denver, Colorado's governor took advantage of a peace campaign led by Cheyenne chief Black Kettle. Promised protection, Black Kettle and other chiefs followed orders to camp at Sand Creek.

Colonel John Chivington, who had so far failed to score a big military victory against the Cheyenne, now saw his chance. On November 29, 1864, his force of 700 men descended upon the encamped Cheyenne and Arapaho. While Black Kettle frantically tried to mount an American flag and a white flag of surrender, Chivington's men slaughtered between 150 and 500 people—largely women and children. The next year, many southern Cheyenne agreed to move to reservations.

> ❝ *Nothing lives long.*
> *Only the earth and the mountains.* ❞
> —Death song sung by a Cheyenne killed at Sand Creek, 1864

This 1864 poster promises cavalry recruits "all horses and other plunder taken from the Indians."

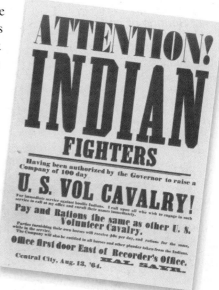

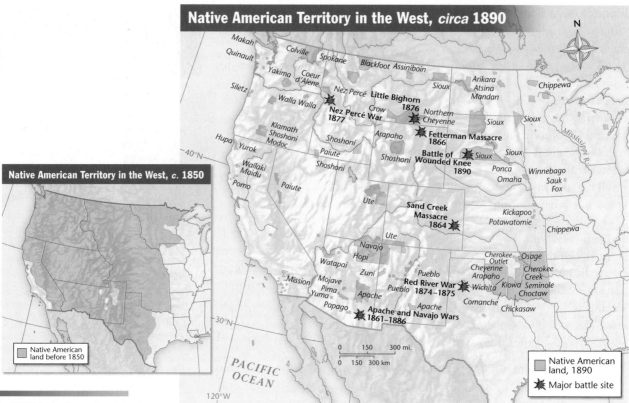

Native American Territory in the West, circa 1890

N

Makah
Quinault
Colville
Spokane
Blackfoot Assiniboin
Yakima
Coeur d'Alene
Siletz
Walla Walla
Nez Percé
Little Bighorn 1876
Sioux
Arikara Atsina Mandan
Chippewa
Nez Percé War 1877
Crow
Northern Cheyenne
Sioux
Sioux
Klamath Shoshoni Modoc
Shoshoni
Arapaho
Fetterman Massacre 1866
Mississippi R.
Hupa
Yurok
Paiute
Shoshoni
Shoshoni
Battle of Wounded Knee 1890
Sioux
Sioux
Wailaki Maidu
Ponca
Omaha
Winnebago Sauk Fox
Pomo
Paiute
Ute
Sand Creek Massacre 1864
Kickapoo Potawatomie
Chippewa
Navajo
Hopi
Ute
Cherokee Outlet
Osage
Watapai
Zuni
Pueblo
Cheyenne Arapaho
Cherokee
Creek
Mission
Mojave
Pima
Apache
Red River War 1874–1875
Wichita
Kiowa
Seminole Choctaw
Yuma
Papago
Pueblo
Apache and Navajo Wars 1861–1886
Comanche
Chickasaw
Apache

PACIFIC OCEAN

120°W

40°N
30°N

0   150   300 mi.
0   150   300 km

Native American land, 1890
✸ Major battle site

Native American Territory in the West, c. 1850

Native American land before 1850

MAP SKILLS The main map at right shows Indian lands in 1890, compared with the land they roamed in 1850, shown in the inset map above. **Regions** *In what directions were Native Americans pushed as they lost territory?*

Sounds of an Era

Listen to *a* Sioux war song and other sounds from the era of western settlement.

The Battle of Little Bighorn, 1876   The Sioux of the northern plains—Dakota, Wyoming, and Montana territories—powerfully resisted white expansion. In 1865, the government enraged the Sioux by deciding to build a road, the Bozeman Trail, through prime Sioux hunting grounds in the Bighorn Mountains.

Sioux chief Red Cloud launched a two-year war to block the project. In 1866, Sioux warriors slaughtered more than 80 soldiers under Captain W. J. Fetterman near Fort Phil Kearny. The war ended in the Fort Laramie Treaty of 1868, under which the United States abandoned the Bozeman Trail and created a large Sioux reservation in what is half of South Dakota today.

Sioux land protected by the treaty included the Black Hills—tall, dramatic, pine-covered mountains in South Dakota and Wyoming territories, held sacred by many Sioux. But in 1874, the government sent Lieutenant Colonel George A. Custer to investigate rumors of gold in the Black Hills. He reported that the hills cradled gold "from the grass roots down." This news was the starting gun in a mining race that overran the region.

The government offered to buy the Black Hills, and Red Cloud entered negotiations. But two Sioux chiefs, Sitting Bull and Crazy Horse, who had never signed the Fort Laramie Treaty, left the reservation. Hostilities resumed.

In June 1876, Custer was sent to round up the Indians. He moved his cavalry toward the Little Bighorn River in what is now Montana. There he met the full fury of the Sioux: nearly 2,000 warriors, the largest Indian force ever gathered on the plains. Custer, expecting a smaller enemy, had split his forces. The Sioux fell on their prey, wiping out Custer and his more than 200 soldiers within an hour.

The **Battle of Little Bighorn,** or "Custer's Last Stand," stunned Americans. The army flooded the area with troops and swiftly forced most of the Sioux back to their reservations. Crazy Horse was killed after surrendering in 1877. Sitting Bull and some remaining Sioux escaped to Canada, but starvation forced them to surrender and return to a reservation four years later.

The Battle of Wounded Knee, 1890 Under stress for a half-century, Native Americans saw the rise of religious prophets predicting danger or prosperity. A prophet of the plains, Wovoka, promised a return to traditional life if people performed purification ceremonies. These included the **Ghost Dance,** a ritual in which people joined hands and whirled in a circle.

The Ghost Dance caught on among the Teton Sioux, who, still struggling to adjust to reservation life, practiced it with great urgency, encouraged by Sitting Bull. In 1890, word spread that the Indians were becoming restless. The government agent at the Pine Ridge Reservation in South Dakota wired the army: "Indians are dancing in the snow and are wild and crazy. . . . We need protection and we need it now." The army dispatched the Seventh Cavalry, Custer's old unit, to the scene.

Hoping to calm the crisis, Indian police officers tried to arrest Sitting Bull. When he hesitated, the officers shot and killed him. His grieving followers, some 120 men and 230 women and children, surrendered and were rounded up at a creek called Wounded Knee. As they were being disarmed, someone fired a shot. Soldiers opened fire, killing more than 200 Sioux. The **Massacre at Wounded Knee** was the last major episode of violence in the Indian wars.

New Policies Toward Native Americans

"I am the last Indian," Sitting Bull is reported to have said. Indeed, he was among the last to have lived the life of a free Native American, roaming with the buffalo herds across unobstructed plains, practicing traditional customs.

Critics of Federal Indian Policies While many white Americans called for the destruction of Native Americans, others, horrified by the government's policies, formed a growing peace movement. It found inspiration in Helen Hunt Jackson's 1881 publication *A Century of Dishonor.* Protesting what she

BIOGRAPHY

George Armstrong Custer
1839–1876

He had the stuff of a legendary hero: charming, fearless, and memorable in his long, golden curls and flamboyant uniform. He was also vain, heedless of authority, and foolhardy—qualities that would prove fatal.

Custer seemed to be born for war. Daring in battle, he achieved great distinction in the Civil War. At the war's end, he was sent to fight Indians, a job he relished. To the Sioux, he was the "chief of thieves" for entering their sacred Black Hills and spreading word of their gold wealth.

Court-martialed twice for various offenses, Custer at last found fame and adoration in his final impulsive act: rushing to his death in 1876 at the Battle of Little Bighorn. At "Custer's Last Stand," he became the heroic victim of legend and song.

Apache chief Geronimo leads a band of renegades. Apache resistance ended with his surrender in 1886, the year of this photograph.

Key Events in the Indian Wars, 1861–1890

Wars / Battles	Native American Nations / Homelands	Key Players	Description / Outcome
Apache and Navajo Wars 1861–1886	Apache in Arizona, New Mexico, and Colorado territories; Navajo in New Mexico, Colorado territories	• Geronimo • Col. Christopher "Kit" Carson	Carson kills or relocates many Apache to reservations in 1862. Clashes drag on until Geronimo's surrender in 1886. Navajo told to surrender in 1863, but before they can, Carson attacks, killing hundreds, destroying homelands. Navajos moved to New Mexico reservation in 1865.
Sand Creek Massacre 1864	Southern Cheyenne, Arapaho, in central plains	• Black Kettle • Col. John Chivington	Cheyenne massacres prompt Chivington to kill up to 500 surrendered Cheyenne and Arapaho led by Black Kettle.
Red River War 1874–1875	Comanche and southern branches of Cheyenne, Kiowa, and Arapaho, in southern plains	• Comanche war parties • Gen. William T. Sherman • Lt. Gen. Philip H. Sheridan	Southern plains Indians relocated to Oklahoma Indian Territory under 1867 Treaty of Medicine Lodge. After buffalo hunters destroy the Indians' food supply, Comanche warriors race to buffalo grazing areas in Texas panhandle to kill hunters. Sherman and Sheridan defeat warriors and open panhandle to cattle ranching.
Battle of Little Bighorn 1876	Northern plains Sioux in Dakota, Wyoming, and Montana territories	• Sitting Bull • Crazy Horse • Red Cloud • Lt. Col. George A. Custer	U.S. tries to buy gold-rich Black Hills from Sioux. Talks fail. Custer's 7th Cavalry is sent to round up Sioux, but meets huge enemy force. Custer and some 200 men perish in "Custer's Last Stand."
Nez Percé War 1877	Largest branch of Nez Percé, in Wallowa Valley of Idaho and Washington territories and Oregon	• Chief Joseph • Gen. Oliver O. Howard • Col. Nelson Miles	Howard orders Nez Percé to Idaho reservation; violence erupts. Joseph leads some 700 men, women, and children on 1,400-mile flight. His 200 warriors hold off Miles's 2,000 soldiers until halted 40 miles short of Canada. Sent to Indian Territory, many die of disease. In 1885, survivors moved to reservation in Washington Territory.
Battle of Wounded Knee 1890	Sioux at Pine Ridge Reservation, South Dakota	• Sitting Bull • U.S. 7th Cavalry	Ghost Dance raises fears of Sioux uprising; Sitting Bull killed in attempted arrest. His followers surrender and camp at Wounded Knee. Shots are fired; some 200 Sioux die.

INTERPRETING CHARTS
This chart provides a brief summary of some of the key battles that were fought in various areas of the western interior. **Making Comparisons** (a) What factors did many of these clashes have in common? (b) In what ways did they differ?

saw as the government's broken promises and treaties, Jackson wrote, "It makes little difference . . . where one opens the record of the history of the Indians; every page and every year has its dark stain."

Attempts to Change Native American Culture As sincere as the reformers may have been, most believed that Native Americans still needed to be "civilized." That is, they should be made to give up their traditions, become Christians, learn English, adopt white dress and customs, and support themselves by farming and trades. Tribal elders were ordered to give up their religious beliefs and rituals. Christian missionaries ran schools on the reservations.

In 1879, Army Captain Richard H. Pratt opened the United States Indian Training and Industrial School in Carlisle, Pennsylvania. Children as young as 5 years old were taken from the reservations by coaxing, trickery, or force, and sent to Carlisle and other such schools to be educated "as Americans." The children were to be integrated into white society. This policy is called **assimilation,** the process by which one society becomes a part of another, more dominant society by adopting its culture.

In 1887, a federal law dismantled the Native American concept of shared land in favor of the principle of private property highly valued by Americans. The **Dawes Act** divided reservation land into individual plots. Each Native American family headed by a man received a plot, usually 160 acres. These landholders were granted U.S. citizenship and were subject to local, state, and federal laws. Many Indian sympathizers believed that the land allocations would make families self-supporting and create pride of ownership.

But the idea of taking up farming offended the beliefs of many Native Americans. Smohalla, a religious teacher from the Northwest, retorted: "You ask me to cut grass and make hay and sell it, and be rich like white men! But how dare I cut off my mother's hair?"

In reality, much reservation land was not suitable for farming. Many Native Americans had no interest or experience in agriculture. Some sold their land to speculators or were swindled out of it. Between 1887 and 1932, some two thirds of the 138 million acres of Indian land wound up in the hands of whites.

The Opening of Indian Territory   For the some 55 Indian nations that had been forced into Indian Territory, worse trouble loomed. The territory contained the largest unsettled farmland in the United States—about 2 million unassigned acres. During the 1880s, as squatters overran the land, Congress agreed to buy out Indian claims to the region.

On the morning of April 22, 1889, tens of thousands of homesteaders lined up at the territory's borders. At the stroke of noon, bugles blew, pistols fired, and the eager hordes surged forward, racing to stake a claim.

> 66 [W]ith a shout and a yell the swift riders shot out, then followed the light buggies or wagons and last the lumbering prairie schooner and freighters' wagons, with here and there even a man on a bicycle and many too on foot—above all a great cloud of dust hovering like smoke over a battlefield. 99
>
> —newspaper reporter, 1889

By sundown, these settlers, called **boomers,** had staked claims on almost 2 million acres. Many boomers discovered that some of the best lands had been grabbed by **sooners,** people who had sneaked past the government officials earlier to mark their claims. Under continued pressure from settlers, Congress created Oklahoma Territory in 1890. In the following years, the remainder of Indian Territory was opened to settlement.

It took a half-century, more than a thousand battles, and the deaths of about 950 United States soldiers to conquer the Native Americans. The clashes also took the lives of countless Indians used by the army as scouts and fighters; of settlers killed in Indian attacks; and of millions of Native American men, women, and children who died in battles or on squalid reservations.

VIEWING HISTORY Officials at the Carlisle, Pennsylvania, Indian school took before-and-after photographs of their students. **Analyzing Visual Information** List details that show the changes undergone by these boys.

Section 2 Assessment

READING COMPREHENSION

1. Describe early changes in the lifestyle of the Plains Indians.

2. Why were Indian treaties often unsuccessful?

3. How did the **Ghost Dance** lead to a tragic conflict?

4. Describe two major federal **assimilation** policies.

CRITICAL THINKING AND WRITING

5. **Identifying Assumptions** What assumptions about Native Americans did sympathetic easterners make when proposing improvements on the reservations?

6. **Writing a News Story** As an eastern reporter traveling with an army unit, report on one of the battles discussed in this section.

Go Online
PHSchool.com

For: An activity on Indian boarding schools
Visit: PHSchool.com
Web Code: mrd-5142

Mining, Ranching, and Farming

READING FOCUS

- How did mining spread in the West?
- What caused the western cattle boom?
- What was life like for a cowboy on the Chisholm Trail?
- How did settlers overcome barriers in farming the plains?

MAIN IDEA

Mining, ranching, and farming developed from individual and family enterprises into major industries, transforming the West.

KEY TERMS

placer mining
long drive
homesteader
soddie
dry farming
bonanza farm
Turner thesis
stereotype

TARGET READING SKILL

Understand Effects As you read, complete this diagram to show the effects of settlement by various groups.

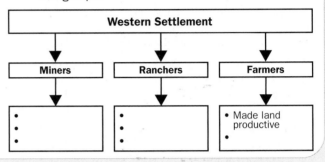

Western Settlement		
Miners	Ranchers	Farmers
•	•	• Made land productive
•	•	•
•		

Setting the Scene

Along with the armies of Custer and Sherman came virtual armies of miners, ranchers, and farmers that descended on the American West from the end of the Civil War to the end of the nineteenth century. Once unleashed, this force would remake the West. One railroad worker saw the transformation coming:

> 66 The time is coming, and fast, too, when, in the sense it is now understood, THERE WILL BE NO WEST. 99
>
> —from the diary of a Union Pacific engineer

VIEWING HISTORY With the arrival of large mining operations, mining sites became sprawling industrial towns, like Virginia City, Nevada, shown here. **Analyzing Visual Information** Describe the character and appearance of this mining site, using details from the photograph.

He was right. By the late 1800s, the West of the Native Americans, of unplowed prairie, of thundering buffalo, had vanished. A new breed of Westerners had come here, they believed, on a mission: to unlock the potential of this land and make it fruitful.

The Spread of Western Mining

After the stunning discovery of gold at Sutter's Mill, California, in 1848, a surge of fortune-hunters, from single men to whole families, set their sights on the West Coast. Little did they know that on the way to California, their wagon wheels rolled over mountains even more rich in precious minerals.

Mining Moves Inland In 1859, rumors of gold "everywhere you stick your shovel" at Pikes Peak, Colorado, brought on a stampede of wagons painted with the slogan "Pikes Peak or Bust!" The rumors turned out to be exaggerated. But later that year, one of the biggest strikes ever, Nevada's Comstock Lode, sent prospectors converging on the ore-laden western mountain ranges. Over the next 30 years, the Comstock Lode would yield $400 million in gold and silver.

Almost simultaneously, a gold strike west of the little town of Denver, in what was then Kansas Territory, threw open the gates to the American interior.

By 1861, the swarm of settlers caused the federal government to carve out Colorado Territory from western Kansas. Homestake Mine, opened in 1877 in the Black Hills of Dakota, was possibly the richest single mine ever uncovered in the world, producing a billion dollars' worth of ore.

One miner, William Parsons, perceived the national significance of the gold rush: "The Atlantic and Pacific coasts, instead of being, as they are now, divided countries, will become parts of a compact whole, joined and cemented together by bonds of mutual interest."

Early Mining and Mining Towns   At first, miners searched for metal in surface soil or in streambeds. The simplest tool was a shallow pan in which the miner scooped dirt and water, and then swished it around. Lighter particles washed over the edge while the gold stayed in the bottom of the pan. A Spanish technique called **placer mining** used this method on a larger scale. Miners shoveled loose dirt into boxes and then ran water over the dirt to separate it from gold or silver particles. (The word *placer*, of Spanish origin, rhymes with *passer*.)

These methods could be used by individuals, small groups of men, or even families. People came at the first whisper of a new strike, and tent communities popped up almost overnight. Larger strikes led to settled towns, even cities. Merchants, farmers, and other entrepreneurs came to supply miners' needs.

The easily gathered precious metal was skimmed off quickly. By the late 1850s and early 1860s, most of the precious metals that remained in the West lay locked in quartz and deeply buried. At that point, many prospectors straggled home, leaving mining settlements deserted ghost towns.

The large, deep veins of ore attracted the money and sophisticated technologies of large corporations. Using large work crews, they diverted streams and dug into the exposed beds. Workers tunneled into mountains and plunged into rickety mine shafts that sometimes became their graves. Huge drills replaced pickaxes. Hydraulic pumps pounded mountainsides with water. With the arrival of dynamite in the 1870s, miners blasted ore out of hillsides. Like other industries, mining had become the realm of big business.

The Cattle Boom

Mexicans taught Americans cattle ranching in the early 1800s. The Americans adopted Mexican ranching equipment and dress. They also learned from Mexican cattlemen the advantages of raising the hardy Texas longhorn cattle that thrived on the dry, grassy plains.

Demand Spurs Growth   Several changes launched the West's legendary cattle industry. Since Spanish colonial times, vast numbers of cattle had roamed wild on the Texas grasslands. After the Civil War, Texans founded ranches and rounded up these herds, which provided ample supplies of beef.

Prior to the war, pork had been Americans' meat of choice. But when cookbooks began snubbing pork as "difficult to digest" and "unwholesome," the nation went on a beef binge. Cattle that had sold for only $3 to $6 a head in Texas at the war's end now brought $40 a head in Illinois and $80 in New York. Soon, however, consumers began to complain about the tough beef from the Texas

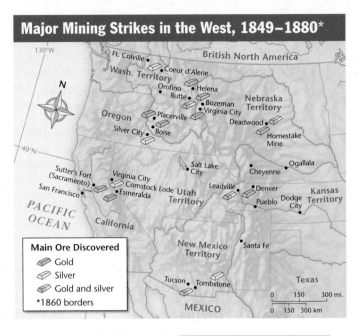

Major Mining Strikes in the West, 1849–1880*

Main Ore Discovered
Gold
Silver
Gold and silver
*1860 borders

MAP SKILLS Mining spread throughout the interior West in the 1860s after a gold strike outside of Denver. **Place** *From the map, what can you tell about the characteristics of places where key mining strikes occurred?*

longhorn, known as "the butcher's nightmare: eight pounds of hamburger on 800 pounds of bone and horn." Breeders then began importing eastern purebreds to make a better-quality longhorn.

Shipping the live cows to the East by rail was expensive. But with the invention of refrigerated railroad cars in the 1870s, animals were slaughtered before shipping. This development cut transportation costs in half.

Destruction of the Buffalo   Widespread cattle ranching became possible with the removal of Native Americans and the near-extinction of the buffalo. Of some 25 million buffalo on the Great Plains in 1840, as few as 1,100 remained in the entire country by 1889. Several factors caused the destruction. Buffalo-fur robes became popular in the East, and buffalo-hide leather made sturdy belts to drive machines in factories. Buffalo hunting became a popular sport, and the huge beasts with poor eyesight made easy targets for individuals or organized hunting groups. "The biggest killing I ever made was 106 buffalo before breakfast," boasted one hunter. The government also sought to wipe out the buffalo, to force Indians to grow their food and to make room for settlers.

Cow Towns   At first, Texas herds were driven north across the open range all the way to the nearest railroad. In 1867, J. G. McCoy established the town of Abilene, Kansas, on the Hannibal & St. Joseph Railroad—the first town built specifically for receiving cattle. Other "cow towns" sprang up along the rail lines: Cheyenne in Wyoming; and in Kansas, Dodge City, Wichita, and Ellsworth.

Cow towns were a truly *wild* part of the West—at least until farmers came along and settled in as year-round residents, determined to make the towns respectable and law-abiding. Cattle trades, banking, and other commerce took place in larger towns.

Abilene thrived for only a few years but saw some 700,000 head of cattle pass through its stockyard gates in 1871 alone. By 1872, the cattle business had shifted to Wichita; but within about three years, that town, like Abilene, had become fenced in by farmers. Dodge City, on the Santa Fe Trail, proclaimed

Cowboys with their herd in the 1880s

itself the "cowboy capital of the world." All told, in the cattle industry's two decades of great prosperity (roughly 1867 to 1887), as many as 8 million Texas cattle were rounded up and shipped east.

A Cowboy's Life: Cattle Drive on the Chisholm Trail

In the year of Abilene's founding, cowboys drove some 35,000 cattle up the Chisholm Trail. Within two decades, 2 million animals had made the trek. The story of the Chisholm Trail typifies the cowboy's experience on the **long drive,** the herding of thousands of cattle to railway centers scattered across the plains.

Geography of the Trail   The Chisholm Trail was one of several trails that linked the good grazing lands of Texas's San Antonio region with cow towns to the north. The trail was a network of routes, many of which converged at Fort Worth, the largest town on the trail. From there, the trail led north to the Red River, one of several rivers that required a hazardous crossing of men, horses, and cows.

The Red River marked the border between Texas and Indian Territory, which had to be crossed to reach Kansas. Cowboys had to be on the lookout for Indian raids. Some enterprising Native Americans set up what were virtually toll booths on the trail, demanding payment in steers for passage through their land. Once into Kansas, the Chisholm Trail branched out to various end-of-the-line towns.

The Cowboy   The men of the Chisholm Trail were a tough lot. They included Americans, Native Americans, and immigrants. About a fifth of all cowboys were African American or Mexican. Cowhands had trail names, like "Busted Snoot Johnny" and "Teddy Blue." They survived on their physical endurance, little need for sleep, sense of humor, and perhaps a touch of eccentricity. Neither Union nor Confederate, the cowboy became a unifying national hero. His past didn't matter; only how he did his job. And what a job!

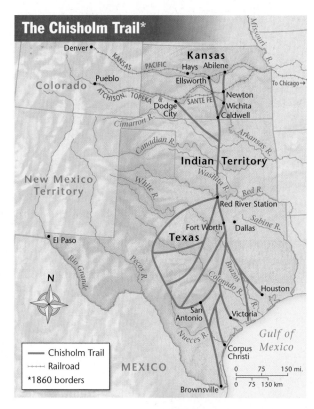

The Chisholm Trail*

> 66 *After you have . . . learned not to dread getting in mud up to your ears, jumping your horse into a swollen stream when the water is freezing, nor . . . trying to stop a stampeded herd, on a dark night, when your course has to be guided by the sound of the frightened steer's hoofs—you command good wages [$25 to $60 a month].* 99
> —cowboy Charles A. Siringo

A cowboy earned more the farther north he worked, partly because he had to buy warmer clothes. A no-frills cowboy outfit cost $77: pony, $25; leggings, $5; saddle, $25; saddle blankets, $5; spurs, bridle, and rope, $5; revolver, $12.

The Long Drive   For all the stories of the supposed joys and freedoms of cowboy life, the job was mostly bone-tiring drudgery; boring and at the same time tense. The men were up at 3:30 A.M. and in the saddle by 4:00. On the trail, the cowhands spread out across tens of miles. As the cattle moved along the trail, two experienced cowboys rode in front of the herd, guiding the animals along the route. Other men rode beside the herd to keep the cattle all together, and still others rode in the dust at the rear, pushing the stragglers along. A cowhand

MAP SKILLS The Chisholm Trail was probably named after Jesse Chisholm, a trader in the region. The trail originated south of San Antonio, Texas, and ended in Kansas cow towns along the railroad lines. **Movement** *Why do you think ranchers risked driving their herds through Indian Territory?*

could spend up to 18 hours a day in the saddle and still had to be on constant alert.

A cowboy's greatest nightmare was the stampede. A mere breath of wind could spook a nervous herd, sending thousands of cattle into crushing, headlong flight. The men learned that singing calmed the cattle at night, and they invented endless lullabies and ballads, accompanied by a harmonica or a fiddle. One of the best known songs was "The Old Chisholm Trail":

> 66 *I'm up in the mornin' afore daylight*
> *And afore I sleep the moon shines bright. . . .*
> *I went to the boss to draw my roll [pay],*
> *He had it figured out I was nine dollars in the hole.* 99
>
> —"The Old Chisholm Trail"

During the era of the cattle drives, the leading cause of cowboy deaths was being dragged by a horse. Diseases such as pneumonia, tuberculosis, fevers, and infections also took many a young life, as did lightning and, of course, stampedes and gunfights. Not the least of the hardships on the trail was loneliness, with only fellow cowhands as company for months on end. In cattle country, men outnumbered women 10 to 1. In the West as a whole, men outnumbered women about 2.5 to 1 in 1870 (not counting Native Americans).

The Cattle Barons As the cattle business grew, a new breed of wealthy ranchers created huge cattle operations. Some of these new lords of the Texas plains owned more than 100,000 cattle that grazed over millions of acres. On such a grand scale, the annual roundup, said one cowhand, was like "a farmer in Massachusetts turning a cow out to graze and finding her months later in Delaware." By 1885, about three dozen cattle barons reigned over more than 20 million acres of rangeland.

Often, these entrepreneurs were cowboys who had struck out on their own. One of the most famous, Charles Goodnight, arrived in Texas as a child. He made a study of ranching. He determined that a cow needed 10 acres of grass in the Texas panhandle to graze for a year, if the soil was good, and it could drink up to 30 gallons of water a day. Thus, success depended on ownership of water sources and plenty of land. He acquired these by clearing out the Native Americans and their buffalo herds in the Palo Duro Canyon and beyond.

After fighting in the Civil War, Goodnight joined the Texas-wide roundup to recover his free-roaming cattle. He built a mighty business with the help of his wife, Mary Ann (who ran the operation after his death). With business partner Oliver Loving, he blazed the Goodnight-Loving Trail through the Southwest all the way up to Cheyenne, Wyoming.

The cattle bonanza ended in the mid-1880s, when a combination of over-expansion, price declines, cold winters, dry summers, and cattle fever drove thousands into bankruptcy. Cattle ranching survived, but on a much smaller scale.

Farming the Plains

Prairie life is romanticized in novels and films. But for most **homesteaders**—those who farmed claims under the Homestead Act—life was relentlessly rugged.

Texas Cattle Driven North, 1867–1881	
Year	**Number of Cattle**
1867	35,000
1868	75,000
1869	350,000
1870	300,000
1871	600,000
1872	350,000
1873	405,000
1874	166,000
1875	151,618
1876	321,998
1877	201,159
1878	265,646
1879	257,927
1880	394,784
1881	250,000

SOURCE: *The Cowboys*, William H. Forbis

VIEWING HISTORY Frederic Remington's famous 1902 painting *The Cowboy* (top) captures the skill and spirit of the cowboy legend. The cowboy's heyday was relatively brief, as the table above shows. **Interpreting Tables** *When did the Texas cattle drives peak?*

Hardships for Homesteaders The first order of business for a homesteader was building a home. In the early days, wood-frame homes were rare on the virtually treeless plains. Most people built either a dugout or a soddie. A dugout was actually carved out of the side of an embankment. The earthen structure cost about $3 to build. It was insulated from winter chill and summer heat. A **soddie**, or sod home, was a structure with the walls and roof made from blocks of sod—strips of grass with the thick roots and earth attached. Construction cost: less than $10.

Once the soddie was up, farmers faced the grim task of sodbusting—plowing the fields for planting. Oscar Micheaux, a black homesteader in South Dakota, tried to plow his whole claim in one season, to prove his ability. But, he noted, "as it had taken a 1,400-mile walk to follow the plow in breaking the 120 acres, I was about 'all in' physically when it was done." Backbreaking labor became heartbreaking when floods, prairie fires, dust storms, or drought left the year's work in ruins.

Then there were the bugs. Grasshoppers, locusts, and boll weevils ravaged fields of wheat, rye, sorghum, and corn. Various sources describe a mammoth column of grasshoppers stretching 150 miles by 100 miles that gnawed its way through Kansas. Mosquitoes and flies showed no mercy to people or animals, and could carry disease. Insects crawled out of the walls of dugouts and soddies.

Like the rattlesnakes that hung from the roof of a soddie, money worries hung on farmers' minds. Creating a livable homestead could cost $1,000, beyond the reach of many newcomers. Some settlers who lacked farming skills could not hold on for five years in order to receive their claim.

Falling crop prices created rising farm debt. Once farmers invested in machines, they had to focus on raising the crop for which the machines were designed. If prices for that crop dipped, farmers could not pay off their debts, which carried crippling interest rates of up to 25 percent or more.

Conditions proved so difficult that in the mid-1880s, following a series of droughts, hordes of prairie schooners took off and headed back east. About 18,000 wagons with returning homesteaders crossed over the Missouri River from Nebraska to Iowa in 1891 alone.

Families Pull Together Among the families who stayed, most husbands and wives had fairly well-defined roles. Yet in a pinch, it didn't much matter what was "men's work" or "women's work."

In general, men did the sodbusting, often walking miles to borrow a neighbor's ox or plow. They "dragged" the field to break up clots; they planted, hoed, and harvested. They did the threshing and binding. In the off-season, or to raise money in a bad year, husbands lent themselves out for labor in construction or other jobs.

In most families, women raised and schooled children, cooked, cleaned, made and washed clothes, and preserved food. They also raised food crops, made soap and butter, raised chickens, milked the cows, spun wool for sale, and managed the money.

Although most homesteaders went west as families, women could file claims on their own. Married or not, farm women often faced long periods of solitude and hardship. "My Husband went a way to find work and came home last night and told me that we would have to Starve he has

VIEWING HISTORY A family of Nebraska homesteaders pose in front of their soddie. **Analyzing Visual Information** *From looking at this photograph, describe what might have been the challenges of building a soddie.*

bin in ten countys and did not Get no work," a desperate Susan Orcutt wrote the governor of Kansas in 1894. "It is Pretty hard for a woman to do with out any thing to Eat. . . ."

Under these conditions, children's labor was crucial to the family's survival. Boys and girls as young as 4 years old collected wood for fuel or carried water. Some parents were forced to hire out their older children for work. In this unforgiving land, settlers relied heavily on each other, raising houses and barns together, sewing quilts, husking corn, and providing other forms of support.

New Technology Eases Farm Labor   The dry climate in parts of the West greatly reduced the land's productivity. In response, farmers practiced water conservation techniques called **dry farming.** These techniques included planting crops that do not require a great deal of water, such as sorghum, keeping the fields free of weeds, and digging deep furrows so water could reach the plant roots.

Farmers welcomed any machines that would save time and effort. During the 1870s, improvements in farm implements multiplied. Soon farmers were riding behind a plow that made several furrows at once. Other inventions included harrows, implements with spring teeth to dislodge debris and break up the ground before planting, and automatic drills to spread grain. Steam-powered threshers arrived by 1875, and cornhuskers and cornbinders by the 1890s.

Knowledge of farming techniques improved during this period as well. In the 1880s and 1890s, the United States Department of Agriculture (USDA), which was created under the 1862 Morrill Land-Grant Act, collected statistics on markets, crops, and plant diseases. The USDA provided information on crop rotation, hybridization (cross-breeding plants), and soil and water conservation.

Farming Becomes Big Business   New farm machines and techniques increased farm output enormously. Owners of large farms hoped to reap a "bonanza" by supplying food to growing eastern populations. They applied to farming the organizational ideas taking hold in industry. As one observer noted:

> 66 It is no longer left to the small farmer, taking up 160 acres of land. . . . Organized capital is being employed in the work, with all the advantages which organization implies. Companies and partnerships are formed for the cultivation precisely as they are for building railroads, manufactures, etc. 99
> —Commercial and Financial Chronicle, 1879

The result was **bonanza farms,** operations controlled by large businesses, managed by professionals, and raising massive quantities of single cash crops. The farms' huge output caused problems, however. When the supply of a crop rose faster than the demand, prices fell. To make up for falling prices, farmers produced ever larger quantities of the product, adding to the oversupply.

Farmers Prevail on the Plains   Large-scale farms absorbed smaller farms in some places, and many employed landless tenant farmers. Still, the Great Plains remained primarily a region of small family farms well into the 1900s. Despite continual setbacks, the farmer's way of life prevailed in the

Farming Innovations on the Prairie, 1860–1900

Mechanized Reaper	Reduces labor force needed for harvest. Allows farmers to maintain larger farms.
Barbed Wire	Keeps cattle from trampling crops and uses a minimal amount of lumber, which was scarce on the plains.
Dry Farming	Allows cultivation of arid land by using drought-resistant crops and various techniques to minimize evaporation.
Steel Plow	Allows farmers to cut through dense, root-choked sod.
Harrow	Smoothes and levels ground for planting.
Steel Windmill	Powers irrigation systems and pumps up ground water.
Hybridization	Cross-breeding of crop plants, which allows greater yields and uniformity.
Improved Communication	Creation of the U.S. Department of Agriculture in 1862 provides farmers with information about improved farming practices.
Grain Drill	Array of multiple drills used to carve small trenches in the ground and feed seed into the soil.

INTERPRETING CHARTS An agricultural revolution took place in the late 1800s with the introduction of farm machinery and new growing techniques. While it took a farmer an average of about 61 hours to harvest an acre of land by hand, a farmer with a machine could do it in about 3 hours. **Drawing Conclusions** *Choose one of the items in the chart and describe the effect it might have had on a farm family on the plains.*

West, as mines closed down and the song of the cowboy slowly faded. Farmers triumphed in a showdown with ranchers that shaped the economy of the West. (See Geography and History: Settling the Great Plains, on pages 286–287.)

Frontier Myths

The "Wild West": Was it the rootin'-tootin', hard-livin', free-for-all of sharp-shootin' marshals, quick-witted outlaws, rough-talkin' women, and handsome Indian fighters? To be sure, the West was all this and more: boxing matches and animal fights; traveling minstrels, jugglers, magicians, and zoos; rodeos and carnivals. Yet in truth, many wild towns of the West calmed down fairly quickly or disappeared.

Taming the Frontier   In Colorado after about 1880, residents had a choice of at least seven church denominations. They might join a social group such as the Masons, the Odd Fellows, or a Civil War veterans' group. Most social clubs had a women's auxiliary devoted to charitable work. There were clubs for railroad engineers, ranchers, teachers; for hunters and equestrians; for lovers of literature, science, and Shakespearean drama. Major theatrical productions toured growing western cities. The East had come West.

The End of the Frontier   In 1870, most of the Great Plains and the Rocky Mountains had a population of less than two people per square mile. (The census did not count Native Americans.) As populations swelled, unorganized lands became U.S. territories, then states. In 1872, the government moved to preserve western lands, establishing Yellowstone National Park in northwest Wyoming, southern Montana, and eastern Idaho. It was the nation's first national park.

Finally, in 1890, the head of the Census Bureau announced the official end of the frontier. The country's "unsettled area has been so broken into by isolated bodies of settlement," he declared, "that there can hardly be said to be a frontier line." The days of free western land were over.

Turner's Frontier Thesis   In 1893, historian Frederick Jackson Turner claimed that the frontier had played a key role in forming the American character. "American intellect owes its striking characteristics [to the frontier]," Turner declared. Frontier life, he said, had created Americans who were socially mobile, ready for adventure, bent on individual self-improvement, and committed to democracy.

Historians have since modified the **Turner thesis,** as his view came to be called. His theory of frontier life did not include the contributions of women and of various ethnic groups. It emphasized the effects of individual effort but played down the effects of federal subsidies and business investments on development and on Native Americans.

Myths in Literature, Shows, and Song   Despite today's deeper understanding of the history of the American West, frontier myths continue to influence how Americans think about themselves. The romantic image of the American cowboy, for example, began as early as the 1870s, in dime novels often based on the lives of real people. Writers celebrated characters such as Wild Bill Hickok, Calamity Jane, and Deadwood Dick. The stories promoted **stereotypes,** exaggerated or oversimplified descriptions of reality. The stereotypical hero might be an

VIEWING HISTORY Buffalo Bill's Wild West shows (above) toured America and Europe. African American cowboy Nat Love (below) became the larger-than-life hero of a novel. **Distinguishing False From Accurate Images** What details in the images above and below might have given Americans a romanticized image of the West?

The 1943 Rodgers and Hammerstein musical *Oklahoma!* is a love story that takes place during the settlement of Oklahoma Territory, where "the corn is as high as an elephant's eye." One song declares that "the farmer and the cowman should be friends," a reference to the frequent land feuds between the two groups.

outlaw, a miner, a gang leader, or a cowboy—anyone who dealt out righteous justice against evil.

Edward Wheeler's novel *Deadwood Dick, The Prince of the Road: or, the Black Rider of the Black Hills* was based on a real person. But the real Deadwood Dick was no outlaw. He was an African American named Nat Love. Entering a rodeo contest in a Dakota Territory mining town named Deadwood, Love won several roping and shooting contests. In his autobiography, Love wrote, "Right there the assembled crowd named me 'Deadwood Dick' and proclaimed me champion roper of the Western cattle country."

In 1883, William F. ("Buffalo Bill") Cody created his fantastically popular Wild West shows, contributing further to frontier myths. These events drew thousands of spectators to steer-roping contests, rodeos, and battle enactments between "good" cavalry regiments and "bad" Native Americans. One season featured the real-life Sitting Bull.

Most stories from the West supported stereotypes about men. The West was the place where a young man could find freedom and opportunity. He could lead a virtuous life and resist the forces of civilization that had made easterners soft. Many writers praised the West for having toughened the bodies and souls of young men. In his histories of the West, future President Theodore Roosevelt urged American men to experience the "strenuous life" of the West before they became too weak from the comforts of modern civilization.

Some male themes also appealed to women. In 1912, Juliette Low founded the American Girl Scouts in part because she feared that civilization had made girls too soft. Praising women homesteaders for their strength and intelligence, she made the scouting techniques of tracking, woodcraft, and wilderness survival the core of her program.

The Wild West remains fixed in popular culture, from the Dallas lawyer in a cowboy hat to western movies. Cowboy songs—"Home on the Range" and "Don't Fence Me In"—celebrate images of wide-open spaces and freedom from civilization. While myths of the Old West are more dramatic than the reality, the era produced many of the nation's most cherished images of itself.

Section 3 Assessment

READING COMPREHENSION

1. What technologies gradually replaced **placer mining?**
2. Why did cattle ranching become so successful after the Civil War?
3. Describe the rise of cow towns.
4. What hardships did **homesteaders** face?
5. What kinds of **stereotypes** were created about the Old West?

CRITICAL THINKING AND WRITING

6. **Analyzing Information** Describe the impact of new technologies and other factors on small entrepreneurs in mining, ranching, and farming.
7. **Writing to Narrate** Create a historical fiction narrative describing the experience of a homesteading family on the Great Plains.

For: An activity on the Chisholm Trail
Visit: PHSchool.com
Web Code: mrd-5143

READING FOCUS

- Why did farmers complain about federal post–Civil War economic policies?

- How did the government respond to organized protests by farmers?

- What were the Populists' key goals?

- What was the main point of William Jennings Bryan's Cross of Gold speech?

- What was the legacy of Populism?

MAIN IDEA

Economic crises led to organized protests by farmers seeking government relief. Economic reform became an election issue and led to the rise of Populism.

KEY TERMS

money supply
deflation
monetary policy
bimetallic standard
free silver
Bland-Allison Act
Sherman Silver Purchase Act
the Grange
Interstate Commerce Act
Populist
Cross of Gold speech

TARGET READING SKILL

Understand Effects Copy the web diagram below. As you read, fill in the blank circles to show the effects of economic instability from 1870 to 1900. Add more circles if needed.

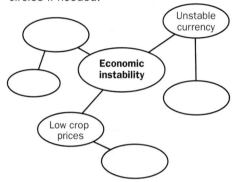

Setting the Scene American farmers have always struggled against two forces: nature and the economy. In the late 1800s, economic perils were as devastating to farmers as locusts or boll weevils. Ever since the end of the Civil War, farm production had risen. So too had debt, as farmers borrowed heavily to purchase the expensive new equipment that made possible such increased productivity.

Indebted farmers found themselves in an increasingly dangerous, even hopeless, position, as competition from abroad increased and crop prices went into a prolonged decline. Tenant farming increased as homesteaders lost their farms when they couldn't make their loan payments. The crisis struck farmers throughout the West and the South, both whites and blacks.

In 1890, a Congregational minister described the plight of the farmer:

> 66 The farmers . . . are the bone and sinew of the nation; they produce the largest share of its wealth; but they are getting, they say, the smallest share for themselves. The American farmer is steadily losing ground. His burdens are heavier every year and his gains are more meager. 99

—Washington Gladden

The Farmers' Complaint

The American economy rested on shaky ground in the post–Civil War era. Twice, in 1873 and 1893, the collapse of a financially ailing railroad led to a cascading national panic. Banks failed. Businesses—which, like farmers, had also

Wheat Prices 1866–1890

SOURCE: *Historical Statistics of the United States, Colonial Times to 1970*

INTERPRETING CHARTS

Farmers often suffered from unpredictable crop prices. **Drawing Conclusions** *(a) What might have caused the sharpest price drop? (b) What happened to prices during the Panic of 1873?*

over-borrowed—went under. Unemployment soared. During both panics, farmers suffered the double disasters of falling crop prices and loans called in by banks desperate for cash.

Historically, the federal government rarely had intervened to stabilize the nation's economy, nor would most people have expected it to. But in their distress, farmers increasingly began to view government help as a right. In small but rapidly growing numbers, they voiced their demands.

Farmers and Tariffs   One federal policy of concern to farmers was tariffs. Tariffs on imported goods discourage people from buying imports by making them more expensive. Thus, tariffs encourage the sale of goods produced at home.

Americans in the late 1800s were divided on the benefit of tariffs. Businesses claimed that tariffs protected American factory jobs—and their own profits. But because tariffs reduced foreign competition, they also encouraged American firms to raise their prices, which harmed workers and consumers in general.

However, tariffs hurt most farmers in two ways. First, they raised the prices of manufactured goods, such as farm machinery. Second, U.S. tariffs on manufactured goods spurred manufacturing nations in Europe to retaliate with their own tariffs against American crops. Thus, tariffs indirectly reduced the world market for American farm products.

Whenever the government raised tariffs to benefit industry, farmers protested. They viewed tariff increases as proof that the government favored eastern manufacturers over western farmers.

The Money Issue   Tariffs were not farmers' only concern in the late 1800s. For many, the key issue was the silver supply. The value of money is linked to the **money supply,** the amount of money in the national economy. If the government increases the money supply, the value of every dollar drops. This drop in value shows up as inflation, a widespread rise in prices on goods of all kinds.

People who borrow money benefit from inflation because the money they eventually pay back is worth less than the money they borrowed. Inflation also helps sellers, such as farmers, because it raises the prices of the goods they sell.

In contrast, if the government reduces the money supply, the value of each dollar becomes greater. This causes **deflation,** or a drop in the prices on goods. People who lend money are helped by deflation because the money they receive in payment of a loan is worth more than the money they lent out.

After the Civil War, the federal government made the first of several attempts to take out of circulation the paper money—greenbacks—issued during the war. This policy created a furor among farmers and others0 who favored inflated prices. **Monetary policy,** the federal government's plan for the makeup and quantity of the nation's money supply, thus emerged as a major political issue. Supporters of inflation pushed for an increase in the money supply. Supporters of deflation wanted a "tight money" policy of less currency in circulation.

Gold Bugs   In 1873—the year of the worst economic panic in U.S. history to that point—supporters of tight money won a victory. Until that time, United States currency had been on a **bimetallic standard.** That is, currency consisted of gold or silver coins or United States treasury notes that could be traded in for gold or silver. In 1873, in order to prevent inflation and stabilize the economy, Congress put the nation's currency on a gold standard. This move reduced the amount of money in circulation because the money supply was limited by the amount of

Focus on
ECONOMICS

Monetary Policy   The federal government's plan for the size of the nation's money supply.

The Historical Context   Farmers in the late 1800s called for an increase in the money supply, which would cause higher prices and thus raise their incomes. Their opponents called for a continued "tight money" policy, in which the money supply is kept low.

The Concept Today   The Federal Reserve System, established in 1913, controls the nation's money supply today. Led by its chairman, the "Fed" seeks to promote steady economic growth without causing high inflation.

gold held by the government. Conservative "gold bugs" were pleased. Many of them were big lenders, and they liked the idea of being repaid in currency backed by the gold standard.

Silverites The move to a gold standard enraged "silverites," mostly silver-mining interests and western farmers. They claimed that ending silver as a monetary standard would depress farm prices. Silverites called for **free silver,** the unlimited coining of silver dollars to increase the money supply. The Greenback Party, founded in 1875 to push for the continued issuing of paper money, joined the silverite cause.

The **Bland-Allison Act** of 1878, was, for the silverites, a step in the right direction. This act required the federal government to purchase and coin more silver, increasing the money supply and causing inflation. Passed by Congress, the Bland-Allison Act was vetoed by President Rutherford B. Hayes because he opposed the inflation it would create. Congress overrode Hayes's veto. Yet the act had only a limited effect, because the Treasury Department refused to buy more than the minimum amount of silver required under the act. The Treasury also refused to circulate the silver dollars that the law required it to mint.

In 1890, Congress passed the **Sherman Silver Purchase Act.** While not authorizing the free and unlimited coinage of silver that silverites wanted, it increased the amount of silver the government was required to purchase every month. During the early 1890s, the government's gold reserves dwindled, and the government nearly went bankrupt in the financial panic of 1893 when frightened foreign investors withdrew gold from the country. President Grover Cleveland blamed the Silver Purchase Act for the loss of gold and the panic, and he oversaw the repeal of the act in 1893.

Gold *vs.* silver: an 1891 silver dime and an 1873 $20 gold coin

COMPARING PRIMARY SOURCES

Gold Bugs *vs.* Silverites

In this famous exchange, one "silverite" proposes the return to a bimetallic standard along with the unlimited coining of silver, while his opponent, a "gold bug," criticizes the proposal.

Analyzing Viewpoints Compare the main arguments made by the two scholars.

In Favor of Free Silver

"Our forefathers showed much wisdom in selecting silver, of the two metals, out of which to make the unit [of currency]. . . . [T]hey were led to adopt silver because it was the most reliable. It was the most favored as money by the people. It was scattered among all the people. . . . Gold was considered the money of the rich. . . . [With the coining of silver,] you increase the value of all property by adding to the number of monetary units in the land. You make it possible for the debtor to pay his debts; business to start anew, and revivify all the industries of the country. . . . The money lenders in the United States, who own substantially all our money, have a selfish interest in maintaining the gold standard."

—*pamphlet by Professor W. H. "Coin" Harvey,
of Coin's Financial School, 1894*

Opposed to Free Silver

"Do you suppose that the farmers of this country really believe that with each ton of silver taken out of the mines by the silver law-makers in the Senate that there are created bushels of wheat [?] . . . Free coinage of silver then is absolutely certain to drive all our gold out of circulation. . . . [Hence] there will be no increase in the quantity of money. . . . The only way it would act would be by increasing the price of everything. . . . A dozen eggs, now selling at 15 cents, would sell for about 30 cents. . . . As [it] would inevitably result in a rise of prices it would immediately result in the fall of wages. . . . Are we willing to sacrifice the interests of the laboring classes to the demands of certain owners of silver mines . . . ?"

—*University of Chicago economist James Laurence
Laughlin, in a public debate with "Coin" Harvey, 1895*

Organizing Farmer Protests

Because farmers lived far from one another and usually relied on their own efforts, they tended not to organize protests against policies they opposed. In the late 1800s, however, farmers took advantage of improvements in communication and transportation to form several powerful protest groups.

The Grange   In 1866, the Department of Agriculture sent Oliver H. Kelley on an inspection tour of southern farms. Disturbed by the farmers' isolation, the following year he founded the Patrons of Husbandry, or **the Grange.**

The Grange soon began helping farmers form cooperatives, through which they bought goods in large quantities at lower prices. The Grange also pressured state legislators to regulate businesses on which farmers depended, such as the operators of grain elevators that stored farmers' crops and the railroads that shipped goods to market.

Farmers' Alliances   Although the Grange was popular (and still exists today), eventually farmers formed other political groups. In the 1880s, many farmers joined a network of Farmers' Alliances that were formed around the nation. The alliances launched harsh attacks on monopolies, such as those that controlled the railroads.

The Farmers' Alliance in the South, formed in Texas in the mid-1870s, grew especially powerful. It called for actions that many of the nation's farmers could support: federal regulation of the railroads, more money in circulation, creation of state departments of agriculture, antitrust laws, and farm credit.

Farmers' Alliances held special importance for women, who served as officers and won support for women's political rights. One of the most popular speakers was Kansas lawyer Mary Elizabeth Lease, who reportedly urged farmers to raise "less corn and more Hell!" African Americans worked through a separate but parallel "Colored Farmers' Alliance." Formed in 1886 in Lovelady, Texas, the group had a quarter of a million members by 1891.

A series of natural disasters gave special urgency to Farmers' Alliance programs. The Mississippi River flooded in 1882. In 1886 and 1887, Texas suffered a 21-month drought. Terrible blizzards, which killed thousands of cattle, struck the West in 1887. Increasingly, farmers wanted to know why the federal government was unwilling to respond to these disasters.

Government Responses   Political power and influence were splintered during this period. Farmers often differed on how much federal help was needed, if any. On the other hand, business interests were not always strong enough to prevent legislation they disliked from becoming law. As one historian put it, "Big business was powerful; it was by no means all-powerful."

Meanwhile, fragmented political parties had difficulty rallying support for controversial proposals among their members in various regions of the country as well as among different economic and ethnic groups. In every election from 1880 to

1892, no candidate won a majority of the popular vote. Only rarely did the President's party command a majority in Congress. Presidents thus lacked the power to take bold action. In addition, some Presidents were influenced by promises of support from powerful business interests.

In 1887, Congress passed the Texas Seed Bill, which provided seed grain to drought victims. But President Cleveland, a Democrat, vetoed the bill, expressing the commonly held view that "though the people support the government, the government should not support the people."

On the issue of railroad regulation, some consensus emerged. Even some railroad owners backed moderate regulations, fearing more drastic measures. In 1887, Cleveland signed the **Interstate Commerce Act.** It regulated the prices that railroads charged to move freight between states, requiring the rates to be set in proportion to the distance traveled. The law also made it illegal to give special rates to some customers. While the act did not control the monopolistic railroad practices that angered farmers, it established the principle that Congress could regulate the railroads, a significant expansion of federal authority. The act also set up the Interstate Commerce Commission (ICC) to enforce the laws.

In 1890, President Benjamin Harrison approved the Sherman Antitrust Act. This act was meant to curb the power of trusts and monopolies. But during its first decade, enforcement was lax.

The Populists

In 1890, the various small political parties associated with the Farmers' Alliances began to enjoy success at the ballot box, especially in the South. In 1891, the Alliances founded the People's Party, a new national party that demanded radical changes in federal economic and social policies. The **Populists,** as followers of the new party were known, built their platform around the following issues:

1. An increased circulation of money.
2. The unlimited minting of silver.
3. A progressive income tax, in which the percentage of taxes owed increases with a rise in income. This tax would place a greater financial burden on wealthy industrialists and a lesser one on farmers.
4. Government ownership of communications and transportation systems.

Seeking the support of urban industrial workers, the Populists endorsed an eight-hour work day. For the same reason, they opposed the use of Pinkertons, the private police force that had been involved in the bloody Homestead Strike of 1892, as strikebreakers. Breaking through deeply rooted racial prejudice, Populists sought a united front of African American and white farmers. The poor of both races had a common cause, they argued. "You are kept apart that you may be separately fleeced of your earnings," said one party leader. In the South, the party often endorsed a common list of candidates with the Republican Party to pool the support of poor black farmers.

During the 1892 campaign, populism generated great excitement among its followers. But the party's presidential candidate, Iowan James B. Weaver, won barely a million votes. Cleveland returned to the presidency.

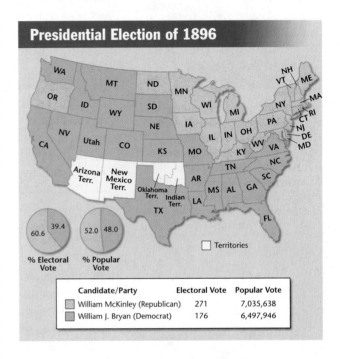

Presidential Election of 1896

Candidate/Party	Electoral Vote	Popular Vote
William McKinley (Republican)	271	7,035,638
William J. Bryan (Democrat)	176	6,497,946

60.6 | 39.4 % Electoral Vote

52.0 | 48.0 % Popular Vote

MAP SKILLS William Jennings Bryan was the candidate of the Democrats and the Populists in 1896. As the map shows, he won most of the western and southern states and nearly half the popular vote, yet he lost the election. **Regions** *Explain the reasons for Bryan's defeat.*

VIEWING HISTORY This cartoon shows William Jennings Bryan holding a crown of thorns and a cross of gold, biblical images that he used in his famous speech. **Analyzing Visual Information** *Does this cartoon present Bryan in a positive or a negative light?*

Bryan's "Cross of Gold"

An ongoing economic depression colored the 1896 presidential campaign. In an election focused mainly on currency issues, the Republicans ran Ohio governor William McKinley on a gold-standard platform. William Jennings Bryan, a former silverite congressman from Nebraska and a powerful speaker, captured the Democratic nomination with an emotional plea for free silver.

Bryan addressed the 1896 Democratic Convention in Chicago on July 8, at the close of the debate over the party platform. Using images from the Bible, he stood with head bowed and arms outstretched and cried out at the climax of his speech, "You shall not press down upon the brow of labor this crown of thorns. You shall not crucify mankind upon a cross of gold!" So stunning was Bryan's speech that both the Democrats and the Populists nominated him for President. The **Cross of Gold speech** is one of the most famous in American history.

The 1896 campaign was one of marked contrasts. Bryan created a whirlwind of activity, traveling all over the country and making speeches at every stop. McKinley ran a more traditional campaign. He remained in his hometown of Canton, Ohio, greeting visitors and making a few speeches from his front porch.

Despite his best efforts, Bryan lost the election. He carried the Democratic West and South but none of the urban and industrial midwestern and northern states. In these states, factory workers feared that free silver might cause inflation, which would eat away the buying power of their wages. Thus, despite populism's broad appeal, it could not bridge the gap between America's cities and farms. Nor could populism slow America's transition from an agricultural nation to an industrial nation.

Populism's Legacy

By 1897, McKinley's administration had raised the tariff to new heights. In 1900, after gold discoveries in South Africa, the Canadian Yukon, and Alaska had increased the world's gold supply by more than $100 million, Congress returned the nation to a gold standard. To the surprise of many farmers, crop prices began a slow rise. The silver movement died, as did populism.

The goals of populism, however, lived on. In the decades ahead, other reformers, known as Progressives, applied populist ideas to urban and industrial problems. In so doing, they launched a new, historic era of reforms.

Section 4 Assessment

READING COMPREHENSION

1. What changes in economic policy did many farmers seek?

2. Explain the difference between a gold standard, a **bimetallic standard,** and **free silver.**

3. What did the government do to address farmers' complaints?

4. To whom did Bryan's **Cross of Gold speech** appeal, and why?

CRITICAL THINKING AND WRITING

5. **Drawing Conclusions** Few strong third parties such as the Populists have arisen in the nation's history. What caused the Populist Party to enjoy relative success in its time?

6. **Writing an Outline** Set up an outline for an analysis of the gold-versus-silver debate. Include facts on the currency plans put forward and who favored and opposed them.

Go Online PHSchool.com

For: An activity on the National Grange
Visit: PHSchool.com
Web Code: mrd-5144

Expressing Problems Clearly

Expressing a problem clearly is the first step toward understanding and solving it. Problems often arise out of situations that have many elements; this makes them complex or puzzling. Other problems are difficult because there are clearly several possible solutions; this makes these problems open to debate. The ability to express a problem clearly means being able to describe a complex situation or body of information so that possible solutions can be evaluated, and the problem can be solved.

In 1877, the United States was in the midst of a depression. On July 14, the Baltimore and Ohio Railroad announced a 10 percent wage cut. The passage below is from an editorial, "The Railroad Strike," which appeared in a business journal.

LEARN THE SKILL

Use the following steps to express problems clearly:

1. **Analyze the information.** Identify the difficulties faced by the persons or groups involved. Consider what led to the problem, including the historical context. Be aware of the point of view of those who are describing the problem.

2. **Identify the basic concepts involved.** Problems usually arise out of a specific set of circumstances. However, they often revolve around a general principle, such as fairness. To identify this concept, try to express the problem in terms of what each side wants for itself.

3. **Identify the function of the supporting details.** Note details that are not basic to the problem. Eliminating them from consideration can help you see the problem more clearly.

4. **Express the problem as simply and completely as possible.** Once you have identified the main area of dispute and have stripped away irrelevant details, you are ready to express the problem clearly.

PRACTICE THE SKILL

Answer the following questions:

1. **(a)** What difficulty were the railroad companies facing? What actions did they take? **(b)** What difficulty were the workers facing? What action did they take? **(c)** Who else may have been affected by the problem? Why? **(d)** How does the historical context affect this situation? **(e)** What is the point of view of the writer of this editorial?

2. **(a)** Explain what each party wants for itself. **(b)** Do you think the writer is interested in fairness, or unfairly favors one side? Explain.

3. **(a)** Is the detail that the Baltimore & Ohio Company is paying 10 percent to its stockholders important to understanding the problem? Explain. **(b)** Are there any details in this excerpt that are irrelevant to the problem? Explain.

4. **(a)** Describe the problem caused by the railroad strike. **(b)** Evaluate the editorial's proposed solution. **(c)** What other solutions might be possible?

"The present strike among the employees of most of our principal railroad lines, is an illustration of errors in judgment . . . committed by the employers as well as by the employees of the railroad companies. None can deny, as a fundamental principle, the absolute necessity of . . . 'making both ends meet.' This principle is as applicable to every line of business, whether small or large, as to every family, whether poor or rich. Now, the railroad companies, in order to make ends meet, had the choice of three different means: 1st, to pay less dividends to the stockholders, in case dividends are paid; 2d, to raise the rates of freight; 3d, to reduce expenses. . . .

Of these three ways to make ends meet, the railroad companies, or rather those who are supposed to have sound judgment enough to be entrusted with their management . . . chose the latter means; and this was unjust to the employees and unfortunate for the stockholders, and especially unfortunate for the community at large, which is highly interested in reliable railroad transportation. . . .

It should not be lost sight of that the railroad on which the strike began (the Baltimore & Ohio) has been paying, and has thus far continued to pay, 10 per cent dividends to its stockholders. We ask if it would not be more just all around to pay only 8 or 9, or even 6 or 7 per cent dividend, and thus, instead of reducing the already too scanty wages of their employees, enable the railroad company to increase their pay. They forget that the interest on the capital invested must be earned by the men they employ, without whom they could not earn anything. . . ."

—*The Manufacturer and Builder*, August 1877

APPLY THE SKILL

See the Chapter Review and Assessment for another opportunity to apply this skill.

creating a CHAPTER SUMMARY

Copy this chart (right) on a piece of paper and complete it by adding information about major influences on western development. Some entries have been completed for you as examples.

For additional review and enrichment activities, see the interactive version of *America: Pathways to the Present*, available on the Web and on CD-ROM.

Forces That Shaped the West		
Cause(s)	**Event**	**Effect(s)**
Gold and silver strikes in California and the western interior	Mining rushes	
	Ranching	
	Homesteading	Immigrants populate the West.
	Indian wars	
	Populism	

★ Reviewing Key Terms

For each of the terms below, write a sentence explaining how it relates to the period of frontier development in the West.

1. Pacific Railway Acts
2. Exoduster
3. reservation
4. Battle of Little Bighorn
5. long drive
6. soddie
7. bonanza farm
8. free silver
9. the Grange
10. Interstate Commerce Act

★ Reviewing Main Ideas

11. Describe four ways that the federal government encouraged the settlement of the West. (Section 1)

12. Why did it take decades for the government to bring the Indian wars to an end? (Section 2)

13. How did large mining, ranching, and farming industries evolve in the West? (Section 3)

14. How did the arrival of American and immigrant settlers change the culture of the West? (Section 3)

15. Which groups supported the gold standard, and which favored free silver? (Section 4)

16. Why did Populism take hold in the late 1800s, and what were its main goals? (Section 4)

17. Identify the key issues, the key players, and the outcome of the 1896 presidential election. (Section 4)

18. Describe the origins of some of the frontier myths around the turn of the century. (Section 4)

★ Critical Thinking

19. **Recognizing Ideologies** Analyze the beliefs of settlers and Native Americans that brought them into conflict.

20. **Drawing Conclusions** Evaluate the impact of the federal government's policy of assimilation of Native Americans in the late 1800s.

21. **Synthesizing Information** Explain the roles played by the following people in the development of the West: (a) Lieutenant Colonel George Armstrong Custer; (b) Chief Joseph of the Nez Percé; (c) Native American sympathist writer Helen Hunt Jackson; (d) cattle baron Charles Goodnight.

22. **Testing Conclusions** Give evidence to support these statements: (a) Private property rights encouraged the settlement of the West. (b) Homesteaders caused the spread of traditional values such as democracy and a strong work ethic.

23. **Recognizing Cause and Effect** Analyze the effects of the federal government's monetary policies, such as tariffs and the gold standard, on the following groups: (a) farmers; (b) businesses and banks.

★ Standardized Test Prep

A PARTY OF PATCHES.
Grand Balloon Ascension—Cincinnati, May 20th, 1891.

Analyzing Political Cartoons ▶

24. This hot-air balloon hold aloft several Populist figures. What does the construction of the balloon imply?

   A That the party has wide support

   B That the party is made up of a patchwork of Populist groups

   C That the party is strong

   D That the party is easy to manipulate

25. Analyze the elements of this cartoon and state the cartoonist's main message.

Analyzing Primary Sources

Reread the two quotations in Comparing Primary Sources in Section 4, and then answer the questions that follow.

26. Which of Harvey's arguments does Laughlin most strongly refute?

   A Gold was considered the money of the rich.

   B Coining silver would increase the money supply.

   C Silver is a more reliable type of currency than gold.

   D Coining silver would result in increased wages and a fall in prices.

27. According to Laughlin, who would be harmed by the coinage of free silver?

   F miners, farmers, and consumers

   G consumers and silver lawmakers

   H laborers, farmers, and consumers

   I mine owners and pro-silver senators

Test-Taking Tip

To answer Question 27, reread the last line of the quote by Laughlin. In it, he states that free silver would "sacrifice the interests of the laboring classes."

Applying the Chapter Skill

Expressing Problems Clearly Review the skill on page 283. Then refer to Section 2 to write a paragraph that addresses these questions:

What was the central conflict between Native American groups and the United States, and how did their goals differ?

(a) What attempts were made to resolve the conflict, and what circumstances usually caused the efforts to fail? (b) What other solutions to the conflict could have been pursued?

Go Online
PHSchool.com

For: Chapter 7 Self-Test
Visit: PHSchool.com
Web Code: mra-5145

Settling the Great Plains

Native Americans once hunted buffalo on the Great Plains and farmed its river valleys. By the 1860s, especially in Texas, cattle ranchers had taken over the open ranges of the Plains. That all changed with the expansion of railroads and the invention of barbed wire.

Transformation of the Plains

In 1870, no railroads crossed the Texas plains. Ranchers drove their cattle over long trails to railroad towns in Kansas and Colorado. This was the heyday of the open range. As railroads expanded, though, farmers settled in areas of higher rainfall and put up barbed-wire fences to keep cattle off their land. Ranchers sometimes responded violently, but the government stood by the farmers. By 1890, railroads crisscrossed the Plains, and ranchers were forced to retreat to their own fenced ranges.

Geographic Connection

Why might farmers prefer areas with more rain?

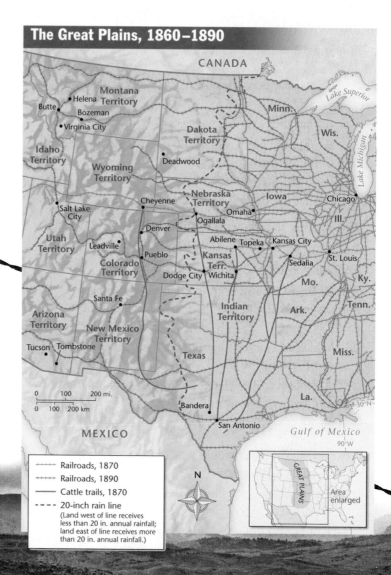

The Great Plains, 1860–1890

Legend:
- Railroads, 1870
- Railroads, 1890
- Cattle trails, 1870
- 20-inch rain line
  (Land west of line receives less than 20 in. annual rainfall; land east of line receives more than 20 in. annual rainfall.)

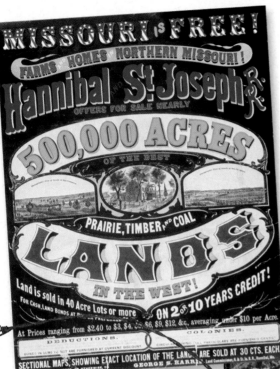

Attracting Farmers

The government gave railroads generous land grants for building lines across unsettled country on the Great Plains and in other parts of the country. Railroads such as the Hannibal and St. Joseph could cover expenses—and win future customers—by recruiting farmers to purchase and settle their land, as advertised in glowing posters like the one shown here.

A Rough Start

The first settlers on the Plains lacked wood for building houses and had to build "soddies," or houses made of sod, which consists of dirt and grass. They also had to contend with hostile, gun-slinging cattlemen, whose herds trampled their crops until the farmers could build barbed-wire fences.

The Nation's Breadbasket

Early explorers had called the treeless Great Plains the "Great American Desert," fit only for buffalo and cattle herds. However, farmers proved them wrong and made the region one of the world's most productive grain belts. This poster contrasts the reputation of Kansas as "drouthy" (or drought-prone) with images of abundant rainfall and crops.

Geographic Connection

How did the physical and human geography of the Great Plains allow farmers to displace ranchers?

Politics, Immigration, and Urban Life
(1870–1915)

Boss Tweed cartoon

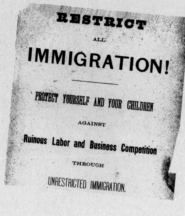

RESTRICT

ALL

IMMIGRATION!

PROTECT YOURSELF AND YOUR CHILDREN

AGAINST

Ruinous Labor and Business Competition

THROUGH

UNRESTRICTED IMMIGRATION.

American Events

1873
New York City's Boss Tweed is sent to prison for corruption in city government.

1882
The Chinese Exclusion Act closes the door to new immigration from China.

1883
In response to scandals, the Pendleton Civil Service Act changes how the federal government hires and promotes workers.

1886
The United States officially accepts the Statue of Liberty as a gift from France.

Presidential Terms: U.S. Grant 1869–1877   R. Hayes 1877–1881   J. Garfield 1881
C. Arthur 1881–1885   G. Cleveland 1885–1889   B. Harrison 1889–1893

1870

1880

1890

World Events

European powers meet at Berlin to divide up Africa.

Sherlock Holmes debuts in *A Study in Scarlet*.

1884

1887

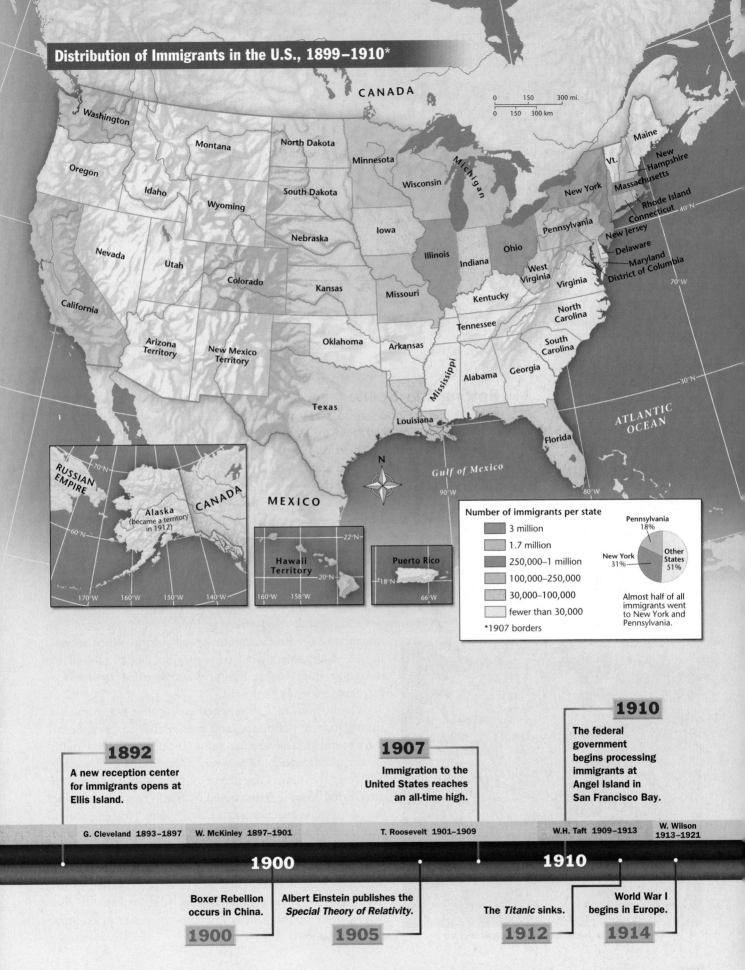

Distribution of Immigrants in the U.S., 1899–1910*

CANADA

0   150   300 mi.
0   150   300 km

Washington

Oregon

Montana

Idaho

Wyoming

Nevada

Utah

California

Arizona
Territory

New Mexico
Territory

North Dakota

South Dakota

Nebraska

Colorado

Kansas

Oklahoma

Texas

Minnesota

Wisconsin

Iowa

Missouri

Arkansas

Louisiana

Michigan

Illinois

Indiana

Ohio

Kentucky

Tennessee

Mississippi

Alabama

Georgia

New York

Pennsylvania

West
Virginia

Virginia

North
Carolina

South
Carolina

Florida

Maine

Vt.

New
Hampshire

Massachusetts

Rhode Island

Connecticut

New Jersey

Delaware

Maryland

District of Columbia

40°N

70°W

30°N

80°W

90°W

ATLANTIC
OCEAN

Gulf of Mexico

N

MEXICO

RUSSIAN
EMPIRE

70°N

60°N

Alaska
(became a territory
in 1912)

CANADA

170°W   160°W   150°W   140°W

Hawaii
Territory

22°N

20°N

160°W   158°W

Puerto Rico

18°N

66°W

Number of immigrants per state

- 3 million
- 1.7 million
- 250,000–1 million
- 100,000–250,000
- 30,000–100,000
- fewer than 30,000

*1907 borders

Pennsylvania
18%

New York
31%

Other
States
51%

Almost half of all
immigrants went
to New York and
Pennsylvania.

1892

A new reception center
for immigrants opens at
Ellis Island.

1907

Immigration to the
United States reaches
an all-time high.

1910

The federal
government
begins processing
immigrants at
Angel Island in
San Francisco Bay.

G. Cleveland 1893–1897   W. McKinley 1897–1901   T. Roosevelt 1901–1909   W.H. Taft 1909–1913   W. Wilson 1913–1921

1900

1910

**Boxer Rebellion
occurs in China.**

1900

**Albert Einstein publishes the
Special Theory of Relativity.**

1905

The *Titanic* sinks.

1912

**World War I
begins in Europe.**

1914

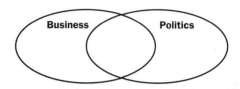

Politics in the Gilded Age

READING FOCUS

- How did business influence politics during the Gilded Age?

- In what ways did government reform the spoils system and regulate railroads?

- What effect did the transition from depression to prosperity have on politics in the 1890s?

MAIN IDEA

From 1877 to 1900, national politics was dominated by issues of corruption and reform.

KEY TERMS

Gilded Age
laissez-faire
subsidy
blue law
civil service
Pendleton Civil
  Service Act
rebate
Munn v. *Illinois*

TARGET READING SKILL

Identify Main Ideas Copy the diagram below. As you read, fill in the two circles with events and issues of the Gilded Age that you can categorize as related to business or politics. Place events and issues that involved both politics and business in the area where the two circles overlap.

Setting the Scene Jay Gould never formally learned how to run a railroad, but he understood the stock market. By 1871, he had become the most powerful railroad man in New York. A decade later he controlled the largest rail network in the nation.

Gould began buying and selling shares of small railways in 1859 and rose to the position of Director of New York's Erie Railroad Company. In 1867, Cornelius Vanderbilt moved to buy stock in the Erie to combine it with his own New York Central Railroad. Gould, seeking to keep control out of Vanderbilt's hands, swiftly issued 50,000 new shares. Knowing the stock issue was illegal, Gould bribed members of the New York State Legislature to legalize his stock sale and to forbid the combination of the New York Central and Erie railroads. Vanderbilt had been stopped.

Now securely in control, Gould directed the Erie to pay his own private construction companies to lay track. No work was done. Gould pocketed the money, and the Erie's share price fell sharply. When several British shareholders tried to stop him, Gould refused to recognize their voting rights. A judge ruled against the shareholders when they sued.

Gould lived in a time when corruption was common among judges, politicians, and presidential advisors. Some corrupt individuals were caught and punished. Jay Gould, on the other hand, died a very wealthy man. His story illustrates the remarkable flavor of politics and business in the **Gilded Age**—a term coined by Mark Twain to describe the post-Reconstruction era. Gilded means "covered with a thin layer of gold," and "Gilded Age" suggests that a thin but glittering layer of prosperity covered the poverty and corruption of much of society. This was a golden period for America's industrialists. Their wealth helped hide the problems faced by immigrants, laborers, and farmers. It also helped cover up the widespread abuse of power in business and government.

INTERPRETING POLITICAL CARTOONS Jay Gould's wealth and social connections gave him tremendous power in the financial world, as this cartoon shows. **Making Inferences** *How did the cartoonist feel about Gould's power? Explain your answer.*

JAY GOULD'S NEW YORK BOWLING ALLEY

The Business of Politics

The United States faced great challenges in Gould's day as it emerged from Reconstruction. Industrial expansion raised the output of the nation's factories and farms. Some Americans, such as speculators in land and stocks, quickly rose "from rags to riches." At the same time, depressions, low wages, and rising farm debt contributed to discontent among working people.

Laissez-faire Policies   In the late 1800s, businesses operated largely without government regulation. This hands-off approach to economic matters, known by the French phrase **_laissez-faire,_** holds that government should play a very limited role in business. Supporters of this strategy maintain that if government does not interfere, the strongest businesses will succeed and bring wealth to the nation as a whole.

The term _laissez-faire_ translates roughly as "allow to be" in French. Although the term probably originated with French economists in the mid-1700s, the theory of _laissez-faire_ economics was primarily developed by Adam Smith in his 1776 book, _The Wealth of Nations._ A university professor in Scotland, Smith argued that government should promote free trade and allow a free marketplace for labor and goods.

In the late 1800s, most Americans accepted _laissez-faire_ economics in theory. In practice, however, many supported government involvement when it benefited them. For example, American businesses favored high tariffs on imported goods to encourage people to buy American goods instead. American businesses also accepted government land grants and subsidies. A **subsidy** is a payment made by the government to encourage the development of certain key industries, such as railroads.

In this political cartoon, monopolies and trusts are depicted as controlling the government.

To ensure government aid, business giants during the Gilded Age supported friendly politicians with gifts of money. Some of these contributions were legal and some were illegal. Between 1875 and 1885, the Central Pacific Railroad reportedly budgeted $500,000 each year for bribes. Central Pacific co-founder Collis P. Huntington explained, "If you have to pay money to have the right thing done, it is only just and fair to do it."

Credit Mobilier Scandal   Washington's generous financial support for railroad-building after the Civil War invited corruption. A notorious scandal developed when Congress awarded the Union Pacific Railroad Company loans and western land to complete the first transcontinental railroad. Like Jay Gould and the Erie Railroad, the owners of the Union Pacific hired an outside company—Credit Mobilier—to build the actual tracks that Union Pacific trains would ride upon. Credit Mobilier charged Union Pacific far beyond the value of the work done, and money flowed from the federal government through the Union Pacific railroad to the shareholders of Credit Mobilier.

Credit Mobilier's managers needed Congress to continue funding the Union Pacific. They gave cheap shares of valuable Credit Mobilier stock to those who agreed to support more funding. Congress did not investigate Credit Mobilier until 1872—three years after the Union Pacific had completed the transcontinental railroad. It was discovered that Credit Mobilier gave stock to representatives of both parties, including a future President, a future Vice President, several cousins of President Grant, and as many as thirty other officials. Unfortunately, Credit Mobilier was only one of many scandals that marked Grant's eight years as President.

READING CHECK

How did the government help private businesses in the Gilded Age?

The Spoils System   Bribery was one consequence of the reliance of American politics on the spoils system. Under this system, elected officials appointed friends and supporters to government jobs, regardless of their qualifications. By the Gilded Age, government swarmed with unqualified, dishonest employees.

The spoils system appealed to many politicians because it ensured them a loyal group of supporters in future elections. Both Democrats and Republicans handed out jobs to pay off the people who had helped them get elected. But the system led to corruption when dishonest appointees used their jobs for personal profit.

Opposing Political Parties   During the Gilded Age, the Democratic and Republican parties had roughly the same number of supporters. They differed greatly, however, in who those supporters were and in their positions on major issues.

Republicans appealed to industrialists, bankers, and eastern farmers. The party was strongest in the North and the upper Midwest and was weak to nonexistent in the South, although it did receive support from southern blacks. In general, Republicans favored a tight money supply backed by gold, high tariffs to protect American business, generous pensions for Union soldiers, government aid to the railroads, strict limits on immigration, and enforcement of **blue laws,** regulations that prohibited certain private activities that some people considered immoral.

As a rule, the Democratic Party attracted those in American society who were less privileged, or at least felt that way. These groups included northern urban immigrants, laborers, southern planters, and western farmers. Claiming to represent the interests of ordinary people, Democrats favored an increased money supply backed by silver, lower tariffs on imported goods, higher farm prices, less government aid to big business, and fewer blue laws.

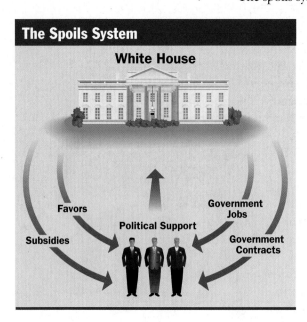

The Spoils System

White House

Favors

Subsidies

Political Support

Government Jobs

Government Contracts

Reforming the Spoils System

Since the two parties had roughly equal strength, presidential candidates needed the votes of almost all members of their party in order to win an election. To avoid offending party members, candidates generally avoided taking well-defined stands on controversial issues. Most states had very strong ties to one party or the other, so candidates often came from the few states that could swing either Democratic or Republican. Seven of the eight presidents who followed Andrew Johnson came from Ohio or New York.

Republicans whipped up support by "waving the bloody shirt." This meant recalling the bloodshed of the Civil War, a conflict they blamed on the Democrats. Southern Democrats had their own "bloody shirt," in this case a reference to the abuses of Radical Reconstruction.

Presidents of this period did make some efforts to exercise leadership. Indeed, the Gilded Age witnessed some important reforms in such areas as the spoils system and the railroads.

Hayes Fights the Spoils System   After his election in 1877, Rutherford B. Hayes surprised many supporters by refusing to use the patronage system. Instead he appointed qualified political independents to Cabinet posts and fired employees who were not needed. By these actions Hayes began to reform the **civil service,** or the government's nonelected workers.

Hayes undertook these reforms without congressional backing, even from members of his own Republican Party. He further angered his party on July 11, 1878, when he removed fellow Republican Chester A. Arthur from an important patronage position in New York. Then, with the help of congressional Democrats, he replaced Arthur with one of his own appointments. These moves especially upset Senator Roscoe Conkling, a supporter of patronage in New York State.

Hayes had announced at the beginning of his presidency that he would not seek a second term. After his bold attack on the spoils system, he probably could not have won his party's nomination in any case. That attack strengthened the government but also helped weaken the Republicans.

Garfield's Term Cut Short

As the 1880 presidential election approached, the Republican Party was split into three factions. The Stalwarts, followers of Senator Conkling, defended the spoils system. The Half-Breeds, who followed Senator James G. Blaine of Maine, hoped to reform the spoils system while remaining loyal to the party. Independents opposed the spoils system altogether.

James A. Garfield, an Ohio congressman and ally of the Half-Breeds, won the party's presidential nomination. To balance the ticket, the Republicans chose as their vice-presidential candidate Chester A. Arthur, a New York Stalwart.

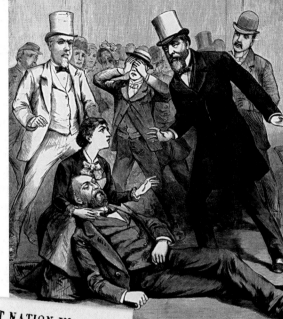

A GREAT NATION IN GRIEF

PRESIDENT GARFIELD SHOT BY AN ASSASSIN.

THOUGH SERIOUSLY WOUNDED HE STILL SURVIVES.

THE WOULD-BE MURDERER LODGED IN PRISON.

President Garfield's assassination made the nation aware of the need for reform of the spoils system.

Garfield won a narrow victory over the Democratic candidate, General Winfield S. Hancock. However, his term was cut short. On July 2, 1881, a mentally unstable lawyer named Charles Guiteau shot Garfield as the President walked through a Washington, D.C., railroad station. When he fired his fatal shot, Guiteau cried out, "I am a Stalwart and Arthur is President now!" Garfield died three months later.

The public later learned that Guiteau, a loyal Republican, had expected a job from Garfield. When Garfield passed him over, Guiteau became so enraged that he decided to murder the President. The murder caused a public outcry against the spoils system.

Arthur Reforms the Civil Service

Upon Garfield's death, Vice President Chester Arthur became President. Arthur had fought for (and benefited from) patronage in New York. Once in office, however, he urged Congress to support reform of the spoils system. With Garfield's assassination fresh in the nation's mind, President Arthur was able to obtain congressional support for this reform. As a result, the **Pendleton Civil Service Act** became law in 1883.

The act created a Civil Service Commission, which classified government jobs and tested applicants' fitness for them. It also stated that federal employees could not be required to contribute to campaign funds and could not be fired for political reasons.

INTERPRETING GRAPHS
Arthur's reforms protected thousands of jobs from political concerns. **Synthesizing Information** *Why did the rapid growth of the government work force encourage the spoils system?*

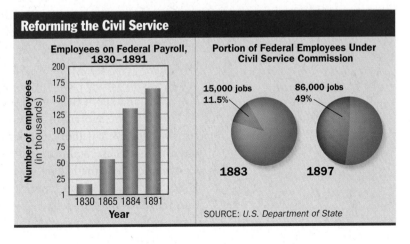

Reforming the Civil Service

Employees on Federal Payroll, 1830–1891

Number of employees (in thousands)

200
175
150
125
100
75
50
25
1

1830 1865 1884 1891
Year

Portion of Federal Employees Under Civil Service Commission

15,000 jobs
11.5%

86,000 jobs
49%

1883   1897

SOURCE: *U.S. Department of State*

Democrats Take Power In 1884, the Republicans nominated James G. Blaine, a former Secretary of State and senator from Maine, for President. The Democrats chose Grover Cleveland, former mayor of Buffalo and governor of New York.

Serious issues confronted the nation that year, such as high tariffs, unfair business practices, and unregulated railroads. Yet the campaign focused mostly on scandals. Had James G. Blaine received railroad stock options in return for favorable votes while he was in Congress? No one could prove that he had. Had Cleveland fathered a child out of wedlock while a bachelor in Buffalo? Cleveland admitted the rumor was true. Republicans jeered, "Ma, Ma, where's my Pa?" Democrats responded, "Going to the White House, ha, ha, ha!"

Cleveland became the first Democratic president since 1856. He owed at least some of his success to Republican independents who decided that Blaine was too corrupt to support. These independents were called "mugwumps," an Algonquin word for "renegade chief." The term stuck when a newspaper editor joked that it really meant "unreliable Republicans," men whose "mugs" were on one side of the fence and "wumps" on the other.

Cleveland favored tight money policies, so most business interests backed him. Yet not all his policies were pro-business. He opposed high tariffs and took back from the railroads and other interests some 80 million acres of federal land that had been granted to them. In addition, Cleveland supported more government regulation of the powerful railroad companies.

Regulating Railroads

Railroad regulation had begun in 1869, when Massachusetts investigated claims that railroad companies were overcharging customers. By 1880, about 14 states had railroad commissions that looked into complaints about railroad practices. One of those practices was charging more for a short haul than for a long haul over the same track. Another practice was to offer **rebates,** or partial refunds, to favored customers. Others included keeping rates secret and charging different rates to different people for the same service.

Some of these practices can be justified by the economics of operating a railroad. For example, a short haul is more costly per mile than a long haul because the cost of loading and unloading the cargo is equal in both cases. Rebates were one legal way that railroads competed for customers. In any event, farmers and businesses opposed them because they favored some customers and kept others from predicting their costs.

In 1877 the Supreme Court, in **Munn v. Illinois,** allowed states to regulate certain businesses within their borders, including railroads. But railroad traffic often crossed state boundaries. Lawyers for the railroads argued that under the Constitution only the federal government could regulate interstate commerce. In 1886, in the *Wabash* case, the Supreme Court agreed. Interstate railroad traffic thus remained unregulated.

Fast Forward to Today

Confederate Battle Flags

Memories of the Civil War still divided Americans after Reconstruction. In 1887, President Cleveland proposed returning captured Confederate battle flags held by the federal government to southern states. Cleveland was the first Democrat and non-veteran President elected since the Civil War, and his request unleashed a firestorm of anger from the 400,000 veterans of the Grand Army of the Republic. Governor Foraker of Ohio said, "The patriotic people of this state are shocked and indignant beyond anything I can express." Shaken by the reaction, Cleveland retreated from his proposal.

Today President Theodore Roosevelt returned the battle flags held by the federal government in 1905, but individual states and societies still hold other battle flags today. In 2000, the Virginia Senate urged the Minnesota Historical Society to return the battered flag of the 28th Virginia Infantry. The Minnesota 1st Volunteer had captured the flag at the Battle of Gettysburg after suffering terrible losses. "Absolutely not," replied Minnesota Gov. Jesse Ventura. "We took it. That makes it our heritage."

? Why were many northerners upset by Cleveland's proposal to return the flags?

Pressure mounted on Congress to curb these abuses. As you read in the last chapter, in 1887 Congress responded by passing the Interstate Commerce Act. The act required that rates be set in proportion to the distance traveled and that rates be made public. It also outlawed the practice of giving special rates to powerful customers. Finally, it set up the nation's first federal regulatory board, the Interstate Commerce Commission (ICC), to enforce the act.

The Interstate Commerce Act did not give the ICC the power to set railroad rates. Also, to enforce its rulings, the ICC had to take the railroads to court, where it usually lost. Of the 16 cases involving the ICC that came before the Supreme Court between 1887 and 1905, the Court ruled against the ICC 15 times.

Depression to Prosperity

Boosted by vigorous industrial growth, American business generally grew during the late 1880s and into the 1890s. But in 1893 a depression struck, and prosperity did not return until around 1900. These ups and downs made the economy the hottest political issue of this period.

Focus on Tariffs Cleveland lost the 1888 presidential election to Republican Benjamin Harrison. The campaign had focused on tariffs. Cleveland favored a minor reduction in tariffs, while Harrison wanted an increase. Harrison's position won him plenty of business support and, ultimately, the presidency.

Among President Harrison's achievements was the signing of the Sherman Antitrust Act in 1890, described earlier. Like the Interstate Commerce Act, however, this seemingly bold action failed to curb the power of the largest corporations until well after the turn of the century.

Meanwhile, Harrison made good his campaign promise to business by approving a huge tariff increase in 1890. He also supported legislation on behalf of special business interests. Although he was thought to be conservative with public funds, Harrison dipped deep into the Treasury to award huge new pensions to dependents of Civil War soldiers.

These actions would later damage the economy, and they did not help Harrison in the election of 1892. Many new immigrants had swelled the ranks of the Democratic Party. Campaigning again for lower tariffs, Grover Cleveland was returned to the presidency.

Cleveland's Second Term Cleveland's second term started badly. A worldwide economic slowdown contributed in part to a financial panic that hit the country in 1893. This began a long depression, during which millions of workers lost their jobs or had their wages slashed. Despite the suffering, the government offered no help.

In 1894, Jacob S. Coxey, a wealthy Ohio quarry owner, demanded that government create jobs for the unemployed. Coxey called on unemployed workers to march on the nation's capital. "We will send a petition to Washington with boots on," he declared.

Many small "armies" started out on the protest march, but only Coxey's army reached Washington. Police arrested him and a few others for illegally carrying banners on the Capitol grounds and for trampling the grass. A song sung by

These campaign ribbons illustrate how presidential candidates attracted support from different groups of people.

Presidential Election of 1892

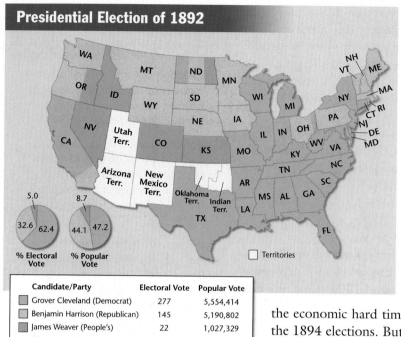

5.0
32.6 | 62.4
% Electoral Vote

8.7
44.1 | 47.2
% Popular Vote

☐ Territories

Candidate/Party	Electoral Vote	Popular Vote
Grover Cleveland (Democrat)	277	5,554,414
Benjamin Harrison (Republican)	145	5,190,802
James Weaver (People's)	22	1,027,329

MAP SKILLS Grover Cleveland returned to the White House after the 1892 election with the support of Southern Democrats and immigrants. **Place** *Compare this map to the map on page 289. How did the states that later attracted many immigrants vote in 1892?*

Coxey's supporters mocked the government for worrying more about its lawns than its citizens.

In his second term Cleveland managed to anger not only the unemployed but almost everyone else. In 1893, he upset farmers by repealing the Sherman Silver Purchase Act, which had become law just three years before. He enraged unions when he sent federal troops to Chicago during the Pullman strike of 1894.

By the time of his party's convention in 1896, Cleveland had turned many fellow Democrats against him. Hence, the President failed to win his party's nomination.

McKinley Wins in 1896 The Populists had emerged as a political power during the economic hard times of the early 1890s and had made gains in the 1894 elections. But in 1896, William Jennings Bryan, the presidential candidate of the Populists and Democrats, lost to the Republican candidate, William McKinley. McKinley was supported by urban workers and the middle class.

President McKinley oversaw a new tariff bill and a stronger gold standard. These actions brought Republicans an even more decisive victory against Bryan in 1900. McKinley won 292 electoral votes while Bryan only won 155. As the economy began to climb out of the 1890s depression, Republicans claimed credit with their slogan "A Full Dinner Pail."

McKinley did not live long enough to enjoy the effects of the returning prosperity. On September 6, 1901, McKinley went on a tour of the Pan-American Exposition in Buffalo, New York. Leon Czolgosz, a mentally ill man who called himself an anarchist, shot the President as he greeted the public there. McKinley died days later.

Section 1 Assessment

READING COMPREHENSION

1. Is the term **Gilded Age** a positive or negative description of this period? Explain.

2. What is the purpose of a **subsidy?**

3. How did the **Pendleton Civil Service Act** address the problems of the spoils system?

4. How did the Interstate Commerce Act affect railroads?

CRITICAL THINKING AND WRITING

5. **Recognizing Cause and Effect** Businesses sought political influence by making large contributions to politicians. How do you think these politicians voted on tariff legislation? Why?

6. **Creating an Outline** Create an outline for an essay in which you explain how economic issues affected the outcome of presidential elections during the Gilded Age.

Go Online
PHSchool.com

For: An activity on civil service jobs
Visit: PHSchool.com
Web Code: mrd-5151

READING FOCUS

- What were the experiences of immigrants in the late 1800s and early 1900s?
- What different challenges did immigrants from Europe, Asia, and Mexico face?

MAIN IDEA

Millions of immigrants, representing many different cultures, arrived in the United States during the late 1800s and early 1900s.

KEY TERMS

pogrom
steerage
quarantine
ghetto
restrictive covenant
Chinese Exclusion Act
Gentlemen's Agreement
alien

TARGET READING SKILL

Recognize Multiple Causes As you read, complete this chart listing the reasons why immigrants came to America and their experiences in their new land.

Place of Origin	Reasons for Immigration	Experiences in the United States
Europe	To escape religious persecution	Settled in cities in the East and the Midwest
Asia		
Mexico		

Setting the Scene   Peter Mossini was born in 1898 into a poor family in Sicily. He shared a small two-bedroom house with his parents and seven brothers and sisters. Peter's parents could not afford to send him to school, so at age ten he went to work in a factory. He earned about ten cents a day for eleven or twelve hours of work.

When Peter was still an infant, his father left home to find work in the coal mines of Pennsylvania. Peter's family survived on the money his father sent back in addition to the children's wages from the factory. Peter's father returned to Sicily in 1913, and the family once again struggled to get by. Following World War I, Peter saw no future for himself in his hometown of Santa Teresa di Riva:

A family of immigrants arrives at Ellis Island in 1905.

> 66 *During the First World War, I was in the army, and I held to my idea about coming to America. Then, in 1919, my sister Josephine came [to America]. I was very close to her . . . She came by herself and she got married. She was doing very well over here. And I wanted to build a new life, better myself. Eventually, all my brothers and sisters came to the United States.* 99
>
> —Peter Mossini

At age 22, Peter boarded a ship, the *Pesaro*, bound for America. Three months later he joined his sister in Portage, Pennsylvania.

It was sometimes said that America's streets were paved with gold. This myth held a grain of truth for the millions of immigrants who left a life of poverty behind. Like Peter, they came to America because it offered, if not instant wealth, then at least the chance to improve their lives. Some immigrants did get rich through hard work and determination. Many more managed to carve out a decent life for themselves and their families. For these immigrants, the chance to come to the United States was indeed a golden opportunity.

The Immigrant Experience

In the late 1800s, people in many parts of the world were on the move from farms to cities and from one country to another. Immigrants from around the globe were fleeing crop failures, shortages of land and jobs, rising taxes, and famine. Some were also escaping religious or political persecution.

Immigrants' Hopes and Dreams The United States received a huge portion of this global migration. In 1860, the resident population of the United States was 31.5 million people. Between 1865 and 1920, close to 30 million additional people entered the country.

Some of these newcomers dreamed of getting rich, or at least of securing free government land through the Homestead Act. Others

yearned for personal freedoms. In America, they had heard, everyone could go to school, young men were not forced to serve long years in the army, and citizens could freely take part in a democratic government. Conditions in two countries, Italy and Russia, illustrate how economic problems and political persecution encouraged millions to immigrate to the United States.

"There [were] two classes of people in Sicily," Peter Mossini said, "the rich and the very poor." A few people owned most of the land and the poor lived as sharecroppers. In the late 1800s, the economy of southern Italy slipped into decline. The land was very poor, but the government of Italy demanded more and more money in taxes. Thousands of farmers lost their livelihood when a parasite killed many of the region's grapevines. Many tenant farmers found they simply could not afford to stay in their homes and still take care of their families. Skilled workers, too, could not find jobs. The United States offered a solution.

In Russia, Jews faced hostility from their Christian neighbors and the government. In the 1880s, a wave of **pogroms,** or violent massacres of Jews, swept across the country. The czar responded to the pogroms by sharply limiting where Jews could live and how they could earn a living. America offered freedom of religion and the opportunity to build a new life.

Crossing the Ocean In the late 1800s, steam-powered ships could cross the Atlantic Ocean in two to three weeks. By 1900, on more powerful steamships, the crossing took just one week. Even this brief journey, however, could be difficult, especially for those who could not afford cabins. Most immigrants traveled in **steerage,** a large open area beneath the ship's deck. Steerage offered limited toilet facilities, no privacy, and poor food, but tickets were relatively cheap.

Crossing the vast Pacific Ocean took much longer, but the arrangements were similar. Passengers traveled in steerage, with few comforts. A person's country of origin, however, could make a difference in the conditions aboard a ship. Immigrants from Japan, whose power in the world was growing, often received better treatment than those from China, which at that time was a weak country.

In the late 1800s, millions of immigrants brought their belongings and their dreams to the United States in a single steamer trunk.

Expanding Cities

But New York was not alone. Philadelphia, Chicago, St. Louis, New Orleans, and many other cities were bursting at the seams with newcomers. While millions of immigrants from around the world were settling in the cities of the United States, growing numbers of native-born Americans were moving there, too. Between 1880 and 1920, 11 million Americans left behind the economic hardship of their farms and headed for the opportunities of the cities. This migration within the country, combined with the new immigration, brought explosive growth to the nation's urban centers.

Women and men alike took part in the migration from rural to urban America. As factories produced more of the goods that farm women had once made, the need for women's labor on farms declined. In addition, as new machines replaced manual labor on many farms, the need for male farmhands shrank. The result was a striking shift in the nation's population. Between 1880 and 1910, the percentage of the nation's population living on farms fell from 72 to 54 percent.

Many African Americans took part in this internal migration. In 1870, fewer than a half million of the nation's 5 million African Americans lived outside the South. But after Reconstruction ended in 1877, segregation and acts of racial violence against African Americans increased. By 1890, partly as a result of these pressures, another 150,000 black southerners had left the South, and many rural African Americans had moved into nearby cities. Then, in the 1910s, the boll weevil destroyed cotton crops and floods ruined Alabama and Mississippi farmlands. These disasters drove several hundred thousand more African Americans out of the South, mostly to northern cities.

How Cities Grew

The arrival of large numbers of newcomers, from both within and outside the nation, radically changed the face of the nation's cities. Between 1865 and 1900 many features of modern city life, both good and bad, first appeared—from subways and skyscrapers to smog and slums.

Before the Civil War, cities were small in area, rarely extending more than three or four miles across. Most people lived near their workplace and walked wherever they had to go. The introduction of public, horse-drawn carriages that traveled on rails began to change this pattern. Appearing in many cities in the 1850s, they allowed people who could afford the fares to move outside the cities. Those people made their homes in the **suburbs,** or residential communities surrounding the cities.

Later in the 1800s, motorized methods of transportation made commuting much easier and advanced suburban growth. The first elevated trains, opened in 1868 in New York,

VIEWING FINE ART These two drawings give a bird's-eye view of Chicago in 1871 and many years later in 1916. **Making Comparisons** *What happened to the farmland at the city's edge between 1871 and 1916? What changes do you observe in the buildings in the city center?*

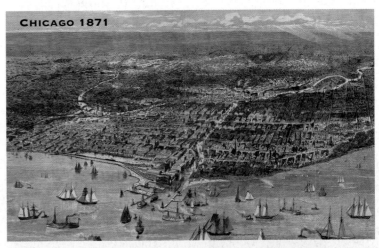

CHICAGO 1871

CHICAGO 1916

Streetcar Suburbs The spread of streetcar lines created a new type of town: the streetcar suburb. Streetcars doubled or tripled the distance people could live from the central city while still traveling there to work each day. In many places, the same company that operated the streetcar line built middle-class homes and apartments in leafy suburbs to create demand for their services. Streetcar suburbs included West Philadelphia; East Cleveland; Piedmont Park near Charlotte, North Carolina; Roxbury and Dorchester near Boston; and Harlem, north of downtown New York. Many of these first suburbs later merged with their parent cities.

allowed commuters to bypass the congested streets. Cable cars, introduced in San Francisco in 1873, allowed quick access to the city's steep hills. Electric trolleys, first used in Richmond, Virginia, in 1888, replaced horse-drawn cars and reached even farther into the suburbs. Subway trains first appeared in Boston in 1897. Finally, the automobile, invented in the 1890s and mass-produced beginning in the 1910s, guaranteed that expansion into the suburbs would continue.

Cities grew upward as well as outward. Before the Civil War, buildings stood no more than five stories high. Yet as urban space became scarce, buildings were made taller and taller. To build these mammoth structures, engineers needed the strength of Bessemer steel girders.

To reach the upper floors, people relied on the speed and efficiency of elevators. In 1852 Elisha Graves Otis, an American, invented a safety device that made passenger elevators possible. The first one went into operation five years later. The first skyscraper, Chicago's Home Insurance Company Building, appeared in 1885. Ten stories tall, it was built with a framework of iron and steel and had four passenger elevators. Architect Louis Sullivan completed the ten-story Wainwright building in St. Louis in 1891. The Wainwright building consisted of a steel skeleton sheathed in red sandstone, granite, brick, and a form of baked red clay called terra cotta.

As cities expanded, specialized areas emerged within them. Banks, financial offices, law firms, and government offices were located in one central area. Retail shops and department stores were located in another central neighborhood. Industrial, wholesale, and warehouse districts formed a ring around the center of the city.

Urban Living Conditions

Some urban workers moved into housing built especially for them by mill and factory owners. The rest found apartments wherever they could. Many middle-class residents who moved to the suburbs left empty buildings behind. Owners converted these buildings into multifamily units for workers and their families.

Speculators also built many **tenements,** low-cost apartment buildings designed to house as many families as the owner could pack in. A group of dirty, run-down tenements could transform an area into a slum.

Conditions in the Slums Before long, because of poverty, overcrowding, and neglect, the old residential neighborhoods of cities gradually declined. Trees and grass disappeared. Hundreds of people were crammed into spaces meant for a few families. Soot from coal-fired steam engines and boilers made the air seem dark and foul even in daylight. Open sewers attracted rats and other disease-spreading vermin.

In 1905, journalist Eleanor McMain quoted a university student who described a block of tenements in the Italian district of New Orleans as "death traps, closely built, jammed together, with no side openings. Twenty-five per cent of the yard space is damp and gloomy. . . . Where the houses are three or more rooms in depth, the middle ones are dark, without outside ventilator. . . . There is no fire protection whatever."

Fire was a constant danger in cities. With tenement buildings so closely packed together, even a small fire could quickly consume a neighborhood. Once a fire started, it leaped easily from roof to roof. As a result, most large cities had major fires during this period. Chicago experienced one of the

Growing cities drew people from rural areas. This woman found work as a porter in a subway.

most devastating: the Great Chicago Fire of 1871. Nobody knows for sure what started it, but before it was over, 18,000 buildings had burned, leaving some 250 people dead and 100,000 homeless. Property damage estimates reached $200 million, the equivalent of $2 billion today. A similar fire in Boston caused the equivalent of nearly $1 billion in damage.

Contagious diseases, including cholera, malaria, tuberculosis, diphtheria, and typhoid, thrived in crowded tenement conditions. Epidemics, such as the yellow fever that swept through Memphis, Tennessee, in the late 1870s and through New Orleans in the early 1900s, took thousands of lives. Children were especially vulnerable to disease. In one district of tenements in New York City, six out of ten babies died before their first birthday.

Diseases spread rapidly, especially during the summer months when apartments heated up like ovens. A heat wave lasting from August 5 to 13, 1896, took the lives of over 400 New Yorkers. The Chicago Health Department found that at least 80 percent of summer deaths among children under two were caused by preventable diseases. Chicago and New York City established fresh-air havens on their waterfronts for sick children to escape the deadly conditions of the slums.

Light, Air, and Water Scientists believed that lack of good ventilation helped disease spread. They pushed for reforms to improve air flow and natural light in tenements. One wrote:

> 66 *Simple ordinary outdoor air is a most valuable health resource . . . a balcony on a city street is a thousand times better than a room in a house closed for fear of drafts, curtained for fear of fading the furniture, and lighted by a lamp.* 99
>
> —Ellen Swallow Richards

INTERPRETING DIAGRAMS
Architects designed the dumbbell tenement to fit as many people as possible into a city block while providing all rooms with light and air. **Drawing Conclusions** *How successful was the dumbbell tenement at meeting these two goals?*

In 1879, a change in New York laws required an outside window in every room. To accommodate windows in rows of buildings, an architect designed the **dumbbell tenement,** named for its dumbbell shape. Each building narrowed in the middle, and gaps on either side formed air shafts to bring light and air to inside rooms.

While an improvement, the gloomy air shaft was certainly not an open balcony. The tenement-dweller looked across the closed space to a brick wall and a neighbor's window only a few feet away. Rotting garbage collected at the bottom of the shaft. Little sunlight or fresh air reached apartments this way.

Scientists also linked diseases like cholera and typhoid to contaminated drinking water, which tenement residents drew from a common pipe or pump in the yard. Authorities feared that polluted city water drawn from local springs and rivers could cause epidemics. Boston, Cincinnati, and New York built reservoirs or waterworks to collect clean water far from the city and filter out impurities. City water companies later introduced chlorination and filtration. A 1901 New York City law required that hallway bathrooms replace

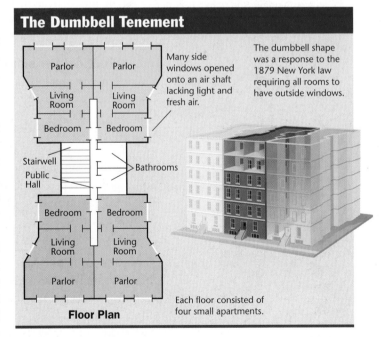

The Dumbbell Tenement

Parlor · Parlor

Living Room · Living Room

Bedroom · Bedroom

Stairwell
Public Hall

Bathrooms

Bedroom · Bedroom

Living Room · Living Room

Parlor · Parlor

Floor Plan

Many side windows opened onto an air shaft lacking light and fresh air.

The dumbbell shape was a response to the 1879 New York law requiring all rooms to have outside windows.

Each floor consisted of four small apartments.

backyard outhouses. Landlords installed small bathtubs and sinks with running water in most apartments.

How the Other Half Lives The American public learned about the horrors of tenement life in 1890 when a reporter named Jacob Riis published *How the Other Half Lives*. Hoping to generate public support for reform of the tenement "system," Riis painted a bleak picture of New York's future:

> ❝ *Today three-fourths of [New York's] people live in the tenements. . . . We know now that there is no way out; that the 'system' that was the evil offspring of public neglect and private greed has come to stay, a storm-centre forever of our civilization. Nothing is left but to make the best of a bad bargain.* ❞
>
> —Jacob Riis, *How the Other Half Lives*, 1890

In order to document his reporting, Riis mastered the new technology of flash photography. Drawings based on these photographs appeared in his book, and he showed the actual photographs of overcrowded rooms and run-down buildings in his lectures on the plight of immigrants. As a result of Riis's work, New York State passed the nation's first meaningful laws to improve tenements.

The Results of City Growth

Some city residents could avoid urban problems simply by leaving the cities. The middle and upper classes began moving to the suburbs in the late 1800s. As a result, the gap between the well-to-do and the poor widened.

A few cities preserved neighborhoods of mansions and luxury townhouses near the city center for the wealthiest residents. These areas included Beacon Hill in Boston, the Gold Coast in Chicago, and Nob Hill in San Francisco. Often, people living in these neighborhoods also owned country estates and were quite isolated from the nearby poverty.

Political Divisions Rapidly growing cities proved difficult to govern. Urban growth put pressure on city officials to improve police and fire protection, transportation systems, sewage disposal, electrical and water service, and health care. To deliver these services, cities raised taxes and set up offices to deal with people's needs.

Increased revenue and responsibilities gave city governments more power. Competition among groups for control of city government grew more intense. Some groups represented those members of the middle and upper classes who still lived in the cities. Other groups represented new immigrants, migrants from the countryside, and workers—people that now made up the majority of the population in most cities.

The Rise of Political Bosses The **political machine** was born out of these clashing interests. A political machine was an unofficial city organization designed to keep a particular party or group in power and usually headed by a single powerful "boss." Sometimes the boss held public office. More often, he handpicked others to run for office and then helped them win.

Political machines worked through the exchange of favors. Machines used an army of ward leaders, each of whom managed a city district, to hand out city jobs and contracts to residents of their ward and do other favors for them. In return, those residents were expected to give their votes to the machine's

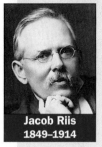

BIOGRAPHY

Jacob Riis
1849–1914

Some reformers worked to improve the lives of the urban poor. One was Jacob Riis. A native of Denmark, Riis had boarded a steamship bound for America in 1870 at the age of 21 and settled in New York City. There he personally experienced the dreadful conditions in which many new Americans lived.

Riis held various jobs before he landed a position as a police reporter in 1873. Riis honed his writing skills while covering New York's Lower East Side, a tenement slum bursting with immigrant families. He worked for the *New York Tribune* from 1877 to 1888 and the *New York Evening Sun* from 1888 to 1899. While working at the *Sun*, Riis wrote *How the Other Half Lives*.

READING CHECK
Why did urban growth change the role of city government?

candidates on election day. Similarly, individuals or companies wanting a favor from the city could get it by first paying some money to the machine. **Graft,** or the use of one's job to gain profit, was a major source of income for the machines.

Many people blamed the success of political machines on the large number of urban immigrants. They charged that corrupt politicians easily took advantage of immigrants who were poorly educated and unfamiliar with democracy. Immigrants tended to support political machines because they helped poor people at a time when neither government nor private industry would.

Cincinnati's George B. Cox, a former saloon owner, was an unusual example of a fairly honest political boss. A Republican, in 1879 he won election to the city council. In true machine fashion he used this post to guarantee election victories and business contracts for the party faithful. But he also worked with local reformers to improve the quality of the police force and city services.

Perhaps the most notorious boss was William Marcy Tweed. "Boss" Tweed controlled Tammany Hall, the political club that ran New York City's Democratic Party. Once Tweed and his pals gained access to the city treasury in 1870, they used various illegal methods to plunder it. Tweed and his friends padded bills for construction projects and supply contracts with fake expenses and kept the extra money for themselves. Through countless such instances of fraud and graft, the Tweed ring amassed many millions of dollars.

The brilliant political cartoons of German immigrant Thomas Nast helped bring Tweed down by exposing his methods to the public. Nast's cartoons depicted Tweed as a thief and a dictator who manipulated New York City politics for his own benefit. Convicted of crimes in 1873, Tweed eventually died in jail. Under new leaders, however, Tammany Hall dominated New York politics for another half century.

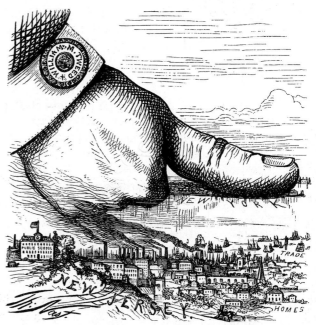

UNDER THE THUMB.

INTERPRETING POLITICAL CARTOONS This cartoon by Thomas Nast illustrates Boss Tweed's total control over New York City. **Recognizing Point of View** *Why did some people believe Boss Tweed's leadership helped New York City?*

Section 3 Assessment

READING COMPREHENSION

1. Describe the living conditions in a **tenement** apartment.

2. What were three technological developments that enabled cities to house more people?

3. What contributed to the rise of **political machines?**

4. Why did some people criticize **graft?**

CRITICAL THINKING AND WRITING

5. **Drawing Inferences** Who benefited most from Boss Tweed's control of New York City? What does this tell you about the effects of political machines?

6. **Writing an Outline** Create an outline of the challenges city dwellers faced in the 1880s and 1890s.

For: An activity on the Lower East Side tenements
Visit: PHSchool.com
Web Code: mrd-5153

Analyzing Tables and Statistics

Statistical tables present large amounts of numerical data concisely and clearly. The patterns suggested by statistics must be carefully analyzed, however, and their sources evaluated for reliability. Once you have analyzed the data, you can draw conclusions about historical periods or trends.

Estimated Number of Immigrants to the United States, by Region, 1871–1920

Years	Northwestern Europe	Central Europe	Eastern Europe	Southern Europe	Asia[1]	The Americas[2]	Africa	Oceania
1871–1875	858,325	549,610	15,580	37,070	65,727	193,345	205	6,312
1876–1880	493,866	254,511	24,052	39,248	58,096	210,690	153	4,602
1881–1885	1,121,477	1,128,528	63,443	120,297	60,432	403,977	331	4,406
1886–1890	1,131,844	729,967	157,749	211,399	7,948	22,990	526	8,168
1891–1895	745,433	762,216	251,405	314,625	19,255	14,734	163	2,215
1896–1900	392,907	432,363	270,421	389,608	51,981	24,238	187	1,750
1901–1905	761,517	1,121,234	711,546	1,061,406	115,941	63,774	1,829	6,134
1906–1910	807,020	1,365,530	1,058,024	1,260,424	127,626	298,114	5,539	6,890
1911–1915	652,189	1,027,138	978,931	1,137,539	123,719	528,098	5,847	6,126
1916–1920	201,304	23,276	33,547	322,640	68,840	615,573	2,596	7,301

[1] No record of immigration from Korea prior to 1948. [2] No record of immigration from Mexico for 1886 to 1893.
SOURCE: *Historical Statistics of the United States, Colonial Times to 1970*

LEARN THE SKILL

Use the following steps to analyze tables and statistics:

1. **Determine what type of information is presented and decide whether the source is reliable.** The title of the table and the labels for the rows and columns tell you what information is presented. The source is most often found below the table. Government publications are usually reliable sources.

2. **Read the information in the table.** Note how the statistics are organized. This table provides the total number of immigrants who came from each region for a given five-year period.

3. **Find relationships among the statistics.** In this case, you can compare the number of immigrants who came to the United States from different regions or trace changes in the pattern of immigration from one region over time.

4. **Use the data to draw conclusions.** You can also use what you know from other sources. Compare patterns in the two sets of data.

5. **Share your data and conclusions.** Present and support your conclusions in a report, or create graphs or charts that help explain your data.

PRACTICE THE SKILL

Answer the following questions:

1. **(a)** What is the title of the table? **(b)** What geographical areas are covered? **(c)** What is the source of the statistics? **(d)** Are the data reliable?

2. **(a)** Between 1871 and 1875, how many immigrants came to the United States from Asia? **(b)** Between 1881 and 1885, which region provided the largest number of immigrants? The smallest number of immigrants?

3. **(a)** Between 1871 and 1920, which region provided the largest total number of immigrants? **(b)** During which five-year period did the Americas show the sharpest drop in the number of immigrants?

4. Between 1891 and 1900, the unemployment rate in the United States averaged 10.5 percent. Between 1901 and 1910, it averaged 4.5 percent. What conclusions can you draw about the relationship between the unemployment rate and the immigration rate for these time periods?

5. **(a)** Write a paragraph summarizing the conclusions you reached in Question 4. Support your conclusions with data from the table. **(b)** Create a line graph showing the pattern of immigration from one region from 1871–1920.

APPLY THE SKILL

See the Chapter Review and Assessment for another opportunity to apply this skill.

Ideas for Reform

READING FOCUS

- How did different movements help the needy?

- How and where did sociology develop?

- What efforts were made to control immigration and personal behavior in the late 1800s?

MAIN IDEA

A variety of groups worked to improve social, economic, and political conditions in the cities.

KEY TERMS

social gospel movement
settlement house
sociology
nativism
temperance movement
prohibition
vice

TARGET READING SKILL

Identify Main Ideas Copy the web diagram below. As you read, fill in each blank circle with important movements that focused on immigration, morality, or both.

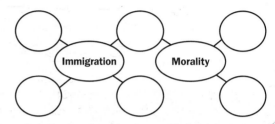

Setting the Scene   During the Gilded Age, saloons, places where men could meet to drink and gamble, could be found in nearly every city and town. Frances Willard paid her first visit to one at the age of 35. Unlike the customers, she arrived with a prayer group. Willard later wrote:

> 66 *The tall, stately lady who led us placed her Bible on the bar and read a psalm . . . and then one of the older women whispered to me softly that the leader wished to know if I would pray. It was strange, perhaps, but I felt not the least reluctance, and kneeling on the sawdust floor, with a group of earnest hearts around me, and behind them . . . a crowd of unwashed, unkempt, hard-looking drinking men, I was conscious that perhaps never in my life, save beside my sister Mary's dying bed, had I prayed as truly as I did then.* 99
>
> —Frances Willard

Temperance advocates pray outside a saloon.

Frances Willard described the experience as her "baptism" in the "Crusade." One week later she became president of the Chicago chapter of the Woman's Christian Temperance Union, an anti-alcohol group. Frances Willard was a reformer. Like many Americans of her time, she observed a problem in society and chose to confront it, motivated by her faith and her concern for the well-being of others. However, not everyone agreed with her wish to ban alcohol. Like many other crusaders, Frances Willard found that her personal goals could lead to conflict.

Helping the Needy

Many middle-class people were genuinely shocked by poor living and working conditions in the slums. Moved by social conscience or religious idealism, thousands of individuals joined groups to improve society by helping the needy. They argued that prosperous Americans should fight poverty and improve unwholesome social conditions in cities.

The Charity Organization Movement In 1882, Josephine Shaw Lowell founded the New York Charity Organization Society (COS). The COS tried to make charity a scientific enterprise. Members kept detailed files on those who received help. In this way, COS leaders could more easily determine how to serve their clients. Yet keeping detailed files also allowed COS leaders to distinguish between the poor whom they considered worthy of help and those whom they deemed unworthy. This attitude sometimes led to unkind treatment of the needy.

Many COS members wanted immigrants to adopt American, middle-class standards of child-raising, cooking, and cleaning. They did not care how strange these customs seemed to people with different cultural backgrounds. This disturbed some immigrants, but others were grateful for the assistance.

The Social Gospel Movement In the 1880s and 1890s, urban churches began to provide social services for the poor who now surrounded them. They also tried to aim some reform campaigns in new directions. Instead of blaming immigrants for drinking, gambling, and other behaviors, the churches sought to treat the problems that drove people into such activities.

Soon a social reform movement developed within religious institutions. It was called the **social gospel movement** and it sought to apply the gospel (teachings) of Jesus directly to society. The movement focused on the gospel ideals of charity and justice, especially by seeking labor reforms. In 1908, followers of such views formed the Federal Council of the Churches of Christ. This organization supported providing improved living conditions and a larger share in the national wealth for all workers. Other religious organizations, including some Jewish synagogues, adapted the social gospel ideal for themselves.

The Settlement Movement Thousands of young, educated women and men put the social gospel into practice in an innovative reform program called the settlement movement. These young reformers settled into a house in the midst of a poor neighborhood. From this **settlement house,** a kind of community center, they eventually offered social services.

The settlement movement had begun in Britain. Its founders believed that simply giving money to the poor never really helped them. In order to find out what would be most helpful, the young settlers had to live in poor neighborhoods. There they could witness the effects of poverty firsthand.

In 1889, inspired by the British settlement movement, Jane Addams and Ellen Gates Starr bought the run-down Charles Hull mansion in Chicago. They repaired it and opened its doors to their immigrant neighbors. At first, Starr and Addams simply wanted to get to know their neighbors, offering help when needed. Soon they began anticipating and responding to the needs of the community as a whole.

Over the decades that followed, Addams and Starr turned Hull House into a center of community activity. At Hull House, neighbors could attend cultural events, take classes, or display exhibits of crafts from their home countries. The

ENGLISH FOR COMING AMERICANS

Series A --- Fourth Lesson

PREPARING BREAKFAST

gets	The wife gets the kettle.
takes off	She takes off the lid.
is	The kettle is empty.
puts on	She puts on the lid.
fills	The wife fills the kettle with water
is placed	The kettle is placed on the fire.
burns	The fire burns brightly.
gets	The water gets hot in the kettle
boils	The water boils.
is taken	The kettle is taken off the stove
pours	The wife pours boiling water on the coffee.
puts	She puts the coffee pot on the stove.
pours	She pours boiling water into a saucepan.
cooks	She cooks the eggs in the pan.
are	The eggs are done.
takes	She takes the eggs out of the pan.
are placed	The eggs are placed on the table.
pours out	The wife pours out the coffee.

VIEWING HISTORY Some reformers focused their efforts on helping immigrants adjust to life in the United States. This immigrant is learning English. **Analyzing Information** *What else is she learning?*

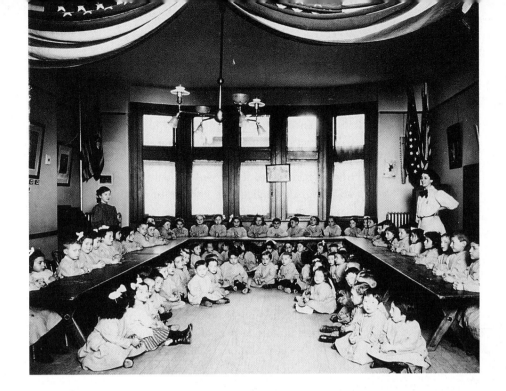

settlement set up child-care centers, playgrounds, clubs, and summer camps for boys and girls; offices to help people find jobs and deal with legal problems; and health-care clinics. It also launched investigations of city economic, political, and social conditions. These actions laid the foundation for many later reforms.

Settlement houses like Hull House sprang up across the country. The Henry Street Settlement, founded by Lillian Wald on New York's Lower East Side, was originally a nurses' settlement to offer home health care to the poor. Its programs soon expanded to resemble many of those at Hull House. Missionaries, too, founded settlement houses, in part to gain converts but also to apply the social gospel in practical ways.

By 1910 there were more than 400 settlement houses. Most were supported by donations and staffed by volunteers or people willing to work for low wages and free room and board. Hundreds of college graduates, especially women excluded from other professions, became settlement workers. Except for leaders, such as Addams and Wald, most workers spent only a few years in these jobs. Many moved on to professional careers in social work, education, or government.

Few ever forgot their settlement experience. "I don't know that my attitude changed," wrote one former settlement worker, "but my point of view certainly did, or perhaps it would be more true to say that now I have several points of view." By helping its workers see social issues in new ways, the settlement houses energized the reform movement while improving the lives of the urban poor.

The Development of Sociology

While settlement workers observed first-hand the problems of the slums, scholars in America and Europe were developing a scientific way of looking at how people lived. Philosopher Auguste Comte coined the term **sociology** to describe the study of how people interact with one another in a society. Sociology is a social science. Like a biologist studying animals, a sociologist collects data on societies, and measures the data against theories of human behavior.

READING CHECK
What were the effects of the settlement movement?

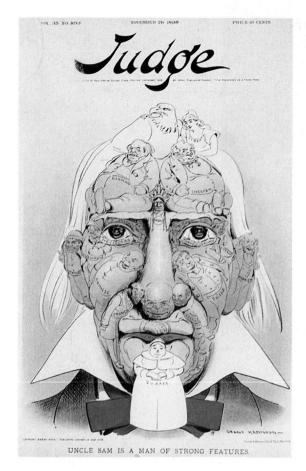

UNCLE SAM IS A MAN OF STRONG FEATURES.

Judge

INTERPRETING POLITICAL CARTOONS The caption on this magazine cover reads, "Uncle Sam is a man of strong features." **Recognizing Point of View** *What does this cartoon suggest about the artist's view of immigration?*

Sociology provided a scientific counterpart to the settlement houses' practical experience.

Sociologists studied cultures around the world to learn what institutions and practices define a society. The institutions in an American community might include houses of worship, local governments, schools, libraries, and museums. Practices might include the way that children relate to their parents or a community teaches students. In the late nineteenth century, many sociologists studied the effects of industrialization and urbanization on established communities. America's rapidly changing population provided them with many examples.

Controlling Immigration and Behavior

Many Americans linked the problems of the cities to the new immigrants. By controlling immigrants, they hoped to restore what they believed had been a past of purity and virtue. Groups were formed to pursue this goal. Some sought to keep immigrants out of the United States, while others wanted to change their behavior.

Nativism   In the 1850s, the Know-Nothing Party had gained many followers by vowing to restrict immigration. Thirty years later this policy of **nativism,** or favoring native-born Americans over immigrants, reappeared. The rise of immigrants to positions of power in the cities helped provoke this new wave of antiforeign bias. Passage of the Chinese Exclusion Act in 1882 showed how politically effective the new nativists were.

Nativists did not oppose only Asian immigration. The American Protective Association, a nativist group founded in 1887, targeted immigrants in general as well as the Catholic Church. It called for the teaching of only American culture and the English language in schools and demanded tighter rules on citizenship and employment of aliens. Members of this secret society took an oath to hire and vote for Protestants alone.

Nativists won a victory in 1885, when Congress repealed the Contract Labor Act. Passed in 1864, the law had allowed employers to recruit foreign laborers. Even after the law's repeal, however, employers often illegally brought in foreign workers to replace striking employees. Such actions only heightened nativist feelings among workers.

There were nativists among the wealthy as well. The Immigration Restriction League was organized in 1894 by some Harvard College graduates. The League hoped to exclude immigrants considered unfit by requiring them to pass literacy tests. Its main targets were immigrants from southern and eastern Europe, whose cultures differed greatly from those of League members.

Prohibition   Like nativism, another movement begun before the Civil War saw a revival later in the 1800s: the **temperance movement,** an organized campaign to eliminate alcohol consumption. Three groups dominated the new temperance movement: the Prohibition party, founded in 1869, the Woman's Christian Temperance Union, founded in 1874, and the Anti-Saloon League, founded in 1893. These groups opposed drinking on the grounds that it led to personal tragedies. They supported **prohibition,** a ban on the manufacture and sale of alcoholic beverages. One activist, Carry Nation, won fame by smashing illegal saloons with a hatchet in her home state of Kansas.

READING CHECK

Why did nativists oppose immigration?

Prohibition groups also opposed drinking because of what they saw as the links among saloons, immigrants, and political bosses. Immigrant men often used saloons as social clubs, where they could relax and also find information about jobs. Prohibitionists believed that saloons undermined public morals. Some prohibitionists even claimed that saloons formed the center of a movement to take over the United States. "Foreign control or conquest is rapidly making us un-Christian, with immorality throned in power," one prohibitionist wrote in 1908.

At first, progress was slow. Early prohibitionists measured their success by towns and counties that agreed to ban alcohol. By 1890, only three states had gone completely "dry" and embraced prohibition: Maine, Kansas, and North Dakota.

Purity Crusaders   As cities grew, drugs, gambling, prostitution, and other forms of vice became big business. **Vice** (immoral or corrupt behavior) was not unique to the cities. But large urban populations made vice highly visible and very profitable. Then as now, many residents fought to rid their communities of unwholesome and illegal activities.

"Purity crusaders" led the way. In 1873, Anthony Comstock founded the New York Society for the Suppression of Vice. The following year he won passage of a law that prohibited sending obscene materials through the United States mail. Material deemed obscene included descriptions of methods to prevent unwanted pregnancy. For decades the Comstock Law, as it came to be known, slowed the distribution of information about birth control.

Other purity crusaders attacked urban political machines, saying that machine-controlled police forces profited from vice. Police were known to demand payment from gamblers in return for ignoring illegal activities. On occasion, purity crusaders joined forces with other reformers to run for public office. By campaigning on an anti-vice platform, some succeeded in throwing machine candidates out of office. Usually the political machines regained power in later elections by mocking the self-righteous tone of many purists and by arguing that morality was a personal issue.

Focus on DAILY LIFE

Mrs. Winslow's Soothing Syrup
The WCTU found a target in the heavily advertised patent medicines that parents bought to cure illness and quiet crying babies. Mrs. Winslow's Soothing Syrup sold very well; it put children to sleep with a mix of alcohol and morphine, a narcotic made from opium. Other childhood remedies based on morphine included Dr. Fahrney's Teething Syrup, Dr. Seth Arnold's Cough Killer, and Carney Common Sense Cure. Although popular, these so-called medicines were addictive and harmful to children's health. The federal government outlawed Mrs. Winslow's Soothing Syrup in 1906.

Section 4 Assessment

READING COMPREHENSION

1. What was the purpose of the New York Charity Organization Society?

2. What is the purpose of **sociology?**

3. What was the goal of **nativist** movements?

4. How did **temperance** groups and purity crusaders differ from charity, **social gospel,** and **settlement** movements?

CRITICAL THINKING AND WRITING

5. **Identifying Assumptions** How might the anti-immigrant arguments of wealthy nativists have differed from those of less-affluent nativists?

6. **Drawing Inferences** What were two possible reasons for people to oppose purity crusaders?

7. **Journal Writing** Write three brief fictional journal entries from the point of view of a settlement house worker.

For: An activity on Hull House
Visit: PHSchool.com
Web Code: mrd-5154

creating a CHAPTER SUMMARY

Copy this chart (right) on a piece of paper and complete it by adding important events and issues that fit each heading. Some entries have been completed for you as examples.

For additional review and enrichment activities, see the interactive version of *America: Pathways to the Present*, available on the Web and on CD-ROM.

Politics, Immigration, and Urban Life in the Gilded Age	
Immigration and Nativism	• More immigrants arrive from eastern and southern Europe. • Mexican immigrants settle in the Southwest. • Asian immigrants face challenges in the West. •
Presidential Politics	
Urban Growth	
Political Machines	
Social Reform	

★ Reviewing Key Terms

For each of the terms below, write a sentence explaining how it relates to the Gilded Age.

1. Gilded Age
2. *laissez-faire*
3. blue law
4. civil service
5. steerage
6. ghetto
7. Chinese Exclusion Act
8. suburb
9. tenement
10. political machine
11. graft
12. settlement house
13. nativism
14. prohibition

★ Reviewing Main Ideas

15. How did business influence politicians during the Gilded Age? (Section 1)

16. What problems did the spoils system create? (Section 1)

17. Why did so many people want to come to the United States between 1870 and 1915? (Section 2)

18. Starting in the 1890s, where did large numbers of immigrants come from? (Section 2)

19. How did slums develop in cities? (Section 3)

20. What were the advantages and disadvantages of political machines for urban residents? (Section 3)

21. How did the settlement movement seek to help the needy? (Section 4)

22. What actions did nativists take to restrict immigration? (Section 4)

★ Critical Thinking

23. **Drawing Inferences** What character trait did President Rutherford B. Hayes exhibit by his actions regarding the spoils system? Explain.

24. **Drawing Conclusions** What conclusion(s) can you draw from the fact that Tammany Hall dominated New York City for more than 50 years?

25. **Predicting Consequences** What might have been the effect if the United States had adopted all the ideas of the nativists?

26. **Making Comparisons** How and why did the experiences of Chinese immigrants differ from the experiences of immigrants from Italy and Russia?

27. **Recognizing Bias** Read the following quote about a charity reformer's visit to an immigrant home: "[they] upset the usual routine of their lives, opening windows, undressing children, giving orders not to eat this and that, not to wrap babies in swaddling clothes." (a) What does this quote reveal about the author's opinions? (b) How might a charity reformer describe the visit?

★ Standardized Test Prep

Analyzing Political Cartoons ▶

28. This scene shows a strength contest once popular at fairs. The goal was to test one's strength in an attempt to ring the bell at the top of the column. The contestants are hammering consumers using a tariff and the bell represents profits. Who are the contestants?

   A Foreigners
   B Congressmen
   C Trust-busters
   D Wealthy trust owners

29. Read the caption. Describe the cartoonist's message in a brief paragraph.

Interpreting Data

Turn to the graph titled "European Immigration, 1870–1920" in Section 2.

30. In which of the following years did immigrants from central Europe outnumber immigrants from every other region?

   A 1870
   B 1880 and 1890
   C 1900 and 1910
   D 1920

31. Which sentence BEST describes immigration from eastern Europe from 1870 to 1920?

   F Immigration increased steadily and then fell to near zero.
   G The number of immigrants declined steadily.
   H The number of immigrants increased steadily every decade.
   I The number of immigrants stayed constant.

TRY YOUR STRENGTH, GENTS!
THE HARDER YOU HIT IT, THE HIGHER IT GOES.

Test-Taking Tip

To answer Question 31, determine which bars on the graph represent Eastern European immigrants. Then note the trend for this group across the time period shown. Select the answer that best describes the trend.

Applying the Chapter Skill

Analyzing Tables and Skills Look back at the table on the Skills for Life page. World War I was fought from 1914 to 1918. How does the table reflect the influence of the war on immigration to the United States?

For: Chapter 8 Self-Test
Visit: PHSchool.com
Web Code: mra-5155

Life at the Turn of the Twentieth Century

(1870–1915)

The justices of the Supreme Court

American Events

1890

Local women's clubs join together to form influential national organizations, such as the General Federation of Women's Clubs.

1895

In his speech at the Atlanta Exposition, Booker T. Washington urges blacks to postpone demands for equality while educating themselves for productive work.

1896

In *Plessy* v. *Ferguson*, the Supreme Court upholds segregation and the concept of "separate but equal."

Presidential Terms: B. Harrison 1889–1893   G. Cleveland 1893–1897   W. McKinley 1897–1901

1890   **1895**   **1900**

World Events

New Zealand grants women the right to vote.

1893

The first motion picture, made by the Lumière brothers, opens in Paris.

1895

The first "foolproof" vacuum cleaner is invented in England.

1901

READING FOCUS

- What new kinds of performances and recreation did Americans enjoy at the turn of the century?
- What were people reading for information and entertainment?
- How was American music changing?

MAIN IDEA

Americans flocked to new forms of entertainment, sports, and music during the period from the late 1880s to 1915.

KEY TERMS

vaudeville
yellow journalism
ragtime

TARGET READING SKILL

Identify Supporting Details Copy the chart below. As you read, add types of entertainment to the first column, and details to the other two columns.

Type of Entertainment	How It Developed	Why People Enjoyed It
• Vaudeville	• Grew out of minstrel shows	• Inexpensive
•	•	• Lots of variety
•	•	•

Setting the Scene You can probably hum the following song, even though it was written in 1908. It has been baseball's "anthem" since that time, and is still sung at the seventh-inning stretch in ballparks today. But "Take Me Out to the Ballgame" also captures the spirit of the turn of the twentieth century in America.

> 66 *Take me out to the ball game*
> *Take me out with the crowd*
> *Buy me some peanuts and Cracker Jack*
> *I don't care if I never get back . . .* 99
> —Jack Norworth

Many of the changes occurring in America at that time are reflected in this verse: more leisure time for working people, more money to spend on entertainment, the craze for sports, the introduction of snack foods, and a spirit of fun. The United States was becoming a more urban nation, and city dwellers began looking for entertainment in their own neighborhoods, as well as for recreation away from the dirty, crowded streets where they lived and worked. These factors would fuel a whole new commercial recreation industry designed to supply inexpensive entertainment for all Americans.

Performances and Recreation

Many kinds of performances attracted audiences at this time. They ranged from live theater to a new medium: the moving picture show, or the "movies."

Vaudeville and Minstrel Shows The most popular kind of live theatrical performance was **vaudeville,** a type of inexpensive variety show that first appeared in the 1870s. Vaudeville performances consisted of comic sketches based on ethnic or racial humor; song-and-dance routines; magic acts; and performances by ventriloquists, jugglers, and animals. In 1899, the actor Edwin Milton Royle wrote, "The vaudeville theatre is an American invention. There is nothing like it anywhere else in the world." Although early vaudeville was geared to male spectators, the shows soon sought a wider audience and presented themselves as family entertainment.

PRICE 10+ CENTS.

REACH'S

1898

OFFICIAL

BASE BALL

GUIDE

PUBLISHED BY
A.J. REACH CO.
PHILADELPHIA, PA.

By 1898, baseball had become the American pastime. From 1891 to 1899, there was one professional league, with teams from Boston to St. Louis. The ball and glove shown above commemorate an 1899 college game.

One of the sources of vaudeville was the minstrel show. A popular form of entertainment from the 1840s, minstrel shows began to die out as vaudeville gained popularity. Minstrel shows featured white actors in "blackface" (exaggerated make-up caricaturing African Americans). The shows perpetuated racial stereotypes with exaggerated imitations of African American music, dance, and humor. Nevertheless, black performers—also wearing blackface—sometimes performed in minstrel shows, as these were often the only stage jobs they could get. Once they were able to, many African American performers switched to vaudeville.

Movies   As the twentieth century began, vaudeville started getting competition from the movies. *The Great Train Robbery*, released in 1903, was a huge success and clearly demonstrated that profits could be made from movies. By 1908, the nation had 8,000 nickelodeons—theaters set up in converted stores or warehouses that charged a nickel admission. They showed short slapstick comedies and other films to as many as 200,000 people a day.

Improving technology and the increasing popularity of films led to longer, better movies and to bigger, more elaborate movie houses. Full-length dramas featured new stars such as Mary Pickford and Douglas Fairbanks. Charlie Chaplin began appearing in comedies. Early movies were silent and often accompanied by a live piano player. Soon audiences flocked to new movie palaces with names like The Empress and The Riviera, which often had full orchestras to accompany their films.

The Circus   While circuses have a long history, it was the introduction of the circus train in 1872 that made the annual visit of the circus an anticipated event all over America. First, "advance men" arrived in a town to promote the performances. They often recruited young boys to hand out printed advertisements. Several days later, the circus train pulled in, and the big top went up. This was a show in itself, and hundreds of people often gathered to watch. Then the circus parade kicked off, and all the circus acts and performers marched through town to great fanfare. After the parade and advertising created great anticipation, the paid performances were held. At the turn of the century, there was hardly a town or a city in America where a youngster did not dream of running away to join the circus.

Amusement Parks   The technology of the trolley—and the trolley lines themselves—led to the development of amusement parks. A similar technology helped to create their main attractions: mechanical rides like the steeplechase, the Ferris wheel, and the roller coaster.

As trolley lines were extended from the central cities out to less populated areas, "trolley parks" began to spring up at the end of the lines. Although many people still worked ten hours a day, a half-holiday on Saturday was becoming more common. Transportation companies encouraged ridership on weekends, and the inexpensive excursion from the city to an amusement park was just what the public wanted. These parks often featured music, games of skill, vaudeville productions, bathing beaches, and exciting rides. The business of the amusement park, according to the manager of Coney Island's Luna Park, was "the business of amusing the million."

Focus on TECHNOLOGY

Snapshots Although professional photographers had been taking portraits for decades, it was not until the 1880s that ordinary people could become their own family photographers—and the snapshot was born. In 1888, George Eastman marketed a handheld camera that he had developed. The Kodak was so easy to use that its motto was, "You press the button—We do the rest." "The rest" included developing the film when the camera was sent to the company, and then returning the camera reloaded and ready to take more pictures. However, at $25 the Kodak was expensive. In 1900, Eastman came out with a new and even simpler camera called the Brownie (below right). It was marketed to children and cost only one dollar. Families all over America began snapping pictures of each other, and the family snapshot album became a staple of American culture.

A GOVERNMENT OF THE PEOPLE BY THE PEOPLE FOR THE PEOPLE

ARE NOT THE WOMEN HALF THE NATION?

★ Standardized Test Prep

Analyzing Political Cartoons ▶

24. In this cartoon, the kneeling woman represents American women who lack the right to vote. How can you tell the cartoonist favors women's suffrage?

   A The cartoonist portrays "Justice" as supporting the kneeling woman.

   B The cartoonist portrays the kneeling woman with shackles.

   C The cartoonist portrays the government as Uncle Sam.

   D The cartoonist includes a quote from the Gettysburg Address at the top of the cartoon

25. Read the words at the bottom of the cartoon. What is the message of the cartoon?

Interpreting Data

Turn to the graph on illiteracy in the United States in Section 1.

26. In which year were illiteracy rates the highest?

   A 1870

   B 1880

   C 1890

   D 1920

27. Which of the following statements BEST summarizes the information in the graph?

   F Few people were able to read and write in the late 1800s.

   G About 10 percent of the United States population was illiterate in 1900.

   H During the period from 1870 to 1920, illiteracy rates dropped in the United States.

   I Literacy was an important requirement for citizenship in the United States.

Test-Taking Tip

Question 27 asks you to choose the statement which BEST summarizes the information in the graph. More than one of the possible answers may seem correct. Be sure to choose the one that summarizes all of the information in the graph—not just one piece of data from the graph.

Applying the Chapter Skill

Analyzing Political Cartoons for Point of View

Look back at the cartoon on page 333. Use the steps presented on the Skills for Life page in this chapter to analyze the cartoon. (a) What subject was the cartoonist commenting on? (b) Do you think his point of view is the same as that of the two men in the cartoon? Explain. (c) What is the point of view of the cartoonist? What action might he advocate?

Go Online
PHSchool.com

For: Chapter 9 Self-Test
Visit: PHSchool.com
Web Code: mra-5165

Living Under Jim Crow

The editors of *American Heritage* magazine have selected this account, published in 1902 and written by an unnamed African American woman living in the South. In it she described the world of Jim Crow—the daily frustrations and humiliations that African Americans had to endure as they struggled to build successful lives.

I AM A COLORED WOMAN, wife and mother. I have lived all my life in the South, and have often thought what a peculiar fact it is that the more ignorant the Southern whites are of us the more vehement they are in their denunciation of us. They boast that they have little intercourse with us, never see us in our homes, churches or places of amusement, but still they know us thoroughly.

They also admit that they know us in no capacity except as servants, yet they say we are at our best in that single capacity. What philosophers they are! The Southerners say we Negroes are a happy, laughing set of people, with no thought of tomorrow. How mistaken they are! The educated, thinking Negro is just the opposite. There is a feeling of unrest, insecurity, almost panic among the best class of Negroes in the South. In

Even well-educated African Americans were often restricted to low-paying jobs.

our homes, in our churches, wherever two or three are gathered together, there is a discussion of what is best to do. Must we remain in the South or go elsewhere? Where can we go to feel that security which other people feel? Is it best to go in great numbers or only in several families? These and many other things are discussed over and over. . . .

I know of houses occupied by poor Negroes in which a respectable farmer would not keep his cattle. It is impossible for them to rent elsewhere. All Southern real estate agents have "white property" and "colored property." In one of the largest Southern cities there is a colored minister, a graduate of Harvard, whose wife is an educated, Christian woman, who lived for weeks in a tumble-down rookery because he could neither rent nor buy in a respectable locality.

Many colored women who wash, iron, scrub, cook or sew all the week to help pay the rent for these miserable hovels and help fill the many small mouths, would deny themselves some of the necessaries of life if they could take their little children and teething babies on the cars to the parks of a Sunday afternoon and sit under trees, enjoy the cool breezes and breathe God's pure air for only two or three hours; but this is denied them. Some of the parks have signs, "No Negroes allowed on these grounds except as servants." Pitiful, pitiful customs and laws that make war on women and babes! There is no wonder that we die; the wonder is that we persist in living.

A NEIGHBORHOOD OF POOR PEOPLE

Fourteen years ago I had just married. My husband had saved sufficient money to buy a small home. On account of our limited means we went to the suburbs, on unpaved streets, to look for a home, only asking for a high, healthy locality. Some real estate agents were "sorry, but had nothing to suit," some had "just the thing," but we discovered on investigation that they had "just the thing" for an unhealthy pigsty. Others had no "colored property." One agent said that he had what we wanted, but we should have to go to see the lot after dark, or walk by and give the place a casual look; for, he said, "all the white people in the neighborhood would be down on me." Finally, we bought this lot. When the house was being built we went to see it. Consternation reigned. We had ruined his neighborhood of poor people; poor as we, poorer in manners at least. The people who lived next door received the sympathy of their friends. When we walked on the street (there were no sidewalks) we were embarrassed by the stare of many unfriendly eyes.

Two years passed before a single woman spoke to me, and only then because I helped one of them when a little sudden trouble came to her. Such was the reception, I a happy young woman, just married, received from people among whom I wanted to make a home. Fourteen years have now passed, four children have been born to us, and one has died in this same home, among these same neighbors. Although the neighbors speak to us . . . , not one woman has ever been inside of my house, not even at the times when a woman would doubly appreciate the slightest attention of a neighbor. . . .

White agents and other chance visitors who come into our homes ask questions that we must not dare ask their wives. They express surprise that our children have clean faces and that their hair is combed. . . .

We were delighted to know that some of our Spanish-American heroes were coming where

Jim Crow laws continued into the second half of the twentieth century, as this woman discovered in a Dallas, Texas, bus station in 1961.

we could get a glimpse of them. Had not black men helped in a small way to give them their honors? In the cities of the South, where these heroes went, the white school children were assembled, flags waved, flowers strewn, speeches made, and "My Country, 'tis of Thee, Sweet Land of Liberty," was sung. Our children who need to be taught so much, were not assembled, their hands waved no flags, they threw no flowers, heard no thrilling speech, sang no song of their country. And this is the South's idea of justice. Is it surprising that feeling grows more bitter, when the white mother teaches her boy to hate my boy, not because he is mean, but because his skin is dark? I have seen very small white children hang their black dolls. It is not the child's fault, he is simply an apt pupil. . . .

Source: Anonymous, *Independent* magazine, 1902.

Understanding Primary Sources

1. At what time of day did this woman and her husband have to go to look at the lot of land they were thinking of buying for their new house?

2. When she refers to her neighbors as "poor people," what does she mean?

American Heritage®
MY BRUSH WITH **HISTORY**™
 Videotapes

For more information about segregation and Jim Crow laws, view "Living Under Jim Crow."

TEST PREPARATION

Write your answers on a separate sheet of paper.

1. Which one of the following was a purpose of the Union naval blockade of the South during the Civil War?

    A To encourage Southerners to move to the North

    B To stop travel to the Confederate capital city

    C To prevent cotton from being sold in Europe

    D To limit the food exports of the South

2. The purpose of the Gettysburg Address was to

    A rally tired Confederate soldiers.

    B remind the nation about the reasons for fighting the Civil War.

    C help Union generals locate a house full of stored weapons.

    D outline Lincoln's reelection platform.

3. After the Civil War, the Radical Republicans believed

    A in completely restructuring society to guarantee equality to blacks.

    B that the North should rebuild the South.

    C that Southern military leaders could serve in the Congress.

    D that violence was the best way to settle social problems in the South.

4. Which one of the following groups provided food, clothing, and education to blacks in the South after the Civil War?

    A Progressives

    B Radical Republicans

    C Tweed Machine

    D Freedmen's Bureau

5. The sharecropping system in the South resulted in

    A higher wages in Southern industries.

    B annual debts for many farm families.

    C the government's giving each black family 40 acres of land.

    D the end of large-scale cotton production.

6. Which one of the following nineteenth-century business leaders is correctly paired with his area of industry?

    A John D. Rockefeller and oil

    B Andrew Carnegie and railroads

    C Edwin Drake and steel

    D Thomas A. Edison and the telephone

7. The Sherman Antitrust Act initially was unsuccessful because

    A it was not passed into law by Congress.

    B it was enforced infrequently by the courts.

    C President Harrison refused to support it.

    D Rockefeller turned his employees against it.

Use the chart and your knowledge of social studies to answer the following question.

Which Early Labor Union?
• Represented skilled workers • Consisted of a network of smaller "craft" unions • Focused on wages, hours, and working conditions • Excluded women and African Americans • Used strikes, boycotts, and collective bargaining • Wanted "closed shops"

8. The chart describes which one of the following early labor unions?

   A National Labor Union

   B Knights of Labor

   C American Federation of Labor

   D Industrial Workers of the World

9. What was the long-term result of the Pullman Strike of 1894?

   A The federal government sided with business against labor unions.

   B The Knights of Labor membership grew after they won the strike.

   C Nonviolent methods helped the unions win the strike.

   D Unskilled workers formed their own labor unions.

10. The Pendleton Civil Service Act

    A limited government assistance to businesses.

    B provided special jobs for Civil War veterans.

    C opened up government jobs to African Americans.

    D helped to end the spoils system.

Use the chart and your knowledge of social studies to answer the following question.

Immigration From Italy	
Year	**Number of Immigrants**
1900	100,135
1901	135,996
1902	178,375
1903	230,622
1904	193,296
1905	221,479

SOURCE: *Historical Statistics of the United States, Colonial Times to 1970*

11. Which one of the following factors contributed to the rise in U.S. immigration from Italy around the turn of the century?

    A Pogroms

    B Steerage and quarantines

    C High taxes and crop failures

    D Revolution and civil war

12. Jane Addams operated Hull House as a center to

    A assist the urban poor.

    B fight immigration from Asia.

    C aid men who fought in the Civil War.

    D support Populist Party candidates.

Writing Practice

13. Describe how the Compromise of 1877 brought an end to Reconstruction.

14. Explain the methods businesses used to limit the power of unions.

15. What actions did the federal government take to encourage people to move to the West following the Civil War?

The United States on the Brink of Change (1890–1920)

> **"Whether they will or no, Americans must begin to look outward."**
>
> Alfred T. Mahan
> *The Interest of America in Sea Power, 1897*

This 1898 painting by Fred Pansing shows part of the U.S. fleet entering New York harbor following the Spanish-American War. ▶

Becoming a World Power
(1890–1915)

$50,000 REWARD.—WHO DESTROYED THE MAINE?—$50,000 REWARD.

EDITION FOR GREATER NEW YORK.

NEW YORK JOURNAL
AND ADVERTISER.

DESTRUCTION OF THE WAR SHIP MAINE WAS THE WORK OF AN ENEMY

1890

Alfred T. Mahan's
The Influence of Sea Power Upon History, 1660– 1783 urges the United States to build a powerful navy to protect markets abroad.

American Events

1893

American business groups, with the help of United States Marines, overthrow Hawaii's Queen Liliuokalani and set up a provisional government.

1898

The U.S.S. *Maine* explodes off the coast of Havana, Cuba, killing more than 250 American sailors. An outraged American public convinces Congress to declare war on Spain.

Presidential Terms: Grover Cleveland 1893–1897   William McKinley 1897–1901

1890   1894   1898

World Events

Cuba rebels against Spanish rule.

1895

The Boxer Rebellion erupts in China.

1900

World Imperialism, *circa* 1900

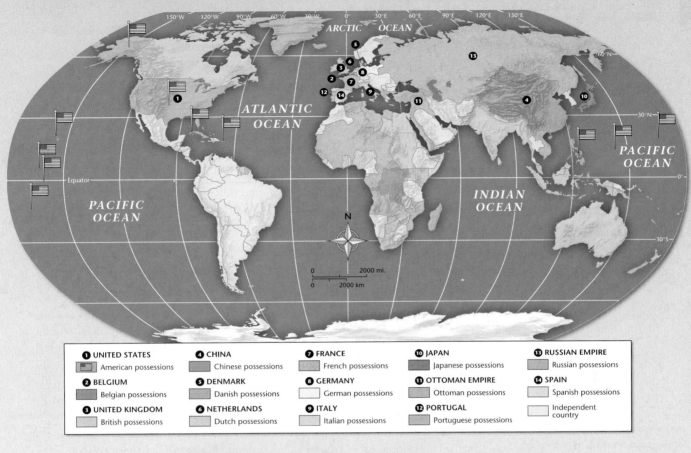

❶ UNITED STATES
American possessions

❷ BELGIUM
Belgian possessions

❸ UNITED KINGDOM
British possessions

❹ CHINA
Chinese possessions

❺ DENMARK
Danish possessions

❻ NETHERLANDS
Dutch possessions

❼ FRANCE
French possessions

❽ GERMANY
German possessions

❾ ITALY
Italian possessions

❿ JAPAN
Japanese possessions

⓫ OTTOMAN EMPIRE
Ottoman possessions

⓬ PORTUGAL
Portuguese possessions

⓭ RUSSIAN EMPIRE
Russian possessions

⓮ SPAIN
Spanish possessions

Independent country

1903
Panama gives the United States control over the Panama Canal Zone for $10 million.

1904
President Roosevelt issues the Roosevelt Corollary to the Monroe Doctrine.

1907
The Great White Fleet tours the world as a display of the impressive naval power of the United States.

1914
President Wilson sends troops to Mexico to assist Mexican revolutionaries.

Theodore Roosevelt 1901–1909

William Howard Taft 1909–1913

Woodrow Wilson 1913–1921

1902   **1906**   **1910**   **1914**

1905
Japan defeats Russia in the Russo-Japanese War.

1908
Austria annexes Bosnia and Herzegovina.

1912
The First Balkan War begins.

1914
World War I begins.

The Pressure to Expand

READING FOCUS

- What factors led to the growth of imperialism around the world?

- In what ways did the United States begin to expand its interests abroad in the late 1800s?

- What arguments were made in favor of United States expansion in the 1890s?

MAIN IDEA

In the late 1800s, as European nations took over vast areas in Africa and Asia, American leaders looked to extend American influence abroad.

KEY TERMS

imperialism
nationalism
annex
banana republic

TARGET READING SKILL

Recognize Multiple Causes As you read, complete the diagram below to show some of the causes that led the United States to adopt a policy of political and economic expansion overseas.

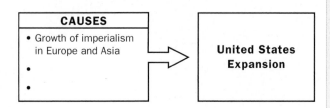

Setting the Scene By the dawn of the twentieth century, industrialization had forever changed the national landscape and the daily lives of all Americans. The rise of cities, the beginnings of mass culture, westward expansion, and new coast-to-coast networks of travel and communications all strengthened the country's national identity. Americans wondered what these changes meant for the future of the country.

The development of the United States into an industrial powerhouse not only revolutionized the lives of all Americans, it also forced them to strengthen their ties to other nations more than ever before. Many Americans began to believe that the country had to protect its economic, political, and social interests internationally. A surge in European conquests for new lands and resources reinforced this new way of thinking about America's role in the world. Some Americans, such as Senator Henry Cabot Lodge, believed that the time was right for the United States to expand its interests abroad.

VIEWING HISTORY This 1902 photograph shows a man in a car overlooking the Grand Canyon. **Determining Relevance** *What does this photograph suggest about the new pressures facing the United States?*

> ❝ *Small States are of the past and have no future. The modern movement is all toward the concentration of people and territory into great nations and large dominions. The great nations are rapidly absorbing for their future expansion and their present defence all the waste places of the earth. . . . As one of the great nations of the world, the United States must not fall out of the line of march.* ❞
> —Senator Henry Cabot Lodge, speech to Congress, 1895

Growth of Imperialism

As the map on the previous page shows, Europe had reached new heights in its quest for territories to rule. The late 1800s marked the peak of European **imperialism,** with much of Africa and Asia under foreign domination. Under imperialism, stronger nations attempt to create empires by dominating weaker nations—economically, politically, culturally, or militarily.

Why Imperialism Grew   Several factors accounted for the burst of imperialistic activity in the late 1800s.

Economic factors The growth of industry in Europe created an increased need for natural resources, such as rubber and petroleum, which came from undeveloped areas of the world. Manufacturing nations also required new markets in which to sell their manufactured goods.

Nationalistic factors Competition among European nations for large empires was the result of a rise in **nationalism,** or devotion to one's nation. Nationalism usually suggests that a nation's people believe themselves, their ideals, and their goals to be superior to those of other nations. In the late 1800s, nationalist feelings grew stronger in many countries, causing several European nations to take strong actions to protect their interests. For example, when France acquired colonies in West Africa in the late 1800s, rival nations Great Britain and Germany seized lands nearby to stop French expansion.

Military factors Advances in military technology produced European armies and navies that were far superior to those in Africa and Asia. Also, Europe's growing navies required bases around the world for taking on fuel and supplies.

Humanitarian factors Humanitarian and religious goals spurred on imperialists. Colonial officials, doctors, and missionaries believed they had a duty to spread the blessings of Western civilization, including its law, medicine, and Christian religion.

Europe Leads the Way   Improved transportation and communication made it easier for Great Britain, France, and Russia, all with long imperialist traditions, to extend their grip over far-flung lands. Great Britain, in particular, acquired so much new territory around the globe that people began to say "the sun never sets on the British Empire." Competition for new territory grew even more intense when Germany, unified in 1871, seized colonies in Africa and Asia.

By 1890, the United States was eager to join the competition for new territories. Supporters of expansion denied that the United States sought to **annex** foreign lands. (To annex is to join a new territory to an existing country.) Yet annexation did take place.

Expanding U.S. Interests

In his Farewell Address in 1796, President George Washington had advised Americans to "steer clear of permanent alliances" with other countries. For the next century, Americans generally followed Washington's advice. The nation's rapid economic growth along with the settlement of the West left the United States with little interest in foreign affairs.

As early as the 1820s, the Monroe Doctrine had been the main principle of foreign policy in the United States. Taking Washington's advice, under this doctrine, the United States had declared itself neutral in European wars and

Focus on WORLD EVENTS

The Sino-Japanese War After the Meiji Restoration in 1868, Japan entered a period of reform and modernization in which it grew to be an imperial power. (See the map, below left.) The Japanese began using Western military techniques, developed an advanced industrial economy, and even Westernized their political system. As Japan expanded economically, socially, and militarily, it experienced a rise in nationalism. In August 1894, conflict between China and Japan over Korea erupted into the Sino-Japanese War.

Japan's more modern military easily defeated China's massive forces. As a result, China ceded Taiwan and other lands to Japan, signaling the status of Japan as a major world power.

warned other nations not to interfere in the Western Hemisphere. There were instances, however, when Americans "looked outward." Over time the Monroe Doctrine would be broadened to support American imperialism.

From the 1830s to 1850s, belief in the idea of Manifest Destiny helped the United States to justify its policies toward Mexico. The annexation of Texas and the acquisition of California and other southwestern lands were early steps toward claiming an American empire.

After the Civil War, American secretaries of state continued to apply the principles of the Monroe Doctrine. Secretary of State William H. Seward advised the president to send 50,000 troops to the Mexican border after France placed an emperor on the Mexican throne. Faced with this army, the French abandoned their colonial venture into Mexico. Then, in 1867, Seward bought Alaska from Russia. In addition to gaining more territory, Seward hoped that the presence of the United States on two sides of Canada would force the British out of that region. Most Americans ridiculed the undertaking. Seward, they said, was buying "walrus-covered icebergs" in a "barren, worthless, God-forsaken region." Seward, however, waged a successful campaign to educate the nation about Alaska's rich resources. In the end, the Senate ratified the purchase, and the United States took possession of what was then called "Seward's Folly."

Americans also showed their interest in the Pacific. In 1853, an American fleet led by Commodore Matthew C. Perry sailed into Tokyo Bay, forcing Japan to start trading with the United States. By the 1860s, the United States and several European countries had signed a series of treaties that allowed for expanded trade with China.

Now the U.S. government wanted control of some Pacific islands to use as refueling and repair stations for its naval vessels. To this end, Seward championed the annexation of the uninhabited Midway Islands in 1867. Eight years later the U.S. government signed a treaty with Hawaii. This agreement allowed Hawaiians to sell sugar in the United States duty-free, as long as they did not sell or lease territory to any foreign power.

COMPARING HISTORIANS' VIEWPOINTS
The Motivation Behind American Imperialism

Historians offer many different explanations for why the United States sought to expand its influence abroad.
Analyzing Viewpoints What factors do these historians describe as contributing to American expansionism?

Expansion to Solve Domestic Problems

"Spurred by a fantastic industrial revolution, which produced ever larger quantities of surplus goods, depressions, and violence, and warned by a growing radical literature that the system was not functioning properly, the United States prepared to solve its dilemmas with foreign expansion. Displaying a notable lack of absent-mindedness, Americans set out to solve their problems by creating an empire whose dynamic and characteristics marked a new departure in their history."
—*Walter LaFeber,* The New Empire: An Interpretation of American Expansion 1860–1898

Expansion to Restore a Sense of Security

"In a period of drastic social change, old maxims lost their sway over people who had good reason to take them for granted no longer; calm and thoughtful Americans, as well as frightened and anxious ones, felt compelled by events to reexamine the precepts of U.S. foreign policy. . . . Perhaps the United States could reaffirm its soundness by thrashing some country in a war or, more subtly, by demonstrating its ability to govern 'inferior' peoples in a colonial empire. Once indifferent to events outside their boundaries, Americans now searched abroad for means to internal salvation."
—*Robert L. Beisner,* From the Old Diplomacy to the New, 1865–1900

Also of great concern to the United States were the Caribbean islands and Latin America. In 1870, President Ulysses S. Grant announced that in the future the Monroe Doctrine would protect all territories in these two regions from "transfer to a European power." Not long after, the United States was playing an active role in several diplomatic and military conflicts in Latin America.

Arguments for U.S. Expansion

By the 1890s, Americans were debating what foreign policy would best serve the United States. Some argued that the country should continue to avoid foreign entanglements. Others offered a variety of reasons for increased American involvement in international affairs.

Promoting Economic Growth   A chief argument in favor of expansion was economic. By the late 1800s, the industrialists, inventors, and workers of the United States had built a powerful industrial economy. Americans alone, however, could not consume everything their nation produced. The overproduction of food and goods led to financial panics and frequent economic depressions. Protesting their plight, workers and farmers helped to convince business and political leaders that the United States must secure new markets abroad.

Many business leaders agreed that the economic problems of the nation could be solved only by expanding its markets. For this reason, they threw their support behind expansionist policies. Some American businesses already dominated international markets. Firms such as Rockefeller's Standard Oil and American Telephone and Telegraph had all become international businesses.

Other American business leaders had gone a step further and invested directly in the economies of other countries. In some cases their investments gave them political influence in those countries. In Central America, for example, an American named Minor C. Keith provided financial services to the Costa Rican government. In return, he won long-term leases for lands and railroad lines. By 1913, Keith's United Fruit Company not only exported 50 million bunches of bananas a year to the United States, it also played a significant role in the governments and economies of Costa Rica, Guatemala, and Honduras. As a result, some people began calling the Central American nations **banana republics.**

Protecting American Security   Lobbyists who favored a strong United States Navy formed a second force pushing for expansion. By the 1880s, U.S. warships left over from the Civil War were rusting and rotting. Naval officers joined with business interests to convince Congress to build modern steam-powered, steel-hulled ships to protect overseas trade.

The most influential of these officers was Captain (later Admiral) Alfred T. Mahan. In his 1890 book, *The Influence of Sea Power Upon History, 1660–1783,* Mahan argued that the nation's economic future hinged on gaining new markets abroad. In his view, the United States needed a powerful navy to protect these markets from foreign rivals.

Influenced by supporters of an expanded navy, Congress established a Naval Advisory Board in 1881. The board pushed to increase the navy's budget. Two years later, Congress authorized the building of three cruisers and two battleships, including the U.S.S. *Maine.* Finally, the Naval Act of 1890 called for the construction of more battleships, gunboats, torpedo boats, and

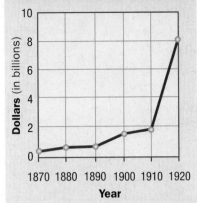

Value of United States Exports, 1870–1920

SOURCE: *Historical Statistics of the United States, Colonial Times to 1970*

INTERPRETING GRAPHS
Businesses eagerly sought new markets abroad in the late 1800s and early 1900s. **Analyzing Information** *By how much did U.S. exports increase between 1870 and 1920?*

INTERPRETING POLITICAL CARTOONS As this 1901 political cartoon suggests, the United States relied on the principles of the Monroe Doctrine to block European involvement in Latin America. **Drawing Inferences** *What is the cartoonist suggesting about the role of the United States in world affairs?*

cruisers. By 1900, the United States had one of the most powerful navies in the world. The expanded fleet suggested that the United States was willing and able to confront an enemy on the open sea.

Preserving American Spirit A third force for expansion consisted of people who feared that the United States was losing its vitality. Among them were Massachusetts Senator Henry Cabot Lodge, historian Frederick Jackson Turner, and a young politician from New York named Theodore Roosevelt. Worried that the closing of the frontier would sap the nation's energy, they argued that a quest for an empire might restore the country's pioneer spirit.

These and other leaders of the day drew on the doctrine of social Darwinism to justify the takeover of new territories, just as they had done earlier to defend the conquest of Native Americans. In the opinion of respected leaders such as Congregationalist minister Josiah Strong and Indiana senator Albert J. Beveridge, the civilizations produced by Anglo-Saxon and Teutonic (Germanic) peoples were superior to the societies they conquered. Social Darwinists believed that expansionism was not only this nation's destiny but also a noble pursuit, for it introduced Christianity and modern civilization to other "heathen" peoples around the world. This was an age when many intellectuals believed that certain racial and national groups were superior to others.

Americans Lean Toward Expansion Gradually public opinion warmed to the idea of expansionism. Although most Americans had accepted the conquest of Native Americans as right and inevitable, they did not see themselves as potential rulers of oppressed foreign peoples. Moreover, they did want new markets abroad and favorable trade relations. What they soon discovered was that political and military entanglements tended to follow. The United States would find itself in difficult, bloody, and painful foreign conflicts.

Section 1 Assessment

READING COMPREHENSION

1. Why did **imperialism** grow in Europe at the end of the 1800s?

2. How did the United States apply the Monroe Doctrine to its foreign policy throughout the 1800s?

3. Why did U.S. policymakers feel the need to secure new markets abroad?

4. Why did some believe that U.S. expansion was needed to preserve the "American spirit"?

CRITICAL THINKING AND WRITING

5. **Recognizing Cause and Effect** What effect did the growth of European imperialism have on United States attitudes toward foreign policy and expansion?

6. **Writing a List** Beginning with the Louisiana Purchase, write a chronological list tracing specific examples of American expansionism before 1880.

For: An activity on Seward's Folly
Visit: PHSchool.com
Web Code: mrd-6171

READING FOCUS

- How did the activities of the United States in Latin America set the stage for war with Spain?

- What were the events leading up to and following the Spanish-American War?

- What challenges did the United States face after the war?

- Why did the United States seek to gain influence in the Pacific?

MAIN IDEA

A swift victory in the Spanish-American War confirmed the status of the United States as a world power, but it left some people arguing over how to govern newly acquired territories.

KEY TERMS

arbitration
jingoism
Platt Amendment
sphere of influence
Open Door Policy

TARGET READING SKILL

Understand Effects As you read, complete this chart listing the effects of United States foreign policies on other nations after the Spanish-American War.

Effects of United States Foreign Policy	
Nation	**Policy and Effects**
Philippines	Annexed by U.S. after Spanish-American War. U.S. soldiers remain there. Fighting between U.S. and Philippines occurs. U.S. occupation continues until 1946.
Cuba	
Puerto Rico	
Hawaii	
China	

Setting the Scene

The United States was poised on the edge of becoming a world power. All that was needed was something to push the country in that direction. The cautious McKinley administration resisted the growing demands of those in Congress and throughout the country who hungered for expansion. The time was not yet right. As they waited for action, Americans woke up to this newspaper headline in October 1897:

> 66 *EVANGELINA CISNEROS RESCUED BY THE JOURNAL: AN AMERICAN NEWSPAPER ACCOMPLISHES AT A SINGLE STROKE WHAT THE RED TAPE OF DIPLOMACY FAILED UTTERLY TO BRING ABOUT IN MANY MONTHS.* 99
>
> —Headline in the *New York Journal,*
> October 10, 1897

Many would have been shocked to read in big, bold letters that a newspaper had acted outside the law to protect liberty and justice abroad. In this instance, the *Journal* staged the rescue of someone they described as a beautiful, young Cuban girl being held prisoner by the Spanish. Vivid headlines such as this attracted readers craving controversy and excitement. The sensational stories that followed increased newspaper circulations and resulted in huge profits for newspaper publishers.

Another year would pass before the United States fought a war that would forever change its role in world affairs. The newspapers did not cause the war, but they did help to reinforce and magnify a new set of assumptions among the American people regarding their place in the world. Americans began to feel that their nation was growing bigger and stronger. They were ready and willing to take action outside U.S. borders. In the process of expanding and becoming a world power, however, the United States increasingly found itself in conflict with other nations.

VIEWING HISTORY This illustration by Thure de Thulstrup depicts Cuban rebels charging into battle with the Spanish. **Analyzing Visual Information** *What do the details in the illustration tell you about the artist's view of the Cuban rebellion?*

Setting the Stage for War

American expansionists paid close attention to the political and economic actions of countries in the Western Hemisphere. In the 1890s, several incidents took place that allowed the United States to strengthen its role in Latin American affairs.

Displays of United States Power   In 1891, an angry Chilean mob attacked a group of American sailors on shore leave in Valparaíso. They killed two Americans and injured seventeen others. The U.S. government reacted strongly, forcing Chile to pay $75,000 to the families of the sailors who were killed or injured. Two years later, when a rebellion threatened the friendly republican government of Brazil, President Cleveland ordered naval units to Rio de Janeiro to protect United States shipping interests. This show of force broke the back of the rebellion.

In the third and most important incident of the era, the United States confronted the nation then considered the most powerful in the world, Great Britain. Since the 1840s, Britain and Venezuela had disputed ownership of a piece of territory located at the border between Venezuela and British Guiana. In the 1880s, the dispute intensified when rumors surfaced of mineral wealth in this border area. President Cleveland's Secretary of State, Richard Olney, demanded in July 1895 that Britain acknowledge the Monroe Doctrine and submit the boundary dispute to **arbitration.** (Arbitration is the settlement of a dispute by a person or panel chosen to listen to both sides and come to a decision.) The British government replied that the doctrine had no standing in international law.

Eventually Britain backed down and agreed to arbitration. Concerned about the rising power of Germany in Africa, the British government realized that it needed to stay on friendly terms with the increasingly powerful United States.

The Cuban Rebellion   By the mid-1890s, not only had the Monroe Doctrine been reaffirmed but the world's most powerful country had bent to it. Events in Cuba soon paved the way for a far more spectacular display of American power.

An island nation off the coast of Florida, Cuba first rebelled against Spain in 1868. After ten years of fighting the rebels, Spain finally put in place a few meager reforms to appease the Cuban people. In 1895, after the island's economy had collapsed, Cubans rebelled again. This time Spain sent 150,000 troops and its best general, Valeriano Weyler, to put down the rebellion. In a desperate attempt to prevent civilians from aiding the rebels, Weyler instituted a policy of "reconcentration." He forced hundreds of thousands of Cubans into guarded camps. The prisoners, including women, children, and the elderly, lived in miserable conditions with little food or sanitation. Over two years, disease and starvation killed an estimated 200,000 Cubans.

Cuban exiles living in the United States, led by the journalist José Martí, urged the United States to intervene. Both Presidents Cleveland and McKinley refused. They were unwilling to spend the money that intervention would require and feared the United States would be saddled with colonial responsibilities it could not handle. Frustrated, Cuban guerrillas turned to the one tactic they knew would attract the U.S. government's attention: the destruction of American sugar plantations and mills in Cuba. As a result, business owners increased their pressure on the government to act.

READING CHECK
How did the 1895 dispute between the United States and Great Britain reaffirm the validity of the Monroe Doctrine?

Focus on WORLD EVENTS

José Martí Fights for Cuban Independence   José Martí (1853–1895) dedicated his life to achieving Cuban independence. A patriot and a revolutionary, Martí had dreamed of *Cuba Libre* (a free Cuba) since the age of 15. A gifted writer, he wrote poems as a teenager and soon founded his own newspaper, *La patria libre (The Free Fatherland)*.

Because of his revolutionary activity, Martí was forced to leave Cuba in 1871. He was deported to Spain, where he received a master's degree and a law degree. Martí finally settled in New York City in 1881, where he led the Cuban Revolutionary Party. In 1895, Martí left New York to stage attacks in Cuba with other revolutionaries. Later that year, he was killed in battle, just a few years before *Cuba Libre* became a reality.

Yellow Journalism Demands for United States intervention in Cuba also came in large part from American newspapers. In the 1890s, a fierce competition for readers broke out between two New York City newspapers, the *New York World* and the *New York Morning Journal*. Both newspapers reported exaggerated and sometimes false stories about the events in Cuba in order to increase circulation. The battle pitted the *World's* established publisher, Joseph Pulitzer, against a newcomer to the city, the *Journal's* William Randolph Hearst.

Hearst bought the *Journal* when it was struggling in 1895. By luring experienced journalists from other papers, including the *World*, he managed to turn it into a success. Hearst used a variety of other techniques to increase the *Journal's* circulation, including printing sensational crime stories, using illustrations and vivid headlines to draw in the reader, and lowering the price to one penny.

Both Hearst and Pulitzer took advantage of the horrifying stories coming from Cuba about the "Butcher" Weyler and his barbed-wire concentration camps. Their sensational headlines and stories, known as yellow journalism, whipped up American public opinion in favor of the rebels. The intense burst of national pride and the desire for an aggressive foreign policy that followed came to be known as **jingoism.** The name came from a line in a British song of the 1870s: "We don't want to fight, yet by Jingo! if we do, We've got the ships, we've got the men, and got the money too."

The Spanish-American War

The stories printed in newspapers such as the *Journal* strengthened American sympathy for the Cuban rebels. Slowly the demand for U.S. intervention began to build.

Steps to War Early in 1898, riots erupted in Havana, the capital of Cuba. In response, President McKinley moved the battleship U.S.S. *Maine* into the city's harbor to protect American citizens and property. Several events followed that pushed the United States to war.

The de Lôme letter A few weeks later, in early February 1898, United States newspapers published a letter stolen from the Spanish ambassador to Washington, Dupuy de Lôme. The de Lôme letter, which described McKinley as "weak and a bidder for the admiration of the crowd," caused an outcry in the United States. The letter raised a commotion not just because it ridiculed McKinley, but mostly because of the sensationalism surrounding it. Because de Lôme was a Spaniard, the press now had a golden opportunity to intensify anti-Spanish sentiments.

The explosion of the U.S.S. Maine Then, on February 15, an explosion sank the *Maine*, killing more than 250 American sailors. The blast had probably been caused by an accidental fire that set off ammunition, but the American public put the blame on Spain. The papers jumped on the chance to arouse more bitter feelings toward Spain. The *New York Morning Journal* asked, "How long shall the United States sit idle and indifferent within sound and hearing of rapine and murder? How long?" The Spanish were willing to enter into arbitration talks to determine more decisively if they were responsible, but that did not matter. An enraged American public called for war. Still, McKinley hesitated.

INTERPRETING TABLES
Sales of Hearst's *New York Morning Journal* soared in 1898. **Synthesizing Information** *What factors led to the increased demand for papers such as the* Journal?

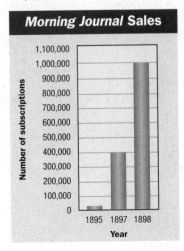

Morning Journal Sales

Number of subscriptions / Year

Preparing in the Philippines On the other side of the world, the people of another of Spain's last remaining possessions, the Philippine Islands, also were rebelling. In the view of Theodore Roosevelt, then Assistant Secretary of the Navy, the Philippines could become a key base from which the United States might protect its Asian trade. On February 25, while his boss, the Secretary of the Navy, was out of the office, Roosevelt cabled naval commanders in the Pacific to prepare for military action against Spain. When President McKinley discovered what Roosevelt had done, he ordered most of the cables withdrawn, but he made an exception in the case of the cable directed to Admiral George Dewey. Dewey was told to attack the Spanish fleet in the Philippines if war broke out with Spain.

McKinley's war message Late in March, in a final attempt at a peaceful solution, McKinley sent a list of demands to Spain. These included compensation for the *Maine,* an end to the reconcentration camps, a truce in Cuba, and Cuban independence. Eager to find a peaceful settlement to the crisis, Spain accepted all but the last. McKinley decided he could not resist the growing cries for war. On April 11, he sent a war message to Congress. A few days later, rallying to the cry of "Remember the *Maine*!" Congress recognized Cuban independence and authorized force against Spain.

"A Splendid Little War"

The war's first action took place not in Cuba but in the Philippines, as shown on the map on this page. On May 1, 1898, Admiral Dewey launched a surprise attack on Spanish ships anchored in Manila Bay, destroying Spain's entire Pacific fleet in just seven hours. In Cuba, meanwhile, United States warships quickly bottled up Spain's Atlantic fleet in the harbor at Santiago.

American army troops gathered in Tampa, Florida, to prepare for an invasion of Cuba. The group that received the most publicity was the First Volunteer Cavalry, known as the Rough Riders. Its leader, Theodore Roosevelt, had resigned his position as Assistant Secretary of the Navy and recruited a diverse group of volunteers that included cowboys, miners, policemen, and college athletes. On July 1, 1898, Roosevelt led the Rough Riders in a charge up San Juan Hill. This charge became the most famous incident of the war.

The Spanish fleet made a desperate attempt to escape Santiago harbor on July 3. In the ensuing battle, the United States Navy sank every Spanish ship,

MAP SKILLS Although the Spanish-American War was fought in two locations on opposite sides of the world, the United States defeated Spain in just nine weeks. **Location** *At what specific sites were the major battles of the war fought?*

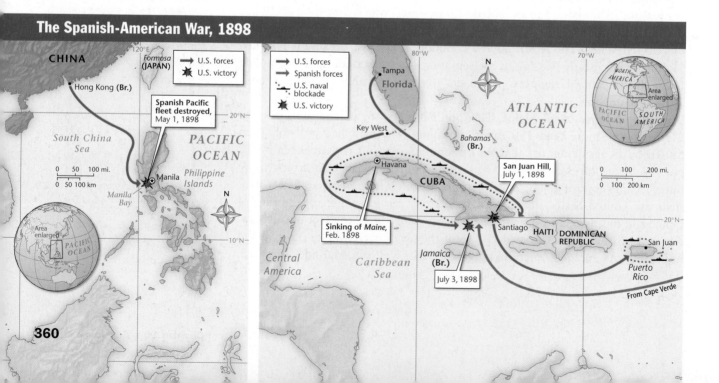

The Spanish-American War, 1898

Using a Time Zone Map

A system of worldwide standard time was devised in 1884. It divides the world into 24 time zones based on meridians of longitude. The time is the same throughout each zone. The Prime Meridian of 0°, which passes through Greenwich, England, is the starting point for calculating the time in each zone. The meridian of 180° longitude, halfway around the world, is the International Date Line. The calendar date to the east of the line is one day earlier than the date to the west.

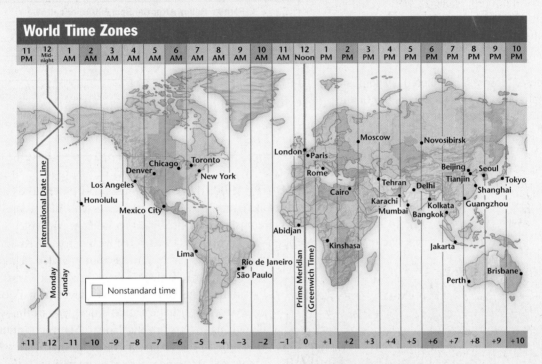

World Time Zones

LEARN THE SKILL

Use the following steps to read a time zone map:

1. **Study the information on the map.** Locate the Prime Meridian and the International Date Line. Study any keys, labels, and color-coding. On this map, the 24 time zones are shown by colored bands. The numbers at the bottom of the map indicate the number of hours each time zone differs from time at the Prime Meridian (Greenwich time). For example, +3 means that local time is three hours later than Greenwich time. The numbers at the top of the map provide examples of how this system works if it is 12:00 noon in Greenwich.

2. **Determine where the time zones and date change.** Notice how closely the time zones correspond to the meridians of longitude and where they vary from these lines. Compare time zones in different areas.

3. **Compare the time in your zone with other zones around the world.** Find your time zone on the map. Determine how it differs from Greenwich time.

PRACTICE THE SKILL

Answer the following questions:

1. **(a)** How does the map indicate which line is the Prime Meridian? **(b)** What time is it at the International Date Line when it is noon in Greenwich? **(c)** How many different time zones does South America have?

2. **(a)** If it is 12:00 noon, Greenwich time, what time is it in Moscow, Russia? In Denver, United States of America? **(b)** If it is 2 P.M. in Abidjan, Côte d'Ivoire, what time is it in the zone labeled +7? In the zone labeled –4? **(c)** Why do you think some of the time zones follow geographical features and political boundaries rather than the meridians of longitude?

3. **(a)** If it is 12:00 noon in Greenwich, what time is it in your time zone? **(b)** If it is 1 A.M. in your time zone, what time is it in Karachi, Pakistan? In Guangzhou, China? **(c)** If it is 12:00 noon in São Paulo, Brazil, what time is it where you live? **(d)** If it is 9 P.M. on Wednesday where you live, what are the day and time in Brisbane, Australia?

APPLY THE SKILL

See the Chapter Review and Assessment for another opportunity to apply this skill.

READING FOCUS

- Why did the United States want to build the Panama Canal?

- What were the goals of Theodore Roosevelt's "big stick" diplomacy?

- In what ways did the foreign policies of Presidents Taft and Wilson differ from those of President Roosevelt?

MAIN IDEA

President Theodore Roosevelt conducted a vigorous foreign policy that suited the new status of the United States as a world power. Presidents Taft and Wilson took a different approach to influencing other nations.

KEY TERMS

concession
Roosevelt Corollary
dollar diplomacy

TARGET READING SKILL

Understand Effects Copy the flowchart below. As you read, fill in the boxes with some of the major effects of the new United States foreign policy.

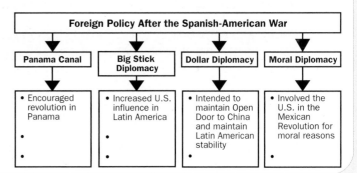

Foreign Policy After the Spanish-American War			
Panama Canal	**Big Stick Diplomacy**	**Dollar Diplomacy**	**Moral Diplomacy**
• Encouraged revolution in Panama • •	• Increased U.S. influence in Latin America • •	• Intended to maintain Open Door to China and maintain Latin American stability	• Involved the U.S. in the Mexican Revolution for moral reasons •

Setting the Scene By 1900, the United States had emerged as a genuine world power. It controlled several overseas territories and had a large and vigorous economy. These circumstances contributed to William McKinley's decisive victory in the presidential election of 1900. One year later McKinley was dead, cut down by an assassin's bullet. Theodore Roosevelt, McKinley's Vice President, was now President. The new President developed a foreign policy to support the nation's new role in the world. Under his leadership, the United States continued to intervene in the affairs of countries that were of economic and strategic interest to the nation.

The Panama Canal

The Spanish-American War brought home to Americans the need for a shorter route between the Pacific and Atlantic oceans. A canal built across Central America would link the two oceans, making global shipping much faster and cheaper. It would also allow the United States Navy to move quickly from one ocean to the other in time of war.

Building the Canal The Isthmus of Panama was an ideal location for such a route. At that time, Panama was a province of the South American nation of Colombia. In 1879, a French company headed by Ferdinand de Lesseps had bought a 25-year **concession** from Colombia to build a canal across Panama. (A concession is a grant for a piece of land in exchange for a promise to use the land for a specific purpose.) Defeated by yellow fever and severe mismanagement, the company abandoned the project ten years later. It offered its remaining rights to the United States for $100 million. When the price fell to $40 million, Congress

Because of the uneven elevation in the Canal Zone, engineers had to design a series of locks to raise and lower the ships so that they could pass through the canal.

passed the Spooner Act in 1902 that authorized the purchase of the French assets. The act required that the United States work out a treaty with Colombia for a lease on the land.

Treaty negotiations went nowhere. Colombia was waiting for the French concession to expire in 1904 so that it could offer the isthmus at a higher price. Roosevelt was enraged by this attempt of Colombian "bandits" to "rob" the United States. Secretary of State John Hay sent a message to the American minister in Colombia in June 1903 essentially threatening Colombia if it did not reconsider.

> 66 *If Colombia should now reject the treaty or unduly delay its ratification, the friendly understanding between the two countries would be so seriously compromised that action might be taken by the Congress next winter which every friend of Colombia would regret.* 99
> —Secretary of State John Hay

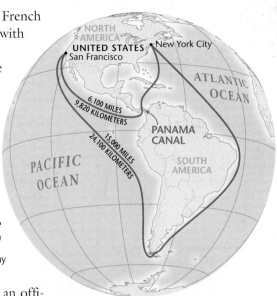

Meanwhile, Roosevelt secretly made it clear to Philippe Bunau-Varilla, an official with the French company, that the United States would not interfere if the company organized a Panamanian revolution against Colombia.

The revolt took place in November 1903 with U.S. warships waiting offshore to provide support for the rebels. The United States immediately recognized an independent Panama and became its protector. In return, Panama signed the Hay-Bunau-Varilla Treaty in November 1903. The treaty gave the United States a permanent grant of a 10-mile-wide strip of land for a Canal Zone over which the United States would have complete sovereignty. In return, the Panamanians received a payment of $10 million.

Construction of the canal began in 1904. To complete this mammoth task, workers were brought in from several countries. Many of them had no construction experience whatsoever. After receiving proper training, the workers surpassed all expectations. They finished the canal in 1914, six months ahead of schedule and $23 million under budget.

Reaction to the Canal   Roosevelt's opponents did not appreciate the methods he had used to secure the Canal Zone. A newspaper published by William Hearst commented, "Besides being a rough-riding assault upon another republic over the shattered wreckage of international law . . . , it is a quite unexampled instance of foul play in American politics."

Most Americans, however, convinced that the canal was vital to national security and prosperity, approved of President Roosevelt's actions in Panama. Two years after leaving office, Roosevelt gave a speech at the University of California at Berkeley in which he justified his methods:

> 66 *If I had followed traditional, conservative methods I would have submitted a dignified State paper of probably 200 pages to Congress and the debates on it would have been going on yet; but I took the Canal Zone and let Congress debate; and while the debate goes on the canal does also.* 99
> —Theodore Roosevelt, 1911

Despite the success of the Panama Canal as a link between the Atlantic and Pacific, its acquisition left a legacy of ill will among Latin Americans toward the United States. In recognition of the illegal means used to acquire the Canal

MAP SKILLS Compare the sea route from New York City to San Francisco (above) with and without the canal. **Movement** *By how many miles did the Panama Canal reduce the journey?*

Workers on the Panama Canal wore identification badges like the ones shown here.

Zone, Congress voted to pay $25 million to Colombia in 1921, two years after Roosevelt had died.

Roosevelt's Big Stick Diplomacy

In 1901, Roosevelt reminded an audience at the Minnesota State Fair of an old African proverb: "Speak softly and carry a big stick; you will go far." In his view, the "big stick" was the United States Navy. Indeed, the threat of military force allowed Roosevelt to conduct an aggressive foreign policy.

The Roosevelt Corollary In December 1904 and 1905, Roosevelt issued messages to Congress that became known as the **Roosevelt Corollary** to the Monroe Doctrine. In this corollary, or extension of a previously accepted idea, Roosevelt denied that the United States wanted any more territory.

INTERPRETING POLITICAL CARTOONS Published after the announcement of the Roosevelt Corollary, this cartoon depicts Roosevelt as the world's police officer, using his "big stick" to maintain order and stability in Latin America. **Making Comparisons** *Compare this cartoon to the others in this chapter. What similarities can you find? What conclusions can you draw?*

KEY DOCUMENTS " *It must be understood that under no circumstances will the United States use the Monroe Doctrine as a cloak for territorial aggression. We desire peace with all the world, but perhaps most of all with the other peoples of the American continent. . . . It is always possible that wrong actions toward this nation . . . may result in our having to take action to protect our rights; but such action will not be taken with a view to territorial aggression.* "

—Roosevelt Corollary to the Monroe Doctrine, Theodore Roosevelt, 1905

The United States wanted only "to see neighboring countries stable, orderly, and prosperous," he said. But if the countries engaged in activities harmful to the interests of the United States or if their governments collapsed, inviting intervention from stronger nations, then the United States would be forced to exercise "an international police power." In other words, the U.S. government would intervene to prevent intervention from other powers. This was the central point of the Roosevelt Corollary.

The first test of the Roosevelt Corollary concerned the small Caribbean island republic of Santo Domingo (now the Dominican Republic). When the island went bankrupt, European nations threatened to intervene to collect their money. Roosevelt moved quickly to establish American supervision of customs collections. Bankers in the United States took over the country's finances and paid its European debt. Congress initially blocked Roosevelt's actions. However, the President was able to get around congressional opposition by creating an executive agreement with Santo Domingo's president.

Under Roosevelt, U.S. intervention in Latin America became common. This development angered many Latin Americans. Congress also was displeased with Roosevelt's single-handed foreign policies that seemed to strengthen the President's powers while weakening their own.

Roosevelt as Peacemaker In Asia, the President's chief concern was to preserve an open door to trade with China. However, growing conflicts between Japan and Russia posed a threat to Asian security. These conflicts came to a head in the Russo-Japanese War, which began in 1904. As the war progressed it was clear that Japan's military power outmatched Russia's. Finally, after a key naval victory for Japan, Japan requested peace talks.

READING CHECK

What were the main points of the Roosevelt Corollary?

Meanwhile, President Roosevelt had grown increasingly concerned over Japan's expanding military power. Japan had crushed China a decade earlier in the Sino-Japanese War and had been growing stronger ever since. He also saw potential problems resulting from certain policies then being proposed in California that would discriminate against and exclude Japanese immigrants. In a letter to his friend Senator Henry Cabot Lodge, Roosevelt wrote:

> 66 *I hope that we can persuade our people on the one hand to act in a spirit of generous justice and genuine courtesy toward Japan, and on the other hand to keep the navy respectable in numbers and more than respectable in the efficiency of its units. If we act thus we need not fear the Japanese. But if, as Brooks Adams says, we show ourselves 'opulent, aggressive, and unarmed,' the Japanese may sometime work us an injury.* 99
>
> —President Theodore Roosevelt, June 1905

Two months later, in August 1905, Roosevelt mediated a peace agreement to the Russo-Japanese War. He invited delegates from the two nations to Portsmouth, New Hampshire, where he persuaded Japan to be satisfied with small grants of land and control over Korea instead of a huge payment of money. He also secured a promise from Russia to vacate Manchuria, which remained part of China. Roosevelt succeeded in keeping trade in China open to all nations. His role as mediator won him the Nobel peace prize.

NOTABLE PRESIDENTS
Theodore Roosevelt

"Speak softly and carry a big stick; you will go far."
—1901 speech at the Minnesota State Fair

Born into a wealthy New York family, Theodore ("Teddy") Roosevelt had asthma as a child, but at his father's insistence he overcame it with rigorous physical exercise. "TR" developed a stocky body, a fighter's toughness, and a love for strenuous living.

As a Republican politician in New York in the 1880s, TR called for a larger government role in the economy, a stand that made him a leader of the Progressives. TR believed in honest as well as active government. During a six-year term on the U.S. Civil Service Commission, he enforced the merit system. TR later attacked corruption as head of the New York City Police Board.

In 1897, TR was appointed Assistant Secretary of the Navy. There he built up a two-ocean fleet and urged a more aggressive American foreign policy. When the Spanish-American War was declared in 1898, TR, though nearly 40 and with poor eyesight, demanded to see combat. He organized the "Rough Riders" and led them on a famous charge up Cuba's San Juan Hill.

The war made TR a national hero. Returning to New York, he won the governorship in 1898. Two years later, President McKinley chose TR as his running mate. In 1901, McKinley was assassinated. Roosevelt became,

26th President 1901–1909

at age 42, the nation's youngest President up to that time.

TR saw the presidency as a "bully pulpit," or a wonderful stage from which to win public support for his brand of strong leadership. His economic policies included regulating big business and supporting labor unions. His foreign policies reflected the "big stick" approach described in the quotation above. Roosevelt was also a vocal conservationist, acting to preserve the nation's natural resources and wildlife. Most importantly, TR's boldness and constant activity helped create the modern image of the President.

Connecting to Today
Do you think that American foreign policy today should be guided by the principle "speak softly and carry a big stick"? Explain your answer.

Go Online PHSchool.com
For: More on Theodore Roosevelt
Visit: PHSchool.com
Web Code: mrd-6177

Foreign Policy After Roosevelt

Under the presidency of Theodore Roosevelt, the United States assumed a forceful new role in foreign affairs. Roosevelt's successors were thrown into a complex mix of political alliances and world events that would require careful and creative policymaking. William Howard Taft and Woodrow Wilson continued the Roosevelt legacy, but each brought with them his own unique methods of diplomacy.

Taft and Dollar Diplomacy William Howard Taft, elected to the presidency in 1908, was not as aggressive as Roosevelt in pursuing foreign policy aims. A distinguished lawyer from Ohio, Taft had served as Roosevelt's Secretary of War and had headed the commission that governed the Philippines.

Taft's main foreign policy goals were to maintain the open door to Asia and preserve stability in Latin America. As for the rest, he preferred "substituting dollars for bullets." By this he meant maintaining orderly societies abroad through increased American investment in foreign economies. Although some of Taft's contemporaries mocked his approach, calling it **dollar diplomacy**, Taft himself later used this term with pride.

Dollar diplomacy did not succeed as well as Taft had hoped. Although it increased the level of United States financial involvement abroad, the results were not always profitable. For example, when Taft's Secretary of State, Philander Knox, persuaded bankers from the United States to invest in railroad projects in China and Manchuria, Russia and Japan united in an effort to block the influence of the Americans. In addition, many U.S. investments in China were lost when the country's government collapsed in revolution in 1911.

Dollar diplomacy also created enemies in Latin America, especially in the Caribbean and Central America, where local revolutionary movements opposed American influence. Although the United States reached new heights as an international power under Roosevelt and Taft, anti-colonialism abroad and anti-imperialism at home provided a growing check to further expansion.

Wilson and the Mexican Revolution American intervention in Mexico under President Woodrow Wilson led to even more anti-American feeling in Latin America. In 1911, a revolution forced Mexico's longtime dictator, Porfirio Diaz, to resign. The new president, Francisco Madero, promised democratic reforms but could not unite his deeply divided and impoverished country. In 1913, General Victoriano Huerta overthrew him and had him killed.

The United States was unsure how to respond to Huerta's illegal action. Americans had invested over $1 billion in Mexican oil, mines, land, and railways. When Huerta promised to protect foreign investments, most European countries recognized him. American investors urged President Wilson to do the same, but he refused. To him, Huerta was a "butcher" ruling without the consent of the

United States Interventions, 1898–1934

U.S. expeditionary force, 1916–1917

UNITED STATES

ATLANTIC OCEAN

N

Parral

MEXICO

U.S. occupation, 1898–1902, 1906–1909, 1912, 1917–1922

U.S. occupation, 1915–1934

Bahamas (Br.)

U.S. possession, 1898

Tampico

U.S. seizure, 1914

Havana

CUBA

DOMINICAN REPUBLIC

Purchased from Denmark, 1917

Mexico City

Guantanamo

Puerto Rico

Virgin Is.

Antigua (Br.)

Veracruz

GUATEMALA

Br. Honduras (Br.)

Jamaica (Br.)

HAITI

Guadeloupe (Fr.)

Dominica (Br.)

Martinique (Fr.)

St. Lucia (Br.)

Grenada (Br.)

Barbados (Br.)

HONDURAS

United Fruit Co. organized for banana trade, 1899

EL SALVADOR

NICARAGUA

U.S. leased naval base, 1903

U.S. occupation, 1924–1925

COSTA RICA

PANAMA

U.S. occupation, 1916–1924

Trinidad (Br.)

VENEZUELA

U.S. occupation, 1909–1910, 1912–1925, 1926–1933. Canal rights secured, 1916

U.S. leased Corn Is., 1914

COLOMBIA

U.S. acquired Canal Zone, 1904. Canal completed, 1914

PACIFIC OCEAN

0 | 250 | 500 mi.

0 | 250 | 500 km

100°W   90°W

—20°N

—10°N

—0°—

Low, a close friend and admirer of Baden-Powell, founded the American Girl Scouts. Low hoped to use the program both to build moral character in girls and to teach them skills that would make them "hardy" and "handy."

Many people were swayed by the practical advantages of imperialism. They agreed with the economic arguments that emphasized the need to gain access to foreign markets. Others embraced the strategic military reasons for expansion.

In December 1907, Roosevelt sent part of the United States Navy on a cruise around the world. The trip was designed to demonstrate the nation's impressive naval power to other nations. The **Great White Fleet,** as the gleaming white ships were called, made a big impression everywhere it sailed. For American citizens, the fleet clearly showed the benefits of having a powerful navy.

Imperialism Viewed From Abroad

Having begun a pattern of international involvement, the United States discovered that these actions frequently took on a life of their own. In the Caribbean and Central America, for example, the United States often had to defend governments that were unpopular with local inhabitants. In Latin America, the cry "Yankee, Go Home!" began to be heard. Even before the Panama Canal was completed in 1914, Panamanians began to complain that they suffered from discrimination.

On the other hand, because the United States was quickly becoming so powerful, other countries—even those fearful about maintaining their independence—began to turn to the United States for help. Both welcomed and rejected, the United States would spend the rest of the century trying to decide the best way to reconcile its growing power and national interests with its relationships with other nations.

Section 4 Assessment

READING COMPREHENSION

1. Why did some people believe that **racism** was at work in imperialism?

2. What were three economic arguments raised by the anti-imperialists?

3. How did imperialism's appeal go beyond what many saw as its practical advantages?

4. What was significant about the tour of the **Great White Fleet?**

CRITICAL THINKING AND WRITING

5. **Identifying Assumptions** How did expansionists and anti-imperialists view imperialism in relation to the original principles of American democracy? What different assumptions did people on the two sides make about the roots and goals of the United States?

6. **Writing an Opinion** Based on the arguments they made against imperialism, what role do you think the anti-imperialists believed the United States should play in world affairs?

Go Online PHSchool.com

For: An activity on the Great White Fleet
Visit: PHSchool.com
Web Code: mrd-6174

creating a CHAPTER SUMMARY

Copy this cause-and-effect diagram (right) on a separate sheet of paper to show some of the causes and effects of American expansion during the late 1800s and early 1900s. Provide at least four causes and four effects.

For additional review and enrichment activities, see the interactive version of *America: Pathways to the Present*, available on the Web and on CD-ROM.

CAUSES
- Pressure to find new markets abroad
-
-
-

AMERICAN EXPANSIONISM

EFFECTS
- Purchase of Alaska from Russia
-
-
-

★ Reviewing Key Terms

For each of the terms below, write a sentence explaining how it relates to the era of imperialism in the United States.

1. imperialism
2. nationalism
3. annex
4. banana republic
5. arbitration
6. jingoism
7. Platt Amendment
8. sphere of influence
9. concession
10. dollar diplomacy
11. racism
12. compulsory
13. Great White Fleet

★ Reviewing Main Ideas

14. Why were the major European powers scrambling to seize new territory in the late 1800s? (Section 1)

15. Briefly explain the arguments of Alfred T. Mahan, Henry Cabot Lodge, and Albert J. Beveridge regarding expansionism. (Section 1)

16. Why did the American public favor war with Spain in 1898? (Section 2)

17. What was the Open Door Policy, and why was it important to the United States? (Section 2)

18. How did the Roosevelt Corollary affect United States policy in Latin America? (Section 3)

19. Describe the foreign policy goals of Taft and Wilson. (Section 3)

20. Explain why anti-imperialists believed that imperialism betrayed basic American principles. (Section 4)

★ Critical Thinking

21. **Synthesizing Information** In what sense were the expansionist policies of the United States in the late 1800s a continuation of the concept of Manifest Destiny?

22. **Identifying Central Issues** How did the popular theory of social Darwinism make it easier for some Americans to embrace imperialist policies in the late 1800s?

23. **Drawing Conclusions** During the late 1800s, the press fanned the flames of the Spanish-American War by publishing sensational stories about Spanish cruelties in Cuba. On what current issues has the press played a major role in influencing public opinion?

24. **Distinguishing Fact From Opinion** President McKinley's Secretary of State, John Hay, referred to the Spanish-American War as "a splendid little war." Can you think of any Americans, in addition to anti-imperialists, who might disagree with Hay's opinion?

★ Standardized Test Prep

Analyzing Political Cartoons ▶

25. The caption to this 1904 political cartoon reads "HIS 128th BIRTHDAY. 'Gee but this is an awful stretch!'" Whose birthday is it?

A The President's
B The United States'
C The American Flag's
D The Bill of Rights'

26. What is the cartoonist's view of United States imperialism?

Analyzing Primary Sources

Read this excerpt, and then answer the questions that follow.

> 66 I hope that we can persuade our people on the one hand to act in a spirit of generous justice and genuine courtesy toward Japan, and on the other hand to keep the navy respectable in numbers and more than respectable in the efficiency of its units. If we act thus we need not fear the Japanese. But if . . . we show ourselves 'opulent, aggressive, and unarmed,' the Japanese may sometime work us an injury. 99
>
> –President Theodore Roosevelt

27. This statement BEST reflects Roosevelt's support for

A the Monroe Doctrine.
B "Speak softly and carry a big stick."
C the Open Door Policy.
D the Roosevelt Corollary.

28. What is the most likely reason for Roosevelt's concern over Japan?

F He knew their military could easily defeat the military of the United States.
G The Japanese threatened to intervene if Western nations pursued trade with China.
H Laws were being proposed in the United States that discriminated against Japanese immigrants.
I The United States was interested in acquiring Japanese land.

Test-Taking Tip

To answer Question 27 use a process of elimination. Three of the four possible answers do not apply to Japan.

Applying the Chapter Skill

Using a Time Zone Map Review the time zone map on page 365. Name two cities on the map that are in the same time zone as New York City.

For: Chapter 10 Self-Test
Visit: PHSchool.com
Web Code: mra-6175

Building the Panama Canal

Constructing the Panama Canal was one of the greatest engineering feats of all time. Panama's physical and human geography presented several obstacles to the canal's planners and builders, but they overcame each challenge. When the canal was completed in 1914, it linked the Atlantic and Pacific Oceans, as well as the East and West Coasts of the United States.

Flooding a River Valley

The greatest challenge was how to move ships across the Continental Divide, with an elevation of 312 feet above sea level. Digging a canal at sea level across the entire isthmus would have been much too expensive and time-consuming. However, the proposed route of the canal partly followed the course of the wild Chagres River, which had a record of violent floods. Engineers solved these problems by damming the Chagres River to create Gatún Lake, 85 feet above sea level. A series of locks would raise ships from the Atlantic Ocean to the lake. Ships could then travel across most of the isthmus at the level of the lake.

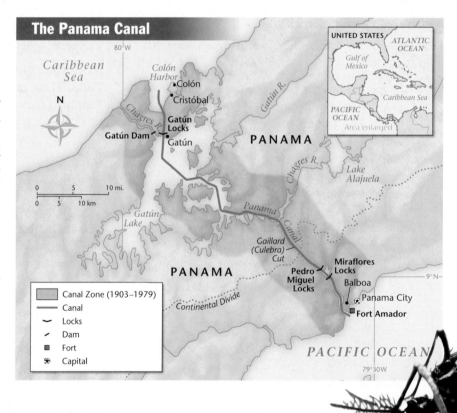

The Panama Canal

Caribbean Sea

80° W

Colón Harbor
• Colón
• Cristóbal

N

Chagres R.

Gatún Locks

Gatún Dam

Gatún

Gatún R.

PANAMA

Chagres R.

Lake Alajuela

0   5   10 mi.
0   5   10 km

Gatún Lake

Panama Canal

Gaillard (Culebra) Cut

PANAMA

Miraflores Locks

Pedro Miguel Locks

Balboa

Panama City

Continental Divide

Fort Amador

9° N

PACIFIC OCEAN

79°30W

UNITED STATES   ATLANTIC OCEAN

Gulf of Mexico

Caribbean Sea

PACIFIC OCEAN

Area enlarged

Canal Zone (1903–1979)
Canal
Locks
Dam
Fort
Capital

Cutting Across the Continental Divide

Workers would cut a deep gorge, later known as the Gaillard Cut (or Culebra Cut), to allow ships to cross the continental divide at the level of Gatún Lake before descending through another set of locks to the Pacific.

Geographical Connection The inset map shows that the Atlantic Ocean lies east of the Pacific Ocean. According to the main map, in what direction do ships passing from the Pacific to the Atlantic actually travel through the Panama Canal?

Solving Problems of Movement

One of the greatest challenges for planners was assembling a labor force to build the canal, because Panama did not have enough workers for the project. As a solution, workers were brought in from overseas, mainly from the United States and the West Indies. Another challenge was removing rock and soil from the canal bed and bringing in machinery and supplies for the workers. The engineers' solution was an extensive rail system.

How Locks Work

The canal's massive locks are an engineering marvel. The locks' lower gates serve as temporary dams to hold water so that ships can float in at the level of the canal above the locks. Then, the upper gates close, the lower gates open, and water flows out of the lock chamber. This lets ships float down to the next-lowest level. When the lower gates close and the gates at the upper end open, water floods in and raises ships. This drawing shows a lock chamber and gates under construction.

Eradicating Disease

Two deadly mosquito-borne diseases—malaria and yellow fever—threatened the canal's work force, but army physician William Gorgas devised an effective mosquito eradication program that saved thousands of lives.

Geographic Connection

What kinds of obstacles did the human and physical geography of Panama pose for the builders of the Panama Canal? How did they overcome those obstacles?

The Progressive Reform Era
(1890–1920)

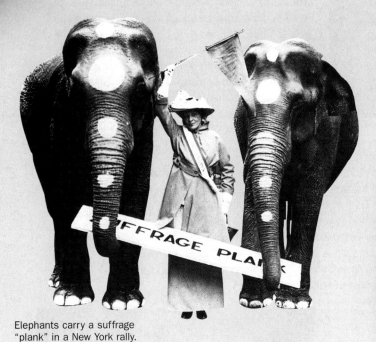

Elephants carry a suffrage "plank" in a New York rally.

American Events

1890
The National American Woman Suffrage Association is founded.

1899
The National Consumers' League is founded.

1900
Hurricane devastates Galveston, Texas; recovery produces new model for city government.

Presidential Terms: B. Harrison 1889–1893   Grover Cleveland 1893–1897   William McKinley 1897–1901   Theodore Roosevelt 1901–1909

1890   **1900**

World Events

The Boxer Rebellion fails to drive foreigners out of China.

Albert Einstein puts forth his special theory of relativity.

1900   **1905**

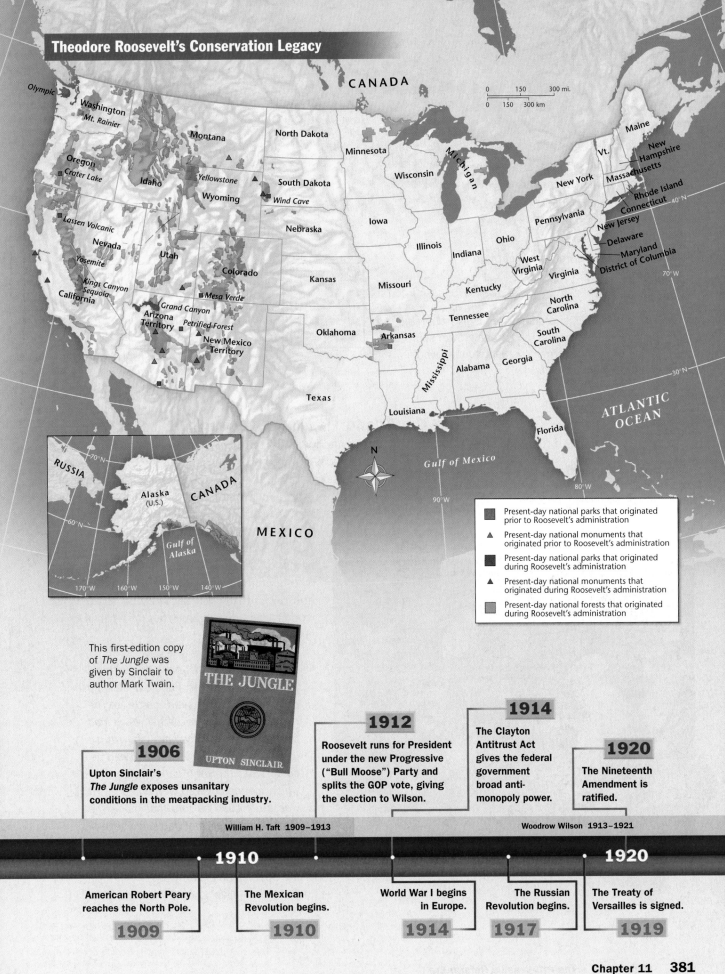

Theodore Roosevelt's Conservation Legacy

CANADA

Olympic

Washington
Mt. Rainier

Oregon
Crater Lake

Montana

North Dakota

Minnesota

Wisconsin

Michigan

Maine

Vt.

New Hampshire

New York

Massachusetts

Idaho

Yellowstone

South Dakota

Wyoming

Wind Cave

Iowa

Rhode Island
Connecticut

Pennsylvania

New Jersey

Delaware

Maryland

District of Columbia

Lassen Volcanic

Nevada

Utah

Nebraska

Illinois

Indiana

Ohio

West
Virginia

Virginia

Yosemite

Colorado

Kansas

Missouri

Kentucky

North
Carolina

Kings Canyon
Sequoia

California

Mesa Verde

Grand Canyon

Arizona
Territory

Petrified Forest

New Mexico
Territory

Oklahoma

Arkansas

Tennessee

Mississippi

Alabama

Georgia

South
Carolina

Texas

Louisiana

Florida

ATLANTIC
OCEAN

Gulf of Mexico

RUSSIA

Alaska
(U.S.)

CANADA

Gulf of
Alaska

MEXICO

0   150   300 mi.

0   150   300 km

Present-day national parks that originated
prior to Roosevelt's administration

Present-day national monuments that
originated prior to Roosevelt's administration

Present-day national parks that originated
during Roosevelt's administration

Present-day national monuments that
originated during Roosevelt's administration

Present-day national forests that originated
during Roosevelt's administration

This first-edition copy
of *The Jungle* was
given by Sinclair to
author Mark Twain.

THE JUNGLE

UPTON SINCLAIR.

1906

Upton Sinclair's
The Jungle exposes unsanitary
conditions in the meatpacking industry.

1912

Roosevelt runs for President
under the new Progressive
("Bull Moose") Party and
splits the GOP vote, giving
the election to Wilson.

1914

The Clayton
Antitrust Act
gives the federal
government
broad anti-
monopoly power.

1920

The Nineteenth
Amendment is
ratified.

William H. Taft 1909–1913

Woodrow Wilson 1913–1921

1910

1920

American Robert Peary
reaches the North Pole.

1909

The Mexican
Revolution begins.

1910

World War I begins
in Europe.

1914

The Russian
Revolution begins.

1917

The Treaty of
Versailles is signed.

1919

The Origins of Progressivism

READING FOCUS

- What were the key goals of Progressives?

- How did the ideas of progressive writers help to inspire new reform movements?

- What reform organizations and what women reformers took up Progressive causes?

- Why did Progressive reforms meet with resistance?

MAIN IDEA

At the end of the 1800s, problems resulting from rapid industrialization, immigration, and urban growth spurred the creation of many reform movements during what is known as the Progressive Era.

KEY TERMS

Progressive Era
muckraker
injunction

TARGET READING SKILL

Identify Supporting Details Copy the chart below. As you read, fill in factors relating to the Progressive Era.

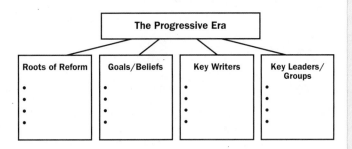

Setting the Scene

In 1906, Upton Sinclair turned the nation's stomachs. That year, the writer and journalist published *The Jungle*, a novel based on his investigations of the turn-of-the-century meatpacking industry. Besides depicting the violent accidents, horrible illnesses, and painful deaths that came to packinghouse workers themselves, Sinclair sickened the public with descriptions of how meat—and what was *called* meat—was processed on the way to their dinner tables.

Workers at a Chicago stockyard package boiled hams on dingy tables. Sinclair and others pressed for tough sanitary standards in meatpacking plants.

The main character in *The Jungle* is a naive, hard-working new immigrant from Lithuania who gratefully takes a job at a meatpacking house. Gradually, Sinclair's readers learn, as the worker does, the ugly secrets of what goes on inside the plant.

> 66 *It seemed they must have agencies all over the country, to hunt out old and crippled and diseased cattle to be canned. There were cattle which had been fed on 'whisky-malt,' the refuse [garbage] of the breweries, and had become what the men called 'steerly'— which means covered with boils. . . . It was stuff such as this that made the 'embalmed beef' that had killed several times as many United States soldiers as all the bullets of the Spaniards [in the Spanish-American War].* 99
> —Upton Sinclair, *The Jungle*, 1906

against Tammany Hall's ward bosses, settlement houses sent children out to post handbills in their neighborhoods. Low lost that election but won in 1901. Still, the Tammany Hall machine returned to power in the next election.

In some cities, however, voter support for reforms prompted machine politicians to work with reformers. Together they improved city services, established public health programs and workplace reforms, and enforced tenement codes.

New Forms of Municipal Government Like the Triangle Shirtwaist fire, other catastrophes served to bring about reforms. On September 8, 1900, a powerful hurricane in the Gulf of Mexico slammed into the city of Galveston, Texas. The storm left more than 6,000 people dead when its 120-mile-per-hour winds and surging waves pounded the unprotected city for 18 hours. To manage the huge relief and rebuilding effort needed, the city created an emergency commission of five appointed administrators to replace the mayor and aldermen. The commission worked so efficiently that Galveston permanently instituted the commission form of government, with later reforms to make it more democratic. Other cities rapidly adopted the Galveston model, adapting it to their needs.

In March 1913, Ohio's Great Miami River Basin flooded the city of Dayton, killing 360 people and causing damage of more than $100 million. In the aftermath, Dayton became the first large city to adopt a council-manager government. Typically, this system includes an elected city council, which sets laws and appoints a professional city manager to run city services.

Cities Take Over Utilities Reformers made efforts to regulate or dislodge the monopolies that provided city utilities such as water, gas, and electricity. Reform mayors Hazen S. Pingree of Detroit (1889–1897), Samuel M. Jones of Toledo (1897–1904), and Tom Johnson of Cleveland (1901–1909) worked within existing government structures to pioneer city control or ownership of utilities. By 1915, nearly two out of three cities had some city-owned utilities.

Providing Welfare Services Some reform mayors led movements for city-supported welfare services. Pingree provided public baths, parks, and a work-relief program for Detroit. Jones opened playgrounds, free kindergartens, and lodging houses for the homeless in Toledo. In his view, all people would become good citizens if social conditions were good.

VIEWING HISTORY The coastal city of Galveston, Texas, lacked a retaining wall to protect it from the powerful hurricanes that blow ashore from the Gulf of Mexico. In 1900, after a huge storm left wind and flood devastation, the city needed a new type of government to manage the relief and rebuilding effort. **Drawing Inferences** *What features or qualities would a municipal government need to handle a reconstruction job of the magnitude seen here?*

Texas

Galveston

State Reforms

Some governors and state legislators also promoted progressive reforms. Like the reform mayors, Progressives at the state level first worked to oust party bosses and give more power to citizens. Then they passed laws to increase the role of government in business regulation and social welfare.

More Power to Voters During the Progressive Era, voters gained somewhat more direct influence in lawmaking and in choosing candidates. Throughout the country, party leaders traditionally had handpicked candidates for public office. In Wisconsin, reform governor Robert M. La Follette instituted a **direct primary,** an election in which citizens vote to select nominees for upcoming elections. Other states later adopted direct primaries for state and local offices. Many states also instituted the **initiative,** a process in which citizens can put a proposed new law directly on the ballot in the next election by collecting voters' signatures on a petition. Another lawmaking reform was the **referendum,** a process that allows citizens to approve or reject a law passed by the legislature. The **recall** procedure permits voters to remove public officials from office before the next election.

In 1904, Oregon began allowing voters, rather than the state legislature, to choose their United States senators. In 1913, the Seventeenth Amendment, requiring the direct election of senators, was ratified by the states.

Reforms in the Workplace Motivated in part by the Triangle Shirtwaist fire, state reformers worked to curb workplace hazards. Some states established labor departments to provide information and dispute-resolution services to employers and employees. Other states developed workers' accident insurance and compensation systems. However, government efforts to control working conditions met legal opposition. Business owners contended that the government could not interfere with their constitutional right to make contracts with their employees. They also maintained that government workplace regulations violated their private property rights by attempting to dictate how they used their property.

The courts generally upheld these views. Reformers argued that the Constitution reserves police powers to the states, and the states could use these powers to intervene in the workplace to protect workers.

In principle, the courts acknowledged the reformers' reasoning. But in the case of *Lochner* v. *New York* (1905), the Supreme Court struck down a law setting maximum hours for bakers. The Court said that since the law had not been shown to protect public health, the law constituted an improper use of the state's police power and "an illegal interference with the rights of individuals . . . to make contracts."

The justices left open the possibility that if such a law *could* be shown to protect workers' health, it would be permissible. Reformers used this strategy in

Progressive Political Reforms

Before	Reforms	After
Party leaders choose candidates for state and local offices.	**Direct Primaries** Voters select their party's candidates.	Power moves to voters.
State legislatures choose U.S. senators.	**17th Amendment** U.S. senators are elected by popular vote.	
Only members of the state legislature can introduce bills.	**Initiative** Voters can put bills before the legislature.	
Only legislators pass laws.	**Referendum** Voters can vote on bills directly.	
Only courts or the legislature can remove corrupt officials.	**Recall** Voters can remove elected officials from office.	

INTERPRETING DIAGRAMS
This diagram shows the effects of some of the major reforms achieved by Progressives at all levels of government. **Synthesizing Information** *What type of reform do all these measures address, and why were such changes so important to Progressives?*

large number of electoral votes in presidential elections, would now be courted by candidates seeking the support of the state's women voters.

Impact of World War I The United States entered World War I in April 1917. Women across the country hastened to do their patriotic duty by volunteering for ambulance corps and for medical work and by taking on jobs left by men. Arguments of separate spheres for women and men were forgotten during wartime.

In addition, Congress adopted the Eighteenth Amendment, prohibiting the sale of liquor. As a result of this action, liquor interests no longer had reason to fight suffrage.

Victory for Suffrage

In 1919, Congress formally proposed the suffrage amendment. Its members finally succumbed to the political forces of states that had passed suffrage and to the unrelenting work of NAWSA. They also had been keenly embarrassed and disturbed by the treatment that the women of Alice Paul's Congressional Union had received in filthy jails, where some hunger strikers were force-fed. After the amendment was proposed in Congress, the ratification battle began. It would end in August, 1920, when Tennessee became the 36th state necessary to ratify the suffrage amendment.

As suffragist Carrie Chapman Catt commented when the exhausting battle of many decades was finally over, "It is doubtful that any man . . . ever realized what the suffrage struggle came to mean to women. . . . It leaves its mark on one, such a struggle." The Nineteenth Amendment marked the last major reform of the Progressive Era.

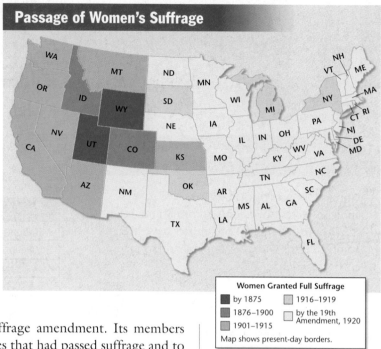

Passage of Women's Suffrage

Women Granted Full Suffrage
- ■ by 1875
- ■ 1876–1900
- ▨ 1901–1915
- ▨ 1916–1919
- ☐ by the 19th Amendment, 1920

Map shows present-day borders.

MAP SKILLS Women's suffrage was already in place in many states by the time the Nineteenth Amendment was ratified. **Analyzing Visual Information** What pattern do you see in the locations of states that did and did not pass suffrage at the state level?

Section 4 Assessment

READING COMPREHENSION

1. Describe how Anthony and Stanton worked together to lead the suffrage movement.

2. Why was the suffrage movement in need of new leadership after the turn of the century?

3. How did the **National American Woman Suffrage Association** and the **Congressional Union** differ in their tactics?

4. (a) How did passage of the Nineteenth Amendment come about? (b) Why did the battle take so long?

CRITICAL THINKING AND WRITING

5. **Drawing Inferences** How do you think the state-by-state efforts of suffragists affected the effort to win a constitutional amendment on suffrage?

6. **Writing an Opinion** Identify the goals, strategies, and tactics of two of the suffrage leaders described in this section. Which leader or group do you think was most effective? Why? Write a brief paragraph expressing your opinion.

Go Online
PHSchool.com

For: An activity on the suffrage movement
Visit: PHSchool.com
Web Code: mrd-6184

creating a CHAPTER SUMMARY

Copy the chart (right) on a piece of paper and complete it by adding information about the Progressive Era. Some entries have been completed for you as examples. Add as many entries as you can.

For additional review and enrichment activities, see the interactive version of *America: Pathways to the Present*, available on the Web and on CD-ROM.

Progressive Era Reforms		
Municipal Level	**State Level**	**Federal Level**
Regulating utilities	.	Pure Food and Drug Act

★ Reviewing Key Terms

For each of the terms below, write a sentence explaining how it relates to the Progressive reforms.

1. Progressive Era
2. muckraker
3. injunction
4. municipal
5. holding company
6. conservationist
7. New Nationalism
8. Bull Moose Party
9. Federal Reserve System
10. civil disobedience

★ Reviewing Main Ideas

11. What people and ideas contributed to the rise of progressivism? (Section 1)

12. What were the typical methods of Progressive reformers? (Section 1)

13. Summarize progressive reforms at the municipal and state levels. (Section 2)

14. Describe progressive reforms at the national level. (Section 2)

15. Why did TR have to proceed with caution on pushing for reforms in his first term? (Section 2)

16. What were the main successes and failures of Taft's presidency? (Section 3)

17. What factors contributed to the election of Wilson in 1912? (Section 3)

18. Why did progressivism decline? (Section 3)

19. What two main approaches did women's organizations take to win suffrage? (Section 4)

20. Choose two leaders of the suffrage movement and describe their contributions to the cause. (Section 4)

★ Critical Thinking

21. **Drawing Conclusions** In what ways did reform movements benefit from the contributions of both men and women? Give examples.

22. **Drawing Inferences** Why do you think reformers at the municipal and state levels began by passing voting reforms and tackling corruption?

23. **Synthesizing Information** How did Roosevelt use the "bully pulpit," and how did his style shape the modern presidency?

24. **Making Comparisons** How did TR, Taft, and Wilson compare in their approaches to reform?

25. **Identifying Central Issues** What was the Clayton Antitrust Act, and why was it important to progressive reformers and labor leaders?

26. **Recognizing Cause and Effect** What kinds of reforms contributed to an increase in the size and role of government?

27. **Analyzing Information** What shift in public attitudes was necessary for social welfare programs to gain support and passage?

★ Standardized Test Prep

Analyzing Political Cartoons ▶

28. Examine this 1904 cartoon on the right. What does the octopus represent?

    A Monopolies

    B Businessmen

    C the Standard Oil Company

    D government

29. Why is the octopus pictured on a globe?

30. (a) What overall point is the cartoonist trying to make? (b) Why was an octopus such a good choice for making this point?

Analyzing Primary Sources

Read the quotation from Jane Addams on page 386, and answer the questions that follow.

31. In comparing the lives of rural and urban women, Addams' main purpose was to point out

    A the problems that united women throughout the country.

    B their differing lifestyles and roles in American society.

    C the ways in which urban living presented new problems for women.

    D the reasons that rural children were healthier.

32. In this quotation, Addams made the argument for

    F better health services for children.

    G more and better government services in cities, to help families survive.

    H the need for garbage collection in rural areas, to prevent the spread of disease.

    I programs to get women and children out of tenement houses.

Test-Taking Tip

To answer Question 32, note that Addams states that "if the garbage is not properly collected and destroyed," disease will result.

Applying the Chapter Skill

Testing Conclusions Based on the results of the election of 1912, is it reasonable to conclude that most Americans favored some amount of progressive reform? Explain.

For: Chapter 11 Self-Test
Visit: PHSchool.com
Web Code: mra-6185

American Pathways
HISTORY

Fighting for Freedom and Democracy

Throughout the nation's history, Americans have stepped forward to risk their lives to protect freedom and democracy. More than 40 million Americans have fought in the nation's wars both at home and abroad, and more than one million have given their lives to preserve their country's cherished ideals.

1 From Colonies to Nation

1565–1783   As Europeans established a presence in North America, conflicts occurred among the competing nations as well as with Native Americans. Ultimately, the colonists' struggle to gain independence from Britain resulted in the creation of a new country built on the foundations of freedom, equality, and self-government.

Emanuel Gottlieb Leutze's *George Washington Crossing the Delaware* (left)

2 The New Nation Asserts Its Authority

1812–1848   In the first half of the nineteenth century, the United States asserted its sovereignty during the War of 1812 and the Mexican-American War, as well as with the proclamation of the Monroe Doctrine.

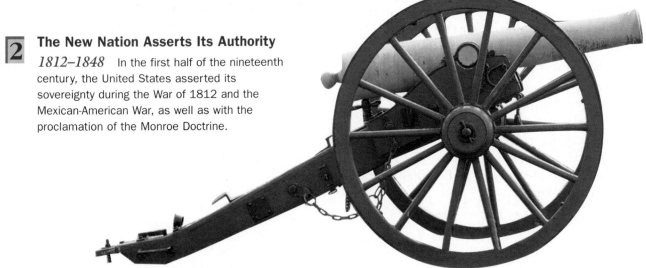

3 Civil War and Reunion

1861–1890   From 1861 to 1865, the Civil War split the nation in two as armies from the North and the South battled over the issues of states' rights and slavery. Although the Union was restored, conflicts developed over the status of freed African Americans during the Reconstruction period. In the West, Native Americans continued to resist the expansion of the United States.

A cannon used in the Battle of Gettysburg (above)

Allied troops fighting in the trenches during World War I (left)

 Becoming a World Power and World War I

1890–1918 As a result of the industrial boom at the turn of the century, the United States expanded its foreign trade. When German submarines attacked neutral American merchant ships, the United States entered World War I and helped the French and English defeat the Germans. In the words of President Wilson, Americans fought "to make the world safe for democracy."

 Isolationism

1920–1940 The horrors of World War I convinced many Americans that the country should end foreign entanglements and curtail military expenditures.

 World War II and the Cold War

1941–1991 Tensions between the United States and the Soviet Union developed at the end of World War II and lasted for 50 years until the collapse of the Soviet Union in 1991. Throughout that time, the goal of U.S. foreign policy was to prevent the spread of communism.

American troops landing in Normandy, France, on D-Day, June 6, 1944 (above)

 Regional Conflicts and Terrorism

1991–Present In the post–Cold War period, the United States played a role in resolving many regional ethnic conflicts. The nation also struggled to preserve its freedoms in the face of terrorism.

Firemen raise an American flag amid the rubble of the World Trade Center following the terrorist attacks on New York and the Pentagon, on September 11, 2001 (above).

Continuity and Change

1. What factors contributed to the country's relative isolationism between the two World Wars?
2. Explain how the Cold War began and ended.

For: A study guide on U.S. foreign policy
Visit: PHSchool.com
Web Code: mrd-6189

The World War I Era

(1914–1920)

Assassination of Archduke
Francis Ferdinand

The New York Times. EXTRA 5:30 A.M.

LUSITANIA SUNK BY A SUBMARINE, PROBABLY 1,260 DEAD;
TWICE TORPEDOED OFF IRISH COAST; SINKS IN 15 MINUTES;
CAPT. TURNER SAVED, FROHMAN AND VANDERBILT MISSING;
WASHINGTON BELIEVES THAT A GRAVE CRISIS IS AT HAND

American Events

1914
President Wilson announces American neutrality in the war.

1915
The sinking of the *Lusitania* angers Americans.

1916
With the Sussex pledge, Germany promises the United States that U-boats will warn ships before attacking.

Presidential Terms: Woodrow Wilson 1913–1921

1912   **1914**   **1916**

World Events

Assassination of Archduke Francis Ferdinand triggers World War I.
1914

Poison gas is first used against the Allies.
1915

Millions of British, French, and German soldiers die in failed offensives at Verdun and the Somme River.
1916

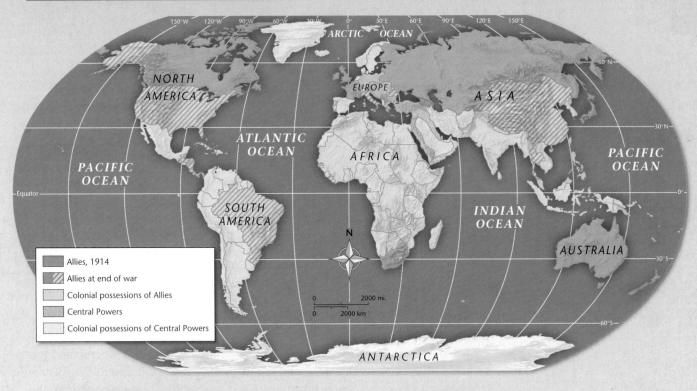

Allies, 1914
Allies at end of war
Colonial possessions of Allies
Central Powers
Colonial possessions of Central Powers

Allied soldiers on the Western Front

Department of Labor poster

1917

Germany ends Sussex pledge and resumes undeclared submarine warfare. Wilson declares war and sends the first units of the AEF to France under General Pershing.

1918

American troops fight at Belleau Wood, Château-Thierry, and the Argonne Forest.

1919

United States Senate rejects the Treaty of Versailles and membership in the League of Nations as American soldiers return from Europe.

Warren G. Harding
1921–1923

1918   **1920**   **1922**

Revolutions in Russia overthrow the czar and bring the Bolsheviks to power.

Central Powers agree to a truce with the Allies.

Germany signs the Treaty of Versailles.

1917   **1918**   **1919**

READING FOCUS

- What were the main causes of World War I?
- How did the conflict expand to draw in much of Europe?
- In what ways did the United States respond to the war in Europe?

MAIN IDEA

As World War I began and then spread to much of Europe, the United States tried to remain neutral as long as possible.

KEY TERMS

militarism
mobilization
Central Powers
Allies
stalemate
propaganda

TARGET READING SKILL

Identify Cause and Effect As you read, complete the following cause-and-effect diagram that shows why World War I began.

CAUSES
• Assassination of Archduke Francis Ferdinand in Sarajevo
• Competition for colonies in Africa, Asia, and the Pacific
•
•

⬇

WORLD WAR I

Setting the Scene On June 28, 1914, Archduke Francis Ferdinand and his wife made a state visit to Sarajevo, the capital of Bosnia. Bosnia was a new province within the Austro-Hungarian Empire, and Francis Ferdinand was heir to the empire's throne. Although many Bosnians were upset with Austro-Hungarian rule, Francis Ferdinand decided to disregard growing tensions and visit his government's soldiers in Sarajevo.

The morning of his visit, a bomb thrown by a terrorist bounced off the archduke's car and exploded, injuring two officers in another car. Unfazed, Francis Ferdinand attended a state ceremony and then rode to the hospital to see the wounded officers. Gavrilo Princip, a second terrorist, just 19 years old, happened to spot the car as it slowly moved down a narrow street. One of Princip's friends saw what happened next:

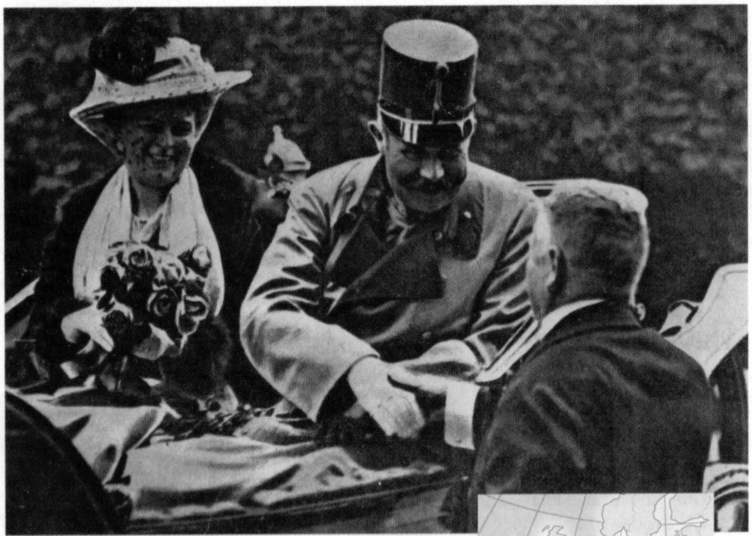

❝ As the car came abreast he stepped forward from the curb, drew his automatic pistol from his coat and fired two shots. The first struck the wife of the Archduke, the Archduchess Sofia, in the abdomen. . . . She died instantly. The second bullet struck the Archduke close to the heart. He uttered only one word; 'Sofia'—a call to his stricken wife. Then his head fell back and he collapsed. He died almost instantly. ❞
—Borijove Jevtic

VIEWING HISTORY The assassination of Archduke Francis Ferdinand and his wife Sofia in Sarajevo triggered a series of events that led to war. **Recognizing Cause and Effect** Which of the four causes of World War I contributed most directly to the murder in Sarajevo?

Princip, a Serbian nationalist, believed that Bosnia should be part of neighboring Serbia, not Austria-Hungary. Little did he know that his act of terrorism in Sarajevo would have grave consequences.

Causes of World War I

The assassination of Archduke Francis Ferdinand ignited what was then called the Great War, later known as World War I. However, the main causes of the war existed well before 1914. Those causes included imperialism, militarism, nationalism, and a tangled system of alliances.

Imperialism   A great scramble for colonies took place in the late 1800s. European powers rushed to claim the remaining uncolonized areas of the world, particularly in Africa, Asia, and the Pacific. Japan joined the roster of colonial powers when it won the Sino-Japanese War in 1895 and moved to acquire Korea, Taiwan, and territory on China's mainland.

By 1910, the most desirable colonies had been taken. Competition for the lands that remained led to conflict among the powers of Europe. Germany's leaders envied Britain and France—two countries that had begun colonizing early and controlled large, resource-rich empires. Leaders in Germany and other countries recognized that they could only expand in Africa by taking land away from other colonizers.

READING CHECK
How did competition for colonies help lead to war?

Militarism   By the early 1900s in Europe, diplomacy had taken a back seat to **militarism.** This policy involved aggressively building up a nation's armed forces in preparation for war and giving the military more authority over the government and foreign policy. The great powers of Europe—Austria-Hungary, France, Germany, Great Britain, and Russia—all spent large sums of money on new weapons and warships for expanding their armed forces. Their endless planning for war made war much more likely.

Nationalism   Two kinds of nationalism contributed to World War I. The first was the tendency for countries such as the great powers to act in their own

The War in Europe, 1914–1918

MAP SKILLS Before the war, Europe was a land of empires and alliances. When Austria-Hungary declared war on Serbia, much of the continent was drawn into the conflict. **Location** *Based on this map, which side, if any, had a geographical advantage in the war? Explain.*

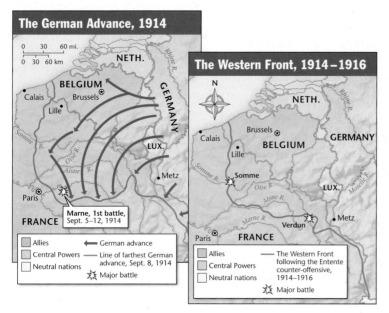

The German Advance, 1914

0   30   60 mi.
0   30   60 km

NETH.
BELGIUM
Calais
Brussels
Lille
GERMANY
Rhine R.
LUX.
Somme R.
Oise R.
Aisne R.
Metz
Paris
Marne, 1st battle,
Sept. 5–12, 1914
FRANCE

Allies
Central Powers
Neutral nations
German advance
Line of farthest German
advance, Sept. 8, 1914
Major battle

The Western Front, 1914–1916

N
NETH.
Calais
Brussels
BELGIUM
GERMANY
Rhine R.
Lille
Somme R.
Somme
Oise R.
LUX.
Moselle R.
Aisne R.
Marne R.
Verdun
Metz
Paris
FRANCE

Allies
Central Powers
Neutral nations
The Western Front
following the Entente
counter-offensive,
1914–1916
Major battle

MAP SKILLS German troops advanced deep into French territory before British and French armies stopped them at the Battle of the Marne. **Movement** *Why did the battle lines change little after 1914?*

As the need for soldiers increased, the British government used powerful national symbols to draw young people into Britain's all-volunteer army.

national interest. When such action went against the national interest of another nation, warfare could result.

One source of trouble was the German region of Alsace-Lorraine, a strip of land along Germany's border with France. The French people considered the return of Alsace-Lorraine, which had been conquered by Germany in 1871, a matter of national pride. German leaders valued the region's strong defenses and historic ties to Germany. These conflicting goals soured relations between France and Germany.

The second kind of nationalism occurred in countries with diverse ethnic populations, particularly those in central and eastern Europe. In Austria-Hungary, Hungarians and German-speaking Austrians governed millions of Czechs, Slovaks, Poles, and others who sought self-government. The empire also included Italians, Romanians, and Serbs who wished to join their compatriots in neighboring lands. Poles in Russia, Germany, and Austria-Hungary wanted to reunite and build an independent Poland. The longing of an ethnic minority for independence often led to violence.

As the most powerful Slavic country, Russia protected Slavs in Serbia and those under Austro-Hungarian rule. Russia's strong ties to the Serbs would play an important role in expanding the conflict beyond Serbia in 1914.

Alliances A complicated system of alliances developed among the nations of Europe during the late nineteenth century. Designed to bolster each nation's security, the alliances bound the great powers to come to each other's aid in the event of attack. Germany and Austria-Hungary were linked by treaty, as were Russia and France. Great Britain and France shared a looser alliance called the Entente Cordiale, or simply Entente. In 1914, this fragile balance of power, which had kept the peace for decades, led its creators into war.

The Conflict Expands

Bosnia was the focus of a nationalist dispute between Austria-Hungary, which had recently annexed Bosnia, and Serbia, which shared a common national identity with one of Bosnia's three major ethnic groups. Austria-Hungary blamed Serbia for the assassination. On July 23, Austria-Hungary demanded that Serbia cease its support for terrorism in Bosnia within two days or risk war. Unsatisfied with Serbia's response, Austria-Hungary declared war on July 28.

This declaration of war set off a chain reaction that rapidly worked its way through Europe's complex web of alliances. On July 29, Russia, as Serbia's protector, began **mobilization**—the readying of troops for war. Germany, Austria-Hungary's chief ally, demanded that Russia stop mobilizing. Russia refused. At that point, Russia's ally, France, began to ready its troops, as did Germany.

On August 1, Germany declared war on Russia. Germany's military leaders had long prepared for this day. Their country lay between France to the west and Russia to the east. To avoid fighting both the French and Russian armies at the same time, Germany had developed a first-strike strategy. Known as the Schlieffen Plan, it called for a quick sweep through France to knock the French out of the war. Then, the German army would turn east and defeat Russia.

The United States Declares War

Setting the Scene   The fighting in Europe continued with no end in sight. In October 1916, *The New York Times* explained why American voters wanted a leader who would keep the United States out of war:

> 66 *The voters . . . have seen lives lost, property ruined, privations suffered, on a greater scale than the world had ever known, and they have seen existence become harder, not only for the men who are fighting, but for all the inhabitants of the stricken countries. They have seen nation after nation drawn in, until the roll of the original combatants has been doubled.* 99

Many Americans hoped that the United States would not be the next country to be drawn in. Nevertheless, friction between the United States and Germany increased from 1914 to 1917. The preparedness movement continued to gain support in the United States, and the pressure to join in the war intensified. Ultimately, actions by the Central Powers pushed Congress and the President into entering the war on the side of the Allies.

German Submarine Warfare

One action that provoked angry calls for war in the United States was the German use of submarine warfare. This tactic was effective militarily, but it cost the Germans dearly in terms of American public opinion.

The German **U-boat,** short for *Unterseeboot,* or submarine, was a terrifying new weapon that changed the rules of naval warfare. Germany deployed them to prevent munitions and food from reaching Britain's ports. At first, U-boats rose to the surface to allow the crew of merchant ships to abandon ship before their ship was attacked. After Britain armed merchant ships to fire on exposed U-boats, Germany abandoned the old rules and permitted U-boats to remain hidden and fire on merchant ships without warning.

The U-boat enabled Germany to break a stalemate at sea. In the years leading up to the war, Britain and Germany competed to build the largest, strongest

This German poster urged U-boats on their mission. The translation is "U-boats: Go out!"

VIEWING HISTORY Germany warned travelers—including passengers on the *Lusitania*—to stay out of the war zone (top, left). Nevertheless, the sinking of the *Lusitania* and the deaths of 1,200 passengers shocked Americans. Germany did not show much remorse and even designed this medal (above) to commemorate the attack. **Drawing Inferences** *How strongly did Wilson respond to the sinking of the* Lusitania?

navy in Europe. When war came, Germany chose not to risk the loss of its ships and kept all but the U-boats in port.

The German High Seas Fleet did make one attempt to enter the North Sea and confront the British fleet in 1916. The British encountered the Germans north of Denmark, where at the ensuing Battle of Jutland both fleets suffered heavy losses. Neither Britain nor Germany could claim victory, and the German fleet returned to port after the battle. This stalemate meant that the U-boat was the only tool the Germans had to fight the British blockade and to target Allied shipping and transport.

Passenger and merchant ships had no defense against the submarine, which could go undetected nearly anywhere in the ocean. Only gradually did the British develop devices called hydrophones that could detect the sound of a submarine underwater. Although Americans generally accepted Britain's blockade of Germany, the German efforts to blockade Britain with submarine attacks struck many as uncivilized.

The British encouraged such anti-German feelings. Shortly after the war began, the British cut the transatlantic cable connecting Germany and the United States. All news of the European front henceforth flowed through London. The pro-Allied bias of news reports helped shape the opinion of the people in the United States in favor of punishing Germany for its use of submarines against Britain.

American public opinion of the Germans declined further on May 7, 1915, when a U-boat sighted the *Lusitania*, a British passenger liner, in the Irish Sea. Suspecting correctly that the ship carried weapons for the Allies, the U-boat fired on the liner. Eighteen minutes later, the *Lusitania* disappeared beneath the waves along with almost 1,200 passengers. Included among the dead were 128 Americans, who had boarded the *Lusitania* in spite of German warnings to stay off British ships. Nevertheless, the American press wildly denounced what they called Germany's act of "barbarism."

Wilson urged patience. He demanded that Germany stop its submarine warfare and make payments to the victims' families. Germany's reply that the *Lusitania* carried small arms and ammunition did not quiet American anger. Wilson sent a second, stronger note of protest. In response, Germany promised to stop sinking passenger ships without warning, as long as the ship's crew offered no resistance to German search or seizure.

Still, U-boats continued to torpedo Allied ships. On March 24, 1916, a German submarine torpedoed the *Sussex*, a French passenger steamship. The attack killed or injured 80 passengers, including two Americans. The United States threatened to cut diplomatic ties to Germany. In what came to be called the **Sussex pledge,** the German government again promised that U-boats would warn ships before attacking.

The series of demands and broken promises that led up to the Sussex pledge frustrated Wilson. He could not threaten force without entering the war. During this time, however, Wilson did embrace the concept of preparedness. He also authorized bankers to make a huge loan to the Allies. American neutrality was beginning to weaken.

Moving Toward War

In the presidential election of 1916, Wilson ran for reelection on the slogan "He kept us out of war." The Republicans, who nominated Supreme Court Justice Charles Evans Hughes, criticized Wilson for not taking a stronger stand against Germany. American voters gave Wilson a narrow victory.

Germany soon tested Wilson's patience. On January 31, 1917, Germany informed the United States that it would end the Sussex pledge and resume unrestricted submarine warfare the following day. German strategists knew that it might bring the United States into the war. But they gambled that they could defeat Britain and win the war in France before American entry could make a difference.

Germany's action dashed Wilson's hope of maintaining freedom of the seas—and American neutrality. On February 3, the United States broke off diplomatic relations with Germany. A few weeks later, Wilson asked Congress for permission to arm American merchant ships.

The Zimmermann Note Despite the announcement, the German Navy avoided attacking American ships in February. As a result, the American public continued to hope for peace. In the Senate, a group of antiwar senators tried to prevent a vote on Wilson's initiative to arm ships. While these senators stalled the initiative, the British revealed the contents of an intercepted German telegram. In the note, Arthur Zimmermann, Germany's foreign secretary, made a secret offer to Mexico. If Mexico declared war on the United States, he wrote, Germany would reward it with American land in the Southwest.

> ❝ We shall endeavor to keep the United States neutral. In the event of this not succeeding, we make Mexico a proposal of alliance. . . : Make war together, make peace together, . . . and . . . Mexico is to reconquer the lost territory in Texas, New Mexico, and Arizona. ❞
>
> —Arthur Zimmermann

READING CHECK
Why did Germany resort to submarine warfare?

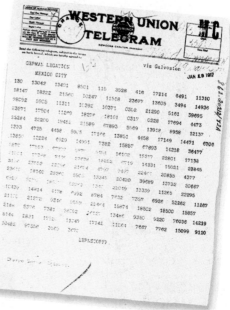

VIEWING HISTORY The Zimmermann note, shown here in its original code, infuriated many Americans with its promise to give American land to Mexico.
Recognizing Cause and Effect *Why did the Zimmermann note threaten Americans more directly than German submarine attacks?*

The Price of Pacifism One of the fifty votes against the House war resolution came from Montana's Representative Jeannette Rankin, the first woman elected to Congress. Elected only a few months earlier, she said, "I want to stand by my country, but I cannot vote for war." Rankin faced a strong backlash over her vote. The Republican Party refused to nominate her for the Senate in 1918. She ran as an independent candidate but lost.

Rankin returned to Congress in 1941. When Japan bombed Pearl Harbor that December and the President asked Congress for a declaration of war, Rankin voted no once again.

Neither Wilson nor Mexico took the **Zimmermann note** seriously. Already divided by civil war, Mexico could not have launched a successful invasion of the United States. The telegram's release, however, scored another public relations victory for Great Britain. The United States edged closer to war.

Revolution in Russia By early 1917, Russia already had suffered enormous casualties in the war: more than 1.5 million killed, roughly 2.5 million taken prisoner, and millions more wounded. Austro-Hungarian and German forces had advanced deep into Russian territory. Poorly fed and miserably equipped, the Russians fell back farther and farther into their country's interior.

Then, in March 1917, Czar Nicholas II of Russia was forced to give up the throne to a republican government. The czar had been an **autocrat**—a ruler with unlimited power. The **Russian Revolution** cheered the pro-war faction in the United States. Concern over being allied with an autocrat had slowed the nation's move toward entering the war. The fall of the czar removed a last stumbling block to joining the Allies.

The War Resolution Between March 16 and March 18, Germany sank the United States ships *City of Memphis, Illinois,* and *Vigilancia.* Wilson's patience had run out. On March 20, the President's Cabinet voted unanimously for war. Casting the issue in idealistic terms, Wilson told Congress on April 2 that "the world must be made safe for democracy." He stated:

> ❝ It is a fearful thing to lead this great peaceful people into war, the most terrible and disastrous of all wars, civilization itself seeming to be in the balance. But the right is more precious than peace. ❞
>
> —Woodrow Wilson

Members of Congress, ambassadors, and Supreme Court justices stood up and cheered the President's call to war. A war resolution passed 82 to 6 in the Senate and 373 to 50 in the House. On April 6, 1917, the President signed it.

Section 2 Assessment

READING COMPREHENSION

1. Why did Germany's use of **U-boats** lead to conflict with the United States?

2. (a) How did the **Sussex pledge** affect relations between the United States and Germany? (b) Why did Germany end the pledge?

3. Why did the **Zimmermann note** enrage Americans?

CRITICAL THINKING AND WRITING

4. Identifying Alternatives Consider the causes that brought the United States into World War I. (a) What would the United States have had to do to avoid the conflict altogether? (b) Why did the United States not take such steps?

5. Writing to Inform Write a paragraph explaining why President Wilson asked Congress to arm American merchant ships.

For: An activity on women's contributions to the war effort
Visit: PHSchool.com
Web Code: mrd-6192

Americans on the European Front

READING FOCUS

- How did the United States prepare to fight in World War I?

- In what ways did American troops help turn the tide of war?

- What were conditions like in Europe and in the United States at the end of the war?

MAIN IDEA

American troops helped the Allies defeat the Central Powers in World War I.

KEY TERMS

Selective Service Act
American Expeditionary
  Force (AEF)
convoy
zeppelin
armistice
genocide

TARGET READING SKILL

Identify Sequence Copy this flowchart. As you read, fill in the boxes with significant events, beginning with the declaration of war by the United States and ending with the Allied victory. The first box has been completed to help you get started.

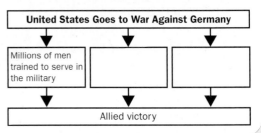

United States Goes to War Against Germany		
Millions of men trained to serve in the military		

Allied victory

Setting the Scene

Woodrow Wilson brought the United States into war with the support of Congress and most of the country. But in April 1917, despite the success of the preparedness movement, the United States was far from ready to send an army to the European front. With a little more than 100,000 men in uniform, the United States army was outranked in size by the armies of 16 other countries. The country's 15,500 marines were far from Europe, patrolling several Central American countries and American possessions in the Pacific. The National Guard, 132,000 strong, needed training. The United States was simply not ready for war.

The Allies desperately needed replacement troops. In June, President Wilson agreed to send a small force to Europe under the command of General John J. Pershing. A veteran of the Spanish-American War, the general had also taught for a time at West Point. Pershing would need all his experience and skills to lead the American forces against a determined German army.

Preparing for War

Instead of a full-sized army, a cautious Congress sent the Allies naval support, supplies, arms, and $3 billion in loans. The token force of 14,500 men led by General Pershing served mainly to boost Allied morale. After landing in France, Pershing realized that he needed more troops. He recommended that the army number 1 million men by 1918 and 3 million the following year.

Draftees and Volunteers Congress passed a **Selective Service Act** in May 1917, authorizing a draft of young men for military service. During the Civil War, the draft had sparked riots. Now, however, the general feeling that this was the "war to end all wars" led to wide acceptance of the draft. By November 1918, more than 24 million men had registered for the draft. From those, a lottery picked 3 million draftees to serve in the war. Volunteers and National Guardsmen made up the remainder of what was called the **American Expeditionary Force (AEF).**

VIEWING HISTORY James Montgomery Flagg's poster called on Americans to join the military. **Drawing Inferences** *Why do you think this poster was effective?*

VIEWING HISTORY New soldiers learn how to attack with bayonets at a training camp in the United States. **Recognizing Cause and Effect** *Why was training important to the war effort?*

Among the Americans who served their country were thousands of women. Some 11,000 women volunteered to serve in uniform as nurses, drivers, and clerks. Another 14,000 women served abroad, as civilians working for the government or for private agencies.

Training for War The military's next challenge was to transform draftees into soldiers who were armed and ready to fight. In September, draftees began to arrive at new and expanded training camps around the country. At these camps, they learned how to use a bayonet and a rifle, dig a trench, put on a gas mask, and throw a grenade. American and British lecturers told them about German crimes in Belgium and the strategies of trench warfare.

The military planned to give new soldiers several months of training in the United States and France before shipping them off to battle. In reality, soldiers did not always receive that much training. The task of building an army of millions and transporting it to France in time to be of help meant that training would sometimes be cut short.

The Convoy System In addition to building a fighting force, the War Department had to worry about transporting its troops overseas safely. In April 1917 alone, German U-boats had sunk more than 400 Allied and neutral ships.

Starting in May 1917, all merchant and troop ships traveled in a **convoy.** A convoy consisted of a group of unarmed ships surrounded by a ring of destroyers, torpedo boats, and other armed naval vessels equipped with hydrophones to track and destroy submarines. Between April and December 1917, merchant marine losses dropped by half.

The convoy system was remarkably successful in carrying American troops to Europe. Despite several scares, U-boats did not sink a single United States troopship traveling to Europe. A relatively small number of Americans lost their lives on the return trip.

American Soldiers in Europe From the time the AEF arrived in France in June 1917, Pershing kept American troops independent of the Allied armies. In Pershing's view, the Allies had become too accustomed to defensive action. He wanted to save his men's strength for offensive moves.

American troops surprised the British and French soldiers on the front lines with their strength, good health, and energy. They resembled the European soldiers who had gone to war in 1914, not the exhausted forces that survived after several years of fighting. By 1918, European armies could only recruit new soldiers among much older men, boys turning 18, and wounded soldiers returning from the hospital.

Members of the American Expeditionary Force were called doughboys, although no one is sure why. The nickname had been in use for years, but it stuck with World War I soldiers. The name could have come from the white adobe dust that stuck to the boots of soldiers during the Mexican War. On the other hand, Civil War soldiers might have picked up the nickname from their uniform buttons, which looked like flour dumplings, or from the white flour they used to keep their belts white.

Focus on
CITIZENSHIP

Conscientious Objectors Some men refused to fight when they were drafted. Most of these men belonged to religious groups that opposed war, such as the Quakers. They were known as "conscientious objectors" because they objected to fighting as a matter of conscience. Most conscientious objectors were allowed to serve in a noncombatant (nonfighting) position. Sometimes they were resented by other soldiers. General Leonard Wood called conscientious objectors "enemies of the Republic, fakers and active agents of the enemy."

The more than 300,000 African Americans who volunteered or were drafted served in segregated units. Most black soldiers never saw combat, though many fought with distinction and nearly 4,000 died or were wounded. The marines refused to accept African Americans altogether, and the navy used them for menial tasks only. The army, too, used African Americans mostly for manual labor.

These assignments distressed many African Americans. The 369th Infantry Regiment, which came to be known as the Harlem Hell Fighters, was especially eager to fight. Its members persuaded their white officers to loan the regiment to the French, who integrated the regiment into the French army. Because of their distinguished service, the entire regiment received France's highest combat medal, the Croix de Guerre.

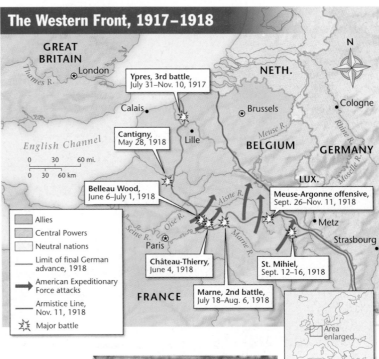

The Western Front, 1917–1918

GREAT BRITAIN

London

Thames R.

Calais

English Channel

0   30   60 mi.

0   30   60 km

NETH.

Brussels

Cologne

Ypres, 3rd battle,
July 31–Nov. 10, 1917

Cantigny,
May 28, 1918

Lille

Meuse R.

BELGIUM

GERMANY

Rhine R.

Moselle R.

LUX.

Belleau Wood,
June 6–July 1, 1918

Meuse-Argonne offensive,
Sept. 26–Nov. 11, 1918

Metz

Aisne R.

Strasbourg

Allies

Central Powers

Neutral nations

Limit of final German advance, 1918

American Expeditionary Force attacks

Armistice Line, Nov. 11, 1918

Major battle

Seine R.

Oise R.

Marne R.

Paris

Château-Thierry,
June 4, 1918

St. Mihiel,
Sept. 12–16, 1918

FRANCE

Marne, 2nd battle,
July 18–Aug. 6, 1918

Area enlarged

N

Turning the Tide of War

As American involvement in the war expanded, events in Russia shook the alliance. In November 1917, followers of Vladimir Lenin, called Bolsheviks, violently overthrew Russia's republican government. Until that spring, Lenin had been living in Switzerland. He had promised to make peace with Germany if he successfully won control of his native land, and for that reason Germany helped arrange his return to Russia.

Lenin signed a truce with Germany in December and a final peace treaty on March 3, 1918. Germany won vast territories in western Russia that included much of the country's industry and richest farmland. More important, Russia's exit from the war freed the Germans from the two-front war they had been forced to fight. Germany sent hundreds of thousands of troops west for one final offensive before American troops could reinforce the British and French armies in large numbers.

German forces attacked British lines on March 21, 1918. For the first time since 1914, they successfully broke through the trenches and advanced deep into Allied territory. Their aim was to split British troops in northern France from French armies to the east, and eventually to capture Paris. From March through May 1918, German forces turned all their energies toward pounding the French and British lines. By the end of May, they were only about 50 miles from Paris.

Americans Save Paris American forces came to the rescue. General Pershing dispatched troops to the front to turn back the German offensive. American troops attacked and recaptured the village of Cantigny on May 28. One week later, soldiers from the Marine Corps and the army stopped German attacks at Belleau Wood and Château-Thierry, east of Paris. Marching out from Paris, the men received this word from their leader, Brigadier General James G. Harbord: "We dig no trenches to fall back on. The Marines will hold where they stand." At the battle of Château-Thierry, they did just that.

MAP SKILLS After the final German offensive faltered, American troops helped the British and French push the Germans back across land Germany had held since the start of the war. General Pershing (above, center) directed American forces in Europe. **Place** In what region of France did American troops have the greatest impact?

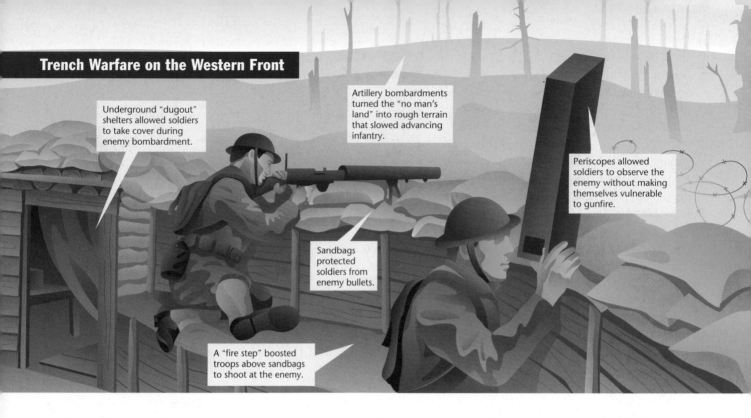

Trench Warfare on the Western Front

Underground "dugout" shelters allowed soldiers to take cover during enemy bombardment.

Artillery bombardments turned the "no man's land" into rough terrain that slowed advancing infantry.

Periscopes allowed soldiers to observe the enemy without making themselves vulnerable to gunfire.

Sandbags protected soldiers from enemy bullets.

A "fire step" boosted troops above sandbags to shoot at the enemy.

INTERPRETING DIAGRAMS Protected by rows of barbed wire, sandbags, and armed soldiers, trenches were very difficult to capture. Neither side could advance on the Western Front without losing thousands of men in the attack.
Drawing Inferences *How did tanks overcome the obstacles of barbed wire, sandbags, and enemy guns?*

READING CHECK

How did American soldiers contribute to the Allied counterattack?

At a loss of over half of their troops, they helped the French save Paris, blunted the edge of the German advance, and began to turn the tide of the war.

In mid-July, the Germans launched a massive attack on French positions on the river Marne. The French were joined by 28,000 American troops in a counter-attack that forced the Germans back across the river and into retreat. The Second Battle of the Marne ended any German hopes for victory.

Allied Counterattack After turning back the Germans outside Paris, the Allies took heart. About 250,000 new American soldiers were arriving in France each month, and thousands more were ready to leave training camps in France for the front line.

Using a new weapon, the tank, which could cross trenches and roll through barbed wire, the Allies began to break the German lines. On August 8, at the battle of Amiens, the Allied armies stopped the German advance in the north and recaptured Germany's gains from earlier in the year. General von Ludendorff, sensing the end was near, called it the "black day of the German army." He advised Kaiser Wilhelm to seek a peace settlement. The Allies, however, insisted on total surrender before peace talks.

In September, some 500,000 American troops, assisted by 100,000 French soldiers, began to hit the final German strongholds. In the battle of St. Mihiel, the first major military effort entirely in American hands, General Pershing and his troops ousted the Germans from a long-held position. The final Allied assault, the Meuse-Argonne Offensive, began on September 26, 1918. Over a million AEF troops began the drive to expel the Germans from France and to cut their supply lines. Soon after, the German army was in full retreat from the Argonne Forest and the region of the Meuse river.

War in the Air The Americans entered the war with only 55 planes, all too primitive to use in war. The United States quickly manufactured hundreds of planes to match the technology used by the Allies. Very different from modern aircraft, World War I planes were built from wooden frames covered with cloth. The pilot, and sometimes a copilot, sat in an open-air cockpit.

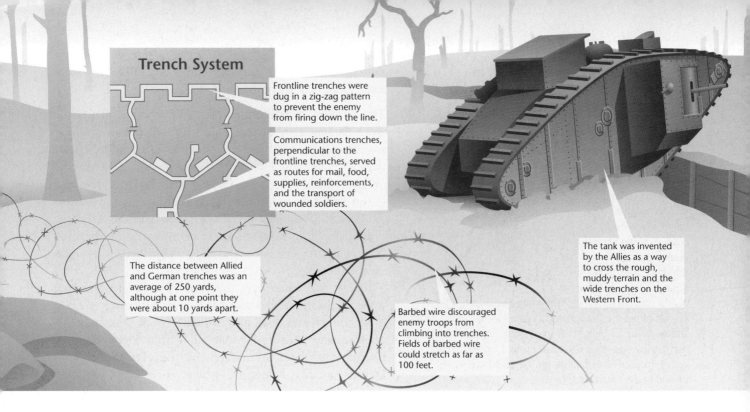

Trench System

Frontline trenches were dug in a zig-zag pattern to prevent the enemy from firing down the line.

Communications trenches, perpendicular to the frontline trenches, served as routes for mail, food, supplies, reinforcements, and the transport of wounded soldiers.

The distance between Allied and German trenches was an average of 250 yards, although at one point they were about 10 yards apart.

Barbed wire discouraged enemy troops from climbing into trenches. Fields of barbed wire could stretch as far as 100 feet.

The tank was invented by the Allies as a way to cross the rough, muddy terrain and the wide trenches on the Western Front.

Aircraft were first used to scout enemy positions, but soon flyers engaged each other in dogfights with pistols and later with machine guns. Each side had its "aces," such as the American Captain Eddie Rickenbacker, who downed 26 enemy fighters. Pilots also shot down hot-air balloons that were used for observation, and fired on individual soldiers on the ground. German **zeppelins,** or floating airships, and German bombers launched more than 100 raids on London, killing almost 1,500 civilians.

The airplane took on a new role in the 1918 offensive. American Colonel Billy Mitchell organized a fleet of more than 1,400 planes to drop bombs on enemy positions and on the railroads that carried supplies to the front. Bombing was not very effective at destroying targets, but frequent bombing raids frightened and confused enemy soldiers. Bombing raids would become a devastating weapon in the future.

Ending the War

The Allies pressed on against their enemy. The Central Powers collapsed, one by one, in the face of Allied attacks and domestic revolutions. Two of Germany's allies, Bulgaria and the Ottoman Empire, made a separate peace with the Allies in autumn. Austria-Hungary splintered in October as Poles, Hungarians, Czechs, and Slovaks declared their independence from the emperor.

The German commanders begged for peace, still hoping to dictate some terms before the fighting crossed onto German soil. The Allies refused. In the last week of October, the German naval command ordered the fleet to leave port and confront the British Navy for one final battle. Sailors in the German port of Kiel recognized that defeat was only a matter of time and further fighting would cause needless loss of life, so they mutinied on October 29. The revolt quickly spread to other ships and ports as well as to factories and industrial cities, pressuring the generals to bring the war to an end. By November 10, the Kaiser had fled to Holland. A civilian representative of the new German

James Cochran was an American soldier from Philadelphia who died in the war at the age of 19. His family honored his memory with a locket containing a photograph and a lock of his hair.

Bomber Planes

Airplanes equipped with bombs came late to the war and played a minor role in the fighting. Early planes were limited by how far and how fast they could fly and how well they could attack other planes. World War I-era planes averaged a speed of 100 miles per hour and carried about 1,750 pounds of bombs. Their guns were only effective on targets up to about 200 yards away.

Today Once a helpful tool for armies, fighter and bomber planes have replaced ground troops altogether in some campaigns. In the 1990s, the United States attacked Yugoslavia with air power alone. Bombers can launch airstrikes against factories, roads, railroads, and enemy positions with a much smaller risk of casualties.

The most advanced bombers are no longer limited by distance from a home base. In March 1999, two

B-2 bombers took off from an air force base in Missouri and flew across the Atlantic to bomb targets in Yugoslavia. They returned to Missouri after the mission was completed—a total of 30 hours in the air without landing.

Modern planes fly faster and higher than their predecessors. B-2 bombers can fly at speeds approaching 600 miles per hour. The B-1B bomber can break the speed of sound, reaching 900 miles an hour, and carry 80,000 pounds of bombs.

? Why does the military rely so heavily on air power today?

Republic signed an **armistice,** or cease-fire, in a French railroad car at 5:00 AM on November 11, 1918. Six hours later, as agreed, the guns finally fell silent.

The Influenza Epidemic The last months of the war were darkened by an epidemic that killed more people worldwide than all of the wartime battles. American troops arriving in France in the spring of 1918 carried with them a new strain of an influenza virus that had been first detected in a military training camp in Kansas in March. The virus swept across the Western Front in June, disabling 500,000 German troops at the peak of their summer offensive, and then it vanished. But worse was to come.

The first cases were followed by a second, deadlier wave in the fall and a third wave in the winter. Unlike other flu viruses, the new variant struck people of all ages equally hard and could kill within a few days. A doctor described the effects of the disease at Fort Devens in Massachusetts, where an average of 100 people died each day:

66 *These men start with what appears to be an attack of LaGrippe or Influenza, and when brought to the [hospital] they very rapidly develop the most viscous type of Pneumonia that has ever been seen. Two hours after admission they have the Mahogany spots over the cheek bones. . . . It is only a matter of a few hours then until death comes, and it is simply a struggle for air until they suffocate. It is horrible.* 99

—Anonymous

The virus spread easily in crowded, unsanitary conditions. Military bases and cities were particularly susceptible to outbreaks of influenza. San Francisco required citizens to wear surgical masks in public. After a parade led to an outbreak in Philadelphia, officials closed all schools, churches, and theaters. At the peak of the second wave in October, so many people died in a short period of time that gravediggers could not dig graves quickly enough.

Conditions were no better among American soldiers in Europe. The AEF suffered 16,000 cases of influenza in the first week of October alone, and the death rate in some units reached 32 percent. In a little under a year, more American soldiers died from influenza than from battle. Over half a million Americans and perhaps 30 million people worldwide died before the epidemic came to an end.

Results of the War The physical and mental scars of the war ran deep. About 50,000 American soldiers died in battle, and many more died of disease, mainly influenza. The toll would have been even greater but for the efforts of volunteer nurses serving their country through the Red Cross and other agencies.

Corporal Elmer Sherwood of Indiana, just 21 years old, wrote after one bloody battle in August 1918:

> 66 *Hundreds of bodies of our brave boys lie on Hill 212, captured with such a great loss of blood. We will never be able to explain war to our loved ones back home even if we . . . live and return.* 99
>
> —Corporal Elmer Sherwood

American losses were tiny compared with those suffered by the Europeans. The total death toll of 8 million soldiers and sailors is only an estimate. Still, this figure averages out to more than 5,000 soldiers killed on each day of the war. Germany, Austria-Hungary, Russia, and France all suffered more than a million dead. About 900,000 troops from Britain and its empire died. While most of the fighting and dying took place in Europe, there were battles in the Middle East and Africa as well. Survivors sensed that the war had destroyed a whole generation of young men. Their deaths were mourned not only by those who knew them, but by their countries, which would suffer the loss of their talents and abilities as well as the loss of future generations.

In every major country, the sick and wounded outnumbered the dead. Thousands of soldiers had lost limbs to bullets and artillery shells. Doctors amputated feet infected with "trench foot," a disease developed from spending too much time in wet, muddy trenches. Poison gas attacks blinded many soldiers permanently and caused long-lasting lung damage.

The suffering extended beyond the battlefields. Millions of civilians died during and immediately after the fighting, from starvation, disease, or war-related injuries. These deaths included hundreds of thousands of Armenian civilians. In a campaign of **genocide,** or the organized killing of an entire people, Ottoman forces deported and murdered Armenians, whom they suspected of disloyalty to the government. The killings of Armenians would continue into the early 1920s.

BIOGRAPHY

Corporal York 1887–1964

Many acts of heroism shone during the final months of the war. But the bravery of Corporal Alvin York during the Meuse-Argonne offensive stood out above the rest. On October 8, York's patrol tried to destroy a German machine-gun nest, losing half its men in the attempt. Facing heavy machine-gun fire, the remaining soldiers took cover. York continued the attack on his own, killing 25 machine-gunners with his rifle and pistol and capturing 132 German soldiers.

When a general asked about his exploits, York replied, "General, I would hate to think I missed any of them shots; they were all at pretty close range—50 or 60 yards." For his heroism above and beyond the call of duty, York received the Congressional Medal of Honor as well as the French Croix de Guerre.

Section 3 Assessment

READING COMPREHENSION

1. Why were **convoys** important to American war efforts?

2. (a) In what ways was the United States unprepared to help the Allies in 1917? (b) In what ways did the United States offer immediate help?

3. Why did Germany agree to an **armistice** in November 1918?

4. How did new weapons change the way that soldiers fought during the war?

CRITICAL THINKING AND WRITING

5. Analyzing Information (a) How did America's losses in the war compare to those of Germany, France, and Britain? (b) How might these losses have affected how the people in these countries remember World War I?

6. Creating a Time Line Create a time line of all the major wartime events that involved the United States.

For: An activity on the influenza epidemic of 1918
Visit: PHSchool.com
Web Code: mrd-6193

Americans on the Home Front

READING FOCUS

- What steps did the government take to finance the war and manage the economy?
- How did the government enforce loyalty to the war effort?
- How did the war change the lives of Americans on the home front?

MAIN IDEA

Americans and their government took extra-ordinary steps at home to support the war effort.

KEY TERMS

Liberty Bond
price controls
rationing
daylight saving time
sedition
vigilante

TARGET READING SKILL

Identify Supporting Details As you read, prepare an outline of this section. Use Roman numerals to indicate the major headings of this section, capital letters for the subheadings, and numbers for the supporting details. The sample below will help you get started.

I. **Financing the War**
II. **Managing the Economy**
   A. **New agencies are founded to organize the economy.**
      1. **War Industries Board oversees production.**
      2. _____
      3. _____
   B. _____

Setting the Scene

> *I hate war, because war is murder, desolation and destruction. If one-tenth of what has been spent on preparedness for war had been spent on the prevention of war the world would always have been at peace.*
>
> —Henry Ford

Henry Ford's words appeared in the *Detroit Free Press* on August 12, 1915, when the United States still practiced neutrality. Ford vowed that he would burn down his factories before allowing them to make goods for the war in Europe.

Two years later, the United States was at war, and Ford had orders to build 16,000 tanks and 20,000 tractors for the United States government. A new Ford factory that would build anti-submarine ships was rising in Dearborn, Michigan, with the help of $10 million in federal aid. Henry Ford and his workers, along with the rest of the nation, had joined the war effort.

Waging war required many sacrifices at home. Despite the efforts of the preparedness movement, the American economy was not ready to meet the demands of modern warfare. War required huge amounts of money and personnel. As President Wilson explained, now "there are no armies . . . ; there are entire nations armed."

Financing the War

The government launched a vigorous campaign to raise money from the American people. It borrowed money by selling **Liberty Bonds,** special war bonds to support the Allied cause. Like all bonds, they could later be redeemed for the original value of the bonds plus interest. By selling war bonds to enthusiastic Americans, Secretary of the Treasury William Gibbs McAdoo raised more than $20 billion. These funds allowed the United States to pay about one quarter of its war costs and still loan more than $10 billion to the Allies during and just after the war.

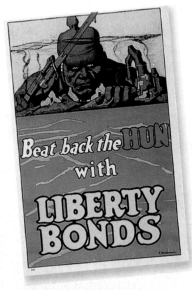

VIEWING HISTORY The United States government used posters to whip up sentiment against the "Huns"—the Germans—and to sell bonds to fund the war effort. **Recognizing Bias** *How does this poster depict German soldiers?*

Responding to the slogan "Every Scout to Save a Soldier," Boy Scouts and Girl Scouts set up booths on street corners and sold bonds. The government hired popular commercial artists to draw colorful posters and recruited famous screen actors to lead public rallies to buy bonds. An army of 75,000 "four-minute men" gave brief (four-minute) speeches before movies, plays, and school or union meetings to persuade audiences to buy bonds.

Buying war bonds was one of several ways that civilians could support Americans at the front and demonstrate their patriotism. Patriotism is the love of one's country and the willingness to fight to defend its ideals and institutions.

Managing the Economy

The government also called on industry to switch from producing commercial goods to war goods. In 1918, Wilson won authority to set up a huge bureaucracy to manage this process. Business leaders flocked to Washington to take up posts in thousands of new agencies. Because they gave their service for a token salary, they were called "dollar-a-year" men and women.

New Agencies A War Industries Board, headed by financier Bernard Baruch, oversaw the nation's war-related production. The board had far-reaching powers. It doled out raw materials, told manufacturers what and how much to produce, and even fixed prices.

A War Trade Board licensed foreign trade and punished firms suspected of dealing with the enemy. A National War Labor Board, set up in April 1918 under former President Taft, worked to settle any labor disputes that might disrupt the war effort. Labor leader Samuel Gompers promised to limit labor problems in war-production industries. A separate War Labor Policies Board, headed by Harvard law professor Felix Frankfurter, set standards for wages, hours, and working conditions in the war industries. Labor unions won limited rights to organize and bargain collectively.

Regulating Food and Fuel Consumption In August 1917, Congress passed the Lever Food and Fuel Control Act. This act gave the President the power to manage the production and distribution of foods and fuels vital to the war effort.

Using the slogan "Food will win the war," the government began to manage how much food people bought. Under the leadership of engineer and future President Herbert Hoover, the Food Administration worked to increase farm output and reduce waste. Hoover had the power to impose **price controls,**

Sounds of an Era

Listen to "Over There" and other sounds from the World War I era.

VIEWING HISTORY At this shipyard, women workers replaced men who left to join the military. **Synthesizing Information** *Based on this photograph, describe some of the changes that wartime brought to the workplace.*

שפײַ וועט געווינען דיא קריעג!

אידער קומט אהער צו געפינען פרײַהײַט.
יעצט מוזט איהר העלפֿען זיא צו בעשיצען
מיר מעגען דיא עלליעס פֿערזארגען מיט ווײַץ.

לאזט קײַן זאַך ניט גיין אין ניוועץ

יוניטעד סטײַטס פֿוד פֿערוואלטונג.

FOOD WILL WIN THE WAR
You came here seeking Freedom
You must now help to preserve it
WHEAT is needed for the allies
Waste nothing

VIEWING HISTORY The poster on the left, written in Yiddish, encouraged Jewish people who had immigrated to the United States from Eastern Europe to conserve food for the war effort. It was also printed in English and other languages to appeal to as many immigrants as possible. **Determining Relevance** *How does this poster link the decision to come to America with aiding the war effort?*

a system of pricing determined by the government, on the sale of food. He also had the power to begin a system of **rationing,** or distributing goods to consumers in a fixed amount. But Hoover thought both these approaches went too far. He hoped instead that voluntary restraint and increased efficiency would accomplish the Food Administration's goals.

Women played a key role in Hoover's program. Writing to women in August 1917, he preached a "Gospel of the Clean Plate." He appealed:

> ❝ *Stop, before throwing any food away, and ask 'Can it be used?' . . . Stop catering to different appetites. No second helpings. Stop all eating between meals. . . . One meatless day a week. One wheatless meal a day. . . . No butter in cooking: use substitutes.* ❞
> —Herbert Hoover

"The American woman and the American home," Hoover concluded, "can bring to a successful end the greatest national task that has ever been accepted by the American people." Eager to take part in the war effort, women across the country responded to this patriotic challenge.

The Lever Food and Fuel Control Act also created an agency called the Fuel Administration. It sponsored gasless days to save fuel. This agency also began the practice of **daylight saving time**—turning clocks ahead one hour for the summer. By shifting an hour of sunlight from the early morning, when most people were asleep, to the evening, it increased the number of daylight hours available for work. Daylight saving time also reduced the need for artificial light and lowered fuel consumption.

Enforcing Loyalty

News and information also came under federal control during World War I. The government imposed censorship on the press and banned some publications from the mails. Even a movie about the American Revolution was banned and its producer jailed because the film showed British troops killing American women and children, and Britain was now America's ally. The government challenged any media influences that threatened the war effort.

In 1917, George Creel, a Denver journalist and former muckraker, was appointed the head of the Committee on Public Information. His job was to rally popular support for the war. Creel's office coordinated the production of short films, pamphlets explaining war aims, and posters advertising recruitment and Liberty Bonds. Some of the slogans used were "Buy Bonds Till It Hurts" and "The Soldier Gives—You Must Lend."

Fear of Foreigners As in all wars, the fear of espionage, or spying, was widespread. A few months after the sinking of the *Lusitania,* a staff member of the German embassy left his briefcase on an American train. Inside the briefcase were plans for turning Americans against the Allies and disrupting the American economy.

The government feared that secret agents might try to undermine the war effort by destroying transportation or communication networks. The possibility of such acts of sabotage put the government on alert. It also generated calls for restrictions on immigration.

The National Security League, having won its battle for preparedness, began to preach "100 Percent Americanism." Early in 1917, the League got Congress to pass, over Wilson's veto, a literacy test for immigrants. This test excluded those who could not read English or any other language. As it turned out, relatively few immigrants failed the test. Still, the test had set the stage for an increase in nativist feelings.

"Hate the Hun!" Once the United States declared war, alertness for spies approached hysteria. The war also spurred a general hostility toward Germans. People began calling them Huns, in reference to a people who had brutally invaded Europe in the fourth and fifth centuries. High schools stopped teaching German. Books by German authors disappeared from library shelves, and German composers and musicians were banned from symphony concerts. German measles became "liberty measles," and a hamburger (which was named after Hamburg, a German city) became a Salisbury steak. Nervous dog-owners even renamed their German shepherds, calling them "police dogs" instead.

Anti-German sentiment had a more serious dimension. In April 1918, a mob lynched a German-born citizen named Robert Prager near St. Louis. Despite his German heritage, Prager had in fact tried to enlist in the navy. His lynching was but one of many wartime attacks on people of German descent.

Repression of Civil Liberties In his 1917 call for war on Germany, Wilson had claimed that the United States would be fighting for liberty and democracy. In that same war message, Wilson warned that disloyalty would be "dealt with with a firm hand of stern repression." His efforts to unite Americans against the enemy often prevailed over his promise to fight for liberty.

In 1917, Congress passed the Espionage Act, which made it illegal to interfere with the draft. The Espionage Act was amended in 1918 by the Sedition Act. (**Sedition** is any speech or action that encourages rebellion.) The Sedition Act made it illegal to obstruct the sale of Liberty Bonds or to discuss anything "disloyal, profane, scurrilous, or abusive" about the American form of government, the Constitution, or the army and the navy. The Sedition Act violated the First Amendment's guarantee of freedom of speech, but many felt that the needs of war required harsh measures.

The government pursued more than 1,500 prosecutions and won more than 1,000 convictions. Socialist and former presidential candidate Eugene V. Debs drew a ten-year jail sentence for criticizing the American government and business leaders and for urging people to "resist militarism."

Controlling Political Radicals Socialists such as Debs argued that the war was merely a fight among imperialist capitalists and that workers had no stake in the outcome. This view became a rallying point for antiwar sentiment. In the elections of 1917 in New York, Ohio, and Pennsylvania, Socialists made impressive gains.

The radical labor organization Industrial Workers of the World (IWW) also won new supporters from among western miners, migrant farm workers, and other unskilled laborers. They supported the IWW's goal of overthrowing capitalism and tried to interfere with copper mining during the war.

The views of Socialists and the IWW upset moderate labor leaders like Samuel Gompers, who had promised that unions would work with the war effort. The police hounded the IWW. Raids in September 1917 led to the conviction of nearly 200 members in trials held in Illinois, California, and Oklahoma. Groups of **vigilantes**, citizens who take the law into their own hands, lynched and horsewhipped others.

The IWW gained strength during World War I. It also became the target of the government's effort to control political radicals.

With the help of workers in the Woman's Land Army, farmers were able to harvest crops despite a labor shortage.

Changing People's Lives

American patriotism and war fever made military styles and activities more acceptable at home. Children joined scouting programs with military-style uniforms, marching, and patriotic exercises. Military drill became part of many school programs. By the summer of 1918, all able-bodied males in colleges and universities had become army privates, subject to military discipline.

Social Mobility for Minorities and Women After the war, Americans would turn away from military trends and other war-related activities. But other social changes that occurred during the war would have more lasting effects. The war virtually stopped the flow of immigrants from Europe, and the armed forces had taken many young men out of the labor pool. Businesses, especially war-related industries, suddenly needed workers. These wartime conditions drew some people into higher paying jobs. Factory owners and managers who had discriminated against African Americans and Mexican Americans now actively recruited them.

The African Americans who had left the South to work in northern factories added to a steady stream of migrants that had already started in the late 1800s. The stream turned into a flood during the war, when some 500,000 African Americans joined what came to be called the Great Migration.

The diminished work force also created new opportunities for women. Some women found jobs on farms, thanks to organizations such as the Woman's Land Army. Others moved into jobs as telegraph messengers, elevator operators, letter carriers, and similar jobs that were previously open only to men. A few earned management positions.

As a result of the war, about 400,000 women joined the industrial work force for the first time. In 1917, a speaker for the Women's Trade Union League proclaimed, "At last, after centuries of disabilities and discrimination, women are coming into the labor and festival of life on equal terms with men." Such pronouncements, while premature, celebrated what seemed to be a major social change.

Section 4 Assessment

READING COMPREHENSION

1. What was the role of **price controls** and **rationing** on the home front in World War I?

2. What were three ways that the government intervened in the economy to help the war effort?

3. How did the government deal with newspapers, magazines, and movies during the war?

CRITICAL THINKING AND WRITING

4. **Drawing Inferences** (a) What was the primary purpose of selling Liberty Bonds? (b) What else did the government's efforts to sell bonds accomplish?

5. **Writing an Opinion** Write a short speech discussing anti-German sentiment. Why do you think people reacted the way they did to the use of German words in the United States?

For: An activity on the financial costs of World War I
Visit: PHSchool.com
Web Code: mrd-6194

Global Peacemaker

READING FOCUS

- What expectations did Wilson and the Allies bring to the Paris Peace Conference?

- What were the important provisions of the peace treaty?

- How did the federal government and ordinary Americans react to the end of war?

MAIN IDEA

When the fighting ended in Europe, President Wilson pressed for a treaty that would bring peace to the postwar world.

KEY TERMS

Fourteen Points
self-determination
spoils
League of Nations
reparations
Versailles Treaty

TARGET READING SKILL

Compare and Contrast Copy this incomplete Venn diagram. As you read, write the key peace proposals offered by President Wilson and the Allied leaders in the appropriate sections. If both sides supported a proposal, include it in the space where the circles overlap.

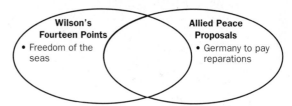

Wilson's Fourteen Points
- Freedom of the seas

Allied Peace Proposals
- Germany to pay reparations

Setting the Scene On January 8, 1918, President Wilson stood before the Congress of the United States. The war had not ended, yet Wilson talked about peace. He hoped that the world could "be made safe for every peace-loving nation which, like our own, wishes to live its own life, determine its own institutions, be assured of justice and fair dealing by the other peoples of the world as against force and selfish aggression."

Wilson's program for reaching these goals came to be called the **Fourteen Points,** for the number of provisions it contained. Wilson's first point called for an end to secret treaties, a key cause of the war. He wrote:

> 66 *Open covenants of peace, openly arrived at, after which there shall be no private international understandings of any kind but diplomacy shall proceed always frankly and in the public view.* 99
>
> —Woodrow Wilson

The remaining provisions of the Fourteen Points dealt with a variety of issues related to keeping the peace after the war. They included the removal of trade barriers among nations and the reduction of military forces. Wilson also called for the right of Austria-Hungary's ethnic groups to **self-determination,** or the power to make decisions about one's own future.

Wilson hoped that these points would form the basis of peace negotiations. Germany assumed that they would. At first, the Allies appeared to cooperate. But it soon became clear that Wilson's colleagues did not share his idealism. The Allies discarded Wilson's proposals one by one as they met to map out a future for Europe.

The Paris Peace Conference

In January 1919, an international peace conference convened in Paris. Wilson decided to head the United States delegation. Although the Republican-controlled Senate would have the final word on the treaty,

VIEWING HISTORY Crowds greet returning soldiers at a victory parade in New York City. **Drawing Inferences** How did American attitudes toward Europe change in 1919 and 1920?

British Prime Minister David Lloyd George (left), French Prime Minister Georges Clemenceau (center), and Wilson negotiated at the Paris Peace Conference.

INTERPRETING TABLES
Many American soldiers died either from disease or in battle, but European countries on both sides of the conflict suffered even greater losses. **Understanding Point of View** *How did high casualties in Britain and France influence how Lloyd George and Clemenceau acted at the Paris Peace Conference?*

Casualties of World War I *

Allies	Killed	Wounded
Russia	1,700,000	4,950,000
France	1,358,000	4,266,000
British Empire	908,000	2,090,000
Italy	462,000	954,000
United States	51,000	206,000
Others	410,000	343,000
Total	**4,889,000**	**12,809,000**

Central Powers	Killed	Wounded
Germany	1,809,000	4,247,000
Austria-Hungary	923,000	3,620,000
Turkey	325,000	400,000
Bulgaria	76,000	152,000
Total	**3,133,000**	**8,419,000**

SOURCE: *Encyclopedia of Military History*
*Numbers rounded to thousands

Wilson chose not to name any senior Republicans to the group, with the exception of one elderly diplomat.

When Wilson arrived in Paris, the Parisians greeted the American President as a conquering hero and threw flowers in his path. Wilson claimed that he was not interested in the **spoils,** or rewards, of war. That is, he did not expect the United States to take money or land from the war's losers. His only goal was to establish a permanent agency where countries could work together to resolve disputes peacefully and guarantee international stability. As Wilson had declared two years earlier, "There must be not a balance of power, but a community of power; not organized rivalries, but an organized common peace."

Wilson Forced to Compromise All would not go Wilson's way. Wilson shared power at the conference with other members of the Big Four: David Lloyd George of Britain, Georges Clemenceau of France, and Vittorio Orlando of Italy. Wilson's three allies were interested in making the Central Powers pay for their part in the war with land, goods, livestock, and money. In particular, they wanted to divide up Germany's colonies.

Russia, although absent from the conference, was still on everyone's mind. Civil war had erupted between Lenin's Bolsheviks and the armies loyal to the old government. British, French, and American forces had become involved in the civil war on the side of Lenin's opponents. Would Lenin's government survive? Would it present a set of war claims? Lenin called for workers everywhere to overthrow their governments, and the Allies feared a Bolshevik Russia as much as they feared Germany. As it turned out, Lenin's government held on to power, but refused to claim any spoils of war. Lenin's government would, in fact, sign a Treaty of Friendship and Cooperation with Germany in 1922.

From the start of the Paris Peace Conference, Wilson was forced to compromise on the principles outlined in the Fourteen Points. He had to give up, for example, the idea of respecting the rights of native peoples in Germany's colonies in Africa, China, and the Pacific. He finally agreed that the Allied powers could simply take over the colonies.

The League of Nations Wilson did, however, convince the other powers to postpone further discussion of Germany's fate and talk about his ideas for global security. After ten days of hard work, he produced a plan for the **League of Nations,** an organization in which the nations of the world would join together to ensure security and peace for all its members. Wilson then left France for home, hoping to persuade Congress and the nation to accept his plan.

For Wilson, the heart of his proposal for the League of Nations was Article 10 of the plan. This provision pledged that members of the League would regard an attack on one country as an attack on all. Since the League would not have any military power, the force of the article depended on the will of members to back it up with their armies. Nevertheless, 39 Republican senators or senators-elect signed a statement rejecting it. They feared that Article 10 could be used to drag the United States into unpopular foreign wars.

The Peace Treaty

In March 1919, Wilson returned to the peace conference. The Big Four dominated the proceedings. Although the Allies accepted Wilson's plan for the League of Nations, opposition to the League from Congress and many Americans had weakened Wilson's position at the conference.

French premier Georges Clemenceau took advantage of that weakness to demand harsh penalties against Germany. Wilson feared that these demands would lead to future wars, but he could not get Clemenceau to budge.

Redrawing the Map of Europe Wilson also had to compromise elsewhere. Self-determination for the peoples of Central Europe proved hard to apply. As the map on the following page shows, the conference created nine new nations out of the territory of Austria-Hungary, Russia, and Germany. Several of these nations were created to form a north-south buffer zone dividing Bolshevik Russia from the rest of Europe. Most borders were drawn with the ethnic populations of the region in mind, but clean divisions were impossible. The boundaries created new ethnic minorities in several countries, including millions of Germans and Hungarians whose homes became part of Poland, Czechoslovakia, or Romania. These arrangements failed to resolve all ethnic tensions.

In the Middle East, the Allies reduced the Ottoman Empire to a small remnant that became the nation of Turkey. Britain took control of Palestine, Transjordan, and Iraq. France was awarded Syria and Lebanon.

Wilson had more luck opposing the demands of Vittorio Orlando, Italy's prime minister. To convince Italy to join the Allies in 1915, Britain had secretly promised Italy several pieces of territory controlled by Austria-Hungary. At the conference, however, Wilson and the other Allied leaders refused to support Italy's claims. As a result, Italy gained less territory than it had expected. Orlando had to resign as prime minister because of his failure at the conference.

War Guilt and Reparations Wilson met his greatest defeat when he gave in to French insistence on German war guilt and financial responsibility. The French, with the support of Britain, wanted to cripple Germany. They insisted that Germany supply **reparations,** or payment for economic injury suffered during a war. In 1921, a Reparations Commission ruled that Germany owed the Allies $33 billion, an amount far beyond its ability to pay. As Wilson had feared, Germany never forgot or forgave this humiliation.

Signing the Treaty The Allies presented the treaty to the Germans on May 7, 1919. Insisting that the treaty violated the Fourteen Points, the Germans at first refused to sign it. They gave in, however, when threatened with a French invasion. On June 28, the great powers signed the treaty at Versailles, the former home of French kings, outside of Paris. Thus, the treaty is known as the **Versailles Treaty.** Even the location offered an opportunity to

---

COMPARING PRIMARY SOURCES
League of Nations

The debate over joining the League of Nations often hinged on the effect that joining would have on American sovereignty or independence.

Analyzing Viewpoints On what basis does each speaker support or oppose American entry into the League?

In Favor of Joining the League of Nations

"The United States will, indeed, undertake . . . to 'respect and preserve as against external aggression the territorial integrity and existing political independence of all members of the League,' and that engagement constitutes a very grave and solemn moral obligation. But it is a moral, not a legal, obligation, and leaves our Congress absolutely free to put its own interpretation upon it."

—*Woodrow Wilson, testifying before the Foreign Relations Committee, August 19, 1919*

Opposed to Joining the League of Nations

"Shall we go there, Mr. President, to sit in judgment, and in case that judgment works for peace join with our allies, but in case it works for war withdraw our cooperation? How long would we stand as we now stand, a great Republic commanding the respect and holding the leadership of the world, if we should adopt any such course?"

—*Senator William Borah (Idaho), testifying in the Senate, November 19, 1919*

READING CHECK

How did Wilson's allies react to the Fourteen Points?

Europe After World War I

New nation

Allied-occupied zone

MAP SKILLS Britain, France, and the United States redrew the map of Europe at the Paris Peace Conference. **Regions** *Which three participants in the war lost the most territory in central and eastern Europe?*

humiliate Germany. In 1871, the new German Empire had been founded in the same hall at Versailles.

Reactions at Home

On July 8, treaty in hand, Wilson returned home to great acclaim. But many legislators had doubts about the results of the peace conference. Some senators opposed the treaty because it committed the United States to the League of Nations. These senators were called the "irreconcilables," because they could not be reconciled to, or made to accept, the treaty. Irreconcilables argued that joining the League would threaten American independence.

Senator Henry Cabot Lodge, chair of the Foreign Relations Committee, led another group called the "reservationists." This group accepted the League of Nations but wanted to impose reservations, or restrictions, on American participation. In particular, they wanted a guarantee that the Monroe Doctrine would remain in force. Wilson's point that compliance with the League's decisions was "binding in conscience only, not in law," failed to persuade them.

Wilson Tours the Country Determined to win grass-roots support for the League, Wilson took to the road in September. In 23 days, he delivered three dozen speeches across the country. After this tremendous effort, he suffered a stroke that paralyzed one side of his body. He would remain an invalid, isolated from his Cabinet and visitors, for the rest of his term.

During his illness, Wilson grew increasingly inflexible. Congress would have to accept the treaty and the League as he envisioned it, or not at all. In November 1919, the Senate voted on the treaty with Lodge's reservations included. The Senate rejected the treaty by a vote of 39 for, 55 against. When the treaty came up without the reservations, it failed again, 38 to 53. In the face of popular dismay at this outcome, the Senate reconsidered the treaty in March 1920, but once again the treaty was rejected.

A Formal End to Hostilities On May 20, 1920, Congress voted to disregard the Treaty of Versailles and declare the war officially over. Steadfast to his principles, Wilson vetoed the resolution. Finally, on July 2, 1921, another joint resolution to end the war passed. By that time, a Republican President, Warren G. Harding, was in office, and he signed it. Congress ratified separate peace treaties with Germany, Austria, and Hungary that October.

Difficult Postwar Adjustments The war spurred the United States economy, giving a big boost to American businesses. The United States was now the world's largest creditor nation. In 1922, a Senate debt commission calculated that European countries owed $11.5 billion to the United States.

The decline of the European powers thrust the United States into a position of unexpected strength. Britain, once the banker to the world and center of the greatest colonial empire, had spent much of its great wealth on the war. Britain's economy never adjusted to peacetime, and the nation's power declined in comparison to that of the United States. The German invasion had devastated France, and Germany was weakened by the Treaty of Versailles. Yet even though the United States enjoyed unparalleled power, it chose to turn away from international affairs and focus on its concerns at home.

The return to peace had caused problems for the country at large. By April 1919, about 4,000 servicemen a day were being mustered out of the armed forces. But nobody had devised a plan to help returning troops merge back into society. The federal agencies that controlled the economy during the war had abruptly canceled war contracts. As a result, jobs proved scarce. The women who had taken men's places in factories and offices also faced readjustment. To free up jobs for returning soldiers, many women left their jobs voluntarily or were fired.

Like white troops, black soldiers came home to a hero's welcome. When they went to find jobs, however, their reception was different. Their contributions to the war had not earned black soldiers more respect from others. African Americans still faced discrimination in housing and employment, and lynchings and race riots continued.

Postwar Gloom   Many artists and intellectuals in the United States entered the postwar years with a sense of gloom or disillusionment. They expressed their feelings in books and other artistic works. Social reformers had been encouraged by the government-business collaboration during the war. For most of them, the end of the war also ended an era of optimism. Alice Lord O'Brian, a military post exchange director from Buffalo who was twice decorated by the French, expressed the views of many who took part in the war. In a letter home she stated:

> " We all started out with high ideals. . . . [A]fter being right up here almost at the front line . . . I cannot understand what it is all about or what has been accomplished by all this waste of youth. "
>
> —Alice Lord O'Brian

Section 5 Assessment

READING COMPREHENSION

1. Describe three of Woodrow Wilson's **Fourteen Points.**

2. How did the Allies both encourage and discourage **self-determination** in Europe?

3. Why did France and Britain demand **reparations** from Germany?

4. How did the United States eventually make peace with Germany?

CRITICAL THINKING AND WRITING

5. **Synthesizing Information** Why do you think many Americans opposed the Versailles Treaty?

6. **Drawing Inferences** Why did the Fourteen Points fail as a basis of peace negotiations?

7. **Writing a List** Compile a list of ten descriptive phrases that characterize the United States and Europe after the war.

Go Online PHSchool.com

For: An activity on the Big Four
Visit: PHSchool.com
Web Code: mrd-6195

creating a CHAPTER SUMMARY

Copy this chart (right) on a piece of paper and complete it by adding important events that occurred in each year. Some entries have been completed for you as examples.

For additional review and enrichment activities, see the interactive version of *America: Pathways to the Present*, available on the Web and on CD-ROM.

Year	Events
1914	• Gavrilo Princip assassinates Archduke Francis Ferdinand. • War breaks out between the Central Powers and the Allies. •
1915	
1916	
1917	
1918	
1919	
1920	

★ Reviewing Key Terms

For each of the terms below, write a sentence explaining how it relates to World War I.

1. militarism
2. Central Powers
3. Allies
4. stalemate
5. U-boat
6. Zimmermann note
7. American Expeditionary Force (AEF)
8. convoy
9. armistice
10. Liberty Bond
11. sedition
12. Fourteen Points
13. League of Nations
14. Versailles Treaty

★ Reviewing Main Ideas

15. What were the main causes of World War I? (Section 1)
16. Describe the first three months of the war in Europe in your own words. (Section 1)
17. What were the reactions in the United States to the outbreak of the war in Europe? (Section 2)
18. Why did the United States declare war on Germany? (Section 2)
19. Name some of the military innovations introduced during World War I. (Section 3)
20. How did American troops help turn the tide of the war on the battlefield? (Section 3)

21. Why and how did the government try to control the economy at home? (Section 4)
22. Why and how did the government influence what people said about the war? (Section 4)
23. What was the American reaction to the Versailles Treaty and to the League of Nations? (Section 5)

★ Critical Thinking

24. **Predicting Consequences** What might have happened on the European front if General Pershing had decided to combine the American troops with other Allied armies instead of keeping them independent?
25. **Drawing Inferences** Do you think that women played a key role in World War I? Why or why not?
26. **Testing Conclusions** Many young people in Europe and the United States felt that they bore the heaviest costs of the war. Cite evidence showing whether they were correct.
27. **Supporting a Position** Do you think the Sedition Act was a good way to deal with critics during wartime? Explain.
28. **Identifying Central Issues** It is often said that Woodrow Wilson won World War I, but then "lost the peace." Explain your understanding of this statement.

★ Standardized Test Prep

Analyzing Political Cartoons ▶

29. In this 1919 cartoon, what is President Wilson trying to persuade the "child" to do?

   A Join the war in Europe
   B Join the League of Nations
   C Stop fighting within Congress
   D Attend a party celebrating the end of World War I

30. Why does the "child" want to play alone?

Interpreting Data

Turn to the table of casualties in Section 5.

31. Which two countries suffered the greatest number of soldiers killed?

   A Russia and France
   B Germany and Austria-Hungary
   C Russia and Austria-Hungary
   D Germany and Russia

32. What can you conclude about casualties in "Other" Allied countries from this table?

   F These countries suffered as many casualties as the British Empire and France.
   G Their casualties were comparable to the total casualties in Bulgaria.
   H Unlike soldiers from France or Russia, soldiers in Romania, Serbia, and other small Allied countries were more likely to be killed in battle than wounded.
   I "Other" Allies suffered fewer casualties because they entered the war in 1916 or later.

THE CHILD WHO WANTED TO PLAY BY HIMSELF.
President Wilson: "Now come along and enjoy yourself with the other nice children. I promised that you'd be the life and soul of the party."

Test-Taking Tip

To answer Question 31, find the two highest numbers in the first column of the table and then look to the left to identify which two countries go with those numbers.

Applying the Chapter Skill

Identifying Alternatives The United States chose to go to war with Germany in 1917 largely because of continued German submarine attacks on neutral shipping. Identify alternative solutions to this problem of U-boat attacks. Discuss your alternative in a written proposal to President Wilson.

Go Online
PHSchool.com

For: Chapter 12 Self-Test
Visit: PHSchool.com
Web Code: mra-6196

A Flyer on the Edge

The dangers of war took a heavy toll on the men who served in uniform, not only the soldiers in the trenches but also those who fought in the skies overhead. The passage below, selected by the editors of *American Heritage* magazine, is from the diary of an unknown pilot in World War I. As you read the following excerpt, think about how the psychological stresses of modern warfare affected those who fought to defend freedom.

WE'VE LOST A LOT OF GOOD MEN. It's only a question of time until we all get it. I'm all shot to pieces. I only hope I can stick it. I don't want to quit. My nerves are all gone and I can't stop. I've lived beyond my time already.

It's not the fear of death that's done it. I'm still not afraid to die. It's this eternal flinching from it that's doing it and has made a coward out of me. Few men live to know what real fear is. It's something that grows on you, day by day, that eats into your constitution and undermines your sanity. I have never been serious about anything in my life and now I know that I'll never be otherwise again. But my seriousness will be a burlesque for no one will recognize it.

Here I am, twenty-four years old, I look forty and I feel ninety. I've lost all interest in life beyond the next patrol. No one Hun will ever get me and I'll never fall into a trap, but sooner or later I'll be forced to fight against odds that are too long or perhaps a stray shot from the ground will be lucky and I will have gone in vain. Or my motor will cut out when we are trench strafing or a wing will pull off in a dive. Oh, for a parachute! The Huns are using them now. I haven't a chance, I know, and it's this eternal waiting around that's killing me. I've even lost my taste for liquor. It doesn't seem to do me any good now. I guess I'm stale. Last week I actually got frightened in the air and lost my head. Then I found ten Huns and took them all on and I got one of them down out of control. I got my nerve back by that time and came back home and slept like a baby for the first time in two months. What a blessing sleep is! I know now why men go out and take such long chances

Airplanes, originally used for reconnaissance, fought in aerial "dogfights" toward the end of the war.

and pull off such wild stunts. No discipline in the world could make them do what they do of their own accord. I know now what a brave man is. I know now how men laugh at death and welcome it. I know now why Ball went over and sat above a Hun airdrome and dared them to come up and fight with him. It takes a brave man to even experience real fear. A coward couldn't last long enough at the job to get to that stage. What price salvation now?

More than 8 million soldiers died in World War I, making it the costliest war in history to that time.

THOUGHTS ABOUT WAR

War is a horrible thing, a grotesque comedy. And it is so useless. This war won't prove anything. All we'll do when we win is to substitute one sort of Dictator for another. In the meantime we have destroyed our best resources. Human life, the most precious thing in the world, has become the cheapest. After we've won this war by drowning the Hun in our own blood, in five years' time the sentimental fools at home will be taking up a collection for these same Huns that are killing us now and our fool politicians will be cooking up another good war. Why shouldn't they? They have to keep the public stirred up to keep their jobs and they don't have to fight and they can get soft berths for their sons and their friends' sons. To me the most contemptible cur in the world is the man who lets political influence be used to keep him away from the front. For he lets another man die in his place.

The worst thing about this war is that it takes the best. If it lasts long enough the world will be populated by cowards and weaklings and their children. And the whole thing is so useless, so unnecessary, so terrible! . . .

The devastation of the country is too horrible to describe. It looks from the air as if the gods had made a gigantic steam roller, forty miles wide and run it from the coast to Switzerland, leaving its spike holes behind as it went. . . .

I've lost over a hundred friends, so they tell me—I've seen only seven or eight killed—but to me they aren't dead yet. They are just around the corner, I think, and I'm still expecting to run into them any time. I dream about them at night when I do sleep a little and sometimes I dream that some one is killed who really isn't. Then I don't know who is and who isn't. I saw a man in Boulogne the other day that I had dreamed I saw killed and I thought I was seeing a ghost. I can't realize that any of them are gone. Surely human life is not a candle to be snuffed out. . . .

Source: Anonymous, *War Birds: Diary of an Unknown Aviator,* Doran, 1926.

Understanding Primary Sources

1. **(a)** What is the writer's attitude toward war? **(b)** How does he feel about politicians and their role in war? **(c)** Why does the writer feel this way?

2. **(a)** In the author's opinion, what are his chances of surviving the war? **(b)** From what you've learned about World War I, is this a reasonable position?

American Heritage®
MY BRUSH WITH **HISTORY**™
Videotapes

For more information about the experience of World War I, view "A Flyer on the Edge."

TEST PREPARATION

Write your answers on a separate sheet of paper.

Use the information in the map to answer the following question.

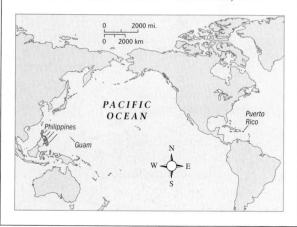

United States Overseas Possessions, 1900

1. How did the United States gain the territories labeled on the map?

   A Through the Monroe Doctrine

   B By treaty after World War II

   C Through a ruling of the United Nations

   D By winning the Spanish-American War

2. Who argued that naval power was crucial to the success of United States involvement overseas?

   A Samuel Gompers

   B William Randolph Hearst

   C Alfred T. Mahan

   D William Howard Taft

3. Which one of these was the main argument for those who supported United States imperialism?

   A Colonies would give the United States a place to sell products.

   B Colonies would provide students for United States colleges and universities.

   C The Constitution must go wherever the flag goes.

   D The United States needed naval bases in China and Japan.

Use the chart and your knowledge of social studies to answer the following question.

?????
• Settled the United Mine Workers' strike
• Passed the Hepburn Act, giving the ICC the power to limit railroad rates
• Created the Department of Labor
• Was a leader in the conservation of natural resources
• Changed the Monroe Doctrine
• Won the Nobel peace prize for ending the Russo-Japanese War

4. Which one of these is a correct title for the information in the chart?

   A Progressive reforms of Woodrow Wilson

   B Accomplishments of Theodore Roosevelt

   C Accomplishments of Admiral Alfred T. Mahan

   D Actions of Roosevelt canceled by Taft

5. What did the Muckrakers do in the Progressive Era?

   A They helped sell war bonds during World War I.

   B They were the leaders in the Red Scare.

   C They exposed problems present in American society.

   D They did not want the United States to have colonies.

6. How did the Clayton Antitrust Act differ from the Sherman Antitrust Act?

   A The Sherman Antitrust Act divided the nation into 12 banking districts.

   B The Clayton Antitrust Act applied equally to businesses and unions.

   C The Sherman Antitrust Act applied only to railroads and transportation.

   D The Clayton Antitrust Act listed specific actions businesses could not do.

Use the information in the chart to answer the following question.

1912 Election Results			
Candidate	**Party**	**Popular Vote**	**Percentage**
Woodrow Wilson	Democrat	6,293,152	41.8%
Theodore Roosevelt	Progressive	4,119,207	27.4
William Howard Taft*	Republican	3,486,333	23.2
Eugene V. Debs	Socialist	900,369	6.0

*Incumbent

SOURCE: *New York Times Almanac 2001*

7. Which one of the following conclusions is correct?

   A Most of the Republican votes came from the Western states.

   B The American people voted for change in 1912.

   C The Democrats spent more money than the Republicans.

   D Taft would have won if Debs had not been in the race.

8. Susan B. Anthony and Carrie Chapman Catt were two of the leaders in the fight for the

   A rejection of prohibition.

   B approval of the Treaty of Versailles.

   C right of women to vote.

   D passage of the Clayton Antitrust Act.

9. Which one of the following contributed to the decision of the United States to enter World War I?

   A Germany's unrestricted submarine warfare

   B Mobilization of their armies by the Central Powers

   C The failure of the convoy system

   D The success of the czar in ending the Russian Revolution

10. Who was the commander of the American Expeditionary Force (AEF) in World War I?

    A Louis D. Brandeis

    B Arthur Zimmermann

    C John J. Pershing

    D David Lloyd George

11. Which of the following best describes Woodrow Wilson's Fourteen Points?

    A A statement of the goals for peace put forth by the United States following World War I

    B The American fighting plan for World War I

    C A list of Progressive Era reforms

    D The constitutional amendments planned by Progressives

Writing Practice

12. What actions did the Progressives take to change the United States government?

13. Describe the major reasons for the entry of the United States into World War I.

14. What steps did the government take to manage the economy during World War I?

Boom Times to Hard Times
(1920–1941)

"We are moving forward to a greater freedom, to greater security for the average man than he has ever known before in the history of America."

Franklin D. Roosevelt
Fireside chat, September 1934

Howard Thain's painting, *The Great White Way, Times Square, 1925,* captures the upbeat mood of the 1920s. ▶

Chapter 13

Postwar Social Change (1920–1929)

SECTION 1   Society in the 1920s

SECTION 2   Mass Media and the Jazz Age

SECTION 3   Cultural Conflicts

The campaign for Prohibition succeeds.

A newspaper headline shows unrest in Chicago.

The Shadow of Danger

U.S. WHISKEY

If you believe that the traffic in Alcohol does more harm than good—*help stop it!*

Strengthen America Campaign

Heavyweight champion Jack Dempsey, sports hero of the 1920s

American Events

1919
Race riots erupt in Chicago and other cities. Marcus Garvey launches the first of his Black Star Line ships for the Universal Negro Improvement Association.

1920
The Eighteenth Amendment takes effect, instituting Prohibition. The Nineteenth Amendment gives women the right to vote.

1923
Louis Armstrong makes his first jazz recording. Duke Ellington begins playing in Harlem's jazz clubs. Jazz is made more popular by a growing radio audience.

1924
Women governors are elected in Wyoming and Texas.

Presidential Terms: Woodrow Wilson 1913–1921   Warren G. Harding 1921–1923   Calvin Coolidge 1923–1929

1918   **1920**   **1922**   **1924**

World Events

Dutch painter Piet Mondrian publishes his ideas on "neoplastic" style.

King Tutankhamen's tomb is discovered in Egypt.

The first Winter Olympic games are held in Chamonix, France.

1920   **1922**   **1924**

The Growth of Urban Areas, 1900–1920

Population by 1900
- Cities over 10,000
- Cities over 100,000

Population by 1920
- Cities over 10,000
- Cities over 100,000

People per Square Mile 1920
- 45–90
- 18–45
- 2–18
- under 2

CANADA

MEXICO

Gulf of Mexico

ATLANTIC OCEAN

90°W   80°W

40°N   30°N

N

0   150   300 mi.
0   150   300 km

Sixth Avenue Elevated at Third Street, 1928, by John Sloan

Actress Lillian Gish, star of silent films and "talkies"

1925
The Scopes trial stirs a national debate on evolution.

1926
Gertrude Ederle becomes the first woman to swim across the English Channel.

1927
Aviator Charles Lindbergh completes the first nonstop transatlantic solo flight.

Herbert Hoover 1929–1933

1926   1928   1930

Japan enacts universal male suffrage.

The Threepenny Opera by Bertolt Brecht and Kurt Weill debuts in Berlin.

The term *apartheid* is introduced in South Africa.

1925   1928   1929

Society in the 1920s

READING FOCUS

- How were women's roles changing during the 1920s?

- How were the nation's cities and suburbs affected by Americans on the move from rural areas?

- Who were some American heroes of the 1920s? What made them popular with the American public?

MAIN IDEA

The 1920s were a time of rapid social change, in which many young people, particularly young women, adopted new lifestyles and attitudes. As its rural population decreased, the United States became an urban nation, and traditional values were increasingly challenged.

KEY TERMS

flapper
demographics
barrio

TARGET READING SKILL

Identify Supporting Details Copy the chart below. As you read, fill in details relating to various social changes of the 1920s.

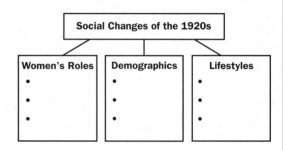

Social Changes of the 1920s		
Women's Roles	**Demographics**	**Lifestyles**
•	•	•
•	•	•
•	•	•

VIEWING HISTORY Flappers defined a new style of dress. **Drawing Inferences** *How does this young woman's attitude reflect the mood of the 1920s?*

Setting the Scene The decade of the 1920s stands out as a time of rapid change in American society. Much of the change had its roots in the previous century. In the late 1800s, industrialization and immigration began transforming the United States into an urban nation. Farm families streamed into the cities. Along with masses of immigrants, the new arrivals helped form a more complex urban culture.

The Great War accelerated those changes. Millions of young people had marched off to war full of enthusiasm. Many returned bearing the scars of that war: shell shock, permanent injury, and the effects of poison gas. Many also came back disillusioned, a condition they shared with others who had stayed home during the war. Together, they questioned the ideas and attitudes that had led to the war. Their challenge of traditional values helped ignite a revolution in manners and morals.

The **flapper** symbolized this revolution. The term described a new type of young woman: rebellious, energetic, fun-loving, and bold. One author depicted the flapper this way:

66 *Breezy, slangy, and informal in manner; slim and boyish in form; covered in silk and fur that clung to her as close as onion skin; with carmined [vivid red] cheeks and lips, plucked eyebrows and close-fitting helmet of hair; gay, plucky and confident.* 99
—Preston Slosson, *The Great Crusade and After,* 1930

Many older Americans held more traditional views of how young women were supposed to behave in public. They disapproved not only of the flappers' display of free manners but also of the behavior of the young men who flocked around them.

Of course, not all young women became flappers, and not everyone questioned traditional values. Still, those who did had a lasting effect on society. They helped create what we think of today as modern America.

Women's Changing Roles

Women stood at the center of much of the social change in the 1920s. Both single and married women had been in the work force for a long time. During the war, their numbers rose and they moved into better, higher-paying jobs. After the Nineteenth Amendment was adopted in 1920, all American women could vote. These experiences made them eager for still greater equality with men. Without intending to, the rebellious flapper brought all women closer to that goal.

The Flapper Image   The flapper represented only a small number of American women, yet her image had a wide impact on fashion and on behavior. Stylish young women began wearing dresses shorter than their mothers did, to the dismay of some guardians of decency. The fashion page of the *New York Times* declared in July 1920 that "the American woman . . . has lifted her skirts far beyond any modest limitation." At that time, hemlines had risen to just nine inches above the ground. By 1927, they would rise to knee-length or even higher. Between 1913 and 1928, the average amount of fabric used to make a woman's outfit shrank from 19.5 yards to just 7 yards.

Women also broke with the past in other ways. While most of their mothers had grown their hair long and then pinned it up, young women bobbed, or cut short, their hair. Instead of wide-brimmed hats, they wore the close-fitting "cloche," whose bell shape accentuated the new hairstyles. They also began wearing heavy makeup, a practice formerly associated only with actresses or prostitutes.

Women's manners changed as well. Before the 1920s, "proper" women rarely drank anything much stronger than wine, much less smoked, in public. By the end of the decade, many women were doing both, in part to defy Prohibition, but also to express their new freedom. Between 1918 and 1928, the number of cigarettes produced in the United States more than doubled. Though men were smoking more (many switching from cigars and pipes to cigarettes), the new woman smoker accounted for a large part of the increase. All these changes shocked American society and enraged many parents.

Women Working and Voting   Although many women bobbed their hair and wore shorter skirts, most did not embrace a flapper lifestyle. Some women adopted the new fashions simply because they were more convenient.

Convenience was an issue for young working women, as they had less time to spend maintaining elaborate wardrobes or hairstyles. During the 1920s, about 15 percent of wage-earning women became professionals and about 20 percent held clerical positions. Generally, these were single white women, although the percentage of married women working increased from 23 percent of the total female work force in 1920 to 29 percent in 1930.

Businesses remained prejudiced against women seeking professional posts. Many hospitals refused to hire female doctors, and many legal firms rejected female lawyers or offered them secretarial jobs. Employers seldom trained women for jobs beyond the entry level or paid them on as high a scale as men. Few women advanced to leadership positions. Employers expected women to quit if they married and became pregnant.

Women in the Workplace

Over time, the nature of women's work has changed to accommodate the needs of the labor market and changes in attitudes about women working outside the home. In a rural setting, women looking for outside work have typically found their choices more limited than in a city. As more and more people moved from rural areas in the 1920s, growing urban economies made room for women to enter the paid work force. The 1920s saw many women securing clerical jobs, work once reserved for men. From the 1920s to today, work available to women in the United States has expanded from jobs women have traditionally held, such as teaching and nursing, to include a range of options never before available.

As shown by the chart below, the percentage of women in the labor force has risen from the 1920s to the 1990s.

? What types of jobs are limited to rural areas or to cities today?

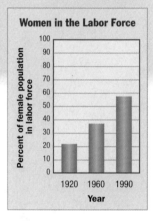

Women in the Labor Force

VIEWING HISTORY In 1920, women in New York City vote after the adoption of the Nineteenth Amendment. **Drawing Conclusions** *Why do you think more women did not turn out to vote in the early 1920s?*

Like the situation of women at work, women's status in politics changed little. As of 1920, women could vote in all elections. At first, some politicians feared that women might vote as a bloc, or special-interest group. That did not happen. Most women voted along the same lines as men. Moreover, relatively few women voted at all, especially in the early years after gaining national suffrage. Only about 35 percent of women voters went to the polls in 1920. In 1923, a survey asked women in Chicago why they did not vote in the mayoral election. Most notably, about a third said that they lacked interest. Another eleven percent said that they did not think women should vote at all.

Early on, women did not exercise their right to vote for a number of reasons. Women who lived in rural areas or had children to look after had to make special arrangements to get to the polls. Sometimes women's families discouraged them from voting. Other women were not comfortable with the idea of voting. In short, women had yet to make voting a habit, and it would take time for the habit to develop.

As the decade wore on, more women voted, but their choices did not change politics greatly. In national elections, women voted in patterns similar to men's. In local elections, however, women's votes often differed from men's, perhaps because women were more familiar with the candidates and issues.

After the Nineteenth Amendment was adopted, the alliance that worked for suffrage split, weakening its ability to push bills through Congress. Progressive reformers did lobby successfully for the Sheppard-Towner Act of 1921, the first major federal welfare measure concerned with women's and children's health. A constitutional amendment calling for an end to child labor failed, however. So did the Equal Rights Amendment (ERA), introduced in Congress for the first time in 1923. The original wording of the ERA stated that "Men and women shall have equal rights throughout the United States and every place subject to its jurisdiction." Some reformers opposed the ERA because it would make the laws requiring special working conditions for women unconstitutional.

Despite their disagreements, women worked together to win political office. Jeannette Rankin of Montana won election to the U.S. House of Representatives in 1916, becoming the first woman to serve in either house of Congress. Miriam A. Ferguson from Texas and Nellie Tayloe Ross of Wyoming, both wives of former governors, were elected governors themselves in 1924. By 1928, there were 145 women in 38 state legislatures. Thus, although women did not increase their political power as quickly as suffragists had hoped, they did lay a foundation for future participation in government on a larger scale.

READING CHECK
How did women influence politics in the 1920s?

Americans on the Move

In addition to social changes, many changes in **demographics** occurred in the 1920s. Demographics are the statistics that describe a population, such as data on race or income. The major demographic change of the 1920s was a movement away from the countryside. The 1920 census showed that for the first time in the nation's history, more Americans lived in urban areas than in rural areas.

Rural-Urban Split The 1920s magnified the gap between rural and urban society. One aspect of that gap was economic. Farmers had done well for the first two decades of the century. After the war, however, market prices dropped while the costs of operation rose. By the early 1920s, many farmers were economically stressed.

Meanwhile, the industrial and commercial economy began to boom. This prosperity bypassed much of rural America. Many farmers reluctantly left the land and headed to cities. During the decade, some 6 million people moved from rural to urban areas.

This migration, combined with urban prosperity, had important effects on society. Attendance at public high schools rose from 2.2 million in 1920 to 4.4 million by 1930. Some of this rise came from an increase in urban population and greater prosperity, but an important part of it resulted from a change in the labor pool. On farms, most older children played vital roles as laborers, so they often had to drop out of school to help their parents. In cities, children needed more education to compete in urban-based industry.

Rural and urban America also split over cultural issues. You read earlier about the change in manners and morals. This general shift away from traditional values took place mainly in the cities. Most rural populations wanted to preserve traditional values, not defy them. They frowned on the flappers and other aspects of society that they deemed immoral or dangerous.

African Americans in the North As you have read, the passage of Jim Crow laws, as well as new job opportunities in the North, produced the Great Migration of blacks from the South to northern cities. This migration continued from the late 1800s through World War I. The boom in northern industries further encouraged this demographic shift.

Throughout the early 1900s, jobs for African Americans in the South had been scarce and low-paying. Many factories refused to hire blacks for anything other than menial jobs. As industries expanded during the 1920s, many jobs opened up for African Americans in the North. In 1860, 93 percent of all African Americans lived in the South. By 1910, this figure had dropped to 89 percent. By 1930, it had fallen far more, to 80 percent.

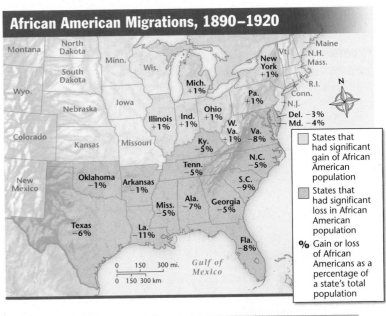

African American Migrations, 1890–1920

States that had significant gain of African American population

States that had significant loss in African American population

% Gain or loss of African Americans as a percentage of a state's total population

MAP SKILLS The migration of African Americans from the South to the North helped alter the populations of both regions. **Movement** *Which states lost the largest percentages of their black populations?*

Yet the North was no promised land. African American factory workers often faced anger and hatred from whites, who believed that migrants would work for lower wages and take their jobs. African American women generally worked for very low wages as household help for whites.

Other Migration After World War I, masses of refugees applied for entry into the United States. During the 1920s, Congress acted to limit immigration, especially from southern and eastern Europe and also from China and Japan. Since the limits did not apply to nations in the Americas, employers turned to immigrants from Mexico and Canada to fill low-paying jobs.

In the West, Mexicans supplied most of this labor, migrating to work on the farms of California and the ranches of Texas. In the Northeast, Canadians from the French-speaking province of Quebec traveled south to work in the paper mills, potato fields, and forests of New England and New York.

Migrants also took jobs in the cities. Los Angeles, for example, became a magnet for Mexicans and developed a distinct **barrio,** or Spanish-speaking neighborhood. New York also attracted a Spanish-speaking population— Puerto Ricans migrating in the hope of a better life in the United States.

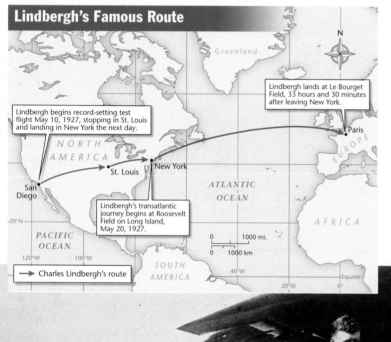
Lindbergh's Famous Route

Lindbergh begins record-setting test flight May 10, 1927, stopping in St. Louis and landing in New York the next day.

Lindbergh lands at Le Bourget Field, 33 hours and 30 minutes after leaving New York.

Lindbergh's transatlantic journey begins at Roosevelt Field on Long Island, May 20, 1927.

→ Charles Lindbergh's route

Growth of the Suburbs   As a result of the migrations of the 1920s, American suburbs grew. Suburban growth had begun to accelerate in the late nineteenth century. Cities built transportation systems that used electric trolleys—cars that ran on rails laid in the streets, and were powered by overhead wires. Trolleys allowed people to get from their suburban homes to jobs and stores in the city cheaply.

During the 1920s, buses replaced trolleys in many areas. Buses did not need rails and overhead wires, and thus were less expensive and easier to route. By the mid-1920s, about 70,000 buses were operating throughout the United States. At the same time, the automobile became more affordable to middle-class families and offered even greater flexibility in travel.

New York City provides a good example of the demographic changes that occurred during the 1920s. The number of residents decreased in Manhattan, the heart of the city, while the suburb of Queens saw its population double.

American Heroes

The changing morals of the 1920s made many Americans hungry for the values of an earlier time. Many in the nation became fascinated with heroes. Some were admired for their bravery and modesty, others for the way they showed Americans how to meet new challenges, with spirit and vitality. Among the decade's heroes, none became more famous than Charles Lindbergh.

"Lucky Lindy"   The sky was drizzling rain at Roosevelt Field on Long Island, New York, on the morning of May 20, 1927. A 25-year-old Minnesotan, Charles Lindbergh, climbed into the cockpit of his plane, the *Spirit of St. Louis,* and revved the engine. He had not slept much, but he did not dare wait any longer. Two other teams were waiting on the airfield, hoping to be the first to fly nonstop from

The Last Flight of Amelia Earhart

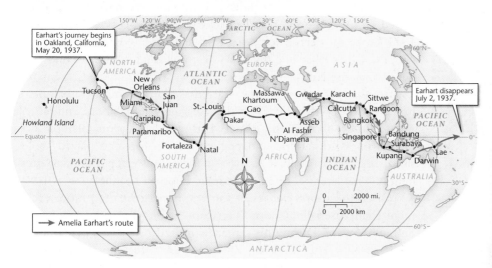

Earhart's journey begins in Oakland, California, May 20, 1937.

Earhart disappears July 2, 1937.

→ Amelia Earhart's route

Amelia Earhart helped open the field of aviation to more women.

New York to Paris. The prize was $25,000, and Lindbergh was determined to capture it.

In those days, flying was an infant science. Orville and Wilbur Wright had achieved the first powered, sustained, and controlled airplane flight only two decades earlier, in 1903. Radio and navigation equipment were primitive at best, and Lindbergh had no autopilot to switch on if he grew tired. Flying solo, he would have to stay awake and alert for the entire flight.

The minute Lindbergh's plane was aloft, the news flashed by telegraph and telephone to news desks around the nation. Americans everywhere took notice and began to wait eagerly for the latest word. The newspapers fed this hunger, printing some 27,000 columns of information about Lindbergh in the first few days after his departure.

After a brutal flight over the Atlantic Ocean, battling icy weather and fighting off sleep, "Lucky Lindy" landed safely in an airfield outside Paris, $33\frac{1}{2}$ hours after he had left New York. America went wild with jubilation. Lindbergh was brought home on a navy cruiser, given the Distinguished Flying Cross, and celebrated with parades throughout the nation.

Yet despite this frenzy of hero-worship, Lindbergh remained modest and calm. He refused offers of millions of dollars in publicity fees. To millions of Americans, Lindbergh was proof that the solid moral values of the old days lived on in the heartland of America. The public's fascination with Lindbergh may have played a role in a great tragedy for him, however, when one night his firstborn son was kidnapped from his crib. The child was later found murdered. Ironically, the murder case brought Lindbergh and his family more media attention than ever before.

Amelia Earhart Lindbergh's feat inspired later flyers, including Amelia Earhart. In 1928, Earhart became the first woman to fly across the Atlantic, although she was only a passenger. In 1932, she made the trip on her own, becoming the first woman to fly solo across the Atlantic. Later Earhart set another record, as the first person to fly solo from Hawaii to California, a challenge that had resulted in the deaths of many aviators before her. In 1937, Earhart and her navigator, Fred Noonan, tried to fly around the world. After completing two thirds of the trip, they disappeared mysteriously while crossing the Pacific Ocean.

Sports Heroes Though spectator sports had long been popular with the American public, they became big business in the 1920s. The new, heavy commercialization of sports led to larger audiences and more revenues. A highly publicized fight between boxers Jack Dempsey and Georges Carpentier in 1921 broke the record for ticket sales, taking in $1 million. Dempsey won the fight to become the heavyweight champion of the world and a new American hero.

Another hero, Jim Thorpe, starred as a professional football player in the 1920s. By then he was in the late stages of his career, and his role was to attract fans to the games. Earlier, he had won Olympic gold medals in the decathlon and pentathlon and had also played professional baseball. Thorpe, a Native American, was elected the first president of what later became the National Football League.

Of all the sports heroes of the era, none generated more excitement than baseball's George Herman "Babe" Ruth, known as "the Sultan of Swat." During his career with the Boston Red Sox and then with the New York Yankees, Ruth hit 714 home runs, a record that was unbroken for nearly 40 years. In 1927, the champion enthralled Americans by setting the legendary record of 60 home runs in a 154-game season.

Women who excelled in sports included Hazel Wightman and Helen Wills, Olympic and Wimbledon tennis stars, and Gertrude Ederle, who smashed record after record in women's freestyle swimming. Ederle won one gold and two bronze medals in the 1924 Olympic Games. Newspapers hailed her as the "bob-haired, nineteen-year-old daughter of the Jazz Age." Her coach explained that her feat was a product of modern times. Thirty years previously, he said, "corsets and other ridiculously unnecessary clothing" would have hampered her physical conditioning. In 1926, Ederle became the first woman to swim the English Channel, having made an unsuccessful attempt the year before. She covered some 35 miles, taking into account crosscurrents and rough water. Her time beat the men's record by nearly two hours.

Besides being eager spectators, more Americans participated in amateur sports during the 1920s. With wide-ranging transportation, such as buses and automobiles, plus more leisure time, people took up golf, tennis, swimming, and many other types of recreation.

VIEWING HISTORY At Cape Gris Nez, France, Gertrude Ederle is greased up in preparation for her swim across the English Channel. **Analyzing Visual Information** *What does the photograph show about the difficulties of a Channel swim and what the feat might mean to the public?*

Section 1 Assessment

READING COMPREHENSION

1. How did the **flapper** symbolize change for women in the 1920s?

2. What conditions brought about the **demographic** shifts of the 1920s?

3. How did a **barrio** develop in Los Angeles during the 1920s?

CRITICAL THINKING AND WRITING

4. **Making Comparisons** How is today's youth culture similar to the youth culture of the 1920s?

5. **Writing a News Brief** Write a short news article and headline reporting on women voting in 1920 after the adoption of the Nineteenth Amendment.

For: An activity on aviators
Visit: PHSchool.com
Web Code: mrd-7201

Mass Media and the Jazz Age

READING FOCUS

- How did the mass media help create common cultural experiences?

- Why are the 1920s called the Jazz Age, and how did the jazz spirit affect the arts?

- How did the writers of the Lost Generation respond to the popular culture?

- What subjects did the Harlem Renaissance writers explore?

MAIN IDEA

In the 1920s, the mass media provided information and entertainment as never before. The decade was an especially creative period for music, art, and literature.

KEY TERMS

mass media
Jazz Age
Lost Generation
Harlem Renaissance

TARGET READING SKILL

Understand Effects Copy the web diagram below. As you read, fill in the blank circles with details on how the mass media affected American life.

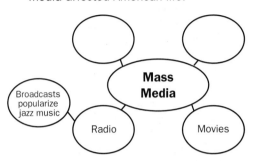

Mass Media

Broadcasts popularize jazz music

Radio

Movies

Setting the Scene

Before 1900, few people outside Los Angeles had even heard of a dusty little subdivision northwest of the city. Its founder, a religious man, hoped that it would remain a quiet town, where citizens valued proper behavior. In the early 1900s, however, filmmakers began moving there. They were attracted by the large work force in nearby Los Angeles; by the variety of landscapes, from desert to snowy mountains; and by the warm climate and the sun they needed to light their films.

These pioneer filmmakers faced many difficulties. Director Cecil B. DeMille set up his first studio in a rented barn, which he shared with horses and a carriage. DeMille later wrote, "I expected to be working like a horse: what did it matter being housed like one?"

In the early 1920s, DeMille became known for his stylish comedies that dealt with the changing romance customs of the time, and for his epics, which were designed to appeal to mass audiences. The barn he rented grew into a huge movie complex and the small suburb it was located in—Hollywood—soon became the center of the entertainment film industry. The town's main avenue displayed a strip of expensive shops and bars. Stars drove the streets in luxurious cars, trailed by reporters. In turn, what grew out of Hollywood in the 1920s—its culture of movies, movie stars, and entertainment reporters—helped create the beginnings of a common national culture.

VIEWING HISTORY Hollywood's Mulholland Drive is shown in this 1924 photo. The now-famous sign in the hills was erected to promote a real-estate development. **Analyzing Visual Information** *What details in the photograph show Hollywood's past and future?*

The Mass Media

Hollywood's new fame reflected a major trend of the 1920s. Before that time, the United States had been largely a collection of regional cultures. Interests, tastes, and attitudes varied widely from one region to another. Most Americans simply did not know much about the rest of the country, talk with people in other regions, or even read the same news as other Americans.

Adding Sound to Movies The system used to record and play sound in *The Jazz Singer* (below) was known as Vitaphone, which used a 16-inch rotating wax disk to record the movie's singing and speech. The sound was then synchronized with the film and amplified by loudspeakers in the theater. The Vitaphone system offered the best sound quality of its time.

Another method of making sound movies involved recording sound directly onto film. Although the early use of this method produced poor sound quality and distortion, by the 1930s it became the preferred technology for making "talkies."

The 1920s changed all that. Films, nationwide news gathering, and the new industry of radio broadcasting produced the beginnings of a national culture. As you have read, early in the decade few American women dressed in the flapper style or smoked and drank in public. Such customs became common cultural experiences because of the growth of the mass media. The **mass media** are print, film, and broadcast methods of communicating information to large numbers of people.

Movies From their beginnings in the 1890s, motion pictures had been a wildly popular mass medium, and through the 1920s, audiences grew. Between 1910 and 1930, the number of theaters rose from about 5,000 to about 22,500. By 1929, when the total population was less than 125 million, the nation's theaters sold roughly 80 million tickets each week. Moviemaking had become the fourth largest business in the country.

This growth occurred throughout the silent film era. In 1927, the success of the first sound film, *The Jazz Singer*, changed the course of the movie industry. Starring vaudeville performer Al Jolson, the movie included speech, singing, music, and sound effects. Audiences loved it. As more theaters played "talkies," the industry's boom continued.

Some actors never made the shift from silent films to sound films. Foreign actors, for example, often faced the choice of learning English or giving up their movie careers. Other actors moved more smoothly to talkies. Greta Garbo, a glamorous star of the silent screen, retained her popularity in speaking roles despite a heavy Swedish accent. Silent screen actress Lillian Gish won renown for playing the part of the delicate heroine. She readily transferred her expressive gestures and heart-rending glances to speaking roles. Charlie Chaplin extended the silent era. Dressed in his famous tattered suit, derby hat, and cane, Chaplin had delighted American audiences since 1914 with his silent comedy. In the era of sound, Chaplin added music to his films and successfully continued his soundless portrayal of the "little tramp."

Newspapers and Magazines Americans followed the off-screen lives of their favorite stars in two other mass media—newspapers and magazines. During the 1920s, newspapers increased both in size and in circulation, or readership. In 1900, a hefty edition of the *New York Times* totaled only 14 pages. By the mid-1920s, however, newspapers even in mid-sized American cities often totaled more than 50 pages a day, and Sunday editions were enormous. In fact, the use of newsprint roughly doubled in the United States between 1914 and 1927.

Even as newspapers grew and gained more readers, the number of independently owned newspapers fell. Many disappeared as a result of mergers. A newspaper chain, owned by a single individual or company, often bought up two of a city's established papers and merged them. Thus they created one newspaper with potentially twice the circulation. The larger the circulation, the more money that advertisers would pay to market their products in the paper and the greater the profits for the publisher. Between 1923 and 1927, the number of chains doubled, and the total number of newspapers they owned rose by 50 percent.

Profits, not quality, drove most of these newspaper chains. To attract readers, especially in the cities, many chains published tabloids. A tabloid is a compact newspaper that relies on large headlines, few words, and many pictures to tell a story. Tabloids of the 1920s replaced serious news with entertainment that focused on fashion, sports, and sensational stories about crimes and scandals. This content sold papers, as publisher William Randolph Hearst knew well. Hearst once said that he wanted his New York tabloid the *Daily Mirror* to be "90 percent entertainment, 10 percent information—and the information without boring you."

During the 1920s, sales of magazines rose, too. By 1929, Americans were buying more than 200 million copies of such popular magazines as the *Saturday Evening Post, Reader's Digest, Ladies' Home Journal,* and *Time.* These magazines provided a variety of information in a form that most people could easily digest. Advertisers, eager to reach so many potential customers, often ran full-page ads promoting their products.

With the rise of newspapers and magazines as mass media, Americans began to share the same information, read about the same events, and encounter the same ideas and fashions. Thus newspapers and magazines helped create a common popular culture.

Radio Italian physicist Guglielmo Marconi invented a means of wireless communication using radio waves in 1896. Twenty years later, relatively few Americans had radio sets, and those they had were all homemade. They used their radios to communicate with each other one-on-one. In 1920, Frank Conrad, an engineer with the Westinghouse Electric Company, set up a radio transmitter in his garage in Pittsburgh. As an experiment, he began sending recorded music and baseball scores over the radio. The response was so great that Westinghouse began broadcasting programs on a regular basis. Soon the nation had its first commercial radio station, Pittsburgh's KDKA.

At first, the only advertising on KDKA was the occasional mention of its sponsor, Westinghouse. Yet even that was enough to increase the sales of Westinghouse products, mainly home appliances. In the coming years, radio would become a profitable medium for advertisers.

Radio enjoyed tremendous growth. By 1922, more than 500 stations were on the air, and Americans eagerly bought radios to listen to them. To reach more people, networks such as the National Broadcasting Company (NBC) linked many individual stations together. Each station in the network played the same programming. Soon much of the country was listening to the same jokes, commercials, music, sports events, religious services, and news.

The Jazz Age

Both the growing radio audience and the great African American migration to the cities helped make a music called jazz widely popular in the 1920s. This music features improvisation, a process by which musicians make up music as they are playing it rather than relying completely on printed scores. It also has a type of off-beat rhythm called syncopation.

Jazz Arrives Jazz grew out of the African American music of the South, especially ragtime and blues. By the early 1900s, bands in New Orleans were

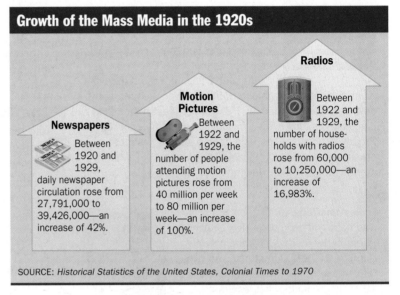

Growth of the Mass Media in the 1920s

Newspapers
Between 1920 and 1929, daily newspaper circulation rose from 27,791,000 to 39,426,000—an increase of 42%.

Motion Pictures
Between 1922 and 1929, the number of people attending motion pictures rose from 40 million per week to 80 million per week—an increase of 100%.

Radios
Between 1922 and 1929, the number of households with radios rose from 60,000 to 10,250,000—an increase of 16,983%.

SOURCE: *Historical Statistics of the United States, Colonial Times to 1970*

INTERPRETING DIAGRAMS
The decade of the 1920s saw an explosion in forms of mass communication. **Making Comparisons** *Why do you think radio grew the most during this decade?*

READING CHECK
What social changes were brought about by the mass media?

BIOGRAPHIES

Duke Ellington
(1899–1974)

Edward Kennedy Ellington was born in Washington, D.C. At 17, "Duke," as Ellington was called, played in Washington's clubs at night and painted signs during the day. In 1923, Ellington and several other musicians moved to New York City and formed a band. This band, under various names and in one form or another, continued to play with Ellington until his death at age 75.

Although Ellington was an excellent pianist, his greatest talents were as a band leader, an arranger, and a composer. He wrote at least a thousand pieces in his long career, including music for concerts, Broadway shows, films, and operas. Among his most memorable tunes are "Mood Indigo," "Solitude," "In a Sentimental Mood," "Blue Harlem," and "Bojangles."

Louis Armstrong, nicknamed "Satchmo," was born and grew up in New Orleans, where he learned to sing and play the trumpet. In 1922, Armstrong was invited to play the trumpet in Chicago, and in 1923, he made his first recordings with King Oliver's Creole Jazz Band. Armstrong's showmanship and virtuosity soon became evident, especially when he performed his improvised extended solos. Because of Armstrong, long solos became key elements of jazz ensemble performances.

Louis Armstrong
(1901–1971)

Armstrong also improvised with his voice, replacing words with nonsense syllables in a style known as "scat" singing. His first scat recording, "Heebie Jeebies," encouraged many jazz vocalists to sing scat. His Hot Five and Hot Seven ensemble recordings are among his most notable early recordings.

Sounds of an Era

Listen to a 1927 recording of "East St. Louis Toodle-oo" by Duke Ellington.

playing the new mix of styles. Although jazz recordings were available in the 1910s, many radio listeners began hearing the new sound for the first time in the 1920s. Soon jazz became a nationwide craze. Younger people in particular loved to dance to the new music. By 1929, a survey of stations showed that two thirds of all radio air time was devoted to jazz.

Some Americans were horrified by jazz. Its syncopated rhythms and improvisations were too suggestive of the free manners and morals of the age. Eventually, however, Americans from many walks of life embraced the music. The great symphony conductor Leopold Stokowski declared that jazz was "an expression of the times, of the breathless, energetic, superactive times in which we are living." The 1920s came to be called the **Jazz Age.**

Jazz Clubs and Dance Halls   One of the most popular places to listen to jazz was Harlem, a district on the northern end of the island of Manhattan. By one count, Harlem had some 500 jazz clubs. A dozen of them, including the Cotton Club, Connie's Inn, and the Saratoga Club, catered to the rich and famous. At clubs such as these, musicians, most of whom were black, performed for audiences that were primarily white.

Nearly all the great jazz musicians played in the Harlem clubs at one time or another. Jelly Roll Morton, a jazz pianist from New Orleans, arranged his band's music in a way that encouraged group improvisation. This gave his band a smooth, modern sound. Benny Goodman, known as the "King of Swing," began playing jazz professionally as a teenager in the early 1920s. His "big band" helped make jazz popular with white audiences. Goodman's 1936 quartet, which included African American musicians Lionel Hampton and Teddy Wilson, was the first popular racially mixed jazz group. Two musicians, in particular, made important contributions to jazz beginning in the 1920s: Louis Armstrong, who wowed audiences with his brilliantly improvised trumpet solos, and Duke Ellington, an arranger, composer, and bandleader, whose works are played widely to this day.

When flappers danced to jazz on the radio or to a live jazz band, most likely they did the Charleston. This dance took over the dance halls and ballrooms in the 1920s and became a national fad. The Charleston embodied the Jazz Age. It was wild and reckless, full of kicks and twists and pivots. Unlike traditional ballroom dancing, the Charleston could be danced with a partner, in a group, or all alone.

The Jazz Spirit   The jazz spirit ran through all the arts of the 1920s. People spoke of "jazz poetry" and "jazz painting." However, jazz most strongly influenced other forms of music. Composers in the Jazz Age, such as George Gershwin, mixed jazz elements into more familiar-sounding music. Gershwin, the son of

reporting to their papers over the ten days of the trial. This was the first trial ever broadcast over American radio.

On the surface, the case was a simple one. The judge ruled that the jury should determine only whether Scopes had taught evolution, which he readily admitted he had. The jury took just a few minutes to find Scopes guilty, and the judge fined him $100. However, more complex issues were at stake, including the clash between the country's modern beliefs and its traditional values.

The dramatic climax of the case came when Darrow put Bryan himself on the stand to testify as an expert on the Bible. Darrow set about testing the logic of Bryan's faith by citing passages from the Bible and forcing him to try to explain them. In the process, Darrow ridiculed fundamentalist beliefs. Under Darrow's intense, often brutal, questioning, Bryan admitted that even he did not believe all of the Bible literally. He kept fighting back, however, at one point saying, "I am simply trying to protect the word of God."

This grueling battle exhausted Bryan, who died just a few days after the trial ended. Fundamentalists saw Bryan as a martyr for their cause. Modernists saw Darrow as a defender of science and reason. Although fundamentalists considered the trial a setback, their movement remained active. In later decades, it would grow in membership and strength.

Racial Tensions

Americans clashed over race in the 1920s. African Americans took part in the Great Migration to the North in the early 1900s for two main reasons. They wanted to take advantage of greater job opportunities in the North, and they wanted to escape the increasing violence against African Americans in the South. Many of them, however, found both racial prejudice and violence in the North.

Violence Against African Americans   During the summer of 1919, mob violence between white and black Americans erupted in about 25 cities. That summer became known as the "Red Summer" for all the blood that was spilled. Omaha, Tulsa, and Washington, D.C., all suffered periods of racial turmoil. The worst of these race riots, however, occurred in Chicago.

The African American population of Chicago had doubled since 1910. This increase led to overcrowded neighborhoods and heightened tensions between blacks and whites. An incident at a beach on Lake Michigan touched off the violence. On one especially hot July day, stone-throwing had erupted between whites and blacks on a beach typically used only by whites. Meanwhile, a 17-year-old black boy, swimming just offshore with his friends, accidentally floated into the "whites only" area. A white man, who had been throwing rocks at the swimmers for some time, struck the boy, and he drowned. Furious blacks accused the whites of killing him, and more fights broke out. The riot spread through the city. For several days, chaos reigned in parts of Chicago. By the end, some 23 African Americans and 15 whites were dead, another 537 people were wounded, and the destruction caused by rioting had left hundreds homeless.

Race riots broke out in several cities in the summer of 1919.

This 1920s poster illustrates the Ku Klux Klan's views on immigration.

Some whites also directed racial violence against specific individuals. During the 1920s, the lynchings of the Jim Crow era continued. Many of these new crimes were the work of an old enemy of racial harmony, the Ku Klux Klan.

Revival of the Klan   During Reconstruction, President Grant's campaign against the Ku Klux Klan had largely eliminated it. However, in 1915 a former Methodist circuit preacher from Atlanta, Colonel William J. Simmons, revived the organization. The Klan used modern fundraising and publicity methods to increase its influence and size. By 1922, Klan membership had grown to about 100,000. Two years later, it had ballooned to 4 million. The new Klan was no longer just a southern organization. In fact, the state with the greatest number of Klansmen was Indiana. The Klan's focus shifted, too. The organization vowed to defend their own white-Protestant culture against any group, not just blacks, that seemed to them un-American:

> 66 *Klansmen are to be examples of pure patriotism. They are to organize the patriotic sentiment of native-born white, Protestant Americans for the defense of distinctively American institutions. Klansmen are dedicated to the principle that America shall be made American through the promulgation [circulation] of American doctrines, the dissemination [spread] of American ideals, the creation of wholesome American sentiment, the preservation of American institutions.* 99
> —Klansman's Manual, 1925

During the early 1920s, Klan members carried out many crimes against African Americans, Catholics, Jews, immigrants, and others. They rode by night, beating, whipping, even killing their victims, terrorizing blacks and whites alike. Then, in 1925, the head of the Klan in Indiana was sentenced to life imprisonment for assaulting a girl who later poisoned herself. The nation was finally shocked into action, and police began to step up enforcement. By 1927, Klan activity had diminished once again.

Fighting Discrimination   Increasing violence against African Americans rallied the efforts of the NAACP. During the 1920s, the NAACP worked in vain to pass federal anti-lynching laws. A proposed law passed the House of Representatives in 1922 but died in the Senate. Law enforcement improved at the state level, and the number of lynchings gradually decreased. Ten lynchings were reported in 1929.

During the 1920s, the NAACP also worked to protect the voting rights of African Americans, but again it had only limited success. For example, the Supreme Court struck down as unconstitutional a Texas law prohibiting blacks from voting in the Democratic primary. Yet the Texas legislature got around the law by giving political parties the right to decide who could vote in primary elections. African Americans in the South still could not exercise their full political rights.

READING CHECK

Where and how did racial issues surface in the 1920s?

The Garvey Movement   Some African Americans, frustrated by continued violence and discrimination, dreamed of a new homeland where they could live in peace. An African American named Marcus Garvey worked to make that dream a reality. Garvey had come to New York City from his native Jamaica in 1916 to establish a new headquarters for his Universal Negro Improvement Association (UNIA).

Through the UNIA, Garvey sought to build up African Americans' self-respect and economic power. African Americans were encouraged to buy shares in Garvey's Negro Factories Corporation, a set of small black-owned businesses. He also urged African Americans to return to "Motherland Africa" to create a self-governing nation. Garvey's message of racial pride and independence attracted a large number of followers to his black nationalist movement. Garvey held regular UNIA meetings in Harlem, and his followers could be seen in military-style uniforms reflecting their status, whether as members of the marching band, the Black Cross Nurses, or the African Legion. Several respected African American leaders, such as W.E.B. Du Bois, criticized the movement, however. They objected to Garvey's call for separation of the races, as well as his careless business practices.

Garvey gathered $10 million for a steamship company, the Black Star Line, that would carry his followers back to the motherland. Corruption and mismanagement plagued the shipping line, however, and in 1925, Garvey was jailed on mail fraud charges relating to the sale of stock in the steamship company. From prison the same year, he wrote in an essay: "Why should we be discouraged because somebody laughs at us today? Who [is] to tell what tomorrow will bring forth? . . . We see and have changes every day, so pray, work, be steadfast and be not dismayed."

Garvey's sentence was later commuted, and he was deported to Jamaica in 1927. Without his leadership, the UNIA in America collapsed. Still, Garvey's ideas remained an inspiration to later "black pride" movements.

VIEWING HISTORY This ship belonged to Marcus Garvey's Black Star Line steamship company, founded in 1919. It was one of many enterprises Garvey (left) hoped would strengthen the African American community. **Drawing Conclusions** *Was Marcus Garvey a successful leader?*

Section 3 Assessment

READING COMPREHENSION

1. What were the goals of Prohibition?

2. How did organized crime profit from **bootleggers** and **speakeasies** during Prohibition?

3. How were religious issues and **fundamentalism** at odds with the teaching of evolution?

4. Which positions did William Jennings Bryan and Clarence Darrow each represent in the **Scopes trial?**

5. Why were many African Americans drawn to Marcus Garvey's message and movement?

CRITICAL THINKING AND WRITING

6. **Predicting Consequences** How might life in the 1920s have been different without Prohibition?

7. **Synthesizing Information** Consider the racial tensions that existed in the 1920s and those that exist today. Why are racial issues difficult to resolve?

8. **Writing a Conclusion** Write a short essay that supports the following conclusion: Differences between traditional and modern beliefs were responsible for the cultural conflicts of the 1920s.

For: An activity on Prohibition
Visit: PHSchool.com
Web Code: mrd-7203

creating a CHAPTER SUMMARY

Copy this chart (right) on a piece of paper and complete it by adding information about the effects of important social changes and conflicts that occurred in the 1920s. Some entries have been completed for you as examples.

For additional review and enrichment activities, see the interactive version of *America: Pathways to the Present*, available on the Web and on CD-ROM.

Conflict and Change in the 1920s	
Change/Conflict	**Impact on Society**
Women win the right to vote.	Their vote influences local politics.
Prohibition takes effect.	
Farm prices drop.	

★ Reviewing Key Terms

For each of the terms below, write a sentence explaining how it relates to the 1920s.

1. flapper
2. demographics
3. barrio
4. mass media
5. Jazz Age
6. Lost Generation
7. bootleggers
8. speakeasies
9. fundamentalism
10. Scopes trial

★ Reviewing Main Ideas

11. How did women's roles change during the 1920s? (Section 1)

12. What types of demographic change occurred during the 1920s? (Section 1)

13. Name two American heroes from the 1920s and tell why they were popular at that time. (Section 1)

14. What types of changes occurred with the rise of mass media in the 1920s? (Section 2)

15. Explain the significance of radio broadcasting in the Jazz Age. (Section 2)

16. What was the Lost Generation? What trends in society did they find troubling? (Section 2)

17. How were the experiences of African Americans reflected by the writers of the Harlem Renaissance? (Section 2)

18. What cultural conflicts did Prohibition highlight? (Section 3)

19. What divisions in American society did the Scopes trial reflect? (Section 3)

20. Describe the racial conflicts experienced in the 1920s. (Section 3)

★ Critical Thinking

21. **Drawing Conclusions** Why did women fail to have an immediate impact on national elections after the passage of the Nineteenth Amendment?

22. **Drawing Inferences** Evaluate the possible impact of racial tensions of the 1920s on the growth of the Universal Negro Improvement Association (UNIA).

23. **Comparing Points of View** Evaluate Prohibition from the point of view of (a) a law officer, (b) a bootlegger, (c) a member of the Woman's Christian Temperance Union.

24. **Demonstrating Reasoned Judgment** Explain the meaning of this statement: "For many African Americans, migration to the North was a mixed success."

★ Standardized Test Prep

Analyzing Political Cartoons ▶

25. Herbert Hoover famously referred to Prohibition as a "noble experiment." Why does the cartoonist show the Woman's Christian Temperance Union (WCTU) as a nurse assisting in the "experiment"?

    A The WCTU opposed the Eighteenth Amendment.

    B Hoover was counting on votes from the WCTU.

    C The WCTU opposed Prohibition.

    D The WCTU had pushed for Prohibition for many years.

26. What is the cartoonist's message?

Analyzing Primary Sources

Reread the poem below, "First Fig" by Edna St. Vincent Millay, from Section 2:

(1) ❝ My candle burns at both ends;

(2)   It will not last the night;

(3)   But ah, my foes, and oh, my friends—

(4)   It gives a lovely light! ❞

27. Which of the following BEST expresses the speaker's meaning in lines one and two?

    A She feels bright.

    B She lives in a dark world.

    C She stays up all night.

    D The pace of her life is dangerously fast.

28. Which of the following BEST expresses the meaning of lines three and four?

    F Her lifestyle is exciting while it lasts.

    G She feels bright and lovely.

    H Her friends and foes approve of her lifestyle.

    I Her life is quiet.

"YES, IT'S A NOBLE EXPERIMENT."

Test-Taking Tip

To answer Question 25, recall that the word *temperance* means "moderation or abstinence from drinking alcoholic liquors."

Applying the Chapter Skill

Supporting a Position Review the steps involved in supporting a position outlined on page 466. Then reread the Comparing Primary Sources quotes on page 468. What reasons does each speaker give as evidence to support his or her position on the Eighteenth Amendment?

For: Chapter 13 Self-Test
Visit: PHSchool.com
Web Code: mra-7204

American Pathways

CULTURE

The Arts in America

Throughout the nation's history, the arts have reflected the era in which they were created. Newspapers and magazines have brought the latest information into American homes. Books, movies, and music often have focused on issues of national concern.

1 Early American Arts and Crafts

1732–1776   The colonial period abounded with artisans such as Paul Revere, news printers such as Benjamin Franklin, and writers such as Franklin, Thomas Paine, and Thomas Jefferson.

A bowl made by Paul Revere (right)

2 A New Nation

1783–1860   A spirit of improvement swept the new nation, leading to increased interest in education and the arts. Transcendental writers Ralph Waldo Emerson and Henry David Thoreau celebrated both the individual and the natural world, and intellectuals like Margaret Fuller sought to raise awareness of women's new roles in society.

Henry David Thoreau (far left) and Ralph Waldo Emerson (left)

3 Civil War to World War I

1861–1918   Following the Civil War, Americans embraced new forms of popular entertainment, including vaudeville, minstrel shows, ragtime music, jazz, and motion pictures.

A poster for the 1903 film *The Great Train Robbery* (right)

4 The Jazz Age

1920–1929 The popularity of jazz soared during the Roaring Twenties, and its spirit ran through many of the other arts of the time.

Louis Armstrong's Hot Five jazz band (below) and record labels from the 1920s (right)

6 Postwar Turmoil and Change

1945–Present After World War II, Americans experienced a time of rapid cultural and social change. Writers and other artists explored subjects such as youthful rebellion, civil rights, environmental issues, and the Vietnam War.

American artist Georgia O'Keeffe (above)

5 The Great Depression and World War II

1929–1945 During this period, serious works of art dealt with the despair of the Depression and the war, while entertainment largely sought to offer a means of escape from these harsh realities.

American author John Steinbeck (above)

Continuity and Change

1. What works of literature created in colonial times helped bring about the American Revolution? Explain.
2. How did Ernest Hemingway and F. Scott Fitzgerald view the era in which they lived?

For: A study guide on the arts in America
Visit: PHSchool.com
Web Code: mrd-7209

Politics and Prosperity
(1920–1929)

SECTION 1   A Republican Decade

SECTION 2   A Business Boom

SECTION 3   The Economy in the Late 1920s

Coolidge backers sang this song to show their support.

American Events

1919

During a Red Scare, the Palmer raids target suspected Communists and other "subversives." Labor strikes are widespread.

1920

Sacco and Vanzetti are arrested and later tried and convicted for murder. They are executed in 1927.

1923

Senate hearings on Teapot Dome reveal corruption in the Harding administration.

Presidential Terms: Woodrow Wilson 1913–1921   Warren G. Harding 1921–1923   Calvin Coolidge 1923–1929

1918   **1920**   **1922**   **1924**

World Events

The Russian civil war ends.

The Chinese Communist Party is founded.

In Germany, Hitler's Beer Hall Putsch fails.

Soviet leader Vladimir Ilyich Lenin dies.

1920   **1921**   **1923**   **1924**

★ Standardized Test Prep

Analyzing Political Cartoons ▶

26. What is this cartoon satirizing?

  A The Teapot Dome Scandal

  B Scandals during President Harding's administration

  C Scandals during President Coolidge's administration

  D Laissez-faire politics

27. Why are Cabinet members advertised as being for sale?

Analyzing Primary Sources

Reread President Harding's quote from the first page of Section 1, and then answer the questions that follow.

28. Which statement BEST represents the meaning of the quotation?

  A Americans need to commit to radical reforms.

  B The nation's problems can be solved with international assistance.

  C The nation should look calmly inward and proceed with caution.

  D The nation's heroes will lead the country to triumph.

29. Harding's message was effective because

  F the heroic actions taken in World War I were no longer admired.

  G Americans were seeking the stability and normalcy Harding promised.

  H voters were looking for Harding to deliver dramatic solutions to their problems.

  I sustaining international ties was important to the American public.

Test-Taking Tip

To answer Question 29, note that Harding says the American people do not need heroics, the dramatic, or internationality.

Applying the Chapter Skill

Analyzing Advertising Turn to the vacuum cleaner ad in Section 2. What does the ad say about life in the 1920s? What does the ad promise that the vacuum cleaner will do for the consumer?

For: Chapter 14 Self-Test
Visit: PHSchool.com
Web Code: mra-7214

Geography & History

Taking to the Highway

Car ownership expanded rapidly during the 1910s and the 1920s. By 1927, some 54 percent of American families owned a car. The growing popularity of car travel and the usefulness of trucks during World War I led to calls for federally funded highways. In 1926, the first nationwide system of numbered highways was introduced, as shown on this map.

Aid for Highways

The first paved highways were built with state and local funding. The Federal Highway Act of 1921 provided federal funding for the first time for a national system of paved highways.

Geographic Connection

How would a federal highway system with uniform route numbers make long-distance travel easier than separate systems of numbered highways in each state?

Principal U.S. Highways, 1926

Washington
Oregon
Idaho
Nevada
California
Montana
Wyoming
Utah
Arizona
New Mexico
Colorado
North Dakota
South Dakota
Nebraska
Kansas
Okla.
Texas

0   100   200 mi.
0   100   200 km

— Principal U.S. highways
(80) Route numbers

The Difficulties of Early Car Travel

When cars were first introduced in the 1890s and early 1900s, they had to travel on poorly maintained dirt roads that often turned to mud when it rained.

Finding the Way

Improved highways helped make auto tourism and car camping popular. To find their way, drivers turned to road maps, which often carried advertisements for car and camping accessories.

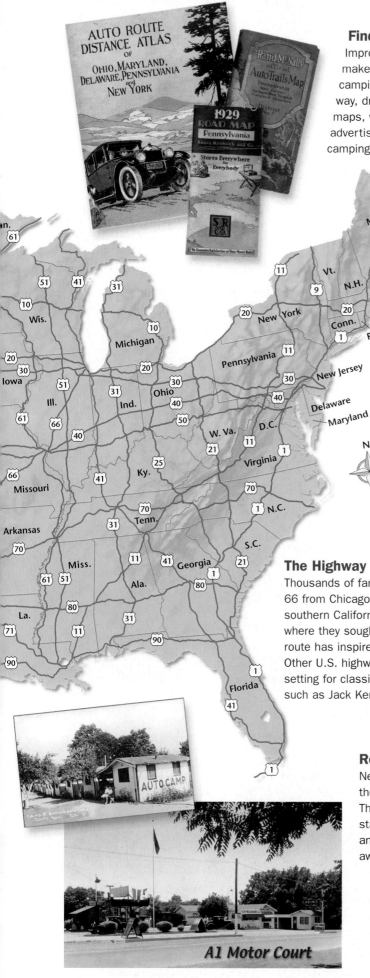

Safe and Reliable

At first, the difficulty of travel made driving more of a sport or hobby than a routine means of transportation. The development of covered cars and a system of paved highways helped carmakers promote cars as family vehicles.

The Highway in Popular Culture

Thousands of families followed Route 66 from Chicago and the Midwest to southern California or the Southwest, where they sought a better life. The route has inspired songs and stories. Other U.S. highways have provided a setting for classic American novels, such as Jack Kerouac's *On the Road.*

Roadside Businesses

New businesses along highways served the growing numbers of car travelers. These postcards show an early service station with a motor court, or motel, and an auto camp, featuring cabins with awnings for cars.

Geographic Connection

How did car travel and highway construction change this country's landscape?

A1 Motor Court

Chapter 15

Crash and Depression
(1929–1933)

SECTION 1 The Stock Market Crash
SECTION 2 Social Effects of the Depression
SECTION 3 Surviving the Great Depression
SECTION 4 The Election of 1932

Tickertape machines delivered investors news about their stocks.

The Long and the Short of it

American Events

1929
Oct. 29: Stock prices tumble in what is known as the Great Crash. Investors lose millions of dollars, and the economy sinks into a devastating depression.

1930
Congress passes the Hawley-Smoot tariff, the highest import tax in American history, in an effort to protect domestic industries. World trade suffers as a result.

1931
The Empire State Building, the world's tallest, opens in New York City.

Presidential Terms: Herbert Hoover 1929–1933

1929   **1930**   **1931**

World Events

The term *apartheid* is introduced in South Africa.

Five nations meet at the London Naval Conference.

Japanese troops occupy Manchuria.

1929   **1930**   **1931**

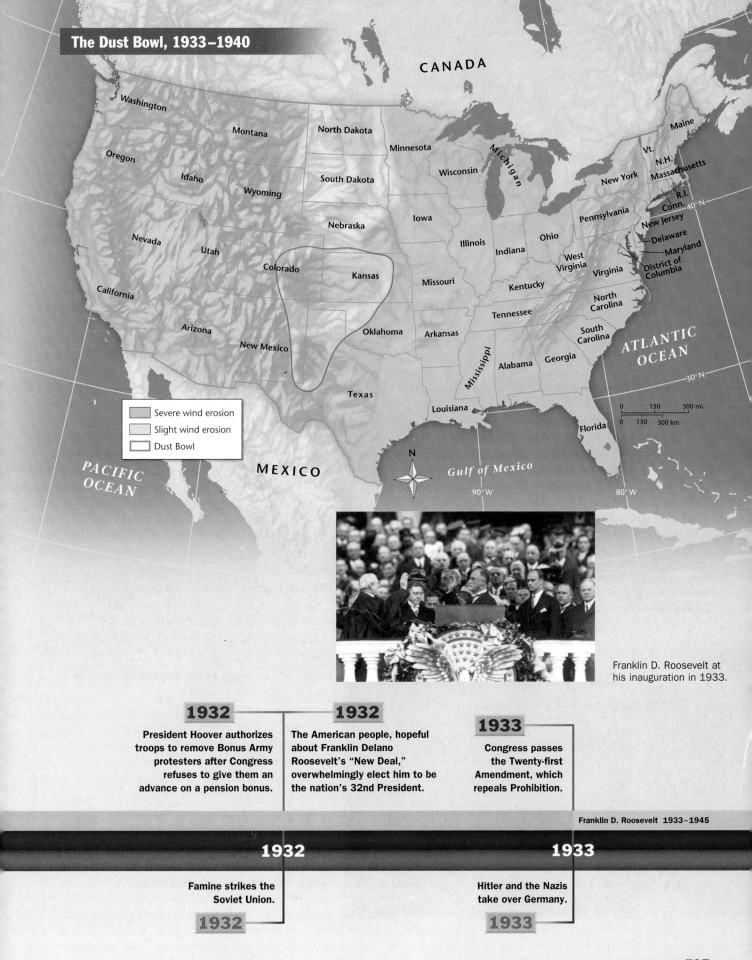

The Dust Bowl, 1933–1940

CANADA

Washington
Montana
North Dakota
Minnesota
Oregon
Idaho
Wyoming
South Dakota
Wisconsin
Michigan
Maine
Vt.
N.H.
New York
Massachusetts
Nevada
Utah
Nebraska
Iowa
Illinois
Indiana
Ohio
Pennsylvania
New Jersey
R.I.
Conn.
40° N
California
Colorado
Kansas
Missouri
Kentucky
West Virginia
Virginia
Delaware
Maryland
District of Columbia
Arizona
New Mexico
Oklahoma
Arkansas
Tennessee
North Carolina
South Carolina
ATLANTIC OCEAN
Texas
Mississippi
Alabama
Georgia
Louisiana
30° N

PACIFIC OCEAN

MEXICO

Florida

Severe wind erosion
Slight wind erosion
Dust Bowl

0   150   300 mi.
0   150   300 km

N

Gulf of Mexico
90° W
80° W

Franklin D. Roosevelt at his inauguration in 1933.

1932

President Hoover authorizes troops to remove Bonus Army protesters after Congress refuses to give them an advance on a pension bonus.

1932

The American people, hopeful about Franklin Delano Roosevelt's "New Deal," overwhelmingly elect him to be the nation's 32nd President.

1933

Congress passes the Twenty-first Amendment, which repeals Prohibition.

Franklin D. Roosevelt 1933–1945

1932

Famine strikes the Soviet Union.

1932

1933

Hitler and the Nazis take over Germany.

1933

READING FOCUS

• What events led to the stock market's Great Crash in 1929?

• Why did the Great Crash produce a ripple effect throughout the nation's economy?

• What were the main causes of the Great Depression?

MAIN IDEA

In October 1929, panic selling caused the United States stock market to crash. The crash led to a worldwide economic crisis called the Great Depression.

KEY TERMS

Dow Jones Industrial Average
Black Tuesday
Great Crash
business cycle
Great Depression

TARGET READING SKILL

Identify Cause and Effect As you read, complete the following diagram to show some of the causes and effects of the Stock Market's Great Crash in 1929.

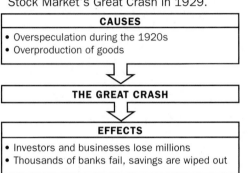

CAUSES
• Overspeculation during the 1920s
• Overproduction of goods

THE GREAT CRASH

EFFECTS
• Investors and businesses lose millions
• Thousands of banks fail, savings are wiped out

Setting the Scene On October 29, 1929, fear gripped the floors of the New York Stock Exchange as investors watched millions of dollars slip away. The "wonderful prosperity" of the 1920s had come to an abrupt end. Writers Gordon Thomas and Max Morgan-Witts captured the scene:

> 66 *A messenger struggling through the crowd suddenly found himself yanked by his hair off his feet. The man who held him kept screaming he had been ruined. He would not let the boy go. The terrified youth at last broke free, leaving the man holding tufts of his hair. Crying in pain, the messenger fled the Exchange. His hair never regrew.*
>
> *Behind, he left a scene of increasing pandemonium. As huge blocks of shares continued to be dumped, . . . 1,000 brokers and a support army of 2,000 page boys, clerks, telephonists . . . and official recorders could sense this was going to be the 'day of the millionaire's slaughter.'*
>
> *William Crawford, swept along helplessly by the great tide of people, would always remember how 'they roared like a lot of lions and tigers. They hollered and screamed, they clawed at one another's collars. It was like a bunch of crazy men.'* 99
>
> —Gordon Thomas and Max Morgan-Witts from *The Day the Bubble Burst*

VIEWING HISTORY As stock market prices fell, the ticker tape could not report market activity fast enough. Nervous investors crowded into Wall Street hoping to hear the latest news. **Identifying Central Issues** Why did investors panic in October 1929?

The Market Crashes

Before the panic on that fateful October day, most people saw no reason to worry. In early 1928, the **Dow Jones Industrial Average,** an average of stock prices of major industries, had climbed to 191. By Hoover's Inauguration

Day, March 4, 1929, it had risen another 122 points. By September 3, the Dow Jones average reached an all-time high of 381.

The rising stock market dominated the news. Keeping track of prices became almost as popular as counting Babe Ruth's home runs. Eager, nervous investors filled brokerage houses to catch the latest news coming in on the ticker tape. Prices for many stocks soared far above their real value in terms of the company's earnings and assets.

Black Thursday   After the peak in September, stock prices fell slowly. Some brokers began to call in loans, but others continued to lend even more. One bank official assured the nervous public: "Although in some cases speculation has gone too far, . . . the markets generally are now in a healthy condition."

When the stock market closed on Wednesday, October 23, the Dow Jones average had dropped 21 points in an hour. The next day, Thursday, October 24, worried investors began to sell, and stock prices fell. Investors who had bought General Electric stock at $400 a share sold it for $283 a share.

Again, business and political leaders told the country not to worry. Another banking executive said that only a nation as rich as the United States could "withstand the shock of a $3 billion paper loss on the Stock Exchange in a single day without serious effects to the average citizen." President Hoover maintained that the nation's business "is on a sound and prosperous basis."

Black Tuesday   To stop the panic, a group of bankers pooled their money to buy stock. This action stabilized prices, but only for a few days. By Monday, prices were falling again. Investors all over the country raced to get their money out of the stock market. On October 29, **Black Tuesday,** a record 16.4 million shares were sold, compared with the average 4 million to 8 million shares a day earlier in the year.

This collapse of the stock market is known as the **Great Crash.** Despite efforts to halt it, the Crash continued beyond Black Tuesday. By November 13, the Dow Jones average had fallen from its September high of 381 to 198.7. Overall losses totaled $30 billion. The Great Crash was part of the nation's **business cycle,** a span in which the economy grows, then contracts.

The Ripple Effect of the Crash

Initially the effects of the Crash were felt only by those who were heavily invested in the stock market. By 1929, that number was about 4 million people out of a population of 120 million. Some investors lost everything. One wealthy Bostonian who lost heavily in the market wrote in his diary, "The profit in my little book melted yesterday to seven thousand. It is probably nil [nothing] today. . . . My dreams of a million—where are they?"

Within a short time, however, the effects of the Great Crash began to ripple throughout the nation's economy. Soon millions of people who had never owned a share of stock were affected. The following list explains how the effects of the Crash spread to all Americans.

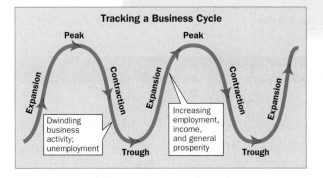

Tracking a Business Cycle

Peak — Expansion — Contraction — Peak

Dwindling business activity; unemployment

Increasing employment, income, and general prosperity

Trough

READING CHECK
Who felt the effects of the Great Crash?

Risky loans hurt banks Banks earn their profits on the interest they earn from lending out their deposits. Throughout the 1920s, banks loaned huge sums of money to many high-risk businesses. When stock prices fell, these businesses were unable to repay their loans.

Consumer borrowing Banks also make money on loans they lend to consumers. Consumers had borrowed heavily from banks throughout the 1920s to purchase consumer goods. When banks called in their loans, customers did not have cash to pay them.

Bank runs The Great Crash resulted in widespread bank runs. Fearful that banks would run out of money, people rushed to make withdrawals from their accounts. To pay back these deposits, banks had to recall loans from borrowers. However, many businesses and consumers hurt by falling stock prices could not repay their loans. Even if loans were repaid, banks could not get the money fast enough to pay all the depositors demanding their money.

Bank failures The combination of unpaid loans and bank runs meant that many banks across the country failed. Thousands of banks closed their doors when they could not return their depositors' money. In just a few years, more than 5,500 banks failed.

Savings wiped out Bank failures wiped out what little savings people had. By 1933, the money from 9 million savings accounts had vanished.

Cuts in production Businesses now could not borrow money to use to produce more goods. In addition, businesses lacked any incentive to spend money producing goods. Few people had money to buy them.

Rise in unemployment As businesses cut back on production, they laid off workers. Unemployment grew.

INTERPRETING DIAGRAMS
After the Great Crash, each sector of the economy experienced a damaging cycle of events. Each cycle also directly influenced the others. **Expressing Problems Clearly** *How did the events following the Great Crash interact and affect one another?*

Effects of the Great Crash, 1929

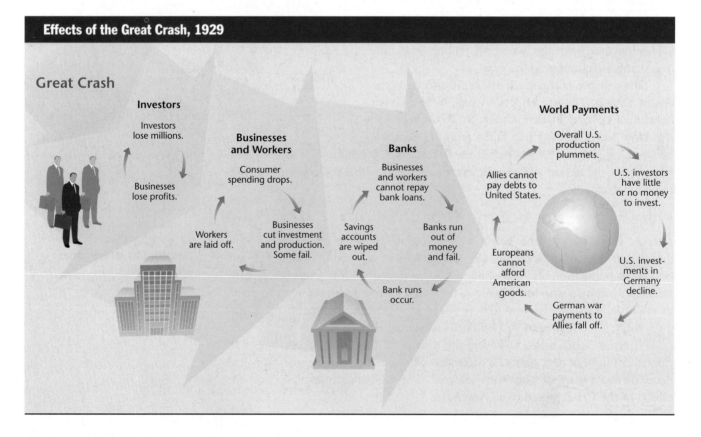

Great Crash

Investors
Investors lose millions.
Businesses lose profits.

Businesses and Workers
Consumer spending drops.
Workers are laid off.
Businesses cut investment and production. Some fail.

Banks
Businesses and workers cannot repay bank loans.
Savings accounts are wiped out.
Banks run out of money and fail.
Bank runs occur.

World Payments
Overall U.S. production plummets.
Allies cannot pay debts to United States.
Europeans cannot afford American goods.
German war payments to Allies fall off.
U.S. investors have little or no money to invest.
U.S. investments in Germany decline.

Further cuts in production As unemployment grew and incomes shrank, consumers spent less and less money and businesses produced still fewer goods. The overall output of goods in the economy dropped.

Economic Contraction

The results of the Great Crash described above are symptoms of a contracting economy. A contraction is an economic decline marked by a falling output of goods and services. A particularly long and severe contraction is called a depression. The economy had begun to show danger signs in the late 1920s; the Great Crash triggered even more serious consequences. The result was the most severe economic downturn in the nation's history—the **Great Depression**—which lasted from 1929 until the United States entered World War II in 1941.

Impact on Workers and Farmers

With no money and little incentive to produce more goods, factories throughout the country began to close. Thousands of workers lost their jobs or endured pay cuts. In August 1931, Henry Ford shut down his Detroit automobile factories, putting at least 75,000 people out of work.

Soon after local factories closed, small local businesses began to suffer as well. Restaurants and other small businesses closed because customers could no longer afford to go to them. Formerly wealthy families dismissed household workers. Farm prices, already low, fell even more, bringing disaster to many families. In 1929, a bushel of wheat had sold for $1.18; in 1932 it brought a mere 49 cents. Cotton dropped from 19 to 6.5 cents a pound.

By 1932, more than 12 million people were unemployed, which accounted for about a quarter of the labor force. (See the graph to the right.) Others worked only part-time or had their wages cut. The Gross National Product (GNP)—the total value of goods and services a country produces annually—dove from $103 billion in 1929 to just $56 billion in 1933.

Impact on the World

By the 1930s, international banking, manufacturing, and trade had made nations around the world interdependent. For example, Latin America depended on U.S. markets for its goods. Europeans depended on the United States for investments and loans. When the world's leading economy fell, the global economic system began to crumble or contract in much the same way the U.S. economy had.

After World War I, the United States had insisted that France and Britain, its wartime allies, repay their war debts. At the same time, Congress kept import taxes high, making it hard for European nations to sell goods in the United States. With economies weakened by the war and little chance of selling goods in the United States, the Allies had to rely on Germany's reparations payments for income.

As long as American companies invested in Germany, reparations payments continued. But with the Depression, investments fell off. German banks failed, Germany suspended reparations, and the Allies, in turn, stopped paying their debts. Industrial production fell by 40 percent in Germany, 14 percent in Britain, and 29 percent in France. Europeans could no longer afford to buy American-made goods. Thus the American stock market crash started a downward cycle in the global economy.

Economic Impact of the Great Depression

Stock Prices 1925–1933

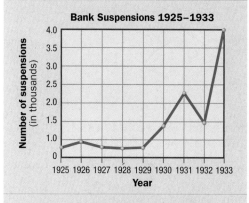

*Based on Standard and Poor's index of common stocks

Bank Suspensions 1925–1933

Unemployment 1925–1933

SOURCE: *Historical Statistics of the United States, Colonial Times to 1970*

INTERPRETING GRAPHS
The stock market crash caused a series of economic disasters.
Analyzing Information *Roughly how many people became unemployed between 1929 and 1933?*

Underlying Causes of the Depression

The stock market crash of 1929 did not cause the Great Depression. Rather, both the Great Crash and the Depression were the result of deep underlying problems with the country's economy.

An Unstable Economy Overall, the seemingly prosperous economy of the 1920s lacked a firm base. National wealth was unevenly distributed, with most money in the hands of a few families who tended to save or invest rather than buy goods. Industry produced more goods than most consumers wanted or could afford. Farmers and many workers had not shared in the economic boom. The uneven prosperity of the 1920s made rapid recovery from an economic downturn impossible.

Overspeculation During the 1920s, speculators bought stocks with borrowed money and then pledged those stocks as *collateral* to buy more stocks. Collateral is an item of value that a borrower agrees to forfeit to the lender if the borrower cannot repay the loan. Brokers' loans went from under $5 billion in mid-1928 to $850 billion in September 1929. The stock market boom was based on borrowed money and optimism instead of real value.

Government Policies Mistakes in monetary policy were also to blame. During the 1920s, the Federal Reserve system, which regulates the amount of money in circulation, cut interest rates to spur economic growth. Then in 1929, worried about overspeculation, the Federal Reserve limited the money supply to discourage lending. As a result, there was too little money in circulation to help the economy recover after the Great Crash.

Section 1 Assessment

READING COMPREHENSION

1. What is the **Dow Jones Industrial Average?**

2. What happened on **Black Tuesday?**

3. Which part of the **business cycle** did the **Great Depression** represent?

4. What could cause a country's Gross National Product to decrease?

5. How did the unstable economy in the 1920s contribute to the Great Depression?

CRITICAL THINKING AND WRITING

6. **Recognizing Cause and Effect** How did the Great Depression have such a huge impact on the economies of other countries?

7. **Making Comparisons** Many people today use credit cards and charge accounts to buy on credit. Is this practice as dangerous now as it was in 1929? Why or why not?

8. **Writing to Inform** It is the day after Black Tuesday. Write a brief newspaper report describing the scene at local banks.

For: An activity on the Great Crash
Visit: PHSchool.com
Web Code: mrd-7221

Social Effects of the Depression

READING FOCUS

- How did poverty spread during the Great Depression?
- What social problems were caused by poverty in the 1930s?
- How did some people struggle to survive hard times?

MAIN IDEA

By the early 1930s, wage cuts and growing unemployment had brought widespread suffering across the United States.

KEY TERMS

Hooverville
Dust Bowl

TARGET READING SKILL

Understand Effects As you read, complete this chart by listing examples of how the Great Depression affected different parts of American society.

Effects of the Great Depression	
Social Groups	**Effects**
City laborers	Many lost their jobs, became homeless, lived in poverty, some resorted to living in "Hoovervilles"
Farmers	
Women	
Children	
Men	
Racial minorities	

Setting the Scene

Many Americans thought the Depression would not last. They were soon proved wrong. Hard times continued and eventually spread to all levels of society. Those who never imagined they would one day have to ask friends, neighbors, or even the government for money found themselves with no other option. In this account from 1934, a "middle-class" college graduate details the awkwardness and pain associated with what she described as "becoming one of them," or joining the ranks of the poor:

    Two years ago I was living in comfort and apparent security. My husband had a good position in a well-known orchestra and I was teaching a large and promising class of piano pupils. When the orchestra was disbanded we started on a rapid down-hill path. My husband was unable to secure another position. My class gradually dwindled away. We were forced to live on our savings.

    In the early summer of 1933 I was eight months pregnant and we had just spent our last twelve dollars on one month's rent for an apartment. . . . [which] lacked the most elementary comforts such as steam heat, bathtubs, sunlight, and running hot water. They usually are infested with mice and bedbugs. Ours was. . . .

    What then, did we do for food when our last money was spent on rent? So strong was the influence of our training that my husband kept looking feverishly for work when there was no work, and blaming himself because he was unable to find it. . . . An application to the Emergency Home Relief Bureau was the last act of our desperation.

—From Ann Rivington [pseudonym],
"We Live on Relief," *Scribner's Magazine*, April 1934

Poverty Spreads

Imagine that the bank where you have a savings account suddenly closes. Your money is gone. Or your parents lose their jobs and cannot pay the rent or mortgage. One day you come home to find your furniture and all of your belongings on the sidewalk—you have been evicted.

VIEWING HISTORY The number of people without jobs rose dramatically after the Crash. **Drawing Inferences** *What can you tell from this man's sign about the social view of charity in the 1930s?*

People at all levels of society faced these situations during the Great Depression. Professionals and white-collar workers, who had felt more secure in their jobs than laborers, suddenly were laid off with no prospects of finding another position. Those whose savings disappeared could not understand why banks no longer had the money they had deposited for safekeeping.

"Hoovervilles"   The hardest hit were those at the bottom of the economic ladder. Some unemployed laborers, unable to pay their rent, moved in with relatives. Others drifted around the country. In 1931, census takers estimated the homeless population in New York City alone at 15,000.

Homeless people sometimes built shanty towns, with shacks of tar paper, cardboard, or scrap material. These shelters of the homeless came to be called **Hoovervilles,** mocking the President, whom people blamed for not resolving the crisis.

A woman living in Oklahoma visited one Hooverville: "Here were all these people living in old, rusted-out car bodies," she noted. "There were people living in shacks made of orange crates. One family with a whole lot of kids were living in a piano box."

Many homeless and jobless people, rather than staying in one place, became drifters, hitchhiking from one "hobo jungle" to another. Thousands rode the rails—or jumped on trains illegally to travel across the country. They slept in boxcars or open freight cars. By 1933, an estimated one million people were on the move, risking jail, injury, or death.

Farm Distress   Farm families suffered as low crop prices cut their income. When they could not pay their mortgages, they lost their farms to the banks, which sold them at auction. In the South, landowners expelled tenant farmers and sharecroppers. In protest against low prices, farmers dumped thousands of gallons of milk and destroyed crops. These desperate actions shocked a hungry nation.

The Dust Bowl   For thousands of farm families in the Midwest, the harsh conditions of the Depression were made even more extreme by another major crisis of the decade. The origin of this one was not economic, but environmental. Between 1931 and 1940, so much soil blew out of the central and southern Great Plains that the region became known as the **Dust Bowl.**

Focus on GEOGRAPHY

Weather in the Dust Bowl The Great Plains is called "America's breadbasket." Deep, fertile soils, a long growing season, and flat land make it ideal for farming. But the region has always experienced severe weather. Hot and humid tropical air masses come from the Gulf of Mexico. Cold polar air masses rush southward from above the Arctic Circle. When these air masses collide, powerful storms with fierce updrafts are created. The complex root systems of the grasslands had protected the soil from weather. As you have read, however, when farmers plowed the land, this natural protection was lost.

The Dust Bowl was created, in part, by dust storms that began in the early 1930s. Farmers said the storms were the result of a severe drought. While drought was a major factor in creating the Dust Bowl, it was not the only factor. Farming practices also contributed.

As long as there was a thick layer of prairie grasses to protect topsoil, severe weather could not harm the land. When farmers plowed the land, however, they stripped the soil of its natural protection. Winds picked up the dark, nutrient-rich topsoil and carried it eastward, sometimes for hundreds of miles, leaving behind barren, shifting dunes of grit and sand. The map below shows the extent of soil erosion across the plains.

The most severe storms of the dry years were called "black blizzards." Time after time, dirt was swept up and dropped by the ton over states and cities far to the east. The dirt darkened the sky in New York City and Washington, D.C. It stained the snows of New England red and dropped on ships hundreds of miles off the Atlantic Coast. The drought and winds persisted for more than seven years, bringing ruin to the farmers.

The combination of terrible weather and low prices for farm products caused about 60 percent of Dust Bowl families to lose their farms. More than 440,000 people left Oklahoma during the 1930s. Nearly 300,000 people left Kansas. Thousands of families in Oklahoma, Texas, Kansas, and other southwestern Plains states migrated to California. Many found work on California's farms as laborers. About 100,000 of the Dust Bowl migrants headed to cities such as Los Angeles, San Francisco, and San Diego. Relief did not come to the Dust Bowl region until the early 1940s, when the rains finally arrived and World War II drove farm prices up.

Poverty Strains Society

As the Depression wore on, it took a serious physical and psychological toll on the entire nation. Unemployment and fear of losing a job caused great anxiety. People became depressed; many considered suicide, and some did take their own lives.

Impact on Health "No one has starved," President Hoover declared, but some did, and thousands more went hungry. Impoverished people who could not afford food or shelter got sick more easily. Children suffered most from the long-term effects of poor diet and inadequate medical care.

"All last winter we never had a fire except about once a day when Mother used to cook some mush or something," one homeless boy recalled. "When the kids were cold they went to bed. I quit high school, of course."

In the country, people grew food. In cities, they sold apples and pencils, begged for money to buy food, and fought over the contents of restaurant garbage cans. Families who had land planted "relief gardens" to feed themselves or so they could barter food for other items. One historian recalled:

Sounds of an Era

Listen to a reading from John Steinbeck's *The Grapes of Wrath* and other sounds from the Great Depression.

MAP SKILLS Drought combined with over-farming to reduce the Great Plains to dust. **Regions** *How did farmers destroy the region's natural protection against severe weather?*

Effects of the Dust Bowl and Depression, 1930–1940

CANADA

North Dakota
−23.8
−47%

South Dakota
−28.9
−57%

Wyoming
+2.5
−40%

Nebraska
−43.6
−61%

Colorado
−16.4
−51%

Kansas
−67.7
−53%

Oklahoma
−93.4
−49%

New Mexico
+17.6
−32%

Texas
+120.5
−45%

Montana Minnesota Wisconsin Michigan Iowa Ohio Illinois Indiana Missouri Kentucky Tennessee Arkansas Mississippi Alabama Georgia Utah

Area enlarged

0   100   200 mi.
0   100 200 km

N

MEXICO

Area affected by wind erosion
−16.4 Shift in number of gainful workers, 1930–1940 (in thousands)
−51% Shift in total value of harvested crops, 1929–1939 (as percent)

❝ *In Detroit nearly one out of every seven persons was on relief [government aid]. Children scavenged through the streets like animals for scraps of food, and stayed away from school. . . . Among high school students in the inner city the incidence of tuberculosis tripled. Each day four thousand children stood in bread lines. With their sunken, lifeless eyes, sallow cheeks, and distended bellies, some resembled the starving children in Europe during the war.* ❞

—Robert Conot

Stresses on Families Living conditions declined as families moved in together, crowding into small houses or apartments. People gave up even small pleasures like an ice cream cone or a movie ticket.

Men who had lost jobs or investments often felt like failures because they could no longer provide for their families. If their wives or children were working, men thought their own status had fallen. Many were embarrassed to be seen at home during normal work hours. They were ashamed to ask friends for help. Some even abandoned their families.

Women faced other problems. Those who had depended on a husband's paycheck worried about feeding their hungry children. Working women were accused of taking jobs away from men. Even in the better times of the 1920s, Henry Ford had fired married women. "We do not employ married women whose husbands have jobs," he explained. During the Depression, this practice became common. In 1931, the American Federation of Labor endorsed it. Most school districts would not hire married women as teachers, and many fired those who got married.

Many women continued to find work, however, because poor-paying jobs such as domestic service, typing, and nursing were considered "women's work." The greatest job losses

VIEWING FINE ART Dorothea Lange's most famous photographs, the "Migrant Mother" series (1936, right), have become a symbol of the Depression. The face of the undernourished mother displays a numbness to her destitute surroundings, yet a certain determination to pull through it all. Above is another of Lange's most famous photographs, "White Angel Breadline." **Determining Relevance** *What effect did Lange's photographs have on the general public?*

of the Depression were in industry and other areas that seldom hired women.

Discrimination Increases Hard economic times put groups of Americans in competition with one another for a shrinking number of jobs. This produced a general rise in suspicions and hostilities against minorities. African Americans, Hispanics, and in the West, Asian Americans all suffered as white laborers began to demand the low-paying jobs typically filled by these minorities. Hispanics and Asian Americans lost not only their jobs but also their country. Thousands were deported—even those born in the United States.

Black unemployment soared—about 56 percent of black Americans were out of work in 1932. Some white citizens declared openly that blacks had no right to jobs if whites were out of work. Gordon Parks, a photographer who rode the rails to Harlem, later wrote:

> 66 *To most blacks who had flocked in from all over the land, the struggle to survive was savage. Poverty coiled around them and me with merciless fingers.* 99

—Photographer Gordon Parks

Because government relief programs often discriminated against African Americans, black churches and organizations like the National Urban League gave private help. The followers of a Harlem evangelist known as Father Divine opened soup kitchens that fed thousands every day. Discrimination was even worse in the South, where African Americans were denied civil rights such as access to education, voting, and health care. Lynchings increased.

The justice system often ignored the rights of minority Americans. In March 1931, near Scottsboro, Alabama, nine black youths who had been riding the rails were arrested and accused of raping two white women on a train. Without being given the chance to hire a defense lawyer, eight of the nine were quickly convicted by an all-white jury and sentenced to die.

The case of the "Scottsboro boys" was taken up, and sometimes exploited, by northern groups, most notably the Communist Party. The party helped supply legal defense and organized demonstrations, which, after many years, helped overturn the convictions, but four of the "boys" spent many years in jail.

Stories of Survival

A generation of Americans would live to tell their grandchildren how they survived the Depression. Wilson Ledford first felt the effects of the Depression in March 1930 when he was 15, living in Chattanooga, Tennessee, with his mother and younger sister. Wilson had worked part time and after school in a grocery store since he was 11. By 1930, his family could no longer afford Chattanooga. They moved back to Cleveland, Tennessee, a nearby small town. They survived on the rent Wilson's mother received on a house and 15 acres of land, which she still owned. The property brought in $6 a month in rent—except when the tenants were out of work. After taxes and insurance, the family had about a dollar a week to live on. Wilson "swapped work with neighbors." He looked after the family horse and cow, chopped wood for the fireplace, tended the garden that provided family food, and raised corn to feed the animals:

BIOGRAPHY

Dorothea Lange
1895–1965

"The camera is an instrument that teaches people how to see without a camera," said photographer Dorothea Lange. Born in New Jersey in 1895, Lange decided at a young age to be a photographer. In 1919, Lange opened a portrait studio in San Francisco where she photographed wealthy clients. Beyond the windows of her studio, she could see the spreading effects of the Depression. She thought about the vast difference "between what I was working on in the printing frames [in the studio] and what was going on in the street."

Lange's first exhibition, in 1934, landed her an assignment to photograph the hundreds of migrant workers streaming into California from the Dust Bowl. Lange's photographs showed the world the desperation and bravery of families displaced by the Depression.

Lange continued to document the suffering and mistreatment of other Americans until her death in 1965. But she will be forever linked in people's minds to the 1930s and the human courage that she made a part of the nation's permanent record.

❝ *We had to raise most of what we ate since money was so scarce. . . . Sometimes I plowed for other people when I could get the work. . . . I got 15 cents an hour for plowing, and I furnished the horse and plow.* ❞

—Wilson Ledford

Nothing was wasted. Wilson's mother kept chickens and traded eggs at the store for things they could not grow or raise. Overalls cost 98 cents; shoes were $2. She bought a pig for $3 and raised it for meat, and she made jelly from wild blackberries. Despite the family's own poverty, she gave extra milk and butter to "some poor people, a woman with three small children who lived in a one-room shack with a dirt floor."

Wilson never got to high school, "as survival was more important." The Ledfords had no radio, but Wilson made his own entertainment. Wilson and some other boys cleaned the rocks off a field, graded it, and made a baseball diamond. Baseballs were precious. "You could buy a pretty good baseball for a quarter and a real good one for 50 cents. . . . If we lost a ball during the game, everyone had to go hunt for it."

In the summer of 1932, when he was 17, Wilson got a job in Chattanooga delivering ice. He worked there again the next summer: "I worked twelve hours a day, six days a week, and made $3.00 a week." When the icehouse closed in the fall, Wilson hitchhiked throughout the Southeast looking for work, but never had any success. "I pumped up so many tires for people I rode with, I had blisters all in my hands. Finally I got back home."

Later Wilson bought a truck to haul coal, cotton, and oranges, then worked nights in a woolen mill while carrying ice during the day. Finally, "I got a call from Chickamauga Dam and I went to work there. That was a good job working on the dam. I made 60 cents an hour. Times were better by then, but did not start booming until World War II started."

Section 2 Assessment

READING COMPREHENSION

1. Who lived in **Hoovervilles?**

2. What factors led to the creation of the **Dust Bowl** in the 1930s?

3. What were some causes and effects of increased discrimination during the Great Depression?

4. What can you learn about the Depression from Wilson Ledford's experiences?

CRITICAL THINKING AND WRITING

5. Identifying Central Issues Explain the effect the Depression had on the psychology of many Americans. Why do you think the Depression changed people's goals and expectations?

6. Writing an Interview In an effort to learn firsthand what it was like to live during the Great Depression, write ten questions that you might ask someone who lived through it.

For: An activity on the Dust Bowl
Visit: PHSchool.com
Web Code: mrd-7222

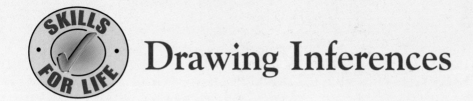

Drawing Inferences

Drawing inferences is a way of interpreting what you read. When you draw inferences about a person's character, you add what you know to what an author tells you, including facts about the person's words and actions, and ideas that are implied but not directly stated in the text.

Gordon Parks eventually became a successful photographer and writer. But when the Great Depression hit, he was only a teenager, on his own and desperately in need of a job and a place to live. When he tried to get a room in a cheap hotel, he was refused because he was black (Passage A). Later, Parks determined to become a photographer (Passage B).

LEARN THE SKILL
Use the following steps to draw inferences:

1. **Identify stated facts.** Identify what the person actually said and did. Determine what information is directly stated.

2. **Identify unstated ideas.** Distinguish between what is implied by the facts and what is suggested by the perspective of the author.

3. **Add what you know.** Use information you know about the historical period and about human nature to help you understand the person's actions.

4. **Draw inferences about the person's character.** Keep the point of view of the author in mind, and be wary of authors who may have a bias.

PRACTICE THE SKILL
Answer the following questions:

1. Summarize the facts in each passage.

2. **(a)** What does Passage A suggest about Parks's reaction to racism? Explain. **(b)** Where does Parks suggest what he wants you to think? **(c)** What do you think the author of Passage B wants you to feel about Parks? Explain.

3. **(a)** How does your knowledge of the Depression help you understand what Parks does in Passage A? **(b)** How does your understanding of human nature help you evaluate Parks's decision to tell the truth in Passage B? Explain.

4. **(a)** From the passages, what inferences can you draw about Parks as a teenager? As an adult? **(b)** How do the two passages help you understand Gordon Parks?

APPLY THE SKILL
See the Chapter Review and Assessment for another opportunity to apply this skill.

A

"Mike tells me you're looking for a room and work. That so?" [the manager] asked, squinting down . . . at me.
"That's right."
"You look like a clean-cut colored boy."
"I'm a boy. I don't know what my color's got to do with it."
"Don't go gittin' your dander up. I think I got a proposition for you." I waited. "How'd you like to have a room and a job both?"
"Where?"
"Right here. I'm needin' a boy to clean this place. You'll git a room in the back and a half a buck a day. . . ."
"I'd like to know why I can't just pay and sleep here?"
"Look, I ain't no expert on race problems," the . . . man said impatiently. "I'm just givin' you a proposition. Whyn't you try it and see how things work out?"
"Give me twenty-five cents more a day and some food."
"Hell, fellow, you'll be makin' a buck a day with all that. That's big dough round these parts."
"Sorry," I said, turning as if I were going.
"Just a second." I had bluffed him into a decision. "Okay. . . ."

—Gordon Parks, *Voices in the Mirror: An Autobiography*

B

"Early in 1938, Parks walked through the door of an upscale women's clothing store in St. Paul and asked if they might need any fashions photographed. The manager wasn't interested, but the fellow's wife convinced him to give Parks a chance. Parks borrowed a Speed Graphic camera on credit, and spent a day photographing models. But when he developed the film, he was devastated to find that he had double-exposed all but one shot. Sally Parks [his wife] suggested he take a chance and blow up the one good picture. When the store manager saw it, he was thrilled. Where were the rest? Parks told the truth. He was allowed to reshoot. Soon his pictures filled the windows of Frank Murphy's store. That was the beginning. . . ."

—Dick Russell, *Black Genius and the American Experience*

Surviving the Great Depression

READING FOCUS

- In what ways did Americans pull together to survive the Great Depression?
- What signs of change did Americans begin to notice in the early 1930s?

MAIN IDEA

Americans survived the Great Depression with determination and even humor. They helped one another, looked for solutions, and waited for the hard times to pass.

KEY TERMS

penny auction
Twenty-first Amendment

TARGET READING SKILL

Identify Supporting Details As you read, prepare an outline of this section. Use Roman numerals to indicate the major headings of this section, capital letters for the subheadings, and numbers for the supporting details.

> **I. Americans Pull Together**
>   **A. Farmers Stick Together**
>   **1. Worked together to minimize impact of Great Depression**
>   2. _____
>   3. _____
>   **B. Young People Ride the Rails**
>   **1. Young people left home to seek a better life.**
>   2. _____
>   3. _____

Setting the Scene No one who lived through the Great Depression ever forgot it. Long after the economy rebounded, many from the "Depression generation," even those who recovered enough to live a very comfortable life, would continue to pinch pennies as if financial ruin were just around the corner. Many Americans avoided buying on credit, instead saving for years to pay cash for needed items. Others even stuffed money under their mattresses rather than trust their life savings to banks.

Americans Pull Together

Not all the memories of the Depression were bad or despairing, as one reporter noted:

> 66 The great majority of Americans may be depressed. They may not be well pleased with the way business and government have been carried on, and they may not be at all sure that they know exactly how to remedy the trouble. They may be feeling dispirited. But there is one thing they are not, and that is—beaten. 99
>
> —Journalist Gerald W. Johnson, 1932

Throughout the country people pulled together to help one another. Tenant groups formed to protest rent increases and evictions. Neighbors, in difficult circumstances themselves, helped those they saw as worse off than themselves. One woman remembered:

> 66 There were many beggars, who would come to your back door, and they would say they were hungry. I wouldn't give them money because I didn't have it. But I did take them in and put them in my kitchen and give them something to eat. 99
>
> —Depression survivor Kitty McCulloch

VIEWING HISTORY Traveling hobos gave each other helpful information about certain areas with symbols such as these. They were usually written on sidewalks, fences, or buildings using chalk or coal. **Drawing Inferences** How did such a symbol system help hobos and the homeless? Why do you think they wanted to help each other?

Hobo Symbols

Kind-hearted woman lives here	Bad-tempered owner
Food for work	Unsafe place
Good place for a handout	Good water
Can sleep in barn	Doctor won't charge

McCulloch also gave one beggar a pinstripe suit belonging to her husband, who, she explained, already had three others.

Farmers Stick Together   Farmers also worked together to minimize the impact of the Depression. When a farmer was unable to pay the mortgage on his farm, the bank would foreclose on the property and then sell it at an auction. In some farm communities, local farmers met secretly and agreed to keep bids low during the auction. In what were known as **penny auctions,** farmers would bid mere pennies on land and machines auctioned by the banks in order to help their struggling neighbors. Buyers then returned the farms and machinery to their original owners. As one farmer recalled about his farming community:

> ❝ *The aim of our organization was pure survival. All the farmer asked was more time to see him through the depression years. If they won, they had saved (temporarily at least) their home and means of livelihood, and the means of paying their just debts. If they lost, they would be no worse off. They knew they had nothing to lose, so they decided to fight. . . .*❞
>
> —Harry Haugland

In the first two months of 1933, more than 70 foreclosure sales on farms were blocked by penny auctions. The success of penny auctions as well as the threat of violence at some farm auctions led some states to pass laws suspending foreclosures on farms. For example, in February 1933, the Iowa state legislature passed a "foreclosure moratorium law," which gave farmers more time to pay back their mortgages.

Young People Ride the Rails   At the height of the Great Depression, many young people left their homes, either out of necessity or the desire to seek a better life. In the mid-1930s roughly 250,000 teenagers were living on the road, illegally riding the rails of freight trains. Some rode the rails to find work; others hungered for adventure. Clarence Lee, who left home when he was 16, recalled:

> ❝ *I wanted to stay home and fight poverty with my family. But my father told me I had to leave. . . . But I didn't have it in my mind to leave until he told me, 'Go fend for yourself. I cannot afford to have you around any longer.'*❞
>
> —Clarence Lee

Jim Mitchell also left home at 16. He was not forced to leave, but he could not deal with the pressures of home life after his father lost his job and was unable to support the family. "The quickest and easiest way to get out," he recalled, "was go jump a train and go somewhere."

Young people riding the rails faced danger every day. They were vulnerable to train-related injuries, the possibility of being arrested by police, or even the threat of being shot at by angry farmers. These hobos, as they are sometimes called, witnessed the Depression in all parts of the country firsthand. Many who rode the rails described their experiences as some of the loneliest times of their

Focus on CULTURE

Monopoly With everyday life so difficult during the Depression, people needed a way to get their minds off their troubles. In response to this need, Charles B. Darrow, an unemployed man living in Germantown, Pennsylvania, created a compelling board game. Called Monopoly®, the game allowed people to live the fantasy of acquiring land, houses, and hotels that they could rent or sell to fellow players. Darrow brought Monopoly to executives at Parker Brothers, a leading board game company, to see if they would produce it. The company rejected Darrow's game, saying that it had 52 design errors. Determined to make the game a success, Darrow worked on correcting the flaws and produced Monopoly on his own. Darrow sold so many sets so quickly that Parker Brothers reconsidered its decision and agreed to produce it. The game was introduced in 1935 and was a bestseller in its first year. Since then, an estimated 500 million people have played Monopoly.

READING CHECK
Why did so many young people ride the rails in the 1930s?

lives. Yet, most managed to survive and pull themselves together when the Depression came to an end.

Seeking Political Solutions   As bad as conditions were, few Americans called for violent political change. In Europe, economic problems brought riots and political upheaval, but in the United States most citizens trusted the democratic process to handle their problems. As one writer wryly observed:

> 66 *Ten million unemployed continue law-abiding. No riots, no trouble, no multi-millionaires cooked and served with cranberry sauce, alas.* 99
> —William Saroyan, 1936

For some Americans, however, radical and reform movements offered new solutions to the country's problems, by promising a fairer distribution of wealth. The Communist Party had about 14,000 members, mainly intellectuals and labor organizers. In the 1932 election, the Communist candidate polled just over 100,000 votes. Socialists, who called for gradual social and economic changes rather than revolution, did better. Their presidential candidate, Norman Thomas, won 881,951 votes in 1932, about 2.2 percent of the total vote.

Voting figures and party membership do not reflect the notable interest in radical and reform movements in the 1930s. Those who were part of those movements remember the decade as a high point of cooperation among different groups of Americans—students, workers, writers, artists, and professionals of all races. They worked together for social justice in cases such as that of the Scottsboro boys.

Depression Humor   For the most part, Americans gritted their teeth and waited out the hard times. Jokes and cartoons helped people through their troubles. The term "Hooverville" was at first a joke. People who slept on park benches huddled under "Hoover blankets"— old newspapers. Empty pockets turned inside out were "Hoover flags." When Babe Ruth was criticized for requesting a salary of $80,000, higher than Hoover's, he joked, "I had a better year than he did."

People fought despair by laughing at it. In 1929, humorist Will Rogers quipped, "When Wall Street took that tail spin, you had to stand in line to get a window to jump out of." A cartoon that showed two men jumping out of a window arm-in-arm was captioned "The speculators who had a joint account."

Signs of Change

Looking back, we know that the Great Depression began to ease when the United States entered into World War II in 1941. Americans suffering through the Depression, of course, had no idea when the hard times would end. They looked for signs of change, and even in the early 1930s there were some.

Prohibition Is Repealed   In February 1933, just 15 years after it passed the Eighteenth Amendment banning the sale of alcoholic beverages, Congress passed the **Twenty-first Amendment**, repealing Prohibition. The amendment was ratified by the end of the year.

Some people, including President Hoover, regretted the repeal, but most welcomed it as an end to a failed social experiment and as a curb on gangsters who profited from bootlegging. Control of alcohol returned to the states, eight of which chose to continue the ban on liquor sales.

READING CHECK
What political solutions did some Americans seek in the 1930s?

INTERPRETING POLITICAL CARTOONS Showing the darker side of Depression humor, an end-of-the-year cartoon in *Life* magazine summed up the hopes and disasters of 1929. **Drawing Conclusions** Why did Americans use humor to fight their despair?

The Empire State Building For many, a dramatic symbol of hope was the new Empire State Building, begun in 1930. John J. Raskob, the developer of the gleaming new skyscraper, won the race to build the world's tallest building. Some 2,500 to 4,000 people worked on its construction on any given day. The cost of the construction was about $41 million (including land). Because of the Depression, projected building costs were cut in half.

The 102-story Empire State Building soared 1,250 feet into the sky and was topped with a mooring mast for blimps. The building's 67 elevators, traveling 1,000 feet per minute, brought visitors to its observation deck. The building officially opened on May 1, 1931, when President Hoover pressed a button in Washington, D.C. that turned on the building lights, illuminating the New York City skyline. On the first Sunday after it opened, more than 4,000 people paid a dollar each to make the trip to the top.

The End of an Era By the mid-1930s, it was clear that an era was ending. One by one, symbols of the 1920s faded away. In 1931, organized crime gangster Al Capone was at last brought down, convicted of tax evasion and sent to prison. The frugal former President Calvin Coolidge, who presided over the freewheeling prosperity of the 1920s, died in January 1933. Baseball legend Babe Ruth retired in 1935. The Depression-era labor policies of automaker Henry Ford, once admired for his efficiency, made him labor's prime enemy.

In 1932, the nation was horrified when the infant son of aviation hero Charles Lindbergh and Anne Morrow Lindbergh was kidnapped and murdered. Somehow this tragedy seemed to echo the nation's distressed condition and its fall from the heights of its energy and heroism in the 1920s.

VIEWING HISTORY Workers like the man shown above looked out over New York City as they labored to complete the Empire State Building. **Determining Relevance** *How was the Empire State Building a symbol of hope?*

Section 3 Assessment

READING COMPREHENSION

1. What were **penny auctions** and how did they help farmers overcome some of the hardships of the Great Depression?

2. Why was there an interest among some Americans in radical and reform movements? How did American involvement in these movements differ from the political movements occurring in some parts of Europe at the same time?

3. Why was the **Twenty-first Amendment** passed? Why do you think it was passed during the Great Depression?

CRITICAL THINKING AND WRITING

4. **Making Comparisons** Cite three events in American history that reflect the same qualities of cooperation and endurance exhibited by Americans during the Depression.

5. **Writing an Opinion** In a time of crisis, the building of an expensive skyscraper such as the Empire State Building might have been seen as wasteful. Instead, many Americans found it inspiring. What might account for this view of the project?

Go Online
PHSchool.com

For: An activity on the Empire State Building
Visit: PHSchool.com
Web Code: mrd-7223

READING FOCUS

- How did President Hoover respond to the Great Depression?

- What did Roosevelt mean when he offered Americans a "new deal"?

- Why was the election of 1932 a significant turning point for American politics?

MAIN IDEA

As the Depression worsened, people blamed Hoover and the Republicans for their misery. The 1932 presidential election brought a sweeping victory for Democrat Franklin D. Roosevelt and profound changes in the role of government.

KEY TERMS

Hawley-Smoot tariff
Reconstruction Finance Corporation (RFC)
Bonus Army

TARGET READING SKILL

Making Comparisons As you read, complete this chart listing some ideas of the presidential candidates in 1932.

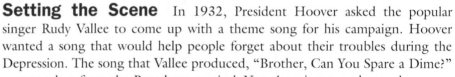

Candidate	Ideas on Government
Herbert Hoover	• Believed in minimal government action • Strict view of government (less government is better) •
Franklin Delano Roosevelt	• Willing to experiment with government roles • Supported broadening the role of government •

Mar. 4, 1933 THE NEW YORKER Price 15 cents

VIEWING HISTORY This *New Yorker* cover drawing of FDR's inauguration in 1933 shows Roosevelt, the new President, in contrast with Hoover. **Recognizing Bias** *Do you think this drawing is being critical of a particular candidate or of the American public's perception of the two candidates?*

Setting the Scene In 1932, President Hoover asked the popular singer Rudy Vallee to come up with a theme song for his campaign. Hoover wanted a song that would help people forget about their troubles during the Depression. The song that Vallee produced, "Brother, Can You Spare a Dime?" was taken from the Broadway musical *New Americana,* and soon became a fitting symbol for the Depression years. Although embraced by Americans, it was not quite the rousing song of optimism Hoover would have preferred as a campaign song.

> **❝** *Once I built a railroad*
> *I made it run*
> *Made it race against time.*
> *Once I built a railroad*
> *Now it's done*
> *Brother, can you spare a dime?* **❞**

In contrast, the Democratic candidate for President in 1932, Franklin Delano Roosevelt, built his campaign around a much different tune:

> **❝** *Happy days are here again,*
> *The skies above are clear again*
> *Let us sing a song of cheer again—*
> *Happy days are here again.* **❞**

As the election approached, Hoover, known as the "great engineer" for his exceptional engineering career, tried desperately to "engineer" the United States out of the Depression. His strict adherence to his political beliefs, however, would put severe limits on what he was able to accomplish.

Hoover's Limited Strategy

For a few months after the stock market crash, President Hoover, along with business leaders, insisted that the key to recovery was confidence. Hoover blamed the Great Depression on "world-wide economic conditions beyond our control"—not on problems in the United States economy. Taking Hoover's advice, business and government leaders tried to maintain public confidence in the economy. Even as factories closed, Hoover administration officials insisted that conditions would improve soon.

Voluntary Action Fails Hoover believed that voluntary controls by businesses in the United States were the best way to end the economic crisis. He quickly organized a White House conference of business leaders and got their promise to maintain wage rates. At first, many firms did keep wages up. By the end of 1931, however, companies were quietly cutting workers' pay.

Hoover held rigidly to his principle of voluntary action. A shy man, he was successful in business but inexperienced in politics. As a result, he showed less flexibility when it came to political compromise. Often unwilling to budge from his views, Hoover was ultimately unable to make his plan attractive to the American people. After a year of misery, the public began to blame him and the Republicans for the crisis.

The Government Acts Despite his staunch beliefs and continual reassurances to the public, Hoover knew that he had to do something to alleviate the suffering of so many Americans. Even before the Depression began, Congress, with the support of Hoover, passed the Agricultural Marketing Act in June 1929. The act provided a form of relief for farmers by creating a Federal Farm Board, which was designed to stabilize the prices of farm crops. The program proved to be a failure, however, losing over $150 million and sending farm prices on another downward spiral.

As a result of the worsening Depression, the Republicans took a beating in the 1930 midterm elections. After the election, Republicans no longer controlled the House, and their majority in the Senate was reduced to

just one seat. As the hardships continued and criticisms increased, Hoover took an even more active approach. To create jobs, the government spent more on new public buildings, roads, parks, and dams. Construction on Boulder Dam (later renamed Hoover Dam) began in 1930. A President's Emergency Committee on Employment advised the President to create local relief programs.

In an attempt to protect domestic industries from foreign imports, in 1930 Congress passed the **Hawley-Smoot tariff,** the highest import tax in history. The tariff backfired. European countries raised their own tariffs, bringing a sudden slowdown in international trade. Hoover suspended the Allies' payments of their war debts, but Europe's economies grew weaker.

In early 1932, Hoover set up the **Reconstruction Finance Corporation (RFC),** which gave government credit to a number of institutions, such as large industries, railroads, and insurance companies. The act also lent money to banks so that they could extend loans. Also that year, Congress passed the

VIEWING HISTORY Boulder Dam, seen here under construction, was built with massive steel bar columns, and used as much steel as the Empire State Building. **Synthesizing Information** *What did Hoover hope to accomplish by spending money to build Boulder Dam?*

Home Loan Bank Act, which, by discounting mortgage rates, helped homeowners save their homes and farmers keep their farms. The RFC reflected the theory that prosperity at the top would help the economy as a whole. To many people, however, it seemed that the government was helping bankers and big business leaders while ordinary people went hungry. Despite the RFC, banks continued to fail.

READING CHECK
What did Hoover think of direct federal relief?

Hoover's Unpopularity Grows Despite his support of these programs, Hoover insisted that state and local governments should handle relief. Hoover argued that direct federal relief would destroy people's self-respect and create a large bureaucracy. His refusal to provide direct aid brought bitter public reaction and negative publicity. Although his World War I relief work had earned him the title "Great Humanitarian," Hoover's attitude toward Depression relief made him seem cold and hard-hearted.

Many people blamed Hoover, not always fairly, for their problems. While people went hungry, newspapers showed a photograph of him feeding his dog on the White House lawn. People booed when he said such things as "Our people have been protected from hunger and cold."

Private charities and local officials could not meet the demands for relief as Hoover wanted. Finally, in 1932, Hoover broke with tradition and let the RFC lend the states money for unemployment relief. But it was too little and too late.

As the Depression deepened, some economists backed the ideas of British economist John Maynard Keynes. Keynes argued that massive government spending could help a collapsing economy and encourage more private spending and production of goods and services. This economic theory was not yet widely accepted, however.

Veterans March on Washington A low point for Hoover came in the summer of 1932, when 20,000 jobless World War I veterans and their families encamped in Washington, D.C. The **Bonus Army,** as they called themselves,

Fast Forward to Today

Philosophy of Government

FDR's New Deal represented the birth of a new philosophy of the government's role in American life. Since the days of FDR, Americans have had differing opinions on what the size and role of the government should be.

1981 Conservatives, who believe in a minimal role for the government, score a victory when President Reagan begins to cut social welfare spending.

1933 Roosevelt's New Deal greatly expands the role of government for social and welfare programs.

1964 In the tradition of FDR, President Johnson promises a "Great Society," which would provide legislation to combat poverty and offer healthcare.

1993 President Clinton promotes a smaller, but active government, which reconciles FDR's activism with Reagan's conservativism.

? What are possible consequences of both a large government role in social welfare and a limited government role?

wanted immediate payment of a pension bonus that had been promised for 1945. The House of Representatives agreed, but the Senate said no. Most of the Bonus Army then went home, but a few thousand stayed, living in shacks.

Although the bonus marchers were generally peaceful, a few violent incidents prompted Hoover to call in the army. Although the President ordered General Douglas MacArthur to clear only Pennsylvania Avenue, MacArthur decided to use force to drive the marchers out of Washington. Armed with bricks and stones, the Bonus Army veterans faced their own country's guns, tanks, and tear gas. Many people were injured. Hoover was horrified, but he took responsibility for MacArthur's actions. In the next election, the lingering image of this ugly scene would help defeat him.

A "New Deal" for America

"I pledge myself to a new deal for the American people," announced presidential candidate Franklin Delano Roosevelt as he accepted the Democratic Party's nomination at its Chicago convention in July 1932. Delegates cheered, and an organ thundered out the song "Happy Days Are Here Again." The Republicans, in June, had again named Hoover as their candidate. As the presidential campaign took shape, the differences between the two candidates became very clear.

In Franklin and Eleanor Roosevelt, the Democrats had a remarkable political couple ready to bring them to victory. Franklin, nicknamed "FDR" by the press, was born in 1882. He graduated from Harvard University and took a job in a law firm, although his main interest was politics. He was elected twice to the New York State Senate before becoming Assistant Secretary of the Navy under President Wilson.

In 1920, FDR ran for Vice President but lost. The following summer, he came down with polio and never walked without help again. He spent much of the 1920s recovering at Warm Springs, Georgia, but with his wife's help kept up his political interests.

Eleanor Roosevelt, a niece of Theodore Roosevelt, was born in 1884 into a wealthy family. She married her distant cousin Franklin in 1905. During the 1920s, in New York State, Eleanor worked for several causes, including public housing legislation, state government reform, birth control, and better conditions for working women. By 1928,

The Twentieth Amendment On March 2, 1932, Congress proposed the Twentieth Amendment to the Constitution. Called the "Lame Duck Amendment," its purpose was to shorten the period between election day in November and the time when congressional representatives and the President take office. Prior to this amendment, elected officials took office on March 4. During this post-election period of over four months, those who had lost the election were "lame ducks," and would spend this time without having much influence or effectiveness. The amendment changed the inauguration date to January 20, cutting the lame duck period in half. By October 15, 1933, every state had ratified the amendment. The first presidential term to be affected would be FDR's second term, which began on January 20, 1937.

when FDR was persuaded to run for governor of New York, Eleanor was an experienced political worker and social reformer.

After FDR's success as governor of New York (1929–1932), his supporters believed him ready to try for the presidency. With his broad smile and genial manner, he represented a spirit of optimism that the country badly needed.

Unlike Hoover, FDR was ready to experiment with governmental roles. Though from a wealthy background, he had genuine compassion for ordinary people, in part because of his disability. He was also moved by the great gap between the nation's wealthy and the poor.

As governor of New York, Roosevelt had worked vigorously for Depression relief. In 1931, he set up an unemployment commission and a relief administration, the first state agencies to aid the poor in the Depression era. When, as a presidential candidate, FDR promised the country a "new deal," he had similar programs in mind.

The Election of 1932

Hoover, the incumbent candidate for President, summed up the choice that voters had in 1932:

> 66 This campaign is more than a contest between two men. . . . It is a contest between two philosophies of government. 99
> —President Herbert Hoover, October 1932

This statement also accurately describes the long-term impact of the 1932 presidential election. It was a historic battle between those who believed that the federal government could not and should not try to fix people's problems, and those who felt that large-scale problems such as the Depression required the government's help. The election would have an enormous effect on public policy for decades to come.

Still arguing for voluntary aid to relieve the Depression, Hoover attacked the Democratic platform. If its ideas were adopted, he said, "this will not be the America which we have known in the past." He sternly resisted the idea of giving the national government more power.

Roosevelt, by contrast, called for "a reappraisal of values" and controls on business:

> 66 I feel that we are coming to a view through the drift of our legislation and our public thinking in the past quarter century that private economic power is . . . a public trust as well. 99
> —Franklin Delano Roosevelt, 1932

While statements like this showed FDR's new approach, many Americans did not support Roosevelt because of his ideas as much as they opposed Hoover because he had been too passive. Even longtime Republicans deserted him. A reserved man by nature, Hoover became grim and isolated. He gave few campaign speeches. Crowds jeered his motorcade.

FDR won the presidency by a huge margin of 7 million popular votes. Much of his support came from groups that had begun to turn to the

---

COMPARING PRIMARY SOURCES
Fighting the Depression

Sharp philosophical differences characterized the presidential campaign of 1932.

Analyzing Viewpoints Compare the statements made by the two candidates.

Against Drastic Measures

"We are told by the opposition that we must have a change, that we must have a new deal. It is not the change . . . to which I object but the proposal to alter the whole foundations of our national life which have been built through generations of testing and struggle."

—Herbert Hoover, speech at Madison Square Garden, October 31, 1932

For Drastic Measures

"I have recounted to you in other speeches, and it is a matter of general information, that for at least two years after the Crash, the only efforts made by the [Hoover administration] to cope with the distress of unemployment were to deny its existence."

—Franklin D. Roosevelt, campaign address, October 13, 1932

READING CHECK
From what groups did FDR receive support in the 1932 election?

Democrats in 1928: urban workers, coal miners, and immigrants of Catholic and Jewish descent.

On a rainy day in 1933, FDR stood before a Depression-weary crowd and took the oath of office of President of the United States. As reporter Thomas Stokes observed, a stirring of hope moved through the crowd when Roosevelt said, "This nation asks for action and action now."

Phrases like this foreshadowed a sweeping change in the style of presidential leadership and government response to its citizens' needs. Ultimately, such changes altered the way many Americans viewed their government and its responsibilities.

In the depths of the Great Depression, many Americans had to give up cherished traditional beliefs in "making it on their own." They turned to the government as their only hope. Thus, as you will read in the next chapter, the Roosevelt years saw the beginning of many programs that changed the role of government in American society.

The words of FDR's Inaugural Address gave much of the country renewed hope for the future:

> 66 *So first of all let me assert my firm belief that the only thing we have to fear is fear itself.* 99
>
> —President Franklin Delano Roosevelt,
> First Inaugural Address, 1933

Having overcome fear in his own life many times, Roosevelt spoke with conviction and confidence, reassuring a frightened nation.

Presidential Election of 1932

11.1 / 88.9
% Electoral Vote

2.9 / 39.7 / 57.4
% Popular Vote

Candidate/Party	Electoral Vote	Popular Vote
Franklin D. Roosevelt (Democrat)	472	22,821,857
Herbert Hoover (Republican)	59	15,761,841
Other		1,160,615

MAP SKILLS Franklin D. Roosevelt and the Democratic Party won the popular vote in 1932 as well as a huge margin of electoral votes. **Location** *Which states' electoral votes did Hoover win?*

Section 4 Assessment

READING COMPREHENSION

1. How did President Hoover hope to end the Depression and its hardships?

2. What was the intent of the **Hawley-Smoot tariff** and the **Reconstruction Finance Corporation?**

3. How did the **Bonus Army** conflict contribute to Hoover's downfall?

4. Describe Franklin Delano Roosevelt's appeal to the American voter in 1932.

CRITICAL THINKING AND WRITING

5. **Distinguishing Fact From Opinion** Do you think the criticisms of Hoover were justified, or might the Depression have brought failure for any President? Explain.

6. **Writing a News Story** Take the position of a reporter covering FDR's inaugural speech. Write a brief newspaper report describing what the President said and how Americans responded to the speech.

Go Online PHSchool.com

For: An activity on FDR's campaign
Visit: PHSchool.com
Web Code: mrd-7224

creating a CHAPTER SUMMARY

Copy this cause-and-effect diagram (right) on a piece of paper and complete it by filling in the major causes and effects of the Great Depression.

For additional review and enrichment activities, see the interactive version of *America: Pathways to the Present*, available on the Web and on CD-ROM.

CAUSES
• Inflated stock prices and uneven economy of the 1920s
• Stock market crash of 1929
•

THE GREAT DEPRESSION

EFFECTS
• Thousands lose their jobs, homes, farms, and other property.
• Discrimination against minorities increases.
•

★ Reviewing Key Terms

For each of the terms below, write a sentence explaining how it relates to the Great Depression.

1. Dow Jones Industrial Average
2. Black Tuesday
3. Great Crash
4. business cycle
5. Great Depression
6. Hooverville
7. Dust Bowl
8. penny auction
9. Twenty-first Amendment
10. Hawley-Smoot tariff
11. Reconstruction Finance Corporation (RFC)
12. Bonus Army

★ Reviewing Main Ideas

13. How did overspeculation in the stock market endanger the economy? (Section 1)

14. Why did the Great Depression in the United States affect countries worldwide? (Section 1)

15. How did the Depression affect those at the bottom of the economic scale? (Section 2)

16. Why were farm families hit particularly hard by the Depression? (Section 2)

17. Give specific examples of Americans helping one another to survive the Depression. (Section 3)

18. In what ways did the end of Prohibition mark the end of an era? (Section 3)

19. Why was President Hoover criticized for his handling of the Great Depression? (Section 4)

20. Compare and contrast Hoover's strategy for ending the Great Depression with Roosevelt's. (Section 4)

★ Critical Thinking

21. **Determining Relevance** During the Depression, some economists turned to the ideas of British economist John Maynard Keynes, who argued that massive government spending could help a collapsing economy. Do you agree with Keynes's approach? To what extent are Keynes's views still at work in the American economy today?

22. **Drawing Conclusions** The Great Depression led to hardships for almost everyone, from the very wealthy to the very poor. Do you think this had an impact on traditional American assumptions regarding the work ethic and the theory of social Darwinism?

23. **Demonstrating Reasoned Judgment** Think about some of the examples of Depression humor in this chapter, such as the cartoon in Section 3, and the use of President Hoover's name to describe certain symbols of the Depression. (a) What is the tone of this "humor"? (b) Would you describe it as funny? (c) Think about examples of humor in today's culture. What differences and similarities can you find between now and then?

24. **Recognizing Ideologies** How did the political ideologies of Hoover and Roosevelt affect their decision making?

★ Standardized Test Prep

Analyzing Political Cartoons ▶

25. This cartoon appeared in 1931. To what does the word "it" refer?

   A The Great Depression

   B A rise in stock prices

   C Consumer borrowing

   D A rise in farm prices

26. What is the crowd doing?

27. Do you think the cartoonist is criticizing Hoover or those who are blaming him? Explain.

Interpreting Data

Turn to the series of three graphs in Section 1.

28. About how many banks suspended their business in 1933?

   A about 2,000

   B about 2,300

   C about 1,500

   D about 4,000

29. Which of the following statements BEST summarizes the data on the unemployment graph?

   F The numbers of unemployed people peaked in 1929.

   G Unemployment was low in 1925.

   H Unemployment increased dramatically between 1929 and 1933.

   I Unemployment decreased after 1933.

30. Which of the following can you NOT tell from these graphs?

   A the percentage of Americans unemployed in 1930

   B the average monthly value of stock prices in 1932

   C the change in stock prices from 1927 to 1932

   D the total number of bank suspensions from 1925 to 1933

Test-Taking Tip

To answer Question 29, be sure to pick the statement which BEST summarizes all of the data on the unemployment graph. More than one statement may be correct, but only one summarizes all of the data.

Applying the Chapter Skill

Drawing Inferences Review the steps needed to draw inferences in the Skills for Life feature on page 519. Then, reread the American Biography on Dorothea Lange on page 517 and study her photographs. Taking into account what you know about the Depression, what inferences can you draw about Lange's attitude toward the Depression? Why do you think she depicts it the way she does?

For: Chapter 15 Self-Test
Visit: PHSchool.com
Web Code: mra-7225

AmericanHeritage®

MY BRUSH WITH HISTORY™

by TOM FLEMING

Afternoon in the Ballpark

Both the boom times of the 1920s and the hard times of the 1930s produced numerous heroes and celebrities. Thanks to advances such as radio, these national heroes were familiar to Americans all across the country. Seeing one in person was a memorable experience. In the passage below, Tom Fleming recalls the day he saw three: the President, the man who would become the next President, and the greatest baseball player of his era.

LIKE EVERY AMERICAN BOY in the twenties and thirties, I revered Babe Ruth as the greatest name in baseball. What made him come alive for me was a genuine American League baseball that my father brought home after one of his trips to New York. Ruth had fouled it off, and Dad had jumped up and caught it one-handed. "Just for you," he said. That was at Yankee Stadium, the "House that Ruth built."

Of course, I wanted to see Babe Ruth play too, but this wasn't easy. Dad and I were Cub fans. Ruth was an American Leaguer with the Yankees, so when they came to Chicago, they played the White Sox in Comiskey Park on the South Side. In the fall of 1932 it became clear that Babe

Babe Ruth in action, 1929

would be coming to Wrigley Field (the Cubs and Yankees had reached the World Series). It was beyond expectation that I would actually get to see those games; I hoped that perhaps I could sneak into the coach's office in the high school locker room and catch a few plays on his radio before the bell rang for afternoon classes.

One evening in September Dad came home in an unusually buoyant mood. I was doing a jigsaw puzzle at the family game table in the den. I watched him take off his suit coat and drape it deliberately over the back of his desk chair. As he unbuttoned his vest, he leaned forward and took a small envelope from his inside coat pocket.

Inside the envelope was a pair of tickets to the October 1 home opener of the World Series—the Cubs and the Yankees at Wrigley Field.

"Now you can see Babe Ruth," he said.

Our beloved Wrigley Field had been transformed for the Series, with red, white, and blue bunting draped everywhere. Temporary stands had been set up in the outfield to accommodate the huge crowd. Our seats were only six rows back from the playing field on the left-field side, between the end of the Cubs' dugout and third base.

"There's your man," Dad said, pointing to left field as we settled in. Sure enough, there he was warming up with his teammates—the Bambino, the Sultan of Swat, the Colossus of Clout—Babe Ruth, all six feet two inches and 215 pounds of him.

When the players left the field, the announcer introduced President Hoover, who was in the stands for the big game. The applause was scattered, and I was shocked to hear boos. (As a Boy Scout I thought you didn't do such a thing to a President.) When Governor Franklin D. Roosevelt was introduced, there was much more applause and fewer boos. Both men were on the campaign trail for the presidential election coming up that November. If I had been politically conscious, I would have known right then that Mr. Hoover was in trouble, for it seemed most fans felt Hoover wasn't having nearly as good a year as Ruth.

Charlie Root took the mound for the Cubs. He was in trouble from the first pitch. With the first two Yankees on base on a walk and a throwing error by the shortstop Billy Jurges, Ruth lumbered up to the plate. He promptly did what he was famous for—lofted one of his patented homers out to the center field seats.

The Cubs lifted our hearts with some good hitting, especially from Kiki Cuyler, but they never seemed to get real control of the game. The score was 4 to 4 when Ruth stepped into the box at the top of the fifth inning.

RUTH CALLS HIS SHOT How lucky we were to be on the third-base side. As a left-handed batter, Ruth faced us, and we could see his every move and gesture. Root was very careful. After each strike the Babe raised his right arm, showing one finger for a strike, then two, to keep the stands posted on the duel between him and the pitcher. The crowd reacted wildly. When the count stood at 2 and 2, Ruth stepped back a bit and then pointed grandly to the outfield, making a big arc with his right hand.

Dad poked me in the ribs.

"Look at him point, son! Look at him point! He's calling a home run!"

The very air seemed to vibrate. I held my breath, digging my fingernails into my palms.

Ruth stepped back into the batter's box, ready for Root's next pitch. It came in knee-high, and the Babe connected solidly with his great swing. The crowd let out a volcanic, spontaneous gasp

of awe. Everybody knew it was gone, gone, gone as it soared high and out over the center-field score board for one of the longest homers ever hit out of Wrigley Field.

The Babe started his trip around the bases. When he rounded second and came toward us, we saw a triumphant smile on his face. Past third, he leaned over and pointed into the Cub dugout. I can only guess what he said to the Cub bench jockeys, although I probably wouldn't have known all the words then.

Root and Hartnett, the Cub battery, later denied that Ruth had called his shot or pointed. I guess that as great competitors they didn't want to give Ruth any more luster than he already had. Dad and I knew that Babe Ruth had pointed though. The Yankees went on to win, 7 to 5, and four of their runs were provided by Babe Ruth. That was the Sultan of Swat at his greatest.

As we were leaving the ballpark, a loud siren wailed just below us, and we rushed over to the ramp railing to see what was going on. Below was the big white touring car of the city greeter, and beside him on the back seat was Governor Roosevelt—gray felt hat and cigarette holder at the jaunty angle cartoonists loved to draw. For a brief moment my eyes locked with his as he looked up at the people lining the railing.

At that moment I realized I was seeing a new star about to enter a more serious arena. That day was a capsule of life. I passed from my boyhood interests to those of the greater game of politics on that bright autumn afternoon of October 1, 1932.

Source: *American Heritage* magazine, November 1990.

Understanding Primary Sources

1. What was the public's reaction when President Herbert Hoover was introduced?

2. Why was this reaction particularly significant in 1932?

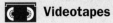

American Heritage®

MY BRUSH WITH **HISTORY**™

▶ **Videotapes**

For more information about life during the Great Depression and the 1932 election, view "Afternoon in the Ballpark."

The New Deal

(1933–1941)

Campaigning in 1932, Roosevelt greets a miner in Elm Grove, West Virginia.

Union poster from an oil painting by Ben Shahn, late 1930s

American Events

1933
FDR's New Deal is launched, creating new legislation and several major federal agencies.

1934
The American Liberty League is founded. Father Coughlin attracts millions of listeners to his radio show.

1935
As the Depression continues, FDR launches the Second New Deal. The Social Security system is created.

1936
Workers stage a sit-down strike at automobile plants in Michigan.

Presidential Terms: Franklin D. Roosevelt 1933–1945

1932   **1934**   **1936**

World Events

Germany opens the first concentration camps.
1933

Communists begin the 6,000-mile "Long March" across China.
1934

The Spanish Civil War begins.
1936

P.W.A. IN ACTION

Bonneville Dam
Washington-Oregon border

Transportation
Trans-Mountain highway to Glacier Park

Indian School
For Sioux in South Dakota

Low-rent Housing
Indianapolis, Indiana

Conservation Project
Tree planting in New York State

Rebuilt Schools
After earthquake in Los Angeles

Art Museum
Wichita, Kansas

Aircraft Carriers
Built in Newport News, Virginia

Flood Control
Along Rio Grande in Texas

State Hospital
Saline County, Arkansas

Navigational Beacons
For air traffic from Washington, D.C., to Nashville, Tennessee

Sea Walls
Storm protection along Florida coast

Pacific Ocean

Atlantic Ocean

Gulf of Mexico

OFF RELIEF ROLLS ON TO PAY ROLLS

A map showing how the Public Works program is building a greater nation, making jobs for men and factories. How it conserves resources and harnesses rivers. How finer transportation is being created and land saved for better use.

Adapted from New Deal-era P.W.A. map

The Wizard of Oz (1939) delighted Depression-era audiences.

1937
San Francisco's Golden Gate Bridge is completed. FDR attempts to "pack" the Supreme Court. The U.S. economy collapses into recession again.

1941
James Agee's *Let Us Now Praise Famous Men* is published.

1938
1940
1942

The Sino-Japanese War breaks out.
1937

Germany invades and annexes Austria.
1938

The United States enters World War II.
1941

Forging a New Deal

READING FOCUS

- How did Franklin and Eleanor Roosevelt work to restore the nation's hope?

- What major New Deal programs were created in the first hundred days, and who were some of FDR's key players in these programs?

- What caused the New Deal to falter?

- What were the key goals and accomplishments of the Second New Deal?

- What did the outcome of the 1936 election indicate?

MAIN IDEA

President Roosevelt sought to end the Great Depression through the federal programs of the New Deal.

KEY TERMS

New Deal
hundred days
public works program
Civilian Conservation
  Corps (CCC)
Agricultural Adjustment
  Administration (AAA)
Tennessee Valley Authority
  (TVA)
Second New Deal
Wagner Act
closed shop
Social Security system

TARGET READING SKILL

Identify Implied Main Idea As you read, fill in the chart below with key goals of the first and second phases of the New Deal.

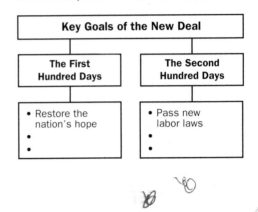

Setting the Scene

A desperate nation anticipating Franklin Delano Roosevelt's "new deal" for America had to wait an agonizingly long time for it to begin. Presidential elections took place in November, but the inauguration of the victor did not occur until the following March 4—a full four-month wait. The lengthy time interval had made sense in earlier days, when vote counting took longer and the President-elect often needed more time to travel to the capital.

By 1933, however, improvements in communication and transportation had eliminated the need for such a long wait, and the disadvantages of the delay were abundantly clear. Hoover remained in office as a "lame duck"—a leader whose authority is weakened because he or she is about to leave office. Meanwhile, the Depression deepened.

The situation prompted Congress to pass the Twentieth Amendment—nicknamed the "lame-duck amendment"—which changed the date of the inaugural to January 20. Ratified in early 1933, the amendment did not take effect until the next election. Roosevelt, therefore, became the last President to be inaugurated in March. While the nation waited, FDR prepared for what would be the biggest change in the federal government since its inception.

Restoring the Nation's Hope

As he prepared plans for rescuing the economy, FDR, along with the new First Lady, Eleanor, went about restoring Americans' sense of hope. Building public confidence in the future was essential to calming panic and creating support for the President's plans.

A test of the new administration's approach to crises came shortly after he took office. World War I veterans staged a second Bonus March on Washington. This time, the White House provided campsites for the veterans. Even more astounding, Eleanor Roosevelt paid them a visit.

VIEWING HISTORY Whenever a presidential administration changes hands from one political party to another, many members of the old administration lose their government jobs. **Drawing Inferences** (a) Who are the elephants in this cartoon, and what are they doing? (b) What point is the cartoonist trying to make?

When she walked up to a group of marchers, "They looked at me curiously and one of them asked my name and what I wanted," she recalled later. By the time she left, the veterans were waving and calling out, "Good-bye and good luck to you!" The First Lady told reporters afterward how polite the marchers had been. By this act, she demonstrated compassion and soothed popular fears about renewed radical agitation.

FDR, in his First Inaugural Address, March 4, 1933, told Americans, "The only thing we have to fear is fear itself." The first Sunday after taking office, Roosevelt spoke to the nation over the radio in the first of what became regular "fireside chats." His easy manner and confidence helped renew people's hopes for the future.

In campaigning for the White House, FDR had promised "bold, persistent experimentation." No one knew exactly what that meant—only that someone was going to do something. As reporter Arthur Krock noted, Washington "welcomes the 'New Deal,' even though it is not sure what the New Deal is going to be."

Even Roosevelt himself had no sure plan for government under his leadership. Nevertheless, the new President's optimism and willingness to experiment won him the support of the American people. He had promised "a new deal for the American people," and he kept his word. The term **New Deal** came to refer to the relief, recovery, and reform programs of FDR's administration that were aimed at combating the Great Depression.

 Sounds of an Era

Listen to excerpts from FDR's First Inaugural Address, one of his fireside chats, and other sounds from the New Deal era.

The First Hundred Days

From his inauguration in March through June 1933, a period known as the **hundred days,** Roosevelt pushed program after program through Congress to provide relief, create jobs, and stimulate economic recovery. He based some of these programs on the work of federal agencies that had controlled the economy during World War I and on agencies set up by states to ease the Depression. Former Progressives figured prominently, inspiring New Deal legislation or administering programs.

Stabilizing Financial Institutions FDR's first step was to restore public confidence in the nation's banks. On March 5, 1933, he ordered all banks to close for the next four days. He then pushed Congress to pass the Emergency Banking Act, which was approved on March 9. The act authorized the government to inspect the financial health of all banks.

Many Americans had been terrified by the prospect of losing all their savings in a bank failure. By his actions, FDR hoped to assure the American people that their banks would not fail. Indeed, government inspectors found that most banks were healthy, and two thirds had reopened by March 15.

After the brief "bank holiday," Americans regained confidence in the banking system. They began to put more money back into their accounts than they took out. These deposits allowed banks to make loans that would help stimulate the economy. Congress increased public confidence further by passing the Glass-Steagall Banking Act of 1933. It established a Federal Deposit Insurance Corporation (FDIC) to insure bank deposits.

VIEWING HISTORY A Detroit, Michigan, bank opens under a new charter following the "bank holiday" ordered by FDR. **Drawing Inferences** *(a) Why do you think the bank is so crowded? (b) How would you react to the bank closings if you were a bank customer in March 1933?*

Congress also moved to correct problems that had led to the stock market crash. The Federal Securities Act, passed in May 1933, required companies to provide information about their finances if they offered stock for sale. The next year Congress set up the Securities and Exchange Commission (SEC) to regulate the stock market. Congress also gave the Federal Reserve Board power to regulate the purchase of stock on margin.

In July 1933, Roosevelt took a further step to stimulate the economy. He decreased the value of U.S. currency by taking it off the gold standard. He hoped that this action would raise the prices of farm products and other goods. He also hoped that a devalued American currency would stimulate export trade. FDR's move pleased many in Congress, who thought it would make paying off New Deal debts easier. Others, including his budget director, Lewis Douglas, thought it was "the end of Western civilization."

Providing Relief and Creating Jobs FDR's next step was to help overburdened local relief agencies. He persuaded Congress in May to establish a Federal Emergency Relief Administration (FERA), which sent funds to these agencies. Harry Hopkins, a former settlement worker and a longtime Roosevelt friend and advisor, directed this agency. Hopkins professed a strong belief in helping people find work:

> 66 Give a man a dole [handout], and you save his body and destroy his spirit. Give him a job and pay him an assured wage and you save both the body and the spirit. 99
>
> —FERA administrator Harry Hopkins

To help people who were out of work, the FERA also put federal money into **public works programs,** government-funded projects to build public facilities. One of these programs, set up in November 1933, was the Civil Works Administration (CWA). The CWA put the unemployed to work building or improving roads, parks, airports, and other facilities. The agency was a tremendous morale booster to its 4 million employees. As a former insurance salesman

VIEWING HISTORY This worker for the Civilian Conservation Corps (right) is planting seedlings in Montana. The poster below proclaims the benefits of CCC labor. **Drawing Conclusions** If you had been a young person during the Depression, what effect might these images have had on you? Why?

"The only thing we have to fear is fear itself."
—First Inaugural Address, 1933

Courage in times of crisis was perhaps Franklin Delano Roosevelt's greatest strength. His first crisis was personal rather than political. In 1921, Roosevelt was stricken with polio, which paralyzed his legs and threatened to destroy what had been a promising political career. (Roosevelt had been the Democratic vice-presidential candidate the year before.)

Roosevelt returned to politics in 1928, running for governor of New York. Despite having to be helped or carried onto podiums to speak, Roosevelt campaigned energetically and won the election. Four years later he ran for President. In a campaign dominated by the gloom of the Great Depression, FDR's confidence helped bring him victory.

As President, Roosevelt fought the Depression through what he called "bold, persistent experimentation." "It is common sense to take a method and try it," he explained. "If it fails, admit it frankly and try another. But above all, try something." This commitment to action gave Americans much-needed hope.

Roosevelt showed a similar commitment as commander in chief during World War II. After the attack on Pearl Harbor in 1941, Roosevelt rallied a shocked nation and oversaw the creation of the greatest

32nd President 1933–1945

military force ever seen up to that time. Elected President for a record fourth time in 1944, Roosevelt died in April 1945, just months before the victorious end of the war.

Connecting to Today

Should government programs to help the elderly and the poor be temporary responses to crises such as the Great Depression, or should such programs be permanent? Defend your position.

Go Online
PHSchool.com

For: More on Franklin Delano Roosevelt
Visit: PHSchool.com
Web Code: mrd-7237

---

from Alabama remarked, "When I got that [CWA identification] card, it was the biggest day in my whole life. At last I could say, 'I've got a job.'"

The **Civilian Conservation Corps (CCC)** became FDR's favorite program. Established in March 1933, the CCC put more than 2.5 million young, unmarried men to work maintaining forests, beaches, and parks. CCC workers earned only $30 a month, but they lived in camps free of charge and received food, medical care, and job training. Eleanor Roosevelt persuaded the CCC to fund similar programs for young women.

Public works programs also helped Native Americans. John Collier, FDR's commissioner of Indian Affairs, used New Deal funds and Native American workers to build schools, hospitals, and irrigation systems. The Indian Reorganization Act of 1934 ended the sale of tribal lands begun under the Dawes Act (1887) and restored some lands to Indian owners.

Regulating the Economy The sharp decline of industrial prices in the early 1930s had caused many business failures and much unemployment. The National Industrial Recovery Act (NIRA) of June 1933 sought to bolster those prices. The NIRA established the National Recovery Administration (NRA), which set out to balance the unstable economy through extensive planning.

This planning took the form of industry-wide codes to spell out fair business practices. The federal codes regulated wages, restraining wage competition. They controlled working conditions, production, and prices, and set a minimum wage. They gave organized labor collective bargaining rights, which allowed workers to negotiate as a group with employers. NRA officials wrote some of the codes, and they negotiated the details of some codes with the affected businesses. Many codes, however, were drawn up by the largest companies in an

The National Recovery Administration (NRA) attempted to stabilize the economy by regulating business practices.

Florida's Overseas Highway: A New Deal Project Like a string of pearls, the Florida Keys dangle from the tip of Florida out into the Gulf of Mexico. In the early 1900s, the Florida East Coast Railroad connected the mainland to the popular island of Key West. But in 1935, the strongest hurricane ever recorded in the Western Hemisphere smacked into the Keys with winds of up to 250 miles an hour, destroying the railroad. The Public Works Administration stepped in with a $3.6 million loan that largely financed the construction of a highway over the old railroad bed. Officially opened on July 4, 1938, the 110-mile-long Overseas Highway is the longest overwater road in the world. Part of U.S. Highway 1, it links the Keys with 42 bridges. FDR celebrated this engineering feat by driving the route from Miami to Key West in 1939.

industry. This practice pleased businesses but drew criticism from people concerned that industry influence would bias the codes against workers.

For a brief time, the codes stopped the tailspin of industrial prices. But by the fall of 1933, when higher wages went into effect, prices rose, too. Consumers stopped buying. The cycle of rising production and falling consumption returned, and many more businesses failed, causing more unemployment. Businesses complained that the codes were too complicated and the NRA's control was too rigid.

To this day, one of the most visible parts of the NIRA's efforts is the work carried out by its Public Works Administration (PWA). Directed by Secretary of the Interior Harold Ickes, the PWA launched projects ranging from the Grand Coulee Dam on the Columbia River in Washington State, to New York City's Triborough Bridge, to the causeway that connects Key West to the Florida mainland.

Assisting Homeowners and Farmers The Depression caused many middle-income homeowners to fall behind in paying their mortgages. The Home Owners' Loan Corporation (HOLC) refinanced mortgages— that is, changed the terms of the mortgages—to make the payments more manageable. Between June 1933 and June 1936, the HOLC made about 1 million low-interest loans. Even with these low-interest-rate loans, however, many owners lost their homes because they could not pay their mortgages.

The National Housing Act of 1934 established the Federal Housing Administration (FHA), a government-owned corporation. The FHA, which exists today, was created to improve housing standards and conditions, to insure mortgages, and to stabilize the mortgage market.

Many farmers were losing their homes and their land because of the low prices they received for their products. The **Agricultural Adjustment Administration (AAA),** set up in May 1933, tried to raise farm prices by paying subsidies, or government financial assistance, to farmers who cut production of certain crops. The AAA hoped that lowering the supply of these farm products would cause their prices to rise. Proceeds from a new tax on the companies that processed agricultural produce were used to pay for the subsidies to farmers.

Under this program, some farmers plowed under crops that were already growing. Many Americans could not understand how the federal government could encourage the destruction of food while so many people were hungry.

The TVA One public works project proved especially popular. The **Tennessee Valley Authority (TVA),** created in May 1933, helped farmers and created jobs in one of the country's least developed regions. By reactivating a hydroelectric power facility started during World War I, the TVA provided cheap electric power (in cooperation with the Rural Electrification Administration), flood control, and recreational opportunities to the entire Tennessee River valley, as shown on the map on the next page.

Key Players in the New Deal

Roosevelt surrounded himself with eager and hard-working advisors. Some became members of the Cabinet or, like Harry Hopkins, headed one of the new agencies. Columbia University Professors Raymond Moley, Adolf A. Berle, and Rexford G. Tugwell became the three key members of FDR's so-called "brain trust," an informal group of intellectuals who helped draft policies.

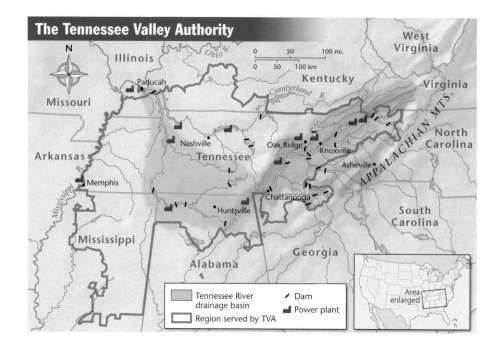

The Tennessee Valley Authority

N

Illinois
Ohio R.
0   50   100 mi.
0   50   100 km

West Virginia

Missouri

Paducah
Kentucky
Cumberland R.
Virginia

Arkansas

Nashville
Tennessee
Oak Ridge
Knoxville
Asheville
APPALACHIAN MTS.
North Carolina

Memphis
Mississippi

Chattanooga
Huntsville

South Carolina

Mississippi
Alabama
Georgia

Tennessee River drainage basin
Region served by TVA
Dam
Power plant

Area enlarged

MAP SKILLS The massive TVA project combined the activities of many government agencies to control flooding of the Tennessee River, provide hydroelectric power and irrigation for farms, improve navigation, and provide recreation. The photograph below shows the interior of a dam in Norris, Tennessee. **Regions** (a) Which states benefited from the TVA? (b) What formed the boundary of TVA activity in the East?

Groundbreaking Appointments Roosevelt was the first President ever to appoint a woman to a Cabinet post. Frances Perkins, a former Progressive who had headed the New York State Industrial Commission, became Secretary of Labor. She held this job until 1945. Perkins successfully pressed for laws that would help both wage earners and the unemployed. Perkins was one of more than two dozen women who held key New Deal positions.

FDR's administration also broke new ground by hiring African Americans in more than a hundred policymaking posts. One of Roosevelt's key appointees, Mary McLeod Bethune, held the highest position of any African American woman in the New Deal. Bethune was a former elementary school teacher, a college president, and the founder of the National Council of Negro Women. She entered government service with a reputation as one of the country's most influential spokespersons for African American concerns.

Appointed director of the Division of Negro Affairs of the National Youth Administration (NYA) in 1936, Bethune advised FDR on programs that aided African Americans. In the process, she increased her level of influence. She forged a united stand among black officeholders by organizing a Federal Council on Negro Affairs. This unofficial group, known as the "black Cabinet," met weekly to hammer out priorities and increase African American support for the New Deal.

Eleanor Roosevelt Among FDR's most important colleagues was his wife, Eleanor. She threw herself into supporting the New Deal and traveled widely for her husband, whose disability made traveling difficult. She reported to him on conditions in the country and on the effects of his programs. At times, the First Lady took stands that posed problems for her husband. For example, in 1938, she attended a Birmingham, Alabama, meeting of the Southern Conference for Human Welfare, an interracial group. She knew she was expected to obey local Jim Crow laws that required blacks and whites to sit on opposite sides of the auditorium. In protest, she sat in the center of the aisle, between the divided races. Her act received wide publicity, and no one missed its symbolism.

READING CHECK

What historic appointments did FDR make to his administration?

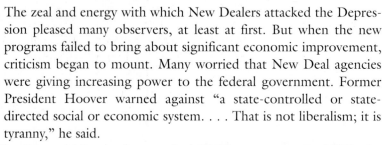

Eleanor Roosevelt 1884–1962

Anna Eleanor Roosevelt, a niece of Theodore Roosevelt, was born in New York City on October 11, 1884. A member of a wealthy family, Eleanor attended private schools. In 1905, she married her distant cousin Franklin, and they had six children.

During World War I, Eleanor Roosevelt joined the war effort as a volunteer for the Red Cross. After the war, she became involved in social and political reforms. In 1922, she joined the Women's Trade Union League and became a leader in the New York State Democratic Party.

Eleanor Roosevelt reshaped the role of First Lady. Besides traveling widely to observe the effects of the New Deal on Americans, she held her own press conferences at the White House, which were for women correspondents only. She lectured widely, and in 1935, she started a newspaper column called "My Day." She used the column to drum up support for the New Deal.

Within a year after Franklin's death in 1945, Eleanor gained further admiration as a delegate to the United Nations. In that role, she led the campaign to approve a Declaration of Human Rights. She worked vigorously for human rights causes until her death in 1962.

Eleanor Roosevelt's activities troubled some Americans. In their view, a First Lady should act only as a gracious hostess at state dinners. Gradually, however, the public got used to her unconventional style, and many came to admire her for her political skills, her humanity, and her idealism.

The New Deal Falters

The zeal and energy with which New Dealers attacked the Depression pleased many observers, at least at first. But when the new programs failed to bring about significant economic improvement, criticism began to mount. Many worried that New Deal agencies were giving increasing power to the federal government. Former President Hoover warned against "a state-controlled or state-directed social or economic system. . . . That is not liberalism; it is tyranny," he said.

The Supreme Court also attacked FDR's programs. In 1935, the Court declared the NIRA unconstitutional because it gave the President lawmaking powers and regulated local, rather than interstate, commerce. The following year, the Court also struck down the tax that funded AAA subsidies to farmers. Two of the most important elements of the New Deal had crumbled. It was time to reassess.

A Second New Deal

Most of the public remained behind Roosevelt. The midterm elections of 1934 showed overwhelming nationwide support for FDR's administration. In 1935, the President launched a new, even bolder burst of activity. Many historians call this period and the legislation it produced the **Second New Deal,** or the Second Hundred Days. In part, it was FDR's response to critics who said he was not doing enough for ordinary Americans. The Second New Deal included more social welfare benefits, stricter controls over business, stronger support for unions, and higher taxes on the rich.

New and Expanded Agencies New agencies attacked joblessness even more aggressively than before. The Works Progress Administration (WPA), an agency set up in 1935 and lasting eight years, provided work for more than 8 million citizens. The WPA built or improved tens of thousands of playgrounds, schools, hospitals, and airfields, and it supported the creative work of many artists and writers. The National Youth Administration, established in June 1935 within the WPA, provided education, jobs, recreation, and counseling for young men and women ages 16 through 25.

The Second New Deal responded to the worsening plight of agricultural workers. The original AAA had caused hardship to many farm workers who did not own land. When large commercial farms cut back their production, these workers often lost their jobs. In the Southwest, Mexican American farm workers struggled to survive. Many of these migrant workers were forced to return to Mexico. Others tried to form unions, causing fierce resistance from farming associations. In the South, when landlords accepted the AAA subsidies and took land out of production, many tenants and sharecroppers were left without land to farm.

In May 1935, Rexford Tugwell, an economist in FDR's Department of Agriculture, set up the Resettlement Administration. The agency loaned money to owners of small farms and helped resettle tenants and sharecroppers on productive land. In 1937, the Farm Security Administration (FSA) replaced

Tugwell's agency. It loaned more than $1 billion to farmers and set up camps for migrant workers.

Rural Electrification The New Deal also brought electricity to the American countryside. By the 1930s, nearly 90 percent of Americans in urban areas had electricity, compared to only about 10 percent in rural areas. The free market did not encourage private companies to provide power because of the high cost of running power lines to remote areas.

Roosevelt believed that the government had an obligation to provide this essential service where private enterprise would not. In 1935, Congress created the Rural Electrification Administration (REA), which offered loans to electric companies and farm cooperatives for building power plants and extending power lines, as well as to farmers and other rural residents to wire their homes and barns.

Within four years, about 25 percent of rural households had electricity. In time, the REA brought power to 98 percent of U.S. farms. Demand for electric appliances grew, benefiting manufacturing companies and local merchants.

New Labor Legislation Labor unions had liked the NIRA provision known as 7a, which granted them the right to organize and bargain collectively. When the NIRA was declared unconstitutional, workers began to demand new legislation to protect their rights.

In July 1935, Congress responded. It passed the National Labor Relations Act, called the **Wagner Act** after its leading advocate, New York Senator Robert Wagner. The Wagner Act legalized such union practices as collective bargaining and **closed shops,** which are workplaces open only to union members. It also outlawed spying on union activities and blacklisting, a practice in which employers agreed not to hire union leaders. The act set up the National Labor Relations Board (NLRB) to enforce its provisions. The

READING CHECK
Why did Roosevelt see a need to launch a second New Deal?

INTERPRETING CHARTS
The New Deal created an alphabet soup of new federal agencies, greatly expanding the bureaucracy and authority of the government. **Synthesizing Information** *Write a statement explaining the major goals of these agencies.*

Major New Deal Agencies

Agency	Purpose
Federal Emergency Relief Act (FERA), 1933	Provided funds to state relief agencies.
Civil Works Administration (CWA), 1933	Provided federal jobs in building and improving roads and public facilities.
Tennessee Valley Authority (TVA), 1933	Provided hydroelectric power, flood control, and recreational opportunities to the Tennessee River Valley and surrounding areas.
Home Owners Loan Corporation (HOLC), 1933	Provided low-cost mortgage refinancing to homeowners facing foreclosure.
Civilian Conservation Corps (CCC), 1933	Provided jobs to young, unmarried men (and, later, women) to work on conservation and resource development projects.
Public Works Administration (PWA), 1933	Sponsored massive public works projects such as dams and hydroelectric plants.
National Recovery Administration (NRA), 1933	Worked with industries to establish codes outlining fair business and labor practices.
Federal Deposit Insurance Corporation (FDIC), 1933	Insured bank deposits up to $5,000.
Agricultural Adjustment Administration (AAA), 1933	Attempted to raise farm prices by paying farmers to lower farm output.
Federal Housing Administration (FHA), 1934	Improved housing standards and conditions and provided home financing.
Securities and Exchange Commission (SEC), 1934	Regulated the stock market and protected investors from dishonest trading practices.
Works Progress Administration (WPA), 1935	Gave the unemployed work in building construction and arts programs.
National Labor Relations Board (NLRB), 1935	Enforced provisions of the Wagner Act, which included the right to collective bargaining and other union rights.
National Youth Administration (NYA), 1935	Provided education, jobs, recreation, and counseling for youth ages 16 to 25.
Rural Electrification Administration (REA), 1935	Provided loans for building power plants, extending power lines to rural areas, and wiring homes.
Social Security Administration (SSA), 1935	Provided old-age pensions, disability payments, and unemployment benefits.

The Social Security system marked a major expansion of the federal government's role as a caretaker of its citizens.

Supreme Court upheld the constitutionality of the Wagner Act in *NLRB* v. *Jones and Laughlin* (1937). The landmark case established the federal government's ability to regulate labor disputes linked to interstate commerce. In 1938, the Fair Labor Standards Act banned child labor and established a minimum wage for all workers covered under the act.

Social Security In 1935, Congress also passed the Social Security Act. The act established a **Social Security system** to provide financial security, in the form of regular payments, to people who could not support themselves. This system offered three types of insurance:

Old-age pensions and survivors' benefits Workers and their employers paid equally into a national insurance fund. Retired workers or their surviving spouses were eligible to start receiving Social Security payments at age 65. The act did not cover farm and domestic workers until it was amended in 1954.

Unemployment insurance Employers with more than eight employees funded this provision by paying a tax. The government distributed the money to workers who lost their jobs. States administered their own programs, with federal guidance and financial support.

Aid for dependent children, the blind, and the disabled The federal government gave grants to states to help support needy individuals in these categories.

The 1936 Election

No one expected the Republican presidential candidate of 1936, Kansas governor Alfred M. Landon, to beat the popular incumbent President. But few could have predicted the extent of FDR's landslide. Roosevelt carried every state except Maine and Vermont, winning 523–8 in the electoral college.

FDR's landslide victory showed that most Americans supported the New Deal. Yet the New Deal still had many critics with their own sizable followings.

Section 1 Assessment

READING COMPREHENSION

1. What steps did FDR take to restore the nation's hope and boost public confidence in economic institutions?

2. What role did **public works programs** play in Roosevelt's plans for economic recovery?

3. What benefits did the **Tennessee Valley Authority** bring about?

4. How was the **Wagner Act** a triumph for organized labor?

CRITICAL THINKING AND WRITING

5. **Making Comparisons** Compare the success of the early New Deal programs with those of the Second New Deal. Explain why the early programs faltered, and how the Second New Deal gave FDR a boost in the 1936 election.

6. **Writing a Conclusion** Write a statement that analyzes the types of programs created under the New Deal and then draws conclusions about FDR's view of the role of government. Give evidence to support your conclusions.

Go Online
PHSchool.com

For: An activity on the TVA
Visit: PHSchool.com
Web Code: mrd-7231

The New Deal's Critics

READING FOCUS

- What were some of the shortcomings and limits of the New Deal?
- What were the chief complaints of FDR's critics inside and outside of politics?
- How did the court-packing fiasco harm FDR's reputation?

MAIN IDEA

A variety of critics pointed out the shortcomings of the New Deal as well as its potential for restricting individual freedom.

KEY TERMS

American Liberty League
demagogue
nationalization
deficit spending

TARGET READING SKILL

Identify Implied Main Idea Copy the chart below. As you read, fill in criticisms of the New Deal.

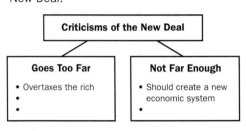

Criticisms of the New Deal

Goes Too Far
- Overtaxes the rich
-
-

Not Far Enough
- Should create a new economic system
-

Setting the Scene To the poor and the jobless who benefited from New Deal programs, Franklin Delano Roosevelt was a true hero. One mill worker expressed the thoughts of many citizens:

> 66 *Roosevelt is the only President we ever had that thought the Constitution belonged to the pore [poor] man too. . . . Yessir, it took Roosevelt to read in the Constitution and find out them folks way back yonder that made it was talkin' about the pore man right along with the rich one.* 99
>
> —Testimony by mill worker George Dobbin in 1939, collected in *These Are Our Lives,* Federal Writers Project of the Works Progress Administration (1939)

Letters thanking the President poured into the White House. One letter read, "There ain't no other nation in the world that would have sense enough to think of WPA and all the other *A's*."

Yet the New Deal inspired its share of critics, and the criticism would swell as the Depression dragged on. One critic wrote, "If you could get around the country as I have and seen the distress forced upon the American people, you would throw your darn NRA and AAA, and every other . . . *A* into the sea."

The Limitations of the New Deal

For all its successes, the New Deal fell short of many people's expectations. The Fair Labor Standards Act, for example, covered fewer than one quarter of all gainfully employed workers. It set the minimum wage at 25 cents an hour, which was well below what most covered workers already made. New Deal agencies also were generally less helpful to women and minority groups than they were to white men.

Women Many aspects of New Deal legislation put women at a disadvantage. The NRA codes, for example, permitted lower wages for women's work in almost a quarter of all cases. In relief and job programs, men and boys received strong preference. In accordance with the social customs of the time, jobs went to male "heads of families," unless the men were unable to work.

"COME ALONG. WE'RE GOING TO THE TRANS-LUX TO HISS ROOSEVELT."

INTERPRETING POLITICAL CARTOONS In this cartoon, rich people are going to a fancy hotel to "hiss"—that is, protest—FDR. **Analyzing Visual Information** *How does the cartoonist depict wealth? Why did some rich people oppose Roosevelt's policies?*

No New Deal provision protected domestic service, the largest female occupation. In 1942, an African American domestic worker in St. Louis pleaded with the President to ask employers, the "rich people," to "give us some hours to rest in and some Sundays off and pay us more wages." Working 14-hour days, she earned only $6.50 per week. A brutally honest official wrote back to her:

> State and Federal labor laws, which offer protection to workers in so many occupations, have so far not set up standards for working conditions in domestic situations. There is nothing that can be done . . . to help you and others in this kind of employment.
>
> —Roosevelt administration official

African Americans   Federal relief programs in the South, including public works projects, reinforced racial segregation. As a rule, African Americans were not offered jobs at a professional level. They were kept out of skilled jobs on dam and electric power projects, and they received lower pay than whites for the same work. Because the Social Security Act excluded both farmers and domestic workers, it failed to cover nearly two thirds of working African Americans. One black American expressed deep disappointment with FDR's policies:

> All the prosperity he had brought to the country has been legislated and is not real. Nothing he has ever started has been finished. My common way of expressing it is that we are in the middle of the ocean like a ship without an anchor. No good times can come to the country as long as there is so much discrimination practiced. . . . I don't see much chance for our people to get anywhere when the color line instead of ability determines the opportunities to get ahead economically.
>
> —Testimony by Sam T. Mayhew in 1939, collected in *Such As Us* (1978)

VIEWING HISTORY This photograph, taken at a relief center in Louisville, Kentucky, highlights the struggle of African Americans to overcome the effects of both the Depression and prejudice. **Analyzing Visual Information** *What contrast was the photographer trying to point out in this picture?*

Nor did the New Deal do anything to end discriminatory practices in the North. In many black neighborhoods, for example, white-owned businesses continued to employ only whites. In the absence of help from the federal government, African Americans took matters into their own hands. Protesters picketed and boycotted such businesses with the slogan "Don't shop where you can't work."

The early Depression had seen an alarming rise in the number of lynchings. The federal government again offered no relief. A bill to make lynching a federal crime was abandoned by Congress in 1938. NAACP leader Walter White recalled in 1948 that FDR had given this explanation for his refusal to support these measures:

> Southerners, by reason of seniority rule in Congress, are chairmen or occupy strategic places on most of the Senate and House committees. If I come out for the anti-lynching bill now, they will block every bill I ask Congress to pass to keep America from collapsing. I just can't take that risk.
>
> —President Franklin Roosevelt

Although African Americans in the North had not supported FDR in 1932, by 1936 many had joined his camp. Often the last hired and first fired, they had experienced the highest unemployment rates of any group during the Depression. For this reason, those who did gain employment appreciated many of the New Deal programs.

Other aspects of Roosevelt's record also had some appeal to many African Americans. He appointed more African Americans to policymaking posts than any President before him. The Roosevelts also seemed genuinely concerned about the fate of African Americans. These factors help to explain FDR's wide support among black voters.

Political Critics

Under the desperate conditions of the Great Depression, reactions to the New Deal ran strong. People with widely differing political views criticized the New Deal, both for what it did and for what it did not do.

New Deal Does Too Much A number of Republicans, in Congress and elsewhere, opposed Roosevelt. They knew something had to be done about the Depression, but they believed that the New Deal went too far.

These critics included many wealthy people who regarded FDR as their enemy. Early in the New Deal, they had disapproved of certain programs, such as the TVA and rural electrification, that they considered to be socialistic. The Second New Deal gave them even more to hate, as FDR pushed through a series of higher taxes aimed at the rich. One of these was the Revenue Act of 1935, also known as the Wealth Tax Act. This act raised the tax rate on individual incomes over $50,000 as well as on the income and profits of corporations.

The Social Security Act also aroused political opposition. Some of FDR's enemies claimed that it penalized successful, hardworking people by forcing them to pay into the system. Others saw the assignment of Social Security numbers as the first step toward a militaristic, regimented society. They predicted that soon people would have to wear metal dog tags engraved with their Social Security numbers.

A group called the **American Liberty League,** founded in 1934, spearheaded much of the opposition to the New Deal. It was led by former Democratic presidential candidate Alfred E. Smith, the National Association of Manufacturers, and leading business figures.

The league charged the New Deal with limiting individual freedom in an unconstitutional, "un-American" manner. To them, programs such as compulsory unemployment insurance smacked of "Bolshevism," a reference to the political philosophy of the founders of the Soviet Union.

New Deal Does Not Do Enough Many Progressives and Socialists also attacked the New Deal. But these critics charged that FDR's programs did not provide enough help.

Muckraking novelist Upton Sinclair believed that the nation's entire economic system needed to be reformed in order to cure what he believed to be a "permanent crisis." A Socialist, he sought solutions that went far beyond New Deal–style reforms. In 1934, Sinclair ran for governor of California on the Democratic ticket. His platform, "End Poverty in California" (EPIC), called for a new economic system in which the state would take over factories and farms.

READING CHECK
What were the main criticisms of the New Deal?

EPIC clubs formed throughout the state, and Sinclair won the primary. Terrified opponents then used shady tactics to discredit him. They produced fake newsreels showing people who spoke with a Russian accent endorsing Sinclair. Associated unfairly with communism, Sinclair lost the election.

The New Deal had only limited success in eliminating poverty. This fact contributed to a revival of progressivism in Minnesota and Wisconsin. Running for the United States Senate, Wisconsin Progressive Robert La Follette, Jr., argued that "devices which seek to preserve the unequal distribution of wealth . . . will retard or prevent recovery." His brother Philip also took a radical stand, calling for a redistribution of income. Philip's ideas persuaded the state Socialist Party to join the Progressives after he won the Wisconsin governorship in 1934.

Other Critics

Some New Deal critics were **demagogues,** leaders who manipulate people with half-truths, deceptive promises, and scare tactics. Two such demagogues attracted strong followings during the Depression.

Father Coughlin One such demagogue was Father Charles E. Coughlin (CAWG-lin), a dynamic speaker who used the radio to broadcast his message. Throughout the 1930s, the so-called Radio Priest held listeners spellbound from his studio in Detroit. In 1934, Father Coughlin's weekly broadcasts reached an audience estimated at more than 10 million people.

Coughlin achieved popularity even though he sometimes contradicted himself. One time he advocated the **nationalization,** or government takeover and ownership, of banks and the redistribution of their wealth. Another time he defended the sanctity of private property, including banks. At first he supported FDR and the New Deal. Later he denounced them, through his radio show and through the organization he formed in 1934 called the National Union for

Social Justice. Coughlin's attacks on FDR grew increasingly reckless. In 1936, he called him "Franklin 'Double-crossing' Roosevelt" and described him as a "great betrayer and liar."

By the end of the 1930s, Coughlin was issuing openly anti-Jewish statements. He also began showering praise on Adolf Hitler and Benito Mussolini, two menacing leaders who were rising to power in Europe. Coughlin's actions alarmed many Americans, and he lost some of his support. In 1942, Roman Catholic officials ordered him to stop broadcasting his show.

Huey Long A powerful figure in Louisiana politics, Huey Long was a different type of demagogue. Long was a country lawyer who had grown up in poverty. He won the governorship of Louisiana in 1928 and became a United States senator in 1932. Unlike many southern Democrats, Long did not build his base of power on racial attacks. Instead, he worked to help the underprivileged by improving education, medical care, and public services. He also built an extraordinarily powerful and ruthless political machine in his home state.

Originally a supporter of FDR, Long broke with him early in the New Deal. "Unless we provide for redistribution of wealth in this country, the country is doomed," he said. While in the Senate, Long developed a program called Share-Our-Wealth. It would limit individual income to $1 million and inheritance to $5 million. The government would take the rest in steep progressive income taxes. Thus the plan would confiscate large fortunes. It would then redistribute that wealth by giving every family a minimum $5,000 "household estate" and a minimum annual income of $2,500. Long also sought other improvements for Americans: shorter working hours, more veterans' benefits, payments for education, and pensions for the elderly.

At top, Father Coughlin addresses some 6,000 members of his National Union for Social Justice in Detroit, 1936. Above, Louisiana's Huey Long gestures in the flamboyant style for which he was famous.

COMPARING PRIMARY SOURCES
Roosevelt and the New Deal

Historians, politicians, and economists disagree on the effectiveness of the New Deal in combating the Depression and improving the lives of Americans.

Analyzing Viewpoints Compare the viewpoints of these two authors.

Criticism of the New Deal

"[New Deal measures] have not been administered with any special care to preserve the best features of private industry and encourage it to bring about recovery. The relief measures have been inefficient and expensive. They have resulted in a tremendous burden of taxation. . . . There has been no effort to preserve conditions under which a man, striving for a private job and doing his job well, shall be encouraged and preferred to the man on WPA. . . . More men have gone out of business in the last five years than have gone into business because of the complete uncertainty whether they can survive a constant Government interference."

—*Robert A. Taft, "A Conservative Critique: The New Deal and the Republican Program"*

Praises for the New Deal

"What then did the New Deal do? . . . [It] expanded the authority of the presidency, recruited university-trained administrators, won control of the money supply, established central banking, imposed regulations on Wall Street, . . . rescued debt-ridden farmers and homeowners, . . . fostered unionization of the factories, drastically reduced child labor, . . . established minimal working standards, enabled thousands of tenants to buy their own farms, built camps for migrants, introduced the Welfare State with old-age pensions, unemployment insurance, . . . subsidized painters and novelists, composers and ballet dancers, . . . [and] gave women greater recognition. . . ."

—*William E. Leuchtenburg, The FDR Years: On Roosevelt and His Legacy*

Deficit and Debt The terms *federal deficit* and *federal debt* (or *national debt*) are often confused. A federal <u>deficit</u> occurs when the government spends more money in its annual budget than it receives in revenues during that year. To cover a deficit, the government borrows money by issuing bonds, which are essentially IOUs to those who buy the bonds. The federal <u>debt</u> is the money the government owes to its bondholders. The government could have a great deal of federal debt, but not be practicing deficit spending. That is, it could be spending no more than it earns each year, yet it still could be paying off old debt, much like individuals who owe money on their credit cards. The chart below, for example, shows the deficit rising and falling during the Depression, as federal revenues and spending varied. The debt chart at the bottom, however, shows steady increases in government borrowing for New Deal programs.

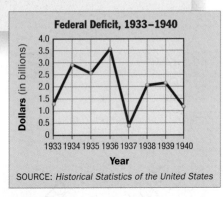

Federal Deficit, 1933–1940

SOURCE: *Historical Statistics of the United States*

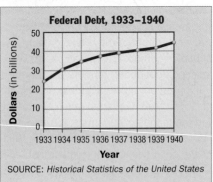

Federal Debt, 1933–1940

SOURCE: *Historical Statistics of the United States*

Although Long's program for helping all Americans achieve wealth was mathematically impossible, it attracted many followers. His success helped push FDR to propose new taxes on wealthy Americans in the Second New Deal. Meanwhile, Long himself began to eye the presidency. But in September 1935, the son-in-law of one of Long's political enemies shot and killed him.

Long and Coughlin's popularity warned Roosevelt that if he failed to solve the nation's problems, he could lose mass support. Coughlin was never a serious threat to FDR, but if Long had lived, he might have influenced the 1936 election.

Modern-Day Critics

Although many of the people who directly benefited from the New Deal are now gone, their children and grandchildren still pass down individual stories of hope and help that came to their families through programs like the WPA. To many Americans, FDR's bold actions place him among the nation's greatest Presidents. Yet some modern-day critics question whether the New Deal achieved the greatest good for the greatest number of Americans.

Some critics have examined this question in recent years and found the New Deal lacking. They say that New Deal programs hindered economic progress, threatened American free enterprise, and encouraged inefficient use of resources. Further, they charge that the programs created a dangerously powerful federal bureaucracy that usurped the historical role of state governments in making public policy.

For example, critics maintain that New Deal employment programs created "make work" jobs instead of allowing the free market to determine what jobs, and how many, were needed. These job programs were financed by heavy tax increases, which took money out of the economy and gave people less money to spend on products that would boost production and create jobs.

Modern critics also attack the policy of paying farmers not to plant. They contend that market demand should have been allowed to determine the supply and price of farm products. In a time of hunger, the program wasted precious resources, they note—from dumped milk to burned wheat. The program encouraged some farmers to plant crops on poor land just so that they could later take the land out of production and get paid for doing so. This caused marginal soil to erode further and become depleted. Farm production quotas penalized efficient and less-efficient farmers equally, while the free market would have weeded out inefficiency and rewarded productivity.

Finally, the New Deal receives criticism from people who oppose **deficit spending**—paying out more money from the annual federal budget than the government receives in revenues. Deficit spending to fund New Deal programs required the government to borrow money. Government borrowing produced what economists call the "crowding-out effect"—making less money available for private borrowing by businesses and consumers.

At the heart of the question is a difference in ideologies. Some people believe that the New Deal violated the free-market system that Americans have traditionally cherished. Others believe that providing direct relief to many of the nation's suffering citizens was worth the compromise. These debates continue today.

The Court-Packing Fiasco

Roosevelt received criticism not only for his programs, but also for his actions. No act aroused more opposition than his attempt to "pack" the Supreme Court.

Throughout the early New Deal, the Supreme Court had caused FDR his greatest frustration. The Court had invalidated the NIRA, the AAA, and many state laws from the Progressive Era. In February 1937, FDR proposed a major court-reform bill.

The Constitution had not specified the number of Supreme Court justices. Congress had last changed the number in 1869. By Roosevelt's time, the number nine had become well established. Arguing that he merely wanted to lighten the burden on the aging justices, FDR asked Congress to allow him to appoint as many as six additional justices, one for each justice over 70 years old. Roosevelt's real intention was to "pack" the Court with judges supportive of the New Deal.

Negative reaction came swiftly from all sides. Critics blasted the President for trying to inject politics into the judiciary. They warned Congress not to let him undermine the constitutional principle of separation of powers. With several dictators ruling in Europe, the world seemed already to be tilting toward tyranny. If Congress let FDR reshape the Supreme Court, critics worried, the United States might head down the same slope.

Strong opposition forced FDR to withdraw his reform bill. He also suffered political damage. Many Republicans and Southern Democrats united against further New Deal legislation. This alliance remained a force for years to come.

In the end, FDR still wound up with a Court that tended to side with him. Some older justices retired, allowing the President to appoint justices who favored the New Deal. Even earlier, however, the Court, acting on lawsuits filed by New Deal adversaries, had begun to uphold measures from the Second New Deal, including the Wagner Act. The Court may have been reacting to public opinion, or it may have decided that those measures were better thought out and more skillfully drafted than earlier ones.

ALL I SAID WAS 'GIMME SIX MORE JUSTICES!'

INTERPRETING POLITICAL CARTOONS FDR's request to Congress to allow him to appoint more Supreme Court justices (friendly to his New Deal programs) caused an uproar that damaged the President politically. **Analyzing Visual Information** *In this cartoon, what do you think the donkey represents, and what is the cartoonist trying to portray?*

Section 2 Assessment

READING COMPREHENSION

1. What effects did the New Deal have on women and minorities?

2. Why did the **American Liberty League** view the New Deal as unconstitutional and un-American?

3. Why did Upton Sinclair and Robert La Follette believe that the New Deal did not go far enough?

4. Describe FDR's "court-packing" maneuver and its outcome.

CRITICAL THINKING AND WRITING

5. Making Comparisons Compare and contrast the criticisms of two New Deal–era demagogues, Father Coughlin and Huey Long.

6. Writing an Opinion Review the arguments made by modern-day supporters and critics of the New Deal, and reread Comparing Historians' Viewpoints. Write a statement explaining which arguments you agree with, and why.

Go Online
PHSchool.com

For: An activity on FDR's court-packing plan
Visit: PHSchool.com
Web Code: mrd-7232

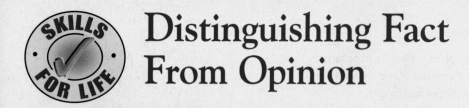

Distinguishing Fact From Opinion

A fact is something that can be proved to be true by checking an encyclopedia or other trusted source. An opinion is a judgment that reflects beliefs or feelings. Historical materials such as speeches, letters, and diaries often contain both facts and opinions. The ability to distinguish between facts and opinions will help you determine the soundness of a writer's ideas and reach your own conclusions about historical events.

In the excerpt below from a speech given at the 1936 Republican National Convention, Herbert Hoover criticizes the New Deal.

LEARN THE SKILL

Use the following steps to distinguish between fact and opinion in historical materials:

1. **Determine which statements are facts.** Remember that facts can be verified in other sources.

2. **Determine which statements are opinions.** Sometimes authors signal opinions with phrases such as "I believe" or "I think," but often they do not. Other clues that indicate opinions are emotion-packed words and sweeping generalizations. (A sweeping generalization is a broad statement about a group of people, things, or events, such as, "Politicians are corrupt.")

3. **Evaluate opinions as you read.** Generally, an opinion is more reliable when the author gives facts to support it.

PRACTICE THE SKILL

Answer the following questions:

1. **(a)** For what reason is Hoover's first statement, about the Supreme Court, easily recognizable as a fact? **(b)** Find two other statements of fact in the excerpt. How might you prove each one is a statement of fact?

2. **(a)** What indicates that the final sentence of the first paragraph is an opinion rather than a fact? **(b)** Find two other statements of opinion in the excerpt. What indicates that they are opinions?

3. **(a)** How does Hoover support his opinion that many New Deal acts "were a violation of the rights of men and of self-government"? **(b)** Does he present any facts to support his statement that the Congress has "abandoned its responsibility"? **(c)** In your opinion, how good a job has Hoover done in supporting his opinions? Explain your answer.

APPLY THE SKILL

See the Chapter Review and Assessment for another opportunity to apply this skill.

"The Supreme Court has reversed some ten or twelve of the New Deal major enactments. Many of these acts were a violation of the rights of men and of self-government. Despite the sworn duty of the Executive and Congress to defend these rights, they have sought to take them into their own hands. That is an attack on the foundations of freedom.

More than this, the independence of the Congress, the Supreme Court, and the Executive are pillars at the door of liberty. For three years the word 'must' has invaded the independence of Congress. And the Congress has abandoned its responsibility to check even the expenditures [spending] of money. . . .

We have seen these gigantic expenditures and this torrent of waste pile up a national debt which two generations cannot repay. . . .

Billions have been spent to prime the economic pump. . . . We have seen the frantic attempts to find new taxes on the rich. Yet three-quarters of the bill will be sent to the average man and the poor. He and his wife and his grandchildren will be giving a quarter of all their working days to pay taxes. Freedom to work for himself is changed into a slavery of work for the follies of government. . . .

We have seen the building up of a horde of political officials. We have seen the pressures upon the helpless and destitute to trade political support for relief. Both are a pollution of the very foundations of liberty."

—Herbert Hoover, *American Ideals Versus the New Deal*

Last Days of the New Deal

READING FOCUS

- What factors led to the recession of 1937, and how did the Roosevelt administration respond?

- What triumphs and setbacks did unions experience during the New Deal era?

- What effects did the New Deal have on American culture?

- What lasting effects can be attributed to the New Deal?

MAIN IDEA

Ultimately, the New Deal did not end the Depression. Yet it had lasting effects on many aspects of American life.

KEY TERMS

recession
national debt
revenue
coalition
sit-down strike

TARGET READING SKILL

Understand Effects Copy the chart below on a piece of paper. As you read, fill in the blanks by listing various effects of the New Deal.

Effects of the New Deal			
Economic	Political	Social	Cultural

Setting the Scene In 1936, writer James Agee and photographer Walker Evans made a six-week journey among the nation's poorest citizens, the tenant farmers of Alabama. Evans's photographs and Agee's descriptions were later published as *Let Us Now Praise Famous Men,* a book that left powerful images of the Great Depression in the nation's consciousness. The book bore witness to the survival of human dignity in the midst of deepest poverty. Here Agee, who shared meager lodgings with families, describes one farmer's revolving door of debt and despair:

66 *Years ago the Ricketts were, relatively speaking, almost prosperous. Besides their cotton farming they had ten cows and sold the milk, and they lived near a good stream and had all the fish they wanted. Ricketts went $400 into debt on a fine young pair of mules. One of the mules died before it had made the first crop; the other died the year after; against his fear . . . Ricketts went into debt for other, inferior mules; his cows went one by one . . . ; he got congestive chills; his wife got pellagra [a disease caused by dietary deficiencies]; a number of his children died; . . . for ten consecutive years now . . . they have not cleared or had any hope of clearing a cent at the end of the year. . . .*

VIEWING HISTORY Walker Evans's photographs captured both the plight and the dignity of the impoverished farm families he visited. **Analyzing Visual Images** *What impressions come to mind when you study this picture? Explain.*

WPA work is available to very few tenants: they are, technically, employed, and thus have no right to it: and if by chance they manage to get it, landlords are more likely than not to intervene. They feel it spoils a tenant to be paid wages, even for a little while. 99

—James Agee, *Let Us Now Praise Famous Men*, 1941

Unemployment, 1933–1940

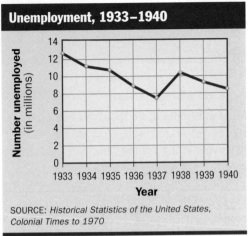

Number unemployed (in millions) vs **Year** (1933–1940), with values ranging from 0 to 14.

SOURCE: *Historical Statistics of the United States, Colonial Times to 1970*

INTERPRETING GRAPHS
Combating unemployment was one of Roosevelt's greatest challenges during the Depression. **Analyzing Visual Information** (a) From your reading of Section 3, explain why unemployment rose during 1937. (b) By about how much did unemployment decline over the course of the New Deal?

CIO chief John L. Lewis addresses 10,000 textile workers in Massachusetts in 1937.

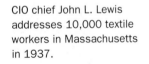

The Recession of 1937

The New Deal was no miracle cure for the Great Depression. While massive government spending led to some temporary economic improvement, in August 1937, the economy collapsed again. Industrial production fell, as did employment levels. The nation entered a **recession,** a period of slow business activity.

Americans had less money because FDR had cut way back on government spending. Many of the biggest cuts targeted programs such as the WPA, which had provided jobs to many workers. At the same time, FDR had increased taxes. FDR wanted a balanced budget, in which the government's revenue and expenses are equal. The President had also become distressed at the rising **national debt,** or the total amount of money the federal government borrows and has to pay back. (See Focus on Economics, page 550.) The government borrows when its **revenue,** or income, does not keep up with its expenses. To fund the New Deal, the government had to borrow massive amounts of money. As a result, the national debt rose from $21 billion in 1933 to $43 billion by 1940.

After 1937, Harry Hopkins and other advisors persuaded FDR to expand the WPA and other programs that had been cut back. The increased spending provided some economic relief. Still, hard times lasted until well into the 1940s.

Unions Triumph

The New Deal changed the way many Americans thought about labor unions. New federal protections for unions under the 1935 Wagner Act made union membership more attractive to workers. Membership rose from about 3 million in 1933 to 10.5 million by 1941, a figure representing 11.3 percent of the nonagricultural work force. By 1945, some 36 percent were unionized, the all-time high for unions in the United States.

A New Labor Organization Activism by powerful union leaders helped increase membership. The cautious and craft-based American Federation of Labor (AFL) had done little to attract unskilled industrial workers during the half-century of its existence. In 1935, United Mine Workers President John L. Lewis joined with representatives of seven other AFL unions to try to change this situation. They created a Committee for Industrial Organization (CIO) within the AFL.

Although the AFL did not support its efforts, the CIO sought to organize the nation's unskilled workers in mass-production industries. It sent organizers into steel mills, auto plants, and southern textile mills and encouraged all workers to join. In response, the AFL suspended CIO unions in 1936.

Two years later, the CIO had 4 million members. In November 1938, this **coalition,** or alliance of groups with similar goals, changed its name to the Congress of Industrial Organizations. John L. Lewis became its first president. The aim of this coalition of industrial unions was to challenge conditions in industry. Their main tool was the strike.

An Era of Strikes The Wagner Act legalized collective bargaining and required companies to bargain in good faith with certified union representatives. But the act did not force companies to accept unions' demands. Although the Wagner Act was designed to bring about industrial peace, in the short term it led to a wave of dramatic strikes.

Many of these work stoppages took the form of sit-down strikes. A weapon often used by the Congress of Industrial Organizations, the **sit-down strike** is a strike in which laborers stop working but refuse to leave the building. Supporters outside the workplace set up picket lines. Together, the strikers and the picket lines prevent the company from bringing in scabs, or non-union substitute workers. In areas where local authorities were New Deal Democrats, the workers' actions sometimes went unchallenged, making the sit-down strike an effective tool.

The first sit-down strikes took place in early 1936 at three huge rubber-tire plants in Akron, Ohio. The success of the sit-downs led to similar strikes later in the year at several General Motors (GM) auto plants. The most famous began on December 31, 1936. In this strike, laborers associated with the United Auto Workers (UAW) occupied GM's main plants in Flint, Michigan, and refused to leave.

GM executives turned off the heat and blocked entry to the plants so that the workers could not receive food. They also called in the police against the picketers outside. Violence erupted. The wife of a striker grabbed a bullhorn and urged other wives to join the picketers.

Women—both workers' wives and female employees—later organized food deliveries to supply the strikers. They set up a speakers' bureau to present the union's position to the public, and formed a Women's Emergency Brigade to take up picket duty. Governor Frank Murphy of Michigan and President Roosevelt refused to use the militia against the strike. By early February General Motors had given in.

Not all labor strikes were as successful. Henry Ford continued to resist unionism. In 1937, at a Ford Motor Company plant near Detroit, his men beat UAW officials when the unionists tried to distribute leaflets. Walter Reuther, a future UAW president, later testified about the incident:

> 66 *They picked me up about eight different times and threw me down on my back on the concrete. While I was on the ground they kicked me in the face, head, and other parts of my body. . . . I never raised a hand.* 99
>
> —Walter Reuther

Companies and the police were not the only instigators of violence. Mobs of striking unionists sometimes attacked strikebreakers trying to enter or leave a plant, or they destroyed company property. Unions generally opposed such actions, instead encouraging passive resistance. Still, strikers often fought back with bottles, bricks, stones, and bats.

Like Ford, the Republic Steel Company refused to sign with steelworkers' unions until war loomed in 1941. At one strike against Republic Steel on May 30, 1937, Chicago police killed several picketers and injured dozens. This Memorial Day tragedy was a sign that labor, despite its triumphs, still faced many challenges. Another sign came in the form of a Supreme Court ruling. In 1939, the Court outlawed the sit-down strike as being too potent a weapon and an obstacle to negotiation.

The New Deal's Effects on Culture

Artists created enduring cultural legacies for the nation during the Great Depression. They were aided by federal funds allocated by Congress to support the popular and fine arts and to provide jobs.

Literature   Several works of literature destined to become classics emerged during this period. One example is Pearl Buck's novel *The Good Earth* (1931), a saga of peasant struggle in China. In 1937, folklorist Zora Neale Hurston published *Their Eyes Were Watching God*, a novel about a strong-willed African American woman and the Florida town in which she lives. John Steinbeck wrote *The Grapes of Wrath* (1939), a powerful tale about Dust Bowl victims who travel to California in search of a better life. Funding from *Fortune* magazine allowed James Agee and Walker Evans to live for weeks with Alabama sharecroppers. The result of their experiences was the nonfiction masterpiece *Let Us Now Praise Famous Men* (1941).

Radio and Movies   The new medium of radio became a major source of entertainment for American families. Comedy shows of the 1930s produced stars such as Jack Benny, Fred Allen, George Burns, and Gracie Allen. The first daytime dramas, called soap operas because soap companies often sponsored them, emerged in this period. These 15-minute stories, designed to provoke strong emotional responses, were meant to appeal to women who remained at home during the day. Symphonic music and opera also flourished on the radio.

By 1933, the movies had recovered from the initial setback caused by the early Depression. Americans needed an escape from hard times, and the movies provided that escape. For a quarter, customers could see a double feature (introduced in 1931) or take the whole family to a drive-in theater (introduced in 1933). Federal agencies used motion pictures to publicize their work. The Farm Security Administration, for example, produced documentaries of American agricultural life.

Some Hollywood studios concentrated on optimistic films about common people who triumphed over evil, such as the Columbia Pictures movie *Mr. Smith Goes to Washington* (1939). Comedies were

Social Security

1935 "Young people have come to wonder what would be their lot when they came to old age," says FDR, signing into law the Social Security Act. It provides retirement pensions financed by a tax on employers and employees. Initally, retirees received a one-time payment, averaging $58.08.

1939 Act is amended to include benefits for spouses, minor children, and survivors, paid in monthly checks.

1950 Act is amended to increase the number of workers covered in the program from about 50 percent to nearly all workers; cost-of-living increases are enacted.

1956 Act is amended to cover disabled Americans.

1965 Creation of Medicare gives Social Security recipients health insurance.

2000 Social Security Trustees report that payment of full benefits can be guaranteed only through 2037. With the huge "baby boom" generation nearing retirement, concern about funding for the system prompts intense debate on proposals to reform Social Security.

? **Why do you think the federal government kept enlarging the Social Security system and extending its benefits?**

very popular, too. In this era, the zany Marx Brothers produced such comic classics as *Monkey Business* (1931) and *Duck Soup* (1933), both of which had first premiered as stage shows.

The greatest box-office hits were movies that distracted Americans from the gloom of the Depression. *The Wizard of Oz*, released in 1939, allowed viewers to escape to a whole different world. Moviegoers flocked to musicals that featured large orchestras and lavishly choreographed dance numbers. No one understood the needs of Depression-era audiences better than Walt Disney, whose Mickey Mouse cartoons delighted moviegoers everywhere. Disney also released the classic cartoon *Snow White and the Seven Dwarfs* (1938) during this period.

The WPA and the Arts   FDR believed that the arts were not luxuries that people should have to give up in hard times. For this reason, he earmarked WPA funds to support unemployed artists, musicians, historians, theater people, and writers. The Federal Writers' Project, established in 1935, assisted more than 6,000 writers, including Richard Wright, Saul Bellow, Margaret Walker, and Ralph Ellison. Historians with the project surveyed the nation's local government records, wrote state guidebooks, and collected life stories from about 2,000 former slaves.

Other government projects supported music and the visual arts. The Federal Music Project started community symphonies and organized free music lessons. It also sent music specialists to lumber camps and small towns to collect and preserve a fast-disappearing folk music heritage.

The Federal Art Project, begun in 1935, put thousands of artists to work. They painted some 2,000 murals, mainly in public buildings. They also produced about 100,000 other paintings, 17,000 sculptures, and many other works of art.

VIEWING FINE ART New Deal support for the arts led to many lasting works, including this mural painted by Thomas Hart Benton in 1930 for the New School of Social Research in New York City. **Analyzing Visual Information** *How does this mural celebrate the values and spirit of the era? Support your answer with specifics from the painting.*

READING CHECK

Why did the federal government fund new arts programs during the Depression?

The Federal Theatre Project, directed by Vassar College Professor Hallie Flanagan, was the most controversial project. Flanagan used drama to create awareness of social problems. Her project launched the careers of many actors, playwrights, and directors who later became famous, including Burt Lancaster, Arthur Miller, John Houseman, and Orson Welles.

Accusing the Federal Theatre Project of being a propaganda machine for international communism, the House Un-American Activities Committee (HUAC) investigated the project in 1938 and 1939. In July 1939, Congress eliminated the project's funding.

Lasting New Deal Achievements

The New Deal attacked the Great Depression with a barrage of programs that affected nearly every American. The New Deal did not end the nation's suffering, but it led to some profound changes in American life. Voters began to expect a President to formulate programs and solve problems. People accepted more government intervention in their lives, and they grew accustomed to a much larger government. Laborers demanded more changes in the workplace.

The New Deal did not vanish completely when the Depression ended. Its accomplishments continued in many forms. This legacy ranges from physical monuments that dot the American landscape to towering political and social achievements that still influence American life.

Public Works and Federal Agencies Many New Deal bridges, dams, tunnels, public buildings, and hospitals exist to this day. These durable public works are visual reminders of this extraordinary period of government intervention in the economy.

Some of the federal agencies from the New Deal era have also endured. The Tennessee Valley Authority remains a model of government planning. The Federal Deposit Insurance Corporation still guarantees bank deposits. The Securities and Exchange Commission continues to monitor the workings of the stock exchanges.

And in rural America, farmers still plant according to federal crop allotment policies adopted after the Supreme Court struck down AAA crop-reduction plans.

Social Security   Despite its enduring support throughout American society, the Social Security system has had many critics. At first, Social Security came under attack because its payments were very low.

For a long time the system discriminated against women. It assumed, for example, that the male-headed household was typical. A mother could lose benefits for her children if a man, whether providing support for her or not, lived in her house. Women who went to work when their children started school rarely stayed in the work force long enough or earned high enough wages to receive the maximum benefits from the system. In addition, when a male recipient died, his benefits ended, leaving his family without an income.

Sample Social Security card, with zeroes representing an individual's Social Security number

In 1939, Congress and the Social Security Administration developed a series of amendments to the system attempted to address some of the weaknesses in the system. The amendments raised benefit amounts and provided monthly benefit checks instead of one-time payments. They also provided benefits for recipients' dependents and survivors. Later amendments included farm workers and others previously excluded from coverage, and added disability coverage.

A Legacy of Hope   Of all of its achievements, perhaps the New Deal's greatest was to restore a sense of hope. People poured out their troubles to the President and First Lady. Eleanor and Franklin Roosevelt received thousands of letters daily during the late Depression era. Every letter contained a story of continued personal suffering. In their distress, people looked to their government for support. Indeed, government programs did mean the difference between survival and starvation for millions of Americans.

Nevertheless, economic recovery in the United States would not come until well into the 1940s, and it did not come through more New Deal programs. The return of a robust economy was set in motion on the battlefields of Europe in the late 1930s, where another test of American character was brewing: a second world war.

Section 3 Assessment

READING COMPREHENSION

1. Why did the United States slide back into a **recession** in 1937?

2. Why did FDR become concerned about the **national debt?**

3. (a) What gains and setbacks did unions experience during the New Deal era? (b) What impact did the Congress of Industrial Organizations (CIO) have on union strategies?

4. What did critics dislike about the Social Security system?

CRITICAL THINKING AND WRITING

5. **Testing Conclusions** FDR's advisors concluded that certain actions were needed to combat the recession of 1937. What actions did they recommend, and what were the consequences?

6. **Writing an Opinion** Write an essay that examines the legacy of the New Deal. In your opinion, what positive or negative effects did it have on the country? Should the federal government have become involved in creating jobs in theater and the other arts?

For: An activity on publicly funded arts projects
Visit: PHSchool.com
Web Code: mrd-7233

creating a CHAPTER SUMMARY

Copy this web diagram (right) on a piece of paper and complete it by adding information about New Deal programs and laws. Add as many circles as you need. Some entries have been completed for you as examples.

For additional review and enrichment activities, see the interactive version of *America: Pathways to the Present*, available on the Web and on CD-ROM.

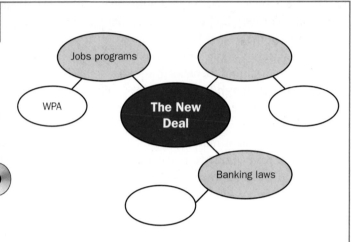

Jobs programs

WPA

The New Deal

Banking laws

★ Reviewing Key Terms

For each of the terms below, write a sentence explaining how it relates to the New Deal era.

1. New Deal
2. hundred days
3. Tennessee Valley Authority (TVA)
4. Second New Deal
5. Wagner Act
6. Social Security system
7. demagogue
8. nationalization
9. national debt
10. sit-down strike

★ Reviewing Main Ideas

11. Why did FDR begin the New Deal by closing the nation's banks? (Section 1)
12. How did the National Industrial Recovery Act aim to help businesses? (Section 1)
13. What did the 1936 election reveal about voters' attitudes toward the New Deal? (Section 1)
14. What were some of the limitations of the New Deal? (Section 2)
15. What was the main criticism of the New Deal by the American Liberty League? (Section 2)
16. Why did President Roosevelt attempt to "pack" the Supreme Court? (Section 2)
17. What factors led to the recession of 1937? (Section 3)

18. What permanent changes took place for labor unions as a result of the New Deal? (Section 3)
19. How did the New Deal support the popular and fine arts in America? (Section 3)

★ Critical Thinking

20. **Identifying Central Issues** Do you think that the New Deal was a success or a failure? Explain, citing information from the chapter.
21. **Comparing Points of View** (a) How did Eleanor Roosevelt view her role as First Lady? (b) How did her critics view that role? (c) How and why did these viewpoints differ?
22. **Demonstrating Reasoned Judgment** (a) Why did the Supreme Court strike down the National Industrial Recovery Act? (b) Do you agree with the court's decision? Why or why not?
23. **Identifying Alternatives** Choose a present-day social or economic problem and state whether a New Deal type of approach would help to solve it. Explain your reasoning.
24. **Recognizing Ideologies** Compare the viewpoints of supporters and critics of the New Deal. Describe the beliefs and values that influenced the opinions of each side.

THIS IS ONE RABBIT THAT NEVER FAILED ME!

SPENDING

OLD RELIABLE!

★ Standardized Test Prep

Analyzing Political Cartoons ▶

25. This cartoon shows President Roosevelt as a magician pulling a rabbit out of his hat. What does the rabbit represent?

A Spending on New Deal programs

B Roosevelt's control of Congress

C Roosevelt's ability to increase consumer spending

D Cuts in government spending

26. Summarize the cartoon's message.

Analyzing Primary Sources

Turn to the quotation from Sam T. Mayhew in Section 2. Then answer the questions that follow.

27. What statement BEST summarizes Mayhew's opinion of the New Deal?

A Roosevelt's policies were harmful to all Americans because they were never put into action.

B Roosevelt should have provided more leadership during the Depression instead of letting the country drift.

C The New Deal failed to bring prosperity to all of America because its benefits were given out by race, not ability.

D Discrimination on the basis of color caused the Great Depression to worsen in the United States.

28. What does Mayhew mean when he says, "All the prosperity he had brought to the country has been legislated and is not real"?

F Laws to relieve the Depression were passed but not carried out.

G Roosevelt used government spending to create prosperity that was not rooted in real economic growth.

H Politicians misled Americans into believing that the New Deal had brought prosperity.

I Roosevelt himself did not bring any real prosperity to the country; Congress did, through the legislation it passed.

Test-Taking Tip

To answer Question 27, note that one of Mayhew's main points is that discrimination has prevented African Americans from prospering.

Applying the Chapter Skill

Distinguishing Fact From Opinion Suppose you could use these three sources for a report on the 1936 election: (a) a speech by Alfred M. Landon, (b) a political encyclopedia, (c) Franklin Roosevelt's diary for 1936. Which source would you turn to for verifiable facts about the election? Why? Which sources would you turn to for opinions? Why?

Go Online PHSchool.com

For: Chapter 16 Self-Test
Visit: PHSchool.com
Web Code: mra-7234

TEST PREPARATION

Write your answers on a separate sheet of paper.

1. Charles Lindbergh was admired by many Americans in the 1920s after he

   A made many popular silent films.

   B set records in Major League baseball.

   C flew alone across the Atlantic Ocean.

   D became a commercial radio announcer.

2. Which one of the following best describes the Harlem Renaissance?

   A A system of registering African Americans to vote

   B A very popular nightclub in New York City

   C A program to end Jim Crow laws in the southern states

   D An African American literary and artistic movement

3. Support for African American businesses and a back-to-Africa movement were part of whose program?

   A Marcus Garvey

   B W.E.B. Du Bois

   C James Weldon Johnson

   D Jim Thorpe

4. Which one of the following best describes the Red Scare of the 1920s?

   A A part of the Ku Klux Klan program

   B A type of popular music, especially among teenagers

   C A period of fear of communism and radical ideas

   D A plan to limit immigration from eastern Europe

Use the information in the graph to answer the following question.

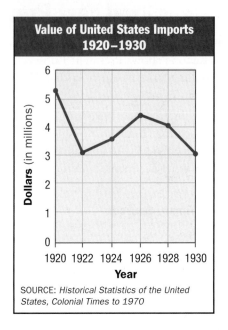

Value of United States Imports 1920–1930

SOURCE: *Historical Statistics of the United States, Colonial Times to 1970*

5. Which one of the following statements best explains the information in the graph?

   A United States tariffs reduced imports into the country during the 1920s.

   B No one had money in the 1920s to buy imports.

   C World War I effectively ended all international trade.

   D New immigrants bought many things from their former countries.

6. The assembly line was made more efficient by

   A J. P. Morgan.

   B Walter Chrysler.

   C A. Mitchell Palmer.

   D Henry Ford.

Use the information in the chart to answer the following question.

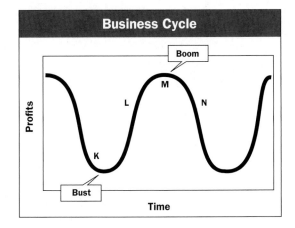

Business Cycle

7. At what point in the business cycle was the U.S. economy just before the Great Crash occurred?

   A K

   B L

   C M

   D N

8. Which one of the following was an action taken by President Hoover to fight the Depression?

   A Giving assistance directly to individuals

   B Closing down all the nation's banks

   C Establishing the Social Security Act

   D Providing jobs through public works programs

9. Which one of the following was one of the first actions taken by Franklin D. Roosevelt when he became President?

   A Ending prohibition in the country

   B Creating the Reconstruction Finance Corporation

   C Closing down all the nation's banks

   D Establishing the 12 Federal Reserve Banks

10. The New Deal–era law that gives money to people who are retired or without work is the

    A Wagner Act.

    B National Youth Administration.

    C Social Security Act.

    D National Industrial Recovery Act.

11. Putting young men to work restoring and maintaining forests, beaches, and parks was the purpose of Roosevelt's

    A Civilian Conservation Corps.

    B American Federation of Labor.

    C Tennessee Valley Authority.

    D Federal Emergency Relief Administration.

12. Which one of the following effectively ended the Depression and restored the U.S. economy?

    A The Public Works Administration

    B The Security and Exchange Commission

    C World War II

    D The Bonus Army march on Washington

Writing Practice

13. Describe the changing role of women in the 1920s.

14. What were the three major causes of the Depression?

15. Describe the actions taken during the New Deal to change the financial system of the United States.

> "It is not enough to fight. It is the spirit which we bring to the fight that decides the issue. It is morale that wins the victory."

George C. Marshall
Military Review, October 1948

U.S. soldiers disembark from Coast Guard landing craft on the shores of Normandy after the main D-Day invasion. ▶

Chapter 17

World War II: The Road to War

(1931–1941)

This German election poster translates to "Our Last Hope: Hitler."

Adolf Hitler

American Events

1934
The United States cuts tariffs on foreign goods to benefit trade and international relations.

1935
Congress passes the first Neutrality Act banning the sale of arms to countries at war.

Presidential Terms: Herbert Hoover 1929–1933   Franklin D. Roosevelt 1933–1945

1931   **1933**   **1935**

World Events

Japanese army overruns Manchuria.

1931

Adolf Hitler is named Chancellor of Germany.

1933

Joseph Stalin begins the Great Purge of Soviet citizens.

1934

Political Regimes in Europe Before World War II

1930
Communist Party banned.

1924–1941
Stalin kills or imprisons millions of Soviets.

Jan. 1933
Adolf Hitler appointed chancellor.

1926–1935
Pilsudski reigns as dictator.

March 1933
Dollfuss established as dictator.

March 1939
Nationalists win Civil War; Franco seizes power.

October 1922
Mussolini seizes power.

1923–1938
Kemal Ataturk modernizes Turkey.

Legend:
- Communist
- Democratic
- Fascist
- Repressive
- 1937 borders

0   200   400 mi.
0   200   400 km

Joseph Stalin

1939
Congress repeals the arms embargo.

1940
Roosevelt sends 50 destroyers to Britain in exchange for military bases in the Western Hemisphere.

1941
Roosevelt proposes lend-lease program to aid the Allies. Japan bombs Pearl Harbor and brings the United States into the war.

1936
Italy conquers Ethiopia.

1937
Marco Polo Bridge incident leads Japan to invade China.

1938
Chamberlain and Hitler meet at the Munich Conference.

1939
Invasion of Poland begins World War II.

1940
Germany defeats France and attacks Britain by air.

READING FOCUS

- How did Stalin change the government and the economy of the Soviet Union?
- What were the origins and goals of Italy's fascist government?
- How did Hitler rise to power in Germany and Europe in the 1930s?
- What were the causes and results of the Spanish Civil War?

KEY TERMS

totalitarian
fascism
purge
Nazism
Axis Powers
appeasement

TARGET READING SKILL

Identify Main Ideas As you read, complete this chart listing the actions of dictators in the Soviet Union, Italy, and Germany in the 1930s.

Country	Actions Taken
Soviet Union	• Combined farms into collectives • Sent millions to labor camps in Siberia •
Germany	
Italy	

MAIN IDEA

Dictators in the Soviet Union, Italy, Germany, and Spain formed brutal, repressive governments in the 1920s and 1930s. They were motivated by their political beliefs and a desire for power.

Adolf Hitler presided over massive party rallies, including this one at Nuremberg.

Setting the Scene In September 1936, German dictator Adolf Hitler called hundreds of thousands of his followers to a week-long rally in the German city of Nuremberg. Included with political meetings and parades was a nighttime ceremony: the Oath under the Cathedral of Light. A Nazi Party booklet described the beginning of the ceremony.

❝ *180,000 people look to the heavens. 150 blue spotlights surge upward hundreds of meters, forming overhead the most powerful cathedral that mortals have ever seen.*

There, at the entrance, we see [Hitler]. He too stands for several moments looking upward, then turns and walks, followed by his aides, past the long, long columns, 20 deep, of the fighters for his idea. An ocean of Heil-shouts and jubilation surrounds him. ❞
—*The Party Rally of Honor*

Amid waving red banners and circling searchlights, Hitler led the audience of 180,000 in a "holy oath" to Germany.

Grand spectacles like the Nuremberg Party Rally were essential to Hitler's **totalitarian** rule. A totalitarian government exerts total control over a nation. It dominates every aspect of life, using terror to suppress individual rights and silence all forms of opposition. The pride and unity of the Nuremberg rally hid the fact that people who disagreed with Hitler were silenced, beaten, or killed. Hitler's power rested on the destruction of the individual.

Hitler and Italy's Benito Mussolini governed by a philosophy called **fascism.** Fascism emphasizes the importance of the nation or an ethnic group and the supreme authority of the leader. In the Soviet Union, Joseph Stalin based his totalitarian government on a vicious form of communism. Like fascism, communism relies upon a strong, dictatorial government that does not respect individual rights and freedoms. Historically, however, Communists and Fascists have been fierce enemies.

Stalin's Soviet Union

While Lenin led the Soviet Union, the worldwide Communist revolution he sought never materialized. Even in his own country, economic failure threatened Communist control of the government. Lenin eased up on the drive to convert all property to public ownership. His New Economic Policy (NEP) allowed some private business to continue. Stalin took over after Lenin's death in 1924. Stalin decided to abandon the NEP and take "one great leap forward" to communism. He launched the first of a series of five-year plans to modernize agriculture and build new industries from the ground up.

Stalin's Economic Plans To modernize agriculture, Stalin encouraged Soviet farmers to combine their small family farms into huge collective farms owned and run by the state. Facing widespread resistance, Stalin began forcing peasants off their land in the late 1920s.

The state takeover of farming was completed within a few years, but with terrible consequences. In the Ukraine and other agricultural regions, Stalin punished resistant farmers by confiscating much or all of the food they produced. Millions of people died from starvation, and millions more fled to the cities. Stalin also sent approximately 5 million peasants to labor camps in Siberia and northern Russia.

Labor Camps in the Western Soviet Union, *circa* 1936

- Canal
- Railroad
- ■ Labor camp

The Belomor (White Sea) Canal was built almost entirely by forced labor.

Camps in the southern, more fertile regions of Russia focused on agriculture.

Millions of people starved when Stalin's policies caused a famine in the Ukraine in the early 1930s.

In addition to the human cost, the collectivization campaign caused agricultural production to fall dramatically. Food shortages forced Stalin to introduce rationing throughout the country.

Stalin pursued rapid industrialization with more success. He assigned millions of laborers from rural areas to build and run new industrial centers where iron, steel, oil, and coal were produced. Because Stalin poured money and labor into these basic industries rather than housing, clothing, and consumer goods, the Soviet people endured severe shortages of essential products, and their standard of living fell sharply. Still, by 1940 Stalin had achieved his goal of turning the Soviet Union into a modern industrial power.

Stalin's Reign of Terror During the economic upheaval, Stalin completed his political domination of the Soviet Union through a series of **purges.** In political terms, a purge is the process of removing enemies and undesirable

MAP SKILLS Stalin presided over a vast expansion of the Soviet Union's system of labor camps. **Place** *What hardships did prisoners experience in the northernmost camps?*

individuals from power. Stalin "purified" the Communist Party by getting rid of his opponents and anyone else he believed to be a threat to his power or to his ideas. The Great Purge began in 1934 with a series of "show trials," in which the only possible verdict was "guilty." Stalin's reign of terror did not stop there, however. He and his followers purged local party offices, collective farms, the secret police, and the army of anyone whom he considered a threat.

By 1939, his agents had arrested more than 7 million people from all levels of society. A million were executed, and millions more ended up in forced labor camps. Nearly all of the people were innocent victims of Stalin's paranoia. But the purges successfully eliminated all threats to Stalin's power, real or imagined.

Fascism in Italy

As in the Soviet Union, Italy's totalitarian government arose from the failures of World War I. Benito Mussolini had fought and been wounded in the war. He believed strongly that the Versailles Treaty should have granted Italy more territory. A talented speaker, Mussolini began to attract followers, including other dissatisfied war veterans, opponents of the monarchy, Socialists, and anarchists. In 1919, Mussolini and his supporters formed the revolutionary Fascist Party.

Calling himself *Il Duce* ("the leader"), Mussolini organized Fascist groups throughout Italy. He relied on gangs of Fascist thugs, called Blackshirts because of the way they dressed, to terrorize and bring under control those who opposed him. By 1922, Mussolini had become such a powerful figure that when he threatened to march on Rome, the king panicked and appointed him prime minister.

Strikes and riots had plagued Italy since World War I. Mussolini and the Fascists vowed to end Italy's economic problems. In the name of efficiency and order, they suspended elections, outlawed all other political parties, and established a dictatorship.

Italy's ailing economy improved under *Il Duce*'s firm command. Other European nations noted his success with the Italian economy and applauded him as a miracle worker. They would soon choke on their words of praise, however, for Mussolini had dreams of forging a new Roman Empire. A Fascist slogan summed up Mussolini's expansionist goals: "The Country Is Nothing Without Conquest."

In October 1935, Mussolini put those words into practice by invading the independent African kingdom of Ethiopia. The Ethiopians resisted fiercely, but the large Italian army, using warplanes and poison gas, overpowered the Ethiopian forces. By May 1936, Ethiopia's emperor had fled to England and the capital, Addis Ababa, was in Italian hands.

VIEWING HISTORY This poster announced, "Italy finally has its empire," after the conquest of Ethiopia. The letters *A.O.* are the Italian abbreviation for East Africa—the site of Mussolini's empire. **Drawing Inferences** *How does this poster glorify Mussolini?*

Hitler's Rise to Power

While Mussolini was gaining control in Italy, a discontented Austrian painter was rising to prominence in Germany. Like Mussolini, Adolf Hitler had been wounded while serving in World War I. He, too, felt enraged by the terms of the peace settlement, which stripped Germany of land and colonies and imposed a huge burden of debt to pay for the damage done to France, Belgium, and Britain. He especially hated the war-guilt clause—the section of the Versailles Treaty that forced Germany to accept the blame for starting the war.

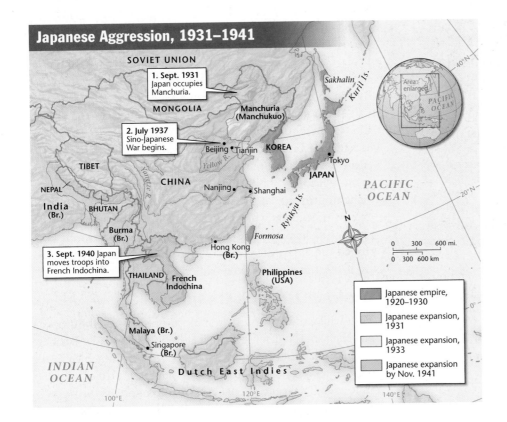

Japanese Aggression, 1931–1941

SOVIET UNION

1. Sept. 1931 Japan occupies Manchuria.

MONGOLIA

Manchuria (Manchukuo)

2. July 1937 Sino-Japanese War begins.

Beijing • Tianjin   KOREA

Yellow R.

TIBET

CHINA   JAPAN

Tokyo

NEPAL

India (Br.)   BHUTAN

Nanjing • Shanghai

PACIFIC OCEAN

Burma (Br.)

3. Sept. 1940 Japan moves troops into French Indochina.

Formosa

Hong Kong (Br.)

THAILAND   French Indochina

Philippines (USA)

Sakhalin

Kuril Is.

Ryukyu Is.

Area enlarged   PACIFIC OCEAN

Malaya (Br.)

• Singapore (Br.)

INDIAN OCEAN

Dutch East Indies

0   300   600 mi.
0   300 600 km

Japanese empire, 1920–1930

Japanese expansion, 1931

Japanese expansion, 1933

Japanese expansion by Nov. 1941

MAP SKILLS Japan's gradual expansion in Asia led to an outright war with China in 1937. **Location** List three countries or colonial possessions that appeared to be likely targets of Japanese aggression in November 1941. Explain your reasoning.

fear for their lives so much that they dared not criticize the military. The new prime minister said:

> The military are like an untamed horse left to run wild. If you try head-on to stop it, you'll get kicked to death. The only hope is to jump on from the side and try to get it under control while still allowing it to have its head to a certain extent.
>
> —Hirota Koki

Japan's military leaders never actually seized control of the government. However, they took a much stronger hand in governing the nation, especially in the area of foreign policy. They began to develop Manchuria as a base for even further Japanese expansion in Asia.

War Against China

In July 1937, Japan resumed its invasion of China. The Japanese army turned a minor clash at the Marco Polo Bridge outside Beijing into a full-scale war. By the end of the month, Japanese forces occupied the major cities of Beijing and Tianjin and threatened the rest of northern China. The Chinese Nationalist army, led by General Jiang Jieshi* (jyawng jeh SHEE), fiercely resisted the invasion. In battle after battle, however, Japan's superior weapons overcame China's huge manpower advantage. Japanese warplanes ruthlessly bombed Chinese cities. During the "Rape of Nanjing," Japanese soldiers brutalized or killed at least 100,000 civilians, including women and children, in the former capital of China.

The United States and other nations condemned Japan's actions. President Roosevelt spoke out against international aggression, saying that "the epidemic of world lawlessness is spreading" and calling for a "quarantine" to protect peaceful nations. Meanwhile, Congress passed a series of Neutrality Acts that prevented the United States from becoming involved in foreign conflicts. The

READING CHECK
How successful was Japan's 1937 invasion of China?

* This name is also spelled Chiang Kai-shek.

An American Partner in the Pacific

Since the 1930s and 1940s, when they competed for control of the Pacific, Japan and the United States have become important allies and trading partners. The two countries share concerns about aggressive moves by North Korea and China.

Japan had renounced war and had limited the use of its much-reduced military to defense purposes after World War II. In 1998, the Japanese government announced that Japan would offer non-combat support to American troops in "areas surrounding Japan." This bill upset many Japanese who were unwilling to send any troops overseas, even in noncombat roles, to avoid association with Japan's wartime past.

 Why did the United States and Japan come into conflict in the 1930s and 1940s?

Soviet Union also voiced its concern and backed up its words with arms, military advisors, and warplanes for China. Later, Britain sent a steady stream of supplies to the Chinese over the **Burma Road,** a 700-mile-long highway linking Burma (present-day Myanmar) to China.

The war brought two longtime enemies together. Jiang and Chinese Communist leader Mao Zedong, who were locked in a bitter struggle for power, put aside their differences to fight the Japanese. When direct resistance failed, Jiang withdrew his armies to the mountains of remote Sichuan province in the south. Mao split his army into small groups of soldiers who organized bands of Chinese guerrilla fighters to harass the Japanese. While Japanese troops controlled the cities, these guerrillas dominated the countryside. By 1939, the war in China had reached a stalemate.

Looking Beyond China

Meanwhile, the start of the war in Europe distracted European powers from the defense of their colonies in East Asia. Japanese leaders took this opportunity to expand their influence in the region to its south. In 1940, Japan's prime minister announced a **Greater East Asia Co-Prosperity Sphere** to be led by the Japanese, extending from Manchuria in the north to the Dutch East Indies in the south. Japan declared it would liberate Asia from European colonizers. In reality, Japan needed the region's natural resources, especially oil and rubber, to carry on its war against China. In this way, Japan's co-prosperity sphere resembled Hitler's invasion of other countries for *lebensraum* ("living space").

In September 1940, Japan allied itself with Germany and Italy through the Tripartite Pact. That same month, Japan moved troops into the northern part of French Indochina, with the reluctant permission of the Vichy government of France. With the Netherlands in German hands, Japan also set its sights on the oil-rich Dutch East Indies. Then, in April 1941, the Japanese signed a neutrality pact with the Soviet Union. The stage was now set for Japan to challenge the Europeans and Americans for supremacy in Asia.

Section 3 Assessment

READING COMPREHENSION

1. (a) Who among the Japanese was responsible for the conquest of Manchuria? (b) How was this invasion different from Germany's invasion of Poland?

2. Why was Japan unable to win the war in China?

3. (a) According to Japan, what was the purpose of the **Greater East Asia Co-Prosperity Sphere?** (b) What was Japan's real goal?

CRITICAL THINKING AND WRITING

4. **Drawing Conclusions** What do Japan's actions indicate about the way economic problems affect foreign policy? Cite evidence from your reading.

5. **Writing an Opinion** Read the quote from Hirota Koki. Write a paragraph defending or criticizing Hirota's response to the military's actions.

4 From Isolationism to War

READING FOCUS

- Why did the United States choose neutrality in the 1930s?
- How did American involvement in the European conflict grow from 1939 to 1941?
- Why did Japan's attack on Pearl Harbor lead the United States to declare war?

MAIN IDEA

United States foreign policy changed slowly from neutrality to strong support for the Allies. Japan's surprise attack on Pearl Harbor immediately brought the United States into the war with the full support of the people.

KEY TERMS

Neutrality Acts
cash and carry
America First Committee
Lend-Lease Act

TARGET READING SKILL

Identify Main Ideas As you read, complete this chart by listing reasons why people supported or opposed the involvement of the United States in the war.

Supported Involvement in the War	Opposed Involvement in the War
• Britain was defending American ideals of freedom and democracy. • The Axis Powers would eventually declare war on the United States. •	

Setting the Scene

During the 1930s, the United States largely turned away from international affairs. Instead, the government focused its energies on solving the domestic problems brought about by the Great Depression. Even as Italy, Germany, and Japan threatened to shatter world peace, the United States clung to its policy of isolationism. The horrors of World War I still haunted many Americans who refused to be dragged into another foreign conflict. President Franklin Roosevelt assured Americans that he felt the same way:

> 66 *I have seen war. I have seen war on land and sea. I have seen blood running from the wounded. I have seen men coughing out their gassed lungs. I have seen the dead in the mud. I have seen cities destroyed. I have seen two hundred limping, exhausted men come out of line—the survivors of a regiment of one thousand that went forward forty-eight hours before. I have seen children starving. I have seen the agony of mothers and wives. I hate war.* 99
>
> —Franklin D. Roosevelt, address at Chautauqua, New York, August 1936

VIEWING HISTORY Franklin Roosevelt used "fireside chats" to speak directly to Americans during the Depression and later as the United States drew closer to war.

Few people in the United States agreed with the actions or the ideas of the Fascists, the Nazis, or the Japanese radicals. Most Americans sympathized with the victims of aggression. Still, nothing short of a direct attack on the United States would propel Americans into another war.

The United States Chooses Neutrality

American isolationism increased in the early 1930s, although President Roosevelt, elected in 1932, favored more international involvement. The demands of carrying out the New Deal kept Roosevelt focused on domestic issues, however. He was more concerned with lifting the United States out of the Depression than with addressing foreign concerns.

THESE SPRING DAYS IT'S HARD TO KEEP YOUR MIND ON YOUR WORK!

In 1930, Congress had passed the Hawley-Smoot tariff to protect American industries from foreign competitors. In response, other nations raised their tariff walls against American goods. Although they were reduced in 1934, these trade barriers prolonged the Depression and isolated the United States.

Congress again prevented international involvement by passing a series of **Neutrality Acts.** The first of these, in 1935, banned the United States from providing weapons to nations at war. The second, in 1936, banned loans to such nations. The third, in 1937, permitted trade with fighting nations in nonmilitary goods as long as those nations paid cash and transported the cargo themselves. This policy became known as **cash and carry.**

The Neutrality Acts prevented the United States from selling arms even to nations that were trying to defend themselves from aggression. By doing this, as FDR pointed out later, the Neutrality Acts encouraged aggression. By the end of 1938, Italy had conquered Ethiopia, Japan had invaded China, and Germany had taken Austria and the Sudetenland. The United States watched warily from a distance, protected by the Atlantic and Pacific oceans.

American Involvement Grows

As the decade wore on, the American economy recovered somewhat. Unemployment and business failures no longer required the nation's full attention. At the same time, Germany and Japan stepped up their aggression against neighboring countries. This combination of events softened Americans' isolationist views.

American opinion shifted even further against the Axis Powers in September 1939, when Germany invaded Poland. At that time, almost no one believed that America should enter the war against Germany. But many people felt that the United States shared Britain's interests, and given the constraints of neutrality, President Roosevelt began to look for ways to send more aid to the Allies.

COMPARING PRIMARY SOURCES
Assistance for Britain

After France fell and Britain stood alone against Germany, Americans debated whether to assist Britain and what form that assistance should take.

Analyzing Viewpoints Compare the statements of the two speakers.

Opposed to Aid

"When England asks us to enter this war, she is considering her own future, and that of her Empire. In making our reply, I believe we should consider the future of the United States and that of the Western Hemisphere. . . . I ask you to look at the map of Europe today and see if you can suggest any way in which we could win this war if we entered it. . . . If we concentrate on our own and build the strength that this nation should maintain, no foreign army will ever attempt to land on American shores."

—Charles Lindbergh, Address to the America First Committee, April 23, 1941

In Favor of Aid

"The Nazi masters of Germany have made it clear that they intend . . . to enslave the whole of Europe, and then to use the resources of Europe to dominate the rest of the world. . . . the Axis not merely admits but proclaims that there can be no ultimate peace between their philosophy of government and our philosophy of government. . . . [Britain is] putting up a fight which will live forever in the story of human gallantry."

—Franklin D. Roosevelt, Arsenal of Democracy speech, December 29, 1940

Debating the American Role Three weeks after the invasion of Poland, Roosevelt asked Congress to revise the Neutrality Acts to make them more flexible. Congress did so by repealing the arms embargo and providing Britain and France with the weapons they needed. A later amendment allowed American merchant ships to transport these purchases to Britain. Neutrality legislation still prevented the United States from lending money to the Allies.

In June 1940, France fell to the Germans, and Hitler prepared to invade Britain. France's rapid collapse shocked Americans, who had expected the Allies to defend themselves effectively against Germany. Now Britain stood alone against Hitler, and many Americans supported "all aid short of war" for Britain. Roosevelt successfully pressed Congress for more aid. On September 3, the United States agreed to send 50 old destroyers to Britain in return for permission to build bases on British territory in the Western Hemisphere. Some Americans saw this exchange as a dangerous step toward direct American military involvement. Two days after the trade, a group of isolationists formed the **America First Committee** to block further aid to Britain. At its height, this group attracted more than 800,000 members, including Charles Lindbergh.

During the presidential campaign of 1940, both Roosevelt and his Republican opponent, Wendell Willkie, supported giving aid to the Allies. They disagreed, however, on how much aid should be given and on what the aid should be. As election day approached, Willkie sharpened his attack, saying that if FDR won, he would plunge the nation into war. To counter this charge, FDR assured all parents: "Your boys are not going to be sent into any foreign wars." In reality, both men knew that war would be hard to avoid.

Lend-Lease In November 1940, Roosevelt won reelection to a third term as President. His easy victory encouraged him to push for greater American involvement in the Allied cause. To continue battling Germany, Britain needed American equipment. Britain, however, faced a financial crisis. Prime Minister Churchill, in a letter to FDR, confessed that his country was nearly bankrupt. "The moment approaches," he wrote in December, "when we shall no longer be able to pay cash for shipping and other supplies."

In December 1940, Roosevelt introduced a bold new plan to keep supplies flowing to Britain. He proposed providing war supplies to Britain without any payment in return. Roosevelt explained his policy to the American people by

READING CHECK
Why did Roosevelt press Congress for aid to Britain?

VIEWING HISTORY Members of the "Mothers' Crusade" knelt and prayed outside the Capitol to stop Congress from passing the Lend-Lease Act, Bill 1776. **Drawing Inferences** *How did these protesters hope to sway votes?*

the use of a simple comparison: If your neighbor's house is on fire, you don't sell him a hose. You lend it to him and take it back after the fire is out.

The America First Committee campaigned strongly against this new type of aid. Nevertheless, Congress passed the **Lend-Lease Act** in March 1941, authorizing the President to aid any nation whose defense he believed was vital to American security. FDR immediately began sending aid to Britain. After Germany attacked the Soviet Union, the United States extended lend-lease aid to the Soviets as well. By the end of the war, the United States had loaned or given away more than $49 billion worth of aid to some 40 nations.

Japan Attacks Pearl Harbor

Although Roosevelt focused his attention on Europe, he was aware of Japan's aggressive moves in the Pacific. In July 1940, Roosevelt began limiting what Japan could buy from the United States. In September, he ended sales of scrap iron and steel. He hoped to use the threat of further trade restrictions to stop Japan's expansion. A year later, however, Japanese forces took complete control of French Indochina. In response, Roosevelt froze Japanese financial assets in the United States. Then he cut off all oil shipments. As you have read, Japan desperately needed raw materials, and this embargo encouraged Japan to look to the lightly defended Dutch East Indies for new supplies of oil. For the next few months, leaders in the United States and Japan sought ways to avoid war with each other.

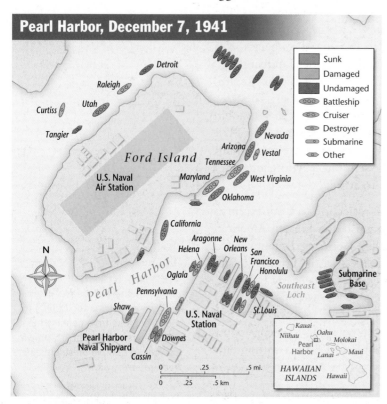

Pearl Harbor, December 7, 1941

Detroit
Raleigh
Curtiss
Utah
Tangier
Ford Island
U.S. Naval Air Station
Nevada
Arizona
Vestal
Tennessee
Maryland
West Virginia
Oklahoma
California
Aragonne
Helena
New Orleans
San Francisco
Honolulu
Oglala
Pennsylvania
St. Louis
Southeast Loch
Submarine Base
Shaw
U.S. Naval Station
Pearl Harbor Naval Shipyard
Downes
Cassin
Pearl Harbor

Sunk
Damaged
Undamaged
Battleship
Cruiser
Destroyer
Submarine
Other

N

0   .25   .5 mi.
0   .25   .5 km

Kauai
Niihau   Oahu
Pearl   Molokai
Harbor   Lanai   Maui
HAWAIIAN ISLANDS   Hawaii

MAP SKILLS The Japanese attack on Pearl Harbor was surprising and swift. **Location** *Where did the Japanese inflict the most damage?*

Final Weeks of Peace While Japanese and American diplomats negotiated, a militant army officer took power in Japan. General Tojo Hideki, who supported war against the United States, became prime minister in October 1941. Yet Roosevelt still hoped for peace, and he continued negotiations.

More than a year earlier, American technicians had cracked a top-secret Japanese code. Knowing this code allowed them to read intercepted diplomatic messages. By November 27, based on decoded messages, American military leaders knew that Japanese aircraft carriers were on the move in the Pacific. They expected an attack, but they did not know where.

Indeed, a Japanese fleet of 6 aircraft carriers and more than 20 other ships was already on the move. Its target was Pearl Harbor, the naval base on the Hawaiian island of Oahu that served as the home of the U.S. Pacific Fleet. Japan's leaders had gambled that they could cripple the American fleet and then achieve their goals in Asia before the United States could rebuild its navy and challenge Japan.

The Attack Shortly after 7:00 on the morning of December 7, an American army radar operator on Oahu noticed a large blip on his radar screen. He called his headquarters to report that planes were headed toward the island. The only officer on duty that Sunday morning believed that the planes were American. "Don't worry about it," the officer told the radar operator, and he hung up the phone. Less than an hour later, more than 180 Japanese warplanes streaked overhead. Half of the Pacific Fleet lay at anchor in Pearl Harbor, crowded into an area less than three miles square.

Japanese planes bombed and strafed (attacked with machine-gun fire) the fleet and the airfields nearby. By 9:45, the attack was over. In less than two hours, some 2,400 Americans had been killed and nearly 1,200 wounded. Nearly 200 American warplanes had been damaged or destroyed; 18 warships had been sunk or heavily damaged, including 8 of the fleet's 9 battleships. Japan had lost just 29 planes.

United States Declares War

The attack on Pearl Harbor stunned the American people. Calling December 7, 1941, "a date which will live in infamy," Roosevelt the next day asked Congress to declare war on Japan:

Wearing a black armband to mourn those killed at Pearl Harbor, Roosevelt signed a declaration of war against Japan on December 8, 1941.

66 *Hostilities exist. There is no blinking at the fact that our people, our territory, and our interests are in grave danger. With confidence in our armed forces—with the unbound determination of our people—we will gain the inevitable triumph—so help us God.* 99
—Franklin D. Roosevelt, December 8, 1941

Within hours after Roosevelt finished speaking, Congress passed a war resolution. Only one of its members, pacifist Jeannette Rankin of Montana, voted against declaring war. Even the America First Committee called on its members to back the war effort.

On December 11, Germany and Italy declared war on the United States. For the second time in the century, Americans had been drawn into a world war. Once more, their contributions would make the difference between victory and defeat for the Allies.

 Sounds of an Era

Listen to Roosevelt's speech and other sounds from World War II.

Section 4 Assessment

READING COMPREHENSION

1. (a) What was required by the **Neutrality Acts?** (b) Did they succeed in keeping the United States neutral? Why or why not?

2. Why did Roosevelt ask Congress to pass the **Lend-Lease Act?**

3. In your own words, describe relations between Japan and the United States before the attack on Pearl Harbor.

CRITICAL THINKING AND WRITING

4. **Recognizing Cause and Effect**
(a) How much did President Roosevelt consider American public opinion when deciding how to respond to the conflict in Europe? (b) Why did he need to consider public opinion at all?

5. **Writing a News Story** Write a short newspaper article on the fall of France from an American point of view. Explain the consequences for the United States.

For: An activity on Pearl Harbor
Visit: PHSchool.com
Web Code: mrd-8244

creating a **CHAPTER SUMMARY**

Copy this diagram (right) on a piece of paper and complete it by adding important events and issues that fit each heading.

For additional review and enrichment activities, see the interactive version of *America: Pathways to the Present,* available on the Web and on CD-ROM.

Time Period	Important Events
The Rise of Dictators	• Stalin takes control of the Soviet Union and nationalizes most of the economy. • Millions die during Stalin's collectivization campaign and Communist purges. • Mussolini overthrows the Italian government shortly after World War I.
Europe Goes to War	
Japan Builds an Empire	
From Isolationism to War	

★ Reviewing Key Terms

For each of the terms below, write a sentence explaining how it relates to the years leading up to the entry of the United States into war.

1. totalitarian
2. fascism
3. Nazism
4. Axis Powers
5. appeasement
6. *blitzkrieg*
7. collaboration
8. Allies
9. Manchurian Incident
10. puppet state
11. Neutrality Acts
12. cash and carry
13. America First Committee
14. Lend-Lease Act

★ Reviewing Main Ideas

15. (a) How did Hitler come to power in Germany? (b) How did Mussolini come to power in Italy? (Section 1)

16. List three ways that individuals in the Soviet Union suffered under Stalin. (Section 1)

17. What role did aircraft play in the German attacks on Poland? (Section 2)

18. (a) How did the Blitz affect life in Britain? (b) Did it succeed in discouraging Britain from resisting? Why or why not? (Section 2)

19. Describe the relationship between the military and the civilian government in Japan in the 1930s. (Section 3)

20. Why was Japan unable to defeat China in 1939 and 1940? (Section 3)

21. What steps did Roosevelt take to help Britain up until the attack on Pearl Harbor? (Section 4)

22. Describe the events leading up to and following the attack on Pearl Harbor. (Section 4)

★ Critical Thinking

23. **Predicting Consequences** If Britain and France had not adopted a policy of appeasement, would Adolf Hitler have been as successful as he was in overrunning Europe?

24. **Making Comparisons** (a) What characteristics did fascism under Mussolini and Hitler have in common with communism under Stalin? (b) What are two important differences between fascism and communism?

25. **Synthesizing Information** In what ways did the Spanish Civil War foreshadow the events that occurred in 1939 and later, throughout Europe?

26. **Recognizing Ideologies** How was the idea of the Greater East Asia Co-Prosperity Sphere designed to appeal to Asians? (b) Why do you think Japan failed to win lasting support from most non-Japanese within this region?

27. **Identifying Central Issues** Why didn't Roosevelt declare war on Germany in 1939?

"Sometimes I wonder -- would we speed things up if we used turtles instead of snails?"

★ Standardized Test Prep

Analyzing Political Cartoons ▶

28. In this cartoon from May 4, 1941, American policy makers and weapons manufacturers are shown riding in a tank. What does the tank represent?

   A The Cash and Carry policy

   B American neutrality

   C Aid to Britain

   D The poor quality of American war machines

29. Why is it significant that the tank is riding on the backs of snails?

30. What point is the cartoonist making by having the men ask this question?

Analyzing Primary Sources

Read the excerpt from Roosevelt's speech asking Congress to declare war on Japan. Then answer the questions below.

31. How would you describe the tone of Roosevelt's speech?

   A serious but optimistic

   B joyful

   C pessimistic

   D angry

32. What is the most likely reason that Roosevelt began this speech with the words, "hostilities exist"?

   F to inform members of Congress that Japan has bombed Pearl Harbor

   G to inform the Japanese that the United States is hostile to the Axis Powers

   H to give Japan an opportunity to make peace with the United States

   I to convince members of Congress that their only option is to declare war

Test-Taking Tip

Question 31, asks you to identify the tone of Roosevelt's speech. Consider the context in which the speech is given—immediately following the attack on Pearl Harbor—and note the following words from the speech: *grave, confidence, unbound determination, triumph.*

Applying the Chapter Skill

Examining Photographs Study the photograph of St. Paul's Cathedral in London on p. 578. (a) What do you think was the purpose of this photo? (b) How did the photographer add drama to a picture of St. Paul's among damaged buildings? (c) Do you think this photo reflects the experiences of ordinary Londoners during the Blitz? Explain your answer.

Go Online
PHSchool.com

For: Chapter 17 Self-Test
Visit: PHSchool.com
Web Code: mra-8245

Chapter 18

World War II: Americans at War
(1941–1945)

Ration cards and points

American troops in the South Pacific

American Events

1941
A. Philip Randolph threatens to march on Washington to end discrimination in war industries. The United States declares war on Japan, Germany, and Italy.

1942
Japan conquers the Philippines. The United States defeats the Japanese navy at the Battle of Midway. Japanese Americans are interned in camps.

Presidential Terms: Franklin D. Roosevelt 1933–1945

1940   **1941**   **1942**

World Events

1941
Hitler invades the Soviet Union. Hong Kong falls to Japan.

1942
Allied troops land in North Africa. The Battle of Stalingrad begins.

Hitler's Europe, 1942

Legend:
- Axis powers
- Occupied by Axis
- Axis satellites
- Allied territory
- Occupied by Allies
- Neutral nations

ATLANTIC OCEAN

20°W   60°N   10°W   0°   10°E

FINLAND

NORWAY

SWEDEN

North Sea

Baltic Sea

DENMARK

Reichskommissariat Ostland

SOVIET UNION

IRELAND   GREAT BRITAIN

50°N

NETH.

BELG.

Rhine R.

GREATER GERMANY

Oder R.

Occupied Poland

Occupied Soviet Union

Dnieper R.

Reichskommissariat Ukraine

OCCUPIED FRANCE

Danube R.

SLOVAKIA

HUNGARY

Bay of Biscay

SWITZ.

VICHY FRANCE

Po R.

CROATIA

SERBIA

ROMANIA

Black Sea

Ebro R.

ITALY

MONT.

BULGARIA

40°N

PORTUGAL

Tagus R.

SPAIN

ALBANIA

GREECE

TURKEY

SPANISH MOROCCO

0   200   400 mi.
0   200   400 km

TUNISIA (Fr.)

Mediterranean Sea

10°E

20°E

LEBANON (Fr.)

MOROCCO (Fr.)

ALGERIA (Fr.)

30°E

PALESTINE (Br.)

A Soviet soldier raises his country's flag over the ruined *Reichstag* in Berlin.

A letter written by Albert Einstein led to the development of the atomic bomb.

1943
Americans help defeat Axis armies in North Africa and invade Italy. Troops in the Pacific take Guadalcanal and begin island-hopping campaign.

1944
American and British troops lead the D-Day invasion of France.

1945
Harry S Truman becomes President after Roosevelt's death. American troops liberate Western Germany. The United States drops atomic bombs on Hiroshima and Nagasaki.

Harry S Truman
1945–1953

1943

1944

1945

Jews in Warsaw ghetto rebel. Germany invades Italy after Mussolini is overthrown.

Japan begins *kamikaze* attacks. De Gaulle leads Allies into Paris.

Hitler commits suicide. Germany and Japan surrender.

1943

1944

1945

Mobilization

READING FOCUS

- How did Roosevelt mobilize the armed forces?

- In what ways did the government prepare the economy for war?

- How did the war affect daily life on the home front?

MAIN IDEA

The United States quickly mobilized millions of Americans to fight the Axis powers. The government organized the economy to supply the military.

KEY TERMS

Selective Training and
Service Act
GI
Office of War Mobilization
Liberty ship
victory garden

TARGET READING SKILL

Understand Effects As you read, complete the following flowchart to show some of the effects that America's entry into war had on the economy of the United States.

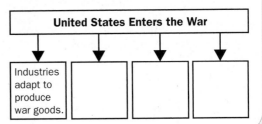

Setting the Scene Well before the Japanese attack on Pearl Harbor, officials in the United States had begun to prepare for war. President Roosevelt made his concerns and worries clear to the American people in a radio address in December 1940. He stated that the Axis nations, especially Germany, posed a direct threat to the security of the United States. He appealed to American business owners and workers to support Britain's defensive efforts or face the ultimate task of defending their own land against the "brute force" of the Axis.

> 66 *We must be the great arsenal of democracy. For us this is an emergency as serious as war itself. We must apply ourselves to our task with the same resolution, the same sense of urgency, the same spirit of patriotism and sacrifice as we would show were we at war.* 99
>
> —Franklin D. Roosevelt, fireside chat, December 29, 1940

Millions of Americans traded their civilian clothes for military fatigues (above) as the United States prepared to fight the Axis.

FDR understood that the outcome of the war in Europe ultimately depended on his country's ability to produce planes, tanks, guns, uniforms, and other war materials for the Allies.

Mobilizing the Armed Forces

FDR realized that a crucial step that he had to take was to strengthen the armed forces if the United States were to enter the war on the side of the Allies. In September 1940, Congress authorized the first peacetime draft in the nation's history. The **Selective Training and Service Act** required all males aged 21 to 36 to register for military service. A limited number of men was selected from this pool to serve a year in the army. The United States also boosted its defense spending from $2 billion at the start of the year to more than $10 billion in September.

As the United States prepared for the possibility of war, thousands of American men received official notices to enter the army. In what came to be known as the "Four Freedoms speech," FDR shared his vision of what these troops would be fighting for:

INTERFERENCE FROM A LOUD VOICE

One evening I was copying KCT with the usual Japanese garbage jamming my frequency. I had my eyes closed, and I was concentrating totally on that faint but distinctive signal: Dit dah dit. I automatically hit the R key on the typewriter (or mill, as the Navy called it). Dah dit dit dit, B. Dit dit dit, S.

Then a loud voice behind me asked, "Are they jamming our station?"

"Yes, sir," I replied, my concentration broken. I hit the space bar of the mill several times to indicate missed letters. I found the signal once again.

"Are you able to copy it?" The voice again. I hit the space bar several more times before finding my signal once more. "Will you be able to get enough for us?" And the space-bar routine again. But this time I blurted out, "Shut up!"

When the transmission was complete, I pulled the message from my machine. Wondering if the blank spaces would ruin our mapmaking effort, I turned in my seat—and looked up at four stars on each lapel of a brown shirt. I had just met Admiral Halsey.

Oh my . . . , I thought. I was an insignificant radioman, third class, and I had told an admiral to shut up.

At nineteen years my life would end. I would be fortunate to get a court-martial for insubordination along with a dishonorable discharge from the Navy.

"Sir, are you the one I told to 'shut up'?"

This tough-looking admiral was standing there with arms folded and legs apart in a mild inverted Y, brown naval field cap pulled to his brow, jaw jutting menacingly with lips pressed firmly together. I could see now why they called him Bull Halsey.

"Yes, lad," he blared.

"I apologize, sir. I did not know it was you. I have no excuse, sir."

The admiral broke his stance and began to pace the floor. "Lad," he bellowed, "when I come into this radio shack and speak to you while you are on that radio, you do not tell me to shut up! Do you understand?"

His voice boomed like the nine 16-inch guns attached to the ship's three main turrets.

Launched in 1944, the battleship USS Missouri was nearly 900 feet long and had a crew of 1,900.

"Yes, sir, I understand." I was frozen at attention and, I am certain, tears were welling in my eyes.

Then, stopping in front of me and looking me straight in the eye, he went on in a very calm and friendly voice. "If I or anyone else ever bothers you while you are on that radio, you do not tell them to shut up. What you tell them is to get the . . . out of here and that's an order. Do you understand, lad?"

I could only look at him and stammer, "Yes, sir."

We saluted. Admiral Halsey went on his way. I never met him again.

Source: *American Heritage* magazine, September 1997.

Understanding Primary Sources

1. How did Admiral Halsey respond when an underling told him to "shut up" under these circumstances?

2. What does this response imply about Halsey's character and leadership ability?

American Heritage®
MY BRUSH WITH **HISTORY**™
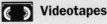 **Videotapes**

For more information about World War II in the Pacific, view "Locking Horns With the Bull."

The Cold War

(1945–1960)

Churchill, Truman, and Stalin (left to right) at the Potsdam Conference

1945

The United States, Britain, and the Soviet Union meet at Yalta, and later at Potsdam, to plan the postwar world. The United Nations is founded.

1947

The Truman Doctrine promises support to nations resisting Communist aggression.

1948

The Marshall Plan provides U.S. aid to Europe. The Berlin airlift brings supplies to West Berlin.

1949

NATO is formed to defend Europe against the Communists.

1950

The Korean War begins. Senator Joseph McCarthy launches his anti-Communist campaign.

American Events

Presidential Terms:
F. D. Roosevelt 1933–1945

Harry S Truman 1945–1953

1944

1946

1948

1950

World Events

Soviet leader Joseph Stalin predicts the worldwide triumph of communism.

1946

Communists win control of China. The Soviets test an atomic bomb.

1949

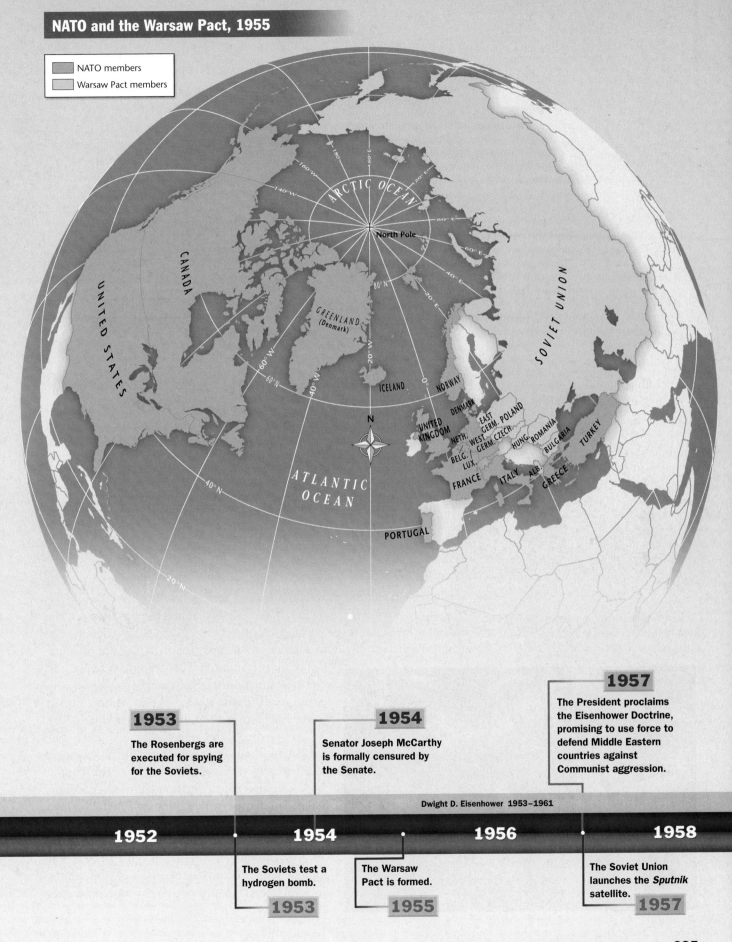

NATO and the Warsaw Pact, 1955

NATO members
Warsaw Pact members

ARCTIC OCEAN

North Pole

CANADA

UNITED STATES

GREENLAND
(Denmark)

ICELAND

NORWAY

UNITED
KINGDOM

DENMARK

NETH.

BELG.

LUX.

FRANCE

WEST
GERM.

EAST
GERM.

POLAND

CZECH.

HUNG.

ITALY

ALB.

ROMANIA

BULGARIA

GREECE

TURKEY

SOVIET UNION

ATLANTIC
OCEAN

PORTUGAL

N

1953

The Rosenbergs are executed for spying for the Soviets.

1954

Senator Joseph McCarthy is formally censured by the Senate.

1957

The President proclaims the Eisenhower Doctrine, promising to use force to defend Middle Eastern countries against Communist aggression.

Dwight D. Eisenhower 1953–1961

| 1952 | 1954 | 1956 | 1958 |

The Soviets test a hydrogen bomb.
1953

The Warsaw Pact is formed.
1955

The Soviet Union launches the *Sputnik* satellite.
1957

Origins of the Cold War

READING FOCUS

- Why was 1945 a critical year in United States foreign relations?

- What were the postwar goals of the United States and the Soviet Union?

- How did the iron curtain tighten the Soviet Union's hold over Eastern Europe?

- How did the Truman Doctrine complement the policy of containment?

MAIN IDEA

At the end of World War II, conflicting goals for the future of Europe led to growing hostility between the United States and the Soviet Union.

KEY TERMS

satellite nation
iron curtain
Cold War
containment
Truman Doctrine

TARGET READING SKILL

Summarize As you read, complete this chart by summarizing how the Soviets tightened their hold on Eastern Europe and how the United States responded to the increasing Soviet threat. Add as many rows as you need.

Soviet Actions	U.S. Actions
Stalin refuses to allow free elections in Poland.	Truman criticizes Soviets for not allowing Polish elections.

Setting the Scene

"I know you will not mind my being brutally frank when I tell you that I can personally handle Stalin," President Roosevelt told Winston Churchill during World War II. "He thinks he likes me better, and I hope he will continue to." By 1944, Roosevelt was so sure of Stalin's cooperation that he began calling the Soviet dictator "Uncle Joe."

A Roosevelt advisor later wrote that the President did not have "any real comprehension of the great gulf that separated [their] thinking." Nor did he understand just what a wily and difficult adversary Stalin would turn out to be. Churchill, however, clearly understood the situation. "Germany is finished," he declared. "The real problem is Russia. I can't get the Americans to see it."

1945—A Critical Year

The wartime cooperation between the United States and the Soviet Union was a temporary arrangement. There had been a history of bad feelings between the two nations ever since the Russian Revolution of 1917. During that revolt, President Wilson had dispatched American troops to Russia to support anti-Communist resistance. The United States had not even recognized the legal existence of the Soviet government until 1933. These actions caused considerable resentment in the Soviet Union.

As wartime allies, the Soviets disagreed bitterly with their American and British partners over battle tactics and postwar plans. The United States was angered by the nonaggression pact that Stalin had signed with Hitler (which Hitler had broken), and Stalin was angry that the Allies had not invaded Europe sooner, to take the pressure off the Russian front. As the end of the war approached, relations between the Communist Soviet Union and the two Western democracies grew increasingly tense.

Churchill, Roosevelt, and Stalin (left to right) met at Yalta to discuss postwar Europe.

Differences at Yalta In February 1945, Roosevelt met with Stalin and Churchill at Yalta to work out the future of Germany and Poland. They agreed on the division of Germany into American, British, French, and Soviet occupation zones. (Later, the American, British, and French zones were combined to create West Germany. The Soviet zone became East Germany.) Roosevelt and Churchill rejected Stalin's demand that Germany pay the Soviet Union $20 billion in war damages.

At the meeting, Roosevelt pressed Stalin to declare war on Japan. The atomic bomb had not yet been tested, and the President wanted Soviet help if an invasion of Japan became necessary. Stalin promised to enter the war against Japan soon after Germany surrendered, in exchange for Soviet control over two Japanese islands.

Poland proved the most difficult issue at Yalta. The Red Army had occupied that country and supported the Communist-dominated government. Stalin opposed the return of Poland's prewar government, then in exile in London. Historically, Poland provided an invasion route into Russia, as Hitler had just demonstrated. The Polish government, Stalin insisted, must be sympathetic to Soviet security needs. The Yalta meeting stalled until Stalin agreed on elections to let Poles choose their government, using the Communist-dominated regime as a framework. However, disputes about Poland were not over; they would continue to strain American-Soviet relations for years to come.

The United Nations One item on which the leaders at Yalta all agreed was the creation of the United Nations (UN), a new international peacekeeping organization. The League of Nations, founded after World War I, had failed largely because the United States refused to join. This time, policymakers got congressional support for the UN.

In April 1945, delegates from 50 nations met in San Francisco to adopt a charter, or statement of principles, for the UN. The charter stated that members would try to settle their differences peacefully and would promote justice and cooperation in solving international problems. In addition, they would try to stop wars from starting and "take effective collective measures" to end those that did break out.

All member nations belonged to the UN's General Assembly. Representatives of 11 countries sat on a Security Council. The United States, the Soviet Union, Great Britain, France, and China had permanent seats on the Security Council and a veto over proposed policies.

VIEWING HISTORY President Truman called the United Nations "a victory against war itself." In this photograph, Truman and representatives from other member nations look on as Secretary of State Edward Stettinius signs the UN charter in June 1945. **Drawing Conclusions** *Why do you think Congress agreed to United States membership in the UN even though it had not supported the League of Nations?*

Truman Takes Command Roosevelt never lived to see his dream of the United Nations fulfilled. On April 12, 1945, just two weeks before the UN's first meeting, the President died while vacationing at Warm Springs, Georgia. Although he was in poor health and noticeably tired, his unexpected death shocked the nation. No one was more surprised than Vice President Harry S Truman, who suddenly found himself President.

Few Vice Presidents have been less prepared to become President. Although he had spent ten years in Congress, Truman had been Vice President for only a few months. Roosevelt had never involved him in major foreign policy discussions. Truman at first seemed willing to compromise with the Soviets. But before long his attitude hardened.

The Potsdam Conference   Truman's first meeting with Stalin occurred in July 1945 in the Berlin suburb of Potsdam. During the conference, Churchill was replaced by Clement Attlee, who had just won the British election. Thus, new representatives from Britain and the United States now faced off against Stalin. They continued to debate the issues that had divided them at Yalta, including the future of Germany and of Poland. Stalin renewed his demand for war payments from Germany, and Truman insisted on the promised Polish elections.

At Potsdam, Truman got word that the atom bomb had been tested in New Mexico. Hoping to intimidate Stalin, Truman told him that the United States had a new weapon of extraordinary force. Stalin, who already knew of the bomb from Soviet spies, simply nodded and said that he hoped it would be put to good use. Stalin's casual manner hid his concern over America's new strategic advantage.

READING CHECK

Summarize what happened at the Potsdam Conference.

Conflicting Postwar Goals

Shortly after Truman took office, he scolded the Soviet Foreign Minister, Vyacheslav Molotov, for the Soviet Union's failure to allow Polish elections. Molotov was offended by Truman's bluntness. "I have never been talked to like that in my life," Molotov protested. "Carry out your agreements and you won't get talked to like that," Truman snapped.

The American View   Tensions over Poland illustrated the differing views of the world held by American and Soviet leaders. Americans had fought to bring democracy and economic opportunity to the conquered nations of Europe and

---

NOTABLE PRESIDENTS
Harry S Truman

33rd President
1945–1953

"We must build a new world, a far better world—one in which the eternal dignity of man is respected."

—**Radio address to the UN conference, 1945**

Harry S Truman has been called the ultimate common man—but he was a common man who became President. Truman tried careers as a bank clerk, a farmer, and a haberdasher, but he was more successful as a military officer during World War I. He entered politics in Missouri in 1922. In spite of his connection to corrupt Democratic Party boss Thomas Pendergast, Truman earned a reputation for personal integrity and skillful management, both as a judge and as a United States senator.

When Vice President Truman was catapulted into the presidency by FDR's death in 1945, he expressed shock and asked reporters to pray for him. He also put a sign on his desk that said, "The buck stops here," and took responsibility for dropping the atomic bombs on Japan that ended World War II, the Truman Doctrine, the Berlin airlift, sending troops to Korea, integrating the military, and initiating other civil rights reforms. His election to a second term surprised the pundits of his day, and the reforms of his Fair Deal were eventually supported by both parties. Today, Truman is regarded as a common man who faced uncommon challenges with considerable success.

Connecting to Today
Truman's reputation for personal integrity no doubt contributed to his reelection in 1948. How did the issue of personal integrity influence the election of 2000, between George W. Bush and Al Gore?

Go Online
PHSchool.com

For: More on Harry S Truman
Visit: PHSchool.com
Web Code: mrd-8267

Recognizing Cause and Effect

History is more than a list of events; it is a study of relationships among events. Recognizing cause and effect means examining how one event or action brings about another—which, in turn, may bring about still more events. Each one becomes a link in a growing chain of events. The statements below deal with the events and attitudes leading to the Cold War.

LEARN THE SKILL
Use the following steps to recognize cause and effect:

1. **Identify the two parts of a cause-effect relationship.** A cause is an event, action, or idea that brings about an effect. As you read, look for key words that signal a cause-effect relationship. Words and phrases such as *because, due to,* and *on account of* signal causes. Words and phrases such as *so, thus, therefore,* and *as a result* signal effects.

2. **Remember that events can have more than one cause and more than one effect.** Several causes can combine to lead to one event. So, too, can a single cause have more than one effect.

3. **Understand that an event can be both a cause and an effect.** A cause can lead to an effect, which in turn can be the cause of another event—forming a chain of related events. You can illustrate the chain by making a cause-effect diagram like this one:

PRACTICE THE SKILL
Answer the following questions:

1. **(a)** Read statements A through C. Which statements contain both a cause and an effect? **(b)** Which is the cause and which is the effect in each statement? **(c)** Which words, if any, signal the cause-effect relationship?

2. **(a)** In Statement D, find an example of a cause that has more than one effect. **(b)** Give an example of an effect that has more than one cause in Statement D.

3. **(a)** What is the chain of related events in Statement D? Explain it in one or two sentences. **(b)** Draw a diagram showing the chain of related events.

APPLY THE SKILL
See the Chapter Review and Assessment for another opportunity to apply this skill.

A

Because President Roosevelt believed that post-war cooperation with the Soviet Union was necessary, he viewed Stalin as a partner—if not an ally—in formulating a peace.

B

Unlike Roosevelt, President Truman was persuaded by advisors that the Soviet Union would become a "world bully" after the war. As a result, he adopted a "get tough" policy whose aim was to block any possibility of Soviet expansion.

C

The Soviets, for their part, believed that the United States was intent on global domination and meant to encircle the Soviet Union with anti-Communist states.

D

Due to mounting distrust between the United States and the Soviet Union, each power came to view the postwar peace negotiations as an opportunity to test the other's global objectives. Thus, negotiating the status of Poland became the first such test. Other tests included the plans for former German satellite states and the policies for the occupation of Germany. Each power regarded its own positions in these negotiations as essentially defensive, but each viewed the other's stances as aggressive and expansionist. Together these tests and stances produced the Cold War, an armed and dangerous truce that lasted for 45 years.

The Cold War Heats Up

READING FOCUS

- How did the Marshall Plan, the Berlin air-lift, and NATO help to achieve American goals in postwar Europe?
- How did Communist advances affect American foreign policy?
- How did the Cold War affect American life at home?

MAIN IDEA

As the Cold War intensified, American foreign policy focused on rebuilding and unifying Western Europe. At home, Americans began to suspect Communist infiltration of their own society and government.

KEY TERMS

Marshall Plan
Berlin airlift
North Atlantic Treaty
 Organization (NATO)
collective security
Warsaw Pact
House Un-American
 Activities Committee
 (HUAC)
Hollywood Ten
blacklist
McCarran-Walter Act

TARGET READING SKILL

Understand Effects Copy the chart below. As you read, fill in details illustrating the effects of the Cold War on American foreign policy and on life at home.

The U.S. Responds to the Cold War		
In Europe	Regarding Nuclear Weapons	At Home

Setting the Scene The end of World War II caused a profound change in the way world leaders and ordinary citizens thought about war. The devastation caused by the atomic bombs dropped on Japan and the efforts of the Soviet Union to acquire similar weapons instilled fear in both East and West. In his last State of the Union address, President Truman declared:

> 66 *[W]e have entered the atomic age and war has undergone a techno-logical change which makes it a very different thing from what it used to be. War today between the Soviet empire and the free nations might dig the grave not only of our Stalinist opponents, but of our own society, our world as well as theirs. . . . Such a war is not a possible policy for rational men.* 99
>
> —President Harry S Truman

A 1946 American atomic bomb test creates the signature mush-room cloud over the Pacific Ocean.

Anxiety about a "hot" and catastrophic nuclear war became a backdrop to the Cold War policies of both the United States and the Soviet Union.

The Marshall Plan

In addition to worrying about the new threat of nuclear war, American policymakers were deter-mined not to repeat the mistakes of the post–World War I era. This time the United States would help restore the war-torn nations so that they might create stable democracies and achieve economic recovery. World War II had devastated Europe to a degree never seen before. About 21 million people had been made homeless. In Poland, some 20 percent of the population had died. Nearly 1 of every 5 houses in France and Belgium had been damaged or destroyed. Across

Europe, industries and transportation were in ruins. Agriculture suffered from the loss of livestock and equipment. In France alone, damage equaled three times the nation's annual income.

These conditions led to two fundamental shifts in American foreign policy that were designed to strengthen European democracies and their economies. The first was the Truman Doctrine. The other was the **Marshall Plan,** which called for the nations of Europe to draw up a program for economic recovery from the war. The United States would then support the program with financial aid.

The plan was unveiled by Secretary of State George C. Marshall in 1947. The Marshall Plan was a response to American concerns that Communist parties were growing stronger across Europe, and that the Soviet Union might intervene to support more of these Communist movements. The plan also reflected the belief that United States aid for European economic recovery would create strong democracies and open new markets for American goods.

Marshall described his plan in a speech at Harvard University in June 1947:

KEY DOCUMENTS 66 *It is logical that the United States should do whatever it is able to assist in the return of normal economic health in the world, without which there can be no political stability and no assured peace. Our policy is directed not against any country or doctrine but against hunger, poverty, desperation, and chaos. Its purpose should be the revival of a working economy in the world so as to permit the emergence of political and social conditions in which free institutions can exist.* 99

—Marshall Plan speech, George C. Marshall, June 5, 1947

Shipments Financed by the Marshall Plan, 1948–1951

Shipment	Total Value (in millions of dollars)
Food, feed, fertilizer	3,209.5
Fuel	1,552.4
Cotton	1,397.8
Other raw materials	2,327.6
Machinery and vehicles	1,428.1
Other	88.9
Total	**10,004.3**

SOURCE: *Statistical Abstract of the United States*

The Soviet Union was invited to participate in the Marshall Plan, but it refused the help and pressured its satellite nations to do so too. Soviet Foreign Minister Vyacheslav Molotov called the Marshall Plan a vicious American scheme for using dollars to "buy its way" into European affairs. In fact, Soviet leaders did not want outside scrutiny of their country's economy.

In 1948, Congress approved the Marshall Plan, which was formally known as the European Recovery Program. Seventeen Western European nations joined the plan: Austria, Belgium, Denmark, France, Greece, Iceland, Ireland, Italy, Luxembourg, the Netherlands, Norway, Portugal, Sweden, Switzerland, Turkey, the United Kingdom, and West Germany. Over the next four years, the United States allocated some $13 billion in grants and loans to Western Europe. The region's economies were quickly restored, and the United States gained strong trading partners in the region.

ANALYZING TABLES The photo shows a parade in Athens, Greece, following the unloading of sacks of flour delivered by the Marshall Plan. The table identifies the kinds of goods the Marshall Plan provided.
Drawing Conclusions *What made up the largest percentage of goods delivered? Why do you think this was so?*

The Berlin Airlift

The Allies could not agree on what to do with Germany following World War II. In March 1948, the Western Allies announced plans to make the zones they controlled in Germany into a single unit. The United States, Britain, and

Divided Germany and Berlin, 1949

North Sea

NETH.

Elbe R.

Oder R.

POLAND

Berlin

EAST GERMANY

Rhine R.

N

LUX.

WEST GERMANY

CZECH.

FRANCE

Danube R.

SWITZ.

AUSTRIA

0 50 100 mi.
0 50 100 km

Berlin

Havel R.

East Berlin

West Berlin

Spree R.

0 5 mi.
0 5 km

EAST GERMANY

MAP SKILLS The map shows the location of West Berlin within East Germany. In the photo below, German children wave to an American airplane during the Berlin airlift. **Location** *How did Berlin's location make it difficult to supply?*

France prepared to merge their three occupation zones to create a new nation, the Federal Republic of Germany, or West Germany. The western part of Berlin, which lay in the Soviet zone, would become part of West Germany. The Soviets responded in 1949 by forming a Communist state, the German Democratic Republic, or East Germany.

Capitalist West Berlin and Communist East Berlin became visible symbols of the developing Cold War struggle between the Soviet Union and the Western powers. Hundreds of thousands of Eastern Europeans left their homes in Communist-dominated nations, fled to East Berlin, and then crossed into West Berlin. From there they booked passage to freedom in the United States, Canada, or Western Europe.

Stalin decided to close this escape route by forcing the Western powers to abandon West Berlin. He found his excuse in June 1948, when a new German currency was introduced in West Germany, including West Berlin. Stalin considered the new currency and the new nation it represented to be a threat. The city of West Berlin—located within East Germany—was a symbol of that threat. The Soviets used the dispute over the new currency as an excuse to block Allied access to West Berlin. All shipments to the city through East Germany were banned. The blockade threatened to create severe shortages of food and other supplies needed by the 2.5 million people in West Berlin.

Truman did not want to risk starting a war by using military force to open the transportation routes. Nor did he want to give up West Berlin to the Soviets. Instead, Truman decided on an airlift, moving supplies into West Berlin by plane. During the next 15 months, British and American military aircraft made

more than 200,000 flights to deliver food, fuel, and other supplies. At the height of the **Berlin airlift,** nearly 13,000 tons of goods arrived in West Berlin daily.

The Soviets finally gave up the blockade in May 1949, and the airlift ended the following September. By that time, the Marshall Plan had helped achieve economic stability in the capitalist nations of Western Europe, including West Germany. Berlin, however, remained a focal point of East-West conflict.

NATO

In the early postwar period, the international community looked to the United Nations to protect nations from invasion or destabilization by foreign governments, and to maintain world peace. However, the Soviet Union's frequent use of its veto power in the Security Council prevented the UN from effectively dealing with a number of postwar problems. Thus it became clear that Western Europe would have to look beyond the UN for protection from Soviet aggression. In 1946, the Canadian foreign minister, Louis St. Laurent, proposed creating an "association of democratic peace-loving states" to defend Western Europe against attack by the Soviet Union.

American officials expressed great interest in St. Laurent's idea. Truman was determined to prevent the United States from returning to pre–World War II isolationism. The Truman Doctrine and the Marshall Plan soon demonstrated his commitment to making America a leader in postwar world affairs. Yet Truman did not want the United States to be the only nation in the Western Hemisphere pledged to defend Western Europe from the Communists. For this reason, a Canadian role in any proposed organization became vital to American support.

Not all Americans agreed that such an organization was a good idea. Ohio Senator Robert Taft thought that the pact was "not a peace program; it is a war program." He continued, "We are undertaking to arm half the world against the other half. We are inevitably starting an armament race." On the other hand, Senator Tom Connally favored joining such an association:

> 66 *From now on, no one will misread our motives or underestimate our determination to stand in defense of our freedom. . . . The greatest obstacle that stands in the way of complete recovery [from World War II] is the pervading and paralyzing sense of insecurity. The treaty is a powerful antidote to this poison. . . . With this protection afforded by the Atlantic Pact, Western Europe can breathe easier again.* 99
>
> —Texas Senator Tom Connally, 1949

In April 1949, Canada and the United States joined Belgium, Britain, Denmark, France, Iceland, Italy, Luxembourg, the Netherlands, Norway, and Portugal to form the **North Atlantic Treaty Organization (NATO).** Member nations agreed that "an armed attack against one or more of them . . . shall be considered an attack against them all." This principle of mutual military assistance is called **collective security.** Having dropped its opposition to military treaties with Europe for the first time since the Monroe Doctrine, the United States now became actively involved in European affairs. In 1955,

Focus on
WORLD EVENTS

Operation Little Vittles The Berlin airlift was called "Operation Vittles," (*vittles* is slang for food) by American servicemen. It provided the necessities of life to Berliners. But one USAF pilot, Lieutenant Gail Halvorsen, felt that the children needed more than necessities, and he began dropping candy to the children of Berlin. Halvorsen rigged up tiny parachutes made of handkerchiefs and fabric scraps. As he flew over groups of children who had gathered to watch the planes, he wiggled the wings of his aircraft to signal that the parachuted candy was about to be dropped. German children began calling him "Uncle Wiggly Wings." Soon other pilots joined this Operation Little Vittles, and donations of handkerchiefs as well as thousands of pounds of candy began arriving at American air bases. Eventually, Operation Little Vittles dropped more than 250,000 miniature parachutes and some 23 tons of candy.

Early Cold War Crises, 1944–1949

Year	Crisis	Significance
1944–1949	Poland, Albania, Bulgaria, Czechoslovakia, Hungary, Romania, and East Germany become Soviet satellite nations.	Communist power grows with the Soviet Union's domination of Eastern Europe.
1948–1949	The Soviet Union blockades West Berlin. Truman initiates Berlin airlift to supply the city with food, fuel, and other necessities.	Tensions increase between the United States and the Soviet Union, with Berlin a focal point of East-West conflict.
1949	The Soviet Union develops nuclear weapons technology. China falls to Communist dictator Mao Zedong.	The United States no longer has the upper hand in weapons technology. Communism spreads to the most populous nation in Asia.

INTERPRETING CHARTS
A series of crises stepped up demands on the American government to deal effectively with the spread of communism. **Making Comparisons** (a) How are the two entries in the last row different from those that came before? (b) How did they affect American public opinion?

READING CHECK
Describe how China fell to the Communists.

the Soviet Union responded to the formation of NATO by creating the **Warsaw Pact,** a military alliance with its satellite nations in Eastern Europe.

Communist Advances

In 1949, two events heightened American concerns about the Cold War. The first was President Truman's terrifying announcement that the Soviet Union had successfully tested an atomic bomb. Then, just a few weeks later, Communist forces took control of China.

The Soviet Atomic Threat "We have evidence that within recent weeks an atomic explosion occurred in the USSR," Truman told reporters in September 1949. The news jolted Americans. New York, Los Angeles, and other American cities were now in danger of suffering the horrible fate of Hiroshima and Nagasaki.

Truman's response to the Soviet atomic threat was to forge ahead with a new weapon to maintain America's nuclear superiority. In early 1950, he gave approval for the development of a hydrogen, or thermonuclear, bomb that would be many times more destructive than the atomic bomb. The first successful thermonuclear test occurred in 1952, reestablishing the United States as the world's leading nuclear power.

At about the same time, Truman organized the Federal Civil Defense Administration. The new agency flooded the nation with posters and other information about how to survive a nuclear attack. These materials included plans for building bomb shelters and instructions for holding air raid drills in schools. Privately, however, experts ridiculed these programs as almost totally ineffective. Not until the late 1950s did civil defense become a more important federal government priority.

China Falls to the Communists The Communist takeover of China also came as a shock to many Americans. However, in actuality the struggle between China's Nationalists and Communists had been going on since the 1920s. (See Section 3.) During World War II, the Communist leader Mao Zedong and the Nationalist leader Jiang Jieshi (also known as Chiang Kai-shek) grudgingly cooperated to resist the invading Japanese. But the war also enabled Mao to strengthen his forces and to launch popular political, social, and economic reforms in the regions of China that he controlled.

As World War II drew to a close, the fighting between the Communists and government forces resumed. The Truman administration at first provided economic and military assistance to Jiang. Despite this aid, by 1947 Mao's forces had occupied much of China's countryside and had begun to take control of the northern cities. When Jiang asked for more American help, Truman and his advisors concluded that Mao's takeover of China probably could not be prevented. While continuing to give some aid to Jiang, the United States decided to focus instead on saving Western Europe from Soviet domination.

In early 1949, China's capital of Peking (now Beijing) fell to the Communists. A few months later, Mao proclaimed the creation of a Communist state, the People's Republic of China. The defeated Jiang and his followers withdrew to the island of Taiwan, off the Chinese mainland. There they continued as the Republic of China, claiming to be the legitimate government of the entire

Chinese nation. With American support, the Republic of China also held on to China's seats in the UN's General Assembly and Security Council.

Many Americans viewed the "loss of China" as a stain on the record of the Truman administration. Members of Congress and others who held this view called for greater efforts to protect the rest of Asia from communism. Some Americans also began to suspect the loyalties of those involved in making military and foreign policy.

The Cold War at Home

Throughout the Great Depression, tens of thousands of Americans had joined the Communist Party, which was a legal organization. Many were desperate people who had developed serious doubts about the American capitalist system, partly because of the economic collapse of the 1930s. Others were intellectuals who were attracted to Communist ideals. After World War II, however, improved economic times, as well as the increasing distrust of Stalin, caused many people to become disillusioned with communism. Most American Communists quit the party, although some remained members, whether active or not. Now, as a new red scare began to grip America, their pasts came back to haunt them.

During the presidencies of Truman and his successor, Dwight D. Eisenhower, concern about the growth of world communism raised fears of a conspiracy to overthrow the government, particularly when a number of Communist spies were caught and put on trial. These fears launched an anti-Communist crusade that violated the civil liberties of many Americans. Anyone who had ever had Communist party ties and many who had never even been Communists were swept up in the wave of persecutions.

The Loyalty Program As the Truman administration pursued its containment policy abroad, government officials launched programs to root out any element of communism that might have infiltrated the United States. Exposure of a number of wartime spy rings in 1946 increased the anxiety of many Americans. (In recent years, new evidence of Soviet infiltration has come to light. It is known, for instance, that Soviet spies gathered information on the United States nuclear program that helped the Soviet Union advance its own atomic development.)

When Republicans made big gains in the 1946 congressional elections, Truman worried that his rivals would take political advantage of the loyalty issue. To head off this possibility, he began his own investigation, establishing a federal employee loyalty program in 1947. Under this program, all new employees hired by the federal government were to be investigated. In addition, the FBI checked its files for evidence of current government employees who might be engaged in suspicious activities. Those accused of disloyalty were brought before a Loyalty Review Board.

While civil rights were supposed to be safeguarded, in fact those accused of disloyalty to their country often had little chance to defend themselves. Rather than being considered innocent until proven guilty, they found that the accusation alone made it difficult to clear their names. The Truman program examined several million government employees, yet only a few hundred were actually removed from their jobs. Nonetheless, the loyalty program added to a climate of suspicion taking hold in the nation.

Focus on CULTURE

The Rise of the Spy Novel The Cold War produced real spies, as well as the fear of spies where none existed. But perhaps the most famous Cold War spies were the fictional espionage agents in spy novels. James Bond, for example, is a postwar British Secret Service agent whose exploits continue in countless movies. The author of the Bond novels, Ian Fleming, had served in British naval intelligence during the war. John Le Carré, who was in the British Foreign Service in West Germany, created another famous British intelligence agent, George Smiley, who battles the Soviet master spy Karla in a series of novels. In Le Carré's classic *The Spy Who Came in From the Cold,* agents and double agents struggle to cross (and get doublecrossed!) at the Berlin Wall. Len Deighton's *Funeral in Berlin* also features a dangerous passage between East and West in the divided city of Berlin, where heroes and villains, secrets and spies, often slipped through the iron curtain on their shadowy missions.

HUAC As the Loyalty Review Board carried out its work, Congress pursued its own loyalty programs. The **House Un-American Activities Committee,** known as **HUAC,** had been established in 1938 to investigate disloyalty on the eve of World War II. Now it began a postwar probe of Communist infiltration of government agencies and, more spectacularly, a probe of the Hollywood movie industry.

Claiming that movies had tremendous power to influence the public, in 1947 HUAC charged that numerous Hollywood figures had Communist leanings that affected their filmmaking. In fact, some Hollywood personalities were or had been members of the Communist Party. Others in the industry had openly supported various causes and movements with philosophical similarities to communism (which, of course, did not make them Communists or disloyal in any way). With government encouragement, Hollywood had also produced some movies favorable to the Soviet Union and its people. These films had been made during the war, when the United States and the Soviet Union had been allies.

Many movie stars protested HUAC's attitude and procedures. Actor Frederic March asked Americans to consider where it all could lead: "Who's next? . . . Is it you, who will have to look around nervously before you can say what's on your mind? . . . This reaches into every American city and town."

The Hollywood Ten In September and October of 1947, HUAC called a number of Hollywood writers, directors, actors, and producers to testify. They were a distinguished group, responsible for some of Hollywood's best films of the previous decade. Facing the committee, celebrities who were accused of having radical political associations had little chance to defend themselves. The committee chairman, Republican Representative J. Parnell Thomas of New Jersey, first called witnesses who were allowed to make accusations based on rumors and other flimsy evidence. Then the accused were called.

Over and over the committee asked, "Are you now or have you ever been a member of the Communist Party?" When some of those called before HUAC attempted to make statements, they were denied permission. Invoking their Constitutional rights, ten of the accused declined to answer the committee's questions. The **Hollywood Ten** were cited for contempt of Congress and served jail terms ranging from six months to a year.

The HUAC investigations had a powerful impact on filmmaking. Nervous motion picture executives denounced the Hollywood Ten for having done a disservice to their industry. The studios compiled a **blacklist,** a list circulated among employers, containing the names of persons who should not be hired. Many other entertainment figures were added to the Hollywood blacklist simply because they seemed subversive or because they opposed *the idea* of a blacklist. The list included actors, screenwriters, directors, and broadcasters.

In the past, Hollywood had been willing to make movies on controversial subjects such as racism and anti-Semitism. Now studios resisted all films dealing with social problems and concentrated on pure entertainment.

The McCarran-Walter Act While HUAC carried out its work in the House, Democrat Pat McCarran led a Senate hunt for Communists in the movie industry, labor unions, the State Department, and the UN. Senator McCarran became convinced that most disloyal Americans were immigrants from Communist-dominated parts of the world.

VIEWING HISTORY Actor Humphrey Bogart protested HUAC's actions against other actors, and then ended up having to clear his own name. *Red Channels* was an index of blacklisted actors published in 1950. **Drawing Inferences** *How do these two items demonstrate the climate of suspicion at that time?*

At his urging, Congress passed the **McCarran-Walter Act** in 1952. This law reaffirmed the quota system for each country that had been established in 1924. It discriminated against potential immigrants from Asia and from Southern and Central Europe. President Truman vetoed McCarran's bill, calling it "one of the most un-American acts I have ever witnessed in my public career." Congress, however, passed the bill over the President's veto.

Spy Cases Inflame the Nation Two famous spy cases helped fuel the suspicion that a conspiracy within the United States was helping foreign Communists gain military and political successes overseas. In 1948, HUAC investigated Alger Hiss, who had been a high-ranking State Department official before he left government service. Whittaker Chambers, a former Communist who had become a successful *Time* magazine editor, accused Hiss of having been a Communist in the 1930s. Hiss denied the charge and sued Chambers for slander. Chambers then declared that Hiss had been a Soviet spy.

Too much time had passed for the spying charge to be pressed. After two trials, Hiss was convicted of lying to a federal grand jury investigating him for espionage, however. In 1950, he went to prison for four years. Not all Americans were convinced that he was guilty, and the case was debated for years. For most people, however, the case seemed to prove that there was a real Communist threat in the United States.

Several months after Hiss's conviction, Julius and Ethel Rosenberg, a married couple who were members of the Communist Party, were accused of passing atomic secrets to the Soviets during World War II. After a highly controversial trial, the Rosenbergs were convicted of espionage and executed in 1953. The case was another event that inflamed anti-Communist passions and focused attention on a possible internal threat to the nation's security.

Like the Hiss case, the Rosenbergs' convictions were debated for years afterward. Careful work by historians in once-classified American records and in secret Soviet records opened at the end of the Cold War indicate that both Alger Hiss and Julius Rosenberg were guilty. While Ethel Rosenberg may have had some knowledge of her husband's activities, it now appears that she was not guilty of espionage.

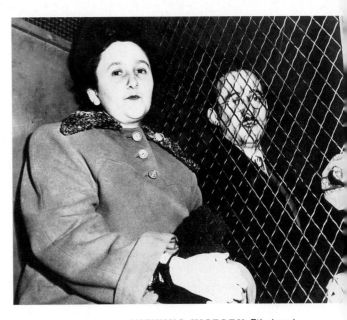

VIEWING HISTORY Ethel and Julius Rosenberg were the first U.S. civilians to be executed for espionage. **Drawing Conclusions** *How did spy cases affect Americans' perception of a Communist threat to society?*

Section 2 Assessment

READING COMPREHENSION

1. What was the **Marshall Plan,** and why was it instituted?

2. What was the importance of the **Berlin airlift?**

3. How did **NATO** demonstrate the principle of **collective security?**

4. What did the **HUAC** hearings and the **McCarran-Walter Act** show about American attitudes?

CRITICAL THINKING AND WRITING

5. **Identifying Central Issues** What dangers to a free society are posed by the kind of tactics used by HUAC and by the creation of blacklists?

6. **Writing a Conclusion** How well did the United States respond to Cold War threats? Support your conclusion with three examples.

Go Online
PHSchool.com

For: An activity on the Marshall Plan
Visit: PHSchool.com
Web Code: mrd-8262

The Korean War

READING FOCUS

- How did Communist expansion in Asia set the stage for the Korean War?

- Who fought in the Korean War, and what were the three stages of the war?

- What were the effects of the Korean War?

MAIN IDEA

To repel a North Korean invasion of South Korea, American and other UN troops fought against Communist forces for three years. The result was a return to prewar Korean borders.

KEY TERMS

38th parallel
Korean War
military-industrial complex

TARGET READING SKILL

Identify Cause and Effect Copy the diagram below. As you read, fill in the causes and effects of the Korean War.

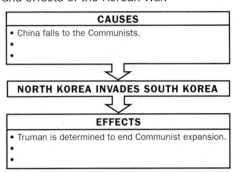

CAUSES
• China falls to the Communists.
•
•

NORTH KOREA INVADES SOUTH KOREA

EFFECTS
• Truman is determined to end Communist expansion.
•
•

Setting the Scene The Korean War is sometimes called America's forgotten war, but the soldiers who fought in Korea never forgot it. In June of 1950, American troops struggled to push back the Communists, who had made huge advances. One American marine recalled the fierce fighting:

> ❝ To push the North Koreans back across the river we had to kick them off a series of ridges. . . . It was straight uphill. No cover. There were machine guns, mortars, grenades going off. The volume of fire was terrific. They were pouring everything they had into us. Guys were cursing and yelling and dropping all around me. . . . ❞
>
> —Arnold Winter

Later in 1950, both sides dug in to hold their positions. Infantryman Tom Clawson said later, "I didn't realize it at the time, but when I got to Korea the war of movement had just ended. What they called the sitting war had taken its place." He described what "the sitting war" was like:

American soldiers dig in during the Korean War.

> ❝ You spent hours every day improving your position, working on the foxholes and trenches and bunkers. But I never liked to get too fancy, because sooner or later we'd be shifted to a different position. . . . Most times [after going on patrol] you'd return to the place you started from, but the day would always come when you wouldn't. You'd come back and move directly to a new position. But all the positions were always somewhere on the same ridgeline. ❞
>
> —Tom Clawson

Although it lacked the glory of World War II and the turmoil of the Vietnam War, the Korean conflict had important effects on the United States.

Communist Expansion in Asia

While the attention of most Americans was focused on the Communist threat in Europe, events were unfolding in Asia that would cause the Cold War to flare up into a "hot" military confrontation. The roots of this armed conflict were found in the Chinese Civil War and in Japanese aggression in both China and Korea before and during World War II.

The Chinese Civil War   As you recall, before World War I, foreign powers exerted considerable influence in China and even held some Chinese territory. One of these powers was Japan. Another was Germany. After Germany was defeated in World War I, the Allies gave Japan control over former German possessions, thus increasing Japanese power in China. In 1919, Chinese protesters began calling for a stronger, more independent China. Some demanded democracy and nationalism. Others, impressed by the results of the Russian Revolution of 1917, thought that communism was the way to build a strong nation.

In the mid-1920s, the Nationalist Party led by Jiang Jieshi gained strength in northern China and captured Beijing. Meanwhile, the Communists had made gains around Shanghai. In 1927, Jiang sent troops to attack the Communists and their supporters. The result was a massacre that would lead to civil war.

The Communists were led by Mao Zedong. He gained support for the Communist cause in southeastern China by redistributing land to the peasants and offering them schooling and health care. Determined to consolidate his power, Jiang continued to pursue the Communists. In 1934, Mao and his followers began retreating before Jiang's forces. After the Long March, Mao began rebuilding his forces in the north of China.

As you read in Section 2, the Nationalists and the Communists had cooperated to resist invading Japanese forces, but after World War II the Chinese Civil War became more intense. The Nationalists lost support because of their harsh treatment of the population, high taxes, and corruption. Mao's land reforms and his promise of equality, as well as his military victories, led the Communists to power in 1949. The Nationalists fled to Taiwan, where they still claimed to be the legitimate government of China.

Dividing Korea   In addition to seeking territory and influence in China before World War I, Japan had also annexed the Korean peninsula. Japanese rule of Korea was harsh, and Koreans hoped that their nation would be restored after the Japanese were finally defeated in World War II. However, the war ended before careful plans for Korean independence could be worked out. In 1945, the Allies agreed on a temporary solution. Soviet soldiers accepted the surrender of Japanese troops north of the **38th parallel,** the latitude line running across Korea at approximately the midpoint of the peninsula; American forces did the same south of the parallel. While the dividing line was never intended to be permanent, Korea was divided—temporarily—into a Soviet-occupied northern zone and an American-occupied southern zone. Soon a pro-American government formed in South Korea and a Communist regime was established in North Korea. Occupying forces withdrew from both zones in 1948 and 1949.

READING CHECK
How did Korea become a divided nation?

The Korean Conflict

Koreans on both sides of the dividing line wanted to unify their nation. In June 1950, the **Korean War** broke out when North Korean troops streamed across the 38th parallel, determined to reunite Korea by force. The invasion took the United States by surprise. It also alarmed Americans, who were sure—wrongly, it turned out—that the action had been orchestrated by the Soviet Union. The fall of China to the Communists had been a shock to the United States; now it seemed as though communism was on the advance again. Faced with what he viewed as a clear case of aggression, President Truman was determined to respond. He recalled earlier instances "when the strong had attacked the weak." Each time that the democracies failed to act, Truman remembered, it had encouraged the aggressors. "If this [invasion of South Korea] was allowed to go unchallenged, it would mean a third world war, just as similar incidents brought on the second world war," Truman said.

The UN Police Action   After the defeat of the Chinese Nationalists in 1949, the United States had blocked Communist China's admission to the United Nations. The Soviet delegation had walked out in protest, and thus could not exercise its veto when President Truman brought the issue of North Korean aggression to the UN. The United States gained unanimous approval for resolutions that branded North Korea an aggressor and that called on member states to help defend South Korea and restore peace.

President Truman wasted no time. He commanded the American Seventh Fleet to protect Taiwan, and he ordered American air and naval support for the South Koreans. Later he sent ground troops as well. Although Truman did not go to Congress for a declaration of war as required by the Constitution, both Democrats and Republicans praised him for his strong action. Members of the House stood and cheered when they heard of it.

The UN set up the United Nations Command and asked the United States to choose the commander of the UN forces. Eventually, 16 member nations contributed troops or arms, but Americans made up roughly 80 percent of the troops that served in the UN police action in Korea.

MAP SKILLS These maps show the back-and-forth nature of the fighting in the Korean War.
Movement Examine the maps and the movements of UN troops. Why do you think China entered the war when it did?

The Korean War, 1950–1953

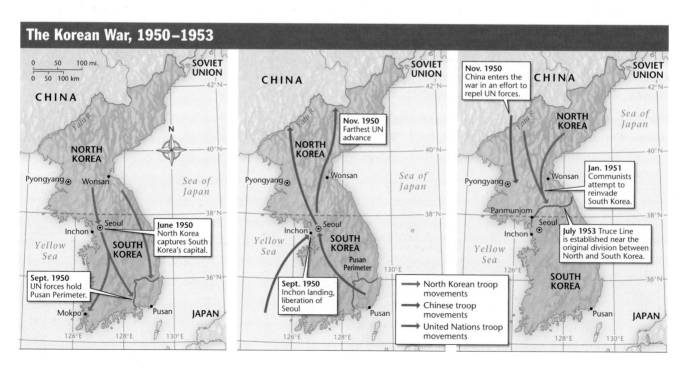

Waging the War A hero of two world wars and a strong anti-Communist, General Douglas MacArthur was Truman's choice to lead the UN forces in Korea. MacArthur was based in Japan, where he headed the postwar occupation. He was responsible for establishing Western democracy there and for creating Japan's new democratic constitution. He had been less successful in implementing democracy in South Korea, where he also commanded American occupation forces. There, MacArthur had supported Korean president Syngman Rhee, despite Rhee's brutal elimination of his opponents.

Despite a difficult personality, MacArthur was an excellent military strategist, and he developed a bold plan to drive the invaders from South Korea. With Soviet tanks and air power, the North Koreans had swept through South Korea in just weeks. Only a small part of the country, near the port city of Pusan, remained unconquered.

MacArthur suspected that the North Koreans' rapid advance had left their supply lines stretched thin. He decided to strike at this weakness. After first sending forces to defend Pusan, in September 1950 he landed troops at Inchon in northwestern South Korea, and attacked enemy supply lines from behind.

MacArthur's strategy worked. Caught between UN forces in the north and in the south, and with their supplies cut off, the invaders fled back across the 38th parallel. UN troops pursued them northward. American and South Korean leaders began to boast of reuniting Korea under South Korean control. Such talk alarmed the Chinese Communists, who had been in power less than a year and who did not want a pro-Western nation next door.

As UN troops approached North Korea's border with China, the Chinese warned them not to advance any farther. MacArthur ignored the warning. On November 24, 1950, the general announced his "Home by Christmas" offensive, designed to drive the enemy across the North Korean border at the Yalu River into China and end the war. However, Chinese troops poured across the Yalu to take the offensive. The Chinese and the North Koreans pushed the UN forces back into South Korea. A stalemate developed.

MacArthur favored breaking the stalemate by opening a second front. He wanted the Chinese opposition forces of Jiang Jieshi on the island of Taiwan to return to the mainland to attack the Chinese Communists. Truman opposed this strategy, fearing it could lead to a widespread war in Asia. Unable to sway Truman, MacArthur sent a letter to House Minority Leader Joseph Martin in March 1951, attacking the President's policies. Martin made the letter public. On April 11, Truman fired MacArthur for insubordination.

MacArthur returned home to a hero's welcome. In an address to a joint session of Congress on April 19, he made an emotional farewell:

> 66 *Since I took the oath at West Point, the hopes and dreams [of youth] have all vanished. But I still remember the refrain of one of the most popular barracks ballads of that day, which proclaimed most proudly that old soldiers never die, they just fade away. And like the old soldier of that ballad, I now close my military career and just fade away, an old soldier who tried to do his duty as God gave him the light to see that duty. Good-bye.* 99

—General Douglas MacArthur, 1951

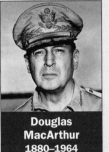

BIOGRAPHY

Douglas MacArthur 1880–1964

The son of an army officer, Douglas MacArthur graduated from West Point at the top of his class. Cited for bravery in World War I, he became a general by the time he was 38, and Army Chief of Staff in 1930.

During World War II, MacArthur commanded American forces in Asia. He organized the defense of the Philippines and the island-hopping campaign against the Japanese in the Pacific. After commanding American Occupation forces in both Japan and South Korea, MacArthur led the UN forces in the Korean War. His dispute with President Truman led the President to fire him for insubordination.

Although a hero to those he commanded and to much of the American public, MacArthur was disliked by many political leaders, who viewed him as overly ambitious. MacArthur, in turn, had little respect for either Roosevelt or Truman; he thought both were soft on communism. His attitude made MacArthur an anti-Communist hero. Yet his characteristic contempt for anyone with authority over him led him to take actions that undermined his otherwise brilliant career.

Sounds of an Era

Listen to MacArthur's speech to Congress and other sounds from the Cold War period.

U.S. Defense Spending, 1941–1961

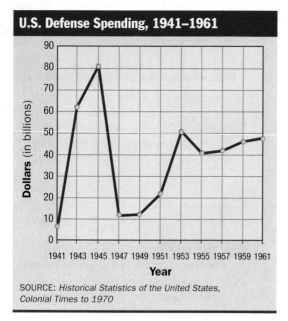

SOURCE: *Historical Statistics of the United States, Colonial Times to 1970*

INTERPRETING GRAPHS
The competition for world leadership led to an arms race between the United States and the Soviet Union. **Recognizing Cause and Effect** *What was the cause of the sharpest rise in American defense spending in the post–World War II era? Why do you think spending did not drop off abruptly again, the way it did after World War II?*

Once tempers cooled, MacArthur did, in fact, fade from view, and Truman was able to keep the war limited. However, the struggle dragged on for over two more years, into the presidency of Dwight D. Eisenhower. When peace talks stalled, Eisenhower's threat to use atomic weapons got the talks going again. Finally, a truce was signed in 1953, leaving Korea divided at almost exactly the same place as before the war, near the 38th parallel.

The Effects of the Korean War

The Korean War caused enormous frustration in the United States. Americans wondered why roughly 54,000 of their soldiers had been killed and 103,000 wounded for such limited results. They questioned whether their government was serious about stopping communism. On the other hand, Communist forces had been pushed back beyond the 38th parallel. What's more, this containment had occurred without nuclear war. It seemed that Americans would have to get used to more limited wars and more limited victories.

Americans would have to get used to other changes as well. One change was in the military itself. Although President Truman had ordered the integration of the armed forces in 1948, the Korean War was the first war in which white Americans and African Americans served in the same units.

The Korean War also led to a huge increase in military spending. The military had taken less than a third of the federal budget in 1950; a decade later, military spending made up about half of federal expenditures. At the same time, the United States came to accept the demands of permanent mobilization. Over a million American soldiers were stationed around the world. At home, the military establishment became more powerful as it developed links to the corporate and scientific communities. These ties created a powerful **military-industrial complex** that employed 3.5 million Americans by 1960.

The Korean War also helped to shape future U.S. policy in Asia. Hoping that Japan could help to maintain the balance of power in the Pacific, the United States signed a peace treaty with that nation in September 1951. In addition, the Korean War further poisoned relations with Communist China, leading to a diplomatic standoff that would last more than 20 years.

Section 3 Assessment

READING COMPREHENSION

1. What was the importance of the **38th parallel?**

2. (a) How did the **Korean War** begin? (b) Who fought on each side?

3. Why did President Truman fire General MacArthur?

4. Name two effects of the war.

CRITICAL THINKING AND WRITING

5. **Drawing Conclusions** Considering containment and the Truman Doctrine, do you think the Korean War was a success or a failure? Why?

6. **Creating a Time Line** Make a time line of the important events of the Korean War.

Go Online PHSchool.com

For: An activity on the Korean War
Visit: PHSchool.com
Web Code: mrd-8263

READING FOCUS

- What were the characteristics of the McCarthy era?

- How was the Cold War waged in Southeast Asia, the Middle East, and Latin America during the 1950s?

- How did the arms race develop?

MAIN IDEA

During the 1950s, the Cold War spread around the world. At home, McCarthyism caused fear and distrust.

KEY TERMS

McCarthyism
arms race
deterrence
brinkmanship
ICBM
Sputnik
U-2 incident

TARGET READING SKILL

Identify Sequence As you read, prepare an outline of the first section. Follow the model below.

> **The McCarthy Era**
>
> **I. McCarthy's Rise to Power**
>   **A. McCarthy needed a popular issue for the 1952 election.**
>   **1.** _____
>   **2.** _____
>   **B.** _____

Setting the Scene Communist aggression in Korea was already heightening Americans' fear of communism when Wisconsin Senator Joseph McCarthy held up a piece of paper and declared, "I have here in my hand a list of 205 [people] who were known to the secretary of state as being members of the Communist Party and who, nevertheless, are still working and shaping policy at the State Department." In the Cold War atmosphere of 1950, McCarthy's charges quickly gained so much support that only the most courageous spoke out against him. One such person was Edward R. Murrow, who concluded his TV show on McCarthy by saying that "[t]his is no time for men who oppose Senator McCarthy to keep silent." He explained:

> 66 *[T]he line between investigating and persecuting is a very fine one and the junior Senator from Wisconsin has stepped over it repeatedly. . . . We must not confuse dissent with disloyalty. We must remember always that accusation is not proof. . . . We can deny our heritage and our history, but we cannot escape responsibility for the result. . . .* 99
>
> —Edward R. Murrow

The McCarthy Era

In 1950, it seemed to many Americans that the events in Asia supported McCarthy's sensational charges. However, the famous list of 205 known State Department Communists turned out to be the names of people who were still employed by the government, even though they had been accused of disloyalty under Truman's loyalty program. When pressed for details, the senator reduced the number from 205 to 57. Nevertheless, McCarthy's accusations sparked an anti-Communist hysteria and national search for subversives that caused suspicion and fear across the nation.

McCarthy's Rise to Power Joseph McCarthy's first term in the Senate had been undistinguished and he needed an issue to arouse public support. He found that issue in the menace of communism. Piling baseless accusations on top of unprovable charges, McCarthy took his crusade to the floor of the Senate and engaged in the smear tactics that came to be called **McCarthyism.** Not only was McCarthy reelected, but he became

ANALYZING POLITICAL CARTOONS The caption of this cartoon cites Senator McCarthy's famous claim to have proof of subversion "in his hand." **Drawing Conclusions** (a) According to the cartoon, what does McCarthy really have, instead of proof? (b) What is the message of the cartoon?

"I Have Here In My Hand—"

VIEWING HISTORY Army counsel Joseph Welch listens as Senator Joseph McCarthy discusses Communist infiltration into the army. **Analyzing Visual Information** *(a) What emotion do you think Welch is experiencing? Why do you think he feels that way? (b) What was the result of the Army-McCarthy hearings?*

chairman of an investigations subcommittee. Merely being accused by McCarthy caused people to lose their jobs and reputations.

McCarthy soon took on larger targets. He attacked former Secretary of State George Marshall, a national hero and a man of unquestioned integrity. McCarthy claimed that Marshall was involved in "a conspiracy so immense and an infamy so black as to dwarf any previous venture in the history of man," because of his inability to stop the Communist triumph in China.

Even other senators came to fear McCarthy. They worried that opposition to his tactics would brand them as Communist sympathizers. But there were a few exceptions. As early as June 1950, Republican Senator Margaret Chase Smith of Maine presented a Declaration of Conscience to the Senate. She denounced McCarthy for having "debased" the Senate "to the level of a forum of hate and character assassination sheltered by the shield of congressional immunity. . . ."

McCarthy's Fall In early 1954, when one of his assistants was drafted, McCarthy charged that even the army was full of Communists. Army officials, in turn, charged McCarthy with seeking special treatment for his aide. As charges and countercharges flew back and forth, the senator's subcommittee voted to investigate the claims.

The Army-McCarthy hearings began in late April 1954. Democrats asked that the hearings be televised, hoping that the public would see McCarthy for what he was. Ever eager for publicity, the senator agreed. For weeks, Americans were riveted to their television sets. Most were horrified by McCarthy's bullying tactics and baseless allegations.

By the time the hearings ended in mid-June, the senator had lost even his strongest supporters. The Senate formally condemned him for his reckless actions. Unrepentant, McCarthy charged his accusers with being tools of the Communists, but he no longer had credibility. Although McCarthy remained in the Senate, his power was gone.

Eventually this second red scare, much like the one that followed World War I, subsided. But the nation was damaged by the era's suppression of free speech and open, honest debate.

The Cold War in the 1950s

American Cold War policy entered a new phase when Republican Dwight D. Eisenhower became President in 1953. Eisenhower's Secretary

---

Focus on
CITIZENSHIP

Declaration of Conscience

Margaret Chase Smith's declaration to the Senate made it clear that Senator McCarthy, far from protecting American values as

he claimed, was really putting American principles in danger:

"Those of us who shout the loudest about Americanism in making character assassinations are all too frequently those who, by our own words and acts, ignore some of the basic principles of Americanism—

The right to criticize;
The right to hold unpopular beliefs;
The right to protest;
The right of independent thought.

The exercise of these rights should not cost one single American citizen his right to a livelihood nor should he be in danger of losing his reputation nor should he be in danger . . . merely because he happens to know someone who holds unpopular beliefs."

of State, John Foster Dulles, was a harsh anti-Communist who considered winning the Cold War to be a moral crusade. Dulles believed that Truman's containment policy was too cautious. Instead, he called for a policy to roll back communism where it had already taken hold.

As a military leader, Eisenhower recognized the risks of confronting the Soviets. He acted as a brake on Dulles's more extreme views. In Eisenhower's judgment, the United States could not intervene in the affairs of the Soviet Union's Eastern European satellites. So when East Germans revolted in 1953, and Poles and Hungarians in 1956, the United States kept its distance as Soviet troops crushed the uprisings. Eisenhower felt that any other response risked war with the Soviet Union. He wanted to avoid that at all costs. Thus containment remained an important part of American foreign policy in the 1950s.

Southeast Asia   In July 1953, Eisenhower fulfilled a campaign promise to bring the Korean War to an end. The sudden death of Stalin in March and the rapid rise of more moderate Soviet leaders contributed to the resolution of this conflict. Meanwhile, the United States continued to provide substantial military aid to France, which was trying to retain control of its colony, Vietnam. When an international conference divided Vietnam, like Korea, into a Communist north and an anti-Communist south, the United States provided aid to South Vietnam, but—for the time being—resisted greater involvement. (See Chapter 24.)

The Middle East   The Cold War was also played out in the historic tensions of the Middle East. In the 1930s and 1940s, the Holocaust had forced many Jews to seek safety in Palestine, the Biblical home of the Jewish people, now controlled by the British. Calls for a Jewish state intensified. In 1947, the British turned the question over to the UN, which created two states in the area, one Jewish and one Arab. In May 1948, the Jews in Palestine proclaimed the new nation of Israel. Israel's Arab neighbors, who also viewed Palestine as their ancient homeland, attacked the Jewish state in 1948. Israel repelled the Arab assault, and the UN mediated new borders. As Arab hostility to the idea of a Jewish state continued, the United States supported Israel, while the Soviet Union generally backed Arab interests.

Meanwhile, the United States also worked to prevent oil-rich Arab nations from falling under the influence of the Soviet Union. In 1952, a nationalist leader gained control in Iran. Fearful that he would be neutral—or worse, sympathetic to Communism— the United States backed groups that overthrew the nationalist government and restored the pro-American Shah of Iran to power.

Next came the Suez crisis of 1956. When Egypt's ruler, Gamal Abdel Nasser, sought Soviet support, the United States and Great Britain cut off their aid to Egypt. Nasser responded by seizing the British-owned Suez Canal. This canal was a vital waterway that passed through Egypt and allowed Middle East oil to reach Europe via the Mediterranean. In late 1956, British and French forces attacked Egypt to regain control of the canal, despite prior assurances they would not rely on force. Reacting to Soviet threats of "dangerous consequences," a furious Eisenhower persuaded his NATO allies to withdraw from Egypt, which retained control of the canal.

To combat further Soviet influence in the Middle East, the President announced the Eisenhower Doctrine in

MAP SKILLS Following the 1948 war, Israel controlled most of what had been Palestine, but Egypt barred all Israeli ships and any ships of any nationality going to or from Israel from using the Suez Canal. **Location** *(a) Why do you think the Suez Canal was important to Israel and to its trading partners? (b) What do you think Egypt's purpose was in denying access to Israel?*

Israel After the 1948 War

Palestine prior to the creation of Israel

Israeli-held territory, 1948

Arab-held territory, 1948

Suez Canal

From *Sputnik* to Space Station

When the Soviets launched *Sputnik* in 1957, they also launched the space race. NASA was established in 1958 to oversee an American space program that could compete with the Soviets. However, in 1961, the Soviets scored another win: the first man in space. Competition continued through the 1960s, but the Americans raised the stakes by landing on the moon in 1969.

The two nations also continued to launch orbiting satellites. In 1973, the American *Skylab* became the first successful space station, but the Soviet *Mir,* launched in 1986, was the most successful, remaining in orbit until 2001. *Mir,* which means "peace" in Russian, also changed the nature of space exploration: it became a cooperative venture. Crews from many nations visited *Mir,* including the United States beginning in 1995. And in 1998, when the United States and Russia began assembling the International Space Station, to which many nations will eventually contribute, a new era of cooperation had truly begun.

? Which kind of "space race" do you think would lead to more progress: competition or cooperation? Explain your reasoning.

January 1957. This policy stated that the United States would use force "to safeguard the independence of any country or group of countries in the Middle East requesting aid against [Communist-inspired] aggression." Eisenhower used his doctrine in 1958 to justify landing troops in Lebanon to put down a revolt against its pro-American government.

Latin America The United States also acted to support pro-American governments and to suppress Communist influences in Latin America, especially where American companies had large investments. Since the mid-1920s, the United States had exercised control over the economies of some ten Latin American nations. In Central America, United States troops had invaded Nicaragua and Honduras to prop up leaders who supported American interests. In 1947, the United States signed the Rio Pact, a regional defense alliance with 18 other nations in the Western Hemisphere. The next year, the United States led the way in forming the Organization of American States (OAS) to increase cooperation among the nations of the hemisphere.

In 1954, the CIA helped overthrow the government of Guatemala on the grounds that its leaders were sympathetic to radical causes. The CIA takeover restored the property of an American corporation, the United Fruit Company, which had been seized by the Guatemalan government. Such actions fueled a Soviet perception that America was escalating the Cold War.

The Arms Race

Throughout the 1950s, the United States and the Soviet Union waged an increasingly intense struggle for world leadership. Nowhere was this competition more dangerous than in the **arms race,** the struggle to gain weapons superiority.

The Growth of Nuclear Arsenals In August 1953, less than a year after the United States exploded its first thermonuclear device, the Soviet Union successfully tested its own hydrogen bomb. As part of the policy of deterrence begun by President Truman, Eisenhower stepped up American weapons development. **Deterrence** is the policy of making the military power of the United States and its allies so strong that no enemy would dare attack for fear of retaliation. Between 1954 and 1958, the United States conducted 19 hydrogen bomb tests in the Pacific. One of these explosions, in March 1954, was over 750 times more powerful than the atomic bomb that had been dropped on Nagasaki in World War II. Japanese fishermen some 90 miles from the blast suffered severe radiation burns. The test was a chilling warning that nuclear war could threaten the entire world with radioactive contamination.

Brinkmanship American policymakers used the fear of nuclear war to achieve their Cold War objectives. In 1956, Secretary of State John Dulles made it clear that the United States was prepared to risk war to protect its national interests. Dulles explained the policy of **brinkmanship** this way: "The ability to get to the verge without getting into the war is the necessary art. If you cannot master it, you inevitably get into war. If you try to run away from it, if you are scared to go to the brink, you are lost." Many Americans agreed with the reaction of Democratic leader Adlai Stevenson: "I am shocked that the Secretary of State is willing to play Russian roulette with the life of our nation." Still, the Eisenhower administration relied on the policy of brinkmanship.

Cold War in the Skies　To carry hydrogen bombs to their targets, American military planners relied mainly on airplanes. Unable to match this strength, the Soviets focused on long-range rockets known as intercontinental ballistic missiles, or **ICBMs.** Americans also worked to develop ICBMs. However, in part because of its dependence on conventional air power, the United States lagged behind the Soviet Union in missile development.

The size of this technology gap became apparent in 1957, when the Soviets used one of their rockets to launch ***Sputnik,*** the first artificial satellite to orbit Earth. The realization that the rocket used to launch *Sputnik* could carry a hydrogen bomb to American shores added to American shock and fear.

In May 1960, the Soviet military again demonstrated its arms capabilities by using a guided missile to shoot down an American U-2 spy plane over Soviet territory. Because these spy planes flew more than 15 miles high, American officials had assumed that they were invulnerable to attack. The **U-2 incident** shattered this confidence, and made Americans willing to expend considerable resources to catch up to—and surpass—the Soviet Union.

One legacy of the Cold War was the creation of what Eisenhower called a "permanent armaments industry of vast proportions." As he left office, he warned that the existence of this military-industrial complex, employing millions of Americans and having a financial stake in war-making, could become a threat to peace:

This 1959 *Newsweek* illustration shows Soviet leader Khrushchev (left) and President Eisenhower (right) using missiles to maintain a balance of power.

66 *Our arms must be mighty, ready for instant action. . . . We recognize the imperative need for this development. Yet we must not fail to comprehend its grave implications. . . . [In] government, we must guard against the acquisition of unwarranted [unnecessary] influence, whether sought or unsought, by the military-industrial complex. The potential for the disastrous rise of misplaced power exists and will persist.* 99

—Dwight D. Eisenhower, Farewell Address, 1961

Section 4 Assessment

READING COMPREHENSION

1. What was **McCarthyism?**

2. What was the **arms race?**

3. How did the policy of **deterrence** influence U.S. actions during the Cold War?

4. How did *Sputnik* and the **U-2 incident** affect American public opinion and policy?

CRITICAL THINKING AND WRITING

5. **Identifying Alternatives** When could President Eisenhower have chosen an alternative to containment and the arms race? How might history have been different if he had done so?

6. **Writing a Letter** Write a letter urging a senator of 1952 to oppose Senator McCarthy.

For: An activity on *Sputnik*
Visit: PHSchool.com
Web Code: mrd-8264

creating a CHAPTER SUMMARY

Copy the diagram (right) onto a piece of paper. Complete it by filling in the the most important causes and effects of the Cold War.

For additional review and enrichment activities, see the interactive version of *America: Pathways to the Present*, available on the Web and on CD-ROM.

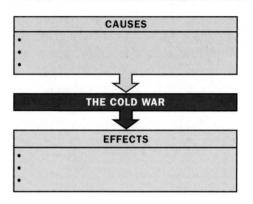

CAUSES
•
•
•

THE COLD WAR

EFFECTS
•
•
•

★ Reviewing Key Terms

For each of the terms below, write a sentence explaining how it relates to the Cold War.

1. satellite nation
2. iron curtain
3. containment
4. Marshall Plan
5. Warsaw Pact
6. HUAC
7. blacklist
8. 38th parallel
9. brinkmanship
10. U-2 incident

★ Reviewing Main Ideas

11. What decisions were reached at Yalta and Potsdam? (Section 1)

12. Summarize the postwar goals of the United States and the Soviet Union. (Section 1)

13. How did the United States hope to use the policy of containment and the Truman Doctrine to respond to the Soviet creation of an iron curtain? (Section 1)

14. What did the Marshall Plan accomplish in Europe? (Section 2)

15. (a) What was the Soviet atomic threat? (b) How did President Truman respond to it? (Section 2)

16. What was the purpose of NATO? (Section 2)

17. What Communist advances worried Americans in 1949? (Section 2)

18. (a) Describe the efforts by the Truman administration and Congress to stop Communist influence in the United States. (b) How did this anti-Communist effort affect the nation? (Section 2)

19. How did the Communists gain control of China? (Section 3)

20. Describe the three phases of the Korean War. (Section 3)

21. Describe the rise and fall of Senator Joseph McCarthy. (Section 4)

22. How did the Cold War play out in Southeast Asia, the Middle East, and Latin America? (Section 4)

23. Describe the arms race of the 1950s. (Section 4)

★ Critical Thinking

24. **Recognizing Ideologies** Explain how the differing ideologies of the Soviets and the United States were reflected in their Cold War policies.

25. **Predicting Consequences** (a) What principles of American foreign policy did the Berlin airlift put into action? (b) What do you think might have happened if the United States and Britain had not tried the airlift or if the airlift had failed?

26. **Identifying Central Issues** Why do you think that Americans were so willing to believe that Communists had infiltrated the movie industry and the American government?

27. **Expressing Problems Clearly** General MacArthur wanted to pursue the Korean War more aggressively, but President Truman was more cautious. Explain the pros and cons of each position.

"FIRE!"

June 17, 1949

★ Standardized Test Prep

Analyzing Political Cartoons ▶

28. In this 1949 cartoon a man is about to douse a flame. What does the flame symbolize?

   A American civil liberties
   B The Statue of Liberty
   C The heating up of the Cold War
   D Communism

29. (a) What does the man represent? (b) How can you tell?

30. What is the cartoonist's message?

Analyzing Primary Sources

Turn to the excerpt from the Truman Doctrine at the end of Section 1.

31. What was the main purpose of Truman's speech?

   A to frighten the Soviet government
   B to make clear how the United States would respond to Communist aggression
   C to win congressional approval of his containment policy
   D to expand the Cold War

32. What group or groups did Truman promise to help?

   F subjugated minorities
   G armed resistance movements
   H majorities whose freedom was threatened
   I all of the above

33. According to Truman, what two groups might try to subjugate free peoples?

   A free peoples and armed minorities
   B subjugated minorities and outside forces
   C the majority and outsiders
   D outside forces and armed minorities

Test-Taking Tip

In answering Question 28, note that you're asked what the flame symbolizes, or what it stands for or represents.

Applying the Chapter Skill

Recognizing Cause and Effect Look back at the Skills for Life page, and review the steps for recognizing cause and effect. Then create a cause-and-effect chain to explain what led to the Marshall Plan and what impact it had.

For: Chapter 19 Self-Test
Visit: PHSchool.com
Web Code: mra-8265

American Pathways
SCIENCE & TECHNOLOGY

American Innovations in Technology

Technological innovation has always spurred the nation's economic growth. From the Industrial Revolution to the Information Age, American inventiveness has resulted in new and improved products for consumers and increased profits for businesses.

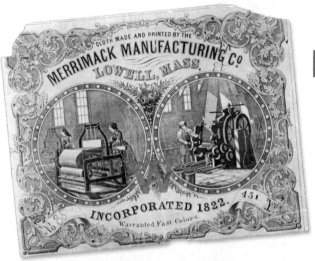

1 A Young and Growing Economy

1790–1850 As the nation expanded westward, a number of innovations such as the cotton gin, the mechanical reaper, and centralized textile factories improved agriculture and encouraged trade.

A textile mill label from Lowell, Massachusetts (left)

2 Industrial Expansion

1850–1890 New inventions such as the telephone and the light bulb, as well as other technological advances such as the first electric power stations, played an important role in the massive industrial expansion that occurred after the Civil War.

Corliss steam engine at the 1876 Centennial Exhibition (left) and the receiving device for Alexander Graham Bell's first telephone call (above)

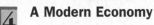

3 Becoming a Superpower

1900–1945   The Allies won two world wars in part because of American technological skills, including the ability to apply assembly-line and other mass-production techniques to the manufacture of war materials.

Boeing B-17 bomber production during the 1940s (above)

4 A Modern Economy

1945–Present   The modern American economy has benefited from a steady stream of innovations, especially in the fields of biotechnology, electronics, plastics, aerospace, and computer science. These scientific advances have also given a boost to the global economy.

High-tech devices (above) and an implantable replacement heart (left)

Continuity and Change

1. How did the Erie Canal encourage the growth of agriculture in the West?
2. How did the assembly line improve productivity in the automobile industry?

Go Online PHSchool.com

For: A study guide on American technology
Visit: PHSchool.com
Web Code: mrd-8269

665

The Postwar Years at Home (1945–1960)

Plastic flamingos were popular lawn ornaments in the 1950s.

A Levittown suburb

This sign sat on President Truman's desk.

American Events

1944
Congress passes the GI Bill of Rights.

1946
Dr. Spock publishes *The Common Sense Book of Baby and Child Care.*

1947
Congress passes the Taft-Hartley Act. The first transistor is invented, spurring growth in computers and electronics.

Presidential Terms: Franklin D. Roosevelt 1933–1945   Harry S Truman 1945–1953

1940   **1945**   **1950**

World Events

Thor Heyerdahl and his crew sail the raft *Kon-Tiki* from Peru to Polynesia.

1947

English novelist George Orwell's *Nineteen Eighty-Four* is published.

1949

In some ways, the economic issues facing the United States at the end of World War II were similar to those at the end of World War I. Workers demanded wage increases that they had forgone for the sake of the war effort. In 1946, nearly 4.6 million workers went on strike, more than ever before in the United States. Strikes hit the automobile, steel, electrical, coal, and railroad industries, and affected nearly everyone in the country.

Although Truman agreed that workers deserved higher wages, he thought that their demands were inflationary. That is, he feared that such increases would push the prices of goods still higher. In his view, workers failed to understand that big wage increases might destroy the health of the economy.

In the spring of 1946, a railroad strike caused a major disruption in the economy. In response, Truman asked Congress for the power to draft the striking workers into the army. He would then be able to order them as soldiers to stay on the job. During his address to Congress, Truman received a note stating that the strike had ended "on terms proposed by the President."

Truman's White House took other steps to limit the power of labor unions as well. When John L. Lewis and his United Mine Workers defied a court order against a strike, the Truman administration asked a judge to serve Lewis with a contempt of court citation. The court fined Lewis $10,000 and his union $3.5 million.

Congress went even further than Truman: In 1947, it passed the **Taft-Hartley Act.** This act allowed the President to declare an 80-day cooling-off period during which strikers had to return to work, if the strikes were in industries that affected the national interest. Reflecting the widespread anti-Communist feelings gripping the United States at the time, the measure also required union officials to sign oaths that they were not Communists. Furious union leaders complained bitterly about the measure, and Truman vetoed it. Congress, however, passed the act over Truman's veto.

Truman's Fair Deal Truman had supported Roosevelt's New Deal, and now, playing on the well-known name, he devised a program he called the Fair Deal. The Fair Deal extended the New Deal's goals.

Truman agreed with FDR that government needed to play an active role in securing economic justice for all American citizens. As the war ended, he introduced a 21-point program that included legislation designed to promote full employment, a higher minimum wage, greater unemployment compensation for workers without jobs, housing assistance, and a variety of other items. Over the next ten weeks, Truman added more proposals to the Fair Deal. By early 1946, he had asked for a national health insurance program and legislation to control atomic energy.

Truman ran into tremendous political opposition in Congress from a coalition of conservative Democrats and Republicans. Opponents rejected the majority of the Fair Deal initiatives. One measure that passed was the Employment Act of 1946, which created a Council of Economic Advisors to advise the President.

As the 1946 midterm elections approached, it seemed to many people that Truman was little more than a bungling bureaucrat. Among the remarks often heard about Truman were, "You just sort of forget about Harry until he makes another mistake," and "To err is Truman," adapted

VIEWING HISTORY Truman sits at his desk in the White House. **Analyzing Information** *Why would Truman place a sign reading "The buck stops here" on his desk?*

The leader of the United Mine Workers, John Lewis (left), opposed the Taft-Hartley Act cosponsored by Senator Robert Taft (right).

from a well-known saying. Truman's support in one poll dropped from 87 percent just after he assumed the presidency to 32 percent in November 1946. The results of the 1946 elections reflected many people's feelings that Truman was not an effective leader. Republicans won majorities of both houses of Congress.

The 80th Congress battered the President for the next two years. Under the leadership of the conservative Republican senator Robert A. Taft of Ohio, commonly known as "Mr. Republican," the Republican Party worked hard to reduce the size and the power of the federal government, to decrease taxes, and to block Truman's liberal goals. On civil rights initiatives, in particular, Truman found opposition throughout his presidency.

VIEWING HISTORY Harry Truman became the first President ever to campaign in Harlem, the heart of New York City's African American community. The campaign button (top) supports his civil rights stance. **Synthesizing Information** *How did Truman's support of civil rights cause a split in the Democratic Party?*

Truman on Civil Rights While holding in private many of the racial prejudices he had learned growing up, Truman recognized that as President he had to take action on civil rights. In a letter to a friend, he wrote, "I am not asking for social equality, because no such things exist, but I am asking for equality of opportunity for all human beings, and, as long as I stay here, I am going to continue that fight."

Truman had publicly supported civil rights for many years. In September 1946, he met with a group of African American leaders to discuss the steps that needed to be taken to achieve their goals. They asked Truman to support a federal anti-lynching law, abolish the poll tax as a voting requirement, and establish a permanent board to prevent discriminatory practices in hiring. Congress refused to address any of these concerns, so in December 1946, Truman appointed a biracial Committee on Civil Rights to look into race relations. This group produced a report demanding action on the concerns listed above. It also recommended that a permanent civil rights commission be established.

With southerners in control of key congressional committees and threatening a filibuster, Congress took no action. In July 1948, Truman banned discrimination in the hiring of federal employees. He also ordered an end to segregation and discrimination in the armed forces. Real change came slowly, however. Only with the onset of the Korean War in 1950 did the armed forces make significant progress in ending segregation.

The Election of 1948

Truman decided to seek another term as President in 1948. He had no reason to expect victory, however, because even in his own party, his support was disintegrating. The southern wing of the Democratic Party, protesting a moderate civil rights plank in the party platform, split off from the main party. These segregationists formed the States' Rights, or Dixiecrat Party and nominated Governor J. Strom Thurmond of South Carolina for President.

Meanwhile, the liberal wing of the Democratic Party deserted Truman to follow Henry Wallace, who headed the Progressive Party ticket. Wallace had been Franklin Roosevelt's second Vice President, and many Democrats believed that he was the right person to carry out the measures begun by Roosevelt. Most recently Wallace had served as Truman's Secretary of Commerce. Wallace had resigned, however, because he did not support Truman's Cold War policies.

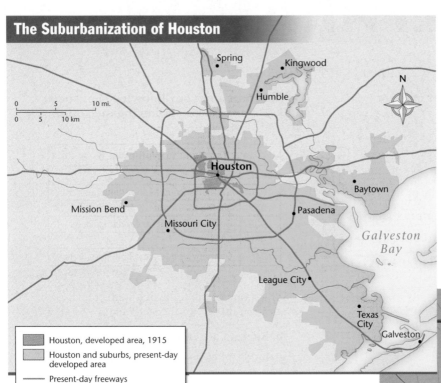

The Suburbanization of Houston

Spring
Kingwood
Humble
Houston
Baytown
Mission Bend
Pasadena
Missouri City
Galveston Bay
League City
Texas City
Galveston

0   5   10 mi.
0   5   10 km

N

Houston, developed area, 1915

Houston and suburbs, present-day developed area

Present-day freeways

One City's Example

In 1915, before most people owned cars, Houston, Texas, was a compact city, and most people walked or took a streetcar to work. With the growth in car ownership and the construction of freeways and suburban developments, Houston has expanded to cover a much larger area, organized around car travel and major highways.

A New Roadside Landscape

Billboards and retail businesses sprang up along suburban highways to serve a growing population of drivers.

Geographic Connection

How did the geography of cities and suburbs change as a result of growth along suburban highways?

New Commercial Centers

At first, suburbs were mainly residential, and people traveled into the city to shop and work. Then open-air malls were built to serve suburban shoppers. By the 1960s, covered malls and office parks had begun to replace traditional downtown city districts as places to shop and work.

Geographic Connection

How do you think the growth of suburban malls and roadside businesses affected traditional downtown businesses?

691

TEST PREPARATION

Write your answers on a separate sheet of paper.

1. Which one of the following is a correct statement about Stalin's "show trials" in the Soviet Union in the 1930s?

   A The rights of the accused were fully protected.

   B The juries always found Communists not guilty.

   C Guilt was determined before the trial began.

   D Few people were actually punished by the trials.

2. Why did British and French leaders follow a policy of appeasement when dealing with Germany?

   A They were not ready to fight a war with Hitler.

   B The two countries were following isolationist policies.

   C As Axis Powers, they could ignore the growing German strength.

   D Their main interests were in East Asia and not Western Europe.

> **"Never . . . was so much owed by so many to so few."**
>
> —Winston Churchill

3. British Prime Minister Winston Churchill was speaking about

   A American military forces who invaded France during D-Day.

   B British pilots who defeated the Germans in the Battle of Britain.

   C British troops who ended German expansion in North Africa.

   D Soviet soldiers who stopped the Germans in central Russia.

Use the chart and your knowledge of social studies to answer the following question.

The Road to World War II	
Year	Event
1936	Germany occupies the Rhineland
1938	Austria taken over by Germany
1938	Germany divides up Czechoslovakia
1939	???
1940	Germany invades and conquers France

4. Which one of the following items replaces the question marks on the chart?

   A England begins bombing raids on Germany.

   B Italy and Germany invade Spain.

   C Germany declares war on the Soviet Union.

   D Germany invades and conquers Poland.

5. During World War II, why did the government ration sugar, butter, and other foods?

   A To stop the Germans from buying up foods and exporting them to Germany

   B To prevent deflation of the nation's money

   C To make sure items in short supply were available for all people

   D To keep the military from getting more food than it needed

6. Which battle in World War II ended Japan's ability to carry out offensive operations in the Pacific?

   A Midway

   B Coral Sea

   C Leyte Gulf

   D Okinawa

Use the information in the map to answer the following question.

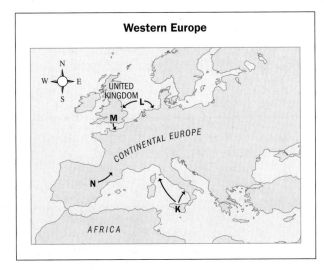

Western Europe

7. Which one of the arrows represents Operation Overlord on D-Day, June 6, 1944, when Western Europe was invaded by Allied forces?

A K

B L

C M

D N

"The President shall be Commander in Chief of the Army and Navy of the United States. . . ."

—Article II, Section 2, United States Constitution

---

8. This part of the United States Constitution provided the basis for President Harry S Truman to

A open up trade with China.

B make General Dwight Eisenhower the next President.

C help rebuild the Soviet Union after World War II.

D fire General Douglas MacArthur.

Use the information in the graph and your knowledge of social studies to answer the following question.

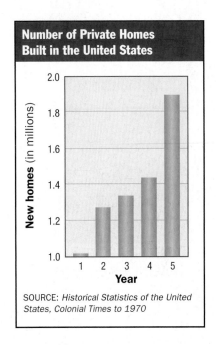

SOURCE: *Historical Statistics of the United States, Colonial Times to 1970*

9. The information on housing best describes which five-year period?

A 1931–1935

B 1936–1940

C 1941–1945

D 1946–1950

Writing Practice

10. What was the intended purpose of the U. S. Neutrality Acts passed during the 1930s? What was their actual effect? Explain why this happened.

11. What promises were made at the Yalta Conference and which of these were kept?

12. Describe three components of the Fair Deal as proposed by President Harry S Truman.

A Period of Turmoil and Change

(1950–1975)

"*In a democratic society like ours, relief must come through an aroused popular conscience that sears the conscience of the people's representatives.*"

Felix Frankfurter, Supreme Court Justice
Baker v. Carr, 1962

Thousands showed their support for the civil rights movement at the March on Washington in 1963. ▶

Chapter 21

The Civil Rights Movement (1950–1968)

This protester picketed a restaurant in Georgia.

American Events

1954
In a unanimous decision, the Supreme Court rules that segregation in public schools is unconstitutional in *Brown* v. *Board of Education of Topeka, Kansas.*

1955
Thousands of African Americans participate in the Montgomery, Alabama, bus boycott to protest discrimination in public transportation.

1957
Eisenhower sends troops to Little Rock, Arkansas, to facilitate integration at Central High School.

Presidential Terms: Harry S Truman 1945–1953   Dwight D. Eisenhower 1953–1961

1950   **1954**   **1958**

World Events
Vietnamese Communists defeat the French at Dien Bien Phu.

1954

Sudan becomes an independent nation.

1956

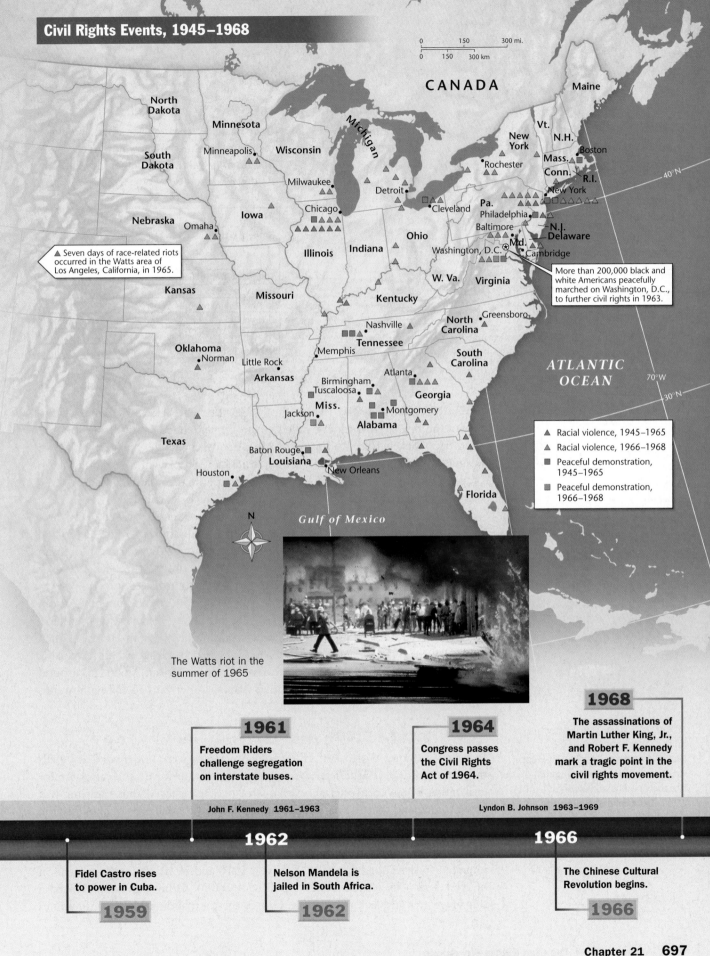

0   150   300 mi.
0   150   300 km

CANADA   Maine

North
Dakota
Minnesota   Vt.   N.H.
                                                     New   Boston
South   York   Mass.
Dakota   Minneapolis   Rochester   Conn.   R.I.
          Milwaukee   New York
                        Detroit   Pa.
Nebraska   Chicago   Cleveland   Philadelphia
          Omaha   Baltimore   N.J.
Iowa   Washington, D.C.   Md. Delaware
                                    Ohio   Cambridge

▲ Seven days of race-related riots
occurred in the Watts area of
Los Angeles, California, in 1965.   W. Va.   Virginia
                                                    More than 200,000 black and
Kansas   Missouri   Kentucky   white Americans peacefully
                                                    marched on Washington, D.C.,
                                   North   to further civil rights in 1963.
                        Nashville   Carolina Greensboro
Oklahoma   South
          Norman   Memphis   Carolina   ATLANTIC
          Little Rock Tennessee   OCEAN
Arkansas   Birmingham   Atlanta
                        Tuscaloosa   Georgia
                Jackson   Miss. Montgomery
Texas   Alabama
                Baton Rouge   ▲ Racial violence, 1945–1965
          Louisiana New Orleans   ▲ Racial violence, 1966–1968
Houston   ■ Peaceful demonstration,
                                                        1945–1965
                                        Florida   ■ Peaceful demonstration,
                                                        1966–1968
          N
                Gulf of Mexico

The Watts riot in the
summer of 1965

1968

The assassinations of
Martin Luther King, Jr.,
and Robert F. Kennedy
mark a tragic point in the
civil rights movement.

1961

Freedom Riders
challenge segregation
on interstate buses.

1964

Congress passes
the Civil Rights
Act of 1964.

John F. Kennedy 1961–1963   Lyndon B. Johnson 1963–1969

1962   **1966**

Fidel Castro rises
to power in Cuba.

Nelson Mandela is
jailed in South Africa.

The Chinese Cultural
Revolution begins.

1959   **1962**   **1966**

Demands for Civil Rights

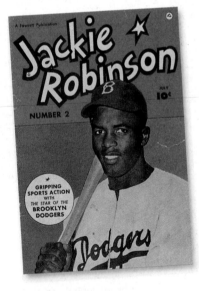

VIEWING HISTORY After his brilliant first season with the Brooklyn Dodgers, Jackie Robinson was featured on baseball cards like the one above, issued in 1951. **Determining Relevance** *How did Robinson's career serve the cause of civil rights?*

Setting the Scene In August 1945, Branch Rickey, the general manager of the Brooklyn Dodgers, called a young man named Jackie Robinson into his office. Rickey told Robinson of his plan to challenge the rule in Major League Baseball that required African Americans to play in a separate Negro League. Rickey wanted Robinson, a promising athlete in college and a World War II veteran, to be the first player to break the color barrier.

To test how Robinson would respond to the pressure he was likely to face, Rickey acted the part of those who might try to discourage him. He roared insults at Robinson and threatened him with violence. "Mr. Rickey," Robinson finally said, "do you want a ballplayer who's afraid to fight back?" Rickey answered, "I want a player with guts enough not to fight back."

In 1947, Robinson joined the Brooklyn Dodgers, becoming the first African American to play in the Major Leagues. Despite many instances of prejudice, Robinson behaved with dignity and had a sparkling first season. He was named Rookie of the Year in 1947. In 1949, he was voted the league's most valuable player. Just as important, Robinson fostered pride in African Americans around the country and paved the way for other African Americans to follow him into professional sports.

The Rise of African American Influence

Before and during World War II, African Americans were not treated as equals by a large portion of American society. After the war, however, the campaign for civil rights began to accelerate. Millions of people believed that the time had come to demand that the nation live up to its creed that all are equal before the law. Several factors contributed to this growing demand.

African American Migration After the Civil War, many African Americans migrated to large northern cities. Between 1910 and 1940, the black population of New York City leaped from 60,000 to 450,000. Other cities experienced a similar growth in black population. Out of these expanding black communities emerged a number of prominent African American citizens, including doctors and lawyers, who gained political influence. They were able to form alliances with political machines. In effect, they could offer their votes in return for social gains.

The New Deal During the Depression, Roosevelt and the Democrats began to court black votes and gain African Americans' support for New Deal policies. Under Roosevelt, the number of African Americans working for the federal government increased significantly.

World War II Perhaps the greatest stimulus to the changing racial climate in the United States was World War II. During the war, increased demands for labor in northern cities led to a rise in the black population in the North. This increase in numbers gave African Americans considerable voting power in some northern cities.

Another impact of World War II was ideological. The end of the war revealed the horrors of the Holocaust, and opened many people's eyes to the racism and discrimination taking place in the United States. This realization did not spread to everyone, nor did it have a sudden impact. Rather, these new ideas crept into the ideological climate of the country.

Rise of the NAACP Amidst these cultural changes, the NAACP—the National Association for the Advancement of Colored People—worked hard in the courts to challenge segregation laws throughout the country. For years the NAACP had tried to get the 1896 *Plessy v. Ferguson* decision overturned. That decision held that segregation of the races in public institutions and accommodations was constitutional as long as facilities were "separate but equal." In practice, equal facilities were rarely—if ever—the case.

One of the NAACP's greatest assets was its legal team. Leading the NAACP's Legal Defense Fund was Thurgood Marshall, who had joined the association in the 1930s. Known as "Mr. Civil Rights," Marshall fought many battles over segregation in the courts and achieved great gains. His success was bolstered by the support of an exceptional team of lawyers.

One lawyer in particular, Oliver Hill, from Virginia, won many civil rights suits that focused on issues of discrimination in education and wages. According to the *Washington Post*, Hill's team of lawyers had succeeded in winning more than $50 million in higher pay and better educational facilities for black students and teachers. Little by little, Marshall and Hill managed to chip away at the "separate but equal" clause of *Plessy v. Ferguson*. Finally, in 1951, they took on the greatest and most important fight of all.

Brown v. Board of Education

In 1951, Oliver Brown sued the Topeka, Kansas, Board of Education to allow his 8-year-old daughter Linda to attend a nearby school for whites only. Everyday, Linda walked past the school on her way to the bus that took her to a distant school for African Americans. After appeals, the case reached the Supreme Court. There, Thurgood Marshall argued on behalf of Brown and against segregation in America's schools.

On May 17, 1954, in ***Brown v. Board of Education of Topeka, Kansas,*** the Supreme Court issued its historic ruling.

READING CHECK
How did World War II affect African Americans in the United States?

VIEWING HISTORY Thurgood Marshall talks to reporters in New York City in 1955, after the Supreme Court ordered the desegregation of public schools. Marshall later became the first African American Supreme Court Justice.
Analyzing Information *How did Marshall's efforts lead to gains in civil rights and prepare him for the* Brown v. Board of Education *case?*

READING CHECK
What did the Supreme Court say about the "separate but equal" clause?

> **"** Does segregation of children in public schools solely on the basis of race . . . deprive the children of the minority group of equal educational opportunities? We believe that it does. . . . To separate them from others of similar age and qualifications solely because of their race generates a feeling of inferiority as to their status in the community that may affect their hearts and minds in a way unlikely to ever be undone. . . . We conclude that in the field of public education the doctrine of 'separate but equal' has no place. Separate educational facilities are inherently unequal. **"**
>
> —Chief Justice Earl Warren

In a unanimous decision, the Court declared that the "separate but equal" doctrine was unconstitutional and could not be applied to public education. A year later, the Court ruled that local school boards should move to desegregate "with all deliberate speed."

Reaction to *Brown* v. *Board of Education*

The public's reaction to the Supreme Court's ruling was mixed. African Americans rejoiced. Many white Americans, even if they did not agree, accepted the decision and hoped that desegregation could take place peacefully. President Eisenhower, who privately disagreed with the *Brown* ruling, said only that "the Supreme Court has spoken and I am sworn to uphold the constitutional processes in this country, and I am trying. I will obey." Not everyone, however, was willing to obey.

The ruling in *Brown* v. *Board of Education* caused many southern whites, especially in the Deep South, to react with fear and angry resistance. In Georgia, Governor Herman Talmadge made it clear that his state would "not tolerate the mixing of the races in the public schools or any other tax-supported institutions." The Ku Klux Klan also became more active, threatening those who advocated acceptance of the *Brown* decision. The congressional representatives of states in the Deep South joined together in March 1956 to protest the Supreme Court's order to desegregate public schools.

More than 90 members of Congress expressed their opposition to the Court's ruling in what was known as the "Southern Manifesto." The congressmen asserted

MAP SKILLS Many states were slow to integrate their public schools after the *Brown* decision. **Place** *Which states had the highest increase in the percentage of African Americans attending integrated schools?*

African Americans Attending Integrated Southern Schools

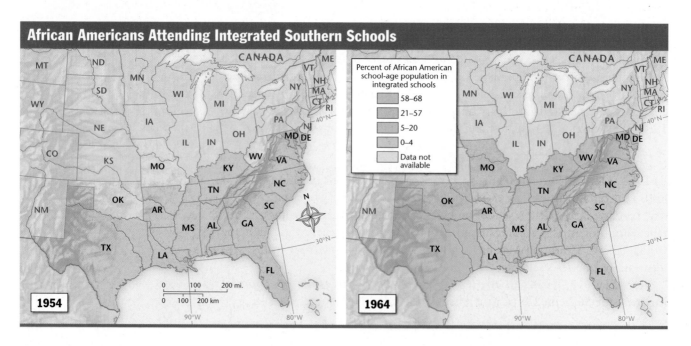

Percent of African American school-age population in integrated schools
- 58–68
- 21–57
- 5–20
- 0–4
- Data not available

1954

1964

that the Supreme Court had overstepped its bounds and had "no legal basis for such action." The decision, they claimed, violated states' rights and was an example of "judicial usurpation." Many believed that desegregation would lead to violence and chaos in several southern states. As a result, they refused to comply with the court's ruling:

> 66 We pledge ourselves to use all lawful means to bring about a reversal of this decision, which is contrary to the Constitution, and to prevent the use of force in its implementation. 99
>
> —From the Congressional Record, 84th Congress, 2nd session

The Montgomery Bus Boycott

In 1955, the nation's attention shifted from the courts to the streets of Montgomery, Alabama. In December, Rosa Parks, a seamstress who had been the secretary of the Montgomery NAACP for 12 years, took a seat at the front of the "colored" section of a bus. The front of the bus was reserved for white passengers. African Americans, however, were expected to give up their seats for white passengers if no seats were available in the "whites only" section. When a white man got on at the next stop and had no seat, the bus driver ordered Parks to give up hers. She refused. Even when threatened with arrest, she held her ground. At the next stop, police seized her and ordered her to stand trial for violating the segregation laws.

Civil rights leaders in Montgomery quickly met and, after Jo Ann Robinson of the Women's Political Council (WPC) suggested the idea, decided to organize the **Montgomery bus boycott.** The plan called for African Americans to refuse to use the entire bus system until the bus company agreed to change its segregation policy. Robinson and other members of the WPC wrote and distributed leaflets announcing the boycott. Martin Luther King, Jr., the 26-year-old minister of the Baptist church where the original boycott meeting took place, soon became the spokesperson for the protest movement. He proclaimed:

Rosa Parks's arrest in 1955 touched off the successful Montgomery bus boycott. Here, one year later, she smiles after the Supreme Court ruled bus segregation to be unconstitutional.

> 66 There comes a time when people get tired . . . tired of being segregated and humiliated, tired of being kicked about by the brutal feet of oppression. We have no alternative but to protest. 99
>
> —Martin Luther King, Jr.

The morning of the first day of the boycott, King roamed the streets of Montgomery. He was anxious to see how many African Americans would participate, and recorded his observations:

> 66 During the rush hours the sidewalks were crowded with laborers and domestic workers, many of them well past middle age, trudging patiently to their jobs and home again, sometimes as much as twelve miles. They knew why they walked, and the knowledge was evident in the way they carried themselves. And as I watched them I knew that there is nothing more majestic than the determined courage of individuals willing to suffer and sacrifice for their freedom and dignity. 99
>
> —Martin Luther King, Jr.

Over the next year, 50,000 African Americans in Montgomery walked, rode bicycles, or joined car pools to avoid the city buses. Despite losing money,

The Boycott

The boycott has often been an effective form of protest throughout United States history. When Britain passed the Stamp Act in 1765, the colonists responded by organizing a boycott of certain British goods. The boycott proved to be effective when the British merchants who had lost profits on their goods pressured Parliament into repealing the act.

The actual term "boycott" did not come into use until the 1880s in Ireland. A land agent there, Charles Boycott, had refused to comply with a new land reform law designed to lower rents. As a result, his tenants and employees turned against him. He soon found himself isolated and poor.

In modern times, boycotts are often initiated to protest the actions of corporations. Recently, a successful boycott was waged on the tuna industry. The nets used to catch tuna had killed many dolphins and raised environmental concerns. Now, almost all commercial tuna fishing is "dolphin-friendly." Other boycotts have centered around religious, political, and civil or human rights issues.

? **Why do you think boycotts are effective? What types of boycotts are the hardest for boycotters to endure? Explain.**

U.S. Department of Commerce

Dolphin Safe

---

the bus company refused to change its policies. Finally, in 1956, the Supreme Court ruled that bus segregation, like school segregation, was unconstitutional.

The Montgomery bus boycott encouraged a new generation of leaders in the African American community, most notably Martin Luther King, Jr. In addition, it gave minority groups hope that steps toward equality could be made through peaceful protest.

Resistance in Little Rock

In the fall of 1957, Arkansas Governor Orval Faubus declared that he could not keep order if he had to enforce **integration,** or the bringing together of different races. In blatant defiance of the Supreme Court's *Brown* decision, Governor Faubus posted Arkansas National Guard troops at Central High School in Little Rock, Arkansas, and instructed them to turn away the nine African American students who were supposed to attend the school that year. Outside the school, mobs of angry protesters gathered to prevent the entry of the black students. One of those students, 15-year-old Elizabeth Eckford, remembered that day:

VIEWING HISTORY African American students like Elizabeth Eckford (below, right) had to endure the insults of white students who disagreed with the the Court's *Brown* v. *Board* decision. **Recognizing Cause and Effect** *What finally caused President Eisenhower to support desegregation?*

66 *[The Arkansas national guardsmen] glared at me with a mean look and I was very frightened and didn't know what to do. I turned around and the crowd came toward me. They moved closer and closer. Somebody started yelling 'Lynch her! Lynch her!' I tried to see a friendly face somewhere in the mob—someone who maybe would help. I looked into the face of an old woman and it seemed a kind face, but when I looked at her again, she spat on me.* 99

—Elizabeth Eckford

Although President Eisenhower was not an ally of the civil rights movement, Faubus's actions were a direct challenge to the Constitution and to Eisenhower's authority as President. Eisenhower acted by placing the National Guard under federal command. He then sent soldiers to Arkansas to protect the nine students. In a speech to the nation on September 24, 1957, Eisenhower told the nation that his actions were necessary to defend the authority of the Supreme Court.

Other Voices of Protest

African Americans were not the only minority group to demand equal rights. The League of United Latin American Citizens (LULAC), founded in 1929, also struggled to achieve equality for Hispanics. When a funeral home in Texas refused to bury Felix Longoria, a World War II veteran, LULAC protested. Longoria was finally buried in Arlington National Cemetery. Other groups, including the Community Service Organization and the Asociación Nacional México-Americana, also worked to bring about improvements for Mexican Americans.

Like African American children in southern states, Mexican American children often attended inferior segregated public schools. Gonzalo and Felicitas Méndez of Orange County, California, sued their school district over this discrimination. In 1947, a Federal District Court judge ruled that segregating Mexican American students was unconstitutional. Soon thereafter, attorney Gus Garcia filed a similar lawsuit in Texas. That case, *Delgado* v. *Bastrop ISD*, made the segregation of Mexican American children in Texas illegal as well. LULAC was involved in both of these lawsuits.

Native Americans faced a unique situation. The federal government managed the reservations where most Native Americans lived in terrible poverty. In 1953, however, the government adopted a new approach, known as "termination," which sought to eliminate reservations altogether. The government's goal was to assimilate Native Americans into the mainstream of American life.

The policy of termination met with resistance, and in time the federal government discarded it. Yet the problems of the Native Americans remained: poverty, discrimination, and little real political representation. For Native Americans, the civil rights advances of the 1950s were mere tokens of the real gains that were needed.

Focus on CITIZENSHIP

Dr. Hector Garcia
When Latino veterans returned to the United States from battle in World War II, they faced discrimination and prejudice at every turn. Latino veterans were often denied employment, housing, and military benefits afforded to white Americans. Many were still denied the right to vote and hold office.

Dr. Hector P. Garcia, who served as a combat surgeon during the war, decided that he had to act. In 1948, with the assistance of LULAC, he organized a group that would protect the rights of Latino veterans: the American G.I. Forum. Through the years, the G.I. Forum worked tirelessly to battle discrimination and improve conditions for Latinos in the United States. The Forum's activities included providing funds for higher education, raising money to help poor Latinos pay poll taxes so they could vote, and winning a Supreme Court case allowing Latinos to serve on juries. Today, the G.I. Forum continues to thrive as it works to promote and protect Latino rights.

Section 1 Assessment

READING COMPREHENSION

1. What was the principle behind the Supreme Court's ruling in **Brown v. Board of Education?**

2. What were the goals of the Southern Manifesto?

3. How did President Eisenhower react to the incident over **integration** in Little Rock, Arkansas?

4. How did Mexican Americans and Native Americans assert their rights in the 1950s?

CRITICAL THINKING AND WRITING

5. Making Comparisons The Montgomery bus boycott proved to be an effective form of nonviolent protest against segregation. Can you find other examples of effective boycotts in American history?

6. Writing a News Story Take the position of a reporter stationed at Central High School in Little Rock, Arkansas, on the day when nine African American students are to be integrated into the school. Write a brief news story describing the scene.

Go Online
PHSchool.com

For: An activity on *Brown* v. *Board of Education*
Visit: PHSchool.com
Web Code: mrd-9281

Leaders and Strategies

READING FOCUS

- How did early groups lay the groundwork for the civil rights movement?

- What was the philosophy of non-violence?

- How did SNCC give students a voice in the civil rights movement?

MAIN IDEA

The civil rights movement of the 1960s consisted of many separate groups and leaders. While the methods used by these groups differed, they shared the same goal of securing equal rights for all Americans.

KEY TERMS

interracial
Congress of Racial
 Equality (CORE)
Southern Christian
 Leadership Conference
 (SCLC)
nonviolent protest
Student Nonviolent
 Coordinating Committee
 (SNCC)

TARGET READING SKILL

Identify Main Ideas As you read, complete the chart below listing the prominent civil rights organizations in the early 1960s and their goals and characteristics.

Civil Rights Group	Features
NAACP	Focused on gaining legal equality. Appealed mainly to middle- and upper-class African Americans.
National Urban League	
CORE	
SCLC	
SNCC	

Setting the Scene

VIEWING HISTORY The NAACP was one of many civil rights groups committed to improving the status of African Americans. **Analyzing Visual Information** *(a) How are the images in this poster intended to rally support for the NAACP? (b) What does the poster tell you about the goals of this organization?*

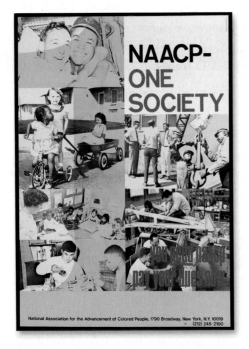

NAACP-
ONE
SOCIETY

National Association for the Advancement of Colored People, 1790 Broadway, New York, N.Y. 10019 • (212) 245-2100

66 *It really hit me when I was fifteen years old, when I heard about Martin Luther King, Jr., and the Montgomery bus boycott. Black people were walking the streets for more than a year rather than riding segregated buses. To me it was like a great sense of hope, a light. . . . That more than any other event was the turning point for me, I think. It gave me a way out.*

When I graduated from high school, I enrolled at the American Baptist Theological Seminary in Nashville. . . . While I was there I began attending these workshops, studying the philosophy and discipline of nonviolence: the life and times of Gandhi, the works of Henry Thoreau, and the philosophy of civil disobedience. And we began to think about how we could apply these lessons to the problem of segregation. 99

—John Lewis

In the 1960s, many young people, like John Lewis, became active in the struggle for civil rights. They knew that battling segregation and gaining civil rights would require organization and strong commitment.

Laying the Groundwork

The civil rights movement of the 1950s and 1960s was a grass-roots effort of ordinary citizens determined to end racial injustice in the United States. Although no central organization directed the movement, several major groups formed to share information and coordinate civil rights activities. Each of these groups had its own priorities, strategies, and ways of operating, but they all helped to focus the energies of thousands of Americans committed to securing civil rights for all citizens.

NAACP Behind the case of *Brown* v. *Board of Education* was the National Association for the Advancement of Colored People (NAACP), one of the oldest civil rights organizations in the United States. The group formed in 1909 as an **interracial** organization—one with both African Americans and white Americans as members.

W.E.B. Du Bois, a prominent African American scholar, was a founding member. Du Bois had been the first African American to receive a doctoral degree from Harvard University. He served as the NAACP's director of publicity and research and also edited the NAACP magazine, *Crisis*. Du Bois summarized the NAACP's goals this way:

> 66 *The main object of this association is to secure for colored people, and particularly for Americans of Negro descent, free and equal participation in the democracy of modern culture. This means the clearing away of obstructions to such participation . . . and it means also the making of a world democracy in which all men may participate.* 99
>
> —W.E.B. Du Bois

From the start, the NAACP focused on challenging the laws that prevented African Americans from exercising their full rights as citizens. The NAACP worked to secure full legal equality for all Americans and to remove barriers that kept them from voting.

In the 1920s and 1930s, lynching was still a threat to African Americans, particularly in the South. Working to end such violence, the NAACP succeeded in getting two anti-lynching bills passed by the House of Representatives in the 1930s. Southern leaders in the Senate prevented the bills from becoming law, but the NAACP continued to keep the issue of lynching in the public eye.

The NAACP was more successful in its lawsuits that challenged segregation laws. In the 1920s and 1930s, it won a number of legal battles in the areas of housing and education.

The NAACP appealed mainly to educated, middle- and upper-class African Americans and some liberal white Americans. Critics charged that it was out of touch with the basic issues of economic survival faced by many poorer African Americans.

National Urban League One organization that took on economic issues was the National Urban League, founded in 1911. The League sought to assist people moving to major American cities. It helped African Americans moving out of the South find homes and jobs and ensured that they received fair treatment at work. League workers also looked for migrant families on ship docks and at train stations and found safe, clean apartments for them. They also insisted that factory owners and union leaders allow African American workers the opportunity to learn the skills that could lead to better jobs.

CORE Founded by pacifists in 1942, the **Congress of Racial Equality (CORE)** was dedicated to bringing about change through peaceful confrontation. It too was interracial, with both African American and white members. During World War II, CORE organized demonstrations against segregation in cities including Baltimore, Chicago, Denver, and Detroit.

In the years after World War II, CORE director James Farmer worked without pay in order to keep the organization alive. The growing interest in civil rights in the 1950s gave him a new base of support and allowed him to

STUDENT NONVIOLENT COORDINATING COMMITTEE
WE SHALL OVERCOME

Focus on CULTURE

"We Shall Overcome" The anthem of the civil rights movement, which brought together activists from all backgrounds, similarly arose through a combination of diverse efforts. "We Shall Overcome" has its roots in an African American spiritual from the days of slavery and from a gospel song called "I'll Overcome Someday," by Minister Charles Albert Tindley.

In 1945, tobacco strikers in South Carolina adopted the song, which had been passed by oral tradition down through the generations. The song later reached white folk singers Pete Seeger and Guy Carawan, who changed the lyrics and altered the melody. They renamed the song "We Shall Overcome," and began teaching it to young activists. The song spread quickly across the nation, unifying all those fighting for civil rights. The successful folk group Peter, Paul, and Mary made the song popular to audiences across the country.

"We Shall Overcome" soon became not only a symbol of the movement, but also a source of pride and determination. An SCLC leader remarked: "You really have to experience it to understand the kind of power it has for us. When you get through singing it, you could walk over a bed of hot coals, and you wouldn't even feel it!"

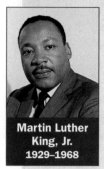

Martin Luther King, Jr.
1929–1968

Born in Atlanta, Georgia, in 1929, King grew up amid all the symbols of southern segregation—separate schools, stores, churches, and public places. Although he had white playmates as a child, those social ties ended when he reached school age. King's father, Martin Luther King, Sr., and his grandfather were both prominent and respected Baptist preachers. He was raised with a sense of personal pride and dignity that went beyond the limitations of segregation.

Even in high school, young Martin was an inspiring and eloquent public speaker. Graduating early from high school, he went to Morehouse College in Atlanta. He earned a divinity degree at Crozer Theological Seminary in Pennsylvania, and then a doctorate in theology at Boston University in 1955. There he met and married Coretta Scott.

King's opponents attacked him physically and verbally, and he often went to jail for his beliefs. Death threats were frequent. As King had sometimes predicted, he did not live to see the success of the movement. He was assassinated in Memphis, Tennessee, in April 1968, at the age of 39. King's accused killer, a white southerner named James Earl Ray, was convicted in 1969 and sentenced to 99 years in prison.

turn CORE into a national organization, one that would play a major role in the confrontations that lay ahead.

The Philosophy of Nonviolence

Growing opposition to the gains made by African Americans through the *Brown* decision and the Montgomery bus boycott resulted in increasing violence and hostility toward African Americans. Even so, rising new leaders such as Martin Luther King, Jr., preached a philosophy of nonviolence. They asked anyone involved in the fight for civil rights not to retaliate with violence out of fear or hate.

The SCLC   In 1957, Martin Luther King, Jr., and other African American clergymen began a new and significant civil rights organization, the **Southern Christian Leadership Conference (SCLC).** SCLC advocated the practice of **nonviolent protest,** a peaceful way of protesting against restrictive racial policies. Nonviolent protesters do not resist even when attacked by opponents. In its first official statement, SCLC set out this principle:

❝ *To understand that nonviolence is not a symbol of weakness or cowardice, but as Jesus demonstrated, nonviolent resistance transforms weakness into strength and breeds courage in the face of danger.* ❞
—SCLC statement

SCLC shifted the focus of the civil rights movement to the South. Earlier organizations had been dominated by northerners. Now southern African American church leaders moved into the forefront of the struggle for equal rights. Among them, Martin Luther King, Jr., became a national figure. (See the American Biography on this page.)

Dr. King Leads the Way   When the Montgomery bus boycott began, Martin Luther King, Jr., was a young Baptist preacher. Within a few years he would become one of the most loved and admired—and also one of the most hated—people in the United States. King became not only a leader in the African American civil rights movement but also a symbol of nonviolent protest for the entire world.

As he became more and more involved in the civil rights movement, King was influenced by the beliefs of Mohandas K. Gandhi. Gandhi had been a leader in India's long struggle to gain independence from Great Britain, an effort that finally succeeded in 1947. Gandhi preached a philosophy of nonviolence as the only way to achieve victory against much stronger foes. Those who fight for justice must peacefully refuse to obey unjust laws, Gandhi taught. They must remain nonviolent, regardless of the violent reactions such peaceful resistance might provoke—a tactic that requires tremendous discipline and courage.

The philosophy of protest advocated by King had other sources as well. American author Henry David Thoreau had been an advocate of civil disobedience in the mid-1800s. Thoreau, who opposed the 1846 war with Mexico, refused to pay his taxes, and as a result, was jailed. He then wrote about this experience and the principles behind his actions in his famous essay "Civil Disobedience."

As the Montgomery boycott ended and boycotters prepared to ride the newly integrated buses, King began training volunteers for what they might expect in the months ahead. Films, songs, and skits showed Gandhi's activities and demonstrated the success of passive resistance in India. Bus riders were advised to follow 17 rules for maintaining a nonviolent approach in case they encountered confrontations on the buses as they traveled through the South. These rules included the following:

> 66 *Pray for guidance and commit yourself to complete nonviolence in word and action as you enter the bus. . . . Be loving enough to absorb evil and understanding enough to turn an enemy into a friend. . . . If cursed, do not curse back. If pushed, do not push back. If struck, do not strike back, but evidence love and good will at all times. . . . If another person is being molested, do not arise to go to his defense, but pray for the oppressor and use moral and spiritual force to carry on the struggle for justice. . . .* 99
>
> —Leaflet distributed throughout the city

As a result of his role in the Montgomery boycott, King gained national prominence. He went on to play a key role in almost every major civil rights event. His work earned him the Nobel peace prize in 1964.

A New Voice for Students

Nonviolent protest was a practical strategy in the civil rights struggle. It also represented a moral philosophy. "To accept passively an unjust system is to cooperate with that system; thereby the oppressed become as evil as the oppressor," King said. "Noncooperation with evil is as much a moral obligation as is cooperation with good."

The Formation of SNCC A new, student organization conceived by the SCLC took a somewhat different approach. The **Student Nonviolent Coordinating Committee,** usually known as **SNCC** (pronounced "snick"), began in 1960 at a meeting in Raleigh, North Carolina, for students active in the struggle. SCLC executive director Ella Baker thought that the NAACP and SCLC were not keeping up with the demands of young African Americans. She wanted to give them a way to play an even greater role in the civil rights movement.

Nearly 200 students showed up for the first SNCC meeting. Most came from southern communities, but some northerners attended as well. Baker delivered the opening address. "The younger generation is challenging you and me," she told the adults present. "They are asking us to forget our laziness and doubt and fear, and follow our dedication to the truth to the bitter end."

Martin Luther King, Jr., spoke next to the young audience, calling the civil rights movement "a revolt against the apathy and complacency of adults in the Negro community. . . ." At the end of the meeting, the participants organized a temporary coordinating committee.

A month later, student leaders met with Baker and other SCLC and CORE leaders and voted to maintain their independence from other civil rights groups. By the end of the year, the Student Nonviolent Coordinating Committee was a permanent and separate organization. It was interracial at first, though that changed in later years.

READING CHECK
What led to the formation of SNCC?

VIEWING HISTORY Robert Moses helped train SNCC volunteers in Ohio in 1964. **Drawing Conclusions** *Why was Bob Moses well suited to be a leader of SNCC?*

SNCC filled its own niche in the American civil rights movement. The focus of the civil rights movement shifted away from church leaders alone and gave young activists a chance to make decisions about priorities and tactics. SNCC also sought more immediate change, as opposed to the gradual change advocated by most of the older organizations.

Robert Moses One of SNCC's most influential leaders was Robert Moses, a Harvard graduate student and a mathematics teacher in Harlem. As the civil rights movement developed, he wanted to be involved. He first went to work for SNCC in Atlanta, and later headed for Mississippi to recruit black and white volunteers to help rural blacks register to vote.

While Martin Luther King, Jr., spoke with eloquence and passion, Moses was more soft-spoken. He took time to gather his thoughts, and then he spoke slowly. Todd Gitlin, a white student-activist leader, later noted that Moses was loved and trusted "precisely because he seemed humble, ordinary, accessible." Gitlin went on to describe Moses's style of oratory:

> 66 *He liked to make his points with his hand, starting with palm down-turned, then opening his hand outward toward his audience, as if delivering the point for inspection, nothing up his sleeve. The words seemed to be extruded [thrust forth], with difficulty, out of his depths. What he said seemed earned. . . . To teach his unimportance, he was wont [accustomed] to crouch in the corner or speak from the back of the room, hoping to hear the popular voice reveal itself.* 99
>
> —Todd Gitlin

With fresh new ideas and strong leaders like Bob Moses, SNCC became a strong and vital organization for students wanting to take part in the civil rights movement. As the struggle intensified, SNCC became a powerful force, and many students found that they would risk almost anything for their beliefs.

Section 2 Assessment

READING COMPREHENSION

1. What functions did the National Urban League and **CORE** serve for African Americans?

2. What was Dr. King's approach to civil rights?

3. What role did **SNCC** play in the movement?

4. Why was Bob Moses an effective leader?

CRITICAL THINKING AND WRITING

5. **Determining Relevance** What do you think are some of the strengths and weaknesses of nonviolent protest as a means to bring about social change?

6. **Writing a List** As a student in the 1960s, you have been asked to help organize a local chapter of SNCC. Write an agenda for organizing such a group, listing strategies you would use to recruit members and to work for change.

For: An activity on civil rights organizations
Visit: PHSchool.com
Web Code: mrd-9282

The Struggle Intensifies

READING FOCUS

- What were the goals of sit-ins and Freedom Rides?

- What was the reaction to James Meredith's integration at the University of Mississippi?

- How did the events in Birmingham, Alabama, affect the nation's attitudes toward the civil rights movement?

MAIN IDEA

The tactics of nonviolent protest, including sit-ins and boycotts, challenged segregation and brought change, but also generated violent confrontations.

KEY TERMS

sit-in
Freedom Ride

TARGET READING SKILL

Identify Main Ideas Copy this flowchart. As you read, fill in the boxes with the tactics and outcomes of the civil rights protests mentioned in this section.

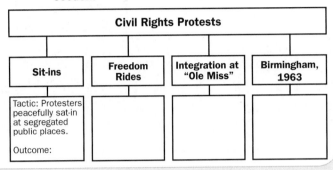

Civil Rights Protests			
Sit-ins	**Freedom Rides**	**Integration at "Ole Miss"**	**Birmingham, 1963**
Tactic: Protesters peacefully sat-in at segregated public places. Outcome:			

Setting the Scene

As a child in the rural Mississippi town of Centreville, Anne Moody grew up wondering what "the white folks' secret" was. "Their homes were large and beautiful with indoor toilets and every other convenience that I knew of at the time," she observed. "Every house I had ever lived in was a one- or two-room shack with an outdoor toilet." Moody was horrified when 14-year-old Emmett Till, visiting from Chicago, was killed in Mississippi supposedly because he had whistled at a white woman.

While in college, Moody became involved in the civil rights movement. She joined the NAACP and also worked with CORE and SNCC. She took part in the first sit-ins in Jackson, Mississippi, in 1963. Like so many other students in the 1960s, Moody was jailed for taking part in civil rights demonstrations.

Worse was the reaction from her family at home. Her mother, afraid for the lives of her relatives, begged Moody to end her involvement with the civil rights movement. The local sheriff had warned that Moody should never return to her hometown. Moody's brother had been beaten up and almost lynched by a group of white boys. Her sister angrily told her that her activism was threatening the life of every African American in Centreville.

Against all that resistance, Moody persevered. She participated in demonstrations, helped force the desegregation of local facilities, and remained determined to do everything she could to make the South a better place for African Americans. But it was never easy, and the gains came at tremendous personal cost. Like many other Americans committed to changing society through nonviolent means, Moody learned that challenging white supremacy often provoked an ugly and violent reaction.

Sit-ins Challenge Segregation

As you read in an earlier chapter, the Congress of Racial Equality (CORE) created the **sit-in** in 1943 to desegregate the Jack Spratt Coffee House in Chicago. In this technique, a group of CORE members simply sat down at a segregated lunch counter or other public place. If they were refused service at first, they simply stayed where they were.

Anne Moody joined a SNCC voter registration drive during her first year at Tougaloo College. She said of her fellow SNCC workers, "I had never known people so willing and determined to help others."

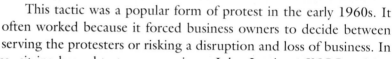

CITY CAFE
COLORED ENTRANCE

This tactic was a popular form of protest in the early 1960s. It often worked because it forced business owners to decide between serving the protesters or risking a disruption and loss of business. In some places, sit-ins brought strong reactions. John Lewis, a SNCC activist, participated in sit-ins in Nashville, Tennessee, in the 1960s. He remembered the experience:

> 66 *It was a Woolworth in the heart of the downtown area, and we occupied every seat at the lunch counter, every seat in the restaurant. . . . A group of young white men came in and they started pulling and beating primarily the young women. They put lighted cigarettes down their backs, in their hair, and they were really beating people. In a short time police officials came in and placed all of us under arrest, and not a single member of the white group, the people that were opposing our sit-in, was arrested.* 99
>
> —John Lewis

Soon, thousands of students were involved in the sit-in campaign, which gained the support of SCLC. Martin Luther King, Jr., told students that arrest was a "badge of honor." By the end of 1960, some 70,000 students had participated in sit-ins, and 3,600 had served time in jail. The protests began a process of change that could not be stopped.

The Freedom Rides

In *Boynton* v. *Virginia* (1960), the Supreme Court expanded its earlier ban on segregation on interstate buses. As a result, bus station waiting rooms and restaurants that served interstate travelers could not be segregated either.

In 1961, CORE, with aid from SNCC, organized and carried out the **Freedom Rides.** They were designed to test whether southern states would obey the Supreme Court ruling and allow African Americans to exercise the rights newly granted to them.

Violence Greets the Riders The first Freedom Ride departed Washington, D.C., on May 4, 1961. Thirteen freedom riders, both African Americans and

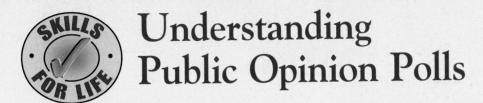

Understanding Public Opinion Polls

Elected officials are always interested in public opinion—first, so they can support the policies their constituents favor; and second, so they can be reelected. Public opinion polls that use scientific polling techniques are a good way of finding out what the public thinks at a particular time and how these opinions change over time. Professional polling organizations follow a complex process to provide reliable public opinion data. In the 1960s, civil rights was a divisive issue. Samples of polling about civil rights conducted by the Gallup Organization appear at right.

LEARN THE SKILL

Use the following steps to understand opinion polls:

1. **Define the universe being polled.** In polling, a *universe* is the whole population that the poll aims to measure—for example, all adults in the country or all the members of a political party or region. After defining the universe, pollsters interview a randomly selected sample of people representing that universe. Unless noted, the universe is assumed to be all the adults in the nation or region being polled.

2. **Examine the questions.** Polling questions should be simply worded and objective, and should not lead toward a particular answer.

3. **Analyze the results.** If they include answers from subgroups of the universe, ask yourself why the pollster chose these groups. What are the differences between the groups? Use your knowledge of the historical period to determine what events might have affected results. Consider how the polling results might be used by a politician or other decision-maker.

PRACTICE THE SKILL

Answer the following questions:

1. **(a)** What is the universe of Poll C? **(b)** Of Poll D? **(c)** What subgroup is singled out in Poll A?

2. **(a)** How is the first question in Poll C different from the questions in the other polls? **(b)** Why do you think the pollster gives "No opinion" or "Don't know" as options? **(c)** Do you think the polls contain any leading questions? Explain.

3. **(a)** Why do you think Poll A breaks out only one region of the country? **(b)** Why do you think the pollster asks the same question in Polls B and D? **(c)** What kind of information can you learn from Poll C that you cannot learn from the others? **(d)** How might decision-makers or candidates use each of these polls?

A. Integration, June 23, 1961

The United States Supreme Court has ruled that racial segregation in the public schools is illegal. This means that all children, no matter what their race, must be allowed to go to the same schools. Do you approve or disapprove of this decision?

		South Only
Approve.............62%		Approve..........24%
Disapprove.........33%		Disapprove.....69%
No opinion...........5%		No opinion........7%

B. Integration, Nov. 14, 1962

Do you think the Kennedy Administration is pushing racial integration too fast, or not fast enough?

Too fast.............42%	About right......31%
Not fast enough...12%	No opinion.......15%

C. Most Important Problem, Oct. 2, 1963

What do you think is the most important problem facing this country today?

Racial problems.............52%
International problems (Russia—threat of war)........25
Unemployment........5
Cost of living...........3
Other problems.....13
Don't know.............5
_____
108%

Which political party do you think can do a better job of handling the problem you just mentioned—the Republican Party or the Democratic Party?

Democratic........30%
Republican........20
No opinion........50

(Note: table [at left] adds to more than 100% since some persons named more than one problem.)

D. Integration, Oct. 13, 1963

Do you think the Kennedy Administration is pushing integration too fast, or not fast enough?

Too fast.............50%	About right......27%
Not fast enough...11%	No opinion.......12%

APPLY THE SKILL

See the Chapter Review and Assessment for another opportunity to apply this skill.

The Political Response

READING FOCUS

- What was President Kennedy's approach to civil rights?

- Why did civil rights leaders propose a march on Washington?

- What were the goals of the Civil Rights Act of 1964?

- How did African Americans fight to gain voting rights?

MAIN IDEA

Continuous civil rights protests in the 1960s gradually made politicians respond to public opinion and move forward with strong civil rights legislation.

KEY TERMS

March on Washington
filibuster
cloture
Civil Rights Act of 1964
Voting Rights Act of 1965
Twenty-fourth Amendment

TARGET READING SKILL

Paraphrase As you read, complete this chart by paraphrasing some of the provisions of major civil rights legislation passed in the 1960s.

Legislation	Provisions
Civil Rights Act of 1964	• Increased Justice Department authority to enforce school desegregation and ensure fair voting practices •
Voting Rights Act of 1965	
Twenty-fourth Amendment	

Setting the Scene

In October 1960, just weeks before the presidential election, John F. Kennedy had an opportunity to make a powerful gesture of goodwill toward African Americans. Martin Luther King, Jr., had been arrested in Georgia and sentenced to four months of hard labor. His family feared for his life in the prison camp. Kennedy called Coretta Scott King, Dr. King's wife, and offered his help. Then, Robert Kennedy, John's younger brother, persuaded the Georgia sentencing judge to release King on bail. Word of the Kennedys' actions spread quickly throughout the African American community, and many switched their votes from Nixon to Kennedy. These votes were crucial in Kennedy's slim margin of victory in the election.

Kennedy on Civil Rights

As a senator from Massachusetts, John F. Kennedy had voted for civil rights measures but had never actively pushed the issue. During his presidential campaign, however, Kennedy had sought and won many African American votes with bold rhetoric. In 1960, he proclaimed, "If the President does not himself wage the struggle for equal rights—if he stands above the battle—then the battle will inevitably be lost."

Once in office, however, Kennedy moved slowly on issues such as fair housing. He did not want to anger southern Democratic senators whose votes he needed on other issues. Yet Kennedy did appoint a number of African Americans to prominent positions. For example, Thurgood Marshall, who would later become the first African American Supreme Court Justice, joined the United States Circuit Court under Kennedy. At the same time, however, Kennedy also named a number of segregationists to federal courts.

As the civil rights movement gained momentum and violence began to spread, Kennedy could no longer avoid the issue. He was deeply disturbed by the scenes of violence in

President Kennedy confers with his brother, Attorney General Robert Kennedy, outside the White House in 1962.

the South that flooded the media. The race riots surrounding the Freedom Rides in 1961 embarrassed the President when he met with Soviet leader Nikita Khrushchev. Observers around the world watched the brutality in Birmingham early in 1963. Aware that he had to respond, Kennedy spoke to the American people on television:

> 66 We preach freedom around the world, and we mean it, and we cherish our freedom, here at home, but are we to say to the world, and much more importantly, to each other that this is the land of the free except for the Negroes? . . . The time has come for this nation to fulfill its promise. 99
>
> —President John F. Kennedy, television address, June 1963

Hours after Kennedy's broadcast, civil rights leader Medgar Evers was gunned down outside his home. Evers had been an NAACP field secretary in Mississippi. He worked on recruiting NAACP members and organized various voter-registration drives throughout the state. Police charged a white supremacist, Byron de la Beckwith, with the murder. After two hung juries failed to convict him, Beckwith was set free in 1964. (Beckwith was convicted of murder in 1994 after the case was reopened.) The timing of the Evers murder made it clear that the government needed to take action.

Earlier in his term, Kennedy had proposed a modest civil rights bill. After the crisis in Birmingham, he introduced a far stronger one. The bill would prohibit segregation in public places, ban discrimination wherever federal funding was involved, and advance school desegregation. Powerful southern segregationists in Congress, however, kept the bill from coming up for a vote.

The March on Washington

To focus national attention on Kennedy's bill, civil rights leaders proposed a march on Washington, D.C. Kennedy feared the march would alienate Congress and cause racial violence. Yet when he could not persuade organizers to call off the march, he gave it his support.

The **March on Washington** took place in August 1963. More than 200,000 people came from all over the country to call for "jobs and freedom," the official slogan of the march. Labor leader A. Philip Randolph directed the march. Participants included religious leaders and celebrities such as writer James Baldwin, entertainer Sammy Davis, Jr., and baseball player Jackie Robinson. Leading folk singers of the early 1960s, such as Joan Baez and Bob Dylan, were also there. Dylan's powerful protest song "Blowin' in the Wind" was performed at the march by the popular group Peter, Paul, and Mary:

> 66 How many years can a mountain exist
> Before it's washed to the sea?
> Yes, 'n' how many years can some people exist
> Before they're allowed to be free.
> Yes, 'n' how many times can a man turn his head,
> Pretending he just doesn't see?
> The answer, my friend, is blowin' in the wind,
> The answer is blowin' in the wind. 99
>
> —Bob Dylan, ©1962

READING CHECK
Why did civil rights violence embarrass Kennedy when he met with world leaders?

VIEWING HISTORY Bob Dylan raised social consciousness about civil rights issues with his songs. Here, he plays on the back porch of the SNCC office in Greenwood, Mississippi, in 1963. **Determining Relevance** Why do you think music played an important role in the civil rights movement?

The march was peaceful and orderly. After many songs and speeches, Martin Luther King, Jr., delivered what was to become his best-known address. With power and eloquence, he spoke to all Americans:

KEY DOCUMENTS 66 *I have a dream that one day this nation will rise up and live out the true meaning of its creed, 'We hold these truths to be self-evident, that all men are created equal.' I have a dream that one day on the red hills of Georgia, the sons of former slaves and the sons of former slave owners will be able to sit down together at the table of brotherhood. . . . I have a dream that my four little children will one day live in a nation where they will not be judged by the color of their skin, but by the content of their character. . . . When we allow freedom to ring, when we let it ring from every village and every hamlet, from every state and every city, we will be able to speed up that day when all of God's children, black men and white men, Jews and Gentiles, Protestants and Catholics, will be able to join hands and sing in the words of the old Negro spiritual: 'Free at last. Free at last. Thank God Almighty, we are free at last.'* 99

—"I Have a Dream" speech, Martin Luther King, Jr., August 28, 1963

King's words echoed around the country. President Kennedy, watching the speech on television, was impressed with King's skill. But still the civil rights bill remained stalled in Congress.

The Civil Rights Act of 1964

Three months after the March on Washington, President Kennedy was assassinated, and his civil rights bill was not much closer to passage. The new President, Lyndon Johnson, was finally able to move the legislation along.

Johnson's Role Lyndon Johnson, a former member of Congress from Texas, had voted against civil rights measures during the Truman administration. As Senate majority leader, however, he had worked successfully to get a civil rights bill passed in 1957. Upon becoming President, he was eager to use his

Martin Luther King, Jr. (above), delivers his famous "I Have a Dream" speech at the March on Washington (below) in 1963.

Sounds of an Era

Listen to Martin Luther King, Jr.'s "I Have a Dream" speech and other sounds from the civil rights movement.

Black Nationalism   Elijah Muhammad, the leader of the Nation of Islam, taught that Allah (the Muslim name for God) would bring about a "Black Nation," a union among all nonwhite peoples. According to Elijah Muhammad, one of the keys to self-knowledge was knowing one's enemy. For him, the enemy of the Nation of Islam was white society.

Members of the Nation of Islam did not seek change through political means but waited for Allah to create the Black Nation. In the meantime, they tried to lead righteous lives and become economically self-sufficient.

Released from prison in 1952, Malcolm Little changed his name to Malcolm X. (The name Little, he said, had come from slaveowners.) He spent the next 12 years as a minister of the Nation of Islam, spreading the ideas of **black nationalism,** a belief in the separate identity and racial unity of the African American community. His fiery speeches won him many followers, including Louis Farrakhan, who would one day head the Nation of Islam.

Opposition to Integration   Malcolm X disagreed with both the tactics and the goals of the early civil rights movement. He called the March on Washington the "Farce on Washington," and voiced his irritation at "all of this non-violent, begging-the-white-man kind of dying . . . all of this sitting-in, sliding-in, wading-in, eating-in, diving-in, and all the rest." Instead of preaching brotherly love, he rejected ideas of integration. Asking why anyone would want to join white society, he noted:

VIEWING HISTORY Malcolm X was a leading minister of the Nation of Islam until 1964. **Making Comparisons** How did black nationalism differ from other kinds of civil rights activism?

66 *No sane black man really wants integration! No sane white man really wants integration! No sane black man really believes that the white man ever will give the black man anything more than token integration. No! The Honorable Elijah Muhammad teaches that for the black man in America the only solution is complete separation from the white man. . . . The American black man should be focusing his effort toward building his own businesses, and decent homes for himself. As other ethnic groups have done, let the black people, wherever possible, however possible, patronize their own kind, hire their own kind, and start in those ways to build up the black race's ability to do for itself. That's the only way the American black man is ever going to get respect.* 99

—Malcolm X

Malcolm X and Elijah Muhammad came to disagree about many things, including political action. In 1964, Malcolm X left the Nation of Islam and formed his own religious organization, called Muslim Mosque, Inc. He then made a pilgrimage, or religious journey, to Mecca, the holy city of Islam, in Saudi Arabia.

Seeing millions of Muslims of all races worshipping together peacefully had a profound effect on Malcolm X. It changed his views about separatism and hatred of white people. When he returned, he was ready to work with other civil rights leaders and even with white Americans on some issues. It seemed as if Malcolm X might become one of the leaders in a unified civil rights movement. His change of heart, however, had earned him some enemies.

Malcolm X had only nine months to spread his new beliefs. In February 1965, he was shot to death at a rally in New York. Three members of the Nation of Islam were charged with the murder. Malcolm X's message of black nationalism lived on, however. He particularly influenced younger members of SNCC, the Student Nonviolent Coordinating Committee.

READING CHECK
How did Malcolm X's views change after his pilgrimage in 1964?

The symbols of the black power movement reflected its call for a strong African American community.

VIEWING HISTORY Members of the Black Panthers marched in New York City in 1968 to protest the trial of Huey P. Newton. Newton had been convicted of voluntary manslaughter in the death of a police officer. His conviction was later overturned. **Identifying Central Issues** *What efforts did the Black Panthers make to improve the quality of life in black communities?*

The Black Power Movement

One SNCC leader who heard Malcolm's message was Stokely Carmichael. Born in Trinidad, in the West Indies, in 1941, Carmichael came to the United States at the age of 11 and was soon involved in protests. At Howard University in Washington, D.C., he and other students became actively involved in the Washington chapter of SNCC.

SNCC Shifts Gears   As Carmichael rose to SNCC leadership, the group became more radical. After being beaten and jailed for his participation in demonstrations, he was tired of nonviolent protest. He called on SNCC workers to carry guns for self-defense. He wanted to make the group exclusively black, rejecting white activists.

The split in the civil rights movement became obvious in June 1966. At a protest march in Greenwood, Mississippi, while King's followers were singing "We Shall Overcome," Carmichael's supporters drowned them out with "We Shall Overrun." Then Carmichael, just out of jail, jumped into the back of an open truck to challenge the moderate leaders:

> ❝ *This is the twenty-seventh time I have been arrested, and I ain't going to jail no more! . . . The only way we gonna stop them white men from whippin' us is to take over. We been saying freedom for six years—and we ain't got nothin'. What we gonna start saying now is 'black power!'* ❞
> —Stokely Carmichael, public address, June 1966

As he repeated "We . . . want . . . black . . . power!" the audience excitedly echoed the new slogan. Carmichael's idea of **black power** resonated with many African Americans. It was a call "to unite, to recognize their heritage, to build a sense of community . . . to begin to define their own goals, to lead their own organizations and support those organizations."

The Black Panthers   In the fall of 1966, a new militant political party, the Black Panthers, was formed by activists Bobby Seale and Huey Newton. The Panthers wanted African Americans to lead their own communities. They demanded that the federal government rebuild the nation's ghettos to make up for years of neglect. The Panthers also wanted to combat what they saw as police brutality in the ghettos. Often, as a result of their monitoring the police, they became engaged in direct confrontation with white authorities. Newton repeated the words of Chinese Communist leader Mao Zedong: "Power flows from the barrel of a gun." Although they did organize some beneficial community programs, the Panthers more often found themselves in violent encounters with police.

Black power gave rise to the slogan "Black is beautiful," which fostered racial pride. It also led to a serious split in the civil rights movement. More radical groups like SNCC and the Black Panthers moved away from the NAACP and other more moderate organizations.

Riots in the Streets

The early civil rights movement focused on battling **de jure segregation,** racial separation created by law. Changes in the law, however, did not address the more difficult issue of **de facto segregation,** the separation caused by social conditions such as poverty. *De facto* segregation was a fact of life in most American cities, not just in the South.

There were no "whites only" signs above water fountains in northern cities, yet discrimination continued in education, housing, and employment. African Americans were kept out of well-paying jobs, job-training programs, and suburban housing. Inner-city schools were run-down and poorly equipped.

Residents of ghetto neighborhoods viewed police officers as dangerous oppressors, not upholders of justice. James Baldwin remarked that a white police officer in one of these neighborhoods was "like an occupying soldier in a bitterly hostile country." Eventually, frustration and anger boiled over into riots and looting. In 1964, riots ravaged Rochester, New York; New York City; and several cities in New Jersey.

One of the most violent riots occurred in the Los Angeles neighborhood of Watts. On August 11, 1965, police in Watts pulled over a 21-year-old black man for drunk driving. At first the interaction was friendly among the police, the suspect, and a crowd of Watts residents that had gathered. When the suspect resisted arrest, however, one police officer panicked and began swinging his riot baton. The crowd was outraged, and the scene touched off six days of rioting.

Thousands of people filled the streets, burning cars and stores, stealing merchandise, and sniping at firefighters. When the national guard and local police finally gained control, 34 people were dead and more than a thousand had been injured. Violence spread to other cities in 1966 and 1967. Cries of "Burn, baby, burn" replaced the gentler slogans of the earlier civil rights movement.

A concerned federal government set up a special National Advisory Commission on Civil Disorders, headed by former Illinois Governor Otto Kerner, to investigate. In 1968, the Kerner Commission report declared flatly that the riots were an explosion of the anger that had been smoldering in the inner-city ghettos. It declared that "our nation is moving toward two societies, one black, one white—separate and unequal."

Tragedy Strikes in 1968

In the troubled decade of the 1960s, the most shattering year was 1968. A series of tragic events hit with such force that, month by month, the nation seemed to be coming apart. Against a backdrop of domestic violence, chaos, and confrontation, many Americans began to believe that the chance of achieving peaceful social change through political activism was hopeless.

For many Americans, the memory of President Kennedy's assassination in 1963 was still vivid and haunting five years later. They looked to other leaders to carry on the spirit and idealism of the Kennedy years. But in 1968, people's hopes were again shattered by the burst of bullets from assassins' guns.

Martin Luther King, Jr., Is Assassinated In 1968, Dr. King turned his attention to economic issues. Convinced that poverty bred violence, he broadened his approach to attack economic injustice. Calling his new crusade the

---

Focus on ECONOMICS

De facto Challenges The fight against *de facto* segregation faced different challenges than the fight against *de jure* segregation. One problem was that the civil rights movement lost much of its political support as the Nixon administration assumed power in 1969. Another had to do with changes taking place within the African American community. Not all civil rights organizations joined in this fight. Some activists believed that the real struggle was against legal barriers and not against residential patterns. Because there was less solidarity among civil rights groups, protests lost much of their strength.

African American solidarity was also weakened as a result of the increasing number of black Americans who had "made it" by the early 1970s. Many began moving to suburbs, attending college, and obtaining better jobs. As a result, some African Americans became disconnected from the intense struggle with poverty in the city ghettos.

Overall, the statistics looked promising. The number of black Americans living in poverty decreased from more than 40 percent in 1959 to about 20 percent in 1968. Between 1960 and 1977, the number of African Americans enrolled in college increased by 500 percent. Yet, for those African Americans living in inner cities, conditions had not improved. For example, in 1970, 60 percent of African Americans living in cities had low-level service jobs, compared to 33 percent of white Americans also living in cities.

Poor People's Campaign, King began planning a Poor People's March on Washington. Traveling around the United States to mobilize support, he went to Memphis, Tennessee, in early April. There he offered his assistance to striking garbage workers who were seeking better working conditions.

King spoke eloquently, referring to threats made against his life:

66 *We've got some difficult days ahead. But it doesn't matter with me now, because I've been to the mountain top. And I don't mind. Like anybody, I would like to live a long life. . . . But I'm not concerned about that now. I just want to do God's will. And He's allowed me to go up to the mountain. And I've looked over. And I've seen the promised land.* 99
—Martin Luther King, Jr., April 3, 1968

The next day, as King stood on the balcony of his motel, a bullet fired from a high-powered rifle tore into him. An hour later, King was dead.

King's assassination sparked violent reactions across the nation. In an outburst of rage and frustration, some African Americans rioted, setting fires and looting stores in more than 120 cities. The riots, and the police response to them, left close to 50 people dead. President Johnson ordered flags on federal buildings to be flown at half mast to honor King, but it took more than 50,000 troops to quell the violence. For many Americans of all races, King's death eroded faith in the idea of nonviolent change.

Robert F. Kennedy Is Assassinated   Since the assassination of President Kennedy, his brother, Senator Robert F. Kennedy, had come to support the civil rights movement and to oppose the Vietnam War. In 1968, he decided to enter the race for the Democratic presidential nomination. President Johnson had lost support from many Democrats because of America's involvement in the Vietnam War. After Senator Eugene McCarthy lost to Johnson in the New Hampshire primary by only a few percentage points, Kennedy realized that Johnson was vulnerable. On March 16, Kennedy entered the campaign. His candidacy received a critical boost on March 31, when Johnson stunned the nation by announcing that he would not run for a second term as President. In the years since his brother's death, Robert Kennedy had reached out to many Americans, including Chicanos, Native Americans, African Americans, and poor white families. He condemned the killing of both Americans and Vietnamese in the Vietnam War. He criticized the Johnson administration for financing a war instead of funding the programs needed to help the poor and disadvantaged at home.

Kennedy spent the spring of 1968 battling McCarthy in the Democratic primary elections. On June 4, he won a key victory in California's primary. But just

VIEWING HISTORY Assassinations in 1968 shocked the nation. Above, Martin Luther King, Jr., lies mortally wounded, while companions point frantically to the direction from which shots were fired. At right, busboy Jay Romero is the first to reach Robert Kennedy after he was shot in a hotel kitchen just after winning the California primary. **Identifying Central Issues** *What effect did these murders have?*

READING CHECK
Why had Robert Kennedy represented a source of hope for many Americans?

after midnight, after giving his victory speech in a Los Angeles hotel, Robert Kennedy was shot by an assassin. He died the next day.

When the shooting was reported, several campaign workers who had watched the speech on TV were waiting for Kennedy in his hotel room. One of them, civil rights leader John Lewis, later said, "We all just fell to the floor and started crying. To me that was like the darkest, saddest moment." Kennedy's death ended many people's hopes for an inspirational leader who could heal the nation's wounds.

Legacy of the Movement

At times, both black and white Americans wondered whether real progress in civil rights was possible. Many young activists felt frustrated and discouraged when the movement failed to bring changes quickly. Lyndon Johnson was devastated by the violence that exploded near the end of his presidency. "How is it possible," he asked, "after all we've accomplished?" Still, the measures passed by his administration had brought tremendous change. Segregation was now illegal. Because of voter registration drives, thousands of African Americans could now vote. The power they wielded changed the nature of American political life.

Between 1970 and 1975, the number of African American elected officials rose by 88 percent. Black mayors were elected in Atlanta, Detroit, Los Angeles, and Newark, New Jersey. Others served in Congress and state legislatures. In 1966, Barbara Jordan became the first African American elected to the Texas state senate since Reconstruction. Six years later she was elected to the United States Congress. Jordan noted what made the movement necessary:

> ❝ *The civil rights movement called America to look at itself in a giant mirror. . . . Do the black people who were born on this soil, who are American citizens, do they really feel that this is the land of opportunity, the land of the free? . . . America had to say no.* ❞
>
> —Texas Representative Barbara Jordan

Shirley Chisholm
b. 1924

In 1968, Shirley Chisholm became the first black woman elected to Congress. Running from New York's twelfth district as a Democrat, Chisholm overcame social obstacles facing both women and African Americans.

Chisholm, born in Brooklyn, New York, in 1924, had long held a deep interest in social welfare, particularly the social welfare of children. In her early 30s, Chisholm was the director for a child-care center in New York. Her career in politics began in 1964 when she was elected to the New York state assembly. Four years later she gained national attention when she won a seat in the U.S. House of Representatives. She would win the next six elections, serving in the House until 1983.

Her early career in politics was marked by her outspoken criticism of the seniority system in Congress and U.S. involvement in the Vietnam War. Her major work involved sponsoring legislation that would help the urban poor and increase funding for child welfare programs.

Section 5 Assessment

READING COMPREHENSION

1. How did **black nationalism** reflect a change from the early days of the civil rights movement?

2. How did the Black Panthers reflect Stokely Carmichael's idea of **black power?**

3. What did the Kerner Commission conclude about the race riots occurring in American cities?

4. What impact did the 1968 assassinations have on the legacy of the civil rights movement?

CRITICAL THINKING AND WRITING

5. **Distinguishing Fact From Opinion** Malcolm X once said that for African Americans "the only solution is complete separation from the white man." Do you believe this statement to be a fact or an opinion? Explain your answer.

6. **Writing to Persuade** Black nationalists believed that African Americans should establish separate communities. Write a brief paper defending or opposing this position.

For: An activity on the civil rights movement in the late 1960s
Visit: PHSchool.com
Web Code: mrd-9285

creating a CHAPTER SUMMARY

Copy this web diagram (right). Add more circles to each of the four categories of civil rights participants. Fill in the circles with details about each person you add.

For additional review and enrichment activities, see the interactive version of *America: Pathways to the Present*, available on the Web and on CD-ROM.

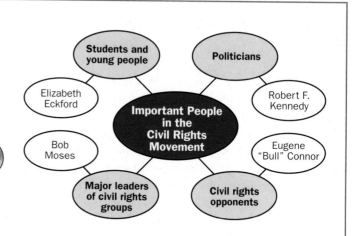

- Students and young people
- Elizabeth Eckford
- Bob Moses
- **Important People in the Civil Rights Movement**
- Politicians
- Robert F. Kennedy
- Eugene "Bull" Connor
- Major leaders of civil rights groups
- Civil rights opponents

★ Reviewing Key Terms

For each of the terms below, write a sentence explaining how it relates to the civil rights movement.

1. Montgomery bus boycott
2. integration
3. interracial
4. nonviolent protest
5. sit-in
6. Freedom Ride
7. filibuster
8. cloture
9. Twenty-fourth Amendment
10. black nationalism
11. black power
12. *de facto* segregation

★ Reviewing Main Ideas

13. How did the Supreme Court's decision in *Brown* v. *Board of Education* set the stage for a civil rights movement? (Section 1)

14. What were three effects of the *Brown* decision? (Section 1)

15. Name two groups that worked for African American rights *before* the 1960s. What did they accomplish? (Section 2)

16. What new approach did Martin Luther King, Jr., bring to the civil rights movement? What was the inspiration for his philosophy? (Section 2)

17. How did activists work to desegregate the interstate bus system? (Section 3)

18. What was President Johnson's role in passing civil rights legislation? (Section 4)

19. What did the Civil Rights Act of 1964 and the Voting Rights Act of 1965 accomplish? (Section 4)

20. What is the Nation of Islam? (Section 5)

21. What major changes occurred in the civil rights movement in the mid- to late 1960s? (Section 5)

★ Critical Thinking

22. **Identifying Assumptions** What assumptions did the federal government make when it created the termination policy to promote Native American assimilation into mainstream American culture?

23. **Formulating Questions** Make a list of five questions that you might ask a student activist from the 1960s to find out his or her reasons for taking part in the civil rights movement.

24. **Synthesizing Information** SNCC began as an alternative to existing civil rights groups. How did SNCC maintain itself as an alternative organization, and how did it change over time?

25. **Demonstrating Reasoned Judgment** Many people who lived through the 1960s would agree that the country lost its sense of hope after the deaths of Martin Luther King, Jr., and Robert F. Kennedy. Do you think that people in the United States today have regained a sense of hope?

★ Standardized Test Prep

Analyzing Political Cartoons ▶

26. Look at both panels of the cartoon. What challenge does this African American face after succeeding in his struggle against racism?

   A economic inequality
   B lack of education
   C more racial discrimination
   D a lack of jobs

27. What is the man's overall goal, and what obstacles does he face?

28. What point is the cartoonist trying to make?

Analyzing Primary Sources

Read the excerpt from Martin Luther King, Jr.'s "I Have a Dream" speech in Section 4. Then answer the following questions.

29. Which of the following BEST summarizes King's dream?

   A that Americans of all religions will be free at last
   B that all Americans will achieve true equality and freedom
   C that African Americans will form a brotherhood
   D that children will not be judged by their color

30. King hopes that his dream will be fulfilled

   F sometime in the future.
   G in his children's lifetime.
   H in the twentieth century.
   I today.

Test-Taking Tip

To answer Question 30, note that King states "I have a dream that my four little children will one day live in a nation where they will not be judged by the color of their skin, but by the content of their character. . . ."

Applying the Chapter Skill

Understanding Public Opinion Polls Look back at the Skills for Life page and review the steps needed for understanding public opinion polls. Think of a poll question relating to the civil rights movement that you would have liked to ask the American public in the 1950s or 1960s. Make sure your question is simply worded and objective. Then, answer the following questions. (a) What is your poll "universe"? (b) What is the purpose of your poll?

For: Chapter 21 Self-Test
Visit: PHSchool.com
Web Code: mra-9286

AmericanHeritage®

MY BRUSH WITH HISTORY™

by BRUCE KILLEBREW and JOAN W. MUSBACH

Encounters With Segregation

COLORED WAITING ROOM

The two passages below describe how two white Americans became aware of the system of racial segregation that existed in many parts of the country. In the first account, Bruce Killebrew recalls the integration of his third-grade class. In the second account, Joan W. Musbach remembers the day that she, as a high school student, came face to face with her own ignorance about segregation.

A VIRGINIA CLASSROOM In 1954 my father was stationed at the Pentagon in Washington, D.C., and we lived on the now-defunct South Post of Fort Myer. My friends and I had a grand time romping through the nearby Civil War battlefields, taking turns being Yankee and Rebel. I couldn't decide whether to favor the Blue or the Gray. At the age of eight I'd really never thought about the issues that fueled the fighting.

Then, one day in the first week of September 1954, at the beginning of the year for our small military elementary school at Fort Myer, there were new faces in my class—and reporters from United Press and *Army Times* taking pictures. They were photographing the class while I led the Pledge of Allegiance for the first integrated class in the formerly Confederate state of Virginia. The two new students were black, and to me and the rest of my third-grade classmates they did not seem any different from the rest of us kids. But I was very proud to have been chosen to lead the Pledge of Allegiance on that day.

The event would help shape this nation's future, and my own. It brought

Bruce Killebrew (far left) leads the Pledge of Allegiance for one of the first integrated classes in Virginia.

home to me the idea that all men are created equal and have the right to equal opportunity. Much of my life as an individual and a social worker has been based on the premise I learned in that classroom in 1954.

A MIDWESTERN CAFÉ On a crisp, cool, sunny Saturday in January, a Midwestern café—a free-standing building with one counter, stools in front, grill behind—became the site of the most memorable experience of my high school years.

It was 1960. I was a senior member of the debate team from John J. Ingels High School, in Atchison, Kansas. I was growing up within sixty miles of the origin of the 1954 Supreme Court case, *Brown* v. *Board of Education*, but, as of 1960, had never heard of Linda Brown or the case that bears her name. I was soon to discover that there was a great deal about which I was unaware.

We finished the Saturday-morning rounds and then went out for lunch before returning to the college to hear the semifinalists announced. We chose an appealing-looking cafeteria near the college. I was the only girl on the trip, and I was still just entering when Mr. Phipps and the boys turned around and came back out. I was busy talking and didn't ask why we had left. I assumed the cafeteria was too crowded. We got into Mr. Phipps's old car and drove a few blocks to a café. Business was sparse, and we spread out down the red-plastic-covered stools along the counter. John, my partner, was seated beside me. The waitress came down the counter distributing menus. John did not get one. We called this to her attention, and she quickly informed us that blacks were not served in there. I was shocked. I had never heard of such a thing. We all got up and went to the car, and Mr. Phipps went to a nearby hamburger stand and bought hamburgers and sodas for us all to eat in the car.

John wouldn't eat. He sat in the corner of the back seat, speechless. We didn't know what to say either. We just ate our hamburgers and went back to the college.

As I thought about the incident, I realized that John was the victim of our ignorance as well as of the prejudice of the management of the cafeteria and the café. He had probably never been exposed to such humiliation before,

The countless small conflicts of a segregated society flared up nationwide in diners and lunchrooms such as this one.

protected by parents or other adults who would have avoided such an incident. Strange as it may seem, a carful of high school students and their teacher were unaware of the segregation of public services just across the river from where they lived.

The look on John's face as we ate our hamburgers ensured that I would never forget that crisp January Saturday or the Kansas City café where I met Jim Crow.

Source: *American Heritage* magazine, April 1991 and April 1994.

Understanding Primary Sources

1. What do Mr. Phipps and the boys do after they go into the first cafeteria near the college?

2. Why might they have done this?

American Heritage®
MY BRUSH WITH **HISTORY**™
Videotapes

For more information about the fight against segregation, view "Encounters With Segregation."

American Pathways

CITIZENSHIP

Expanding Civil Rights

When the Constitution was written, only white male property owners had the right to vote. Over the past two centuries, though, the term "government by the people" has become more of a reality. Civil rights have been expanded for many groups, including Native Americans, African Americans, women, and young adults.

 The Bill of Rights

1791 The first ten amendments to the United States Constitution were added in 1791. Known as the Bill of Rights, these amendments guaranteed freedom of belief and expression, freedom and security of the person, and fair and equal treatment before the law. Throughout American history, many people have worked to make these constitutional guarantees a reality for all Americans.

President Washington's cabinet (right)

 Rights for African Americans

1868 and 1870 Two amendments ratified during the Reconstruction period sought to improve the civil rights of African Americans. The Fourteenth Amendment, ratified in 1868, granted citizenship to African Americans and declared that states could not "deprive any person of life, liberty, or property, without due process of law" or "deny to any person . . . the equal protection of the laws." The Fifteenth Amendment, ratified in 1870, was intended to protect any citizen from being denied the right to vote because of race or color. Still, for nearly another century, African Americans were systematically prevented from voting.

African American voters casting ballots in the 1876 election (left)

 **Suffrage for Women**

1900–1920 Women made important civil rights gains with the ratification of the Nineteenth Amendment in 1920, which gave all American women the right to vote.

An American suffragist (left)

Rights for Native Americans

1924 As European settlers migrated westward, they pushed many Indian groups off their lands. The result for many Native Americans was the loss of their sovereignty, culture, and territory. To help prevent further losses, Congress ratified the General Citizenship Act in 1924. It granted Native Americans the rights of citizenship, including the right to vote in federal elections.

The Civil Rights Era

1954–1968 In the period following World War II, thousands of ordinary Americans worked to end racial and ethnic injustice in the United States. The civil rights movement, especially, won significant victories in the battle to secure equal rights for all Americans, including African Americans, Latinos, Native Americans, and women.

Martin Luther King, Jr., and his wife, Coretta Scott King, lead a protest march from Selma to Montgomery, Alabama, in 1965 (above).

Suffrage for Young Adults

1971 Ratified in 1971, the Twenty-sixth Amendment set the minimum voting age at 18. Many of those who backed the amendment began to work for its passage during World War II. Its ratification was spurred by the Vietnam War.

An 18-year-old voter (left)

Rights for the Disabled

1990 The Americans with Disabilities Act guarantees disabled Americans equal opportunity in employment and public accommodations. The act has succeeded in breaking down many of the barriers that prevented the disabled from achieving equality.

Continuity and Change

1. How long did the system of Jim Crow, or legal segregation, last? What finally ended it?
2. What did minority groups do to try to gain their civil rights?

Go Online
PHSchool.com

For: A study guide on civil rights
Visit: PHSchool.com
Web Code: mrd-9289

733

The Kennedy and Johnson Years

(1961–1969)

SECTION 1   The New Frontier

SECTION 2   The Great Society

SECTION 3   Foreign Policy in the Early 1960s

The Kennedys host renowned cellist Pablo Casals at a White House gala in 1961.

Lyndon Johnson rides his horse, Lady B, at his Texas ranch in 1963.

American Events

1960
Kennedy and Johnson win election by a razor-thin margin.

1961
Kennedy launches his New Frontier program. The first U.S. astronaut goes into space. The failed Bay of Pigs invasion is a U.S. foreign policy disaster.

1962
The Cuban Missile Crisis brings the superpowers to the brink of nuclear war.

1963
On November 22, Kennedy is assassinated in Dallas; Johnson becomes President.

1964
Johnson wins election. He launches a "war on poverty" with a series of programs known as the Great Society.

Presidential Terms: John F. Kennedy 1961–1963   Lyndon B. Johnson 1963–1969

1960   **1962**   **1964**

World Events

In a showdown with Kennedy, Soviets build the Berlin Wall.

1961

Algeria wins independence from France, a colonial power in Africa.

1962

UN peacekeepers are sent to Cyprus amid Greek-Turk hostilities.

1964

Nuclear Threat From Cuba

CANADA

0   150   300 mi.
0   150   300 km

2,843 miles

2,000 miles, 17 minutes

Seattle

Chicago

New York

Washington, D.C.

ATLANTIC OCEAN

N

40°N

Denver

1,819 miles

1,333 miles

1,317 miles

Los Angeles

1,500 miles, 15 minutes

2,299 miles

Atlanta

1,139 miles

30°N

1,000 miles, 12 minutes

761 miles

Houston

924 miles

Miami

About 5,000 miles

UNITED STATES

SOVIET UNION

Gulf of Mexico

243 miles

Havana   CUBA

80°W

Nuclear Threat From the U.S.S.R.

MEXICO

1,103 miles

90°W

Mexico City

Teacher and students in the federal Head Start program begun under Johnson

1965

Johnson sends the Marines to support a U.S.-backed government in the Dominican Republic. U.S. involvement in Vietnam deepens. Medicare and Medicaid programs are created.

1966

The Warren Court's landmark *Miranda* ruling gives rights to persons accused of crimes.

1968

Amid race riots and Vietnam War protests, Johnson's popularity plummets. He announces he will not run for reelection.

1966

1968

Rhodesia declares independence from Britain.

China's Cultural Revolution begins.

1965

1966

The New Frontier

READING FOCUS

- What factors affected the election of 1960?
- What domestic programs did President Kennedy pursue?
- What circumstances surrounded Kennedy's assassination?

MAIN IDEA

Following a narrow election victory, President John F. Kennedy proposed a number of changes in domestic policy, many of which were defeated in Congress.

KEY TERMS

mandate
New Frontier
Warren Commission

TARGET READING SKILL

Identify Supporting Details Copy the chart below. As you read, fill in details relating to Kennedy's New Frontier program.

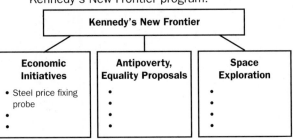

Kennedy's New Frontier

Economic Initiatives	Antipoverty, Equality Proposals	Space Exploration
• Steel price fixing probe • •	• • • •	• • • •

Setting the Scene On September 26, 1960, American politics changed forever. From a CBS television studio in Chicago, two presidential candidates—Republican Richard Nixon and Democrat John F. Kennedy—faced off in the first of four live, televised debates broadcast by all the networks. This debate focused on domestic issues.

Nixon was a tough, veteran campaigner who had gained plenty of political experience as a member of Congress and as Eisenhower's Vice President. Yet he was not in peak form. He had kept a grueling campaign schedule and had been sidelined in the hospital for two weeks with a serious knee injury. Nixon arrived at the studio 10 pounds underweight, having ignored advice to get a new shirt with a collar that fit. He refused makeup, except for a pasty beard stick called "Lazy Shave" to cover his perpetual "five o'clock shadow." According to biographer Stephen A. Ambrose, Nixon stood under the hot studio lights "half slouched, his 'Lazy Shave' powder faintly streaked with sweat, his eyes exaggerated hollows of blackness, his jaw, jowls, and face dropping with strain." Nixon had prepared his mind for the battle, but not his appearance.

Senator Kennedy, on the other hand, arrived in Chicago after a campaign swing through California that included plenty of rest and sunshine. Tanned, relaxed, and smiling, he breezed into the studio. The camera favored his young, handsome face, and Kennedy spoke directly to the camera, paying little attention to his opponent and addressing the viewing voters instead.

Who won the debate? Surveys showed that most of the 70 million TV viewers thought Kennedy won. Yet many radio listeners gave the victory to Nixon. Analysts still disagree over whether the debate was the turning point in the election.

The undisputed winner that night was television itself. The presidential debates of 1960 put TV in the national spotlight and made it the communications vehicle of choice for politicians.

In a CBS studio in Chicago, a relaxed John Kennedy (seated) browses his notes as he prepares to meet Richard Nixon (at the podium) in the first of their four televised debates in the fall of 1960.

The Election of 1960

Kennedy, a Massachusetts Democrat, had served in the United States House of Representatives and Senate for 14 years, following distinguished service in the United States Navy in World War II. Yet the senator faced serious obstacles in his quest for the presidency.

A New Type of Candidate   John Kennedy was only 43 years old, and many questioned whether he had the experience needed for the nation's highest office. (While he was the youngest person ever to be *elected* President, Kennedy was not the youngest ever to serve. Theodore Roosevelt became President at age 42 when William McKinley was assassinated.) In addition, Kennedy was a Roman Catholic, and no Catholic had ever been elected President. Kennedy helped put an end to the religion issue when he won the primary of the largely Protestant state of West Virginia.

With that hurdle behind him, he campaigned hard, promising to spur the sluggish economy. During the last years of the Eisenhower administration, the Gross National Product (GNP) had grown very slowly, and the economy had suffered several recessions. During the campaign, Kennedy proclaimed that it was time to "get America moving again."

A Narrow Kennedy Victory   Kennedy and his running mate, Lyndon Baines Johnson, won the election by an extraordinarily close margin. Although the electoral vote was 303 to 219 in Kennedy's favor, he won by fewer than 119,000 popular votes out of nearly 69 million cast. In Illinois, Nixon could have inched by Kennedy with just a few thousand more votes, and accusations were made that the Democrats had won the state through fraud.

As a result of this razor-thin victory, Kennedy entered office without a strong **mandate**, or public endorsement of his proposals. Without a mandate, Kennedy would have difficulty pushing his more controversial measures through Congress.

Senator John F. Kennedy, the 1960 Democratic presidential candidate, greets supporters during a campaign stop.

 Sounds of an Era

Listen to John F. Kennedy's Inaugural Address and other sounds from the Kennedy-Johnson era.

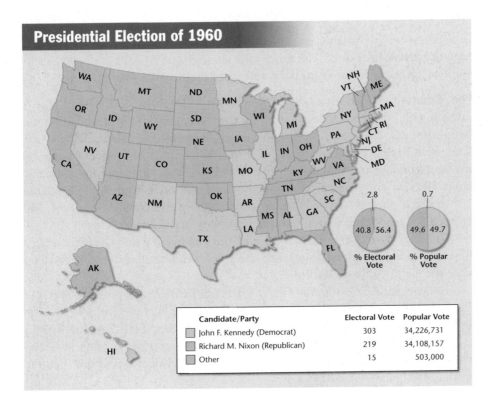

Presidential Election of 1960

Candidate/Party	Electoral Vote	Popular Vote
John F. Kennedy (Democrat)	303	34,226,731
Richard M. Nixon (Republican)	219	34,108,157
Other	15	503,000

2.8

0.7

40.8 56.4

49.6 49.7

% Electoral Vote

% Popular Vote

MAP SKILLS Kennedy and Nixon fought a head-to-head contest in the 1960 presidential election. **Regions** *(a) From what areas did each candidate draw the most votes? (b) Compare the popular vote and the electoral college vote, and explain the election outcome.*

The President's children, Caroline Kennedy and John F. Kennedy, Jr., created an atmosphere of fun and family life in the Oval Office.

Kennedy nevertheless took office with vigor and confidence. In his Inaugural Address, he inspired a generation of young people by urging them to put patriotism before personal interests:

> 66 My fellow Americans, ask not what your country can do for you; ask what you can do for your country. 99
>
> —John F. Kennedy, Inaugural Address, 1961

Kennedy's Domestic Programs

In a speech early in his presidency, Kennedy said that the nation was poised at the edge of a **"New Frontier."** The name stuck. It referred to Kennedy's proposals to improve the economy, assist the poor, and speed up the space program.

The Economy Concerned about the continuing recession, Kennedy hoped to work with business leaders to promote economic growth. Often, however, he faced resistance from executives who were suspicious of his plans. Their worst fears were realized in the spring of 1962. When the U.S. Steel Company announced that it was raising the price of steel by $6 a ton, other firms did the same. Worried about inflation, Kennedy called the price increase unjustifiable and charged that it showed "utter contempt for the public interest." He ordered a federal investigation into the possibility of price fixing.

Under that pressure, U.S. Steel and the other companies backed down. Business leaders remained angry, and the stock market fell in its steepest drop since the Great Crash of 1929.

To help end the economic slump, in 1963 Kennedy proposed a large tax cut over three years. At first, the measure would reduce government income and create a budget deficit. Kennedy believed, however, that the extra cash in taxpayers' wallets would stimulate the economy and eventually bring in added tax revenues. However, as often happened, the President's proposal became stuck in Congress.

READING CHECK

What domestic issues did President Kennedy attempt to address?

Combating Poverty and Inequality   Kennedy also was eager to take action against poverty and inequality. In his first two years in office, he hoped that he could help the poor simply by stimulating the economy. In 1962, though, author Michael Harrington described the lives of the poor in his powerful book, *The Other America*. Harrington's book revealed that while many Americans were enjoying the prosperity of the 1950s, a shocking one fifth of the population was living below the poverty line. Kennedy became convinced that the poor needed direct federal aid.

Kennedy's ambitious plans for federal education aid and medical care for the elderly both failed in Congress. Some measures did make it through Congress, however. Congress passed both an increase in the minimum wage and the Housing Act of 1961, which provided $4.9 billion for urban renewal. Congress also approved the Twenty-fourth Amendment, which outlawed the poll tax. In June 1963, Congress passed the Equal Pay Act. Added into the Fair Labor Standards Act of 1938, a New Deal program, the Equal Pay Act stated that all employees doing substantially the same work in the same workplace must be given equal pay.

Other Kennedy Initiatives   In the face of congressional roadblocks, Kennedy, like many Presidents, sought to achieve his goals through executive orders. Among them were orders on providing equal opportunity in housing and establishing an expanded program of food distribution to needy families. Other orders established the President's Committee on Equal Employment, the President's Commission on the Status of Women, and the President's Council on Aging.

Other acts in Kennedy's shortened presidency—some carried out in collaboration with Congress—included the following:

1. an executive order providing high-quality surplus food to unemployed Americans;
2. the largest, fastest defense buildup in peacetime history, as Kennedy boosted missile programs;
3. an Area Redevelopment law to help communities plagued with long-term unemployment;
4. changes in Social Security extending benefits to 5 million people and allowing Americans to retire and collect benefits at age 62;
5. a law doubling federal resources to combat water pollution;
6. the creation of National Seashore Parks, a part of the National Park System;
7. the expansion and increase of the minimum wage;
8. the creation of the first federal program to address juvenile delinquency;
9. changes in the welfare system aimed at helping ailing families instead of encouraging dependency on government benefits;
10. the construction of the world's largest nuclear power plant, in Hanford, Washington;
11. tightening of food and drug laws to protect against untested drugs;
12. signing of a Trade Expansion Act to reduce American protectionism and encourage free trade;
13. signing of the Nuclear Test Ban Treaty, the first nuclear weapons agreement.

INTERPRETING GRAPHS
At bottom, Defense Department workers inspect the *Friendship 7* capsule after John Glenn's historic flight and splashdown. The graph below shows changes in NASA funding over seven years. **Analyzing Visual Information** *What accounts for the sudden surge in funding during the late 1950s?*

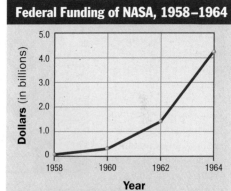

Federal Funding of NASA, 1958–1964

Dollars (in billions) — Year

SOURCE: *Historical Statistics of the United States, Colonial Times to 1970*

Camelot The name *Camelot* came to represent the energetic, idealistic image of the Kennedy White House. The Broadway musical *Camelot,* which opened in 1960, portrayed the legendary kingdom of the British King Arthur. Arthur dreamed of transforming medieval Britain from a country in which "might makes right," or the strong always get their way, into one in which power would be used to achieve what is right.

The Kennedys themselves embodied the royal, romantic spirit of Camelot. The President and First Lady made the White House a stage for high culture, inviting the best artists, musicians, and thinkers. Jacqueline Kennedy, an intelligent and beautiful woman, brought an atmosphere of style and grace to the White House. She personally supervised its renovation and redecoration, acquiring tasteful furnishings that reflected the Kennedys' interest in American cultural history.

The couple's young children, Caroline and John, Jr., added to the lively atmosphere. They played with their father in the Oval Office and in a swimming pool and treehouse on the White House lawn. The fact that the Kennedys had young children made it all the more tragic when Camelot came to a sudden end.

The Space Program Kennedy was also successful in his effort to breathe life into the space program. Following the Soviet Union's launch of the *Sputnik* satellite in 1957, government agencies and private industries had been working furiously with the National Aeronautics and Space Administration (NASA) to place a manned spacecraft in orbit around Earth. As part of the Mercury program, seven test pilots were chosen to train as astronauts in 1959. Government spending and the future of NASA became uncertain, however, when a task force appointed by Kennedy recommended that NASA concentrate on exploratory space missions without human crews.

All of that changed in April 1961. The Soviet Union announced that Yuri Gagarin had circled Earth on board the Soviet spacecraft *Vostok,* becoming the first human to travel in space. Gagarin's flight rekindled Americans' fears that their technology was falling behind that of the Soviet Union.

On May 5, 1961, the United States made its own first attempt to send a person into space. Astronaut Alan Shepard made a 15-minute flight that reached an altitude of 115 miles. Unlike Gagarin's flight, Shepard's flight did not orbit Earth. Nevertheless, its success convinced Kennedy to move forward. On May 25, Kennedy issued a bold challenge to the nation. He said the United States "should commit itself to achieving the goal, before this decade is out, of landing a man on the moon."

The nation accepted the challenge, and funding for NASA was increased. Less than a year later, on February 20, 1962, John Glenn successfully completed three orbits around Earth and landed in the Atlantic Ocean near the Bahamas. Later that year Kennedy outlined the reasons for American space exploration:

" We set sail on this new sea because there is new knowledge to be gained, and new rights to be won, and they must be won and used for the progress of all people. . . . [O]nly if the United States occupies a position of preeminence can we help decide whether this new ocean will be a sea of peace or a new, terrifying theater of war. "
—John F. Kennedy, speech at Rice University, Houston, Texas, 1962

Over the course of the decade, NASA flights brought the country closer and closer to its goal. Finally, on July 20, 1969, astronaut Neil Armstrong became the first person to walk on the moon. Unfortunately, Kennedy would not live to see the fulfillment of the goal he set in motion.

Kennedy Is Assassinated

On November 22, 1963, as Kennedy looked ahead to the reelection campaign the following year, he traveled to Texas to mobilize support. Texas Governor John Connally and his wife, Nelly, met the President and the First Lady, Jacqueline Kennedy, at the airport in Dallas. Together they rode through the streets of downtown Dallas in an open limousine, surrounded by Secret Service agents. Newspapers had published the parade route ahead of time, and it was jammed with thousands of supporters hoping for a glimpse of the President.

The motorcade slowed as it turned a corner in front of the Texas School Book Depository. Its employees had been sent to lunch so they could watch the event outside. Yet one man stayed behind. From a sixth-floor window, he aimed his rifle.

Suddenly shots rang out. Bullets struck both Connally and Kennedy. Connally would recover from his injuries. The President, slumped over in Jacqueline's lap, was mortally wounded.

The motorcade sped to nearby Parkland Memorial Hospital, where doctors made what they knew was a hopeless attempt to save the President. Kennedy was pronounced dead at 1:00 P.M. An aide delivered the news to a dazed Lyndon Johnson, addressing him as "Mr. President."

As the news spread by radio and TV bulletins, the country came to a halt in stunned disbelief. By the time Air Force One arrived in Washington, thousands of people had gathered in the streets. They stood in near silence, except for the sounds of weeping. America was shattered. Millions remained glued to their televisions for days as the impact of the tragedy sank in.

The prime suspect in Kennedy's murder was Lee Harvey Oswald, a former marine and supporter of Cuban leader Fidel Castro. He was apprehended within an hour of the President's death, but revealed little information to the police.

Two days after Kennedy's assassination, the TV cameras rolled as Oswald was being transferred from one jail to another. As the nation watched, a Dallas nightclub owner, Jack Ruby, stepped through the crowd of reporters and fatally shot Oswald.

On November 29, President Johnson appointed The President's Commission on the Assassination of President John F. Kennedy. It was better known as the **Warren Commission,** after its chairman, Supreme Court Chief Justice Earl Warren. After months of investigation, the Warren Commission determined that Oswald had acted alone in shooting the President. Neither Oswald, Jack Ruby, nor any other American or foreigner was involved in a conspiracy to commit the crime, the commission concluded.

Since then, the case has been explored in millions of pages of books, magazine and newspaper accounts, and formal and informal reports. It continues to be the topic of reenactments and television documentaries. Some investigations support the theory that Oswald was involved in a larger conspiracy, and that he was killed in order to protect others who had helped plan Kennedy's murder.

On his third birthday, November 25, 1963, John F. Kennedy, Jr., salutes as his father's casket passes by in the funeral procession for President Kennedy. Other family members, from left, are JFK's brother Edward M. Kennedy; the late President's daughter, Caroline, almost age 6; his wife, Jacqueline Kennedy; and his brother Robert F. Kennedy.

Section 1 Assessment

READING COMPREHENSION

1. Explain the role of television in the 1960 presidential election, and describe the election outcome.

2. How did lack of a **mandate** affect Kennedy's administration?

3. Describe some of the successes and failures of Kennedy's **New Frontier.**

4. What were the conclusions of the **Warren Commission?**

CRITICAL THINKING AND WRITING

5. **Making Comparisons** Compare the advantages and disadvantages that Richard Nixon had going into the 1960 debates with John F. Kennedy.

6. **Writing a Conclusion** Why do you think the goal of a moon landing was so important to Kennedy? What effects do you think the successful NASA mission had on the country?

Go Online
PHSchool.com

For: An activity on JFK
Visit: PHSchool.com
Web Code: mrd-9291

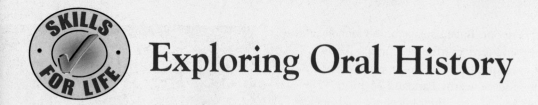

Exploring Oral History

Oral history is made up of people's verbal accounts and recollections of former times and events. Historians collect oral history through interviews, which may take place at the time of an event or at some later date, perhaps even decades later. These interviews are primary sources that record not only facts about the past, but also people's opinions, feelings, and impressions—all important for putting together a picture of the past.

The excerpt below is from an interview with John Lewis on the twentieth anniversary of President Kennedy's death. In 1963, Lewis was chairperson of the Student Nonviolent Coordinating Committee and one of the leaders of the civil rights March on Washington.

LEARN THE SKILL
Use the following steps to analyze an oral history:

1. **Identify the nature of the oral account.** Determine who was interviewed, that person's relationship to the event, and any factors that might have influenced the person's recollection of the event.

2. **Determine the reliability of the evidence.** Consider whether the person was in a position to observe events first-hand, or to judge events impartially. Also consider the length of time between the event and the interview.

3. **Study the evidence to learn more about the historical event.** Note any new facts you learn from the interview, as well as new insights into people's attitudes at the time of the event.

PRACTICE THE SKILL
Answer the following questions:

1. **(a)** Who was interviewed? **(b)** When did the interview take place? **(c)** What was Lewis's attitude toward Kennedy at the time of his death? Why? **(d)** Did that attitude change in any way over time?

2. **(a)** What was Lewis's relationship to the event he is describing? **(b)** How might Lewis's role in the civil rights movement have affected his interpretation of the event? **(c)** How might events after Kennedy's death have affected the account? **(d)** What do Lewis's views reveal about his political perspective?

3. **(a)** What impact does Lewis think Kennedy's presidency had on government policy and the nation? **(b)** What can you learn about Kennedy's presidency from Lewis's account?

APPLY THE SKILL
See the Chapter Review and Assessment for another opportunity to apply this skill.

An Interview with John Lewis: Remembering President Kennedy's Assassination

"I was living in Atlanta then, but I had gone back to Nashville for a trial. I was getting into a car to go to the Nashville airport when I heard it on the radio. And to me, it was the saddest moment in my life. I had grown up to love and to admire President Kennedy. I remember crying on the plane.

I saw him as a sort of guy that listened. Sincere. Caring. People argue and say that he didn't really do anything. But he did listen, and during that period from 1961 to 1963, I'll tell you, I think probably for the first time in modern American history, we felt, 'Well, we have a friend in the White House.' On some things we disagreed. We'd call them up and argue and debate with them on some issue, and we said a lot of different things, and sometimes it was harsh. But we saw the Kennedy administration during that period as a sympathetic referee in the whole struggle for civil rights.

His campaign had created a sense of hope, a sense of optimism for many of us. When someone asked him about the civil rights sit-ins that year, he said, 'By sitting down, these young people are standing up for the very best in American tradition.'"

—*Newsweek*, November 28, 1983

READING FOCUS

- What was Lyndon Johnson's path to the presidency?
- What were some of the goals and programs of the Great Society?
- What were some of the cases that made the Warren Court both important and controversial?

MAIN IDEA

President Johnson's Great Society programs aimed to improve America's economy and provide substantial government aid to its citizens, especially the poor.

KEY TERMS

Great Society
Head Start
Volunteers in Service to America (VISTA)
Medicare
Medicaid
Immigration Act of 1965
Miranda rule
apportionment

TARGET READING SKILL

Identify Supporting Details Copy the web diagram below. As you read, fill in details relating to President Johnson's Great Society programs.

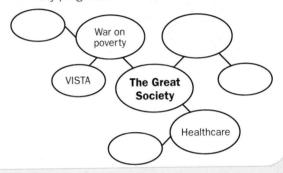

Setting the Scene At 2:35 P.M. on November 22, 1963, about 90 minutes after John F. Kennedy was pronounced dead, Lyndon Baines Johnson stood inside Air Force One on an airstrip at Dallas's Love Field. He was flanked by his wife, Lady Bird, and by Jacqueline Kennedy, who was bearing up with "amazing strength and calm," according to an account by the *Houston Chronicle*. According to the Constitution, LBJ had *immediately* become the thirty-sixth President from the moment of Kennedy's death. Johnson, however, insisted on taking the oath of office before leaving Dallas.

Federal District Judge Sarah T. Hughes was rushed to the airport to administer the oath. "The President and Mrs. Johnson were very serious and very calm," Judge Hughes told the *Chronicle* afterward. "He thanked us and told us he would rely on God's help."

Two minutes later, Air Force One took off for the capital, bearing Kennedy's body. Lady Bird Johnson, the new First Lady, began her White House diary that day.

"Friday, November 22, 1963 DALLAS

"It all began so beautifully. . . ."

LBJ's Path to the White House

The grief of a nation, and the responsibility for healing it, hung heavily upon the new President. Johnson began the recovery process in a speech to Congress:

A sad and solemn Lyndon Johnson is sworn in as President aboard Air Force One shortly after President Kennedy's assassination. On Johnson's right is his wife, Lady Bird, and on his left is Kennedy's grief-stricken widow, Jacqueline.

> ❝ All I have I would have given gladly not to be standing here today. . . . No words are sad enough to express our sense of loss. No words are strong enough to express our determination to continue the forward thrust of America that [Kennedy] began. . . . [T]he ideas and the ideals which he so nobly represented must and will be translated into effective action. ❞
>
> —Lyndon Johnson, address to a joint session of Congress, November 27, 1963

Johnson's nose-to-nose form of persuasion could be intimidating.

Although he came to the Oval Office through tragedy, Johnson found himself in a job he had long sought. LBJ's road to the presidency was laid carefully and cunningly, through years of skillful political maneuvering and strong leadership.

Lyndon Johnson arrived in the United States House of Representatives in 1937 as a New Deal Democrat from Texas. In 1948, he won a seat in the Senate, but only by a tiny margin of 87 votes. He was jokingly dubbed "Landslide Lyndon"—a nickname that stuck for the rest of his career.

In the Senate, Johnson demonstrated both political talent and an unstoppable ambition. In 1953, he became the youngest Senator ever to be elected Minority Leader. When the Democrats won control of the Senate the following year, LBJ became Majority Leader. In this powerful post he became famous for his ability to use the political system to accomplish his goals. He controlled the legislative agenda and the votes to get bills passed by rewarding his friends and punishing his enemies. Johnson inspired fear and awe among his colleagues.

He was "not a likeable man," former Secretary of State Dean Acheson once told him. But Johnson was more concerned with accomplishment than popularity, and his single-minded intensity enabled him to get his way. Other senators marveled at the "Johnson treatment," in which he carefully researched a bill, and then approached in a hallway or office the legislator whose vote he needed. If he thought it was the best way to persuade the legislator, he would attack, "his face a scant millimeter from his target, his eyes widening and narrowing, his eyebrows rising and falling," according to columnists Rowland Evans, Jr.,

NOTABLE PRESIDENTS
Lyndon Baines Johnson

36th President
1963–1969

"In a land of great wealth, families must not live in hopeless poverty."
—**Inaugural Address, January 20, 1965**

Lyndon Johnson rose to the presidency under the worst of circumstances—the assassination of President John F. Kennedy—and governed during one of the nation's most divisive periods. President Johnson waged war on poverty in America. But another war, half a world away, drained funds from his ambitious domestic agenda.

Born to a financially struggling political family in Texas, Johnson became a school teacher during the 1920s, witnessing the harsh poverty of his students, mostly Mexican Americans. His concerns led him into politics. Johnson served for nearly 12 years in the House as a New Deal Democrat. In 1948, he won election to the Senate. Shrewd and determined, LBJ fought his way up to become, at age 46, the youngest-ever Senate Majority Leader.

In the 1960 Democratic primaries, Johnson had to settle for the No. 2 spot on Kennedy's ticket. As Vice President, Johnson was restless and powerless. But power came all too soon, when Kennedy's death launched him into the Oval Office.

LBJ moved quickly to pursue his Great Society programs, designed to lift Americans out of poverty and promote equal rights. But Johnson had inherited a problem: the escalating war against communism in Vietnam. The conflict was political and military quicksand.

In the 1968 primaries, facing low public support and a growing challenge from Robert F. Kennedy, a war-weary LBJ withdrew his candidacy. At the end of his term, he retired to his beloved Texas ranch with his wife, Claudia "Lady Bird" Johnson.

Connecting to Today
Have crises overseas had a strong effect on any recent presidencies? Why or why not?

  **For:** More on Lyndon Baines Johnson
Visit: PHSchool.com
Web Code: mrd-9297

and Robert Novak. Johnson might grab his victim by the lapels or by the shoulders, flattering, cajoling, and shouting in turn. Nearly without fail, he got the vote he wanted.

When Johnson's bid for the Democratic nomination failed in 1960, he accepted Kennedy's invitation to run for the vice presidency. Once elected, however, Johnson was frustrated with the job, which lacked any real power. He was also unhappy being away from Congress, where he had been so effective.

Yet Johnson was not powerless for long. While it had been a long journey to the vice presidency, it was a tragically short trip to the Oval Office in 1963.

The Great Society

Johnson was aware that the American people needed some action that would help heal the wound caused by the loss of their President. To that end, he used all the talents he had developed as Senate Majority Leader to push through Congress an extraordinary program of reforms on domestic issues.

Johnson's agenda included Kennedy's civil rights and tax-cut bills. It also embraced laws to aid public education, provide medical care for the elderly, and eliminate poverty. By the spring of 1964, he had begun to use the phrase *Great Society* to describe his goals. In a speech that year he told students:

> 66 Your imagination, your initiative, and your indignation will determine whether we build a society where progress is the servant of our needs, or a society where old values and new visions are buried under unbridled [unrestrained] growth. For in your time we have the opportunity to move not only toward the rich society and the powerful society, but upward toward the Great Society. 99
>
> —Lyndon Johnson, speech at the University of Michigan, May 1964

Johnson's **Great Society** was a series of major legislative initiatives that continued into his second term. The Great Society programs included major poverty relief, education aid, healthcare, voting rights, conservation and beautification projects, urban renewal, and economic development in depressed areas.

The Election of 1964 Johnson's early successes paved the way for his landslide victory over Republican Barry Goldwater in the election of 1964. Goldwater, a senator from Arizona, held conservative views that seemed excessive to many Americans, as well as to many members of his own party.

For example, he opposed civil rights legislation, and he believed that military commanders should be allowed to use nuclear weapons as they saw fit on the battlefield. The Johnson campaign took advantage of voters' fears of nuclear war. It aired a controversial television commercial in which a little girl's innocent counting game turned into the countdown for a nuclear explosion.

Johnson received 61 percent of the popular vote and an overwhelming 486 to 52 tally in the electoral college. The Democrats won majorities in both houses of Congress: 295 Democrats to 140 Republicans in the House of Representatives and 68 to 32 in the Senate. "Landslide Lyndon" now had the mandate to move ahead even more aggressively.

Sounds of an Era

Listen to Lyndon Johnson's Great Society speech and other sounds from the Kennedy-Johnson era.

Focus on GOVERNMENT

The "Daisy" Campaign Commercial
It aired only once, on September 7, 1964. Yet the Johnson campaign's chilling, black-and-white "daisy" commercial became one of the most famous in history. The camera zeroes in on a little girl holding a daisy. She counts the petals as she pulls them off: "One, two, three, four . . ." At "nine," a man's voice begins counting down to zero: ". . . three, two, one . . ." The image of the girl fades to the mushroom cloud of a nuclear blast.

The ad made no mention of Johnson's opponent, Barry Goldwater, but its message was clear: America in the hands of Goldwater risked nuclear war. Republicans cried foul. "This horror-type commercial is designed to arouse basic emotions and has no place in the campaign," the head of the Republican National Committee complained.

The protest backfired. Although the ad was pulled, the controversy caused TV news shows to play it over and over. The little girl with the daisy appeared on the cover of *Time* magazine.

The Tax Cut Like Kennedy, Johnson believed that a budget deficit could be used to improve the economy. Not everyone agreed. To gain conservatives' support for Kennedy's tax-cut bill, which was likely to bring about a deficit, Johnson also agreed to cut government spending. With that agreement, the measure passed and worked just as planned. When the tax cut went into effect, the Gross National Product (GNP) rose by 7.1 percent in 1964, by 8.1 percent in 1965, and by 9.5 percent in 1966. The deficit, which many people feared would grow, actually shrank because the renewed prosperity generated new tax revenues. Unemployment fell, and inflation remained in check.

The War on Poverty Growing up in an impoverished area of rural Texas, Johnson had experienced the pain of poverty firsthand. He now pressed for the antipoverty program that Kennedy had begun to consider.

In his 1964 State of the Union message, Johnson vowed, "This administration today, here and now, declares unconditional war on poverty in America." The Economic Opportunity Act, passed in the summer of 1964, was created to combat several causes of poverty, including illiteracy and unemployment. The act gave poor people a voice in defining housing, health, and education policies in their own neighborhoods. The act also provided nearly $950 million for ten separate projects, including education and work-training programs such as the Job Corps.

Two of the best-known programs created under the act were Head Start and VISTA. **Head Start** is a preschool program for children from low-income families that also provides healthcare, nutrition services, and social services. **Volunteers in Service to America (VISTA)** sent volunteers to help people in poor communities. Under Presidents Bush and Clinton, VISTA was merged with other national service programs.

Aid to Education Johnson's education initiatives moved through Congress as well. The Elementary and Secondary Education Act of 1965 provided $1.3 billion in aid to states, based on the number of children in each state from low-income homes. The funds went to public and private schools, including parochial schools. Johnson signed the Education Act into law in the small Texas school he had attended as a child. The graph at left shows federal aid to schools from 1959 to 1972.

Medicare and Medicaid President Johnson also focused attention on the increasing cost of medical care. Harry Truman had proposed a medical assistance plan as part of his Fair Deal program, but it had never been passed into law. In 1965, Johnson used his leadership skills to push through Congress two new programs, Medicare and Medicaid.

Medicare provides hospital and low-cost medical insurance to most Americans age 65 and older. "No longer will older Americans be denied the healing miracle of modern medicine," Johnson declared. "No longer will illness crush and destroy the savings that they have so carefully put away." **Medicaid** provides low-cost health insurance coverage to poor Americans of any age who cannot afford their own private health insurance.

INTERPRETING GRAPHS
The cartoon above depicts Johnson playing Congress like a piano, with Great Society programs flowing forth like music. One of those programs, the Elementary and Secondary Education Act, was passed by Congress in 1965. **Analyzing Visual Information** How did the legislation affect federal funding of public schools?

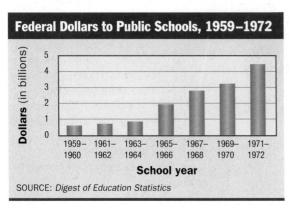

Federal Dollars to Public Schools, 1959–1972

SOURCE: *Digest of Education Statistics*

Great Society Legislation, 1964–1966

Legislation	Purpose
Economic Opportunity Act, 1964	Created to combat causes of poverty such as illiteracy. Set up community action programs to give the poor a voice in defining local housing, health, and education policies.
Volunteers in Service to America (VISTA), 1964	Sent volunteers to help people in poor communities.
Medicare, 1965	Provided hospital and low-cost medical insurance for most Americans age 65 and older.
Medicaid, 1965	Provided low-cost health insurance for poor Americans of any age who could not afford their own private health insurance.
Elementary and Secondary Education Act of 1965	Provided education aid to states based on the number of children from low-income homes.
Immigration Act of 1965	Eliminated strict quotas for individual countries and replaced them with more flexible limits.
The Department of Housing and Urban Development (HUD), 1965	Established to oversee the nation's housing needs and to develop and rehabilitate urban communities. HUD also provided money for rent supplements and low-income housing.
The National Foundations of the Arts and Humanities, 1965	Offered grants to artists and scholars.
Water Quality Act, 1965; Clean Water Restoration Act, 1966	Brought about water and air quality standards and provided funding for environmental research.
The National Traffic and Motor Vehicle Safety Act, 1966	Established safety standards for all vehicles to protect consumers.

INTERPRETING CHARTS As this chart shows, Great Society legislation addressed a wide range of topics. **Synthesizing Information** *Which pieces of legislation attempted to combat poverty?*

These broad-based healthcare programs were the most important pieces of social welfare legislation since the passage of the Social Security Act in 1935. They demonstrated the government's commitment to provide help to needy Americans.

Immigration Reform   The Great Society also revised the immigration policies that had been in place since the 1920s. Laws passed in 1921 and 1924 had set quotas, or numerical limits, for newcomers from each foreign nation. Low quotas—based on the 1890 census, before the arrival of new waves of immigrants—had been established for countries from southern and eastern Europe.

The **Immigration Act of 1965** replaced the varying quotas with a limit of 20,000 immigrants per year from any one country outside the Western Hemisphere. In addition, the act set overall limits of 170,000 immigrants from the Eastern Hemisphere and 120,000 from the Western Hemisphere. Family members of United States citizens were exempted from the quotas, as were political refugees. In the 1960s, some 350,000 immigrants entered the United States each year; in the 1970s, the number rose to more than 400,000 a year.

The Warren Court

The Kennedy-Johnson years featured many of the landmark decisions of the Supreme Court, often called the Warren Court after its Chief Justice, Earl Warren. As it had in earlier civil rights cases, the Supreme Court under Chief

READING CHECK
Under President Johnson, how did the role of the federal government change?

The members of the Warren Court, shown here on Nov. 22, 1965, are: (standing, left to right) Byron White, William Brennan, Potter Stewart, Abe Fortas; (seated, left to right) Tom Clark, Hugo Black, Earl Warren, William Douglas, and John Marshall Harlan.

VIEWING HISTORY The Warren Court issued rulings that angered many Americans, as this popular sign below shows. **Recognizing Ideologies** *What beliefs might have caused critics to oppose some of these rulings?*

Justice Earl Warren overturned many old laws and rulings and established new legal precedents.

Social Issues   The Warren Court made the first attempt to define obscenity in the 1957 case *Roth* v. *United States,* ruling that obscene materials were "utterly without redeeming social importance." In an explosive 1962 case, the Court ruled that religious prayer in public schools was unconstitutional according to the First Amendment principle of separation of church and state *(Engel* v. *Vitale).* In 1965, the Court struck down a Connecticut law that prohibited the use of birth control *(Griswold* v. *Connecticut).*

Criminal Procedure   The Warren Court was concerned with safeguarding the constitutional rights of the individual against the power of the government. In particular, the Court handed down several decisions protecting the rights of persons accused of crimes.

Mapp v. *Ohio* (1961) established the exclusionary rule, which states that evidence seized illegally cannot be used in a trial. The Court's decision in *Gideon* v. *Wainwright* (1963) stated that suspects in criminal cases who could not afford a lawyer had the right to free legal aid. In *Escobedo* v. *Illinois* (1964), the justices ruled that accused individuals had to be given access to an attorney while being questioned.

The Court's decision in *Miranda* v. *Arizona* (1966) stated that a suspect must be warned of his or her rights before being questioned. As a result of this **Miranda rule,** police must inform accused persons that they have the right to remain silent; that anything they say can be used against them in court; that they have a right to an attorney; and that if they cannot afford an attorney, one will be appointed for them.

"One Man, One Vote"   The Warren Court also handed down a series of decisions on **apportionment,**

or the distribution of the seats in a legislature among electoral districts. Over the years, many Americans had moved from rural to urban areas, but most state governments had not reapportioned their electoral districts to reflect that fact. As a result, in many states, rural areas had more power in state legislatures—and urban areas had less power—than their populations should have given them.

The Warren Court's decision in the case of *Baker* v. *Carr* (1962) declared that state legislative districts had to be divided on the basis of "one man, one vote." In other words, each person's vote should carry the same weight, regardless of where in the state the person lived. This decision prevented the party in power from drawing district lines in unfair ways to give itself more potential votes. In *Reynolds* v. *Sims* (1964), the Supreme Court held that state legislative districts not based on the "one man, one vote" formula violated the equal protection clause of the Fourteenth Amendment.

Many of these decisions were, and remain, controversial. Some people argued that the justices had gone too far in their "loose construction" of the Constitution. A number of Warren Court rulings are under vigorous attack from conservatives today.

Effects of the Great Society

At first, the Great Society seemed enormously successful. Opinion polls taken in 1964 showed Johnson to be more popular than Kennedy had been at a comparable point in his presidency.

In time, however, criticisms began to surface. New programs raised expectations that often could not be met. From 1965 through 1968, bloody race riots erupted in poor areas of major cities, giving urgency to Johnson's plans for Great Society programs. But military spending on Vietnam took ever-bigger bites out of the federal budget.

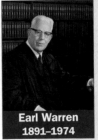

Earl Warren
1891–1974

One of the most important chief justices in history, Earl Warren led a Supreme Court that brought sweeping changes to American law and society. His decisions delighted liberals but surprised and angered many in his own Republican Party.

Earl Warren earned his law degree at the University of California at Berkeley. From 1925 to 1953, he won various posts in California: Alameda County district attorney, state attorney general, and finally governor. Warren's only election defeat was as Thomas E. Dewey's vice presidential running mate in 1948. In 1953, President Eisenhower appointed him the fourteenth Chief Justice of the United States—a choice Ike would later regret. Warren served as Chief Justice until he retired in 1969.

COMPARING HISTORIANS' VIEWPOINTS
The Great Society

Historians disagree about the effectiveness of President Johnson's Great Society programs.

Analyzing Viewpoints Compare the main arguments made by the two writers.

In Support of the Great Society

"In 1965 and early 1966 . . . the President and his economic advisors gratefully accepted the fiscal dividends provided by the booming economy as a means of bringing the Great Society closer to reality. Prosperity helped in two vital ways: by creating new jobs and by generating additional federal income that could be used to fund new social programs. Congress, which frequently approves new federal activities but then starves them to death by providing little or no money for their operation, funded the programs it authorized during 1965 and 1966 quite generously."

—Jim F. Heath,
The Decade of Disillusionment:
The Kennedy-Johnson Years

In Opposition to the Great Society

"In fact the war on poverty was destined to be one of the great failures of twentieth-century liberalism. Most of its programs could be grouped under two strategies. One of these emphasized opening new opportunities for poor people. . . . The other strategy, recognizing that mere opportunity would not be enough for many of the poor, provided subsidies to increase their consumption of food, shelter, and medical care. . . . Taken together, the programs spawned by these two strategies did little to diminish inequality and therefore, by definition, failed measurably to reduce poverty."

—Allen J. Matusow,
The Unraveling of America:
A History of Liberalism in the 1960s

VIEWING HISTORY A teacher instructs young students in the Head Start program. **Predicting Consequences** What long-term effects do you think the Johnson administration hoped to achieve through the Head Start program?

Meanwhile, some Americans complained that too many of their tax dollars were being spent on poor people. For decades following the Great Society, a major political debate continued over the criticism that antipoverty programs encouraged poor people to become dependent on government aid and created successive generations of families on welfare instead of in jobs. Other critics argued that Great Society programs put too much authority into the hands of the federal government. They opposed the expansion of the federal bureaucracy that accompanied the new programs.

Nevertheless, the number of Americans living in poverty in the United States was cut in half during the 1960s and early 1970s. Michael Harrington, author of *The Other America,* argued that the federal government should have allocated even more public funds to fight poverty. He noted, "What was supposed to be a social war turned out to be a skirmish and, in any case, poverty won."

In the midst of praise and criticism, Johnson himself was proud of his Great Society programs. In his view, they were "major accomplishments without equal or close parallel in the present era."

Before his death, John Kennedy had focused more on foreign affairs than domestic. When Johnson took office, he threw his energies into problems at home. The next section describes Kennedy's actions on the world stage and, after JFK's death, the beginnings of the conflict in Southeast Asia that would eventually consume the resources that Johnson had hoped to spend on domestic programs. LBJ's inability to contain that conflict undermined and finally ended the Great Society.

Section 2 Assessment

READING COMPREHENSION

1. Briefly outline LBJ's rise to the presidency.

2. List the key goals of the **Great Society** and some of the programs created to meet those goals.

3. Describe the changes made by the **Immigration Act of 1965.**

4. How did the **Miranda rule** change law enforcement in the United States?

CRITICAL THINKING AND WRITING

5. **Demonstrating Reasoned Judgment** Do you think Johnson's Great Society programs were a success? What questions would you ask yourself in order to make this judgment?

6. **Writing an Opinion** What positive or negative effects do you think the Warren Court has had on society today? Use examples to support your opinion.

For: An activity on Jacqueline Kennedy and Lady Bird Johnson
Visit: PHSchool.com
Web Code: mrd-9292

Foreign Policy in the Early 1960s

READING FOCUS

- What were the goals of the Bay of Pigs invasion, and what was the outcome?

- What events led to the Berlin crisis and to the Cuban Missile Crisis?

- What were the goals of the Alliance for Progress and the Peace Corps?

- Which Cold War conflicts did Johnson become involved in?

MAIN IDEA

The Cold War intensified as President Kennedy and President Johnson became involved in anti-Communist conflicts in Latin America, Europe, and Southeast Asia.

KEY TERMS

Bay of Pigs invasion
Berlin Wall
Cuban Missile Crisis
Limited Test Ban Treaty
Alliance for Progress
Peace Corps

TARGET READING SKILL

Summarize Copy the chart below. As you read, summarize facts about the outcomes of Cold War crises under Kennedy and Johnson.

Cold War Crises Under Kennedy and Johnson	Outcomes
Bay of Pigs	Failed invasion; United States humiliated

Setting the Scene Although they would have liked to dedicate more of America's resources to improving conditions at home, both Kennedy and Johnson found themselves in the front lines of the Cold War. It was a dangerous and expensive battle, but, as Kennedy argued, it was one worth fighting:

> 66 *Let every nation know, whether it wishes us well or ill, that we shall pay any price, bear any burden, meet any hardship, support any friend, oppose any foe to assure the survival and the success of liberty.* 99
> —John F. Kennedy, Inaugural Address, 1961

As President at the height of the Cold War between the Soviet Union and the United States, Kennedy spoke boldly. In the crises he faced as President, though, Kennedy found that he had to act more cautiously to prevent a local conflict from sparking a global war.

The Bay of Pigs Invasion

Kennedy's first foreign crisis arose in Cuba, an island about 90 miles off the Florida coast. The United States had been concerned about Cuba ever since 1959, when Fidel Castro overthrew the U.S.-backed dictator Fulgencio Batista. Some Cubans had supported Castro because he promised to improve the lives of poor people. Castro claimed that the poor were being exploited by wealthy Cubans and by United States companies operating in Cuba.

Once in power, the Castro government seized large, privately owned plantations and property owned by foreign corporations, including some U.S. businesses. The United States broke diplomatic relations with Cuba and refused to accept Castro as the country's legitimate leader. When Castro developed ties to the Soviet Union, American officials began to fear that Cuba could become a model for revolutionary upheaval throughout Latin America.

A Plan to Overthrow Castro After Kennedy became President, he was informed about a plan that President Eisenhower had approved in 1960. Under

Cuba's Fidel Castro (left) poses with his ally and supporter, Soviet leader Nikita Khrushchev, at a United Nations meeting.

this plan, the Central Intelligence Agency (CIA) was training a group of Cubans to invade Cuba and overthrow Castro. The training took place in Guatemala, a nearby Central American country. Kennedy and his advisors expected the Cuban people to help the invaders defeat Castro.

Resistance to the plan soon surfaced, however. When Democratic Senator J. William Fulbright, head of the Foreign Relations Committee, learned of the scheme, he called it an "endless can of worms." He warned the President:

> 66 To give this activity even covert [secret] support is of a piece with the hypocrisy and cynicism for which the United States is constantly denouncing [condemning] the Soviet Union in the United Nations and elsewhere. This point will not be lost on the rest of the world—nor on our own consciences. . . . The Castro regime is a thorn in the flesh; but it is not a dagger in the heart. 99
> —Senator J. William Fulbright, memorandum to Kennedy, March 29, 1961

Despite such reservations and those of some military leaders, Kennedy accepted the advice of the CIA and agreed to push ahead with the invasion plan.

A Military Catastrophe The **Bay of Pigs invasion**, shown on the map below, took place on April 17, 1961. It was a total disaster. An airstrike failed to destroy Cuba's air force, and Cuban troops were more than a match for the 1,500 U.S.-backed invaders. When Kennedy's advisors urged him to use American planes to provide air cover for the attackers, he refused. Rather than continue a hopeless effort, he chose simply to accept defeat.

The United States lost a great deal of prestige in the disastrous attack. To begin with, the invasion was clumsy and incompetent. Furthermore, America's support of an effort to overthrow another nation's government was exposed to the world. The United States faced anger from other countries in Latin America for violating agreements not to interfere in the Western Hemisphere. European

MAP SKILLS This map traces the ill-fated Bay of Pigs invasion authorized by President Kennedy in 1961. The photo below shows a Cuban beachfront resort littered with artillery shells following the invasion. **Regions** (a) How many countries played a role in the incident in some form? (b) How do you think this complexity affected the outcome of the operation?

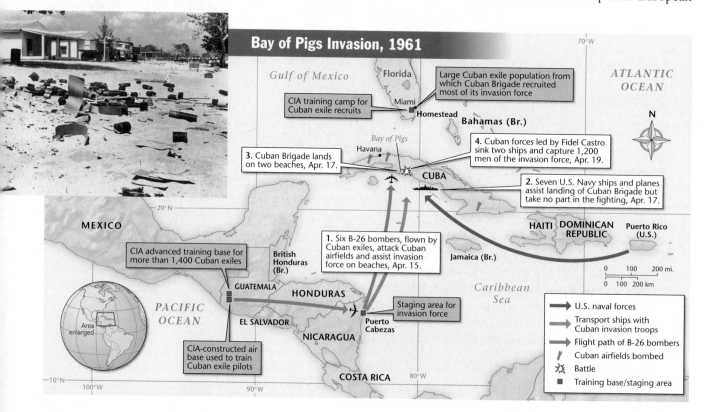

Bay of Pigs Invasion, 1961

CIA training camp for Cuban exile recruits

Large Cuban exile population from which Cuban Brigade recruited most of its invasion force

3. Cuban Brigade lands on two beaches, Apr. 17.

4. Cuban forces led by Fidel Castro sink two ships and capture 1,200 men of the invasion force, Apr. 19.

2. Seven U.S. Navy ships and planes assist landing of Cuban Brigade but take no part in the fighting, Apr. 17.

CIA advanced training base for more than 1,400 Cuban exiles

1. Six B-26 bombers, flown by Cuban exiles, attack Cuban airfields and assist invasion force on beaches, Apr. 15.

Staging area for invasion force

CIA-constructed air base used to train Cuban exile pilots

Gulf of Mexico · Florida · Miami · Homestead · Bahamas (Br.) · Bay of Pigs · Havana · CUBA · ATLANTIC OCEAN · MEXICO · British Honduras (Br.) · GUATEMALA · HONDURAS · EL SALVADOR · NICARAGUA · Puerto Cabezas · COSTA RICA · HAITI · DOMINICAN REPUBLIC · Puerto Rico (U.S.) · Jamaica (Br.) · Caribbean Sea · PACIFIC OCEAN · Area enlarged

0   100   200 mi.
0   100   200 km

— U.S. naval forces
— Transport ships with Cuban invasion troops
— Flight path of B-26 bombers
✈ Cuban airfields bombed
⚔ Battle
■ Training base/staging area

The Berlin Wall

Electrified fence

33 - 109 yards

Interior wall

EAST BERLIN

Barbed wire was the first barrier used to divide East and West Berlin in 1961.

Observation bunker

Siren signals

Trip wires activated **automatic guns** that fired at violators.

Antitank obstacles

Lights

Observation tower

Viewing stands were built by West Berlin to allow visitors to look over the wall.

Round **tubes** were placed at the top of the wall to make it difficult to scale.

WEST BERLIN

By 1975, the 7.5 mile **Wall** consisted of two 12–15 foot walls of concrete and steel.

Steel **anti-vehicle traps** and **mines** prevented escape attempts by car.

Patrols could drive along the paved **control track** to check potential violations quickly.

A strip of **gravel and sand** along the control track was kept smooth to show footprints.

leaders, who had high hopes for the new President, were concerned about the kind of leadership he would provide.

The Berlin Crisis

Upset by the failure at the Bay of Pigs, Kennedy was now even more determined to prove his toughness against communism. Later in 1961, he had another opportunity when a new crisis arose over a familiar issue: Berlin.

Rekindled Tensions Over Germany   After World War II, the Allies had divided Germany into zones. The United States, Great Britain, the Soviet Union, and France each controlled one sector of the country. While the zones were meant to be temporary, the lines between them had hardened as Cold War tensions increased among the former Allies. In time, the western regions had been combined to form the nation of West Germany. The sector controlled by the Soviet Union became East Germany. The city of Berlin, although located completely inside East Germany, had also been divided among the World War II victors.

The Soviet attempt to cut off access to Berlin in 1948 had failed as a result of President Truman's successful Berlin airlift. Now the Soviets made another effort to resolve problems in Berlin on their own terms. They demanded a peace treaty that would make the division of the city permanent. Their goal was to cut off the large flow of East Germans escaping into West Germany, particularly through Berlin.

Kennedy feared that the Soviet effort in Germany was part of a larger plan to take over the rest of Europe. Adding to his fears, his first meeting with Soviet leader Nikita Khrushchev, in Vienna, Austria, in June 1961, went poorly. When Khrushchev made a public ultimatum regarding Germany, Kennedy felt bullied by the Soviet leader.

Kennedy Takes Action   Upon returning home, Kennedy decided to show the Soviets that the United States would not be intimidated. He asked Congress for a huge increase of more than $3 billion for defense. He doubled the number of young men being drafted into the armed services and called up reserve forces for active duty. At the same time, he sought more than $200 million for a

INTERPRETING DIAGRAMS
Below, West Berliners peer through the newly built Berlin Wall into East Berlin near Checkpoint Charlie. Initially, tubes on the top of the wall were supposed to prevent escapees from getting a grip to pull themselves over. Later, as shown in the diagram of a typical checkpoint in the 1980s (top), a whole range of deadly deterrents were installed. **Analyzing Visual Information** As depicted in the diagram, what other hazards were added to prevent escape?

program to build fallout shelters across the country. He argued that the United States had to be prepared if the crisis led to nuclear war.

Kennedy appeared on television to tell the American people that West Berlin was "the great testing place of Western courage and will, a focal point where our solemn commitments . . . and Soviet ambitions now meet in basic confrontation." The United States, he said, would not be pushed around: "We do not want to fight—but we have fought before."

In August 1961, the Soviets responded by building a wall to separate Communist and non-Communist Berlin. The **Berlin Wall** became a somber symbol of the Cold War. Still, by stopping the flow of East Germans to the West, the Soviet Union had found a way to avoid a showdown over East Berlin.

Although the immediate crisis was over, the tensions of the Cold War continued. Speaking in Frankfurt, Germany, in June 1963, Kennedy declared that the United States "will risk its cities to defend yours because we need your freedom to protect ours." Two days later, the President addressed a cheering crowd near the Berlin Wall. To symbolize his commitment to the city, he concluded his speech with the rousing words, *"Ich bin ein Berliner,"* or "I am a Berliner."

The Cuban Missile Crisis

Kennedy also had a chance to restore American prestige in another crisis with Cuba. The Soviet Union, disturbed by the attempted Bay of Pigs invasion, had pledged to support Castro's government. On October 16, 1962, photographs taken from an American spy plane revealed that the Soviets were building missile bases on Cuban soil—only about 90 miles from the island of Key West, Florida. What followed was the **Cuban Missile Crisis,** a terrifying standoff between the United States and the Soviet Union that brought the superpowers to the brink of nuclear war.

Kennedy's Options The Soviet missiles in Cuba did not radically change the military balance between the United States and

MAP SKILLS U.S. spy plane photographs such as the one at right showed missile bases under construction in Cuba. The map shows the naval blockade of Cuba, put in place during tense diplomatic negotiations to avert a nuclear disaster. Khrushchev offered to withdraw the missiles from Cuba if Kennedy promised not to invade the island. **Location** *What details in the map help to explain (a) why the Soviet Union wanted a military presence in Cuba, and (b) why Kennedy was determined to prevent that from happening?*

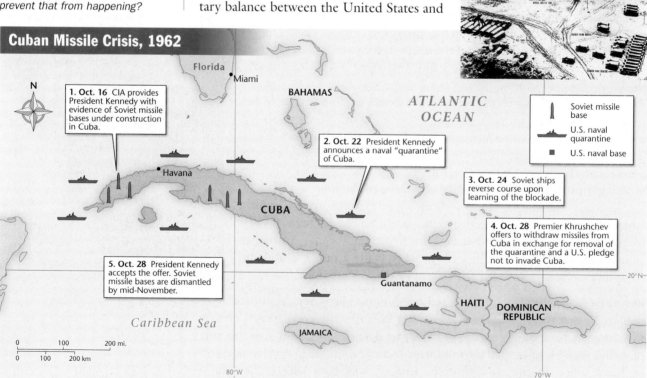

Cuban Missile Crisis, 1962

1. **Oct. 16** CIA provides President Kennedy with evidence of Soviet missile bases under construction in Cuba.

2. **Oct. 22** President Kennedy announces a naval "quarantine" of Cuba.

3. **Oct. 24** Soviet ships reverse course upon learning of the blockade.

4. **Oct. 28** Premier Khrushchev offers to withdraw missiles from Cuba in exchange for removal of the quarantine and a U.S. pledge not to invade Cuba.

5. **Oct. 28** President Kennedy accepts the offer. Soviet missile bases are dismantled by mid-November.

	Soviet missile base
	U.S. naval quarantine
	U.S. naval base

Florida
Miami
BAHAMAS
ATLANTIC OCEAN
Havana
CUBA
Guantanamo
HAITI
DOMINICAN REPUBLIC
JAMAICA
Caribbean Sea

0   100   200 mi.
0   100   200 km

20°N
80°W   70°W

the Soviet Union. Yet installing missiles so close to the United States seemed to be an effort by the Soviets to intimidate the Americans. In addition, the Soviets intended their missiles in Cuba to counter American missiles close to the USSR in Turkey. Kennedy was convinced that the missiles presented a direct challenge to which he must respond.

But how? The President quickly assembled his top advisors in a series of secret meetings. They outlined four possible responses:

1. Engage in further negotiations with Khrushchev. This option, although peaceful, would give the Soviets more time to finish building the missile bases. It also risked making Kennedy look hesitant and weak in the face of the bold Soviet move.

2. Invade Cuba. This would eliminate the missile threat and achieve the additional goal of ousting Fidel Castro. A Cuban invasion had failed before, though, and this plan risked all-out nuclear war with the Soviets.

3. Blockade Cuba. This action would prevent Soviet ships from making further missile deliveries. It would force Khrushchev either to back off or to take aggressive action against U.S. warships. However, no one knew how the Soviet leader might react to this step.

4. Bomb the missile sites. A series of airstrikes could quickly knock out the missiles. Yet would the Soviets launch a counterstrike, and where?

Attorney General Robert Kennedy argued against the airstrike option. It seemed, he said, too much like the Japanese attack on Pearl Harbor that had launched the United States into World War II. At one point former Secretary of State Dean Acheson joined the discussions and declared that the United States had to knock out the Soviet missiles. He was asked what would happen next. His response points out the very real danger of a local conflict escalating, or expanding, into a widespread war:

Acheson: I know the Soviet Union well. I know what they are required to do in the light of their history and their posture around the world. I think they will knock out our missiles in Turkey.

An advisor: Well, then what do we do?

Acheson: I believe under our NATO treaty . . . we would be required to respond by knocking out a missile base inside the Soviet Union.

Another advisor: Then what do they do?

Acheson: That's when we hope that cooler heads will prevail, and they'll stop and talk.

Kennedy Decides President Kennedy ordered United States forces on full alert. U.S. bombers were armed with nuclear missiles. The navy was ready to move, and army and marine units prepared to invade Cuba.

Kennedy listened to the different views of his advisors, grilling them with questions. Then, in solitude, he weighed the options, facing one of the most dangerous and agonizing decisions any President has had to make.

On Monday, October 22, Kennedy went on television and radio to confirm the press reports that had begun to circulate about Cuba. "[U]nmistakable evidence has established the fact that a series of offensive missile sites is now in

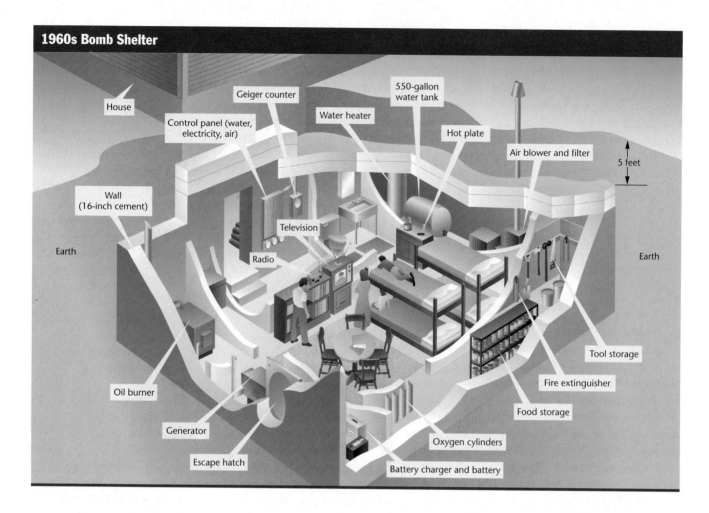

House

Geiger counter

550-gallon water tank

Control panel (water, electricity, air)

Water heater

Hot plate

Air blower and filter

5 feet

Wall (16-inch cement)

Television

Radio

Earth

Earth

Tool storage

Fire extinguisher

Oil burner

Food storage

Generator

Oxygen cylinders

Escape hatch

Battery charger and battery

INTERPRETING DIAGRAMS
Many Americans hoped they could survive a nuclear war in a basement shelter that would protect them from radioactive fallout, the deadly particles that rain down after an atomic blast. **Analyzing Visual Information** Which features of this fallout shelter are intended to provide safety for the family, and which provide comfort and necessities for living?

preparation on that imprisoned island," he said. The President then announced his decision: He had authorized a naval "quarantine" around Cuba. He was careful not to call the action a "blockade" because a blockade is an act of war. He demanded that Khrushchev "halt and eliminate this clandestine, reckless and provocative threat. . . ."

America did not desire confrontation, Kennedy said, but neither would it shrink from aggression. He told Americans:

> **❝** The path we have chosen for the present is full of hazards. . . . The cost of freedom is always high—and Americans have always paid it. And one path we shall never choose, and that is the path of surrender or submission. **❞**
>
> —President Kennedy, television and radio address to the nation, October 22, 1962

The World Waits The two most powerful nations in the world stood teetering on the brink of disaster. "The immediate public reaction was a mixture of anger and fear—but no panic—as they rallied in support of the president," one reporter later recalled. Some people huddled in their bomb shelters, expecting the worst.

The naval quarantine went into effect on Wednesday, October 24. On October 25, a Soviet ship reached the quarantine line and was stopped by the navy. Because it was carrying only oil, it was allowed to proceed. Meanwhile, a dozen more Soviet cargo ships were steaming toward the blockade. Then, to everyone's great relief, the Soviet ships suddenly reversed direction. Khrushchev had called them back.

Disaster Avoided   The crisis was not yet over, however. In Cuba, construction on the existing missile sites continued. On October 26, Khrushchev sent Kennedy a long letter in which he pledged to remove the missiles if Kennedy promised that the United States would end the quarantine and stay out of Cuba. A second letter delivered the next day demanded that the United States remove its missiles from Turkey in exchange for the withdrawal of Soviet missiles in Cuba. Kennedy publicly accepted the terms of the first note. He responded to the second note through secret negotiations and eventually met the demand.

As a U.S. Navy patrol plane flies overhead, the American destroyer USS *Barry* pulls alongside the Soviet freighter *Anesov* during the American naval blockade of Cuba.

With that, the crisis ended. As Secretary of State Dean Rusk observed to President Kennedy, "We have won a considerable victory. You and I are still alive."

The Cuban Missile Crisis brought the world closer than ever before to nuclear war. Such a war would have caused unimaginable death and destruction—far more, for example, than the atomic bombings of Japan in 1945, in part because more-powerful hydrogen bombs had replaced those early atomic weapons.

Kennedy emerged from the confrontation as a hero. He had stood up to the Soviets and shown that the United States would not be pushed around. His reputation, and that of the Democratic Party, improved just in time for the midterm congressional elections that were only weeks away.

The Aftereffects   The Cuban Missile Crisis led to a number of efforts to reduce the risk of nuclear war. Once the confrontation was over, Kennedy and Khrushchev established a "hot line" between their two nations to allow the Soviet and American leaders to communicate quickly in the event of a future crisis. In addition, in the summer of 1963 the two countries (along with Great Britain) signed the first nuclear treaty since the development of the atomic bomb.

This agreement, the **Limited Test Ban Treaty,** banned nuclear testing above the ground. By doing so, it sought to eliminate the radioactive fallout that threatened to contaminate human, animal, and plant life.

The treaty still permitted underground nuclear testing, and the United States and the Soviet Union continued to build bigger and bigger bombs. Nonetheless, as Kennedy noted, the treaty marked "an important first step toward peace, a step toward reason, a step away from war."

The Alliance for Progress

The Soviet Union and the United States competed not only by building up their military forces, but also by seeking allies in the developing countries of Latin America, Asia, and Africa. Many of these countries were terribly poor. Communist revolutionary movements in some of these countries were gaining support by promising people a better future.

To counter these revolutionary movements, Kennedy tried to promote "peaceful revolution"—that is, to help build stable governments that met the needs of their citizens and also were allied with the democratic countries of the West. Two months after taking office, Kennedy called on all the people of the Western Hemisphere to join in a new **Alliance for Progress,** or *Alianza para Progreso.* The Alliance would be a vast cooperative effort to satisfy the basic needs of people in North, Central, and South America for homes, work, land, health, and schools.

The task was a huge undertaking. The administration pledged $20 billion over ten years to promote economic development and social reform and to prevent revolution. All citizens in the Western Hemisphere, Kennedy declared, had "a right to social justice," and that included "land for the landless, and education for those who are denied education."

Soon, however, Latin Americans began to question the benefits of the Alliance. Some viewed it simply as a tool of the United States to stop the spread of communism. Because of such doubts, the Alliance for Progress never lived up to Kennedy's expectations.

The Peace Corps

Kennedy's hope for a world in which nations worked together peacefully to solve problems was also reflected in his establishment of the **Peace Corps** in 1961. This program sent volunteers abroad as educators, health workers, and technicians to help developing nations around the world.

Paul Cowan was typical of many Peace Corps volunteers. After graduating from college in 1963, he worked in the civil rights movement, tutoring African American children in Maryland. In 1965, Cowan and his wife, Rachel, joined the Peace Corps and prepared to work in South America. After a training program at the University of New Mexico, they went to the city of Guayaquil in Ecuador to do community development work. Their job was to raise the standard of living in

The Peace Corps

The idea for an overseas voluntary service organization began late at night on October 14, 1960. Kennedy, in an unscheduled speech to students at the University of Michigan, challenged them to devote two years of their lives helping people in developing countries. The idea took off. With the official creation of the Peace Corps a year later, the first volunteers accepted assignments in a handful of countries.

The mission of the Peace Corps, as set by Congress in 1961, was to meet the need for trained workers in participating countries and to promote mutual understanding between Americans and other peoples. "Life in the Peace Corps will not be easy," President Kennedy said in authorizing the organization. The more than 163,000 Peace Corps volunteers who served during the last four decades discovered the truth of Kennedy's statement. They have served in 135 countries, working side by side with local citizens—for low wages and only basic provisions—to improve impoverished areas of the world.

The mission and reach of the Peace Corps has expanded in recent years. In 1990, President George Bush celebrated the "talented Americans who are . . . to become the first Peace Corps volunteers to serve in Eastern Europe"—in Hungary and Poland. A special "Crisis Corps," created in 1995, provided workers who were trained to respond to humanitarian and natural disasters such as hurricanes. And in 2000, the Peace Corps announced that volunteers in Africa and in the Crisis Corps would be trained to provide education on HIV/AIDS. A "domestic Peace Corps," Americorps, founded in 1994, trains workers in local community service projects in the United States. Volunteers receive various benefits, including money for college, in return for their service.

 What is the meaning of the Peace Corps slogan, "The toughest job you'll ever love"?

poor areas and to work with local governments to provide services such as garbage removal and clean water.

Johnson's Foreign Policy

In 1963, Lyndon Johnson assumed the presidency upon Kennedy's death. His foreign policy, like Kennedy's, focused on containing communism around the world.

The Dominican Republic In 1965, Johnson received word that the military-backed government in the Dominican Republic, a Caribbean nation close to Cuba, had been attacked by rebels. Johnson feared that the disruption might endanger American citizens living there. Arguing (wrongly, it turned out) that Communist elements were causing the disruption, Johnson sent 22,000 marines to the Dominican Republic. Their presence tipped the balance away from the rebels. Within a few months a provisional government backed by the United States was put in place. Elections were held the following year.

Vietnam   Johnson also became deeply involved in the ongoing conflict in Southeast Asia between Communist North Vietnam and non-Communist South Vietnam. Like Kennedy, Johnson was determined to prevent the spread of communism there. By 1963, about 16,000 American military advisors were in South Vietnam. The United States was also contributing economic aid to the South Vietnamese government.

In his 1964 campaign for President, Johnson opposed more direct United States involvement in the war. Yet, before long he faced the prospect of a Communist takeover of South Vietnam, which he could not tolerate. During 1965, American involvement in the conflict deepened as more and more troops and money were sent to prop up the South Vietnamese government.

COMPARING PRIMARY SOURCES
The Cold War

The United States and its allies continued to battle Communist expansion in the 1960s.

Analyzing Viewpoints What strategy did each of the speakers below want to pursue during the Cold War?

For Moderation in the Cold War

"The issues called the cold war . . . must be met with determination, confidence, and sophistication. . . . [C]hannels of communication should be kept open. . . . Our discussion, public or private, should be marked by civility; our manners should conform to our own dignity and power and to our good repute throughout the world."

—Secretary of State Dean Rusk, speech at the University of California, Berkeley, March 20, 1961

For Aggressiveness in the Cold War

"[I]t is really astounding that our government has never stated its purpose to be that of complete victory over the tyrannical forces of international communism. . . . And we need an official act, such as the resumption of nuclear testing, to show our own peoples and the other freedom-loving peoples of the world that we mean business."

—Arizona Senator Barry Goldwater, address to the United States Senate, July 14, 1961

Section 3 Assessment

READING COMPREHENSION

1. Describe the causes and effects of the **Bay of Pigs invasion.**

2. (a) Why did tensions reignite over the division of Germany? (b) Why was the **Berlin Wall** built?

3. What goals did the **Alliance for Progress** and the **Peace Corps** attempt to fulfill?

4. In what ways did Johnson continue Kennedy's approach to the Cold War?

CRITICAL THINKING AND WRITING

5. **Drawing Inferences** What can you infer about the Soviet Union's foreign policy goals from its actions in the Cold War crises of the 1960s?

6. **Journal Writing** Write a fictional entry from a personal journal of President Kennedy during the Cuban Missile Crisis. Include details that demonstrate your understanding of the difficulties Kennedy faced.

For: An activity on the Peace Corps
Visit: PHSchool.com
Web Code: mrd-9293

creating a CHAPTER SUMMARY

Copy this chart (right) on a piece of paper and complete it by adding information about key events and policies of the Kennedy and Johnson administrations. Some entries have been completed for you as examples.

For additional review and enrichment activities, see the interactive version of *America: Pathways to the Present*, available on the Web and on CD-ROM.

Major Events/ Actions	Kennedy	Johnson
Domestic Policy	• Housing Act of 1961 •	• Tax cut •
Foreign Policy	• Bay of Pigs • •	• Dominican Republic uprising • •

★ Reviewing Key Terms

For each of the terms below, write a sentence explaining how it relates to the Kennedy-Johnson years.

1. mandate
2. New Frontier
3. Great Society
4. Medicare
5. Medicaid
6. Immigration Act of 1965
7. Miranda rule
8. apportionment
9. Limited Test Ban Treaty
10. Peace Corps

★ Reviewing Main Ideas

11. Describe the outcome of the first Nixon-Kennedy debate and the reasons for that outcome. (Section 1)

12. What domestic programs did Kennedy propose, and why were they largely unsuccessful? (Section 1)

13. What actions were taken to investigate Kennedy's assassination? (Section 1)

14. What domestic programs did Johnson propose? (Section 2)

15. Describe three landmark decisions handed down by the Supreme Court under Chief Justice Earl Warren. (Section 2)

16. Identify the major effects of the Great Society. (Section 2)

17. What consequences to President Kennedy and the United States resulted from the failed Bay of Pigs invasion? (Section 3)

18. Describe the Berlin crisis of 1961. (Section 3)

19. Why did Kennedy establish the Peace Corps? (Section 3)

20. What was Johnson's approach to foreign policy? (Section 3)

★ Critical Thinking

21. **Making Comparisons** What policies and programs would you recommend as part of an effort to eliminate poverty? How would they be similar to, or different from, the programs of Johnson's Great Society?

22. **Predicting Consequences** How did the beliefs of Presidents Kennedy and Johnson about the spread of communism influence their foreign policy decisions?

23. **Drawing Inferences** In what ways did the Warren Court help to uphold the principle that a person is "innocent until proven guilty"?

24. **Drawing Conclusions** Would you characterize Johnson as a weak or a powerful politician? Explain your reasoning.

★ Standardized Test Prep

Analyzing Political Cartoons ▶

25. This cartoon was printed in November 1962. It depicts John F. Kennedy and Nikita Khrushchev. What are the two men trying to do?

A Prevent a third country from starting a nuclear war

B Prevent each other from starting a nuclear war

C Contain the threat of nuclear war

D Lock nuclear weapons in their silos

26. (a) What is the message of the cartoon? (b) What event do you think inspired the cartoon?

Analyzing Primary Sources

Reread the two quotations in Comparing Primary Sources in Section 3 and then answer the questions that follow.

27. Which statement BEST describes Secretary of State Dean Rusk's view of the Cold War?

A The Cold War is not a serious threat to the United States and does not require a strong American response.

B The United States should be cautious in its discussions with the Soviet Union.

C The United States should be firm but honorable in its Cold War diplomacy.

D The United States must live up to its reputation as a superpower by being tough on communism.

28. Which statement BEST describes Senator Barry Goldwater's view of the Cold War?

F A strong statement of America's goal of eliminating communism should be backed up by military action.

G The United States should use nuclear weapons to protect people's freedom.

H The United States government has waged a tyrannical fight against communism.

I American businesses should help fight communism and protect freedom-loving peoples.

Nov. 1, 1962   HERBLOCK

LET'S GET A LOCK FOR THIS THING.

Test-Taking Tip

To answer Question 27, note the following words from Rusk's quotation: *determination, confidence, civility, dignity.*

Applying the Chapter Skill

Exploring Oral History Interview one or two adults who remember Kennedy's assassination. Ask them if they can recall what they were doing when they heard the news. Have them describe their reaction to the tragedy as well as its impact on the nation.

For: Chapter 22 Self-Test
Visit: PHSchool.com
Web Code: mra-9294

An Era of Activism

(1960–1975)

1966

The National Organization for Women is formed.

1963

The Feminine Mystique by Betty Friedan inspires the women's movement.

1965

Ralph Nader's *Unsafe at Any Speed* is published, initiating the consumer protection movement.

1967

César Chávez's United Farm Workers organize a nationwide boycott of grapes picked on nonunion farms.

1962

Rachel Carson's book *Silent Spring* launches the environmental movement.

American Events

Presidential Terms: D. Eisenhower 1953–1961   John F. Kennedy 1961–1963   Lyndon B. Johnson 1963–1969

1960

1965

World Events

In Ceylon (now Sri Lanka), Sirimavo Bandaranaike is elected the world's first female prime minister.

1960

Soviet cosmonaut Valentina Tereshkova becomes the first woman in space.

1963

Indira Gandhi becomes prime minister of India.

1966

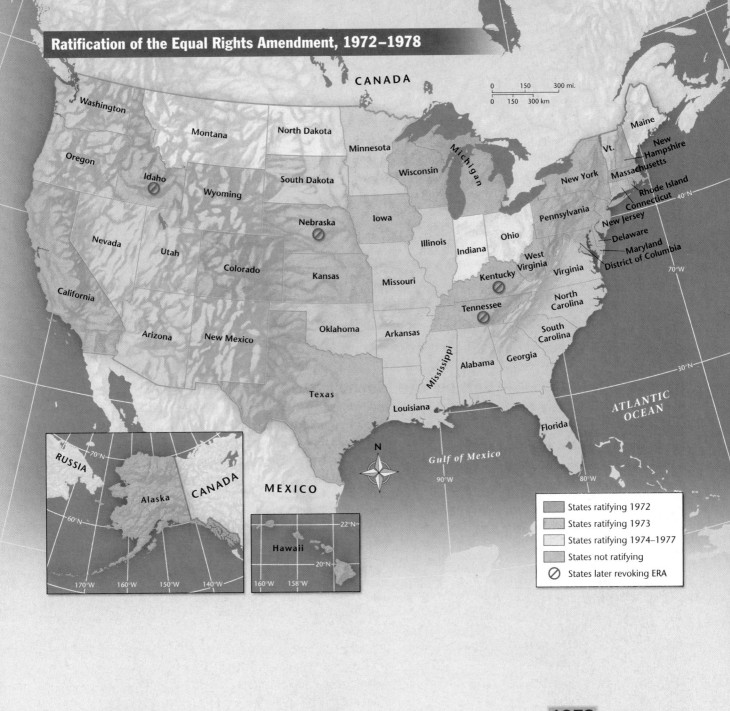

Ratification of the Equal Rights Amendment, 1972–1978

CANADA

Washington
Montana
North Dakota
Minnesota
Oregon
Idaho
Wyoming
South Dakota
Wisconsin
Michigan
Maine
New Hampshire
Vt.
New York
Massachusetts
Rhode Island
Connecticut
New Jersey
Delaware
Maryland
District of Columbia
Nevada
Utah
Colorado
Nebraska
Iowa
Illinois
Indiana
Ohio
Pennsylvania
California
Kansas
Missouri
West Virginia
Kentucky
Virginia
North Carolina
Arizona
New Mexico
Oklahoma
Arkansas
Tennessee
South Carolina
Texas
Mississippi
Alabama
Georgia
Louisiana
Florida

ATLANTIC OCEAN

N

Gulf of Mexico

RUSSIA
Alaska
CANADA
MEXICO

Hawaii

	Legend
	States ratifying 1972
	States ratifying 1973
	States ratifying 1974–1977
	States not ratifying
⊘	States later revoking ERA

0   150   300 mi.
0   150   300 km

70°N
60°N
170°W 160°W 150°W 140°W
160°W 158°W
22°N
20°N
70°W
40°N
30°N
80°W
90°W

1969
The Woodstock festival celebrates rock music and the counterculture.

1970
The first Earth Day is celebrated, the Environmental Protection Agency is established, and Congress passes the Clean Air Act.

1973
The Supreme Court legalizes abortion in *Roe* v. *Wade*. Protesters from the American Indian Movement take over the reservation at Wounded Knee.

Richard M. Nixon 1969–1974   Gerald R. Ford 1974–1977

1970   1975

1970
Greenpeace is founded in Vancouver, Canada.

1971

1973
U.S. involvement in the Vietnam War ends with the signing of a formal peace agreement in Paris.

1975

The Women's Movement

READING FOCUS

- What was the background of the women's movement?
- How did women organize to gain support and to effect change?
- What was the impact of feminism?
- Which groups opposed the women's movement and why?

MAIN IDEA

The women's movement, which was dedicated to ending discrimination based on gender, found inspiration in the civil rights movement and other activist causes.

KEY TERMS

feminism
National Organization for Women (NOW)
Roe v. *Wade*
Equal Rights Amendment (ERA)

TARGET READING SKILL

Identify Cause and Effect Copy the web diagram below. As you read, write the conditions that led to the women's movement in the bubbles on the left. Write the effects on the right.

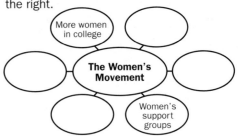

Setting the Scene Songwriter Bob Dylan's 1964 hit "The Times They Are A-Changin'" reflected the atmosphere of the sixties. The fifties had been primarily a time of unprecedented prosperity and security, but not all groups had participated equally. The sixties ushered in an era of activism, as these groups and their supporters seized the opportunity to make their voices heard. One demand for change came from women who did not want to be limited to the traditional roles of wife and mother. These women demanded the same opportunities as men. Pop singer Helen Reddy's 1971 song exemplified this new point of view:

> " *I am woman, hear me roar*
> *In numbers too big to ignore,*
> *And I know too much to go back*
> * and pretend. . . .*
> *Yes, I've paid the price*
> *But look how much I gained.*
> *If I have to, I can do anything.*
> *I am strong, I am invincible,*
> *I am woman.* "
>
> —Ray Burton and Helen Reddy

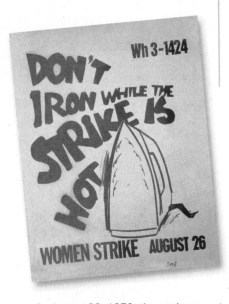

On August 26, 1970, the anniversary of the passage of the constitutional amendment granting women suffrage, thousands of women took the day off from jobs and household chores to observe Women's Equality Day.

These lyrics reflect the sense of self-confidence and strength that helped to create the new women's movement in the 1960s and continued to drive it forward into the 1970s.

Background of the Women's Movement

The crusade for women's rights was not new in 1960. In the late 1800s, particularly, women had worked for the right to vote and for equality in education and in jobs. The term **feminism,** which came to be associated with the 1960s, had first come into recorded use in 1895 to describe the theory of political, economic, and social equality of men and women. Feminists were those who believed in this equality or took action to bring it about.

While much progress had been made since the 1890s, the full equality sought by feminists had not been achieved. The women's movement of the 1960s sought to change aspects of American life that had been accepted for decades. The 1950s stereotype of women still placed them in the home, married and raising children. For many women, this stereotype did not reflect either reality or necessity. As had been the case in earlier decades, many women needed to work in order to support themselves or to help support their families. Furthermore, World War II had opened many new employment opportunities for women. During and after the war, more and more women entered the labor force. By the beginning of the 1960s, about 38 percent of all women held jobs. In addition, many women were educated, and looked forward to putting their education to use in professional careers.

The new women's movement chose symbols of power to represent its cause.

Education and Employment An increasing number of women began going to college after World War II. In 1950, only 25 percent of all Bachelor of Arts degrees were earned by women. Twenty years later, in 1970, the number was 43 percent. Better-educated women had high hopes for the future, but they were often discouraged by the discrimination they faced when they looked for jobs or tried to advance in their professions.

In many cases, employers were reluctant to invest in training women because they expected female employees to leave their jobs after a few years to start families. Other employers simply refused to hire qualified women because they believed that home and family should be a woman's only responsibility.

Women who did enter the work force often found themselves underemployed, performing jobs and earning salaries below their abilities. Working women earned less than working men doing similar or even identical jobs. In 1963, women, on average, were paid only 59 cents for each dollar that men earned. By 1973, this figure had dropped to 57 cents. This financial inequality created a growing sense of frustration among women and led to renewed demands for equal pay for equal work.

The Impact of the Civil Rights Movement While social, educational, and economic conditions set the scene for the women's movement, the civil rights movement provided a "how-to" model for action. It also provided inspiration. Black and white women had joined in the struggle for civil rights and gained valuable skills from their work in the movement. At the same time, they had endured frustration over their second-class status in civil rights organizations. As they worked to end racial discrimination, women were expected to make coffee and do clerical work while men made most of the policy decisions. Frustrated over their assigned roles, women began to apply the techniques that had been successful in the civil rights movement to a new movement that would address their own concerns.

The civil rights movement also provided women with legal tools to fight discrimination. One such tool was the 1964 Civil Rights Act. Originally, the section of the act called Title VII prohibited discrimination based on race, religion, or national origin. When Congress debated the bill, however, some opponents of civil rights added an amendment to outlaw discrimination on the basis of sex. This action was a strategy to make the entire bill look ridiculous, so that it would fail in the final vote. To the dismay of its opponents, both the amendment and the bill passed. The

INTERPRETING GRAPHS
Women's incomes continued to lag behind men's earnings, partly because many low-paying jobs were traditionally considered "women's work." **Making Comparisons** *How did the gap change between 1950 and 1975?*

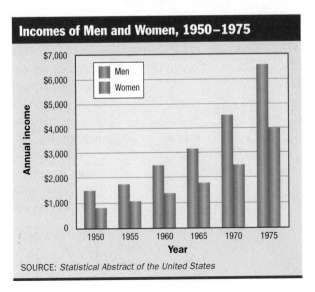

Incomes of Men and Women, 1950–1975

SOURCE: *Statistical Abstract of the United States*

new Civil Rights Act now had a provision that gave women a legal framework to challenge discrimination.

Even with the added boost of the new legislation, progress took time. Women soon discovered that the Equal Employment Opportunity Commission (EEOC) set up by the bill did not take women's discrimination claims seriously. Nevertheless, Title VII would be tremendously important as the women's movement gained strength.

Women's Groups Organize

As the 1960s unfolded, women began to meet in groups to compare experiences. Women active in the civil rights movement met to look for ways in which they could play a larger role in that struggle. Soon they went beyond politics, exploring other aspects of their lives. The growing movement drew women who were active in other forms of protest and reform. They included student radicals, opponents of the Vietnam War and the draft, and workers for welfare rights and other social issues. Another important influence was Betty Friedan's 1963 book *The Feminine Mystique*. The dissatisfied housewives that Friedan described in her book began meeting, too, to discuss their lives and their roles in society.

Support Groups Meeting in kitchens and living rooms, women began gathering in consciousness-raising groups, which were dedicated to increasing their members' awareness of women's situation in society. One participant, Nancy Hawley, who was a community activist in Boston, Massachusetts, was troubled by patterns she saw at work. "Though many of us were working harder than the men," she noted, "we realized we were not listened to and often ignored." Growing numbers of women recognized the negative attitudes, or sexism, directed toward them. Many told of being ridiculed for attending women's groups. Such lack of support outside the group made their bond stronger within the group.

Organizing NOW In 1966, a group of 28 professional women, including Betty Friedan, established the **National Organization for Women (NOW)**. These women were frustrated that existing women's groups were unwilling to pressure the Equal Employment Opportunity Commission to take women's grievances more seriously. The goal of NOW was "to take action to bring American women into full participation in the mainstream of American society now."

NOW sought fair pay and equal job opportunities. It attacked the "false image of women" in the media, such as advertising that used sexist slogans or photographs. NOW also called for more balance in marriages, with men and women sharing parenting and household responsibilities. A year after NOW was founded, it had 1,000 members. Only four years later, some 15,000 women had joined.

For some women, NOW seemed too extreme; for others, it was not extreme enough. Some saw NOW—and the women's movement in general—as mainly benefiting white, middle-class women. Nonetheless, NOW served as a rallying point to end sex discrimination and to promote equality for all women.

The Impact of Feminism

The women's movement came of age in the early 1970s. In August 1970, a New York City march celebrating the fiftieth anniversary of women's suffrage drew

tens of thousands of demonstrators supporting women's equality. More women began identifying themselves as feminists. Even those who did not join feminist groups could now find new kinds of information and opinions on women's issues. One new source was a book called *Our Bodies, Ourselves*. This handbook, published in 1970 by a women's health collective in Boston, encouraged women to understand their own health issues. It sold 200,000 copies in the first several years after its publication and three million by 1990.

In 1972, journalist Gloria Steinem and several other women founded *Ms.* magazine. Devoted to feminist issues, *Ms.* provided women with viewpoints that were decidedly different from those in *Good Housekeeping, Ladies' Home Journal,* and other women's magazines of the day. All 300,000 copies of the preview issue sold out in eight days. Only one year later, *Ms.* had nearly 200,000 subscribers. While not all readers considered themselves feminists, the magazine familiarized its audience with the arguments and issues of the women's movement.

A Shift in Attitudes Slowly the women's movement brought a shift in attitudes and in the law. For example, in 1972, Congress passed a prohibition against sex discrimination as part of the Higher Education Act. A survey of first-year college students revealed a significant change in career goals—and opportunities. In 1970, men interested in fields such as business, law, engineering, and medicine outnumbered women by eight to one. Five years later, the margin had dropped to three to one. More women entered law school and medical school. Women were finally admitted to military academies to be trained as officers.

In 1971, the National Women's Political Caucus was formed to expand women's participation in politics. By working from within the system, women were able to gain broader support for the goals of the women's movement. Women also became more influential in politics. New Yorker Shirley Chisholm, who was a founder of the National Women's Political Caucus, served in the House of Representatives from 1969 to 1983. In 1972, she ran for President, winning 152 delegates to the Democratic National Convention before she withdrew from the race. Chisholm's candidacy demonstrated that an African American woman

READING CHECK
What were some of the effects of the women's movement?

COMPARING PRIMARY SOURCES

Working Mothers

In the early years of the women's movement, experts disagreed over the issue of working mothers.

Analyzing Viewpoints What assumptions and biases about women and about children are revealed by each author? What reasonable argument does each author use?

In Favor of Working Mothers

"At the present time, one can say anything—good or bad—about children of employed mothers and support the statement by some research finding. But there is no definitive evidence that children are less happy, healthy, adjusted, because their mothers work. The studies that show working women to be happier, better, more mature mothers do not get much publicity."

—Betty Friedan,
The Feminine Mystique, *1963*

Opposed to Working Mothers

"To work or not to work? Some mothers have to work to make a living. Usually their children turn out all right, because some reasonably good arrangement is made for their care. But others grow up neglected and maladjusted. . . . It doesn't make sense to let mothers go to work making dresses in a factory or tapping typewriters in an office, and have them pay other people to do a poorer job of bringing up their children."

—Benjamin Spock, M.D.,
Baby and Childcare, *1957 (first published in 1946)*

VIEWING HISTORY Gloria Steinem, above, was one of the founders of *Ms.* magazine. The first issue is shown at right.
Analyzing Visual Information *How does the* Ms. *cover show the many roles women were expected to fill?*

could gain support for national office. And she paved the way for Geraldine Ferraro's selection as the Democratic Party's vice presidential candidate in 1984.

Many women did not actively participate in or support the women's movement. Still, most agreed with NOW's goal to provide women with better job opportunities. Many were also pleased that the women's movement brought a greater recognition of issues important to women. These issues included the need for child-care facilities, shelters for homeless women, more attention to women's health concerns, and increased awareness of sexual harassment.

Despite many shared concerns, the women's movement continued to be divided regarding some of its goals and strategies. Radical feminists emphasized the need to end male domination, sometimes even rejecting men, marriage, and childbearing. Other women rejected the strong opinions of the radicals, fearing they would cause a split in the women's movement. These women emphasized that they sought only equality with men, not rejection of them.

Roe* v. *Wade One issue that had the potential to divide the movement was abortion. NOW and other groups worked to reform the laws governing a woman's decision to choose an abortion instead of continuing an unwanted pregnancy. Many states outlawed or severely restricted access to abortion. Women who could afford to travel to another state or out of the country could usually find legal medical services, but poorer women often turned to abortion methods that were not only illegal but unsafe.

A landmark social and legal change came in 1973, when the Supreme Court legalized abortion in the controversial ***Roe* v. *Wade*** decision. The justices based their decision on the constitutional right to personal privacy, and struck down state regulation of abortion in the first three months of pregnancy. However, the ruling still allowed states to restrict abortions during the later stages of pregnancy. The case was, and remains, highly controversial, with radical thinkers on both sides of the argument.

The Equal Rights Amendment Many women also took part in the campaign for a change to the Constitution that would make discrimination based on a person's sex illegal. In 1972, Congress approved passage of the **Equal Rights Amendment (ERA)** to the Constitution:

Many women demonstrated in favor of ratification of the ERA.

KEY DOCUMENTS
❝*Equality of rights under the law shall not be denied or abridged by the United States or by any State on account of sex.*❞
—Equal Rights Amendment, 1972

To become law, the amendment had to be ratified by 38 states. Thirty states did so quickly. When a few others also ratified it, approval seemed certain. By 1977, 35 states had ratified the amendment, but opposition forces were gaining strength. The effort to add the ERA to the Constitution limped along until the 1982 deadline for ratification and then died.

Opposition to the Women's Movement

It was a woman, conservative political activist Phyllis Schlafly, who led a national campaign to block ratification of the ERA. She said this about the amendment:

> ❝ It won't do anything to help women, and it will take away from women the rights they already have, such as the right of a wife to be supported by her husband, the right of a woman to be exempted from military combat, and the right . . . to go to a single-sex college. ❞
>
> —Phyllis Schlafly

VIEWING HISTORY Phyllis Schlafly spoke out against the ERA. **Determining Relevance** *Do you think the fact that Schlafly was a woman made her a more effective or less effective advocate for her point of view? Explain your answer.*

Women already had legal backing for their rights, Schlafly argued. ERA supporters contested Schlafly's charges about the supposed effects of the ERA, such as the establishment of coed bathrooms and the end of alimony. Nevertheless, arguments such as Schlafly's were instrumental in preventing the ERA from being ratified before the deadline.

Schlafly was not alone in her opposition to the ERA and to the women's movement in general. Many men were also hostile to the feminist movement, which was sometimes scornfully called "women's liberation" or "women's lib."

Nor were all women sympathetic to the goals of the women's movement. Some women responded by stressing their desire to remain at home and raise children. They were happy with women's traditional roles and resented being told that they should feel dissatisfied. These women felt that their roles as wives, and particularly as mothers, were being undervalued by the women's movement. The result, as these women saw it, was less rather than more respect for women and for the important task of raising the next generation.

Opposition came from other quarters as well. Some African American women felt that combating racial discrimination was more important than battling sex discrimination. In 1974, NOW's African American president, Aileen Hernandez, acknowledged that "Some black sisters are not sure that the feminist movement will meet their current needs." Many working-class women felt removed from the movement, too. They believed they were being encouraged to give up homemaking in order to take up undesirable paid labor.

Nevertheless, the women's movement continued to make gains, to change minds, and to expand opportunities for women. In so doing, it became one of several important strands of reform in the era of activism.

Section 1 Assessment

READING COMPREHENSION

1. What is **feminism**?
2. (a) When was **NOW** formed? (b) What was its purpose?
3. Who was Shirley Chisholm?
4. Explain the **Roe v. Wade** decision.
5. (a) What was the **ERA**? (b) How many states eventually ratified it?

CRITICAL THINKING AND WRITING

6. **Identifying Assumptions** (a) What beliefs led many women to support the women's movement? (b) What beliefs led others to oppose it?
7. **Writing an Opinion** Would there have been a successful women's movement without the example of the civil rights movement? Support your opinion in a paragraph.

Go **Online**
PHSchool.com

For: An activity on the ERA
Visit: PHSchool.com
Web Code: mrd-9301

Recognizing Bias

Recognizing bias means being aware of information and ideas that are one-sided or that present only a partial view of a subject. Bias may be stated or unstated. A writer may admit partisanship, or bias, and then support one side of an issue. Unstated bias—when a source presents only one side of an issue while suggesting that it presents the whole picture—is more difficult to detect. The ability to spot bias will help you analyze information and make sound judgments about the reliability of sources.

Bias is often attached to issues that have emotional impact—issues that also inspire strong expressions of different points of view. One such issue was the Equal Rights Amendment (ERA).

LEARN THE SKILL

Use the following steps to recognize bias:

1. **Decide whether or not the source presents only one side of an issue.** Writing from a single viewpoint signals imbalance—and bias.

2. **Look for unstated as well as stated bias.** Look for clear statements of a position that signal stated bias. Also look for indications that a source is presenting only one side of the issue while suggesting it covers all sides; that is unstated bias.

3. **Determine whether the presentation of the issue is supported by opinions or verifiable facts.** Sometimes what appear to be facts are actually opinions disguised as facts. Remember, you can check the accuracy of facts in other sources.

4. **Examine the source for hidden assumptions or generalizations that are not supported by facts.** Look for sweeping generalizations and for claims that opposing opinions are worthless.

PRACTICE THE SKILL

Answer the following questions:

1. **(a)** What is the overall message of each passage? **(b)** Does either passage present both sides of the issue? Explain.

2. **(a)** Is the bias in Passage A stated or unstated? Explain. **(b)** Is the bias in Passage B stated or unstated? Explain.

3. **(a)** Which details in the passages can be checked for accuracy? **(b)** Are any opinions presented as though they were facts? Give an example.

4. **(a)** What hidden assumptions or generalizations do you find in the passages? **(b)** Which passage ridicules the opposing point of view? How does it do so? **(c)** How much would you rely on each passage for information about the ERA? Explain your reasoning.

APPLY THE SKILL

See the Chapter Review and Assessment for another opportunity to apply this skill.

A.

"My primary objection to ERA is that it's a broad, general amendment which is open to interpretation. I think only an absolute fool would give an open amendment to the Supreme Court in light of what the Court has done in the last twenty-five years.

The ERA is a power grab by Washington. States' rights pertaining to women will go to the national government. We've already given up power to the feds in other Constitutional amendments. Why give up more power?"

—Opponent of ERA, in *The Politics of the Equal Rights Amendment,* 1979

B.

"The 14th and 15th amendments, written in 1868 and 1870, said: 'All persons born or naturalized in the U.S. are citizens and have the right to vote.'

Susan B. Anthony, considering herself to be a person, registered and voted in 1872. She was arrested, brought to trial, convicted of the crime of voting—because she was a woman, and the word *persons* mentioned in our Constitution did not mean women. . . . If she were alive today, Susan B. Anthony might vote, but she would still see 1000 legal discriminations against women upon various state statute books. . . .

The solution of the problem of giving women 100 per cent protection of the Constitution . . . is the adoption of the Equal Rights for Women Amendment which reads: Equality of rights under law shall not be denied or abridged by the United States or by any state on account of sex."

——Proponent of ERA, in *Delta Kappa Gamma Magazine,* Fall 1969

READING FOCUS

- How did Latinos seek equality during the 1960s and early 1970s?

- How did Asian Americans fight discrimination during this period?

- In what ways did Native Americans confront their unique problems?

MAIN IDEA

Inspired by the civil rights movement, Latinos, Asian Americans, and Native Americans organized to seek equality and to improve their lives.

KEY TERMS

Latino
migrant farm worker
United Farm Workers (UFW)
Japanese American Citizens League (JACL)
American Indian Movement (AIM)
autonomy

TARGET READING SKILL

Identify Main Ideas As you read, complete the chart below to describe each group's struggle for equality.

Actions and Accomplishments

Latinos	Asian Americans	Native Americans
• Students boycott L.A. schools to demand better conditions. • • •	• JACL wins compensation for internees. • •	• • •

Setting the Scene

Inspired by the civil rights and women's movements, other ethnic and racial groups began to fight for equality during the 1960s and 1970s. In May 1970, journalist Rubén Salazar predicted the future of one of these new movements, the Chicano movement in Los Angeles, California. "We are going to overthrow some of our institutions," he said. "But in the way Americans have always done it: through the ballot, through public consensus. That's a revolution." Three months later, Salazar was killed in the rioting that broke out after police tried to stop a Chicano anti–Vietnam War demonstration.

After his death, Salazar became a martyr to the Chicano movement. His ideals and his death also point to the connection between the Chicano movement and other activist causes of the era, such as the antiwar and civil rights movements. In addition, Salazar's words show how these movements of the 1960s and 1970s fit into the long tradition of American reform—a tradition that is marked by change "through the ballot, through public consensus"—and occasionally marred by violence.

Latinos Fight for Change

People whose family origins are in Spanish-speaking Latin America, or **Latinos,** come from many different places, but they share the same language and some elements of culture. Whether their origins are in Puerto Rico, Cuba, Mexico, or other parts of the Americas, Latinos have often been regarded as outsiders by other Americans. They have frequently been denied equal opportunities in many important areas, including employment, education, and housing.

The Latino Population Spanish-speaking people lived in many parts of the present-day United States before English-speaking settlers arrived, and their numbers have grown steadily. In the late 1960s and early 1970s, for example, immigration from Central and South America increased, and between 1970 and 1980, census figures for people "of Spanish origin" rose from 9 million to 14.6 million. Specific groups

VIEWING HISTORY César Chávez leads a United Farm Workers Union march in 1965. **Checking Consistency** *Does this peaceful protest by Latino migrant workers correspond to the description of the "revolution" described by Rubén Salazar? Explain your answer.*

VIEWING HISTORY Mexico's northern neighbors, California and Texas, traditionally received the majority of Mexican immigrants. This mural is located in Los Angeles. **Analyzing Visual Information** *What elements does the mural use to show Chicano cultural pride?*

tended to settle in certain areas. In the 1960s, Cubans, fleeing Fidel Castro's Communist rule, went first to Florida. Many of these refugees were educated professionals, and they became successful citizens of Miami and other American cities. The Puerto Ricans who moved to the Northeast, and the Mexicans who settled in the West and Southwest, usually had less education and found it harder to succeed in American society.

Mexican Americans, also known as Chicanos, have always made up the largest group of Latinos in the United States. In the 1960s, they began to organize against discrimination in education, employment, and the legal system, leading to *el Movimiento Chicano*—the Chicano movement.

Cultural Identity   Activists such as Americo Parédes, a noted folklorist and author from Texas, began encouraging Mexican Americans to take pride in their culture and its dual heritage from Spain and the ancient cultures of Mexico. Some of these activists also claimed that Anglos—white, English-speaking non-Latinos—had undermined Mexican Americans' control over their lives through economic pressure and through institutions such as the Roman Catholic Church, the media, and the schools.

This claim was supported by conditions in barrios, or Latino neighborhoods, across the United States. In many barrios, schools were crowded and run-down, with high dropout rates. In March 1968, 10,000 Mexican American students walked out of five such Los Angeles high schools to protest their unequal treatment. Latino students in other parts of California, and in the states of Colorado and Texas, followed their example. They demanded culturally sensitive courses, better facilities, and Latino teachers and counselors.

Organizing to Fight Discrimination   Throughout the 1960s, organizers struggled to unite Latino farm workers. César Chávez became a hero to millions of Americans, both Latino and Anglo, in his effort to improve conditions for migrant workers. Moving from farm to farm, and often from state to state to provide the labor needed to plant, cultivate, and harvest crops, **migrant farm workers** were some of the most exploited workers in the country. They spent long hours doing backbreaking work for low pay, and their children had little opportunity for education.

Growing up among these farm workers, Chávez came to believe that unions offered them the best opportunity to gain bargaining power and

Focus on
WORLD EVENTS

The Cuban Revolution In the 1950s, a young Cuban lawyer began organizing opposition to the corrupt regime of the Cuban dictator Fulgencio Batista. By 1959, Fidel Castro and his small band of guerrilla fighters had driven Batista from the country. When he took power, Castro promised an honest administration, full civil and political liberties, and moderate reforms. Instead, he imposed a one-party dictatorship, nationalized farms and industries, and suppressed all political dissent. Many Cubans—skilled workers, educated professionals, wealthy owners of businesses and farms, intellectuals and journalists—felt betrayed by Castro and chose to emigrate. Hundreds of thousands left Cuba, and many settled in the United States.

to resist the economic power of their employers. In the 1960s, he and fellow-activist Dolores Huerta began to organize Mexican field hands into what became the **United Farm Workers (UFW).** They went from door to door and field to field. By 1965, the union had 1,700 members. They soon proved how effective "brown power"—the use of Latino political and economic strength—could be.

The UFW's first target was the grape growers of California. Chávez, like Martin Luther King, Jr., believed in nonviolent action. In 1967, when growers refused to grant more pay, better working conditions, and union recognition, Chávez organized a successful nationwide consumer boycott of grapes picked on nonunion farms. Later boycotts of lettuce and other crops also won consumer support across the country.

Chávez's efforts generated angry opposition and even brought him death threats. He responded this way:

> 66 *It's not me who counts, it's the Movement. And I think that in terms of stopping the Movement—this one or other movements by poor people around the country—the possibility is very remote. . . . The tide for change now has gone too far.* 99
>
> —César Chávez

In 1975, California passed a law requiring collective bargaining between growers and union representatives. Workers finally had a legal basis to ask for better working conditions. By demanding equality, Latino migrant farm workers had joined the movement for civil rights.

While Chávez was organizing farm workers, other Chicanos took a different approach: they sought political power. In 1961, voters in San Antonio, Texas, elected Henry B. González to Congress. Another Texan, Elizo "Kika" de la Garza, went to the House of Representatives in 1964. Joseph Montoya of New Mexico was elected to the Senate in 1962. At the same time, new political groups formed to support Latino interests. In Texas, José Angel Gutiérrez spearheaded the formation of the political party *La Raza Unida* in 1970. This new party worked for better housing and jobs, and also backed Latino political candidates.

Yet a different approach was taken by Reies López Tijerina, who argued that the Anglo culture had stolen the Chicanos' land and heritage. To call attention to broken treaties, his *Alianza Federal de Mercedes* ("Federal Alliance of Land Grants") marched on the New Mexico state capital, Santa Fe, in 1966. At about the same time, the Mexican American Legal Defense and Educational Fund (MALDEF) began providing legal aid to help Mexican Americans defend their rights. It also encouraged Mexican American students to become lawyers.

Asian Americans Fight Discrimination

Ever since they first arrived in the United States, Americans of Chinese and Japanese ancestry have faced racial discrimination. Prejudice against Japanese Americans reached a peak during World War II, and the Communist takeover of China in 1949 caused negative feelings toward Chinese Americans. Still, the years after the war brought positive changes for Asian Americans.

Japanese Americans After the War As you have read, Japanese American citizens living along the West Coast were interned in camps during World War II. The government had feared that they were a risk to American security following Japan's attack on Pearl Harbor. Not only had they been unjustly detained and deprived of their rights as citizens, but they had also lost hundreds of millions of

BIOGRAPHY

**César Chávez
1927–1993**

Before the Depression, César Chávez's father was a successful farmer and a local postmaster in Yuma, Arizona. In 1937, when César was 10, the family lost their farm because they could not afford the taxes. They became migrant workers in California. Because the family was always on the move, young César attended more than 30 different schools while working part time in the fields. Even so, the Chávez family fostered a powerful sense of independence. Chávez recalled, "I don't want to suggest we were that radical, but I know we were probably one of the strikingest families in California." After serving in the Navy, Chávez returned to California and worked as an organizer for the Community Services Organization before launching his own farm workers union.

Sounds of an Era

Listen to a speech by César Chávez and other sounds from the activist movements of the 1960s and 1970s.

dollars in homes, farms, and businesses. After the war, many of those who had been interned sought compensation for these losses through the **Japanese American Citizens League (JACL).** In 1948, the JACL won passage of the Japanese American Claims Act. Under this act, Congress eventually paid relatively small amounts for property losses, with some claims not being settled until 1965. (It was not until 1988, however, that the United States apologized to Japanese American internees and paid them further monetary compensation.)

Economic and Political Advances   Although Asian Americans as a group were well educated, in 1960 they earned less than white Americans. In California, for example, for each $51 a white man was paid, a Chinese man would earn $38 and a Japanese man, $43. College graduates faced prejudice when they tried to move into management positions. In the 1960s and 1970s, Asian Americans made economic gains faster than other minorities. Nonetheless, they still faced discrimination and relied on the example of the civil rights movement to push for change.

When Hawaii became a state in 1959, Asian Americans gained a voice in Congress. The new state sent Hiram Leong Fong, a Chinese American, to the Senate, and Daniel K. Inouye, a Japanese American, to the House of Representatives.

Asian Immigration, 1951–1978

Number of immigrants (in thousands)

Legend:
- 1951–1960
- 1961–1970
- 1971–1978

Place of origin: India, China, Hong Kong, Vietnam, Korea, Japan, Philippines

SOURCE: *Statistical Abstract of the United States*

INTERPRETING GRAPHS
The photo above shows the JACL participating in the 1963 Civil Rights March in Washington, D.C. Patterns of immigration from Asia changed dramatically from the 1950s to the 1970s. **Analyzing Information** *(a) Which two countries did the greatest number of Asian immigrants come from in the 1950s? In the 1970s? (b) What do you think might have accounted for this change?*

Native Americans Face Unique Problems

As the original inhabitants of North America, Native Americans have always occupied a unique social and legal position in the United States. Although the cultures and languages of Indian peoples varied, white society tended to view all Native Americans as one group. By 1871, the United States government no longer recognized Indian nations as independent powers. At the same time, it did not extend full citizenship to Native Americans, either. Instead, state and federal agencies limited self-government for Native Americans and often worked to destroy their traditional lifestyles. In 1924, the Snyder Act granted citizenship to all Native Americans born in the United States, but they continued to be recognized as citizens of their own nations or tribal groups as well. Even then, many states denied suffrage to Native Americans. It was not until 1948 that Arizona and New Mexico granted Indians the right to vote.

As a whole, Native Americans have routinely been denied equal opportunities. They have had higher rates of unemployment, alcoholism, and suicide, as well as a shorter life expectancy, than white Americans. Many communities have suffered from poverty and poor living conditions. Like other nonwhite groups, Native Americans have been the victims of centuries-old stereotypes reinforced by the images in movies and other media.

Native Americans also have had some grievances unique to their situation. The land now occupied by the United States was once theirs, and treaties made between Indian nations and the United States have repeatedly been broken by the American government.

Land Claims   Traditional lands have a special role in most Native American cultures. "Everything is tied to our homeland," declared D'Arcy McNickle, a

Native American anthropologist, in 1961. Yet, many years after pioneers first moved onto Native American territory, state and federal governments continued to take over traditional tribal lands. In 1946, Congress created a special Indian Claims Commission to investigate land claims by Native Americans. In the decades that followed, the federal government paid the Cherokee, Crow, Nez Percé, and other tribes millions of dollars in compensation for lost lands.

Some tribes refused government offers of money. They wanted their land back instead. In 1971, after more than 60 years of effort, the Taos Pueblo of New Mexico finally regained their sacred Blue Lake and 48,000 acres of land around it. The Lakota Sioux also pressed the government to return sacred lands—the Black Hills region of South Dakota, acquired by treaty in 1877. Like the Taos Pueblo, the seven Lakota tribes refused a large monetary settlement. The Lakota claim was denied. The Black Hills, which include Mount Rushmore, later became the scene of several protests by Native American activists.

The American Indian Movement   In 1968, two Chippewa activists, Dennis Banks and George Mitchell, set out the goals of a new activist organization, the **American Indian Movement (AIM).** Banks called it "a new coalition that will fight for Indian treaty rights and better conditions and opportunities for our people." Following the example of militant black groups, AIM focused first on the special problems of Native Americans living in cities by setting up patrols and encouraging racial and cultural pride in young people. Eventually, AIM also fought for Native American legal rights, including **autonomy,** or self-government. It also sought control of natural resources on Native American lands, and the restoration of lands illegally taken from Indian nations. Many people, both white and Native American, criticized AIM's militant approach. Nevertheless, AIM continued to confront the government over Indian-rights issues.

Confronting the Government   Native American activists used standoffs with the federal government to call attention to issues that mainstream America had long ignored. In 1972, demonstrators protesting the violation of treaties between the United States and various Indian groups formed the Broken Treaties Caravan. They traveled to Washington, D.C., and occupied the Bureau of Indian Affairs' offices for six days. Other protests were even more dramatic.

In 1969, more than 75 Native American protesters landed on Alcatraz Island in San Francisco Bay. They claimed the 13-acre rock under the terms of the Fort Laramie Treaty of 1868, which allowed male Native Americans to file homestead claims on federal lands. Others joined the group, planning to turn the deserted island into an educational and cultural center. The occupation failed. Federal marshals eventually removed the last protesters after a year and a half. But the episode drew national attention to Native American grievances.

An even more dramatic confrontation came in 1973 at the Oglala Sioux village of Wounded Knee, South Dakota. In 1890, the army's Seventh Cavalry had massacred more than 200 Sioux men, women, and children there. The Pine Ridge reservation around the village was one of the country's poorest, with half of its families living on welfare. In February 1973, AIM leader Russell Means directed the takover of the village and

VIEWING HISTORY AIM leader Dennis Banks leads a protest march in South Dakota. **Drawing Inferences** *Why do you think Banks chose to pose in front of Mount Rushmore?*

READING CHECK
Describe two Native American protests.

VIEWING HISTORY Echoes of history surrounded the Sioux village of Wounded Knee during the AIM protest there. **Identifying Alternatives** (a) Why did some people who sympathized with AIM's goals object to the organization's tactics? (b) What other tactics might AIM have used? Do you think they would have been as effective?

refused to leave until the United States government agreed to investigate the treatment of Indians and the poor conditions on the reservation, and to review more than 300 treaties. Other Native American leaders supported the occupation. Onondaga Chief Oren Lyons, speaking for the Iroquois, said:

66 We support the Oglala Sioux Nation or any Indian Nation that will fight for its sovereignty. . . . The issue here at Wounded Knee is the recognition of the treaties between the United States Government and the sovereign nations that were here before. 99

—Onondaga Chief Oren Lyons

Federal marshals and FBI agents put the village under siege, and agents arrested some 300 people, including news reporters and outside supporters. The standoff finally ended in May, when protesters agreed to surrender their weapons and to leave the reservation. In exchange, the government consented to reexamine Indian treaty rights. But during the siege, two AIM members had been killed and about a dozen people hurt, including two federal marshals.

Government Response Native American activism brought some positive government action. The Kennedy and Johnson administrations tried to bring jobs and income to some reservations by encouraging industries to locate there and by leasing reservation lands to energy and development corporations. But many Native Americans worried about the effects that these projects would have on the land, and later sought to renegotiate or cancel many of the leases.

A number of laws passed in the 1970s favored Native American rights. The Indian Education Act of 1972 gave parents and tribal councils more control over schools and school programs. The Indian Self-Determination and Education Assistance Act of 1975 upheld Native American autonomy and let local leaders administer federally supported social programs for housing and education. Native Americans also continued to win legal battles to regain land, mineral, and water rights.

Section 2 Assessment

READING COMPREHENSION

1. What are the family origins of **Latinos** and of Chicanos?

2. How did the **UFW** help **migrant farm workers**?

3. What was the purpose of the **Japanese American Citizens League**?

4. Which Native American group led the protest at Wounded Knee?

CRITICAL THINKING AND WRITING

5. **Making Comparisons** How and why was the Native Americans' struggle for equality different from that of Latinos and Asian Americans?

6. **Writing to Inform** Write a paragraph about one protest covered in this section. Include its purpose and its effect.

For: An activity on César Chávez
Visit: PHSchool.com
Web Code: mrd-9302

The Counterculture

READING FOCUS

• What social changes were promoted by the counterculture?

• How did music both reflect and contribute to the cultural changes of this era?

MAIN IDEA

In the 1960s, a youth culture blossomed that promoted freedom and individuality. The counterculture's new attitudes toward personal relationships, drugs, and music shocked many Americans but ultimately changed American society.

KEY TERMS

counterculture
Woodstock festival

TARGET READING SKILL

Identify Supporting Details Copy the web diagram below. As you read, fill in the characteristics of the counterculture and the changes they caused.

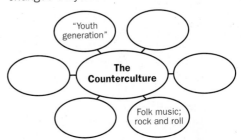

Setting the Scene If the man in the gray flannel suit was the symbol of the 1950s, then the long-haired hippie dressed as outrageously as possible in bright colors, beads, and flowers was the symbol of the 1960s. The former looked adult and responsible, and was clearly dressed for nine-to-five success. He was the organization man, and conformed to the culture of his time. The latter, the hippie, rejected the gray flannel suit and the regimented life it represented. The hippie generation favored "flower power" over corporate and military power, and eventually influenced the dominant culture.

A Time of Change

In the 1960s, many young people adopted values that ran counter to, or against, the mainstream culture that they saw around them. Members of this **counterculture** valued youth, spontaneity, and individuality. Also called hippies, these young people promoted peace, love, and freedom. And they experimented with new styles of dress and music, freer attitudes toward sexual relationships, and the recreational use of drugs. The result was often a "generation gap," or a lack of understanding and communication between the older and younger generations.

The so-called youth generation had an enormous influence on American society. First of all, it was the largest generation in American history. The "baby boom" that followed World War II resulted in a huge student population in the 1960s. By sheer numbers, the baby boomers became a force for change. The music industry rushed to produce the music they liked; clothing designers copied the styles they

The hippie (seated below) is doing his best *not* to look like the man of the fifties (at left).

VIEWING HISTORY The Andy Warhol painting (above) and the Op Art poster (at right) show the irreverence of 1960s artists.
Making Comparisons *What do the two art works have in common? How are they different?*

introduced; universities changed college courses and rules to accommodate them. Politicians, too, found that they could not ignore the voice of the baby boom generation.

Sixties Style   The look of the 1960s was distinctive, frivolous, and free. But it was also a signal of changing attitudes. The counterculture rejected restrictions and challenged authority. Many young women gave up the structured hairstyles of the 1950s and began wearing their hair long and free. They also chose freer fashions, such as loose-fitting dresses. Men, too, let their hair grow long and wore beards. Their clothing was as different from a gray flannel suit as they could make it—and that was the point. These styles announced a rejection of the corporate world and its uniform. Of course, hippie dress itself became a kind of uniform for the youth generation.

Many members of the counterculture identified with the poor and downtrodden around the world and at home. They fought for the civil rights of minority groups in the United States, and sided with those they believed were oppressed abroad. Hippies often adopted the dress of working people, including blue jeans, plain cotton shirts, peasant blouses, and other simple garments. They also sought out apparel of indigenous peoples, such as ponchos from South America, dashikis from Africa, jewelry made by Native Americans, and other hand-made items.

The colorful look of the sixties was not confined to clothing. Hippies painted their cars—and their bodies. And this spirit of fun and irreverence also invaded the art world. The Pop Art of the 1960s, such as paintings by Andy Warhol and Roy Lichtenstein, featured realistic depictions of the artifacts of modern life. Scorned at the time, these satirical paintings of soup cans and comic books now hang in art museums. Another style, Op Art, captured the spirit of the sixties with its fluorescent colors and dizzying optical illusions. Many of the images were—or looked as though they were—created under the influence of psychedelic drugs. Op Art was especially popular for posters and album covers showcasing popular rock groups.

The Sexual Revolution   Just as participants in the counterculture demanded more freedom to make personal choices in how they dressed, they also demanded more freedom to choose how they lived. Their new views of sexual conduct, which rejected many traditional restrictions on behavior, were labeled "the sexual revolution." Some of those who led this revolution argued that sex should be separated from its traditional ties to family life. Many of them also experimented with new living patterns. Some hippies rejected traditional relationships and lived together in communal groups, where they often shared property and chores. Others simply lived together as couples, without getting married.

The sexual revolution in the counterculture led to more open discussion of sexual subjects in the mainstream media. Newspapers, magazines, and books published articles that might not have been printed just a few years earlier. The 1962 book by Helen Gurley Brown, *Sex and the Single Girl*, became a bestseller. In 1966, William H. Masters and Virginia E. Johnson shocked many people when they published *Human Sexual Response,* a report on their scientific studies of sexuality.

The Drug Scene   Some members of the 1960s counterculture also turned to psychedelic drugs. These powerful chemicals cause the brain to behave abnormally. Users of psychedelic drugs experience hallucinations and other altered perceptions of reality. The beatniks of the 1950s, who were an inspiration to the 1960s counterculture, had experimented with drugs, but the beatniks had been relatively few in number. In the 1960s, the use of drugs, especially marijuana, became much more widespread among the nation's youth.

One early proponent of psychedelic drug use was researcher Timothy Leary. Leary worked at Harvard University with Richard Alpert on the chemical compound lysergic acid diethylamide, commonly known as LSD. The two men were fired from their research posts in 1963 for involving undergraduates in experiments with the drug. Leary then began to preach that drugs could help free the mind. He advised listeners, "Tune in, turn on, drop out."

Leary's view presented just one side of the drug scene. On the other side lay serious danger. The possibility of death from an overdose or from an accident while under the influence of drugs was very real. Three leading musicians of the 1960s—Janis Joplin, Jim Morrison, and Jimi Hendrix—died of complications from drug overdoses. And they were not the only ones. Their deaths represented the tragic excesses to which some people were driven by their reliance on drugs to enhance or to escape from reality.

The Music World

Music both reflected and contributed to the cultural changes of the 1960s. The rock and roll of the 1950s had begun a musical revolution, giving young people a music of their own that scandalized many adults. The early 1960s saw a new interest in folk music. Members of the counterculture turned to traditional songs that had been passed down from generation to generation of "folk," or ordinary people around the world. They also favored songs of protest against oppression; songs of laborers, such as sailors and railroadmen, and songs that originated under slavery.

The year 1964 marked a revolution in rock music that some called the British Invasion. It was the year that the Beatles first toured America. The "Fab Four" had already taken their native England by storm. They became a sensation in the United States as well, not only for their music but also for their irreverent sense of humor and their "mop top" long hair. The Beatles heavily influenced the music of the period, as did another British group, the Rolling Stones. Mick Jagger of the Stones was a dramatic and electrifying showman. Another exciting performer was Texan Janis Joplin, a hard-drinking singer whose powerful interpretations of classic blues songs catapulted her to superstardom.

Woodstock   The diverse strands of the counterculture all came together at the Woodstock Music and Art Fair in August 1969. About 400,000 people gathered for several days in a large pasture in Bethel, New York, to listen to the major bands of the rock world. Despite brutal heat and rain, those who attended the **Woodstock festival** recalled the event with something of a sense of awe for the fellowship they experienced there. Police avoided confrontations with those

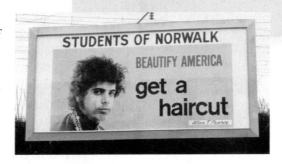

STUDENTS OF NORWALK
BEAUTIFY AMERICA
get a haircut

READING CHECK
Describe some influences on American music of the sixties.

VIEWING HISTORY This group of hippies lived together in a commune and traveled around in their outrageously painted bus. **Drawing Inferences** *How are they showing their rejection of traditional social customs?*

attending by choosing not to enforce drug laws. The crowd remained under control. Tom Law was at Woodstock:

> 66 *The event was so much bigger than the music. It was a phenomenon. It was absolutely a phenomenon. And it was also the most peaceful, civilized gathering that was probably happening on the planet at the time.* 99
>
> —Tom Law

Other Americans, however, viewed both the festival and the mood it reflected with disgust. Even as some of the older generation began growing their hair longer and wearing "hipper" clothing, they were alarmed at the changes they saw around them. These changes also disturbed many in the younger generation. In particular, some in the mainstream culture deplored the drugs, sex, and nudity they saw at the Woodstock festival and around the country. To them, the counterculture represented a rejection of morals and honored values, and seemed a childish reaction to the problems of the era.

Altamont The fears of those who criticized Woodstock came true at another rock festival held at the Altamont Speedway in California in December 1969. There, 300,000 people gathered for a concert by the Rolling Stones. When promoters of the concert failed to provide adequate security, the Stones hired a band of Hell's Angels, an infamous and lawless motorcycle gang, to keep order. The cyclists ended up beating one man to death when he approached the stage with a gun. This ugly violence contradicted the values preached by the counterculture. It also signaled that the era of "peace and love" would not last forever.

Despite their celebration of simple lifestyles, most hippies were children of the comfortable middle class. American corporations marketed such items as bell-bottom blue jeans and stereo equipment to them, and they eagerly bought the products. When the counterculture fell apart, the hippies melted right back into the mainstream. By the 1980s, many baby boomers who had protested the values of 1950s and 1960s mainstream America would hold executive positions in the same corporations they had once denounced.

Section 3 Assessment

READING COMPREHENSION

1. What was the **counterculture?**

2. What are Pop Art and Op Art?

3. What new attitudes toward sexual activity and drugs were promoted by the counterculture?

4. How was the Altamont concert different from the **Woodstock festival?**

CRITICAL THINKING AND WRITING

5. **Identifying Assumptions** (a) What assumptions about mainstream culture were made by the counterculture? (b) Were they fair? Explain.

6. **Writing a Letter to the Editor** It is 1967, and you are the parent of a teenager. Write a letter to the editor either for or against a rule banning "hippie dress" at your child's school.

Go Online
PHSchool.com

For: An activity on sixties folk music
Visit: PHSchool.com
Web Code: mrd-9303

The Environmental and Consumer Movements

READING FOCUS

- What efforts were begun in the 1960s to protect the environment?

- How did the government try to balance jobs and environmental protection?

- How did the consumer movement begin, and what did it try to accomplish?

MAIN IDEA

Conditions that came to light in the 1960s as well as the activist mood of the period helped to create movements for preserving the environment and for ensuring the safety of consumer products.

KEY TERMS

Nuclear Regulatory Commission (NRC)
Environmental Protection Agency (EPA)
Clean Air Act
Clean Water Act

TARGET READING SKILL

Compare and Contrast Copy the diagram below. As you read, fill in the two circles with the goals and accomplishments of each movement. Place items that apply to both where the circles overlap.

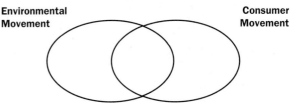

Environmental Movement   Consumer Movement

Setting the Scene

In 1958, a woman in Massachusetts wrote a letter to a friend—and set off a revolution. The letter writer was Olga Owens Huckins, and the friend was Rachel Carson. An airplane had sprayed Huckins's neighborhood with DDT to control mosquitoes, and the next day she had found dead birds in her yard. She asked Carson, a biologist, to look into the connection. The result was *Silent Spring*, the 1962 book that started the environmental movement.

Carson begins *Silent Spring* with "A Fable for Tomorrow." In the fable, she describes a lovely country town surrounded by farms and wilderness, by beauty and the sounds of wildlife. She continues:

> 66 *Then a strange blight crept over the area and everything began to change. Some evil spell had settled on the community: mysterious maladies swept the flocks of chickens; the cattle and sheep sickened and died. Everywhere was a shadow of death. The farmers spoke of much illness among their families. . . . There was a strange stillness. The birds, for example—where had they gone? . . . [T]here was now no sound; only silence lay over the fields and woods and marsh. . . . No witchcraft, no enemy action had silenced the rebirth of new life in this stricken world. The people had done it themselves.* 99
>
> —Rachel Carson in *Silent Spring*

Protecting the Environment

Carson's fable links two protest movements of the 1960s and 1970s. Both the environmental movement and the consumer movement demanded honesty and accountability from industry and government. Consumer advocates insisted upon safety for customers and workers. Environmentalists went further: they called for actions that would preserve and restore the earth's environment and resources. According to environmental activists, the very products that people used in an effort to improve their world and their lives—to control mosquitoes, for example—were damaging not only the health of the environment but the health of the people as well.

Like the women's movement, the environmental movement of the 1960s had roots in the American past. In the late 1890s and early 1900s,

Rachel Carson was already recognized as a distinguished naturalist when she wrote *Silent Spring*.

The Return of the Bald Eagle

In 1963, a year after *Silent Spring* was published, bald eagles were near extinction, with only 417 breeding pairs in the lower 48 states. They were declared an endangered species in 1967. In 1972, DDT was banned, and a year later the Endangered Species Act was passed. The eagles were put under the protection of this act in 1978. Efforts to save the bald eagle included bringing young eaglets from Canada and Alaska and then releasing them in the continental United States, and breeding eagles in captivity and then releasing their offspring into the wild. By 1999, the eagles had made a strong recovery; there were more than 5,000 breeding pairs, and the species was removed from the endangered list. Posing with an eagle named Challenger at an Independence Day ceremony, President Bill Clinton said, "It's hard to think of a better way to celebrate the birth of a nation than to celebrate the rebirth of our national symbol."

? What does the return of the bald eagle suggest about saving other endangered species? Explain your answer.

Progressives had worked to make public lands and parks available for the enjoyment of the population. New Deal programs of the 1930s included tree-planting projects in an effort to put people back to work—and to conserve forests and farmlands. The modern environmental movement, however, would not have started without Rachel Carson.

Rachel Carson Marine biologist Rachel Carson grew up wanting to become a writer. Her mother taught her to appreciate nature and encouraged Carson's growing interest in zoology. In the 1930s and 1940s, Carson combined her talents and began to write about scientific subjects for general audiences. In 1951, she published *The Sea Around Us,* which was an immediate bestseller and won the National Book Award. This book, and her next, *The Edge of the Sea,* made her famous as a naturalist. One of Carson's main themes was that human beings are part of nature, and that all parts of nature interact. She also believed that people carry a great responsibility for the health of nature because they have the power to change the environment. *Silent Spring,* her most influential book, warned against the abuse of that power.

In *Silent Spring,* Carson spoke out against the use of chemical pesticides, particularly DDT. She argued that DDT had increased agricultural productivity but killed various other plants and animals along with the insect pests that were its target. She stated:

66 *The most alarming of all man's assaults upon the environment is the contamination of air, earth, rivers, and sea with dangerous and even lethal materials. This pollution is for the most part irrecoverable. . . . In this now universal contamination of the environment, chemicals are the sinister and little-recognized partners of radiation in changing the very nature of the world.* 99

—Rachel Carson in *Silent Spring*

As Carson explained, chemicals sprayed on crops enter into living organisms and move from one to another in a chain of poisoning and death. Specifically, in the 1960s, the lingering effects of DDT threatened to destroy many species of birds and fish, including the national symbol, the bald eagle.

Silent Spring caused a sensation. The chemical industry fought back vigorously, arguing that Carson confused the issues and left readers "unable to sort fact from fancy." The public, however, was not persuaded by this attack on Carson. So great was national concern that a special presidential advisory committee was appointed. It called for continued research and warned against the widespread use of pesticides. Eventually DDT was banned in the United States, and other chemicals came under stricter control. (For more on the impact of *Silent Spring,* see the "Geography and History" feature that follows this section.)

It was not only DDT that worried people. They became more conscious of poisonous fumes in the air, oil spills on beaches, and toxic wastes buried in the ground. In the mid-1960s, President Lyndon Johnson addressed environmental concerns in his plans for the Great Society:

READING CHECK
What was Rachel Carson's main argument in *Silent Spring?*

Attorney Ralph Nader spearheaded the new consumer effort. Nader had been a serious activist all his life. While a student at Princeton University in the early 1950s, Nader protested the spraying of campus trees with DDT. His interest in automobile safety began while he was attending Harvard Law School. In 1964, Daniel Patrick Moynihan, then Assistant Secretary of Labor, hired Nader as a consultant on the issue of automobile safety regulations. The government report Nader wrote developed into a book, *Unsafe at Any Speed: The Designed-in Dangers of the American Automobile,* published the next year. It began:

> 66 *For over half a century the automobile has brought death, injury, and the most inestimable sorrow and deprivation to millions of people. . . . [T]his mass trauma began rising sharply four years ago reflecting new and unexpected ravages by the motor vehicle. A 1959 Department of Commerce report projected that 51,000 persons would be killed by automobiles in 1975. That figure will probably be reached in 1965, a decade ahead of schedule.* 99

—Ralph Nader in *Unsafe at Any Speed*

Like the muckrakers of the Progressive Era, Nader drew attention to the facts with passionate arguments. He called many cars "coffins on wheels," pointing to dangers such as a tendency of some models to flip over. The automobile industry, he charged, knew about these problems but continued to build over one million cars before confronting the safety problems.

Nader's book was a sensation. In 1966, he testified before Congress about automobile hazards. That year, Congress passed the National Traffic and Motor Vehicle Safety Act. The *Washington Post* noted, "Most of the credit for making possible this important legislation belongs to one man—Ralph Nader. . . . A one-man lobby for the public prevailed over the nation's most powerful industry."

Nader broadened his efforts and investigated the meatpacking business, helping to secure support for the Wholesome Meat Act of 1967. He next looked into problems in other industries. Scores of volunteers, called "Nader's Raiders," signed on to help. They turned out report after report on the safety of such products as baby food and insecticides, and they inspired consumer activism. As ordinary Americans began to stand up for their rights, consumer protection offices began to respond to their many complaints.

VIEWING HISTORY Ralph Nader was a "one-man lobby" for consumer safety. **Making Comparisons** *How were the tactics of Ralph Nader and his "raiders" different from those of other activists of the 1960s?*

Section 4 Assessment

READING COMPREHENSION

1. What is Earth Day?

2. When was the **Environmental Protection Agency** formed and what is its purpose?

3. Describe the **Clean Air Act** and the **Clean Water Act.**

4. Explain the importance of *Unsafe at Any Speed.*

CRITICAL THINKING AND WRITING

5. **Recognizing Cause and Effect** Explain how Rachel Carson's concern with DDT initiated the environmental movement.

6. **Writing an Opinion** Do you think the United States should rely more on nuclear power plants? Write a paragraph that supports your opinion.

For: An activity on the EPA and NRC
Visit: PHSchool.com
Web Code: mrd-9304

creating a CHAPTER SUMMARY

Copy the chart (right) on a piece of paper. Use it to organize information about some of the groups that challenged the status quo in the 1960s and 1970s.

Interactive Textbook

For additional review and enrichment activities, see the interactive version of *America: Pathways to the Present*, available on the Web and on CD-ROM.

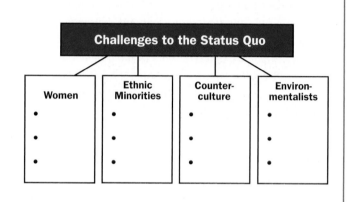

Challenges to the Status Quo

Women	Ethnic Minorities	Counter-culture	Environ-mentalists
•	•	•	•
•	•	•	•
•	•	•	•

★ Reviewing Key Terms

For each of the terms below, write a sentence explaining how it relates to the activism of the 1960s and 1970s.

1. feminism
2. *Roe* v. *Wade*
3. Latino
4. migrant farm worker
5. United Farm Workers (UFW)
6. autonomy
7. counterculture
8. Woodstock festival
9. Nuclear Regulatory Commission (NRC)
10. Environmental Protection Agency (EPA)

★ Reviewing Main Ideas

11. What were the goals of NOW? (Section 1)
12. Describe the effort to ratify the ERA. (Section 1)
13. What opposition did the women's movement encounter? (Section 1)
14. What role did César Chávez play in the Chicano struggle for equal rights? (Section 2)
15. What did the JACL accomplish? (Section 2)
16. What were the goals of the American Indian Movement? (Section 2)
17. Describe three new attitudes of the youth culture of the 1960s and 1970s. (Section 3)
18. What happened at the Altamont festival? (Section 3)
19. Describe how Rachel Carson influenced the environmental movement. (Section 4)

20. What were two of the targets of Ralph Nader's consumer movement? (Section 4)

★ Critical Thinking

21. **Determining Relevance** (a) How did the civil rights movement affect groups as diverse as women, Native Americans, and environmentalists? (b) Do you think that these groups would have been as successful without the example of the civil rights activists? Explain your answer.

22. **Identifying Central Issues** (a) What underlying problem in American society did the women's movement, the Chicano movement, and the American Indian Movement try to address? (b) What kinds of changes were all three groups fighting for?

23. **Making Comparisons** What was the attitude of the counterculture toward "the establishment" (institutions such as government and big business) and how did they show it? Compare their attitudes and actions to those of the environmental and consumer movements.

24. **Demonstrating Reasoned Judgment** Balancing the demands of economic development and environmental protection often involves making trade-offs. Choose a current environmental issue or use one that was discussed in the chapter, and write a paragraph suggesting how to balance those demands.

★ Standardized Test Prep

Analyzing Political Cartoons ▶

25. Examine the images in the cartoon. What do the ships represent?

   A The arrival of Europeans in the Americas

   B The arrival of Puritans in the Americas

   C The arrival of the Spanish in the Americas

   D The departure of Europeans from the Americas

26. Who are the people standing on the shore, and what do they represent?

27. Explain the humor in the dialogue, as well as the serious point it is making.

Analyzing Primary Sources

Dennis Banks restated the goals of the American Indian Movement in a speech marking the group's second anniversary. Read the following excerpt from his speech, and answer the questions that follow.

> 66 *The government and churches have demoralized, dehumanized, massacred, robbed, raped, promised, made treaty after treaty, and lied to us. . . . We must now destroy this political machine that man has built to prevent us from self-determination.* 99
>
> —Dennis Banks

28. Which of the following was one of AIM's goals as expressed by Dennis Banks?

   A to join the government

   B to make no changes to Native American lifestyles

   C to make radical changes in order to gain self-determination

   D to enter into a new treaty with the government

29. How did Banks suggest that AIM achieve its goals?

   F through peaceful demonstration

   G by destroying the political machine built by the government and churches

   H by joining churches

   I by ignoring the problem

Test-Taking Tip

To answer Questions 28 and 29, note Banks' use of the word *destroy*.

Applying the Chapter Skill

Recognizing Bias Look back at the Skills for Life page. Then choose a quoted passage in this chapter, and use the steps for recognizing bias to evaluate that passage.

For: Chapter 23 Self-Test
Visit: PHSchool.com
Web Code: mra-9305

The Environmental Movement

The publication of Rachel Carson's book *Silent Spring* in 1962 helped spark an awareness of environmental problems during the 1960s. A growing environmental movement led to the first Earth Day in 1970—which featured demonstrations like the one shown here—to raise public awareness of environmental problems.

Environmental Legislation

Concerned citizens pressed the federal government to protect the environment. The 1963 Clean Air Act was followed by the tougher Clean Air Acts of 1970 and 1990, which required states to reduce high levels of pollution. In response to air quality concerns, carmakers and other industries acted to produce more fuel-efficient cars and to reduce harmful emissions. A 1980 law established a trust fund (known as the Superfund) to clean up hazardous waste sites.

Geographic Connection

In the image to the left, areas shaded in blue have below-normal ozone levels. Based on this image, what areas suffer from ozone loss?

Growing Concerns

While they continued to fight pollution in the 1980s and 1990s, scientists also addressed the thinning ozone layer and a growing "ozone hole" over Antarctica, shown in the remote sensing image on the right. Certain chemicals cause ozone in the atmosphere to break down, exposing Earth to higher levels of harmful ultraviolet radiation from the sun. An international accord in 1987 committed the world's nations to reducing gases that harm the ozone layer. Another concern was the accumulation of "greenhouse gases" released by industry and motor vehicles (right), which could raise temperatures globally.

Protecting the Mojave

Environmental scientists have worked to protect open space and to preserve wildlife diversity and habitat. In 1994, Congress created the Mojave National Preserve, which protects part of the Mojave Desert from development.

One State's Example

This map of California shows just a few of that state's environmental achievements. The Sacramento and San Joaquin rivers feed canals and aqueducts that provide water to California's farms and cities as well as the Sacramento–San Joaquin Delta—a network of wetlands and inland waterways that flow into San Francisco Bay. Environmental organizations and the government have acted to ensure that enough fresh water flows into the delta and bay to protect fish and other species in danger of extinction. Meanwhile, air quality districts covering the state's largest cities have imposed strict air pollution standards.

Geographic Connection
Why might tougher air quality standards be needed in urban areas?

California Environmental Progress

Legend:
- Air quality management or air pollution control district
- Mojave Desert Ecosystem
- Canal
- Aqueduct
- California condor protection site
- Dam

Oregon · Idaho · Nevada · Utah · Arizona · MEXICO

California

Sacramento R.
Sacramento Metropolitan AQMD
Sacramento
Bay Area AQMD
Oakland · Stockton
San Francisco
San Francisco Bay
San Jose
Delta-Mendota Canal
San Joaquin R.
Friant Dam
Fresno
San Joaquin Valley Unified APCD
Friant Kern Canal
California Aqueduct
Bakersfield
Mojave Desert Ecosystem
Mojave National Preserve
Joshua Tree National Park
Sespe Condor Sanctuary
Los Angeles Zoo
Los Angeles
Riverside · San Bernardino
Long Beach
South Coast AQMD
San Diego APCD
San Diego Wild Animal Park
San Diego

PACIFIC OCEAN

0 50 100 mi.
0 50 100 km

40°N · 35°N · 120°W

Geographic Connection
Why do environmentalists seek protection of nature preserves and wild areas?

Saving the California Condor

When California condors were almost extinct in the wild in the 1980s, scientists began a program to breed young condors in captivity at the Los Angeles Zoo and the San Diego Wild Animal Park. They have since released these birds in protected areas such as the Sespe Condor Sanctuary.

789

Chapter 24

The Vietnam War

(1954–1975)

President Kennedy (left) and Vice President Johnson at the 1961 inauguration.

American Events

1954
After the French defeat in Vietnam, the United States starts to support the newly established nation of South Vietnam with military advisors and aid.

1963
U.S. involvement in Vietnam increases. President Kennedy is assassinated.

1964
The Gulf of Tonkin Resolution gives President Johnson complete authority to escalate the war in Vietnam.

1968
A year of crises unfolds with the assassinations of Martin Luther King, Jr., and Robert Kennedy. Violence erupts at the Democratic National Convention in Chicago.

Presidential Terms: Dwight D. Eisenhower 1953–1961   John F. Kennedy 1961–1963   Lyndon B. Johnson 1963–1969

1954   **1960**   **1966**

World Events

The Berlin Wall is built.
1961

The Six-Day War takes place in the Middle East.
1967

The Tet Offensive begins.
1968

Major Players in the Vietnam Conflict

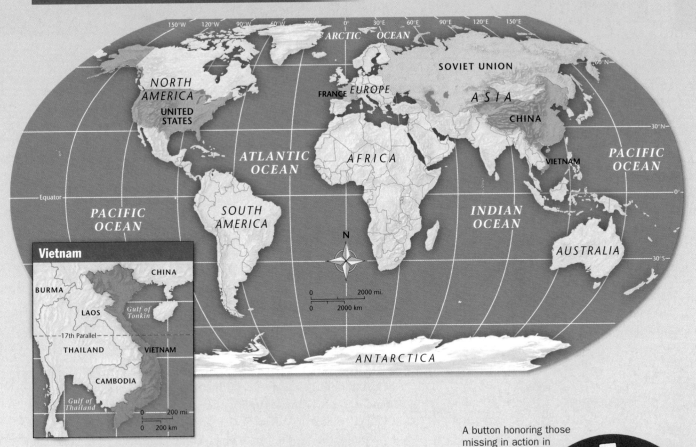

A button honoring those missing in action in Vietnam.

Antiwar protests sweep the nation.

1971

The Twenty-sixth Amendment lowers the voting age to 18. Proponents argue that if 18-year-olds can fight in Vietnam, they should be able to vote.

1973

American troops withdraw from Vietnam, but returning veterans receive a mixed welcome at home.

1970

National Guardsmen at Kent State and police forces at Jackson State open fire on unarmed students during antiwar demonstrations, killing six.

Richard M. Nixon 1969–1974　　　　Gerald R. Ford 1974–1977　　Jimmy Carter 1977–1981

1972

1978

India and Pakistan go to war.

The Vietnam War ends with the signing of a formal peace agreement in Paris.

Communists take over South Vietnam, Cambodia, and Laos.

1971

1973

1975

The War Unfolds

READING FOCUS

- What events led to the war between North Vietnam and South Vietnam?

- What were the Vietnam policies of President Kennedy and Robert McNamara?

- How did President Johnson change the course of the war?

MAIN IDEA

The United States entered the Vietnam War to defeat Communist forces threatening South Vietnam.

KEY TERMS

domino theory
Vietminh
Geneva Accords
Viet Cong
National Liberation Front
Gulf of Tonkin Resolution

TARGET READING SKILL

Identify Cause and Effect Copy the chart below. As you read, fill in some of the causes of the Vietnam War and its early effects on the United States.

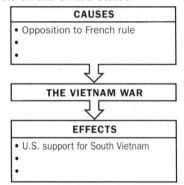

CAUSES
• Opposition to French rule
•
•

↓

THE VIETNAM WAR

↓

EFFECTS
• U.S. support for South Vietnam
•
•

Setting the Scene American involvement in Vietnam began during the early years of the Cold War. It was based on President Harry S Truman's policy of containment, which called for the United States to resist Soviet attempts to spread communism around the world. At a news conference in 1954, President Dwight D. Eisenhower described the principle that became associated with American involvement in Southeast Asia:

> 66 *You have a row of dominoes set up, you knock over the first one, and what will happen to the last one is the certainty that it will go over very quickly.* 99
>
> —Dwight D. Eisenhower

The **domino theory,** described above, refers to the fear that if one Southeast Asian nation fell to the Communists, the others would also fall. A Communist takeover of Vietnam, because of its geographic location, posed a threat to Cambodia, Laos, Burma, and Thailand.

Background of the War

Vietnam had a history of nationalism that extended back nearly 2,000 years. The Vietnamese spent much of that time resisting attempts by neighboring China to swallow their small country. In the 1800s, France established itself as a new colonial power in Vietnam, and the French met similar resistance from the Vietnamese.

Ho Chi Minh, who sympathized with Communist ideas, fought for independence before, during, and after World War II. He was head of the League for the Independence of Vietnam, commonly called the **Vietminh.**

Ho Chi Minh aroused his people's feelings of nationalism against French control. The French opposed the Vietminh by forming the Republic of Vietnam, headed by the emperor Bao Dai. War between these opposing forces continued until May 1954, when the Vietminh defeated the French after a long siege at a fortress in Dien Bien Phu.

A Divided Vietnam In April 1954, an international conference met in Geneva, Switzerland. After the French defeat in Vietnam, representatives of Ho Chi Minh, Bao Dai, Cambodia, Laos, France, the United States, the Soviet Union, China, and Britain arranged a peace settlement. As a result of the **Geneva Accords,** Vietnam was divided near the 17th parallel into two separate nations in July 1954. Two months later, the United States and seven other nations formed the Southeast Asia Treaty Organization (SEATO). The goal of this alliance was to stop the spread of communism.

Ho Chi Minh became president of the new Communist-dominated North Vietnam, with its capital in Hanoi. Ngo Dinh Diem, a former Vietnamese official who had been living in exile in the United States, became president of anti-Communist South Vietnam, with its capital in Saigon. The Geneva agreements called for elections to be held in 1956 to unify the country. South Vietnam refused to support this part of the agreement, claiming that the Communists would not hold fair elections. As a result, Vietnam remained divided.

United States Involvement After World War II, President Truman had pledged American aid to any nation threatened by Communists. Beginning in 1950, the United States provided economic aid to the French effort in Vietnam as a way of gaining French support for the policy of containment in Europe. After the French defeat, the United States began to support anti-Communist South Vietnam.

President Eisenhower pledged his support to South Vietnam's Diem. By 1960, about 675 United States military advisors were in South Vietnam to assist in that country's struggle against the North. Thus the United States became involved in the Vietnam War.

Kennedy's Vietnam Policy

When President John F. Kennedy took office in 1961, he was determined to prevent the spread of communism at all costs. This meant strengthening

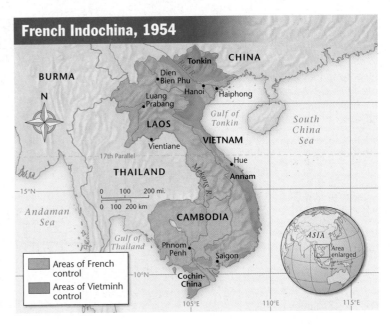

French Indochina, 1954

Areas of French control

Areas of Vietminh control

MAP SKILLS After World War II, France struggled to keep control of its colonies in Southeast Asia. The Vietminh was fighting for Vietnamese independence.
Regions In early 1954, where was the largest region of Vietminh (Ho Chi Minh's) control?

"Personally, I find it a rather unrewarding job."

INTERPRETING POLITICAL CARTOONS This cartoon uses an open sedan chair, similar to a kind of personal transportation popular in Southeast Asia, to make a political point. **Drawing Inferences** (a) Who are the two men "carrying" President Diem of South Vietnam? (b) What has brought Diem's progress to a halt? (c) Why is the man in front complaining? (d) Explain the point the cartoonist is making.

and protecting the government that the United States had helped create in South Vietnam.

Kennedy sent Vice President Lyndon Johnson to Vietnam to assess the situation there. Diem told Johnson that South Vietnam would need even more aid if it was to survive. In response, Kennedy increased the number of American military advisors to Vietnam. By the end of 1963, that number had grown to more than 16,000.

Military aid by itself could not ensure success. Diem lacked support in his own country. He imprisoned people who criticized his government and filled many government positions with members of his own family. United States aid earmarked for economic reforms went instead to the military and into the pockets of corrupt officials.

Diem's Downfall   Diem launched an unpopular program which relocated peasants from their ancestral lands to "strategic hamlets." These government-run farming communities were intended to isolate the peasants from Communist influences seeping into South Vietnam.

In addition, Diem was a Catholic in a largely Buddhist country. When Diem insisted that Buddhists obey Catholic religious laws, serious opposition developed. In June 1963, a Buddhist monk burned himself to death on the streets of Saigon. Photographs showing his silent, grisly protest appeared on the front pages of newspapers around the world. Other monks followed the example, but their martyrdom did not budge Diem.

Kennedy finally realized that the struggle against communism in Vietnam could not be won under Diem's rule. United States officials told South Vietnamese military leaders that the United States would not object to Diem's overthrow. With that encouragement, military leaders staged a coup in November 1963. They seized control of the government and assassinated Diem as he tried to flee.

McNamara's Role   One of the American officials who helped create the Kennedy administration's Vietnam policy was Robert McNamara, President Kennedy's Secretary of Defense. A Republican with a strong business background, McNamara became one of Kennedy's closest

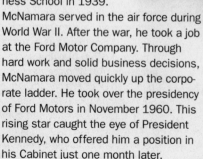

BIOGRAPHY

Robert McNamara was born in San Francisco, California, and grew up across the bay in Oakland. He attended the University of California at Berkeley and went on to earn a graduate degree at Harvard Business School in 1939.

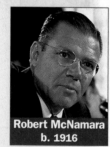

Robert McNamara
b. 1916

McNamara served in the air force during World War II. After the war, he took a job at the Ford Motor Company. Through hard work and solid business decisions, McNamara moved quickly up the corporate ladder. He took over the presidency of Ford Motors in November 1960. This rising star caught the eye of President Kennedy, who offered him a position in his Cabinet just one month later.

advisors on Vietnam. Later he helped shape the policies that drew the United States deeper into the war.

As Secretary of Defense, McNamara applied his business knowledge, managing to cut costs while modernizing the armed forces. He turned the Pentagon's thinking away from reliance on the threat of nuclear bombs toward the development of a "flexible response" to military crises. He also began to focus his attention on how to handle the conflict in Vietnam.

Later, under Lyndon Johnson, McNamara pushed for direct American involvement in the war. In 1963, however, he still questioned whether a complete withdrawal was not the better alternative. Looking back on that period later, McNamara revealed his feelings:

> 66 I believed that we had done all the training we could. Whether the South Vietnamese were qualified or not to turn back the North Vietnamese, I was certain that if they weren't, it wasn't for lack of our training. More training wouldn't strengthen them; therefore we should get out. The President (Kennedy) agreed. 99
>
> —Robert McNamara

As you will read later in this chapter, the United States did not withdraw. It continued to back South Vietnam and the military leaders who took over the government.

Johnson Commits to Containment

Three weeks after Diem's assassination, President Kennedy himself fell to an assassin's bullet in Dallas, Texas. Lyndon Johnson assumed the presidency and faced an escalating crisis in Vietnam. Johnson believed strongly in the need for containment:

> 66 The Communists' desire to dominate the world is just like the lawyer's desire to be the ultimate judge on the Supreme Court. . . . You see, the Communists want to rule the world, and if we don't stand up to them, they will do it. And we'll be slaves. Now I'm not one of those folks seeing Communists under every bed. But I do know about the principles of power, and when one side is weak, the other steps in. 99
>
> —Lyndon Johnson

Communist Advances Diem's successors established a new military government in South Vietnam that proved to be both unsuccessful and unpopular. The ruling generals bickered among themselves and failed to direct the South Vietnamese army effectively. Communist guerrillas in the south, known as **Viet Cong,** and their political arm, called the **National Liberation Front,** gained control of more territory and earned the loyalty of an increasing number of the South Vietnamese people. Ho Chi Minh and the North Vietnamese aided the Viet Cong throughout the struggle.

Just after Johnson assumed office, he met with Henry Cabot Lodge, who was the United States ambassador to South Vietnam. Lodge told the new President that he faced some tough choices if he wanted to save Vietnam.

Focus on GOVERNMENT

The Powers of the President The United States Constitution divides military power between the executive and legislative branches. It makes the President commander in chief of the army and navy, but gives Congress the power to declare war and the power to raise an army and navy.

Throughout American history, Presidents have used their extensive authority as commander in chief to order military operations without a formal declaration of war. The Gulf of Tonkin Resolution, passed by Congress in 1964, was not a declaration of war, but it gave the President expanded powers to conduct the war in Vietnam.

The nation's anguish over the Vietnam War led Congress to pass the War Powers Act in 1973. The act places close limits on the President's war-making powers: If there is no declaration of war by Congress, it requires the President to

1. notify Congress within 48 hours of committing American troops to combat, and
2. end the combat within 60 days unless Congress authorizes a longer period.

In addition, the act gives Congress the power to end the combat at any time by passing a resolution to that effect.

READING CHECK

Describe the new military government in South Vietnam.

GULF OF TONKIN RESOLUTION

Joint Resolution of Congress
H.J. RES 1145 • August 7, 1964
Public Law 88-408; 78 Stat. 384 • August 10, 1964

Resolved by the Senate and House of Representatives of the United States of America in Congress assembled,

That the Congress approves and supports the determination of the President, as Commander in Chief, to take all necessary measures to repel any armed attack against the forces of the United States and to prevent further aggression.

Section 2. The United States regards as vital to its national interest and to world peace the maintenance of international peace and security in southeast Asia. Consonant with the Constitution of the United States and the Charter of the United Nations and in accordance with its obligations under the Southeast Asia Collective Defense Treaty, the United States is, therefore, prepared, as the President determines, to take all necessary steps, including the use of armed force, to assist any member or protocol state of the Southeast Asia Collective Defense Treaty requesting assistance in defense of its freedom.

Section 3. This resolution shall expire when the President shall determine that the peace and security of the area is reasonably assured by international conditions created by action of the United Nations or otherwise, except that it may be terminated earlier by concurrent resolution of the Congress.

The Gulf of Tonkin Resolution tipped the balance of power between Congress (upper photo) and the White House (lower photo).

Johnson replied to Lodge: "I am not going to be the President who saw Southeast Asia go the way China went." Johnson did not want the Southeast Asian "dominoes" to be set in motion by the fall of Vietnam. At the same time, conversations between Johnson and his advisors reveal that Johnson was skeptical about the war. While he did not wish to pursue a full-scale war, he also did not want to risk damaging the authority of the United States by pulling out. In the end, Johnson was convinced of the need to escalate the war.

Expanding Presidential Power In August 1964, Johnson made a dramatic announcement: North Vietnamese torpedo boats had attacked United States destroyers in the international waters of the Gulf of Tonkin, 30 miles from North Vietnam. This announcement would change the course of the war.

Although details were sketchy, it was later shown that the attacks did not occur. In any case, Johnson used the Gulf of Tonkin incident to deepen American involvement in Vietnam. The President asked Congress for and obtained a resolution giving him authority to "take all necessary measures to repel any armed attack against the forces of the United States and to prevent further aggression."

Congress passed this **Gulf of Tonkin Resolution** on August 7 by a vote of 416 to 0 in the House of Representatives and 88 to 2 in the Senate. Johnson had been waiting for some time for an opportunity to propose the resolution, which, he noted, "covered everything." The President now had nearly complete control over what the United States did in Vietnam, even without an official declaration of war from Congress.

Section 1 Assessment

READING COMPREHENSION

1. How did the **domino theory** explain American involvement in Southeast Asia?

2. What were (a) the **Vietminh,** (b) the **Viet Cong,** and (c) the **National Liberation Front?**

3. What were the results of the **Geneva Accords?**

4. Why did American officials support the overthrow of Diem's government?

CRITICAL THINKING AND WRITING

5. Drawing Conclusions Write a paragraph explaining how the Gulf of Tonkin Resolution affected the balance of power between the President and Congress.

6. Writing an Outline Write an outline for an essay from the perspective of Robert McNamara in 1963 in which you present President Kennedy with two options—withdraw from Vietnam or fully support Diem.

For: An activity on the early years of the Vietnam War
Visit: PHSchool.com
Web Code: mrd-9311

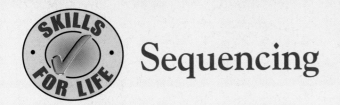 Sequencing

The order in which events occur is called sequence. When you are using several sources to gather information, each source may tell only part of the story. You will need to use sequencing to understand the order in which events took place. And when you are preparing your own report, presenting facts in sequence will help your audience understand your message.

These passages describe events in the 1950s and early 1960s that led to increased American involvement in Vietnam.

LEARN THE SKILL

Use the following steps to present information in sequence:

1. **Identify the order in which events happened.** Look for time-order words such as *later, earlier, now, then, finally, before,* and *after.* Also note any dates, including specific days, months, or parts of the year.

2. **Use visual aids to organize the information.** Make a list of events from all your sources, and the dates the events occurred. Then sort the events by date, and write them in a flowchart or a time line. Now you can add the events that don't have specific dates by inserting them according to clues given by time-order words.

3. **Explain how events are connected.** Present the information in your own words, using dates and time-order words to help your audience understand the sequence of events.

PRACTICE THE SKILL

Answer the following questions:

1. **(a)** Which years are identified in Source A, and what events occurred during those years? **(b)** Which years are identified in Source B, and what events occurred during those years? **(c)** Which time-order words in the sources help you understand the order of events?

2. **(a)** According to both sources, what events occurred in 1961? **(b)** What other event is described in both sources? **(c)** What information not given in Source A is provided by Source B?

3. Create a flowchart or a time line that shows all the events that are described in both sources. Include dates.

APPLY THE SKILL

See the Chapter Review and Assessment for another opportunity to apply this skill.

A

"When Kennedy took office in early 1961 he continued the policies of Truman and Eisenhower in Southeast Asia. . . .

One day in June 1963, a Buddhist monk sat down in the public square in Saigon and set himself afire. More Buddhist monks began committing suicide by fire to dramatize their opposition to the Diem regime. Diem's police raided the Buddhist pagodas and temples, wounded thirty monks, arrested 1,400 people, and closed down the pagodas. . . .

Earlier in 1963, Kennedy's Undersecretary of State, U. Alexis Johnson, was speaking before the Economic Club of Detroit: '. . . Why is [Southeast Asia] desirable, and why is it important? First, it provides a lush climate, fertile soil, rich natural resources, a relatively sparse population in most areas, and room to expand. . . .'

This is not the language that was used by President Kennedy in his explanations to the American public. He talked of Communism and freedom. In a news conference February 14, 1962 he said: 'Yes, as you know, the U.S. for more than a decade has been assisting the government, the people of Vietnam, to maintain their independence.'"

—Howard Zinn,
A People's History of the United States

B

"In 1961, Diem asked for more U.S. assistance, saying, 'The level of their [the Communists] attacks is already such that our forces are stretched to their utmost.'

Kennedy was willing to help, but he was wary of sending in combat troops. Instead, he took measures to enhance the fighting ability of the [South Vietnamese]. . . .

In late August [1963], disapproval of Diem intensified when he declared martial law in South Vietnam and ordered a military crackdown on Communist activists. Once again his troops also targeted Buddhists. . . .

Though the raids momentarily halted the Buddhist uprisings, they infuriated many South Vietnamese and millions of Americans. Kennedy, in response to mounting public outrage over the crackdown, temporarily halted all economic and military aid to South Vietnam on October 2, 1963."

—John M. Dunn,
The Vietnam War: A History of U.S. Involvement

Fighting the War

READING FOCUS

- How did battlefield conditions in Vietnam affect American soldiers?
- How would you describe the course of the war between 1965 and 1968?
- Why was the Tet Offensive a turning point in the war?

MAIN IDEA

The violence and brutality of the Vietnam War affected civilians as well as soldiers.

KEY TERMS

land mine
saturation bombing
fragmentation bombs
Agent Orange
napalm
escalation
Ho Chi Minh Trail
hawks
doves
Tet Offensive

TARGET READING SKILL

Summarize As you read, prepare an outline of this section. Use Roman numerals for the major headings of the section, capital letters for the subheadings, and numbers for the supporting details. The sample below will help you get started.

> **I. Battlefield Conditions**
> **A. One Soldier's Story**
>   1. _____
>   2. _____
> **B. The Ground War**
>   1. _____
>   2. _____

Setting the Scene Nearly 3 million Americans served in the Vietnam War. These soldiers found themselves thousands of miles from home, fighting under conditions that were far different from those they had seen in films. Marine Corps officer James Webb served as rifle platoon and company commander in the An Hoa Basin near Da Nang:

> 66 *We moved through the boiling heat with 60 pounds of weapons and gear, causing a typical Marine to drop 20 percent of his body weight while in the bush. When we stopped we dug chest-deep fighting holes and slit trenches for toilets. We slept on the ground under makeshift poncho [tents]. . . . Sleep itself was fitful, never more than an hour or two at a stretch for months at a time as we mixed daytime patrolling with night-time ambushes, listening posts, foxhole duty, and radio watches. Ringworm, hookworm, malaria, and dysentery were common, as was trench foot when the monsoons came.* 99

—James Webb

American soldiers encountered unfamiliar terrain and conditions when they landed in Vietnam.

The Vietnam Veterans Memorial Aside from the Civil War, the Vietnam War divided the nation more than any other conflict in American history. The issues were so difficult and emotional that for many years something was forgotten—that the Americans who died in Vietnam should be honored with a national monument.

In 1979, a group of veterans began making plans for a Vietnam Veterans Memorial. They wanted to recognize the courage of American GIs during the Vietnam ordeal and to help heal the wounds the war had caused. A Vietnam veteran named Jan Scruggs started a fund for the memorial. Eventually, he won support from Congress to build a monument in Washington, D.C., near the Lincoln Memorial. The question quickly arose: How could the memorial honor the people who gave their lives, while avoiding the hard political issues surrounding the war?

Scruggs's committee held a contest. Famous architects and artists submitted their ideas. Many were surprised when the winner was a 21-year-old college student named Maya Ying Lin. Her idea was to build a long wall of black granite, cut down into the ground. This wall would display the names of every American man and woman who died in the Vietnam War.

Lin had a reason for each element of the memorial. She chose black granite because it reflects light like a mirror, allowing visitors to see reflections of themselves and the nature around them. She put the memorial on a slope that led below ground level to create a quiet place where visitors could think about life and death and sorrow. She placed the names in the order people died, rather than in alphabetical order, so that the individual passing of each life would be emphasized. The memorial was to be long, but not tall, so that visitors could easily see and touch every name.

Lin's concept suited the needs of a nation that needed to heal. Her simple, abstract design would allow visitors to carry their own beliefs to the memorial, without creating images that might disturb or distract them. The Vietnam Veterans Memorial was completed in 1982, and ever since, people have added to it by leaving personal tokens at the wall in memory of their loved ones.

VIEWING HISTORY A Vietnam veteran holds a flower as he points to a name on the Memorial, which was designed by Maya Lin (lower photo). **Determining Relevance** *How do you think listing the names on the wall has contributed to the Memorial's popularity?*

Section 4 Assessment

READING COMPREHENSION

1. What terms were finally agreed to at the **Paris peace talks?**

2. What event led to American withdrawal from Vietnam?

3. Why was President Nixon's policy known as **Vietnamization?**

4. Who are **POWs** and **MIAs?**

CRITICAL THINKING AND WRITING

5. Determining Relevance How did violence at Kent State and Jackson State affect American public opinion? Explain your answer.

6. Making a List Do you think the United States made every effort to win the war in Vietnam? List reasons why or why not.

For: An activity on Vietnam since 1974
Visit: PHSchool.com
Web Code: mrd-9314

creating a CHAPTER SUMMARY

Copy this chart (right) on a piece of paper and complete it by adding information about U.S. involvement in Vietnam under each President from Truman through Nixon.

For additional review and enrichment activities, see the interactive version of *America: Pathways to the Present*, available on the Web and on CD-ROM.

U.S. Involvement in Vietnam		
President	**Action (date)**	**Result**
Truman	Sent economic aid to French in Vietnam (1950)	U.S. began to fight the spread of communism.
Eisenhower	Provided military advisors to South Vietnam (1960)	U.S. became involved in the Vietnam War.
Kennedy	• Increased military aid • Supported overthrow of Diem (1963)	
Johnson		
Nixon		

★ Reviewing Key Terms

For each of the terms below, write a sentence explaining how it relates to the Vietnam War.

1. domino theory
2. Viet Cong
3. Gulf of Tonkin Resolution
4. land mine
5. Agent Orange
6. escalation
7. Ho Chi Minh Trail
8. conscientious objector
9. Middle America
10. Vietnamization

★ Reviewing Main Ideas

11. How did the Vietnam War escalate under President Johnson? (Section 1)

12. How did the Gulf of Tonkin Resolution expand presidential power? (Section 1)

13. Why was the Tet Offensive a turning point in the war? (Section 2)

14. Why was the war so hard on American soldiers fighting in Vietnam? (Section 2)

15. What advantages did the Viet Cong have in the war? (Section 2)

16. What methods did student activists use during the 1960s to oppose the war in Vietnam? (Section 3)

17. How did the war influence the election of 1968? (Section 3)

18. Why did Richard Nixon authorize the invasion of Cambodia in 1970? (Section 4)

19. What happened in Southeast Asia after American withdrawal from Vietnam? (Section 4)

★ Critical Thinking

20. **Comparing Points of View** Evaluate American involvement in Vietnam from the point of view of the following: a hawk, a dove, a conscientious objector, and a soldier.

21. **Drawing Conclusions** If you had been a student during the Vietnam War, do you think your views of the conflict would have changed or remained the same throughout the course of the war? What factors might have influenced your views?

22. **Checking Consistency** President Nixon promised to end the war in Vietnam. Yet he authorized the heaviest bombing raids of the war, and he expanded the war into Cambodia. Were these actions consistent with his promise? Explain.

23. **Drawing Inferences** Why do you think Vietnam veterans came home to a different reception than the ones veterans of the two World Wars received?

24. **Predicting Consequences** Since the end of the Vietnam War, government officials have advised caution in global affairs. How do you think Americans would react to United States involvement in "another Vietnam"? Explain your answer.

★ Standardized Test Prep

Analyzing Political Cartoons ▶

©1972 *HERBLOCK*

25. This cartoon from the 1972 election refers to Nixon's claim during the 1968 election that he had a secret plan to end the war in Vietnam. What does the gravestone refer to?

A The number of lives that could have been saved by Nixon's plan

B The number of Americans killed in Vietnam since 1968

C The number of Americans killed in anti-war demonstrations

D A new plan to end the war in Vietnam

26. What is the message of the cartoon?

Analyzing Primary Sources

Read this excerpt, and then answer the questions that follow.

> 66 *You have a row of dominoes set up, you knock over the first one, and what will happen to the last one is the certainty that it will go over very quickly.* 99
>
> —Dwight D. Eisenhower

27. Which statement BEST represents the meaning of the quotation?

A Southeast Asian nations will support one another in the fight against communism.

B If one Southeast Asian nation falls to communism, others will also fall.

C The strongest Southeast Asian nation will remain standing after the others fall to communism.

D No one can predict what will happen if communism spreads in Southeast Asia.

28. Which of the following events supports the idea expressed in the quotation?

F American forces could not bring about victory in Vietnam.

G After decades of fighting, Vietnam became a single nation under a Communist government.

H Laos and Cambodia became Communist nations.

I The Vietnam War divided the American people.

Test-Taking Tip

In answering Question 27, which statement matches the image of a line of dominoes all falling in order?

Applying the Chapter Skill

Sequencing Look back at the Skills for Life page. Write a paragraph telling, in sequence, the events described in the sources.

Go Online
PHSchool.com

For: Chapter 24 Self-Test
Visit: PHSchool.com
Web Code: mra-9315

TEST PREPARATION

Write your answers on a separate sheet of paper.

1. The United States Supreme Court, in *Brown* v. *Board of Education* (1954), ended

   A mandatory poll taxes and literacy tests.

   B racial segregation in public schools.

   C discrimination in employment and housing.

   D separation of the races in buses and trains.

2. Which one of the following African Americans became known nationally as a result of the Montgomery, Alabama, bus boycott?

   A Martin Luther King, Jr.

   B James Meredith

   C Malcolm X

   D Barbara Jordan

3. Which one of the following issues was addressed by the Civil Rights Act of 1964?

   A Racial discrimination in public colleges and universities

   B Racial discrimination in voter registration standards

   C Racial segregation in public schools

   D Racial segregation in buses and taxis

4. Which decision of the United States Supreme Court requires police officials to inform suspects of their constitutional rights before questioning them?

   A *Mapp* v. *Ohio* (1961)

   B *Baker* v. *Carr* (1962)

   C *Engel* v. *Vitale* (1962)

   D *Miranda* v. *Arizona* (1966)

Use the table and your knowledge of social studies to answer the following question.

African American Elected Officials*	
Year	Number
1970	1,469
1980	4,890
1985	6,016
1990	7,335

*National, state, and local governments
SOURCE: *Statistical Abstract of the United States, 1995*

5. Which one of the following was the primary cause of the trend shown in the table?

   A *Brown* v. *Board of Education*, 1954

   B Southern Manifesto, 1956

   C Civil Rights Act, 1964

   D Voting Rights Act, 1965

6. Which one of the following events during the Cold War almost led to war between the United States and the Soviet Union?

   A The Bay of Pigs invasion

   B The Cuban Missile Crisis

   C The Gulf of Tonkin incident

   D The Tet Offensive

7. Which one of the following helped to further the women's movement of the 1960s and 1970s?

   A The failed social welfare policies of President Lyndon Johnson

   B The perceived threat to the suffrage movement

   C The high rate of inflation throughout the 1960s

   D The publication of *The Feminine Mystique* by Betty Friedan

Use the graph and your knowledge of social studies to answer the following question.

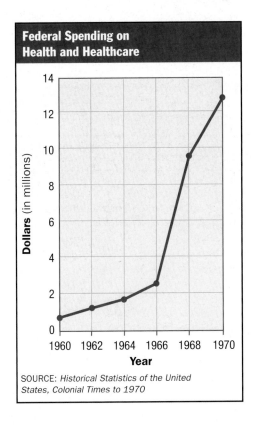

Federal Spending on Health and Healthcare

SOURCE: *Historical Statistics of the United States, Colonial Times to 1970*

8. Which one of the following caused the trend shown in the line graph?

  A Policies of the New Frontier

  B Demands of the civil rights movement

  C Programs of the Great Society

  D The war in Vietnam

9. United States public opinion shifted against the Vietnam War following

  A the battle of Dien Bien Phu.

  B the assassination of President Ngo Dinh Diem.

  C Operation Rolling Thunder.

  D the Tet Offensive.

10. Which President established the Environmental Protection Agency (EPA), the federal agency designed to set and enforce national pollution-control standards?

  A John Kennedy

  B Lyndon Johnson

  C Richard Nixon

  D Jimmy Carter

11. Which one of the following was the legal basis for the involvement of the United States in Vietnam?

  A A declaration of war by Congress

  B The Geneva Accords

  C The Gulf of Tonkin Resolution

  D The Paris agreement

12. President Nixon's policy of Vietnamization was designed to

  A replace Americans in Vietnam with South Vietnamese soldiers.

  B bomb North Vietnam until it surrendered.

  C stop the use of the Ho Chi Minh Trail.

  D extend the fighting into Laos and Cambodia.

Writing Practice

13. Describe the major social programs of President Johnson's "Great Society."

14. Describe the role of César Chávez in the fight against discrimination.

15. How did Rachel Carson affect the movement for a cleaner environment?

Continuity and Change
(1969 to the Present)

"*The challenge . . . is to make and keep our communities places where we can tolerate, even celebrate, our differences, while pulling together for the common good. 'Of many, one' is the main challenge, I believe; it is my hope for our country and the world.*"

Ruth Bader Ginsburg,
Supreme Court Justice, 1998

Americans across the nation celebrated the arrival of the new century with fireworks and festivities, like this celebration in San Francisco, California. ▶

25 Nixon, Ford, Carter (1969–1981)

An intercontinental ballistic missile (ICBM)

Apollo 11 astronaut
Buzz Aldrin

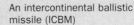

American Events

1969

The United States achieves the first moon landing.

1972

Nixon travels to China and the Soviet Union to pursue détente. The United States and the Soviet Union sign the SALT I treaty.

1973

Senate investigation of the Watergate scandal reveals White House involvement.

1974

Nixon becomes the first U.S. President to resign. Ford becomes the first nonelected Vice President to assume office as President.

Presidential Terms: Richard M. Nixon 1969–1974

1968   **1970**   **1972**   **1974**

World Events

China joins the United Nations.

OPEC imposes an embargo on oil shipments.

1971

1973

OPEC Nations, 1975

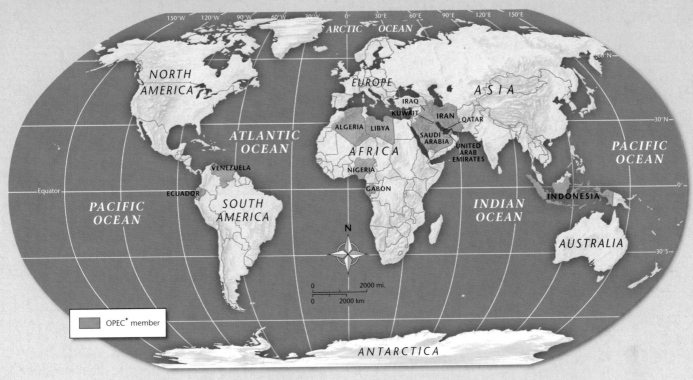

*Organization of Petroleum Exporting Countries

A 1976 bicentennial quarter

Jimmy Carter's less aggressive leadership style challenged the idea of an "imperial presidency."

1975

Ford signs the Helsinki Accords on European security.

1976

The United States celebrates the bicentennial of the signing of the Declaration of Independence.

1978

President Carter negotiates the Camp David Accords to promote peace in the Middle East.

1980

The United States leads a boycott of the Moscow summer Olympics.

1981

American hostages held in Iran are returned to the United States.

Gerald R. Ford 1974–1977   Jimmy Carter 1977–1981   Ronald Reagan 1981–1989

1976   **1978**   **1980**   **1982**

Cambodia captures the *Mayaguez,* an American merchant ship.

The Soviet Union invades Afghanistan.

A rescue attempt fails to free American hostages in Iran.

1975   **1979**   **1980**

Nixon's Domestic Policy

READING FOCUS

- How did Richard Nixon's personality affect his relationship with his staff?

- How did Nixon's domestic policies differ from those of his predecessors?

- How did Nixon apply his "southern strategy" to the issue of civil rights and to his choice of Supreme Court justices?

- Describe the first manned moon landing.

MAIN IDEA

President Richard Nixon relied on several close advisors to help him move the country in a new direction.

KEY TERMS

deficit spending
Organization of Petroleum Exporting Countries (OPEC)
embargo
New Federalism

TARGET READING SKILL

Identify Supporting Details Copy the chart below. As you read, fill in details about the Nixon administration. Add more boxes as needed.

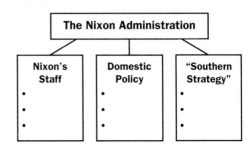

Setting the Scene Richard Nixon's victory in 1968 was, for him, particularly sweet. His earlier bid for the presidency, in 1960, had failed. Two years later he had lost another election, for governor of California. Deeply unhappy, Nixon had vowed to retire from politics. Instead, he came back from those bitter defeats to win the nation's highest office at a time when the country sorely needed strong leadership.

Nixon grew up in a low-income family in Whittier, California. He never got over his sense of being an outsider. In 1963, he described how that feeling drove him to achieve:

❝ What starts the process really are laughs and slights and snubs when you are a kid. Sometimes it's because you're poor or Irish or Jewish or Catholic or ugly or simply that you are skinny. But if you are reasonably intelligent and if your anger is deep enough and strong enough, you learn that you can change those attitudes by excellence, personal gut performance. . . . ❞

—Richard Nixon, 1963

Although he was a private man, Nixon loved the applause of a crowd.

Nixon in Person

Unlike most politicians, Richard Nixon was a reserved and remote man. Uncomfortable with people, he often seemed stiff and lacking in humor and charm. He overcame these drawbacks by using modern campaign techniques to get his message across.

Many Americans looked beyond Nixon's personality traits. They respected him for his experience and his service as Vice President under Eisenhower. Many others, though, neither trusted nor liked him.

According to Patrick Buchanan, then a Nixon speech writer, there was "a mean side to his nature." He was willing to say or do anything to defeat his enemies. Those enemies included his political opponents, the government bureaucracy, the press corps, and leaders of the antiwar movement.

Nixon was fully prepared to confront these forces. He wrote, "I believe in the battle, whether it's the battle of the campaign or the battle of this office, which is a continuing battle. It's always there wherever you go."

Insulating himself from people and the press, Nixon had few close friends. He found support and security in his family: his wife Pat and their two daughters. He also established lasting associations with several activists in his political campaigns. Away from the White House, he stayed far from crowds by spending time at his estates in Florida and California.

Nixon believed the executive branch of government had to be strong to be successful. When he took office, he gathered a close circle of trusted advisors around him to pursue that goal.

Nixon's Staff

Cabinet members, representatives of the executive branch departments, have historically been a President's top advisors. Many have been independent-minded people. More than most other post–World War II Presidents, Nixon avoided his Cabinet and preferred to rely on his White House staff to develop his policies. Staff members were team players. They gave him unwavering loyalty.

Two key appointees had direct access to Nixon. They shielded him from the outside world and carried out his orders. One was H. R. Haldeman, an advertising executive who had campaigned tirelessly for Nixon. He became chief of staff. Haldeman once summarized how he served the President: "I get done what he wants done and I take the heat instead of him." The other key staffer was lawyer John Ehrlichman. Ehrlichman served as Nixon's personal lawyer and rose to the post of chief domestic advisor.

Haldeman and Ehrlichman framed issues and narrowed options for the President. They also stood between the President and anybody else who wanted to speak to him. Together they became known as the "Berlin Wall" for the way they protected Nixon's privacy.

A third trusted advisor was John Mitchell, a lawyer. Mitchell had worked with Nixon in New York and had managed his presidential campaign. Nixon asked him to be Attorney General just after the 1968 election. Mitchell had great influence with the President, often speaking with him several times a day.

Another of Nixon's closest advisors did not fit the mold of Haldeman, Ehrlichman, and Mitchell. Henry Kissinger, a Harvard government professor, had no previous ties to Nixon. Still, he acquired tremendous power in the Nixon White House. Nixon first appointed Kissinger to be his national security advisor, and then, in 1973, to be Secretary of State. Kissinger played a major role in shaping foreign policy, both as an advisor to the President and in behind-the-scenes diplomacy.

Domestic Policy

The Vietnam War and domestic policy had both been important in the 1968 political campaign. As you have read, restoring law and order was one element of Nixon's domestic policy. Other domestic issues also required attention, and on these, Nixon broke with many of the policies of Presidents Kennedy and Johnson.

VIEWING HISTORY The Oval Office in the White House saw many meetings of Nixon and his inner circle of advisors. Left to right in this photo are Kissinger, Ehrlichman, the President, and Haldeman. **Synthesizing Information** *What role did Nixon's advisors play in his presidency?*

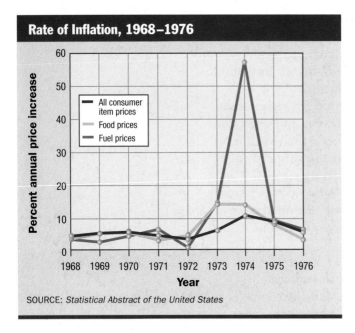

Rate of Inflation, 1968–1976

Percent annual price increase

- All consumer item prices
- Food prices
- Fuel prices

Year

SOURCE: *Statistical Abstract of the United States*

INTERPRETING GRAPHS
Rising oil prices in the 1970s had a strong impact on all parts of the American economy. **Analyzing Information** *When did fuel prices reach their peak? What caused fuel prices to rise so dramatically?*

READING CHECK
What was the state of the nation's fuel supply before the oil embargo?

Inflation   The economy was shaky when Nixon took office. Largely because of rising spending for the Vietnam War, inflation had doubled between 1965 and 1968. In addition, the government was spending more than it was taking in from taxes, so the budget deficit was growing. Unemployment was also growing.

Nixon's first priority was to halt inflation. He wanted to bring federal spending under control, even if it led to further unemployment. He was determined, though, to avoid imposing government controls on wages and prices. He had seen such controls in action while working for the Office of Price Administration during World War II. "I will not take the nation down the road of wage and price controls, however politically expedient [helpful] they may seem," he said in 1970.

During Nixon's first few years in office, however, federal spending proved difficult to control. Unemployment and inflation both continued to rise. Although Republicans traditionally aimed for a balanced budget, Nixon began to consider **deficit spending,** or spending more money in a year than the government receives in revenues. In this way he hoped to stimulate the economy. Proposed by British economist John Maynard Keynes, deficit spending had restored prosperity during World War II. "I am now a Keynesian in economics," Nixon announced in 1971, to many people's surprise.

Finally, in an attempt to slow the high rate of inflation, the President imposed a 90-day freeze on wages, prices, and rents in August 1971, and a 60-day general price freeze in June 1973. Pressure from business and labor, however, led him to lift these controls, and inflation again soared.

Oil Crisis   In some ways, the United States had been heading toward an energy crisis long before Nixon took office. The nation's growing population and economy used more energy each year. Coal was plentiful, but environmental concerns discouraged its use. Federal regulations imposed in the mid-1950s kept the price of natural gas low, which meant producers had little incentive to raise their output. Furthermore, the nation's oil production began to decline in 1972. At the time, Americans depended on cheap, imported oil for about a third of their energy needs.

Nixon's oil price controls served to aggravate the energy problem. Refineries let supplies run so low during the price freezes that demand could not be met after the controls were lifted.

Unrest in the Middle East turned the energy problem into a crisis. In 1973, Israel and the Arab nations of Egypt and Syria went to war. The United States backed its ally Israel. In response, the Arab members of the **Organization of Petroleum Exporting Countries (OPEC)** imposed an **embargo,** or ban, on the shipping of oil to the United States. OPEC, a group of nations that cooperates to set oil prices and production levels, also quadrupled its prices. The cost of foreign oil skyrocketed.

Higher oil prices, in turn, worsened inflation. A loaf of bread that had cost 28 cents earlier in the 1970s now cost 89 cents. Americans had paid 25 cents a gallon for gas but now paid 65 cents. Consumers reacted to the higher prices by cutting back on spending. The result was a recession.

Social Programs President Nixon hoped to halt the growth of government spending by cutting back or shutting down some of the social programs that had mushroomed under Johnson's Great Society. Critics claimed that these programs were wasteful, encouraged "welfare cheaters," and discouraged people from seeking work.

Nixon had voiced similar complaints in his campaign, but he now faced a dilemma. On the one hand, he wanted to please conservative voters who demanded cutbacks. On the other hand, he hoped to appeal to traditionally Democratic blue-collar voters and others who favored social programs.

Nixon called for a new partnership between the federal government and the state governments known as the **New Federalism.** Under this policy, states would assume greater responsibility for the well-being of their own citizens. Congress passed a series of "revenue-sharing" bills that granted federal funds to state and local governments to use as they wished.

The "Southern Strategy"

Nixon believed he had little to gain by supporting advances in civil rights. Few African Americans had voted for him in the 1960 race against John Kennedy, and in 1968, he had won just 12 percent of the black vote. Besides, he reasoned, any attempt to appeal to black voters might cost him the support of many white southern voters.

Explaining his position, Nixon once observed that "there are those who want instant integration and those who want segregation forever. I believe that we need to have a middle course between those two extremes." In effect, this meant a slowdown in desegregation.

Nixon's aim was to find the proper "southern strategy" to win over white southern Democrats. Republican Senator Strom Thurmond of South Carolina, who had left the Democratic Party in 1948, became Nixon's strongest southern

Energy Shortages

Oil shortages caused enormous frustration in the United States during the 1970s. As shown in the photo left, lines at gas stations were long, often extending for blocks. Many people began to buy energy-efficient foreign cars instead of the "gas-guzzling" American models. Midwestern farmers had difficulty finding fuel to dry out their crops before they spoiled. Winter heating-oil shortages led to school closings in Colorado.

Interruptions in electricity supply can also cause hardships. When disruption is minor, an area may experience a brownout, a temporary reduction in electrical power. Blackouts, complete cuts to power, are more serious. Recently, "rolling blackouts" in California shut off power to selected areas at hours of peak usage. Homes and businesses without alternate energy sources, such as gas-powered generators, could not operate computers or appliances. Causes of the California energy crisis were threefold: energy deregulation leading to steeply rising prices, increased demand for electricity, and the financial instability of the state's major utility companies. Demonstrators (above) protested high prices by burning their electricity bills.

 How are oil shortages of the 1970s similar to more recent energy shortages?

VIEWING HISTORY In 1974, police escorts help Boston schools to comply with court-ordered busing. **Drawing Conclusions** *Why did Nixon oppose busing?*

supporter. To keep Thurmond and his colleagues happy, Nixon sought to cut funding for the enforcement of fair housing laws. He also made it easier to meet desegregation requirements.

The Justice Department, headed by John Mitchell, tried to prevent the extension of certain provisions of the Voting Rights Act of 1965 that were due to expire in 1970. This law had greatly increased the number of African Americans who could vote in the South. Congress went ahead with the extension, but through the efforts of his Attorney General, Nixon had made his point to white southern voters.

Another controversial racial issue was the use of busing to end school segregation. In several cities, federal courts ordered school systems to bus students to other schools in order to end the pattern of all-black or all-white schools. Particularly in northern cities, such as Detroit and Boston, some white students and their parents responded to busing with boycotts or violent protests.

In 1971, the Supreme Court issued guidelines for busing that went against Nixon's views. A federal judge in North Carolina had ruled that voluntary integration was not working. In *Swann* v. *Charlotte-Mecklenburg Board of Education*, the Court agreed, saying that busing was one possible option for ending school segregation.

Nixon, who had long opposed busing, then went on television to say he would ask Congress to halt it. He also allowed the Department of Health, Education, and Welfare to restore federal funding to school districts that were still segregated. Nixon's refusal to enforce the Court ruling did not halt busing in the country, but his opposition did limit it.

Nixon's Supreme Court

During the election campaign, Nixon had criticized the Supreme Court for being too liberal and easy on criminals. In his first term, four of the nine justices either died, resigned, or retired. This gave him the extraordinary opportunity to name four new justices and thus reshape the Court. Nixon first named Warren Burger as Chief Justice, replacing Earl Warren. Burger, a moderate, was easily confirmed by the Senate in 1969.

Focus on GOVERNMENT

The Imperial Presidency Nixon took a broad view of his powers as President of the United States and is counted among several Presidents, including Andrew Jackson and Theodore Roosevelt, who sought to expand the powers of the office. Nixon worked to extend executive privileges to include rights historically reserved for kings and emperors, such as the right to use public funds at his discretion and the right to shield himself from prosecution. Because of these efforts, Nixon contributed to what came to be called the "imperial presidency." The term is sometimes used by critics who think the powers of the presidency have become too strong.

Later nominations reflected Nixon's southern strategy and conservative views. The Senate rejected his first two nominees from the South, with opponents charging the men showed racial bias. Nixon successfully appointed Harry A. Blackmun (1970); Lewis F. Powell, Jr. (1972); and William H. Rehnquist (1972). All three were respected jurists who generally tilted the Court in a more conservative direction. As Justice Blackmun's tenure continued, however, he became increasingly liberal in his decisions.

The First Moon Landing

The Nixon years witnessed the fulfillment of President Kennedy's commitment in 1961 to achieve the goal, "before this decade is out, of landing a man on the moon." That man was *Apollo 11* astronaut Neil A. Armstrong.

On July 20, 1969, at 10:56 P.M. Eastern Daylight Time, Armstrong descended from the *Eagle* lunar landing craft and set foot on the moon's surface. Armstrong radioed back the famous message: "That's one small step for man, one giant leap for mankind."

Television viewers around the world witnessed this triumph of the *Apollo* program, carried out by the National Aeronautics and Space Administration (NASA). The *Apollo 11* crew included Edwin E. "Buzz" Aldrin, Jr., who landed with Armstrong in the *Eagle*, and Michael Collins, who remained in the *Apollo 11* command module circling the moon.

Aldrin joined Armstrong in the two-hour moon walk, during which they collected rock and soil samples and set up scientific instruments to monitor conditions on the moon. They also photographed the landing site, a dusty plain in an area called the Sea of Tranquillity.

The *Eagle* and its crew stayed on the moon for 21 hours and 36 minutes before lifting off to rejoin Collins for the return trip. After a safe splashdown, the astronauts were quarantined for 18 days to ensure that they had not picked up any unknown lunar microbes. They emerged to a hero's welcome.

VIEWING HISTORY Astronaut Buzz Aldrin takes a walk on the moon. **Drawing Inferences** *Why was the government so committed to the space program?*

Section 1 Assessment

READING COMPREHENSION

1. What is **deficit spending?** How did Nixon attempt to control inflation?

2. Why was the United States vulnerable to **OPEC?**

3. How did the 1973 oil **embargo** affect the United States?

4. What was the **New Federalism?**

5. Describe the busing issues and events of the 1970s.

CRITICAL THINKING AND WRITING

6. **Recognizing Bias** How was Nixon's image of himself as an outsider reflected in the way he ran the White House? Use specific examples in your explanation.

7. **Writing to Persuade** Write an outline for a persuasive essay either supporting or opposing Nixon's domestic policies.

For: An activity on Nixon's domestic policy
Visit: PHSchool.com
Web Code: mrd-0321

Nixon's Foreign Policy

READING FOCUS

- What role did Henry Kissinger play in relaxing tensions between the United States and the major Communist powers?
- What was Nixon's policy toward the People's Republic of China?
- How did Nixon reach an agreement with the Soviet Union on limiting nuclear arms?

MAIN IDEA

President Nixon's foreign policy led to more positive relationships with China and the Soviet Union.

KEY TERMS

realpolitik
détente
SALT I

TARGET READING SKILL

Identify Supporting Details Copy the web diagram below. Include three or four blank circles. As you read, fill in each blank circle with important facts about U.S. relations with China and the Soviet Union during Nixon's presidency.

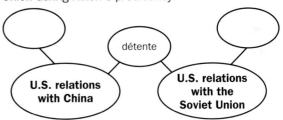

détente

U.S. relations with China

U.S. relations with the Soviet Union

Setting the Scene As President, Richard Nixon's greatest achievements came in the field of foreign policy. "I've always thought this country could run itself domestically without a President," he observed. In his first Inaugural Address, Nixon set the stage for a new direction in foreign relations:

> 66 *After a period of confrontation, we are entering an era of negotiation. Let all nations know that during this administration our lines of communication will be open. We seek an open world. Open to ideas, open to the exchange of goods and people. A world in which no people, great or small, will live in angry isolation. We cannot expect to make everyone our friend, but we can try to make no one our enemy.* 99
> —Nixon's First Inaugural Address, January 20, 1969

Nixon's creative approach to foreign affairs helped ease Cold War tensions. Aided by the skillful diplomacy of Henry Kissinger, Nixon helped establish ties with China and crafted stronger relations with the Soviet Union.

Henry Kissinger

While Nixon had a keen understanding of foreign policy, he relied heavily on Henry Kissinger in charting his course. Kissinger quickly gained the President's confidence. By the time Nixon appointed Kissinger Secretary of State in 1973, he was a dominant figure in the administration.

Practical Politics Kissinger had written his doctoral dissertation on Klemens von Metternich, an Austrian statesman and diplomat in the nineteenth century who had helped maintain stability in Europe amid liberal change. Kissinger's studies in European history gave him an admiration for *realpolitik*, a German term meaning "practical politics." Nations that follow this policy make decisions based on maintaining their own strength rather than following moral principles. Kissinger would later apply this approach to his dealings with China and the Soviet Union.

VIEWING HISTORY President Nixon owed the success of much of his foreign policy to his national security advisor, and later, Secretary of State, Henry Kissinger. **Demonstrating Reasoned Judgment** *Why did Nixon rely so heavily on Kissinger's advice?*

Nixon liked to be flattered, and he liked people who could talk tough. Kissinger, who understood what Nixon wanted from an advisor, soon became the man Nixon talked to most. "Henry, of course, was not a personal friend," Nixon later said, but the two spoke five or six times a day, sometimes in person, sometimes by phone, and often for hours at a time.

Both men were suspicious and secretive. They tended not to seek consensus, or general agreement with others, but to keep information to themselves. "They tried not to let anyone else have a full picture, even if it meant deceiving them," noted Lawrence Eagleburger, a State Department official.

Kissinger's actual influence in shaping American foreign policy was broader than his official role as Secretary of State. He knew how to frame questions in ways the President wanted. He could condense complex foreign policy issues into briefing papers that gave Nixon clear options for making decisions. In his memoirs, Kissinger wrote:

> 66 *Nixon could be very decisive. Almost invariably during his Presidency, his decisions were courageous and strong and often taken in loneliness against all expert advice. But wherever possible Nixon made these decisions in solitude on the basis of memoranda or with a few very intimate aides.* 99

—Henry Kissinger, *The White House Years*

Public Opinion Kissinger also understood the power of the press. He had a remarkable ability to use the media to shape public opinion. Journalists depended on him for stories, so they were afraid to anger him. "You know you are being played like a violin," a *Time* magazine reporter observed, "but it's still extremely seductive."

Kissinger's efforts in ending the Vietnam War and easing Cold War tensions made him a celebrity. He shared the 1973 Nobel peace prize with North Vietnam's Le Duc Tho (who refused it); he appeared on 21 *Time* magazine covers; and in a 1973 Gallup poll, he led the list of the most-admired Americans. Kissinger's efforts in the Nixon administration left a lasting mark on American foreign policy.

Relaxing Tensions

Nixon and Kissinger's greatest accomplishment was in bringing about **détente,** or a relaxation in tensions, between the United States and the world's two Communist giants. China and the Soviet Union were sworn enemies of the United States. Nixon's willingness to conduct talks with them stunned many observers. In the 1950s, Nixon had been one of the most bitter and active anti-Communists in government. He had made his reputation by demanding that the United States stand firm against the Communist threat.

As President, however, Nixon dealt imaginatively with both China and the Soviet Union. Nixon distrusted government bureaucracy, so he kept much of his diplomacy secret. Bypassing Congress, and often bypassing his own advisors, he and Kissinger reversed the direction of postwar American foreign policy.

Nixon drew on Kissinger's understanding that foreign affairs were more complex than a simple standoff between the United States and communism.

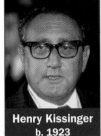
READING CHECK
What were some obstacles to achieving détente?

VIEWING HISTORY Chinese premier Zhou Enlai and President Richard Nixon congratulate each other on the new ties between their nations. **Determining Relevance** *Why was it important for the press to capture such moments?*

The Soviet Union and China, once allies, had become bitter enemies. This stunning development had the potential to reshape global politics. "The deepest international conflict in the world today," Kissinger noted, "is not between us and the Soviet Union but between the Soviet Union and Communist China."

A New Approach to China

The most surprising policy shift was toward China. In 1949, the Communists had taken power and established the People's Republic of China. Many Americans saw all Communists as part of a united plot to dominate the world. As a result, the United States did not formally recognize the new Chinese government. In effect, the United States officially pretended that it did not exist.

Even when the Chinese-Soviet alliance crumbled, the United States clung to its position. It insisted that the government of Jiang Jieshi, which was set up on the island of Taiwan when the Nationalists fled the Chinese mainland, was the rightful government of all China.

Opportunity for Change Quietly, Nixon began to prepare the way for a new policy of *realpolitik*. His first foreign policy report to Congress in 1970 began:

❝ *The Chinese are a great and vital people who should not remain isolated from the international community. . . . United States policy is not likely soon to have much impact on China's behavior, let alone its ideological outlook. But it is certainly in our interest, and in the interest of peace and stability in Asia and the world, that we take what steps we can toward improved practical relations with Peking [Beijing].* ❞

—Richard Nixon, report to Congress, 1970

Focus on WORLD EVENTS

Cultural Revolution As the United States reconsidered its China policy, Chinese society was engulfed in chaos. In 1966, China's leader, Mao Zedong, had launched the Cultural Revolution, an attempt to revive the country's revolutionary spirit by "smashing the four olds"—old ideas, old culture, old customs, and old habits. High school and university students led the way, forming a radical group known as the Red Guards. Operating mainly in the cities, they destroyed temples, books, and works of art while terrorizing teachers and government officials. Their campaign soon spiraled out of control, and Mao had to direct the military to restore order. In the resulting clashes between bands of Red Guards and the army, thousands of Chinese died. The Cultural Revolution ended with Mao's death in 1976. However, the damage to China's society would linger for many years.

The administration undertook a series of moves designed to improve the relationship between the United States and China:

1. In January and February 1970, American and Chinese ambassadors met in Warsaw, Poland.
2. In October 1970, in a first for an American President, Nixon referred to China by its official title, the People's Republic of China.
3. In March 1971, the United States government lifted restrictions on travel to China.
4. In April 1971, an American table-tennis team accepted a Chinese invitation to visit the mainland, beginning what was called "ping-pong diplomacy."
5. In June 1971, the United States ended its 21-year embargo on trade with the People's Republic of China.

In July 1971, after extensive secret diplomacy by Kissinger, Nixon made the dramatic announcement that he planned to visit China the following year. He would be the first United States President ever to travel to that country.

Nixon understood that the People's Republic was an established government that would not simply disappear. Other nations had recognized the government, and it was time for the United States to do the same. Similarly, other countries wanted to give China's seat in the United Nations to the People's Republic. The United States could no longer convince the world to oppose this change. In October 1971, Taiwan lost its seat in the United Nations to the People's Republic of China.

Benefiting From Friendship Nixon had other motives as well. He recognized that he could use Chinese friendship as a bargaining chip in his negotiations with the Soviet Union. (In other words, the Soviet Union might compromise with the United States in order to keep the United States and China from developing too close a relationship.) Press coverage of the trip would give Nixon a boost at home. Also, he believed that he could take this action without suffering political damage, because of his reputation as a strong anti-Communist.

Nixon traveled to China in February 1972. He met with Mao Zedong, the Chinese leader who had led the revolution in 1949. He spoke with Premier Zhou Enlai about international problems and ways of dealing with them. He and his wife Pat toured the Great Wall and other Chinese sights, all in front of television cameras that sent the historic pictures home.

When he returned to the United States, Nixon waited in his plane until prime time so that his return would be seen by as many television viewers as possible. Formal relations were not yet restored—that would take a few more years—but the basis for diplomatic ties had been established. While some members of Congress remained outspoken in their opposition to Communist China, most members—and most Americans—applauded Nixon for taking a more realistic approach to Asia.

NOTABLE PRESIDENTS
Richard M. Nixon

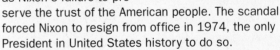

37th President
1969–1974

"In trusting too much in government, we have asked of it more than it can deliver."
—**Second Inaugural Address, 1973**

Born in Yorba Linda, California, in 1913, Richard Milhous Nixon spent his early years in southern California. He worked at his family's gas station and grocery store while attending Whittier College, and then moved to North Carolina, where he graduated from the Duke University School of Law.

Nixon returned to California to practice law. A few years later, in 1940, he married Patricia Ryan. Nixon served as a naval officer during World War II. When the war was over, Nixon began his political career, winning a seat as a Republican in the U.S. House of Representatives. During this time, Nixon gained national prominence for his lead role within the House Un-American Activities Committee (HUAC) in 1948. While serving on HUAC, Nixon showed himself to be an aggressive politician, while gaining many admirers, as well as critics, for his anti-Communist zeal.

After two terms in the House, Nixon was elected to the United States Senate, and then served as Vice President during the Eisenhower administration, from 1953 to 1961.

Many believe Nixon's greatest successes while President were in the field of foreign relations. However, his foreign policy achievements are often overshadowed by the Watergate scandal, and what many saw as Nixon's failure to preserve the trust of the American people. The scandal forced Nixon to resign from office in 1974, the only President in United States history to do so.

After leaving office, Nixon wrote several books and traveled to many countries, including China and the Soviet Union, where he continued his work on foreign relations. He died in 1994.

Connecting to Today
Examine recent U.S. foreign policy decisions. How do they compare to Nixon's approach to foreign relations?

Go Online
PHSchool.com

For: More on Richard M. Nixon
Visit: PHSchool.com
Web Code: mrd-0327

SLBM Submarine-Launched Ballistic Missile

Average range: 600–3,500 miles. These missiles, launched by submarines beneath the surface, are a type of IRBM (Intermediate-Range Ballistic Missile) with smaller warheads and a shorter range than ICBMs. The advantage of submarine-launched missiles is that they are difficult for the enemy to locate and destroy.

Poseidon C-3 Introduced in 1971, the Poseidon had a range of about 2,800 miles and could carry multiple warheads.

ICBM Intercontinental Ballistic Missile

Range: Up to 8,000 miles. These are missiles fired from underground silos. After an initial burst of power, they travel most of the distance to their target by momentum.

Minuteman III This missile was the most widely deployed ICBM around the time of the SALT talks. It was the first missile to carry Multiple Independent Re-entry Vehicles (MIRVs), meaning that a single Minuteman missile can send warheads to several targets.

ABM Anti-Ballistic Missile

In the late 1960s, both the United States and the Soviet Union deployed interceptor missile systems meant to destroy incoming ballistic missiles. The United States built these missiles mainly to protect ICBM launch sites. Safeguard, the ABM program created under Nixon, was shut down in 1975 because it was judged to be unreliable.

Spartan The Spartan missile had a range of 465 miles.

Sprint This smaller missile had a 25-mile range.

INTERPRETING DIAGRAMS
The SALT I Treaty limited the stockpiling of missiles in various categories. **Synthesizing Information** *Which type of missile is used to ward off other missiles?*

Limiting Nuclear Arms

Several months after his 1972 China trip, Nixon visited the Soviet Union. He received as warm a welcome in Moscow as he had in Beijing. In a series of friendly meetings between Nixon and Premier Leonid I. Brezhnev, the two nations reached several decisions. They agreed to work together to explore space, eased longstanding trade limits, and completed negotiations on a weapons pact.

Balancing the Superpowers Nixon viewed arms control as a vital part of his foreign policy. Like many Americans, he was worried about the superpowers' growing stockpiles of nuclear weapons. The Limited Test Ban Treaty of 1963 had ended testing of new bombs in the atmosphere, but underground testing continued. The two superpowers were making bigger and more powerful bombs all the time. Some people feared that the world might be destroyed unless these weapons were brought under control.

Nixon was determined to address the nuclear threat and to deal creatively with the Soviet Union at the same time. He had taken office with the intention of building more nuclear weapons to keep ahead of the Soviet Union, but he came to believe that this kind of arms race made little sense. Each nation already had more than enough weapons to destroy its enemy many times over. The nuclear age demanded balance between the superpowers.

Weapons Talks To address the issue, the United States and the Soviet Union had begun the Strategic Arms Limitation Talks in 1969. In 1972, the talks produced a treaty that would limit offensive nuclear weapons. This treaty was ready for Nixon to sign during his visit to Moscow.

The first Strategic Arms Limitation Treaty, known as **SALT I,** included a five-year agreement that froze the number of intercontinental ballistic missiles (ICBMs) and submarine-launched ballistic missiles (SLBMs) at 1972 levels. The treaty also included an agreement restricting the development and deployment of antiballistic missile defense systems (ABMs), which were designed to shoot down attacking missiles.

While Congress approved SALT I and the treaty went into effect, some government officials were troubled by the agreement. They worried that the treaty's limitation on missiles might leave the United States unprepared to defend itself in an emergency. One solution was to improve conventional weapons, which were not limited by the treaty. Therefore, Secretary of Defense Melvin Laird made the Pentagon's approval contingent on a commitment to move ahead with plans to build a better bomber and a larger submarine. At the same time, both the United States and the Soviet Union began to develop a new technology that used multiple nuclear warheads on a single missile, and was correspondingly more destructive.

SALT I was a triumph for the Nixon administration and an important step forward. Yet it did not reduce the number of warheads the two nations possessed. Nor did it stop them from improving nuclear weapons in other ways. Still, it helped to ease what had been growing concerns about the arms race, and it demonstrated the willingness of the United States and the Soviet Union to work together toward a common goal. In showing that arms control agreements between the superpowers were possible, SALT I paved the way for more progress in the future.

About a year before the signing of SALT I, Nixon pointed out that the potential benefits of negotiating with the Soviet Union went beyond the issue of limiting nuclear arms:

> 66 *Perhaps for the first time, the evolving strategic balance allows a Soviet-American agreement which yields no unilateral [one-sided] advantages. The fact [that] we have begun to discuss strategic arms with the USSR is in itself important. Agreement in such a vital area could create a new commitment to stability, and influence attitudes toward other issues.* 99
>
> —Richard Nixon

Focus on GOVERNMENT

Shuttle Diplomacy After the Arab-Israeli War in 1973, Kissinger undertook what came to be known as shuttle diplomacy, traveling back and forth between Middle Eastern capitals to arrange peace. In April 1974, he secured a cease-fire agreement between Israel and Syria, whose forces had been fighting on the Golan Heights. In June, President Nixon visited the Middle East to recognize the success of Kissinger's efforts to reduce tensions in the region. Others holding the office of Secretary of State since Kissinger have followed his lead, using shuttle diplomacy to further U.S. foreign policy goals.

Section 2 Assessment

READING COMPREHENSION

1. How did Kissinger use *realpolitik* to carry out Nixon's foreign policy?

2. What is the meaning of **détente?** Why was it difficult to achieve détente with Communist nations?

3. What did the term "ping-pong diplomacy" refer to in the Nixon administration? What steps were taken to improve the relationship between the United States and China?

4. What were Nixon's concerns about nuclear weapons?

5. What was **SALT I?**

CRITICAL THINKING AND WRITING

6. **Identifying Central Issues** What were Nixon's policies toward China and the Soviet Union? Why were they so surprising at the time?

7. **Drawing Conclusions** Why did Nixon and Kissinger believe it was important to relax the tensions between the United States and both China and the Soviet Union?

8. **Writing an Opinion** Considering the limitations of SALT I, do you think it was an important treaty? Make a list of reasons to support your opinion.

Go Online
PHSchool.com

For: An activity on Nixon's foreign policy
Visit: PHSchool.com
Web Code: mrd-0322

READING FOCUS

- How did the Nixon White House battle its political enemies?

- How did the Committee to Reelect the President conduct itself during Nixon's reelection campaign?

- What was the Watergate break-in, and how did the story of the scandal unfold?

- What events led directly to Nixon's resignation?

MAIN IDEA

The break-in at the Watergate apartment complex started a scandal that led to President Nixon's resignation.

KEY TERMS

wiretap
Watergate scandal
special prosecutor
impeach

TARGET READING SKILL

Identify Cause and Effect Copy the cause-and-effect diagram below. As you read, add information about the Watergate scandal and Nixon's resignation.

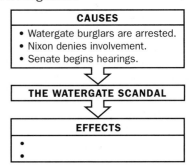

CAUSES
• Watergate burglars are arrested.
• Nixon denies involvement.
• Senate begins hearings.

⬇

THE WATERGATE SCANDAL

⬇

EFFECTS
•
•

INTERPRETING POLITICAL CARTOONS This 1973 cartoon pokes fun at Nixon for compiling an "enemies list." **Drawing Inferences** *What message is conveyed by the two lists in the cartoon?*

" YOU THOUGHT OF ANOTHER NAME? OH, GOOD, SIR... FOR WHICH LIST? "

Setting the Scene President Nixon was determined to win an overwhelming victory in the 1972 election. With such a mandate, he would be in a strong position to move his programs through Congress. Fiercely loyal aides carried out schemes to help ensure that the President would win, some of them committing crimes in the process. When Nixon tried to hide their illegal actions, he involved himself in a scandal that ended his presidency and shook the foundations of American government.

In a detailed chronicle of the events surrounding the fall of Richard Nixon, author Theodore H. White observed:

> ❝ The true crime of Richard Nixon was simple: he destroyed the myth that binds America together, and for this he was driven from power.
>
> The myth he broke was critical—that somewhere in American life there is at least one man who stands for law, the President. . . . It was that faith that Richard Nixon broke, betraying those who voted for him even more than those who voted against him. ❞
> —Theodore H. White, *Breach of Faith*

Battling Political Enemies

The President's suspicious and secretive nature caused the White House to operate as if it were surrounded by political enemies. Nixon's staff tried to protect him at all costs from anything that might weaken his political position.

The Enemies List One result of this mind-set was what became known as the "enemies list." Special counsel Charles W. Colson helped develop a list of prominent people who were seen as unsympathetic to the administration. It included politicians such as Senator Edward Kennedy, reporters such as Daniel

Schorr, and a number of outspoken performers such as comedian Dick Gregory and actors Jane Fonda and Steve McQueen. Aides then considered how to harass these White House "enemies." One idea, for example, was to arrange income tax investigations of people on the list.

Wiretaps In 1968, Nixon had campaigned as a man who believed in law and order. Sometimes, however, he was willing to take illegal actions. In 1969, someone in the National Security Council appeared to have leaked secret information to the *New York Times.* In response, Nixon ordered Henry Kissinger to install **wiretaps,** or listening devices, on the telephones of several members of his own staff. He also ordered wiretaps on some news reporters' phones. These wiretaps, installed for national security reasons, were legal at the time. Yet they would lead to other, illegal wiretaps, many of them for political purposes.

The Plumbers In the spring of 1971, Daniel Ellsberg, a former Defense Department official, handed the *New York Times* a huge, secret Pentagon study of the Vietnam War. In June 1971, as you have read, the *New York Times* began to publish this study, which became known as the Pentagon Papers. The documents showed that previous Presidents had deceived Congress and the American people about the real situation in Vietnam.

Nixon was furious that Ellsberg could get away with leaking secret government information. He was even more furious when leaks to the press continued. He and Kissinger were in the midst of secret discussions with China and the Soviet Union, and he did not want those talks to become public.

Nixon approved a plan to organize a special White House unit to stop government leaks. The group, nicknamed the Plumbers, included E. Howard Hunt, a spy novelist and former CIA agent, and G. Gordon Liddy, a former FBI agent. In September 1971, with approval from White House chief domestic advisor John Ehrlichman, the undercover unit broke into the office of Ellsberg's psychiatrist. The Plumbers hoped to find and disclose damaging information about Ellsberg's private life. Their goal was to punish Ellsberg for leaking the Pentagon Papers.

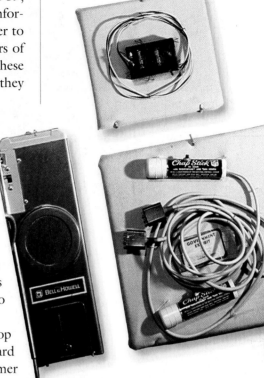

These types of illegal listening devices were later linked to the Nixon administration.

Nixon's Reelection Campaign

Determined to ensure Nixon's victory in 1972, the Committee to Reelect the President used similarly questionable tactics. Headed by John Mitchell, who resigned as Attorney General to assume command, the Committee launched a special fund-raising campaign. It wanted to collect as much money as possible before a new law made it necessary to report such contributions. The money would fund both routine campaign activities and unethical actions hidden from the public.

Though a few of the Committee's actions might have been considered annoying pranks, others were damaging. In 1972, people on the Committee payroll made up a letter attempting to discredit Edmund Muskie, a Democratic senator from Maine and a leading presidential contender. Then they leaked the letter to a conservative New Hampshire newspaper.

Charging Muskie with making insulting remarks about French Canadians living in the state, the letter was timed to arrive two weeks before the New Hampshire primary. The letter also claimed that Muskie's wife was an alcoholic. The normally composed Muskie broke down in tears in front of TV cameras, seriously hurting his candidacy.

READING CHECK
Why did the press leaks infuriate Nixon?

VIEWING HISTORY Security guard Frank Willis discovered the break-in at Washington's Watergate apartment complex. **Identifying Central Issues** What did Nixon do to become ensnared in the scandal?

A May 1973 *Time* magazine cover shows some players in the Watergate scandal, from left, John Ehrlichman; John W. Dean III; H. R. Haldeman; James McCord, Jr.; E. Howard Hunt; and G. Gordon Liddy.

Attempts such as this to sabotage Nixon's political opponents came to be known as "dirty tricks." They included sending hecklers to disrupt Democratic campaign meetings and assigning spies to join the campaigns of major candidates.

The Watergate Break-In

Within the Committee to Reelect the President, a group formed to gather intelligence. The group, which included "Plumbers" Liddy and Hunt, masterminded several outlandish plans.

One scheme called for wiretapping top Democrats to try to find damaging information about delegates at their convention. Twice, Committee leader John Mitchell refused to go along—not because the plan was illegal, but because it was too expensive. Finally, in March 1972, he approved a different idea. Liddy would oversee the wiretapping of phones at Democratic National Committee headquarters in the Watergate apartment complex in Washington, D.C.

The first break-in to install illegal listening devices failed. A second attempt early on the morning of June 17, 1972, ended with the arrest of the five men involved. One suspect was James McCord, a former CIA employee working as a security officer for the Committee to Reelect the President. The Watergate burglars carried money that could be linked to the Committee, thus tying the break-in directly to Nixon's reelection campaign.

When the FBI traced the money carried by the Watergate burglars to the reelection committee, Nixon contacted the CIA. He authorized that organization to try to persuade the FBI to stop its investigation on the grounds that the matter involved "national security."

This action would come back to haunt the President. Although he had not been involved in planning the break-in, Nixon was now part of the illegal coverup. The break-in and the coverup became known as the **Watergate scandal.**

In the months following the Watergate break-in, the incident barely reached the public's notice. Behind the scenes in the White House, some of the President's closest aides worked feverishly to keep the truth hidden.

In the summer of 1972, Nixon advisors H. R. Haldeman, John Ehrlichman, John Mitchell, and others launched a scheme to bribe the Watergate defendants. They distributed hundreds of thousands of dollars in illegal "hush money" to buy their silence. Also, to shield the President, Mitchell and other top officials coached the defendants about how to commit perjury by lying under oath in court.

In the election, Nixon trounced Senator George McGovern of South Dakota by 520 to 17 electoral votes. McGovern had been unable to unify Democrats sufficiently to offer an effective campaign and was perceived as too liberal by much of the country. Nixon had the mandate he wanted, though he did not get a Republican majority in Congress.

The Scandal Unfolds

Despite Nixon's victory in the election, the Watergate story refused to go away. Newspapers such as the *Washington Post* continued to ask probing questions of administration officials. Nixon himself had proclaimed publicly that "no one in the White House staff, no one in this administration, presently employed, was involved in this very bizarre incident." Not everyone believed him.

The Watergate Trial The trial of the Watergate burglars began in January 1973 before Judge John J. Sirica. All the defendants either pleaded guilty or were found guilty. Meanwhile, the White House and the President himself were becoming more deeply involved. In March 1973, just before the judge handed down the sentences, Nixon personally approved the payment of "hush money" to defendant E. Howard Hunt.

At sentencing time, Judge Sirica was not convinced that the full story had yet been told. Criticizing the prosecution, he said:

> ❝ I have not been satisfied, and I am still not satisfied that all the pertinent facts that might be available—I say might be available—have been produced before an American jury. . . . I would hope that the Senate committee is granted the power by Congress . . . to try to get to the bottom of what happened in this case. ❞
>
> —Judge John J. Sirica

To prompt the burglars to talk, Sirica sentenced them to long prison terms, up to 40 years. Their sentences could be reduced, he suggested, if they cooperated with the upcoming Senate hearings on Watergate.

Watergate Chronology

1972

June: Five men linked to Nixon's reelection campaign are arrested for breaking into the Democratic National Committee headquarters.

1973

April: Nixon denies knowledge of the break-in.

May: The Senate Select Committee on Presidential Campaign Activities begins hearings (right).

June: Former Nixon counsel John Dean tells the committee that Nixon authorized a coverup.

July: The committee discovers that Nixon had been secretly recording presidential conversations since 1971 and orders Nixon to release certain tapes. Nixon refuses.

August: Special Prosecutor Archibald Cox sues Nixon for the tapes.

October: Nixon offers summaries of the tapes, which Cox rejects. Nixon fires Cox, setting off a series of firings known as the "Saturday Night Massacre." The House takes steps to impeach Nixon. Nixon releases all but two of the requested tapes.

November: An 18½-minute gap is found on one of the tapes.

1974

January: Nixon claims "executive privilege."

April: Nixon is ordered to surrender more tapes and related documents. Nixon supplies 1,254 pages of edited transcripts. Special Prosecutor Leon Jaworski sues Nixon for the originals.

July: The Supreme Court orders Nixon to surrender the tapes and documents. The House Judiciary Committee recommends impeachment.

August: Nixon releases transcripts that prove he learned of the break-in as early as June 23, 1972, and ordered the coverup. Nixon resigns August 9. His resignation speech is televised (right).

INTERPRETING TIME LINES
As the investigation unfolded, it became increasingly clear that Nixon had something to hide.
Analyzing Information *How was the investigation an example of the federal system of checks and balances?*

VIEWING HISTORY Reporters Carl Bernstein (left) and Bob Woodward of the *Washington Post* persisted in tracking down information to uncover the Watergate story.
Recognizing Cause and Effect
How did their reporting affect the official investigation?

Woodward and Bernstein Meanwhile, two *Washington Post* reporters were following a trail of leads. Bob Woodward and Carl Bernstein, both young and eager, sensed that the trail would lead to the White House.

Even before the election, Woodward and Bernstein had learned about the secret funds of the Committee to Reelect the President. They had written about the political spying and sabotage. As they began to realize who was involved, they called John Mitchell and asked him to verify their story. He denied it angrily.

The Senate Investigates In February 1973, a Senate Select Committee on Presidential Campaign Activities had begun to investigate the Watergate affair. James McCord, one of the convicted Watergate burglars, responded to his lengthy prison sentence by testifying before the committee in secret session. He gave members a vague sense of what had gone on, and he suggested that Nixon staffers were involved. The stories by Woodward and Bernstein helped the probe. In turn, leaks from the Senate committee aided these and other reporters.

As rumors of White House involvement grew, Nixon tried to protect himself. In April 1973, he forced Haldeman and Ehrlichman, his two closest aides, to resign. On national television he proclaimed that he would take final responsibility for the mistakes of others, for "there can be no whitewash at the White House."

The investigation ground on. In May 1973, the Senate committee, chaired by Senator Sam Ervin of North Carolina, began televised public hearings on Watergate. Millions of Americans watched, fascinated, as the story unfolded like a mystery thriller. John Dean, the President's personal legal counselor, sought to save himself by testifying that Nixon knew about the coverup. Other staffers described illegal activities at the White House.

COMPARING PRIMARY SOURCES
Should Nixon Be Impeached?

In July 1974, the House Judiciary Committee debated the possible impeachment of President Richard Nixon.
Analyzing Viewpoints Compare the main arguments made by the two speakers.

In Favor of Impeachment

"My faith in the Constitution is whole, it is complete, it is total, and I am not going to sit here and be an idle spectator to the diminution [lessening], the subversion [undermining], the destruction of the Constitution. . . . The Framers confided in the Congress the power if need be to remove . . . a President swollen with power and grown tyrannical."

—*Texas Representative Barbara Jordan, Democrat*

Opposed to Impeachment

"As the trust is placed in Congress to safeguard the liberties of the people through the . . . powers to remove a President, so must Congress's vigilance be fierce in seeing that the trust is not abused. . . . Not only do I not believe that any crimes by the President have been proved beyond a reasonable doubt, but I do not think the proof even approaches the lesser standards of proof which some of my colleagues . . . suggested we apply."

—*Michigan Representative Edward Hutchinson, Republican*

The most dramatic moment came when Alexander Butterfield, a former presidential assistant, revealed the existence of a secret taping system in the President's office that recorded all meetings and telephone conversations. The system had been set up to provide a historical record of Nixon's presidency. Now those audiotapes could show whether or not Nixon had been involved in the coverup.

The "Saturday Night Massacre" In an effort to demonstrate honesty, Nixon agreed in May 1973 to the appointment of a special Watergate prosecutor. A **special prosecutor** works for the Justice Department but conducts an independent investigation of claims of wrongdoing by government officials. Archibald Cox, a Harvard law professor, took the post and immediately asked for the tapes. Nixon refused to release them. When Cox persisted, Nixon ordered him fired on Saturday, October 20, 1973. This action triggered a series of resignations and firings that became known as the "Saturday Night Massacre."

An Administration in Jeopardy By that time, Nixon was in serious trouble. His public approval rating plummeted. After Cox's firing, *Time* magazine declared, "The President Should Resign."

Leon Jaworski of Texas, Cox's replacement as special prosecutor, also asked for the tapes. Nixon then tried to demonstrate innocence by releasing edited transcripts of some of his White House conversations. He carefully cut out the most damaging evidence. Still, many people were angry and disillusioned when they read even the edited comments of some of the conversations in the Oval Office.

Meanwhile, a subplot had emerged in the troubled White House. Vice President Spiro Agnew stood accused of evading income taxes and taking bribes. Early in October 1973, just ten days before the "Saturday Night Massacre," he resigned in disgrace. To succeed Agnew, Nixon named Gerald R. Ford, the House Minority Leader. For nearly two months, until the Senate confirmed Ford, the nation had a President in big trouble—and no Vice President.

Hearings Begin Nixon had to make another move. After the "Saturday Night Massacre," Congress had begun the process to help them determine if they should **impeach** the President—to charge him with misconduct while in office.

In July 1974, the House Judiciary Committee, which included 21 Democrats and 17 Republicans, began to hold hearings to determine if there were adequate grounds for impeachment. This debate, like the earlier hearings, was broadcast on national television. The country watched anxiously as even Republicans deserted the President. Representative M. Caldwell Butler of Virginia spoke for many of them when he said:

> 66 For years we Republicans have campaigned against corruption and misconduct. . . . But Watergate is our shame. Those things have happened in our house and it is our responsibility to do what we can to clear it up. . . . In short, power appears to have corrupted. It is a sad chapter in American history, but I cannot condone what I have heard; I cannot excuse it; and I cannot and will not stand for it. 99
>
> —Representative M. Caldwell Butler, 1974

American BIOGRAPHY

**Barbara Jordan
1936–1996**

Born in Houston, Texas, Barbara Jordan grew up in a segregated society. She graduated from Texas Southern University, and then earned a law degree from Boston University.

Barbara Jordan's political career included many "firsts." In 1966, she became the first African American in the Texas state senate since Reconstruction. In 1972, Jordan became the first African American woman from Texas elected to the House of Representatives.

As a member of the House Judiciary Committee, Jordan took part in the Watergate hearings in July 1974. Her strong opinions were based on her belief that Nixon's actions threatened the Constitution.

Jordan was reelected to the House in 1974 and 1976. Retiring from politics in 1978, she taught political ethics at the Lyndon B. Johnson School of Public Affairs (University of Texas). Jordan was the keynote speaker at the Democratic conventions in 1976 and 1992.

VIEWING HISTORY In this famous photograph, former President Richard Nixon offers the crowd his familiar salute as he leaves Washington, D.C., following his resignation. **Drawing Conclusions** *Why is the Watergate scandal an important part of American political history?*

By sizable tallies, the House Judiciary Committee voted to impeach the President on charges of obstruction of justice, abuse of power, and refusal to obey a congressional order to turn over his tapes. To remove him from office, a majority of the full House of Representatives would have to vote for impeachment, and the Senate would then have to hold a trial, with two thirds of the senators present voting to convict. The outcome seemed obvious.

Nixon Resigns

On August 5, after a brief delay, Nixon finally obeyed a Supreme Court ruling and released the tapes. They contained a disturbing gap of 18½ minutes, during which the conversation had been mysteriously erased. Still, the tapes gave clear evidence of Nixon's involvement in the coverup.

Three days later, Nixon appeared on television and painfully announced that he would leave the office of President the next day. On August 9, 1974, Nixon resigned, the first President ever to do so. That same day, in a smooth constitutional transition, Vice President Gerald Ford was sworn in. "Our long national nightmare is over," he said.

The Watergate scandal still stands as a low point in American political history. Government officials abused the powers granted to them by the people. A President was forced to resign in disgrace. Many Americans lost a great deal of faith and trust in their government.

However, the scandal also proved the strength of the nation's constitutional system, especially its balance of powers. When members of the executive branch violated the law instead of enforcing it, the judicial and legislative branches of government stepped in and stopped them. As President Ford said upon taking office, "Our constitution works. Our great republic is a government of laws, not of men."

Section 3 Assessment

READING COMPREHENSION

1. Why did Nixon keep an "enemies list"? How was the list used?

2. Describe the use of **wiretaps** within the Nixon White House.

3. How did the public learn about Nixon's role in the **Watergate scandal?**

4. What role did the **special prosecutor** play in the Watergate investigation?

5. Describe what became known as the "Saturday Night Massacre."

6. What does it mean to **impeach?**

CRITICAL THINKING AND WRITING

7. **Posing Questions** Write three questions you would want to ask President Richard Nixon if you were a member of the House Judiciary Committee preparing for impeachment hearings.

8. **Writing an Opinion** Write an outline for an essay in which you evaluate Nixon's role in the Watergate scandal, and state your opinion as to whether or not he should have resigned.

For: An activity on Watergate
Visit: PHSchool.com
Web Code: mrd-0323

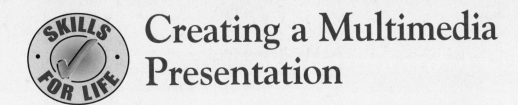

Creating a Multimedia Presentation

The Space Age helped launch new technologies as well as put men on the moon. Today, "reports" are no longer limited to handwritten or typewritten papers. With the help of computers, audio recorders, scanners, VCRs, and more, you can add graphics, photos, and maps; intersperse a written report with audio segments and video clips; and even make your own Web site with quizzes and links.

LEARN THE SKILL
Use the following steps to create a multimedia presentation:

1. **Define your topic.** Multimedia presentations are best suited to topics that have a variety of aspects or subtopics and that lend themselves to visual or audio segments. But your topic should not be so broad that you cannot cover it thoroughly.

2. **Make a "blueprint"—a written plan—for your project.** Find out what media are available to you. Brainstorm! List main subtopics, key sources of information, and the sequence and description of segments. If you are working with a team, assign roles to all team members.

3. **Develop your presentation.** Set deadlines for each main task. Do research, write scripts, and gather materials. Collecting more material than you need will give you flexibility in editing and assembling your work. As in a written report, make sure your ideas flow logically.

4. **Present your work.** The best presentations are interactive, so try to involve your audience in the presentation.

PRACTICE THE SKILL
Answer the following questions:

1. **(a)** Do you think the history of space flight would be too broad or too narrow a topic, or would it be manageable? Explain. **(b)** Evaluate the first moon landing as a topic. **(c)** What audio or video segments might you use for each of these topics?

2. **(a)** Suppose your topic is the first moon landing. What might your subtopics be? **(b)** Besides NASA's Web site (www.nasa.gov), what other sources might be helpful? (Don't forget "stills," such as magazine photographs, newspaper headlines, or diagrams. You might also do your own research by taping interviews with people who watched the moon landing on television as it happened.) **(c)** Create a blueprint for your presentation.

3. **(a)** How much time will you need to gather or create materials? **(b)** How much time will you need to write a script? **(c)** Create a schedule and assign tasks.

4. **(a)** Who is your audience? It might be your classmates, a community group, or younger students. **(b)** How will you involve your audience in the presentation?

APPLY THE SKILL
See the Chapter Review and Assessment for another opportunity to apply this skill.

READING FOCUS

- How did Gerald Ford become President, and why did he pardon Richard Nixon?

- What economic problems did the Ford administration face?

- What actions in foreign policy did President Ford take during his term?

- How did Americans celebrate the nation's bicentennial?

MAIN IDEA

After becoming President, Gerald Ford worked to reunite the country while facing economic problems at home and challenges abroad.

KEY TERMS

stagflation
War Powers Act
Helsinki Accords
bicentennial

TARGET READING SKILL

Identify Sequence As you read, prepare an outline of this section. Use Roman numerals to indicate the major headings, capital letters for the subheadings, and numbers for the supporting details.

> **The Ford Administration**
> I. Ford Becomes President
>   A. Background
>   1. Served in House of Representatives
>   2. _____

Setting the Scene The new President, Gerald R. Ford, faced a difficult job. In his autobiography he recalled the situation he faced when he took office in August 1974:

> 66 *The years of suspicion and scandal that had culminated in Nixon's resignation had demoralized our people. They had lost faith in their elected leaders and in their institutions. I knew that unless I did something to restore their trust, I couldn't win their consent [approval] to do anything else. . . . The New Frontier and Great Society promises of the 1960s had been partly responsible for the national disillusionment. The country didn't need more promises. It yearned for performance instead.* 99
>
> —Gerald R. Ford, *A Time to Heal*

President Gerald Ford is shown with his wife Betty Ford, the new First Lady, after taking the oath of office.

Ford had to help the United States emerge from its worst political scandal. At the same time, the economy was in trouble, and the divisions over the Vietnam War had hardly begun to heal.

Ford Becomes President

"Jerry" Ford was one of the most popular politicians in Washington when he was appointed Vice President in October 1973, following Spiro Agnew's resignation. A football star at the University of Michigan, Ford had played on the national championship teams of 1932 and 1933, and had been a college all-star. After earning a law degree and serving in the navy during World War II, he entered politics. In 1948, he won election to the House of Representatives, where he rose to become Minority Leader in 1965. He was an unassuming man who believed in hard work and self-reliance.

Ford described himself as "conservative in fiscal affairs, moderate in domestic affairs, internationalist in foreign affairs." Over the years, he had opposed much government spending—federal aid to education, the antipoverty program, and spending for mass transit. He had supported defense spending and measures for law and order.

Nixon saw Ford as a noncontroversial figure who might bolster his own support in Congress. When Ford was confirmed as Vice President, Congress and the public were interested mainly in his reputation for honesty, integrity, and stability. Some, however, questioned whether he was qualified to take over the presidency if that became necessary. Despite Ford's long experience in Congress, he had little experience as an administrator or in foreign affairs. Ford acknowledged his own limitations when he was sworn in, saying, "I am a Ford, not a Lincoln."

When Nixon resigned in August 1974, Ford became the first nonelected President. Other Vice Presidents who had moved into the White House had been elected to the vice presidency as part of the national ticket. To fill the vice-presidential vacancy, Ford named former New York Governor Nelson Rockefeller. This created the unique situation of having both a President and a Vice President who had been appointed, not elected.

The Nixon Pardon

Ford became President at the end of a turbulent time in the country's history. The nation was disillusioned by Watergate. During the scandal, many Americans had wondered whether the Constitution would survive Nixon's actions. Few people looked forward to the prospect of an impeachment trial. It would have been only the second in United States history; the first was that of Andrew Johnson in 1868. When Ford assumed the presidency, the nation needed a leader who could take it beyond the ugliness of Watergate.

In response to this public mood, President Ford declared that it was a time for "communication, conciliation, compromise and cooperation." Americans were on his side. *Time* magazine noted "a mood of good feeling and even exhilaration in Washington that the city had not experienced for many years."

All too quickly, Ford lost some popular support. Barely a month after Nixon had resigned, Ford pardoned the former President for "all offenses" he might have committed, avoiding further prosecution. On national television, Ford explained that he had looked to God and his own conscience in deciding "the right thing" to do about Nixon and "his loyal wife and family":

> 66 Theirs is an American tragedy in which we have all played a part. It could go on and on and on, or someone must write the end to it. I have concluded that only I can do that, and if I can I must. . . . My conscience tells me that only I, as President, have the constitutional power to firmly shut and seal this book. My conscience tells me that it is my duty not merely to proclaim domestic tranquility but to use every means that I have to ensure it. 99
>
> —Gerald R. Ford, September 8, 1974

Ford expected criticism of the pardon, but he underestimated the widespread negative reaction. Many of Nixon's loyalists were facing prison for their role in Watergate. The former President, however, walked away without a penalty. Although some people supported Ford's action, his generous gesture

VIEWING HISTORY Betty Ford described her husband as "an accidental Vice President, and an accidental President, and in both jobs he replaced disgraced leaders." **Predicting Consequences** What political risks did President Ford take when he pardoned Richard Nixon?

READING CHECK
Describe the public mood during the Watergate scandal. How did Ford respond to this mood?

Granting Pardons The President's power to "grant reprieves and pardons for offenses against the United States, except in cases of impeachment," is provided by Article II, Section 2 of the Constitution. Most often, pardons are given to individuals who have been convicted in court. President Ford's pardon of Nixon was unusual in that it was awarded before a trial ever took place. Whoever is granted a pardon must, in turn, accept it in order for that pardon to be carried out. Though Nixon was never convicted of his alleged crimes, he was seen to have admitted guilt when he accepted his pardon.

backfired. Some people suggested that a bargain had been made when Nixon resigned. Many also criticized the new President's judgment. Ford was occasionally booed when he made public speeches, just as Johnson and Nixon had been for their stands on the Vietnam War. To counter the reactions, he went before a House committee in October to explain his reasons. The public, angry both at Watergate and the pardon, voted a number of Republicans out of office in the 1974 congressional elections.

Economic Problems

While focusing on the Watergate scandal, the nation had paid less attention to other issues. In the meantime, some conditions had grown worse. Now, facing a hostile Congress, the new administration found it hard to provide direction.

The Economy Stalls Months of preoccupation with Watergate had kept Nixon from dealing with the economy. By 1974, inflation was at about 11 percent, much higher than it had been in the past. Unemployment climbed from about 5 percent in January 1974 to just over 7 percent by the year's end. Home building, usually a sign of a healthy economy, slowed as interest rates rose. The fears of investors brought a drop in stock prices.

Usually, federal policymakers had to deal with either inflation (the result of a rapidly growing economy) or unemployment (the result of a slow economy). Most economists believed that each of those trends could balance out the other. For example, a moderate rise in inflation would help lower the rate of unemployment. Now, however, inflation and unemployment both rose, while the economy remained stalled and stagnant. Economists named this new situation **stagflation.**

By the time Ford assumed the presidency, the country was in a recession, a period in which the economy is shrinking. Not since Franklin Roosevelt took office during the Great Depression had a new President faced such harsh economic troubles.

Ford's approach—like Herbert Hoover's in the early 1930s—was to try to restore public confidence. Early in October 1974, he sent Congress an economic program called "WIN," or "Whip Inflation Now." The President asked Americans to wear red and white "WIN" buttons; to save money, not spend it; to conserve fuel; and to plant vegetable gardens to counter high grocery store prices. The WIN campaign

INTERPRETING GRAPHS
Ford's administration saw the worst economic slump in the United States since the Great Depression. **Analyzing Information** *Describe how consumer prices changed throughout the 1970s. When did unemployment peak in this decade?*

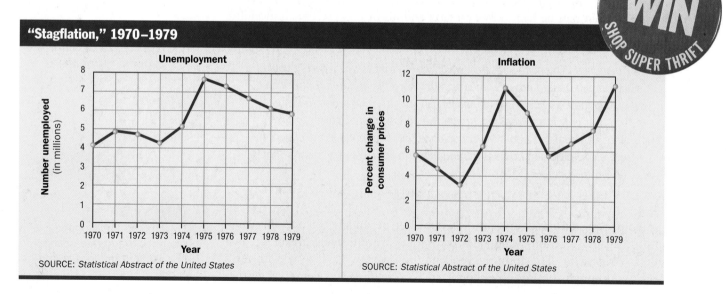

"Stagflation," 1970–1979

SOURCE: *Statistical Abstract of the United States*

SOURCE: *Statistical Abstract of the United States*

In a complex ruling in *Regents of the University of California* v. *Bakke*, the Court ordered that Bakke be admitted to the California medical school. It also upheld the school's right to consider race as one factor in admission decisions, but it did not allow the use of numerical quotas. While the Court decision supported the concept of affirmative action, the case signaled the start of a backlash against the policy.

Carter's Foreign Policy

Although Jimmy Carter had little diplomatic experience when he took office, his personal beliefs greatly influenced his decisions on foreign affairs. Support for human rights was the cornerstone of Carter's foreign policy.

Camp David Accords   Carter's commitment to finding ethical solutions to complicated problems was most visible in the Middle East. In that unstable region, Israel and the Arab nations had fought several wars, most recently in 1967 and 1973. In 1977, though, Egypt's President Anwar el-Sadat made a historic visit to Israel to begin negotiations with Prime Minister Menachem Begin. The two men had such different personalities, however, that they had trouble compromising. Carter intervened, sending Secretary of State Cyrus Vance to invite them to Camp David, the presidential retreat in the Maryland hills.

At Camp David in September 1978, Carter assumed the role of peacemaker. He practiced highly effective personal diplomacy to bridge the gap between Sadat and Begin. They finally agreed on a framework for peace that became known as the **Camp David Accords.** Under the resulting peace treaty, Israel would withdraw from the Sinai peninsula, which it had occupied since 1967. Egypt, in return, became the first Arab country to recognize Israel's existence as a nation.

The Camp David Accords, of course, did not solve all the problems in the Middle East. Among the remaining problems were issues concerning the Palestinians. Many had fled their homes when Arab nations declared war on Israel immediately after that country was established in 1948. Still, as Secretary of State Vance noted:

> 66 *The Camp David Accords rank as one of the most important achievements of the Carter administration. First, they opened the way to peace between Egypt and Israel, which transformed the entire political, military, and strategic character of the Middle East dispute. Genuine peace between Egypt and Israel meant there would be no major Arab-Israeli war, whatever the positions of [other Arab groups].* 99
>
> —Cyrus Vance, *Hard Choices*

VIEWING HISTORY President Carter congratulates Egypt's President Sadat (left) and Israel's Prime Minister Begin (right) on the signing of the Camp David Accords. **Drawing Conclusions** *What were the major achievements of the accords?*

Soviet-American Relations   Several issues complicated the relationship between the United States and the Soviet Union. Détente was at a high point when Carter took office. However, Carter's stand on human rights angered Soviet leaders, undermining the efforts of the two nations to work together. The Soviets were especially annoyed when the President spoke in support of Soviet **dissidents**—writers and other activists who criticized the actions of their government. Soviet citizens were denied the right to speak freely or to criticize their political leaders. Carter believed that such rights were essential

The Panama Canal In the early 1900s, President Theodore Roosevelt had been proud of the way the United States had gained control of land for the Panama Canal. Many Latin Americans, though, resented the continuing United States presence in Panama.

In spite of bitter debate in Congress, in 1978 President Carter convinced the Senate to ratify two treaties dealing with the canal. One treaty was an agreement to return the canal to Panama by the year 2000. The other gave the United States the right to take military action to keep the canal open. The pacts protected American interests while improving relations with Latin America.

and was outspoken in defending them, even when such a defense caused international friction.

In spite of the discord, a second round of Strategic Arms Limitation Talks (SALT II) led Carter and Soviet leader Leonid Brezhnev to sign a new treaty in June 1979. More complicated than SALT I, this agreement limited the number of nuclear warheads and missiles held by each superpower.

Late in 1979, before the Senate could ratify SALT II, the Soviet Union invaded Afghanistan, a country on its southern border, to bolster a Soviet-supported government there. Carter telephoned Brezhnev and told him that the invasion was "a clear threat to the peace." He added, "Unless you draw back from your present course of action, this will inevitably jeopardize the course of United States–Soviet relations throughout the world." A United Nations resolution also called for Soviet withdrawal.

Carter halted American grain shipments to the Soviet Union and took other steps to show United States disapproval of Soviet aggression. Realizing that SALT II surely would be turned down, he removed the treaty from Senate consideration. (Although SALT II was never approved by the Senate, both countries followed the terms of the treaty based on its signing.) Carter also imposed a boycott on the 1980 summer Olympic Games to be held in Moscow. Eventually, some 60 other nations joined the Olympic boycott. Détente was effectively dead.

The Iran Hostage Crisis
Iran, Afghanistan's neighbor to the west, was the scene of the worst foreign policy crisis of the Carter administration. For years the United States had supported the shah (or king) of Iran, Mohammad Reza Shah Pahlavi. The shah had taken many steps to modernize Iran. He was also a reliable supplier of oil and a pro-Western force in the region. For these reasons, Americans overlooked the corruption and harsh repression of the shah's government.

In January 1979, revolution broke out in Iran. It was led by Muslim fundamentalists, who wanted to bring back traditional ways, and by liberal critics of the shah, who wanted more political and economic reforms. As the revolution spread, the shah fled the country. He was replaced by an elderly Islamic leader, the Ayatollah Ruholla Khomeini, who had been in exile. Khomeini and his followers were aggressively anti-Western and planned to make Iran a strict Islamic state.

In October, out of concern for the shah's health, Carter let him enter the United States for medical treatment. Many Iranians were outraged. On November 4, 1979, angry followers of Khomeini seized the American embassy in Tehran and took Americans, mostly embassy workers, hostage.

For 444 days, revolutionaries imprisoned 52 hostages in different locations. The prisoners were blindfolded and moved from place to place. Some were tied up and beaten. Others spent time in solitary confinement and faced mock executions intended to terrorize them. One of the hostages, Kathryn Koob, described part of her experiences:

VIEWING HISTORY Iranian protestors express anti-American sentiment in Tehran, where the American embassy was seized. **Identifying Central Issues** What events led to the hostage crisis?

66 [T]he sounds outside the embassy were nerve-wracking. . . . There seemed to be a continuous crowd of people shouting anti-American slogans, listening to the exhortations [cries] of the students and mullahs [clergymen] who were always on hand. In addition to the crowd noises, there were three or four loudspeakers blaring newscasts. . . . As I sat confined in my chair I thought . . . I just can't take this. 99

—Kathryn Koob, *Guest of the Revolution*

Meanwhile, the American public became more impatient for the hostages' release. President Carter tried many approaches to secure the hostages' freedom. He broke diplomatic relations with Iran and froze all Iranian assets in the United States. Khomeini held out, insisting that the shah be sent back for trial. In April 1980, Carter authorized a risky commando rescue mission. It ended in disaster when several helicopters broke down in the desert. In the retreat, two aircraft collided, killing eight American soldiers. The government was humiliated, and Carter's popularity dropped further. Even after the shah died in July, the standoff continued. Carter's chances for reelection appeared dim.

The 1980 Election

Despite Carter's achievements in the Middle East and his commitment to serious goals, his administration had lost the confidence of many Americans. Rising inflation in early 1980 dropped his approval rating to 21 percent in public opinion polls. Unemployment was still over 7 percent. At times Carter himself seemed to have lost confidence. In two speeches in July, he spoke of a national "crisis of confidence" and a "national malaise."

In the Democratic primaries leading up to the 1980 elections, Massachusetts Senator Edward M. Kennedy won a large number of delegate votes. Kennedy withdrew just as the Democratic National Convention began, however, and Carter was nominated again. Nonetheless, many people were ready for the optimism of the Republican candidate, Ronald Reagan. A leading conservative, Reagan had failed to win his party's nomination in 1976. In 1980, however, Reagan won the nomination, and went on to win the election by a landslide.

After months of secret talks, the Iranians agreed to release the 52 hostages in early 1981. Not until the day Carter left office, however, were they allowed to come home. Newly elected President Reagan sent Carter, as a private citizen, to greet the hostages as they arrived at a U.S. military base in West Germany.

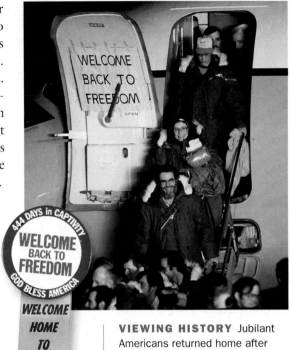

VIEWING HISTORY Jubilant Americans returned home after being held hostage by Iranians. **Drawing Conclusions** *How did Carter's handling of the hostage crisis affect his career?*

Section 5 Assessment

READING COMPREHENSION

1. What is an **incumbent?**

2. What issues concerning **deregulation, amnesty,** and **affirmative action** came up during Carter's presidency?

3. What were the **Camp David Accords?**

4. Why did the United States and the Soviet Union clash over Soviet **dissidents?**

CRITICAL THINKING AND WRITING

5. **Making Comparisons** List examples of the positive and negative results of Carter's approach to foreign policy.

6. **Writing a Letter to the Editor** Write a letter in which you support or oppose Carter's program to conserve energy.

For: An activity on the Iran Hostage Crisis
Visit: PHSchool.com
Web Code: mrd-0325

creating a **CHAPTER SUMMARY**

Copy this chart (right) on a piece of paper and complete it by adding information about the issues and policies under each President's administration. Some entries have been completed for you as examples.

Interactive Textbook

For additional review and enrichment activities, see the interactive version of *America: Pathways to the Present*, available on the Web and on CD-ROM.

Presidents and Issues, 1969–1981

President	Economic Issues	Foreign Policy	Civil Rights	Energy Issues
Nixon				Oil crisis
Ford	Stagflation			
Carter		Camp David Accords		

★ Reviewing Key Terms

For each of the terms below, write a sentence explaining how it relates to the Nixon, Ford, or Carter administration.

1. deficit spending
2. embargo
3. *realpolitik*
4. détente
5. special prosecutor
6. impeach
7. Helsinki Accords
8. incumbent
9. deregulation
10. amnesty
11. affirmative action
12. Camp David Accords

★ Reviewing Main Ideas

13. How did the New Federalism fit into Nixon's approach to domestic policy? (Section 1)

14. What was Nixon's "southern strategy"? (Section 1)

15. How did Henry Kissinger affect American foreign policy under President Nixon? (Section 2)

16. How did the Nixon administration change United States policy toward China? (Section 2)

17. What measures did the Committee to Reelect the President take to win the 1972 election? (Section 3)

18. What illegal actions did Nixon take in attempting to cover up the Watergate break-in? (Section 3)

19. Why did Ford grant Nixon a pardon? (Section 4)

20. What programs did Ford propose to solve the nation's economic problems? (Section 4)

21. How did Carter's lack of Washington experience affect his administration? (Section 5)

22. Evaluate the impact of the Iran hostage crisis on the 1980 presidential election. (Section 5)

★ Critical Thinking

23. **Synthesizing Information**   How did the Watergate scandal shape politics in the 1970s?

24. **Drawing Conclusions**   In 1975, Congress refused President Ford's request to send military aid to South Vietnam. Which do you think played a larger role in Congress's decision—the War Powers Act or public opinion? Why?

25. **Checking Consistency**   Although Americans complained about fuel shortages during the 1970s, many did not support Carter's energy program or try to conserve oil and gas. How do you explain this inconsistent behavior?

26. **Identifying Central Issues**   How did the relationship between the United States and the Soviet Union evolve during the 1970s?

27. **Making Comparisons**   In what ways was "Nixon the President" different from "Nixon the Congressman"? How can you account for this change?

★ Standardized Test Prep

Analyzing Political Cartoons ▶

28. This cartoon, which appeared during the Watergate scandal, shows Richard Nixon caught in a spider's web. What do the reels of tape represent?

   A Recordings of the Watergate hearings

   B Recordings of Nixon's impeachment hearings

   C The White House tapes that Nixon was ordered to surrender

   D The confusing Watergate investigation

29. What is the cartoon's message? Write a caption that could be used with the cartoon.

Interpreting Data

Turn to the line graph on page 828 titled "Rate of Inflation, 1968–1976," in Section 1.

30. In what year was the inflation rate for consumer goods highest?

   A 1972

   B 1973

   C 1974

   D 1975

31. What is the BEST description of the rate of inflation during the period from 1968 to 1972?

   F stayed about the same

   G rose steadily

   H dropped steadily

   I rose and dropped wildly from year to year

32. **Writing** Using this graph and the information in this chapter, examine the relationship between food and fuel prices. Write a paragraph that explains how food prices might be affected by changes in fuel prices.

Test-Taking Tip

To answer Question 31, look at the lines on the graph between the years 1968 and 1972. Describe the overall trend shown for these years only, then identify the best answer.

Applying the Chapter Skill

Creating a Multimedia Presentation Review the major topics discussed in this chapter. Develop a blueprint for a multimedia presentation on a topic you have not yet explored. Consider using information from previous chapters to provide a background for your topic.

For: Chapter 25 Self-Test
Visit: PHSchool.com
Web Code: mra-0326

AmericanHeritage®

MY BRUSH WITH HISTORY™

by CRAIG B. GREENFIELD

A Cold War Test

A Poseidon missile is launched from a submarine.

The Cold War decades were a boom time for the American defense industry. The billions spent each year to develop and produce modern weapons not only helped protect the nation, but also boosted its economy. In the passage below, Craig B. Greenfield, whose father worked for a defense contractor, describes a visit to see his father's handiwork in action.

⟫•≪

IT WAS 1974. As your average twelve-year-old, my world was one of mischievous after-school activities, mixed with the usual sandlot sports, awkward encounters with girls, and homework. With the exception of the trendy peace-sign belt buckle and fingers-gesturing peace-sign T-shirt that I owned, I had only a faint familiarity with the politics of peace and war in faraway Vietnam. In fact, my only real exposure to those events came from those television voices that came between "Gilligan's Island" and "Adam 12," who spoke of the specter of nuclear holocaust that losing to communism in Asia might invite.

All that changed one winter with a brief but profound encounter with the inner workings and realities of the Cold War.

My family had taken a vacation that December. With my father employed as an electrical engineer by the Sperry Corporation, a leading Long Island defense contractor, and my mother keeping busy with her family at home, we set out for Fort Lauderdale to combine some sunshine with the duty of visiting all our recently retired relatives. A much-anticipated highlight of this trip for me was to be a visit to the newly opened Disney World. But compared with the show I was to see, that children's mecca turned out to be just a roadside attraction.

We were relaxing in the cool comfort of my uncle's condominium when my father proudly announced that he had arranged for a side trip to Cape Canaveral for what he called, in the acronymistic vernacular of the defense industry, a DASO, or "daytime at sea operation," wherein a Poseidon missile would be launched from an actual submarine. Although I viewed this

The nuclear-powered strategic missile submarine USS Lafayette underway

860

Cape Canaveral

development as one more dreaded lengthy car ride full of slap fighting with my brother, to my father, who had worked hard on developing submarine navigation systems, it was a rare and valuable chance to see his engineering achievement at work—a demonstration otherwise possible only in an apocalyptic armed launch situation.

With a quick good-bye we set off on our three-hour journey to Port Canaveral, neighboring the cape, where so many televised space shots originated, my father's excitement manifesting itself in driving at a clip that ultimately got him ticketed.

THE MISSILE LAUNCH We arrived at Cape Canaveral and were processed in true Cold War fashion: security clearance, identification cards, and a short, sharp admonishment to stay only in certain areas of the host Navy ship during our day at sea. Then we proceeded up the gangplank and onto the huge auxiliary ship *Compass Island* (EAG 153), which had seen action over the years as a part of the U.S. Military Sealift Command.

I spent the hours-long voyage out to sea exploring the ship and listening to a succession of lectures about this and that capability, guidance system, and the like on both the *Compass Island* and the day's feature attraction, the five-hundred-foot long Poseidon submarine USS *Lafayette* (SSBN 616), which rode regally beside us until it majestically submerged into the sparkling Atlantic water, trailed only by its perfect wake and the indiscreet presence of an antenna-laden Soviet "fishing trawler."

At dusk, with the Florida sun low on the horizon, everyone aboard became aware of the countdown that had actually been going on all day. With fifteen seconds left and our formidable companion well hidden under the sea, the boat buzzed with anticipation and excitement.

At about five seconds to launch, our immense host ship began to rock to and fro, despite the relative tranquillity of the Atlantic shortly before. At four seconds to launch the boat was heaving so violently that all of us had to brace ourselves. At three seconds to launch the rumbling became so loud that I imagined myself being in the center of a thunderclap. At two seconds to launch, with the blocks-long ship in its turbulent pitch and roll and the noise of eruption becoming ever

louder, the inside missile hatch of the submarine blew open explosively far below. Finally, rising on a column of fire, the thirty-four-foot body of the C-3 Poseidon missile emerged from the boiling sea and, with a zig right and a zag left, rocketed skyward and headed toward its destination in the Indian Ocean, nearly three thousand miles away. As I gazed awestruck, my jaw opened wide, that image implanted itself indelibly in my memory.

Today, more than twenty years later, with the disintegration of Soviet communism receding into history, what occurred on that winter day at sea seems almost to have been staged for a movie rather than the profound and scary reality that it was.

However, that vivid childhood memory allows me as an adult to appreciate fully the magnitude of the resources involved in that endeavor called the Cold War. Having personally lived with the practical realities of the Cold War—and having been fed, clothed, and educated with the money that the employment of thousands like my father in the defense industry brought—I greet these new historical developments with both a sense of hope for a peaceful future and a sense of what brought them about.

Source: *American Heritage* magazine, July 1995.

Understanding Primary Sources

1. What was the Soviet "fishing trawler" carrying?

2. How would these items be used?

American Heritage®
MY BRUSH WITH **HISTORY**™
Videotapes

For more information about the Cold War, view "A Cold War Test."

The Conservative Revolution (1980–1992)

Nancy Reagan and Ronald Reagan

Space Shuttle *Columbia*

American Events

1980
Conservatives sweep the 1980 federal elections. Ronald Reagan is elected President, and Republicans win control of the Senate.

1981
President Reagan cuts income tax rates and announces plans to curb government spending.

1982
Unemployment reaches a 40-year high of 10.8 percent during a sharp recession.

1984
Reagan wins a second term in office aided by an economic boom.

Presidential Terms:
Jimmy Carter 1977–1981

Ronald Reagan 1981–1989

1980   **1982**   **1984**

World Events

1982
Argentina and Great Britain battle for control of the Falkland Islands.

1984
Indira Gandhi, prime minister of India, is assassinated.

Cold War Events, 1980–1991

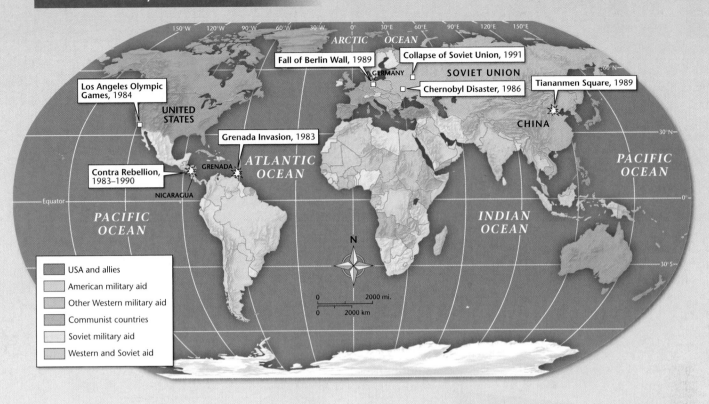

Fall of Berlin Wall, 1989
GERMANY

Collapse of Soviet Union, 1991
SOVIET UNION

Chernobyl Disaster, 1986

Tiananmen Square, 1989

Los Angeles Olympic Games, 1984

UNITED STATES

CHINA

Grenada Invasion, 1983

ATLANTIC OCEAN

PACIFIC OCEAN

Contra Rebellion, 1983–1990

GRENADA

NICARAGUA

ARCTIC OCEAN

Equator

PACIFIC OCEAN

INDIAN OCEAN

N

0   2000 mi.
0   2000 km

Legend:
- USA and allies
- American military aid
- Other Western military aid
- Communist countries
- Soviet military aid
- Western and Soviet aid

1986

Americans learn that presidential aides illegally sold arms to Iran and sent money to support anti-Communist rebels in Nicaragua.

1990

President Bush agrees to raise taxes to fight budget deficits.

1991

American troops lead an international force to liberate Kuwait and defeat Iraq in Operation Desert Storm.

George H. W. Bush 1989–1993

1986

1988

1990

1992

Britain and the United States ban most trade with South Africa over apartheid.

1985

Palestinians rebel against Israel.

1987

China crushes Beijing protests.

1989

Germany is reunified.

1990

Gorbachev resigns, and the Soviet Union dissolves into 15 republics.

1991

Roots of the New Conservatism

READING FOCUS

- What were the major events in Ronald Reagan's political career?

- How did conservatism evolve in the years between the 1930s and the 1970s?

- Why did the 1980 election mark a turning point in United States history?

KEY TERMS

Reagan Democrat
New Right
televangelism

TARGET READING SKILL

Identify Sequence Copy this flowchart. As you read, fill in the boxes with some of the major events in the history of the conservative movement. The first box has been completed to help you get started.

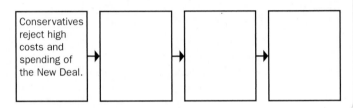

MAIN IDEA

After decades of federal government expansion and social and cultural change, a conservative movement gained strength during the 1970s. In 1980, it brought Ronald Reagan to power.

Setting the Scene Two weeks after Ronald Reagan won the presidency in 1980, Richard Nixon wrote to the president-elect to recommend advisors for top positions:

> 66 *Washington needs new men and new ideas. By your appointments, you can give the country a sense of excitement, hope and drive to government which we have not seen since FDR.* 99
> —Richard Nixon

By most accounts, Reagan succeeded. Six years after the Watergate scandal drove Nixon from the White House, Reagan arrived in Washington at the head of a more conservative and powerful Republican Party. Reagan achieved many of his goals through the strength of his administration and the appeal of his warm personality and firm beliefs.

Although the 1980 election appeared to mark a sudden shift in American politics, the roots of change lay deep in the past. The new President voiced the growing frustrations of voters around the country who believed that government had grown too large and had lost touch with the needs of the people. Reagan's own political journey reflected the growing conservatism of millions of Americans.

With this 1980 campaign poster, Ronald Reagan appealed to voters' patriotism and their unhappiness with the direction of the country.

Reagan's Political Career

Reagan was originally a Democrat who considered Franklin D. Roosevelt, architect of the New Deal, his political hero. When Reagan began his career as a movie actor in Hollywood, he became actively involved in the political affairs of the actors' union.

After World War II, Reagan found himself less comfortable with the Democratic Party, and he joined the Republican Party in the 1950s. He served as a spokesman for General Electric, making speeches that praised capitalism and attacked government regulation. He also spoke out strongly against

Communists in the United States. Ronald Reagan was now clearly in the conservative camp.

Reagan gained national attention in 1966, when he was elected governor of California. Likable, photogenic, and committed to conservative values, he gained support for cutbacks in social programs in his state. During his eight years as governor, Reagan eliminated California's budget deficit by modestly increasing taxes and reforming state spending. He called for similar reforms of social programs run by the federal government.

The Evolution of Conservatism

Reagan's political transition took place against the backdrop of a national debate over the proper size and scope of government. During the prosperous 1920s, conservative Republicans had won national elections by promising to keep taxes low and minimize spending. The Great Depression reshaped the debate with Franklin Roosevelt's introduction of New Deal programs that greatly enlarged the size and cost of the federal government.

New Deal Opponents New Deal agencies, which provided banking regulation, assistance to farmers, aid for the unemployed, and a great deal more, changed the role of the President and the federal government. Critics argued that in a capitalist country, government should not undertake these tasks. They said that the nation could not afford the high federal spending and substantial budget deficits that resulted.

Some of these critics joined to form the American Liberty League. Established in 1934, this organization included both industrialists and politicians. The Liberty League sought to teach respect for the rights of individuals and property and to underscore the importance of individual enterprise. All of these values, members claimed, were being undermined by FDR's large government programs.

In 1937, an attempt by Roosevelt to "pack" the Supreme Court by adding new justices caused a backlash. Conservatives in both major political parties formed a coalition that opposed further New Deal legislation. Nevertheless, Republicans struggled to overcome Roosevelt's enduring popularity as President. Led by Roosevelt and later by Harry S Truman, the Democrats kept control of the White House for twenty years.

From Eisenhower to Goldwater The election of Dwight D. Eisenhower as President in 1952 began eight years of Republican rule. Eisenhower called his approach to government "modern Republicanism." He accepted the basic outlines of the New Deal and never attempted to dismantle the federal bureaucracy. The federal bureaucracy even expanded, as it did in 1953 with the creation of a Department of Health, Education, and Welfare, headed by Oveta Culp Hobby.

In 1964, the Republican candidate for President, Senator Barry Goldwater of Arizona, ran on a staunchly conservative platform. Facing Democrat Lyndon B. Johnson, Goldwater opposed government activism, including social security, federal civil rights

Evolution of Conservatism

1934
The American Liberty League is founded to defend conservative values of private property and individual enterprise.

1937
Roosevelt's attempt to "pack" the Supreme Court causes conservative backlash in Congress.

1952
Dwight Eisenhower is elected President as a moderate Republican.

1964
Barry Goldwater runs on a conservative platform and loses to Johnson in a landslide.

1973
The Supreme Court angers social conservatives with its decision to legalize abortion in *Roe* v. *Wade*.

1980
Conservative Republicans sweep the historic 1980 election.

Liberal Republicans

Historically, the Democratic Party and Republican Party have included coalitions of both liberals and conservatives. Liberal Republicans dominated their party's presidential nominations from the 1930s to the 1960s. However, Goldwater defeated a liberal Republican in the primaries to win the nomination with conservative support. At the 1964 convention, Goldwater denounced "moderation" in a fiery speech that inspired his followers but upset many liberals and moderates in the GOP.

Today Old coalitions have broken up, and the two major parties are clearly divided by philosophy on a national level. The conservative wing of the Republican Party, strengthened by conservative ex-Democrats, controls most leadership positions in the GOP. Some liberal Republicans and conservative Democrats still flourish at state and local levels, but they face difficulties running for Congress or the presidency. One of the few liberal Republicans in the Senate, James Jeffords of Vermont (above), broke his life-long ties to his party in 2001 to become an Independent aligned with Democrats. He said,

"Looking ahead, I can see more and more instances where I will disagree with [President George W. Bush] on very fundamental issues: the issues of choice [abortion rights], the direction of the judiciary, tax and spending decisions, missile defense, energy and the environment, and a host of other issues, large and small."

 How did Goldwater's 1964 campaign lay the foundation for later Republican victories?

laws and antipoverty programs. He also demanded a military buildup against a possible Soviet attack.

Many members of the Republican Party, particularly in the Northeast, felt Goldwater was too conservative to lead their party. Johnson portrayed Goldwater as a dangerous extremist and crushed him in the 1964 election. Goldwater only won his home state of Arizona and several southern states that were unhappy with federal desegregation initiatives. Some analysts concluded that Goldwater's conservatism would never gain wide support. His victory in the South, however, showed that southern conservatives might break their historic ties to the Democrats if a Republican candidate better represented their conservative views.

The Great Society Conservatives found themselves silenced for a time following Goldwater's decisive defeat in 1964. The Democratic landslide in the election gave liberals the political upper hand in the mid-1960s. Congress cooperated as President Johnson pushed ahead with his Great Society program, an extension of the New Deal, starting in 1965.

"Is a new world coming?" Johnson asked. "We welcome it, and we will bend it to the hopes of man."

The Great Society promised something for everyone. The Office of Economic Opportunity helped the poor and gave them a voice in handling their own affairs. Medicare provided medical care for the elderly, while Medicaid gave similar aid to the poor. The Great Society included the most far-reaching school support program in American history. In 1965, a new Department of Housing and Urban Development gave Cabinet-level visibility to the effort to revive the nation's cities and provide good housing for all Americans. However, the Great Society cost billions of dollars annually and raised expectations beyond what the government could meet.

Nixon and the Welfare State In 1968, Richard Nixon won the presidency, bringing Republicans back to power. Nixon wanted to trim social welfare programs, which he believed encouraged people not to work, and to bring the budget under control.

Yet in fact, the federal government continued to grow during Nixon's presidency. The Occupational Safety and Health Act (OSHA) of 1970 provided for employee rights in the workplace and demanded that safety standards be maintained with federal enforcement regulation. Also in 1970, the Environmental Protection Agency (EPA) was created to oversee federal antipollution laws. Opponents of government growth criticized these efforts for interfering with private enterprise.

Social Issues Many conservatives were deeply troubled by rapid cultural changes of the period. Rock music was becoming increasingly shocking, its lyrics more openly sexual and drug-oriented. The use of illegal drugs became widespread, and a wave of radical and often violent student protests swept

READING CHECK
How did conservatives feel about Johnson's Great Society?

proved weaker than Bush's advisors had thought, and he remained in power.

Domestic Issues

Bush's leadership during the Persian Gulf War drove his approval rating up to an astounding 89 percent. Yet while his foreign policy generally won him praise, Americans began to believe that Bush did not have a clear plan for handling domestic problems. In the end, this perception helped usher him out of office.

Bush angered many moderates and liberals with his nomination of Clarence Thomas, a conservative black judge, to the Supreme Court in 1991 when Thurgood Marshall retired. Thomas faced grilling about his views on civil rights and about charges of past sexual harassment. Thomas won confirmation after stormy televised Senate hearings that ignited public debate on the issue of sexual harassment.

Budget deficits continued to swell during Bush's presidency. Bush countered by slowing spending for social programs. Finally, he agreed to a deficit reduction plan that included new taxes. The tax hike broke Bush's 1988 campaign promise and generated public anger.

Bush's real undoing was a recession that began in the early 1990s. Turmoil in the Persian Gulf led gasoline prices to rise rapidly, creating unexpected costs for businesses and consumers alike. The end of the Cold War enabled the United States to spend less on defense. As a result, firms that supplied planes, ships, and military hardware laid off workers. Companies in several other industries also laid off workers to cut costs in a process called **downsizing.** By 1991, the jobless rate reached 7 percent, the highest level in nearly five years. The recession was felt unevenly across the country. States that relied heavily on defense spending, including California and Connecticut, were hit much harder than others.

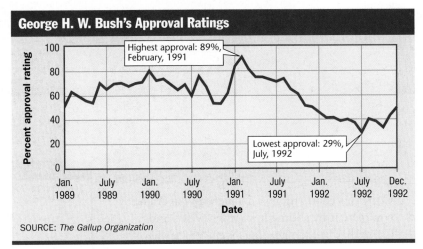

George H. W. Bush's Approval Ratings

Highest approval: 89%, February, 1991

Lowest approval: 29%, July, 1992

SOURCE: *The Gallup Organization*

INTERPRETING GRAPHS
The percentage of Americans who believed Bush was doing a good job plunged from a high of 89 percent during the Gulf War to only 29 percent 17 months later.
Analyzing Information *What were Bush's approval ratings in early 1990, before the Gulf War and the recession?*

Section 4 Assessment

READING COMPREHENSION

1. What factors helped George Bush win the 1988 presidential election?

2. List two reasons why Communist regimes in Eastern Europe collapsed in 1989.

3. How did China's Communist government react to democracy protests in 1989?

4. What domestic issues damaged Bush's popularity?

CRITICAL THINKING AND WRITING

5. **Making Comparisons** How was the Persian Gulf War fought differently from the Vietnam War?

6. **Demonstrating Reasoned Judgment** Was it reasonable for Americans to believe that the Cold War would be followed by international peace and cooperation? Why or why not?

7. **Defending a Position** Some people describe George Bush's presidency as Reagan's third term. Explain whether you agree or disagree.

For: An activity on the Persian Gulf War
Visit: PHSchool.com
Web Code: mrd-0334

creating a CHAPTER SUMMARY

Copy this chart (right) on a piece of paper and complete it by adding important events and issues that fit each heading. Some entries have been completed for you as examples.

For additional review and enrichment activities, see the interactive version of *America: Pathways to the Present*, available on the Web and on CD-ROM.

Time Period	Important Events
Evolution of Conservatism (1934–1981)	• American Liberty League is founded to oppose the New Deal. • Barry Goldwater runs for President as a staunch conservative. •
Ronald Reagan's First Term (1981–1985)	
Ronald Reagan's Second Term (1985–1989)	
George H. W. Bush's Administration (1989–1993)	

★ Reviewing Key Terms

For each of the terms below, write a sentence explaining how it relates to the presidencies of Ronald Reagan and George Bush.

1. Reagan Democrat
2. New Right
3. televangelism
4. supply-side economics
5. New Federalism
6. Strategic Defense Initiative (SDI)
7. AIDS
8. Sandinista
9. Contra
10. Iran-Contra affair
11. INF Treaty
12. entitlement
13. Strategic Arms Reduction Treaty
14. Persian Gulf War
15. downsizing

★ Reviewing Main Ideas

16. List three conservative criticisms of society in the 1960s and 1970s. (Section 1)
17. How did the New Right help Ronald Reagan win the 1980 presidential election? (Section 1)
18. How did supply-side economics change the federal government's tax policy? (Section 2)
19. Did Reagan's tax cuts achieve all of his economic and budgetary goals? (Section 2)
20. How did Reagan view Communist governments in other countries? (Section 2)
21. What role did Supreme Court appointments have in Reagan's conservative strategy? (Section 3)

22. Describe four economic trends of the 1980s. (Section 3)
23. What was the impact on Eastern Europe of Gorbachev's call for *perestroika* and *glasnost*? (Section 4)
24. How did President Bush change America's foreign policy at the end of the Cold War? (Section 4)

★ Critical Thinking

25. **Recognizing Ideologies** (a) How did conservative beliefs affect Reagan's policies? (b) How did they affect Bush's policies?
26. **Identifying Assumptions** Read the selection from Ronald Reagan's first inaugural speech in Section 2. (a) What words does Reagan use to describe government regulations and taxes? (b) What does his choice of words say about his view of government?
27. **Synthesizing Information** During his first term, Reagan called the Soviet Union an "evil empire." In his second term, he developed a working relationship with Gorbachev. What do you think accounts for this change in strategy?
28. **Understanding Cause and Effect** Was Reagan responsible for all the changes in the American economy in the 1980s? Explain your answer.
29. **Drawing Conclusions** Why did President Bush respond differently to the crisis in Panama than he did to the crisis in China?

★ Standardized Test Prep

Analyzing Political Cartoons ▶

30. This cartoon shows President Ronald Reagan aboard a ship. What does the ship represent?

   A The nation's economy
   B The nation's foreign policy
   C Reagan's Cold War policies
   D Government regulations

31. (a) Where is the ship headed? (b) What is the man's attitude about the ship's course?

32. Summarize the cartoonist's message.

Interpreting Data

Turn to the Federal Budget Deficit graph in Section 2.

33. During the Reagan years, what happened to the overall course of the budget deficit?

   A It rose steadily.
   B It fell.
   C It increased by about $210 billion.
   D It increased, and then fell back to its original level.

34. What was the major cause of deficit increases during the period shown in the graph?

   F the cost of the Persian Gulf War
   G the Strategic Defense Initiative
   H increased defense spending and tax cuts under Reagan
   I Bush's pledge not to raise taxes

35. **Writing** Do you think the government should be allowed to spend more money in any given year than it earns in revenues from taxes and other sources? Why or why not?

Test-Taking Tip

To answer Question 30, note the words on the ship's life preserver, "S.S. Reaganomics." Which of the possible answers is related to "Reaganomics"?

Applying the Chapter Skill

Analyzing Trends in the Electoral College Map
Review the information on the Skills for Life page. (a) Which regions of the country lost political clout between 1948 and 1980? (b) Did this change affect the outcome of the 1980 presidential election? Explain your answer.

For: Chapter 26 Self-Test
Visit: PHSchool.com
Web Code: mra-0335

Geography & History

The Rise of the Sunbelt

During the second half of the twentieth century, people and jobs moved on a massive scale from northern portions of the United States to the Sunbelt, a region encompassing states in the South and the Southwest.

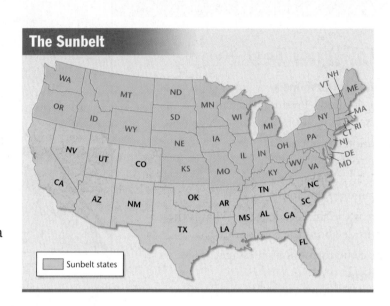

The Sunbelt

Sunbelt states

Why People Left

Cold, snowy winters, and older, declining industries made life challenging in the Midwest and the Northeast. In the 1970s and 1980s, many factories in these regions shut down, and jobs moved south or overseas.

The Appeal of the Sunbelt

Many new jobs became available in the Sunbelt. Employers chose to locate in this region because of lower labor and energy costs. Also, some Sunbelt states had lower business taxes. Families and individuals were drawn to the Sunbelt both by abundant jobs and by its warmer climate and opportunities for year-round outdoor recreation.

Geographic Connection

Why did many Americans move from the Northeast and the Midwest to the Sunbelt?

READING FOCUS

- What political changes took place in the post-Cold War world?

- What conflicts proved difficult to resolve during the post-Cold War years?

- How did Americans respond to the terrorist attacks of September 11, 2001?

KEY TERMS

proliferation
apartheid
economic
  sanctions

MAIN IDEA

The United States faced new challenges in the post–Cold War world, including the collapse of communism, increased ethnic tensions in several countries, and the threat of terrorism.

TARGET READING SKILL

Identify Supporting Details As you read, complete this chart showing the role of the United States in events around the world.

Nation or Region	U.S. Role
Africa	Economic sanctions encourage South Africa to end apartheid. Troops in Somalia aid in famine relief.
China	
Yugoslavia	
Northern Ireland	
Israel and Palestine	
Afghanistan	
Iraq	

Setting the Scene Witnessing the collapse of communism in the Soviet Union and Eastern Europe, President George H. W. Bush had spoken hopefully of the dawn of a "New World Order" in 1990. By this he meant a more stable and peaceful world in which "the strong respect the rights of the weak." Actually, however, the world seemed to grow less stable in the post–Cold War years. Nations that had thrown off repressive governments faced political and economic uncertainty. Racial, cultural, and religious strife tore apart other nations. Even Americans confronted a grim, new reality—living with the continual threat of terrorism.

Post–Cold War Politics

In the 1980s, during the Cold War years, communism seemed a permanent aspect of the Soviet Union. The collapse of communism there and throughout Eastern Europe came as a shock to the world. Similarly unexpected changes occurred in South Africa and, to a lesser extent, China. In each case the United States stood ready to assist the transition from an oppressive system to one that valued political and economic freedom.

Russia As the old Soviet empire crumbled, the United States tried to promote the move toward Western-style democracy in the former Soviet republics. For example, it applauded the election that brought Boris Yeltsin to power as president of Russia.

    To help Russia create a free market economy, the international community offered billions in aid, but it was far from enough. Goods remained in short supply and the Russian economy remained unstable. In the fall of 1993, the Russian parliament resisted reforms that Yeltsin argued were necessary. In response, he dissolved the parliament and tightened censorship in a bid to silence his political opponents.

VIEWING HISTORY Russian president Boris Yeltsin addresses a crowd in 1993. **Identifying Central Issues** *How did Russia change after the Cold War?*

Russian reformers, upset by these curbs on freedom, soon grew angry. In 1994, Yeltsin ordered troops into Chechnya, a largely Muslim republic that sought independence from Russia. After nearly two years of fierce fighting, a cease-fire was finally reached, and the Russian troops were withdrawn. With an already ailing economy, charges of government corruption, and thousands of people killed in Chechnya, Yeltsin lost much of his public support.

In 1999, the conflict over Chechnya became the source of great public support for Vladimir Putin, whom Yeltsin had appointed Russia's prime minister. A series of Chechen terrorist attacks in Russia that year prompted Putin to order air raids against Chechnya and a full-scale ground invasion. Most Russians applauded these actions. Yeltsin, in poor health, resigned his post at the end of the year, making Putin the acting president of Russia. In the next presidential election, Russian voters officially elected Putin their new president.

Taking advantage of his popularity, Putin pushed for reforms that would streamline Russia's bloated government bureaucracy and encourage economic growth. He also worked to strengthen Russia's ties with the international community. In 2001, Russia signed a 20-year treaty of friendship and cooperation with China. The next year Russia agreed to work jointly with the NATO alliance on specific issues of concern, including the **proliferation,** or spread, of nuclear weapons. The United States was particularly eager to shut down Russia's ongoing transfer of nuclear materials and technology to Iran.

Eastern Europe   Political changes also continued to occur in Eastern Europe. Poland, for example, undertook bold economic reforms in the early 1990s to create a free market. It also established a democratic system of government. Other former Communist nations in the region, including Hungary and the Czech Republic, followed Poland's lead. The road to political and economic change was often bumpy, but progress toward a stable democracy and a functioning market economy continued at a steady pace in these and other Eastern European countries.

In a clear sign that there was no returning to the past, Poland, Hungary, and the Czech Republic all joined NATO in 1999. In 2003, seven more former Communist nations of Eastern Europe were set to join the NATO alliance.

F. W. de Klerk and Nelson Mandela shared the 1993 Nobel peace prize for their work in ending apartheid.

South Africa   The collapse of communism shocked the world. Just as stunning was South Africa's rejection of **apartheid,** the systematic separation of people of different racial backgrounds. South Africa's white minority, which made up only about 15 percent of the population, had long denied equal rights to the black majority. To encourage reform, the United States and other nations had used **economic sanctions,** or trade restrictions and other economic measures intended to punish another nation. Finally, in 1990, Prime Minister F. W. de Klerk released anti-apartheid leader Nelson Mandela from jail. Mandela had been held prisoner for 27 years.

Former rivals de Klerk and Mandela worked together to end apartheid. In 1994, South Africa held its first elections in which blacks as well as whites voted. These democratic elections produced a new government, led by President Nelson Mandela and his anti-apartheid organization, the African National Congress (ANC). Despite fears of civil war, South Africa made a peaceful transition to black majority rule.

From 1996 to 1998, a government-appointed Truth and Reconciliation Commission investigated the brutal crimes of the apartheid era. Its final report, published in 1998, won international praise for addressing wrongdoings on both sides and for continuing the nation's move toward peace. That move continued with the democratic election in 1999 of another ANC leader, Thabo Mbeki, as president. Under Mbeki, South Africa pursued the role of peacemaker in Africa. It tried to apply its own model of power-sharing and reconciliation to resolve conflicts in Burundi, Congo, and Zimbabwe.

China While the United States supported democratic change within other nations, it also sought to remain on peaceful terms with Communist China. China's economic growth, combined with its size, made it an increasingly important power in the 1990s. As a result, the United States began working more closely with China on various issues, including trade and regional security. However, underlying tensions between the two nations remained just below the surface.

Probably the greatest source of tension was the issue of Taiwan. China viewed Taiwan as a province of China and refused to rule out the use of force to gain control of the island. In particular, China warned Taiwan not to declare its independence from the mainland. The United States opposed any military action by China against Taiwan and, against China's wishes, sold fighter jets and other weapons to Taiwan.

In 1996, as Taiwan prepared for elections, China held missile tests and military exercises nearby to try to frighten voters away from supporting a pro-independence candidate. President Clinton responded by sending warships to the area to show the American commitment to Taiwan.

Tensions between the two nations slowly lessened, thanks in part to mutual economic interests. In 2000, President Clinton signed the U.S.-China Relations Act, permanently normalizing trade relations with China. The act also lowered tariffs on exports from the United States, further opening China's huge market to American businesses.

In 2003, George W. Bush and China's new president, Hu Jintao, met in France. The two leaders talked about trade and the status of Taiwan, but perhaps their most important discussion involved nuclear weapons. North Korea, an economically unstable, Communist ally of China, had recently backed out of a treaty banning the spread of nuclear weapons. Now it threatened to restart its program to develop nuclear bombs. Hu agreed with Bush that North Korea should join discussions aimed at resolving this issue peacefully.

VIEWING HISTORY In April 1999, the United States and China agreed to expand commercial air service between the two nations. Here, Secretary of State Madeleine Albright shakes hands with Chinese Foreign Minister Tang Jiaxuan after signing the agreement. **Drawing Conclusions** *Why was the United States interested in expanding trade with China?*

Post–Cold War Conflicts

For the United States, spreading democracy and decreasing world tensions were satisfying challenges. Far less satisfying was the task of trying to stop the terrifying violence that erupted in several different regions of the world. The government had to balance Americans' desire to promote peace with their fear of costly commitments—a fear magnified by memories of the Vietnam War.

Africa Conflicts in Africa demonstrated how hard it was to maintain this balance. In the early 1990s, the East African nation of Somalia suffered from a devastating famine, made worse by a civil war. President George H. W. Bush sent American troops to Somalia in 1992 to assist a United Nations (UN) relief effort. The food crisis eased, but Somalia's government remained unable to control the armed groups that ruled the countryside. The following year, after

The Former Yugoslavia, 1998

MAP SKILLS This map shows the regions of Bosnia and Herzegovina controlled by various groups. At the right, U.S. soldiers patrol a village in Kosovo, as part of a NATO peacekeeping operation. *Regions How does the map demonstrate the problems facing the former Yugoslavia?*

READING CHECK
Why did it seem that peace-keeping in the former Yugoslavia would be especially difficult?

more than a dozen U.S. soldiers were killed in a battle with Somali rebels, President Clinton recalled the troops without having restored order.

In April 1994, the Hutu government of Rwanda set out to exterminate the rival Tutsi minority. Haunted by the Somalia episode, the United States failed to intervene. Some 800,000 Tutsis died in the genocidal rampage by Hutu militias, soldiers, and ordinary citizens. Finally, in June, a French-led UN force moved in to stop the bloodshed.

Yugoslavia The United States did play a key role in the peacekeeping process elsewhere. One place in which peace seemed especially difficult to achieve was Yugoslavia, a nation of several distinct ethnic and religious groups. Tensions among these groups had remained below the surface for several decades, while a Communist government ruled Yugoslavia. After the collapse of communism, however, these underlying problems erupted into violent conflict.

Some Yugoslav republics, including Bosnia, wanted to become independent nations. The republic of Serbia—and its leader, Slobodan Milosevic—wanted to preserve a unified Yugoslavia, dominated by Serbia. A minority of Bosnians were ethnic Serbs; they, too, opposed independence for Bosnia.

Thus, when Bosnia declared its independence in 1991, the Bosnian Serbs took military action. Backed by Serbia, the Bosnian Serbs began a siege of Sarajevo, Bosnia's major city, and carried on a ferocious "ethnic cleansing" campaign to remove non-Serbs from the republic. Millions were forced to flee their homes, and more than 200,000 people were killed in the most brutal violence seen in Europe since World War II.

When Clinton campaigned for President in 1992, he promised to take strong action in Bosnia. Once in office, however, he hesitated, partly because America's European allies resisted the use of force. Finally, in mid-1995, an American-led NATO bombing campaign pushed the Bosnian Serbs into peace talks. These talks, held in Dayton, Ohio, produced a cease-fire and the commitment to allow foreign peacekeeping troops, including thousands of U.S. soldiers, to monitor the region.

Although these steps toward peace had been taken, none of the underlying problems had gone away. New troubles began in Kosovo, another part of the former Yugoslavia. As in Bosnia, the majority population of Kosovo was not Serbian. Most people living there were ethnic Albanians, and they wanted more self-rule. That demand led to another brutal round of violence, this time between Serbs and Kosovar Albanians. Ethnic cleansing by Serbs forced many Kosovar Albanians to flee their homes.

In 1999, after Serbs refused to commit to a peace conference, the United States and NATO launched a series of airstrikes against Serbia. These forced Serbian leader Milosevic to allow international peacekeepers into Kosovo. The UN took over the running of Kosovo, helping the province prepare for the day when it could govern itself as an independent state.

Meanwhile, Serbian opposition to Milosevic was growing. In 2000, voters overwhelmingly rejected Milosevic's bid for another term as president. When

Milosevic refused to accept the election results, Serbs organized a revolt and forced him from power. The next year, an international tribunal indicted Milosevic for war crimes and took him to the Netherlands to stand trial.

In 2003, the two remaining republics of the former Yugoslavia joined in a loose federation called Serbia and Montenegro. Both republics planned to hold a referendum on independence in 2006.

Northern Ireland In the British province of Northern Ireland, the United States encouraged renewed efforts in the 1990s to end decades of violence between Protestants and Catholics. Catholic nationalists there wanted to reunite the province with the nation of Ireland, while Protestant unionists wanted to remain a part of Britain. In 1996, President Clinton asked former U.S. Senator George Mitchell to lead talks that included representatives of the warring factions and the British and Irish governments.

After months of tense negotiations, Mitchell's efforts paid off. In 1998, all major parties to the peace process signed the Good Friday Accords. They agreed to major reforms in Northern Ireland, including power-sharing between Catholics and Protestants and the demilitarization of the province. Voters in both Northern Ireland and Ireland later approved the agreement.

Sporadic violence and confrontations between unionists and nationalists slowed the implementation of the agreement. In 2002, the newly created Northern Ireland Assembly was suspended and later dissolved when the Irish Republican Army (IRA), a nationalist group, was accused of spying within government offices. The IRA also refused to destroy all its weapons and end its paramilitary activities, as required by the Good Friday Accords. As a result, the British government postponed the Assembly elections scheduled for spring 2003. Still, to aid the peace process, Britain made plans to withdraw most of its troops from Northern Ireland over a three-year period.

Israel and Palestine In September 1993, Palestine Liberation Organization (PLO) leader Yasir Arafat and Israeli Prime Minister Yitzhak Rabin signed a historic peace agreement in Washington, D.C. It was an extremely difficult step for both sides. The pact provided for Palestinian self-rule in the Gaza Strip (between Israel and Egypt's Sinai Peninsula) and in the town of Jericho on the West Bank of the Jordan River. The agreement also set the stage for talks on the status of the rest of the West Bank. Israel had seized these areas in the Six-Day War of 1967. Also in the agreement, the PLO formally recognized Israel's right to exist.

Radicals on both sides, however, tried to destroy the agreement by carrying out terrorist attacks. In 1995, a Jewish extremist assassinated Prime Minister Rabin. The prospects for peace declined. Then, in 1999, newly elected Prime Minister Ehud Barak called for a greater commitment to peace talks. The next year, President Clinton invited Barak and Arafat to Camp David to try to settle the issues that still divided them. Although the two sides had made great progress since their 1993 agreement, they were unable to solve all the remaining issues, such as control of the holy city of Jerusalem.

Hopes for peace then faded rapidly, and violence again increased. Ariel Sharon—a fierce critic of the concessions Israel had made in the search for peace—became Israeli prime minister in 2001. Palestinian extremists stepped up their suicide bombings, killing Israelis in restaurants, buses, and other public places. Israel regularly countered these terrorist attacks with military strikes on Palestinian targets, often killing civilians in the process. After a wave of suicide

Despite the continued fighting between Israelis and Palestinians, efforts to promote peace continue. At this youth camp, Israeli and Palestinian kids work together to resolve conflicts.

bombings in 2002, Israeli troops reoccupied the West Bank and completely cut off Arafat's headquarters, trapping him in his offices.

In 2003, new hopes for peace emerged when the United States, the European Union, the UN, and Russia presented the Israelis and Palestinians with a "road map" to peace. Both sides approved the plan, a three-step approach to establishing a Palestinian state in the West Bank and Gaza Strip. In accepting the plan, the Israeli government for the first time formally recognized the Palestinians' right to a state. The world waited to see if these positive events would result in a lasting peace or in yet another disappointment.

The War on Terrorism

In the 1990s, most Americans believed that their country was immune to the kind of violence against civilians that wracked Israel and other parts of the world. That opinion changed radically with an attack launched against the United States in late summer 2001. That attack would result in a broad-based war on terrorism.

Attack on America   On September 11, 2001, Americans reacted with horror when terrorists struck at targets in New York City and just outside Washington, D.C. Using hijacked commercial airplanes as their weapons, the terrorists crashed into both towers of New York's World Trade Center and plowed into part of the Pentagon. A fourth plane crashed in a field near Pittsburgh, Pennsylvania. A total of 266 passengers and crew on the four planes lost their lives.

The attack on the Pentagon took place less than an hour after the first plane hit New York. Damage was contained to a newly renovated section of the building, but fires raged for hours, preventing emergency workers from entering the wreckage. More than 180 people in the Pentagon were killed.

In New York, the impact of the fully fueled jets caused both towers to burst into flames. Debris rained down on employees evacuating the buildings and on emergency workers rushing to respond to the scene. The fires led to the catastrophic collapse of both 110-story buildings as well as other buildings in the World Trade Center complex. Emergency workers battled fires and began a search-and-rescue operation.

Tragically, the speedy response to the disaster led to the deaths of hundreds of firefighters and police officers who were in and around the buildings when they collapsed. The number of people missing and presumed dead after the assault was estimated to be 2,800.

Law-enforcement agencies immediately began an intensive investigation. Countries around the world pledged to support efforts to hunt down the criminals responsible for the attacks. Within days, government officials named Osama bin Laden, a wealthy Saudi dissident, as "a prime suspect" for masterminding the plot. Bin Laden, the head of a terrorist network of Muslim extremists known as Al Qaeda, was believed to be hiding in Afghanistan.

Afghanistan   After the Soviet Union withdrew from Afghanistan in 1989, the civil war there continued, as several private armies vied for power. In 1996, one of those militias, a group of Islamic fundamentalists called the Taliban, seized the Afghan capital of Kabul.

Rescue workers raise the American flag amidst the rubble of the fallen World Trade Center towers.

Sounds of an Era

Listen to President Bush's speech to Congress following the attacks of September 11, 2001, and other recordings from recent years.

Taliban leaders sought to set up their version of a pure Islamic state, banning such things as television and music. The Taliban also provided sanctuary for Osama bin Laden, who established terrorist training camps in the countryside. The United States demanded that the Taliban shut down the training camps and turn over bin Laden and other terrorist leaders. The Taliban refused to meet those demands. As a result, President Bush vowed that they would "pay a price."

On October 7, 2001, the United States, along with Great Britain, launched a bombing campaign known as "Operation Enduring Freedom" on Taliban military and communications bases. After just two months, United States and rebel Afghan forces defeated the Taliban, ending their five-year rule. By the end of the year, those forces had established an interim government in Kabul.

Though bin Laden was not found, defeating the Taliban was the first victory in the war on terrorism. This war, according to Bush, would not be limited to "instant retaliation and isolated strikes" but would be "a lengthy campaign, unlike any other we have seen." The President stressed the importance of global cooperation in this campaign. "Every nation, in every region, now has a decision to make," Bush warned. "Either you are with us or you are with the terrorists."

Homeland Security The President also moved quickly to combat terrorism at home. Less than a month after the 9/11 attacks, Bush created the Office of Homeland Security, to be headed by Pennsylvania Governor Tom Ridge. Ridge took office amidst a new wave of mysterious attacks. Anthrax spores, which can be deadly if inhaled, began turning up in letters mailed to the media and government officials. This rare organism is considered a possible agent of biological warfare—the use of deadly viruses, bacteria, or other microorganisms against humans. By December, the anthrax attacks had come to an end, after a total of 18 people had been infected, five of whom died. The attacks opened Americans' eyes to the dangers of bioterror. How could we stop a foreign terrorist from bringing a small amount of anthrax or smallpox or even plague into the country and dispersing it in a public place?

The attacks of September 11 and the potential for further, more sophisticated assaults pointed to a need for more safeguards against terrorism. The Bush administration responded to this need by establishing a new, Cabinet-level Department of Homeland Security, with Ridge as its first secretary. The department, approved by Congress in November 2002, represented a major government reorganization. It merged 22 existing agencies, including the Customs Service, the Immigration and Naturalization Service (along with the Border Patrol), the Coast Guard, and the Secret Service. The agencies would work together to prevent terrorist attacks, to reduce the country's vulnerability to terrorism, and to design ways of dealing with the potential damage of an attack.

The Department of Homeland Security set to work to make Americans feel more secure. Perhaps the most obvious effects of the department's efforts could be found at airports across the country. Thorough screening of passengers and baggage caused lengthy waits for air travelers, although most people welcomed the tighter security. The new department also tried to keep Americans informed of the risk of terrorist attacks through a color-coded terror alert

READING CHECK
Why did Afghanistan become a focal point for the United States after the September 11 terrorist attacks?

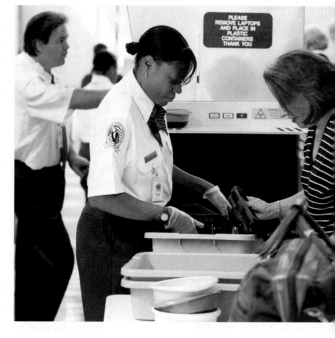

Federally employed security workers took over screening work at the nation's airports following the September 11 terrorist attacks.

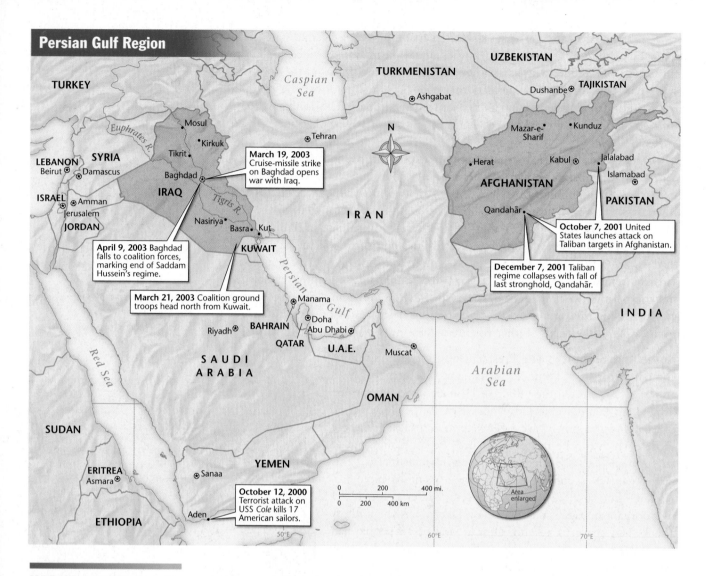

March 19, 2003 Cruise-missile strike on Baghdad opens war with Iraq.

April 9, 2003 Baghdad falls to coalition forces, marking end of Saddam Hussein's regime.

March 21, 2003 Coalition ground troops head north from Kuwait.

October 7, 2001 United States launches attack on Taliban targets in Afghanistan.

December 7, 2001 Taliban regime collapses with fall of last stronghold, Qandahār.

October 12, 2000 Terrorist attack on USS *Cole* kills 17 American sailors.

MAP SKILLS This map shows the area of the Middle East surrounding the Persian Gulf. *Regions Why has this region been of special concern to the United States since 2000?*

system. Alert levels changed based on reports from the FBI and other intelligence-gathering agencies.

War With Iraq Following the terrorist attacks on the United States in 2001, President Bush sent a warning to hostile nations to stop developing weapons of mass destruction. "The United States of America," Bush said, "will not permit the world's most dangerous regimes to threaten us with the world's most destructive weapons." Bush declared Iraq, Iran, and North Korea to be part of an "axis of evil," recalling the United States' enemies in World War II, the Axis Powers.

With the conflict in Afghanistan winding down, President Bush turned his attention to Iraq. Despite Iraq's defeat in the Gulf War, Iraqi leader Saddam Hussein continued his brutal oppression of the Iraqi people. He also refused to cooperate fully with UN inspectors sent to Iraq to ensure that the nation destroyed its most dangerous weapons. In 1998, Saddam had put a halt to all UN monitoring activities. Bush pointed to these actions as he sought support in Congress and among America's allies for a possible attack on Iraq. He also linked Iraq to international terrorist organizations.

In October 2002, Congress passed a joint resolution authorizing the President to use force against Iraq. Under mounting pressure, Saddam allowed UN inspectors to return to his country in November. Two months later, they reported that they had found no banned chemical or biological weapons or any sign of a nuclear-weapons program. Despite this report and a lack of support from several key allies, Bush went ahead with a massive buildup of troops and weapons in the Persian Gulf region. Great Britain, Poland, and several other nations provided soldiers and other support, forming what Bush called "a coalition of the willing."

The war, which the military called "Operation Iraqi Freedom," started on March 19, 2003. An American ship in the Persian Gulf launched a cruise-missile strike on a building in which senior Iraqi leaders were suspected of meeting. Precision-guided missiles and bombs continued to hit key targets, paving the way for ground troops. By March 21, those troops had begun to move toward Baghdad. Coalition tanks and armored personnel carriers rumbled north out of Kuwait, while U.S. Special Operations forces slipped quietly into Iraq from the west.

Battered by the airstrikes, the Iraqi army put up only spotty resistance, bolstered at times by irregular militias and suicide bombers. Three weeks after the start of the war, American tanks arrived in Baghdad. Saddam's regime had fallen. Within days, all areas of the country were in coalition hands, although violent resistance continued. At the same time, a frenzy of looting and general lawlessness broke out in the larger Iraqi cities.

On May 1, President Bush declared that major combat operations in Iraq had ended, but Saddam's supporters continued to attack coalition soldiers and others involved in rebuilding Iraq. The attacks resulted in numerous casualties. In the months that followed, coalition troops continued their search for Saddam and his supporters. Saddam was finally captured by coalition troops in December and many people hoped that his capture would help put an end to the violence. Meanwhile, American officials worked to restore Iraq's basic services and began putting the pieces in place for the Iraqis to establish their own democratic system of government.

Iraqi children cheer while running beside a United States armored vehicle in Baghdad on April 11, 2003.

Iraq's brutal dictator, Saddam Hussein, is shown here shortly after his capture by coalition troops in December 2003.

Section 2 Assessment

READING COMPREHENSION

1. Why did the United States impose **economic sanctions** on South Africa during **apartheid?**

2. What has been the greatest source of tension between China and the United States?

3. How did the United States try to end post-Cold War conflicts around the world?

4. How did President Bush respond to the terrorist attacks on America?

CRITICAL THINKING AND WRITING

5. **Drawing Conclusions** A new sense of patriotism swept the nation in the months following the 9/11 terrorist attacks. American flags appeared on many cars and store fronts. Why do you think the attacks brought about this response?

6. **Writing to Persuade** Write a letter to the Secretary of the Department of Homeland Security describing three steps you think the department should take to improve security in the United States.

Go Online
PHSchool.com

For: An activity on the Department of Homeland Security
Visit: PHSchool.com
Web Code: mrd-0342

Americans in the New Millennium

READING FOCUS

- What factors contributed to the growing diversity of the nation's population?
- In what ways did Americans disagree over how to make diversity work?
- How did the technological revolution at the end of the twentieth century affect American life?
- What was the impact of the expanding global economy?

MAIN IDEA

In the 1990s and beyond, the United States sought new ways to create unity out of its diversity and to deal with the consequences of a technological revolution and an increasingly global economy.

KEY TERMS

bilingual education
Internet
North American Free Trade Agreement (NAFTA)
World Trade Organization (WTO)
multinational corporation

TARGET READING SKILL

Identify Supporting Details As you read, complete the flowchart below to show the many changes occurring in the United States.

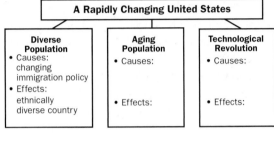

A Rapidly Changing United States		
Diverse Population	**Aging Population**	**Technological Revolution**
• Causes: changing immigration policy	• Causes:	• Causes:
• Effects: ethnically diverse country	• Effects:	• Effects:

This California road sign warns drivers to be on the lookout for undocumented aliens who might have crossed the border from Mexico.

Setting the Scene The Latin motto of the United States, found on American coins, is *e pluribus unum,* meaning "from many, one." This short phrase reflects the patterns of the nation's past and the possibilities for its future. The United States was created when 13 separate colonies agreed to form a single union. Since then, people from an astonishing variety of lands have immigrated to the United States and have enriched this nation's culture. That process continues today. Creating unity out of diversity remains one of the nation's greatest challenges and a key to its future.

A Nation of Diversity

In the early 1900s, most immigrants came from various places in Europe. A fresh wave of immigration at the end the century made the United States more diverse than at any time in its history. Close to 80 percent of all legal immigrants during this time came from Asia and Latin America. As a result, as the twenty-first century began, some 30 percent of the nation's people were either African American, Latino, Asian American, or Native American. This expanding diversity meant that the United States was becoming, in the words of writer Ben J. Wattenberg, "the first universal nation."

Changing Immigration Policies Changes to immigration policies contributed to the nation's growing diversity. Laws passed in the 1920s had strictly limited immigration and had given preference to immigrants from northern and western Europe. The Immigration Act of 1965, though, eliminated this bias of favoring European immigrants. In 1986, the Immigration Reform and Control Act sought to reduce illegal immigration, in part by forbidding employers to hire illegal aliens. At the same time, however, it permitted illegal aliens who had lived in the United States since 1982 to register to become citizens. The Immigration Act of 1990 increased immigration quotas by 40 percent. It also erased restrictions that had denied entrance to many people in the past.

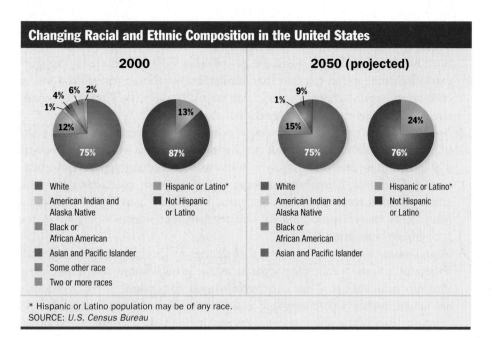

Changing Racial and Ethnic Composition in the United States

2000

- 4%
- 1%
- 6%
- 2%
- 12%
- 75%

- 13%
- 87%

2050 (projected)

- 1%
- 9%
- 15%
- 75%

- 24%
- 76%

- ■ White
- ■ American Indian and Alaska Native
- ■ Black or African American
- ■ Asian and Pacific Islander
- ■ Some other race
- ■ Two or more races

- ■ Hispanic or Latino*
- ■ Not Hispanic or Latino

* Hispanic or Latino population may be of any race.
SOURCE: *U.S. Census Bureau*

INTERPRETING GRAPHS
These graphs show the recent and projected ethnic makeup of the United States. **Analyzing Information** *According to the graphs, which group in the United States will experience the most dramatic rate of growth between 2000 and 2050?*

Changing Population Patterns   Changes in immigration affected the nation's demographics, or population patterns. Earlier immigrants who crossed the Atlantic from Europe had settled mainly on the East Coast. Many of the new arrivals, who crossed the Pacific from Asia or came north from Latin America, chose the Sunbelt. Like earlier immigrants, most immigrants of the 1990s settled in urban areas.

In 2000, minorities accounted for 56 percent of the total population of the nation's 100 largest cities. In 48 of those cities they made up at least half the population. African Americans formed a majority of the residents in Detroit, Baltimore, Memphis, and Washington, D.C. Latinos were most heavily concentrated in El Paso, Santa Ana, and Miami. Large numbers of Asian Americans settled in San Francisco.

The 2000 Census revealed dramatic growth and change in the Latino population since 1990. Latinos surpassed African Americans as the country's largest minority. Established Latino communities in California, Texas, and New York continued to grow and diversify, while non-traditional destinations such as Georgia and North Carolina welcomed hundreds of thousands of new residents.

Growth in minority populations has affected the demographics of some states more than others. By 2000, minorities represented the majority of the people in California, New Mexico, and Hawaii. Texas, too, had nearly joined the ranks of "minority-majority" states.

Making Diversity Work

As American society became more diverse, government, private organizations, and individual citizens all undertook efforts to make diversity work. Some of these efforts aroused controversy.

The Debate Over Immigration   In the 1990s, as in earlier periods of rising immigration, Americans disagreed over how immigration would affect the nation. The debate, which continues today, centers on economic and social issues.

Focus on
CULTURE

Understanding the New Census Data The 2000 Census began a new system for reporting race in the United States. In the 1990 census, respondents could identify their race by choosing one of four racial categories. The 2000 Census expanded these categories to six. The most significant change in 2000, however, was a new set of directions, which allowed respondents to choose more than one racial category by which to identify themselves. In the chart above, the "Two or more races" category represents those respondents who chose to identify themselves in such a way.

Analysts point out that the American system of racial classification has undergone considerable changes in the past. Asian Indians, for example, were included in the white race in 1970, but beginning in 1980, became a part of the Asian and Pacific Islander race. As the nation's racial makeup continues to change, the Census will continue to work to find new and better ways of reporting race.

1. *Jobs.* People who favor restricting immigration point out that immigrants are willing to work for low wages. For this reason, they take jobs away from native-born Americans and drive down the pay of other workers. Those who support expanded immigration respond that immigrants contribute to the economy as consumers, small-business owners, and taxpayers. Also, they say, immigrants take jobs that few native-born Americans want.

2. *Services.* People who favor restrictions note that the federal government sets immigration policy but does not pay for all the services immigrants require. This problem is particularly costly in states with a huge immigrant population, such as California. Those who support expansion point out that most immigrants do not receive public assistance. Around 22 percent of immigrant households receive some kind of welfare, compared with 15 percent of the native-born population.

3. *Assimilation.* Some people believe that immigrant groups fragment American society by staying within their separate ethnic groups rather than assimilating into American culture. They criticize **bilingual education,** in which students are taught in their native language as well as English while their English skills improve. They argue that it encourages new immigrants to continue relying on their native language. California, Arizona, and Massachusetts have all passed anti–bilingual education initiatives. Those who support expanding immigration say that immigrants, especially young people, are assimilating at a rapid rate. They are eager to learn English, and many of them prefer it to their native language. Also, they say, about one third of immigrants intermarry outside their ethnic group.

Affirmative Action   Another heated debate concerned affirmative action. President Johnson introduced the first affirmative action policies in the 1960s. His goal was to improve employment and educational opportunities by giving preference to African Americans and to other minorities and women who had been discriminated against in the past. Some people argued, however, that giving special treatment to some groups was unfair to everyone else.

Claims of "reverse discrimination" led to lawsuits and ballot initiatives that steadily weakened affirmative action. In 1978 the Supreme Court, in the *Bakke* case, ruled that educational institutions could not set fixed quotas for admitting minority applicants. However, it allowed race to be one of the factors used in the admissions process. In 1996, California voters passed Proposition 209, ending affirmative action in state hiring and education. The state of Washington passed a similar ban two years later. In 2003, the Supreme Court reaffirmed its opposition to the use of quotas by educational institutions in two cases involving the University of Michigan (*Gratz* v. *Bollinger* and *Grutter* v. *Bollinger*). However, the court upheld the "narrowly tailored" use of race as a factor in admissions.

America's Aging Population   As the United States entered the twenty-first century, its population was older than ever before. Advances in medical care increased the average life expectancy of newborns from 47 to 77 years during the 1900s. In 2000, more than 12 percent of all Americans were 65 or older, compared with 4 percent in 1900.

The "graying of America" had important political and economic effects. The Social Security system, for example, faced difficulties

VIEWING HISTORY   The elderly population of the United States is increasing at a rapid rate. Almost all Americans aged 65 and over are insured by Medicare. **Expressing Problems Clearly** *What challenges does the Medicare system face?*

because the number of retirees receiving benefits from the program was rising faster than the number of workers paying taxes into it. In fact, polls showed that many young Americans doubted that the Social Security system would even exist when they reached retirement age.

There was similar pressure on the nation's medical system. Medicare, a federal program established during the Great Society of the 1960s, paid for many of the medical expenses of older Americans. As the number of recipients and the price of healthcare rose, however, Medicare costs exploded from $7.5 billion in 1970 to more than $225 billion in 2002. As with Social Security, federal lawmakers agreed that long-term changes were needed but disagreed on what those changes should be.

A Technological Revolution

The modern communications revolution began more than a century ago when Samuel Morse developed the telegraph. Since then, communications technology has made major advances with the invention of the telephone, radio, and television. In the last several decades, the invention of many more ways to store, retrieve, and transmit information has created a new era in communications known as the Information Age.

Communication and Information The centerpiece of the Information Age is the computer. Between 1984 and 2001, the percentage of American households with a computer jumped from 8 percent to 56 percent. Originally the size of a room, computers have decreased in size as they have grown in their ability to store and retrieve information. Advances in wireless technology have also made computers more flexible and convenient.

The **Internet,** a computer network that links millions of people around the world, has revolutionized many areas of American life. Today, more than half of American households and nearly all public schools and libraries have an Internet connection. In several regions of the world, however, countries lacked the wealth or infrastructure to become active participants in this global network. In 2002, only about 10 percent of the world population had access to the Internet.

The "New Economy" The United States enjoyed the greatest period of economic expansion in its history during the 1990s, thanks in large part to the technological boom. Businesses, seeing the Internet as a way to reach a global audience of millions, scrambled to set up their own Web sites. Investors and entrepreneurs, excited about the opportunities offered by the Internet and other digital technologies, created new businesses and worked on ways to improve old ones. Waves of what came to be called "dot-com" companies appeared, each trying to corner a unique market of online business.

Those companies relied for survival on the growing investment in technology by large corporations. In 2001, however, businesses sharply cut their spending on technology. In the resulting recession, many dot-coms failed. The long economic boom ended, but by then the new, computer-based economy had been established.

How has this "new economy" affected employment? High-tech industries demand workers with advanced skills. Fewer positions exist for unskilled workers. Education, therefore, has never been as important to economic success as it is now.

READING CHECK
What factors caused a huge increase in Medicare costs in recent years?

BIOGRAPHY

Bill Gates
b. 1955

In 1975, Bill Gates envisioned the future of computers and set to work turning that vision into reality. That year, at the age of 19, Gates dropped out of Harvard University to join his high school friend Paul Allen in establishing a new company. During high school, Gates had used his computer knowledge to help create a company that sold traffic data to local governments. In 1975, the two friends first read about a kit computer in *Popular Electronics* magazine. "Paul and I didn't know exactly how it would be used, but we were sure it would change us and the world of computing."

At first, people couldn't make the kit computer do much. Gates and Allen changed that by writing software, or the coded instructions for performing specific tasks, to run on the computer. Their efforts transformed it from a device with limited uses into a general-purpose computer that was similar to (though much less powerful than) those we use today. The company that the two friends started for marketing their software, later named Microsoft, grew to become a giant in the computer industry. Located near Seattle, Washington, where Gates was born, Microsoft's success made Gates a billionaire by the age of 31.

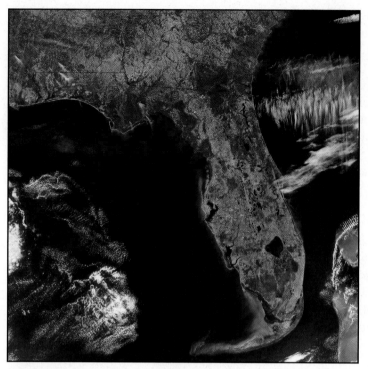

MAP SKILLS According to reports from the Southern Area Fire Coordination Center of the U.S. Department of Agriculture Forest Service, both prescribed fires and wildfires were burning across the southern United States on February 12, 2003. This Moderate Resolution Imaging Spectroradiometer (MODIS) image from the Aqua satellite on February 12 shows the active fires marked with red dots. Regions *Based on the smoke plumes showing in this image, in which direction do you think the prevailing winds were blowing in northeastern Florida?*

Impact on Education Computers and the Internet have become essential parts of American society, but their place in schools is still being determined. An important task for schools will be to find the right balance between traditional teaching and the use of new technology. For many schools, an even bigger challenge will be to find enough money to fund the new and ever-changing technology.

In addition, as the Internet becomes more important as a research tool, students will have to learn how to evaluate the information that is available online. While some of this information is of very high quality, much of it is unreliable.

Impact on Government The federal government also had to confront domestic issues raised by the Internet and other new technologies. One concern was privacy. Many people worried that the privacy of e-mail conversations or online purchases was not being sufficiently protected.

Another controversial issue concerned ownership rights. One company, Napster, grew popular because its software allowed users to trade song files over the Internet for free. Many record companies and musicians—the owners of this music—believed that such trading was illegal because they did not make any money when these song files were shared. Record companies successfully sued Napster, and the company later went out of business.

The government also faced a problem with the giant software company Microsoft. By 1998, Microsoft had become the world's second most valuable company, worth some $200 billion. However, Microsoft's size and success gave it great power in the marketplace. Several competitors argued that Microsoft was trying to drive them out of business.

In 1998, the federal government and 20 states sued Microsoft for violating the Sherman Antitrust Act of 1890. They accused Microsoft of using its power to gain a monopoly over the market for software needed to browse the Internet. In 2000, a federal judge ruled that Microsoft was indeed a monopoly and had used unfair business practices, and he ordered that the company be split apart. The following year, an appeals court reversed this order but upheld the judgment that Microsoft had acted improperly. In 2002, Microsoft and the Department of Justice settled the antitrust case.

Impact on Daily Life The new communications technologies left their mark on Americans' daily lives. Many people kept in touch with friends and family through e-mail more than through letters or telephone calls. They took cell phones or hand-held computers along with them on daily errands and vacations. They used the Internet to shop, to look for jobs, or to check the weather forecast or sports results. Everything they needed to know about the products they bought, the movies they watched, and the companies they invested in was only a few "clicks" away.

Trade and the Global Economy

The new communications technologies helped the development of a global economy by making it easier to conduct business internationally. Economic cooperation among nations proved to be another vital ingredient in the expansion of world trade.

The European Union In 1957, six European nations set up the European Economic Community (EEC) to coordinate their economic and trade policies. Over time, other nations joined them. Member nations agreed to move toward dismantling the tariffs on one another's exports, thereby creating a single market.

In 1993, the EEC nations formed the European Union (EU) to begin coordinating their political and monetary policies. The EU established a parliament and a council in which all member nations are represented. In the late 1990s, member nations agreed to replace their individual monetary systems gradually with a single new currency called the eurodollar, or euro. In 2002 the EU, now with 15 members, voted to invite 10 additional European nations to join. The following year, they drafted a constitution designed to suit a greatly expanded union.

One important goal of the EU is to create a European economic unit that rivals the size and strength of the American economy. After expansion, the union will have reached at least part of that goal. The size of the EU economy will nearly match that of the United States.

NAFTA Meanwhile, the United States encouraged greater economic cooperation within the Western Hemisphere. In 1992, the United States, Canada, and Mexico signed the **North American Free Trade Agreement (NAFTA),** which called for a gradual removal of trade restrictions among the three nations. The resulting free trade zone created a single market similar to the market of the European Union. The goal of NAFTA was to stimulate economic growth. Many economists predicted that free trade would accomplish that goal by encouraging foreign investment, reducing prices, and raising exports.

The U.S. Senate ratified NAFTA, but only after a bruising battle. Its opponents worried that American jobs would move to Mexico, where wages were lower and government regulations (such as environmental controls) were less strict. In the years since NAFTA went into effect, supplemental agreements have dealt with such issues as worker rights, occupational safety, and environmental protection.

In 2002, President Bush, calling NAFTA a success, vowed to continue negotiations to build a Free Trade Area of the Americas that would link the markets of 34 countries. Bush said, "America is back in the business of promoting open trade to build our prosperity and to spur economic growth."

GATT and the WTO Bush's support for free trade reflected a longstanding American foreign policy goal. In 1994, the United States had joined many other countries in adopting a revised version of the **General Agreement on Tariffs and Trade (GATT).** The goal of GATT, originally established in 1948, was to reduce tariffs and expand world trade. The 1994 meeting reinforced that goal by replacing GATT with the **World Trade Organization (WTO)** officially established in 1995. The WTO would have more power to negotiate new trade agreements, resolve trade disputes, and ensure that countries complied with earlier GATT agreements.

As with NAFTA, many people complained that the WTO favored big business over workers and the environment. At a meeting of the WTO in

Focus on
ECONOMICS

Tariffs *Taxes on foreign goods imported into a country.*

The Historical Context In the 1980s and 1990s, a number of governments worked together to reduce tariffs in the hope that expanded trade would stimulate economic growth. These efforts resulted in regional trade agreements, such as NAFTA, and the formation of the World Trade Organization to resolve trade disputes.

The Concept Today Tariffs remain a controversial issue. Some Americans worry that as American tariffs are lowered, jobs will shift from the United States to less-developed nations. Other Americans, in contrast, argue that lower tariffs worldwide will boost American exports and create new jobs.

Seattle in 1999, protesters attacked the growing power and influence of giant worldwide corporations. They called for greater attention to the rights of workers, the welfare of poorer nations, and the global environment. WTO officials countered that labor and environmental standards can be improved through freer trade, especially in developing countries.

Rise of Multinationals   The debate over the WTO stemmed in part from the growing importance of **multinational corporations,** businesses that operate in more than one country. Multinationals benefit consumers and workers around the world by providing new products and jobs and by introducing advanced technologies and production methods. On the other hand, these powerful big businesses sometimes skirt the law by using their economic clout to unduly influence politicians or by devising dishonest ways to keep profits growing.

One multinational, the Enron Corporation, owned energy-related businesses in the United States and throughout the world. When it filed for bankruptcy in 2001, Enron was the seventh-largest American corporation. A congressional investigation into the bankruptcy turned up improper accounting practices. Several Enron executives faced charges of overstating profits and enriching themselves at the expense of investors. The resulting scandal led to the collapse of Arthur Andersen, the global accounting firm that monitored Enron's finances.

Similar accounting-fraud charges stung several other multinationals, including the huge telecommunications company WorldCom. The scandals led many investors to pull out of the stock market, deepening the lingering recession that had started in 2001.

American Economy   Early in the recession, President Bush proposed to stimulate the economy through a tax cut. In response, Congress passed a record $1.35 trillion tax-cut package, to be spread out over 10 years. Still, the economy remained shaky through the next two years, with unemployment rising to its highest level in 10 years.

In May 2003, Bush signed another tax cut into law, this one for $350 billion. The President insisted that this "bold package of tax relief" would add a million jobs in the first year and boost the stock market. Critics charged that the tax cuts would create huge budget deficits far into the future.

COMPARING PRIMARY SOURCES
Stimulating the Economy Through Tax Cuts

The debate in Congress over Bush's tax-cut policies generally split along party lines.
Analyzing Viewpoints   How do these senators' economic philosophies differ?

In Favor of Large Tax Cuts

"We all agree the economy needs a shot in the arm. Although our economy is growing, it's not growing fast enough to create jobs. . . . This bill will . . . help create jobs and grow the economy. It will put money back into the hands of families, consumers, investors, and businesses that will help fuel our economic engines. . . . The people will spend and invest their money in more productive ways than the government ever will."

—*Iowa Senator Chuck Grassley,*
Republican, May 22, 2003

Opposed to Large Tax Cuts

"The economy is floundering. Economists are warning that it could begin to contract in the months ahead, raising the risk of a disastrous double-dip recession. . . . We hear the cry for stimulus through tax cuts. I say bunk! . . . If all we had to do was to pass massive tax cuts every time the economy began to stumble, if it was just that simple, we would have done away with recessions in the last century."

—*West Virginia Senator Robert C. Byrd,*
Democrat, April 11, 2003

Facing the Future

Near the end of his life, Thomas Jefferson wrote, "If a nation expects to be ignorant and free . . . it expects what never was and never will be." Freedom, in other words, does not maintain itself. We must all commit ourselves to its preservation by working to understand and participate in the events around us.

The wealth and power our nation now enjoys might cause some of us to lose sight of this lesson. Yet as changes occur increasingly quickly in the years ahead, bringing advances—and challenges—we can hardly imagine, Jefferson's words could become more true than ever before.

Section 3 Assessment

READING COMPREHENSION

1. What effects did increasing immigration have on the United States?

2. Explain the debate over **bilingual education.**

3. What challenges did the **Internet** pose for the federal government?

4. What were the goals of the European Union, **NAFTA,** and the **WTO?**

CRITICAL THINKING AND WRITING

5. **Drawing Inferences** How can the country's immigration policies affect its economy?

6. **Predicting Consequences** Why is it important for Americans to create unity out of diversity?

7. **Writing to Persuade** Write a letter to your senator either supporting or opposing a free trade area of the Americas.

For: An activity on global organizations
Visit: PHSchool.com
Web Code: mrd-0343

creating a CHAPTER SUMMARY

Copy the web diagram (right) on a separate sheet of paper to summarize international events in recent years.

For additional review and enrichment activities, see the interactive version of *America: Pathways to the Present*, available on the Web and on CD-ROM.

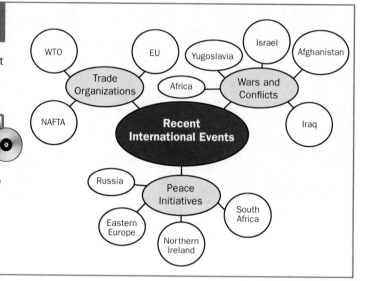

★ Reviewing Key Terms

For each of the terms below, write a sentence explaining how it related to the United States at the end of the twentieth century.

1. Contract with America
2. Whitewater affair
3. apartheid
4. economic sanctions
5. North American Free Trade Agreement
6. World Trade Organization
7. multinational corporation
8. proliferation
9. Internet

★ Reviewing Main Ideas

10. What were some domestic successes and failures for Bill Clinton in the 1990s? (Section 1)

11. After the 1994 elections, why did Republicans believe that they had a mandate to reduce the size of the federal government? (Section 1)

12. What role did the United States play in producing cease-fires in Bosnia and Kosovo? (Section 2)

13. How did the United States government react to the terrorist attacks of September 11, 2001? (Section 2)

14. How did government policy contribute to the diversity of the United States? (Section 3)

15. Give reasons why some people supported NAFTA and others opposed it. (Section 3)

★ Critical Thinking

16. **Demonstrating Reasoned Judgment** The United States intervened in some foreign conflicts during the 1990s and launched a war on terrorism in 2001. What do you think should be the role of the United States in future overseas conflicts?

17. **Identifying Assumptions** What arguments might supporters and opponents of affirmative action give in defense of their different positions?

18. **Drawing Inferences** President Bush laid out the case against Iraq in a televised speech in March 2003 as a way of rallying public support for war. What benefits and drawbacks does television offer to Presidents?

19. **Predicting Consequences** Think about how technology affects our daily lives. What changes might take place as a result of technological advances in the next five to ten years?

20. **Synthesizing Information** What various factors and events in the late 1990s helped cause the election of 2000 to be so close?

★ Standardized Test Prep

Analyzing Political Cartoons ▶

21. Which of the following statements BEST summarizes the message of this cartoon?

    A Beaches are not as relaxing as they used to be.

    B Technology has created more work rather than freeing us from work.

    C Laws should be passed reducing noise pollution.

    D Technology has simplified life for families.

22. What comment is the cartoonist making about 1990s lifestyle?

Interpreting Data

Turn to the racial and ethnic composition graphs in Section 3.

23. Which of the following groups made up 12 percent of the United States population in 2000?

    A White

    B Black or African American

    C American Indian and Alaskan Native

    D Asian and Pacific Islander

24. Which of the following groups will more than double its percentage of the United States population by 2050?

    F White

    G Black or African American

    H Asian and Pacific Islander

    I Hispanic or Latino Origin

25. What percentage of the United States population reported that they belonged to one racial category in 2000?

    A 98 percent

    B 6 percent

    C 94 percent

    D 13 percent

Test-Taking Tip

Question 25 requires that you compare the two left-hand graphs carefully to determine which group will double its percentage of the population. Do this by comparing the percentages on both graphs one color at a time. When you find which color more than doubles its percentage from 2000 to 2050, consult the key to see which group it is.

Applying the Chapter Skill

Predicting Consequences Review the steps needed to predict consequences on page 902. Then describe the consequences of the nation's aging population.

For: Chapter 27 Self-Test
Visit: PHSchool.com
Web Code: mra-0345

American Pathways

ECONOMICS

Free Enterprise and the American Economy

In 1776, Scottish economist Adam Smith published *The Wealth of Nations*, a book that promoted capitalism, an economic system based on free enterprise and little government interference. Capitalism has suited independent, industrious, and competitive Americans, who have enjoyed the fruits of a productive economy for two centuries.

Currency issued by state-chartered banks and individual companies from the Free Banking Era, 1837–1863 (above)

1 The Market Revolution

1793–1824 The new nation's abundant natural resources and its political and legal systems, which protected patent and property rights, allowed hard-working Americans to bring about a "market revolution." New, profitable manufacturing enterprises sprang up throughout the Northeast and the Ohio Valley.

Title page of Adam Smith's *The Wealth of Nations* (above right)

2 Nationalism and Sectionalism

1816–1865 In the ongoing power struggle between the federal government and the states, Congress and the Supreme Court worked to strengthen nationalism. The economy, especially the northern industrial economy, expanded. At the same time, slavery was becoming the economic cornerstone of the agricultural South. This issue and other sectional tensions eventually sparked the Civil War.

Currency issued by state-chartered banks and individual companies from the Free Banking Era, 1837–1863 (above)

3 Industrial Expansion and Progressive Reforms

1865–1914 After the Civil War, industry thrived in a free market, with little interference from the government. During the Progressive Era, reformers concerned about low pay and harsh working conditions in the nation's factories pressed government officials to regulate corporations more closely.

An early Ford Motor Company assembly line (above)

The record of many decades stands as proof that our people and their Government have, in the main, understood these truths and have responded to them well in the face of threat and stress. . . .

Until the latest of our world conflicts, the United States had no armaments industry. American makers of plowshares could, with time and as required, make swords as well. But now we can no longer risk emergency improvisation of national defense; we have been compelled to create a permanent armaments industry of vast proportions. Added to this, three and a half million men and women are directly engaged in the defense establishment. We annually spend on military security more than the net income of all United States corporations.

This conjunction of an immense military establishment and a large arms industry is new in the American experience. The total influence—economic, political, even spiritual—is felt in every city, every Statehouse, every office of the Federal government. We recognize the imperative need for this development. Yet we must not fail to comprehend its grave implications. Our toil, resources and livelihood are all involved; so is the very structure of our society.

In the councils of government, we must guard against the acquisition of unwarranted influence, whether sought or unsought, by the military-industrial complex. The potential for the disastrous rise of misplaced power exists and will persist.

We must never let the weight of this combination endanger our liberties or democratic processes. We should take nothing for granted. Only an alert and knowledgeable citizenry can compel the proper meshing of the huge industrial and military machinery of defense with our peaceful methods and goals, so that security and liberty may prosper together. . . .

Down the long lane of the history yet to be written America knows that this world of ours, ever growing smaller, must avoid becoming a community of dreadful fear and hate, and be, instead, a proud confederation of mutual trust and respect.

Such a confederation must be one of equals. The weakest must come to the conference table with the same confidence as do we, protected as we are by our moral, economic, and military strength. That table, though scarred by many past frustrations, cannot be abandoned for the certain agony of the battlefield.

Disarmament, with mutual honor and confidence, is a continuing imperative. Together we must learn how to compose differences, not with arms, but with intellect and decent purpose. Because this need is so sharp and apparent I confess that I lay down my official responsibilities in this field with a definite sense of disappointment. As one who has witnessed the horror and the lingering sadness of war—as one who knows that another war could utterly destroy this civilization which has been so slowly and painfully built over thousands of years—I wish I could say tonight that a lasting peace is in sight. . . .

You and I—my fellow citizens—need to be strong in our faith that all nations, under God, will reach the goal of peace with justice. May we be ever unswerving in devotion to principle, confident but humble with power, diligent in pursuit of the Nations' great goals.

To all the peoples of the world, I once more give expression to America's prayerful and continuing aspiration:

We pray that peoples of all faiths, all races, all nations, may have their great human needs satisfied; that those now denied opportunity shall come to enjoy it to the full; that all who yearn for freedom may experience its spiritual blessings; that those who have freedom will understand, also, its heavy responsibilities; that all who are insensitive to the needs of others will learn charity; that the scourges of poverty, disease and ignorance will be made to disappear from the earth, and that, in the goodness of time, all peoples will come to live together in a peace guaranteed by the binding force of mutual respect and love.

Now, on Friday noon, I am to become a private citizen. I am proud to do so. I look forward to it.

Thank you, and good night.

Analyzing Documents

Use the passage on these pages to answer the following questions.

1. For what ends, according to Eisenhower, should the United States use its economic and military strength?
   A fighting terrorism and fascism
   B promoting world peace and human betterment
   C increasing arts and sciences education
   D promoting balance and proper posture

2. To what specific "hostile ideology global in scope, atheistic in character, ruthless in purpose, and insidious in method" was Eisenhower referring in his speech?
   A terrorism
   B secular humanism
   C communism
   D religious fundamentalism

3. Critical Thinking: Making Comparisons
   Does America face any global "hostile ideologies" today? What are they? How are we responding to them?

 Primary Source CD-ROM Find additional American historical documents on the *Exploring Primary Sources in U.S. History* CD-ROM.

Address to the Forty-Third UN General Assembly Session

December 7, 1988

By MIKHAIL GORBACHEV

VOCABULARY Before you read the selection, find the meaning of these words in a dictionary:
ubiquitous
ideological
immutable
prerequisites
infringing
inertia
tenet

On December 7, 1988, Soviet General Secretary Mikhail Gorbachev addressed the United Nations General Assembly. After speaking about the recent changes in the Soviet Union, Gorbachev announced drastic cuts in the Soviet military presence in Eastern Europe and along the Chinese border—a move that ultimately allowed Soviet satellite nations to choose their own paths. In the following excerpts from that speech, Gorbachev reflects on a "new world order" and United States–Soviet relations.

. . . Today we have entered an era when progress will be based on the interests of all mankind. Consciousness of this requires that world policy, too, should be determined by the priority of the values of all mankind.

The history of the past centuries and millennia has been a history of almost ubiquitous wars, and sometimes desperate battles, leading to mutual destruction. They occurred in the clash of social and political interests and national hostility, be it from ideological or religious incompatibility. All that was the case, and even now many still claim that this past—which has not been overcome—is an immutable pattern. However, parallel with the process of wars, hostility, and alienation of peoples and countries, another process, just as objectively conditioned, was in motion and gaining force: The process of the emergence of a mutually connected and integral world.

Further world progress is now possible only through the search for a consensus of all mankind, in movement toward a new world order. We have arrived at a frontier at which controlled spontaneity leads to a dead end. The world community must learn to shape and direct the process in such a way as to preserve civilization, to make it safe for all and more pleasant for normal life. It is a question of cooperation that could be more accurately called "co-creation" and "co-development." The formula of development "at another's expense" is becoming outdated. In light of present realities, genuine progress by infringing upon the rights and liberties of man and peoples, or at the expense of nature, is impossible. . . .

. . . Behind differences in social structure, in the way of life, and in the preference for certain values, stand interests. There is no getting away from that, but neither is there any getting away from the need to find a balance of interests within an international framework, which has become a condition for survival and progress. As you ponder all this, you come to the conclusion that if we wish to take account of the lessons of the past and the realities of the present, if we must reckon with the objective logic of world development, it is necessary to seek—and to seek jointly—an approach toward improving the international situation and building a new world. If that is so, then it is also worth agreeing on the fundamental and truly universal prerequisites and principles for such activities. It is evident, for example, that force and the threat of force can no longer be, and should not be, instruments of foreign policy. . . .

Gorbachev addresses the United Nations.

The compelling necessity of the principle of freedom of choice is also clear to us. The failure to recognize this . . . is fraught with very dire consequences, consequences for world peace. Denying that right to the peoples, no matter what the pretext, no matter what the words are used to conceal it, means infringing upon even the unstable balance that is, has been possible to achieve.

Freedom of choice is a universal principle to which there should be no exceptions. We have not come to the conclusion of the immutability of this principle simply through good motives. We have been led to it through impartial analysis of the objective processes of our time. The increasing varieties of social development in different countries are becoming an ever more perceptible feature of these processes. This relates to both the capitalist and socialist systems. The variety of sociopolitical structures which has grown over the last decades from national liberation movements also demonstrates this. This objective fact presupposes respect for other people's views and stands, tolerance, a preparedness to see phenomena that are different as not necessarily bad or hostile, and an ability to learn to live side by side while remaining different and not agreeing with one another on every issue.

. . . We are not giving up our convictions, philosophy, or traditions. Neither are we calling on anyone else to give up theirs. Yet we are not going to shut ourselves up within the range of our values. That would lead to spiritual impoverishment, for it would mean renouncing so powerful a source of development as sharing all the original things created independently by each nation. In the course of such sharing, each should prove the advantages of his own system, his own way of life and values, but not through words or propaganda alone, but through real deeds as well. That is, indeed, an honest struggle of ideology . . .

Finally, being on U.S. soil, but also for other, understandable reasons, I cannot but turn to the subject of our relations with this great country. . . . Relations between the Soviet Union and the United States of America span $5\frac{1}{2}$ decades. The world has changed, and so have the nature, role, and place of these relations in world politics. For too long they were built under the banner of confrontation, and sometimes of hostility, either open or concealed. But in the last few years, throughout the world people were able to heave a sigh of relief, thanks to the changes for the better in the substance and atmosphere of the relations between Moscow and Washington.

No one intends to underestimate the serious nature of the disagreements, and the difficulties of the problems which have not been settled. However, we have already graduated from the primary school of instruction in mutual understanding and in searching for solutions in our and in the common interests. The U.S.S.R. and the United States created the biggest nuclear missile arsenals, but after objectively recognizing their responsibility, they were able to be the first to conclude an agreement on the reduction and physical destruction of a proportion of these weapons, which threatened both themselves and everyone else. . . .

We are not inclined to oversimplify the situation in the world. Yes, the tendency toward disarmament has received a strong impetus, and this process is gaining its own momentum, but it has not become irreversible. Yes, the striving to give up confrontation in favor of dialogue and cooperation has made itself strongly felt, but it has by no means secured its position forever in the practice of international relations. Yes, the movement toward a nuclear-free and nonviolent world is capable of fundamentally transforming the political and spiritual face of the planet, but only the very first steps have been taken. Moreover, in certain influential circles, they have been greeted with mistrust, and they are meeting resistance.

The inheritance of inertia of the past are continuing to operate. Profound contradictions and the roots of many conflicts have not disappeared. The fundamental fact remains that the formation of the peaceful period will take place in conditions of the existence and rivalry of various socioeconomic and political systems. However, the meaning of our international efforts, and one of the key tenets of the new thinking, is precisely to impart to this rivalry the quality of sensible competition in conditions of respect for freedom of choice and a balance of interests. In this case it will even become useful and productive from the viewpoint of general world development; otherwise, if the main component remains the arms race, as it has been till now, rivalry will be fatal. Indeed, an ever greater number of people throughout the world, from the man in the street to leaders, are beginning to understand this. . . .

Analyzing Documents

Use the passage on these pages to answer the following questions.

1. Gorbachev did not call for nations to give up their own traditions, but issued a reminder that remaining isolated "within the range" of one's own values would lead to
   A world war.
   B unilateral disarmament.
   C spiritual impoverishment.
   D economic rivalry.

2. According to the speech, what quality should the rivalry between conflicting nations and interests have?
   A fierce and punishing aggression
   B a friendly playfulness
   C sensible competition and respect for freedom of choice
   D the underlying threat of military force

3. **Critical Thinking: Making Comparisons** To what extent have the nations of the world lived up to Gorbachev's ideals since his 1988 speech? Support your claim with historical events from the text.

 Primary Source CD-ROM Find additional American historical documents on the *Exploring Primary Sources in U.S. History* CD-ROM.

Illustrated Databank

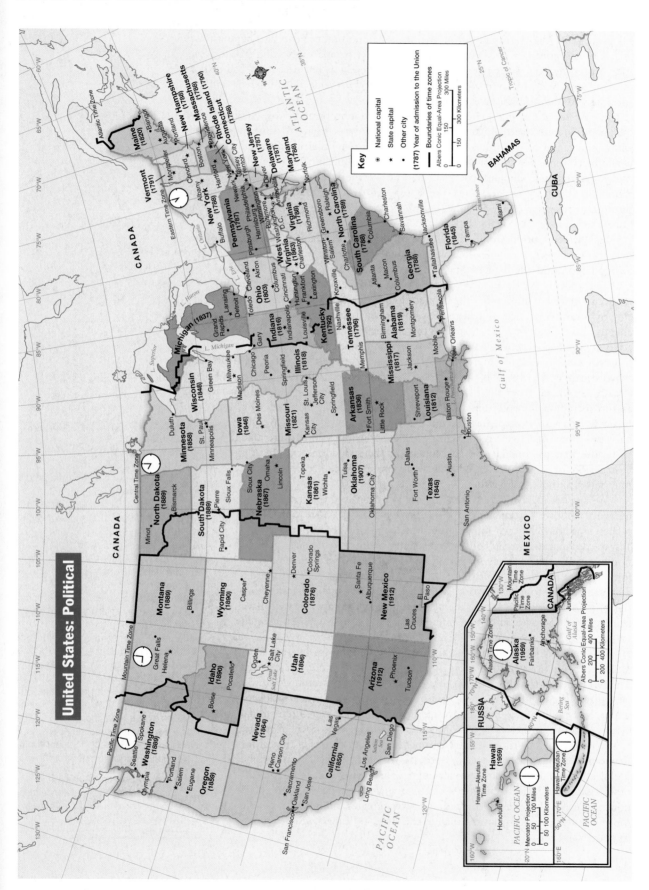

United States: Political

United States Population, 1800–2000

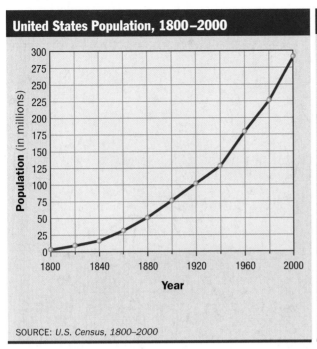

SOURCE: *U.S. Census, 1800–2000*

United States Median Age, 1840–2040

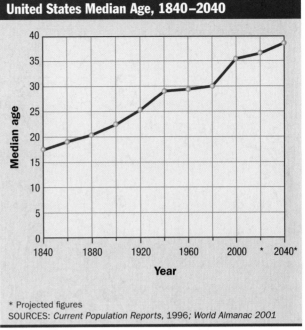

* Projected figures
SOURCES: *Current Population Reports, 1996; World Almanac 2001*

United States Birthrate, 1910–2000

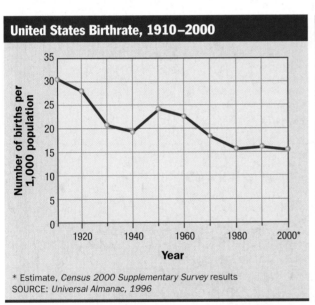

* Estimate, *Census 2000 Supplementary Survey* results
SOURCE: *Universal Almanac, 1996*

United States Population by Race, 2000

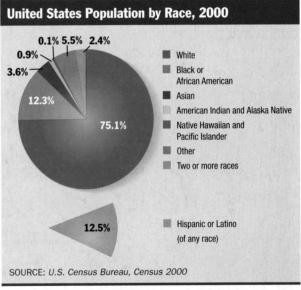

SOURCE: *U.S. Census Bureau, Census 2000*

United States Hispanic or Latino Population, 2000

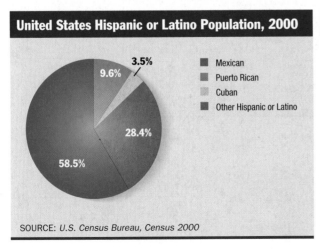

SOURCE: *U.S. Census Bureau, Census 2000*

United States Asian Population, 2000

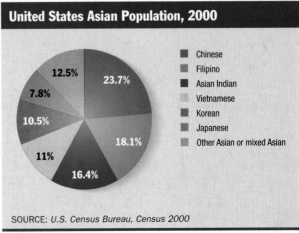

SOURCE: *U.S. Census Bureau, Census 2000*

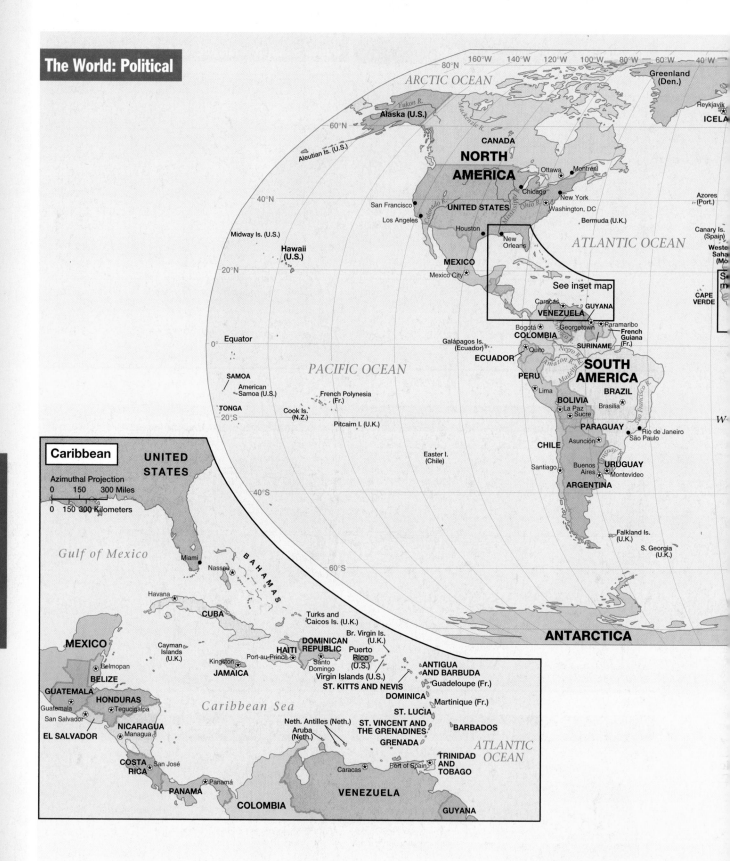

Illustrated Databank

Caribbean

Azimuthal Projection

0   150   300 Miles

0   150   300 Kilometers

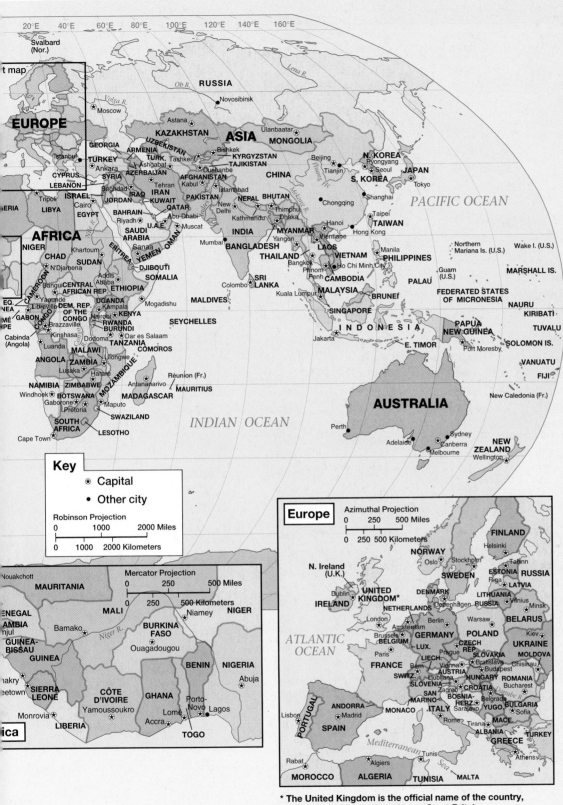

* The United Kingdom is the official name of the country, but it is more often referred to as Great Britain.

Profile of the Fifty States

State	Capital	Entered Union	Population (2000)	Population Rank	Land Area (Sq. Mi.)	Land Area Rank
Alabama	Montgomery	1819	4,447,100	23rd	50,744	28th
Alaska	Juneau	1959	626,932	48th	571,951	1st
Arizona	Phoenix	1912	5,130,632	20th	113,635	6th
Arkansas	Little Rock	1836	2,673,400	33rd	52,068	27th
California	Sacramento	1850	33,871,648	1st	155,959	3rd
Colorado	Denver	1876	4,301,261	24th	103,718	8th
Connecticut	Hartford	1788	3,405,565	29th	4,845	48th
Delaware	Dover	1787	783,600	45th	1,954	49th
Florida	Tallahassee	1845	15,982,378	4th	53,927	26th
Georgia	Atlanta	1788	8,186,453	10th	57,906	21st
Hawaii	Honolulu	1959	1,211,537	42nd	6,423	47th
Idaho	Boise	1890	1,293,953	39th	82,747	11th
Illinois	Springfield	1818	12,419,293	5th	55,584	24th
Indiana	Indianapolis	1816	6,080,485	14th	35,867	38th
Iowa	Des Moines	1846	2,926,324	30th	55,869	23rd
Kansas	Topeka	1861	2,688,418	32nd	81,815	13th
Kentucky	Frankfort	1792	4,041,769	25th	39,728	36th
Louisiana	Baton Rouge	1812	4,468,976	22nd	43,562	33rd
Maine	Augusta	1820	1,274,923	40th	30,862	39th
Maryland	Annapolis	1788	5,296,486	19th	9,774	42nd
Massachusetts	Boston	1788	6,349,097	13th	7,840	45th
Michigan	Lansing	1837	9,938,444	8th	56,804	22nd
Minnesota	St. Paul	1858	4,919,479	21st	79,610	14th
Mississippi	Jackson	1817	2,844,658	31st	46,907	31st
Missouri	Jefferson City	1821	5,595,211	17th	68,886	18th
Montana	Helena	1889	902,195	44th	145,552	4th
Nebraska	Lincoln	1867	1,711,263	38th	76,872	15th
Nevada	Carson City	1864	1,998,257	35th	109,826	7th
New Hampshire	Concord	1788	1,235,786	41st	8,968	44th
New Jersey	Trenton	1787	8,414,350	9th	7,417	46th
New Mexico	Santa Fe	1912	1,819,046	36th	121,356	5th
New York	Albany	1788	18,976,457	3rd	47,214	30th
North Carolina	Raleigh	1789	8,049,313	11th	48,711	29th
North Dakota	Bismarck	1889	642,200	47th	68,976	17th
Ohio	Columbus	1803	11,353,140	7th	40,948	35th
Oklahoma	Oklahoma City	1907	3,450,654	27th	68,667	19th
Oregon	Salem	1859	3,421,399	28th	95,997	10th
Pennsylvania	Harrisburg	1787	12,281,054	6th	44,817	32nd
Rhode Island	Providence	1790	1,048,319	43rd	1,045	50th
South Carolina	Columbia	1788	4,012,012	26th	30,110	40th
South Dakota	Pierre	1889	754,844	46th	75,885	16th
Tennessee	Nashville	1796	5,689,283	16th	41,217	34th
Texas	Austin	1845	20,851,820	2nd	261,797	2nd
Utah	Salt Lake City	1896	2,233,169	34th	82,144	12th
Vermont	Montpelier	1791	608,827	49th	9,250	43rd
Virginia	Richmond	1788	7,078,515	12th	39,594	37th
Washington	Olympia	1889	5,894,121	15th	66,544	20th
West Virginia	Charleston	1863	1,808,344	37th	24,078	41st
Wisconsin	Madison	1848	5,363,675	18th	54,310	25th
Wyoming	Cheyenne	1890	493,782	50th	97,100	9th

SOURCE: *World Almanac, Census 2000*

Presidents of the United States

George Washington
(1732–1799)
Years in Office: 1789–1797
No political party
Elected from: Virginia
Vice President: John Adams

John Adams
(1735–1826)
Years in Office: 1797–1801
Federalist
Elected from: Massachusetts
Vice President: Thomas Jefferson

Thomas Jefferson
(1743–1826)
Years in Office: 1801–1809
Democratic Republican
Elected from: Virginia
Vice Presidents: Aaron Burr,
    George Clinton

James Madison
(1751–1836)
Years in Office: 1809–1817
Democratic Republican
Elected from: Virginia
Vice Presidents: George Clinton,
    Elbridge Gerry

James Monroe
(1758–1831)
Years in Office: 1817–1825
National Republican
Elected from: Virginia
Vice President: Daniel Tompkins

John Quincy Adams
(1767–1848)
Years in Office: 1825–1829
National Republican
Elected from: Massachusetts
Vice President: John Calhoun

Andrew Jackson
(1767–1845)
Years in Office: 1829–1837
Democrat
Elected from: Tennessee
Vice Presidents: John Calhoun, Martin
    Van Buren

Martin Van Buren
(1782–1862)
Years in Office: 1837–1841
Democrat
Elected from: New York
Vice President: Richard Johnson

William Henry Harrison*
(1773–1841)
Year in Office: 1841
Whig
Elected from: Ohio
Vice President: John Tyler

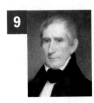

John Tyler
(1790–1862)
Years in Office: 1841–1845
Whig
Elected from: Virginia
Vice President: none

James K. Polk
(1795–1849)
Years in Office: 1845–1849
Democrat
Elected from: Tennessee
Vice President: George Dallas

Zachary Taylor*
(1784–1850)
Years in Office: 1849–1850
Whig
Elected from: Louisiana
Vice President: Millard Fillmore

Millard Fillmore
(1800–1874)
Years in Office: 1850–1853
Whig
Elected from: New York
Vice President: none

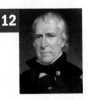

Franklin Pierce
(1804–1869)
Years in Office: 1853–1857
Democrat
Elected from: New Hampshire
Vice President: William King

James Buchanan
(1791–1868)
Years in Office: 1857–1861
Democrat
Elected from: Pennsylvania
Vice President: John Breckinridge

Abraham Lincoln**
(1809–1865)
Years in Office: 1861–1865
Republican
Elected from: Illinois
Vice Presidents: Hannibal Hamlin,
    Andrew Johnson

Andrew Johnson
(1808–1875)
Years in Office: 1865–1869
Democrat[†]
Elected from: Tennessee
Vice President: none

Ulysses S. Grant
(1822–1885)
Years in Office: 1869–1877
Republican
Elected from: Illinois
Vice Presidents: Schuyler Colfax,
Henry Wilson

Rutherford B. Hayes
(1822–1893)
Years in Office: 1877–1881
Republican
Elected from: Ohio
Vice President: William Wheeler

James A. Garfield**
(1831–1881)
Year in Office: 1881
Republican
Elected from: Ohio
Vice President: Chester A. Arthur

Chester A. Arthur
(1830–1886)
Years in Office: 1881–1885
Republican
Elected from: New York
Vice President: none

Grover Cleveland
(1837–1908)
Years in Office: 1885–1889
Democrat
Elected from: New York
Vice President: Thomas Hendricks

Benjamin Harrison
(1833–1901)
Years in Office: 1889–1893
Republican
Elected from: Indiana
Vice President: Levi Morton

Grover Cleveland
(1837–1908)
Years in Office: 1893–1897
Democrat
Elected from: New York
Vice President: Adlai Stevenson

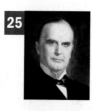

William McKinley**
(1843–1901)
Years in Office: 1897–1901
Republican
Elected from: Ohio
Vice Presidents: Garret Hobart,
Theodore Roosevelt

Theodore Roosevelt
(1858–1919)
Years in Office: 1901–1909
Republican
Elected from: New York
Vice President: Charles Fairbanks

William Howard Taft
(1857–1930)
Years in Office: 1909–1913
Republican
Elected from: Ohio
Vice President: James Sherman

Woodrow Wilson
(1856–1924)
Years in Office: 1913–1921
Democrat
Elected from: New Jersey
Vice President: Thomas Marshall

Warren G. Harding*
(1865–1923)
Years in Office: 1921–1923
Republican
Elected from: Ohio
Vice President: Calvin Coolidge

Calvin Coolidge
(1872–1933)
Years in Office: 1923–1929
Republican
Elected from: Massachusetts
Vice President: Charles Dawes

Herbert C. Hoover
(1874–1964)
Years in Office: 1929–1933
Republican
Elected from: New York
Vice President: Charles Curtis

Franklin D. Roosevelt*
(1882–1945)
Years in Office: 1933–1945
Democrat
Elected from: New York
Vice Presidents: John Garner,
Henry Wallace, Harry S Truman

Illustrated Databank

 **33** **Harry S Truman**
(1884–1972)
Years in Office: 1945–1953
Democrat
Elected from: Missouri
Vice President: Alben Barkley

 **34** **Dwight D. Eisenhower**
(1890–1969)
Years in Office: 1953–1961
Republican
Elected from: New York
Vice President: Richard M. Nixon

 **35** **John F. Kennedy****
(1917–1963)
Years in Office: 1961–1963
Democrat
Elected from: Massachusetts
Vice President: Lyndon B. Johnson

 **36** **Lyndon B. Johnson**
(1908–1973)
Years in Office: 1963–1969
Democrat
Elected from: Texas
Vice President: Hubert Humphrey

 **37** **Richard M. Nixon*****
(1913–1994)
Years in Office: 1969–1974
Republican
Elected from: New York
Vice Presidents: Spiro Agnew,
Gerald R. Ford

 **38** **Gerald R. Ford**
(1913–)
Years in Office: 1974–1977
Republican
Elected from: Michigan
Vice President: Nelson Rockefeller

 **39** **James E. Carter**
(1924–)
Years in Office: 1977–1981
Democrat
Elected from: Georgia
Vice President: Walter F. Mondale

 40 **Ronald W. Reagan**
(1911–)
Years in Office: 1981–1989
Republican
Elected from: California
Vice President: George H. W. Bush

 41 **George H. W. Bush**
(1924–)
Years in Office: 1989–1993
Republican
Elected from: Texas
Vice President: J. Danforth Quayle

 **42** **William J. Clinton**
(1946–)
Years in Office: 1993–2001
Democrat
Elected from: Arkansas
Vice President: Albert Gore Jr.

 **43** **George W. Bush**
(1946–)
Years in Office: 2001–
Republican
Elected from: Texas
Vice President: Richard Cheney

* Died in office
** Assassinated
*** Resigned
† Elected Vice President on the coalition
Union Party ticket

Key Supreme Court Cases

These pages provide summaries of key Supreme Court rulings over the course of the nation's history. For additional material and links to Supreme Court cases, see the **America: Pathways to the Present** *companion Web site at* **www.phschool.com**

Baker v. Carr, 1962

(14th Amendment) Rapid population growth in Nashville and reluctance of the rural-dominated Tennessee legislature to redraw state legislature districts led Mayor Baker of Nashville to ask for federal court help. The federal district court refused to enter the "political thicket" of redistricting, and the case was appealed. The Court directed a trial to be held in a Tennessee federal court. The case led to the 1964 *Wesberry* decision, which created the "one man, one vote" equal representation concept.

Bethel School District #403 v. Fraser, 1986

(1st Amendment, freedom of speech) A high school student gave a sexually suggestive political speech at a high school assembly to elect student officers. The school administration strongly disciplined the student, Fraser, who argued that school rules unfairly limited his freedom of political speech. Fraser's view was upheld in Washington State court. The Supreme Court, however, found that "it does not follow . . . that simply because the use of an offensive form of expression [is permitted by] adults making . . . a political point, the same latitude must be permitted to children in a public school."

Bob Jones University v. United States, 1983

(14th and 1st amendments) Bob Jones University, a private school, denied admission to applicants in an interracial marriage or who "espouse" interracial marriage or dating. The Internal Revenue Service then denied tax-exempt status to the school because of racial discrimination. The university appealed, claiming that its policy was based on the Bible. The Court upheld the IRS ruling, stating that "Government has a fundamental overriding interest" in ending racial discrimination in education.

Brown v. Board of Education of Topeka, 1954

(14th Amendment) Probably no twentieth-century Supreme Court decision so deeply stirred and changed life in the United States as *Brown*. An 8-year-old girl from Topeka, Kansas, was not permitted to attend her neighborhood school because she was an African American. The Court found that segregation itself was a violation of the Equal Protection Clause, commenting that "in the field of public education the doctrine of 'separate but equal' has no place. . . . Segregation is a denial of the equal protection of the laws." The decision overturned *Plessy,* 1896.

City of Philadelphia v. New Jersey, 1978

The Court decided that New Jersey may not restrict the importation of solid or liquid waste that originated outside the State. The Commerce Clause protects all objects of interstate trade, including waste. A State may not discriminate against items that are identical except for their origin, and thus may not prohibit out-of-state waste that is no different from domestically produced waste. Although waste disposal is a problem in many locations, States may not constitutionally deal with the problem by erecting a barrier against the movement of interstate trade.

The Civil Rights Cases, 1883

(14th Amendment) The Civil Rights Acts of 1875 included punishments for businesses that practiced discrimination. The Court ruled on a number of cases involving the Acts in 1883, finding that the Constitution, "while prohibiting discrimination by governments, made no provisions . . . for acts of racial discrimination by private individuals." The decision limited the impact of the Equal Protection Clause, giving tacit approval to segregation in the private sector.

Cruzan v. Director, Missouri Dept. of Health, 1990

(9th Amendment, right to die) A Missouri woman was in a coma from an automobile accident in 1983. Her family, facing astronomical medical bills and deciding that "her life had ended in 1987," directed the healthcare providers to end intravenous feeding. The State of Missouri opposed the family's decision, and the family went to court. The Court ruled that states could require "clear and convincing" evidence that Cruzan would have wanted to die. However, the Court did not require other states to meet the Missouri standard. At a subsequent hearing, "clear and convincing evidence" was presented. The intravenous feeding was ended, and Cruzan died on December 26, 1990.

Dennis v. United States, 1951

(1st Amendment) The Smith Act of 1940 made it a crime for any person to work for the violent overthrow of the United States in peacetime or war. Eleven Communist party leaders, including Dennis, had been convicted of violating the Smith Act, and they appealed. The Court upheld the Act. Much modified by later decisions, the Dennis case focused on anti-government speech as an area of controversy.

Dred Scott v. Sandford, 1857

(6th Amendment) This decision upheld property rights over human rights by saying that Dred Scott, a slave, could not become a free man just because he had traveled in "free soil" states with his master. A badly divided nation was further fragmented by the decision. "Free soil" federal laws and the Missouri Compromise line of 1820 were held unconstitutional because they deprived a slave owner of the right to his "property" without just compensation. This narrow reading of the Constitution, a landmark case of the Court, was most clearly stated by Chief Justice Roger B. Taney, a states' rights advocate.

Edwards v. South Carolina, 1963

(1st Amendment, freedom of speech and assembly) A group of mostly African American civil rights activists held a rally at the South Carolina State Capitol, protesting segregation. A hostile crowd gathered, and the rally leaders were arrested and convicted of "breach of the peace." The Court overturned the convictions, saying, "The Fourteenth Amendment does not permit a State to make criminal the peaceful expression of unpopular views."

Engel v. Vitale, 1962

(1st Amendment) The state Board of Regents of New York required the recitation of a 22-word nonsectarian prayer at the beginning of each school day. A group of parents filed suit against the required prayer, claiming it violated their 1st Amendment rights. The Court ruled New York's action unconstitutional, observing, "There can be no doubt that . . . religious beliefs [are] embodied in the Regents' prayer."

Escobedo v. Illinois, 1964

(6th Amendment) A person known to Chicago-area police confessed to a murder but had not been provided with a lawyer while under interrogation. The Court's decision in the case extended the "exclusionary rule" to illegal confessions in state court proceedings. Carefully defining an "Escobedo Rule," the Court said, "where . . . the investigation is no longer a general inquiry . . . but has begun to focus on a particular suspect . . . (and where) the suspect has been taken into custody . . . the suspect has requested . . . his lawyer, and the police have not . . . warned him of his right to remain silent, the accused has been denied . . . counsel in violation of the Sixth Amendment."

Everson v. Board of Education, 1947

(1st Amendment) In a case known as "the New Jersey School Bus Case," the Court considered New Jersey's use of public funds to operate school buses that carried some students to parochial schools. The Court permitted New Jersey to continue the payments, saying that the aid to children was not governmental support for religion. The decision, however, strongly stated that the wall separating church and state must be kept "high and impregnable." This was a clear incorporation of 1st Amendment limits on states.

Ex parte Milligan, 1866

(Article II) An Indiana man was arrested, treated as a prisoner of war, and imprisoned by a military court during the Civil War under presidential order. He claimed that his right to a fair trial was interfered with and that military courts had no authority outside of "conquered territory." The Court ordered him to be released on the grounds that the Constitution "is a law for rulers and people, equally in war and peace" and covers all people "at all times, and under all circumstances." The Court held that presidential powers in time of war did not extend to creating another court system run by the military.

Furman v. Georgia, 1972

(8th Amendment) Three death penalty cases, including *Furman*, raised the issue of racial imbalances in the use of death sentences by state courts. Furman had been sentenced to death in Georgia. Overturning state death penalty laws, the Court noted an "apparent arbitrariness of the use of the sentence." Many states rewrote their death penalty statutes, and these were generally upheld in *Gregg*, 1976.

Gibbons v. Ogden, 1824

(Article I, Section 8) This case examined the power of Congress to regulate interstate commerce. Ogden's exclusive New York ferry license gave him the right to operate steamboats to and from New York. Ogden claimed that Gibbons's federal license did not give him landing rights in New York City. Federal and state regulation of commerce conflicted. The Court strengthened the power of the United States to regulate interstate business. Federal controls on television, pipelines, and banking are based on *Gibbons*.

Gideon v. Wainwright, 1963

(14th Amendment) Gideon was charged with breaking into a poolroom. He could not afford a lawyer, and Florida refused to provide counsel for trials not involving the death penalty. Gideon defended himself poorly and was sentenced to five years in prison. The Court called for a new trial, arguing that the Due Process Clause of the 14th Amendment applied to the 6th Amendment's guarantee of counsel for all poor persons facing a felony charge. Gideon later was found not guilty with the help of a court-appointed attorney.

Gitlow v. New York, 1925

(1st and 14th amendments) For the first time, the Court considered whether the 1st and 14th amendments had influence on state laws. The case, involving "criminal anarchy" under New York law, was the first consideration of what came to be known as the "incorporation" doctrine, under which, it was argued, the provisions of the 1st Amendment were "incorporated" by the 14th Amendment. Although New York law was not overruled in the case, the decision clearly indicated that the Court could make such a ruling. Another important incorporation case is *Powell*, 1932.

Goss v. Lopez, 1975

(14th Amendment, Due Process Clause) Ten Ohio students were suspended from their schools without hearings. The students challenged the suspensions, claiming that the absence of a preliminary hearing violated their 14th Amendment right to due process. The Court agreed with the students, holding that "having chosen to extend the right to an education . . . Ohio may not withdraw that right on grounds of misconduct, absent fundamentally fair procedures to determine whether the misconduct has occurred, and must recognize a student's legitimate entitlement to a public education as a property interest that is protected by the Due Process Clause."

Gregg v. Georgia, 1976

(8th Amendment) In the 1970s, activists tried to get the death penalty reinstated. Several test cases failed when the Court found the sentence had been motivated by racism, issued arbitrarily, or handed down without due process. The case of Gregg, convicted of murdering two men, was considered to be free from such problems. Finding that his conviction and death sentence were fair and consistent with state law, the Court ruled that Georgia's death penalty did not violate the "cruel and unusual punishment" clause of the 8th Amendment. For the first time, the Court clearly affirmed that "punishment of death does not invariably violate the Constitution."

Griswold v. Connecticut, 1965

(14th Amendment) A Connecticut law forbade the use of "any drug, medicinal article, or instrument for the purpose of preventing conception." Griswold, director of Planned Parenthood in New Haven, was arrested for counseling married couples. After conviction, he appealed. The Court overturned the Connecticut law, saying that "various guarantees (of the Constitution) create zones of privacy" and asking, "would we allow the police to search the sacred precincts of marital bedrooms . . . ?" The decision is significant for examining the concept of "unenumerated rights" in the 9th Amendment, later central to *Roe*, 1973.

Hazelwood School District v. Kuhlmeier, 1988

(1st Amendment, freedom of speech) In 1983, the principal of Hazelwood East High School in Missouri removed two articles from the upcoming issue of the student newspaper, deeming their content "inappropriate, personal, sensitive, and unsuitable for student readers." Several students sued the school district, claiming that their 1st Amendment right to freedom of expression had been violated. The Court upheld the principal's action, stating that "a school need not tolerate student speech that is inconsistent with its basic educational mission, even though the government could not censor similar speech outside the school." School officials had full control over school-sponsored activities "so long as their actions are reasonably related to legitimate pedagogical concerns. . . ."

Heart of Atlanta Motel, Inc. v. United States, 1964

(Article I, Section 8) The Civil Rights Act of 1964 outlawed race discrimination in "public accommodations," including motels that refused rooms to blacks. Although local desegregation appeared to fall outside federal authority, the government argued that it was regulating interstate commerce. The Court agreed, declaring, "The power of Congress to promote interstate commerce also includes the power to regulate the local incidents thereof, including local activities . . . which have a substantial and harmful effect upon that commerce." Racial segregation of private facilities engaged in interstate commerce was found unconstitutional.

In re Gault, 1966

(14th Amendment) Before *Gault*, proceedings against juveniles were generally handled as "family law," not "criminal law," and offenders received few due process rights. Gault was sentenced to six years in state juvenile detention for an alleged obscene phone call. He was not provided counsel and not permitted to confront or cross-examine the key witness. The Court overturned the juvenile proceedings and required that states provide juveniles "some of the due process guarantees of adults," including a right to a phone call, to counsel, to cross-examine, to confront the accuser, and to be advised of the right to silence.

Ingraham v. Wright, 1977

(8th Amendment) A majority of the Supreme Court concluded that the 8th Amendment historically protected people convicted of crimes, and does not apply to public school students. If authorized by local law or custom, public schools have the right to administer reasonable discipline, and students do not have a due process right to notice or a hearing before punishment administered in accordance with law or custom.

Johnson v. Santa Clara Transportation Agency, 1987

(Discrimination) Under its affirmative action plan, the Transportation Agency in Santa Clara, California, was authorized to "consider as one factor the sex of a qualified applicant" in an effort to combat the significant underrepresentation of women in certain job classifications. When the Agency promoted Diane Joyce, a qualified woman, over Paul Johnson, a qualified man, for the job of road dispatcher, Johnson sued, claiming that the Agency's consideration of the sex of the applicants violated Title VII of the Civil Rights Act of 1964. The Court upheld the Agency's promotion policy, arguing that the affirmative action plan created no "absolute bar" to the advancement of men but rather represented "a moderate, flexible, case-by-case approach to effecting a gradual improvement in the representation of minorities and women . . . in the Agency's work force, and [was] fully consistent with Title VII."

Korematsu v. United States, 1944

(5th Amendment) Two months after Japan attacked Pearl Harbor, President Roosevelt ordered the internment of more than 110,000 Japanese Americans living on the West Coast. Although many Japanese Americans were United States citizens, they had to abandon their property and live in primitive camps far from the coast. Korematsu refused to report to an assembly center and was arrested. The Court rejected his appeal, noting that "pressing public necessity [World War II] may sometimes justify the existence of restrictions which curtail the civil rights of a single racial group" but added that "racial antagonism" never can justify such restrictions. The *Korematsu* decision has been widely criticized, particularly since few Americans of German or Italian descent were interned.

Lemon v. Kurzman, 1971

(1st Amendment, Establishment Clause) In overturning state laws regarding aid to church-supported schools in this and a similar Rhode Island case, the Court created the *Lemon* test, limiting "excessive government entanglement with religion." The Court noted that any state law about aid to religion must meet three criteria: (1) the purpose of the aid must be clearly secular, not religious; (2) its primary effect must neither advance nor inhibit religion; and (3) it must avoid "excessive entanglement of government with religion."

Mapp v. Ohio, 1961

(4th and 14th amendments) Before *Mapp*, the admission of evidence gained by illegal searches was permitted by some state constitutions. Cleveland police raided Mapp's home without a warrant and found obscene materials. She appealed her conviction, saying that the 4th and 14th amendments protected her against improper police behavior. The Court agreed, extending "exclusionary rule" protections to citizens in state courts. The Court said that the prohibition against unreasonable searches would be "meaningless" unless evidence gained in such searches was excluded. The case developed the concept of "incorporation" begun in *Gitlow*, 1925.

Marbury v. Madison, 1803

(Article III) Chief Justice Marshall established "judicial review" as a power of the Supreme Court. After his defeat in the 1800 election, President Adams appointed many Federalists to the federal courts, but the commissions were not delivered. New Secretary of State James Madison refused to deliver them. Marbury sued in the Supreme Court. The Court declared a portion of the Judiciary Act of 1789 unconstitutional, thereby establishing the Court's power to find acts of Congress unconstitutional.

Massachusetts v. Sheppard, 1984

(4th Amendment) A search in Massachusetts was based on a warrant issued on an improper form. Sheppard argued that the search was illegal and the evidence was inadmissible under *Mapp*, 1961. Massachusetts argued that the police acted in "good faith," believing that the warrant was correct. The Court agreed with Massachusetts, noting that the exclusionary rule should not be applied when the officer conducting the search had acted with the reasonable belief that he was following proper procedures.

McCulloch v. Maryland, 1819

(Article I, Section 8) Called the "Bank of the United States" case. A Maryland law required federally chartered banks to use only a special paper to print money, which amounted to a tax. McCulloch, the cashier of the Baltimore branch of the bank, refused to use the paper, claiming that states could not tax the federal government. The Court declared the Maryland law unconstitutional, commenting ". . . the power to tax implies the power to destroy."

Miller v. California, 1973

(1st Amendment) In *Miller*, the Court upheld a stringent application of California obscenity law by Newport Beach, California, and attempted to define what is obscene. The "Miller Rule" included three criteria: (1) that the average person would, applying contemporary community standards, find that the work appealed to the prurient interest; (2) that the work depicts or describes, in an offensive way, sexual conduct defined by state law; and (3) that "the work, taken as a whole, lacks serious literary, artistic, political or scientific value. . . ."

Miranda v. Arizona, 1966

(5th, 6th, and 14th amendments) Arrested for kidnapping and sexual assault, Miranda signed a confession including a statement that he had "full knowledge" of his legal rights. After conviction, he appealed, claiming that without counsel and without warnings, the confession was illegally obtained. The Court agreed with Miranda that "he must be warned prior to any questioning that he has the right to remain silent, that anything he says can be used against him in a court of law, that he has a right to . . . an attorney and that if he cannot afford an attorney one will be appointed for him. . . ." Although later modified, *Miranda* firmly upheld citizens' rights to a fair trial in state courts.

Mueller v. Allen, 1983

(1st and 14th amendments) Minnesota law allowed taxpayers to deduct the costs of tuition, textbooks, and transportation for children in elementary and secondary schools. Several taxpayers sued to prevent parents with children in religious schools from claiming this deduction, arguing that this would constitute state sponsorship of religion. The Court disagreed, ruling that the deduction was not intended to promote religion and was available to all parents with school-age children. The Court argued that a law must have the advancement of religion as its primary purpose to be found unconstitutional.

New Jersey v. T.L.O., 1985

(4th and 14th amendments) After T.L.O., a New Jersey high school student, denied an accusation that she had been smoking in the school lavatory, a vice-principal searched her purse and found cigarettes, marijuana, and evidence that T.L.O. had been involved in marijuana dealing at the school. T.L.O. was then sentenced to probation by a juvenile court, but appealed on the grounds that the evidence against her had been obtained by an "unreasonable" search. The Court rejected T.L.O.'s arguments, stating that the school had a "legitimate need to maintain an environment in which learning can take place," and that to do this "requires some easing of the restrictions to which searches by public authorities are ordinarily subject." The Court thus created a "reasonable suspicion" rule for school searches, a change from the "probable cause" requirement in the wider society.

New York Times v. United States, 1971

(1st Amendment) In June 1971, the *New York Times* published the first in a series of secret government documents known as the "Pentagon Papers," which detailed how the United States became involved in the Vietnam War. The Justice Department obtained a court order forbidding the newspaper from printing more documents. The *New York Times* and other newspapers challenged the order. The Court cited the 1st Amendment guarantee of a free press and refused to uphold the ban, noting that the government must prove that publication would harm the nation's security. The decision limited "prior restraint" of the press.

Nix v. Williams, 1984

(4th Amendment, illegal evidence) A man was convicted of murdering a 10-year-old girl after he led officers to the body. He had been arrested, but not advised of his rights, in a distant city. During a conversation with a police officer while in transit, Williams agreed that the child should have a proper burial and directed the officer to the body. Later, on appeal, Williams's attorneys argued that the body should not be admitted as evidence because the questioning was illegal. The Court disagreed, observing that search parties were within 2.5 miles of the body. "Evidence otherwise excluded may be admissible when it would have been discovered anyway." The decision was one of several "exceptions to the exclusionary rule" handed down by the Court in the 1980s.

Nixon v. Fitzgerald, 1982

In 1968, A. Ernest Fitzgerald, an Air Force management analyst, testified against the government before a congressional subcommittee about cost overruns and problems with the development of an airplane. In 1970, he lost his job in a "reorganization," but he blamed President Nixon's office for firing him in retaliation for his testimony. A long series of official complaints and investigations turned up incriminating evidence against Nixon and two of his aides, including a memo about Fitzgerald recommending that Nixon "let him bleed." Nixon initially took responsibility for the firing at a press conference, but he retracted his admission the next day. Eventually, he offered to settle out of court for a large sum. Fitzgerald persisted, and a final Nixon appeal on the grounds of presidential immunity from prosecution was dismissed by a Federal District Court.

Just as the case seemed about to go to trial, more than ten years after the fact, the Supreme Court intervened. It ruled that a President or former President is entitled to absolute immunity from liability based on his official acts. The President must be able to act forcefully and independently, without fear of liability. Diverting the President's energies with concerns about private lawsuits could impair the effective functioning of government. The President's absolute immunity extends to all acts within the "outer perimeter" of his duties of office, since otherwise he would be required to litigate over the nature of the acts and the scope of his duties in each case. The remedy of impeachment, the vigilant scrutiny of the press, the Congress, and the public, and presidential desire to earn reelection and concern with historical legacy all protect against presidential wrongdoing.

Nixon v. Shrink Missouri Government PAC, 2000

In *Buckley* v. *Valeo*, 1976, the Supreme Court had upheld a $1000 limit on contributions by individuals to candidates for federal office. In *Nixon* v. *Shrink Missouri Government PAC*, the Court concluded that large contributions will sometimes create actual corruption, and that voters will inevitably be suspicious of the fairness of a political process that allows wealthy donors to contribute large amounts. The Court concluded that the Missouri contribution limits were appropriate to correct this problem and did not impair the ability of candidates to communicate their messages to the voters and to mount an effective campaign.

Plessy v. Ferguson, 1896

(14th Amendment, Equal Protection Clause) A Louisiana law required separate seating for white passengers and black passengers on public railroads. Plessy argued that the policy violated his right to "equal protection of the laws." The Court disagreed, saying that segregation was permissible if facilities were equal. It ruled that the 14th Amendment was "not intended to give Negroes social equality but only political and civil equality. . . ." The Louisiana law was seen as a "reasonable exercise of (state) police power. . . ." This "separate but equal" ruling allowed the segregation of public facilities throughout the South until *Plessy* was overturned by the *Brown* v. *Board of Education* case of 1954.

Powell v. Alabama, 1932

(6th Amendment, right to counsel) The case involved the "Scottsboro Boys," seven black men accused of rape. The men were quickly prosecuted without counsel and sentenced to death. The Court overturned the decision, stating that poor people facing the death penalty in state courts must be provided counsel, saying that "there are certain principles of Justice which . . . no [state] may disregard." The case was a step toward incorporating the Bill of Rights into state constitutions.

Printz v. United States, 1997

The Supreme Court ruled that the Brady Act's interim provision requiring certain State or local law enforcement agents to perform background checks on prospective handgun purchasers was unconstitutional. Although no provision of the Constitution deals explicitly with federal authority to compel State officials to execute federal law, a review of the Constitution's structure and of prior Supreme Court decisions leads to the conclusion that Congress does not have this power.

Regents of the University of California v. Bakke, 1978

(14th Amendment) Under an affirmative action program, the medical school of the University of California at Davis reserved 16 of 100 slots in each class for "disadvantaged citizens." When Bakke, who is white, was not accepted by the school, he claimed racial discrimination in violation of the 14th Amendment. The Court ruled narrowly, requiring Bakke's admission but not overturning affirmative action, preferring to review such questions on a case-by-case basis.

Reno v. ACLU, 1997

The Supreme Court ruled that the "indecent transmission" provision and the "patently offensive display" provision of the Communications Decency Act violated the 1st Amendment's freedom of speech. The Internet does not have the special features (such as historical governmental oversight, limited frequencies, and "invasiveness") that have justified allowing greater regulation of content in radio and television.

Reno v. Condon, 2000

The Court upheld the federal law that forbids States from selling addresses, telephone numbers, and other information that drivers put on license applications. They agreed with the Federal Government that information, including motor vehicle license information, is an "article of commerce" in the interstate stream of business and therefore is subject to regulation by Congress. The Court emphasized that the statute did not impose on the States any obligation to pass particular laws or policies and thus did not interfere with the States' sovereign functions.

Reynolds v. Sims, 1964

Most states have constitutional provisions to reapportion representation in their state legislatures every ten years, based on the U.S. Census. By the 1950s, however, it had become clear that some states were ignoring these laws. The United States was becoming more urban, and one-time rural majorities—now minorities—were holding on to political power at the state

level by refusing to reapportion. A complaint was filed by a group of residents, taxpayers, and voters of Jefferson County, Alabama, challenging the apportionment of the Alabama legislature, which was still based on the 1900 federal census. The Court supported the "one person, one vote" formula, and applied it to this case, calling for reapportionment based on current census data.

Roe v. Wade, 1973

(9th Amendment) A Texas woman challenged a state law forbidding the artificial termination of a pregnancy, saying that she "had a fundamental right to privacy." The Court upheld a woman's right to choose, noting that the state's "important and legitimate interest in protecting the potentiality of human life" became "compelling" at the end of the first trimester, but that before then "the attending physician, in consultation with his patient, is free to determine, without regulation by the state, that . . . the patient's pregnancy should be terminated." The decision struck down state regulation of abortion in the first three months of pregnancy and was later modified by *Webster,* 1989.

Rostker v. Goldberg, 1981

(5th Amendment) In 1980, President Carter reinstated draft registration. For the first time, both sexes were ordered to register. When Congress refused to fund the registration of women, several men sued, arguing that a selective draft violated their due process rights. The Court disagreed, noting that "the purpose of registration was to prepare for draft of combat troops" and that "Congress and the Executive have decided that women should not serve in combat."

Roth v. United States, 1957

(1st Amendment) A New York man named Roth operated a business that used the mail to invite people to buy materials considered obscene by postal inspectors. The Court, in its first consideration of censorship of obscenity, created the "prevailing community standards" rule, which required a consideration of the work as a whole. In its decision, the Court defined as obscene that which offends "the average person, applying contemporary community standards."

Schenck v. United States, 1919

(1st Amendment) Schenck, a member of an antiwar group, had urged men who were drafted into military service in World War I to resist and to avoid induction. He was charged with violating the Espionage Act of 1917, which outlawed active opposition to the war. The Court limited free speech in time of war, stating that Schenck's words presented a "clear and present danger. . . ." Although later decisions modified this one, the *Schenck* case created a precedent that 1st Amendment rights are not absolute.

School District of Abington Township, Pennsylvania v. Schempp, 1963

(1st Amendment) Some Pennsylvania parents challenged a state law that required Bible readings each day at school. The Court agreed with the parents, saying that the Establishment Clause and Free Exercise Clause forbade states from engaging in religious activity. The Court ruled that if the purpose and effect of a law "is the advancement or inhibition of religion," it "exceeds the scope of legislative power."

Sheppard v. Maxwell, 1966

(14th Amendment) Sam Sheppard was convicted of murdering his wife in a trial sensationalized by the national media. Sheppard appealed, claiming that the pretrial publicity had made it impossible for him to get a fair trial. Rejecting arguments about freedom of the press, the Court overturned the conviction and ordered a new trial. Because of *Sheppard*, judges have issued "gag" orders limiting pretrial publicity.

South Dakota v. Dole, 1986

In 1984, Congress voted to withhold five percent of federal highway funds from any state that did not set a minimum drinking age at 21. South Dakota, which would lose money under the new law, challenged the government's right to coerce states to adopt specific policies through funding cuts. The Court ruled that highway funding was not an entitlement, and the national government could impose reasonable conditions upon the states in the interest of the "general welfare." All states that wished to continue to receive full federal highway aid were required to raise the legal age to purchase and consume alcohol to 21 years. In recent years, the threat of spending cuts has become a powerful tool of federal policy.

Tennessee Valley Authority v. Hiram G. Hill, Jr., et al., 1978

The Tellico Dam was nearly completed—and $100 million had been spent on it—when local residents succeeded in halting construction to save a tiny, nearly extinct fish called the snail darter. The fish's only habitat would have been flooded by the dam. The Court found the injunction against the TVA's completion of the nearly finished dam to be proper to prevent violation of the Endangered Species Act. Congress had declared the value of endangered species "incalculable." The Court refused to overrule Congress's judgment. The ruling affirmed the Environmental Protection Agency's power to protect the environment.

Texas v. Johnson, 1989

(1st Amendment) To protest national policies, Johnson doused a United States flag with kerosene and burned it outside the 1984 Republican National Convention in Dallas. He was arrested and convicted under a Texas law prohibiting the desecration of the Texas and United States flags. The Court ruled that the Texas law placed an unconstitutional limit on "freedom of expression," noting that ". . . nothing in our precedents suggests that a state may foster its own view of the flag by prohibiting expressive conduct relating to it."

Thompson v. Oklahoma, 1988

(8th Amendment, capital punishment) A 15-year-old from Oklahoma was convicted of murder and was sentenced to death at age 16. The Court overturned the death sentence, holding that "[t]he Eighth and Fourteenth Amendments prohibit the execution of a person who was under 16 years of age at the time of his or her offense." A death penalty was deemed cruel and unusual punishment for someone so young.

Tinker v. Des Moines School District, 1969

The Court upheld school students' 1st Amendment rights. Because students do not "shed their constitutional rights to freedom of speech or expression at the schoolhouse gate," schools must show a possibility of "substantial disruption" before free speech can be limited at school. Students may express personal opinions as long as they do not materially disrupt classwork, create substantial disorder, or interfere with the rights of others. In this case, the wearing of black armbands was a "silent, passive expression of opinion" without these side effects, and thus constitutionally could not be prohibited by the school.

United States v. Eichman, 1990

The Court agreed with the trial courts' rulings that the Flag Protection Act violated the 1st Amendment. Flag-burning constitutes expressive conduct, and thus is entitled to constitutional protection. The Act prevents protesters from using the flag to express their opposition to governmental policies and activities. Although the protesters' ideas may be offensive or disagreeable to many people, the government may not prohibit them from expressing those ideas.

United States v. Lopez, 1990

(Article I, Section 8, Commerce Clause) Alfonzo Lopez, a Texas high school student, was convicted of carrying a weapon in a school zone under the Gun-Free School Zones Act of 1990. He appealed his conviction on the basis that the Act, which forbids "any individual knowingly to possess a firearm at a place that [he] knows . . . is a school zone," exceeded Congress's legislative power under the Commerce Clause. The Court agreed that the Act was unconstitutional, stating that to uphold the legislation would "bid fair to convert congressional Commerce Clause authority to a general police power of the sort held only by the States."

United States v. Nixon, 1974

President Nixon was widely suspected of participating in the coverup of the Watergate break-in. After journalists discovered that he had recorded all of his conversations in the White House, Congress demanded that Nixon hand over the tapes. The President cited executive privilege, arguing that his office placed him above the law. The Court overruled Nixon and ordered him to surrender the tapes. Limiting executive privilege, it ruled that the President's "generalized interest in confidentiality" was subordinate to "the fundamental demands of due process of law in the fair administration of criminal justice." The tapes implicated Nixon in the coverup and led to his resignation.

Wallace v. Jaffree, 1985

(1st Amendment, Establishment Clause) An Alabama law authorized a one-minute period of silence in all public schools "for meditation or voluntary prayer." A group of parents, including Jaffree, challenged the constitutionality of the statute, claiming it violated the Establishment Clause of the 1st Amendment. The Court agreed with Jaffree and struck down the Alabama law, determining that "the State's endorsement . . . of prayer activities at the beginning of each schoolday is not consistent with the established principle that the government must pursue a course of complete neutrality toward religion."

Walz v. Tax Commission of the City of New York, 1970

(1st Amendment, Establishment Clause) State and local governments routinely exempt church property from taxes. Walz claimed that such exemptions were a "support of religion." The Court disagreed, noting that such exemptions constituted a "benevolent neutrality" between government and churches, not a support of religion. Governments must avoid taxing churches, because taxation would give government a "control" over religion prohibited by the "wall of separation of church and state" noted in *Everson*, 1947.

Webster v. Reproductive Health Services, 1989

(9th Amendment) A 1986 Missouri law stated that (1) life begins at conception; (2) unborn children have rights; (3) public funds could not be used for abortions not necessary to save the life of the mother; and (4) public funds could not be used for abortion counseling. Healthcare providers in Missouri filed suit, challenging the law, claiming that it was in conflict with *Roe*, 1973, and that it intruded into "privacy questions." A 5–4 Court upheld the Missouri law, stating that the people of Missouri, through their legislature, could put limits on the use of public funds. The *Webster* decision narrowed the *Roe* decision.

Weeks v. United States, 1914

(4th Amendment) A search without proper warrant was conducted in San Francisco, and the evidence collected was used by a postal inspector to prosecute Weeks. Weeks claimed that the evidence was gained by an illegal search, and thus was inadmissible. The Court agreed, applying for the first time an "exclusionary rule" for illegally gained evidence in federal courts.

The decision stated ". . . if letters and private documents can thus be seized and used as evidence . . . his right to be secure against such searches . . . is of no value, and . . . might as well be stricken from the Constitution." See also *Mapp v. Ohio*, 1961; *Massachusetts v. Sheppard*, 1984; and *Nix v. Williams*, 1984.

West Virginia Board of Education v. Barnette, 1943

The beliefs of Jehovah's Witnesses forbid them to salute the United States flag. In the patriotic climate of World War II, thousands of children who refused to salute were expelled from public schools. The Court ruled that a compulsory flag salute violated the 1st Amendment's exercise of the religion clause and was therefore unconstitutional. "No official, high or petty, can prescribe what shall be orthodox in politics, nationalism, religion, or other matters of opinion."

Westside Community Schools v. Mergens, 1990

(1st Amendment, Establishment Clause) A request by Mergens to form a student Christian religious group at school was denied by an Omaha high school principal. Mergens took legal action, claiming that a 1984 federal law required "equal access" for student religious groups. The Court ordered the school to permit the formation of the club, stating, "a high school does not have to permit any extracurricular activities, but when it does, the school is bound by the Act of 1984. Allowing students to meet on campus and discuss religion is constitutional because it does not amount to a 'State sponsorship of a religion.' "

Wisconsin v. Yoder, 1972

(1st Amendment, Free Exercise Clause) Members of the Amish religious sect in Wisconsin objected to sending their children to public schools after the eighth grade, claiming that such exposure of the children to another culture would endanger the group's self-sufficient agrarian lifestyle essential to their religious faith. The Court agreed with the Amish, while noting that the Court must move carefully to weigh the State's "legitimate social concern when faced with religious claim for exemption from generally applicable educational requirements."

Glossary

A

abolitionist movement Movement to end slavery (p. 129)

abstinence Refraining from some activity, such as drinking (p. 128)

Adams-Onís Treaty 1819 treaty between the United States and Spain in which Spain ceded Florida to the United States; also called the Transcontinental Treaty (p. 109)

administration Term of office; also the members and agencies of the executive branch as a whole (p. 64)

affirmative action Policy that gives special consideration to women and members of minority groups to make up for past discrimination (p. 854)

Agent Orange An herbicide used as a chemical weapon during the Vietnam War to kill vegetation and expose enemy hiding places (p. 801)

Agricultural Adjustment Administration (AAA) Established in 1933 to raise farm prices through government financial assistance (p. 540)

AIDS Acquired immuno-deficiency syndrome, a virus that killed many people starting in the early 1980s (p. 878)

alien A noncitizen (p. 302)

Alliance for Progress President Kennedy's proposal for cooperation among nations of the Western Hemisphere to meet the basic needs of their people (p. 757)

Allies In World War I, Russia, France, Serbia, and Great Britain; in World War II, the alliance of Great Britain, the United States, the Soviet Union, and other nations (pp. 417, 578)

America First Committee Group formed in 1940 by isolationists to block further aid to Britain (p. 587)

American Expeditionary Force (AEF) Name given to American troops in Europe in World War I (p. 425)

American Indian Movement (AIM) Organization formed in 1968 to help Native Americans (p. 775)

American Liberty League Organization founded in 1934 to oppose the New Deal (p. 547)

amnesty A general pardon for certain crimes (p. 854)

anarchist A radical who opposes all government (p. 251)

annex To join or attach, as in the joining of a new territory to an existing country (pp. 135, 353)

anti-Federalists Opponents of the Constitution during the debate over ratification; opposed to the concept of a strong national government (p. 61)

anti-Semitism Hostility or discrimination toward Jews (p. 609)

apartheid (uh PAHR tayt) The systematic segregation of people of different racial backgrounds (p. 902)

appeasement Policy of giving in to a competitor's demands in order to preserve the peace (p. 573)

apportionment Distribution of seats in a legislative body (p. 748)

arbitration Settlement of a dispute by a person or panel chosen to listen to both sides and come to a decision (p. 358)

armistice A cease-fire or truce (p. 430)

arms race A contest between nations to gain weapons superiority (p. 660)

Articles of Confederation Plan that established, in 1781, a limited national government in the United States, later replaced by the Constitution of the United States (p. 55)

assembly line Manufacturing process in which each worker does one specialized task in the construction of the final product (p. 494)

assimilation Process by which people of one culture merge into and become part of another culture (pp. 266, 321)

Atlantic Charter Agreement signed by President Franklin Roosevelt and Prime Minister Winston Churchill in 1941 outlining the two nations' war aims (p. 600)

autocrat Ruler with unlimited power (p. 418)

autonomy Self-government, with respect to local matters (p. 775)

Axis Powers In World War II, Germany, Italy, and Japan (p. 573)

B

baby boom Dramatic increase in birthrate, especially in the years following World War II (p. 672)

balance of trade Difference in value between imports and exports (p. 25)

banana republic Term used to describe a Central American nation dominated by United States business interests (p. 355)

barrio A Spanish-speaking neighborhood (pp. 455, 625)

barter To trade goods or services without money (p. 6)

Bataan Death March Brutal march of American and Filipino prisoners by Japanese soldiers in 1942 (p. 615)

Battle of Antietam Civil War battle in Maryland in 1862 (p. 165)

Battle of the Bulge World War II battle in which German forces launched a final counterattack in the west (p. 607)

Battle of Chancellorsville Civil War battle in 1863 in Virginia, won by the Confederacy (p. 179)

Battle of Cold Harbor Civil War battle in 1864 in Virginia (p. 187)

Battle of the Coral Sea 1942 World War II battle between American and Japanese aircraft (p. 616)

Battle of Fredericksburg Civil War battle in 1862 in Virginia, won by the Confederacy (p. 179)

Battle of Gettysburg Civil War battle in 1863 in Pennsylvania, won by the Union (p. 180)

Battle of Guadalcanal (gwahd ul kuh NAL) 1942–1943 World War II battle between the United States and Japan (p. 617)

Battle of Iwo Jima 1945 World War II battle between the United States and Japan (p. 619)

Battle of Leyte Gulf 1944 World War II naval battle between the United States and Japan (p. 618)

Battle of Little Bighorn 1876 Sioux victory over army troops led by George Custer (p. 265)

Battle of Midway 1942 World War II battle between the United States and Japan, a turning point in the war in the Pacific (p. 617)

Battle of Okinawa 1945 World War II battle between the United States and Japan (p. 619)

Battle of Shiloh Civil War battle in Tennessee in 1862 (p. 162)

Battle of Spotsylvania Civil War battle in 1864 in Virginia (p. 187)

Battle of the Wilderness Civil War battle in 1864 in Virginia, won by the Confederacy (p. 187)

Battles of Lexington and Concord First battles of the Revolutionary War, on April 19, 1775 (p. 45)

Bay of Pigs invasion Failed invasion of Cuba by a group of anti-Castro forces in 1961 (p. 752)

beatnik In the 1950s, a person who criticized American society as apathetic and conformist (p. 679)

Berlin airlift Operation that moved supplies into West Berlin by American and British planes during a Soviet blockade in 1948–1949 (p. 647)

Berlin Wall Barrier built by the East German government to separate Communist and non-Communist Berlin (p. 754)

Bessemer process A process for making steel more efficiently, patented in 1856 (p. 233)

bicentennial 200th anniversary (p. 850)

bilingual education The teaching of students in their native language, as well as in English (p. 912)

Bill of Rights First ten amendments to the Constitution (p. 62)

bimetallic standard Currency of the United States, prior to 1873, which consisted of gold or silver coins as well as U.S. treasury notes that could be traded in for gold or silver (p. 278)

black codes Laws that restricted freedmen's rights (p. 206)

black nationalism A belief in the separate identity and racial unity of the African American community (p. 723)

black power African American movement seeking unity and self-reliance (p. 724)

Black Tuesday October 29, 1929, the day on which the Great Crash of the stock market began (p. 509)

blacklist List that circulated among employers, beginning in 1947, containing the names of persons who should not be hired (p. 650)

Bland-Allison Act 1878 law that required the federal government to purchase and coin more silver, increasing the money supply and causing inflation (p. 279)

blitzkrieg (BLITS kreeg) Kind of warfare emphasizing rapid and mechanized movement; used by Germany during World War II (p. 576)

blue law Regulation that prohibited certain private activities people considered immoral, such as drinking alcohol on Sundays (p. 292)

bonanza farm Farm controlled by large businesses, managed by professionals, and raising massive quantities of single cash crops (p. 274)

Bonus Army A group of World War I veterans and their families who protested in Washington, D.C., in 1932, demanding immediate payment of a pension bonus that had been promised for 1945 (p. 526)

boomers Settlers who ran in land races to claim land upon the 1889 opening of Indian Territory for settlement (p. 267)

bootlegger Term used to describe a supplier of illegal alcohol during Prohibition (p. 468)

Border States In the Civil War, the states between the North and South: Delaware, Maryland, Kentucky, and Missouri (p. 142)

Boston Massacre Incident on March 5, 1770, in which British soldiers in Boston killed five colonists (p. 43)

boycott Refusal to buy a certain product, or use a certain service (p. 43)

bracero A term used in 1942 to describe Mexican farm laborers brought to the United States (p. 625)

brinkmanship A 1956 term used by Secretary of State John Dulles to describe a policy of risking war in order to protect national interests (p. 660)

Brown v. Board of Education of Topeka, Kansas 1954 Supreme Court case in which racial segregation in public schools was outlawed (p. 699)

Bull Moose Party Nickname of the Progressive Party (p. 398)

Burma Road A 700-mile-long highway linking Burma (present-day Myanmar) to China (p. 584)

business cycle Periods in which a nation's economy grows, then contracts (p. 509)

buying on margin An option that allows investors to purchase a stock for only a fraction of its price and borrow the rest (p. 500)

C

Camp David Accords 1978 agreement between Israel and Egypt that made a peace treaty between the two nations possible (p. 855)

canister A special type of shell filled with bullets (p. 160)

capital Wealth that can be invested to produce goods and make money (p. 117)

carpet bombing Method of aerial bombing in which large numbers of bombs are dropped over a wide area (p. 605)

carpetbagger Negative nickname for a northern Republican who moved to the South after the Civil War (p. 211)

cartel Loose association of businesses that make the same product (p. 240)

cash and carry World War II policy requiring nations at war to pay cash for all nonmilitary goods and to be responsible for transporting the goods from the United States (p. 586)

casualty Military term for a person killed, wounded, captured, or missing in action (p. 158)

Central Powers In World War I, Germany and Austria-Hungary (p. 417)

charter Certificate of permission given by a government (p. 17)

checks and balances System in which each of the branches of the federal government can check the actions of the other branches (p. 59)

Chinese Exclusion Act Law passed in 1882 that prohibited Chinese laborers from entering the country, but did not prevent entry of those who had previously established U.S. residence (p. 302)

civil disobedience Nonviolent refusal to obey a law in an effort to change that law (p. 404)

civil rights Citizens' personal liberties guaranteed by law, such as voting rights and equal treatment (p. 207)

Civil Rights Act of 1964 Law that made discrimination illegal in a number of areas, including voting, schools, and jobs (p. 719)

civil service The government's nonelected workers (p. 292)

Civil War War between the Union states of the North and the Confederate states of the South; fought from 1861 to 1865 (p. 156)

Civilian Conservation Corps (CCC) Established by Congress in 1933, this program put more than 2.5 million young men to work restoring and maintaining forests, beaches, and parks (p. 539)

clan Groups of families who are all descended from a common ancestor (p. 5)

Clayton Antitrust Act Law passed in 1914 to strengthen the Sherman Antitrust Act of 1890; specified big business activities that were forbidden (p. 400)

Clean Air Act Law passed in 1970 that aimed to control pollution caused by industrial and auto emissions (p. 784)

Clean Water Act Law passed in 1972 that aimed to control pollution caused by the discharge of industrial and municipal wastewater, and provided for grants to build better sewage-treatment facilities (p. 784)

closed shop Workplace open only to union members (p. 543)

cloture (KLOH chur) In the Senate, a three-fifths vote to limit debate and call for a vote on an issue (p. 719)

coalition Alliance of groups with similar goals (p. 554)

Cold War The competition that developed after World War II between the United States and the Soviet Union for power and influence in the world, lasting until the collapse of the Soviet Union in 1991 (p. 640)

collaboration Close cooperation (p. 578)

collective bargaining Process in which workers negotiate as a group with employers (p. 249)

collective security The principle of mutual military assistance among nations (p. 647)

colony An area of land settled by immigrants who continue to be ruled by their parent country (p. 15)

Columbian Exchange The transatlantic trade of crops, technology, and culture between the Americas and Europe, Africa, and Asia that began in 1492 with Columbus's first voyage to the Americas (p. 11)

communism Official ideology of the Soviet Union, characterized there by complete government ownership of land and property, single-party control of the government, the lack of individual rights, and the call for worldwide revolution (p. 481)

Compromise of 1850 Agreement designed to ease tensions caused by the expansion of slavery into western territories (p. 138)

Compromise of 1877 Agreement in which Democrats agreed to give Rutherford B. Hayes the victory in the presidential election of 1876, and Hayes, in return, agreed to remove the remaining federal troops from southern states (p. 221)

compulsory Required (p. 374)

concentration camp A place where political prisoners are confined, usually under harsh conditions (p. 610)

concession A grant for a piece of land in exchange for a promise to use the land for a specific purpose (p. 366)

Confederate States of America Association of seven seceding southern states, formed in 1861 (p. 143)

conglomerate Corporation made up of three or more unrelated businesses (p. 669)

Congress of Racial Equality (CORE) Organization founded by pacifists in 1942 to promote racial equality through peaceful means (pp. 625, 705)

Congressional Union (CU) Radical organization formed in 1913 and led by Alice Paul that campaigned for a constitutional amendment guaranteeing women's suffrage (p. 406)

conquistador A Spanish conqueror (p. 15)

conscientious objector A person who opposes war on moral or religious grounds (p. 807)

conservationist A person who favors the protection of natural resources (p. 397)

consumer economy An economy that depends on a large amount of spending by consumers (p. 491)

containment American policy of resisting further expansion of communism around the world (p. 641)

Contra Spanish for "counterrevolutionary," a rebel opposed to Nicaragua's Communist government in the 1980s (p. 880)

contraband Items seized from the enemy during wartime (p. 172)

Contract with America Pledge, made by Republican candidates in the 1994 election campaign, to scale back government, eliminate some regulations, cut taxes, and balance the budget (p. 896)

convoy Group of unarmed ships surrounded by a ring of armed naval vessels (p. 426)

Copperhead During the Civil War, an antiwar Northern Democrat (p. 169)

cotton gin Machine that separates the seeds from raw cotton fiber (p. 112)

counterculture Group of young Americans in the 1960s who rejected conventional customs and mainstream culture (p. 777)

craft union A union for laborers devoted to a specific craft (p. 249)

Cross of Gold Speech William Jennings Bryan's 1896 address at the Democratic Convention; one of the most famous speeches in American history (p. 282)

Cuban Missile Crisis 1962 crisis that arose between the United States and the Soviet Union over a Soviet attempt to deploy nuclear missiles in Cuba (p. 754)

D

Dawes Act 1887 law that divided reservation land into private family plots (p. 266)

daylight savings time Turning clocks ahead by one hour for summer (p. 434)

D-Day Code name for the allied invasion of France on June 6, 1944 (p. 606)

death camp In World War II, a German camp created solely for the purpose of mass murder (p. 611)

Declaration of Independence 1776 statement, issued by the Second Continental Congress, explaining why the colonies wanted independence from Britain (p. 46)

de facto **segregation** Separation caused by social conditions such as poverty (p. 725)

deferment Official postponement, as in a postponement of compulsary military service (p. 808)

deficit spending Paying out more money from the annual federal budget than the government receives in revenues (pp. 550, 828)

deflation A drop in the prices of goods (p. 278)

de jure **segregation** Racial segregation created by law (p. 725)

demagogue (DEHM uh gawg) A leader who manipulates people with half-truths, deceptive promises and scare tactics (p. 548)

democracy Government by the people (p. 55)

demographics The statistics that describe a population, such as data on race or income (p. 454)

denomination A religious subgroup (p. 114)

department store Large retail establishment that carries a wide variety of goods and sells in large quantities (p. 338)

depression A severe economic downturn marked by a decrease in business activity, widespread unemployment, and falling prices and wages (p. 98)

deregulation The reduction or removal of government controls (p. 853)

détente A relaxation in political tensions between nations (p. 833)

deterrence The policy of making the military power of the United States and its allies so strong that no enemy would attack for fear of retaliation (p. 660)

direct primary Election in which all citizens vote to select nominees for upcoming elections (p. 392)

disarmament Program in which the nations of the world voluntarily give up their weapons (p. 486)

discrimination Unequal treatment of a group of people because of their nationality, race, sex, or religion (p. 133)

dissident A person who criticizes the actions of his or her government (p. 855)

division of labor Way of producing in which different tasks are performed by different persons (p. 245)

dollar diplomacy President Taft's policy of encouraging American investment in foreign economies (p. 370)

domino theory Belief that if one country fell to communism, neighboring countries would likewise fall (p. 792)

dove Nickname for a person who opposes war, as in the Vietnam War (p. 802)

Dow Jones Industrial Average Measure of average of stock prices of major industries (p. 508)

downsizing Laying off workers to cut costs (p. 887)

draft Required military service (p. 167)

dry farming Techniques used to raise crops in areas that receive little rain; water conservation techniques (p. 274)

dumbbell tenement A tenement building that narrowed in the middle, forming air shafts on either side and allowing light and air into the rooms (p. 307)

Dust Bowl Term used to describe the central and southern Great Plains in the 1930s, when the region sustained a period of drought and dust storms (p. 514)

E

economic sanctions Trade restrictions and other economic measures intended to punish another nation (p. 902)

economies of scale Phenomenon that as production increases, the cost of each item produced is often lowered (p. 241)

Emancipation Proclamation A presidential decree by President Lincoln, effective January 1, 1863, that freed slaves in Confederate-held territory (p. 171)

embargo A ban or a restriction on trade (pp. 95, 828)

Enforcement Act of 1870 Passed by Congress to ban the use of terror, force, or bribery to prevent people from voting because of their race (p. 219)

entitlement Government program that guarantees

payments to a particular group, such as the elderly (p. 881)

Environmental Protection Agency (EPA) Government organization formed in 1970 to set and enforce national pollution-control standards (p. 784)

Equal Rights Amendment Proposed constitutional amendment, never ratified, to prohibit discrimination on account of sex (p. 768)

escalation Expansion by stages, as from a local to a national conflict (p. 801)

Exoduster An African American who migrated to the West after the Civil War (p. 260)

F

fascism Political philosophy that emphasizes the importance of the nation or an ethnic group, and the supreme authority of the leader over that of the individual (p. 568)

Federal Reserve System The nation's central banking system, established in 1913 (p. 400)

federal system of government System in which power is shared among state and national authorities (p. 59)

Federal Trade Commission (FTC) 1914 commission established by President Wilson and Congress to enforce the Clayton Act and establish fair-trade laws (p. 400)

Federalists Supporters of the Constitution during the debate over its ratification; favored a strong national government (p. 61)

feminism Theory favoring the political, economic, and social equality of men and women (p. 764)

Fifteenth Amendment Constitutional amendment, ratified in 1870, that guaranteed voting rights to all male citizens (p. 210)

filibuster A tactic in which senators prevent a vote on a measure by taking the floor and refusing to stop talking (p. 719)

First Battle of Bull Run First major battle of the Civil War, won by the Confederates in July 1861 (p. 158)

First Continental Congress Assembly of representatives from the colonies that first met in Philadelphia in September 1774 (p. 44)

flapper A 1920s term used to describe a new type of young woman; rebellious, energetic, fun-loving, and bold (p. 452)

Fourteen Points President Wilson's proposal in 1918 for a postwar European peace (p. 437)

Fourteenth Amendment Constitutional amendment, ratified in 1868, to guarantee citizens equal protection under the law (p. 207)

fragmentation bomb A type of bomb that, upon explosion, causes pieces of its thick metal casings to be thrown in all directions (p. 801)

franchise A business that contracts with a large parent company to offer certain goods and services (p. 669)

free enterprise system Economic system characterized by private or corporate ownership of capital goods (p. 117)

free silver The unlimited coining of silver dollars (p. 279)

Freedmen's Bureau Created by Congress in 1865, the first major federal relief agency in the United States (p. 205)

Freedom Ride 1961 event organized by CORE and SNCC in which an interracial group of civil rights activists tested southern states' compliance to the Supreme Court ban of segregation on interstate buses (p. 710)

French and Indian War War from 1754 to 1763 between France, with allied Indian nations, and Britain and its colonists, for control of eastern North America (p. 41)

fundamentalism Set of religious beliefs including traditional Christian ideas about Jesus Christ, the belief that the Bible was inspired by God and does not contain contradictions or errors, and is literally true (p. 470)

G

generation gap A term used to describe the widening difference in values between a younger generation and their parents (p. 806)

Geneva Accords A 1954 international conference in which Vietnam was divided into two nations (p. 793)

Geneva Convention A set of international standards of conduct for treating prisoners of war, established in 1929 (p. 615)

genocide Organized killing of an entire people (p. 431)

Gentlemen's Agreement 1907 agreement between the United States and Japan that restricted Japanese immigration (p. 302)

Gettysburg Address A famous speech by President Lincoln on the meaning of the Civil War, given in November 1863 at the dedication of a national cemetery on the site of the Battle of Gettysburg (p. 185)

ghetto Area in which one ethnic or racial group dominates (p. 300)

Ghost Dance A Native American purification ritual (p. 265)

GI Term used for American soldiers in World War II, derived from the term "Government Issue" (p. 595)

GI Bill of Rights Law passed in 1944 to help returning veterans buy homes and pay for higher education (p. 672)

Gilded Age Term coined by Mark Twain to describe the post-Reconstruction era (p. 290)

graft Use of one's job to gain profit; a major source of income for political machines (p. 309)

grandfather clause Passage in a law that exempts a group of people from obeying the law if they had met certain conditions before the law was passed (p. 333)

Grange, the Established in 1867, this organization helped farmers form cooperatives and pressured state legislators to regulate businesses on which farmers depended (p. 280)

Great Awakening Religious revival in the American colonies during the 1730s and 1740s (p. 32)

Great Crash The collapse of the American stock market in 1929 (p. 509)

Great Depression The most severe economic downturn in the nation's history, which lasted from 1929 to 1941 (p. 511)

Great Plains Vast grassland between the Mississippi River and the Rocky Mountains (p. 261)

Great Society President Lyndon Johnson's proposals for aid to public education voting rights, conservation and beautification projects, medical care for the elderly, and elimination of poverty (p. 745)

Great White Fleet A force of United States Navy ships that undertook a world cruise in 1907 (p. 375)

Greater East Asia Co-Prosperity Sphere As announced in 1940 by Japan's prime minister, the area extending from Manchuria to the Dutch East Indies in which Japan would expand its influence (p. 584)

greenback Name given to the national paper currency created in 1862 (p. 169)

Gross National Product (GNP) Total annual value of goods and services a country produces (p. 493)

guerrilla (guh RIL uh) A soldier who uses surprise raids and hit-and-run tactics (p. 192)

Gulf of Tonkin Resolution 1964 Congressional resolution authorizing President Johnson to take military action in Vietnam (p. 796)

H

Harlem Renaissance African American literary awakening of the 1920s, centered in Harlem (p. 464)

hawk Nickname for a supporter of war, as in the Vietnam War (p. 802)

Hawley-Smoot tariff The highest import tax in history, passed by Congress in 1930 (p. 525)

Haymarket Riot 1886 labor-related violence in Chicago (p. 252)

Head Start A preschool program for children from low-income families that also provides healthcare, nutrition services, and social services (p. 746)

Helsinki Accords Series of agreements on European security made in 1975 (p. 850)

Ho Chi Minh Trail A supply route used to carry troops and supplies from North Vietnam to South Vietnam (p. 802)

holding company Firm that buys up stocks and bonds of smaller companies (p. 394)

Hollywood Ten Group of people in the film industry who were jailed for refusing to answer congressional questions regarding Communist influence in Hollywood (p. 650)

Holocaust Nazi Germany's systematic attempt to murder all European Jews (p. 609)

home rule System that gives cities a limited degree of self-rule (p. 390)

Homestead Act 1862 law that gave 160 acres of land to citizens who met certain conditions (p. 259)

Homestead Strike 1892 strike in Pennsylvania against Carnegie Steel (p. 252)

homesteader One who farmed claims under the Homestead Act (p. 272)

Hooverville Term used to describe a makeshift homeless shelter during the early years of the Great Depression (p. 514)

horizontal consolidation The process of bringing together many firms in the same business to form one large company (p. 241)

House Un-American Activities Committee (HUAC) Established in 1938 to investigate disloyalty in the United States (p. 650)

hundred days Period at the start of Franklin Roosevelt's presidency in 1933, when many New Deal programs were passed by Congress (p. 537)

I

ICBM Intercontinental ballistic missile (p. 661)

immigrant Person who enters a new country to settle (p. 31)

Immigration Act of 1965 Law that ended quotas for individual countries and replaced them with more flexible limits (p. 747)

impeach To charge a public official with wrongdoing in office (pp. 209, 843)

imperialism Policy by a stronger nation to attempt to create an empire by dominating weaker nations economically, politically, culturally, or militarily (p. 352)

incumbent Person currently in office (p. 851)

indentured servant A person who works for another person for a specified period of time, usually seven years, under a contract, in exchange for transportation, food, and shelter (p. 18)

Industrial Revolution Effort, beginning in Britain in the late 1700s, to increase production by using machines powered by sources other than humans or animals (p. 111)

industrial union Union that organizes workers from all crafts in a given industry (p. 251)

industrialization Growth of industry (p. 119)

INF Treaty Intermediate-Range Nuclear Forces, an agreement signed in 1987 by Ronald Reagan and Mikhail Gorbachev that provided for the destruction of about 2,500 Soviet and American missiles in Europe (p. 881)

infrastructure The public property and services that a society uses (p. 215)

initiative A process in which citizens can put a proposed new law directly on the ballot in the next election by collecting voters' signatures on a petition (p. 392)

injunction Court order prohibiting a certain activity (p. 385)

installment plan A payment plan that allows customers to make payments at set intervals over a period of time until the total debt is paid (p. 492)

integration Process of bringing people of different races together (p. 702)

interchangeable parts A system of manufacturing in which all parts are made to an exact standard for easy mass-assembly (p. 112)

interned Confined (p. 626)

Internet A computer network that links millions of people around the world (p. 913)

interracial Between, among, or involving people of different races (p. 705)

Interstate Commerce Act 1887 law passed to regulate railroad and other interstate businesses (p. 281)

Iran-Contra affair Scandal during the Reagan administration involving the use of money from secret Iranian arms sales to support the Nicaraguan Contras (p. 880)

iron curtain Term coined by Winston Churchill to describe the division between Communist and non-Communist life (p. 640)

island-hopping A military strategy used during World War II that involved selectively attacking specific enemy-held islands and bypassing others (p. 618)

isolationism Policy of avoiding political or economic alliances with foreign countries (p. 486)

J

Japanese American Citizens League (JACL) Organization of Japanese Americans working to promote the rights of Asian Americans (p. 774)

Jazz Age Term used to describe the 1920s (p. 462)

Jim Crow Statutes, beginning in the 1890s, that required segregation of public services by race (p. 333)

jingoism A feeling of strong national pride and a desire for an aggressive foreign policy (p. 359)

judicial review Power of federal courts to review state laws and state court decisions to determine if they are constitutional (p. 94)

K

kamikaze (kah mih KAH zee) In World War II, a Japanese suicide plane (p. 618)

Kansas-Nebraska Act 1854 law that called for the creation of these two new territories, and stated that the citizens in each territory should decide whether slavery would be allowed there (p. 139)

Kellogg-Briand Pact Agreement signed in 1928 in which nations agreed not to pose the threat of war against one another (p. 489)

Korean War Conflict over the future of the Korean peninsula, fought between 1950 and 1953 and ending in a stalemate (p. 654)

Kristallnacht The name given to the night of violence on November 9, 1938, when Nazi storm troopers looted and destroyed Jewish homes, businesses, and synagogues and arrested thousands of Jews in Germany and Austria (p. 610)

L

labor union Organization of workers formed to protect the interest of its members (p. 119)

laissez-faire (LES ay FAYR) Doctrine stating that government generally should not interfere in private business (p. 291)

land mine An explosive device planted in the ground (p. 800)

land speculator Person who buys up large areas of land in the hope of selling them later for a profit (p. 259)

Latino Person whose family origins are in Spanish-speaking Latin America (p. 771)

League of Nations International organization formed after World War I that aimed to ensure security and peace for all its members (p. 438)

Lend-Lease Act 1941 law that authorized the President to aid any nation whose defense he believed was vital to American security (p. 588)

Liberty Bond Special war bond sold by the government to support the Allied cause during World War I (p. 432)

Liberty ship A type of large, sturdy merchant ship built in World War II (p. 596)

Limited Test Ban Treaty 1963 treaty in which the United States and the Soviet Union agreed not to test nuclear weapons above the ground (p. 757)

literacy The ability to read and write (p. 321)

long drive Moving of cattle from distant ranges to busy railroad centers that shipped the cattle to market (p. 271)

loose construction Belief that the government can do anything that the Constitution does not prohibit (p. 90)

Lost Generation Group of writers in the 1920s who shared the belief that they were lost in a greedy, materialistic world that lacked moral values, and who often chose to flee to Europe (p. 464)

Louisiana Purchase Purchase by the United States of the Louisiana Territory from France in 1803 (p. 95)

lynching Murder of an accused person by a mob without a lawful trial (p. 334)

M

Magna Carta A "great charter" signed by King John in 1215 that granted certain rights to English nobles and became the foundation for future American ideals of liberty and justice (p. 7)

mail-order catalog Printed material advertising a wide range of goods that can be purchased by mail (p. 339)

Manchurian Incident Situation in 1931, when Japanese troops, claiming that Chinese soldiers had tried to blow up a railway line, took matters in their own hands by capturing several southern Manchurian cities and by continuing to take over the country even after Chinese troops had withdrawn (p. 582)

mandate A public endorsement, expressed to a candidate by voters (p. 737)

Manhattan Project Secret American program during World War II to develop an atomic bomb (p. 620)

manifest destiny Argument that it was the undeniable fate of the United States to expand across North America (p. 135)

manufacturing The making of goods by machinery (p. 116)

Marbury v. *Madison* 1803 Supreme Court case that established the principle of judicial review (p. 94)

March on Washington 1963 civil rights demonstration in Washington, D.C., in which protesters called for "jobs and freedom" (p. 717)

Market Revolution Shift from a home-based, often agricultural, economy to one based on money and the buying and selling of goods (p. 116)

Marshall Plan Program of American economic assistance to Western Europe, announced in 1947 (p. 645)

martial law Emergency rule by military authorities, during which some Bill of Rights guarantees are suspended (p. 170)

mass media Print and broadcast methods of communicating information to large numbers of people (p. 460)

mass production Production of goods in great amounts (p. 234)

Massacre at Wounded Knee 1890 shooting of a group of unarmed Sioux by army troops (p. 265)

Mayflower Compact Agreement in which settlers of Plymouth Colony agreed to obey their government's laws (p. 20)

McCarran-Walter Act Passed by Congress in 1952, this law reaffirmed the quota system that had been established for each country in 1924 (p. 651)

McCarthyism Term used to describe Senator Joseph McCarthy's anti-Communist smear tactics (p. 657)

Medicaid Federal program that provides low-cost health insurance to poor Americans of any age (p. 746)

Medicare Federal program that provides hospital and low-cost medical insurance to most Americans age 65 and older (p. 746)

mercantilism Economic theory that a country should try to get and keep as much bullion, or gold and silver, as possible, by exporting more goods than it imported (p. 25)

Mexican War Conflict between the United States and Mexico from 1846 to 1848, ending with a United States victory (p. 136)

MIA Missing in action (p. 816)

Middle America Term sometimes used to describe mainstream Americans (p. 811)

middle class A new class of merchants, traders, and artisans that arose in Europe in the late Middle Ages; in modern times, the social class between the very wealthy and the lower working class (p. 7)

Middle Passage One leg of the triangular trade; term also used to refer to the forced transport of slaves from Africa to the Americas (p. 28)

migrant farm worker Person who works long hours for low wages moving from farm to farm, often from state to state, to provide the labor needed to plant, cultivate, and harvest crops (p. 772)

migration Movement of people for the purpose of settling in a new place (p. 5)

militarism Policy of aggressively building up a nation's armed forces in preparation for war, as well as giving the military more authority over the government and foreign policy (p. 415)

military-industrial complex The military establishment as it developed links to the corporate and scientific communities, employing 3.5 million Americans by 1960 (p. 656)

Miranda rule Rule that police must inform persons accused of a crime of their legal rights (p. 748)

missionary A person sent out by his or her church to spread religion (p. 16)

Missouri Compromise 1820 agreement calling for the admission of Missouri as a slave state and Maine as a free state, and outlawing slavery in future states to be created north of 36° 30' N latitude (p. 98)

mobilization The readying of troops for war (p. 416)

Modern Republicanism President Eisenhower's approach to government, described as "conservative when it comes to money, liberal when it comes to human beings" (p. 685)

monarch One who rules over a territory, state, or kingdom (p. 7)

monetary policy The federal government's plan for the makeup and quantity of the nation's money supply (p. 278)

money supply The amount of money in the national economy (p. 278)

monopoly Complete control of a product or service (p. 240)

Monroe Doctrine Declaration by President Monroe in 1823 that the United States would oppose efforts by any outside power to control a nation in the Western Hemisphere (p. 121)

Montgomery bus boycott Protest in 1955–1956 by African Americans against racial segregation in the bus system of Montgomery, Alabama (p. 701)

Morrill Land-Grant Act Passed by Congress in 1862, this law distributed millions of acres of western lands to state governments in order to fund state agricultural colleges (p. 259)

muckraker Journalist who uncovers wrongdoing in politics or business (p. 384)

multiculturalism Movement calling for greater attention to non-European cultures in such areas as education (p. 914)

multinational corporation A corporation that operates in more than one country (p. 910)

municipal Relating to a city, as in municipal government (p. 390)

Munn v. Illinois 1877 Supreme Court decision that allowed states to regulate certain businesses within their borders (p. 294)

N

napalm (NAY pahm) Highly flammable chemical dropped from U.S. planes in firebombing attacks during the Vietnam War (p. 801)

Nation of Islam Organization, also called the Black Muslims, dedicated to black separation and self-help (p. 722)

National Aeronautics and Space Administration (NASA) Created in 1958 by the United States government as an independent agency for space exploration (p. 686)

National American Woman Suffrage Association (NAWSA) Organization formed in 1890 to continue the pursuit of women's rights, especially the right to vote (p. 405)

National Association for the Advancement of Colored People (NAACP) Organization founded in 1909 to abolish segregation and discrimination, to oppose racism, and to gain civil rights for African Americans (p. 335)

national debt Total amount of money that the federal government borrows and has to pay back (p. 554)

National Defense Education Act 1958 measure designed to improve science and mathematics instruction in schools (p. 686)

National Liberation Front Political arm of the Viet Cong (p. 795)

National Organization for Women (NOW) Organization formed in 1966 to promote the full participation of women in American society (p. 766)

nationalism Devotion to one's nation (p. 353)

nationalization Government takeover and ownership of banks, and the redistribution of their wealth (p. 548)

nativism A policy of favoring native-born Americans over immigrants (pp. 140, 314)

Nazism An extreme form of fascism shaped by Adolf Hitler's fanatical ideas about German nationalism and racial superiority (p. 571)

Neutrality Acts 1939 laws designed to keep the United States out of future wars (p. 586)

New Deal Term used to describe President Franklin Roosevelt's relief, recovery, and reform programs designed to combat the Great Depression (p. 537)

New Federalism President Nixon's call for a new partnership between the federal government and state governments; President Reagan's plan to cut back the role of the federal government while giving more responsibility to state and local governments (pp. 829, 873)

New Frontier President Kennedy's proposals to improve the economy, to assist the poor, and to advance the space program (p. 738)

New Left New political movement of the late 1960s that called for radical changes to fight poverty and racism (p. 806)

New Nationalism Theodore Roosevelt's plan for greater federal regulation of business and workplaces, income and inheritance taxes, and electoral reforms (p. 398)

New Right A political coalition of conservative groups formed in 1980 (p. 867)

Niagara Movement Founded in 1905, a group of African Americans that called for full civil liberties, an end to racial discrimination, and recognition of human brotherhood (p. 325)

Nisei (nee SAY) A Japanese American whose parents were born in Japan (p. 627)

nomadic People who move their homes regularly, usually in search of available food sources (pp. 5, 261)

nonviolent protest A peaceful way of protesting against restrictive policies (p. 706)

North American Free Trade Agreement (NAFTA) Agreement calling for the removal of trade restrictions among the United States, Canada, and Mexico (p. 915)

North Atlantic Treaty Organization (NATO) 1949 alliance of nations that agreed to band together in the event of war and to support and protect each nation involved (p. 647)

Nuclear Regulatory Commission (NRC) Government organization formed in 1974 to oversee the civilian uses of nuclear materials (p. 783)

nullify A state's rejection of a federal law (p. 123)

Nuremberg Trials Series of trials in 1945 conducted by an International Military Tribunal in which former Nazi leaders were charged with crimes against peace, crimes against humanity, and war crimes (p. 613)

O

Office of War Mobilization Federal agency formed to coordinate issues related to war production during World War II (p. 596)

oligopoly A market structure dominated by only a few large, profitable firms (p. 240)

Open Door Policy American approach to China around 1900, favoring open trade relations between China and other nations (p. 364)

Organization of Petroleum Exporting Countries (OPEC) Group of nations that work together to regulate the price and supply of oil (p. 828)

P

Pacific Railway Acts Laws passed in 1862 and 1864 giving large land grants to the Union Pacific and Central Pacific railroads (p. 259)

pardon An official forgiveness of a crime (p. 202)

Paris peace talks Negotiations between the United States and North Vietnam, beginning in 1968 (p. 812)

patent A license that gives an inventor the exclusive right to make, use, or sell an invention for a set period of time (p. 227)

patriotism Love of one's country; the passion which aims to serve one's country, either in defending it from invasion, or in protecting its rights and maintaining its laws and institutions in vigor and purity (p. 49)

Peace Corps Federal program established to send volunteers to help developing nations (p. 758)

Pendleton Civil Service Act 1883 law that created a Civil Service Commission and stated that federal employees could not be required to contribute to campaign funds or be fired for political reasons (p. 293)

penny auction Farm auctions during the Great Depression at which neighbors saved each other's property from foreclosure by bidding low (p. 521)

per capita income Average annual income per person (p. 668)

Persian Gulf War In 1991, a limited military operation to drive Iraqi forces out of Kuwait (p. 886)

philanthropist A person who gives donations to worthy causes (p. 323)

Pickett's Charge Unsuccessful charge by Confederate infantry during the Battle of Gettysburg (p. 182)

piecework System in which workers are paid not by the time worked, but by the number of items they produce (p. 244)

placer mining A mining technique in which miners shoveled loose dirt into boxes and then ran water over the dirt to separate it from gold or silver particles (p. 269)

plantation Large farm on which crops are raised mainly for sale (p. 12)

Platt Amendment An addition to the 1900 Cuban constitution by the American government that gave the United States the right to establish naval bases in Cuba and to intervene in Cuban affairs whenever necessary (p. 362)

Plessy v. Ferguson 1896 Supreme Court decision that segregation was legal as long as the separate facilities provided for blacks were equal to those provided to whites (p. 334)

pocket veto Type of veto a chief executive may use after a legislature has adjourned; it is applied when the chief executive does not formally sign or reject a bill within the time period allowed to do so (p. 203)

pogrom Violent massacre of Jews (p. 298)

political machine An unofficial city organization designed to keep a particular party or group in power and usually headed by a single, powerful boss (p. 308)

political party Group of people who seek to win elections and to hold public office in order to control government policies and programs (p. 91)

poll tax A special fee that must be paid before a person can vote (p. 333)

Populist Follower of the People's Party (or Populist Party) formed in 1891 to advocate a larger money supply and other economic reforms (p. 281)

POW Prisoner of war (p. 816)

prejudice An unreasonable, usually unfavorable opinion of another group that is not based on fact (p. 139)

price controls System of pricing determined by the government (p. 433)

productivity The amount of goods and services created in a given period of time (p. 227)

Progressive Era The period from about 1890 to 1920, during which a variety of reforms were enacted at the local, state, and federal levels (p. 383)

prohibition A ban on the manufacture and sale of alcoholic beverages (p. 314)

propaganda Information intended to sway public opinion (p. 418)

Proprietary colony A colony granted by a king or queen to an individual or a group who has full governing rights (p. 22)

public works program Government-funded projects to build public facilities (p. 538)

Pullman Strike 1894 railway workers' strike that spread nationwide (p. 253)

puppet state A supposedly independent country under the control of a powerful neighbor (p. 582)

purge In political terms, the process of removing enemies and undesirable individuals from power (p. 569)

Puritans People who favored the purification of England's Anglican Church (p. 19)

push-pull factors Events and conditions that either force (push) people to move elsewhere or strongly attract (pull) them to do so (p. 258)

Q

quarantine A time of isolation to prevent the spread of a disease (p. 299)

quota A numerical limit (p. 487)

R

racism Belief that differences in character or intelligence are due to one's race; asserting the superiority of one race over another or others (p. 373)

Radical Republicans Group of congressmen from within the Republican Party who believed that the Civil War had been fought over the moral issue of slavery, and insisted that the main goal of Reconstruction should be a total restructuring of society to guarantee blacks true equality (p. 203)

ragtime A type of music featuring melodies with shifting accents over a steady, marching-band beat that originated among black musicians in the South and Midwest in the 1880s (p. 331)

rationing Distribution of goods to consumers in a fixed amount (p. 434)

Reagan Democrat Democratic, blue-collar workers who tended to vote Republican during the 1980s (p. 867)

realpolitik (ray AHL poh lih teek) A German term meaning "practical politics," or foreign policy based on interests rather than moral principles (p. 832)

rebate A partial refund (p. 294)

recall Procedure that permits voters to remove public officials from office before the next election (p. 392)

recession A period of slow business activity (p. 554)

recognition Official acceptance as an independent nation (p. 168)

Reconstruction Program implemented by the federal government between 1865 and 1877 to repair the damage to the South caused by the Civil War and to restore the southern states to the Union (p. 200)

Reconstruction Finance Corporation (RFC) Corporation set up by President Hoover in 1932 to give government credit to a number of institutions, such as large industries and insurance companies (p. 525)

reconversion The social and economic transition from wartime to peacetime (p. 680)

Red Scare Intense fear of communism and other politically radical ideas (p. 482)

referendum Process that allows citizens to approve or reject a law passed by their legislature (p. 392)

religious tolerance Idea that people of different religions should live in peace together (p. 20)

reparations Payment from an enemy for economic injury suffered during a war (p. 439)

republic Government run by the people through their elected representatives (p. 55)

republican virtues Virtues the American people would need to govern themselves, such as self-reliance, industry, frugality, harmony, and the ability to sacrifice individual needs for the good of the community (p. 110)

reservation Federal land set aside for Native Americans (p. 262)

Resistance Movement in France that opposed German occupation during World War II (p. 578)

restrictive covenant Agreement among homeowners not to sell real estate to certain groups of people, such as Jews or African Americans (p. 301)

revenue Income (p. 554)

Revolutionary War American colonists' war of independence from Britain, fought from 1775 to 1783 (p. 45)

rock-and-roll Music popular in the 1950s that grew out of rhythm and blues (p. 678)

Roe v. *Wade* 1973 Supreme Court decision that legalized abortion (p. 768)

Roosevelt Corollary President Theodore Roosevelt's 1904 extension of the Monroe Doctrine in which he asserted the right of the United States to intervene in Latin American nations (p. 368)

rural free delivery (RFD) Beginning in 1896, free delivery offered by the U.S. Post Office to farm families in rural areas (p. 339)

Russian Revolution Collapse of the czar's government in Russia in 1917, after which the Russian monarchy was replaced with a republican government (p. 424)

S

SALT I Strategic Arms Limitation Treaty, a 1972 agreement between the United States and the Soviet Union on limiting nuclear weapons (p. 836)

Sandinista In the 1980s, a member of the ruling Marxist group in Nicaragua (p. 880)

satellite nation A country dominated politically and economically by another nation, especially by the Soviet Union during the Cold War (p. 639)

saturation bombing The dropping of a large concentration of bombs over a certain area (p. 801)

scab Negative term for a worker called in by an employer to replace striking laborers (p. 251)

scalawag Negative nickname for a white southern Republican after the Civil War (p. 211)

Scopes trial 1925 court case argued by Clarence Darrow and William Jennings Bryan in which the issue of teaching evolution in public schools was debated (p. 470)

secede To withdraw formally from membership in a group or organization (p. 123)

Second Great Awakening Religious movement of the early 1800s (p. 114)

Second New Deal Period of legislative activity launched by President Franklin Roosevelt in 1935 (p. 542)

sedition Any speech or action that encourages rebellion (p. 435)

segregation Forced separation, oftentimes by race (p. 333)

Selective Service Act Law passed in 1917 authorizing a draft of young men for military service in World War I (p. 425)

Selective Training and Service Act 1940 law requiring all males aged 21 to 36 to register for military service (p. 594)

self-determination The power to make decisions about one's own future (p. 437)

Seneca Falls Convention The first women's rights convention in United States history, held in 1848 (p. 132)

separation of powers The Constitutional allotting of powers within the federal government among the legislative, executive, and judicial branches (p. 59)

settlement house Community center organized to provide various services to the urban poor (p. 312)

sharecropping System of farming in which a farmer tends some portion of a planter's land and receives a share of the crop at harvest time as payment (p. 213)

shell Device that explodes in the air, or when it hits a solid target (p. 160)

Sherman Antitrust Act Law passed by Congress in 1890 that outlawed any combination of companies that restrained interstate trade or commerce (p. 242)

Sherman Silver Purchase Act Law passed by Congress in 1890 to increase the amount of silver the government was required to purchase every month (p. 279)

siege Tactic in which an enemy is surrounded and starved in order to make it surrender (p. 184)

silent majority Term used by President Nixon to describe Americans who opposed the counterculture (p. 814)

sit-down strike Labor protest in which laborers stop working but refuse to leave the workplace (p. 555)

sit-in Form of protest in which protesters seat themselves and refuse to move (p. 709)

social Darwinism Derived from Darwin's theory of natural selection, the belief that society should do as little as possible to interfere with people's pursuit of success (p. 239)

social gospel movement A social reform movement that developed within religious institutions and sought to apply the teachings of Jesus directly to society (p. 312)

Social Security System System established by the 1935 Social Security Act to provide financial security, in the form of regular payments, to people who cannot support themselves (p. 544)

social welfare program Program designed to ensure a basic standard of living for all citizens (p. 390)

socialism An economic and political philosophy that favors public (or social) instead of private control of property and income (p. 247)

sociology Term coined by philosopher Auguste Comte to describe the study of how people interact with one another in a society (p. 313)

soddie A home whose walls and roof are made from blocks of grass with the thick roots and earth attached (p. 273)

solid South Term used to describe the domination of post–Civil War southern politics by the Democratic Party (p. 220)

sooners In 1889, people who illegally claimed land by sneaking past government officials before the land races began (p. 267)

Southern Christian Leadership Conference (SCLC) Civil rights organization that advocated nonviolent protest; formed in 1957 by Dr. Martin Luther King, Jr., and other leaders (p. 706)

speakeasies Bars that operated illegally during the time of Prohibition (p. 468)

special prosecutor An attorney appointed by the Justice Department to investigate wrongdoing by government officials (p. 843)

speculation The practice of making high-risk investments in hopes of getting a huge return (p. 500)

sphere of influence Area of economic and political control exerted by one nation over another nation or other nations (p. 364)

spiritual A folk hymn (p. 115)

spoils Rewards gained through military victory (p. 438)

Sputnik The first artificial satellite to orbit Earth, launched by the Soviets in 1957 (p. 661)

stagflation Combination of high inflation and high unemployment, with no economic growth (p. 848)

stalemate Situation in which neither side in a conflict is able to gain the advantage (p. 417)

states' rights The powers that the Constitution neither gives to the federal government nor denies to the states (p. 123)

steerage A large open area beneath the ship's deck, often used to house traveling immigrants (p. 298)

stereotype An exaggerated or oversimplified description of reality held by a number of people (p. 275)

Strategic Arms Reduction Treaty Agreement signed in 1991 and known as START, that called for the reduction in the supplies of long-range nuclear weapons in Russia and the United States (p. 885)

Strategic Defense Initiative (SDI) President Reagan's proposed defense system against a Soviet missile attack, popularly known as "Star Wars" (p. 873)

strict construction Belief that the government should only use the implied powers of the Constitution when it is absolutely necessary (p. 90)

strike A work stoppage intended to force an employer to meet certain demands, as in the demand for higher wages (p. 119)

Student Nonviolent Coordinating Committee (SNCC) Founded in 1960, a student civil rights organization and an offshoot of the SCLC (p. 707)

subsidy A payment made by the government to encourage the development of certain key industries (p. 291)

suburb Residential community surrounding a city (p. 305)

suffrage The right to vote (p. 132)

supply-side economics Theory that tax reductions will increase investment and thereby encourage business growth (p. 871)

Sussex pledge Pledge by the German government in 1916 that its submarines would warn ships before attacking (p. 423)

sweatshop Factory where employees work long hours at low wages and under poor working conditions (p. 244)

T

Taft-Hartley Act Law passed by Congress in 1947 that allowed the President to declare an 80-day cooling-off period when strikes impacted industries that affected the national interest, and required strikers to return to work while the government conducted a study of the situation (p. 681)

teach-in Special session of lecture and discussion on a controversial topic that often occurred during the Vietnam War era (p. 807)

Teapot Dome scandal Scandal during the Harding administration involving the granting of oil drilling rights on government land in return for money (p. 488)

televangelism The use of television by evangelists to reach millions of people, especially for fund-raising (p. 868)

temperance movement An organized campaign to eliminate alcohol consumption (pp. 128, 314)

tenant farming System of farming in which a person rents land to farm from a planter (p. 214)

tenement A low-cost apartment building that often has poor standards of sanitation, safety, and comfort, and is designed to house as many families as possible (p. 306)

Tennessee Valley Authority (TVA) Federal project to provide inexpensive electric power, flood control, and recreational opportunities to the Tennessee River valley (p. 540)

Tet Offensive 1968 attack by Viet Cong and North Vietnamese forces throughout South Vietnam (p. 803)

Thirteenth Amendment Constitutional amendment, ratified in 1865, abolishing slavery (p. 190)

38th parallel Latitude line that divided North and South Korea at approximately the midpoint of the peninsula (p. 653)

totalitarian A government that exerts total control over the nation and citizens' lives (p. 568)

Trail of Tears The forced movement of Cherokees in 1838 to land west of the Mississippi River (p. 124)

transcendentalism Philosophical movement of the mid-1800s that emphasized spiritual discovery and insight rather than reason (p. 127)

transcontinental railroad Railway extending from coast to coast (p. 230)

transistor A tiny circuit device invented in 1947 that amplifies, controls, and generates electrical signals (p. 670)

triangular trade Trade between the Americas, Europe, and Africa (p. 27)

Truman Doctrine Harry Truman's 1947 speech before a joint session of Congress, calling for the United States to take a leadership role in the world, and declaring that the United States would support nations threatened by communism (p. 642)

trust A group of separate companies that are placed under the control of a single managing board (p. 242)

Turner thesis 1893 theory of Frederick Jackson Turner that claimed the frontier had played a key role in forming the American character (p. 275)

Twenty-first Amendment Constitutional amendment ratified in 1933 to repeal Prohibition (p. 522)

Twenty-fourth Amendment Constitutional amendment ratified in 1964 to outlaw the poll tax (p. 721)

U

U-boat A German submarine (p. 421)

U-2 incident A 1960 incident in which the Soviet military used a guided missile to shoot down an American U-2 spy plane over Soviet territory (p. 661)

Underground Railroad A network of escape routes that provided protection and transportation for slaves fleeing north to freedom (p. 130)

United Farm Workers (UFW) Union created by César Chávez to organize Mexican field hands in the West (p. 773)

United States Constitution Plan of government that describes the different parts of the government and their duties and powers, established in 1787 (p. 57)

utopian community A small society dedicated to perfection in social and political conditions (p. 129)

V

vaudeville A type of variety show that first appeared in the 1870s, often consisting of comic sketches, song-and-dance routines, and magic acts (p. 327)

Versailles Treaty 1919 treaty that ended World War I (p. 439)

vertical consolidation Process of gaining control of the many different businesses that make up all phases of a product's development (p. 241)

vice Immoral or corrupt behavior (p. 315)

victory garden A home vegetable garden created to boost food production during World War II (p. 599)

Viet Cong Communist guerrillas in South Vietnam (p. 795)

Vietminh Common name for the League for Independence of Vietnam (p. 792)

Vietnamization President Nixon's policy of replacing American military forces with those of South Vietnam (p. 813)

vigilante A citizen who takes the law into his or her own hands (p. 435)

Volunteers in Service to America (VISTA) Federal program to send volunteers to help people in poor communities (p. 746)

Voting Rights Act of 1965 Law aimed at reducing the barriers that prevented African Americans from voting, in part by increasing the federal government's authority to register voters (p. 721)

W

Wagner Act Law passed in 1935 that aided unions by legalizing collective bargaining and closed shops, and by establishing the National Labor Relations Board (p. 543)

Wannsee Conference 1942 conference in Germany concerning the plan to murder European Jews (p. 611)

war of attrition A type of war in which one side inflicts continuous losses on the other in order to wear down its strength (p. 159)

War of 1812 War between the United States and Great Britain (p. 96)

War Powers Act 1973 law limiting a President's ability to involve the United States in foreign conflicts without receiving a formal declaration of war from Congress (p. 849)

War Refugee Board (WRB) Federal agency created in 1944 to try to help people threatened with murder by the Nazis (p. 612)

Warren Commission Commission, headed by Chief Justice Earl Warren, that investigated the assassination of President Kennedy (p. 741)

Warsaw ghetto An area of Warsaw sealed off by the Nazis to confine the Jewish population, forcing them into poor, unsanitary conditions (p. 611)

Warsaw Pact Military alliance between the Soviet Union and nations of Eastern Europe, formed in 1955 (p. 648)

Watergate scandal Scandal involving illegal activities that led ultimately to the resignation of President Nixon in 1974 (p. 840)

welfare capitalism An approach to labor relations in which companies meet some of their workers' needs without prompting by unions, thus preventing strikes and keeping productivity high (p. 499)

Whitewater affair Charges that President Clinton had engaged in improper business transactions before becoming President (p. 898)

wiretap A listening device used to intercept telephone information (p. 839)

Woodstock festival 1969 music festival in upstate New York (p. 779)

World Trade Organization (WTO) International organization formed in 1995 to encourage the expansion of world trade (p. 915)

writ of *habeas corpus* Legal protection requiring that a court determine if a person is lawfully imprisoned (p. 171)

Y

yellow journalism Sensational news coverage, emphasizing crime and scandal (p. 329)

Z

zeppelin A German floating airship (p. 429)

Zimmermann note A telegram sent by Germany's foreign secretary in 1917 to Mexican officials proposing an alliance with Mexico and promising U.S. territory if Mexico declared war on the United States (p. 424)

Spanish Glossary

A

abolitionist movement/movimiento abolicionista
Movimiento para acabar con la esclavitud (pág. 129)

abstinence/abstinencia Acción de abstenerse de alguna
actividad, como consumir bebidas alcohólicas
(pág. 128)

Adams-Onís Treaty/Tratado Adams-Onís Tratado firmado en 1819 entre los Estados Unidos y España en
el que España le cedió la Florida a los Estados
Unidos; también se conoce como Tratado Transcontinental (pág. 109)

administration/administración Plazo para ejercer un
cargo; también se refiere al conjunto de miembros y
entidades de la rama ejecutiva (pág. 64)

affirmative action/discriminación positiva Política que
concede consideración especial a las mujeres y a los
miembros de grupos minoritarios para compensarlos
por discriminaciones pasadas (pág. 854)

Agent Orange/agente naranja Herbicida que se utilizó
como arma química durante la Guerra de Vietnam
para exterminar la vegetación y poner al descubierto
zonas enemigas ocultas (pág. 801)

**Agricultural Adjustment Administration (AAA)/
Administración de Ajuste Agrícola (AAA)** Se
estableció en 1933 para elevar los precios de los
productos agrícolas a través apoyo económico del
gobierno (pág. 540)

AIDS/SIDA Síndrome de inmunodeficiencia adquirida;
causado por un virus que ha matado a muchas
personas desde principios de la década de 1980
(pág. 878)

alien/extranjero Alguien que no es ciudadano (pág. 302)

Alliance for Progress/Alianza para el Progreso Propuesta del presidente Kennedy para la cooperación
entre las naciones del hemisferio occidental con el fin
de satisfacer las necesidades básicas de sus habitantes
(pág. 757)

Allies/aliados En la Primera Guerra Mundial: Rusia,
Francia, Serbia y Gran Bretaña; en la Segunda Guerra
Mundial: la alianza de Gran Bretaña, los Estados
Unidos de América, la Unión Soviética y otras
naciones (págs. 417, 578)

**America First Committee/Primer Comité
Estadounidense** Grupo formado en 1940 por aisla-
cionistas para bloquear la ayuda a Gran Bretaña
(pág. 587)

**American Expeditionary Force (AEF)/Cuerpo Expedi-
cionario Estadounidense (AEF)** Nombre que se le
dio a las tropas estadounidenses en Europa durante la
Primera Guerra Mundial (pág. 425)

**American Indian Movement (AIM)/Movimiento Indio
Estadounidense (AIM)** Organización formada en
1968 para ayudar a los indígenas (pág. 775)

**American Liberty League/Asociación para la Libertad
de los Estados Unidos** Organización fundada en
1934 en oposición al Nuevo Trato (pág. 547)

amnesty/amnistía Perdón general para ciertos crímenes
(pág. 854)

anarchist/anarquista Persona radical que se opone a todo
tipo de gobierno (pág. 251)

annex/anexar Incorporar o unir, refiriéndose al caso de la
unión de un territorio nuevo a un país determinado
(págs. 135, 353)

anti-Federalists/antifederalistas Personas que se oponían
a la Constitución durante el debate sobre la ratificación; en contra del concepto de un gobierno
nacional sólido (pág. 61)

anti-Semitism/antisemitismo Hostilidad o discriminación hacia los judíos (pág. 609)

apartheid/*apartheid* La discriminación sistemática de personas con diferentes antecedentes raciales (pág. 902)

appeasement/pacificación Política de aceptación de las
demandas de un competidor con el fin de preservar la
paz (pág. 573)

apportionment/distribución de las asignaciones
Distribución de escaños en un cuerpo legislativo
(pág. 748)

arbitration/arbitraje Conciliación de una disputa a través
de una persona o grupo de expertos que escuchan a
ambas partes y toman una decisión (pág. 358)

armistice/armisticio Cese al fuego o tregua (pág. 430)

arms race/carrera armamentista Competencia entre
naciones para obtener la superioridad de armamento
(pág. 660)

**Articles of Confederation/Artículos de la Confed-
eración** Plan que estableció en 1781 un gobierno
nacional limitado en los Estados Unidos; más tarde
fue reemplazado por la Constitución de los Estados
Unidos (pág. 55)

assembly line/línea de montaje Proceso de fabricación en
el cual cada trabajador realiza una tarea determinada
en la construcción del producto final (pág. 494)

assimilation/asimilación Proceso por el cual las personas
de una cultura se incorporan y se vuelven parte de
otra (págs. 266, 321)

Atlantic Charter/Carta del Atlántico Acuerdo firmado
en 1941 por el presidente Franklin Roosevelt y el
primer ministro Winston Churchill en el que se
resumen los objetivos de guerra de las dos naciones
(pág. 600)

autocrat/autócrata Mandatario con poder ilimitado
(pág. 424)

autonomy/autonomía Capacidad de un pueblo de gobernarse a sí mismo con respecto a asuntos locales
(pág. 775)

Axis Powers/Potencias del Eje En la Segunda Guerra
Mundial: Alemania, Italia y Japón (pág. 573)

B

baby boom/*baby boom* Aumento dramático en la tasa de natalidad, sobre todo en los años que siguieron a la Segunda Guerra Mundial (pág. 672)

balance of trade/balanza comercial Diferencia del valor entre las importaciones y las exportaciones (pág. 25)

banana republic/república bananera Término utilizado para describir a una nación centroamericana que esté dominada por los intereses financieros de los Estados Unidos (pág. 355)

barrio/barrio Un vecindario de hispanohablantes (págs. 455, 625)

barter/canjear Comerciar con productos o servicios sin utilizar dinero (pág. 6)

Bataan Death March/Marcha de la muerte de Bataán Marcha brutal de prisioneros norteamericanos y filipinos dirigida por soldados japoneses en 1942 (pág. 615)

Battle of Antietam/Batalla de Antietam Batalla de la Guerra Civil; ocurrió en Maryland en 1862 (pág. 165)

Battle of the Bulge/Batalla de las Ardenas Batalla de la Segunda Guerra Mundial en la que fuerzas alemanas lanzaron un contraataque final en el oeste (pág. 607)

Battle of Chancellorsville/Batalla de Chancellorsville Batalla de la Guerra Civil; tuvo lugar en Virginia, en 1863, y la ganó la Confederación (pág. 179)

Battle of Cold Harbor/Batalla de Cold Harbor Batalla de la Guerra Civil; ocurrió en 1864 en Virginia (pág. 187)

Battle of the Coral Sea/Batalla del Mar del Coral Batalla de la Segunda Guerra Mundial entre aviones norteamericanos y japoneses; tuvo lugar en 1942 (pág. 616)

Battle of Fredericksburg/Batalla de Fredericksburg Batalla de la Guerra Civil; ocurrió en Virginia, en 1862, y la ganó la Confederación (pág. 179)

Battle of Gettysburg/Batalla de Gettysburg Batalla de la Guerra Civil; tuvo lugar en Pennsylvania, en 1863, y la ganó la Unión; representó un momento crucial en la guerra (pág. 180)

Battle of Guadalcanal/Batalla de Guadalcanal Batalla de la Segunda Guerra Mundial que fue librada de 1942 a 1943 entre los Estados Unidos y Japón (pág. 617)

Battle of Iwo Jima/Batalla de Iwo Jima Batalla de la Segunda Guerra Mundial que ocurrió en 1945 entre los Estados Unidos y Japón (pág. 619)

Battle of Leyte Gulf/Batalla del Golfo Leyte Batalla naval de la Segunda Guerra Mundial librada en 1944 entre los Estados Unidos y Japón (pág. 618)

Battle of Little Bighorn/Batalla de Little Bighorn Victoria de la tribu Sioux sobre las tropas armadas dirigidas por George Custer; ocurrió en 1876 (pág. 265)

Battle of Midway/Batalla de Midway Batalla de la Segunda Guerra Mundial librada en 1942 entre los Estados Unidos y Japón; fue un momento crucial en la guerra en el Pacífico (pág. 617)

Battle of Okinawa/Batalla de Okinawa Batalla de la Segunda Guerra Mundial librada en 1945 entre los Estados Unidos y Japón (pág. 619)

Battle of Shiloh/Batalla de Shiloh Batalla de la Guerra Civil; tuvo lugar en Tennessee en 1862 (pág. 162)

Battle of Spotsylvania/Batalla de Spotsylvania Batalla de la Guerra Civil; ocurrió en 1864, en Virginia (pág. 187)

Battle of the Wilderness/Batalla de Wilderness Batalla de la Guerra Civil; tuvo lugar en Virginia, en 1864, y la ganó la Confederación (pág. 187)

Battles of Lexington and Concord/Batallas de Lexington y Concord Primeras batallas de la Guerra Revolucionaria que tuvieron lugar el 19 de abril de 1775 (pág. 45)

Bay of Pigs invasion/Invasión a la Bahía de Cochinos Invasión fallida a Cuba realizada por un grupo de fuerzas anticastristas en 1961 (pág. 752)

beatnik/*beatnik* Persona que, en la década de 1950 criticaba y consideraba a la sociedad estadounidense como indiferente y conformista (pág. 679)

Berlin airlift/puente aéreo de Berlín Operación en la que aviones norteamericanos e ingleses transportaron provisiones a Berlín Occidental durante un bloqueo soviético de 1948 a 1949 (pág. 647)

Berlin Wall/Muro de Berlín Barrera construida por el gobierno de Alemania Oriental para separar la zona comunista de Berlín de la no comunista (pág. 754)

Bessemer process/proceso Bessemer Proceso patentado en 1856 para elaborar acero de manera más eficiente (pág. 233)

bicentennial/bicentenario Fecha en que se cumplen 200 años de un acontecimiento (pág. 850)

bilingual education/educación bilingüe La enseñanza a los estudiantes en su lengua materna y en inglés (pág. 912)

Bill of Rights/Declaración de Derechos Las primeras diez enmiendas a la Constitución (pág. 62)

bimetallic standard/patrón bimetálico Moneda de los Estados Unidos, antes de 1873, que constaba de monedas de oro o de plata, así como de bonos fiscales que podían ser intercambiados por oro o plata (pág. 278)

black codes/*black codes* o códigos negros Leyes que restringían los derechos de los libertos (pág. 206)

black nationalism/nacionalismo negro Creencia en la identidad propia y la unidad racial de la comunidad estadounidense de raza negra (pág. 723)

black power/poder negro Movimiento estadounidense de raza negra que busca la unión y la independencia (pág. 724)

Black Tuesday/Martes Negro El 29 de octubre de 1929, día en que empezó la gran caída de la bolsa de valores (pág. 509)

blacklist/lista negra Lista que a principios de 1947 circulaba entre los empleadores y que contenía los nombres de las personas que no debían ser contratadas (pág. 650)

Bland-Allison Act/Ley de Bland-Allison Ley promulgada en 1878 que exigía al gobierno federal comprar y acuñar más plata, lo que aumentó la oferta monetaria y causó inflación (pág. 279)

blitzkrieg/blitzkrieg o Guerra Relámpago Tipo de guerra que enfatiza el movimiento rápido y mecanizado; utilizada por Alemania durante la Segunda Guerra Mundial (pág. 576)

blue law/leyes azules Reglamentos que prohibían ciertas actividades privadas que se consideraban inmorales, como ingerir bebidas alcohólicas los domingos (pág. 292)

bonanza farm/granja "la bonanza" Granja controlada por empresas grandes y manejada por profesionales, en la que se cultivan inmensas cantidades de cosechas que se venden al contado (pág. 274)

Bonus Army/Armados para la Bonificación Un grupo de veteranos de la Primera Guerra Mundial y sus familias que protestaron en Washington, D.C., en 1932, exigiendo el pago inmediato de la bonificación de retiro prometida en 1945 (pág. 526)

boomers/pioneros Colonos que corrían para ganar un pedazo de tierra cuando el territorio indio se abrió para la colonización, en 1889 (pág. 267)

bootlegger/contrabandista de licores Término para describir a un vendedor de alcohol ilegal durante el período de Prohibición (pág. 468)

Border States/Estados fronterizos En la Guerra Civil, los estados entre el norte y el sur: Delaware, Maryland, Kentucky y Missouri (pág. 142)

Boston Massacre/Masacre de Boston Incidente ocurrido el 5 de marzo de 1770 en el que los soldados británicos mataron a cinco colonos (pág. 43)

boycott/boicot Rechazo a comprar un producto determinado o utilizar un servicio determinado (pág. 43)

bracero/**bracero** Término utilizado en 1942 para describir a los campesinos mexicanos traídos a los Estados Unidos (pág. 625)

brinkmanship/brinkmanship Término utilizado en 1956 por el secretario de estado John Dulles para describir la habilidad de llegar al borde de una guerra sin participar en ella, con el fin de proteger los intereses nacionales (pág. 660)

Brown v. Board of Education of Topeka, Kansas/Brown **vs.** *la Junta de Educación de Topeka, Kansas* Caso de la Suprema Corte ocurrido en 1954 en el que se prohibió la discriminación racial en las escuelas públicas (pág. 699)

Bull Moose Party/Partido Bull Moose Sobrenombre del Partido Progresista (pág. 398)

Burma Road/Carretera Birmania Autopista de 700 millas de largo que une Birmania (hoy en día Myanmar) con China (pág. 584)

business cycle/ciclo comercial Períodos en los que la economía de una nación crece y luego disminuye (pág. 509)

buying on margin/compra de valores a crédito Opción que permite a los inversionistas adquirir al contado valores por tan sólo una parte de su precio y pedir un préstamo para el resto (pág. 500)

C

Camp David Accords/Acuerdos de Camp David Convenio firmado en 1978 entre Israel y Egipto que hizo posible un tratado de paz entre las dos naciones (pág. 855)

canister/bote de metralla Tipo especial de recipiente lleno de balas (pág. 160)

capital/capital Riqueza que se puede invertir para producir bienes y hacer dinero (pág. 117)

carpet bombing/bombardeo masivo Método de bombardeo aéreo en el que se arrojan muchas bombas sobre un área extensa (pág. 605)

carpetbagger/norteño en busca de dinero fácil Sobrenombre negativo para referirse a un republicano del norte que se iba al sur después de la Guerra Civil (pág. 211)

cartel/cartel Asociación eventual de empresas que elaboran el mismo producto (pág. 240)

cash and carry/pago al contado y transporte propio Política de la Segunda Guerra Mundial que exigía a las naciones en guerra pagar en efectivo todos aquellos productos que no fueran militares y encargarse de su transporte desde los Estados Unidos (pág. 586)

casualty/baja Término militar para una persona asesinada, herida, capturada o perdida en el campo de batalla (pág. 158)

Central Powers/potencias centrales En la Primera Guerra Mundial: Alemania y Austria-Hungría (pág. 417)

charter/carta Certificado de un permiso dado por el gobierno (pág. 17)

checks and balances/pesos y contrapesos Sistema en el que cada rama del gobierno federal revisa las acciones de las otras ramas (pág. 59)

Chinese Exclusion Act/Ley de Exclusión de los Chinos Ley aprobada en 1882 que prohibía a los trabajadores chinos entrar al país; sin embargo, no impedía la entrada a aquellos que habían establecido con anterioridad su residencia en los Estados Unidos (pág. 302)

civil disobedience/desobediencia civil Rechazo pacífico a obedecer una ley en un esfuerzo por cambiarla (pág. 404)

civil rights/derechos civiles Libertades individuales de los ciudadanos garantizadas por la ley, como el derecho al voto y el mismo trato a todos los habitantes (pág. 207)

Civil Rights Act of 1964/Ley de los Derechos Civiles de 1964 Ley que declaró ilegal la discriminación en un gran número de asuntos, tales como el voto, las escuelas y los empleos (pág. 719)

civil service/administración pública Los trabajadores del gobierno no elegidos (pág. 292)

Civil War/Guerra Civil Guerra entre los estados de la Unión del norte y los estados Confederados del sur que tuvo lugar de 1861 a 1865 (pág. 156)

Civilian Conservation Corps (CCC)/Asociación para la Conservación Civil (CCC) Este programa, establecido por el Congreso en 1933, puso a más de 2.5 millones de jóvenes a trabajar en la restauración y el mantenimiento de bosques, playas y parques (pág. 539)

clan/clan Grupos de familias que descienden de un antepasado común (pág. 5)

Clayton Antitrust Act/Ley Antimonopolista Clayton Ley aprobada en 1914 para fortalecer la Ley Antimonopolista Sherman de 1890; especificaba las actividades que estaban prohibidas en las grandes empresas (pág. 400)

Clean Air Act/Ley de Protección de la Calidad del Aire Ley aprobada en 1970 con el fin de controlar la contaminación causada por la emisión de gases de las industrias y los automóviles (pág. 784)

Clean Water Act/Ley de Protección de la Calidad del Agua Ley aprobada en 1972 con el fin de controlar la contaminación causada por la eliminación de aguas de desecho industriales y municipales, y de otorgar concesiones para construir mejores instalaciones para el tratamiento de aguas negras (pág. 784)

closed shop/obligación de reclutar trabajadores sindicados Lugar de trabajo abierto sólo a miembros del sindicato (pág. 543)

cloture/votación calificada para cerrar el debate En el Senado, el voto de las tres quintas partes para limitar el debate y pedir un voto para un asunto determinado (pág. 719)

coalition/coalición Alianza de grupos con metas similares (pág. 554)

Cold War/Guerra Fría La competencia que se desarrolló después de la Segunda Guerra Mundial entre los Estados Unidos y la Unión Soviética por el poder y la influencia en el mundo; duró hasta la caída de la Unión Soviética en 1991 (pág. 640)

collaboration/colaboración Cooperación cercana (pág. 578)

collective bargaining/acuerdo colectivo Procedimiento en el cual los trabajadores negocian como grupo con los patrones (pág. 249)

collective security/seguridad colectiva El principio de apoyo militar mutuo entre las naciones (pág. 647)

colony/colonia Un área de tierra poblada por inmigrantes que siguen siendo regidos por su país natal (pág. 15)

Columbian Exchange/intercambio colombino El comercio trasatlántico de cosechas, tecnología y cultura entre América y Europa, África y Asia; comenzó en 1492 con el primer viaje de Cristóbal Colón a América (pág. 11)

communism/comunismo Ideología oficial de la Unión Soviética, caracterizada por la posesión total de la tierra y las propiedades por parte del gobierno, el control del gobierno a través de un solo partido, la falta de derechos individuales y la exigencia de una revolución mundial (pág. 481)

Compromise of 1850/Acuerdo de 1850 Acuerdo diseñado para disminuir las tensiones de la expansión de la esclavitud en territorios occidentales (pág. 138)

Compromise of 1877/Acuerdo de 1877 Acuerdo en el que los demócratas acordaron otorgar a Rutherford B. Hayes la victoria en la elección presidencial de 1876, y en el que Hayes acordó, a su vez, retirar las tropas federales de los estados del sur (pág. 221)

compulsory/obligatorio Requerido (pág. 374)

concentration camp/campo de concentración Lugar donde se confinan prisioneros políticos, por lo general bajo condiciones muy severas (pág. 610)

concession/concesión La cesión de un pedazo de tierra a cambio de la promesa de utilizarla para un fin específico (pág. 366)

Confederate States of America/Estados Confederados de América Asociación de siete estados del sur formada en 1861 (pág. 143)

conglomerate/conglomerado Corporación formada por tres o más empresas que no se relacionan entre sí (pág. 669)

Congress of Racial Equality (CORE)/Congreso para la Igualdad Racial (CORE) Organización fundada por pacifistas en 1942 para promover la igualdad racial por medios pacíficos (págs. 625, 705)

Congressional Union (CU)/Unión Congresional (CU) Organización radical formada en 1913 y dirigida por Alice Paul, cuya campaña era en favor de una enmienda constitucional que garantizara el sufragio de las mujeres (pág. 406)

conquistador/conquistador Conquistador español (pág. 15)

conscientious objector/objetor de conciencia Persona que se opone a la guerra por motivos morales o religiosos (pág. 807)

conservationist/conservacionista Persona que apoya la protección de los recursos naturales (pág. 397)

consumer economy/economía de consumo Economía que depende de una gran cantidad de gastos por parte de los consumidores (pág. 491)

containment/contención Política estadounidense que se opone a una mayor expansión del comunismo en el mundo (pág. 641)

Contra/contra Término utilizado en español para referirse a un "contrarrevolucionario", o sea, un rebelde que se oponía al gobierno comunista de Nicaragua en la década de 1980 (pág. 880)

contraband/contrabando Artículos confiscados al enemigo durante el período de guerra (pág. 172)

Contract with America/Contrato con América Garantía ofrecida por los candidatos republicanos en la campaña electoral de 1994 de limitar el gobierno, eliminar algunas leyes, reducir impuestos y equilibrar el presupuesto (pág. 896)

convoy/convoy Grupo de barcos sin armas rodeados por un anillo de buques navales armados (pág. 426)

Copperhead/"cabeza de cobre" Apodo que se les daba durante la Guerra Civil a los demócratas pacifistas del norte (pág. 169)

cotton gin/despepitadora de algodón Máquina para separar las semillas de la fibra de algodón en bruto (pág. 112)

counterculture/contracultura Grupo de jóvenes estadounidenses que en la década de 1960 rechazaban las costumbres convencionales y la cultura tradicional (pág. 777)

craft union/gremio de artesanos Sindicato formado por trabajadores dedicados a un oficio específico (pág. 249)

Cross of Gold Speech/Discurso de la Cruz de Oro Discurso pronunciado en 1896 por William Jennings Bryan en la Asamblea Demócrata; uno de los discursos más famosos de la historia de los Estados Unidos (pág. 282)

Cuban Missile Crisis/crisis de los misiles cubanos Crisis que surgió en 1962 entre los Estados Unidos y la Unión Soviética a raíz de un intento soviético por desplegar misiles nucleares en Cuba (pág. 754)

D

Dawes Act/Ley de Dawes Ley promulgada en 1887 que dividió las reservaciones en lotes familiares privados (pág. 266)

daylight savings time/horario de verano Horario en el que se adelantan los relojes una hora durante el verano (pág. 434)

D-Day/Día D Nombre en clave para referirse a la invasión de los aliados a Francia el 6 de junio de 1944 (pág. 606)

death camp/campo de la muerte Campo alemán creado durante la Segunda Guerra Mundial con el único propósito del asesinato en masa (pág. 611)

Declaration of Independence/Declaración de la Independencia Declaración promulgada en 1776 por el Segundo Congreso Continental, que explica por qué las colonias querían independizarse de Gran Bretaña (pág. 46)

de facto segregation/segregación de facto o de hecho Separación causada por condiciones sociales como la pobreza (pág. 725)

deferment/postergación Aplazamiento oficial de un evento, como el servicio militar (pág. 808)

deficit spending/gastos en exceso de los ingresos Cuando se gasta más dinero del presupuesto federal anual en comparación con los ingresos que recibe el gobierno (págs. 550, 828)

deflation/deflación Caída de los precios de los productos (pág. 278)

de jure segregation/segregación de jure o de ley Segregación racial creada por ley (pág. 725)

demagogue/demagogo Líder que manipula a las personas con verdades a medias, falsas promesas y tácticas de intimidación (pág. 548)

democracy/democracia Forma de gobierno en que la autoridad reside en el pueblo (pág. 55)

demographics/estadísticas demográficas Estadísticas que describen una población, como los datos sobre la raza o los ingresos (pág. 454)

denomination/grupo religioso Un subgrupo religioso generalmente mayor que una secta (pág. 114)

department store/tienda por departamentos Establecimiento grande que vende al menudeo, ofrece una amplia variedad de productos y vende en grandes cantidades (pág. 338)

depression/depresión Una baja severa en la economía marcada por la disminución en la actividad empresarial, el desempleo general y la caída de precios y salarios (pág. 98)

deregulation/desregulación La reducción o revocación del control del gobierno (pág. 853)

détente/distensión Moderación de las tensiones políticas entre las naciones (pág. 833)

deterrence/disuasión Política de fortalecer el poder militar de los Estados Unidos y de sus aliados a tal grado que el enemigo desista por temor a las represalias (pág. 660)

direct primary/elección primaria directa Elección en la que todos los ciudadanos votan para elegir a los candidatos para las próximas elecciones (pág. 392)

disarmament/desarme Programa en el que las naciones del mundo entregan voluntariamente sus armas (pág. 486)

discrimination/discriminación Trato desigual a un grupo de personas debido a su nacionalidad, raza, sexo o religión (pág. 133)

dissident/disidente Persona que critica las acciones del gobierno (pág. 855)

division of labor/distribución del trabajo Forma de producción en la que diferentes personas realizan diferentes tareas (pág. 245)

dollar diplomacy/diplomacia del dólar Política establecida por el presidente Taft que consiste en estimular la inversión estadounidense en economías extranjeras (pág. 370)

domino theory/teoría del dominó Creencia de que si un país cae en manos del comunismo, los países vecinos también lo hacen (pág. 792)

dove/paloma Sobrenombre para una persona que se opone a la guerra, como en el caso de quienes se oponían a la Guerra de Vietnam (pág. 802)

Dow Jones Industrial Average/promedio industrial Dow Jones Medida promedio de los precios de las acciones de las principales industrias (pág. 508)

downsizing/reducción de personal Despido de empleados para reducir costos (pág. 887)

draft/reclutamiento Servicio militar obligatorio (pág. 167)

dry farming/cultivo seco Técnicas utilizadas para cultivar productos en áreas con poca lluvia; técnicas de conservación del agua (pág. 274)

dumbbell tenement/*dumbbell tenement* Construcción formada por dos edificios cuya separación es muy angosta, lo que produce corrientes de aire en cada lado y permite que entre luz y aire en las habitaciones (pág. 307)

Dust Bowl/tazón de polvo, el Término que describía las grandes praderas del centro y del sur de los Estados Unidos en la década de 1930, cuando la región sufrió un período de sequía y tolvaneras (pág. 514)

E

economic sanctions/sanciones económicas Restricciones comerciales y otras medidas económicas planeadas para castigar a otra nación (pág. 902)

economies of scale/economías de escala Fenómeno en que a medida que aumenta la producción, el costo de cada artículo producido generalmente disminuye (pág. 241)

Emancipation Proclamation/Proclamación de la Emancipación Decreto presidencial del presidente Lincoln que empezó a regir el 1 de enero de 1863, en el que se liberaba a los esclavos del territorio que estaba bajo el poder de los confederados (pág. 171)

embargo/embargo Prohibición o restricción en el comercio (págs. 95, 828)

Enforcement Act of 1870/Ley Contra la Coacción de 1870 Ley aprobada por el Congreso en la que se prohíbe el uso del terror, la fuerza o el soborno para impedir que las personas voten debido a su raza (pág. 219)

entitlement/programa de ayuda social Programa gubernamental que garantiza un pago a un grupo social determinado, por ejemplo, a las personas de la tercera edad (pág. 881)

Environmental Protection Agency (EPA)/Agencia para la Protección Ambiental (EPA) Organización gubernamental formada en 1970 para establecer y hacer cumplir los estándares nacionales de control de contaminantes (pág. 784)

Equal Rights Amendment/Enmienda para la Igualdad de Derechos Enmienda constitucional propuesta, que nunca se ratificó, en la que se prohíbe la discriminación de las personas a causa de su sexo (pág. 768)

escalation/escalamiento Expansión por etapas, por ejemplo, de un conflicto local a uno nacional (pág. 801)

Exoduster/*exoduster* Estadounidense de raza negra que emigró al Oeste después de la Guerra Civil (pág. 260)

F

facism/fascismo Filosofía política que enfatiza la importancia de una nación o grupo étnico, así como la autoridad suprema del líder sobre la del individuo (pág. 568)

Federal Reserve System/sistema de la reserva federal El sistema bancario central de la nación, establecido en 1913 (pág. 400)

federal system of government/sistema federal de gobierno Sistema en el que las autoridades nacionales y estatales comparten el poder (pág. 59)

Federal Trade Commission (FTC)/Comisión Federal de Comercio (FTC) Comisión establecida en 1914 por el presidente Wilson y el Congreso para hacer cumplir el Ley Clayton y establecer leyes para un comercio recíproco (pág. 400)

Federalists/federalistas Partidarios de la Constitución durante el debate sobre su ratificación; en favor de un gobierno nacional sólido (pág. 61)

feminism/feminismo Teoría que apoya la igualdad política, económica y social entre hombres y mujeres (pág. 764)

Fifteenth Amendment/Decimoquinta enmienda Enmienda constitucional, ratificada en 1870, que garantiza a todos los ciudadanos el derecho al voto (pág. 210)

filibuster/obstruccionismo Táctica en la que los senadores obstruyen un voto al tomar la palabra y prolongar excesivamente su discurso (pág. 719)

First Battle of Bull Run/Primera Batalla de Bull Run Primera y más grande batalla de la Guerra Civil, en la que triunfaron los Confederados en julio de 1861 (pág. 158)

First Continental Congress/Primer Congreso Continental Asamblea de representantes de las colonias que se reunieron por primera vez en Filadelfia en septiembre de 1774 (pág. 44)

flapper/*flapper* Término utilizado en la década de 1920 para describir a un nuevo tipo de jovencita; rebelde, llena de energía, amante de las diversiones y atrevida (pág. 452)

Fourteen Points/Propuesta de los Catorce Puntos Propuesta del presidente Wilson en 1918 para lograr la paz europea durante la posguerra (pág. 437)

Fourteenth Amendment/Decimocuarta enmienda Enmienda constitucional, ratificada en 1868, para garantizar a los ciudadanos igualdad en la protección otorgada por la ley (pág. 207)

fragmentation bomb/bomba de fragmentación Un tipo de bomba que al explotar lanza en todas direcciones los fragmentos de su cubierta metálica (pág. 801)

franchise/franquicia Empresa que firma un contrato con una compañía más grande para ofrecer algunos bienes y servicios (pág. 669)

free enterprise system/sistema de libre empresa Sistema económico caracterizado por la propiedad privada o empresarial de los elementos utilizados en la producción (pág. 117)

free silver/acuñación libre de plata Acuñación ilimitada de dólares de plata (pág. 279)

Freedmen's Bureau/Agencia de libertos Primera organización principal de auxilio federal de los Estados Unidos, creada por el Congreso en 1865 (pág. 205)

Freedom Ride/Paseo de la Libertad Evento organizado en 1961 por el CORE y el SNCC, en el que un grupo interracial de activistas de los derechos civiles puso a prueba el acatamiento de los estados del sur a la prohibición de la segregación racial en autobuses interestatales, dictada por la Corte Suprema (pág. 710)

French and Indian War/Guerra francesa e indígena Guerra que tuvo lugar de 1754 a 1763 entre Francia, las naciones indias aliadas, y Gran Bretaña y sus colonizadores, por el control del este de Norteamérica (pág. 41)

fundamentalism/fundamentalismo Conjunto de creencias religiosas, entre ellas, las ideas cristianas tradicionales sobre Jesucristo, la creencia de que la Biblia fue inspirada por Dios y carece de contradicciones o errores y es literalmente verdadera (pág. 470)

G

generation gap/brecha generacional Término que describe la gran diferencia entre los valores de una generación más joven y la de sus padres (pág. 806)

Geneva Accords/Acuerdos de Ginebra Conferencia internacional que tuvo lugar en 1954 y en la que se dividió a Vietnam en dos naciones (pág. 793)

Geneva Convention/Convención de Ginebra Conjunto de normas de conducta internacionales para el trato de los prisioneros de guerra, establecidas en 1929 (pág. 615)

genocide/genocidio Matanza organizada de un pueblo entero (pág. 431)

Gentlemen's Agreement/Pacto de los caballeros Acuerdo firmado en 1907 entre los Estados Unidos y Japón para resstringir la inmigración japonesa (pág. 302)

Gettysburg Address/Discurso de Gettysburg Un discurso famoso que dio el presidente Lincoln en noviembre de 1863 sobre el significado de la Guerra Civil, durante la dedicatoria de un cementerio nacional en la zona donde se libró la Batalla de Gettysburg (pág. 185)

ghetto/*ghetto* Área en la que domina un grupo étnico o racial (pág. 300)

Ghost Dance/Danza de los espíritus Un ritual de purificación realizado por los indígenas estadounidenses (pág. 265)

GI/soldado de infantería Término utilizado para describir a los soldados estadounidenses en la Segunda Guerra Mundial, se deriva del término "Asunto gubernamental" (pág. 595)

GI Bill of Rights/Declaración de los Derechos de los Soldados de Infantería Ley aprobada en 1944 que ayudaba a los veteranos que regresaban a adquirir una casa y costear su educación superior (pág. 672)

Gilded Age/Edad Dorada Término acuñado por Mark Twain para describir la era posterior a la reconstrucción (pág. 290)

graft/corrupción Utilizar el empleo para obtener una ganancia; una de las principales fuentes de ingreso para los aparatos políticos (pág. 309)

grandfather clause/cláusula del abuelo Pasaje que exime a un grupo de personas de obedecer una ley si reunen ciertas condiciones antes de la aprobación de la misma (pág. 333)

Grange, the/ Granja, la Organización establecida en 1867 y también conocida como los Mecenas de la Agricultura; ayudaba a los granjeros a formar cooperativas y presionaba a los legisladores del estado para que regularan las empresas de las que dependían estos campesinos (pág. 280)

Great Awakening/Gran Despertar, el Renacimiento religioso de las colonias norteamericanas durante la década de 1730 y 1740 (pág. 32)

Great Crash/Gran *Crash*, el El derrumbe de la bolsa de valores estadounidense que tuvo lugar en 1929 (pág. 509)

Great Depression/Gran Depresión, la La baja económica más severa en la historia de la nación; duró de 1929 a 1941 (pág. 511)

Great Plains/ Grandes Llanuras, las Llanura de gran tamaño entre el río Mississippi y las montañas Rocosas (pág. 261)

Great Society/Gran Sociedad, la Propuestas del presidente Lyndon Johnson para el apoyo a la educación, el derecho al voto, los proyectos de conservación y embellecimiento, la atención médica para las personas de la tercera edad y la eliminación de la pobreza (pág. 745)

Great White Fleet/Gran Flota Blanca, la Un grupo de barcos de la Marina de los Estados Unidos que realizó una excursión por todo el mundo en 1907 (pág. 375)

Greater East Asia Co-Prosperity Sphere/esfera de prosperidad de Asia Oriental Proclamada en 1940 por el ministro de Japón; área que se extendía de Manchuria a las Indias Orientales Holandesas en las que Japón extendería su influencia (pág. 584)

greenback/papel moneda Nombre que se le da al dinero en forma de billetes creado en 1862 (pág. 169)

Gross National Product (GNP)/Producto Nacional Bruto (GNP) Valor anual total de los bienes y servicios que produce un país (pág. 493)

guerrilla/guerrillero Soldado que utiliza ataques sorpresivos y tácticas que consisten en atacar y huir (pág. 192)

Gulf of Tonkin Resolution/Acuerdo del golfo de Tonkín Resolución del Congreso autorizada en 1964 por el presidente Johnson para emprender una acción militar en Vietnam (pág. 796)

H

Harlem Renaissance/Renacimiento de Harlem Despertar literario estadounidense de raza negra durante la década de 1920, centrado en Harlem (pág. 464)

hawk/halcón Sobrenombre para un partidario de la guerra, como en el caso de los partidarios de la Guerra de Vietnam (pág. 802)

Hawley-Smoot tariff/tarifa Hawley-Smoot El impuesto de importación más alto de la historia, aprobado por el Congreso en 1930 (pág. 525)

Haymarket Riot/disturbios de Haymarket Trifulca laboral violenta que ocurrió en Chicago en 1886 (pág. 252)

Head Start/*Head Start* Un programa preescolar para niños de familias de escasos recursos que también proporciona servicios sociales, de salud y de nutrición (pág. 746)

Helsinki Accords/Acuerdos de Helsinki Serie de acuerdos sobre la seguridad europea firmados en 1975 (pág. 850)

Ho Chi Minh Trail/Sendero de Ho Chi Minh Ruta de abastecimiento que transportaba tropas y provisiones de Vietnam del Norte a Vietnam del Sur (pág. 802)

holding company/compañía tenedora Empresa que compra acciones y títulos de compañías más pequeñas (pág. 394)

Hollywood Ten/el grupo de los diez de Hollywood Grupo de personas de la industria del cine que fueron encarceladas por negarse a responder preguntas del Congreso relacionadas con la influencia comunista en Hollywood (pág. 650)

Holocaust/Holocausto Intento sistemático de la Alemania Nazi de asesinar a todos los judíos europeos (pág. 609)

home rule/autonomía Sistema que le da a las ciudades un grado limitado de gobierno autónomo (pág. 390)

Homestead Act/Ley de Posesión de Tierras Ley promulgada en 1862 que otorgaba 160 acres de tierra a los ciudadanos que reunían ciertas condiciones (pág. 259)

Homestead Strike/Huelga por la Posesión de Tierras Huelga que tuvo lugar en 1892 en Pennsylvania en contra de Carnegie Steel (pág. 252)

homesteader/colono Persona que tramitaba los títulos bajo la ley de posesión de tierras (pág. 272)

Hooverville/*Hooverville* Término que describía un albergue temporal para personas sin hogar durante los primeros años de la Gran Depresión (pág. 514)

horizontal consolidation/integración horizontal El proceso de reunir muchas compañías dentro de la misma empresa para formar una compañía grande (pág. 241)

House Un-American Activities Committee (HUAC)/Comité del Congreso para la Investigación de Actividades Antiestadounidenses (HUAC) Establecido en 1938 para investigar acciones desleales en los Estados Unidos (pág. 650)

hundred days/Cien Días, los Período inicial de la presidencia de Franklin Roosevelt, en 1933, cuando el Congreso aprobó muchos programas del Nuevo Trato (pág. 537)

I

ICBM/ICBM Misil balístico intercontinental (pág. 661)

immigrant/inmigrante Persona que ingresa a un nuevo país para establecerse (pág. 31)

Immigration Act of 1965/Ley de Inmigración de 1965 Ley que eliminó el número fijo de inmigrantes que se podían admitir en los Estados Unidos, provenientes de diferentes países, y los reemplazó con límites más flexibles (pág. 747)

impeach/incapacitación (presidencial) Someter a un funcionario público (generalmente el presidente) a un proceso de incapacitación por un mal desempeño de sus funciones (págs. 209, 843)

imperialism/imperialismo Política practicada por una nación más fuerte en un intento de crear un imperio mediante el dominio económico, político, cultural o militar de las naciones más débiles (pág. 352)

incumbent/titular Funcionario público actual (pág. 851)

indentured servant/siervo obligado por contrato Alguien que trabaja para otra persona por contrato durante un período de tiempo específico, por lo general siete años, a cambio de transporte, alimento y un lugar donde vivir (pág. 18)

Industrial Revolution/Revolución Industrial Esfuerzo que se inició en Gran Bretaña a finales de la década de 1700 para aumentar la producción utilizando máquinas que funcionaban por medios distintos a la fuerza humana o animal (pág. 111)

industrial union/sindicato industrial Sindicato que organiza a los trabajadores de todos los oficios en una industria determinada (pág. 251)

industrialization/industrialización Crecimiento de la industria (pág. 119)

INF Treaty/Tratado INF Acuerdo firmado en 1987 por Ronald Reagan y Mikhail Gorbachev que tenía como objetivo la destrucción de aproximadamente 2,500 misiles soviéticos y estadounidenses en Europa (pág. 881)

infrastructure/infraestructura La propiedad pública y los servicios que utiliza una sociedad (pág. 215)

initiative/iniciativa Procedimiento por el cual los ciudadanos pueden someter un ley directamente a votaciòn por elevar una petición pública (pág. 392)

injunction/interdicción Orden judicial que prohíbe la realización de una actividad determinada (pág. 385)

installment plan/pago a plazos Plan de pago a plazos que permite a los clientes realizar pagos en intervalos establecidos durante un período de tiempo hasta cubrir la deuda total (pág. 492)

integration/integración Proceso que reúne a personas de diferentes razas (pág. 702)

interchangeable parts/sistema de partes intercambiables Un sistema de fabricación en el que todas las partes están hechas de acuerdo con un patrón para facilitar el montaje en masa. (pág. 112)

interned/confinado Encerrado (pág. 626)

Internet/Internet Red de computadoras que une a millones de personas alrededor del mundo (pág. 913)

interracial/interracial Que comprende personas de diferentes razas o su participación (pág. 705)

Interstate Commerce Act/Ley de Comercio Interestatal Ley aprobada en 1887 para regular la empresa ferroviaria y otras empresas interestatales (pág. 281)

Iran-contra affair/caso Irán-contras Escándalo durante la administración de Reagan por el uso de dinero obtenido de la venta secreta de armas iraníes para apoyar a los contras nicaragüenses (pág. 880)

iron curtain/cortina de hierro Término acuñado por Winston Churchill para describir la división entre la vida comunista y la no comunista (pág. 640)

island-hopping/estrategia de isla a isla Estrategia militar utilizada durante la Segunda Guerra Mundial que consistía en atacar selectivamente ciertas islas bajo el dominio del enemigo y pasar por alto las demás (pág. 618)

isolationism/aislacionismo Política que consiste en evitar alianzas políticas o económicas con otros países (pág. 486)

J

Japanese American Citizen League (JACL)/Asociación de Ciudadanos Estadounidenses de Origen Japonés (JACL) Organización de estadounidenses de origen japonés que trabajan para promover los derechos de los estadounidenses de origen asiático (pág. 774)

Jazz Age/Época del *jazz* Término para describir la década de 1920 (pág. 462)

Jim Crow/*Jim Crow* Estatutos que, a principios de la década de 1890, exigían la segregación racial en la prestación de los servicios públicos (pág. 333)

jingoism/jingoísmo Sentimiento de orgullo nacional arraigado y deseo de tener una política exterior agresiva (pág. 359)

judicial review/revisión judicial Poder de las cortes federales para revisar las leyes estatales y las decisiones de la corte federal con el fin de determinar si son constitucionales (pág. 94)

K

kamikaze/kamikaze Avión suicida japonés en la Segunda Guerra Mundial (pág. 618)

Kansas-Nebraska Act/Ley Kansas-Nebraska Ley promulgada en 1854 que exigía la creación de estos dos territorios nuevos y les pedía a los ciudadanos que decidieran sobre la esclavitud en su territorio (pág. 139)

Kellogg-Briand Pact/Pacto Kellogg-Briand Acuerdo firmado en 1928 en el que las naciones acordaron no representar una amenaza de guerra entre ellas (pág. 489)

Korean War /Guerra Coreana Conflicto sobre el futuro de la peninsula coreana, luchado entre 1950 y 1953, que llegó a punto muerto (pág. 654)

Kristallnacht/ Kristallnacht Nombre que se le da a la noche violenta del 9 de noviembre de 1938 en Alemania y Austria, cuando milicianos nazis saquearon y atacaron hogares, negocios y sinagogas judías, además de arrestar a miles de judíos (pág. 610)

L

labor union/sindicato laboral Organización de trabajadores formada para proteger los intereses de sus miembros (pág. 119)

laissez-faire/laissez-faire Doctrina que establece que, por lo general, el gobierno no debe interferir en las empresas privadas (pág. 291)

land mine/mina terrestre Dispositivo explosivo enterrado en el suelo (pág. 800)

land speculator/especulador de tierras Persona que compra grandes áreas de tierra con la esperanza de venderlas para obtener una ganancia (pág. 259)

Latino/latino Persona cuyo origen familiar está en la América Latina hispanohablante (pág. 771)

League of Nations/Liga de las Naciones Organización internacional formada después de la Primera Guerra Mundial, cuyo objetivo es asegurar la seguridad y la paz de todos sus miembros (pág. 438)

Lend-Lease Act/Ley de Préstamos y Arriendos Ley promulgada en 1941 que autorizó al Presidente a apoyar a cualquier nación cuya defensa considerara vital para la seguridad de los Estados Unidos (pág. 588)

Liberty Bond/Garantía de libertad Garantía especial de guerra concedida por el gobierno para apoyar la causa de los aliados durante la Primera Guerra Mundial (pág. 432)

Liberty ship/buque "Liberty" Un tipo de barco mercante, grande y fuerte, construido en la Segunda Guerra Mundial (pág. 596)

Limited Test Ban Treaty/Tratado de Prohibición Limitada de Pruebas Nucleares Tratado firmado en 1963, en el que los Estados Unidos y la Unión Soviética acordaron abstenerse de realizar pruebas con armas nucleares en tierra (pág. 757)

literacy/alfabetismo La capacidad de una persona de leer y escribir (pág. 321)

long drive/paseo largo Desplazamiento del ganado de praderas distantes a centros ferroviarios activos que lo transportaban para venderlo (pág. 271)

loose construction/interpretación libre Creencia de que el gobierno puede hacer todo lo que la Constitución no prohíbe (pág. 90)

Lost Generation/Generación Perdida, la Grupo de escritores de la década de 1920 que compartían la idea de que estaban perdidos en un mundo codicioso, materialista y sin valores morales; a menudo decidían huir a Europa (pág. 464)

Louisiana Purchase/Compra de Luisiana Compra del territorio de Louisiana que los Estados Unidos le hicieron a Francia en 1803 (pág. 95)

lynching/linchamiento Asesinato de un acusado, efectuado por una multitud sin que se realice un juicio legal (pág. 334)

M

Magna Carta/Carta Magna Una "gran carta" firmada por el rey Juan en 1215 que concedía algunos derechos a los nobles ingleses y que se convirtió en la base para futuros ideales de libertad y justicia en los Estados Unidos (pág. 7)

mail-order catalog/catálogo de ventas por correo Material impreso que muestra una variedad de productos que se pueden ser adquirir por correo (pág. 339)

Manchurian Incident/incidente de Manchuria Situación en 1931 cuándo las tropas japonesas, que alegaban que los soldados chinos habían tratado de hacer explotar una vía férrea, se hicieron cargo del problema al tomar varias ciudades de Manchuria del sur para después apoderarse del país, incluso después de que las tropas chinas se habían retirado (pág. 582)

mandate/delegación Declaración pública de apoyo que los votantes expresan a un candidato (pág. 737)

Manhattan Project/Proyecto Manhattan Programa estadounidense secreto durante la Segunda Guerra Mundial para desarrollar una bomba atómica (pág. 620)

manifest destiny/destino manifiesto Argumento que establece que los Estados Unidos estaban destinados a expandirse a lo largo de América del Norte (pág. 135)

manufacturing/manufactura La fabricación de productos mediante maquinaria (pág. 116)

Marbury v. Madison/Marbury vs. Madison Caso de la Suprema Corte presentado en 1803 que establecía el principio de la revisión judicial (pág. 94)

March on Washington/Marcha en Washington Manifestación por los derechos civiles realizada en 1963 en Washington, D.C., en la cual los inconformes exigían empleos y libertad (pág. 717)

Market Revolution/revolución del mercado Cambio de una economía basada en el hogar y por lo general agrícola a una economía basada en el dinero, y en la compra y venta de productos (pág. 116)

Marshall Plan/Plan Marshall Programa de apoyo económico estadounidense a Europa Occidental, anunciado en 1947 (pág. 645)

martial law/ley marcial Ley de emergencia dictada por autoridades militares, durante la cual se suspenden algunas garantías de la Declaración de Derechos (pág. 170)

mass media/medios masivos de comunicación Métodos, impresos y transmitidos para difundir información a un gran número de personas (pág. 460)

mass production/producción en masa Fabricación de productos en grandes cantidades (pág. 234)

Massacre at Wounded Knee/masacre en Wounded Knee Tiroteo realizado en 1890 por tropas militares contra un grupo de indigenas Sioux desarmados (pág. 265)

Mayflower Compact/Acuerdo Mayflower Convenio en el que los colonos de Plymouth acordaron acatar las leyes de su gobierno (pág. 20)

McCarran-Walter Act/Ley McCarran-Walter Ley aprobada por el Congreso en 1952 que reafirmó el sistema de cupos que había sido establecido para cada país en 1924 (pág. 651)

McCarthyism/macartismo Término para describir las tácticas de difamación anticomunista del senador Joseph McCarthy (pág. 657)

Medicaid/Medicaid Programa federal que proporciona seguro médico a muy bajo costo a estadounidenses de escasos recursos y de cualquier edad (pág. 746)

Medicare/Medicare Programa federal que proporciona atención hospitalaria y seguro médico a muy bajo costo a la mayoría de los estadounidenses de 65 años en adelante (pág. 746)

mercantilism/mercantilismo Teoría económica que sostiene que un país debe tratar de adquirir y conservar el mayor número posible de lingotes de oro y plata mediante el aumento de exportaciones en comparación con las importaciones (pág. 25)

Mexican War/Guerra entre México y los Estados Unidos Conflicto entre los Estados Unidos y México que ocurrió de 1846 a 1848 y que terminó con la victoria de los Estados Unidos (pág. 136)

MIA/desaparecido en combate Perdido en el campo de acción (pág. 816)

Middle America/estadounidense promedio Término utilizado a veces para describir la persona estadounidense típica de clase media (pág. 811)

middle class/clase media Una clase nueva de mercaderes, comerciantes y artesanos que surgió a finales de la Edad Media; en nuestros días, la clase social ubicada entre la clase muy acaudalada y la clase obrera (pág. 7)

Middle Passage/el cruce del Atlántico Una parte del comercio triangular; término que también se refiere al transporte forzado de esclavos de África a América (pág. 28)

migrant farm worker/campesino migratorio Persona que trabaja muchas horas a cambio de un salario muy bajo y que va de una granja a otra, generalmente de un estado a otro, para trabajar en las plantaciones (pág. 772)

migration/migración Desplazamiento de personas con el fin de establecerse en otro lugar (pág. 5)

militarism/militarismo Política que consiste en la acumulación agresiva de las fuerzas militares de una nación como preparativo para una guerra, así como en otorgar a los militares más autoridad sobre el gobierno y las políticas extranjeras (pág. 415)

military-industrial complex/complejo militar-industrial El establecimiento militar de 1960 en el que se desarrollaron vínculos con las comunidades empresariales y científicas, y se emplearon 3.5 millones de estadounidenses (pág. 656)

Miranda rule/regla Miranda Regla que establece que la policía debe informar a las personas acusadas de un crimen sobre sus derechos constitucionales (pág. 748)

missionary/misionero Persona que ha sido enviada por su iglesia a difundir su religión (pág. 16)

Missouri Compromise/Concesión de Missouri Acuerdo firmado en 1820 que demanda el reconocimiento de Missouri como un estado esclavista y de Maine como un estado libre, así como la prohibición de la esclavitud en futuros estados que se crearían al norte de la latitud de 36° 30' N (pág. 98)

mobilization/movilización El alistamiento de las tropas para una guerra (pág. 416)

Modern Republicanism/republicanismo moderno Propuesta del presidente Eisenhower al gobierno, descrita como "conservadora cuando se trata de dinero y liberal cuando se trata de seres humanos" (pág. 685)

monarch/monarca Quien gobierna un territorio, estado o reino (pág. 7)

monetary policy/política monetaria Plan del gobierno federal de la composición y la cantidad del suministro nacional de dinero (pág. 278)

money supply/masa monetaria La cantidad de dinero con la que cuenta la economía nacional (pág. 278)

monopoly/monopolio Control total de un producto o servicio (pág. 240)

Monroe Doctrine/Doctrina Monroe Declaración realizada en 1823 por el presidente Monroe que establecía que los Estados Unidos se opondrían a los esfuerzos de cualquier potencia externa por controlar una nación en el hemisferio occidental (pág. 121)

Montgomery bus boycott/boicot a los autobuses Montgomery Protesta realizada por estadounidenses de raza negra de 1955 a 1956 en contra de la segregación racial en el sistema de transporte de Montgomery, Alabama (pág. 701)

Morrill Land-Grant Act/Ley Morill para la Concesión de Tierras Ley aprobada por el Congreso en 1862 que distribuía millones de acres de tierras del occidente del país a los gobiernos estatales para financiar corporaciones agrícolas estatales (pág. 259)

muckraker/descubridor de escándalos Periodista que descubre actos ilícitos en la política o en las empresas (pág. 384)

multiculturalism/multiculturalismo Movimiento que demanda mayor atención a las culturas no europeas en áreas como la educación (pág. 914)

multinational corporation/corporación multinacional Corporación que opera en más de un país (pág. 910)

municipal/municipal Que pertenece a una ciudad, por ejemplo, el gobierno municipal (pág. 390)

Munn* v. *Illinois*/ *Munn* vs. *Illinois Decisión de la Suprema Corte tomada en 1877 que permitía a los estados regular algunas empresas dentro sus límites fronterizos (pág. 294)

N

napalm/*napalm* Substancia química altamente inflamable lanzada por aviones estadounidenses en bombardeos durante la Guerra de Vietnam (pág. 801)

Nation of Islam/Nación del Islam Organización dedicada a la lucha por la separación de la raza negra y el esfuerzo propio; también llamada los Musulmanes Negros (pág. 722)

National Aeronautics and Space Administration (NASA)/Administración Nacional de la Aeronáutica y el Espacio (NASA) Creada en 1958 por el gobierno de los Estados Unidos como una agencia independiente para la exploración del espacio (pág. 686)

National American Woman Suffrage Association (NAWSA)/Asociación Estadounidense para el Sufragio de la Mujer (NAWSA) Organización formada en 1890 para continuar la obtención de los derechos de las mujeres, especialmente el de votar (pág. 405)

National Association for the Advancement of Colored People (NAACP)/Asociación Nacional para el Progreso de las Personas de Color (NAACP) Organización fundada en 1909 para abolir la segregación y discriminación, luchar contra el racismo y lograr que los estadounidenses de raza negra gozaran de derechos civiles (pág. 335)

national debt/deuda nacional Cantidad total de dinero que debe el gobierno federal y que tiene que pagar (pág. 554)

National Defense Education Act/Ley para la Mejoría de la Educación en Defensa de la Nación Medida tomada en 1958 para mejorar la enseñanza de las ciencias y matemáticas en las escuelas (pág. 686)

National Liberation Front/Frente de Liberación Nacional Arma política del Viet Cong (pág. 795)

National Organization for Women (NOW)/Organización Nacional para las Mujeres (NOW) Organización formada en 1966 para fomentar la participación total de las mujeres en la sociedad estadounidense (pág. 766)

nationalism/nacionalismo Devoción por la nación a la que uno pertenece (pág. 353)

nationalization/nacionalización Adquisición por parte del gobierno de instituciones como bancos, con redistribución de sus recursos económicos (pág. 548)

nativism/nativismo Una política que favorece a los nativos de los Estados Unidos frente a los inmigrantes (págs. 140, 314)

Nazism/nazismo Una especie extrema de fascismo delineada por las ideas fanáticas de Adolfo Hitler sobre el nacionalismo alemán y la superioridad racial (pág. 571)

Neutrality Acts/Leyes de Neutralidad Leyes promulgadas en 1939 diseñadas para mantener a los Estados Unidos fuera de futuras guerras (pág. 586)

New Deal/Nuevo Trato Término que describe los programas de apoyo, recuperación y reforma diseñados por el presidente Franklin Roosevelt para combatir la Gran Depresión (pág. 537)

New Federalism/nuevo federalismo Llamado del Presidente Nixon a una asociación nueva entre el gobierno federal y los gobiernos de los estados; plan del Presidente Reagan para reducir el papel del gobierno federal y otorgar más responsabilidad a los gobiernos estatales y locales (págs. 829, 873)

New Frontier/nueva frontera Propuestas del Presidente Kennedy para mejorar la economía, ayudar a los pobres y desarrollar el programa de exploración espacial (pág. 738)

New Left/nueva izquierda Nuevo movimiento político que tuvo lugar a finales de la década de 1960 y que demandaba cambios radicales para combatir la pobreza y el racismo (pág. 806)

New Nationalism/nuevo nacionalismo Plan de Theodore Roosevelt para lograr una mayor regulación federal de las empresas y lugares de trabajo, de los impuestos a las utilidades e impuestos de sucesión, y de las reformas electorales (pág. 398)

New Right/nueva derecha Una coalición política de grupos conservadores formada en 1980 (pág. 867)

Niagara Movement/movimiento Niágara Grupo de estadounidenses de raza negra fundado en 1905, que demandaba libertad civil, eliminación de la discriminación racial y reconocimiento de la hermandad (pág. 325)

Nisei/*Nisei* Estadounidense de origen japonés cuyos padres nacieron en Japón (pág. 627)

nomadic/nómadas Personas que cambian de hogar con regularidad, generalmente en busca de fuentes de alimento disponibles (págs. 5, 261)

nonviolent protest/protesta pacífica Una forma pacífica de protestar en contra de las políticas restrictivas (pág. 706)

North American Free Trade Agreement (NAFTA)/Tratado de Libre Comercio de Norteamérica (TLCN) Acuerdo que demanda la eliminación de las restricciones comerciales entre los Estados Unidos, Canadá y México (pág. 915)

North Atlantic Treaty Organization (NATO)/Organización del Tratado del Atlántico Norte (OTAN) Alianza de naciones que en 1949 acordaron agruparse en caso de guerra, además de apoyar y proteger a cada nación participante (pág. 647)

Nuclear Regulatory Commission (NRC)/Comisión Nuclear Reguladora (NRC) Organización gubernamental formada en 1974 para examinar el uso civil de los materiales nucleares (pág. 783)

nullify/anulación Rechazo de una ley federal por parte del estado (pág. 123)

Nuremberg Trials/Juicios de Nuremberg Serie de juicios realizados en 1945 por un Tribunal Militar Internacional en los que antiguos líderes nazis fueron acusados de crímenes de guerra y crímenes contra la paz y la humanidad (pág. 613)

O

Office of War Mobilization/Oficina de Movilización de Guerra Agencia federal formada para coordinar cuestiones relacionadas con la producción de la guerra durante la Segunda Guerra Mundial (pág. 596)

oligopoly/oligopolio Una estructura de mercado dominada sólo por unas cuantas compañías grandes y lucrativas (pág. 240)

Open Door Policy/política de libre acceso Propuesta que realizó Estados Unidos a China alrededor de 1900 y que apoya las relaciones de libre comercio entre China y otras naciones (pág. 364)

Organization of Petroleum Exporting Countries (OPEC)/Organización de Países Exportadores de Petróleo (OPEP) Grupo de naciones que trabajaron de manera conjunta para regular el precio y el suministro del petróleo (pág. 828)

P

Pacific Railway Acts/Leyes para el Ferrocarril del Pacífico Leyes aprobadas en 1862 y 1864 que otorgaron grandes concesiones de tierra para la construcción de las vías férreas Union Pacific y Central Pacific (pág. 259)

pardon/perdón Exoneración oficial de un crimen (pág. 202)

Paris peace talks/diálogos de paz de París Negociaciones entre los Estados Unidos y Vietnam del Norte que se iniciaron en 1968 (pág. 812)

patent/patente Licencia expedida a un inventor que le da el derecho exclusivo de fabricar, utilizar o vender su invento durante un período de tiempo establecido (pág. 227)

patriotism/patriotismo Amor por el país al que uno pertenece; pasión que tiene como objetivo servir al propio país, ya sea defendiéndolo de una invasión o protegiendo sus derechos y manteniendo sus leyes e instituciones en vigor y transparencia (pág. 49)

Peace Corps/Cuerpo de Paz Programa federal establecido para enviar voluntarios a auxiliar países en vías de desarrollo (pág. 758)

Pendleton Civil Service Act/Ley Pendleton del Servicio Civil Ley promulgada en 1883 que creó una Comisión de Servicio Civil y estableció que los empleados federales no estaban obligados a contribuir al financiamiento de las campañas ni podían ser despedidos por razones políticas (pág. 293)

penny auction/subasta de a centavo Subastas de granjas durante la Gran Depresión en las que los vecinos salvaban a los demás de perder su propiedad a través de ofertas muy bajas (pág. 521)

per capita income/ingreso per capita Ingreso anual promedio por persona (pág. 668)

Persian Gulf War/Guerra del Golfo Pérsico Operación militar limitada que tuvo lugar en 1991 y cuyo objetivo era sacar a las fuerzas iraquíes de Kuwait (pág. 886)

philanthropist/filántropo Persona que hace donaciones para buenas causas (pág. 323)

Pickett's Charge/ataque de Pickett Ataque fallido de la infantería de los confederados durante la Batalla de Gettysburg (pág. 182)

piecework/trabajo por pieza Sistema en el que el pago de los trabajadores no se basa en el tiempo trabajado sino en el número de artículos que producen (pág. 244)

placer mining/explotación de placeres Técnica minera en la que los mineros echaban en cajas tierra de los placeres y luego le vertían agua para separarla de las partículas de oro o plata (pág. 269)

plantation/plantación Granja de gran extensión en la que se cultivan cosechas principalmente para la venta (pág. 12)

Platt Amendment/enmienda Platt Anexo a la constitución cubana de 1900 realizado por el gobierno estadounidense que le dio a los Estados Unidos el derecho de establecer bases navales en Cuba e intervenir en los asuntos de Cuba cuando fuera necesario (pág. 362)

Plessy v. *Ferguson/Plessy* vs. *Ferguson* Decisión tomada en 1896 por la Suprema Corte que consistía en la legalidad de la segregación siempre y cuando las instalaciones asignadas a la gente de color fueran iguales a las asignadas a los de raza blanca (pág. 334)

pocket veto/veto indirecto Tipo de veto que puede utilizar un presidente después de que se haya suspendido una legislatura; se aplica cuando el presidente no firma o rechaza formalmente una propuesta dentro del tiempo permitido (pág. 203)

pogrom/pogrom Masacre de judíos (pág. 298)

political machine/aparato político Organización urbana extraoficial diseñada para mantener un partido o grupo particular en el poder y bajo la dirección de un solo jefe poderoso (pág. 308)

political party/partido político Grupo de personas que buscan ganar las elecciones y tener un puesto público con el fin de controlar las políticas y los programas del gobierno (pág. 91)

poll tax/impuesto sobre el padrón electoral Un gravamen especial que debe ser pagado para que una persona pueda votar (pág. 333)

Populist/populista Seguidor del Partido del Pueblo (o Partido Populista) formado en 1891 para apoyar una oferta monetaria más grande y otras reformas económicas (pág. 281)

POW/prisionero de guerra Prisionero capturado durante una guerra (pág. 816)

prejudice/prejuicio Una opinión irracional y sin fundamentos, por lo general desfavorable, acerca de otro grupo (pág. 139)

price controls/control de precios Sistema determinado por el gobierno para el establecimiento de precios (pág. 433)

productivity/productividad Cantidad de bienes y servicios creada en un período de tiempo (pág. 227)

Progressive Era/período progresista El período entre 1890 y 1920 durante el cual se aprobaron diversas reformas a nivel local, estatal y federal (pág. 383)

prohibition/prohibición Una restricción en la producción y venta de bebidas alcohólicas (pág. 314)

propaganda/propaganda Información orientada a influir en la opinión pública (pág. 418)

Proprietary colony/colonia sujeta a derechos de propiedad Colonia que un rey o reina otorga a un individuo o grupo que tiene todos los derechos de gobernar (pág. 22)

public works program/programa de obras públicas Proyectos financiados por el gobierno para construir instalaciones públicas (pág. 538)

Pullman Strike/huelga Pullman Huelga de los trabajadores ferroviarios que tuvo lugar en 1894 y que se extendió por toda la nación (pág. 253)

puppet state/estado títere Un país supuestamente independiente que se encuentra bajo el control de un vecino poderoso (pág. 582)

Puritan/puritano Personas que favorecieron la purificación de la Iglesia Anglicana de Inglaterra (pág. 19)

purge/purga En términos políticos, el proceso de sacar del poder a los enemigos e individuos indeseables (pág. 569)

push-pull factors/factores de expulsión del país de origen y de atracción por otro país Sucesos y condiciones que fuerzan a las personas a irse a otra parte o las atraen fuertemente a hacerlo (pág. 258)

Q

quarantine/cuarentena Período de aislamiento para prevenir la propagación de una enfermedad (pág. 299)

quota/cuota Límite numérico (pág. 487)

R

racism/racismo Creencia en que la raza determina las diferencias de carácter o inteligencia; afirmar la superioridad de una raza sobre otra u otras (pág. 373)

Radical Republicans/republicanos radicales Grupo de congresistas miembros del Partido Republicano que creían que en la Guerra Civil se había luchado por el problema moral de la esclavitud; insistía en que la principal meta de la Reconstrucción debía ser una reestructuración total de la sociedad para garantizar a la gente de color la verdadera igualdad (pág. 203)

ragtime/*ragtime* Tipo de música que se califica de melodías con acentos que cambian contra un ritmo constante, que tuvo su orígen entre los músicos negros en la región central y el sur en el década de 1880 (pág. 331)

rationing/racionamiento Distribución de una cantidad fija de productos a los consumidores (pág. 434)

Reagan Democrat/demócratas Reagan Obreros demócratas que tendían a votar por el partido Republicano durante la década de 1980 (pág. 867)

realpolitik/realpolitik Término alemán que significa "política práctica" o política extranjera basada en los intereses más que en los principios morales (pág. 832)

rebate/reembolso Devolución parcial (pág. 294)

recall/revocación Procedimiento que permite a los votantes destituir a funcionarios públicos de su puesto antes de la siguiente elección (pág. 392)

recession/recesión Período de poco movimiento en el negocio (pág. 554)

recognition/reconocimiento Aceptación oficial como nación independiente (pág. 168)

Reconstruction/Reconstrucción Programa puesto en práctica por el gobierno federal entre 1865 y 1877 para reparar el daño al sur causado por la Guerra Civil y restituir los estados del sur a la Unión (pág. 200)

Reconstruction Finance Corporation (RFC)/Corporación Financiera para la Reconstrucción (RFC) Corporación establecida por el presidente Hoover en 1932, que otorgó crédito público a varias instituciones, entre ellas, industrias grandes, compañías ferroviarias y compañías de seguros (pág. 525)

reconversion/reconversión Transición social y económica de los tiempos de guerra a los tiempos de paz (pág. 680)

Red Scare/amenaza roja Miedo intenso al comunismo y a otras ideas políticamente radicales (pág. 482)

referendum/referéndum Proceso que permite a los ciudadanos aprobar o rechazar una ley aprobada por su legislatura (pág. 392)

religious tolerance/tolerancia religiosa Idea de que las personas de diferentes religiones deben convivir en paz (pág. 20)

reparations/compensaciones Pagos que realiza un enemigo por el daño económico ocasionado durante la guerra (pág. 439)

republic/república Gobierno manejado por el pueblo a través de los representantes elegidos (pág. 55)

republican virtues/virtudes republicanas Virtudes que el pueblo estadounidense necesitaría para gobernarse a sí mismo, tales como confianza en uno mismo, destreza, sobriedad, armonía y capacidad para sacrificar las necesidades individuales por el bien de la comunidad (pág. 110)

reservation/reservación Territorio federal reservado para las tribus de indígenas estadounidenses (pág. 262)

Resistance/Resistencia Movimiento en Francia que se opuso a la ocupación alemana durante la Segunda Guerra Mundial (pág. 578)

restrictive covenant/cláusula de prohibición de competencia Acuerdo entre los dueños de fincas para no vender sus propiedades a ciertos grupos de personas, como judíos o estadounidenses de raza negra (pág. 301)

revenue/ingreso Entrada económica (pág. 554)

Revolutionary War/guerra revolucionaria Guerra de los colonos norteamericanos para independizarse de la Gran Bretaña; tuvo lugar de 1775 a 1783 (pág. 45)

rock-and-roll/*rock-and-roll* Música que surgió del rhythm and blues y que se volvió popular en la década de 1950 (pág. 678)

Roe* v. *Wade/Roe* vs. *Wade Decisión tomada en 1973 por la Suprema Corte para legalizar el aborto (pág. 768)

Roosevelt Corollary/Corolario Roosevelt Extensión de la Doctrina Monroe realizada por el presidente Theodore Roosevelt en 1904, en la que hacía valer el derecho de los Estados Unidos de intervenir en las naciones de América Latina (pág. 368)

rural free delivery (RFD)/entrega postal rural gratuita (RFD) En 1896, el Sistema Postal de los Estados

Unidos ofreció entregar el correo de manera gratuita a las familias campesinas en los estados rurales centrales (pág. 339)

Russian Revolution/revolución rusa Colapso del gobierno zarista de Rusia en 1917, después del cual la monarquía rusa fue reemplazada por un gobierno republicano (pág. 424)

S

SALT I/Primer Tratado sobre Limitación de Armas Estratégicas *(SALT I)* Tratado firmado en 1972 entre los Estados Unidos y la Unión Soviética para restringir las armas nucleares (pág. 836)

Sandinista/sandinista En la década de 1980, un miembro del grupo marxista prevaleciente en Nicaragua (pág. 880)

satellite nation/nación satélite Un país dominado política y económicamente por otra nación, sobre todo por la Unión Soviética durante la Guerra Fría (pág. 639)

saturation bombing/bombardeo de saturación El lanzamiento de una gran concentración de bombas sobre un área determinada (pág. 801)

scab/rompehuelgas Término negativo para un obrero que ha sido llamado por un empleador para que reemplace a los trabajadores que están en huelga (pág. 251)

scalawag/caballo piojoso o sureño pro-yanqui Sobrenombre ofensivo utilizado para referirse a un republicano blanco del sur después de la Guerra Civil (pág. 211)

Scopes trial/juicio de Scopes Caso presentado ante los tribunales en 1925 por Clarence Darrow y William Jennings Bryan, en el que se debatía la enseñanza de la evolución en las escuelas públicas (pág. 470)

secede/separarse Dejar de ser miembro formalmente de un grupo u organización (pág. 123)

Second Great Awakening/el Segundo Gran Despertar Movimiento religioso que tuvo lugar a principios del siglo XIX (pág. 114)

Second New Deal/segundo Nuevo Trato Período de actividad legislativa iniciado por el presidente Franklin Roosevelt en 1935 (pág. 542)

sedition/sedición Cualquier discurso o acción que fomente la rebelión (pág. 435)

segregation/segregación Separación forzada, frecuentemente por las diferencias de raza (pág. 333)

Selective Service Act/Ley del Servicio Militar Obligatorio Ley aprobada en 1917 que autoriza el reclutamiento de jóvenes para el servicio militar en la Primera Guerra Mundial (pág. 425)

Selective Training and Service Act/Ley del Servicio y Capacitación Militar Obligatorios Ley promulgada en 1940 que exige que todos los hombres de 21 a 36 años deben realizar el servicio militar (pág. 594)

self-determination/autodeterminación El poder de tomar decisiones sobre el futuro de uno mismo (pág. 437)

Seneca Falls Convention/Convención Seneca Falls La primera convención sobre los derechos de las mujeres en la historia de los Estados Unidos, presidida en 1848 (pág. 132)

separation of powers/división de poderes El reparto constitucional de poderes dentro del gobierno federal entre las ramas legislativa, ejecutiva y judicial (pág. 59)

settlement house/casa del pueblo Centro comunitario organizado para proporcionar varios servicios a las personas de escasos recursos que viven en zonas urbanas (pág. 312)

sharecropping/aparcería Sistema practicado en la agricultura en el que un campesino trabaja un pedazo de tierra del propietario y recibe como pago una parte de la cosecha (pág. 213)

shell/granada Aparato que explota en el aire o cuando golpea un objetivo sólido (pág. 160)

Sherman Antitrust Act/Ley Antimonopolista Sherman Ley aprobada por el Congreso en 1890 que prohibía cualquier combinación de empresas que limitara el intercambio o comercio interestatal (pág. 242)

Sherman Silver Purchase Act/Ley Sherman para la Adquisición de Plata Ley aprobada por el Congreso en 1890 para aumentar la cantidad de plata que el gobierno debía comprar cada mes (pág. 279)

siege/sitio Táctica que consiste en cercar a un enemigo y dejarlo sin alimentos para que se rinda (pág. 184)

silent majority/mayoría silenciosa Término utilizado por el presidente Nixon para describir a los estadounidenses que se oponían a la contracultura (pág. 814)

sit-down strike/huelga de brazos caídos Protesta laboral en la que los trabajadores dejan de trabajar pero se niegan a abandonar el lugar de trabajo (p. 555)

sit-in/sentada Forma de protesta en la que los inconformes se sientan y se niegan a irse (pág. 709)

social Darwinism/darwinismo social Idea que se deriva de la teoría de Darwin de la selección natural; consiste en que la sociedad debe interferir lo menos posible en la búsqueda del éxito de las personas (pág. 239)

social gospel movement/movimiento evangélico social Una reforma social que se desarrolló en las instituciones religiosas y buscó aplicar las enseñanzas de Jesús directamente a la sociedad (pág. 312)

Social Security System/sistema de seguridad social Sistema establecido por el Ley de Seguridad Social de 1935 para proporcionar seguridad económica, a manera de pagos regulares, a quienes no pueden mantenerse por sí mismos (pág. 544)

social welfare program/programa de bienestar social Programa diseñado para asegurar una norma de vida o de subsistencia básica a todos los ciudadanos (pág. 390)

socialism/socialismo Filosofía económica y política que apoya el control público (o social), en lugar del control privado, de la propiedad y los ingresos (pág. 247)

sociology/sociología Término acuñado por el filósofo Auguste Comte para describir el estudio de la forma en que las personas interactúan en una sociedad (pág. 313)

soddie/casa de tepes Casa cuyas paredes y techo están hechas de bloques de pasto compuesto por gruesas raíces y tierra (pág. 273)

solid South/sur sólido Término que describe el dominio del Partido Demócrata sobre las políticas del sur posteriores a la Guerra Civil (pág. 220)

sooners/*sooners* En 1889, personas que exigían ilegalmente un pedazo de tierra escabulléndose de las autoridades antes de que empezaran las carreras por la tierra (pág. 267)

Southern Christian Leadership Conference (SCLC)/Conferencia del Liderazgo Cristiano del Sur (SCLC) Organización de los derechos civiles que apoyaba las protestas pacíficas; formada en 1957 por el Dr. Martin Luther King Jr. y otros líderes (pág. 706)

speakeasies/tabernas clandestinas Bar que operaba ilegalmente durante el período de la Prohibición (pág. 468)

special prosecutor/fiscal especial Un abogado designado por el Departamento de Justicia para investigar actos ilegales de funcionarios públicos (pág. 843)

speculation/especulación Práctica que consiste en hacer inversiones de alto riesgo con la esperanza de obtener una enorme ganancia (pág. 500)

sphere of influence/esfera de influencia Área de control económico y político ejercido por una nación sobre otra u otras (pág. 364)

spiritual/espiritual Himno folklórico (pág. 115)

spoils/botín Ganancias obtenidas en una victoria militar (pág. 438)

Sputnik/Sputnik El primer satélite artificial en entrar en la órbita de la Tierra, lanzado por los soviéticos en 1957 (pág. 661)

stagflation/estanflación Combinación de un alto nivel de inflación y desempleo sin ningún crecimiento económico (pág. 848)

stalemate/estancamiento Situación en la que ninguna de las partes del conflicto logra obtener ventaja (pág. 417)

states' rights/derechos de los estados Los poderes que la Constitución le niega al gobierno y les confiere a los estados (pág. 123)

steerage/entrecubierta Un área abierta muy grande debajo de la cubierta de un barco, por lo general utilizada para alojar inmigrantes (pág. 298)

stereotype/estereotipo Descripción exagerada o demasiado simplificada de la realidad arraigada en ciertas personas (pág. 275)

Strategic Arms Reduction Treaty/Tratado para la Reducción de Armas Estratégicas Acuerdo firmado en 1991 y conocido como START, que demandaba la reducción del suministro de armas nucleares de largo alcance en Rusia y los Estados Unidos (pág. 885)

Strategic Defense Initiative (SDI)/Iniciativa de Defensa Estratégica (SDI) Sistema de defensa propuesto por el presidente Reagan en contra de ataques soviéticos con misiles, popularmente conocido como la "Guerra de las Galaxias" (pág. 873)

strict construction/interpretación estricta Idea de que el gobierno no debe hacer nada que la Constitución no especifique que pueda hacer (pág. 90)

strike/huelga Un paro laboral con el propósito de forzar a los empleadores a cumplir algunas demandas, por ejemplo, un aumento en los salarios (pág. 119)

Student Nonviolent Coordinating Committee (SNCC)/Comité Coordinador Estudiantil Pacifista (SNCC) Organización de los derechos civiles de los estudiantes fundada en 1960, como rama del SCLC (pág. 707)

subsidy/subsidio Un pago realizado por el gobierno para fomentar el desarrollo de ciertas industrias clave (pág. 291)

suburb/área suburbana Comunidad residencial que rodea una ciudad (pág. 305)

suffrage/sufragio El derecho al voto (pág. 132)

supply-side economics/economía de oferta Teoría que establece que la reducción de impuestos aumentará la inversión y, por lo tanto, estimulará el crecimiento de las empresas (pág. 871)

Sussex pledge/promesa Sussex Compromiso adquirido por el gobierno alemán en 1916 de que sus submarinos advertirían a los barcos antes de atacarlos (pág. 423)

sweatshop/fábrica explotadora Fábrica donde los empleados trabajan muchas horas a cambio de salarios muy bajos y en malas condiciones de trabajo (pág. 244)

T

Taft-Hartley Act/Ley Taft-Hartley Ley aprobada por el Congreso en 1947 que permitió al Presidente declarar un período de calma de 80 días cuando las huelgas golpearon las industrias y afectaron los intereses nacionales; asimismo, pedía a los huelguistas que volvieran a su trabajo mientras el gobierno estudiaba la situación (pág. 681)

teach-in/asamblea especial Sesión especial de disertación y discusión sobre un tema controversial utilizada durante la época de la Guerra de Vietnam (pág. 807)

Teapot Dome scandal/escándalo Teapot Dome Escándalo durante la administración de Harding que involucraba la concesión de los derechos de explotación petrolera en el territorio público a cambio de dinero (pág. 488)

televangelism/televangelismo El uso de la televisión por los predicadores para ganarse a millones de personas, especialmente para recaudar dinero (pág. 868)

temperance movement/movimiento de moderación Una campaña organizada para eliminar el consumo de bebidas alcohólicas (págs. 128, 314)

tenant farming/agricultura por arrendamiento Sistema agrícola en el que el propietario de una plantación le arrienda la tierra a un agricultor para que la trabaje (pág. 214)

tenement/casa de vecindad Edificio de apartamentos de bajo costo y por lo regular con normas de sanidad, seguridad y comodidad deficientes; diseñado para alojar el mayor número posible de familias (pág. 306)

Tennessee Valley Authority (TVA)/Autoridad del valle de Tennessee (TVA) Proyecto federal para proporcionar energía eléctrica, control de inundaciones y oportunidades recreativas, a muy bajo precio, al valle del río Tennessee (pág. 540)

Tet Offensive/Ofensiva Tet Ataque realizado en 1968 por el Viet Cong y las fuerzas vietnamitas del Norte a través de Vietnam del Sur (pág. 803)

Thirteenth Amendment/Decimotercera enmienda Enmienda constitucional ratificada en 1865 para abolir la esclavitud (pág. 190)

38th parallel/paralelo 38 Línea de latitud que dividía Corea del Norte y Corea del Sur aproximadamente en el punto céntrico de la península (pág. 653)

totalitarian/totalitario Un gobierno que ejerce un control total sobre la nación y la vida de los ciudadanos (pág. 568)

Trail of Tears/ ruta de las lágrimas El traslado forzado de la tribu Cherokee en 1838 hacia el territorio oeste del río Mississippi (pág. 124)

transcendentalism/trascendentalismo Movimiento filosófico de mediados del siglo XIX que enfatizaba el descubrimiento espiritual y la perspicacia por encima de la razón (pág. 127)

transcontinental railroad/ferrocarril transcontinental Vía férrea que se extiende de costa a costa (pág. 230)

transistor/transistor Circuito diminuto inventado en 1947 que amplifica, controla y genera señales eléctricas (pág. 670)

triangular trade/comercio triangular Comercio entre América, Europa y África (pág. 27)

Truman Doctrine/Doctrina Truman Discurso emitido por Harry Truman en 1947 antes de una sesión conjunta del Congreso, en el que pedía que los Estados Unidos asumieran un papel de liderazgo en el mundo y declaraba que apoyarían a las naciones amenazadas por el comunismo (pág. 642)

trust/consorcio Un grupo de empresas distintas que están bajo el control de un solo consejo administrativo (pág. 242)

Turner thesis/tesis Turner Teoría desarrollada en 1893 por Frederick Jackson Turner, que afirmaba que la región fronteriza había jugado un papel clave en la formación del carácter de los estadounidenses (pág. 275)

Twenty-first Amendment/Vigésima primera enmienda Enmienda constitucional ratificada en 1933 para anular el período de la Prohibición (pág. 522)

Twenty-fourth Amendment/Vigésima cuarta enmienda Enmienda constitucional ratificada en 1964 para prohibir el impuesto sobre el padrón electoral (pág. 721)

U

U-boat/*U-boat* Submarino alemán (pág. 421)

U-2 incident/incidente U-2 Incidente ocurrido en 1960 en el que las fuerzas armadas soviéticas utilizaron un misil guiado para derribar un avión espía U-2 estadounidense que volaba en territorio soviético (pág. 661)

Underground Railroad/vía férrea subterránea Una red de rutas de escape que protegían y transportaban a los esclavos que huían al norte en busca de la libertad (pág. 130)

United Farm Workers (UFW)/Agricultores Unidos (UFW) Sindicato creado por César Chávez para organizar a los agricultores mexicanos en el Oeste (p. 773)

United States Constitution/Constitución de los Estados Unidos Plan de gobierno establecido en 1787 que describe las diferentes partes del gobierno, así como sus deberes y poderes (pág. 57)

utopian community/comunidad utópica Pequeña sociedad que busca la perfección en el ámbito social y político (pág. 129)

V

vaudeville/*vaudeville* Un tipo de teatro de variedades que apareció por primera vez en la década de 1870; generalmente consta de diálogos cómicos, números de música y baile, y actos de magia (pág. 327)

Versailles Treaty/Tratado de Versalles Tratado firmado en 1919 que dio fin a la Primera Guerra Mundial (pág. 439)

vertical consolidation/consolidación vertical Proceso para obtener el control de las diferentes empresas que componen todas las fases del desarrollo de un producto (pág. 241)

vice/vicio Comportamiento inmoral o corrupto (pág. 315)

victory garden/jardín de la victoria Un jardín doméstico de hortalizas creado para apoyar la producción de

alimentos durante la Segunda Guerra Mundial
(pág. 599)

Viet Cong/Viet Cong Guerrillas comunistas de Vietnam
del Sur (pág. 795)

Vietminh/Vietminh Nombre común de la Liga para la
Independencia de Vietnam (pág. 792)

Vietnamization/vietnamización Política del presidente
Nixon para reemplazar las fuerzas militares estadounidenses por las de Vietnam del Sur (pág. 813)

vigilante/miembro de un grupo de autodefensa Ciudadano que hace justicia por su propia cuenta
(pág. 435)

**Volunteers in Service to America (VISTA)/Voluntarios
al Servicio de Norteamérica (VISTA)** Programa
federal que envía voluntarios a las comunidades
pobres para brindarles ayuda (pág. 746)

**Voting Rights Act of 1965/Ley de Derecho al Voto de
1965** Ley cuyo objetivo era reducir los obstáculos
que tenían los estadounidenses de raza negra para
votar, mediante el aumento de la autoridad federal
para registrar a los votantes (pág. 721)

W

Wagner Act/Ley Wagner Ley aprobada en 1935 para
apoyar a los sindicatos mediante la legalización de
acuerdos colectivos y el establecimiento del Consejo
Nacional para las Relaciones Laborales (pág. 543)

Wannsee Conference/Conferencia Wannsee Conferencia
celebrada en 1942 en Alemania, cuyo tema principal
era la elaboración del plan para asesinar a los judíos
europeos (pág. 611)

war of attrition/guerra por desgaste Tipo de guerra en
el que una de las partes causa a la otra continuas pér-
didas para mermar su fuerza (pág. 159)

War of 1812/guerra de 1812 Guerra entre los Estados
Unidos y Gran Bretaña (pág. 96)

War Powers Act/Ley de Poderes de Guerra Ley promulgada en 1973 que limita la capacidad de un presidente para involucrar a los Estados Unidos en
conflictos externos sin recibir una declaración de
guerra formal expedida por el Congreso (pág. 849)

**War Refugee Board (WRB)/Consejo para los Refugia-
dos de Guerra (WRB)** Agencia federal creada en
1944 para ayudar a las personas amenazadas de
muerte por los nazis (pág. 612)

Warren Commission/Comisión Warren Comisión
encabezada por el presidente de la Corte Suprema,
Earl Warren, que investigaba el asesinato del presidente Kennedy (pág. 741)

Warsaw ghetto/ghetto de Varsovia Área de Varsovia cer-
rada por los nazis para confinar a los judíos y obligar-
los a vivir en condiciones malas e insalubres
(pág. 611)

Warsaw Pact/Pacto de Varsovia Alianza militar formada
en 1955 entre la Unión Soviética y las naciones de
Europa Oriental (pág. 648)

Watergate scandal/escándalo de Watergate Escándalo
que involucró actividades ilegales que llevaron final-
mente a la renuncia del presidente Nixon en 1974
(pág. 840)

welfare capitalism/capitalismo benefactor Una
propuesta de relaciones laborales en la cual las empresas cubrían algunas de las necesidades de sus trabajadores sin la presión de los sindicatos, y así prevenían
huelgas y mantenían una productividad elevada
(p. 499)

Whitewater affair/caso Whitewater Cargos que se le
imputaron al presidente Clinton por realizar transac-
ciones empresariales inadecuadas antes de subir a la
presidencia (pág. 898)

wiretap/conectador para interceptar líneas telefónicas
Un aparato auditivo que se utiliza para interceptar las
llamadas telefónicas (pág. 839)

Woodstock festival/festival de Woodstock Festival de
música que tuvo lugar en 1969 en la región norte del
estado de Nueva York (pág. 779)

**World Trade Organization (WTO)/Organización
Mundial de Comercio (OMC)** Organización internacional formada en 1995 para fomentar la expansión
del comercio mundial (pág. 915)

writ of *habeas corpus*/auto de *habeas corpus* Protección
legal que exige que una corte determine si una
persona debe ser encarcelada o no (pág. 171)

Y

yellow journalism/amarillismo Cobertura de noticias
sensacionalistas, centradas en crímenes y escándalos
(pág. 329)

Z

zeppelin/zepelín Globo dirigible alemán (pág. 429)

Zimmermann note/nota Zimmermann Telegrama del
ministro de Relaciones Exteriores alemán a funcionarios mexicanos, enviado en 1917, que proponía
una alianza con México y prometía ceder territorio
estadounidense a cambio de una declaración de
guerra a los Estados Unidos (pág. 424)

Biographical Dictionary

A

Adams, Abigail First Lady, 1797–1801; as the wife of Patriot John Adams, she urged him to promote women's rights at the beginning of the American Revolution (p. 44)

Adams, John Second President of the United States, 1797–1801; worked to relieve increasing tensions with France; lost reelection bid to Jefferson in 1800 as the country moved away from Federalist policies (p. 91)

Adams, John Quincy Sixth President of the United States, 1825–1829; proposed greater federal involvement in the economy through tariffs and improvements such as roads, bridges, and canals (p. 122)

Addams, Jane Cofounder of Hull House, the first settlement house, in 1889; remained active in social causes through the early 1900s (p. 312)

Agnew, Spiro Vice President under President Richard Nixon until forced to resign in 1973 for crimes committed before taking office; known for his harsh campaign attacks (p. 810)

Anthony, Susan B. Political activist and women's rights leader in the late 1800s (p. 404)

Armstrong, Louis Jazz musician famous for his long trumpet solos and "scat" singing (p. 462)

Arthur, Chester A. Twenty-first President of the United States, 1881–1885; signed 1883 Pendleton Act, which instituted the Civil Service (p. 293)

Askia, Muhammad Ruler of the African empire of Songhai, 1493–1528; promoted Islamic culture (p. 10)

Austin, Stephen Leader of first American group of Texas settlers in 1822 (p. 109)

B

Bakke, Allan Student who won a suit against the University of California in 1978 on the grounds that the affirmative action program had denied him admission (p. 854)

Baldwin, James African American author and spokesperson for the civil rights movement during the 1960s (p. 722)

Banks, Dennis Native American leader in the 1960s and 1970s; helped organize American Indian Movement (AIM) and the 1973 Wounded Knee occupation (p. 775)

Barton, Clara Volunteer known as the "angel of the battlefield" during the Civil War; founded the American Red Cross (p. 175)

Clara Barton

Beecher, Lyman Revivalist during the Second Great Awakening; feared the rise of selfishness in the United States (p. 127)

Begin, Menachem Israeli leader during the 1970s; began the Middle East peace process by reaching the 1978 Camp David Accords with Egypt (p. 855)

Bell, Alexander Graham Inventor; developed the telephone in 1876; one of the founders of American Telephone & Telegraph (AT&T) (p. 230)

Bellamy, Edward Author of the novel *Looking Backward* (1888), which proposed nationalizing trusts to eliminate social problems (p. 384)

Bethune, Mary McLeod African American educator, New Deal worker; founded Bethune Cookman College in the 1920s, advised the National Youth Administration (p. 541)

Beveridge, Albert J. Indiana senator in the early 1900s; saw United States imperialism as a duty owed to "primitive" societies (p. 356)

Booth, John Wilkes Southern actor who assassinated President Abraham Lincoln in 1865 (p. 193)

Breckinridge, John C. Presidential candidate of the southern wing of the Democratic Party in 1860 (p. 142)

Brown, John Abolitionist crusader who massacred proslavery settlers in Kansas before the Civil War; hoped to inspire slave revolt with 1859 attack on Virginia arsenal; executed for treason against the state of Virginia (p. 142)

Bruce, Blanche African American senator from Mississippi during Reconstruction (p. 210)

Bryan, William Jennings Advocate of silver standard and proponent of Democratic and Populist views from the 1890s through the 1910s; Democratic candidate for President in 1896, 1900, and 1908 (p. 282)

Buchanan, James Fifteenth President of the United States, 1857–1861; supported by the South; attempted to moderate fierce disagreement over expansion of slavery (p. 140)

Bush, George H. W. Forty-first President of the United States, 1989–1993; continued Reagan's conservative policies; brought together United Nations coalition to fight the Persian Gulf War (p. 882)

Bush, George W. Forty-third President of the United States, took office in 2001; led efforts to unite world against terrorism (p. 899)

C

Calhoun, John C. Statesman from South Carolina who held many offices in the federal government; supported slavery, cotton exports, states' rights; in 1850 foresaw future conflicts over slavery (p. 138)

Carnegie, Andrew Industrialist who made a fortune in steel in the late 1800s through vertical consolidation; as a philanthropist, he gave away some $350 million (p. 238)

Carson, Rachel Marine biologist, author of *Silent Spring* (1962), which exposed harmful effects of pesticides and inspired concern for the environment (p. 781)

Carter, James Earl, Jr. Thirty-ninth President of the United States, 1977–1981; advocated concern for human rights in foreign policy; assisted in mediating the Camp David Accords (p. 855)

Castro, Fidel Revolutionary leader who took control of Cuba in 1959; ally of Soviet Union through the 1980s (p. 751)

Catt, Carrie Chapman Women's suffrage leader in the early 1900s; helped secure passage of Nineteenth Amendment in 1920; headed National American Woman Suffrage Association (p. 406)

Champlain, Samuel de French explorer who founded the city of Quebec in 1608 (p. 19)

Chávez, César Latino leader from 1962 to his death in 1993; organized the United Farm Workers (UFW) to help migratory farm workers gain better pay and working conditions (p. 772)

Cheney, Richard Vice President under George W. Bush (p. 900)

Chisholm, Shirley New York Representative from 1969–1983; a founder of the National Women's Political Caucus (p. 767)

Churchill, Winston Leader of Great Britain before and during World War II; powerful speechmaker who rallied Allied morale during the war (p. 575)

Clark, William Leader, with Meriwether Lewis, of expedition through the West beginning in 1804; brought back scientific samples, maps, and information on Native Americans (p. 95)

Clay, Henry Statesman from Kentucky; accused by Jackson of giving votes to John Q. Adams in return for post as Secretary of State; endorsed government promotion of economic growth; advocate of Compromise of 1850 (p. 122)

Cleveland, Grover Twenty-second and twenty-fourth President of the United States, 1885–1889, 1893–1897; supported railroad regulation and a return to the gold standard (p. 294)

Clinton, William J. Forty-second President of the United States, 1993–2001; advocated economic and healthcare reform; second President to be impeached (p. 894)

Columbus, Christopher Explorer whose voyage for Spain to North America in 1492 opened the Atlantic World (p. 11)

Coolidge, Calvin Thirtieth President of the United States, 1923–1929; promoted big business and opposed social aid (p. 488)

Coughlin, Father Charles E. "Radio Priest" who supported and then attacked President Franklin Roosevelt's New Deal; prevented by the Catholic Church from broadcasting after he praised Hitler (p. 546)

Coxey, Jacob S. Populist who led Coxey's Army in a march on Washington, D.C., in 1894 to seek government jobs for the unemployed (p. 295)

Custer, George Armstrong General who directed army attacks against Native Americans in the 1870s; commanded army forces killed in 1876 at Little Bighorn in Montana (p. 265)

D

Davis, Jefferson President of the Confederate States of America; ordered attack on Fort Sumter, the first battle of the Civil War (p. 143)

de Tocqueville, Alexis French writer; wrote *Democracy in America* following a visit to the United States in the 1830s (p. 122)

Dewey, George Officer in United States Navy, 1861–1917; led a surprise attack in the Philippines during the Spanish-American War that destroyed the entire Spanish fleet (p. 360)

Diem, Ngo Dinh Leader of South Vietnam, 1954–1963; supported by United States, but not by Vietnamese Buddhist majority; assassinated in 1963 (p. 793)

Dix, Dorothea Advocate of prison reform and of special institutions for the mentally ill in Massachusetts before the Civil War (p. 128)

Dole, Robert Senator from Kansas, 1969–1996; challenged William Clinton for the presidency in 1996 (p. 897)

Douglas, Stephen Illinois senator who introduced the Kansas-Nebraska Act, which allowed new territories to choose their own position on slavery; debated Abraham Lincoln on slavery issues in 1858 (p. 139)

Douglass, Frederick African American abolitionist leader who spoke eloquently for abolition in the United States and Britain before the Civil War (p. 130)

Du Bois, W.E.B. African American scholar and leader in early 1900s; encouraged African Americans to attend colleges to develop leadership skills (p. 325)

Frederick Douglass

E

Edison, Thomas A. Inventor; developed the light bulb, the phonograph, and hundreds of other inventions in the late 1800s and early 1900s (p. 228)

Ehrlichman, John Advisor on domestic policy to President Richard Nixon; deeply involved in Watergate (p. 827)

Einstein, Albert Physicist who fled Nazi persecution and later encouraged President Roosevelt to develop the atomic bomb (p. 620)

Albert Einstein

Eisenhower, Dwight D. Thirty-fourth President of the United States, 1953–1961; leader of Allied forces in World War II; as President, he promoted business and continued social programs (p. 684)

Ellington, Duke African American musician, bandleader, and composer of the 1920s and 1930s (p. 462)

Ellsberg, Daniel Defense Department official; leaked Pentagon Papers to the *New York Times* in 1971, revealing government lies to public about Vietnam (p. 839)

Emerson, Ralph Waldo Leader in the Transcendental movement; lecturer and writer (p. 127)

Equiano, Olaudah Antislavery activist who wrote an account of his enslavement (p. 28)

F

Father Divine African American minister; his Harlem soup kitchens fed the hungry during the Great Depression (p. 517)

Fillmore, Millard Thirteenth President of the United States, 1850–1853; promoted the Compromise of 1850 to smooth over disagreements about slavery in new territories (p. 965)

Finney, Charles Grandison Revivalist during the Second Great Awakening; emphasized religious conversion and personal choice (p. 127)

Fitzgerald, F. Scott Novelist who depicted the United States and the world during the 1920s in novels such as *The Great Gatsby* (p. 464)

Ford, Gerald R. Thirty-eighth President of the United States, 1974–1977; succeeded and pardoned Nixon; failed to establish strong leadership (p. 846)

Ford, Henry Pioneering auto manufacturer in the early 1900s; made affordable cars for the masses using assembly line and other production techniques (p. 493)

Franklin, Benjamin Colonial inventor, printer, writer, statesman; contributed to the Declaration of Independence and the Constitution (p. 24)

Frémont, John C. Explorer, military officer, and politician; led United States troops in 1846 Bear Flag Revolt when the United States took California from Mexico; ran for President as a Republican in 1856 (p. 136)

Friedan, Betty Feminist author; criticized limited roles for women in her 1963 book *The Feminine Mystique* (p. 766)

G

Garfield, James A. Twentieth President of the United States, 1881; his assassination by a disappointed office seeker led to the reform of the spoils system (p. 293)

Garrison, William Lloyd White leader of radical abolition movement based in Boston; founded *The Liberator* in 1831 to work for an immediate end to slavery (p. 130)

Garvey, Marcus African American leader from 1919 to 1926 who urged African Americans to return to their "motherland" of Africa; provided early inspiration for "black pride" movements (p. 472)

Gates, Bill Founder of Microsoft; revolutionized personal computing, investigated for questionable business practices (p. 915)

George III King of England during the American Revolution (p. 42)

George, Henry Author of *Progress and Poverty* (1879) linking land speculation and poverty; proposed a single tax based on land value (p. 384)

Gingrich, Newt Representative from Georgia, 1979–1998; called on Republican congressional candidates in 1994 elections to endorse "Contract with America" (p. 896)

Goodnight, Charles Texas cattle baron who helped blaze the Goodnight-Loving Trail through the Southwest (p. 272)

Gorbachev, Mikhail Soviet leader whose bold reforms led to the breakup of the Soviet Union in the late 1980s (p. 881)

Gore, Albert A. Senator from Tennessee; Vice President under President William Clinton, 1993–2001 (p. 899)

Graham, Billy Evangelist and presidential advisor; known for leading large-scale crusades, or religious rallies (p. 676)

Grant, Ulysses S. Eighteenth President of the United States, 1869–1877; commander of Union forces who accepted Lee's surrender in 1865 (p. 160)

H

Haldeman, H. R. Chief of Staff under President Richard Nixon; deeply involved in Watergate (p. 827)

Hamilton, Alexander Officer in the War for Independence; delegate to the Constitutional Convention; Federalist and first Secretary of the Treasury (p. 89)

Harding, Warren G. Twenty-ninth President of the United States, 1921–1923; presided over a short administration marked by corruption (p. 480)

Harrington, Michael Author; wrote *The Other America* in 1962, which described areas of poverty in the otherwise prosperous United States (p. 739)

Harrison, Benjamin Twenty-third President of the United States, 1889–1893; signed 1890 Sherman Antitrust Act later used to regulate big business (p. 295)

Harrison, William Henry Ninth President of the United States, 1841; died of pneumonia after only a month in office (p. 125)

Hayes, Rutherford B. Nineteenth President of the United States, 1877–1881; promised to withdraw Union troops from the South in order to end dispute over his election; attacked spoils system (p. 220)

Hearst, William Randolph Newspaper publisher from 1887 until his death in 1951; used "yellow journalism" in the 1890s to stir up sentiment in favor of the Spanish-American War (p. 359)

Hiss, Alger Former State Department official investigated as a possible Communist spy by House Un-American Activities Committee after World War II; convicted of perjury in 1950 (p. 651)

Hitler, Adolf German leader of National Socialist (Nazi) party 1933–1945; rose to power by promoting racist and nationalist views (p. 570)

Ho Chi Minh Leader of the Communist Party in Indochina after World War II; led Vietnamese against the French, then North Vietnamese against the United States in the Vietnam War (p. 792)

Hoover, Herbert Thirty-first President of the United States, 1929–1933; worked to aid Europeans during World War I; responded ineffectively to 1929 stock market crash and Great Depression (p. 498)

Houston, Sam Leader of Texas troops in war for independence from Mexico in 1836; elected first president of independent Texas (p. 110)

Hughes, Langston Writer active during the Harlem Renaissance (p. 465)

Humphrey, Hubert Democratic presidential candidate in 1968; lost narrowly to Nixon in an election bid hurt by support for the Vietnam War and by third-party candidate George Wallace (p. 809)

Hutchinson, Anne Critic of Puritan leadership of Massachusetts Bay Colony; banished for her religious beliefs (p. 21)

I

Isabella Ruler of Spanish Christian kingdoms with Ferdinand in late 1400s; sponsored Columbus's voyage to North America (p. 11)

J

Jackson, Andrew Seventh President of the United States, 1829–1837; supported minimal government and the spoils system; vetoed rechartering of the national bank; pursued harsh policy toward Native Americans (p. 123)

Jackson, Stonewall Confederate general known for his swift strikes against Union forces; earned nickname Stonewall by holding his forces steady under extreme pressure at the First Battle of Manassas (p. 157)

Jefferson, Thomas Third President of the United States, 1801–1809; main author of the Declaration of Independence; a firm believer in the people and decentralized power; reduced the federal government (p. 93)

Thomas Jefferson

Johnson, Andrew Seventeenth President of the United States, 1865–1869; clashed with Radical Republicans on Reconstruction programs; was impeached, then acquitted, in 1868 (p. 203)

Johnson, Lyndon B. Thirty-sixth President of the United States, 1963–1969; expanded social assistance with his Great Society program; increased United States commitment during Vietnam War (p. 744)

Jordan, Barbara Member of Congress from Texas; first African American and woman to represent her state in Congress; gave keynote addresses at 1976 and 1992 Democratic National Conventions (p. 843)

Joseph, Chief Leader of Nez Percé; forced to give up his home by United States army, fled toward Canada; captured in 1877 (p. 263)

K

Kelley, Florence Progressive reformer active from 1886 to 1920; worked in state and federal government for laws on child labor, workplace safety, and consumer protection (p. 386)

Kennedy, John F. Thirty-fifth President of the United States, 1961–1963; seen as youthful and inspiring; known for his firm handling of the Cuban Missile Crisis; assassinated in 1963 (p. 740)

Kennedy, Robert F. Attorney General under his brother, President John Kennedy, in the early 1960s; supported civil rights; assassinated while running for President in 1968 (p. 809)

Keynes, John Maynard British economist who believed that government spending could help a faltering economy; his theories helped shape New Deal legislation (p. 526)

Khomeini, Ayatollah Ruholla Islamic fundamentalist leader of Iran after the 1979 overthrow of the Shah; approved holding of American hostages (p. 856)

Khrushchev, Nikita Soviet leader from 1953 to 1964; opposed President Kennedy in the Cuban Missile Crisis (p. 753)

King, Martin Luther, Jr. African American civil rights leader from the mid-1950s until his assassination in 1968; used nonviolent means such as marches, boycotts, and legal challenges to win civil rights (p. 706)

Kissinger, Henry Secretary of State under Presidents Richard Nixon and Gerald Ford; used *realpolitik* to open relations with China, to end the Vietnam War, and to moderate Middle East conflict (p. 833)

L

Lafayette, Marquis de French officer who assisted American forces in the War for Independence (p. 48)

Dorothea Lange

Lange, Dorothea Photographed migrant farm workers during the Great Depression; inspired government aid programs and Steinbeck's *The Grapes of Wrath* (p. 517)

Lee, Robert E. Brilliant general of Confederate forces during the Civil War (p. 164)

Lenin, Vladimir I. Revolutionary leader in Russia; established a Communist government in 1917 (p. 427)

Levitt, William J. Built new communities in the suburbs after World War II, using mass-production techniques (p. 672)

Lewis, John L. Head of United Mine Workers through World War II; used strikes during the war to win pay raises (p. 597)

Lewis, Meriwether Leader with William Clark of expedition through the West beginning in 1804; brought back scientific samples, maps, and information on Native Americans (p. 95)

Lincoln, Abraham Sixteenth President of the United States, 1861–1865; known for his effective leadership during the Civil War and his Emancipation Proclamation declaring the end of slavery in Confederate-held territory (p. 170)

Lindbergh, Charles A. Aviator who became an international hero when he made the first solo flight across the Atlantic Ocean in 1927 (p. 456)

Lodge, Henry Cabot Massachusetts senator of early 1900s; supported United States imperialism (p. 356)

Long, Huey Louisiana politician in 1930s; suggested redistributing large fortunes by means of grants to families; assassinated in 1935 (p. 549)

M

MacArthur, Douglas United States general during the Great Depression, World War II, and Korean War; forced by Truman to resign in 1951 (p. 655)

Madison, James Fourth President of the United States, 1809–1817; called the Father of the Constitution for his leadership at the Constitutional Convention (p. 57)

Mahan, Alfred T. Author who argued in 1890 that the economic future of the United States rested on new overseas markets protected by a larger navy (p. 355)

Malcolm X African American leader during the 1950s and 1960s; eloquent spokesperson for African American self-sufficiency; assassinated in 1965 (p. 722)

Mann, Horace School reformer and supporter of public education before the Civil War; devised an educational system in Massachusetts later copied by many states (p. 128)

Mao Zedong Leader of Communists who took over China in 1949; remained in power until his death in 1976 (p. 653)

Marshall, George C. Army Chief of Staff during World War II and Secretary of State under President Harry Truman; assisted economic recovery in Europe after World War II and established strong allies for the United States through his Marshall Plan (p. 645)

Marshall, John Chief Justice of the Supreme Court appointed by John Adams; set precedents that established vital powers of the federal courts (p. 94)

Marshall, Thurgood First African American Supreme Court Justice; as a lawyer, won landmark school desegregation case *Brown* v. *Board of Education* in 1954 (p. 699)

McCarthy, Eugene Candidate in the 1968 Democratic presidential race who opposed the Vietnam War; convinced President Lyndon Johnson not to run again through his strong showing in the primaries (p. 809)

McCarthy, Joseph R. Republican senator from Wisconsin in the late 1940s and early 1950s; led a crusade to investigate officials he claimed were Communists; discredited in 1954 (p. 657)

McClellan, George Early Union army leader in the Civil War; careful organizer and planner who moved too slowly for northern politicians; ran against President Abraham Lincoln in the election of 1864 (p. 160)

McKinley, William Twenty-fifth President of the United States, 1897–1901; supported tariffs and a gold standard; expanded the United States by waging the Spanish-American War (p. 296)

McNamara, Robert Secretary of Defense under Presidents Kennedy and Lyndon Johnson; expanded American involvement in Vietnam War (p. 794)

Meade, George G. Union commander at Battle of Gettysburg in 1863; defended the high ground and forced the Confederate army to attack, causing great casualties (p. 181)

Metacom Leader of Pokanokets in Massachusetts; also known by his English name, King Philip; led Native Americans in King Philip's War, 1675–1676 (p. 21)

Mitchell, John Attorney General under President Richard Nixon; deeply involved in Watergate scandal (p. 827)

Monroe, James Fifth President of the United States, 1817–1825; acquired Florida from Spain; declared Monroe Doctrine to keep foreign powers out of the Americas (p. 121)

Morse, Samuel F. B. Artist and inventor; patented telegraph in 1844 (p. 229)

Mott, Lucretia Women's rights leader; helped organize first women's convention in Seneca Falls, New York, in 1848 (p. 132)

Mussolini, Benito Italian fascist leader who took power in the 1920s; called Il Duce ("the leader"); known for his brutal policies (p. 570)

N

Nader, Ralph Consumer advocate; published *Unsafe at Any Speed* in 1965 criticizing auto safety and inspiring new safety laws; Green Party candidate for president in the 2000 election (p. 784)

Nimitz, Chester Leader of American naval forces in World War II Battle of Midway, during which several Japanese aircraft carriers were destroyed (p. 617)

Nixon, Richard M. Thirty-seventh President, 1969–1974; known for his foreign policy toward the Soviet Union and China and for illegal acts he committed in the Watergate affair that forced his resignation (p. 835)

O

O'Connor, Sandra Day First woman Supreme Court Justice; appointed by President Reagan in 1981 (p. 878)

Oppenheimer, J. Robert Physicist who led American effort in World War II to develop first atomic bomb (p. 620)

P

Pahlavi, Muhammed Reza Shah, leader of Iran, from 1941 until his overthrow in 1979; supported by the United States; brought modernization to his country along with repression and corruption (p. 856)

Paine, Thomas Author of political pamphlets during 1770s and 1780s; wrote *Common Sense* in 1776 (p. 45)

Parks, Rosa Civil rights worker whose arrest in 1955 touched off the Montgomery bus boycott (p. 701)

Paul, Alice Women's suffrage leader of early 1900s; her Congressional Union used aggressive tactics to push the Nineteenth Amendment (p. 406)

Penn, William English Quaker who founded the colony of Pennsylvania in 1681 (p. 22)

Perkins, Frances Secretary of Labor 1933–1945 under President Franklin Delano Roosevelt; first woman Cabinet member (p. 541)

Pershing, John Leader of the American Expeditionary Forces during World War I (p. 425)

Perot, H. Ross Billionaire businessman who challenged William Clinton and George H. W. Bush for the presidency in 1992; strong opponent of NAFTA (p. 894)

Pierce, Franklin Fourteenth President of the United States, 1853–1857; signed the Kansas-Nebraska Act, which renewed conflicts over slavery in the territories (p. 965)

Polk, James K. Eleventh President of the United States, 1845–1849; led expansion of United States to southwest through war against Mexico (p. 136)

Polo, Marco Venetian traveler to China in the late 1200s; his book about the journey helped make Europeans aware of trade opportunities in eastern Asia (p. 7)

Popé Medicine man who led Pueblos and Apaches against Spanish rule in the Pueblo Revolt of 1680 (p. 16)

Pulitzer, Joseph Early 1900s newspaper publisher; used "yellow journalism" to stir up public sentiment in favor of the Spanish-American War (p. 329)

R

Randolph, A. Philip Civil rights activist from the 1930s to the 1950s; planned the Washington march that pressured President Franklin D. Roosevelt into opening World War II defense jobs to African Americans (p. 624)

Reagan, Ronald Fortieth President of the United States, 1981–1989; popular conservative leader who promoted supply-side economics and created huge budget deficits (p. 870)

Ronald Reagan

Riis, Jacob Reformer who wrote *How the Other Half Lives,* describing the lives of poor immigrants in New York City in the late 1800s (p. 308)

Robinson, Jackie Athlete who in 1947 became the first African American to play baseball in the major leagues (p. 698)

Rockefeller, Nelson Vice President appointed by President Gerald Ford in 1974; the nation's only nonelected Vice President to serve with a nonelected President (p. 847)

Roosevelt, Eleanor First Lady 1933–1945; tireless worker for social causes, including women's rights and civil rights for African Americans and other groups (p. 541)

Roosevelt, Franklin D. Thirty-second President of the United States, 1933–1945; fought the Great Depression through his New Deal social programs; battled Congress over Supreme Court control; proved a strong leader during World War II (p. 539)

Roosevelt, Theodore Twenty-sixth President of the United States, 1901–1909; fought trusts, aided Progressive reforms, built Panama Canal, and increased United States influence overseas (p. 369)

Theodore Roosevelt

Rosenberg, Julius and Ethel Husband and wife convicted and executed in 1953 for passing atomic secrets to the Soviet Union; records opened after the end of the Cold War suggest Julius was guilty, but that Ethel did not take part in espionage (p. 651)

S

Sacco, Nicola Immigrant and anarchist executed, in a highly controversial case, for a 1920 murder at a Massachusetts factory (p. 483)

Sadat, Anwar el- Egyptian leader in the 1970s; began the Middle East peace process by reaching the 1978 Camp David Accords with Israel (p. 855)

Salinger, J. D. Author of 1951 novel *The Catcher in the Rye*, which criticized 1950s conformity (p. 678)

Santa Anna, Antonio López de Mexican dictator who led government and troops in war against Texas; won the battle of the Alamo (p. 109)

Schlafly, Phyllis Conservative activist; led campaign during the 1970s and 1980s to block the Equal Rights Amendment (p. 769)

Seward, William Henry Republican antislavery leader during the 1860s; acquired Alaska in 1867 as Secretary of State (p. 219)

Sherman, William Tecumseh Union general in the Civil War; known for his destructive march from Atlanta to Savannah in 1864 (p. 189)

Sirica, John J. Washington judge who presided over the Watergate investigation in the 1970s; gave tough sentences to convicted participants and ordered President Richard Nixon to release secret tapes (p. 841)

Sitting Bull, Chief Leader of Sioux in clashes with United States Army in Black Hills in 1870s (p. 264)

Slater, Samuel English textile worker who brought the Industrial Revolution to the United States by duplicating British textile machinery from memory (p. 111)

Smith, John Leader of the Jamestown, Virginia, colony in the early 1600s (p. 18)

Smith, Joseph Founder of Church of Jesus Christ of Latter-day Saints, or Mormons, in New York in 1830; killed by a mob in Illinois in 1844 (p. 115)

Spock, Benjamin Pediatrician and author of *The Common Sense Book of Baby and Child Care* (1946), which encourages mothers to stay home with their children rather than work (p. 677)

Stalin, Joseph Leader of the Soviet Union from 1924–1953; worked with Roosevelt and Churchill during World War II but afterward became an aggressive participant in the Cold War (p. 569)

Stanton, Elizabeth Cady Women's rights leader in the 1800s; helped organize first women's convention; wrote the Declaration of Sentiments on women's rights in 1848 (p. 132)

Starr, Ellen Gates Cofounder of Chicago's Hull House, the first settlement house, in 1889 (p. 312)

Steinem, Gloria Journalist, women's rights leader since 1960s; founded *Ms.* magazine in 1972 to cover women's issues (p. 767)

Stevenson, Adlai Governor of Illinois and Democratic candidate for President in 1952 and 1956 against Eisenhower (p. 684)

Stilwell, Joseph World War II general active in the campaign against Japan in Southeast Asia (p. 615)

Stowe, Harriet Beecher Author of the novel *Uncle Tom's Cabin* (1852), which contributed significantly to anti-southern feelings among Northerners before the Civil War (p. 132)

Sumner, Charles Abolitionist and senator from Massachusetts; beaten badly with a cane in the Senate by a southern congressman after making an antislavery speech (p. 140)

T

Taft, William Howard Twenty-seventh President of the United States, 1909–1913; continued Progressive reforms of President Theodore Roosevelt; promoted "dollar diplomacy" to expand foreign investments (p. 370)

Taylor, Zachary Twelfth President of the United States, 1849–1850; Mexican War officer (p. 136)

Thoreau, Henry David Transcendentalist author known for his work *Walden* (1854) and other writings (p. 127)

Travis, William Leader in Texas's bid for independence from Mexico in 1836; died at the Alamo after appealing to the United States for help (p. 109)

Truman, Harry S Thirty-third President of the United States, 1945–1953; authorized use of atomic bomb; signed Marshall Plan to rebuild Europe (p. 638)

Truth, Sojourner Abolitionist and women's rights advocate before the Civil War; as a former slave, she spoke effectively to white audiences on abolition issues (p. 130)

Tubman, Harriet "Conductor" on the Underground Railroad, which helped slaves escape to freedom before the Civil War (p. 131)

Turner, Frederick Jackson Historian who wrote an essay in 1893 emphasizing the western frontier as a powerful force in the formation of the American character (p. 275)

Turner, Nat African American preacher who led a slave revolt in 1831; captured and hanged after the revolt failed (p. 120)

Tweed, William Marcy Boss of the Tammany Hall political machine in New York City; convicted of forgery and larceny in 1873 and died in jail in 1878 (p. 309)

Tyler, John Tenth President of the United States, 1841–1845; accomplished little due to quarrels between Whigs and Jacksonian Democrats (p. 125)

V

Van Buren, Martin Eighth President of the United States, 1837–1841; Jacksonian Democrat; was voted out of office after the Panic of 1837 brought widespread unemployment and poverty (p. 125)

Vance, Cyrus Secretary of State under President Jimmy Carter; invited Israelis and Egyptians to Camp David in 1978 to begin Middle East peace process (p. 855)

Vanzetti, Bartolomeo Immigrant and anarchist executed, in a highly controversial case, for a 1920 murder at a Massachusetts factory (p. 483)

Vesey, Denmark African American who planned 1822 South Carolina slave revolt; captured and hanged after revolt failed (p. 120)

W

Walker, Madam C. J. African American leader and businesswoman in the early 1900s; she spoke out against lynching (p. 336)

Wallace, George C. Third-party candidate for President in 1968; focused his campaign on issues of blue-collar anger in the North and racial tension (p. 811)

Warren, Earl Chief Justice of the United States Supreme Court 1953–1968; investigated President Kennedy's assassination; led in many decisions that protected civil rights, rights of the accused, and right to privacy (p. 749)

Washington, Booker T. African American leader from the late 1800s until his death in 1915; founded Tuskegee Institute in Alabama; encouraged African Americans to learn trades (p. 324)

Washington, George First President of the United States, 1789–1797; led American forces in the War for Independence; set several federal precedents, including the two-term maximum for presidential office (p. 63)

Booker T. Washington

Whitney, Eli Inventor; developed the cotton gin in 1793, which rapidly increased cotton production in the South and led to a greater demand for slave labor (p. 112)

Wilhelm, Kaiser Emperor of Germany during World War I; symbol to the United States of German militarism and severe efficiency (p. 418)

Wilson, Woodrow Twenty-eighth President of the United States, 1913–1921; tried to keep the United States out of World War I; proposed League of Nations (p. 399)

Y

Yeltsin, Boris Leader of Russia in late 1980s and 1990s; took over from Mikhail Gorbachev as reforms continued and Communist Party control ended (p. 903)

York, Alvin American soldier who was awarded the Congressional Medal of Honor for bravery during World War I (p. 431)

Z

Zenger, Peter Colonial printer arrested for libel, his landmark trial established truth as a defense against libel (p. 28)

Index

Note: Entries with a page number followed by a *c* indicate a chart or graph on that page; *go* indicates a graphic organizer; *m* indicates a map; *p* indicates a picture; and *q* indicates a quotation.

barter, 6
Barton, Bruce, 499
Baruch, Bernard, 433
baseball, 327, 327*p*, 329, 532–533
basketball, 329
Bataan Death March, 615
Batista, Fulgencio, 751, 772
Bay of Pigs invasion, 751–753, 752*m*, 752*p*
Bear Flag Revolt, 136–137
Beat Generation, 679
Beatles, the, 678, 779
beatniks, 679
Beauregard, P.G.T., 144, 157
Beecher, Lyman, 127
Begin, Menachem, 855, 855*p*
Bell, Alexander Graham, 230, 664
Bellamy, Edward, 384, 384*q*, 385
Bellow, Saul, 557
Bell Telephone Laboratories, 670
Benin, 9–10, 10*m*
Berkeley, William, 19
Berlin 571, 608
    divided Germany and (1949), 646*m*
    occupation zones of, 646, 753
Berlin airlift, 638, 645–647, 646*p*, 753
Berlin, Irving, 598
Berlin Wall, 753*c*, 753*p*, 754
    fall of, 884, 884*p*
Bernstein, Carl, 842, 842*p*
Berry, Chuck, 678
Bessemer, Henry, 233
Bessemer process, 233–234, 240
    used for skyscrapers, 306
Bethune, Mary McLeod, 541
Beveridge, Albert J., 356, 373*q*
bicentennial, 850, 850*p*
big business, 237–238, 239–242, 245
    advertising becomes, 491
    under Eisenhower, 686–687
    farming becomes, 274
    mining becomes realm of, 269
    spectator sports become, 458
    stocks plummet, 509. See also Great Crash; Great Depression
bilingual education, 912
Bill of Rights, 62, 80–88, 170–171, 732
bimetallic standard, 278, 279
bin Laden, Osama, 897, 906–907
biological weapons, 907, 909
Birmingham, Alabama
    civil rights protests in, 713–714
    desegregation of city facilities in, 714
    protests and boycotts in, 712*c*, 714*p*
Bismarck, Otto von, 167
black codes, 206
    Congress outlaws, 207
Black Kettle, Chief, 263
blacklist, 650
Blackmun, Harry A., 831
Black Muslims, 722–723
black nationalism, 723. See also Malcolm X; Nation of Islam
Black Panthers, 724, 724*p*
black power movement, 722*go*, 724, 724*p*
Black Star Line steamship company, 473*p*. See also Garvey, Marcus
Black Thursday, 509. See also Great Crash

Black Tuesday, 509. See also Great Crash
Blaine, James G., 293, 294
Bland-Allison Act, 279
"Bleeding Kansas," 140, 141*m*
blitzkrieg, 576, 577, 601, 603, 606–607
Blitz, the, 579, 579*p*, 605
blockade, Union, 159, 160, 162*m*, 163, 168, 174, 180, 188*m*
blue laws, 292
blues, 331, 461
Bolsheviks, 438, 481. See also Russian Revolution
bomber planes
    World War I, 430
    World War II, 605, 616, 619, 665*p*
bombing raids
    World War I, 429
    World War II, 605, 616, 618
bonanza farms, 274. See also farming
Bonus Army, 526–527
Book of Mormon, The, 115
boomers. See homesteaders
Boone, Daniel, 106
Booth, John Wilkes, 193, 203
bootleggers, 467–468, 469. See also Prohibition
Border States, 142, 144
Bosnia, 416, 904–905
Boston Massacre, 43–44, 43*p*, 91
Boston, siege of, 46
Boston Tea Party, 44
Boulder Dam, 525*p*
Bowie, James, 109
Boxer Rebellion, 364
boycott, 253. See also civil rights; civil rights movement
    colonial, of British goods, 43
    First Continental Congress agrees to, 44
    historic use of, 702
    of Olympic Games, 856, 876, 907
Boycott, Charles, 702. See also boycott
Boynton v. Virginia, 710
Boy Scout movement, 374–375
Bozeman Trail, 264
Bradford, William, 20
Bradley, Omar N., 607
Bradwell v. Illinois, 405
Brady, Matthew, 157, 182
Brandeis, Louis D., 393, 401
Braun, Wernher von, 686*p*
Breckinridge, John C., 142
Brezhnev, Leonid I., 836, 849*p*, 856
brinkmanship, 660–661
Britain, Battle of, 578–579, 578*p*
British East India Company, 44
Broken Treaties Caravan, 775. See also American Indian Movement (AIM)
Brooklyn Bridge, 234–235, 235*p*
Brown, John, 142, 142*q*
"brown power," 773
Brown v. Board of Education, 699–700, 712*c*, 867
    reaction to, 700–701, 702–703
Broz, Josip. See Tito
Bruce, Blanche K., 210*p*, 211
Bryan, William Jennings, 281, 282*p*, 296, 372, 396, 470–471, 470*p*
Buchanan, James, 140, 143, 965
Buchanan, Patrick, 826

Buck, Pearl, 556
budget deficit, 550, 738
    need for reduction of, 895–896
    use of, to improve economy, 746
buffalo, 258*p*, 261, 286
    destruction of, 270
Buffalo Chase—Single Death, 261*p*
Bulgaria, 639
Bulge, Battle of the, 607
Bull Moose Party, 398, 398*p*. See also Progressive Party
Bull Run
    First Battle of, 156–158
    Second Battle of, 164–165
bully pulpit, 369. See also Roosevelt, Theodore
Bunau-Varilla, Philippe, 367
Bunker Hill, Battle of, 46
Bunyan, John, 384
Bureau of Indian Affairs (BIA), 262
    occupation of, 775
Burger, Warren, 830
Burma Road, 584, 615
Burnside, Ambrose, 178–179
Burr, Aaron, 89*p*, 92–93
    duel of Hamilton and, 89
Bush, George H. W., 882*p*, 886*q*, 967
    1992 election and, 894–895
    approval ratings of, 887*c*
    background of, 882
    campaign of (1988), 882–883
    domestic policy of, 887
    events affecting policies of, 882*go*
    foreign policy of, 883–887
    "New World Order" of, 903
Bush, George W., 899, 899*p*, 908*p*, 967
    changes in presidency under, 899–900
    domestic policy of, 900
    foreign policy of, 908
    tax cut of, 900
    and terrorist attack on America, 901
Bush, Laura (Mrs. George W.), 900*p*
Bush v. Gore, 898
business boom, 1920s, 491*go*
business cycle, 509, 563*c*. See also Great Crash
    tracking a, 509*c*
businesses
    closure of, during Great Depression. See also Great Crash; Great Depression
    international, 355
    sell products to youth market, 676
Butler, Andrew, 140
Byrnes, James F., 596, 641*p*

C

Cabeza de Vaca, Alvar Núñez, 16
Cabot, John, 17
Calhoun, John C., 138
California, 956*m*, 964
    Asian Americans in, 301, 774, 912
    Bear Flag Revolt in, 136–137
    civil rights movement in, 725
    environmental achievements, 789*m*
    gains statehood, 257*m*
    Golden Gate Bridge, 535*p*
    gold rush, 137, 137*p*, 262, 268
    during Great Depression, 515, 556

Index

Index

Index

Index

Index

Index

Acknowledgments

STAFF CREDITS

Leann Davis Alspaugh, Mary Ann Barton, Suzanne Biron, Margaret Broucek, Sarah M. Carroll, Siobhan Costello, Anne Drowns, Alex Crumbley, Deborah Dukeshire, Deborah Feldheim, **Thomas Ferreira, Gabriela Pérez Fiato, Mary Ann Gundersen,** Lance Hatch, Kerri Hoar, Kate House, Katharine Ingram, Nancy Jones, Tim Jones, Kevin Keane, Suzanne Klein, Michael Locker, Meredith Mascola, **Constance McCarty,** Anne McLaughlin, Terri Mitchell, Mark O'Malley, Jen Paley, Elizabeth Pearson, Jill Ratzan, Lynn Robbins, **Luess Sampson-Lizotte,** Hope Schuessler, Mark Staloff, Susan Swan, Jerry Thorne, Stacy Tibbetts, Bernadette Walsh, Roberta Warshaw, **Merce Wilczek,** Matthew Wilson, Amy Winchester, Helen Young

COVER IMAGE

Front Cover Vietnam Memorial: Lelia Hendren/Folio, Inc. Flag background: Jim Barber/The StockRep, Inc. **Back Cover** Stone

MAPS

XNR Productions Inc.: 3, 10, 15, 22, 27, 32, 36, 37, 39, 41, 42, 47, 92, 95, 97, 98, 105, 108, 109, 136, 138, 141, 149, 155, 161, 162, 171, 179, 180, 183, 188, 199, 208, 217, 220, 225, 236, 257, 264, 269, 271, 281, 286, 289, 296, 300, 319, 351, 353, 360, 363, 365, 367, 370, 378, 381, 391, 399, 400, 407, 413, 414, 415, 416, 427, 440, 446, 451, 455, 456, 457, 479, 504–505, 507, 515, 529, 535, 540, 541, 567, 569, 572, 577, 583, 588, 593, 601, 603, 606, 612, 616, 635, 641, 646, 654, 659, 667, 673, 691, 693, 697, 700, 711, 735, 737, 752, 754, 763, 789, 791, 793, 802, 811, 813, 825, 863, 869, 883, 890, 891, 899, 906, 909, 960; **Mapping Specialists Limited:** 956, 957, 958, 962–963

ILLUSTRATION

Leann Davis Alspaugh: 865; **argosypublishing.com:** 159, 241, 244, 292, 293, 307, 333, 392, 461, 485, 487, 492, 500, 816, 871, 873, 874, 875, 880; **Kenneth Batelman:** 61, 112, 118, 234, 428–429, 494–495, 510, 753, 756, 800, 836, 854; **Matt Mayerchak & Laura Glassman:** 2–3, 38–39, 104–105, 154–155, 156, 166, 175, 178, 186, 192, 194, 198–199, 200, 206, 212, 218, 221, 222, 224–225, 256–257, 258, 261, 266, 268, 272, 277, 284, 288–289, 318–319, 320, 322, 327, 332, 334, 337, 342, 350–351, 380–381, 382, 389, 396, 403, 412–413, 414, 421, 425, 432, 437, 438, 450–451, 478–479, 506–507, 534–535, 566–567, 592–593, 634–635, 666–667, 672, 696–697, 734–735, 762–763, 790–791, 824–825, 862–863, 892–893; **Jen Paley:** 4, 13, 14, 24, 34, 40, 54, 59, 89, 100, 106, 111, 116, 121, 126, 128, 130, 134, 135, 139, 146, 150, 151, 213, 214, 219, 226, 237, 243, 247, 254, 274, 290, 297, 299, 304, 310, 311, 316, 322, 347, 352, 355, 357, 359, 366, 372, 376, 388, 394, 408, 442, 446, 447, 452, 453, 459, 467, 474, 480, 491, 498, 502, 508, 509, 511, 513, 520, 524, 530, 536, 543, 545, 550, 553, 554, 560, 562, 563, 568, 575, 581, 585, 590, 594, 597, 600, 609, 614, 618, 623, 630, 636, 643, 644, 645, 648, 652, 656, 657, 662, 668, 670, 672, 675, 677, 680, 688, 692, 693, 698, 704, 709, 712, 716, 720, 722, 728, 736, 739, 743, 746, 747, 751, 760, 764, 765, 771, 774, 777, 781, 784, 786, 792, 796, 798, 803, 805, 812, 818, 820, 821, 826, 828, 832, 838, 846, 848, 851, 858, 864, 870, 876, 882, 887, 888, 894, 902, 903, 911, 912, 918, 922, 923, 960, 961, 964; **Hope Schuessler:** 841

PICTURE RESEARCH

Paula Wehde

PHOTOGRAPHY

Front Matter ii T, Courtesy, Andrew Cayton, Ph.D.; **ii TM,** Courtesy, Elisabeth Israels Perry, Ph.D.; **ii BM,** Courtesy, Linda Reed, Ph.D.; **ii B,** Courtesy, Allan M. Winkler, Ph.D.; **iii,** Shelburne Museum

Table of Contents iv T, Dukes County Historical Society/photo by Robert Schellhammer ©1994; **iv B,** The Granger Collection, NY; **v T,** Culver Pictures, Inc.; **v M,** National Museum of American Art, Smithsonian Institution, Washington, D.C., Gift of Mrs. Joseph Harrison, Jr. Art Resource, NY; **v B,** Corbis; **vi TL,** Panama Canal Museum; **vi ML,** Library of Congress; **vi MR,** The Granger Collection, NY; **vi B,** National Archives; **vii BL,** Franklin D. Roosevelt Library; **vii TR,** Corbis; **vii MR,** FDR Library; **vii BR,** Gary Waltz/The Image Works; **viii TL,** The Granger Collection, NY; **viii ML,** Harry S. Truman Presidential Library; **viii BL,** J.R. Eyerman/TimePix; **viii BL inset,** Russ Lappa; **viii BM,** Corbis; **viii BR,** © 1959 Newsweek Inc. All rights reserved. Reprinted by permission.; **ix BL,** Lambert/Hulton/Archive/Getty Images; **ix TR,** Don Uhrbrock *LIFE Magazine* © Time Warner; **ix TM,** Al Freni/*LIFE Magazine* © Time Warner; **ix BM,** David J. Frent; **ix BR,** Guido Rossi/Hulton Archive/Getty Images; **x T,** Steve Northup, © Time Inc. *Time Magazine;* **x M,** David J. Frent; **x B,** Stone; **xi TL,** New Holland Machine Company; **xi BL,** Thomas E. Franklin/Bergen Record/Corbis SABA; **xi TR,** Hulton/Liaison Agency/Getty Images; **xii,** Collection of Ryan Brown; **xiv L,** UPI/Bettmann Archives/Corbis; **xiv R,** Art Resource, NY; **xx T,** Greg E. Mathieson/MAI Photo News Agency, Inc.; **xx M,** Library of Congress; **xx B,** Terry Donnelly/Stone; **xxi T all,** Courtesy of the Federal Reserve Bank of San Francisco; **xxi M,** AP/Wide World Photos; **xxi B,** Brown Brothers; **xxii TL,** Bob Adelman/Magnum Photos, Inc.; **xxii TR,** Hulton/Liaison/Getty Images; **xxii M inset,** Hulton/Archive/Getty Images; **xxii BR,** Time Life Books; **xxiii T,** American Textile History Museum; **xxiii M,** Library of Congress; **xxiii B,** Jewish Hospital/University of Louisville; **xxiv,** Corel Corp.; **xxv all,** Corel Corp.

Reading and Writing Handbook xxviii Michael Newman/PhotoEdit; **xxix** Walter Hodges/Getty Images, Inc.; **xxxi** T Tom Stewart/Corbis; **xxxi B** Getty Images, Inc.; **xxxii** Jose L. Pelaez, Inc./Corbis; **xxxiii** David Young-Wolff/PhotoEdit; **xxxiv** Getty Images, Inc.; **xxxvii** Arthur Tilley/Getty Images, Inc.; **xxxix** Mary Kate Denny/PhotoEdit

Unit Openers xi–1, Architect of the Capitol; **152–153,** The Andrew J. Russell Collection, The Oakland Museum of California; **348–349,** Museum of the City of New York; **448–449,** New York Historical Society/Bridgeman Art Library; **564–565,** Corbis; **694–695,** Corbis; **822–823,** Brad Perks

Chapter 1 2 L, Corbis Sygma; **2 R,** The Pilgrim Society; **3 R,** Laurie Minor-Penland, Smithsonian Institution; **3 L,** Courtesy, American Antiquarian Society; **4,** David Gallery, Philadelphia/SuperStock; **5,** Courtesy The Edward E. Ayer Collection, The Newberry Library; **6 T,** Courtesy of the National Museum of the American Indian/Smithsonian Institution; **6 M,** Etowah Indian Mounds Historic Site; **6 B,** Giraudon/Art Resource, NY; **7,** The Granger Collection, NY; **8 T,** Louvre, Paris, France/Art Resource, NY; **8 B,** The Granger Collection, NY; **9,** Photograph by Jeffrey Ploskonka, National Museum of African Art, Eliot Elisofon Archive, Smithsonian Institution; **11,** The Metropolitan Museum of Art, Gift of J. Pierpont Morgan, 1900 (10.18.2); **12,** London Science Museum. Phot G Michael Holford; **14,** The Granger Collection, NY; **16,** Texas Memorial Museum, Austin; **17,** National Maritime Museum; **18,** Fairholt, F.W.,Tobacco: It's history, London, 1859 (detail) Arents Collection, The New York Public Library, Astor, Lenox and Tilden Foundations; **19 T,** Library of Congress; **19 B,** Peabody & Essex Museum. Photo by Mark Sexton; **20,** The Pilgrim Society; **21,** Culver Pictures, Inc.; **23,** NC Division of Archives and History; **24 T,** Corbis; **24 B,** The Library Company of Philadelphia; **25,** National Portrait Gallery, London/SuperStock; **26,** Library of Congress; **28,** Royal Albert Memorial Museum, Exeter/Bridgeman Art Library, London/New York; **29,** National Maritime Museum; **30 L,** Courtesy Linda O. King/Coastal Islands Historical Society; **30 R,** H.L. Miller/Stock South/PictureQuest; **33 T,** Library of Congress; **33 B,** Library of Congress; **35,** Steve Kelley/ Copley News Service

Chapter 2 38 L, Shelburne Museum; **38 R,** Corbis; **39,** Library of Congress; **40,** Geoffrey Clements/Corbis; **43 T,** Colonial Williamsburg Foundation; **43 B,** The Granger Collection, NY; **44,** Massachusetts Historical Society; **45,** Corbis; **46,** Tom Stack & Associates; **48,** The Granger Collection, New York; **49,** Private Collection; **53 Declaration of Independence,** Library of Congress; **54,** SuperStock; **56,** Culver Pictures, Inc.; **57,** Independence National Historic Park; **58,** Free Library of Philadelphia; **62 B,** Courtesy, American Antiquarian Society; **62 T,** The Library Company of Philadelphia; **63,** Art Resource, NY; **64,** The Granger Collection, NY; **89 B,** Art Resource, NY; **89 T,** New York Historical Society/The Bridgeman Art Library; **89 M,** Special Collection/Dartmouth College Library; **90,** "An Exciseman" (detail) Atwater Kent Museum; **91,** National Portrait Gallery, Smithsonian Institution, Washington, D.C./Art Resource NY; **93,** ©White House Historical Association/Photo by National Geographic Society; **94,** Missouri Historical Society; **95,** Duke University Archives; **96,** National Portrait Gallery, Smithsonian Institution, Washington, DC #83-7221; **101,** Prentice Hall

Chapter 3 104 L, Library of Congress; **104 R,** Archives Division-Texas State Library; **105 L,** The Granger Collection, NY; **105 R,** Women's Rights Collection, Sophia Smith Archives; **106–107 B,** Panoramic Images; **107 T,** Pearson Education/Prentice Hall College; **109,** San Jacinto Museum of History Association; **110,** Corbis; **111,** Library of Congress; **113 T,** Corbis; **113 B,** The Granger Collection, NY; **114,** The New York Historical Society; **115,** Library of Congress; **116,** Museum of American Folk Art; **117,** Lowell Historical Society; **119,** Library of Congress; **122,** The Metropolitan Museum of Art; **123,** Museum of the City of New York; **124,** Woolaroc Museum, Bartlesville, OK; **125,** The New York Historical Society; **126–127 B,** Corbis; **127 T,** The Granger Collection, NY; **128,** Boston Athenaeum; **129,** Library of Congress; **131,** Sophia Smith Collection, Smith College; **132,** The Granger Collection, NY; **134,** Harper's Weekly; **135,** Corbis; **136,** The Granger Collection, NY; **137,** American Antiquarian Society; **138,** Library of Congress; **140,** The New York Public Library; **142,** The New York Public Library Prints Division; **143 T,** The Granger Collection, NY; **143 B,** National Geographic Society; **144 L,** State Historical Society of Wisconsin; **144 R,** National Civil War Museum; **147,** The New York Historical Society

Chapter 4 154 R, Greg E. Mathieson/MAI Photo News Agency, Inc.; **154 L,** Artist: Douglas Volk, Minnesota Historical Society; **155,** Brown University Library; **156,** Culver Pictures, Inc.; **157,** Culver Pictures, Inc.; **160 L,** Rick Vargas and Richard Strauss, SI; **160 R,** Collection of David & Kevin Kyle; **161,** Collection of Michael J. McAfee. Courtesy William Gladstone. Photo © Seth Goltzer; **163,** The Collection of Jay P. Altmayer; **164,** Museum of the Confederacy; **165,** Museum of the Confederacy; **166,** Rick Vargas and Richard Strauss, Smithsonian Institution; **168,** John G. Johnson Collection, Philadelphia Museum of Art; **170,** McLellan Lincoln Collection, John Hay Library, Brown University; **172,** Corbis; **173,** Chicago Historical Society; **174,** Culver Pictures, Inc.; **176,** Corbis; **176 inset,** American Antiquarian Society; **178,** Courtesy of Museum of the Confederacy, Richmond, Virginia; **181,** The Granger Collection, NY; **182 TR,** National Archives; **182 BR,** ABC News/Getty Images, Inc. **182 L,** Philip Jones Griffiths/MP, Zenith Electronics Corporation; **183,** The Beverly R. Robinson Collection, U.S. Naval Academy Museum; **185,** Brown University Library; **186,** The Granger Collection, NY; **189,** The Granger Collection, NY; **190,** The Granger Collection, NY; **191,** Rob Crandall/Folio, Inc.; **192,** Virginia Historical Society; **193,** Anne S.K. Brown Military Collection, Brown University Library, Providence, RI; **195,** Culver Pictures, Inc.

Chapter 5 198 L, The Granger Collection, NY; **198 R,** Library of Congress; **200,** Brown Brothers; **201,** The Granger Collection, NY; **202 B,** Library of Congress; **202 T,** Courtesy of the Museum of the Confederacy/Library of Congress; **204 I,** Collection of William Gladstone; **204 R,** Collection of William Gladstone; **205,** The Granger Collection, NY; The Granger Collection, NY; **208 T,** The Granger Collection, NY; **208 B,** Corbis; **209,** Russ Lappa; **210,** Library of Congress; **211,** Collection of Nancy Gewirz, Antique Textile Resource, Bethesda, Maryland; **212,** Los Angelos County Museum of Art: Acquisition made possible through museum trustees; **213,** The New York Historical Society; **215 T,** Courtesy of the Witte Museum; **215 B,** Library of Congress; **216,** Prentice Hall; **218 inset,** Collection of State Historical Museum/Mississippi Department of Archives and History; **218,** Rutherford B. Hayes Presidential Center; **221,** The Granger Collection, NY; **223,** Library of Congress

Chapter 6 224 L, Library of Congress; **224 R,** Light-Foot Collection; **225,** The Granger Collection, NY; **226,** The Granger Collection, NY; **226 B,** The Granger Collection, NY; **227 T,** Courtesy of the Federal Reserve Bank of San Francisco; **227 B,** Archive Photos; **228 T,** Library of Congress; **228 B,** National Geographic Society; **229,** Hulton Archive/Getty Images; **231,** Index Stock Imagery, Inc.; **231 inset,** The Granger Collection, NY; **232,** The Oakland Museum History Department; **233,** Hulton Archive/Getty Images; **234,** Chicago Historical Society; **235,** Museum of the City of New York; **237,** Corbis; **238,** Museum of American Textile History; **239,** Library of Congress; **240,** Library of Congress; **243,** Brown Brothers; **245,** Putman County Historical Society, Cold Spring, N.Y.; **246 L,** Library of Congress; **246 R,** Library of Congress; **247 L,** Library of Congress; **247 R,** Picture Research Consultants, Inc.; **248 L,** The Granger Collection, NY; **248 R,** Collection of Ralph J. Brunke; **251,** Brown Brothers; **252,** Corbis; **253,** Brown Brothers; **255,** Library of Congress

Chapter 7 256 L, National Anthropological Archives/Smithsonian Institution; **256 R,** Thomas Moran, Grand Canyon of the Yellowstone, 1872, oil on canvas, The U.S. Department of the Interior Museum, Washington, D.C.; **256 M,** Corbis; **258–259,** Jake Rajs/Stone; **260,** Corbis; **261,** National Museum of American Art, Smithsonian Institution, Washington, D.C. Gift of Mrs. Joseph Harrison, Jr. Art Resource, NY; **263 T,** Library of Congress; **263 B,** Colorado Historical Society; **264–265 B,** National Anthropological Archives/Smithsonian Institution; **265 T,** SuperStock; **267 T,** Cumberland County Historical Society; **267 B,** Cumberland County Historical Society; **268,** California State Library; **270,** Library of Congress; **272,** Amon Carter Museum of Western Art; **273,** Denver Public Library; **275 T,** Buffalo Bill Historical Center, Cody WY; **275 B,** Library of Congress; **276,** Photofest; **279,** American Gold Exchange, Austin, TX; **279,** American Gold Exchange, Austin, TX; **280 T,** Kansas State Historical Society; **280 B,** East

Carolina Manuscript Collection, J.Y. Joyner Library, East Carolina University; **282,** Library of Congress; **285,** Library of Congress

Chapter 8 288 M, Division of Political History, Smithsonian Institution; **288 R,** Visions of America; **288 L,** The Granger Collection, NY; **290,** The Granger Collection, NY; **291,** *Puck,* March 10, 1897; **293 T,** Library of Congress; **293 B,** Library of Congress; **295 R,** Collection of David J. Frent and Janice L. Frent; **295 L,** Collection of David J. Frent and Janice L. Frent; **297,** Courtesy George Eastman House; **298 T,** The Museum of the City of New York; **298 BR,** Chermayeff & Geisma; **298 BL,** National Park Service Collection, Gift of Angelo Forgione; **301,** Library of Congress; **302,** California Department of Parks and Recreation, courtesy Fred Wasserman; **303,** El Paso Border Heritage Center; **304,** Brown Brothers; **305 T,** Library of Congress; **305 B,** Library of Congress; **306,** Library of Congress; **308,** Museum of the City of New York, Gift of Joseph Varner Reed; **309,** Thomas Nast; **311,** Library of Congress; **312,** Library of Congress; **313,** California Museum of Photography; **314,** Chermayeff & Geisma; **315,** Corbis; **317,** *Puck,* 1909

Chapter 9 318, Culver Pictures, Inc.; **319 L,** The Kobal Collection; **319 R,** Chicago Historical Society; **319 M, TR,** Wood River Gallery, Mill Valley, California; BR, Wood; **320,** Kansas State Historical Society; **321,** The McGuffy Museum; **322,** Oldest Wooden School House, St. Augustine, Florida; **323,** Sophia Smith Collection; **324,** Brown Brothers; **325,** The New York Public Library; **327 L,** Rick Vargas, Smithsonian Institution; **327 R,** National Baseball Library and Archive, Cooperstown, NY; **328,** Barbara Puorro Galasso/George Eastman House; **329,** Brooklyn Museum; **330,** Corbis; **331,** Fisk University Special Collections; **332,** Corbis; **333,** Mauldin/© 1962 *St. Louis Post-Dispatch;* **335,** The Granger Collection; **336,** Corbis; **337,** Corbis; **338,** Courtesy of The Maytag Company; **339 L,** The Granger Collection, NY; **339 M,** Tony Freeman/PhotoEdit; **339 R,** Bob Daemmrich Photography; **340,** Kansas State Historical Society; **341,** Charles Dana Gibson; **343,** Library of Congress

Chapter 10 350 L, National Portrait gallery, Smithsonian Institution/Art Resource, NY; **350 TR,** New York Historical Society; **350 BR,** Chicago Historical Society; **351 R,** Schalkwijk/New York Historical Society, NY; **351 L,** Courtesy of the U.S. Naval Academy Museum; **352,** Library of Congress; **355,** The Oakland Museum of California; **356,** Library of Congress; **357,** The Granger Collection, NY; **359,** Corbis; **361,** *Puck* magazine 1898; **362 L,** Library of Congress; **362 M,** National Archives; **362 R,** AP/Wide World Photos; **364,** Culver Pictures; **366,** Corbis; **367 BL,** Panama Canal Museum; **367 BR,** Panama Canal Museum; **367 T,** Panama Canal Museum; **368,** Library of Congress; **369,** Theodore Roosevelt Collection Harvard College Library; **372,** The Granger Collection, NY; **374,** Courtesy of the U.S. Naval Academy Museum; **375,** Prentice Hall; **377,** *Puck,* June 29, 1904

Chapter 11 380 L, Sophia Smith College Archives; **380 R,** Texas State Library & Archives Commission; **381,** Dartmouth College College Library, Special Collection; **382,** Brown Brothers; **382 inset,** Courtesy of the Decorative & Industrial Arts Collection of the Chicago Historical Society; **383,** Corbis Sygma; **384,** Culver Pictures, Inc.; **385,** Brown Brothers; **385 inset,** Library of Congress; **386,** Labor Management Documentation Center, Cornell University; **387 T,** Corbis; **387 B,** Corbis; **389,** Corbis; **390–391,** Texas State Library & Archives Commission; **393,** State Historical Society of Wisconsin; **395,** Hulton/Archive/Getty Images; **396,** White House Historical Association; **397,** The Granger Collection, NY; **398 T,** Museum of American Political Life; **398 B,** Theodore Roosevelt Collection Harvard College Library; **401 T,** Bettmann/Corbis; **401 B,** David J.Frent; **402 T,** National Association for the Advancement of Colored People; **402 B,** Schomburg Center for Research in Black Culture; **403,** Courtesy of the Women's Voters of the United States; **404,** Meserve-Kunhardt Collection; **406 T,** Library of Congress; **406 B,** "Vote Yes" suffrage poster/Smithsonian Institution; **409,** Library of Congress

Chapter 12 412 L, Culver Pictures, Inc.; **412 R,** The Granger Collection, NY; **413 R,** Library of Congress; **413 M,** Corbis; **413 L,** Hulton/Archive/Archive Photos; **414,** Hulton/Archive/Archive Photos; **416,** Museum of the City of New York; **417 T,** Collection of Stuart S. Corning, Jr. Photo © Rob Huntley/Lightstream; **417 B,** Bayerisches Haupstaatsarchiv; **419,** Culver Pictures, Inc.; **421,** The Granger Collection, NY; **422 TL,** Library of Congress; **422 R,** The Granger Collection, NY; **422 BL,** From the publication "My Four Years in Germany"; **423,** National Archives; **424,** Library of Congress; **425,** Library of Congress; **426,** Hulton/Archive/Archive Photos; **427,** Hulton/Archive/Archive Photos; **429,** Russ Lappa; **430 T,** Culver Pictures, Inc.; **430 B,** Corbis; **431,** Brown Brothers; **432,** Library of Congress; **433,** National Archives; **434 B,** Museum of the City of New York; **434 T,** Museum of the City of New York; **435,** Wayne State University, Archives of Labor and Urban Affairs; **436,** Museum of the City of New York; **437,** SuperStock; **438,** Hulton/Archive/Archive Photos; **443,** Stock Montage

Chapter 13 450 L, *Chicago Daily Tribune;* **450 M,** Corbis; **450 R,** Corbis; **451 L,** John Sloan Sixth Avenue Elevated at Third Street, 1928 (detail). Collection of Whitney Museum of American Art, Purchase 36. 154. Photograph 1998: Whitney Museum of American Art, NY; **451 R,** Superstock; **452,** Corbis; **454,** Brown Brothers; **456,** Culver Pictures, Inc.; **457,** Corbis; **458,** Corbis; **459,** SuperStock; **460,** Culver Pictures, Inc.; **462 T,** Corbis; **462 B,** SuperStock; **463,** Purchased with funds from the Edmunson Art Foundation, Inc. Des Moines Art Center Permanent Collections, 1958.2; **464 L,** Corbis; **464 R,** Beinecke Library, Yale University; **464 M,** Brown Brothers; **465,** Cartier Bresson/Magnum Photos; **467,** The Michael Barson Collection/ Past Perfect. RH/LS; **468,** Library of Congress; **469,** Chicago Historical Society; **470 T,** Corbis; **470 B,** Brown Brothers; **471,** *Chicago Daily Tribune;* **472,** Chermayeff & Geisma; **473 B,** Brown Brothers; **473 T,** Schomburg Center for Black Research; **475,** Historical Society of Wisconsin

Chapter 14 478 L, UPI/Bettmann Archives/Corbis; **478 R,** Calvin Coolidge Memorial Foundation; **479 L,** Gary Waltz/The Image Works; **479 R,** Corbis; **480,** Hulton/Archive/Getty Images; **481,** Hulton/Archive/Getty Images; **482,** The Granger Collection, NY; **484,** Corbis; **486,** Ohio Historical Society; **488,** David J. Frent; **489,** *LIFE* Magazine December 10,1925; **491,** Western Historical Manuscript Collection–Kansas City; **492,** Courtesy of Speigel; **493,** The Granger Collection, NY; **494,** Henry Ford Museum; **496 B,** Schnectady Museum; **496 T,** Hulton /Liaison /Getty Images; **497,** Culver Pictures Inc./PictureQuest; **498,** Culver Pictures Inc.; **499,** Boston Athenaeum; **503,** The Granger Collection, NY

Chapter 15 506 L, Library of Congress; **506 R,** Museum of the City of New York/Hulton/Archive/Getty Images; **507,** Hulton/Archive/Getty Images; **508,** Hulton/Archive/Getty Images; **512,** The Granger Collection, NY; **513,** *Detroit News;* **514,** Museum of the City of New York. Photograph by Bernice Abbott, Federal Arts Project; **516 L,** Library of Congress; **516 R,** Library of Congress; **517,** Library of Congress; **518,** Corbis; **521,** Collection of Ryan Brown; **522,** Culver Pictures, Inc.; **523,** Corbis; **524,** Corbis/Bettmann; **525,** Corbis; **526 L,** Corbis; **526 M,** The White House Photo Office; **526 R,** Karl Gehring/Liaison /Getty Images; **527,** Corbis; **531,** Reprinted from the *Albany Evening News,* 6/7/31 with permission of the *Times Union,* Albany, NY

Chapter 16 534 L, Library of Congress; **534 R,** The Granger Collection, NY; **535 L,** Richard Berenholtz/Corbis Stock Market; **535 R,** The Kobal Collection; **536,** Hoover Presidential Library; **537,** FDR Library; **538 R,** U.S. Forest Service; **538 L,** Library of Congress; **539 T,** Corbis; **539 B,** Corbis; **541,** FDR Library; **542,** Hulton/Archive/Getty Images; **544,** Library of Congress; **545,** The *New Yorker* Collection, 1963, Peter Arno from www.cartoonbank.com. All rights reserved.; **546,** Margaret Bourke-White, *LIFE* Magazine © Time Warner; **547,** Corbis; **548,** ©1935,1963 by the Conde Nast Publications Inc.; **549 T,** Corbis; **549 B,** UPI/Bettman Archives/Corbis; **551,** The Granger Collection, NY; **553,** Corbis; **554,** Corbis; **555,** Library of Congress; **556,** Corbis; **557 L,** Corbis; **557 R,** Corbis; **558,** James Prigoff; **559,** PTC; **561,** Franklin D. Roosevelt Library

Chapter 17 566 R, Hulton/Archive/Getty Images; **566 L,** A.K.G., Berlin/SuperStock; **567,** Sovfoto/Eastfoto; **568,** Holocaust Museum; **570,** Moro Roma; **571 T,** AP/Wide World Photos; **571 M,** Collection of Chester Stott/, ©Rob Huntley/Lightstream; **571 B,** Corbis; **572,** Liaison/Getty Images; **573 T,** Corbis; **573 B,** Corbis; **574,** Estate of Pablo Picasso/Artists Rights Society (ARS), New York/Art Resource, N.Y.; **575,** Corbis; **576,** The Granger Collection, NY; **577,** The Granger Collection, NY; **578 B,** Library of Congress; **578 T,** Corbis; **579,** Corbis; **580,** Admiral Nimitz Museum; **582 T,** Paul Dorsey/TimePix; **582 B,** Corbis; **585,** Corbis; **586,** Brown Brothers; **587,** Corbis; **589,** Bettman/Corbis; **591,** Dr. Seuss

Chapter 18 592 R, The Granger Collection, NY; **592 L,** Jeff Tinsley, Smithsonian Institution; **593 L,** Liaison/Getty Images; **593 R,** Library of Congress; **594,** Collection of Chester H. Stott, ©Rob Huntley/Lightstream; **595 B, 595 T,** National Archives; **596 inset,** Jeff Tinsley, Smithsonian Institution; **596,** The Bancroft Library, Kaiser Pictorial Collection; **597,** Lawrence Thornton/Hulton/Archive/Getty Images; **598 inset,** National Museum of American History, Smithsonian Institution, Washington D.C.; **598,** H. Armstrong Roberts; **599,** Pearson Education/PH College; **600,** The Granger Collection, NY; **601,** Photographic Collection, Florida State Archives; **602 T,** U.S. Army; **602 B,** Imperial War Museum; **604,** Liaison/Getty Images; **605,** National Portrait Gallery, Smithsonian Institution, Washington D.C., Art Resource, NY; **607,** Corbis; **608,** U.S. Army; **609,** Hulton/Archive/Getty Images; **610 T,** Courtesy of U.S. Holocaust Memorial Museum Archives; **610 B,** Rijksinstituut voor Oorlogsdocumentatie, courtesy of U.S. Holocaust Memorial Museum Archives; **611 T,** U.S. Holocaust Memorial Museum; **611 M,** U.S. Holocaust Memorial Museum; **611 B,** U.S. Holocaust Memorial Museum; **612,** U.S. Holocaust Memorial Museum; **613,** U.S. Holocaust Memorial Museum; **614,** Liaison/Getty Images; **615,** Liaison/Getty Images; **617,** Keystone/Hulton/Archive/Getty Images; **619,** AP Photo/Joe Rosenthal; **620 B,** The Art Archive; **620 T,** Hulton/Archive/Getty Images; **621,** SuperStock; **623,** Hulton/Archive/Getty Images; **624,** National Portrait Gallery, Gift of the Harmon Foundation/Art Resource, NY; **625 inset,** Collection of Jeff Ikler/ © Huntley,Lightstream; **625,** Library of Congress; **626,** National Archives; **627,** Photri Inc.; **628 T,** Collection of Col. Stuart S. Corning, Jr., © Rob Huntley/Lightstream; **628 B,** Library of Congress; **629,** Ellen Kaiper Collection, Oakland; **631,** *Des Moines Register*

Chapter 19 634 L, Corbis; **634 R,** Hulton/Archive/Getty Images; **636,** U.S. Army; **637,** Harry S. Truman Presidential Library; **638,** Harry S. Truman Presidential Library; **640 T,** The Michael Barson Collection/Past Perfect; **640 B,** UPI/Bettman Archives/Corbis; **641,** Courtesy of the J.N. Ding Darling Foundation; **642,** © 1949 Time, Inc. Reprinted with permission; **644,** American Stock/Hulton/Archive/Getty Images; **645,** AP/Wide World Photos; **646,** Corbis; **647,** AP/Wide World Photos; **649,** GP Putnam's Sons; **650 B,** The Michael Barson Collection/Past Perfect, ©Rob Huntley/Lightstream; **650 T,** The Michael Barson Collection/Past Perfect, © Rob Huntley/Lightstream; **651,** Brown Brothers; **652,** Corbis; **653,** Eastfoto; **655,** Culver Pictures; **657,** *Herblock/Washington Post;* **658 T,** Corbis; **658 B,** The Granger Collection, NY; **660,** Corbis; **661,** © 1959 Newsweek Inc. All rights reserved. Reprinted by permission.; **663,** From *Herblock: A Cartoonist's Life* (Macmillan Publishing, 1993)

Chapter 20 666 L, Van Bucher/Photo Researchers, Inc.; **666 BR,** Harry S. Truman Presidential Library; **666 TR,** Russ Lappa; **667,** Michael Ochs Archive; **668,** Brown Brothers; **669 T,** The McDonald's Corporation; **669 B,** Mike Pattisall; **671 ML,** Russ Lappa; **671 B,** Hulton/Archive/Getty Images; **671 TL,** Russ Lappa; **671 TR,** Corbis Digital Stock; **672,** Dan Weiner, Courtesy Sandra Weiner; **673,** Van Bucher/Photo Researchers, Inc.; **674,** Barson Collection/Hulton/Archive/Getty Images; **675,** J.R. Eyreman/TimePix; **676,** Leo Chopin/Black Star; **677,** Hagley Museum and Library; **678 B,** Corbis; **678 T,** Corbis; **679 T,** Fred W. McDarrah; **679 B,** Courtesey of Ken Lopez-Bookseller; **680,** AP/Wide World Photos; **681 B,** AP/Wide World Photos; **681 T,** Harry S. Truman Library; **682 T,** David J. Frent; **682 B,** Corbis; **683,** Corbis; **684 T,** Division of Political History, Smithsonian Institution; **684 B,** AP/Wide World Photos; **685,** Dwight D. Eisenhower Library; **686,** Corbis; **689,** ©The *New Yorker* Collection, 1954, Robert J. Day from cartoonbank.com. All Rights Reserved.

Chapter 21 696 L, Grey Vieten *LIFE* Magazine © Time Warner; **696 R,** Don Uhrbrock *LIFE* Magazine © Time Warner; **697,** Co Rentmeester *LIFE* Magazine © Time Warner; **698,** The Michael Barson Collection/Past Perfect, © Rob Huntley/Lightstream; **699,** AP/Wide World Photos; **701,** Corbis; **702 B,** AP/Wide World Photos; **702 T,** Dept. of Commerce; **703,** Dr. Hector P. Garcia papers, Special Collections, Texas A&M University-Corpus Christi, Bell library; **704,** Library of Congress; **705,** David J. Frent; **706,** AP/Wide World Photos; **707,** Danny Lyon/Magnum Photos; **708,** Steve Schapiro/Black Star; **709,** Dial Juvenile Books,1968, a Divison of Penguin Books USA, Inc.; **710 L,** Danny Lyons/Magnum Photos; **710 R,** Rapho/Photo Researchers, Inc.; **711,** Corbis; **713,** Corbis; **714,** Charles Moore/Black Star; **716,** AP/Wide World Photos; **717,** Danny Lyon/Magnum Photos, Inc.; **718 T,** Bob Adelman/Magnum Photos, Inc.; **718–719 B,** Fred Ward/Black Star; **719 T,** Pullen Library at Georgia State University; **720,** AP/Wide World Photos; **721,** Bob Adelman/Magnum Photos, Inc.; **722,** Corbis; **723,** Eve Arnold/Magnum Photos, Inc.; **724 B,** Corbis; **724 T,** Russ Lappa; **726 T,** Joseph Louw *LIFE* Magazine © Time Warner; **726 B,** Bill Eppridge *LIFE* Magazine © Time Warner; **727,** Corbis; **729,** David Horsey/*The Seattle-Post Intelligencer*

Chapter 22 734 L, Hulton/Archive/Getty Images; **734 M,** John F. Kennedy Library; **734 R,** Magnum Photos, Inc.; **735,** Jacques Chenet/Woodfin Camp & Associates; **736,** John F. Kennedy Library; **737,** John F. Kennedy Library; **738,** Bettmann/Corbis; **739,** NASA; **740,** Black Star; **741,** by Dan Farrell/Daily News Pix; **743,** Corbis; **744 B,** Dennis Brack/Black Star; **744 T,** New York Times Pictures; **745 T,** Political Communication Center, The University of Oklahoma; **745 B,** Political Communication Center, The University of Oklahoma; **746,** Estate of Karl Hubenthal; **748 T,** National Archives; **748 B,** AP/Wide World Photos; **749,** Supreme Court Historical Society; **750,** Jacques Chenet/Woodfin Camp & Associates; **751,** AP/Wide World Photos; **752,** AP/Wide World Photos; **753,** Liaison/Getty Images; **754,** John F. Kennedy Library; **755,** New York Times Pictures; **757,** AP/Wide World Photos; **758 L,** Courtesy of The Peace Corps; **758 R,** Courtesy of The Peace Corps; 761, © 1962 Herblock in *The Washington Post*

Chapter 23 762 L, Picture Research Consultants, Inc.; **762 M,** Russ Lappa; **762 R,** Matt Heron/Take Stock; **764,** Radcliffe College Archives, Schlesinger Library; **765,** Al Freni/*LIFE* Magazine © Time Warner; **p 766,** Werner Wolff/Black Star; **768 T,** ©Bettye Lane; **768 M,** Courtesy Lang Communications; **768 B,** C. Gatewood/The Image Works; **769,** Corbis; **771 inset,** David J. Frent; **771,** Matt Heron/Take Stock; **772,** Craig Auerness/Woodfin Camp & Associates; **773,** Michael Nichols/Magnum Photos, Inc.; **774,** Japanese American National Museum, Gift of K. Patrick and Liby A. Okura; **775,** Rick Smolan/Against All Odds; **776,** Dirck

Halstead/*TIME* Magazine; **777 L,** H. Armstrong Roberts; **777 R,** Lambert/Hulton/Archive/Getty Images; **778 T,** Barry Burstein/Corbis; **778 B,** Prentice Hall; **779,** Barry Burstein/Corbis; **780,** Lisa Law/The Image Works; **781,** Alfred Eisenstaedt/*LIFE* Magazine© Time Warner; **782,** Jeff Lepore/Photo Researchers, Inc.; **783,** Mark Downey/PhotoDisc/Getty Images, Inc.; **785,** Corbis; **787,** Mike Peters

Chapter 24 790 L, Black Star; **790 R,** Hulton/Archive/Getty Images; **791 L,** Stock Boston; **791 R,** David J. Frent; **792,** Russ Lappa; **793,** Bill Mauldin; **794 T,** AP/Wide World Photos; **794 B,** Dennis Brack/Black Star; **795,** Corbis; **796 B,** PhotoDisc, Inc.; **796 T,** PhotoEdit; **798–799,** Jim Pickerell/Black Star; **799T,** www.manchu.org; **800,** Larry Burrows/Life; **801,** Corbis; **804,** Courtesy of the Lyndon B. Johnson Presidential Library; **805,** Stock Boston; **807 L,** AP/Wide World Photos; **807 R,** Russ Lappa; **808,** Goffynd/Archive/Getty Images; **809 T,** Philip Jones Griffiths/MP, Zenith Electronics Corporation; **809 B,** Bryson/Corbis Sygma; **810,** Corbis; **812,** Mark Godfrey/The Image Works; **814,** John Filo; **815 L,** Corbis; **815 R,** Thai Khad Chuon/Corbis; **817 B,** Richard Howard/TimePix; **817 T,** AP/Wide World Photos; **819,** From *Herblock on All Fronts* (New American Library, 1980)

Chapter 25 824 M, John T. Barr/Liason/Getty Images; **824 L,** NASA; **824 R,** AP/Wide World Photos; **825 L,** Russ Lappa; **825 R,** Hulton/Liaison/Getty Images; **826,** Rodney E. Mims/Corbis; **827,** Nixon Presidential Materials Project; **829 R,** AP/Wide World Photos; **829 L,** AP/Wide World Photos; **830,** AP/Wide World Photos; **831,** NASA; **832,** Steve Northup, ©Time Inc. *Time Magazine;* **833,** Corbis Sygma; **834 T,** John Dominis *LIFE* Magazine ©Time Warner; **835,** Hulton/Archive/Getty Images; **838,** Wayne Stayskal/Tribune Media Service; **839,** Margaret McCullough, Smithsonian Institution, courtesy of the National Archives & Records Administration; **840 B,** TimePix; **840 TL,** Dennis Brack/Black Star; **840 TR,** Richard Ellis/Corbis Sygma; **841 M,** Tony Auth. Reprinted by permission/Tribune Media Services; **841 T,** Mark Godfrey/The Image Works; **841 B,** AP/Wide World Photos; **842,** AP/Wide World Photos; **843,** Dennis Brack/Black Star; **844,** Roland Freeman/Magnum Photos; **845 B,** NASA; **845 T,** NASA Headquarters; **846,** Corbis; **847,** AP/Wide World Photos; **847 inset,** Copyright © 1974 by The New York Times Company; **848,** Russ Lappa; **849,** Gerald Ford Presidential Library; **850,** Joseph Pobereskin Photography; **851,** Jimmy Carter Presidential Library; **852,** Dennis Brack/Black Star; **855,** Jimmy Carter Presidential Library; **856,** Alain Mingam/Liasion/Getty Images; **857,** Peter Marlow/Magnum Photos; **857 inset,** David J.Frent; **859,** Cartoon by Robert Pryor. Courtesy of John Locke Studios, Inc.

Chapter 26 862 L, Corbis Sygma; **862 R,** CNP/Hulton/Archive/Getty Images; **863,** Abbas/Magnum Photos, Inc.; **864,** David J. Frent; **865 TL,** Wendell H. Ford Research Center, University of Kentucky; **865 ML,** Popperfoto/Hulton/Archive/Getty Images; **865 TR,** The Granger Collection, NY; **865 MR,** Sally Anderson Bruce; **865 inset,** Heritage House; **865 BL,** Planned Parenthood; **865 BR,** Russ Lappa; **866,** AP/Wide World Photos; **867 T,** Corbis; **867 B,** John Troha/Black Star; **868,** Les Schofer/Corbis Sygma; **870,** Corbis; **872,** Corbis; **874,** Courtesy of the United States Coast Guard; **876,** Arthur Grace/Corbis Sygma; **877,** Pat Rogers/AP/Wide World Photos; **878 T,** Diana Walker/*Time Magazine;* **878 B,** Zimberhoff/Corbis Sygma; **879,** Bruce Weaver/AP/Wide World Photos; **881,** AP/Wide World Photos; **882,** Atlan/Corbis Sygma; **884,** R. Bossu/Corbis Sygma; **885,** AP/Wide World Photos; **886,** Langevin/Corbis Sygma; **889,** Bob Englehard/*The Hartford Courant*

Chapter 27 892 L, Ira Wyman/Corbis Sygma; **892 R,** ©1993 Time Inc., Reprinted by permission; **893 l,** Doug Mills/AP/Wide World Photos; **893 r,** Christophe Calais/In Visu/Corbis; Team at NASA GSFC; **894,** John C. Sykes Jr.; **895 T,** Ira Wyman/Corbis Sygma; **895 B,** ©Rolling Stone Inc.; **895 inset,** Smithsonian Institution; **897,** John Harrington/ Black Star; **898,** Terry Ashe/Liaison/Getty images; **899 M,** Corbis Sygma; **899 B,** AP Photo/Wilfred Lee; **899 T,** AP Photo/LM Otero; **900,** Corbis Sygma; **901,** Thomas E. Franklin/*Bergen Record*/Corbis SABA; **903,** Peter Turnley/Corbis; **904,** Corbis; **905,** Courtesy of Seeds of Peace; **906,** Thomas E. Franklin/Bergen Record/Corbis Saba **907,** Tim Boyle/Getty Images, Inc.; **909 t,** David Leeson/Dallas Morning News/Corbis; **909 inset,** AP Photo/U.S. Army HO; **914,** Image courtesy Jacques Descloitres, MODIS Rapid Response **915,** Corbis Sygma; **916,** University of North Carolina at Wilmington; **917,** Stone; **919,** Mike Smith/Reprinted by permission of United Features Syndicate

American Heritage 102, Francis G. Mayer/Corbis; **103,** Visions of America; **344,** Kansas State Historical Society; **345,** Hulton/Archive/Getty Images; **444,** Hulton/Liaison Agency/Getty Images; **445 T,** Hulton/Liaison Agency/Getty Images; **445 B,** Corbis; **532,** AP/Wide World Photos; **533,** National Baseball Hall of Fame and Museum; **632 B,** U.S. Naval Historical Foundation; **632 T,** U.S. Naval Historical Foundation; **633,** Hulton/Archive/Getty Images; **730 B,** Corbis; **730 T,** Library of Congress; **731,** Corbis; **860 T,** AP/Wide World Photos; **860 B,** Corbis; 861, Prentice Hall

American Pathways 148 BR, Library of Congress; **148 L,** New Holland Machine Company; **148 TR,** Shelburne Museum; **149,** Terry Donnelly/Stone; **196 T,** The Granger Collection, NY; **196 M,** The Granger Collection, NY; **196 B,** Archives of Atlanta Historical Society; **197 L,** AP/Wide World Photos; **197 R,** Brown Brothers; **410 T,** Emanuel Gottlieb Leutze, The Metropolitan Museum of Art, Gift of John S. Kennedy, 1897. (97.34); **410 B,** Greg E. Mathieson/MAI Photo News Agency, Inc.; **411 R,** Hulton/Liaison/Getty Images; **411 BL,** Thomas E. Franklin/*Bergen Record*/Corbis SABA; **411 TL,** Corbis; **476 T,** Yale University Art Gallery, Mabel Brady Garven Collection; **476 MR,** Library of Congress; **476 ML,** The Granger Collection, NY; **476 B,** The Kobal Collection; **477 ML,** Hulton/Archive/Getty Images; **477 T,** Time Life Books; **477 B,** Hulton/Archive/Getty Images; **477 MR,** Corbis; **664 TL,** American Textile History Museum; **664 BL,** The Granger Collection, NY; **664 R,** AT&T Archives; **665 T,** Library of Congress; **665 B,** Jewish Hospital/University of Louisville; **665 M,** Intel Corporation Museum Archives & Collection; **732 B,** Hulton/Liaison/Getty images; **732 T,** The Granger Collection, NY; **732 M,** The Granger Collection, NY; **733 B,** Bob Daemmrich Photography, Inc.; **733 T,** Bob Adelman/Magnum Photos; **920 TR,** Prentice Hall; **920 L (all),** Courtesy of the Federal Reserve Bank of San Francisco; **920 BR,** Ford Motor Company; **921 T,** Corbis; **921 B,** AP/Wide World Photos; **921 M,** Picture Research Consultants

Skills for Life 490, Saturday Evening Post, June 30, 1928, Curtis Archives; **326,** John McCutcheon; **580,** AP/Wide World Photos; **845 B,** NASA; **845 T,** NASA Headquarters

Geography & History 36 L, Skyscan; **36 R,** Pilgrim Hall Museum; **37 B,** Curtis B. Johnson; **37 T,** Corbis; **37 inset,** American Antiquarian Society; **286–287 M,** Russ Lappa; **286–287 B,** Brown Brothers; **287 T,** Corbis; **287 MR,** Corbis; **287 B,** Kansas State Historical Society; **378 T,** Corbis; **378–379 B,** LHSIM/Stone; **379 B,** The Metropolitan Museum of Art; **379 M,** Archive Photos; **379 T,** Corbis; **504,** Brown Brothers; **505 BL,** Walts Postcards; **505 M,** Corbis; **505 TR,** Library of Congress; **505 TL,** Harold Kramer, mapsofpa.com; **505 TL,** Harold Kramer, mapsofpa.com; **505 TL,** Harold Kramer, mapsofpa.com; **505 BR,** Walts Postcards; **690 M,** Josef Scaylea/Corbis; **690 T,** SuperStock; **690 B,** Donovan Marks Photography; **691 B,** Robert Brenner/PhotoEdit; **691 T,** Michael Dwyer/Stock Boston; **788 T,** Ken Regan/Camera 5; **788 B,** Mark Richards/PhotoEdit; **788 M,** NASA/Science Photo Library/Photo Researchers, Inc.; **789 B,** Isaac Hernandez/Mercury Press International; **789 T,** Tom Bean; **789 M,** Tom Brownold; **890 t,** Frank Frisk/GreatLakesPhotos.com; **890 b,** Spencer Grant/PhotoEdit; **891 t,** Buddy Mays/Corbis; **891 bl,** Corbis; **891 br,** PhotoDisc/Getty Images, Inc.

American Literature 924, Library of Congress; **926,** Corbis; **927,** Nichipor Collection, Courtesy of Minuteman National Historic Park. Rob Huntley/Lightstream; **928,** Courtesy, American Antiquarian Society; **929,** The Granger Collection, NY; **930,** The Granger Collection, NY; **931,** The Granger Collection, NY; **932,** Library of Congress; **934,** Corbis; **937,** Margaret Bourke-White, *LIFE* Magazine; **938,** US Holocaust Memorial Museum; **940,** Don Uhrbrock *LIFE* Magazine © Time Warner; **941,** Corbis Bettman; **942,** Dan Farrell/Daily News Pix

American Documents 944, Getty Images, Inc.; **945,** Peabody & Essex Museum. Photo by Mark Sexton; **946,** The Pilgrim Society; **948 R,** Hulton/Liaison/Getty Images; **948 T,** Hulton/Liaison/Getty Images; **950,** United Nations; **951 R,** United Nations; **951 L,** Impact Visuals Photo & Graphics, Inc.; **952,** White House Historical Association; **954,** AP/Wide World Photos

Illustrated Databank 965–967 (Presidents), 1, 2, 4, 5, 6, 9, 10, 12, 13, 14, 15, 16, 18, 20, 21, 25, 26, 27, 35, Art Resource; 3, 7, 8, 11, 17, 19, 22, 23, 24, 28, 29, 30, 31, 32, 33, 34, 36, 37, 38, 39, 40, 41, 42, White House Historical Association; 43, Corbis Sygma; **967** (seal), White House

Biographical Dictionary 1008, American Antiquarian Society; **1009,** Library of Congress; **1010,** Library of Congress; **1011,** White House Historical Association/Photo by National Geographic Society; **1012,** Library of Congress; **1013,** Corbis; **1014,** Theodore Roosevelt Collection Harvard College Library; **1015,** Brown Brothers

PRIMARY SOURCES BIBLIOGRAPHY

Chapter 1 John Smith: Lankford, John, ed. *Captain John Smith's America: Selections from His Writings.* Harper Torchbooks, Harper and Row, 1967, p. 105; **Mayflower Compact:** Caffrey, Kate. *The Mayflower.* Stein and Day, 1974, p. 340; **Miantonomo:** Cronon, William. *Changes in the Land: Indians, Colonists, and the Ecology of New England.* Hill and Wang, 1983, p. 162; **Olaudah Equiano:** Edwards, Paul, ed. *Equiano's Travels.* Heinemann Educational Books, 1967, p. 32; **Jonathan Edwards:** Kupperman, Karen Ordahl, ed. *Major Problems in American Colonial History: Documents and Essays.* D.C. Heath, 1993, p. 369.

Chapter 2 Henry Wadsworth Longfellow: "Paul Revere's Ride," www.paulreverehouse.org; **Declaration and Resolves of the First Continental Congress:** Commager, Henry Steele, ed. *Documents of American History,* Eighth Edition, Appleton-Century-Crofts, 1968, p. 83; **Patrick Henry:** Commager, Henry Steele, and Richard B. Morris, eds. *The Spirit of 'Seventy-Six: The Story of the American Revolution as Told by Participants.* New York: Bonanza Books, 1983, pp. 108-109; **Thomas Paine, Common Sense:** Curti, Merle, et al., eds. *American Issues: The Social Record,* 4th ed. rev. New York: J.B. Lippincott, 1971, vol. 1, pp. 82, 84; **George Washington:** Commager, Henry Steele, ed. *Documents of American History,* Eighth Edition, Appleton-Century-Crofts, 1968, p. 169; **Thomas Jefferson's First Inaugural Address:** Ravitch, Diane, ed. *The Democracy Reader.* HarperPerennial, 1992, p. 140; **Francis Scott Key:** "The Star-Spangled Banner." www.bcpl.net.

Chapter 3 Morris Birkbeck: Birkbeck, Morris. "Notes on a Journey in America from the Coasts of Virginia to the Territory of Illinois." Philadelphia, 1817, p. 34; **Noah Webster:** Wood, Gordon S. *The Rising Glory of America, 1760–1820.* Northeastern University Press, 1990, p. 169; **The Monroe Doctrine:** Commager, Henry Steele, ed. *Documents of American History, Eighth Edition.* Appleton-Century-Crofts, 1968, pp. 236–237; **Germantown Mennonites:** Commager, p. 37; **Henry David Thoreau:** Walden. Princeton University Press, 1971, p. 326; **William Lloyd Garrison:** Wilentz, Sean, ed. *Major Problems in the Early Republic, 1787–1848.* D. C. Heath, 1992, p. 477; **Elizabeth Cady Stanton:** Stanton, Elizabeth Cady, et al. *History of Woman Suffrage, Vol. 1.* Fowler and Wells, 1889, pp. 58–59; **Sojourner Truth:** Anti-Slavery Bugle, Salem, Ohio, June 21, 1851, 4: p. 81–82; **Lincoln's First Inaugural Address:** Ravitch, Diane, ed. *The Democracy Reader.* HarperPerennial, 1992, p. 165; **Abraham Lincoln:** *Selected Speeches and Writings.* The Library of America, 1992, p. 131; **John Brown:** Oates, Stephen B. *To Purge This Land with Blood: A Biography of John Brown.* Harper Torchbooks, 1970, p. 351; **Augusta, Georgia, newspaper editor:** Holt, Michael F. *The Political Crisis of the 1850's.* John Wiley and Sons, 1978, p. 241.

Chapter 4 Sallie Hunt: B. A. Botkin, ed. *A Civil War Treasury of Tales, Legends and Folklore.* Random House, 1960, p. 21; **Abraham Lincoln:** Ward, Geoffrey C. *The Civil War: An Illustrated History.* Alfred A. Knopf, 1990, p. 110; **Elisha Stockwell:** Murphy, Jim. *The Boys' War.* Clarion Books, 1990, p. 33; **Louis Wigfall:** McPherson, James M. *Battle Cry of Freedom.* Oxford University Press, 1998, p. 430; **Abraham Lincoln:** McPherson, p. 510; **Emancipation Proclamation:** Boorstin, Daniel, ed. *An American Primer.* University of Chicago Press, 1968, p. 431; **Lewis Douglass:** Chang, Ina. *A Separate Battle: Women and the Civil War.* Lodestar Books, 1991, p. 65; **Frederick Douglass:** *Douglass' Monthly,* August, 1863; **Cornelia Hancock:** *South After Gettysburg.* University of Nebraska Press, 1998; **Civil War drummer boy:** Murphy, p. 43; **soldier at Gettysburg:** E. B. Long. *The Civil War Day by Day.* Da Capo Press, 1971, p. 377; **Mary Ann Loughborough:** Gragg, Rod, *The Illustrated Confederate Reader.* Harper and Row, 1989, p.82; **Abraham Lincoln:** *Selected Speeches and Writings.* First Vintage Books, Library of America, p. 450; **R.B. Prescott:** Meltzer, Milton, ed. *Voices from the Civil War.* Thomas Y. Crowell, 1989, pp. 179–181; **Henrietta Lee:** Gragg, p. 88; **Abraham Lincoln:** Lincoln, p. 450.

Chapter 5 Val C. Giles: Lasswell, Mary, and ed., *Rags and Hope: The Memoirs of Val C. Giles,* New York: Coward-McCann, 1961. **Abraham Lincoln:** *Selected Speeches and Writings.* First Vintage Books, Library of America, p. 450; **Charlotte Forten:** "Life on the Sea Islands," *Atlantic Monthly,* Vol. 13 (May and June) 1864, pp. 588–589, 591–594, 666–667; **Black Union Soldier:** Litwack, Leon F. *Been in the Storm So Long, The Aftermath of Slavery.* Vintage Books, 1979, Chapter 7.

Chapter 6 Samuel F.B. Morse: Morse, Edward Lind, ed., *Samuel F.B. Morse, His Letters and Journals,* 2 vols., Houghton Mifflin, 1914, quoted in Ambrose, Stephen and Douglas Brinkley. *Witness to America: An Illustrated Documentary History of the United States from the Revolution to Today.* Harper Collins, 1999, p. 96; **Abram Stevens Hewitt:** *Address Delivered on the Occasion of the Opening of the New York and Brooklyn Bridge, May 24th, 1883,* John Polemus, 1883, quoted in Graebner, William, and Leonard Richards, eds., *The American Record: Images of the Nation's Past,* Vol. 2, Alfred Knopf, 1982, p. 50; **Andrew Carnegie:** "How I Served My Apprenticeship." *Youth's Companion,* April 23, 1896, quoted in Ambrose, pp. 301–305; **Andrew Carnegie:** *The Empire of Business.* Doubleday, 1902, pp. 138–140, quoted in Kirkland, Edward Chase. *Dream and Thought in the Business Community, 1860–1900.* Cornell, 1956, pp. 156–157; **Sadie Frowne:** "The Story of a Sweatshop Girl," *The Independent* 54, September 25, 1902, pp. 2279–2282, quoted in Bailey, Thomas A., and David M. Kennedy. *The American Spirit: United States History as Seen by Contemporaries,*

Acknowledgments

Vol. 2, 8TH ed. D.C. Heath and Company, 1994, pp. 80–85; **Frederick Winslow Taylor:** *The Principles of Scientific Management.* W.W. Norton and Company, 1911, p. 39; **Samuel Gompers:** Letter from *American Federationist,* Vol. 1, September 1894, pp. 150–152, quoted in Hofstadter, Richard, ed., *Great Issues in American History From Reconstruction to the Present Day, 1864–1969,* Vintage Books, 1969, pp. 187–191; **Eugene V. Debs:** *Declaration of Principles, American Railway Union,* 1893, quoted in Salvatore, Nick. *Eugene V. Debs: Citizen and Socialist.* University of Illinois Press, 1982, p. 116; **August Spies:** Kogan, B. R. "The Chicago Haymarket Riot," 1959 (a reproduction of the circular in the Chicago Historical Society collection).

Chapter 7 Mary Clark: Nelson, Paula M. *After the West Was Won: Homesteaders and Town-Builders in Western South Dakota, 1900–1917.* University of Iowa Press, 1986, quoted in Jones, Mary Ellen. *Daily Life on the 19th-Century Frontier.* The Greenwood Press, 1998, p. 187; **death song sung by a Cherokee:** Thomas, David hurst, et al. *The Native Americans: An Illustrated History.* Turner Publishing, 1993, p. 332; **newspaper reporter:** Fite, Gilbert. *The Farmer's Frontier, 1865–1900.* University of New Mexico Press, 1974, p. 205; **diary of a Union Pacific engineer:** Ward, Geoffrey C. *The West: An Illustrated History.* Little, Brown and Company (The West Book Project), 1996, p. 222; **cowboy Charles A. Siringo:** Jones, Mary Ellen. *Daily Life on the 19th-Century Frontier.* The Greenwood Press, 1998, p. 167; **"The Old Chisholm Trail":** Forbis, William H. *The Old West: The Cowboys.* Time-Life Books, 1973, p. 154; **"Commercial and Financial Chronicle,"** September 21, 1879: quoted in Fite, p. 82; **Washington Gladden:** *The Annals of America. Vol. 11, 1884–1894: Agrarianism and Urbanization.* Encyclopedia Britannica, 1968, p. 356.

Chapter 8 Peter Mossini: Coan, Peter M. *Ellis Island Interviews: In Their Own Words.* Facts on File, 1997, p. 45; **Fiorello LaGuardia:** *The Making of an Insurgent.* J. B. Lippincott Co., 1948, pp. 64–65; **Emily Dinwiddie:** "Some Aspects of Italian Housing and Social Conditions in Philadelphia," Charities and the Commons, Vol. 12, 1904, p. 490; **Pedro Martínez:** Hoobler, Dorothy and Thomas Hoobler. *The Mexican American Family Album.* Oxford University Press, 1994, p. 34; **Council of Hygiene and Public Health:** Dolkart, Andrew S. and Ruth Limmer. "The Tenement As History And Housing." Lower East Side Tenement Museum, New York; **Ellen Swallow Richards:** *Conservation by Sanitation; Air and Water Supply; Disposal of Waste.* Wiley, 1911; **Jacob Riis:** *How the Other Half Lives.* Penguin, 1997, p. 6; **Frances Willard:** *Glimpses of Fifty Years: The Autobiography of an American Woman.* H.J. Smith & Co., 1889, pp. 339–341.

Chapter 9 Mary Antin: Levinson, Nancy Smiler. *Turn of the Century: Our Nation One Hundred Years Ago.* Lodestar Books, 1994, pp. 54-55. **Tony Longo:** Loeper, John J. *Going to School in 1876.* Atheneum, 1984, pp. 64-65; **Pauli Murray:** *Proud Shoes.* Harper and Row, 1956, pp. 269–270; **Booker T. Washington:** *Address of Booker T. Washington, principal of the Tuskegee Normal and Industrial Institute, Tuskegee, Alabama, delivered at the opening of the Cotton States and International Exposition, at Atlanta, Ga., September 18, 1895.* Daniel A. P. Murray Pamphlet Collection, Library of Congress, 1894, pp. 7–9; **W.E.B. Du Bois:** Du Bois, W.E.B. *The Negro Problem: A Series of Articles by Representative American Negroes of Today.* J. Pott and Company, 1903, pp. 33-75; **Jack Norworth:** "Take Me Out to the Ball Game." Words by Jack Norworth, music by Albert Von Tilzer. www.geocities.com; **Albon Holsey:** Litwack, Leon F. *Trouble in Mind: Black Southerners in the Age of Jim Crow.* Alfred A. Knopf, 1998; p. 16; **Frederick Howe:** Levinson, p. 95.

Chapter 10 Henry Cabot Lodge: "Our Blundering Foreign Policy," *The Forum,* Vol. 19, March 1895, pp. 14–17, quoted in Hofstadter, Richard, ed., *Great Issues in American History From Reconstruction to the Present Day, 1864–1969,* Vintage Books, 1969, pp. 187–191; **New York Journal Headline:** *New York Journal,* October 10, 1897, quoted in Bailey, Thomas A. and David M. Kennedy. *The American Spirit: United States History as Seen by Contemporaries,* Vol. 2, 8TH ed. D.C. Heath and Company, 1994, pp. 171–172; **William McKinley:** Interview at the White House, November 21, 1899, *Christian Advocate,* January 22, 1903, quoted in Olcott, C.S. *The Life of William McKinley,* Vol. 2, 1916, pp. 110–111, quoted in Bailey, pp. 179–180; **John Hay:** Telegram to U.S. minister in Bogotá. *Foreign Relations of the United States, 1903.* Washington D.C.: Government Printing Office, 1904, p. 146, quoted in Bailey, pp. 190–191; **Theodore Roosevelt:** Hart, Albert Bushnell and Herbert Ronald Ferleger, eds. *Theodore Roosevelt Cyclopedia.* Roosevelt Memorial Association, 1941, p. 407; **Theodore Roosevelt's Corollary to the Monroe Doctrine:** "Roosevelt's Annual Message, December 5, 1905," quoted in Commager, Henry Steele, ed. *Documents of American History,* vol. 2, Eighth Edition. Appleton-Century Crofts, 1968, p. 34; **Theodore Roosevelt:** Letter to Henry Cabot Lodge, from Morison, Elting E., ed. *The Letters of Theodore Roosevelt,* Vol. 2, Harvard University Press, 1951, quoted in Bailey, pp. 197–198; **Carl Schurz Platform of the Anti-Imperialist League:** "The Policy of Imperialism," Liberty Tracts No. 4, Address by Carl Schurz to Anti-Imperialist Conference in Chicago, October 17, 1899, quoted in Hofstadter, pp. 202–204; **Carl Schurz:** Ibid.; **Bishop Alexander Walters:** "Wisconsin Weekly Advocate," August 17, 1899, quoted in Gatewood, Willard B., Jr. *Black Americans and the White Man's Burden, 1898–1903.* University of Illinois Press, 1975, p. 200; **Walter Hines Page:** "The War With Spain And After," *Atlantic Monthly,* Vol. 81, June 1898, pp. 725–727, quoted in Hofstadter, p. 201.

Chapter 11 Upton Sinclair: *The Jungle.* Doubleday, 1906, pp. 96–97; **Edward Bellamy:** Bellamy, Edward. *Looking Backward.* River City Press, 1888, p. 56; **Jane Addams:** Addams, Jane. "Why Women Should Vote." Ladies Home Journal, Vol. XXVII, January 1910, pp. 21–22; **Rose Schneiderman:** Mitelman, Bonnie. "Rose Schneiderman and the Triangle Shirtwaist Fire." American History Illustrated, July 1981; **Robert M. La Follette:** La Follette, Robert M. *A Personal Narrative of Political Experiences,* 1913, published online at the Library of Congress's American Memory Web site www.lcweb2.loc.gov; **Woodrow Wilson campaign speech:** Wilson, Woodrow. *The New Freedom: A Call for the Emancipation of the Generous Energies of a People.* Double Day, Page and Company, 1913, pp. 163-191, published online at www.1912.history.ohio-state.edu; **Lyman Abbott:** Abbott, Lyman. "Why Women DO Not Wish the Suffrage." The Atlantic Monthly, September 1903, published online at www.theatlantic.com; **Susan B. Anthony:** Sherr, Lynn. *Failure Is Impossible: Susan B. Anthony in Her Own Words.* Times Books, 1995, pp. 110-112.

Chapter 12 Borijove Jevtic: Carey, John. *Eyewitness to History.* Faber and Faber, 1987, p. 443; *The New York Times:* "He Kept Us out of War." October 21, 1916; **Arthur Zimmermann:** Leckie, Robert. *The Wars of America.* Harper and Row, 1968, p. 628; **Woodrow Wilson:** Cooper, John Milton, Jr. *Pivotal Decades: The United States, 1900–1920.* W. W. Norton and Company, 1990, p. 265; **Anonymous:** Grist, N R. "A Letter from Camp Devens 1918," *British Medical Journal,* December 22-29, 1979; **Corporal Elmer Sherwood:** Berger, Dorothy and Josef, eds. *Diary of America.* Simon and Schuster, 1957, p. 536; **Henry Ford:** Conot, Robert. *American Odyssey.* William Morrow and Co., 1974, p. 181; **Herbert Hoover:** "Gospel of the Clean Plate." *Ladies Home Journal,* August 1917, p. 25; **Woodrow Wilson:** Commager, Henry Steele, ed. *Documents of American History,* vol. II, Eighth Edition. Appleton-Century-Crofts, 1968, p. 138; **Alice Lord O'Brian:** *No Glory: Letters from France, 1917–1919.* Airport Publishers, 1936, pp. 8, 141, 152-153.

Chapter 13 Preston Slosson: *The Great Crusade and After, 1914–1928.* Macmillan, 1930, p. 157; **George Gershwin:** Colbert, David, ed. *Eyewitness to America.* Pantheon, 1997, p. 347; **Sinclair Lewis:** *Main Street.* Harcourt, Brace and Company, 1920, p. 265; **Edna St. Vincent Millay:** Allison, Alexander W., et al., eds. *The Norton Anthology of Poetry,* Third Edition. W. W. Norton & Company, 1983, p. 1032; **Langston Hughes:** *I, Too* from THE COLLECTED POEMS OF LANGSTON HUGHES by Langston Hughes, copyright © 1994 by the Estate of Langston Hughes.; Used by permission of Alfred A. Knopf, a division of Random House, Inc. **Alice Longworth:** *Crowded Hours: Reminiscences of Alice Roosevelt Longworth.* Charles Scribner's Sons, 1933, p. 324; **Paul Morand:** Colbert, p. 364; **Klansman's Manual:** Marcus, Robert D., and David Burner. *America Firsthand,* Vol. II. St. Martin's Press, 1989, p. 238.

Chapter 14 Warren G. Harding, Boston, May 14, 1920: Schortemeier, Frederick E. *Rededicating America: Life and Recent Speeches of Warren G. Harding.* Bobbs-Merrill, 1920, p. 223; **Warren G. Harding, October 26, 1929:** Russell, Francis. *President Harding: His Life and Times, 1865–1923.* Eyre & Spottiswoode, 1969, pp. 471–472. **Earnest Elmo Calkins:** *Business the Civilizer.* Little, Brown, and Company, 1928, quoted in Marcus, Robert D. and David Burner. *America Firsthand,* Vol. II. St. Martin's Press, 1989, p. 225; **Herbert Hoover, New York City, October 1928:** Birley, Robert, ed. *Speeches and Documents in American History,* Vol. IV. Oxford University Press, p. 89, first published in *The World's Classics,* 1942.

Chapter 15 Gordon Thomas and Max Morgan-Witts: *The Day the Bubble Burst.* Doubleday & Company, 1979, quoted in Cary, John H. and Julius Weinberg, eds. *The Social Fabric: American Life from the Civil War to the Present.* 4ᵗʰ ed. Little, Brown and Company, 1984, p. 299; **Ann Rivington:** "We Live on Relief." *Scribner's Magazine 95,* April 1934, pp. 282–285, quoted in Kutler, Stanley I. *Looking for America: The People's History.* 2ⁿᵈ ed., Vol. 2. W.W. Norton and Company, 1979, pp. 360–361; **Robert Conot:** *American Odyssey.* William Morrow and Company, 1974, p. 283; **Gordon Parks:** *Voices in the Mirror: An Autobiography.* Doubleday, 1990; **Wilson Ledford:** "How I Lived During the Depression." Interview taped and transcribed by Reuben Hiatt, November 7, 1982, quoted in Snell, William R. ed. *Hard Times Remembered: Bradley County and the Great Depression.* Bradley County Historical Society, 1983, pp. 117–121; **Gerald W. Johnson:** "The Average American and the Depression." *Current History,* February 1932; **Kitty McCulloch:** Terkel, Studs. *Hard Times: An Oral History of the Great Depression.* Pantheon Books, 1970; **Harry Haugland:** "The Right to Live." Unpublished, quoted in Kutler, pp. 373–374; **Clarence Lee:** Quoted in *Riding the Rails.* Dirs. Michael Uys and Lexy Lovell, WGBH Educational Foundation, 1998, Transcript; **William Saroyan:** *Inhale and Exhale.* Random House, 1936, p. 81; **"Brother Can You Spare a Dime?":** *Brother, Can You Spare A Dime?* Lyrics by E.Y. "Yip" Harburg and Music by Jay Gorney. Copyright © 1932, 1960 (Renewed) by Glocca Morra Music (ASCAP) and Gorney Music (ASCAP). Reprinted by permission of Next Decade Entertainment, Inc. All Rights Reserved.; **"Happy Days Are Here Again":** *Happy Days Are Here Again* Words by Jack Yellin & Music by Milton Ager.; Copyright © 1929 Warner Bros. Inc. (Renewed).; All rights reserved.; Used by permission of Warner Bros. Publications, Miami, FL; **Herbert Hoover:** Myers, William S., ed. *The State Papers and Other Public Writings of Herbert Hoover.* Doubleday, Doran and Company, Inc., Vol. II, 1934, pp. 408–413; **Franklin D. Roosevelt:** *The New York Times,* September 24, 1932; **Roosevelt's First Inaugural Address:** Commager, Henry Steele, ed. *Documents of American History,* vol. 2, Eighth Edition. Appleton-Century-Crofts, 1968, p. 240.

Chapter 16 Harry Hopkins: Dawley, Alan. *Struggles for Justice: Social Responsibility and the Liberal State.* Harvard University Press, 1991, p. 367; testimony by George Dobbin: Federal Writers' Project. *These Are Our Lives.* University of North Carolina Press, 1939; **Roosevelt administration official:** Markowitz, Gerald, and David Rosner, eds. "Slaves of the Depression." Workers' Letters About Life on the Job. Cornell, 1987, p. 154; **Sam T. Mayhew:** Terrill, Tom E., and Jerrold Hirsch, eds. *Such As Us: Southern Voices of the Thirties.* University of North Carolina Press, 1978; **Franklin Roosevelt:** White, Walter. *A Man Called White: The Autobiography of Walter White.* Viking Press, 1948, pp. 179–180; **James Agee:** Agee, James, and Walker Evans. *Let Us Now Praise Famous Men.* Boston: Houghton Mifflin Company, 1941, pp. 118–120; **Walter Reuther:** Madison, Charles A. *American Labor Leaders, Personalities and Forces in the Labor Movement.* Ungar, 1950, p. 382.

Chapter 17 The Party Rally of Honor: *Der Parteitag der Ehre vom 8. bis 14. September 1936.* Zentralverlag der NSDAP, 1936, pp. 170-177; **Nazi Poster:** Hitler, Adolf. *Mein Kampf.* Reynal & Hitchcock, 1940, p. 527; **Alfred Duff Cooper:** Churchill, Winston. *The Gathering Storm.* Vol. 1 of *The Second World War.* Houghton Mifflin, 1948, pp. 291-292. **Winston Churchill:** Baldwin, Hanson W. *The Crucial Years: 1939–1941.* Harper and Row, 1976, p. 127; **Hirota Koki:** Brendon, Piers. *The Dark Valley.* Alfred A. Knopf, 2000, p. 455; **Franklin D. Roosevelt:** Davis, Kenneth S. *FDR: The New Deal Years, 1933–1937.* Random House, 1986, p. 640; **Franklin D. Roosevelt:** Commager, Henry Steele, ed. *Documents of American History,* vol. II, Eighth Edition. Appleton-Century-Crofts, 1968, p. 452.

Chapter 18 Franklin D. Roosevelt: Rosenman, Samuel I., comp. *The Public Papers and Addresses of Franklin D. Roosevelt, 1940 Volume: War—And Aid to Democracies.* MacMillan, 1941, p. 643; **Franklin D. Roosevelt:** Commager, Henry Steele, ed. *Documents of American History,* vol. II, Eighth Edition. Appleton-Century-Crofts, 1968, p. 449; **Franklin D. Roosevelt and Winston S. Churchill:** Curti, Merle, Isidore Starr, and Lewis Paul Todd, eds. *Living American Documents.* Harcourt, 1961, p. 304; **German infantryman:** Carey, John, ed. *Eyewitness to History.* Harvard University Press, 1987, p. 576; **Lieutenant Robert Edlin:** Colbert, Robert, ed. *Eyewitness to America.* Pantheon, 1997, p. 420; **Adolf Hitler:** *Mein Kampf.* Reynal & Hitchcock, 1940, p. 826; **Leon Bass:** *Holocaust and Human Behavior.* Facing History and Ourselves National Foundation, p. 414; **Hiroshima survivor:** Cook, Haruko Taya, and Theodore Cook. *Japan at War: An Oral History.* The New Press, 1992, p. 397; **A. Philip Randolph:** Anderson, Jervis. *A. Philip Randolph.* Harcourt, 1973, p. 249; **Lloyd Brown:** Blum, John Morton. *V Was for Victory: Politics and American Culture During World War II.* Harcourt Brace Jovanovich, 1976, p. 191; **Henry Murakami:** Harris, Mark Jonathan, et al. *The Homefront: America During World War II.* G. P. Putnam's Sons, 1984, p. 113.

Chapter 19 Winston Churchill: *The Annals of America,* vol. 16, 1940–1949: *The Second World War and After.* Encyclopedia Britannica, 1968, p. 367; **Harry Truman:** Commager, Henry Steele, ed. *Documents of American History,* vol. II, Eighth Edition. Appleton-Century-Crofts, 1968, p. 525; **Harry Truman:** "Race for the Superbomb," *The American Experience.* www.pbs.org; **George C. Marshall:** Commager, Henry Steele, ed. *Documents of American History,* vol. II, Eighth Edition. Appleton-Century-Crofts, 1968, p. 532; **Arnold Winter:** Tomedi, Rudy. *No Bugles, No Drums: An Oral History of the Korean War.* John Wiley and Sons, 1993, p. 26; **Tom Clawson:** Tomedi, pp. 147-148; **Douglas MacArthur:** Phillips, Cabell. *The Truman Presidency: The History of a Triumphant Succession.* The Macmillan Company, 1966, p. 348; **Edward R. Murrow:** See It Now broadcast, March 29, 1954, published online at www.indiana.edu; **Margaret Chase Smith:** "Declaration of Conscience," Margaret Chase Smith Library, published online at www.mcslibrary.org; **Dwight D. Eisenhower:** Commager, Henry Steele, ed. *Documents of American History,* vol. II, Eighth Edition. Appleton-Century-Crofts, 1968, p. 667.

Chapter 20 Harry Henderson: "The Mass-Produced Suburbs, Part I: How People Live in America's Newest Towns," *Harper's Magazine,* November 1953, Vol. 207, No. 1242, p. 26; **Malvina Reynolds:** *Little Boxes* by Malvina Reynolds. Copyright © 1962, 1990 (Renewed) by Schroder Music Company (ASCAP). Reprinted by permission; **Geoffrey Perrett:** *A Dream of Greatness: The American People, 1945–1963.* Coward, McCann & Geoghegan, 1979, p. 307; **Betty Friedan:** *The Feminine Mystique.* W.W. Norton & Company, 1963; **Allen Ginsberg:** *Howl* from HOWL & OTHER POEMS by Allen Ginsberg. Copyright © 1956, 1959 by Allen Ginsberg. Reprinted by permission of City Lights Books; **Richard Nixon:** Wicker, Tom. *One of Us: Richard Nixon and the American Dream.* Random House, 1991, p. 98; **Dwight Eisenhower:** Holbo, Paul S., and Robert W. Sellen, eds. *The Eisenhower Era.* Dryden Press, 1974, p. 113.

Chapter 21 Chief Justice Warren: Opinion of the Court in *Brown* v. *Board of Education of Topeka,* quoted in Commager, Henry Steele, ed. *Documents of American History,* vol. 2, Eighth Edition. Appleton-Century-Crofts, 1968, pp. 607–608; **84th Congress's Southern Manifesto:** from *Congressional Record,* 84th Congress, 2nd session, March 12, 1956, pp. 4515–4516, quoted in Bailey, Thomas A., and David M. Kennedy. *The American Spirit: United States History as Seen by Contemporaries,* Vol. 2, 8th ed. D.C. Heath and Company, 1994, pp. 463–464; **Martin Luther King, Jr.:** Sitkoff, Harvard. *The Struggle for Black Equality: 1954–1980.* Hill and Wang, 1981, p. 50; **Martin Luther King, Jr.:** *Stride Toward Freedom: The Montgomery Story.* Harper and Row, 1958, pp. 53–55; **Elizabeth Eckford:** Bates, Daisy. *The Long Shadow of Little Rock.* David McKay, 1962, quoted in Raskin, Jamin B. *We the Students: Supreme Court Decisions for and about Students.* Congressional Quarterly Press, 2000, p. 178; **Dwight D. Eisenhower:** Address of September 24, 1957, from *Vital Speeches,* vol. 24, October 15, 1957, pp. 11–12, quoted in Bailey, pp. 465–466; **John Lewis:** Morrison, Joan, and Robert K. Morrison. *From Camelot to Kent State: The Sixties Experience in the Words of Those Who Lived It.* Times Books, 1987, pp. 25–26; **W.E.B. DuBois:** Aptheker, Herbert, ed. *Pamphlets and Leaflets* by W.E.B. DuBois. Kraus-Thomason Organization Limited, 1986, p. 116; **Southern Christian Leadership Conference:** Sitkoff, p. 65; **SCLC leaflet:** Sitkoff, p. 59; **Todd Gitlin:** *The Sixties: Years of Hope, Days of Rage.* Bantam Books, 1987, pp. 148–149; **John Lewis:** Hampton, Henry, et al. *Voices of Freedom: An Oral History of the Civil Rights Movement from the 1950's Through the 1980's.* Bantam Books, 1990, p. 58; **James Farmer:** Hampton, p. 78; **James Meredith:** "I'll Know Victory or Defeat," *The Saturday Evening Post,* November 10, 1962, p. 17, quoted in Katz, William Loren. *Eyewitness: The Negro in American History,* 3rd ed. David S. Lake Publishers, 1974, pp. 496–497; **Martin Luther King, Jr.:** "Letter From Birmingham Jail." *Essay Series.* A. J. Muste Memorial Institute, p. 18; **John F. Kennedy:** *Radio and Television Report to the American People on Civil Rights,* June 11, 1963; **Bob Dylan:** *Blowin' In The Wind* by Bob Dylan. Copyright © 1962 by Warner Bros. Inc. Copyright Renewed © 1990 by Special Rider Music. All rights reserved. International Copyright Secured. Reprinted by permission; **Martin Luther King, Jr.:** "I Have a Dream." Speech in Washington, D.C., August 1963, quoted in Winkler, Allan M. *The Recent Past: Readings on America Since World War II.* Harper and Row, 1989, p. 275; **Fannie Lou Hamer:** Harley, Sharon, et al. *The African American Experience: A History.* Globe Book Company, 1992, p. 336; **Malcolm X:** *The Autobiography of Malcolm X.* Ballantine Books, 1990, pp. 245–246; **Stokely Carmichael:** Nash, Gary B., et al., eds. *The American People.* Harper and Row, 1986, p. 1001; **Martin Luther King, Jr.:** Kaiser, Charles. *1968 in America: Music, Politics, Chaos, Counterculture, and the Shaping of a Generation.* Weidenfeld and Nicolson, 1988, p. 144; **Barbara Jordan:** Harley, et al., p. 343.

Chapter 22 John F. Kennedy's Inaugural Address: Commager, Henry Steele, ed. *Documents of American History,* 8th ed. Appleton-Century-Crofts, 1968, pp. 668–670; **Kennedy speech at Rice University:** Swenson, Lloyd S., James M. Grimwood, and Charles C. Alexander. *This New Ocean, A History of Project Mercury.* NASA, 1966, frontispiece and p. 470; **Lyndon Johnson:** "Address Before a Joint Session of Congress, November 27, 1963." National Archives and Records Administration, The Lyndon B. Johnson Library and Museum, published online at www.lbjlib.utexas.edu; **John F. Kennedy's Inaugural Address:** Commager, pp. 668–670; **Senator J. William Fulbright:** Schlesinger, Arthur M. *A Thousand Days: John F. Kennedy in the White House.* Houghton Mifflin, 1965, p. 251; **Kennedy:** "Radio and Television Report to the American People on the Soviet Arms Buildup in Cuba, October 22, 1962." John Fitzgerald Kennedy Library, published online at www.jfklibrary.org.

Chapter 23 Helen Reddy: *I Am Woman* Words and Music by Helen Reddy & Ray Burton. Copyright © 1971 Irving Music, Inc. o/b/o itself & Buggerlugs Music Co. (BMI). International Copyright Secured. All Rights Reserved.; **Phyllis Schlafly:** Nash, Gary B. *The American People: Creating a Nation and a Society.* Harper and Row, 1986, p. 1008; **César Chávez:** Levy, Jacques E. *César Chávez: Autobiography of La Causa.* W. W. Norton, 1975, p. 293; **Onondaga Chief Oren Lyons:** *Voices from Wounded Knee: The People Are Standing Up.* Akwesasne Notes, 1974, p. 96; **Tom Law:** Makower, Joel. *Woodstock: The Oral History.* Doubleday, 1989, p. 333; **Rachel Carson:** *Silent Spring.* Houghton Mifflin, 1962, pp. 2–3; **Rachel Carson:** *Silent Spring.* p. 6; **Lyndon Johnson:** Archer, Jules, *The Incredible Sixties: The Stormy Years That Changed America.* Harcourt Brace Jovanovich, 1986, p. 172; **Ralph Nader:** *Unsafe at Any Speed: The Designed-in Dangers of the American Automobile.* Grossman Publishers, 1972, preface.

Chapter 24 Dwight Eisenhower: Press conference of April 7, 1954. *The Columbia World of Quotations.* Columbia University Press, 1996, no. 18606. **Robert McNamara:** Shapley, Deborah. *Promise and Power: The Life and Times of Robert McNamara.* Little, Brown and Company, 1993, p. 263; **Lyndon B. Johnson:** Kearns, Doris. *Lyndon Johnson and the American Dream.* Harper and Row, 1976, p. 316; **A People's History of the United States 1492-Present:** Excerpt from pp. 464-466 from *A People's History of the United States 1492-Present* by Howard Zinn. Copyright © 1980 by Howard Zinn. Reprinted by permission of HarperCollins Publishers, Inc.; **The Vietnam War: A History of U.S. Involvement:** Excerpt from *The Vietnam War: A History of U.S. Involvement* by John M. Dunn. Copyright © 2001 by Lucent Books, Inc. Reprinted by permission.; **James Webb:** "Heroes of the Vietnam Generation," *The American Enterprise,* September 2000, p. 22; **Letter home from an American soldier:** Edelman, Bernard, ed. *Dear America: Letters Home from Vietnam.* New York Veterans Memorial Commission; **Le Thanh:** Chanoff, David, and Van Toai Doan. *Portrait of the Enemy.* Random House, 1986, pp. 62–63; **Vietnamese peasant:** Trullinger, James Walker, Jr. *Village at War: An Account of Revolution in Vietnam.* Longman, 1980, p. 118; **Ballad of the Green Berets:** *Ballad of the Green Berets* by Robert L. Moore, Jr. & Barry A. Sadler. Copyright © 1966, 1994 (Renewed) by Eastaboga Music Co. (ASCAP). Reprinted by permission.; **Private Paul Meadlo:** *The New York Times,* November 25, 1969, p. 16; **Dean Rusk:** *Vietnam: A Television History: The Tet Offensive (1968),* transcript. www.pbs. org; **John McNaughton:** Karnow, Stanley, *Vietnam: A History.* Viking, 1983, p. 479; **Port Huron Statement:** Hayden, Tom. Students for a Democratic Society. Quoted in Winkler, Allan. *The Recent Past: Readings on America Since World War II.* Harper and Row, 1989, pp. 218–219; **Robert F. Kennedy:** Holland, Gini, *A Cultural History of the United States Through the Decades: The 1960s.* Lucent Books, 1999, p. 54; **Lyndon Johnson:** King, Larry L. "LBJ and Vietnam" from *A Sense of History: The Best Writing from the Pages of American Heritage.* American Heritage/Houghton Mifflin Company, 1985, p. 801; **Theodore H. White:** *The Making of the President 1968.* Atheneum, 1969, p. 298; **Richard Nixon:** "Nixon's 'Silent Majority' speech," *Vietnam War History, Speeches, Commentary.* www.geocities.com; **Richard Nixon:** Address to the Nation on the Situation in Southeast Asia. April 30, 1970.

Chapter 25 Richard Nixon: Wicker, Tom. *One of Us: Richard Nixon and the American Dream.* Random House, 1991, p. 9; **Richard Nixon's First Inaugural Address:** *Inaugural Addresses of the Presidents of the United States.* Washington, D.C.: U.S. G.P.O.: for sale by the Supt. of Docs., U.S. G.P.O., 1989; Bartleby.com, 2001. www.bartleby.com/124/. [November 6, 2001]; **Henry Kissinger:** *The White House Years.* Little, Brown and Company, 1979, p. 45; **Richard Nixon, report to Congress, 1970:** *The Memoirs of Richard Nixon.* Grosset & Dunlap, 1978, p. 545; **Richard Nixon:** *Public Papers of the Presidents of the United States: Richard Nixon,* p. 320; **Theodore H. White:** *Breach of Faith.* Atheneum Publishers, Reader's Digest Press, 1975, p. 322; **John J. Sirica:** Bernstein, Carl, and Bob Woodward. *All the President's Men.* Warner Paperback Books, 1975, p. 268; **M. Caldwell Butler:** Burns, James MacGregor. *The Crosswinds of Freedom.* Alfred A. Knopf, 1989, p. 507; **Gerald R. Ford:** *A Time to Heal.* Harper and Row, 1979, pp. 124–125; **Gerald R. Ford:** *A Time to Heal,* pp. 177–178; **Jerald F. terHorst:** P. Goldman, et al. "How Good a President?" October 18, 1976, p. 31; **Jimmy Carter's Inaugural Address:** *Inaugural Addresses of the Presidents of the United States.* Washington, D.C.: U.S. G.P.O.: for sale by the Supt. of Docs., U.S. G.P.O., 1989; Bartleby.com, 2001. www.bartleby.com/124/. [November 6, 2002]; **Cyrus Vance:** *Hard Choices: Critical Years in America's Foreign Policy.* Simon and Schuster, 1983, pp. 228–229; **Kathryn Koob:** *Guest of the Revolution.* Thomas Nelson Publishers, 1982, p. 73.

Chapter 26 Richard Nixon: Cannon, Lou. *Role of a Lifetime.* Simon & Schuster, 1991, p.71; **Ronald Reagan:** Willis, Henry. "Reagan Rejects Debate With Carter." *Eugene Register-Guard,* September 26, 1980, p. 7; **Ronald Reagan:** *Speaking My Mind.* Simon & Schuster, 1989. p. 64; **Ronald Reagan:** "Putting America Back to Work," January 20, 1981. *Vital Speeches of the Day,* Vol. XLVII, No. 9, February 15, 1981; **Kevin Phillips:** "Reagan's America: A Capital Offense." *The New York Times Magazine,* June 24, 1990; **George Bush:** "Open Letter to College Students on the Persian Gulf Crisis," January 9, 1991.

Chapter 27 Bill Clinton's First Inaugural Address: *The New York Times,* January 22, 1993, p. A13.

Skills for Life Christopher Columbus: Phillips, William D. Jr., and Carla Rahn Phillips. *The Worlds of Christopher Columbus.* Cambridge University Press, 1992, p. 111; **Harry Smith:** Smith, G.C. Moore, ed. *The Autobiography of Lieutenant-General Sir Harry Smith.* E.P. Dutton and Company, 1902, p. 20; **Dolley Madison:** Colbert, David, ed. *Eyewitness to America: 500 Years of America in the Words of Those Who Saw It Happen.* Pantheon Books, 1997; **Henry Clay:** *Speech of Mr. Henry Clay, of Kentucky, on the Measures of Compromise.* Jno. T. Towers, 1850, p. 24; **Dr. Samuel McGill:** Barrett, John G. *Sherman's March Through the Carolinas.* The University of North Carolina Press, 1956, p. 95; **William Tecumseh Sherman:** *Memoirs of General William T. Sherman.* Greenwood Press, 1974, pp. 249, 254; **The Railroad Strike:** *The Manufacturer and Builder,* August 1877, p. 170; **Woodrow Wilson:** Appeal for Neutrality, Message to the Senate, August 18, 1914; **Theodore Roosevelt:** *America and the World War.* C. Scribner's Sons, 1915; **Irving N. Fisher:** Grunwald, Lisa, and Stephen J. Adler. *Letters of the Century: America, 1900–1999.* The Dial Press, 1999; **Gordon Parks:** *Voices in the Mirror: An Autobiography.* Doubleday, 1990, p. 35; **Dick Russell:** *Black Genius and the American Experience.* Carroll and Graf, 1998, p. 146; **Herbert Hoover:** *American Ideals Versus the New Deal.* Scribner Press, 1936; **Harry S Truman:** Truman, Margaret, ed. *Where the Buck Stops: The Personal and Private Writings of Harry S. Truman.* Warner Books, 1989, pp. 205–206; **Harry S Truman:** Merrill, Dennis. *Documentary History of the Truman Presidency,* vol. 9. University Publications of America, 1996, pp. 444, 446–447; **Alton R. Lee:** *Truman and Taft-Hartley: A Question of Mandate.* University of Kentucky Press, 1966, pp. 93–95; **John Lewis:** Interview in *Newsweek,* November 28, 1983; **Opponent of ERA:** Boles, Janet K. *The Politics of the Equal Rights Amendment.* Longman, 1979, p.121; **Proponent of Era:** Longwell, Marjorie. "The American Woman—Then and Now," *Delta Kappa Gamma Magazine,* Fall, 1969; **Howard Zinn:** Excerpt from *A People's History of the United States 1492–Present* by Howard Zinn. Copyright © 1980, 1995 by Howard Zinn. Reprinted by permission of HarperCollins Publishers, Inc.; **John M. Dunn:** Excerpt from *The Vietnam War: A History of U.S. Involvement* by John M. Dunn. Copyright © 2001 by Lucent Books, Inc. Reprinted by permission.

SOURCE READINGS ACKNOWLEDGMENTS/LITERATURE

Unit 1 *Of Plymouth Plantation, 1640–1647:* From *Of Plymouth Plantation,*1640–1647 by William Bradford. Ed. Samuel Eliot Morison. New York: Knopf, 1952. ***April Morning:*** From *April Morning* by Howard Fast. Copyright ©1961 by Howard Fast. Copyright renewed 1989. **Unit 2 *Incidents in the Life of a Slave Girl:*** Hariet Ann Jacobs, *Incidents in the Life of a Slave Girl: Written by Herself.* (Cambridge, MA: Harvard University Press, 1987). ***Slavery in Massachusetts:*** Henry David Thoreau. From *The Norton Anthology of American Literature,* Second Edition, Vol. 1. Ed. Nina Baym, et al. New York: W.W. Norton and Company, 1985. **Unit 3 *Hungry Hearts:*** Anzia Yezierska. Permission granted by Ayer Company Publishers. ***A Farewell to Arms:*** Ernest Hemingway. New York: Charles Scribner's Sons, 1957. **Unit 4 *Growing Up:*** From *Growing Up,* by Russell Baker. Copyright © 1982 by Russell Baker. **Unit 5 *Night:*** Excerpt from *NIGHT* by Eli Wiesel, translated by Stella Rodway. Copyright © by MacGibbon & Kee. Copyright renewed © 1988 by the Collins Publishers Group. **Unit 6 "Letter from Birmingham Jail":** Excerpt from *Letter From Birmingham Jail* by Martin Luther King, Jr. Copyright © 1963 Martin Luther King, Jr. Copyright renewed 1991 by Coretta Scott King. Reprinted by arrangement with the Estate of Martin Luther King, Jr. c/o Writer's House as agent for the proprietor New York, NY. **Unit 7** Excerpt from *American History* by Judith Ortiz Cofer. Copyright © 1993 By Judith Ortiz Cofer. Used by permission of The University of Georgia Press.

SOURCE READINGS ACKNOWLEDGMENTS/DOCUMENTS

The Iroquois Constitution: by Dekanawidah. Published online at The University of Oklahoma Law Center www.law.ou.edu/hist/iroquois.html; **The Mayflower Compact:** Published online at The University of Oklahoma Law Center www.law.ou.edu/hist/mayflow.html; **An Act for the Gradual Abolition of Slavery:** Pennsylvania,1780. Published online at The Avalon Project at the Yale Law School www.yale.edu/lawweb/avalon/states/statutes/pennst01.htm. Spelling updated.; **President Wilson's Address to Congress:** April 2, 1917. Published online at The World War I Document Archive www.lib.byu.edu/~rdh/wwi/1917/wilswarm.html; **The Universal Declaration of Human Rights:** The United Nations. Published online at The United Nations www.un.org/Overview/rights.html; **President Eisenhower's Farewell Address to the Nation:** January 17, 1961. Published online at University of Houston History Department http://vi.uh.edu/pages/buzzmat/ikefarewell.htm; **Mikhail Gorbachev's Address to the Forty-Third UN General Assembly Session:** December 7, 1988. Published online at CNN Interactive www.cnn.com/SPECIALS/cold.war/episodes/23/documents/gorbachev/

Note: Every effort has been made to locate the copyright owner of material used in this textbook. Omissions brought to our attention will be corrected in subsequent editions.